"*My Soul Has Grown Deep* is a devastatingly important work that deserves a place in every library and personal collection. This is a provocative anthology that will surely become a classic for anyone who wants a true record of the brilliant black writers and scholars who helped shape America. Wideman has struck gold once again."

—LAWRENCE OTIS GRAHAM
Author of *Our Kind of People:*
Inside America's Black Upper Class

"No one bears keener witness to stony paths and impassable obstacles of United States black history than John Edgar Wideman. He is an intellectual of the first magnitude."

—HOUSTON BAKER
Author of *Singers of Daybreak:*
Studies in Black American Literature

"*My Soul Has Grown Deep*, an appropriately reflective title for the history it encapsulates, is a superb tribute to the efforts of visionary African-American women and men who laid the foundation of the literary/cultural journey of blacks in America. Masterfully conceived, the collection includes a complement of writers, some who are now household names in the academy, others who are only familiar to scholars in the field, and many unknown to readers outside of those worlds. One of the great gifts of this anthology is that it will be welcome to all three groups."

—NELLIE MCKAY, coeditor
The Norton Anthology of
African-American Literature

"This instructive volume, ably edited by John Wideman, contains generous selections from major African-American texts of the eighteenth, nineteenth, and early twentieth centuries. Narrative, poetry, and essay are all well represented in this valuable compendium of early African-American literature."

—WILLIAM L. ANDREWS
Editor of *Classic Fiction of the Harlem Renaissance*

MY SOUL
HAS
GROWN
DEEP

Classics of Early African-American Literature

JOHN EDGAR WIDEMAN

ONE WORLD

BALLANTINE BOOKS • NEW YORK

*Dedicated to Danny, Jake,
Jamila, and Qasima, the next generations.*

CONTENTS

A NOTE ON THE TEXTS

The texts in this book are based on the original printed editions. We have made no attempt to modernize the authors' own distinct usage, spelling, or punctuation, or to make the texts consistent with each other in this regard. In some cases, we have relied on texts published a few years after the first editions, and containing few or no differences from those original texts. Paul Laurence Dunbar's *Lyrics of Lowly Life* appears as it did in the book produced in 1908 by Dodd, Mead and Company. The text of *The Souls of Black Folk* by W.E.B. DuBois is that published in 1909 by A.C. McClurg & Co. In the case of Phillis Wheatley's poems, the text derives from the 1909 edition published by R.R. and C.C. Wright and based almost entirely on the original 1773 edition.

The Editors

INTRODUCTION

*I*T IS A NEW CENTURY. In *The Souls of Black Folk*, written as the 19th century ended and the 20th began, W.E.B. DuBois prophesized that the problem for the new/old century we have just escaped would be the problem of the colorline: "the relation of the darker to the lighter races of man in Asia and Africa, in America and the islands of the sea." To understand if progress has been achieved toward resolution of these race matters, it's necessary to read backward. Place ourselves in the world as W.E.B. DuBois might have understood it, poised at the edge of the unknown, just as we are today, experiencing the transition from one epoch to another, epochs demarcated arbitrarily by 100-year cycles, as if the unknown, the unfathomable configures itself more accessibly, more transparently at such designated junctures. DuBois attempted to gauge the future by looking backward first. In a meditation optimistically entitled "The Dawn of Freedom," he begins the Negro's story in ancient Egypt and brings the tale forward swiftly to concentrate on the last decades of the 19th century, detailing the formation and failure of the Freedman's Bureau, one of the nation's first answers-in-progress to the still unresolved question: How should radically unequal, African-descended ex-slaves—impoverished, landless, stigmatized, disenfranchised, without civil rights, lacking formal education, with little or no previous experience of citizenship—be incorporated into a society whose announced creed is democracy, a democracy in theory open and fair that guarantees all its citizens an equal opportunity to compete in the struggle for a decent life?

Are we closer today to answering this question? How can progress be measured unless we reconstruct and reanimate the past? Put another way, the past is eternally with us, present as the arc of our personal experience follows us, fills us, defines us. Doesn't any step forward depend on invisible footprints anchoring, locating, echoing, connecting, validating the instant

motion by rooting it in time? To be visible in time, visible to ourselves, we imagine the unseen, the unseeable, the trail of footprints evaporating behind each step we take. We imagine a narrative, births and deaths, imagine names for immaterial persons, places, things, for lives we may or may not have lived or never lived.

Language is one form of this moving, recycling energy driving us forward by directing us back through its museum of invisible footprints, its archeology of traces. Language is a medium for constructing histories, both personal and collective. Written language conjures an appearance, inscribes for us the invisible, the intangible. Words are dreams. A spectral means of perceiving what things are and what they might be. Words dream history. History is the bed where words sleep and awaken and sleep again and dream. When we read history, we don't discover some hard, permanent past; we interrogate our present. Jeopardize it, tease it into instability, experience it as one precarious possibility among many possibilities. Reading history permits us to confront what Ralph Ellison in *Invisible Man* calls the "uncertainties that live within our certainties."

Writing our stories, writing our lives reveals them as dream, only as substantial or unsubstantial as the words narrating them. Words resonate and accentuate while they also chip away at each other, just as when we watch a movie or listen to music, the tapestry of one realityscape segues into another. There is no concrete past, no material reality intact, solid, available somewhere for us to dust off and take down off the shelf. History exists as a work in progress, problematic, made up word by word. Even the stories of ancient monuments, like the scattered fragments of Ozymandias, strewn on the desert sand, tell different stories, sing different songs depending on whose words, whose eyes you see them through.

"The past is not simply 'out there,' an objective history to be researched or forgotten at will, but lives most vividly in all of us, deep inside, and needs constantly to be given expression and interpretation." (Richard Holmes, *Footsteps*, 1985.) The narratives in this book have been gathered to stimulate expression and interpretation. All stories are true and, therefore, none is dispensable, nor impervious to the truth of the others. What should we think of an African American cowboy, Nat Love, who has internalized his white fellow cowpokes' hate of Indians and Mexicans? Or of Ida B. Wells, a black woman, armed only with her pen and her convictions, who confronted a city full of murderous racists? "You got to go there to know there," Zora Neale Hurston tells us, and that's exactly why it's necessary to travel with these sto-

rytellers from the 18th and 19th centuries. Each journey rewards the effort with a unique perspective, an expansion of the possible, an expansion, ultimately, of ourselves. Just as importantly, the narratives enfold and unfold the personal within a context of collective significance, a ground of meaning that supports the idea that we may dream alone but we're not alone.

The act of expression and interpretation is sharing a dream. If our present lives and former lives didn't interpenetrate, weren't interdependent, weren't mutually empowering, what would interest us about the spilled milk of the past? Shared dreaming of history creates family, clan, tribe, nation, and as the Igbo say, a man without a clan is like a butterfly without wings.

The mythic African bird Sankofu that flies forward with its head tucked backward, the double-faced Greek God Janus, Sartre's passenger on a train rushing forward down the tracks in a seat facing the caboose are figurations of simultaneity, of time's mysterious, impenetrable perpetual weave of present, past and future—Great Time. In Great Time, the voices of long-dead witnesses embodied in this collection can enter the present, alter it. The reason for attending to the dead is not an obligatory, obsequious accumulation of facts and figures, nor to acquire some nodding, cocktail party acquaintance with a pantheon of former heroines and heroes. The voices of the dead can be revived through imaginative encounters each reader constructs. Just as the rituals of Haitian voodoo attempt to summon the spirits of powerful ancestors so their wisdom can possess the living, strengthen and guide the living, the point of attending to the dead who speak in this book is life, more life. Examined, expanded life for those who were here before and for us, at this moment, here and now, this moment also and always bedded in Great Time.

❧

THE PURPOSE of my introduction is to enhance the reader's imaginative encounter with the works of the writers presented in these pages. But that's almost like drawing a map of a country neither reader nor this writer has seen. A map like all maps, the result of decisions about what to leave out as much as what to include. One conventional strategy for introducing an anthology is briefly describing each selection, sketching its historical, cultural, political setting, detailing vignettes about authors' lives, quoting scholarly analyses of the work, perhaps a word or two about its original reception or publishing history. Their wide availability on the internet has transformed

the value of such information. Facts are less authoritative, less valuable, less hard. They are constantly changing—updated, subjected to revision and challenge. Facts remain pertinent, but setting down frozen packets of data in the permanency of print seems as antiquated and wasteful as the notion of bound encyclopedias. Truth does not reside in information, no matter how high it is piled. As information proliferates, it becomes inflated currency, more likely a sign that a point of view is being constructed than a sign that a definitive representation of some subject has been achieved.

A conventional approach—footnoting, attaching rap sheets to each piece of writing and writer—for all its virtues also serves as a form of mediation, endangering the frame of Great Time, the immediacy of spontaneous, improvised, call-and-response between readers and writers of those texts. The entries in this collection (mildly annotated by short biographical profiles of each author) have been chosen because they can speak for themselves, because they stimulate dialogue, because individually and as a group they address the bottom-line issue of survival, the still unresolved question of America's identity. If we read attentively, listen to the voices preserved here, perhaps we'll learn how each of us, consciously or not, is implicated, enmeshed in the contradictions, ironies, the precarious successes and heart-breaking, body-crushing failures of a so-called "democracy" in which some are always more equal than others.

Life or death is the bottom line that the narratives address. Life or death not only in the metaphorical sense that prompts images of suffering, rebirth and salvation. Literal life or death in the struggles recorded day by day to escape slavery, a lynch mob, the oppression and enforced ignorance of an unexamined existence in which one's thoughts and labor are consumed serv-icing someone else's life, someone else's dream. The social deaths of submis-sion or slavery versus the ever-receding promise of emancipation, the hope-less compromise of dependency versus the crisis of independence—these were the stakes during the periods when the narratives in this collection were composed. These issues, these choices and all the uncharted space between we must define and negotiate are still what's at risk, what we confront as we turn the pages of this book and talk to it while it talks to us.

What is to be the fate of African-descended people in this New World society called America? By living certain kinds of lives and leaving behind a record of them, Sojourner Truth, Nat Love, Ida B. Wells, etc. have forestalled a final answer, a final solution to the conundrum of African-American iden-tity. They are witnesses, fellow sufferers who resisted the bestial otherness

inscribed by slavery, resisted social and economic deprivation, resisted the Manichean dichotomies of black and white, the harrowing, internalized doubleness that felt inescapable if you were both a Negro and an American. The writers transcended identities that attempted to determine and circumscribe what it means to be an African-American. To read them reminds us that words can count as much as deeds, that words are deeds, and that you can dream your way through bars your hands can't bend. Collectively, the authors formulate and keep alive possibilities; individually each reveals the costs and benefits of particular survival strategies, the pain, courage, glory of resistance and subversion, the triumphs of creating a particular path just when darkness and peril appear thickest.

What are the odds against the career of a Sojourner Truth? How did Frederick Douglass escape the systemic degradations and violence that obscured the lives of those many thousands lost and gone who were born like him into slavery? How does the battle Douglass waged relate to the life of James Weldon Johnson, world traveler, artist, sophisticated man about town? What might they say to each other? What would they say about your way, my way of constructing an American identity?

It is necessary to ask such questions because America continues to refuse its Creole identity, its multi-layered, multi-valent, combative, up-for-grabs culture. Denies its stubborn, healthy indeterminancy. Prefers to cling to self-deception. It's either/or, reductive categories of race. Pretends not to notice (except to condemn or prohibit or manipulate for profit) the continuous cross-over traffic between mainstream and marginal cultures, cross-over producing diversity and a rainbow of skin colors, crossings back and forth and back again that keep the country vital, rigorous, competitive in the world's marketplace. The nation chooses instead to blind itself systematically to its many colors, doesn't acknowledge its brutal slide into political and moral repression. Power has been seized by a cynical, wealthy few who manage to convince the majority that everybody benefits from the excess dribbling off the oligarch's plates and that the system promising these trickle-down goodies is worth preserving by any means necessary. Including discriminatory legislation and policies—drug wars, wars on crime, AIDS, welfare, the juvenile justice system, women's rights—policies justified by vicious myths of race, gender and class that divide the country and doom a good proportion of its citizenry to second-class or no-class lives.

Obviously the version of America I've just drawn is one story of many possible stories, my story of what I find revealed, confirmed when I engage

the voices in this collection and blend their testimony with my own experience. Of course other stories could be constructed and that's the beauty, the utility of this volume: providing witness, direct, first-hand materials for piecing together an account of what happened to Africans who crossed an ocean and found themselves beleaguered strangers in a strange land. Africans whose voices have been muted, mediated far too long. Africans who problematize the question of American identity and American experience as profoundly, provocatively as every other group of immigrants who arrived on these New World shores.

In the preface to her book about the religious significance of food to medieval women, Caroline Walker Bynum claims, "Her work has implications for modern problems and obsessions that will not be lost on many of its readers," but then hastens to add, "the book is about then, not about now . . . I intend to reveal the past in its strangeness as well as familiarity." So DuBois, Dunbar, Equiano strike us sometimes as contemporaries and peers, yet often they also wear the shimmering, impenetrable aura of otherness, disrupt and unsettle our expectations, surprise and frighten us as much as visitors from another planet. Remember, it's a two-way street. Some of the most instructive insights available here follow from asking the question, what would Jarena Lee or Booker T. Washington think of us?

As I suggested earlier, introducing a collection such as this inevitably involves accounting and perhaps apologizing for what's been left out. In spite of its 1,300 pages, this collection lays no claim to being comprehensive or exhaustive; it merely samples, ideally in a creative fashion, over two hundred years of writing in English by African-descended people. The pieces chosen for inclusion are the map's visible contours and should speak for themselves. The main criterion for inclusion is simple: each narrator must tell a good story, one that entertains and instructs. Rather than excerpts from many authors, a few works are presented in their entirety. Most selections have attained "classic" status—they've been around a long time, reprinted often, attracted many readers, received positive critical scrutiny, scholarly attention, appeared in university classes. Some, Jarena Lee's narrative, for instance, are relatively unknown. Variety (of point of view, geographical setting, style, genre, date, length, voice) has been sought in order to symbolize the range, the immensely rich potential within the field of African American writing from which these particular examples have been culled.

Though non-fiction seems to dominate and fiction and poetry may appear under-represented, one can argue that in effect all writing fits into a

single genre: autobiography. The choice of subject matter or form, the perspective from which writers view their material, are always self-revelatory no matter how conventional a form the author chooses, no matter how cunningly he disguises or dreams his origins and intentions. This inevitable subjectivity, neither good nor bad in itself, is simply a fact the notion of genre tends to override or hide, perhaps so readers can pretend to have their cake and eat it, too: experience the reality of the fake moment without being unsettled by the radical reevaluation of experience that follows from recognizing real and fake are not mutually exclusive categories. Genre functions as a protection against too much reality and/or too little. Not acknowledging the play, the pretense, the lies inherent in any species of writing can be dangerous. Aren't historians novelists who haven't come out of the closet?

Though this is a gathering of narratives written for publication and printed for the most part in standard English, they also address the artful, unwritable orality of the folk voice, the Africanized Creole vernacular of American speech, the tension between written and spoken, the cross-fertilization of literate and non-literate, the aesthetic, political and moral issues of "dialect" writing. Oral tradition becomes not so much a missing link in this volume but one more salient dimension of African American culture the narrators express and interpret. To find more extensive representations of the spoken word—that indispensable complement to the written in any literary tradition but especially among African Americans since for hundreds of years learning to read and write, let alone breaking into print, was legally forbidden—the reader should look elsewhere, to folklore anthologies, the WPA ex-slave narratives, to music, preaching and other vernacular arts of black oral culture. Yet the power and beauty of oral tradition is embedded in the style of these written voices—their syntax, rhythms, vocabulary, aphorisms, incorporation of call and response, direct address, the mimicking or quoting of vernacular speakers. In addition the writers praise, analyze, describe the presence and meaning of the folk voice in their communities, in their lives.

❧

PAUL LAURENCE DUNBAR chafes at the artistic limitations imposed on the Negro poet by a "dialect tradition" of broken, comic English. Frederick Douglass ("their songs follow me") and DuBois pay extensive homage to the anonymous folk musicians that James Weldon Johnson immortalizes as "black and unknown bards." Living in a highly segregated society doesn't pre-

vent Richard Allen and Jarena Lee from preaching to whites they mesmerize with sermons forged in African traditions of chant and oratory.

One last omission that's not exactly an omission the closer we look. Where's the erotic dimension in these narratives? Surely our ancestors were as aware as we are now of private parts. Why are no signs of that awareness, that erotic energy visible in this collection? Partly, of course, the narratives reflect the period in which they were published. Americans in the 18th and 19th century constructed a distinction between public and private that required writers (unless they chose the demi-monde of pornography) to be mum about matters as basic as the body and sexual desire. Victorian romance was essentially bodyless, relations between men and women reduced to a representation of manners, etherealized sensibility, to social and economic arrangements leading to marriage.

Look again. During the 18th and 19th century, on stage in books and songs, lithographs, knick knacks, the black body was minstrelized as absurd, laughable and entertaining, monkey cute maybe, but sexless, bumbling, essentially harmless. Simultaneously the semi-official spectacles of lynching, rape, prostitution and chain gangs constructed another version of the Negro body for public consumption, creating a racialized pornography that exposed black bodies to the white viewers' gaze as desirable and dangerous, as deadly and dead.

Ida B. Wells obviously was aware of these paradoxical attitudes, of the busy underground crossing-over of black bodies and white:

"Ebenezer Fowler, the wealthiest colored man in Issaguena County, Mississippi, was shot down on the street in Mayersville, January 30, 1885, just before dark by an armed body of white men who filled his body with bullets. They charged him with writing a note to a white woman of the place, which they intercepted and which proved there was an intimacy existing between them.

"Hundreds of such cases might be cited to prove the assertion that there are white women in the South who love the Afro-American's company, even as there are white men notorious for their preference for African American women.

"There is hardly a town in the South that has not an instance of this kind that is well known."

In an apartheid system based on white supremacy, doesn't the denial of

full humanity to black people repress and distort everybody's humanity, including everyone's libidinal energy, channeling erotic desire towards the darkness of what's unspeakable and forbidden? Apart from their outraged condemnation of violations perpetuated upon black bodies, the authors in this collection maintain a disciplined silence about eroticism. In a climate of fear and oppression, the absence of writing about body pleasure may not be surprising, but might it also express the presence of a positive survival strategy. Because they understand how minstrelsy's ridicule and oppression's violence ruled the perceptions of their primarily white readership, African American writers may have chosen to leave the black body unobserved while it performed quietly, privately, patiently, its work of play and propagation.

What does the old school silence of this anthology tell us about rap music's exuberant, over-the-top celebration of black body pleasure? Foucault in his *History of Sexuality* predicted that excessive talk (*discours*) about sex would banalize eroticism, open the door for the state to colonize those once private, interior spaces where gender and racial identities form. Does our culture's noisy obsession, our endless prattle, our worrying and broadcasting and commodifying and commercializing and medicalizing of the most intimate details of our sexual lives mute eroticism's disruptive edge, its Dionysian challenge to the social order?

Part suggestive survey, part offering of indispensable highlights of the first centuries of African-American writing, the unique blend achieved herein seeks to provide materials for substantial conversations, for informed interrogation of a developing culture. The selections map the complex interfaces of oral and written, of pop and high styles, of personal and communal, African and European, tradition and innovation. The writing illustrates the eclectic, creative synthesizing power of Creole ambivalence, of Creole omniverousness that percolate at the culture's core, and generate its universal appeal.

RICHARD ALLEN

(1760-1831)

ichard Allen was born into slavery on February 14, 1760 where he and his family were owned by Benjamin Chew, the Chief Justice of the Commonwealth of Pennsylvania. Allen lived with his parents and three siblings in Philadelphia until they were sold to Stokeley Sturgis, the owner of a plantation outside of Dover, Delaware. He would live there until he was about twenty years of age. Though Sturgis was "an unconverted man," he was, in Allen's opinion, "a good master . . . more like a father to his slaves than anything else."

Sturgis permitted Allen and his siblings to attend meetings at the Methodist Society, where Allen accepted Christ as his savior, and in 1777, he and his brother joined the Methodist Church, beginning what would become a lifelong devotion to God's work. However, slaves attending church meetings were not met with overwhelming approval, as Sturgis' neighbors were of the opinion that Sturgis' "Negroes would soon ruin him."

Allen and his brother held a council together and determined that they would attend to their master's business with great diligence so that no one could state that religion made them worthless servants. Allen writes that he and his brother would "work night and day to get our crops forward, so that they should be disappointed." They even made it a point to miss church meetings if there was work to be done, even to the disapproval of Sturgis himself.

"Boys," Sturgis would say, "I would rather you would go to your meeting: if I am not good myself, I like to see you striving yourselves to be good."

Still, Allen and his brother would resist if the crops needed tending to, and their diligence resulted in Sturgis' public boasting of his slaves as being "better" because of religion. This arrangement suited the Allen brothers, and with the support of Sturgis, they began to invite preachers to the Sturgis house to preach. The meetings and sermons soon became regular events at

the home, as Sturgis himself converted to Methodism.

His own involvement in the Methodist Church led Sturgis to come to the realization that slavery was wrong. He went to Allen and his brother with a proposition—they could purchase their freedom with sixty pounds gold and silver, or two thousand dollars. It took Allen five years of wood chopping and other manual labor to raise the money, but in 1786, he paid his last install-ment to Sturgis and became a free man. But Allen never lost sight of what he felt was his true mission—spreading the word of God to the benefit of the black condition. That same year, he accepted an invitation to preach at a mixed-race congregation of Methodists—St. George's Church in Philadelphia. Quickly, Allen increased the black membership at the church to such an extent that the building could no longer accommodate the growth in the congregation. Worshipers decided to build a balcony on the church to accommodate this growth in membership, but Allen was discouraged when he discovered that the black members would be forced to sit only in the gallery they helped to build. He argued for a separate place of worship instead, but when the church refused, Allen decided to join the Rev. Absalom Jones to found the Free African Religious Society.

In 1792, Jones decided to challenge the segregated seating requirements imposed on black members at St. George's church by praying in the front of the church with the white members. Two trustees of the church forced Jones to leave, and the incident prompted Allen and other black congregation members seated in the balcony to leave the church as well. Before this incident, Allen and Jones did not have overwhelming support among black Methodists for a separate congregation. But in 1794, members of the Free African Society founded the African Church of Philadelphia. Because of the dis-criminatory practices regarding seating arrangements in the Methodist Church, the African Church of Philadelphia was consecrated as part of the Protestant Episcopal Church, and Jones became the denomination's first deacon.

Allen's community involvement in the late 18th century also extended beyond the religious and spiritual. In spite of his lack of medical training, Allen was considered a prestigious "Bleeder" which was the equivalent of modern day surgeon. In 1793, the Black Plague claimed the lives of thou-sands in the Philadelphia area, and Allen was praised for his services by some of the most prominent members of the medical community, including Benjamin Rush, one of the signers of the Declaration of Independence. Allen also operated a station on the Underground Railroad for over thirty years, right up to his death in 1831—work that was continued by the Bethel

Church until the emancipation.

Toward the end of the 18th century, Allen was solicited to be a minister in the African Church, but despite the segregation of black parishioners at St. George's, he remained faithful to the Methodist Church, and felt that he could not accept the African Church's offer. He would later write, "I informed them that I could not be anything else but a Methodist, as I was born and awakened under them, and I could go no further with them, for I was a Methodist."

With his own money, Allen purchased a plot of land in Philadelphia, as well as an old frame that was formerly a blacksmith shop, and had carpenters renovate it, making it a fit place for worship. In 1794, Allen solicited Bishop Asbury to open the church, which ultimately became known as Bethel African Church and would become the oldest parcel of real estate owned continuously by black people in the United States.

After Bethel was officially introduced into the Methodist conference, Allen became embroiled in a decade-long struggle with the Methodist conference over control of the church. Although most white Methodists supported the emancipation of blacks, they were a long way from treating free blacks as equals. Blacks were not allowed burial in congregational cemeteries and were often segregated in Methodist churches. The Trustees of St. George's insisted on imposing hefty fees and mandating white preacher appearances at the church, which Allen opposed vigorously.

Bethel's membership continued to expand under Allen's leadership, reflecting the growth of the black population in Philadelphia. Newly freed African Americans were participating in "love feasts" which were ceremonies at the church permitting the full expression of emotions that were repressed under the slavery system. The strict Methodist system, with sanctions against alcohol consumption, gambling and infidelity, also appealed to many blacks seeking to structure their lives after slavery. Allen's preaching was also a significant factor in the church's growth. His sermons were so renowned, that he was recognized, in 1799, when Bishop Asbury ordained him as the first black deacon of the Methodist Church.

Still, the Trustees of Bethel Church were constantly on the defensive against the more formidable white Methodists, who were still seeking to control Bethel by threatening to have them "expelled from the connexion." It ultimately took a Pennsylvania Supreme Court ruling in 1807, which declared that the black Methodist congregation owned the property and the church, and they could determine who would preach there. Over the years,

however, Allen and other African Americans became disillusioned with Methodism, mostly because white ministers began distancing themselves from their anti-slavery preachings and principles, putting more effort into halting the autonomy of black congregations.

In 1807, the Bethel Church added an "African Supplement" to its incorporation, and nine years later, it obtained legal status as an independent church. Allen organized representatives from four other black Methodist congregations in the northeast to form a new denomination. In 1816, under Allen's leadership, the African Methodist Episcopal Church was formed, and Allen was chosen as the first bishop of the first independent black denomination in the United States. Those meetings at Bethel Church were the groundwork for what ultimately developed into a separate religious identity for black Americans.

In addition to his religious work, Allen was also instrumental in African American educational advancement throughout his life. In 1795 he opened a day school for over sixty children and later on, founded the "Society of Free People of Colour for Promoting the Instruction and School Education of Children of African Descent." By 1811, the city of Philadelphia had more than eleven black schools in the area.

In the late 1800s, there was considerable debate about the future of the African-American community within the community itself. William Thornton was in the midst of proposing a plan originated by anti-slavery groups in England which would settle free black Americans, as well as emancipated slaves in the West Indies. They would sail back to Sierra Leone, an independent state founded on the west coast of Africa, and prominent blacks on the east coast of the United States had endorsed the plan. Allen and the Free African Society did not agree with the principles of the scheme and rejected it, opting instead to promote advancement in the United States as the alternative. By introducing "African" churches, benevolent societies and schools, the black community in Philadelphia embraced their culture and heritage and affirmed their American identity.

In 1827, Allen implored African Americans to remain in the United States and not resettle to colonies such as Sierra Leone. In an essay published in *Freedom's Journal*, the country's first black newspaper, Allen wrote, "this land which we have watered with our tears and our blood is now our mother country."

Richard Allen was recognized as a leading voice of free African Americans in the first part of the 19th century right up to his death in 1831. He fought

to abolish slavery and to elevate the living conditions of free slaves through religious and political channels, as well as through his writings, and the lasting impact on black communities of the northeast is his legacy.

The Life, Experience, and Gospel Labours of the Rt. Rev. Richard Allen

Mark the perfect man, and behold the upright: for the
end of that man is peace.—Ps. xxxvii. 37.

PREFACED

A GREAT part of this work having been written many years after events
actually took place; and as my memory could not exactly point out the
exact time of many occurrences; they are, however, (as many as I can recol-
lect) pointed out; some without day or date, which, I presume, will be of no
material consequence, so that they are confined to the truth.

Could I but recollect the half of my trials and sufferings in this life, with
the many meetings I have held, and the various occurrences that have taken
place in my travelling to and fro, preaching the Gospel of our Lord and
Saviour Jesus Christ to Adam's lost race, they would swell this little book far
beyond my inclination, and weary perhaps those into whose hands it may
chance to come; and as I have been earnestly solicited by many of my friends
to leave a small detail of my life and proceedings, I have thought proper, for
the satisfaction of those who (after I am dead and in the grave) may feel an
inclination to learn the commencement of my life, to leave behind me this
short account for their perusal.

RICHARD ALLEN.

LIFE, &C.

I WAS BORN in the year of our Lord 1760, on February 14th, a slave to Benjamin Chew, of Philadelphia. My mother and father and four children of us were sold into Delaware State, near Dover, and I was a child and lived with him until I was upwards of twenty years of age, during which time I was awakened and brought to see myself poor, wretched and undone, and without the mercy of God must be lost. Shortly after I obtained mercy through the blood of Christ, and was constrained to exhort my old companions to seek the Lord. I went rejoicing for several days, and was happy in the Lord, in conversing with many old experienced Christians. I was brought under doubts, and was tempted to believe I was deceived, and was constrained to seek the Lord afresh. I went with my head bowed down for many days. My sins were a heavy burden. I was tempted to believe there was no mercy for me. I cried to the Lord both night and day. One night I thought hell would be my portion. I cried unto Him who delighteth to hear the prayers of a poor sinner; and all of a sudden my dungeon shook, my chains flew off, and glory to God, I cried. My soul was filled. I cried, enough for me—the Saviour died. Now my confidence was strengthened that the Lord, for Christ's sake, had heard my prayers, and pardoned all my sins. I was constrained to go from house to house, exhorting my old companions, and telling to all around what a dear Saviour I had found. I joined the Methodist society, and met in class at Benjamin Wells's, in the forest, Delaware State. John Gray was the class-leader. I met in his class for several years.

My master was an unconverted man, and all the family; but he was what the world called a good master. He was more like a father to his slaves than any thing else. He was a very tender, humane man. My mother and father lived with him for many years. He was brought into difficulty, not being able to pay for us; and mother having several children after he had bought us, he sold my mother and three children. My mother sought the Lord and found favour with him, and became a very pious woman. There were three children of us remained with our old master. My oldest brother embraced religion, and my sister. Our neighbours, seeing that our master indulged us with the privilege of attending meeting once in two weeks, said that Stokeley's negroes would soon ruin him; and so my brother and myself held a council together that we would attend more faithfully to our master's business, so that it should not be said that religion made us worse servants, we would work

night and day to get our crops forward, so that they should be disappointed. We frequently went to meeting on every other Thursday; but if we were likely to be backward with our crops we would refrain from going to meeting. When our master found we were making no provision to go to meeting, he would frequently ask us if it was not our meeting day, and if we were not going. We would frequently tell him, "no, sir, we would rather stay at home and get our work done." He would tell us, "Boys, I would rather you would go to your meeting: if I am not good myself, I like to see you striving yourselves to be good." Our reply would be, "Thank you, sir; but we would rather stay and get our crops forward." So we always continued to keep our crops more forward than our neighbours; and we would attend public preaching once in two weeks, and class meeting once a week. At length our master said he was convinced that religion made slaves better and not worse, and often boasted of his slaves for their honesty and industry. Some time after I asked him if I might ask the preachers to come and preach at his house. He being old and infirm, my master and mistress cheerfully agreed for me to ask some of the Methodist preachers to come and preach at his house. I asked him for a note. He replied, if my word was not sufficient, he should send no note. I accordingly asked the preacher. He seemed somewhat backward at first, as my master did not send a written request; but the class-leader (John Gray) observed that my word was sufficient; so he preached at my old master's house on the next Wednesday. Preaching continued for some months; at length Freeborn Garrison preached from these words, "Thou art weighed in the balance, and art found wanting." In pointing out and weighing the different characters, and among the rest weighed the slave-holders, my master believed himself to be one of that number, and after that he could not be satisfied to hold slaves, believing it to be wrong. And after that he proposed to me and my brother buying our times, to pay him sixty pounds gold and silver, or two thousand dollars continental money, which we complied with in the year 17—.

We left our master's house, and I may truly say it was like leaving our father's house; for he was a kind, affectionate, and tender-hearted master, and told us to make his house our home when we were out of a place or sick. While living with him we had family prayer in the kitchen, to which he frequently would come out himself at time of prayer, and my mistress with him. At length he invited us from the kitchen to the parlour to hold family prayer, which we attended to. We had our stated times to hold our prayer meetings and give exhortations at in the neighbourhood.

I had it often impressed upon my mind that I should one day enjoy my freedom; for slavery is a bitter pill, notwithstanding we had a good master. But when we would think that our day's work was never done, we often thought that after our master's death we were liable to be sold to the highest bidder, as he was much in debt; and thus my troubles were increased, and I was often brought to weep between the porch and the altar. But I have had reason to bless my dear Lord that a door was opened unexpectedly for me to buy my time, and enjoy my liberty. When I left my master's house I knew not what to do, not being used to hard work, what business I should follow to pay my master and get my living. I went to cutting of cord wood. The first day my hands were so blistered and sore, that it was with difficulty I could open or shut them. I kneeled down upon my knees and prayed that the Lord would open some way for me to get my living. In a few days my hands recovered, and became accustomed to cutting of wood and other hardships; so I soon became able to cut my cord and a half and two cords a day. After I was done cutting, I was employed in a brick-yard by one Robert Register, at fifty dollars a month, continental money. After I was done with the brick-yard I went to days' work, but did not forget to serve my dear Lord. I used oftimes to pray sitting, standing, or lying; and while my hands were employed to earn my bread, my heart was devoted to my dear Redeemer. Sometimes I would awake from my sleep preaching and praying. I was after this employed in driving of wagon in time of the continental war, in drawing salt from Rehobar, Sussex county, in Delaware. I had my regular stops and preaching places on the road. I enjoyed many happy seasons in meditation and prayer while in this employment.

After peace was proclaimed I then travelled extensively, striving to preach the Gospel. My lot was cast in Wilmington. Shortly after I was taken sick with the fall fever and then the pleurisy. September the 3d, 1783, I left my native place. After leaving Wilmington, I went into New-Jersey, and there travelled and strove to preach the Gospel until the spring of 1784. I then became acquainted with Benjamin Abbot, that great and good apostle. He was one of the greatest men that ever I was acquainted with. He seldom preached but what there were souls added to his labour. He was a man of as great faith as any that ever I saw. The Lord was with him, and blessed his labours abundantly. He was as a friend and father to me. I was sorry when I had to leave West Jersey, knowing I had to leave a father. I was employed in cutting of wood for Captain Cruenkleton, although I preached the Gospel at nights and on Sundays. My dear Lord was with me, and blessed my

labours—glory to God—and gave me souls for my hire. I then visited East Jersey, and laboured for my dear Lord, and became acquainted with Joseph Budd, and made my home with him, near the new mills—a family, I trust, who loved and served the Lord. I laboured some time there; but being much afflicted in body with the inflammatory rheumatism, was not so successful as in some other places. I went from there to Jonathan Bunn's, near Bennington, East Jersey. There I laboured in that neighbourhood for some time. I found him and his family kind and affectionate, and he and his dear wife were a father and mother of Israel. In the year 1784 I left East Jersey, and laboured in Pennsylvania. I walked until my feet became so sore and blistered the first day, that I scarcely could bear them to the ground. I found the people very humane and kind in Pennsylvania. I having but little money, I stopped at Cæsar Water's, at Radnor township, twelve miles from Philadelphia. I found him and his wife very kind and affectionate to me. In the evening they asked me if I would come and take tea with them; but after sitting awhile, my feet became so sore and painful that I could scarcely be able to put them to the floor. I told them that I would accept of their kind invitation, but my feet pained me so that I could not come to the table. They brought the table to me. Never was I more kindly received by strangers that I had never before seen, than by them. She bathed my feet with warm water and bran; the next morning my feet were better and free from pain. They asked me if I would preach for them. I preached for them the next evening. We had a glorious meeting. They invited me to stay till Sabbath day, and preach for them. I agreed to do so, and preached on Sabbath day to a large congregation of different persuasions, and my dear Lord was with me, and I believe there were many souls cut to the heart, and were added to the ministry. They insisted on me to stay longer with them. I stayed and laboured in Radnor several weeks. Many souls were awakened, and cried aloud to the Lord to have mercy upon them. I was frequently called upon by many inquiring what they should do to be saved. I appointed them to prayer and supplication at the throne of grace, and to make use of all manner of prayer, and pointed them to the invitation of our Lord and Saviour Jesus Christ, who has said, "Come unto me, all ye that are weary and heavy laden, and I will give you rest." Glory be to God! and now I know he was a God at hand and left not afar off. I preached my farewell sermon, and left these dear people. It was a time of visitation from above. Many were the slain of the Lord. Seldom did I ever experience such a time of mourning and lamentation among a people. There were but few coloured people in the neighbour-

hood—the most of my congregation was white. Some said, this man must be a man of God; I never heard such preaching before. We spent a greater part of the night in singing and prayer with the mourners. I expected I should have had to walk, as I had done before; but Mr. Davis had a creature that he made a present to me; but I intended to pay him for his horse if ever I got able. My dear Lord was kind and gracious to me. Some years after I got into business, and thought myself able to pay for the horse. The horse was too light and small for me to travel on far. I traded it away with George Huftman for a blind horse, but larger. I found my friend Huftman very kind and affectionate to me, and his family also. I preached several times at Huftman's meeting house to a large and numerous congregation.

I proceeded on to Lancaster, Pennsylvania. I found the people in general dead to religion, and scarcely a form of godliness. I went on to Little York and put up at George Tess, a saddler, and I believed him to be a man that loved and served the Lord. I had comfortable meetings with the Germans. I left Little York and proceeded on to the State of Maryland, and stopped at Mr. Benjamin Grover's; and I believed him to be a man that loved and served the Lord. I had many happy seasons with my dear friends. His wife was a very pious woman; but their dear children were strangers to vital religion. I preached in the neighbourhood for some time, and travelled Hartford circuit with Mr. Porters, who travelled that circuit. I found him very useful to me. I also travelled with Jonathan Forest and Leari Coal.

December, 1784, General Conference sat in Baltimore, the first General Conference ever held in America. The English preachers just arrived from Europe, Rev. Dr. Coke, Richard Watcoat, and Thomas Vasses. This was the beginning of the Episcopal Church amongst the Methodists. Many of the ministers were set apart in holy orders at this Conference, and were said to be entitled to the gown; and I have thought religion has been declining in the church ever since. There was a pamphlet published by some person which stated that when the Methodists were no people, then they were a people; and now they have become a people, they were no people, which had often serious weight upon my mind.

In 1785 the Rev. Richard Watcoat was appointed on Baltimore circuit. He was, I believe, a man of God. I found great strength in travelling with him—a father in Israel. In his advice he was fatherly and friendly. He was of a mild and serene disposition. My lot was cast in Baltimore, in a small meeting-house called Methodist Alley. I stopped at Richard Mould's, and was sent to my lodgings, and lodged at Mr. McCannon's. I had some happy meetings

in Baltimore. I was introduced to Richard Russell, who was very kind and affectionate to me, and attended several meetings. Rev. Bishop Asberry sent for me to meet him at Henry Gaff's. I did so. He told me he wished me to travel with him. He told me that in the slave countries, Carolina and other places, I must not intermix with the slaves, and I would frequently have to sleep in his carriage, and he would allow me my victuals and clothes. I told him I would not travel with him on these conditions. He asked me my reason. I told him if I was taken sick, who was to support me? and that I thought people ought to lay up something while they were able, to support themselves in time of sickness or old age. He said that was as much as he got, his victuals and clothes. I told him he would be taken care of, let his afflictions be as they were, or let him be taken sick where he would, he would be taken care of; but I doubted whether it would be the case with myself. He smiled, and told me he would give me from then until he returned from the eastward to make up my mind, which would be about three months. But I made up my mind that I would not accept of his proposals. Shortly after I left Hartford Circuit, and came to Pennsylvania, on Lancaster Circuit. I travelled several months on Lancaster Circuit with the Rev. Peter Moratte and Irie Ellis. They were very kind and affectionate to me in building me up; for I had many trials to pass through, and I received nothing from the Methodist connexion. My usual method was, when I would get bare of clothes, to stop travelling and go to work, so that no man could say I was chargeable to the connexion. My hands administered to my necessities. The autumn of 1785 I returned again to Radnor. I stopped at George Giger's, a man of God, and went to work. His family were all kind and affectionate to me. I killed seven beefs, and supplied the neighbours with meat; got myself pretty well clad through my own industry—thank God—and preached occasionally. The elder in charge in Philadelphia frequently sent for me to come to the city. February, 1786, I came to Philadelphia. Preaching was given out for me at five o'clock in the morning at St. George's Church. I strove to preach as well as I could, but it was a great cross to me; but the Lord was with me. We had a good time, and several souls were awakened, and were earnestly seeking redemption in the blood of Christ. I thought I would stop in Philadelphia a week or two. I preached at different places in the city. My labour was much blessed. I soon saw a large field open in seeking and instructing my African brethren, who had been a long forgotten people and few of them attended public worship. I preached in the commons, in Southwark, Northern Liberties, and wherever I could find an opening. I frequently preached twice

a day, at 5 o'clock in the morning and in the evening, and it was not uncommon for me to preach from four to five times a day. I established prayer meetings; I raised a society in 1786 of forty-two members. I saw the necessity of erecting a place of worship for the coloured people. I proposed it to the most respectable people of colour in this city; but here I met with opposition. I had but three coloured brethren that united with me in erecting a place of worship—the Rev. Absalom Jones, William White, and Dorus Ginnings. These united with me as soon as it became public and known by the elder who was stationed in the city. The Rev. C— B— opposed the plan, and would not submit to any argument we could raise; but he was shortly removed from the charge. The Rev Mr. W— took the charge, and the Rev L— G— . Mr. W— was much opposed to an African church, and used very degrading and insulting language to us, to try and prevent us from going on. We all belonging to St. George's church Rev. Absalom Jones, William White and Dorus Ginnings. We felt ourselves much cramped; but my dear Lord was with us, and we believed, if it was his will, the work would go on, and that we would be able to succeed in building the house of the Lord. We established prayer meetings and meetings of exhortation, and the Lord blessed our endeavours, and many souls were awakened; but the elder soon forbid us holding any such meetings; but we viewed the forlorn state of our coloured brethren, and that they were destitute of a place of worship. They were considered as a nuisance.

A number of us usually attended St. George's Church in Fourth street; and when the coloured people began to get numerous in attending the church, they moved us from the seats we usually sat on, and placed us around the wall, and on Sabbath morning we went to church and the sexton stood at the door, and told us to go in the gallery. He told us to go, and we would see where to sit. We expected to take the seats over the ones we formerly occupied below, not knowing any better. We took those seats. Meeting had begun, and they were nearly done singing, and just as we got to the seats, the elder said, "let us pray." We had not been long upon our knees before I heard considerable scuffling and low talking. I raised my head up and saw one of the trustees, H— M—, having hold of the Rev. Absalom Jones, pulling him up off of his knees, and saying, "You must get up—you must not kneel here." Mr. Jones replied, "wait until prayer is over." Mr. H— M— said "no, you must get up now, or I will call for aid and I force you away." Mr. Jones said, "wait until prayer is over, and I will get up and trouble you no more." With that he beckoned to one of the other trustees, Mr. L— S— to come to his

assistance. He came, and went to William White to pull him up. By this time prayer was over, and we all went out of the church in a body, and they were no more plagued with us in the church. This raised a great excitement and inquiry among the citizens, in so much that I believe they were ashamed of their conduct. But my dear Lord was with us, and we were filled with fresh vigour to get a house erected to worship God in. Seeing our forlorn and distressed situation, many of the hearts of our citizens were moved to urge us forward; notwithstanding we had subscribed largely towards finishing St. George's Church, in building the gallery and laying new floors, and just as the house was made comfortable, we were turned out from enjoying the comforts of worshiping therein. We then hired a store room, and held worship by ourselves. Here we were pursued with threats of being disowned, and read publicly out of meeting if we did continue worship in the place we had hired; but we believed the Lord would be our friend. We got subscription papers out to raise money to build the house of the Lord. By this time we had waited on Dr. Rush and Mr. Robert Ralston, and told them of our distressing situation. We considered it a blessing that the Lord had put it into our hearts to wait upon those gentlemen. They pitied our situation, and subscribed largely towards the church, and were very friendly towards us, and advised us how to go on. We appointed Mr. Ralston our treasurer. Dr. Rush did much for us in public by his influence. I hope the name of Dr. Benjamin Rush and Mr. Robert Ralston will never be forgotten among us. They were the two first gentlemen who espoused the cause of the oppressed, and aided us in building the house of the Lord for the poor Africans to worship in. Here was the beginning and rise of the first African church in America. But the elder of the Methodist church still pursued us. Mr. J— M— called upon us and told us if we did not erase our names from the subscription paper, and give up the paper, we would be publicly turned out of meeting. We asked him if we had violated any rules of discipline by so doing. He replied, "I have the charge given to me by the Conference, and unless you submit I will read you publicly out of meeting." We told him we were willing to abide by the discipline of the Methodist church; "and if you will show us where we have violated any law of discipline of the Methodist church, we will submit; and if there is no rule violated in the discipline, we will proceed on." He replied, "we will read you all out." We told him if he turned us out contrary to rule of discipline, we should seek further redress. We told him we were dragged off of our knees in St. George's church, and treated worse than heathens; and we were determined to seek out for ourselves, the Lord being our helper. He

told us we were not Methodists, and left us. Finding we would go on in rais-
ing money to build the church, he called upon us again, and wished to see
us all together. We met him. He told us that he wished us well, and that he
was a friend to us, and used many arguments to convince us that we were
wrong in building a church. We told him we had no place of worship; and
we did not mean to go to St. George's church any more, as we were so scan-
dalously treated in the presence of all the congregation present; "and if you
deny us your name, you cannot seal up the scriptures from us, and deny us
a name in heaven. We believe heaven is free for all who worship in spirit and
truth." And he said, "so you are determined to go on." We told him—"yes,
God being our helper." He then replied, "we will disown you all from the
Methodist connexion." We believed if we put our trust in the Lord, he would
stand by us. This was a trial that I never had to pass through before. I was
confident that the great head of the church would support us. My dear Lord
was with us. We went out with our subscription paper, and met with great
success. We had no reason to complain of the liberality of the citizens. The
first day the Rev. Absalom Jones and myself went out we collected three hun-
dred and sixty dollars. This was the greatest day's collection that we met with.
We appointed a committee to look out for a lot—the Rev. Absalom Jones,
William Gray, William Wilcher, and myself. We pitched upon a lot at the
corner of Lombard and Sixth streets. They authorized me to go and agree for
it. I did accordingly. The lot belonged to Mr. Mark Wilcox. We entered into
articles of agreement for the lot. Afterwards the committee found a lot in
Fifth street, in a more commodious part of the city, which we bought; and
the first lot they threw upon my hands, and wished me to give it up. I told
them they had authorized me to agree for the lot, and they were all well sat-
isfied with the agreement I had made, and I thought it was hard that they
should throw it upon my hands. I told them I would sooner keep it myself
than to forfeit the agreement I had made. And so I did.

We bore much persecution from many of the Methodist connexion; but
we have reason to be thankful to Almighty God, who was our deliverer. The
day was appointed to go and dig the cellar. I arose early in the morning and
addressed the throne of grace, praying that the Lord would bless our endeav-
ours. Having by this time two or three teams of my own—as I was the first
proposer of the African church, I put the first spade in the ground to dig a
cellar for the same. This was the first African church or meeting house that
was erected in the United States of America. We intended it for the African
preaching house or church; but finding that the elder stationed in this city

was such an opposer to our proceedings of erecting a place of worship; though the principal part of the directors of this church belonged to the Methodist connexion, the elder stationed here would neither preach for us, nor have any thing to do with us. We then held an election, to know what religious denomination we should unite with. At the election it was determined—there were two in favour of the Methodist, the Rev. Absalom Jones and myself, and a large majority in favour of the Church of England. The majority carried. Notwithstanding we had been so violently persecuted by the elder, we were in favour of being attached to the Methodist connexion; for I was confident that there was no religious sect or denomination would suit the capacity of the coloured people as well as the Methodist; for the plain and simple gospel suits best for any people, for the unlearned can understand, and the learned are sure to understand; and the reason that the Methodist is so successful in the awakening and conversion of the coloured people, the plain doctrine and having a good discipline. But in many cases the preachers would act to please their own fancy, without discipline, till some of them became such tyrants, and more especially to the coloured people. They would turn them out of society, giving them no trial, for the smallest offence, perhaps only hearsay. They would frequently, in meeting the class, impeach some of the members of whom they had heard an ill report, and turn them out, saying, "I have heard thus and thus of you, and you are no more a member of society"—without witnesses on either side. This has been frequently done, notwithstanding in the first rise and progress in Delaware State, and elsewhere, the coloured people were their greatest support; for there were but few of us free; but the slaves would toil in their little patches many a night until midnight to raise their little truck and sell to get something to support them more than what their masters gave them, but we used often to divide our little support among the white preachers of the Gospel. This was once a quarter. It was in the time of the old revolutionary war between Great Britain and the United States. The Methodists were the first people that brought glad tidings to the coloured people. I feel thankful that ever I heard a Methodist preach. We are beholden to the Methodists, under God, for the light of the Gospel we enjoy; for all other denominations preached so high-flown that we were not able to comprehend their doctrine. Sure am I that reading sermons will never prove so beneficial to the coloured people as spiritual or extempore preaching. I am well convinced that the Methodist has proved beneficial to thousands and ten times thousands. It is to be awfully feared that the simplicity of the Gospel that was among them

fifty years ago, and that they conform more to the world and the fashions thereof, they would fare very little better than the people of the world. The discipline is altered considerably from what it was. We would ask for the good old way, and desire to walk therein.

In 1793 a committee was appointed from the African Church to solicit me to be their minister, for there was no colored preacher in Philadelphia but myself. I told them I could not accept of their offer, as I was a Methodist. I was indebted to the Methodists, under God, for what little religion I had; being convinced that they were the people of God, I informed them that I could not be any thing else but a Methodist, as I was born and awakened under them, and I could go no further with them, for I was a Methodist, and would leave you in peace and love. I would do nothing to retard them in building a church as it was an extensive building, neither would I go out with a subscription paper until they were done going out with their subscription. I bought an old frame that had been formerly occupied as a blacksmith shop from Mr. Sims, and hauled it on the lot in Sixth near Lobard street, that had formerly been taken for the church of England. I employed carpenters to repair the old frame, and fit it for a place of worship. In July, 1794, Bishop Asbury being in town I solicited him to open the church * for us which he accepted. The Rev. John Dickins sung and prayed, and Bishop Asbury preached. The house was called bethel agreeable to the prayer that was made. Mr. Dickins prayed that it might be a bethel** to the gathering in of thousands of souls. My dear Lord was with us, so that there was many hearty Amen's echoed through the house. This house of worship has been favored with the awakening of many souls, and I trust they are in the kingdom both white and colored. Our warfare and troubles now began afresh. Mr. C. proposed that we should make over the church to the conference. This we objected to, he asserted that we could not be Methodists unless we did, we told him he might deny us their name, but they could not deny us a seat in Heaven. Finding that he could not prevail with us so to do, he observed that we had better be incorporated, then we could get any legacies that were left for us, if not, we could not. We agreed to be incorporated, he offered to draw the incorporation himself, that it would save us the trouble of paying for to get it drawn. We cheerfully submitted to his proposed plan. He drew the incorporation, but incorporated our church under the Conference, our property was then all consigned to the Conference for the present Bishops, Elders,

* This church will at present accommodate between 3 and 4000 persons.
** See Gen. chapt. 28.

and Ministers, &c., that belonged to the white Conference, and our property was gone. Being ignorant of incorporations we cheerfully agreed thereto, we labored about ten years under this incorporation, until J— S— was appointed to take the charge in Philadelphia, he soon waked us up by demanding the keys and books of the church, and forbid us holding any meetings except orders from him, these propositions we told him we could not agree to. He observed he was elder appointed to the charge, and unless we submitted to him, he would read us all out of meeting, we told him the house was our's, we had bought it, and paid for it. He said he would let us know it was not our's, it belonged to the Conference, we took council on it; council informed us we had been taken in, according to the incorporation, it belonged to the white connexion. We asked him if it could'nt be altered, he told us it two thirds of the society agreed to have it altered, it could be altered. He gave me a transcript to lay before them, I called the society together and laid it before them. My dear Lord was with us. It was unanimously agree to by both male and female, we had another incorporation drawn that took the church from Conference, and got it passed before the elder knew any thing about it. This raised a considerable rumpus, for the elder contended that it would not be good unless he had signed it. The elder with the Trustees of St. George's called us together, and said we must pay six hundred dollars a year for their services, or they could not serve us. We told them we were not able so to do. The Trustees of St. George's insisted that we should, or should not be supplied by their preachers, at last they made a move that they would take four hundred, we told them that our house was considerable in debt, and we poor people, and we could not agree to pay four hundred, but we agreed to give them two hundred. It was moved by one of the Trustees of St. George's that the money should be paid into their treasury, we refused paying it into their treasury, but we would pay it to the preacher that served, they made a move that the preacher should not receive the money from us. The bethel Trustees made a move that their funds should be shut and they would pay none, this caused a considerable contention, at length they withdrew their motion, the elder supplied us with preaching five times in a year for two hundred dollars. Finding that they supplied us so seldom, the Trustees of Bethel church passed a resolution that they would pay but one hundred dollars a year, as the elder only preached five times in a year for us, they called for the money, we paid him twenty-five dollars a quarter, but he being dissatisfied, returned the money back again, and would not have it unless we paid him fifty dollars. The Trustees concluded it was

enough for five sermons, and said they would pay no more, the elder of St. George's was determined to preach for us no more, unless we gave him two hundred dollars, and we were left alone for upwards of one year.

Mr. S— R— being appointed to the charge of Philadelphia, declared unless we would repeal the Supplement neither he nor any white preacher travelling or local, should preach any more for us; so we were left to ourselves, at length the preachers and stewards belonging to the Academy, proposed serving us on the same terms that we had offered to the St. George's preachers, and they preached for us better than a twelve month; and then demanded $150 per year; this not being complied with, they declined preaching for us, and we were once more left to ourselves, as an edict was passed by the elder that if any local preacher should serve us, he should be expelled from the connexion. John Emory, then elder of the Academy, published a circular letter in which we were disowned by the Methodists. A house was also hired and fitted up for worship not far from Bethel, and an invitation given to all who desired to be Methodists to resort thither. But being disappointed in this plan, Robert R. Roberts, the resident elder, came to Bethel, insisted on preaching to us, and taking the spiritual charge of the congregation, for we were Methodists. He was told he should come on some terms with the Trustees: his answer was that, "He did not come to consult with Richard Allen or other trustees, but to inform the congregation that on next Sunday afternoon, he would come and take the spiritual charge." We told him he could not preach for us under existing circumstances. "However, at the appointed time he came, but having taken previous advice we had our preacher in the pulpit when he came, and the house was so fixed that he could not get but more than half way to the pulpit. Finding himself disappointed he appealed to those who came with him as witnesses that "That man (meaning the preacher) had taken his appointment." Several respectable white citizens who knew the colored people had been ill used were present, and told us not to fear for they would see us righted, and not suffer Roberts to preach in a forcible manner, after which Roberts went away.

The next elder stationed in Philadelphia was Robert Birch, who following the example of his predecessor, came and published a meeting for himself. But the method just mentioned was adopted, and he had to go away disappointed. In consequence of this he applied to the Supreme Court for a writ of Mandamus, to know why the pulpit was denied him. Being elder, this brought on a law suit, which ended in our favor. Thus by the Providence of God we were delivered from a long, distressing and expensive suit which

could not be resumed, being determined by the Supreme Court. For this mercy we desire to be unfeignedly thankful.

About this time our colored friends in Baltimore were treated in a similar manner by the white preachers and Trustees, and many of them drove away; who were disposed to seek a place of worship, rather than go to law.

Many of the colored people in other places were in a situation nearly like those of Philadelphia and Baltimore, which induced us in April 1816 to call a general meeting, by way of Conference. Delegates from Baltimore and other places which met those of Philadelphia, and taking into consideration their grievances, and in order to secure the privileges, promote union and harmony among themselves, it was resolved, "That the people of Philadelphia, Baltimore, &c. &c., should become one body, under the name of the African Methodist Episcopal Church." We deemed it expedient to have a form of discipline, whereby we may guide our people in the fear of God, in the unity of the Spirit, and in the bonds of peace, and preserve us from that spiritual despotism which we have so recently experienced— remembering that we are not to lord it over God's heritage, as greedy dogs that can never have enough. But with long suffering, and bowels of compassion to bear each other's burthens, and so fulfil the Law of Christ, praying that our mutual striving together for the promulgation of the Gospel may be crowned with abundant success.

> The God of Bethel heard her cries,
> He let his power be seen;
> He stop'd the proud oppressors frown,
> And proved himself a King.

> Thou sav'd them in the trying hour,
> Ministers and councils joined
> And all stood ready to retain
> That helpless church of thine.

> Bethel surrounded by her foes,
> But not yet in despair,
> Christ heard her supplicating cries;
> The God of Bethel heard.

AFRICAN SUPPLEMENT

ARTICLES improving, amending, and altering the articles of association, of the "African Methodist Episcopal Church, commonly called, and known by the name of Bethel Church," of the City of Philadelphia, by and with consent of two thirds of the male members of said church.

ART. 1ST. It is hereby provided, and declared, That so much of the fourth article of association, as requires the consent of the elder for the time being, to grant alienations or conveyances of the estate, real or personal in this corporation, vested, or to be vested, be altered and repealed, provided that no grant, alienation, conveyance, mortgage or pledge of the estate, real or personal, in the said corporation, vested, or to be vested, shall be made by the said trustees or their successors, unless with consent of two thirds of the regular male members of the church, of at least twenty one years of age, and one year's standing.

ART. 2D. Whereas some persons, members of Bethel Church, having been duly suspended, upon complaint made of their having walked, or having been expelled from the said church, have afterwards been received as members of the Methodist Episcopal Church elsewhere, and notwithstanding their suspension, or expulsion as aforesaid, have claimed to be admitted into the private and close meetings of the said "Bethel Church," by reason of notes of admission obtained in some other church, of which they have been received as members—it is hereby declared, that no such person or persons whatever, while so suspended, or have been so expelled, nor any other person or persons, not being members of the said Methodist Episcopal Church, shall be admitted to commune, or to the love feasts, or any other close or private meeting whatever, held in said Bethel Church, or any other church or churches, which may hereafter become the property of this corporation, unless with the consent of two thirds of the trustees of said church for the time being.

ART. 3D. It is hereby further provided and declared, that a majority of the trustees and official members, convened agreeably to notice, given at least one Sabbath day previously to such meeting, shall and may nominate, and appoint, one or more persons of the African race, to exhort and preach in

Bethel church, and any other church or churches, which may hereafter become the property of this corporation, for such time and on such conditions as may be agreed on—provided that the exhorters and preachers so nominated and appointed, shall have been regularly licensed by the Quarterly Meeting Conference of the Bethel church, or some one of the Methodist Episcopal Churches elsewhere, and provided also, that the Elder of the Methodist Episcopal Church for the time being, may as heretofore claim, and shall have and possess, a right to preach once on every Sunday, and once during the course of the week, and no more, in any or all the houses set apart, by the aforesaid trustees or their successors of the said Bethel Church.

ART. 4TH. It is hereby provided and declared, that the trustees of Bethel Church, and their successors, or a majority of them, may open the said church or any church or churches, that may hereafter become the property of this corporation, and may appoint and hold a religious meeting or meetings there, provided that no person or persons, be admitted at such meeting or meetings to exhort or preach, unless they shall have been duly licensed thereto, conformably to the rules and discipline of the M. E. Church, or have leave of a majority of said trustees.

ART. 5TH. It is hereby further ordered and declared, that the Elder of the Methodist Episcopal Church for the time being in Philadelphia, shall in no case receive any person as a member of Bethel Church, nor shall any person be received as a member thereof, or being a member thereof, be suspended or expelled therefrom, unless by a majority of the trustees of said church, or their successors:—and that in case said elder shall refuse, or neglect to preach and exhort in the said church or churches, which shall hereafter become the property of this corporation, once every Sunday, and once during the course of the week, as is herein before provided, or shall neglect or refuse to attend therein, to administer the ordinances of baptism and the Lord's supper, in that case a majority of the trustees or their successors, may appoint any other person duly qualified, according to the rules and discipline of the Methodist Episcopal Church, to officiate in the place instead of the elder so refusing or neglecting—and if the said elder shall neglect or refuse to attend any quarterly conference, love feast, or meeting, for the trial of a disorderly member of said church, or any other meeting public or private, duly appointed by a majority of the trustees or their successors, it shall be lawful for them never-

theless, with the concurrence of one or more of their colored brethren, duly licensed to exhort or preach by the quarterly meeting conference of Bethel church—or with the concurrence of any other person or persons, so licensed by the Methodist Episcopal Church, to hold such quarterly meeting conference or love feast—and to proceed in the trial of such disorderly members, and to suspend or expel him or her, as may be right and just, to license qualified persons to exhort and preach; and, finally, to transact all business, and to proceed in their affairs, temporal and spiritual with the same effect, to all intents and purposes, as if the said elder was personally present, and consented thereto.

ART. 6TH. It is hereby further agreed and declared, that the elder of the Methodist Episcopal Church, for the time being, of the city of Philadelphia, shall in no case nominate any person to preach in Bethel church, or in any church or churches, which shall hereafter become the property of said corporation; unless with the concurrence of a majority of the trustees of the said church, or their successors—and that any nomination made without the concurrence of said trustees or a majority of them, shall be void.

ART. 7TH. And it is hereby agreed, provided, and declared, that any article or provision in the "articles of association," of the trustees and members of the African Methodist Episcopal Church, called Bethel church, heretofore made and agreed on, inconsistent with, or altered by these present articles, shall be deemed and taken to be repealed and absolutely void, so far as they may be inconsistent or altered.

The subscribing trustees and members of the African Methodist Episcopal Church, called Bethel church, heretofore incorporated under the style and title of The African Methodist Episcopal Church, of the city of Philadelphia, in the Commonwealth, which the said corporation as aforesaid, formed and established, having herein specified the improvements, amendments, and alterations which are desired, respectfully exhibit and present the same, to Joseph B. McKean, Esq. Attorney General of the Commonwealth of Pennsylvania, and to the honourable Judges of the Supreme Court of the said Commonwealth; in pursuance of an act of Assembly, entitled, "An act to confer on certain Associations of the citizens of this Commonwealth, the powers and immunities of corporation, or bodies politic in law." Passed the 6th day of April, 1791.

ACTS OF FAITH.

I believe, O God, that thou art an eternal, incomprehensible spirit, infinite in all perfections, who didst make all things out of nothing, and dost govern them all by thy wise providence.

Let me always adore thee with profound humility, as my Soverign Lord; and help me to love and praise thee with godlike affections, and suitable devotion.

I believe that in the unity of the Godhead there is a trinity of persons, that thou art perfectly one and perfectly three; one essence and three persons. I believe O blessed Jesus, that thou art of one substance with the father, the very and eternal God, that thou didst take upon thee our frail nature, that thou didst truly suffer, and wert crucified, dead and buried, to reconcile us to thy Father, and to be a sacrifice for sin.

I believe, that according to the types and prophecies which went before of thee, and according to thy own infallible prediction, thou didst by thy own power rise from the dead the third day, that thou didst ascend into Heaven, that there thou sittest on thy throne of glory adored by angels, and interceding for sinners.

I believe, that thou hast instituted and ordained holy mysteries as pledges of thy love, and for a continual commemoration of thy death; that thou hast not only given thyself to die for me, but to be my spiritual food and sustenance in that holy sacrament, to my great and endless comfort. O may I frequently approach thy altar with humility and devotion, and work in me all those holy and Heavenly affections, which become the remembrance of a crucified Saviour.

I believe, O Lord, that thou hast not abandoned me to the dim light of my own reason, to conduct me to happiness; but that thou hast revealed in the holy Scriptures whatever is necessary for me to believe and practice, in order to my eternal salvation.

O how noble and excellent are the precepts; how sublime and enlightening the truth; how persuasive and strong the motives; how powerful the assistances of thy holy religion, in which thou hast instructed me; my delight shall be in thy statutes, and I will not forget thy word.

I believe, it is my greatest honour and happiness to be thy disciple: how miserable and blind are those that live without God in the world, who despise the light of thy holy faith. Make me to part with all the enjoyments of life; nay, even life itself, rather than forfeit this jewel of great price. Blessed are the sufferings which are endured, happy is the death which is undergone

for Heavenly and immortal truth! I believe that thou hast prepared for those that love thee, everlasting mansions of glory; if I believe thee, O eternal happiness; Why does any thing appear difficult that leads to thee? Why should I not willingly resist unto blood to obtain thee? Why do the vain and empty employments of life take such fast hold of us? O perishing time! Why doest thou thus bewitch and deceive me? O blessed eternity! When shalt thou be my portion for ever?

ACTS OF HOPE.

O, my God! in all my dangers temporal and spiritual I will hope in thee who art Almighty power, and therefore able to relieve me, who art infinite goodness, and therefore ready and willing to assist me.

O precious blood of my dear Redeemer! O gaping wounds of my crucified Saviour! Who can contemplate the sufferings of God incarnate, and not raise his hope, and not put his trust in him. What though my body be crumbled into dust, and that dust blown over the face of the earth, yet I undoubtedly know my Redeemer lives, and shall raise me up at the last day; whether I am comforted or left desolate; whether I enjoy peace or am afflicted with temptations, whether I am healthful or sickly, succoured or abandoned by the good things of this life, I will always hope in thee, O my chiefest, infinite good.

Although the fig-tree shall not blossom, neither shall fruit be in the vines; although the labor of the olive shall fail, and the fields yield no meat; although the flock shall be cut off from the fold, and there shall be no herd in the stalls, yet I will rejoice in the Lord, I will joy in the God of my salvation.

What though I mourn and am afflicted here, and sigh under the miseries of this world for a time, I am sure that my tears shall one day be turned into joy, and that joy none shall take from me. Whoever hopes for the great things in this world, takes pains to attain them; how can my hopes of everlasting life be well ground, if I do not strive and labor for that eternal inheritance? I will never refuse the meanest labors, while I look to receive such glorious wages; I will never repine at any temporal loss, while I expect to gain such eternal rewards. Blessed hope! be thou my chief delight in life, and then I shall be steadfast and immoveable, always abounding in the work of the Lord, be thou my comfort and support at the hour of death, and then I shall contentedly leave this world, as a captive that is released from his imprisonment.

ACTS OF LOVE.

O infinite amiableness! When shall I love thee without bounds, without coldness or interruption which, alas! so often seize me here below? Let me never suffer any creature to be thy rival, or to share my heart with thee; let me have no other God, no other love, but only thee.

Whoever loves, desires to please the beloved object; and according to the degree of love is the greatness of desire; make me O God diligent and earnest in pleasing thee; let me cheerfully discharge the most painful and costly duties; and forsake friends, riches, ease and life itself, rather than disobey thee.

Whoever loves, desires the welfare and happiness of the beloved object; but thou, O dear Jesus, can'st receive no addition from my imperfect services; what shall I do to express my affection towards thee? I will relieve the necessities of my poor brethren, who are members of thy body; for he that loveth not his brother whom he has seen, how can he love God whom he hath not seen?

O crucified Jesus in whom I live, and without whom I die; mortify in me all sensual desires, inflame my heart with thy holy love, that I may no longer esteem the vanities of this world, but place my affections entirely on thee.

Let my last breath, when my soul shall leave my body, breathe forth love to thee, my God; I entered into life without acknowledging thee, let me therefore finish it in loving thee; O let the last act of life be love, remembering that God is love.

A NARRATIVE.

*O*f *the proceedings of the Coloured People during the awful calamity in Philadelphia, in the year 1793; and a refutation of some censures thrown upon them in some publications. By Absalom Jones and Richard Allen.*

In consequence of a partial representation of the conduct of the people who were employed to nurse the sick in the calamitous state of the city of Philadelphia, we were solicited by a number of those who felt themselves injured thereby, and by the advice of several respectable citizens, to step forward and declare facts as they really were; and seeing that from our situation, on account of the charge we took upon us, we had it more fully and gener-

ally in our power to know and observe the conduct and behaviour of those that were so employed.

Early in September, a solicitation appeared in the public papers, to the people of colour, to come forward and assist the distressed, perishing, and neglected sick; with a kind of assurance, that people of our colour were not liable to take the infection; upon which we and a few others met and consulted how to act on so truly alarming and melancholy an occasion. After some conversation, we found a freedom to go forth, confiding in him who can preserve in the midst of a burning fiery furnace. Sensible that it was our duty to do all the good we could to our suffering fellow mortals, we set out to see where we could be useful. The first we visited was a man in Emsley's Alley, who was dying, and his wife lay dead at the time in the house. There were none to assist but two poor helpless children. We administered what relief we could, and applied to the overseers of the poor to have the woman buried. We visited upwards of twenty families that day—they were scenes of woe indeed! The Lord was pleased to strengthen us, and remove all fear from us, and disposed our hearts to be as useful as possible. In order the better to regulate our conduct, we called on the mayor next day, to consult with him how to proceed, so as to be most useful. The first object he recommended was a strict attention to the sick, and the procuring of nurses. This was attended to by Absalom Jones and William Gray; and in order that the distressed might know where to apply, the mayor advertised the public that upon application to them they would be supplied. Soon after, the mortality increasing, the difficulty of getting a corpse taken away was such, that few were willing to do it, when offered great rewards. The coloured people were looked to. We then offered our services in the public papers, by advertising that we would remove the dead and procure nurses. Our services were the production of real sensibility; we sought not fee nor reward, until the increase of the disorder rendered our labour so arduous that we were not adequate to the service we had assumed. The mortality increasing rapidly, obliged us to call in the assistance of five hundred men in the awful charge of interring the dead. They, with great reluctance, were prevailed upon to join us. It was very uncommon, at this time, to find any one that would go near, much more, handle, a sick or dead person.

When the sickness became general, and several of the physicians died, and most of the survivors were exhausted by sickness or fatigue, that good man, Dr. Rush, called us more immediately to attend upon the sick, knowing that we could both bleed. He told us that we could increase our utility

by attending to his instructions, and accordingly directed us where to pro-
cure medicine duly prepared, with proper directions how to administer
them, and at what stages of the disorder to bleed; and when we found our-
selves incapable of judging what was proper to he done, to apply to him, and
he would, if able, attend them himself, or send Edward Fisher, his pupil,
which he often did; and Mr. Fisher manifested his humanity by an affec-
tionate attention for their relief. This has been no small satisfaction to us; for
we think that when a physician was not attainable, we have been the instru-
ments in the hands of God, for saving the lives of some hundreds of our suf-
fering fellow mortals.

We feel ourselves sensibly aggrieved by the censorious epithets of many
who did not render the least assistance in the time of necessity, yet are liber-
al of their censure of us, for the prices paid for our services, when no one
knew how to make a proposal to any one they wanted to assist them. At first
we made no charge, but left it to those we served in removing their dead, to
give what they thought fit. We set no price until the reward was fixed by
those we had served. After paying the people we had to assist us, our com-
pensation was much less than many will believe.

We do assure the public that all the money we received for burying, and
for coffins which we ourselves purchased and procured, has not defrayed the
expense of wages which we had to pay those whom we employed to assist us.
The following statement is accurately made:

Cash received.—The whole amount of cash
 received for burying the dead, and for £233 10 4
 burying beds, is

Cash paid for coffins, for which we received 33 00 0
 nothing
For the hire of five men, three of them 70 days
 each, and the other two 63 days each, at 378 00 0
 22s. 6d. per day 411 00 0

Debts due us, for which we expect but little, 110 00 0
From this statement, for the truth of which
we solemnly vouch, it is evident, and we
sensibly feel the operation of the fact, that
we are out of pocket 177 9 8

Besides the cost of hearses, the maintainance of our families for seventy days, (being the period of our labours) and the support of the five hired men, during the respective times of their being employed; which expenses, together with sundry gifts we occasionally made to poor families, which might reasonably and properly be introduced, to show our actual situation with regard to profit; but it is enough to exhibit to the public, from the above specified items, of cash paid and cash received, without taking into view the other expenses, that by the employment we were engaged in we lost £177 9s. 8d. But if the other expenses, which we have actually paid, are added to that sum, how much then may we not say we have suffered! We leave the public to judge.

It may possibly appear strange to some who know how constantly we were employed, and that we should have received no more cash than £233 10s. 4d. But we repeat our assurance that this is the fact; and we add another, which will serve the better to explain it: we have buried several hundreds of poor persons and strangers, for which service we have never received nor never asked any compensation.

We feel ourselves hurt most by a partial, censorious photograph, in Mr. Carey's 2d edition of his account of the sickness, &c. in Philadelphia, pages 76 and 77, where he asperses the blacks alone, for having taken the advantage of the distressed situation of the people.

That some extravagant prices were paid we admit; but how came they to be demanded? The reason is plain. It was with difficulty persons could be had to supply the wants of the sick as nurses; applications became more and more numerous, the consequence was, when we procured them at six dollars per week, and called upon them to go where they were wanted, we found they were gone elsewhere. Here was a disappointment. Upon inquiring the cause, we found they had been allured away by others who offered greater wages, until they got from two to four dollars per day. We had no restraint upon the people. It was natural for people in low circumstances to accept a voluntary, bounteous reward; especially under the loathsomeness of many of the sick, when nature shuddered at the thought of the infection, and the task assigned was aggravated by lunacy, and being left much alone with them. Had Mr. Carey been solicited to such an undertaking, for hire, quere—what would he have demanded? But Mr. Carey, although chosen a member of that band of worthies who have so eminently distinguished themselves by their labours for the relief of the sick and helpless; yet, quickly after his election, left them to struggle with their arduous and hazardous task, by leaving the city. 'Tis true

Mr. Carey was no hireling, and had a right to flee, and upon his return, to plead the cause of those who fled; yet, we think, he was wrong in giving so partial and injurious an account of the coloured nurses; if they have taken advantage of the public distress, is it any more than he hath done of its desire for information? We believe he has made more money by the sale of his "Scraps" than a dozen of the greatest extortioners among the coloured nurses. The great prices paid did not escape the observation of that worthy and vigilant magistrate, Matthew Clarkson, mayor of the city, and president of the committee. He sent for us, and requested we would use our influence to lessen the wages of the nurses. But on informing him of the cause, i. e. that of the people over-bidding one another, it was concluded unnecessary to attempt any thing on that head; therefore it was left to the people concerned. That there were some few coloured people guilty of plundering the distressed we acknowledge; but in that they only are pointed out, and made mention of, we esteem partial and injurious. We know as many whites who were guilty of it; but this is looked over, while the blacks are held up to censure. Is it a greater crime for a black to pilfer than for a white to privateer?

We wish not to offend; but when an unprovoked attempt is made to make us blacker than we are, it becomes less necessary to be over-cautious on that account; therefore we shall take the liberty to tell of the conduct of some of the whites.

We know that six pounds was demanded by and paid to a white woman, for putting a corpse into a coffin; and forty dollars was demanded and paid to four white men, for bringing it down the stairs.

Mr. and Mrs. Taylor both died in one night. A white womon had the care of them. After they were dead she called on Jacob Servoss, Esq. for her pay, demanding six pounds for laying them out. Upon seeing a bundle with her, he suspected she had pilfered. On searching her, Mr. Taylor's buckles were found in her pocket, with other things.

An elderly lady, Mrs. Malony, was given into the care of a white woman. She died. We were called to remove the corpse. When we came, the woman was lying so drunk that she did not know what we were doing; but we knew that she had one of Mrs. Malony's rings on her finger.

It is unpleasant to point out the bad and unfeeling conduct of any colour; yet the defence we have undertaken obliges us to remark, that although hardly any of good character at that time could be procured; yet only two coloured women were at that time in the hospital; and they were retained, and the others discharged, when it was reduced to order and good government.

The bad consequences many of our colour apprehend from a partial rela-
tion of our conduct are, that it will prejudice the minds of the people in gen-
eral against us; because it is impossible that one individual can have knowl-
edge of all; therefore at some future day, when some of the most virtuous that
were upon most praiseworthy motives, induced to serve the sick, may fall
into the service of a family that are strangers to him or her, and it is discov-
ered that it is one of those stigmatised wretches, what may we suppose will
be the consequence? Is it not reasonable to think the person will be abhorred,
despised, and perhaps dismissed from employment, to their great disadvan-
tage? would not this be hard? and have we not therefore sufficient reason to
seek for redress? We can with certainty assure the public that we have seen
more humanity, more real sensibility from the poor coloured than from the
poor whites. When many of the former, of their own accord, rendered serv-
ices where extreme necessity called for it, the general part of the poor white
people were so dismayed, that instead of attempting to be useful, they, in a
manner, hid themselves. A remarkable instance of this.—A poor, afflicted,
dying man stood at his chamber window, praying and beseeching every one
that passed by to help him to a drink of water. A number of white people
passed and instead of being moved by the poor man's distress, they hurried
as fast as they could out of the sound of his cries, until at length a gentleman,
who seemed to be a foreigner, came up. He could not pass by, but had not
resolution enough to go into the house. He held eight dollars in his hand,
and offered it to several as a reward for giving the poor man a drink of water;
but was refused by every one, until a poor coloured man came up. The gen-
tleman offered the eight dollars to him, if he would relieve the poor man with
a little water. "Master," replied the good-natured fellow, "I will supply the
gentleman with water, but surely I will not take your money for it;" nor
could he be prevailed upon to accept his bounty. He went in, supplied the
poor object with water, and rendered him every service he could.

A poor coloured man, named Sampson, went constantly from house to
house where distress was, and no assistance, without fee or reward. He was
smitten with the disorder, and died. After his death his family were neglect-
ed by those he had served.

Sarah Bass, a coloured widow woman, gave all the assistance she could, in
several families, for which she did not receive any thing; and when any thing
was offered her, she left it to the option of those she served.

A coloured woman nursed Richard Mason and son. They died. Richard's
widow, considering the risk the poor woman had run, and from observing

the fears that sometimes rested on her mind, expected she would have demanded something considerable; but upon asking her what she demanded, her reply was, "fifty cents per day." Mrs. Mason intimated it was not sufficient for her attendance. She replied that it was enough for what she had done, and would take no more. Mrs. Mason's feelings were such, that she settled an annuity of six pounds a year on her for life. Her name was Mary Scott.

An elderly coloured woman nursed —— with great diligence and attention. When recovered, he asked what he must give her for her services—she replied, "a dinner, master, on a cold winter's day." And thus she went from place to place, rendering every service in her power, without an eye to reward.

A young coloured woman was requested to attend one night upon a white man and his wife, who were very ill. No other person could be had. Great wages were offered her—she replied, "I will not go for money: if I go for money, God will see it, and may be make me take the disorder and die; but if I go and take no money, he may spare my life." She went about 9 o'clock, and found them both on the floor. She could procure no candle or other light; but staid with them about two hours, and then left them. They both died that night. She was afterwards very ill with the fever. Her life was spared.

Cæsar Cranchal, a man of colour, offered his services to attend the sick, and said, "I will not take your money—I will not sell my life for money." It is said he died with the flux.

A coloured lad, at the widow Gilpin's, was entrusted with his young master's keys, on his leaving the city, and transacted his business with the greatest honesty and dispatch: having unloaded a vessel for him in the time, and loaded it again.

A woman that nursed David Bacon charged with exemplary moderation, and said she would not have any more.

It may be said in vindication of the conduct of those who discovered ignorance or incapacity in nursing, that it is, in itself, a considerable art, derived from experience as well as the exercise of the finer feelings of humanity. This experience nine tenths of those employed, it is probable, were wholly strangers to.

We do not recollect such acts of humanity from the poor white people, in all the round we have been engaged in. We could mention many other instances of the like nature, but think it needless.

It is unpleasant for us to make these remarks, but justice to our colour

demands it. Mr. Carey pays William Gray and us a compliment; he says our services and others of our colour, have been very great, &c. By naming us, he leaves those others in the hazardous state of being classed with those who are called the "vilest." The few that were discovered to merit public censure were brought to justice, which ought to have sufficed, without being canvassed over in his "Trifle" of a pamphlet; which causes us to be more particular, and endeavour to recall the esteem of the public for our friends and the people of colour, as far as they may be found worthy; for we conceive, and experience proves it, that an ill name is easier given than taken away. We have many unprovoked enemies, who begrudge us the liberty we enjoy, and are glad to hear of any complaint against our colour, be it just or unjust; in consequence of which we are more earnestly endeavouring all in our power, to warn, rebuke, and exhort our African friends to keep a conscience void of offence towards God and man; and, at the same time, would not be backward to interfere, when stigmas or oppression appear pointed at, or attempted against them, unjustly; and we are confident we shall stand justified in the sight of the candid and judicious for such conduct.

We can assure the public that there were as many white as black people detected in pilfering, although the number of the latter, employed as nurses, was twenty times as great as the former, and that there is, in our opinion, as great a proportion of white as of black inclined to such practices; and it is rather to be admired that so few instances of pilfering and robbery happened, considering the great opportunities there were for such things. We do not know of more than five coloured people suspected of any thing clandestine, out of the great number employed. The people were glad to get any person to assist them. A coloured person was preferred, because it was supposed they were not so likely to take the disorder. The most worthless were acceptable; so that it would have been no cause of wonder if twenty causes of complaint had occurred for one that hath. It has been alledged that many of the sick were neglected by the nurses; we do not wonder at it, considering their situation: in many instances up night and day, without any one to relieve them, worn down with fatigue and want of sleep, they could not, in many cases, render that assistance which was needful. Where we visited the causes of complaint on this score were not numerous. The case of the nurses, in many instances, were deserving of commisseration: the patient raging and frightful to behold. It has frequently required two persons, to hold them from running away; others have made attempts to jump out of a window; in many chambers they were nailed down, and the door kept locked, to prevent them

from running away or breaking their necks; others lay vomiting blood, and screaming enough to chill them with horror. Thus were many of the nurses circumstanced, alone, until the patient died; then called away to another scene of distress, and thus have been for a week or ten days left to do the best they could, without any sufficient rest, many of them having some of their dearest connexions sick at the time, and suffering for want, while their husband, wife, father, mother, &c. have been engaged in the service of the white people. We mention this to show the difference between this and nursing in common cases. We have suffered equally with the whites; our distress hath been very great, but much unknown to the white people. Few have been the whites that paid attention to us, while the coloured persons were engaged in others' service. We can assure the public that we have taken four and five coloured people in a day to be buried. In several instances, when they have been seized with the sickness while nursing, they have been turned out of the house, wandering and destitute, until they found shelter wherever they could (as many of them would not be admitted to their former homes)—they have languished alone, and we know of one who even died in a stable. Others acted with more tenderness: when their nurses were taken sick, they had proper care taken of them at their houses. We know of two instances of this. It is even to this day a generally received opinion in this city, that our colour was not so liable to the sickness as the whites. We hope our friends will pardon us for setting this matter in its true state.

The public were informed that in the West Indies and other places where this terrible malady had been, it was observed that the blacks were not affected with it. Happy would it have been for you, and much more so for us, if this observation had been verified by our experience.

When the people of colour had the sickness and died, we were imposed upon, and told it was not with the prevailing sickness, until it became too notorious to be denied; then we were told some few died, but not many. Thus were our services extorted at the peril of our lives. Yet you accuse us of extorting a little money from you.

The bill of mortality for the year 1793, published by Matthew Whitehead and John Ormrod, clerks, and Joseph Dolby, sexton, will convince any reasonable man that will examine it, that as many coloured people died in proportion as others. In 1792 there were 67 of our colour buried, and in 1793, it amounted to 305: thus the burials among us have increased more than fourfold. Was not this in a great degree the effects of the services of the unjustly vilified coloured people?

Perhaps it may be acceptable to the reader to know how we found the sick affected by the sickness. Our opportunities of hearing and seeing them have been very great. They were taken with a chill, a head-ache, a sick stomach, with pains in their limbs and back. This was the way the sickness in general began; but all were not affected alike. Some appeared but slightly affected with some of those symptoms. What confirmed us in the opinion of a person being smitten was the colour of their eyes. In some it raged more furiously than in others. Some have languished for seven and ten days, and appeared to get better the day, or some hours before they died, while others were cut off in one, two, or three days; but their complaints were similar. Some lost their reason, and raged with all the fury madness could produce, and died in strong convulsions; others retained their reason to the last, and seemed rather to fall asleep than die. We could not help remarking that the former were of strong passions, and the latter of a mild temper. Numbers died in a kind of dejection: they concluded they must go, (so the phrase for dying was,) and therefore in a kind of fixed, determined state of mind went off.

It struck our minds with awe to have application made by those in health, to take charge of them in their sickness, and of their funeral. Such applications have been made to us. Many appeared as though they thought they must die and not live; some have lain on the floor to be measured for their coffins and graves.

A gentleman called one evening to request a good nurse might be got for him when he was sick, and to superintend his funeral, and gave particular directions how he would have it conducted. It seemed a surprising circumstance; for the man appeared at the time to be in perfect health; but calling, two or three days after, to see him, found a woman dead in the house, and the man so far gone, that to administer any thing for his recovery was needless—he died that evening. We mention this as an instance of the dejection and despondence that took hold on the minds of thousands, and are of opinion that it aggravated the case of many; while others who bore up cheerfully, got up again, that probably would otherwise have died.

When the mortality came to its greatest stage, it was impossible to procure sufficient assistance; therefore many whose friends and relations had left them, died unseen and unassisted. We have found them in various situations—some lying on the floor, as bloody as if they had been dipped in it, without any appearance of their having had even a drink of water for their relief; others lying on a bed with their clothes on, as if they had come

fatigued, and lain down to rest; some appeared as if they had fallen dead on the floor, from the position we found them in.

Surely our task was hard; yet through mercy we were enabled to go on.

One thing we observed in several instances: when we were called, on the first appearance of the disorder, to bleed, the person frequently, on the opening of a vein, and before the operation was near over, felt a change for the better, and expressed a relief in their chief complaints; and we made it a practice to take more blood from them than is usual in other cases. These, in a general way, recovered; those who omitted bleeding any considerable time, after being taken by the sickness, rarely expressed any change they felt in the operation.

We feet a great satisfaction in believing that we have been useful to the sick, and thus publicly thank Doctor Benjamin Rush for enabling us to be so. We have bled upwards of eight hundred people, and do declare we have not received to the value of a dollar and a half therefor. We were willing to imitate the doctor's benevolence, who, sick or well, kept his house open day and night, to give what assistance he could in this time of trouble.

Several affecting instances occurred when we were engaged in burying the dead. We have been called to bury some, who, when we came, we found alone; at other places we found a parent dead, and none but little innocent babes to be seen, whose ignorance led them to think their parent was asleep; on account of their situation, and their little prattle, we have been so wounded, and our feelings so hurt, that we almost concluded to withdraw from our undertaking; but seeing others so backward, we still went on.

An affecting instance.—A woman died; we were sent for to bury her. On our going into the house, and taking the coffin in, a dear little innocent accosted us with—"mamma is asleep—don't wake her!" but when she saw us put her into the coffin, the distress of the child was so great, that it almost overcame us. When she demanded why we put her mamma in the box, we did not know how to answer her, but committed her to the care of a neighbour, and left her with heavy hearts. In other places where we have been to take the corpse of a parent, and have found a group of little ones alone, some of them in a measure capable of knowing their situation; their cries, and the innocent confusion of the little ones, seemed almost too much for human nature to bear. We have picked up little children that were wandering they knew not where, (whose parents had been cut off,) and taken them to the orphan house; for at this time the dread that prevailed over people's minds was so general, that it was a rare instance to see one neighbour visit another,

and friends, when they met in the streets, were afraid of each other; much less would they admit into their houses the distressed orphan that had been where the sickness was. This extreme seemed in some instances to have the appearance of barbarity. With reluctance we call to mind the many opportunities there were in the power of individuals to be useful to their fellow men, yet through the terror of the times were omitted.

A coloured man, riding through the street, saw a man push a woman out of the house; the woman staggered and fell on her face in the gutter, and was not able to turn herself. The coloured man thought she was drunk, but observing she was in danger of suffocation, alighted, and taking the woman up, found her perfectly sober, but so far gone with the disorder that she was not able to help herself. The hard hearted man that threw her down, shut the door and left her. In such a situation she might have perished in a few minutes. We heard of it, and took her to Bush Hill. Many of the white people, who ought to be patterns for us to follow after, have acted in a manner that would make humanity shudder. We remember an instance of cruelty, which, we trust, no coloured man would be guilty of: Two sisters, orderly, decent white women, were sick with the fever. One of them recovered, so as to come to the door. A neighbouring white man saw her, and in an angry tone asked her if her sister was dead or not? She answered, "no;" upon which he replied, "damn her, if she don't die before morning, I will make her die!" The poor woman, shocked at such an expression from this monster of a man, made a modest reply, upon which he snatched up a tub of water, and would have dashed it over her, if he had not been prevented by a coloured man. He then went and took a couple of fowls out of a coop, (which had been given them for nourishment) and threw them into an open alley. He had his wish—the poor woman that he would make die, died that night.

A white man threatened to shoot us, if we passed by his house with a corpse. We buried him three days after.

We have been pained to see the widows come to us, crying and wringing their hands, and in very great distress, on account of their husbands' death; having nobody to help them, they were obliged to come and get their husbands buried. Their neighbours were afraid to go to their help, or to condole with them. We ascribe such unfriendly conduct to the frailty of human nature.

Notwithstanding the compliment Mr. Carey hath paid us, we have found reports spread of our taking between one and two hundred beds from houses where people died. Such slanderers as these, who propagate such wilful

lies, are dangerous, although unworthy; and we wish, if any person hath the least suspicion of us, they would endeavour to bring us to the punishment which such attrocious conduct must deserve; and by this means the innocent will he cleared from reproach, and the guilty known.

We shall now conclude with the following proverb, which we think applicable to those of our colour, who exposed their lives in the late afflicting dispensation:

> God and a soldier all men do adore
> In time of war, and not before;
> When the war is over, and all things righted,
> God is forgotten, and the soldier slighted.

To Matthew Clarkson, Esq. Mayor of the City of Philadelphia.

SIR—For the personal respect we bear you, and for thee satisfaction of the mayor, we declare, that to the best of our remembrance we had the care of the following beds, and no more.

Two belonging to James Starr we buried; upon taking them up, we found one damaged, the blankets &c. belonging to it were stolen. It was refused to be accepted of by his son Moses. It was buried again, and remains so for aught we know; the other was returned, and accepted of.

We buried two belonging to Samuel Fisher, merchant; one of them was taken up by us, to carry a sick person on to Bush Hill, and there left; the other was buried in a grave, under a corpse.

Two beds were buried for Thomas Willing—one six feet deep in his garden, and lime and water thrown upon it; the other was in the potter's field, and further knowledge of it we have not.

We burned one bed, with other furniture and clothing, belonging to the late Mayor, Samuel Powell, on his farm on the west side of Schuylkill river. We buried one of his beds.

For—Dickinson we buried a bed in a lot of Richard Allen, which we have good cause to believe was stolen.

One bed was buried for a person in Front street, whose name is unknown to us—it was buried in the potter's field by a person employed for the purpose. We told him he might take it up again, after it had been buried a week, and apply it to his own use, as he said that he had lately been discharged from the hospital, and had none to lie on.

Thomas Leiper's two beds were buried in the potter's field, and remained there a week, and was then taken up by us, for the use of the sick that we took to Bush Hill, and left there.

We buried one for—Smith, in the potter's field, which was returned, except the furniture, which we believe was stolen.

One other we buried for—Davis, in Vine street; it was buried near Schuylkill, and we believe continues so.

A bed from—Guest, in Second street, was buried in the potter's field, and is there yet for any thing we know.

One bed we buried in the Presbyterian burial ground, the corner of Pine and Fourth streets, and we believe was taken up by the owner, Thomas Mitchell.

—Milligan, in Second street, had a bed buried by us in the Potter's field. We have no further knowledge of it.

This is a true statement of matters respecting the beds, as far as we were concerned. We never undertook the charge of more than their burial, knowing they were liable to be taken away by evil minded persons. We think it beneath the dignity of an honest man, (although injured in his reputation by wicked and envious persons) to vindicate or support his character by an oath or legal affirmation. We fear not our enemies—let them come forward with their charges—we will not flinch; and if they can fix any crime upon us, we refuse not to suffer.

Sir, you have cause to believe our lives were endangered in more cases than one, in the time of the late mortality, and that we were so discouraged, that had it not been for your persuasion, we would have relinquished our disagreeable and dangerous employments; and we hope there is no impropriety in soliciting a certificate of your approbation of our conduct, so far as it hath come to your knowledge.

With an affectionate regard and esteem,
 We are your friends,
 ABSALOM JONES,
 RICHARD ALLEN.
January 7th, 1794.

———

Having, during the prevalence of the late malignant disorder, had almost daily opportunities of seeing the conduct of Absalom Jones and Richard

Allen, and the people employed by them to bury the dead—I with cheerful-
ness give this testimony of my approbation of their proceedings, so far as they
came under my notice. Their diligence, attention, and decency of deport-
ment, afforded me, at the time, much satisfaction.

MATTHEW CLARKSON, Mayor.
Philadelphia, Jan. 23d, 1794.

AN ADDRESS.

To those who keep slaves, and approve the practice.
The judicious part of mankind, will think it unreasonable, that a supe-
rior good conduct is looked for from our race, by those who stigmatize us as
men, whose baseness is incurable, and may therefore be held in a state of
servitude, that a merciful man would not doom a beast to; yet you try what
you can, to prevent our rising from a state of barbarism you represent us to
be in, but we can tell you from a degree of experience, that a black man,
although reduced to the most abject state human nature is capable of, short
of real madness, can think, reflect, and feel injuries, although it may not be
with the same degree of keen resentment and revenge, that you who have
been, and are our great oppressors would manifest, if reduced to the pitiable
condition of a slave. We believe if you would try the experiment of taking a
few black children, and cultivate their minds with the same care, and let
them have the same prospect in view as to living in the world, as you would
wish for your own children, you would find upon the trial, they were not
inferior in mental endowments. I do not wish to make you angry, but excite
attention to consider how hateful slavery is, in the sight of that God who
hath destroyed kings and princes, for their oppression of the poor slaves.
Pharoah and his princes with the posterity of king Saul, were destroyed by
the protector and avenger of slaves. Would you not suppose the Israelites to
be utterly unfit for freedom, and that it was impossible for them, to obtain
to any degree of excellence? Their history shews how slavery had debased
their spirits. Men must be wilfully blind, and extremely partial, that cannot
see the contrary effects of liberty and slavery upon the mind of man; I truly
confess the vile habits often acquired in a state of servitude, are not easily
thrown off; the example of the Israelites shews, who with all that Moses
could do to reclaim them from it, still continued in their habits more or less;

and why will you look for better from us, why will you look for grapes from thorns, or figs from thistles? it is in our posterity enjoying the same priviledges with your own, that you ought to look for better things.

When you are pleaded with, do not you reply as Pharoah did, "Wherefore do ye Moses and Aaron let the people from their work, behold the people of the land now are many, and you make them rest from their burthens." We wish you to consider, that God himself was the first pleader of the cause of slaves.

That God who knows the hearts of all men, and the propensity of a slave to hate his oppressor, hath strictly forbidden it to his chosen people, "Thou shalt not abhor an Egyptian, because thou wast a stranger in his land." Deut. 23. 7. The meek and humble Jesus, the great pattern of humanity, and every other virtue that can adorn and dignify men, hath commanded to love our enemies, to do good to them that hate and despitefully use us. I feel the obligations, I wish to impress them on the minds of our colored brethren, and that we may all forgive you, as we wish to be forgiven, we think it a great mercy to have all anger and bitterness removed from our minds; I appeal to your own feelings, if it is not very disquiting to feel yourselves under dominion of wrathful disposition.

If you love your children, if you love your country, if you love the God of love, clear your hands from slaves, burthen not your children or your country with them, my heart has been sorry for the blood shed of the oppressors, as well as the oppressed, both appear guilty of each others blood, in the sight of him who hath said, he that sheddeth man's blood, by man shall his blood be shed.

Will you, because you have reduced us to the unhappy condition our color is in, plead our incapacity for freedom, and our contented condition under oppression, as a sufficient cause for keeping us under the grevious yoke. I have shown the cause,—I will also shew why they appear contented as they can in your sight, but the dreadful insurrections they have made when opportunity has offered, is enough to convince a reasonable man, that great uneasiness and not contentment, is the inhabitant of their hearts. God himself hath pleaded their cause, he hath from time to time raised up instruments for that purpose, sometimes mean and contemptable in your sight, at other times he hath used such as it hath pleased him, with whom you have not thought it beneath your dignity to contend. Many have been convinced of their error, condemned their former conduct, and become zealous advocates for the cause of those, whom you will not suffer to plead for themselves.

TO THE PEOPLE OF COLOUR.

FEELING an engagement of mind for your welfare, I address you with an affectionate sympathy, having been a slave, and as desirous of freedom as any of you; yet the bands of bondage were so strong that no way appeared for my release; yet at times a hope arose in my heart that a way would open for it; and when my mind was mercifully visited with the feeling of the love of God, then these hopes increased, and a confidence arose that he would make way for my enlargement; and as a patient waiting was necessary, I was sometimes favoured with it; at other times I was very impatient. Then the prospect of liberty almost vanished away, and I was in darkness and perplexity.

I mention experience to you, that your hearts may not sink at the discouraging prospects you may have, and that you may put your trust in God, who sees your condition; and as a merciful father pitieth his children, so doth God pity them that love him; and as your hearts are inclined to serve God, you will feel an affectionate regard towards your masters and mistresses, so called, and the whole family in which you live. This will be seen by them, and tend to promote your liberty, especially with such as have feeling masters; and if they are otherwise, you will have the favour and love of God dwelling in your hearts, which you will value more than any thing else, which will be a consolation in the worst condition you can be in, and no master can deprive you of it, and as life is short and uncertain, and the chief end of our having a being in this world is to be prepared for a better, I wish you to think of this more than any thing else; then you will have a view of that freedom which the sons of God enjoy; and if the troubles of your condition end with your lives, you will be admitted to the freedom which God hath prepared for those of all colours that love him. Here the power of the most cruel master ends, and all sorrow and fears are wiped away.

To you who are favoured with freedom—let your conduct manifest your gratitude toward the compassionate masters who have set you free; and let no rancour or ill-will lodge in your breast for any bad treatment you may have received from any. If you do, you transgress against God, who will not hold you guiltless. He would not suffer it even in his beloved people Israel; and you think he will allow it unto us? Many of the white people have been instruments in the hands of God for our good; even such as have held us in captivity, are now pleading our cause with earnestness and zeal; and I am

sorry to say, that too many think more of the evil than of the good they have received, and instead of taking the advice of their friends, turn from it with indifference. Much depends upon us for the help of our colour—more than many are aware. If we are lazy and idle, the enemies of freedom plead it as a cause why we ought not to be free, and say we are better in a state of servitude, and that giving us our liberty would be an injury to us, and by such conduct we strengthen the bands of oppression, and keep many in bondage who are more worthy than ourselves. I entreat you to consider the obligations we lie under to help forward the cause of freedom. We who know how bitter the cup is of which the slave hath to drink, O how ought we to feel for those who yet remain in bondage! will even our friends excuse—will God pardon us—for the part we act in making strong the hands of the enemies of our colour?

A short Address to the friends of him who hath no helper.

I FEEL an inexpressible gratitude towards you who have engaged in the cause of the African race; you have wrought a deliverance for many from more than Egyptian bondage; your labours are unremitted for their complete redemption from the cruel subjection they are in. You feel our afflictions— you sympathize with us in the heart-rending distress, when the husband is separated from the wife, and the parents from the children, who are never more to meet in this world. The tear of sensibility trickles from your eye to see the sufferings that keep us from increasing. Your righteous indignation is roused at the means taken to supply the place of the murdered babe; you see our race more effectually destroyed than was in Pharaoh's power to effect upon Israel's sons; you blow the trumpet against the mighty evil; you make the tyrants tremble; you strive to raise the slave to the dignity of a man; you take our children by the hand to lead them in the path of virtue, by your care of our education; you are not ashamed to call the most abject of our race brethren, children of one Father, who hath made of one blood all the nations of the earth. You ask for this, nothing for yourselves, nothing but what is worthy the cause you are engaged in; nothing but that we would be friends to ourselves, and not strengthen the bands of oppression by an evil conduct, when led out of the house of bondage. May He who hath arisen to plead our cause, and engaged you as volunteers in the service, add to your numbers, until the princes shall come forth from Egypt, and Ethiopia stretch out her hands unto God.

RICHARD ALLEN.

Ye ministers that are called to preaching,
 Teachers and exhorters too,
Awake! behold your harvest wasting;
 Arise! there is no rest for you.

To think upon that strict commandment
 That God has on his teachers laid:
The sinners' blood, who die unwarned,
 Shall fall upon their shepherd's head.

But, O dear brethren, let's be doing—
 Behold the nations in distress;
The Lord of hosts forbid their ruin,
 Before the day of grace is past.

We read of wars and great commotions,
 Before the great and dreadful day:
Oh! sinners, turn your sinful courses,
 And trifle not your time away.

But oh! dear sinners, that's not all that's dreadful;
 You must before your God appear,
To give an account of your transactions,
 And how you spent your time when here.

Our Saviour's first and great work was that of the salvation of men's souls; yet we find that of the multitudes who came or were brought to him labouring under sickness and disorders, he never omitted one opportunity of doing good to their bodies, or sent away one that applied to him without a perfect cure; though sometimes, for the trial of their faith, he suffered himself to be importuned. And that he also often administered to the necessities of the poor in money, is plain from several passages of his life, one of which may suffice for the present, viz. When satan had entered into Judas, and our blessed Saviour had said, "That thou doest do quickly;" none of the other

disciples knew for what intent he had so spoken; for some of them thought, because Judas had the bag or common purse, that either he had ordered him to buy what was necessary against the feast, or (as was usual, no doubt, otherwise they could not have supposed it) that he should give something to the poor.

To this unanswerable proof from our Saviour's practice maybe added his repeated precepts and exhortations; for his examples and doctrines were always of a piece. A new commandment, says he, I give unto you, that ye love one another. By this shall all men know that ye are my disciples, if ye have love one to another. This is my commandment, that ye love one another as I have loved you. Greater love hath no man than this, that a man lay down his life for his friends. I say unto you which hear, love your enemies, and do good to them which hate you; bless them that curse you, and pray for them which despitefully use you. Love your enemies, and do good and lend, hoping for nothing again; and your reward shall be great, and ye shall be the children of the Highest; for he is kind to the unthankful and to the evil. Be ye therefore merciful as your father also is merciful. From these few passages may be collected the nature, extent, and necessity of Christian charity. In its nature it is pure and disinterested, remote from all hopes or views of worldly return or recompence from the persons we relieve. We are to do good and lend, hoping for nothing again. In its extent it is unlimited and universal; and though it requires that an especial regard be had to our fellow Christians, is confined to no persons, countries, or places, but takes in all mankind, strangers as well as relations or acquaintances, enemies as well as friends, the evil and unthankful, as well as the good and grateful. It has no other measure than the love of God to us, who gave his only begotten Son, and the love of our Saviour, who laid down his life for us, even whilst we were his enemies. It reaches not only to the good of the soul, but also to such assistance as may be necessary for the supply of the bodily wants of our fellow creatures.

And the absolute necessity of practising this duty is the very same with that of being Christians; this being the only sure mark by which we may be known and distinguished from such as are not Christians or disciples of Christ. By this shall all men know that ye are my disciples, if ye have love one to another.

Hearken to St. Paul, speaking of this most excellent way or duty, and then judge ye, my brethren, of the necessity of putting it in practice. Though I speak with the tongue of men and angels, and have not charity, I am become as a sounding brass or a tinkling cymbal. And though I have the gift of

prophecy, and understand all mysteries, and all knowledge, and though I have all faith, so that I could remove mountains, and have not charity, I am nothing. And though I bestow all my goods to feed the poor, and though I give my body to be burned, and have not charity, it profiteth nothing.

But these articles will receive a considerable light from the consideration of the second point, viz. the benefits and advantages arising from the practice of Christian charity.

In which, as the present occasion more especially points out to us, we may take a short general view of the advantages and benefits attending the exercise of that particular branch of Christian charity, which consists in the applying and bestowing some part of our substance, or the produce of our labours, towards the relief and support of the poor and needy; or in contributing towards such works of piety and mercy as are intended and contrived for the real good and bettering the condition of our indigent brethren, either by public or private ways of charity. And by this we improve our talents to the glory of God and the welfare of our own immortal souls.

Consider, my brethren, that all we have and are is entrusted to us by Almighty God. In him we live, move, and have our being. The earth is the Lord's, and the fullness (or plenty) thereof. We are consequently no more than his servants or stewards; the talents are all his; it is his substance that is distributed by him among us, to some more, to some less, as it has pleased him to entrust us with our own several portions or dividends; and to him we must give an account at the great day of reckoning, for every penny—for the improvement as well as for the principal.

Our blessed Lord has not committed his goods to us as a dead stock, to be boarded up, or to lie unprofitably in our own hands. He expects that we shall put them out to proper and beneficial uses, and raise them to an advanced value by doing good with them, as often as we have opportunity of laying them out upon the real interest and welfare of his poor children and subjects. By doing acts of mercy and charity we acknowledge our dependence upon God and his absolute right to whatever we possess through his bounty and goodness; we glorify him in his creatures, and reverence him by a due and cheerful obedience to his commands. By applying our substance to the pomps and vanities of this wicked world or the gratification of the sinful lusts of the flesh, we deny God's right to what he hath thought fit to place in our hands; and disown him as our master by laying out his substance in ways expressly contrary to his orders; we thereby glorify satan, whom we renounced at our baptism, and most shamefully dishonour our Maker by the

abuse of his talents. When, therefore, we are called to a reckoning at that awful tribunal before which the most wealthy and powerful upon earth shall appear as naked and friendless as the poorest beggar, and when nothing but the goodness of our cause, and the mercy of our judge, can afford us the least support, if in that strict and solemn examination we have no better accounts to give in, than—so much laid out in luxury and extravagance, rapine and oppression; so much in a vexatious, litigious law-suit, or other idle, useless diversions, but little or nothing in charity. Shillings and pounds upon our vanity and folly, but scarce a few pence upon doing good! With what shame and confusion shall we hang down our heads, and wish for rocks and mountains to cover us, not only from the view of our justly offended master, but from the eyes of angels and men, all witnesses of our disgrace!

Some may perhaps say, "Well, I have refrained from debauchery, folly, and idleness; I have earned my honest penny, and kept it, and laid up a comfortable provision for my family." Be it so—this is laudable and praiseworthy, and it were to be wished that many more in this country would do so much. But may not such a one be asked, have you been charitable withal? have you been as industrious in laying up treasures in heaven, as you have been in hoarding up the perishable riches of this world? Have you stretched out your hand, as you had opportunity, beyond the circle of your own house and family? Have your poorer neighbours cause to bless you for your kind and charitable assistance? Have you dedicated any portion of your labours to God who blessed them, by doing good to any besides your own? Has the stranger, the widow, or the fatherless ever tasted of your bounty? If you have never done things of this kind, but have hitherto slighted, overlooked, or put off occasions of this sort, your talent is as yet hid in a napkin, it lies yet buried in the ground, huddled up within yourself. And consider farther, that the real poor and needy are Christ's representatives. We cannot, surely, doubt of this, if we look into our Saviour's own account of the last judgment, 25th chap. of St. Matthew's Gospel, which plainly shows us that the inquiry at that great and solemn day will be very particular about our works of mercy and charity: "Inasmuch as ye have done, or inasmuch as ye have not done it to the least of these my brethren, ye have done, or ye have not done it to me." When, therefore, an object of charity, or an opportunity of doing good, presents itself, the prudent Christian will not once deliberate, shall I relieve this man or this woman? shall I assist this widow, this orphan, or this poor child? No: he rather considers it as a demand made upon him by Christ himself, and would be as much afraid to delay or refuse payment in such case, as if he saw

his Lord and Saviour to ask it of him in person. The question, therefore, with him is this: Do not the holy Scriptures expressly teach me that whatsoever I do to my brethren who stand in need, will be reckoned to me as if I had done it to Christ himself? Can I relieve them without relieving him, or can I neglect them without slighting him? What hope could I have of being received and accepted of him at the last day, or that he will then hearken to my cries for mercy and forgiveness, should I be regardless of the requests he now makes to me by his members and representatives? I earnestly desire my Lord may have mercy upon me; therefore will I cheerfully show mercy to this his brother, however little or contemptible he may appear. I ardently wish my Lord may show goodness to me at the great day of reckoning; therefore will I seize the present opportunity of doing good, which he, in his good will towards me, now offers to my acceptance.

The accustoming ourselves to those acts, separates our affections from earthly things, learns us to sit loose to the world, and secures us treasures in heaven.

To people who are heartily in love with this world, who can see no greater happiness than wealth or power upon earth can afford them, such advantages, I own, are in no sort alluring. To talk of placing their affections upon possessions beyond the grave, or of lessening their present gains, in hopes of future benefits, is much to the same purpose as setting a most beautiful prospect before a blind man, or the most delicate meats before one who has lost his palate.

The person who has a due regard to his eternal salvation; who knows by experience how apt the love of earthly things is to draw off his affections from those of a heavenly nature; who remembers that he ought not to love the world, nor the things that are in the world, because the friendship of this world is enmity with God, and that whosoever will be a friend (or lover) of the world is the enemy of God; who reflects that a time will come when he must part with all that is dear to him here: how necessary it is, therefore, to wean his mind from these perishable things, that they may give him no pain or uneasiness in quitting them, and is convinced that the whole world is of infinitely less value than the least inheritance in the kingdom of heaven. Such a one is always prepared to exercise himself in acts of mercy and charity; giving up a part, whenever opportunity offers of doing good, in token of his readiness to give up the whole whensoever God shall please to call upon him for it; and rejoices in the means afforded him of laying up treasures subject to no waste, rapine, or corruption, at the small expense of a trifling sum here;

nay, is ready, should it appear necessary, to follow the advice of our Saviour to his little flock, "Sell that ye have, and give alms; provide yourselves bags which wax not old, a treasure in the heavens which faileth not."

In short, the love of this world is a heavy weight upon the soul, which chains her down, and prevents her flight towards heaven. Habitual acts of charity loosen her from it by degrees, and help her in her struggle to disengage herself and mount upwards.

A dying person would give the whole world, were it in his possession, for any rational assurance of acceptance with God, and an inheritance in the kingdom of heaven; why then will any man, who knows he must one day die, neglect the insuring it to himself by such works of mercy in his health and strength, as he may be assured will help him to mercy in a dying hour? Blessed are the merciful, saith our dear Redeemer, for they shall obtain mercy.

Another advantage arising from acts of mercy and charity is, that they secure us the blessing and protection of heaven.

Blessed is he, saith King David, who considereth the poor and the needy; the Lord will deliver him in the time of trouble. The Lord will reserve him and keep him alive, and he shall be blessed upon the earth, and thou wilt not deliver him into the will of his enemies. The Lord will strengthen him upon the bed of languishing: thou wilt make all his bed in his sickness. To be slow and uneasy at almsgiving, argues a strong distrust in providence, either that God cannot or will not make up to us what we thus bestow. To suppose he cannot, is to deny his Almighty power, and consequently that he is God. To imagine he will not, is to suspect his truth, who has not only promised eternal treasures in heaven, but has also engaged his sure word that he will repay it, even upon earth, as if it were lent to himself. He that hath pity upon the poor lendeth to the Lord; and that which he hath borrowed, he will repay him again.

With how great reason did our Saviour so solemnly charge his disciples to beware of covetousness, since we see it borders so nearly upon infidelity? How strangely inconsistent is the narrow-hearted man with himself, with his own settled principles! He desires a blessing upon all that he has; he earnestly wishes for wealth and prosperity, yet cannot find in his heart to lay out a little of what he has to secure that blessing, that prosperity he aims at for himself and family, in doing these good and charitable actions which Providence throws in his way, and which God has assured him will purchase it! How much more rationally does the open-hearted benevolent Christian

act, and upon what sure and steady principles does he proceed! This trifle, says he to himself, which I now bestow, may possibly be of some small present inconvenience to me; but it is given to God, and he will never suffer me to feel the want of it. My Saviour has kindly insured to me whatever is necessary in this world, by promising, that if I first seek the kingdom of God and his righteousness, and these things, which others are toiling and sweating after, often to no purpose but vexation and disappointment, shall be added unto me. Here are both earthly and heavenly blessings laid before me, so that I cannot fail of a return from God, though he hath expressly ordered me to hope for nothing again from those I give to. I shall therefore assuredly reap according to my sowing—in this world, if God sees it good for me, but most certainly in the blessings of the next, if I grow not faint or impatient. My alms will ascend up before God for a memorial; and as he has taken the payment upon himself, I am convinced that even a cup of cold water thus bestowed, by those who have no more to give, will not lose its reward; for Jesus has promised, and in him all the promises of God are yea and amen.

Having thus gone through the proposed heads, and shewn the nature, the extent, and necessity of Christian charity; having pointed out the benefits and advantages arising from the practice of it, and how it secures to us the blessings both of this world and the world to come, it now remains that some common objections be considered, with a short application to the present design. Objections, I know, are many; and each person unwilling to contribute towards a charitable proposal will find out one of some kind or other, to ward off the blow that seems to aim at his very heart. Numerous, however, as they are, they appear so trifling, as to deserve little particular consideration, and might well enough be examined in bulk.

All objections to charitable contributions may well be supposed to arise from covetousness, or an unwillingness to part with the present penny. Covetousness is indeed a Goliah, a giant of the first magnitude, which is always ready to defy and set at nought the best formed arguments and motives drawn from reason and Scripture, all the armies of the living God. All the common pretences to prudence in the manner or time of giving charity, all hints of reserving it for better purposes, generally centre in covetousness, in the love of money: and how wretched a fruit is to be expected from the root of all evil, as St. Paul expressly calls it, let every one judge for himself.

But the answer to all such pretences of prudence in bestowing, in short, is this: you may be deceived in the object, but you never can be deceived in

your intention of charity, be the object ever go undeserving; nay, should I bestow money upon one in apparent necessity, who might abuse it to ill purposes, yet the good intention sanctifies my gift, consecrates it to God, and insures me a blessing, because it was done in his name and for his sake; while the whole abuse of it rests upon the guilty head of the vile person who thus basely misapplies my good deed. It may indeed be a reasonable objection against my giving a second time to that same person, but can be no excuse to me for withholding my hand from the relief of any other object which may appear another time to be in real want of charity.

And O! consider what a joyful thing it must be for a person in a dying hour to have a conscience free from offence, and to see their blessed Saviour, with his arms stretched out, ready to receive them when their breath leaves the body, and saying, "Well done, thou good and faithful servant; thou hast been faithful over a few things, I will make thee ruler over many things; enter thou into the joy of thy Lord." Are not these, my brethren and sisters, pleasures worth seeking after? are not these privileges, this freedom, and these possessions of far more value than thousands of worlds like this we live in, which we must all leave in a short time, and cannot carry with us into another life? And can you ever sufficiently admire the goodness of God, or ever be thankful enough to him for his loving kindness, who hath set these glories and these enjoyments as much within the reach of the poorest slave as of the greatest prince alive? For it is not power and high station that can purchase these heavenly possessions: they are only to be gained by goodness and serving of God; and the lowest of us can serve God as well as the richest person here below, and, by that means may adorn the doctrine of the Lord your God in all things, and bring more honour to Christ than many of higher rank and condition, who are not so careful of their souls as you may be.

When, therefore, we shall leave this impertinent and unsociable world, and all our good old friends that are gone to heaven before us, shall meet us as soon as we are landed upon the shore of eternity, and with infinite congratulations for our safe arrival, shall conduct us into the company of patriarchs, prophets, apostles and martyrs, and introduce us into an intimate acquaintance with them, and with all those brave and generous souls, who, by their glorious examples, have recommended themselves to the world; when we shall be familiar friends with angels and archangels; and all the courtiers of heaven shall call us brethren, and bid us welcome to their master's joy, and we shall be received into their glorious society with all the tender endearments and caresses of those heavenly lovers. What a mighty addi-

tion to our happiness will this be! There are indeed some other additions to the happiness of heaven, such as the glory and magnificence of the place, which is the highest heaven, or the upper and purer tracts of the æther, which our Saviour calls Paradise.

In the temper of every wicked mind there is a strong antipathy to the pleasures of Heaven, which being all chaste, pure and spiritual, can never agree with the vitiated palate of a base and degenerate soul. For what concord can there be between a spiteful and devilish spirit, and the fountain of all love and goodness? between a sensual and carnalized one, that understands no other pleasures but only those of the flesh, and those pure and virgin spirits that neither eat nor drink but live forever upon wisdom, holiness, love and contemplation? Certainly till our mind is contempered to the Heavenly state, and we are of the same disposition with God and angels and saints, there is no pleasure in Heaven that can be agreeable to us. For as in the main we shall be of the same temper and disposition when we come into the other life as we are when we leave this, it being unimaginable how a total change should be wrought in us merely by passing out of one world into another, and therefore as in this world it is likeness that does congregate and associate beings together, so doubtless it is in the other world too, so that if we carry with us thither our wicked and devilish dispositions, (as we shall certainly do, unless we subdue and mortify them here) there will be no company fit for us to associate with, but only the devilish and damned ghost of wicked men, with whom our wretched spirits being already joined by a likeness of nature, will mingle themselves as soon as ever they are excommunicated from the society of mortals.

For whither should they flock but to the birds of their own feather, with whom should they associate but with those malignant spirits, to whom they are already joined by a community of nature? So that supposing that when they land in eternity? it were left to their own choice to go to Heaven or hell, into the society of the blessed or the damned, it is plain that Heaven would be no place for them; that the air of that bright region of eternal day, would never agree with their black and hellish natures, for alas! what should they do among those blessed beings that inhabit it? To whose godlike natures divine contemplation and Heavenly employments, they have so great a repugnancy and aversion? So that, besides the having a right to Heaven, it is necessary to our enjoying it, that we should be antecedently disposed and qualified for it. And it being thus, God hath been graciously pleased to make those very virtues, the condition of our right to Heaven, which are the proper disposi-

tions and qualifications of our spirits for it, that so, with one and the same labour, we might entitle ourselves, and qualify ourselves to enjoy it.

THE END.

PHILLIS WHEATLEY

(1753–1784)

Born in Senegal, West Africa in 1753, a young girl was kidnapped at the age of seven, put aboard a slave ship, and sold to a prosperous family, John and Susannah Wheatley of Boston, with whom she would spend the majority of her remarkable yet brief life. The girl was named Phillis for the ship which transported her, and she took the last name of the family she would serve. From an early age, it became clear that she was a gifted child. Though she received no formal schooling, her talents did not escape the Wheatleys, and Susannah took an interest in tutoring her.

As Phillis grew up, she demonstrated a passion for language that was stunning, considering her origins. She learned English with remarkable speed, and was so taken with reading and writing that she learned Greek and Latin too. Influenced by the devout Christianity of the Wheatleys, Phillis was captivated by the Bible, which, in turn, became a strong influence on her verse, along with the works of three English poets, John Milton, Alexander Pope and Thomas Gray.

She began writing poetry at the age of 14, and became something of a sensation in Boston in the 1760s, as an audience of British and Americans were struck by the literary talent and intelligence of someone so young who had seemingly triumphed over the circumstances of her birth. Writing in heroic couplets, many of her poems are elegies, such as her poem, "An Elegiac Poem, on the Death of the Celebrated Divine George Whitefield," and published in 1770, which attracted her much attention. Whitefield was a great evangelical preacher who spoke frequently in New England, and happened to be a good friend of Countess Selina of Huntington, who would later invite Phillis to London, helping her publish her poetry.

Perhaps owing to her early capture and time spent on a slave ship, Wheatley was asthmatic, and was frail and sickly for much of her life. In 1773, in an effort to improve her health, she was sent to England, where she

had once recuperated with the Wheatleys. She wrote "A Farewell to America" before departing, and dedicated it to Susannah Wheatley. The poem acknowledges her frailty—she hopes that England's "misty vapours" might help counteract her asthma.

> In vain for me the flow'rets rise,
> And boast their gaudy pride,
> While here beneath the Northern skies
> I mourn for *health* deny'd.

But it is also a heartfelt goodbye to Susannah, whose grief, she believes, will be greater than her own upon departure.

> *Susannah* mourns, nor can I bear,
> To see the crystal flow'r,
> Or mark the tender falling tear
> At sad departure's hour;
>
> Not unregarding can I see
> Her soul with grief opprest
> So let no sigh, nor groans for me,
> Steal from her pensive breast.

The Wheatleys helped secure Phillis a publisher for her poetry, and her collection, *Poems on Various Subjects* was the first published book of poetry by an African American. Her gift of language caused some skepticism, perhaps because of her age and their racism, and to rebut such skeptics, Wheatley's publisher included a letter from Mr. Wheatley, as well as signed testimony from sixteen other notables, including the Governor of Massachusetts, Thomas Hutchinson, and even John Hancock, to vouch for the authenticity of her writings. The letter states:

As it has been repeatedly suggested to the Publisher, by Persons, who have seen the Manuscript, that Numbers would be ready to suspect they were not really the Writings of Phillis, he has procured the following Attestation, from the most respectable Characters in Boston, that none might have the least Ground for disputing their Original.

We whose Names are underwritten, do assure the World, that the

Poems specified in the following Page, were (as we verily believe) written by Phillis, a young Negro Girl, who was but a few Years since, brought an uncultivated Barbarian from Africa, and has ever since been, and now is, under the Disadvantage of serving as a Slave in a Family in this Town. She has been examined by some of the best Judges, and is thought qualified to write them.

The impact of the Wheatleys and their devotion to Christianity is a theme that runs throughout Phillis Wheatley's poetry. She speaks of the salvation message of Christianity as being available to men and women, regardless of race or class. She was a product of her times and her New England education is evident in much of her writings. Wheatley viewed her capture and enslavement as the work of a merciful God rescuing her from "my pagan land."

In one of her most well-known poems, "To the University of Cambridge, in New–England," she writes:

> While an intrinsic ardor prompts to write,
> The muses promise to assist my pen;
> 'Twas not long since I left my native shore
> The land of errors, and Egyptian gloom:
> Father of mercy, 'twas thy gracious hand
> Brought me in safety from those dark abodes.

For Phillis Wheatley, religion was the passageway to freedom and the ultimate triumph. Her poems say little about life in Africa or her slave status in America, yet in spite of her privileged upbringing in comparison to the overwhelming majority of slaves, she also demonstrated frustration with the institution of slavery. Often cloaked in gentle language, she, at times, wrote openly about race:

> Some view our sable race with scornful eye,
> "Their color is a diabolic die."
> Remember *Christians, Negroes,* black as *Cain,*
> May be refined, and join th' angelic train.

After a stay in London, Phillis would return to Boston with the

Wheatleys, and John gave her her freedom. Nevertheless, she stayed with the Wheatleys, caring for them in their declining years. In 1776, when the Revolution broke out, she wrote a letter and poem offering praise and support to George Washington, who replied with an invitation to visit, which Wheatley did, prior to Boston's evacuation by the British. The poem was published in the *Virginia Gazette* later that year, which brought her even further acclaim.

But the very start of what would seem to be an extraordinary American life in the making took a turn for the worse, beginning with the death of John Wheatley in 1778, which left Phillis free, but impoverished. She would go on to marry another free African-American, John Peters, and the couple would have three children together. But Peters seemingly failed in business and Phillis struggled to support her family as a seamstress and poet.

Wheatley's children all died young, and at the end of her life, Phillis was working mainly as a servant until she died in poverty at the age of 31 in 1784. There was a second volume of poetry that has never been recovered.

Though the bulk of Wheatley's poetry was largely concerned with morality and piety, it was conventional for its time. If some critics at the time failed to praise the quality of her poetry, they were more than offset by the number of people who turned to Wheatley's work for inspiration. The political significance stems from the attention she drew to her successful education, and her poems were reissued in the 1830s by Abolitionists who were eager to use Wheatley and her work as an example of the human potential of blacks.

Selections from
Poems on Various Subjects

To Maecenas

Maecenas, you, beneath the myrtle shade
Read o'er what poets sung, and shepherds play'd.
What felt those poets but you feel the same?
Does not your soul possess the sacred flame?
Their noble strains your equal genius shares
In softer language, and diviner airs.

 While *Homer* paints, lo! circumfus'd in air,
Celestial Gods in mortal forms appear;
Swift as they move hear each recess rebound,
Heav'n quakes, earth trembles, and the shores
 resound.
Great sire of verse, before my mortal eyes,
The lightnings blaze across the vaulted skies,
And, as the thunder shakes the heav'nly plains,
A deep felt horror thrills through all my veins.
When gentler strains demand thy graceful song,
The length'ning line moves languishing along.
When great *Patroclus* courts *Achilles'* aid,
The grateful tribute of my tears is paid;
Prone on the shore he feels the pangs of love,
And stern *Pelides* tend'rest passions move.

 Great *Maro's* strain in heav'nly numbers flows,
The *Nine* inspire, and all the bosom glows,
O, could I rival thine and *Virgil's* page,
Or claim the *Muses* with the *Mantuan* sage;
Soon the same beauties should my mind adorn,

And the same ardors in my soul should burn;
Then should my song in bolder notes arise,
And all my numbers pleasingly surprise;
But here I sit, and mourn a grov'ling mind,
That fain would mount, and ride upon the wind.

 Not you, my friend, these plaintive strains become,
Not you, whose bosom is the *Muses'* home;
When they from tow'ring *Helicon* retire,
They fan in you the bright immortal fire,
But I less happy, cannot raise the song,
The fault'ring music dies upon my tongue.

 The happier *Terence* all the choir inspired,
His soul replenish'd, and his bosom fir'd;
But say, ye *Muses*, why this partial grace
To one alone in *Afric's* sable race;
From age to age transmitting thus his name
With the first glory in the rolls of fame?

 Thy virtues, great *Maecenas!* shall be sung
In praise of him, from whom those virtues sprung;
While blooming wreaths around thy temples spread,
I'll snatch a laurel from thine honor'd head,
While you indulgent smile upon the deed.

 As long as *Thames* in streams majestic flows,
Or *Naiads* in their oozy beds repose,
While *Phoebus* reigns above the starry train
While bright *Aurora* purples o'er the main,
So long, great Sir, the muse thy praise shall sing,
So long thy praise shall make *Parnassus* ring;
Then grant *Maecenas*, thy paternal rays,
Hear me propitious, and defend my lays.

ON VIRTUE

O Thou bright jewel in my aim I strive
To comprehend thee. Thine own words declare
Wisdom is higher than a fool can reach.

I cease to wonder, and no more attempt
Thine height t' explore, or fathom thy profound,
But, O, my soul, sink not into despair,
Virtue is near thee, and with gentle hand
Would now embrace thee, hovers o'er thine head.
Fain would the heav'n-born soul with her converse,
Then seek, then court her for her promis'd bliss,
 Auspicious queen, thine heav'nly pinions spread,
And lead celestial *Chastity* along;
Lo! now her sacred retinue descends,
Array'd in glory from the orbs above.
Attend me, *Virtue*, thro' my youthful years!
O leave me not to the false joys of time!
But guide my steps to endless life and bliss.
Greatness, or *Goodness*, say what I shall call thee,
To give an higher appellation still,
Teach me a better strain, a nobler lay,
O thou, enthron'd with Cherubs in the realms of day.

To the University of Cambridge, in New-England

While an intrinsic ardor prompts to write,
The muses promise to assist my pen;
'Twas not long since I left my native shore
The land of errors, and Egyptian gloom:
Father of mercy, 'twas thy gracious hand
Brought me in safety from those dark abodes.
 Students, to you 'tis giv'n to scan the heights
Above, to traverse the ethereal space,
And mark the systems of revolving worlds.
Still more, ye sons of science, ye receive
The blissful news by messengers from heav'n
How Jesus' blood for your redemption flows.
See Him with hands outstretched upon the cross;
Immense compassion in His bosom glows;

He hears revilers, nor resents their scorn;
What matchless mercy in the Son of God!
When the whole human race by sin had fall'n,
He deign'd to die that they might rise again,
And share with Him in the sublimest skies,
Life without death, and glory without end.
 Improve your privileges while they stay,
Ye pupils, and each hour redeem, that bears
Or good or bad report of you to heav'n.
Let sin, that baneful evil to the soul,
By you be shunned, nor once remit your guard;
Suppress the deadly serpent in its egg.
Ye blooming plants of human race divine,
An *Ethiop* tells you 'tis your greatest foe;
Its transient sweetness turns to endless pain,
And in immense perdition sinks the soul.

To S.M., a Young African Painter, on Seeing His Works

To show the lab'ring bosom's deep intent,
And thought in living characters to paint.
When first thy pencil did those beauties give,
And breathing figures learnt from thee to live,
How did those prospects give my soul delight,
A new creation rushing on my sight?
Still, wond'rous youth! each noble path pursue,
On deathless glories fix thine ardent view:
Still may the painter's and the poet's fire
To aid thy pencil, and thy verse conspire!
And may the charms of each seraphic theme
Conduct thy footsteps to immortal fame!
High to the blissful wonders of the skies
Elate thy soul, and raise thy wishful eyes.
Thrice happy, when exalted to survey
That splendid city, crown'd with endless day,

Whose twice six gates on radiant hinges ring:
Celestial *Salem* blooms in endless spring.
 Calm and serene thy moments glide along,
And may the muse inspire each future song!
Still, with the sweets of contemplation bless'd,
May peace with balmy wings your soul invest!
But when these shades of time are chas'd away,
And darkness ends in everlasting day,
On what seraphic pinions shall we move,
And view the landscapes in the realms above?
There shall thy tongue in heav'nly murmurs flow,
And there my muse with heav'nly transport glow:
No more to tell of *Damon's* tender sighs,
Or rising radiance of *Aurora's* eyes,
For nobler themes demand a nobler strain,
And purer language on th' ethereal plain.
Cease, gentle muse! the solemn gloom of night
Now seals the fair creation from my sight.

JARENA LEE

(1783-?)

ARENA LEE WAS born on February 11, 1783 in Cape May, New
Jersey. Believed to have been born free, she left home at the age of
seven to work as a maid sixty miles away from her parents. What fol-
lowed was a life devoted to spreading her religious message, and she
often traveled miles on foot, up and down the East Coast and to the
Midwest, on what was known as the Gospel Circuit. She kept a journal
while traveling, which she later published in combination with her autobi-
ography, and the expanded volume was published in 1849. But it was her
work in Philadelphia, under the tutelage of Richard Allen, the co-founder of
the African Methodist Episcopal Church, which established Jarena Lee as
one of the most prolific preachers of her time.

Admittedly, Lee was not born into a religious family. She describes her
parents as being "wholly ignorant of the knowledge of God" and declares
herself a "wretched sinner" before the Spirit of God entered her conscience
when she was about twenty-one years old. She writes passionately about that
moment, when her life was forever changed. She had gone to hear a mis-
sionary of the Presbyterian order preach in a schoolroom, and his reading of
the Psalms seemed to describe perfectly Lee's present state of mind. The effect
on her was powerful. She became overwhelmed by the "weight of my sins"
and ultimately found herself beside a brook, contemplating suicide by
drowning herself.

Sitting beside the brook, she claims to have heard someone speaking to
her, telling her to put her head under the water. But for some reason, with-
out explanation, she returned to her house and credits the "unseen arm of
God" for preventing her "self-murder." After being treated by a physician
because "her mind was not at rest," Lee traveled to Philadelphia and was so
inspired by the preachings of Rev. Richard Allen that she "gloriously" con-
verted to God and dedicated herself to the spreading of his word. She imme-

diately volunteered her services, holding prayer meetings at the church with the blessing of Rev. Allen, but so strong was her desire to preach, that she approached Allen many times, only to be denied. Allen informed her that his discipline did not call for female preachers, but Lee was persistent. In her journal, one of the earliest cries for feminist rights, she wrote:

> O how careful ought we to be, lest through our by-laws or church government and discipline, we bring into disrepute even the word of life. For as unseemly as it may appear now-a-days for a woman to preach, it should be remembered that nothing is impossible with God. And why should it be thought impossible, heterodox, or improper for a woman to preach? seeing the Saviour died for the woman as well as for the man. If the man may preach, because the Saviour died for him, why not the woman? seeing he died for her also . . . Did not Mary first preach the risen Saviour, and is not the doctrine of the resurrection the very climax of Christianity—hangs not all our hope on this, as argued by St. Paul? Then did not Mary, a woman, preach the gospel? for she preached the resurrection of the crucified Son of God.

In 1811, Jarena Lee married Joseph Lee, a pastor from Snow Hill outside of Philadelphia. With her passion to preach stifled by the church, Lee's health was poor, and her faith would be greatly tested in the coming years, as tragedy struck her family harshly. Within a six-year period after her marriage, five members of her family would die, including her husband, leaving Lee with only a two year-old child and a six month-old baby.

At a sermon at Bethel Church, as Lee was listening to the Rev. Richard Williams, whom she believed had "lost the spirit," she sprang to her feet and gave a passionate exhortation. Upon sitting down afterward, she was frightened that she might be expelled from the church, but instead, Allen, now Bishop of the African Episcopal Methodist Church, told the congregation how he had put Lee off for eight years, but that he now believed she was "called to the work, as any of the preachers present." From that moment on, Lee's evangelical life never wavered, and she continued to champion the woman's right to preach.

The power of the call Lee felt to preach was so great that she soon took to the road to "do my Master's will." She left a very sick child with friends so that she could make a week-long journey to preach to lawyers, doctors and

magistrates, then returned home to find her son recovering well. Richard Allen helped to arrange preaching appointments for her, and she also attended Methodist conferences with him. Allen also took care of Lee's son for two years while she was on her preaching journeys, and some scholars have noted that Allen was something of a father figure to Lee.

Lee's courage often goes unwritten about, even in her own journal. The vulnerability she must have felt, traveling great distances, often by herself or in the company of another woman, is a testament to the strength she must have felt in her faith. Her need to preach was so strong that she insisted on leaving her children behind, often in poor health, to accomplish what she believed was her life's calling. The threat of assault, robbery, or even possible kidnapping surely loomed over Lee's head on her travels, especially when she journeyed to Maryland, which was still a slave state when she arrived. Lee seemed to be more moved by the slaves, who had sometimes walked up to seventy miles to hear her preach, only to return to their plantations before work began the next morning.

Her journal is filled with poignant entries, both emotional and bittersweet. One such entry finds Lee in Snow Hill on Sabbath morning. She writes:

> I was to preach in the Church of which I was a member, and although much afflicted in body, I strove, by the grace of God, to perform the duty. This was once the charge of JOSEPH LEE. In this desk my lamented husband had often stood up before me, proclaiming the "acceptable year of the Lord"—here he labored with zeal and spent his strength to induce sinners to be "reconciled to God"—here his toil ended. And could it be, his a poor unworthy being like myself should be called to address his former congregation, and should stand in the same pulpit! The thought made me tremble. My heart sighed when memory brought back the image, and the reminiscences of other days crowded upon me. But why, my heart, dost thou sigh? He has ceased from his labor, and I here see his works do follow. It will be enough, if these, the people of his care, press on and gain the freedom.

Lee continued to travel the east coast, speaking wherever she could for months at a time, before returning to Philadelphia. Upon her return in 1830, she discovered that Richard Allen was in poor health, despite taking a keen interest in educating her son while she was away. Allen would die the fol-

lowing year, and Lee would find it more difficult to find places to preach. She was no longer preaching under his guiding hand, yet she continued to persevere, walking to sermons despite being in bad health herself, "poor and destitute."

By 1832, she regained her health and continued to preach. By her own account, she had logged well over 2,000 miles while over the age of forty, and a great deal of the mileage on foot. She would sell her book along the Gospel circuit to raise money for her church back in Philadelphia, which was ironic given that the all-male members of the A.M.E. did not support the book, since it questioned sexism in the church. Her autobiography and journal left a blueprint for women activists to follow, even centuries later. Jarena Lee died in 1850.

Religious Experience and Journal of Mrs. Jarena Lee

"And it shall come to pass . . . that I will pour out my Spirit upon all flesh; and your sons, and your daughters shall prophecy." —Joel ii. 28.

I WAS BORN FEBRUARY 11TH, 1783, at Cape May, State of New Jersey. At the age of seven years I was parted from my parents, and went to live as a servant maid, with a Mr. Sharp, at the distance of about sixty miles from the place of my birth.

My parents being wholly ignorant of the knowledge of God, had not therefore instructed me in any degree in this great matter. Not long after the commencement of my attendance on this lady, she had bid me do something respecting my work, which in a little while after she asked me if I had done, when I replied, Yes—but this was not true.

At this awful point, in my early history, the Spirit of God moved in power through my conscience, and told me I was a wretched sinner. On this account so great was the impression, and so strong were the feelings of guilt, that I promised in my heart that I would not tell another lie.

But notwithstanding this promise my heart grew harder, after a while, yet the Spirit of the Lord never entirely forsook me, but continued mercifully striving with me, until his gracious power converted my soul.

The manner of this great accomplishment, was as follows: In the year 1804, it so happened that I went with others to hear a missionary of the Presbyterian order preach. It was an afternoon meeting, but few were there, the place was a school room; but the preacher was solemn, and in his countenance the earnestness of his master's business appeared equally strong, as though he were about to speak to a multitude.

At the reading of the Psalms, a ray of renewed conviction darted into my soul. These were the words, composing the first verse of the Psalms for the service:

> "Lord, I am vile conceived in sin,
> Born unholy and unclean.
> Sprung from man, whose guilty fall
> Corrupts the race, and taints us all."

This description of my condition struck me to the heart, and made me to feel in some measure, the weight of my sins, and sinful nature. But not knowing how to run immediately to the Lord for help, I was driven of Satan, in the course of a few days, and tempted to destroy myself.

There was a brook about a quarter of a mile from the house, in which there was a deep hole, where the water whirled about among the rocks; to this place it was suggested, I must go and drown myself.

At the time I had a book in my hand; it was on a Sabbath morning, about ten o'clock; to this place I resorted, where on coming to the water I sat down on the bank, and on my looking into it, it was suggested that drowning would be an easy death. It seemed as if some one was speaking to me, saying put your head under, it will not distress you. But by some means, of which I can give no account, my thoughts were taken entirely from this purpose, when I went from the place to the house again. It was the unseen arm of God which saved me from self-murder.

But notwithstanding this escape from death, my mind was not at rest— but so great was the labor of my spirit and the fearful oppressions of a judgement to come, that I was reduced as one extremely ill, on which account a physician was called to attend me, from which illness I recovered in about three months.

But as yet I had not found Him of whom Moses and the prophets did write, being extremely ignorant: there being no one to instruct me in the way of life and salvation as yet. After my recovery, I left the lady, who during my sickness, was exceedingly kind, and went to Philadelphia. From this place I soon went a few miles into the country, where I resided in the family of a Roman Catholic. But my anxiety still continued respecting my poor soul, on which account I used to watch my opportunity to read in the Bible; and this lady observing this, took the Bible from me and hid it, giving me a novel in its stead—which when I perceived, I refused to read.

Soon after this I again went to the city of Philadelphia, and commenced going to the English Church, the pastor of which was an Englishman, by the name of Pilmore, one of the number who at first preached Methodism in America, in the city of New York.

But while sitting under the ministration of this man, which was about three months, and at the last time, it appeared that there was a wall between me and a communion with that people, which was higher than I could possibly see over, and seemed to make this impression upon my mind, *this is not the people for you.*

But on returning home at noon I inquired of the head cook of the house respecting the rules of the Methodists, as I knew she belonged to that society, who told me what they were; on which account I replied, that I should not be able to abide by such strict rules not even one year—however, I told her that I would go with her and hear what they had to say.

The man who was to speak in the afternoon of that day, was the Rev. Richard Allen, since bishop of the African Episcopal Methodists in America. During the labors of this man that afternoon, I had come to the conclusion, that this is the people to which my heart unites, and it so happened, that as soon as the service closed he invited such as felt a desire to flee the wrath to come, to unite on trial with them—I embraced the opportunity. Three weeks from that day, my soul was gloriously converted to God, under preaching, at the very outset of the sermon. The text was barely pronounced, which was "I perceive thy heart is not right in the sight of God." When there appeared to *my* view, in the centre of the heart, *one* sin; and this was malice against one particular individual, who had strove deeply to injure me, which I resented. At this discovery I said, *Lord* I forgive *every* creature. That instant, it appeared to me as if a garment, which had entirely enveloped my whole person, even to my fingers' ends, split at the crown of my head, and was stripped away from my, passing like a shadow from my sight—when the glory of God seemed to cover me in its stead.

That moment, though hundreds were present, I did leap to my feet and declare that God, for Christ's sake, had pardoned the sins of my soul. Great was the ecstacy of my mind, for I felt that not only the sin of *malice* was pardoned, but all other sins were swept away together. That day was the first when my heart had believed, and my tongue had made confession unto salvation—the first words uttered, a part of that song, which shall fill eternity with its sound, was *glory to God*. For a few moments I had power to exhort sinners, and to tell of the wonders and of the goodness of Him who had

clothed me with *His* salvation. During this the minister was silent, until my soul felt its duty had been performed, when he declared another witness of the power of Christ to forgive sins on earth, was manifest in my conversion.

From the day on which I first went to the Methodist Church, until the hour of my deliverance, I was strangely buffeted by that enemy of all right-eousness—the devil.

I was naturally of a lively turn of disposition; and during the space of time from my first awakening until I knew my peace was made with God, I rejoiced in the vanities of this life, and then again sunk back into sorrow.

For four years I had continued in this way, frequently laboring under the awful apprehension that I could never be happy in this life. This persuasion was greatly strengthened during the three weeks, which was the last of Satan's power over me, in this peculiar manner, on which account had come to the conclusion that I had better be dead than alive. Here I was again tempted to destroy my life by drowning; but suddenly this mode was changed—and while in the dusk of the evening, as I was walking to and fro in the year of the house, I was beset to hang myself with a cord suspended from the wall enclosing the secluded spot.

But no sooner was the intention resolved on in my mind, that an awful dread came over me, when I ran into the house; still the tempter pursued me. There was standing a vessel of water—into this I was strangely impressed to plunge my head, so as to extinguish the life which God had given me. Had I done this, I have been always of the opinion, that I should have been unable to have released myself; although the vessel was scarcely large enough to hold a gallon of water. Of me may it not be said as written by Isaiah. (chap. 65, verses 1,2.) "I am sought of them that asked not for me; I am found of them that sought me not." Glory be to God for his redeeming power, which saved me from the violence of my own hands, from the malice of Satan, and from eternal death; for had I have killed myself, a great ransom could not have delivered me; for it is written—"No murderer hath eternal life abiding in him." How appropriately can I sing—

> "Jesus sought me when a stranger,
> Wandering from the fold of God;
> He to rescue me from danger,
> Interposed his precious blood"

But notwithstanding the terror which seized upon me, when about to end

my life, I had no view of the precipice on the edge of which I was tottering, until it was over, and my eyes were opened. Then the awful gulf of hell seemed to be open beneath me, covered only, as it were, by a spider's web, on which I stood. I seemed to hear the howling of the damned, to see the smoke of the bottomless pit, and to hear the rattling of those chains, which hold the impenitent under clouds of darkness to the judgement of the great day.

I trembled like *Belshazzar*, and cried out in the horror of my spirit, "God be merciful to me a sinner." That night I formed a resolution to pray; which, when resolved upon, there appeared, sitting in one corner of the room, Satan, in the form of a monstrous dog, and in a rage, as if in pursuit, his tongue protruding from his mouth to a great length, and his eyes looked like two balls of fire; it soon, however, vanished out of my sight. From this state of terror and dismay, I was happily delivered under the preaching of the Gospel as before related.

This view which I was permitted to have of Satan, in the form of a dog, is evidence, which corroborates in my estimation, the Bible account of a hell of fire, which burneth with brimstone, called in Scripture the bottomless pit; the place where all liars, who repent not, shall have their portion; as also Sabbath breaker, the adulterer, the fornicator, with the fearful, the abominable, and the unbelieving, this shall be the portion of their cup.

This language is too strong and expressive to be applied to any state of suffering in *time*. Were it to be thus applied, the reality could no where be found in human life; the consequence would be, that this scripture would be found a false testimony. But when made to apply to an endless state of perdition, in eternity, beyond the bounds of human life, then this language is found not to exceed our views of a state of eternal damnation.

During the latter part of my state of conviction, I can now apply to my case, as it then was, the beautiful words of the poet:

> "The more I strove against its power,
> I felt its weight and guilt the more;
> 'Till late I heard my Saviour say,
> Come hither soul, I am the way."

This I found to be true, to the joy of my disconsolate and despairing heart, in the hour of my conversion to God.

During this state of mind, while sitting near the fire one evening, after I had heard Rev. Richard Allen, as before related, a view of my distressed con-

dition so affected my heart, that I could not refrain from weeping and cry-
ing aloud; which caused the lady with whom I then lived, to inquire, with
surprise, what ailed me; to which I answered, that I knew not what ailed me.
She replied that I ought to pray. I arose from where I was sitting, being in an
agony, and weeping convulsively, requested her to pray for me; but at the
very moment when she would have done so, some person wrapped heavily at
the door for admittance; it was but a person of the house, but this occurrence
was sufficient to interrupt us in our intentions; and I believe to this day, I
should then have found salvation to my soul. This interruption was, doubt-
less, also the work of Satan.

Although at this time, when my conviction was so great, yet I knew not
that Jesus Christ was the Son of God, the second person in the adorable
Trinity. I knew him not in the pardon of my sins, yet I felt a consciousness
that if I died without pardon, that my lot must inevitably be damnation. If
I would pray—knew not how. I could form no connexion of ideas into
words; but I knew the Lord's prayer; this I uttered with a loud voice, and
with all my might and strength. I was the most ignorant creature in the
world; I did not even know that Christ had died for the sins of the world,
and to save sinners. Every circumstance, however was so directed as still to
continue and increase the sorrows of my heart, which I now know to have
been a Godly sorrow which wrought repentance, which is not to be repent-
ed of. Even the falling of the deal leaves from the forests, and the dried spires
of the mown grass, shown me that I too must die in like manner. But my case
was awfully different from that of the grass of the field, or the wide spread
decay of a thousand forests, as I felt within me a living principle, an immor-
tal spirit, which cannot die, and must forever either enjoy the smiles of its
Creator, or feel the pangs of ceaseless damnation.

But the Lord led me on; being gracious, he took pity on my ignorance;
he heard my wailings, which had entered into the ear of the Lord of Sabaoth.
Circumstances so transpired that I soon came to a knowledge of the being
and character of the Son of God, of whom I knew nothing.

My strength had left me. I had become feverish and sickly through the
violence of my feelings, on which account I left my place of service to spend
a week with a colored physician, who was a member of the Methodist socie-
ty, and also to spend this week in going to places where prayer and supplica-
tion was statedly made for such as me.

Through this means I had learned much, so as to be able in some degree
to comprehend the spiritual meaning of the text, which the minister took on

the Sabbath morning, as before related, which was "I perceive thy heart is not right in the sight of God."—Acts, chap. 8 verse 21.

This text, as already related, became the power of God unto salvation to me, because I believed. I was baptized according to the direction of our Lord, who said, as he was about to ascend from the mount, to his disciples, "Go ye into all the world and preach my gospel to every creature, he that believeth and is baptized shall be saved."

I have now passed through the account of my conviction, and also of my conversion to God: and shall next speak of the blessings of sanctification.

A time, after I had received forgiveness, flowed sweetly on; day and night my joy was full, no temptation was permitted to molest me. I could say continually with the psalmist, that "God had separated my sins from me as far as the east is from the west." I was ready continually to cry,

"Come all the world, come sinner thou,
All things in Christ are ready now."

I continued in this happy state of mind for almost three months, when a certain colored man, by name William Scott, came to pay me a religious visit. He had been for many years a faithful follower of the Lamb; and he had also taken much time in visiting the sick and distressed of our color, and understood well the great things belonging to a man of full stature in Christ Jesus.

In the course of our conversation, he inquired if the Lord had justified my soul. I answered yes. He then asked me if he had sanctified me. I answered no; and that I did not know what that was. He then undertook to instruct me further in the knowledge of the Lord respecting this blessing.

He told me the progress of the soul from a state of darkness, or of nature, was three-fold; or consisted in three degrees, as follows: First, conviction for sin. Second, Justification from sin. Third, the entire sanctification of the soul to God. I thought this description was beautiful, and immediately believed in it. He then inquired if I would promise to pray for this in my secret devotions. I told him yes. Very soon I began to call upon the Lord to show me all that was in my heart, which was not according to his will. Now there appeared to be a new struggle commencing in my soul, not accompanied with fear, guilt, and bitter distress, as while under my first conviction for sin, but a laboring of the mind to know more of the right way of the lord. I began now to feel that my heart was not clean in his sight; that there yet remained the roots of bitterness, which if not destroyed, would ere long sprout up from

these roots, and overwhelm me in a new growth of the brambles and brush-wood of sin.

By the increasing light of the Spirit, I had found there yet remained the root of pride, anger, self-will, with many evils, the result of fallen nature. I now became alarmed at this discovery, and began to fear that I had been deceived in my experience. I was now greatly alarmed, lest I should fall away from what I knew I had enjoyed; and to guard against this I prayed almost incessantly, without acting faith on the power and promises of God to keep me from falling. I had not yet learned how to war against temptation of this kind. Satan well knew that if he could succeed in making me disbelieve my conversion, that he would catch me either on the ground of complete despair, or on the ground of infidelity. For if all I had passed through was to go for nothing, and was but a fiction, the mere ravings of a disordered mind, that I would naturally be led to believe that there is nothing in religion at all.

From this snare I was mercifully preserved, and led to believe that there was yet a greater work than that of pardon to be wrought in me. I retired to a secret place, (after having sought this blessing, as well as I could, for near-ly three months, from the time brother Scott had instructed me respecting it,) for prayer, about four o'clock in the afternoon. I had struggled long and hard, but found not the desire of my heart. When I rose from my knees, there seemed a voice speaking to me, as I yet stood in a leaning posture—"Ask for sanctification." When to my surprise, I recollected that I had not even thought of it in my whole prayer. It would seem Satan had hidden the very object from my mind, for which I had purposely kneeled to pray. But when this voice whispered in my heart, saying, "Pray for sanctification," I again bowed in the same place, at the same time, and said "*lord sanctify* my soul for Christ's sake." That very instant, as if lightning had darted through me, I sprang to my feet, and cried, "The Lord has sanctified my soul!" There was none to hear this but the angels who stood around to witness my joy—and Satan, whose malice raged the more. That Satan was there, I knew; for no sooner had I cried out "The Lord has sanctified my soul," than there seemed another voice behind me, saying "No, it is too great a work to be done." But another spirit said "Bow down for the witness—I received it—*thou art sanctified!*" The first I knew of myself after that, I was standing in the yard with my hands spread out, and looking with my face toward heaven.

I now ran into the house and told them what had happened to me, when, as it were a new rush of the same ecstacy came upon me, and caused me to feel as if I were in an ocean of light and bliss.

During this, I stood perfectly still, the tears rolling in a flood from my eyes. So great was the joy, that it is past description. There is no language that can describe it, except that which was heard by St. Paul, when he was caught up to third heaven, and heard words which it was not lawful to utter.

MY CALL TO PREACH THE GOSPEL.

Between four and five years after my sanctification, on a certain time, an impressive silence fell upon me, and I stood as if some one was about to speak to me, yet I had no such thought in my heart.—But to my utter surprise there seemed to sound a voice which I thought I distinctly heard, and most certainly understand, which said to me, "Go preach the Gospel!" I immediately replied aloud, "No one will believe me." Again I listened, and again the same voice seemed to say—"Preach the Gospel; I will put words in your mouth, and will turn your enemies to become your friends."

At first I supposed that Satan had spoken to me, for I had read that he could transform himself into an angel of light for the purpose of deception. Immediately I went into a secret place, and called upon the Lord to know if he had called me to preach, and whether I was deceived or not; when there appeared to my view the form and figure of a pulpit, with a Bible lying thereon, the back of which was presented to me as plainly as if it had been a literal fact.

In consequence of this, my mind became so exercised, that during the night following, I took a text and preached in my sleep. I thought there stood before me a great multitude, while I expounded to them the things of religion. So violent were my exertions and so loud were my exclamations, that I awoke from the sound of my own voice, which also awoke the family of the house where I resided. Two days after I went to see the preacher in charge of the African Society, who was the Rev. Richard Allen, the same before named in these pages, to tell him that I felt it my duty to preach the gospel. But as I drew near the street in which his house was, which was in the city of Philadelphia, my courage began to fail me; so terrible did the cross appear, it seemed that I should not be able to bear it. Previous to my setting out to go to see him, so agitated was my mind, that my appetite for my daily food failed me entirely. Several times on my way there, I turned back again; but as often I felt my strength again renewed, and I soon found that the nearer I

approached to the house of the minister, the less was my fear. Accordingly, as soon as I came to the door, my fears subsided, the cross was removed, all things appeared pleasant—I was tranquil.

I now told him, that the Lord had revealed it to me, that must preach the gospel. He replied, by asking, in what sphere I wished to move in? I said, among the Methodists. He then replied, that a Mrs. Cook, a Methodist lady, had also some time before requested the same privilege; who, it was believed, had done much good in the way of exhortation, and holding prayer meetings; and who had been permitted to do so by the verbal licence of the preacher in charge at the time. But as to women preaching, he said that our Discipline knew nothing at all about it—that it did not call for women preachers. This I was glad to hear, because it removed the fear of the cross—but no sooner did this feeling cross my mind, than I found that a love of souls had in a measure departed from me; that holy energy which burned within me, as a fire, began to be smothered. This I soon perceived.

O how careful ought we to be, lest through our by-laws of church government and discipline, we bring into disrepute even the word of life. For as unseemly as it may appear now-a-days for a woman to preach, it should be remembered that nothing is impossible, with God. And why should it be thought impossible, heterodox, or improper for a woman to preach? seeing the Saviour died for the woman as well as for the man.

If the man may preach, because the Saviour died for him, why not the woman? seeing he died for her also. Is he not a whole Saviour, instead of a half one? as those who hold it wrong for a woman to preach, would seem to make it appear.

Did not Mary *first* preach the risen Saviour, and is not the doctrine of the resurrection the very climax of Christianity—hangs not all our hope on this, as argued by St. Paul? Then did not Mary, a woman, preach the gospel? for she preached the resurrection of the crucified Son of God.

But some will say that Mary did not expound the Scripture, therefore, she did not preach, in the proper sense of the term. To this I reply, it may be that the term *preach* in those primitive times, did not mean exactly what it is now *made* to mean; perhaps it was a great deal more simple then, than it is now—if it were not, the unlearned fishermen could not have preached the gospel at all, as they had no learning.

To this it may be replied, by those who are determined not to believe that it is right for a woman to preach, that the disciples, though they were fishermen and ignorant of letters too, were inspired so to do. To which I would

reply, that though they were inspired, yet that inspiration did not save them from showing their ignorance of letters, and man's wisdom this the multitude soon found out, by listening to the remarks of the envious Jewish priests. If then, to preach the gospel, by the gift of heaven, comes by inspiration solely, is God straitened; must he take the man exclusively? May he not, did he not, and can he not inspire a female to preach the simple story of the birth, life, death and resurrection of our Lord, and accompany it too with power to the sinner's heart. As for me, I am fully persuaded that the Lord called me to labor according to what I have received, in his vineyard. If he has not, how could he consistently bear testimony in favor of my poor labors, in awakening and converting sinners?

In my wanderings up and down among men, preaching according to my ability, I have frequently found families who told me that they had not for several years been to a meeting, and yet, while listening to hear what God would say by his poor female instrument, have believed with trembling—tears rolling down their cheeks, the signs of contrition and repentance towards God. I firmly believe that I have sown seed, in the name of the Lord, which shall appear with its increase at the great day of accounts, when Christ shall come to make up his jewels.

At a certain time, I was beset with the idea, that soon or late I should fall from grace and lose my soul at last. I was frequently called to the throne of grace about this matter, but found no relief; the temptation pursued me still. Being more and more affected with it, till at a certain time, when the spirit strongly impressed it on my mind to enter into my closet and carry my case once more to the Lord; the Lord enabled me to draw nigh to him, and to his mercy seat, at this time, in an extraordinary manner; for while I wrestled with him for the victory over this disposition to doubt whether I should persevere, there appeared a form of fire, about the size of a man's hand, as I was on my knees; at the same moment there appeared to the eye of faith a man robed in a white garment, from the shoulders down to the feet; from him a voice proceeded, saying: "Thou shalt never return from the cross." Since that time I have never doubted, believe that God will keep me until the day of redemption. Now I could adopt the very language of St. Paul, and say, that nothing could have separated me from the love of God, which is in Christ Jesus. Since that time, 1807, until the present, 1833, I have not even doubted the power and goodness of God to keep me from failing, through the sanctification of the spirit and belief of the truth.

MY MARRIAGE.

I N THE YEAR 1811, I changed my situation in life, having married Mr. Joseph Lee, pastor of a Society at Snow Hill, about six miles from the city of Philadelphia. It became necessary therefore for me to remove. This was a great trial at first, as I knew no person at Snow Hill, except my husband, and to leave my associates in the society, and especially those who composed the band of which I was one. None but those who have been in sweet fellowship with such as really love God, and have together drank bliss and happiness from the same fountain, can tell how dear such company is, and how hard it is to part from them.

At Snow Hill, as was feared, I never found that agreement and closeness in communion and fellowship, that I had in Philadelphia, among my young companions, nor ought I to have expected it. The manners and customs at this place were somewhat different, on which account I became discontented in the course of a year, and began to importune my husband to remove to the city. But this plan did not suit him, as he was the Pastor of the Society, he could not bring his mind to leave them. This afflicted me a little. But the Lord showed me in a dream what his will was concerning this matter.

I dreamed that as I was walking on the summit of a beautiful hill, that I saw near me a flock of sheep, fair and white, as if but newly washed; when there came walking toward me a man of a grave and dignified countenance, dressed entirely in white, as it were in a robe, and looking at me, said emphatically, "Joseph Lee must take care of these sheep, or the wolf will come and devour them." When I awoke I was convinced of my error, and immediately, with a glad heart, yielded to the right spirit in the Lord. This also greatly strengthened my faith in his care over them, for fear the wolf should by some means take any of them away. The following verse was beautifully suited to our condition, as well as to all the little flocks of God scattered up and down this land:

> "Us into Thy protection take,
> And gather with Thine arm;
> Unless the fold we first forsake,
> The wolf can never harm."

After this, I fell into a state of general debility, and in an ill state of health,

so much so, that I could not sit up; but a desire to warn sinners to flee the wrath to come, burned vehemently in my heart, when the Lord would send sinners into the house to see me. Such opportunities I embraced to press home on their consciences the things of eternity, and so effectual was the word of exhortation made through the Spirit, that I have seen them fall to the floor crying aloud for mercy.

From this sickness, I did not expect to recover, and there was but one thing which bound me to earth, and this was, that I had not as yet preached the gospel to the fallen sons and daughters of Adam's race, to the satisfaction of my mind. I wished to go from one end of the earth to the other, crying, Behold, behold the lamb! To this end I earnestly prayed the Lord to raise me up, if consistent with his will. He condescended to hear my prayer, and to give me a token in a dream, that in due time I should recover my health. The dream was as follows: I thought I saw the sun rise in the morning, and ascend to an altitude of about half an hour high, and then become obscured by a dense black cloud, which continued to hide its rays for about one-third part of the day, and then it burst forth again with renewed splendor.

This dream I interpreted to signify my early life, my conversion to God, and this sickness, which was a great affliction, as it hindered me, and I feared would forever hinder me from preaching the gospel, was signified by the cloud; and the bursting forth of the sun, again, was the recovery of my health, and being permitted to preach.

I went to the throne of grace on this subject, where the Lord made this impressive reply in my heart, while on my knees: "Ye shall be restored to thy health again, and worship God in full purpose of heart."

This manifestation was so impressive, that I could but hide my face as if some one was gazing upon me; to think of the great goodness of the Almighty God to my poor soul and body. From that very time, I began to gain strength of body and mind, glory to God in the highest, until my health was fully recovered.

For six years from this time I continued to receive from above, such baptisms of the Spirit as mortality could scarcely bear. About that time I was called to suffer in my family, by death—five, in the course of about six years, fell by his hand; my husband being one of the number, which was the greatest affliction of all.

I was now left alone in the world, with two infant children, one of the age of about two years, the other six months, with no other dependence than the promise of Him who hath said—I will be the window's God, and a father to

the fatherless. Accordingly, he raised me up friends, whose liberality comforted and solaced me in my state of widowhood and sorrows, I could sing with the greatest propriety the words of the poet.

> "He helps the stranger in distress,
> The window and the fatherless,
> And grants the prisoner sweet release."

I can say even now, with the Psalmist, "Once I was young, but now I am old, yet I have never seen the righteous forsaken, nor his seed begging bread." I have ever been fed by his bounty, clothed by his mercy, comforted and healed when sick, succored when tempted, and every where upheld by his hand.

THE SUBJECT OF MY CALL TO PREACH RENEWED.

IT WAS NOW eight years since I had made application to be permitted to preach the gospel, during which time I had only been allowed to exhort, and even this privilege but seldom. This subject now was renewed afresh in my mind; It was as a fire shut up in my bones. About thirteen months passed on, while under this renewed impression. During this time, I had solicited of the Rev. Bishop, Richard Allen, who at this time had become Bishop of the African Episcopal Methodists in America, to be permitted the liberty of holding prayer meetings in my own hired house, and of exhorting as I found liberty, which was granted me. By this means, my mind was relieved, as the house soon filled when the hour appointed for prayer had arrived.

I cannot but relate in this place, before I proceed further with the above subject, the singular conversion of a very wicked young man. He was a colored man, who had generally attended our meetings, but not for any good purpose; but rather to disturb and to ridicule our denomination. He openly and uniformly declared that he neither believed in religion, nor wanted anything to do with it. He was of a Gallio disposition, and took the lead among the young people of color. But after a while he fell sick, and lay about three months in a state of ill health; his disease was a consumption. Towards the close of his days, his sister who was a member of the society, came and desired me to go and see her brother, as she had no hopes of his recovery, perhaps the Lord might break into his mind. I went alone, and found him very low.

I soon commenced to inquire respecting his state of feeling, and how he found his mind. His answer was, "O tolerable well," with an air of great indifference. I asked him if I should pray for him. He answered in a sluggish and careless manner, "O yes, if you have time." I then sung a hymn, kneeled down and prayed for him, and then went my way.

Three days after this, I went again to visit the young man. At this time there went with me two of the sisters in Christ. We found the Rev. Mr. Cornish, of our denomination, laboring with him. But he said he received but little satisfaction from him. Pretty soon, however, brother Cornish took his leave; when myself with the other two sisters, one of which was an elderly women named Jane Hutt, the other was younger, both colored, commenced conversing with him, respecting his eternal interest, and of his hopes of a happy eternity, if any be had. He said but little; we then kneeled down together and besought the Lord in his behalf, praying that if mercy were not clear gone for ever, to shed a ray of softening grace upon the hardness of his heart. He appeared now to be somewhat more tender, and we thought we could perceive give some tokens of conviction, as he wished us to visit him again, in a tone of voice not quite as indifferent as he had hitherto manifested.

But two days had elapsed after this visit, when his sister came to me in haste, saying that she believed her brother was then dying, and that he had sent for me. I immediately called on Jane Hutt, who was still among us as a mother in Israel, to go with me. When we arrived there, we found him sitting up in bed, very restless and uneasy, but he soon laid down again. He now wished me to come to him, by the side of his bed. I asked him how he was. He said, very ill; and added, "Pray for me, quick? We now perceived his time in this world to be short. I took up the hymn-book, and opened to a hymn suitable to his case, and commenced to sing, but there seemed to be a horror in the room—a darkness of a mental kind, which was felt by us all; there being five persons, except the sick young man and his nurse. We had sung but one verse, when they all gave over singing, on account of this unearthly sensation, but myself. I continued to sing on alone, but in a dull and heavy manner, though looking up to God all the while for help. Suddenly I felt a spring of energy awake in my heart, when darkness gave way in some degree. It was but a glimmer from above. When the hymn was finished, we all kneeled down to pray for him. While calling on the name of the Lord, to have mercy on his soul, and to grant him repentance unto life; it came suddenly into my mind never to rise from my knees until God should hear prayer in this behalf, until he should convert and save his soul.

Now, while I thus continued importuning heaven, as I felt I was led, a ray of light, more abundant, broke forth among us. There appeared to my view, though my eyes were closed, the Saviour in full stature, nailed to the cross, just over the head of the young man, against the ceiling of the room. I cried out, brother look up, the Saviour is come, he will pardon you, your sins he will forgive. My sorrow for the soul of the young man was gone; I could no longer pray—joy and rapture made it impossible. We rose up from our knees, when lo, his eyes were gazing with ecstacy upwards; over his face there was an expression of joy; his lips were clothed in a sweet and holy smile; but no sound came from his tongue; it was heard in its stillness of bliss; full of hope and immortality. Thus, as I held him by the hand, his happy and purified soul soared away, without a sigh or a groan, to its eternal rest.

I now closed his eyes, straightened out his limbs, and left him to be dressed for the grave. But as for me, I was filled with the power of the Holy Ghost—he very soon seemed filled with glory. His sister and all that were in the room rejoiced, nothing doubting but he had entered into Paradise; and I believe I shall see him at the last and great day, safe on the shores of salvation.

But to return to the subject of my call to preach. Soon after this, as above related, the Rev. Richard Williams was to preach at Bethel Church, where I with others were assembled. He entered the pulpit, gave out the hymn, which was sung, and then addressed the throne of grace; took his text, passed through the exordium, and commenced to expound it. The text he took is in Jonah, 2d chap. 9th verse,—"Salvation is of the Lord." But as he proceeded to explain, he seemed to have lost the spirit; when in the same instant, I sprang, as by altogether supernatural impulse, to my feet, when I was aided from above to give an exhortation on the very text which my brother Williams had taken.

I told them I was like Jonah; for it had been then nearly eight years since the Lord had called me to preach his gospel to the fallen sons and daughters of Adam's race, but that I had lingered like him, and delayed to go at the bidding of the Lord, and warn those who are as deeply guilty as were the people of Ninevah.

During the exhortation, God made manifest his power in a manner sufficient to show the world that I was called to labor according to my ability, and the grace given unto me, in the vineyard of the good husbandman.

I now sat down, scarcely knowing what I had done, being frightened. I imagined, that for this indecorum, as I feared it might be called, I should be expelled from the church. But instead of this, the Bishop rose up in the

assembly, and related that I had called upon him eight years before, asking to be permitted to preach, and that he had put me off; but that he now as much believed that I was called to the work, as any of the preachers present. These remarks greatly strengthened me, so that my fears of having given an offence, and made myself liable as an offender, subsided, giving place to a sweet serenity, a holy joy of a peculiar kind, untasted in my bosom until then.

The next Sabbath day, while sitting under the word of the gospel, I felt moved to attempt to speak to the people in a public manner, but I could not bring my mind to attempt it in the church. I said, Lord, anywhere but here. Accordingly, there was a house not far off which was pointed out to me; to this I went. It was the house of a sister belonging to the same society with myself. Her name was Anderson. I told her I had come to hold a meeting in her house, if she should call in her neighbors. With this request she immediately complied. My congregation consisted of but five persons. I commenced by reading and singing a hymn; when I arose I found my hand resting on the Bible, which I had not noticed till that moment. It now occurred to me to take a text. I opened the Scripture, as it happened, at the 14st Psalm, fixing my eye on the third verse, which reads: "Set a watch, O Lord, before my mouth, keep the door of my lips." My sermon, such as it was, applied wholly to myself, and added an exhortation. Two of my congregation wept much, as the fruit of my labor this time. In closing, I said to the few, that if any one would open a door, I would hold a meeting the next sixth-day evening: When one answered that her house was at my service. Accordingly I went, and God made manifest his power among the people. Some wept, while others shouted for joy. One whole seat of females, by the power of God, as the rushing of a wind, were all bowed to the floor, at once, and screamed out. Also a sick man and woman in one house, the Lord convicted them both; one lived and the other died. God wrought a judgement some were well at night, and died in the morning. At this place I continued to hold meetings about six months. During that time I kept house with my little son, who was very sickly. About this time I had a call to preach at a place about thirty miles distant, among the Methodists, with whom I remained one week, and during the whole time, not a thought of my little son came diverted from the work I hid from me, lest I should have been diverted from the work I had to do to look after my son. Here by the instrumentality of a poor coloured woman, the Lord poured forth his spirit among the people. Though, as I was told, there were lawyers, doctors and magistrates present, to hear me speak, yet there was mourning and crying among sinners, for the Lord scattered fire

among them of his own kindling. The Lord gave him hand-maiden power to speak for his great name, for he arrested the hearts of the people, and caused a shaking amongst the multitude, for God was in the midst.

I now returned home, found all well; no harm had come to my child, although I left it very sick. Friends had taken care of it which was of the Lord. I now began to think seriously of breaking up housekeeping, and forsaking all to preach the everlasting Gospel. I felt a strong desire to return to the place of my nativity, at Cape May, after an absence of about fourteen years. To this place, where the heaviest cross was to be met with, the Lord sent me, as Saul of Tarsus was sent to Jerusalem, to preach the same gospel which he had neglected and despised before his conversion. I went by water, and on my passage was much distressed by sea sickness, so much so that I expected to have died, but such was not the will of the Lord respecting me. After I had disembarked, I proceeded on as opportunities offered, toward where my mother lived. When within ten miles of that place, I appointed an evening meeting. There were a goodly number came out to hear. The Lord was pleased to give me light and liberty among the people. After meeting, there came an elderly lady to me and said, she believed the Lord had sent me among them; she then appointed me another meeting there two weeks from that night. The next day I hastened forward to the place of my mother who was happy to see me, and the happiness was mutual between us. With her I left my poor sickly boy, while I departed to do my Master's will. In this neighborhood I had an uncle, who was a Methodist, and who gladly threw open his door for meetings to be held there. At the first meeting which I held at my uncle's house, there was, with others who had come from curiosity to hear the woman preacher, an old man, who was a Deist, and who said he did not believe the coloured people had any souls—he was sure they had none. He took a seat very near where I was standing, and boldly tried to look me out of countenance. But as I labored on in the best manner I was able, looking to God all the while, though it seemed to me I had but little liberty, yet there went an arrow from the bent bow of the gospel, and fastened in his till then obdurate heart. After I had done speaking, he went out, and called the people around him, said that my preaching might seem a small thing, yet he believed I had the worth of souls at heart. This language was different from what it was a little time before, as he now seemed to admit that colored people had souls, as it was to these I was chiefly speaking; and unless they had souls, whose good I had in view, his remark must have been without meaning. He now came into the house, and in the most friendly manner shook

hands with me, saying, he hoped God had spared him to some good purpose. This man was a great slave holder, and had been very cruel; thinking nothing of knocking down a slave with a fence stake, or whatever might come to hand. From this time it was said of him that he became greatly altered in his ways for the better. At that time he was about seventy years old, his head as white as snow; but whether he became a converted man or not, I never heard.

The week following, I had an invitation to hold a meeting at the Court House of the Country, when I spoke from the 53d chap. of Isaiah, 3d verse. It was a solemn time, and the Lord attended the word; I had life and liberty, though there were people there of various denominations. Here again I saw the aged slaveholder, who notwithstanding his age, walked about three miles to hear me. This day I spoke twice, and walked six miles to the place appointed. There was a magistrate present, who showed his friendship, by saying in a friendly manner, that he had heard of me: he handed me a hymn–book, pointing to a hymn which he had selected. When the meeting was over, he invited me to preach in a schoolhouse in his neighborhood, about three miles distant from where I then was. During this meeting one backslider was reclaimed. This day I walked six miles, and preached twice to large congregations, both in the morning and evening. The Lord was with me, glory be to his holy name. I next went six miles and held a meeting in a coloured friend's house, at eleven o'clock in the morning, and preached to a well behaved congregation of both coloured and white. After service I again walked back, which was in all twelve miles in the same day. This was on Sabbath, or as I sometimes call it, seventh day; for after my conversion I preferred the plain language of the Friends. On the fourth day, after this, in compliance with an invitation received by note, from the same magistrate who had heard me at the above place I preached to a large congregation, where we had a precious time: much weeping was heard among the people. The same gentleman, now at the close of the meeting, gave out another appointment at the same place, that day week. Here again I had liberty, there was a move among the people. Ten years from that time, in the neighborhood of Cape May, I held a prayer meeting in a school house, which was then the regular place of preaching for the Episcopal Methodists, after service, there came a white lady, of great distinction, a member of the Methodist society, and told me that at the same school house ten years before, under my preaching, the Lord first awakened her. She rejoiced much to see me, and invited me home with her, where I staid till the next day. This was bread cast upon the water, seen after many days.

From this place I next went to Dennis Creek Meeting house, where at the invitation of an elder, I spoke to a large congregation of various and conflicting sentiments, when a wonderful shock of God's power was felt, shown everywhere by groans, by sighs, and loud and happy amens. I felt as if aided from above. My tongue was cut loose, the stammerer spoke freely; the love of God, and of his service, burned with a vehement flame within me—his name was glorified among the people.

I had my little son with me, and was very much straitened for money—and not having means to procure my passage home, I opened a school, and taught eleven scholars, for the purpose of raising a small sum. For many weeks I knew not what to do about returning home, when the Lord came to my assistance as I was rambling in the fields meditating upon his goodness, and made known to me that I might go to the city of Philadelphia, for which place I soon embarked with a very kind captain. We had a perilous passage—a dreadful storm arose, and before leaving the Delaware bay, we had a narrow escape from being run down by a large ship. But the good Lord held us in the hollow of his hand, and in the afternoon of Nov. 12, 1821, we arrived at the city.

Here I held meetings in the dwelling house of sister Lydia Anderson, and for about three months had as many appointments as I could attend. We had many precious seasons together, and the Lord was with his little praying band, convincing and converting sinners to the truth. I continued in the city until spring, when I felt it impressed upon my mind to travel, and walked fourteen miles in company with a sister to meet with some ministers, there to assemble, from Philadelphia. Satan tempted me while on the way, telling me that I was a fool for walking so far, as I would not be permitted to preach. But I pursued my journey, with the determination to set down and worship with them. When I arrived, a goodly number of people had assembled, and no preacher. They waited the time to commence the exercises, and then called upon me. I took the 3d chapter John, 14th verse for my text. I had life and liberty, and the Lord was in the camp with a shout. Another meeting was appointed three miles from there, when I spoke from Psalms cxxxvii, 1, 2, 3, 4. My master was with me, and made manifest his power. In the country House, also, we held a meeting, and had a sweet waiting upon the Lord. I spoke from Hebrews ii, 3, when the Lord gave me peculiar liberty. At a dwelling house one night I spoke from John vii, 46, when six souls fell to the floor crying for mercy. We had a blessed outpouring of the spirit among us—the God of Jacob was in our midst—and the shout of heaven-born souls was

like music to our ears.

About the month of February my little son James, then in his sixth year, gave evidence of having religious inclinations. Once he got up in a chair, with a hymn book in his hand, and with quite a ministerial jesture, gave out a hymn. I felt the spirit move me to sing with him. A worthy sister was in the room, who I asked to pray for him. I invoked the Lord to answer and seal this prayer in the courts of heaven. I believed He would and did, and while yet on our knees I was filled with the fulness of God, and the answer came. I cried out in the joy of my heart—"The dead is alive"—and ran down stairs to inform a neighbor. Tears ran down the cheeks of my now happy boy, and great was our rejoicing together. He had been the subject of many prayers, and often had I thought I would rather follow him to his grave than to see him grow up an open and profane sinner like many children I had seen. And here let me say, the promise of the Lord is, "ask and ye shall receive." Dear parents; pray for your children in childhood—carry them in the arms of faith to the mercy seat, and there present them an offering to the Lord. I can say from my own experience, the Lord will hear prayer. I had given James the Bible as Haman gave Samuel to God in his youth, and by his gracious favor he was received. For the further encouragement of fathers and mothers to engage in this blessed work, let me refer them to Ecclesiastes xi, 6; "In the morning sow thy seed, and in the evening withhold not thy hand, for thou knowest not whether shall prosper either this or that, or whether they both shall be alike good."

> "Sow it in the youthful mind,
> Can you have a fairer field?
> Be it but in faith consigned.
> Harvest, doubtless, it shall yield,
> Fruits of early piety,
> All that God delights to see."

In November I journeyed for Trenton, N. J. At Burlington I spoke to the people on the Sabbath, and had a good time among them, and on Monday the 12th, in a School house. Sister Mary Owan, who had laid aside all the cares of the world, went with me. We had no means of travelling but on foot, but the Lord regarded us, and by some means put it into the heart of a stranger, to convey us to the Trenton bridge. We fell in with the elder of the circuit, who spoke to me in a cold and formal manner, and as though he

thought my capacity was not equal to his. We went into the sister's house, where we expected to stay, and waited a long while with our hats and cloaks on, before the invitation to lodge there was given. In the morning I had thought to visit Newhope, but remained to discharge my duty in visiting the sick and afflicted three or four days in the neighborhood. I was invited to a prayer meeting, and was called upon by a brother to speak. I improved the offer, and made some remarks from Kings xviii, 21. One of the preachers invited me to approach for them on sixth day evening, which I complied with much power, and before an attentive congregation; when God followed the word with much power, and great was our joy. On the 17th I spoke in the morning at 11 o'clock. I felt my weakness and deficiency for the work, and thought "Who is able for these things," and desired to get away from the task. My text was Timothy vi, 2-7. The Lord again cut loose the stammering tongue; and opened the Scriptures to my mind, so that, glory to God's dear name, we had a most melting, sin-killing, and soul-reviving time. In the afternoon I assisted in leading a class, when we found the Lord faithful and true—and on the same evening I spoke from Hebrews ii, 3.

The next day, sister Mary Owan and Myself set out for Newhope, where we arrived, after walking sixteen miles, at about six o'clock in the evening. Though tedious, it was a pleasant walk to view the high mountain and towering hills, and the beauty and variety of nature around us, which powerfully impressed my mind with the greatness and wisdom of my Maker. At this place I stopped at the house of the gentleman with whose wife's mother I was brought up, and by whom we were agreeably received. The next evening we called upon brother Butler, where I addressed a small company, and God, through his words, quickened some. The next night I spoke in an Academy to a goodly number of people, from John iii, 14. Here I found some ever ill-behaved persons, who talked roughly, and said among other things, "I was not a woman, but a man dressed in female clothes." I labored one week among them, and went next to Lambertsville, where we experienced kindness from the people, and had a happy time and parted in tears.

I now returned to Philadelphia, where I stayed a short time, and went to Salem, West Jersey. I met with many troubles on my journey, especially from the elder, who like many others, was averse to a woman's preaching. And here let me tell that elder, if he has not gone to heaven, that I have heard that as far back as Adam Clarke's time, his objections to female preaching were met by the answer—"If an ass reproved Balaam, and a barn-door fowl reproved Peter, why should not a woman reprove sin?" I do not introduce this for its

complimentary classification of women with donkeys and fowls, but to give the reply of a poor woman, who had once been a slave. To the first companion she said—"May be a speaking woman is like an ass—but I can tell you one thing, the ass seen the angel when Balaam didn't."

Not withstanding the position, we had a prosperous time at Salem. I had some good congregations, and sinners were cut to the heart. After speaking in the meeting house, two women came up into the pulpit, and falling upon my neck cried out "What shall I do to be saved?" One said she had disobeyed God, and she had taken her children from her—he had called often after her, but she did not hearken. I pointed her to the all-atoning blood of Christ, which is sufficient to cleanse from all sin, and left her, after prayer, to his mercy. From this place I walked twenty-one miles, and preached with difficulty to a stiff-necked and rebellious people, who I soon left without any animosity for their treatment. They might have respected my message, if not the poor weak servant who brought it to them with so much labor.

"If they persecute you in one city, flee into another," was the advice I had resolved to take, and I hastened to Greenwich, where I had a lively congregation, had unusual life and liberty in speaking, and the power of God was there. We also had a solemn time in the meeting house on Sabbath day morning, and in a dwelling house in the evening; a large company assembled, when the spirit was with us, and we had a mighty shaking among the dry bones.

On second day morning, I took stage and rode seven miles to Woodstown, and there I spoke to a respectable congregation of white and colored, in a school house. I was desired to speak in the colored meeting house, but the minister could not reconcile his mind to a woman preacher he could not unite in fellowship with me even to shaking hands as Christians ought. I had visited that place before, when God made manifest his power "through the foolishness of preaching," and owned the poor old woman. One of the brothers appointed a meeting in his own house, and after much persuasion this minister came also. I did not feel much like preaching, but spoke from Acts viii, 35. I felt my inability, and was led to complain of weakness—but God directed the arrow to the hearts of the guilty—and my friend the minister got happy, and often shouted "Amen," and "as it is, sister." We had a wonderful display of the spirit of God among us, and we found it good to be there. There is nothing too hard for the Lord to do. I committed the meeting into the hands of the elder, who afterwards invited me to preach in the meeting house. He had said he did not believe that ever a soul was con-

verted under the preaching of a woman—but while I was laboring in his place, conviction seized a woman, who fell floor crying for mercy. This meeting held till 12 or 1 o'clock. O how precious is the sound of Jesus' name! I never felt a doubt at this time of my acceptance with God, but rested my soul on his every promise. The elder shook hands, and we parted.

Nov. 22, 1822, I returned to Philadelphia, and attended meetings in and out of the city. God was still my help, and I preached and formed a class, and tried to be useful. The oppositions I met with, however, were numerous—so much so, that I was tempted to withdraw from the Methodist Church, lest some might go into ruin by their persecutions of me—but this was allowed only to try my faithfulness to God. At times I was pressed down like a cart beneath its shafts—my life seemed as at the point of the sword—my heart was sore and pained me in my body. But the Lord knows how to deliver the godly out of temptation, and to reserve the unjust till the day of judgement to be punished. While relating the feelings of my mind to a sister who called to see me, joy sprang up in my bosom that I was not overcome by the adversary, and I was overwhelmed with the love of God and souls. I embraced the sister in my arms, and we had a melting time together. Oh how comforting it is to have the spirit of God bearing witness with our spirits that we are his children in such dark hours!

> When Satan appears to stop up our path,
> And fill us with fears, we triumph by faith;
> He cannot take from us, (tho' oft he has tried,)
> The soul cheering promise the Lord will provide.
> He tells us we're weak, our hope is in vain,
> The good that we seek we ne'er shall obtain;
> But when such suggestions our graces have tried,
> This answers all questions, the Lord will provide.

I felt a greater love for the people than ever. It appeared to me that they erred through ignorance of my desire to do them good; and my prayer was that nothing but love might appear in my ways, and actuate my heart. Religion is love—God is love. But it was nothing less than the Divine power that brought me through, for it appeared that the hosts of darkness were arrayed against me to destroy my peace and lead me away from the throne of love.

June 24, I left the city of Philadelphia to travel in Delaware state. I went with captain Ryal, a kind gentleman, who took me to his house in

Wilmington, and himself and lady both treated me well. The first night of my arrival, I preached in the stone Methodist meeting house. I tried, in my weak way, to interest the assembly from the 2d chapter of Hebrews, 3d verse—"How shall we escape, if we neglect so great salvation." God was there, as we had the most delightful evidence—and many had their eyes opened to see there was no escape from the second death while out of Christ, and cried unto God for his saving grace. I would that all who have not embraced the salvation offered in the gospel, might examine the question candidly and seriously, ere the realities of the other world break up their fancied security.

In July, I spoke in a School house to a large congregation, from Numbers xxix, 17. Here we had a sweet foretaste of heaven—full measure, and running over—shouting and rejoicing—while the poor errand-bearer of a free gospel was assisted from on high. I wish my reader had been there to share with us the joyous heavenly feast. On the 15th of July I gave an exhortation in the meeting house again to a listening multitude—deep and solemn were the convictions of many, and good, I trust, was done.

The next place I visited was Newcastle. The meeting house could not be obtained, and two young gentleman interested themselves to get the Court house, but the Trustees objected, wishing to know why the Methodists did not open their Church. The reason was "I was not licensed," they said. My two friends waited on me to speak in the Market house, where I attended at early candlelight, and had the pleasure of addressing a few plain truths to a crowded but respectful congregation, from John vii, 46—"Never man spoke like this man." On Sunday the same young gentlemen invited me to give another discourse, to which I consented, before a large gathering of all descriptions.

From here I proceeded to Christine, where we worshipped in a dwelling house, and I must say was well treated by some of my colored friends. I then returned to Wilmington, where in a few days I had a message to return again to C. My friends said I should have the Meeting house, for which Squire Luden interested himself, and the appointment was published. When the people, met at the proper time, the doors remained locked. Amid cries of "shame" we left the Church steps—but a private house was opened a short distance up the road, and though disappointed in obtaining egress to a Church, the Lord did not disappoint his people, for we were fed with the bread of life, and had a happy time. Mr. and Mrs. Lewelen took me to their house, and treated me, not as one of their hired servants, but as a compan-

ion, for which I shall ever feel grateful. Mr. Smith, a doctor, also invited me to call upon them—he was a Presbyterian, but we prayed and conversed together about Jesus and his love, and parted without meddling with each others creeds. Oh, I long to see the day when Christians will meet on one common platform—Jesus of Nazareth—and cease their bickerings and contentions about non-essentials—when "our Church" shall be less debated, but "our Jesus" shall be all in all.

Another family gave me the invitation to attend a prayer meeting. It was like a "little heaven below." From here I walked about four miles that evening, accompanied by the house maid of Mrs. Ford, a Presbyterian, who said she knew her mistress would be glad to see me. Mrs. F. gave me a welcome—said she felt interested in my speaking, and sent a note to a Methodist lady, who replied that my labor would be acceptable, no doubt, in her Church that afternoon. When I came in, the elder was in the pulpit. He gave us a good sermon. After preaching, this lady spoke of me to the elder; in consequence, he invited me to his pulpit, saying "he was willing that every one should do good." My text was Hebrew ii, 3. Though weak in body, the good Master filled my mouth and gave me liberty among strangers, and seldom have I spent so happy a Sabbath. Mrs. F. had a colored woman in her family one hundred and ten years of age, with whom I conversed about religion—how Christ had died to redeem us, and the way of salvation, and the poor old lady said "she wished she could hear me every day." I also called upon another, one hundred and sixteen years old, who was blind. We talked together about Jesus—she had a strong and abiding evidence of her new birth, and in a few weeks went home to heaven. Here she was long deprived of the light of the sun, and the privilege of reading God's blessed word; but there her eyes are unsealed, and the Sun of righteousness has risen with healing in his wings.

> There glory beams on all the plains,
> Which sight to her is given—
> There music rolls in sweetest strains,
> And spotless beauty ever reigns,
> And all is love in heaven.

I left Mrs. Ford's and walked about three miles to St. George, with a recommend to a Mrs. Sutton, a noble-minded lady of the Presbyterian order, where I was generously treated. Here I preached in the School house to a

respectable company—had considerable weeping and a profitable waiting upon the Lord. I accepted an invitation from a gentleman to preach in a Methodist Church three miles distant—found there a loving people, and was highly gratified at the order and decorum manifested while I addressed them. Mrs. Smith took me home with her, who I found to be a christian both in sentiment and action. By invitation, I went next to Port Penn, and spoke with freedom, being assisted of the Lord, to a full house, and had a glorious feast of the Spirit. The next night found me at Canton Bride, to which place I had walked—spoke in a School house, from Math xxii, 41—"What think ye Christ?" The presence of the Lord overshadowed us—believers rejoiced—some were awakened to belive well of Master, and I trust are on their way to glory. In Fieldsborough, also, we had gracious meetings.

At Smyrna I met brother C.W. Cannon, who made application for the Friend's Meeting house for me, where the Lord blessed us abundantly. We attended a Camp-meeting of the old connexion, and got greatly refreshed for the King's service. I rode ten miles and delivered a message from the Lord to a waiting audience—the Master assisted, and seven individuals, white and colored, prostrated themselves for prayer. Next day I rode to Middletown— spoke in a School house to a white congregation from Isaiah lxiii, 1, and a good time it was. In the morning at 11 o'clock, I addressed a Methodist Society, and in the afternoon at 3 o'clock, spoke under a tree in the grave yard, by the road side, to a large audience. Squire Maxwell's lady, who was present, invited me home to tea with herself and nieces, and a Quaker lady showed her benevolence by putting into my hand enough to help me on my journey. The Lord is good—what shall I do to make it known? I rode seven miles that night, and gave an exhortation after the minister had preached, and felt happier than a King.

I now travelled to Cecil country, Md., and the first evening spoke to a large congregation. The pastor afterwards baptized some adult persons—and we all experienced the cleansing and purifying power. We had a baptism within and without. I was next sent for by the servant of a white gentleman, to hold a meeting in his house in the evening. He invited the neighbors, colored and white, when I spoke according to the ability God gave me. It was pleasant to my poor soul to be there—Jesus was in our midst—and we gave glory to God. Yes, glory—glory be to God in the highest. "God forbid that I should glory, save in the cross of our Lord Jesus Christ." I boast not myself. Paul may plant and Apollos water, but God giveth the increase. I tried also to preach three times at a place 14 miles from here—had good meetings—

backsliders were reclaimed and sinners convicted of sin, who I left in the hands of God, with the hope of meeting and recognizing again "When we arrive at home."

Returned back to Middletown. The next day the preacher of the circuit conveyed me to his place of appointment at Elkton. We had a wonderful outpouring of the spirit. At Frenchtown I spoke at 11 o'clock, where I realized my nothingness, but, God's name be praised, he helped me in the duty. Went again to Middletown, and from there to Canton's Bridge, and talked to the people as best I could. Seven miles from this place I found, by the direction of a kind Providence, my own sister, who had been separated from me some thirty three years. We were young when last we met, with less of the cares of life than now. Each heart then was buoyant with mild hopes and pleasures— and little did we expect at parting that thirty three years would pass over us, with its changes and vicissitudes, ere we should see each other's face. Both were much altered in appearance, but we knew each other, and talked over the dealings of the Lord with us, retracing our wanderings in the world and "the days when life was young."

> "Our days of childhood quickly pass,
> And soon our happiest years are run—
> As the pure dew that gems the grass the grass
> Is dried beneath the summer sun.
> There's such decent—such guile in men,
> Who would not be a child again?"

During this visit I had three meetings in different directions in gentlemen's houses, and a prayer meeting at my brother's, who did not enjoy religion. My good old friends Mr. Lorton happened to be there, who told the people that she had been to my house—that he knew Mr. Lee (my husband) intimately, and that he had often preached for him while pastor of the Church at Snow Hill, N.J.

I next attended and preached several times at a camp meeting, which continued five days. We had Pentecostal showers—sinners were pricked to the heart, and cried mightily to God for succor from impending judgment, and I verily believe the Lord was well pleased at our weak endeavors to serve him in the tented grove. The elder in charge, on the last day of the camp, appointed a meeting for me in a dwelling house. Spoke from Acts ii, 11. The truth fastened in the hearts of two young women, who, after I was seated, came

and fell down at my side, and cried for God to have mercy on them—we prayed and wrestled with the Lord, and both were made happy in believing, and are alive in the faith of the gospel. The next morning a brother preacher took me to St. Georgetown. From there I took stage to Wilmington, and called on my friend Captain Rial, in whose family I spent two days and nights. Went to Philadelphia to attend a camp-meeting. Returned again to W— where I was taken sick with typhus fever, was in the doctor's hands for some days—but the Lord rebuked the disease, gave me my usual health again, and I returned back to Philadelphia.

The Bishop gave me an invitation to speak in Bethel Church; but here my heart fluttered with fear at the commencement, in manner known but to those who feel their unworthiness in addressing new and large assemblies. My text was in Isaiah x. 10,11. Previous to dismission, the Bishop gave me another appointment in Wesley Church for first day morning. Where I labored to encourage believers, from Ephesians ii, 19. The comforter was with us—we were sprinkled as with clear water from above—the hands of those that were hanging down were lifted up, and we truly had a refreshing season. Glory to God for the manifestation of His Spirit. "Now therefore ye are no more strangers and foreigners, but fellow-citizens with the saints, and of the household of God."

On the ensuing Thursday night, in Union Church, I had the opportunity of speaking a word for my Saviour again, and recommended the impenitent to see to it that they took the advice of my text, in Rev. iii, 18. The Lord searched the heart as he did Jerusalem with a lighted candle, and there was a moving of the Spirit among the people.

From Philadelphia I travelled on foot thirty miles to Downingtown, and gave ten sermons while there, and remember the cold day in December I walked sixteen miles from the above place to brother Wells, where I staid one week, and labored both among colored and white. They had one class there. Three miles further, I talked on Lord's day to an apparently hardened people, and next night preached in a School-house, after a ride of ten miles. The call of the Lord was for me now to go to West Chester, N. Y., where I remained a little period with brother Thomas Henry and brother Miller; preached in a School-house and in the Wesleyan Methodist Meeting-house. When prepared to go home, a request was sent me to preach in the Court-house of the country, to which I rode ten miles, and addressed the citizens on two evenings. The Lord strengthened his feeble instrument in the effort to win souls to Christ, for which my heart at this time was heavily burthened.

Next morning I left for Westhaven, where I visited a School of boys and girls, and was much pleased to see them engaged and improving in their studies. How great the difference now, thought I, for the mental and moral culture of the young than when I was a child!

In the month of June, 1823, I went on from Philadelphia to New York with Bishop Allen and several Elders, (including our present Rev. Bishop Brown,) to attend the New York Annual Conference of our denomination, where I spent three months of my time. We arrived about nine o'clock in the evening. As we left the boat, a person fell into the dock, and notwithstanding the effort made to save and find him, he was seen no more. 'In the midst of life we are in death.' On the 4th of June I spoke in the Asbury Church, from Psalms c, 33.

I think I never witnessed such a shouting and rejoicing time. The Church had then but recently adopted the African M.E. discipline. On the 5th I brought my master's message to the Bethel Church—Text Isaiah lviii, 1. "Cry aloud, spare not; lift up they voice like a trumpet, and show my people their transgressions, and the house of Jacob their sins." The spirit of God came upon me; I spoke without fear of man, and seemed willing even there to be offered up; the preachers shouted and prayed, and it was a time long to be remembered.

June 6, Spoke in the Church in High Street, Brooklyn, from Jer. ix, 1— "Oh that my head were waters, and mine eyes a fountain of tears, that I might weep day and night for the slain of the daughter of my people." In these days I felt it my duty to travel up and down in the world, and promulgate the gospel of Christ, especially among my own people, though I often desired to be released from the great task. The Lord had promised to be with me, and my trust was in his strong arm.

> Renouncing every worldly thing,
> Safe 'neath the shadow of thy wing
> My Sweetest thought henceforth shall be
> That all I want I find in thee,
> In them, my God, In Thee.

I left my friend in Brooklyn, and went to Flushing, L.I. Here we had quite a revival feeling, and two joined society. Visited Jamaica and Jericho; spoke in brother B's dwelling, in the church, and under a tree. Went to White Plains to the camp-meeting; the Lord was with us indeed; believers

were revived, backsliders reclaimed, and sinners converted. Returned and spent a little time in Brooklyn, where I addressed the people from Rev. iii, 18, and John iii, 15.

July 22. Spoke in Asbury Church from Acts xiii, 41—"Behold ye despisers, and wonder and perish." I pointed out the portion of the hypocrite, the liar, the Sabbath-breaker, and all who do wickedly and die in their sins; they shall be to the judgment bar of Jehovah, and before an assembled universe hear their awful sentence, "Depart from me, ye cursed, into everlasting fire, prepared for the devil and his angels," while the righteous shall be received "into life eternal." On the 28th I went to Dutch Hill, L.I., and spoke before a congregation of white and colored, in a barn, as there was no other suitable place. I felt happy when I thought of my dear Redeemer, who was born in a stable and cradled in a manger, and we had a precious season. Brother Croker, of Brooklyn, and father Thompson were with me, at whose feet I desired rather to sit and learn, they being experienced "workmen that needed not to be ashamed." But the Lord sends by whom he will.

The next Sabbath I weakly attempted to address my friends in New York again. Took the words in Math. xxviii, 13, for my text—"Say ye, his disciples came by night, and stole him away while we slept." The place was greatly crowded, and many came who could not get in. A class met here, to which the preacher invited all who desired to remain, and thirty persons tarried. He called upon me to lead, but He who led Israel over the Red Sea assisted, and it was a gracious time with us. Some who remained from curiosity were made, like Belshazzar, to tremble and weep, while the spirit strove powerfully with them. One experienced religion and joined society. I expect in the resurrection morning to meet many who were in that little company, in my Father's house, where we shall strike hands no more to part; where our song of redemption shall be raised to God and the Lamb forever. Dear reader, if you have not, I charge you to make your peace with God while time and opportunity is given, and be one of that number who shall take part and lot in the first resurrection. Though I may never see you in the flesh, I leave on this page my solemn entreaty that you delay not to obtain the pardoning favor of God; that you leave not the momentous subject of religion to a sick bed or dying hour, but now, even one, seek the Lord with full purpose of heart, and he will be found of thee. "If any man sin, he had advocate with the Father, Jesus Christ the righteous."

> "Oh that the world might taste and see
> The riches of his grace;
> The arms of love that compass me,
> Would all mankind embrace."

I visited a woman who was laying sick upon her death-bed. He told me "she had once enjoyed religion, but the enemy had cheated her out of it." She knew that she must die in a very little while, and could not get well, and her agony of soul, in view of its unprepared state for a judgment to come, awoke every feeling of sympathy within me. Oh ! how loud such a scene calls upon us to be "faithful unto death"—then shall we "receive a crown of life." Also visited Mrs. Miller, who once "tasted that the Lord was good," but had ceased now to follow him. She had been a Methodist for many years—got her feelings injured through some untoward circumstance—had fallen from grace, and now was sick. A good sister accompanied me? we conversed with Mrs. M., sung an appropriate hymn, and my friend supplicated the throne of grace in her behalf. She had frequently felt the need of returning Saviour, and during prayer her heart became melted into tenderness. She cried aloud for mercy, wrestled like Jacob for the witness, and the Lord, faithful and the Lord, faithful and true, "healed her backslidings," and we left her happy in his father. Praise the Lord for his matchless grace. I entertained no doubt of her well-grounded hope; and on seeing such a display of God's power, I was lost in wonder, love and praise. Let the backslider hear and take courage.

Let all who are out of Christ hear the invitation—"Repent ye and be converted, for God hath called all men everywhere to repent."

> "Without reserve give Christ your heart,
> Let him his righteousness impart—
> Then all things else he'll freely give,
> With him you all things shall receive."

With a serene and tranquil mind I now returned to Philadelphia. The Bishop was pleased to give me an appointment at Bethel Church, but a spirit of opposition arose among the people against the propriety of female preaching. My faith was tried—yet I felt my call to labor for souls none the less. "Shall the servant be above his Master?" The ministers of Jesus must expect persecution, if they would be faithful witnesses against sin and sinners—but shall they, "awed by a mortal's form, conceal the word of God?"

Thou God knowest my heart, and that they glory is all I have in view. Shall I cease from sounding the alarm to an ungodly world, when the vengeance of offended heaven is about to be poured out, because my way is sometimes beset with scoffers, or those who lose sight of the great Object, and stop on the road to glory to contend about non-essentials? Rather let the messengers of God go on—let them not be hindered by the fashioned and customs of a gainsaying and mis-loving generation, but with the crown in view, which shall deck the brow of those only who are "faithful unto death"—let them "cry aloud and spare not." Who regarded the warnings of Noah? who believed in his report? Who among the antidiluvians, that witnessed the preparations of this righteous man to save himself and family from a deluge of waters, believed him any thing else than a fanatic, deluded, and beside himself? Let the servants of Christ gird on the armor, and listen to the Captain's voice: "Lo I am with you always, even unto the end." With the promise of my Lord impressed upon my mind, I remained at home only a week, and walked twenty-one miles to Lumbertown, and preached in the Old Methodist Church and our African Church. Brother Joshua Edely was then a deacon there, and held a quarterly meeting soon after my reaching the place. He also appointed a lovefeast in the morning, when the love that true believers enjoy at such scenes made the place akin to heaven. While here I spoke as the Spirit taught me from Solomon's Songs. It was a happy meeting—refreshing to the thirsty soul—and we had a shout of the king in the camp. I shall never forget the kindness I received here from dear sister G.B. May the blessings of heaven be hers in this and the world to come.

I travelled seven miles from the above place to Snow Hill on Sabbath morning, where I was to preach in the Church of which I was a member, and although much afflicted in body, I strove, by the grace of God, to perform the duty. This was once the charge of JOSEPH LEE. In this desk my lamented husband had often stood up before me, proclaiming the "acceptable year of the Lord"—here he labored with zeal and spent his strength to induce sinners to be "reconciled to God"—here his toils ended. And could it be, his a poor unworthy being like myself should be called to address his former congregation, and should stand in the same pulpit! The thought made me tremble. My heart sighed when memory brought back the image, and the reminiscences of other days crowded upon me. But why, my heart, dost thou sigh? He has ceased from his labor, and I here see his works do follow. It will be enough, if these, the people of his care, press on and gain the kingdom. It will be enough, if, on the final day, "for which all other days were made," we

pass through the gates into the city, and live again together where death cannot enter, and separations are unknown. Cease then, my tears—a little while, my fluttering heart! and the turf that covers my companion, perchance, may cover thee—a little while, my soul! if faithful, and the widow's God will call thee from this valley of tears and sorrows to rest in the mansions the Saviour has gone to prepare for his people. "Good what God gives—just what he takes away."

My mind was next exercised to visited Trenton, N.J. I spoke for the people there, but soon had felt the cross so heavy. Perhaps it was occasioned through grieving over the past, and my feelings of loneliness in the world. A sister wished me to go with her to Bridgeport—where I found brother or win, then elder over that church. He gave me an appointment. We had a full house, and God's power was manifest among the people, and I returned to the elder's house rejoicing. The following day I walked fourteen miles to a meeting, where also we were greatly favored with the presence of God. Soon after this, I thought of going home to Philadelphia. I got about three miles on foot, when an apparent voice said "if thou goest home thou wilt die." I paused for a moment, and not comprehending what it meant, pursued my journey. Again I was startled by something like a tapping on my shoulder, but, on turning round, I found myself alone, which two circumstances created a singular feeling I could not understand. I thought of Balaam when met by the angel in the way. I was taken sick and it seemed I should die in the road. I said I will go back, and walked about four miles to Bridgeport. Told a good sister my exercise, who was moved with sympathy, and got brandy and bathed me. On Wednesday night I spoke to the people at Trenton Bridge, and notwithstanding the opposition I had met with from brother Samuel R—then on the circuit, the Lord supported the "Woman preacher" and my soul was cheered. On Thursday I walked fourteen miles, when the friends applied to the elder to let me talk for them, but his prejudices also, against women preaching were very strong, and tried hard to disaffect the minds of the people. The dear man has since gone to stand before that God who knows the secrets of all hearts—and where, I earnestly pray, he may find some who have been saved by grace through the instrumentality of female preaching.

> "Then here, O God, thy work fulfil;
> And from thy mercy's throne
> O grant me strength to do thy will,
> And to resist my own."

Norristown, Bucks county, January 6, 1824. Brother Morris conveyed me here at his own expense, and made application for places for me to speak. Addressed a large congregation on the fourth day after my introduction into the place, in the court-house, from Isaiah liiii. 1,—"Who hath believed our report? and to whom is the arm of the Lord revealed?" I felt embarrassed in the commencement, but the Spirit came, and "helped our infirmities"— good attention, and some weeping. On the 18th I spoke in the academy—it was a solemn time, and the people came out in numbers to hear. I then walked four miles to brother Morris's—spoke twice in the school house, and once in a dwelling house.

On the 14th April, I went with Bishop Allen and several elders to Baltimore, on their way to attend Conference; at the end of which the Bishop gave me permission to express a few thoughts for my Lord. On leaving the city of B., I travelled about 100 miles to Eastern Shore, Maryland. Brother Bailey was then laboring on that circuit, who received and treated me very kindly. We had several good meetings, and twice I spoke in Bethel Church, when the outpouring of the Spirit was truly great. In company with a good sister, who took a gig and horse, I travelled about three hundred miles, and labored in different places. Went to Denton African Church, and on the first Sabbath gave two sermons. The Church was in a thriving, prosperous condition, and the Lord blessed the word to our comfort. During the week I labored in the court-house before a large concourse of hearers. The Lord was unspeakably good, and one fell to the floor under the power.

By request, I also spoke in the Old Methodist Church in Denton, which was full to overflowing. It was a happy meeting. My tongue was loosened, and my heart warm with the love of God and souls—a season yet sweet to my memory. From there I went to Greensboro—the elder gave a sermon, after which I exhorted the poor sinner to prepare to meet the Lord in peace, before mercy was clear gone forever. The Old Methodist connexion gave an invitation for me to speak in their house, which I embraced, feeling thankful that the middle wall of partition had, thus far, been broken down. "He that feareth God and worketh righteousness shall be accepted of him"—not he who hath a different skin—not he who belongs to this denomination, or, to that—but "he that feareth God." My Master is no respecter of persons. May the partition walls that divide His sincere followers be broken down by the spirit of love.

In Whitehall Chapel I spoke to a respectable congregation, from Isaiah iii. 1. Though in a slave country, I found the Omnipresent one was with us.

Dr. Clarke took us home to dine with his family—for which uncommon attention I felt highly gratified. I believe him a Christian in heart, and one, no doubt, who has read the words of the Saviour: "Whosoever shall give to drink unto one of these little ones a cup of cold water only, shall in no wise lose his reward." And, notwithstanding the doctor was a Presbyterian, Mr. Buly had the privilege of baptizing two of their colored children.

I stopped next at Concord, and in the Old Methodist connexion tried to encourage the Lord's people to persevere. God displayed His power by a general outpouring of the Spirit—sinners cried for mercy, while others shouted for joy. Spoke also to a congregation of colored and white at Stanton Mills; and arrived again at Eastern Shore, where I spoke in Bethel Church during Quarterly Meeting. Attended their love-feast, where several joined society, and many encouraging testimonies were given by young converts that "God hath power on earth to forgive sins." May they be faithful stewards of the manifold gifts of God—and never be ashamed to confess what the Lord had done for them. Many lose the witness out of the heart by withholding their testimony from their friends and neighbors of the power of God to save. They run well for a season, but the tempter whispers "not now"—and by and by the soul becomes barren and unfruitful. May God help the young converts to "Watch," and tell around what a dear Saviour they have found.

> "Ashamed of Jesus!—yes, I may,
> When I've no guilt to wash away—
> No tears to wipe—no good to crave—
> No fears to quell—no soul to save."

June 10th, 1824. Left Eastern Shore for a journey to Bath, and went around the circuit with brother J.B., the elder. In the Old Methodist Church, at Fory's Neck, I had the privilege of speaking to a large congregation, which was made the power of God unto salvation. Visited Lewistown, and had a blessed meeting in the Methodist Church. The tears of the penitent flowed sweetly, which always encourages me to persevere in proclaiming the glad tidings of a risen Saviour to my fellow beings. When the heart is thus melted into tenderness, I feel assured the Lord sanctions the feeble effort of His poor servant—it is a good omen to my mind that the mourner is not forsaken of God, and that he yet stands knocking at the door for admittance. Oh! that those who weep for an absent Jesus may be comforted by hearing Him say—"Thy sins, which were many, are all forgiven thee: go in peace and sin no more."

Elder J.B. preached in Greensboro, where I attended, and had a quickening time. Some enmity had existed among the brethren, but the spirit of love got the ascendancy, and the lion became as the lamb. The gospel is the best remedy to subdue the evil passions of men that has ever been discovered. Dear Master, let Thy gospel spread to earth's remotest bounds.

I have travelled, in four years, sixteen hundred miles and of that I walked two hundred and eleven miles, and preached the kingdom of God to the falling sons and daughters of Adam, counting it all joy for the sake of Jesus. Many times cast down but not forsaken; willing to suffer as well as love. I spoke at Harris's Mills, in a dwelling house, to a large concourse of people, from Paul's Epistle to the Ephesians, xviii.19-20. I felt much drawn out, in the Spirit of God, meanwhile from my feelings. I observed there were some present that never would meet me again. Mr. J.B., the elder, then requested me to lead the class. Much mourning, weeping and rejoicing. Four days afterwards, a man that sat under this sermon, (a shoemaker by occupation) fell dead from his bench without having any testimony of a hope in Christ. How dreadful to relate the wicked shall not live out half their days. In Easton I spoke from the Evan. John, I chap. 45 ver., the Lord's time. Then proceeded to Dagsberry, 25 miles, preached in Bethel Church to a multitude of people, it being to them a new thing, but only the old made more manifest. Bless God for what my heart feels, for a good conscience is better than a sacrifice. Two sermons preached in said Church, I spoke from Acts 13 chap., 41 ver.,—the power of God filled the place—some shouted, others mourned, some testified God for Christ's sake had forgiven sin, whilst others were felled to the floor. From thence we went to Sinapuxom, spoke on Sabbath day to a large congregation from Num. 24 chap., 17 ver—the Lord gave light, life and liberty on that portion of Scripture, Great time. The elder filled the appointment, and while preaching, there were 10 or 11 white men came and said they wanted to see the preacher; he sent for them to come into the house, but they seemed afraid or refused; after he had finished, they came to the door to know by what authority he was preaching—but it was me they were after, but I was fortified, for their laws, by my credentials, having the United States seal upon them,—they tried to get him out of the house, they said, on business. But he told them he would meet them at 9 o'clock in the morning before the magistrate, seven miles distant. Brother J. B. then took my credentials and also showed his own, and, upon examination, the magistrate said, she is highly recommended and I am bound to protect her. An under-officer, anxious to get hold of my papers, very much opposed to our

being in the State, tried hard to frighten us out of it, and went to lay his hands on it, but was rebuked by the magistrate; and two days after the magistrate sent word to me to go on and preach, he did not care if I preached till I died. I never met them but before one year. My mind led me to Solsbury and to Snow Hill—the brother, through persuasion, did not go, for fear of some difficulty, under which consideration I declined going for that time, I then returned to Easton, but my mind still led me to pay that religious visit, which was still accomplished by a sister and myself. I called on brother Massey, a preacher, who conducted us to Snow Hill and Solsbury. In the afternoon, the elder and one of the Trustees of the white Methodist Church, called on me to know of my faith and doctrine, and, while conversing, the spirit of the Lord breathed upon us—we had groans and shedding of tears— that evening the Elder gave me an appointment in the colored church to a large congregation, and we had a powerful time, sinners awakened and backsliders reclaimed. So great was the time that the meeting lasted until three or four o'clock in the morning. It was like a Camp meeting, they came seven miles distance from only three or four hours' notice. Next morning we left for Snow Hill, the Elder sent down for the friends to take care of us all, and our board, with the horses, should be paid for, consequently we were treated with great hospitality. I preached in the Old Methodist Church to an immense congregation of both the slaves and the holders, and felt great liberty in word and doctrine; the power of God seemed without intermission. We left there and rode 16 miles, spoke to a small company of people. In the afternoon to a large congregation, chiefly Presbyterians, and at many other places too tedious for me to mention, I preached twenty-seven sermons and then returned to Easton again, where I was informed that the constable who was so enraged against me before was then dying; the other white man who came and set at the end of the table twice while I was laboring, thinking I would say something to implicate myself and wanted me arrested so bad, had been sold and his family broke up; it is thus the Lord fights for Israel.

I then made an appointment at a place called the Hole in the Wall, it was a little settlement of coloured people, but we had no Church, but used a dwelling house, and had a large congregation. I had no help but an old man, one hundred and odd years of age; he prayed, and his prayers made us feel awful, he died in the year 1825, and has gone to reap the reward of his labor; freed from the toils and cares of life, no more to labor under a hard task master, but to rest where the slave is freed from his master, I strove then to fill the appointment at 11 o'clock in the morning, from Daniel 5 chap. 27 ver. the

declaration was, there is no other way under heaven that men can be saved only through Jesus Christ; the Lord gave me great light on this subject. At 3 o'clock, in the afternoon, we stood in the open air in the woods, and I spoke from 12 chap. 2-3 ver. I felt greater liberty on this subject than the other; the Lord was with me; of a truth I felt the force of it now. Glory to God. Who can constrain against the power of God? We had people of all descriptions, from the true Christian to the Devil, and from slave-holder to slave. We had two white men and two colored; one of the white men, by the name of Sharp had killed all his family, except his oldest daughter; she conversed with them. Sharp treated it with contempt, but the other answered with a degree of humility; but they were hung according to the laws of their state.

> But O, their end,
> Their dreadful end!

I was invited by one of the Trustees of the Old Methodist Church to pay them a visit on the ensuing Sabbath morning. I made the appointment for said day. I left Georgetown on the morning early, half past ten o'clock we arrived in Milford; Church bell was ringing. We were conducted into the Church; a local preacher was in the pulpit and had prayed, but was asked to come down by another who invited me there. I spoke for them and afterwards they gave out for another appointment at night, but it caused a controversy among themselves, and they threw it on him to come and see if I would fill it. Previous to this coloured preachers told me there was controversy about woman preaching. But he came and asked me how long I had been preaching the Gospel. I answered, rising, 5 or 6 years. He said it was something new. I told him it seemed to be supposed so. I referred him to Mrs. Fletcher, of England, an able preacher and wife of Mr. Fletcher, a great and worthy minister of the Parish. He asked why I did not go to the Quakers. I told him I if he had a sister in the Church, and she witnessed a Christian life, and was called and qualified to preach, do you think you would be justified before God, to stop her? He has not answered me yet. I found it was prejudice in his mind. He talked as if he had not known what the operation of the Spirit of God was. We may say, with propriety, he had not tarried at Jerusalem long enough. When about to part, he asked me if I would come, but I could not then promise. At night, the people came in their carriage from the country, but were disappointed, for I spoke in a colored Church. The doors and windows were opened on account of the heat, but were

crowded with people; pride and prejudice were buried. We had a powerful time. I was quite taken out of myself—the meeting held till day-break; but I returned to my home. They told me that sinners were converted, backsliders reclaimed, mourners comforted, and believers built up in the most holy faith. Then they wished us to stay until next night to preach again; but I thought it best to leave them hungry. Previous to this I was sent for by a slave-holder to come to his house to preach three funeral sermons, all at one time, two grown persons and one child; they had been dead about a year, but their graves were only filled up even with the earth. I spoke standing in the door of his dwelling to a great congregation, from the 2 Book of Samuel, 12 chap. 23 very—dwelling much on the certainty of the child's happiness, through the redemption of Christ—shewing how men might be saved living in accordance with the truth. When finished we fell in procession and moved to the graves of the departed. Brother Massey rehearsed the funeral ceremony, then the graves were raised and made oval, as usual, a most affecting scene, one of the deceased being the mother of two little girls there present. They were so affected, it seemed they would go in fits; several persons tried to pacify them, but in vain. It was a solemn time; many were deeply affected that day at the graves, and mourning of the whites in the house, but they treated us kindly, and we left them, visiting my places too tedious to mention. I met a Camp meeting of the African Methodist Episcopal Church at Denton. The Elder was much encouraged in commencing the Camp. Although in a slave State, we had every thing in order, good preaching, a solemn time, and long to be remembered. Some of the poor slaves came happy in the Lord; walked from 20 to 30, and from that to seventy miles, to seventy miles, to worship God. Although through hardships they counted it all joy for the excellency of Christ; and, before day, they, or a number of them, had to be at home, ready for work; but some said they came as sinners before God, but went away as new creatures in Christ; and they could not be disputed. My heart glows with joy while I write; truly God is inscrutable. The Elder, J.B. then appointed a Camp meeting within five miles of Easton, too near the town, but it was done to glorify God. Yet it seemed there was not that general good done like the previous time. He gave me an appointment on Sunday afternoon; to myself I appeared lost though I was doing nothing, but the south wind from the hill of the Lord began to blow upon the spices of his garden. The power of God arrested a person who started to run, but fell in the flight, and begged God for mercy and obtained it. After the sermon, which was the first of my being apprized of it, but no merit to me, but all glory to God for mercy and

obtained it. After the sermon, which was the first of my being apprized of it, but no merit to me, but all glory to God, for the good done at Camp meetings, though much persecuted, but they are a glorious meeting to me. I pray God to protect the camp-meetings while I thank him for the invention. Various are the operations of the Spirit of God on the human family. We must believe in the truth of God, and then we can behold the mysteries and enjoy the truth of them with joy and thanksgiving. I went to speak about 10 miles from Centreville at early candle light—warm weather—in a dwelling house, the largest congregation being out-of-doors. I felt an open mind, the power of God fell upon the assembly in open air, and I heard an awful cry. A woman had started, jumped over the fence and run, but fell and rose again; that woman contended until she found redemption in Jesus Christ. I went to a place called Beaver Dams and spoke there; left there for Hillsborough, and spoke there to a large congregation; from there to Greensborough, and preached in white Methodist Church. The visit not so prosperous; from there to Boomsborough. We were much favoured and approbated by the people, and blessed with the presence of the Lord in power. I then preached at Cecil Cross roads in an old meeting house, almost down, to a large congregation, and it was warm. I was informed a gentleman rode fourteen miles to attend that meeting. Previous to this the Methodists had almost died away, a very few excepted at that place, but from that time they took a rise as I was informed by two young ladies from there. In about 5 years after I left they built a large Church on that same spot where the old one stood, and had a fine congregation; from there brother J. B. appointed a Quarterly Meeting on Mr. John Peaker's Island, for a society of 60 members, which was composed altogether of the said gentleman's slaves. We were entertained in the best of style, had a powerful meeting, and a great manifestation of the power of God. From there we returned to Easton a second time, and were entertained by the overseer very highly at Mr. John Peakey's Island. Went to Baltimore, from there I visited Hales' Mills, and preached three sermons, much favored the sermons, much favored of the Lord by his presence, after which I returned to Baltimore. The elder gave me an appointment and collection, and I returned to Philadelphia. And on Sunday morning collection, Bishop Allen gave me an appointment in Bethel church, and we had a shout in the Camp of Israel.

I had spent six months in Maryland and I only remained in this city three or four weeks, during which time the Lord was with me, and opened my way through opposition, but I felt willing to suffer cheerfully.

> Through tribulations deep
> The way to glory is.

I also preached in the Union Church, the Lord verified his promise according to what he told Mary, to go, he would meet her, whomsoever I will put forth I will go before, so there was a shaking among the dry bones. My mind soon became oppressed and craved to travel. In 1825 I left Philadelphia for a journey through Pennsylvania. I spoke first at Weston; we had an elder on West Chester Circuit, named Jacob Richardson. We had buried a young Christian before preaching the sermon, and gave me the sacrament sermon in the afternoon. I spoke from Matt. 26 chap. 26-27 ver. I felt as solemn as death; much weeping in the Church, tears stole down the faces of the people.

Jacob Richardson was a spiritual preacher. God attended the word with power, and blessed his labors much on his circuit. From there a friend carried me to Downingtown, where I took stage and went on to Lancaster; but prospect not so good there; they had a new Church but not paid for; the proprietor took the key in possession and deprived them of worshipping God in it. But I spoke in a dwelling house, and I felt a great zeal for the cause of God to soften that man's heart, or kill him out of the way one had better die than many. Brother Israel Williams, a few days, called to converse with him on the subject, and he gave him the key; he was then on his death-bed, and died in a short time afterwards, and we must leave him in the hands of God, for he can open and no man can shut. I went on to Columbia and spoke in the Church, and my tongue fails to describe the encouragement I met with. The Lord converted poor mourners, convicted sinners, and strengthened believers in the most holy faith. God's name be glorified for the display of his saving power. I led class, held prayer meetings, and left with a good conscience for little York. The first sermon I preached was in the Church at 10 o'clock in the morning, from Mat. xxvi, 26, 27, to a large congregation. My faith it seemed almost failed me, for when I got in the stand, so hard was the task that I trembled, and my heart beat heavy, but in giving out the hymn I felt strength of mind, and before I got through, I felt so much of life and liberty in the word, I could but wonder, and in the doctrine of Christ it was a sacramental sermon indeed to my soul. I spent some weeks there, and we enjoyed good meetings and powerful outpourings of the Spirit. I truly met with both good and bad; my scenes were many and my feelings various. I bless the Lord that the prayers of the righteous availeth much. After freeing my mind, I

passed on to York Haven, and preached in a School-house to a white congregation. I was not left alone, but was treated very well by a white Methodist lady. I took lodgings at her house all night; next afternoon took stage for Harrisburg, and when I stopped at the Hotel a gentleman introduced me to the Steward, who took charge of me and escorted me to Mr. Williams, where I took supper. It was on a New Year's evening; the colored congregation had expected me and made a fire in our Church, but being late when I arrived, they had gone to hear a sermon in a white Methodist Church, and I had retired to rest a while in the evening. When they returned they came after me, taking no excuse, and I had to come down stairs, go to the Church, and preach a sermon for them, then 10 o'clock at night. The text from Acts xv, 36. Hymn 250th, as follows:

> And now my soul another year
> Of thy short life is past,
> I cannot long continue here,
> And this may be the last.

The effects of the gospel of Christ was no less than at other great seasons, but was wonderful—backsliders reclaimed and sinners converted—there was mourning, weeping, shouting and praising of God for what he had done. I preached several sermons, and was well treated by all circles of people. We had large congregations of well-behaved people; and feeling my work done in this part, I proceeded to Carlisle, Pa. There was a small body of members; I spoke and led class for them during the time I was there, which was ten days; felt my discharge of God, and took stage to Shippensburg. There was great success at this place; fifteen joined the Church; some of the most hardened sinners became serious and reformed. I was astonished at the wonderful operations of the Spirit, and the immense congregations. At the first sermon the house was crowded, and I had the good attention of the people. A man came into the house intoxicated, and offered to interrupt by speaking, but a gentleman put him out so quietly that it had no effect upon the meeting. When I contemplate the goodness of God to the human family, in putting them in a proper capacity of choosing the way of salvation, I feel sometimes almost lost, to think that God has called such a worm as I to spread the common Saviour's name. But said the Lord, "I will send by whom I will"—praise the Lord who willeth not the death of sinners—"as I live, saith the Lord, I have no pleasure in the death of the wicked, but that they turn and live."

I then proceeded on to Chambersburg by stage, and met with one Rev. Winton, who displayed much of a christian disposition, and conversed freely with me on the most particular points of the God-Head, for my instruction, showing his benevolence. He knew I was a stranger—he had friends to go to at that place, but he offered to pay my bill for a room at the Inn. I never have forgot the goodness of that gentleman, who, I believe, to be a great gospel minister. I stopt at brother Snowden's, who were very kind to me. The Lord continued to pour out His Spirit and clear the way for me, and also continued to convict, convert, and reclaim the backsliders in heart. There were very large congregations, both in and out of doors, and great revivals throughout the circuit. The elders generally treated me well, for which may the Lord bless them and their labors in his vineyard, and add to the Church such as shall be forever saved from the power of sin—may I take heed lest I fall, while I teach others. Saith the Apostle: "Paul may plant and Apollos water, but God must give the increase," for which I feel thankful. I remained in this place for some weeks, but being debilitated in body, I left for Philadelphia about the middle of April. On my return, I met with such a severe trial of opposition, that I thought I never would preach again, but the Apostle says, "ye are not your own but are bought with a price." I feel glad that God is able to keep all that put their trust in him, though the mis-steps of others often interrupt our own way—I always found friends on different parts of Globe. I preached and led classes on my return. Praise God for his delivering grace—"Oh the depth of the riches" of the glory of God, how unsearchable are his ways; they are past finding out—a sea without bottom or shore. One thing is encouraging, "When he who is my life shall appear, I shall be like him." "I know my Redeemer liveth, and shall stand on the latter day upon the earth, and though worms destroy this body, yet in my flesh shall I see God." Lord help me to keep this confidence. Rev. Richard Williams, a gentle and christian-minded man, treated me well. God would not suffer me to be destroyed. It is not by might or by power, but by the Spirit, saith the Lord of hosts. Dear reader, give ear to the truth, for the mouth of the Lord has spoken it.

> If such a worm as I can spread
> The common Saviour's name,
> Let him who raised thee from the dead,
> Quicken my mortal frame.

On my return I stopped at Lancaster; the Church was opened, and I

preached to large congregations, and with powerful success; the dead were brought to life by the preaching of the cross of Christ. From there I left for Philadelphia.

In July, 1824, I felt an exercise of mind to take a journey to Reading, Pa., to speak to the fallen sons and daughters of Adam. I left the city and stopped at Norristown on my way to Reading. I spoke in the Academy to a respectable congregation, the same evening I arrived there. I felt a degree of liberty in speaking, though it was a quiet meeting, and I also felt thankful that the Lord would manifest himself through such a worm as me. Next morning I walked four miles and stopped at Littleton Morris's, and preached two sermons on the Sabbath day, and God struck a woman, and she had liked to have fallen to the floor; I spoke in the Dunkard's meeting house. This ended my visit with them at this time. On Tuesday I walked three miles to Schuylkill, to take the Canal boat on Wednesday morning. I met in company with a Presbyterian minister and lady on the boat; they treated me very kindly indeed. We arrived in Reading about 7 o'clock in the evening. I was recommended to a family in that place, the man of which had once confessed religion, but had fallen from grace, and they were very kind to me. The next morning I enquired for other respectable families of color, and an elderly lady of color that belonged to the white connexion, and the only colored Methodist in the place at that time, conveyed me to Mrs. Murray's, where I remainded a while; then the elderly lady, just mentioned, feeling interested for me, went to the proprietors of the Court-house with me, to see if we could get it to preach in, and like Esther the Queen, who fasted and prayed, and commanded the men of Jerusalem and the women of Zion to pray; as she approached the king the sceptre was bowed to her, and her request was answered to the saving of Mordica, and all the Jewish nation. When we approached this gentleman, who was the head Trustee of the Protestant Church, I showed him my recommendation, and he answered me, "Madam, you can have it," and I felt humble to God for the answer. I felt it my duty to preach to the citizens, and accordingly made an appointment for Sunday afternoon at 4 o'clock. Rev. James Ward, a colored Presbyterian, assembled with us, although he was so prejudiced he would not let me in his pulpit to speak; but the Lord made a way where there was no way to be seen; there was no person to intercede until this sister tried to open the way; the men of color, with no spirit of christianity, remained idle in the enterprise, but we got possession and we had a large concourse of people. I spoke with the ability God gave me. I met with a family of color, but very respectable, that for-

merly had belonged to our Church in Baltimore; they invited me to their house, and it was a home to me, praise God. I held a meeting in their house previous to holding meetings in the Court-house; the white brethren and sisters assembled with us. We called on a minister's lady, and she treated me very kindly, while he, like a Christian, united and helped to go through with the meetings. I visited the Quaker friends (amounting to four only) then in the place, and very pleasant visits they were. A great number of Christian friends called on me, among the rest this minister's lady, who left a donation in my hand, consequently the way was made where there was no way, but I left in friendship. Praise God I feel the approbation now. It is to be lamented, that James Ward, colored, with his over-ruling prejudice, which he manifested by saying no women should stand in his pulpit, and with all the advantages of a liberal education, was in a few weeks after I left there, turned out of the Church.

On returning to Philadelphia, I stopped at Pottsgrove and found a Society of colored persons, christians I believe. We had solemn meetings there; I met kind friends there, and visited a Church about six miles off; preached in the morning; the Lord was with us; of this truth my soul is a witness; in the afternoon I preached to a large congregation. Next morning I left for Philadelphia. I continued to preach, paid some short visits about, and was welcomed home again.

I left Philadelphia again for Lewistown, Del., to attend a camp meeting of the African Methodist Episcopal connexion, of which I was a member, to be held in Gov. Paynter's Woods. There was immense large congregations, and a greater display of God's power I never saw. The people came from all parts, without distinction of sex, size, or color, and the display of God's power commenced from singing; I recollect a brother Camell standing under a tree singing, and the people drew high to hear him, and a large number were struck to the ground before preaching began, and signs and wonders followed. There appeared to be a great union with the white friends. James Towson was the Elder holding the camp; he was in the bloom of the gospel of Christ. But poor brother, may the Lord give him a Peter's look by the way of mercy. Right Rev. Bishop Allen was present. The ministry were all for me, and the Elder gave me an appointment, and the Governor with a great concourse came to hear the weak female. My heart beat, my limbs trembled, and my voice was faint, but I spoke from Eccles. xi, 9, 10. After I took my text, it appeared to me as if I had nothing to do but open my mouth, and the Lord filled it, consequently I was much encouraged: it was an immense assembly of people.

Content with beholding his face,
I all to his pleasure resigned.

After the camp-meeting was over, the Elder visited another campmeeting, and left me in liberty to preach around the circuit, which I did, and afterwards returned to Lewiston, and spoke in the old Methodist meeting-house; I had a great time among my colored brethren. I feel thankful to my friends for their kindness to me, especially to brother Peter Lewis, whose house was a home to me. I had much happiness in leading class and prayer meetings; preaching the gospel seemed to be the great task. Brother Lewis conveyed me to Georgetown; I spoke in our colored people's Church, and we enjoyed ourselves very much; the Lord drew people from all quarters; a wonderful outpouring of the Spirit indeed; weeping in all directions. It is a good sign to see tears of contrition stealing down the cheeks of the hearers; it makes me believe the word is sanctioned. The last place was at the head of the river; I then returned to Lewiston, and in a few days I left for Philadelphia. I had a very uncomfortable passage; very sea-sick indeed—the vessel could not come out of the mouth of the creek for a couple of days, in consequence of a severe storm, after which we arrived in the city on Tuesday morning. After a short stay in the city, I took a visit to Trenton, Dec. 25. I spoke as usual, for there we had lively meetings, after which I had no home, but the Lord provides, for sister Roberts and family were my friends and took me in, and we often had sweet counsel together. From there I went to Princeton. The Elder, Joseph Harper, of our connexion, was a friend to me, but I had to withstand a beast at Princeton, in opposition, like the one I had to front on Bucks county circuit; the former named Thomas Voris, a local preacher, and using the language of the Psalmist prophesying in reference to the Saviour, "mine equal my guide hath lifted up his heel against me." We had preached—he invited me to come to his house to hold meetings the next week, but I was taken sick for a few days, but in the interval, S.R., of Attleborough Circuit, had a Quarterly meeting. They consulted together to stop me from preaching in Princeton; so his door was shut, but bless the Lord, another was opened, Brother Thomas Vinsant, his sister's husband, a Christian man, opened his house. We had a powerful time. I came in the town on Saturday, the next day I walked two miles and spoke twice. It was Thomas' appointment on Sabbath morning, and he had but two persons to meet him in class. An invitation came to me to make an appointment for Wednesday night in the Coloured Presbyterian Church, upon the grant of Rev. Mr. Woodhall,

elder of that order in Princeton. Thos. Vorris, though a Methodist, was like a roaring lion—went to Elder Woodhall for him to stop it, as I was informed. But the meeting went on, it was a respectable, and comfortable congregation. I preached and led class and prayer meetings, and read, and explained the Scriptures. We had mourning and rejoicing, and I saw the kingdom of Satan fall. When Brother J. H. came round again, from some cause, he removed Thomas from that class, as they would not meet him, and placed him over one of five or six persons; also impeached him, taking his license from him, and left him only verbally licenced. Glory to God for his Divine power. I do not rejoice for his downfall, but for God's grace which enables me to stand against the enemies of the Cross. Glory to God, I am not ashamed of the Gospel of Christ, for it is the power of God unto salvation. I spoke from Ephe. 2d chap. 8th ver. I felt life and liberty in word and doctrine. Thank God for the victory, Brother Oakham, one of the Elders of the Coloured Presbyterian Church, invited me to their house, and himself and wife treated me like Christians, which, I believe, they were; my heart glows toward them. I held a meeting in a dwelling house.

Jan., 1827. Contemplating on the greater responsibility I owe to my God for my stewardship, I fain would go round the Cross or shrink beneath the load, but I rest upon the promises of God, which are as firm of the pillars of heaven. My labors here cease a little.

April, 1827. My health having been bad, I have not travelled so largely, and in this, as in some other moments of reflection, I felt somewhat oppressed, and I resorted to the Hymn Book for something to suit my feelings; the poetry as follows:

> 1. Soon as I heard my Father say,
> Ye children seek my grace,
> My heart replies, without delay,
> I'll seek my father's face.
>
> 2. Let not thy face be hid from me,
> Nor frown my soul away,
> God of my life I fly to thee
> In a distressing day.
>
> 3. Should friends and kindred, near and dear,
> Leave me to want and die.

My God will make my life his care,
 And all my wants supply.

4. My fainting flesh had died with grief,
 Had not my soul believed
To see thy grace prove a relief,
 Nor was my hope deceived.

5. Wait on the Lord, ye trembling Saints,
 And keep your courage up,
He'll raise your spirit when it faints,
 And far exceed your hope.

However I went to Baltimore in the same month with the Bishop and Elders, and enjoyed myself under great preaching, and preached several sermons. Praise God, and the slain of the Lord appeared to be many. After Conference, my mind led me over to Eastern Shore the second time; spent a few days with the Church. (Peter D. Schuman, Elder of the charge) and then returned to Baltimore, from there to the city of Philadelphia, and then made some short visits from 40 to 60, and from that to 100 miles round about; then down to Lewistown Camp-meeting, the second time; then to a Camp-meeting at Mount Ephraim, N.J. The last of August I left for New York Camp, on arriving there I spoke once or twice. The same at to other places, our Camp-meeting was not as great as I have seen before. I spoke in both the Churches. We had a good time together, rejoicing in the Lord. I left then for Albany; had a pleasant passage up the North river, one hundred and sixty miles; the mountains and their stupendous looks preached to me in my journey through. Oh, the wisdom of God, and how marvellous in our eyes; enough to convince the infidel, yea, the Atheist, that there is some first cause. From the effects produced, look at the ingenuity of mankind, which actually comes from God, and is displayed in building steamboats, and other great novelties in mechanism. We accomplished the route the same day we started, and I found myself entirely among strangers. But I made inquiry for Methodist friends, and found brother Streeter, a coloured family, very respectable. They treated me very kind; they were under the white Bishop, and I under the coloured. But the same faith, same doctrine, same Baptism, same spirit. Glory to God. Among the coloured people, the Baptists had the ascendancy. There was a large hall prepared for me, and we had a large con-

gregation of different denominations. I spoke from these words and this Gospel of the kingdom shall be preached unto all the world as for a witness, and then shall the end come. God owned the word, sinners screamed; some fell to the floor, others wept, while Christians rejoiced. A lady of color was present, though she was a member of the Dutch Presbyterian Church; her husband belonged to no Church, but was under an exercise of mind. The Lord reached his heart, he mourned more than three days. They sent for me to come to their house. I paid them a visit, and held prayer meeting at their house. That Sabbath two weeks he joined the Methodist Church. I spoke three times the first Sabbath afternoon; we had a large congregation, at night still larger. Text. Never man spoke like this man. God's spirit was poured out in a miraculous manner. On the ensuing third day evening I spoke again, from these words. And came seeking fruit on the tree and found none. To all appearance there was nothing done, but God directed the word to the heart of a little girl, a gentleman's daughter, between eleven and twelve years of age. She joined the Church before I left there. A good old Missionary, by the name of Mitchell, came to the city before I left, and preached three sermons, in which there was a great revival. The Elder appointed prayer meetings, north and south of the city of Albany. I preached two or three sermons in a school house, the last I spoke was in Brother Streeter's house, from St. Matt. Chap. 21 ver. 12th. I thank God for the comfortable visit I had there in the discharge of my duty. This Methodist preacher, Mitchell, had a book with him called the Essence of John Steward, a coloured man, with his miraculous call to the ministry, the first one who succeeded in Christianizing the Methodist Indians in Sandusky and that province, and he sold them in Albany, and it seemed to have its desired effect also with the revival, in encouraging us to hold a fast.

How good to contemplate or to think the heathen has caught the sound of salvation through the name of Jesus, our Lord. I saw a goodly number added to the Church on Sabbath-day. I still continued engaged in my mind with the Lord, in their behalf, when I was informed that they had three and four of an evening at their prayer meetings, then my mind felt at liberty to leave for Schenectady. Sister Streeter rode with fourteen miles; I stopped eleven days, at which place there was a large upper room that was appropriated for a preaching place, where I spoke to a small number of coloured persons several times. They were under the white elder, he was a friend to me, and appointed a meeting for me in the white Brother's house to speak for them. We had a favourable time. But the people, feeling an uninterested spir-

it in propagating the religion of Jesus Christ, I left the dust with them. Got on board a Canal boat for Utica, there I met with my own connexion, African Methodist Episcopal Church, we had a prosperous time. I spoke and had prayer meetings on board of the Canal boat. There was a pasture there notwithstanding the difficulties of this life and the people being hunted like partridges on the mountain. It deprives a man's usefulness among the people, but the work of the Lord went on, and there is no weapon formed by the enemy that can stop the work of God. Therefore we have nothing to fear. We have large and respectable congregations, and I felt strengthened in warning man to flee from the wrath to come. If signs and wonders did not follow sometimes, I must certainly die, but glory to God for refreshing showers. I led class, had prayer meetings, and took my passage on another canal boat for Rochester; had a pleasant passage. I soon found some Methodists, and our local Elder was then a smart preacher. I was there three or four weeks, and he treated me very kindly and opened my way. They erected a new brick church, basement for schools; the corner-stone was laid while I was there. The elder was a man of good repute; people of color of different denominations, but much united together. The elder held the charge from there to Buffalo, he had then a Quarterly Meeting on hand. I left Rochester with him and rode about seventy miles. Next morning I left Lewistown and rode seven miles, crossed the Lakes, on the British side. When we left Rochester the snow was ankle deep, when ten mile from Lewistown, it became dry and hard, and when we crossed the Lakes it was clear and cold, and the air very pure. I told the elder this was the first time I ever breathed pure air. I walked about a mile and the first house I stopped at was sister Holmes'. I felt strange and lonely. I waited to see if the peace of God would abide on the house. Previous to my being introduced, I arose from my chair and the power of God fell upon the people, and, it seemed to me, that God answered me. I was fully convinced that God would make bare his arm, in this part of his moral vineyard. We had a Church in Niagara; the elder made an appointment there, and forty or fifty miles round the circuit, being now about six hundred miles from Philadelphia. I felt the loss of my former companions and friends, the elder and deacon, in two days time left for Buffalo, to hold a quarterly meeting in York state about seventy miles. I commenced to speak for the people, and God owned the word, and I saw many displays of his power—the people in Niagara seemed to me to be a kind and Christian like people. The white inhabitants united with us, and ladies of great renown. The slaves that came there felt their freedom, began to see the necessity of

education, and hired a white man to teach them to read and write among themselves, and have Sabbath schools. I am astonished to see so many there that came from a free state, and not take more interest in instilling the science of education among their fellow beings. The winter was cold—I never had experienced such—but very healthy. I went to a town called Niagara. I spoke in a dwelling house. The next night I spoke in the Old Methodist Church to a large congregation of respectable people. There were three ladies, one the widow of a great Judge, and one daughter and sister of first education; they sympathized with me in this important work of the Gospel of Christ. They assembled with us in our meeting. A little girl about 8 or 9 years of age experienced religion and prayed in public, and attended to their private devotion, so much for early piety. Teach the child the way he should go and when he gets old he will not depart from it. But, it is to be lamented, that so few of our children experience this early piety; the cause we must try to find out and avoid the evil effects, and not bring up our children in so much pride and heathenism. We, as a people, are generally poor and cannot support so many changes of fashion; they grow up and crave it, and oftimes substitute evil practices to support themselves, either girls or boys, and often bring a stigma upon; their parents and family connexions, though very respectable. Let us bring up our children in industry, for work is honorable, and it is the way to get riches and to keep them. I travelled back and forward again from Niagara to Buffalo, and had regular appointments in our Churches. We had a great opposition among the coloured people, one trying to excel the other in point of eminence. One of our preachers left us on the promise of forty dollars per year. Poor man, he was like Simon Magus who perished with his money. Our Circuit rider was absent on the Sunday of the split, but the Lord was with us. I spoke three times to the remaining part of the congregation, which was increased much by a large body of bystanders, and great good followed; and we continued to sow and gather for two or three months, and the Lord blessed our labors abundantly. Feeling I had discharged my duty, I left and crossed the Lake from Buffaloes to Fort George, and spoke about eight miles from there, it was cold and snowed very fast— it was four o'clock in the afternoon—the congregation had been there and gone. We were in a sleigh, and the driver got lost; we all brought up in a swamp, among the fallen tree tops, but we turned about and found a house and lodged all night; and spoke next morning at eleven o'clock to a quiet congregation, and the Lord was with us, though composed of all denominations. I appointed another meeting and rode about eight miles on horse-

back—it snowed and was very sleety—after I spoke to the people I left them for good and made an appointment for the Indians; two of the chiefs called at where I stopped to see me. I asked them to pray for us; they complied, but done it in their own tongue. I felt the power of God in my own heart. Then they held a council about it, and granted my visit at Buffalo village, about three miles from Buffalo city. We rode and got there before their worshipping hour, their school had not dismissed, after a while they dismissed school—of 50 children—and as they gathered to worship I saw an old chief come, he stood and prayed very devoutly, tears running down his cheek. I told them I had not come to worship with them, and wanted to preach for them after their worship ended. They held a council and they agreed I should preach for them, but I could not help admiring the ways as well as gestures of the children. The teachers bring them up in the English language and dress some of them in the English style, but the greatest number are clad in the Indian style; those of the old Indians in their blankets. Some of them met me from seven or eight miles round—they filled the house. It was in the month of March—it rained and snowed—yet they walked in their moccasins, and some bare-headed—they made a large congregation. Their Elder or missionary had gone to teach another tribe that day, and he only taught them very plainly, and read out of pamphlets the experiences of others. I commenced by giving out the hymn in our language, and the interpreter spoke in their tongue. Hymn thus, O for a thousand tongues to sing, &;c. They sung it beautiful,—two long benches of them sung by note (their books printed in their own language) a very familiar note tune, such as we use in congregations. I spoke plain and deliberate and very pointed, the interpreter spoke it after me in the Indian tongue, and one of the women cried out Amen Much weeping among them, dear reader, take notice, notwithstanding they are a nation revolted from Israel, and would not be governed. Yet they can be civilized and Christianized. We might call them heathens, but they are endowed with a Christian spirit. I felt happy in my visit; the missionary wished me to speak for them that evening; but I had an appointment that night at Buffalo, after which my mind was calm and serene. I left on Tuesday, 1st of April, on my return for Philadelphia, and arrived home May 18th.

That year I travelled two thousand three hundred and twenty-five miles, and preached one hundred and seventy-eight sermons. Praise God for health and strength, O my soul, and magnify his name for protection through various scenes of life.

> God of my life whose gracious power
>> Through various deaths my soul has led,
> Or turned aside the fated hour,
>> Or lifted up my sinking head.

While I was in Buffalo, a journey to the West was shewed to me so plain that I could not stop in the city of Philadelphia but five weeks only, then left for the western country. I started in a mail stage, and stopped first at Westtown and spoke in our own connexion Church, and then at West Chester in the old Methodist Episcopal white connexion. We had a large congregation of quiet hearers. I felt liberty but no great displays of God's power. I had several meetings in different places, visiting the sick. Having discharged my duty I left there and proceeded on to Old Lancaster and spent some days. We have a good Church there, and great meetings—the word of the Lord grew and was multiplied. God poured out his spirit upon us, and we had a shout in the camp. I then started for Columbia, Pa. The people are much divided, and it looked very gloomy, but God directed me and he commanded his disciple to be a sheep among wolves, and harmless as doves, notwithstanding the darkness, God aided me in speaking to the people, and aided them in hearing, and his name was praised. The people united, temptations and clouds were vanished away. Then we sung, prayed, spake, and shouted in the spirit, this is true Methodism. I led class, visited the sick and was much favoured with the presence of the Lord. Our faith was increased, our hopes confirmed. The preachers were kind and treated me well, and by their help I travelled on my journey to Harrisburg. Feeling thankful for the visit I had paid it seemed gloomy here, but I spoke there next day. I took stage and rode to Chambersburg, and spent some days there, and proceeded on to Fredericktown, Maryland, and, spoke there from there to Hagerstown, Macallansburg, and, I must confess, I do not remember of ever seeing such a people, for, it seemed strong drink had been their ruin. The circuit minister was there, and we had some signs and wonders to follow after the preaching of the cross of Christ, and I trust to meet some of them on the banks of deliverance, and help to swell the notes of redeeming love. After the preacher left me I took stage for Pittsburgh, at eight in the evening, rode all night until eight in the morning. I was kindly treated, there were other persons in the stage, four of them gentlemen, as I thought there was one who talked a great deal, wise in his own conceit, about religion, and from that he displayed a quantity of degraded principle, with disgusting language, at which I made

several sharp replies, and in my way, reprimanded him and the other gentle-men looked on him with silent contempt, at which he got ashamed, and afterwards treated me with great politeness, and I was comfortable and arrived in Pittsburgh at 5 o'clock in the afternoon. I went to Church that night and heard a sermon from one of my brothers. I met with six or seven ministers, very friendly, and treated me like Christians. I remained in Pittsburgh six weeks, there had been one or two revivals previous to my visit, especially the winter before I arrived, last day of August, 1820. My labors commenced—the field was large—but the Lord was with us—this gave me much encouragement, I was not ashamed of the Gospel—it is the power of God unto salvation, to every one that believes, both Jew or Gentile. We had very good meetings, the Elder and preachers, all received me with one accord—thanks to God for his divine goodness—I felt moved by the Lord to pay Wheeling a visit although we had no society there, I arrived and found but a small class of coloured people with the whites, an old gentleman of color with the elder in charge granted me the Church—the elder being a great preacher of college order. We had a large congregation; I spoke for them once, and gave an exhortation at another time, and felt no difficulty on that head, and after that they could not treat me well enough. And, on the ensuing Sabbath, I helped to lead class; and we all enjoyed ourselves, and on Tuesday I left for Washington, according as I had promised our elder before I left him. On my arrival there I met kind friends, and a large congregation of coloured people. On Lords day I met the class; the people spoke with humility—it was a melting down time—in the Spirit of God I preached sev-eral sermons, visited the sick, and, in this spirit strove to uphold the aged. Feeling a discharge of my duty I left for Steubensville, Ohio, and met a small society—some true Christians there; no Church there; the Baptists granted their Church; we had meetings there, and the Lord was with us—quiet con-gregations—and the word had effect in the hearts of sinners—and believers were established. I stopped a few days and left in the name of the Lord. I pro-ceeded on to Mt. Pleasant, and arrived on seventh day evening, and the trustee gave me an appointment on Sabbath morning. At 11 o'clock I was feeble in both body and mind, but the Lord was with us according to prom-ise, think not what ye shall say, but open thy mouth and I will fill it saith the Lord, he caused a shaking among the dry bones, that morning. I think if any creature has a right to praise God I have, and that in thankfulness, and I love him because he first loved me. Bless his name. I preached several sermons to large gatherings, but revivals not so manifest as at other places. I had some

difficulty in that journey, but only what is common among us; for many times deceitful persons will set the Church on fire but can't burn it up.

Moses saw it as a bush in a flame, yet not consumed. We have to be tried as gold in the fire. After my visit was out a brother (leader in the Church) conveyed me ten miles on my way, I stopped at Sinclairsville; there was an appointment published on the next evening. At 7 o'clock I spoke in the Court house to a large concourse of well behaved and respectable citizens. I felt at liberty and left in peace of mind which makes the work sweet. I was aided on to Cap-teen, a settlement of coloured people; some from the lower counties; but they are industrious, and have a Church of their own, and were about to send their children to school, I held several meetings and there was some very respectable people of colour—and the Lord was with us—I stopped with an aged family, very respectable, they treated me very kind, and between 2 and 3 weeks, I left in peace with God and man, and went to Barnsborough and spoke in the white Methodist Episcopal Church, from thence to Zanesville, at which place I felt much discouraged from the appearance of things. I did not think of tarrying there, but at the first appointment I chose the words "I am not ashamed of the Gospel."—Paul. The room was very small for the number of people, after which an old man well scented with ardent spirits, tried to give an exhortation. I was astonished at the scene, the people laughed, I got up and went out. I tried to labor again at night and exhort the young ladies to the evil consequences of ill-behavior in the Church of God; after which we had better order, and the old gentleman was discovered to be intoxicated with spirituous liquor, and was disowned from the Church, after which there was a great revival took place among the white Methodists, both rich and poor.

Mrs. Dillin, who once was a Friend, and now a member of the Church, spoke to the Trustees and Ministers, and they opened the Church and I spoke twice in that Church, and after that I spoke in west Zanesville, back of that place, and I still remained among my colored friends, and they seemed much revived; after which they formed a Resolution to build themselves a Meeting House. A Quaker Friend, so called, presented them with a piece of ground to build one on, which they did. Glory to God, for his glory stood over the doors of the Tabernacle. Many were convicted, and converted, and many added to the old Methodist Church and I left there on New-years day for New-Lancaster, where we had a Church, standing on a frame of a house for three or four years, and had not been used to preach in; but the Lord opened the way, and a great revival took place among the people, and their eyes being

opened, they with willing minds commenced and built a new Church, and God blessed their labors. I preached several Sermons and led class, &c. My common way is to visit the sick and afflicted in whatsoever city I may stop in, that I may get my spiritual strength renewed in the Lord. Although I preached the Gospel through the Commission of my Lord, yet I have nothing to boast of.

I opened a Love-Feast in the said Church in New Lancaster. We held Prayer Meetings. I spoke in the White's Church also. The people were very friendly. I met them in Class, and after the lapse of eleven days, I left for Columbus. The Preachers generally were very kind to me. Both white and colored. A worthy brother conducted me on further. It snow'd, and I was very cold, but the Lord was with us, and my mind was free'd. But notwithstanding, I met an antagonist, who was ready to destroy my character, and the principles of the work that God saw good to make me instrumental of doing in his name, which caused me to open the case to the Trustees and Preaches, who were much astonished at him to be preaching four or five years with malice in his heart. I was favored to see him in the morning before he went away, that was the first time he had spoke to me anything like a Christian in that time. He knew from the first period I went to him to satisfy his mind. But his heart was bitter. I felt his spirit like a viper. But the word of the Lord was verified at that time also. "When the Tempter raise a flood against you, I will set up a standard against him." He told me he had sent a letter to Pittsburg to stop me, although I had my Licence from the Bishop, with his own signature. I told him he was a worse enemy to me than I was aware of, and I was ashamed of him, professing to be a Preacher in charge, and setting such an example in a strange land, and begged him to throw away his prejudices, or he would never obtain the Kingdom of Heaven. He left me in a flash, and I saw him no more until conference. I wrote a letter to Bishop Allen to let him know of my grievances, as I was innocent of any crime. I felt under no obligation to bear the reproaches of progressing Preachers; and I wanted it settled at Conference. But it was looked upon with little effect by the Preachers and Leaders. I laid it before the Conference, and it was settled. But I tarried all winter. Preached, led Class, visited the sick, &c., with great success. I bless God for the witness of a good conscience. Old sinners were awakened, and constrained to come trembling, and enquiring the way to Zion.

L. W., a respectable brother from Chillicothe, had never heard a woman preach, and was much opposed to it. An appointment was given me, and

when I went into the desk and commenced reading the hymn to commence the worship, he looked at me a while, then got up and went out and stood until I had nearly got through the hymn, and then he came in, when I asked him to pray for us but he refused. I prayed myself, after which I took my text, and felt much liberty in speaking in the spirit indeed. And after meeting he came and shook hands with me in the spirit of a Christian, and next day he came and confessed to me his prejudices had been so great, so much like his father, that he could not unite with me, but now he believed that God, was no respecter of persons, and that a woman as well as a man, when called of God, had a right to preach. He afterwards became a licensed preacher, and we parted in peace. I took the stage and left for Chillicothe, but there was but one house that would open for me in the city, although I had my recommendation with me. As soon as that friend heard of me she met me in christian bonds, and her house was my home, her husband being a man of christian qualifications, and I went of my mission doing my Father's will. I spoke once in the week and on Sabbath afternoon, to crowded houses; it was like a camp-meeting, and twenty-one lay upon the power of God at one time; after preaching, we called them to be prayed for; some got religion that day and some on the next Sabbath, and the father L. W. became one of my best friends, and a doer of the work. There was large fields of labor open to my view, and I visited both colored and white, and many were concerned about sanctification. I was with them about six weeks, during which time I had an interview with a lady, who informed me she had a call to preach the everlasting gospel of Christ. She was a Presbyterian by profession, and she told me she feared the church government. But the greatest objection, was her husband was a Deist by profession; she also told me of her experience she passed through; it was a broken heart and a contrite spirit. God answers the prayers of such a supplicant, but she could not enjoy that sweet fulness of religion in that situation of life, although very rich as regards this world's goods; also knowing that gold and silver should vanish away, but the word of God should endure forever. And some feel their labors a long time before it comes to perfection. Our Methodist sisters established a prayer meeting, and the people worked in the unity of the spirit, and much good was done in the name of the Holy child. Glory to God for what my heart feels while I use my pen in hand. I felt peace of conscience and left Chilicothe for Hillsborough to meet a quarterly meeting of W.C., he being Elder at that place; the Governor and his family residing there, six in number, were all Methodists, and one son a preacher; they had the spirit of christians. The trustee of the

Methodist church opened their doors and gave us liberty to hold our quar-
terly meeting and love feast in their small donation, which was very thank-
ful; after which I left there for Cincinnati, where I spoke to a large congre-
gation. I stop't at Williamsport and spoke in the white Methodist church to
a respectable congregation. I felt liberty in the spirit of God, and we left there
about daybreak in the morning. All nature seemed in silence (except the
chirping notes of a little bird.) A few rods from us a Panther screamed very
loud and sudden, but we could not see him, it being a dense thicket on either
side of the road, but the unseen arm of God sheltered us from harm; one of
the gentlemen seemed quite used to hearing them. We arrived safe in
Cincinnati about 11 o'clock; the Elder W.C. was very liberal in giving me
appointments, and the friends were very affectionate to me, and largest con-
gregations attended. I remained there some time, feeling to be blessed in my
weak endeavors to a great extent. The next day after I arrived there, one of
our sisters fell sick and I had the pleasure of visiting her on her death-bed and
in her last hour she told me in presence of others, her peace was made, and
raised her hands toward heaven and told us she was going. This is the end of
sister Crosby; who can doubt this faithful saying; by grace ye are saved. A
month or more previous, she had buried a daughter, who was a member of
our church; before she left the world, she called her young companions and
caused them to promise to meet her in heaven, and then closed her eyes tri-
umphing in death. Brother Crosby laid the heavy task on me to preach their
funeral sermons, which I did, as feeble a worm as I am, on Sabbath morn-
ing. Words of my choice were found in 2d Ephe. 8th v.—"For by grace ye
are saved through faith, and that not of yourselves, it is the gift of God."
Which of itself is a sermon to all that believe—glory to God, Christ has over-
come the world. And while laboring many tears were shed both in joy and
sorrow. But it's better to be one day in the house of the Lord than a thousand
in the tents of the wicked.

Another circumstance worthy of notice, was a young man whose heart
was in the world and in worldly affairs, or the pursuits of nature, and divert-
ed much of his time on Sabbath days on the Mississippi River, fighting
against all impressions of the Spirit of grace, until God stopped him by the
heavy hand of his power, in a death-bed affliction. After some time he began
to inquire the way to Zion. His mother was also a stranger to the blood of
Jesus, but wished me to come and see her son; being conducted to the house,
I found him looking like an anatomy. I asked him if he believed in Christ
and his all sufficiency to save; his answer was in the affirmative. We had

prayers with him and there was a display of God's power; a white woman screamed and nearly fell to the floor, but strove hard to keep from it. And on that day he acknowledged his Saviour to be reconciled to his poor soul. Praise God! my soul replied. Afterwards he wished me to hold a meeting with as many persons as the room would contain with him, which I accepted; one day and night after, he departed this life, and requested me to preach his funeral sermon at the house before the procession moved to the ground. I spoke from the 14th chap. 13 v., and we had a solemn time; you may anticipate the weight of that important task, but we had joy in the midst of sorrow, and this was the last of James Thompson. I also left his sisters in the last stage of consumption, and she confessed to be in favour with the Lord. Having finished my visit, I left in steamboat for Dayton. I spoke three times, and tried to preach the whole salvation, God the Father, God the Son, and God the Holy Ghost. The members of the New-light church deny the divinity of Christ. Once I spoke in a large dwelling of Dr. Esley, after which himself and wife went on a journey to Indiana and wished me to go with them, but I was deprived by a previous engagement, having to attend a camp meeting at Cap-teen. After my return to Urbanna, Ohio, I took stage for Springfield, and from there to Columbus, and spoke several times. The Elder's class consisted of about twenty; a young man and myself led the class in 1829. The Elder W.C. ordered a camp-meeting for the Cincinnati people, and the brother at Cap-teen and Rev. Bishop Brown, held a conference, and we had a very large camp-meeting, and manifestations of great good, and at the close of the Love-feast, there were thirty-two or three testified that they experienced the love of God. The people of color came out forcibly, and the preachers preached in power. My health was much destroyed by speaking so often and laboring so very hard, having a heavy fever preying upon my system. I was called upon to speak at a camp-meeting, I could scarcely accomplish the task, and I was obliged to take my bed (having also lost my appetite) as soon as my sermon was over. After a while my particular friends conveyed me to Mount Pleasant in a carriage; the day was pleasant, but in the woods at night we were overtaken by a dreadful storm of thunder, wind and rain, but through the will of Providence I escaped the inclemency of the weather and stopped at brother and sister Hance's; after being medically renovated, I fulfilled an appointment, and commenced to visit the sick in that place, but was arrested by a heavy fever. A physician was called, and by day break my sense left me, so severe was the disease, which caused the physician to visit me two and three times a day, which proved to be the bilious fever. After my

mind returned and became calm, I was convinced that it would not termi-
nate in death at that time. I had faith in the Lord. Eleven days I lived on rice
water and chicken tea without salt, at the end of which time I felt an appetite
to eat. I had been under a deep salvation which proved a blessing in effect-
ing a cure. After a lapse of four weeks I was enabled to get out of that house,
but very weak; my money was short; I left seven dollars with them hoping
the Lord may bless them; then I returned to brother Hence, and was well
treated. I commenced preaching, though very weak, and I accepted an
appointment on Sabbath in the white Methodist Episcopal church, to a well-
behaved congregation, about ten miles distance. I had to be carried to the
carriage in a blanket and returned the same way, and was well taken care of
by brother and sister Moor and family, for which may the Lord bless them
in the basket and store. Elder Jones gave me an invitation to go to Pittsburg
and try to gather a little strength, which I accepted, and was kindly taken
care of by brother Lewis and wife, which I very much profited by the assis-
tance of his family doctor, which he called in amid the blessings of
Providence; this was in May, 1830. I then taken care of by brother and sister
Moor and family, for which may the Lord bless them in basket and store.
Elder Jones gave me an invitation to go to Pittsburgh and try to gather a lit-
tle strength; which I accepted, and was kindly taken care of by brother Lewis
and life, which I very much profited by the assistance of his family doctor,
which he called in amid the blessings of Providence; this was in May, 1830.
I then commenced to labor amid the souls of the people, which are precious.
After gaining strength in body and mind in my recovery, I spoke to a good
number of colored friends on the Hill, and they were about to build a church
for worship as they owned the property. When I was able to travel, one of the
preacher's wives and a kind brother conducted me on to Washington, from
which I took stage for Mount Pleasant; labored for them, enjoyed a love-feast
with them, and in a few days left for St. Clairsville and the next successive
place; then took stage for Zanesville, continuing to labor around the circuit,
and then went to Columbus. I was invited to attend a quarterly meeting at
Urbana; we had quite a profitable waiting upon the Lord; it makes me glad
when they say let us go up to the house of the Lord. After trying to rest
myself four or five weeks, a brother preacher, in company with brother
Steward's widow and myself, visited the Indians, she having lived nine years
in Sandusky. We heard them preach in their own language, but I could only
understand when he said Jesus Christ of God, and the interpreter had gone
to conference. I spoke to them in English, was entertained in an Indian fam-

ily, and that very kindly after which I shook the dust off my feet and left them in peace. Thank the Lord for Urbana. The Elder appointed a camp meetings at Hillsborough; it was nothing to boast off; after which I turned towards Philadelphia. Brother Rains paid my stage fare on to Springfield; from thence endeavored to speak to a small and very quiet congregation; from thence to Columbus and paid seven dollars and a half, and left for Wheeling; stopped at a camp-meeting at the request of the Wheeling friends, but it seemed that both the golden wedge and Babalonish garment was there, as the wheel could not turn, for Christ said I could not do may mighty works on account of your unbelief; the Devil was at work, but the Lord was above.

I spoke at Wilkesbarre to both white and colored, Baptists and Methodists, and had an invitation to preach in the afternoon, had good congregations, and tears of contrition were visible in many places. I had life and liberty. I next visited Wheeling, stopped a few days and labored several times, which was much blessed, and the Elder organized a new class of twenty-one young men, brother and myself led them the first time, and they seemed very zealous. But in a few months the severity of the Laws stopped their privileges, which is an honor to any people; while sin is a reproach to any Nation. I then paid $10 and took passage to Hagerstown. My health was poor. Passengers consisted of three white ladies, members of the Episcopal Church, and one old gentleman, (a Deist) 73 years of age who would reproach Religion, until I told him that Solomon spoke of a man 70 years of ages, and called him a fool,—and exhorted him to get religion; for God's name is name is worthy to be praised by all intelligent beings. I have found Him to be a strong hold in the day of trouble. We arrived at Hagerstown in eight or ten days. We had a Meeting House there. I met the Elder, Joseph Harper, Deacon John Cornish. Had good Meetings; a visit of the Holy Ghost. The house was crowded, and many hundred sinners struck to the heart,—back-sliders were reclaimed—and believers built up in the most Holy Faith. Praise God for so much. I spoke to a very respectable congregation of white people about eleven miles distant.

> "Go, preach my Gospel, saith the Lord,
> Bid the whole world my grace receives;
> He shall be sav'd that trusts my word,
> He shall be damn'd that won't believe."

I then took my passage for Fredericktown. The Society was small, but

willing to encourage the Gospel of Christ. We had meeting in a large upper room of a building; the congregation was of both white and colored persons. I felt life and liberty, and an increase of my labors. In about ten days sinners were awakened—backsliders reclaimed—and believers built up in the most Holy Faith. The white Preachers threatened to turn them out of their Church for going to the African Methodist Episcopal Church. I thought when war commenced it was time to run. Oh! what prejudice and stupidity; for love is the fulfilment of the Law.

We had a remnant of our Connexion from Virginia, years before, but through some contention among themselves, the owner of the Church took it from them, run up a chimney in the centre of the house, and rented it out to different families to live in. He also went into the yard, kick'd over the head and foot boards of the graves, and levelled them down, and made a garden of the grave-yard. But the Lord afflicted him even unto death, and he was buried a day or two before I arrived at Frederick-town.

But God has a people everywhere; a remnant that never has bowed their knee to Baal. A Lutheran brother, (minister), interceded in their behalf, (the Church being offered for sale,) and receiving One Hundred Dollars from the Trustees' hands, bought it in for them, and a firm Deed being made of the Trustees, the Elder taking charge of it. So much, for Delivering Grace.

> "God moves in a mysterious way
> His wonders to perform;
> He plants His foot-steps in the sea
> And rides upon the storm."

I next started for Washington City; took passage in the stage about 1 o'clock in the afternoon, and arrived about 1 o'clock in the morning, and the clerk of the office conveyed me to a very respectable colored family, (Mr. Adam's') who kindly received me, and continued so to do, but I met my antagonist in that place, who strove to stop my Ministerial Mission; but Right is more than Might. Bishop Allen being a man of renown, and having Grace abounding in his heart, he sent a letter to his son-in-law who resided in that place, to intercede of me during my stay, which he did. Truly, the way seemed somewhat dark at first. I saw revivals among the members, though the congregation was small, the Lord raised me up plenty of friends among them for letter to his son-in-law who resided in that place, to intercede for me during my stay, which he did—Truly, the way seemed somewhat dark at

first. I saw revivals among the members, though the congregation was small, the Lord raised me up plenty of friends among them, for God is all in all. The Elder in charge was not to be seen until the last Sabbath I was there. He preached in the morning, but I was ashamed of his conduct towards me, through prejudice, while he was a leading man for the people. Reader, judge for thyself. But my God gave me a part and lot in this matter, saying, "Behold, I send you as Sheep among Wolves, be not afraid—Lo! I am with you always—even unto the end of the world." Praise God for his endurable promises. In a few days I left for Baltimore in stage. Some part of the rout was by Rail Road. Pleasant journey; arrived safe in Baltimore, engaged a colored man's back, which conveyed me to Mrs. A.H.'s., to whom I ever shall feel indebted; for herself and family were some of my warmest-hearted friends. Truly, I must say "the Lord remembered me in my lowest state. The Elder and Preachers of Baltimore with one accord, gave me appointment, and we had prosperous Meetings. We had a female speaker there, who seemed very zealous I asked permission to take her into the pupil, which was granted, and she spoke much in the spirit of God—which was attended with power. She being a woman of God; deportment graceful, and her ideas in Scripture very correct, and they were all very much pleased with her. She was a Teacher in the Sabbath School, at which place she often took occasion to extend her usefulness in speaking for the cause of God, for which she suffered much opposition, ever from her husband; although he was a Preacher of the Gospel, she encountered severe trials. Next I left Baltimore for Philadelphia, my home, and found my friends all well; and my only son also, was well, and remained with Rev. Bishop Allen, where I left him before I went away. After being absent for two years and six months, I found Bishop Allen in very ill health, but he ever had continued with unwearied interest in my son's welfare, by sending to school, and otherwise improving him in education; by which he has made considerable improvements therefrom, which give me great reconciliation of mind; one thing lacking, which was a trade. But finally, Rev. Bishop grew nearer and nearer his time of departure—prior to which he was much interested for the good of my son in getting a trade, but it being the winter of 1830, he concluded to keep him until spring; but the Rev. Bishop coming to the steep of time, departed this life March 26th, 1832, after seeing 72 years in a world of affliction. Immediately afterwards I placed my son with a French gentlemen, with whom he stayed and learned my son the Cabinet-making business in this city This is the way I have got along after getting my son to a trade. Felt myself to do like a poor pilgrim indeed,

wandering through this world so wide; having to travel among strangers, and being poor and destitute; I was sorely tempted. My money was gone, my health was gone, and I measurably without a home. But I rested on the promises of God. "They that put their trust in me shall never be confounded." Without having a dollar to help myself, I saw the Lord would verify his promise, bless his name for it.

I stopped a few weeks with my sister and Dr. Burton; boarded with her, and he seeing my debilitation of body, rendered medical assistance, which helped me much; but I was unable to labor and preach for some months. After my business of 1831 had been accomplished, I felt it my duty to visit my aged parent, whom I had not seen for eleven years. At length I started on my journey for Cape May, West Jersey, in the following way: By Steam Boat to Salem, N.J., and preached in the African M.E. Church to a good congregation, and we had a comfortable waiting upon the Lord. Some signs followed the preaching of the Cross of Christ; the people were very kind. From thence by Stages to Greenwich, and spoke with the Elder to a very humble people; a great display of God's power, six joined the Church, seven were baptized, and others fell to the floor and cried for mercy; thank God for it.

On Monday morning I left for Bridgeton; we having no Society there, I preached in the Court House to a large assembly of different denominations. I felt a degree of liberty in speaking, and I then stopped a few days with them, and was kindly received and entertained. I then proceeded on to Fairfield, and endeavored to labor for them at 11 o'clock, Sabbath morning, and at 3 o'clock, P.M. to crowded houses of respectable and quiet congregations, and the Lord poured out his spirit upon us and we had a solemn waiting in his presence, for which my soul rejoices even now.

I next went on to Port Elizabeth, which was very thinly inhabited, some two or three very respectable families there with only three persons belonging to Church; among them a Sqr. Brick, a man of ability. Through him the Church was opened for me, and I preached two Sermons to large congregations of respectable inhabitants of the place, in which I placed myself as in my Saviour's hand, and staying there as clay in the hands of the Potter. I had liberty, whilst I could hear the humble groans of the people, which cause my breast to swell as with pure Serephic joy. I bless the Lord, that the Gospel has never been left without a witness. Wisdom is justified of her children saith our Lord; if it was not so, thousands of Christians would have sunk in despair; but now and then I come across a great many whose sins were cancelled, and in whom pride was destroyed, and respecters of persons were not

known. Among such, God will prosper the labors of his servants. "God knows the proud afar off, but his Saints are beloved in his sight." I next proceeded to Goshen; there I found my aged mother, who I had not seen for eleven years, well in health and very active. But above all the rest, enjoying Religion, the love of God in the soul; which is more than the Gold of Opher; though poor, making many rich. Truly she dropped many aged tears on account of my exposures in travelling, but I strove to compose her by the word of God, which tells us "in this world we shall have tribulation, but in him we shall have peace." 'Tis there, the Christian's warfare ends, and sorrow cannot come. We dropped a few tears of gratitude with uplifted hearts to Almighty God for bringing us together once more in the flesh.

But my work soon again commenced. I preached in a dwelling house the next; in Goshen School-house, to both white and colored; and was assisted by the prayers of some humble souls, and felt both life and liberty. My colored brethren held a protracted meeting. some were Baptists and some Methodist. But all one in Christ. I think I never saw a greater display of God's eternal power; it was somewhat inexpressible: Glory to God for it. Four miles from there I preached in the Court House to a congregation of different denominations, and the house was crowded. Text—28th Chap. of St. Matt. 18th and 19th verses. On the following Sabbath I spoke in a School-house to a white Methodist congregation. We had a weeping time in the afternoon of the same day. Spoke to my own people, and the Lord blessed several souls. It was a time long to be remembered. Truly a sword that is so often whetted, must keep sharp, but in the midst of difficulties it appeared the word had its more perfect effect. After feeling I had discharged my duty towards God in that part of his vineyard, I returned home and spent the winter in Philadelphia, but very much afflicted. But in the midst of it my peace was like a river.

Some time in February 1832, the Lord sent two friends to take me out of town to visit a part of his vineyard, and they thought it would improve my health. I rode about twenty miles,—grew worse again—but medicine was applied which proved effectual. I spent a few weeks, preached in the Free Church in Norristown, three or four times, built by a lady of the Church of England, for all, or any that preach Christ and Him crucified.

Having gained my health, I returned in peace to Philadelphia, where I labored under some difficulties until the middle of May: After which I took a journey with a sister preacher for about two or three weeks, and truly the Lord blessed her labors abundantly, and my heart rejoiced to witness the out-

pouring of the Spirit of that Gospel visit with a Hand-Maiden of the Lord. The Scriptures are fulfilled as spoken of by the Prophet Joel, Chap. 27th, 2nd verse. "Ye shall know that I am in he midst of Israel, and that I am the Lord, your God, and none else, and my people shall never be ashamed. And it shall come to pass afterwards, that I will pour out my spirit upon all flesh, and your sons and your daughters shall Prophecy. "Your old men shall dream dreams, and your young men shall see vision." In 1831, a young man who professed to be righteous, says he saw in the sky men, marching like armies, whether it was with the naked eye, or a Vision by the eye of Faith, I cannot tell. But the wickedness of the people certainly calls for the lowering Judgements of God to be let loose upon the Nation and Slavery, that wretched system that eminated from the bottomless pit, is one of the greatest curses to any Nation.

June 1832, my mind was led to travel towards the east part of New Jersey, through Trenton, N. J., &c., and I preached three or four times, and found considerable consolation; The Elder made me appointments about two or three miles in the country, where there were a class of Methodists. There was a white came next morning to invite me to speak for them the next Sobbath afternoon, and himself proposed to make me a collection. I thus, truly, saw a way made for me I knew not, for I had but three or four cents in my pocket. Yet I had not mentioned it; but according to promise, after I had spoken, their contribution for me amounted to four or five Dollars; which added me on my journey. So much for trusting in God. I then went to Princeton. Not much success there, the Society being small. Preached three or four times there. Left for New Brunswick, and had very good meetings; more praying people, and had more life and power among them, and the Word of God had its effect. And the Judgements of God was in the land, the Cholera was taking away the people by scores. An awful day to them that had no God with them in death. It carried a sword with two edges, it cut right and left, took Saint and sinner, noble and ignoble, white and colored. It showed equality in my god's decree; where he speaks of "all men." I next left for Rahway,—still coming among strangers, but was kindly received by friends, both colored and white, of different orders, without distinction. I saw a large field open before me, and a plenty of labourers wanted in that part of God's moral Vineyard. I commenced to obey the Spirit of God, and had great liberty, both in word and Doctrine. I stopped six weeks, and the Elder only once preached. The people dying fast: News came into town from New York that great mortality was prevailing,—the people dying at the rate of 120 to 160 a

day. It was truly alarming, but we were highly favored in Rahway, there being only about four or five cases; and among them it clearly shown that God had no respect for persons. One poor colored man, who had used too much ardent spirits, was boasting about 8 o'clock that Cholera could do nothing with him; but while harnessing the horse for the family to go to church only two hours after, being 10 o'clock, A.M., he was seized with cramps, carried into the barn, and several Doctors sent for who remained with him, he having no friends. But at last, there being no hope for him by 8 o'clock P.M., the Doctors requested some colored Methodist family to let him die in their house, which was cheerfully acceded to, and he died about 12 o'clock, and was buried before day-light the same morning. A very rich man also died who was buried in splendor in day light, but the poor beggar was hurried away at night; yet they both died wicked. A short notice indeed. But Oh! their end, their dreadful end.

I still continued to labor, and witnessed good revivals. When the President's Proclamation went out for a General fasting throughout the United States on account of the Judgement of God, it was obeyed by all denominations, and of course came under our notice—and we having no Elder in that place, held it ourselves,—and it fell to my lot to give a sermon on that occasion, which I did through some embarrassment, from St. Matt. chap. 24th, 21st and 22d vrs. and the Spirit of the Lord was upon me, and the Scriptures opened to my mind. The stammering tongue was loosed, and the feast truly glorious. At night we held Prayer-meetings, and so continued until I felt at liberty to leave them. I then proceeded on to New York. On my arrival I called on the Elder, S.T.—, and was kindly received by him, and after a few days he gave me an appointment in Brooklyn Church, it having been near six years since I had spoken to that people. But while filling several successive appointments I saw signs of much good being done in the name of the Holy Child Jesus, which was owned with one accord. When entering the pulpit, the Bible being-torn, I was deprived of finding the Text. A young gentleman of the Episcopal Methodist Church being present, took occasion on my next appointment to present the Church being present, took occasion on my next appointment to present the Church with large new Bible. So much for the principles of Christianity. The Elder also gave me three appointments in the Bethel Church, New York, at Asberry, in Allen. st. upper part of the city—several times in Flushing Church, and attended a Loves-Feast, where the people spoke In the Spirit. Praise God for it.

I then returned to New York again, feeling my strength much renewed in

the inward man Christ Jesus. I saw a large want of labor there, as the Prophet Ezekiel said: "I saw the river rise to the Joins of a man."

After laboring about six weeks and seeing it was not in vain; with the approbation of the Brethren and in answer to a good conscience. Oh! that I had language to express my mind while I hold my pen in hand. But had I the tongue of an Hannah, whilst she spoke to Eli! I could not express the revelation of Jesus; but the bodily strength seemed to fail fast. I then returned to Philadelphia, rested four days, and was called to Salem, N.J., and after preaching two or three times crossed the Bay for St. Georges, a town in the State of Delaware, and preached twice by invitation of the citizens, and also by request I spoke in Delaware City. Here a horse, gig and driver being provided for me, I rode four or five miles in the evening and preached to a large congregation of white and colored persons. Good behaviour, but no particular display of God's power. I returned the same night to St. Georges, and spent a few days with my sister, whom I had not seen for eleven years previous. I left there a few days before Christians for Philadelphia, where I remained until January 1, 1833. After which I started, in company with another sister for New Hope, Pa. We held meetings in Frankford, then I proceeded to Ben-salem; from thence to Attleboro'. The Elder, P.S., was on that circuit, he cordially gave me appointments, and we were caused to rejoice. The Devil was also at work, setting up difficulties like mountains high, but having a skilful Pilot! I steered between the rocks. The Church, having been in a seven years law suit, was gained by the African M.E. Connexion. A brother, L.I.—, conveyed us seven mils, and I attended an appointment which was visited by the spirit of the Holy Ghost. Sister C— followed in exhortation and the meeting was closed by a brother—a crowded house— and were requested to hold another. But we appointed the next in Holmesburgh, which was a like prosperous. After which I returned to Philadelphia, and there remained until July 2, at which time I left for Canada, being a second visit to my scattered nation, for which time I felt a painful impression. For more than six years the first stop was in New York, from there to Albany, where I remained three or four weeks, but the Church was wading through deep waters. I had, long before, felt a great anxiety to publish my religious experience and exercise to a dying world, but, laboring under the disadvantages of education, I thought it a favour to pay $5 to have a portion of it taken from the original of my own registering, and corrected for press. By special request I visited Troy and found a christian spirited minister, Rev. Wm. Bishop, with a lively society, and I spoke for them—the Lord

was with us, and gave seed to the sower and bread to the eater, at different times; and, the next Sabbath I preached my Farewell sermon, and so Sunday night I heard prayer meeting in the Church, and on the next Saturday I left for Schenectady, preached in the Presbyterian Church twice on Sunday, and was kindly entertained; after which I left on Monday for Utica, and arrived there next morning about sunrise. I spoke for them on Thursday evening, also on Sunday afternoon to crowded houses of lively christians, and they administered to my necessities to assist me in travelling. I felt a great liberty in the gospel. From there I proceeded to Rochester, where I arrived, after being two days and a night on the canal, and found elder Graham with a prosperous church, which seemed a though his labors were much blessed. But, alas! the Devil crept in—has left them—they became scattered, the old trustees died, and the other connexion caught them. But during my stay they added several to the church. I then left for Little York in Canada, which was one day's sail across the Lakes; the passage was very rough that day. I was directed to Brother Brown's the preacher, and was kindly received by himself and wife. I preached on Sabbath morning and afternoon, and that day we had a shout in the Camp of Israel. Praise God, the mission was both owned and received. After speaking several times and holding prayer meetings, I left them for Niagara, spoke three times. From there to St. David, and preached to a respectable congregation of whites and colored persons. Six years before this I visited Niagara and there was a large society of the A.M.E. Connexion, but at this time the very Chapel was gone, the minister dead, the people scattered and backslid. I finding only two or three members at this time and no school, and children coming up in sin, then left for St. Catharine; spoke three times, but no particular revival, there were some who wished to be lords among God's heritage, and the work seemed stagnated, but they used me well, and I left them with peace of mind, in discharging my duty, fort George, and spoke on Sabbath morning to a white and colored congregation in a school house—wonderful time indeed—some shouted, some mourned, other sought for mercy, and I felt the Holy Ghost upon me, glory, glory, to God. After I helped to lead the class, I was insisted upon specially to preach a child's funeral sermon, before the corps left the house, a curious circumstance, which was caused by the following incident; seven years before I had preached in the neighborhood, to a great mixed multitude, after which I was invited to dine by this person, on which visit this child was born, or on that day; after some little hesitation on my part, I accepted the invitation and preached from the 2d Book of Samuel, "I shall go to him, but he shall not

return to me." It was a very solemn time—the corps was then taken to the Church of England, and laid before the altar, the clergy spoke over it, and very much to the purpose, without partiality, and then committed it to the breathless grave. On Thursday night I filled an appointment at a brother's house, the Lord was there. On the next Sabbath I rode seven miles, preached and helped to lead class, and the next week I left in stage for Little York, but stopped in Niagara, preached several times and paid a visit to a new society of Wesleyan Methodists, also then returned to York again and preached for a society of Baptists, a very quiet and attentive congregation, with one exception. Text by grace ye are saved through faith, that's not of yourselves, it's the gift of God. The Devil is always busy in his agency as in the following: a school-teacher was present in the congregation who, after I concluded my subject, arose to contradict my argument, he became very much excited and red in his face, but while he was on his feet I expressed a desire of the congregation not to notice his replay, and they accordingly treated it with contempt, which caused him to desist with all his prejudices against women. The people were very kind. From thence by steamboat, I proceeded to Hambleton, which was 50 miles; I found no colored society in that place, but the children went to school; about two miles from there I found a class, and, by permission of the trustees, on Wednesday evening, I spoke in the Methodist Chapel, to a small congregation, from a very short notice, but the Lord owned His Word. After the close of the meeting, and English gentleman and his lady invited me to go home and lodge one night at their house, which I did, and they exhibited a great degree of benevolence towards me; may God reward them for it. On Sabbath morning I spoke to my own people, and afterwards led class and found the same one God owned them in worship also. I saw that seed must be sown accordingly. I spoke in the afternoon, and the Lord made himself manifest by His Spirit in great display; the people, though very poor, were exceedingly kind; one of the brother preachers, conveyed me to Dundas and Flamburg, west. I preached to a large congregation in the white Methodist Chapel. We had an humble waiting upon the Lord. From there I went to Ancaster, there the Lord prepared a friend to take care of me through the winter. I preached several times and met many friends whom I had seen in Cincinnati; some gifted preachers there, but no elder to preside. There were many of our society there, called from place to place, which had been scattered like sheep without a shepherd—it truly was heart-rending to hear them lamenting the loss of their shepherd who was deceased. The brethren kept a watch meeting on Christmas eve. We enjoyed

the meeting and spent the night like St. Paul; the next day it fell to my lot to
fill an appointment which I did with both life and liberty, (praise God for it)
from the 2nd chap. of St. Like, verses 10, 11. I felt my mind lead me to a vil-
lage called Ammonsburg, on Lake Ontario, on what was called the Bush side,
but I kept it with myself and the Lord, and kept travelling and preaching as
the Lord gave ability. Brother S. Lewis was much interested at my anxiety for
that people's welfare, and also Brother Wm. Edwards, a gospel preacher, who
had been instrumental in civilizing and christianizing many of the natives
whom I saw in Brentford, an Indian town on the Mohawk river, where a
number of the natives lived along the river side, in the woods formed church-
es of societies of different denominations, hours excepted, and having no
Methodist Church, a gentleman, seeing the necessity of a place of worship
for us, gave us the privilege of a large house to worship in several times; truly
it was cold, but we had many comfortable meetings, and very many solemn
impressions made on a number of the minds of those present; afterwards I
left for Buffalo. The road was so rough that it caused me to be quite sick. I
could not stand it to ride 200 miles that cold weather, and I continued to
preach in and out of town to different denominations through frost and
snow. A gentlemen came to me after the sermon was over, and wished me
God's speed in a very friendly manner, then quietly withdrew with his ladies
in company with him, with politeness. My mind was on Buffalo, Brother
Edwards had not yet formed any society. I particularly desired him to take
my appointment, which he did, and also read the discipline with proper
explanations, wishing to know who would be subject to the government of
the same, and there were ten persons came forward and consented to be sub-
ject as members of our Discipline. I went to Ancaster, stopped at brother
Lewis' and wife, and although she was a young married woman, she was very
much like a mother to me. My mind was exercised to go to Ammonsburg,
through a gloomy winter; that night, after serious meditation, I fell asleep,
and suddenly awoke and received the witness that I must go. Next morning
I informed brother Lewis that I must go, and, he, feeling interested for me,
had me conveyed, in a private carriage, that I might travel comfortably. In
the middle of February I left for Chatham, and arrived there no the 26th of
the same month, where I found a society scattered, without a shepherd; some
living in the faith of Christ, while others had gone back to the beggarly ele-
ments of the world. Mr. Lightfoot received me very kindly; his house was
open for worship, where I had large gatherings come five or six times, for a
new place. The house being quite commodious, and Mr. Lightfoot used

every endeavor to send me on with the gospel to others. In April I left for Ammonsburg, there the believers seemed much strengthened; backsliders reclaimed, and sinners converted to God. Among which was a woman that had belonged to the Methodists by profession, having the form of godliness but was destitute of the power, until, the Spirit of God arrested her at this time. After which she ceased her carnal amusements; quit dancing and went to praying, at which time she arose on her feet and said that she never saw that dancing was wrong before now—but she had resolved to serve God in spirit and truth—praise God for the victory. For three days in Ammonsburg we could scarcely get any rest, from the effects of the outpouring of the spirit of God, on both white and colored. I was still more confirmed in mind that my visit was accepted of my God, who gave me this mission in Christ Jesus. I stopped with a brother, Jas. Jesus. I stopped with a brother, Jas. McKenney, and his affectionate wife, who had suffered much in the fear of Jesus. Brother made an appointment for the next evening for me, which I tried to fill. Text as follows: 16th chap. of St. Matthew's Gospel, 26th verse. I was in a strange part of God's vineyard, but his power was manifest even there; after which another appointment was made for Sunday morning, which was alike prosperous, and I helped to lead class; then spoke in the afternoon and at night with equal success. My mind was much exercised, seeing the need of schools. I counted 25 children and some young people whom I loved. I lamented their obscurity, and advised them to get a white man to reach them, and endeavored to shew them, that, without the advantages of education they never would be a moral people, and, in the course of time, their own children could, by proper advancement, become teachers for themselves. So I continued in all the towns, finally they caught the spirit and commenced in the following places; in Ancaster they chose their trustees to build a house for school, and likewise to preach in, at Brantford, at Chatham, and St. Catharine. Some went to St. David's and Toronto, to Sabbath schools, and in the week also; colored and white, all went together. After the course of two or three weeks, a colored teacher came to the last named place and established a school of between 30 or 40 scholars (after being examined and found competent) which improved the manners of the people very much, and they worshipped in their own Chapels. Their own preachers, exhorters, and class-leaders (colored.) There was a young sister that wished to travel with me a little way, and brother McKenny furnished us with a driver and conveyance, and the friends received us very kindly, and, to my astonishment, we were given appointments by the trustees of the Church. I spoke

from the following text, By grace ye are saved through faith, that is not of yourselves, but it is the gift of God. A Friend, W— God. A Friend W— was there, who was ever ready to oppose the Methodists; he was a Baptist preacher, and would invite the Methodists to preach for them, and then get up contradict them; he wished me to come and preach for them, but I felt no spirit of contention in religion and I declined. Our own people were talking of forming a union with the Canadian Methodists who were a branch of the Old Episcopal Methodists, that was raised by the missionaries from America; this being the time of the split, but some would leave to the Wesleyan Methodists. I preached five or six different times in this village for several Sabbaths two sermons a day, in which the Lord gave ability. We continued our meetings as usual, and invited the old ministers to visit us, which they did; and one of them gave an exhortation after me, and God's power filed the house and the guilty were alarmed, while believers rejoiced in hope of a better resurrection. I left that morning, rode five miles with a friend, and on Wednesday afternoon preached again—signs and wonders followed—after which I continued to visit the sick the remainder of the week, and on Sabbath day I rode five miles again to the Chapel, and filled an appointment in the afternoon for the last time as I thought, but the Lord seen best, and I was retained another week; the next Sabbath I filled an appointment from the following text; Finally, brethren, pray for us that the word of the Lord have free course and be glorified even as it is with you which was my Farewell Sermon. After which I returned to Ammonsburg in the fear of God where I preached several times and saw many manifestations of the operations of the Spirit of grace, and, on the following Sabbath, Brother A— made an appointment for me six miles distant, and one also for 6 o'clock in the evening; we had a very hard ride through the swamp, and met a large gathering both in and out of doors, and sinners were cut to the heart, and cried aloud for mercy, which was a joyful sound to believers in Christ Jesus. The next evening I spoke again from Isaiah, chap. 59 ver. 1; and several of the nobility taking into consideration my necessities, contributed to me the sum of $5. We had a quiet waiting upon the Lord; after which I and a sister that was with me, called on Mr. Gardiner and he collected some subscriptions and added to the former sum, for which, I trust, God will reward all the cheerful givers, as they were very generous. I held prayer-meetings, visited the sick, and passed many joyful moments of sweet communion especially in one sister's company, who was a member of the National Church in Ammonsburg.

But in affliction she enjoyed the Spirit's grace, and, in May, 1834, we parted as for eternity, and I trust to meet her where parting will be no more, neither will any of us shake the parting hand, for we have had sweet communion together, in spiritual exercises. Dear reader, think not that I am going to heaven as in golden slippers, for I have various trials to encounter while travelling over this world so wide, but I feel willing to suffer for the cause of God, after which I shall (if faithful) meet many of my friends that have communed with me in the spirit, where we never, never, shall shake the parting hand—these are the consolations in affliction as described in Rev. chap.12, 11th verse. And they overcame him by the Blood of the Lamb, and by the word of their testimony, and they loved not their lives unto death; and whilst I move my pen my soul rejoices in God my Redeemer. Having filled my mission I parted with my friends on joy. I sailed for Detroit city, 18 miles, then build adieu to British shores, not knowing that I should ever step on them again. I was kindly received on American possessions by a respectable family from Cincinnati, a Mr. D——. I felt there was a work for me to do in that part of God's vineyard. I arrived on Tuesday and on Thursday evening we had a comfortable meeting at the usual place. I met with much encouragement in laboring for the Lord, and many impressions were made on the minds of the hearers. The evening previous to my landing I saw some of the American affliction towards the people of color, such as mobbing, theft and destruction. To unto the inhabitants of the earth and the sea, for the Devil is come down unto you. On the following Sabbath morning, 10 o'clock, I preached again, then lead class—a soul reviving time, indeed—at 7 o'clock, P.M. I preached again, and the house was crowded to overflowing, it not being sufficient to hold the people. Text as follows: And the gospel of the kingdom shall be preached unto all the world for a witness, and then shall the end come. After which we visited a prayer meeting held by the stationed minister in the white Church, which was truly comfortable. On the next Sabbath I had an appointment made for me on the British side in a dwelling house, but, it not being sufficient to hold the people, the Episcopal Methodists opened their session-room which was larger and well crowded with various denominations. Text, 1st chap. St. John; ver. 45. The Lord touched my tongue as with a live coal from his altar, and we had a good time as from the hand of the Lord, and the Amens of the preachers, elders, and leaders, helped to swell the theme of rejoicing. Glory to God, we had all things common. But now feeling my mission ended I waited for the first opportunity and took passage for Buffalo. Three hundred and sixty miles on

Lake Ontaria, and, I must say, the most uncomfortable passage I ever experienced, although the boat was commodious, yet they treated the people of color very indifferently indeed, as regards their accommodation, and yet charged them a high price, I having paid $4.50. After two uncomfortable days' and nights' sail, me arrived at Buffalo wharf about six o'clock, A.M. Six years had elapsed since I had been in Buffalo, which was the first time, but during my absence many changes had taken place, the loss of some of my particular friends by death and other moveable causes. But I found a Mrs. Davis, who was a great friend indeed to the people of God. I felt my mission truly in this part of His vineyard—there were a few of the Episcopal Methodists, but no established society. The Baptist denomination had the majority of the people, they opened their places of worship and I preached and held prayer meetings three or four times among them, which was attended with considerable success. I also had the pleasure of meeting an anti-slavery society where I heard some very able discussions on the rights of the oppressed, and also clear demonstrations of the cruelty of the slaveholder, which was exposed with all its horror by a young man by the name of L— but was greatly opposed by the Judge of the city, after which the young man arose to his feet the second time in which it seemed nothing escaped his exposure. I, about this time had written from Buffalo to Philadelphia (as it was shown me by the Spirit that my son had embraced religion) to know the fact of the matter, as I was some hundred miles from home and received the satisfactory answer by letter from his own hand, which explained his conviction—the length of the distress of his mind—the severity of which had caused him to seek opportunity to put an end to his own existence, but in the act he was told to try and pray once more, by the voice of the Spirit, which he consented to do, but concealed his intention from the people, which had been suggested by the Devil, to take his own life, and it would be all over. In this extremity it was God's opportunity by his act of obedience to convert his soul, after bringing him to the ground like a Soul of Tarsus, and now stands as a living witness that God has power on earth to forgive sin.

O Reader, you may only imagine the joy of my heart at such language as this from my only son, whom, it seemed, God had left as a comfort to me in my old age, more especially after not having had any communication from him for eight months, and then he was very ill which made my cross seem very heavy, but I trusted in God, although I expected to hear of his death when I did hear anything, but, on my knees at a brother and sister L's— at family prayer was shown these things by revelation of spirit, which caused me

to get up off my knees and I exclaimed aloud, the Lord has converted the soul of my son, for which we had a shout around the room, and then comes the letter as a witness of the same from his own written composition. I scarcely knew how to praise the Lord enough, and for another reason when I thought that God granted what I had prayed for, from the days of his childhood, while I travelled the barren wilds, of lonesome hills, and gloomy vales. But so much for trusting in God who will not let the prayers of his people pass unnoticed, but is bound to hear and answer when they pray aright. Praise the Lord, O my soul, magnify his name.

> With joy let Judah stand
> On Zion's chosen hill,
> Proclaim the wonders of thy hand,
> And councils of thy will.

I now began to feel my mission somewhat complete as regards distance, and therefore concluded to return towards home. A brother and his wife crossed the Lakes with me for company, I then took the cars, and bid them adieu. I remained in Rochester a while after my arrival, but, to my sorrow and surprise, a society that, twelve months previous, was large and seemed every way prosperous, had nearly dwindled away—the preacher gone and the people scattered except a resolute few, who were bound to go through, and that at the risk of their all; and to them I endeavored to fulfil my mission. I also spoke for the Wesleyan Methodists—they treated me with christian fellowship. Our Lord said, they that are for us are not against us, forbid them not—it truly was uncomfortable. There was seed to the sower and bread to the eater. I also stopped at Palmyra, visited the sick and otherwise endeavored to fill my mission. A little difficulty existed, relative to a slave girl being concealed and taken away, but while we were at worship the Justice of the Peace was in the house and everything seemed quiet. After service, the congregation quietly withdrew—this was on the 6th of August. On the next day a lady of color paid for a seat for herself and me, and we took passage on to Canondagua, 16 miles; there I found a Church and people prosperous. They received me kindly—my first appointment, 11 o'clock, Sabbath morning; the word had some impressions, in the afternoon still better, at night God was his own interpreter, the hallowed fire began to run to sin's confusion. I had several appointments through the week, which were alike prosperous. Although I felt my inability, yet the answer to a good conscience strength-

ened me, even in a strange land, and, with Paul, I can say I am not ashamed of the Gospel of Christ, for it is the power of God to every one that believes. I then took stage for Geneva, having recommendations to these little towns or villages, I found a few members of the Episcopal Methodists, and also of the Presbyterian denomination; they were very friendly and opened their house to entertain me—the colored gentlemen of the vicinity around were building a house for the Travelling Missionaries to preach in it was opened for me, and I felt great liberty in endeavoring to labour for the Lord; tears of contrition dropped freely; a sister there shewed great hospitality towards me. After filling three appointments, I left on the third day of the week. I took stage for Ithaca, having had an invitation from the Rev. H. J— who had the charge. I arrived about 4 o'clock in the afternoon and was taken to Elder H. J— Before I entered the town I felt, according to the movings of the Spirit, that the Lord would pour out his Spirit upon the people, for which I yet rejoice in hope of a better resurrection. We met in the unity of the Spirit and continued so with humility—the friends were kind indeed to me, in and from the noble edifices of the large conveniences, to the humble cottage of Christian inmates. But an humble heart is better than a sacrifice. The society was young but was composed of some very respectable people, and useful citizens. Congregations large, class lively, and the Spirit of God visited us in abundant measure, which made the people speak with great confidence in the Lord. Though hard toiling, yet duty makes labor light some backsliders reclaimed, sinners converted, and believers strengthened; while many joined the Church, which was a sign of some good in the name of the holy child Jesus. After which my visit closed in peace with God, peace with all men, and the answer of good conscience. I was next conveyed by carriage to the steam boat, and took passage for Albany. Crossing the Seneca river or lake, where passengers meet the canal boat for Albany, which was my next stopping place. I was recommended by a gentleman to the captain; took passage; and after a pleasant voyage of two days and nights, we arrived at Schenectady, and the next morning we arrived at Albany. The Rev. Mr. Williams was stationed there; I payed him a visit; the preachers generally professed a Christian Spirit. The task seemed as though laid on a Jonah; I preached twice on Sabbath day; and through the aid of Bro. S.S.— I was able to get to New York. Rev. R. W— was one of the oldest Elders in the African Methodist Episcopal Church, who has since that fell in the battle-field, declaring war against the power of Darkness, and his bones were buried with all the honors of war. Let me live the life of the righteous and let my last end be like his. On my arrival

at New York, I found the Rev. S. S.—, Elder, stationed there; I spent three weeks in that city; I preached in Bethel; in Allen Church several times; good congregations for that part of the town, but the other was crowded. I only mention a few texts, 1st Sam. 2d chap. 6th ver; 3d chap. Hebrews, 3 first verses. Brother Jacob Matthews gave me an appointment in Zion Church, and I felt the Lord, as before mentioned, to be very close to me. The Rev. T. E— gave me an appointment in Asbury Church on Sabbath night, text, 3d chap. of St. Matthew, 12th verse, which was a night long to be remembered by all present; the Lord made bare his arm; some were arrested under the power of God, and fell to the floor crying for mercy, while believers were strengthened in the faith of Christ. I also had appointments in Brooklyn, L. I; there we were much favored with good meetings; a number of Old Methodists, with faithful preachers who kept the flock of Christ alive; and our labors were crowned with success, and additions to the Church. In the midst of life we are in death. Since I had been last at this place, previous to my tour in British America, the young gentleman that manifested such friendship for the Church by presenting it with a Bible for my appointment, had bid adieu to time and had gone to the mansions of bliss. The day previous to my arrival, I stopped at Bro. T—'s, one of the oldest standard families that celebrated the Church of God; his wife a mother and sister upwards of seventy years of ages; whose character was unblemished, faith firm, although afflicted, yet cheerful, with a short illness, in September, 1835, left the world in triumph. I commenced my journey of Canada, in 1832. From the second day of July to the fifteenth day of October, years following, 1833, I had preached 138 sermons, and travelled between 27 and 28 hundred miles. Returned from Brooklyn, and attended a quarterly meeting at Flushing; Bro. J. S— elder in charge. Saturday evening I gave man exhortation, and preached Sunday afternoon at 3 o'clock, the Lord accompanied the word, and, be it remembered, it will be either a savor of life unto life or of death unto death. Having finished my visit I felt anxious to go to Philadelphia; feeling my labors to come to a close for the present. I arrived safe at home, found my son and friends all well, and then heard the truth of his conversion, for which I yet give glory to God. I was three days in the city and left for Salem, N.J., on business; finding the doors opened to me I preached in the Church; we had a comfortable waiting upon the Lord, but no particular display of his power. After which I crossed the bay to New Castle, Del. and then proceeded to see my long lost sister; this being the second time in forty-two or forty-three years—there I found a large field of labor. Preached in a

school-house by permission of Mr. S.— he being a man of authority, and chief owner of a large part of the town. I was also sent for to speak in Delaware—a horse and gig and dinner prepared—I was taken five or six miles, blessed with a full house and I felt the power from the upper world, and the Lord was with me. After two days visit my mind being and the easy, I rested, and on the third day I left for Philadelphia; finding all well, I remained for a few days, and then left for the Rev. R. R—'s circuit, and found him a Christian and a gentleman. I first hailed Burlington, and met the ministerial order of Brethren, who received me with joy.

THE VINEYARD OF THE
LORD BEFORE THE LABORER LIES.

WE HAD SEVERAL very good meetings: I then crossed over to Bristol and spoke once or twice in a dwelling-house, at which time the Lord verified his promises, which are, I will hearken unto. I proceeded on my journey to Trenton, which was Elder Robinson's Circuit. Two or three days after this he arrived in the city. On Sabbath morning he preached and was much favored by the Spirit of the Lord. At night I preached and felt joy in my soul; from there he gave me other appointments. My mind was cleared and the Scriptures opened themselves to my mind and I felt strengthened; some shouted, others wept. I feel the holy influence of that fire now, while my pen makes record of the same to a dying world. Let the inhabitants of the rocks sing, and let them shout as from the top of the mountains. I preached another sermon from the 59th chap. of Isaiah, 12th verse. The fire kindled some where, and the hearty amens that ascended the hill of the Lord seemed to strike guilt to the hearts of sinners. I helped to lead class. O, the worth and value of precious souls which cause me oft to mourn. I preached again from the 22d chap. of Rev. 1st ver. The prayers of God's people helped me, and the power of God, like the dew of heaven, was let down upon us, and the sower and reaper rejoiced together, independent of various opposition. I also spoke from Romans, 1st chap. 16th ver., and spoke three times on Sabbath day; and I felt more strength at the last appointment than I did at the first, which proves the assertion of Scripture, freely give and freely receive. I also visited the sick, after which they gave me some appointments at Princeton, a

hard part of the vineyard. I had my talent and to use it I was not ashamed, although the substance seemed to be lost—full houses. The Presbyterian friends were very kind to me and received me with Christian friendship. The weather cold, and travelling hard, through wintry storms to pass. The first text, Let the dead bury the dead. It seemed a little astonishing, especially to the brethren. I continued, and on different times filing appointments. From thence to Brunswick; and one of the coldest days, rode sixteen miles; the Lord was with me, and I had great liberty of speech; a church and a large congregation; and the power of God was more fully manifest than at Princeton; and the Lord added such to the Church as, I trust, will be eternally saved. I remained there to labor for the Lord two or three weeks, and there was a general revival throughout in prayer meetings, both of male and female, and in class meetings; not my labors, reader, but the merit belongs to God alone.

> Praise the Lord, ye heavens adore him;
> Praise him all ye stars of light;
> Sun and moon rejoice before him,
> Praise him, angels in your heights.

After my return to Philadelphia in December, 1835, I saw a large field open to my view, it being a strong place, and many different spirits to contend with, I endeavored to commend this portion of sacred Writ: Job, 22d chap. 10th ver., But he knoweth the way I take; when he hath tried me I shall come forth as gold; again, Rev. 3d chap., 8th ver., and I seemed much troubled, as being measurably debarred from my own Church as regards this privilege I had been so much used to; I could scarcely tell where to go or stay in my own house. I said, Lord, where shall I go? and was directed to brother Murray, Elder then of Little Wesley Church, and when coming to his house he expressed his astonishment at my coming out through the inclemency of such weather, I paused, then told him I was sent to him and knew not for what; he said I know—then he gave me an appointment on Sunday night, and on the following Wednesday evening; from there I received an appointment at Zoar Church, by the elder, and the Lord converted one soul, which caused me still more to rejoice in God my Saviour; from that the elder of Wesley Church gave me an appointment and I preached to a large congregation, and felt strong in the cause of my God. My call seemed chiefly in Philadelphia. In the year 1835 I travelled 721 miles, and preached 692 sermons; I also spoke in Bethel Church; some false

brethren. They that are not for us are against us, and are against God's ministry, whether male or female, they are against God, who says I send by whom I will, for all are one in Christ Jesus. May the Lord pardon their errors, and make them be careful how they handle edged tools. In 1836 I travelled 556 miles, and preached 11 sermons; and felt under much exercise to print a book, and I had some friends to encourage me, such as the Rev. R.R.—and the Bishop, with others; and every circumstance was so favorable that I finally succeeded, and when they were brought home, I sat down in the house and wondered how I should dispose of them; to sell them appears too much like merchandize. While in this situation it was suggested to my mind, you must pay for them, or it will do more harm to the Gospel than if you had not printed them. But to myself, (if not printed) would be the encourage of a guilty conscience before the Lord. At 4 o'clock, P.M., my mind was directed to a Presbyterian sister, and on my way I met Bishop Allen's widow who bought one, and that afternoon I sold one dollar and fifty cents' worth. The Lord so blessed the offering of that work to the world, that in less than four months I paid sixty dollars through God's assistance, for the expenses which gave me great tranquility of mind, and caused me to feel still more like wearing out in the service of God. Various are the ways through the interposition of Providence that I succeeded in disposing of that little work, viz: camp-meetings, quarterly meetings, in the public streets, &;c. Praise God for his mercies as well as his graces.

After this I started for a Camp-meeting, near Baltimore. On my arrival I received two appointments, and after the Bishop came, still more was given to me, and at one time the power of God arrested an individual and he cried aloud, fell out of the door and was reclaimed. I preached three sermons in the African M.E. Church, and God gave us souls at every meeting, and my heart rejoiced to see sinners coming to God. Notwithstanding I had my opposers I out-live them through the strength of Him, that yet loves His faithful followers. After seeing so many displays of the miraculous power of God, I returned to the city of Baltimore, with peace of conscience. After which my mind was exercised to go to Elicott's Mills to preach in the African M.E. Church, and was accompanied by a dear sister, previously having had conversation with Bishop Walters he sent a letter to the preacher in charge, who received me with christian spirit. In the morning I led class and in the afternoon I had an appointment. and preached from the 5th Chapter of St. Luke, 18th & 19th verses. A full house, with attentive hearers,—praise God for a visitation of His Spirit. An humble groan is better than a sacrifice. At

night I spoke from the 7th Chapter of Hebrews, 12th & 13th verses, and wonderful to relate, if language could, the power of feeling. And well may it be said that feeling has no fellow. On Thursday night I spoke from the 61st Chapter of Isaiah, 1st verse: And truly I was appointed. And one visible sign of the manifestation of the Spirit of God was, an aged lady was caused to cry aloud, under the distress of mind, and many more, too tedious to mention. During the whole week, I continued to visit the sick, &&;c. One case I here mention as a caution to those who procrastinate the day of Salvation holder of a tyrannical turn, said to be very wicked. But he had received a summons, served by the officer Death, and I saw it pictured in his faces; which is as follows. By request, I called to see a Slave-holder of a tyranical turn, said to be very wicked. But he had received a summons, served by the officer Death, and I saw it pictured in his face; previous to which I had heard of his selling two men from their wives, recently. I asked him what he thought of dying; if he was prepared to meet the change. He told me he was not. He was very ill, could not recover, but wanted religion and could not get it; but wished me to have prayers with him. This I did, but it was of no avail, although it was truly solemn. I then exhorted him to have faith in the merits of the blood of Christ and then left him, a repining subject for eternity.

"Don't you see how unexpected in my chariot I do ride,
Convulsion fits, Plagues and Fevers, are the weapons by my side."
Death.

After this, I returned to Baltimore, and from thence I was conducted to Springtown, and spoke in the morning, Sunday, 11 o'clock. Text, in Psalms. No extra display in the afternoon. Brother H. U., held forth to a very large congregation. At night I preached again.

By this time there was inroads made upon the minds of the people,—they caught the Hallowed Flame, and some shouted, while others were convicted and reclaimed, and I was lifted up in Word and Doctrines of our Lord and Saviour Jesus Christ. On Monday night I held a Prayer-meeting,—next morning I started for Baltimore, quite indisposed, but being once more restored to health, I preached on the following Sabbath night in Bethel Church, Baltimore, appointment by Bishop Walters. Text, Acts 18th Chapter, 9th & 10th verses, with special references, from Chapter 20; 19th, 20th, 21st & 22d verses. On the ensuing Wednesday night I preached again from Prophet Joel, Chapter 1st & 1st vers. The slain of the Lord truly was

many. Again I spoke from Hebrews, Chapter 7th; 12th & 13th verses, at 3 o'clock, P.M. and God's name was glorified. I had great liberty of speech— bless the Lord. It is a good cause to live in, but better to die in. It is sweeter than life and stronger than death.

The Bishop gave me an appointment on the following Sabbath night. Text, from one of Peters' Epistles, 5th verse. The word preached had its effect. Three persons were arrested under the power of God and felled to the floor at once. The grand-mother and her daughter and grand-daughter cried aloud for mercy. In the meanwhile a gentleman fell on his face and cried for Sanctification; and there was a general rumbling among the dry bones. Praise God, for I feel the unction from on high, while I hold my pen.

I next started for Long Green, a distance of sixteen miles. A sister I— who had been travelling with me, as also brother Dunn, accompanied us. I spoke from Acts 17, verse 31. Three persons found peace, several under serious impressions. The word still had a lasting effect, and they sent for us again We complied, accompanied by our Rev. brother; although the morning was very cold, we were blest to get there in time for Church, and by the help of God, I tried to speak to the people from these words. "Although you tread upon scorpions and serpents, they shall not hurt you, having faith." The word went out and did not return void; for two found peace that day, and we left some on the floor mourning for redemption in Christ, while others wore deep symptoms of serious impressions for the welfare of their souls. We left at 4 o'clock in the afternoon, but the meeting continued until night. May God continue to water every plant in Zion. I preached and sold my books, and paid my own way. I returned to Philadelphia in December. After I arrived my health was much impaired, and I had a severe spell of sickness. So ended 1836.

I commenced travelling March 11th, 1837. Eight miles from Philadelphia, I preached three Sermons. Two at Blaketown, N.J., after which I took Steamboat for St. Georges, Del. to see my sister, at the request of Doct. ———, he being the main proprietor of the town, I accepted an appointment and filled it. I then spent a few days with my sister, and left for Salem, N.J. Preached two Sermons on Sabbath day, two miles from Salem, and we had a good meeting,—for, where the Lord is, there is liberty. On Wednesday I left for Greenwich, preached three times, and the Lord was there in power, and my soul witnessed it. From thence I proceeded to ——— and there truly was a revival among the people, which gave me encourage- ment to trust in God. From there I proceeded on to Port Elizabeth, and

spoke in the Ebenezer Church, to a very large and respectable congregation from seventh chapter, Hebrews, 12th & 13th verses. On Sunday 3 o'clock, P.M., I preached at the same Church, then I proceeded six miles further and preached one Sermon to the Forgemen, and tried to give them the Gospel, but I did not feel that liberty of Spiritual fellowship as I did at many places, to see professing Christians working hard on the Sabbath at the forge, and then walk into Church, to keep the Holy is, in my opinion, altogether out of the question. However I returned from that place the same night, and on Monday I left for Goshen, Cape May, to see my aged mother, then 78 years of age. I found her happy in the Lord, and my sister also. I preached three sermons on Cape May and left them as I found them, in the hands of God. I arrived on my return, at Port Elizabeth on the next Sabbath morning, filled an appointment both morning and night. Next morning I took stage for Philadelphia, where I arrived on June 5th, found all well. Our Conference being held in May, I concluded I must have some of the Feast. Three or four days after this I proceeded to New York, from there on to Albany, Elder Williams having charge of the Church. I preached nine sermons. Some revivals, some joined the Church, and members strengthened in the Faith of Christ. I also visited Troy, preached three Sermons there, one for a white congregation. We had a good meeting; and I was well treated by the friends. On my return to Albany I preached two sermons—and truly enjoyed myself in the Lord. I then returned to New York with an appeal to the conscience of every man, as regards my endeavors to do good,—bless the Lord. Duty makes labor light. My visit was to be accomplished in New York and Brooklyn. Rev. Wm. C.—, having charge at both places, gave me appointments. Preached four sermons in New York, five in Brooklyn and two in Flushing and one in Williamsburg.

Knowing my religious visits were nearly closed for the presents I availed myself of the opportunity of visiting the different Schools, the most impressive was that of Mr. Louis Tappan, which I think exceeded all I had ever seen; the principles in different branches which had been, and in some instances, are yet hid from the people of color, to deprive them of their enjoyments, were here taught them, which greatly helped to elevate them to a position that would command respect through the short voyage of life. These are the proceeds of vital piety. "Do unto all men, as ye would they should do unto you." Love, truly, is the fulfilment of the Law. O! may the day speedily come when the yoke of oppression shall be finally destroyed. Under a striking impulse of gratitude, and at the request of Mr. Tappan, I delivered a short

address and then left the School with the answer to a good conscience. Then leaving New York, I arrived at New Brunswick, where I was kindly received. Preached three sermons, truly, the Lord was there in power. Next I proceeded to Rahway, preached four sermons, and some were added to the church. From that to Princeton, and preached four sermons. No particular display of God's power; yet my soul rejoices in hope of the promise. "If Israel is not gathered, Jacob shall not lose his reward." I then left for Trenton, met a Quarterly Meeting, and the Elder gave me two appointments. His labors had been very successful on his circuit. I then left for Philadelphia, and found my friends well. This being the month of November, I remained a-while in the city. I preached in Bethel Church and the Union also. Dec. 2nd I left for New-Hope, with a sister speaker. She and myself attended two churches by the permission of the Elder, R. R.— I preached five sermons before Christmas, 1st at brother's house, 2nd at the Mountain, and 3rd in the new church; praise God for it. "Long expected, seen at last." The 1st text as follows: "Wisdom is justified of her children," &c. it was a time long to be remembered. I preached the Watch-Night sermon Christmas Eve, from Matt. 2nd chap. and 10th verse, and during my stay until New-Years Eve, there was great good done in the name of the Holy Child Jesus. In travelling towards Frankford I stopped at Holmesburg for the purpose of warning some persons of approaching danger, but finding an intimate friend of mine very ill, I paid her a religious visit, which gave me much satisfaction to see her resignation unto death. I purposed leaving next morning for Frankford at 9 o'clock, but she died, and the Elder and preacher being at a far distance from there, by special request I attended the funeral, and after a short sermon at the house I had to commit the body to the earth, as no other person was present to do it. I then left for Frankford, preached four sermons which was profitable through God's grace.

Feb'ry. 16th, I started for Attleboro. I spoke from the Following passages: Romans 6th chap. 21st 22nd 23rd verses. Also from the 8th Chapter, 36th & 37th verses. At first it seemed like seed sown in stony ground, but the deadness began to remove, and life, light and immortality was come to pass through the preaching of the Cross of Christ. I preached one sermon in Ben-Salem, and held a prayer meeting, and the Lord smiled upon us, and truly some had in a measure lost their first love, and others who had not defiled their garments, but contended for the fulfilment of the promise. Now, coming towards Philadelphia, I found my son and my friends all well. After preaching one hundred and forty-six sermons and travelling nine hundred

and ninety-nine miles.

In April, I felt impressed to visit Reading, Pa., which I did, and met some that I had met with years before, testifying that God is God, and changes not. I preached five sermons, and truly I must say that the Gospel is prevailing. Some few years previous there was not one member of church, now there is a good church and a large society. I now went to Norristown, spoke five times and led class. A man formerly lived there that played on the violin, but leaving his place of residence went to Philadelphia and embraced religion, and was called to go to the people of that town to preach the gospel to them, and the Lord blessed his labors, and they now live in hope of a better resurrection.

July 15th, 1838, I left for Westchester, preached two sermons. From there I went to Chichester, from that to the Valley, laboring as I passed along to lively congregations. On the 23rd I left for Colombia, calling on Rev. S. S.— he gave me three appointments. God revived his work in the hearts of his people, and while my pen moves my heart burns with love to God. Next I left for West-town and visited some aged friends, such as could not get to the church, and two remarkable once in particular, which were regarded as pillars of the church. I was conducted on board the canal boat for Lewistown. I had a pleasant passage, arrived at 1 or 2 o'clock, A.M. and was kindly treated by them. Preached four sermons to a hard people. I was sick during my stay, my system was much debilitated before I reached Pittsburg; however, I pressed on to Huntingdon, found a small society suffering for want of help. I was received by all the brethren, preached five sermons, rode 11 miles and spoke to the Forgemen, but through bad management the congregation was small, but the word had its effect; the souls of the redeemed are precious. I next proceeded to Hollidaysburg. Took passage by stage at night, arrived at 8 o'clock A.M. I was kindly received by a gentleman belonging to Wesley church, and entertained in a friendly manner. Preached two sermons to a comfortable congregation, and then left for Johnstown. After I got out of the car I thought it almost the last end of the world as regards accommodations. I had to stand near one hour before I could get a person to carry my trunk. The Captain was kind and offered to send me a person, but I got a man at last to take my trunk there. His wife was kind, although I introduced myself to her, knowing her to be the Barber's wife. She sent for him to coming, and then introduced me to her husband. When he sat down he said, "you preach do you?" I try, said I. "Do you understand the Scriptures?" Some parts of it, was my answer. He appointed a meeting, and the time arrived, congregation

gathered. When I commenced I felt a little confusion in the house, but in a few minutes every thing was still, and we had a solemn waiting upon the Lord; after which the Barber closed the service. So I left them. A brother informed me that the chief Magistrate of the town said we must hold another meeting and he would attend it, but the preacher did not seem to feel interested for the welfare of souls; for this cause I took passage on steam boat for Pittsburg, which was pleasant although crowded. The last day being Sabbath, I sat in serious meditation on the beauties of Creation and the plan of Redemption. There were some lady passengers from Charleston that enjoyed religion would come and sit by me to read. When about to leave, one of them requested me to pray for her husband and daughter. I hope the Elijah's God will prosper her desire for their welfare. We arrived at Pittsburg about 8 o'clock, P.M. I was conducted to the house of a worthy Father in Israel, where I remained a while, preached four or five sermons in Pittsburg. My mind still urging me on to Brownsville; and the Lord opened the way. The Elder of the circuit coming into Pittsburg, made a way for me, and provided me with a sister to accompany me. The Lord blessed the labors of his servants. In three months time there were one hundred and ten added to his circuit Some converts, some mourners. Five out of one family fell in love with this Heaven-born plan. I commenced my winter journey the 10th of December. I left Pittsburgh for a Quarterly Meeting at Williamsport; it was a tedious journey. We had to walk seven miles, and on entering the town we met a brother coming to meet us with a conveyance. That night the meeting commenced, and truly the battle was the Lord's. Six were slain by his mighty power, and the faith of believers strengthened. I spoke at 11 o'clock from the 12th Chapter of Isaiah, 5th & 6th verses, and at night again, to a crowded house of well-believed people. Elder Clemens, a successful laborer for the Lord was on this circuit. After preaching, the mourner's bench was erected, and the slain of the Lord were many. This meeting continued two days and nights, after which our Love-feasts took place. The Lord was in the midst, and the people were crying for mercy in every direction. The Wesleyan Methodists opened their church and gave me an appointment on Monday at 3 o'clock, P.M., after which the Elder gave us privilege to hold prayer meetings, which continued all night, was very successful, and a revival took place with both white and colored people, and one of the members informed me there were thirty persons added to the church that time. Praise God for the Victory.

> The world cannot withstand
> Its ancient conqueror;
> It sure must fail beneath the hand
> That arms us for the war:

We then rested a few days and started for Uniontown, a female travelling with me; and we were received very kindly by Bro. Jackson and wife, and the friends generally. I preached out at the forge to an attentive people and felt both life and liberty. The Elder returning from his circuit, preached again, and five united with us in the Church, after which the Elder formed a new Society, Fourteen miles distant. I then preached in the white M. E. Church to a very attentive congregation, whose groans ascended the hill of the Lord, and I felt his presence in a powerful manner—text, Isaiah lix. 1 v. On 24th of December the Elder held a watch-night, and on the 25th we started for Ridge Port again. I received the morning appointment and the Elder preached at night, and the Lord continued to pour out his Spirit upon the people, which caused a general revival. Ten joined the Church on trial. Some we left mourning for the redemption in Christ, while others seemed to be in all stretch for the Kingdom of God. I had a previous invitation to a church five miles distant on the turnpike, and I spoke in the morning at 11 o'clock, and just closed the sermon, when a gentleman came with a swift horse and vehicle on express for me to come and fill an appointment for them at 3 o'clock P.M., and accordingly went. We arrived between 2 and 3 o'clock. I met a large congregation of very respectable people, and preached from these words: "The Spirit of the Lord God is upon me," &c. The next Wednesday I attended an appointment in Greenfield in the old M. E. church; it was a very stormy night, and I thought from the inclemency of the weather there would be no person out; but through the perseverance of the Brother and his wife that came for me, there was quite a large congregation gathered, after which he handed me up in the pulpit, and I endeavored to preach from these words: "We have found him of whom Moses and the Prophets did write," and I must say that the Christian groans that were uttered, and the hearty Amens that ascended the hill of Zion, were answered seemingly as with coals of fire from God's holy altar, which warmed every heart. Pray God to carry on the work.

> Thy banner unfurl,
> Bid the nation surrender;

And own Thee their God,
Their King, and Defender.

Some hundred were added to that circuit that year, ending February, 1839. In a few days I left for Williamsport, Where I remained a few days at Bro. C's, and attended several very good meetings at Washington, Pa. I had an appointment given me by the Elder of the white M. E. Church, which I accepted. By special request, I visited a white young lady in the last stage of consumption, and after conversing with her about the salvation of her soul, I received great satisfaction, who I trust new rests in Abraham's bosom. I attended a quarterly meeting at Washington, and I heard some powerful exhortations—God owned the word and by his infinite power arrested a woman who formerly kept a dance house, and with her, her family also, (saving her husband who had lately died,) and they, five in number, cried aloud for mercy at the hand of God, and afterwards joined the church; the old lady appeared very serious, and they all spoke well in Love-feast.

I had a special invitation, by letter, to go to Waynesburg, which I received, and spoke in the old Methodist church, after being conveyed there by a brother that was sent for me expressly. On Wednesday evening I spoke in the Court house; it was in the month of February, and the walking was very difficult; the friends were very kind; but few colored persons, only two members of the church, and six joined. I spoke for them five times—after discharging my duty I left in peace with God and man. On my return to Washington, I spent a week or ten days, and preached on Sabbath day, and at night three sermons. The Mayor of the city declared his intention to impose a heavy punishment upon any person or persons disturbing any church, and it had the effect to make some of the wildest of the rabble behave themselves in the church with respect, while I endeavored to declare the oracles of truth. After which I left for Meconnoburg, and preached eleven sermons.

In March I left for Pittsburg, and we met in joy; and at my first appointment I spoke from Isaiah c. 50, v. 31. I then rested three or four weeks, during which time my mind become much exercised to go to Cincinnati—it was difficult to travel, but God always makes a way for his people. A friend both to God and me, got a passage for me on board of a Steamboat, with a preacher and his family, and on my arrival, I was recommended to friends there, Elder King and wife, and I found them. I told them it was my business to preach. An appointment was given me. I spoke several times, and the Lord approbated the efforts of the feeble worm, and believers were built up in the

most holy faith. My visit was joyous. My pamphlets went off as by a wind, the Elder recommending them very highly, and also encouraged me to have the 2d edition printed, which I had done—there being then one thousand more for sale, in which I was successful. Five joined the church after the last sermon.

I then left for Dayton, Ohio, and found a large church and building. The colored population there was very large—there I preached six sermons, and one in the other church. I was aided by both churches. I then took steam-boat for Hambleton, a well situated place, and preached two sermons; had a good visit, much favored of the Lord, although the members were much scattered abroad. But a worthy brother, a man of God, had settled there and formed a Society of some twenty persons, which was still prosperous. After preaching two sermons, I took passage in steamboat for Cincinnati; remained there awhile until I had some new direction opened to my mind, where I might call the people to the arms of Christ. The recent printing of my tracts, had caused me to be very scarce of money, (price of printing 1000 copies, $38.) There were individuals who helped me in a way for travelling. The Elder being absent that Sabbath morning, there was some disorder prevailed amount some who seemed double minded, yet they were officers. But God can make a way where there appears to be no way. Mrs. E.J., her husband and children, made me a present of seven dollars, and another friend interceded for me in getting a good cabin passage in a comfortable boat, and no distinction—captain was a gentleman. I enjoyed sweet communion with the spirit of the Lord. But a painful circumstance took place near our journey's end, which seemed to me awful in the extremes. There was a woman on board of the boat who was called insane. I thought she was laboring under a despair of mind. She had seen herself a dreadful sinner, and set in a melancholy position, at times only she would seemingly arouse and ask us not to let them hurt her. On one occasion I asked her how she felt. She answered, "I hear some persons talking; they will hurt me—I would drown myself, but it is such a sin." A lady and myself strove to comfort her, after which the lady read to her respecting the storms. She set very quiet, then she suddenly arose to her feet, and said she must pray. I told her to kneel down by my side, which she did very orderly; she first prayed in Dutch; I could not understand her only as she said God or Jesus, and then she prayed in English very feeling, then clapped her hands and said he has taken a load off me—this was about 10 or 11 o'clock, A.M. She arose, washed her face and hands, combed her hair, and then put on a cap and looked like another person, and thus

remained until candle-light, she and the young lady walking and talking. I was reading and felt greatly relieved from the care of her. Suddenly the chambermaid came in and asked me for her, and it seemed only five minutes since I missed her. The captain made search, went down on the deck and there found her, but she begged so hard to stay there that he left her. The boat arrived at Portsmouth next morning at sunrise, and that morning at 8 o'clock, she was seen to jump overboard. They lowered a boat and tried to save her, but before they reached her she sank to rise no more; and on the authority of God's word, I say, no self-murderer hath eternal life. Reader, be careful, exceedingly careful, how you trifle with the spirit of God, lest it should take its flight and leave thee to undergo eternal punishment.

> Take the warning, turn and live,
> And God will his Spirit give.

After landing, I felt to be a stranger in a strange land, but the Lord ever provides in time of need. Accordingly I was conducted by a gentleman and introduced to a friend who received me and treated me kindly, and in a few days introduced me to one of the Trustees, who welcomed me to the Church. Now I began to feel the spirit of my station. On Thursday night I filled an appointment. It was altogether a strange thing to hear a woman preach there, so it made quite an excitement, which made my labor very heavy, as the people were all eyes and prayed none. But on Sabbath day we had a crowded house, and an old backslider fell to the floor like Dagon before the Ark. Six joined the church on probation. On next Sabbath, Elder Peters' quarterly meeting took place, which was greatly enjoyed by all present. I met many of my friends from Pittsburg and other places, and we rejoined together. One day in the house of the Lord is more than a thousand in the courts of the wicked. The first Sabbath I spoke to the class, five fell to the floor under the influence of God's power. Two days afterward we left for Galloper quarterly meeting; took passage on board of steamboat, which was very pleasant without distinction. When we arrived, it being night, a gentleman conducted us to our lodgings and introduced us, where we were kindly received. I preached one sermon to a small society that seemed almost without a shepherd to look to their welfare. I was astonished at the situation of the church—after which time the Elder came. A Baptist society occupied the house in the morning, and in the afternoon the Elder preached—it was a dull time indeed, none joined. At night I tried to preach, but could not tell what the Lord had done

for them people, for they seemed both barren and unfruitful.

I felt an anxiety to go to Chilicothe, for which place I took passage and arrived on Wednesday; found a large field of labor open. I preached on the next night (Thursday) to a very large and well informed congregation. I then took passage via canal, and my mind was much exercised, indeed, some what uncommon. Text 1st, Thessalonions: "Because iniquity abounds the love of many waxed cold, but they that endure to the end the same shall be saved." Text 2d: "For Christ sent me not to baptize, but to preach the gospel lest the cause of Christ should be made of non effect." Text 3d. Prov. 5th c. 6th v., I preached again from these words: "All flesh is as grass." Fifth and last: "I am the true Vine," &c. My visit being out, I left for Williamsport in peace with God, likewise the brethren, as the friends had used the very kind. After the quarterly meeting, we all took passage with the Elder for Pittsburg, to meet the conference. I there met the Rt. Rev. Bishop, and others I was glad to see. I remained there two or three weeks, and preached four sermons. Both preachers and people used me like Christians. The conference was largely attended with ministers from every direction. The Bishop granted an open house for persons to visit and hear the arrangements and appointments on the circuits. The preaching was very good, and it seemed as if the word fell heavy upon the hearts of the King's enemies; a general revival took place. The Bishop gave me an appointment during the conference. After my visit came to a close, I was exercised to leave for Philadelphia. A lady, named Mrs. Dorsey, being acquainted with one of the captains of the boats, succeeded in procuring a comfortable passage for me for $15, and $3 for board; making $18 in all, when it was $48 from Philadelphia to Pittsburgh. I felt grateful towards God for his mindfulness of me. The captain was a gentleman, and the passengers of the first circle, and I enjoyed their company When we changed boats at Hollidaysburg, the captain put me on the fast line that I might arrive at Philadelphia in the day. There was a white lady on the boat with me, bound to Philadelphia, who had travelled from New Orleans. A gentleman who was coming to the city, seeing her lonely situation and also mine, he never left the cars until he saw each of our baggages in the omnibus and starting for our doors—a gentleman indeed. Thus ended this journey, Sept. 1839.

After my arrival, my first inquiry was after the state of health of my son and his family, and to my great disappointment I found that my little grandson had died. This was startling news to me, you may think, but the Lord removed him for some wise purpose of his providence, and in this I felt per-

fectly resigned to his will, with a heart of gratitude for my protection and safe arrival at home. I remained in the city about three months and received appointments in our churches on Thursday nights, although in years past I always had them at any time, Sunday afternoons not excepted. In Philadelphia, N. York, Baltimore, and all the principal cities, from 100 to 1000 miles distant, as I travelled under the reign of the first Bishop Rt. Rev. Richard Allen, I have been instrumental in the hands of God of gaining many hundreds of dollars for the connection, buy raising societies where there never had been any, since which time they have grown to such a mass as to build large churches, and that in different places, and likewise have spent hundreds, but don't regret it, as I was about the work of Him that sent me, for which my reward is promised if I but hold out faithful.

> Now, pray for me,
> That while on earth I roam;
> That with the joyful Jubilee,
> I may arrive at home.

I again was impressed upon to go into the western part of the State of Pennsylvania and labor for the Lord, as the field appeared large before me. About this time sister Elaw, a speaker belonging under the jurisdiction of the E. Methodist connection, coming to this place, she received an appointment which had been given to me, and I closed the meeting after her, and we enjoyed good seasons together. The greatest display of God's power seemed visible in a Protestant and congregation; sister preached, and I gave an exhortation and closed, in which there was a great shout for victory. I was informed by those that were in the spirit, that they saw the glory of God like a sun over the pulpit, and a face shone after it, thus the battle was the Lord's.

My sister leaving for England to visit the world's convention, I started alone. My first appointment was over Schuylkill—then I was conveyed nine miles farther, preached three sermons, and then returned to the city; on the following week I left again for Lancaster, Pa., but meeting friends going to Columbia I went with them. The meetings were attended by the spirit of God, and the speakers felt the spirit of their station, and the feast was glorious; over thirty were added to the church in less than a week, and many of them found peace with God. From thence I went to Marietta, preached two sermons, and then left for Lancaster. The Lord owned the word spoken, and after preaching, ten joined the church. "Praise the Lord, for He only doeth

great wonders."—Psalms. I then proceeded on the Carlisle Seemingly the wolf had got in among the fold and had scattered some clear away. But God's word will have its effect where it is promulgated in its purity. The consequence was, we had a great rejoicing. I preached six sermons, including one for the Protestant Methodists. I employed my time, as usual, endeavoring to explain the effects of the everlasting gospel of the kingdom even in common conversation. The happy seasons I have seen are ever memorable to me, and my prayers is, that all Israel may be saved, not only form the trials of life, but from the power of hell. I then proceeded to Harrisburg, preached one sermons to a good congregation, and felt considerable liberty in speaking. I left next morning for Marietta; it was a very cold day; sometimes I rode in a slay and sometimes in a carriage. I preached one sermon on Sabbath, and next day took passage in a slay for Penningtonville. I preached there on Sabbath day to a good congregation of different denominations—it was a glorious day to my soul. Upon the authority of God's word, there need be no doubt about religion, for they that have it carry the witness within themselves. Thus, having finished my visit with a peace of conscience, I returned to Philadelphia, March 1st, and found all my friends well. I waited in the temple of the Lord and preached several times. I felt anxious to go to Baltimore on a visit to the general conference, being the first of that kind held there for many years. After mentioning it to the Bishop, he said I should be paid for it if I wished to go, for which I felt very grateful. After making the necessary preparations by arranging my clothes, &c., the morning came for to start; the boat was to leave Philadelphia at 6 o'clock, A.M. My mind had been somewhat divided about going to N. York, as I wanted to see the convention for the American Anti-Slavery Society. But on my way to the Baltimore boat, in company with a young sister, my mind was suddenly arrested by a strange sensation, which proceeded form some supernatural cause, followed by a voice which seemingly spoke thus: "a watery grave! a watery grave! !" I told the sister what had been revealed to me, yet not half a square from the house. She believed as I did, and I consequently turned back with an impression I should be drowned if I went as I seemingly saw the water. "How unsearchable are God's judgments, and his ways are past finding out."

The same month, April, I was sent for in great haste to visit Cape May, to see my aged mother, as it was thought for the last time, as she was very ill, at the advanced age of 82 years. I went and remained with her several weeks, when she nearly recovered. I then filled several appointments unexpectedly. But my way was I know not where. During my stay there I lost a nephew 12

years of age, whom I trust rests. But I should have mentioned, the day I returned from the Baltimore boat, I took passage at 2 o'clock, P.M. for Burlington, and preached for them on Sabbath day at quarterly meeting and second day after I left for New York and arrived the first day, the convention sat which I attended in company with Mrs. H. Lane, who was ever zealous in the good cause of liberty and the rights of all and I heard some very eloquent speeches which pleased me very much and my heart responded with this instruction: "Do unto all men as you would they should do unto you;" and as we are all children of one parent, no one is justified in holdings slaves. I felt that the spirit of God was in the work and also felt it my duty to unite with this Society. Doubtless the cause is good, and I pray God to forward on the work of abolition until it fills the world, and then the gospel will have free course to every motion and in every clime.—After the convention was over I returned to Philadelphia, and prepared for a long journey. But previously I visited a part of Rev. Turner's circuit—Jersey, Viz. of Burlington, Trenton, &c. His charge was extensive and laborers were much wanted. I endeavored to preach two sermons in Burlington, and in the other places nine more, and then visited Allentown and preached three sermons. I visited a camp meeting and never saw a greater display of God's power, for truly signs and wonders followed the preaching of the cross of Christ, while the voice of prayer made sinners stare and filled them with awe and wonder. I also preached to a small society five miles farther, called Lawrenceville, after which I returned to Trenton, Princeton, &c., and in a few days I left for Brunswick. I left for this journey in 1843, in one of the brother's own conveyance, for which I felt very thankful. I filled several appointments, and then left for New York where I remained several weeks, and proposed the holding of a protracted meeting to the Elder Boggs, in charge and he thought well of it, and appointed one, and it seemed that the people truly had a mind to work, and the Lord blessed our labors. I preached on two Sabbath nights and once in the middle of the week. A revival broke out and twenty-one were added to the church, and it concluded with a victorious Love-feast, glory to God. During my absence my son was taken very ill with a severe disease, and I felt very anxious to see him after an absence if several months. Consequently in December I left N. York in my return, and I found him much better then I expected, which greatly relieved my mind. I preached once in the Bethel, once in the Wesley church, which came in the connexion, Hurst St., and other places, but soon finished my work in this city, and notwithstanding the severity of the winter I returned to Rahway, and found

the friends very kind to me. I thank the Lord for giving them hearts to be so, as the winter was trying. I preached ten sermons during my stay, in which time a great revival took place in the church, and many were added, amongst whom was a Rev. father E.— who had that very appropriate phrase; "The dead is alive and the lost is found," and the brother rejoiced much, seeing the Providence of God. Now I began of feel my labors nearly, completed in that part. I returned to N. York (as my visit was not accomplished in that city) on the 1st of March, 1841, and tarried some time, after which I took passage on steamboat for New Haven and arrived there at 1 o'clock, P.M. I was conducted by carriage to Mr. B's and his-family was kind; on next Wednesday I was taken to a brother's house, near the meeting house, near the meeting house, which they commenced in January, and I preached in it in March. Being a people there whose minds were much cultivated, I felt at liberty to speak, believing God would own his word, which he did and we had a revival. But Lucifer had prepared an engine to play upon it and put it out. But we had some firm members that turned neither to the right or left, as the scripture saith "the righteous shall hold on their way." Ah! reader many scenes I have passed through but I yet live by faith in the Son of God. I preached twenty-one sermons, and made my home at brother white's near the church; this saved me from a great deal of exposure in going to and returning from the church. I perceived their slothfulness in coming out to Sabbath morning services. My first text was Rev. i, 10. God was with us truly for signs and wonders followed, and we commenced a protracted meeting, and on the fifth night there were forteen mourning souls at the anxious bench. After a stay of seven weeks, I felt at liberty to leave them, which I did, and arrived in New York on the 24th of April. Elder B. gave me an appointment the ensuring Sabbath morning in Bethel church. After that I went over to Brooklyn and spoke three or four times, but my heart mourned to see such a great falling off that had taken place in a few months past. But the conference sit there, and they had good preaching, and the congregation soon began to increase. The brothers were kind to me and gave me appointments at different places. I continued to travel round about, and spoke a number of times in Flushing, eight sermons in Jamaica, three in Flatbush, three in Huntingdon south, three in Glen-cove, and then returned to Brooklyn again and remained a while with a sister who was ever kind to me, for which I hope God will reward her, with others. There was a camp-meeting to commence that week of my return, to be held by Rev. Boggs, near Harvest Straw, and I through invitation went in company—it was a very rainy time, but we had a

great meeting, and I received two appointments. We caught no cold, and the Christians rejoiced in the victories of the Cross, for we believed the Lord would shelter us even in the midst of storm.

Having a great desire to go to Massachusetts, I paid my way to Harvest Straw to take the boat, but was disappointed not being in time, after which I had to pay a gentleman to convey me ten miles and conduct me safe on board of the boat for Albany. I had a pleasant cabin passage for $1 50. On my arrival I employed a person to convey me and my baggage to a friend's house, and when I got there, they being absent, I did not stop even for breakfast; but returned to a N. York boat that stopped at Hudson, and there to take passage by Railroad. On my arrival, I found the cars did not start until 4 o'clock, ᴘ.ᴍ. It then occurred to my mind that I was in Hudson unexpectedly and truly the hand of the Lord must be in it, as I wanted to visit that place some time before. I then went out in search of some of my own people of color, trying to find out if I could get a place to preach in on my return, as I felt anxious to call the fallen sons and daughters of Adam. When about to start in the cars for Stockbridge, one of the brothers of the church went in company with me to the camp. By 7 o'clock we were safely landed and found the meeting prosperous and I felt warm for the battle, as though I must press through fire or water. We had one mile to walk or pay 25 cents—after walking the distance, we found the tent that the Albany friends were accommodated at; soon after which the Elder heard of it and called upon me, which seemed to approbate my coming to his camp. I felt a great degree of liberty, believing my self to be in the right place. After several other strangers had labored in their turn, the Elder gave me another appointment on Saturday night. I endeavored to speak as God gave ability, and a brother closed meeting after me. On Sabbath morning at 10 o'clock, I tried to speak again to a large congregation. It rained very heavy, but they gave the best attention and withstood the storm in all quietness; I felt free, the tongue was loosed, the lip was touched, and the heart was warm, which seemed to operate with the language of the text, in Rev.: "I was in the spirit on the Lord's day". The Lord owned the word, and the hearty Amens that went up, caused the woods to echo. A white Methodist gentleman was present, who had become almost choked to death with the glutted case of this world; while sitting, God through his mercy, sent his awakening power to his heart, and he rejoiced louder than others, telling me he was glad the Lord had sent me, that his mind had been overcharged with the cares of this life truly, and all of this while Israel shouted for the battle. The wicked were somewhat rude on

Sunday night, and the Elder gave a very appropriate address to the gentlemen of the State of Massachusetts, showing how our rights were invaded, after which the gentlemen took it on themselves to guard the camp ground, and we had good order. The breaking up was a time long to be remembered, and on that day at 12 o'clock I left for Hudson. I there preached one or two sermons, visited the sick, &;c., and was then taken to Pittsfield, preached one sermon, and then proceeded by stage to Hudson city, where I remained a while with a kind sister and her daughter. I attended the church on Sabbath morning and enjoyed a good sermon delivered by the Elder.

At 2 o'clock, P.M., I tried to preach in the same church to a full congregation. Text from the general epistle of James, 1st Chapter & 25th verse. At night I spoke in the old Methodist church for the first time, from these words; "We have found him of whom Moses and the Prophet's did write, Jesus of Nazareth, the son of Joseph." My mind was much exercised on the subject; receiving light from Heaven. I preached one sermon in the School-House at Catskill from these words; "I will give you power to tread on serpents and scorpions, and they shall not harm you." The Lord was there of a truth. After this, by request, I spoke in the white Methodist church from these words: "Therefore, cast not away your confidence, which has great recompense of reward." The Lord was there, and assisted the clay to speak in his name. On Monday night I spoke from these words of Paul to the Hebrews: "If the words spoken by Angels, are steadfast," &;c., which had its desired effect. On Saturday I left for Albany, taking with me a good report for the Elder of our connection; after which, we wrote for him to come and form a Society, which he did sometime afterwards. The Elder was kind, and gave me appointments frequently. He held a Protracted Meeting, at which all of our laborers were successful. I preached seven sermons in Albany and one in Troy; after which I felt moved upon to visit Binghampton, and sister Tilghman was on her way to the same place to visit her father and mother, from whom she had been absent for some time, Preaching the Everlasting Gospel of the Kingdom. But we were detained on the canal some time; but the Captain was kind and treated us well. After five days sail we arrived safe, and found our friends well; but not well in the Lord.

As soon as I enter a city I can feel the spirit that I may have to contend with; but by the permission of the Elder I filled appointments for a week or two, and then left for Montrose Quarterly Meeting. Preached five sermons, and passed through many things that were not agreeable, but duty makes labor light. I also spoke to a white congregation. After riding five or six miles

and back the same night, and preaching two sermons in the town, I returned again to Binghampton, and held the Christmas Watch-Night meeting, as I found it was about to be omitted, and feeling interested, made application to the Trustees the Elder being absent, and thus Lord was with us, while we rejoiced in the light that had come into the world. Glory to God for the gift of his Son. In the morning three of us attended the Episcopal church, and associated with them in receiving the Lord's Supper. At night I preached again, and I felt zealous in the cause of God, who was and is ever faithful to his promise; "Lo! I am with you always, even to the end of the world."

The Elder then returned and urged me to stay, but I saw my way was onward. After preaching once more, I was aided on my way to Owego, where I found the enemies were many, standing in opposition to female preaching, or preachers of any kind; but God always clears the way for his people. While they were preparing to have a dance rather than come to hear preaching, and boasting that they would invite the Elder to come to it, God laid his heavy hand upon the man that was to play the fiddle for them; he fell sick on the floor; but he was determined to carry it out, and sent for another man, and he refused, and at last this Goliah-like man was glad to send for the Elder to come and pray for him. "O! sinner, thou cans't not measure arms with Jehovah! He is a man of war, and the Lord is his name." In this very place, God worked miracles among them. I preached on Friday night, Sabbath morning, afternoon and night—and God worked wonders; converting some of the most wicked among them.

After this, I left for Smithboro; it seemed truly a hard place, and my labors were attended with but little success. There were a few scattering Methodists that assembled to worship, and seemed profited thereby. After I delivered my message I left for Towanda; and there we had very comfortable meetings. I then proceeded ten miles further and preached; there were eight persons, there one being an exhorter. They met us in the spirit of the gospel. After doing my duty I returned to Towanda, and on Wednesday I left for Athens; remained two days preaching two sermons in the Academy. Next morning I rode about two miles, but we had to wait until the next Tuesday, in consequence of the flood being so great. I now was among strangers, with very little money; but finding the lady was a christian, I ventured to open my mind to her, telling her the nature of my mission. She told her husband, who said he would charge me only six shillings. I sewed three spreads together for her to quilt. She then informed me of a lady preacher in the neighborhood, one mile distant. I was kindly received by her, and met another person there

also that seemed greatly wrought upon. After a seasonable word of exhortation, I took tea with them. In three days time I left for Towanda again, and met with great success by preaching in private houses. There was a gentleman that seemed as if he never thought of God in all his life, but was arrested by the conviction of God's spirit, and sent for me to come and pray for him and his family. In this my soul greatly rejoiced, leaving him with a promise to call again, which I did. After inquiring my manner of travelling, and what I depended upon for support. I replied by giving him a statement. Of how I travelled, when he kindly aided me by a donation and wished me success, requesting me to pray for him and his family before I left them, and I believe I saw him then fast ripening for eternal blessedness.

I was then sent for to return again to Owego, a distance of 38 miles, and they would pay my way on to Montrose, on my way to Philadelphia. I obeyed the request and found things very prosperous indeed. At night we had prayer meetings, and the Lord continued to pour out his spirit upon the people, and we had a meeting every night. Mr. J. H., formerly of Columbia, whose lot was cast as in a strange land, where there were only for a few people that were members of the M.E. Church; several husbands, strangers to God until now, and their wives, servants of the most High God, and two daughters of Mr. J.H., were justified through faith—three joined the church previously. I was selected to make a class book, and did so, as I wanted to see how many were for us. The Baptists had held an anxious meeting, after which five joined them. I made the trial by special invitation, and thirteen joined us. I had preached on Sabbath morning and night, and then held prayer meetings every night afterwards that week, except Saturday night; a man and his wife fell to the floor and cried for mercy, and both arose in the same hour soundly converted, giving God the glory. I preached on the next Sabbath morning and then led class, and at night again—text, Judges iv. 25, 26. They all marvelled at a woman taking such a deep subject, but the Lord assisted the organ of clay, and we had the victory, as there were twenty-one persons joined from that revival, and nearly all of them evinced justifying grace. On 3d day night we wound up, as I was to start on my journey on next day, which I did—brother paid my passage. I rode 28 miles in good company with a lady and gentleman who were going to New York. She said she was sorry to part; we had a heavy thunder storm with rain, and it was very dark, but we had a very careful driver, and we arrived safe at Montrose and took supper—between 12 and 1 o'clock at night I took stage for Wilkesbarre and arrived there at 8 next morning, and there I crossed the Susquehanna; I was

very hungry, having a little time I went to the house and asked the lady for breakfast and I would pay her. She said she had nothing, but would try and get me a good breakfast and take no pay, which she did. I truly feel thankful to God that he has proved himself a table in the wilderness. About 4 o'clock in the afternoon I arrived safe and was kindly received, and preached on Sabbath morning and night. Between the two appointments I rode two miles and preached in the afternoon. That day the Lord was in the house in power. Tuesday evening we had a glorious prayer meeting. I rode all night around the mountain, and some walked and appeared to be a quarter of a mile off. But the Lord preserved me in the mail stage alone. I adore his name now and I shall for evermore. The preacher in charge arrived the next day after I did, and spent his labors of love among the people. On the Wednesday following he went away and left me in charge of the class, (eight persons) to regulate them, and by the permission of the elder I addressed them. After I had relieved my mind and taken my seat the preacher formed them into a class and appointed a leader, who but three months before, was unconverted; but being so interested for the prosperity of Zion, seemed worthy of the appointment. After this I endeavored to hold prayer meetings through the week; preached twice on Sabbath day and helped to lead class, as the brother was young,—but they were all willing people, and truly it seemed to be the day of God's power among them, and "Peace abided at our House."

At the expiration of three weeks and four days I left them fifteen names on their class book. I then rode a distance of sixty miles over a hard road, hills and mountains, (there being no turn-pike or rail-road on that rout from Wilksbarre to Easton;)—some part of the way there was good sleighing. Through the help of Providence we arrived at Easton about 8'clock, P.M. I took supper and lodging in the Hotel, where I was well accommodated; after which I found a small number of colored friends. We had a meeting, and "it was good for us to be there." After this I called at New Hope, thirty-two miles I think from Philadelphia; visited the family I was brought up in, stopped and rested myself, as I felt much exhausted from travelling, so much winter and summer. I preached two or three times. Brother J. B.— was holding a protracted meeting. I gained strength; thank the Lord, and then left for home, and arrived in the city the last day of March 1842, having been two years, wanting a few days, almost incessantly travelling. I found my son, together with the rest of my family connections quite well; yet I could hear of the ravages of death, the relentless murderer, who never takes denials; my little grand-daughter, a promising child indeed, was taken with the rest. O!

how soon delights may perish, and my heart responds—"The Lord's will be done."

My health being very much impaired, I knew not but that I should be the next one called away, but the Lord spared me for some other purpose, and upon my recovery I commenced travelling again, feeling it better to wear out than to rust out—and so expect to do until death ends the struggle—knowing, if I lose my life for Christ's sake, I shall find it again.

I now conclude—by requesting the prayers of God's people everywhere, who worship in His holy fear, to pray for me, that I ever may endeavor to keep a conscience void of offence, either towards God or man—for I feel as anxious to blow the Trumpet in Zion; and sound the alarm in God's Holy Mount, as ever;—

> Though Nature's strength decay,
> And earth and hell withstand—
> To Canaan's land I'l urge my way,
> At HIS Divine command.

But here I feel constrained to give over; as from the smallness of this pamphlet I cannot go through with the whole of my journal, as it would probably make a volume of two hundred pages; which, if the Lord be willing, may at some future day be published. But for the satisfaction of such as may follow after me, when I am no more, I have recorded how the Lord called me to his work, and how he has kept me from falling from grace, as I feared I should. In all things he has proved himself a God of truth to me; and in his service I am now as much determined to spend and be spent, as at the very first. My ardour for the progress of his cause abates not await, so far as I am able to judge, though I am now something more than fifty years of age.

As to the nature of uncommon impressions, which the reader cannot but have noticed, and possibly sneered at in the course of these pages, they may be accounted for in this way: It is known that the blind have the sense of hearing in a manner much more acute than those who can see: also their sense of feeling is exceedingly fine, and is found to detect any roughness on the smoothest surface, where those who can see find none. So it may be with such as I am, who has never had more than three months schooling; and wishing to know much of the way and law of God, have therefore watched the more closely, the operations of the Spirit, and have in consequence been led thereby. But let it be remarked that I have never found that Spirit lead me

contrary to the scriptures of truth, as I understand them. "For as many as are led by tha Spirit of God are the sons of God."—Rom. viii. 14.

I have now only to say, May the blessing of the Father, and of the Son, and of the Holy Ghost, accompany the reading of this poor effort to speak well of his name, wherever it may be read. AMEN.

P. S. Please to pardon errors, and excuse all imperfections, as I have been deprived of the advantages of education (which I hope all will appreciate) as I am measurably a self-taught person. I hope the contents of this work may be instrumental in leaving a lasting impression upon the minds of the impenitent; may it prove to be encouraging to the justified soul, and a comfort to the sanctified.

Though much opposed, it is essential in life, as Mr. Wesley wisely observes. Thus ends the Narrative of Jarena Lee, the first female preacher of the First African Methodist Episopal Church.

Bethel At Philadelphia, Penn., United States Of America.

FINIS.

OLAUDAH EQUIANO

(?-1797)

Olaudah Equiano was born around the year 1745 in northeast Nigeria, West Africa. The son of a chief, Equiano, at the age of eleven, was kidnapped along with his sister and transported to the coast, where he was sold into slavery. He was then put on board a slave ship bound for the West Indies, where he was sold to a Virginia planter, then shipped to Virginia where he was sold again, this time to a British naval Officer, Captain Michael Henry Pascal.

Pascal intended to bring Equiano to England and present him as a gift to his cousins, renaming him Gustavas Vassa, after a sixteenth-century Swedish nobleman who led the Swedes into a war of independence from the Danes. As Pascal's slave, Equiano was introduced to life at sea, giving him opportunities he would not have had as a plantation slave. He sailed to England and ultimately saw many parts of the world aboard Pascal's ship. More importantly, Equiano was sent to school in London between naval actions, where he learned to read and write.

In the late 1750s when Britain was engaged in the Seven Years' War with France, fighting over control of North America and the Caribbean, Equiano spent much of his time at sea with Pascal, often working as a gunpowder carrier. Since the Royal Navy did not recognize slavery on board its ships, Equiano reasoned that, having seen a great deal of action in Canada and the Mediterranean, he was entitled to his share of the prize money that was dispersed to sailors.

However, Equiano was cheated of his money and sold to another sea-captain, who took him to Monserrat in the Caribbean and ultimately sold him to a Quaker by the name of Robert King. He feared he'd be sold yet again and subjected to a life on the plantations, but by this point, Equiano was well-educated and deemed far too valuable for field work. King had him trained as a gauger—something of a quality control manager, and he was

paid wages for three years until he was able to buy his own freedom with 40 pounds he managed to save.

Shortly afterward, after making a few voyages with King, this time as a "freeman" and hired for his labor, Equiano returned to England. Upon his arrival, he managed to obtain payment for the wages he was owed by the Royal Navy for his service years earlier, but was unsuccessful with Captain Pascal, who refused to pay him his share of prize money.

Because he had proven himself a worthy seaman, Equiano continued to procure work aboard ships as either a hairdresser or a steward. Some of his voyages were quite pleasant, others rife with adventure. In 1773 he joined a voyage aboard a ship named "Racehorse" under the command of John Phipps. The expedition was an attempt to find a passage to India across the North Pole, which would save British ships a great deal of time, and consequentially, strengthen its imperial claims on India. Ultimately, Equiano's voyage proved there was no north-east passage to India, and when he returned to London, Equiano would begin the next significant stage of his life— becoming a key figure in the British abolitionist movement.

As was a common threat to freemen at the time, Equiano's friend and former slave, John Annis, was kidnapped by his former owner, who wanted to have him sent to the Caribbean. The previous year (1772), this practice of reclaiming freed slaves had been proclaimed illegal by Lord Mansfield, and Equiano went to Granville Sharp, the first prominent abolitionist, for help. He and Sharp fought to save Annis, but were unable to regain his freedom. However, his efforts helped Equiano establish contact with the most important English crusader against slavery.

Aside from beginning his own campaign against slavery, Equiano also converted to Christianity around this time. He had been studying scriptures for some time, but it was on a voyage to Spain that Equiano writes of being "born again." In 1775, he set out for the Caribbean again, this time with the notion of setting up a new plantation or colony on the coast of Central America—probably Nicaragua today. It is on this adventure that Equiano engaged in two projects which were more closely associated with European colonization. First, he became a Christian missionary with the hope that he would be able to convert native Americans in this part of Central America. And secondly, he and his associates purchased slaves to work the plantation. Equiano clearly participated in these purchases, but he did point out that he made every effort to make their conditions bearable.

It is important to realize that in the mid 1770s, abolition was not yet a

movement, and very few individuals even held such ideas. However, there were a growing number of individuals who believed that slaves had the right to be treated humanely, with access to decent medical care, housing and food.

These individuals, called "ameliorationists," also believed in putting an end to corporal punishment, and Equiano was considered one at this point in his life, since he had not yet become an abolitionist.

His experience on the colony in Central America may have made actually sealed his move toward abolition, as he was once again cheated of the money he was owed, and nearly reenslaved by a slave owner, only to escape capture in a canoe. These experiences led to his decision to return to London where he spent the next seven years as a servant and activist.

However, Equiano also became involved with another project—this time, the Sierra Leone resettlement project. In 1786, an eccentric amateur botanist named Henry Smeathman, taken by the sheer number of unemployed Africans on the streets of London, came to the conclusion that since they'd been brought to England from Africa against their will, the humane thing to do would be to round them up and return them to their native land. Many anti-slavery advocates supported Smeathman's sentiments, including Equiano himself, who was given the job of Commissary of Provisions and Stores, putting him in charge of food and equipment purchases. Some historians believe Equiano became the first black civil servant in England when he accepted this position on the Sierra Leone resettlement project.

Equiano soon discovered that corrupt officials were stealing money, which would have a direct effect on the colonists as they attempted to survive until the first harvest. He went to great measures to alert the proper authorities about this problem, as well as other abuse at the expense of blacks, but despite of the Navy Board's support of him, Equiano was ultimately fired for speaking up. As he had warned, only 60 of the 374 shipped to Sierra Leone were able to survive the first four years because of lack of provisions.

Equiano then set his efforts to writing the book on which he made his name. In the spring of 1789, the abolition movement had gained significant momentum and he became one of the major voices in this movement. Equiano's *The Interesting Narrative* was only one of over one hundred books on the subject of slavery to appear that year. However, Equiano's autobiography is much different from "slave narratives," published because it was not an oral account, spoken to a white amanuenses as many narratives of the time were. Not only had he written it himself, but he had also published it and

sold it by subscription—a way of getting people to support the book before it was printed.

The Interesting Narrative draws its strength not only from its powerful description of the European slave trade and the horrors and oppression inflicted on Africans, but also from the literary style and quality of Equiano's writing. He begins his story with beauty and poignancy, describing a rich childhood in his native land as the youngest son of the village chief, with a mother who adored him. Equiano heartbreakingly describes the evening when he is pried from his sisters' arms as they sleep.

> But alas! we were soon deprived of even the small comfort of weeping together. The next day proved one of greater sorrow than I had yet experienced; for my sister and I were separated, while we lay clasped in each others arms. It was in vain that we besought them not to part us; she was torn from me, and immediately carried away, while I was left in a state of distraction not to be described. I cried and grieved continually; and for several days did not eat any thing but what they forced into my mouth.

The days and weeks that follow are filled with horror for the young boy, as he encounters the strange and rough slave traders who chain him below the decks of the ship with hundreds of other prisoners with little regard for their health or safety. As excruciating as it is to learn of Equiano's numerous heartbreaking sagas and those of the Africans in his narrative, Equiano also compels the reader to understand his joy at the moment when he buys his freedom from Robert King and receives his manumission.

> I thought this was the happiest day I had ever experienced; and my joy was still heightened by the blessings and prayers of many of the sable race, particularly the aged, to whom my heart had ever been attached with reverence.

Equiano also demonstrated considerable genius in terms of marketing, building up a significant and influential list of subscribers, such as the Prince of Wales and no fewer than eight dukes. And once the book was published, he set out on a vigorous lecture tour around England, Scotland, Ireland and Wales, and in effect, he was not only promoting the sale of his autobiography, but the abolition of slavery as well. By the early 1790s, Equiano's life

story was not only a book opposing slavery, but Equiano himself had become a symbol of anti-slavery.

Financially, *The Interesting Narrative* was a success, rivaling Defoe's *Robinson Crusoe* in sales, and the book was published in nine different editions before his death.

The coming of the end of the 18th century also brought personal changes for Equiano as well. In 1792, he married an Englishwoman by the name of Susanna Cullen, and had two daughters, one of whom survived to inherit a substantial estate from her father. Olaudah Equiano died in March 1797, a decade before the slave trade was abolished among British ships and forty years before slavery was abolished in the British colonies. It would be 28 years after that before the United States ended slavery. Equiano never lived to see it, but it is impossible to underestimate the importance of his narrative and the impact it had on the world's conscience at the time.

The Interesting Narrative
of the Life of Olaudah Equiano,
or Gustavas Vassa, the African

Behold, God is my salvation; I will trust, and not be afraid for the Lord Jehovah is my strength and my song; he also is become my salvation.

And in that day shall ye say, Praise the Lord, call upon his name, declare his doings among people.

<div align="right">Isa. xii. 2. 4.</div>

DEDICATION

To the Lords Spiritual and Temporal, and the Commons of the Parliament of Great Britain.

My Lords And Gentlemen,

Permit me, with the greatest deference and respect, to lay at your feet the following genuine narrative; the chief design of which is to excite in your august assemblies a sense of compassion for the miseries which the Slave-Trade has entailed on my unfortunate countrymen. By the horrors of that trade was I first torn away from all the tender connections that were naturally dear to my heart; but these, through the mysterious ways of Providence, I ought to regard as infinitely more than compensated by the introduction I have thence obtained to the knowledge of the Christian religion, and of a nation which, by its liberal sentiments, its humanity, the glorious freedom of its government, and its proficiency in arts and sciences, has exalted the dignity of human nature.

I am sensible I ought to entreat your pardon for addressing to you a work so wholly devoid of literary merit; but, as the production

of an unlettered African, who is actuated by the hope of becoming an instrument towards the relief of his suffering countrymen, I trust that such a man, pleading in such a cause, will be acquitted of boldness and presumption.

May the God of Heaven inspire your hearts with peculiar benevolence on that important day when the question of Abolition is to be discussed, when thousands, in consequence of your determination, are to look for Happiness or Misery!

I am,
My Lords and Gentlemen,
Your most obedient,
And devoted humble servant,
OLAUDAH EQUIANO,
OR
June 1792. *GUSTAVUS VASSA.*

CHAPTER I

The Author's account of his country.—The manners and customs of the Inhabitants—Administration of justice—Embrenche-Marriage ceremony, and public entertainments—Mode of living—Dress—Manufactures—Buildings— Commerce—Agriculture—War and religion—Superstition of the natives— Funeral ceremonies of the Priests or Magicians—Curious mode of discovering Poison—Some hints concerning the origin of the author's countrymen, with the opinions of different writers on that subject.

I.

I BELIEVE it is difficult for those who publish their own memoirs to escape the imputation of vanity. Nor is this the only disadvantage under which they labour: it is also their misfortune, that whatever is uncommon is rarely, if ever, believed, and from what is obvious we are apt to turn with disgust, and to charge the writer of it with impertinence. People generally think those memoirs only worthy to be read or remembered which abound in great or striking events; those in short, which, in a high degree, excite either admira-

tion or pity: all others they consign to contempt and oblivion. It is therefore, I confess, not a little hazardous in a private and obscure individual, and a stranger too, thus to solicit the indulgent attention of the public, especially when I own I offer here the history of neither a saint, a hero, nor a tyrant. I believe there are a few events in my life which have not happened to many. It is true the incidents of it are numerous; and did I consider myself an European, I might say my sufferings were great: but when I compare my lot with that of most of my countrymen, I regard myself as a particular favourite of Heaven, and acknowledge the mercies of Providence in every occurrence of my life. If, then, the following narrative does not appear sufficiently interesting to engage general attention, let my motive be some excuse for its publication. I am not so foolishly vain as to expect from it either immortality or literary reputation. If it affords any satisfaction to my numerous friends, at whose request it has been written, or in the smallest degree promotes the interests of humanity, the ends for which it was undertaken will be fully attained, and every wish of my heart gratified. Let it therefore be remembered that, in wishing to avoid censure, I do not aspire to praise.

II.

That part of Africa, known by the name of Guinea, to which the trade of slaves is carried on, extends along the coast above 3,400 miles, from Senegal to Angola, and includes a variety of kingdoms. Of these the most considerable is the kingdom of Benin, both as to extent and wealth, the richness and culture of the soil, the power of its king, and the number and warlike disposition of its inhabitants. It is situated nearly under the line, and extends along the coast about 170 miles, but runs back into the interior of Africa to a distance hitherto, I believe, unexplored by any traveller; and seems only terminated at length by the empire of Abyssinia, near 1,500 miles from its beginning. This kingdom is divided into many provinces or districts; in one of the most remote and fertile of which, named Essaka, situated in a charming fruitful vale, I was born, in the year 1745. The distance of this province from the capital of Benin and the sea coast must be very considerable: for I had never heard of white men or Europeans, nor of the sea; and our subjection to the king of Benin was little more than nominal. Every transaction of the government, as far as my slender observation extended, was conducted by the chiefs or elders of the place. The manners and government of a people who have little commerce with other countries, are gener-

ally very simple; and the history of what passes in one family or village, may serve as a specimen of the whole nation. My father was one of those elders or chiefs of whom I have spoken, and was stiled Embrenche; a term, as I remember, importing the highest distinction, and signifying in our language "a mark of grandeur." This mark is conferred on the person entitled to it by cutting the skin across at the top of the forehead, and drawing it down to the eyebrows; and applying a warm hand to it, while in this situation, and rubbing it until it shrinks up into a thick wale across the lower part of the forehead. Most of the judges and senators were thus marked; my father had long borne this badge: I had seen it conferred on one of my brothers, and I also was destined to receive it by my parents. Those Embrenche, or chief men, decided disputes, and punished crimes; for which purpose they always assembled together. The proceedings were generally short; and in most cases the law of retaliation prevailed. I remember a man was brought before my father, and the other judges, for kidnapping a boy; and, although he was the son of a chief, or senator, he was condemned to make recompense by a man or woman slave. Adultery, however, was sometimes punished by slavery or death; a punishment which, I believe, is inflicted on it throughout most of the nations of Africa;* so sacred among them is the honour of the marriage bed, and so jealous are they of the fidelity of their wives. Of this I recollect an instance;—A woman was convicted, before the judges, of adultery, and delivered over, as the custom was, to her husband to be punished. Accordingly he determined to put her to death; but it being found, just before the execution, that she had an infant at her breast; and no woman being prevailed on to perform the part of a nurse, she was spared on account of the child. The men, however, do not preserve the same constancy to their wives, which they expect from them; for they indulge in a plurality, though seldom in more than two. Their mode of marriage is this:—Both parties are usually betrothed when young by their parents, though I have known the males betroth themselves. On this occasion a feast is prepared, and the bride and bridegroom stand up in the midst of all their friends, who are assembled for the purpose, while he declares she is henceforth to be looked upon as his wife, and that no person is to pay any addresses to her. This is also immediately proclaimed in the vicinity, on which the bride retires from the assembly. Some time after she is brought home to her husband, and then another feast is made, to which the relations of both parties are invited. Her parents

*See Anthony Benezet's "Some Account of Guinea, with an Inquiry into the Slave Trade" (1771) throughout.

then deliver her to the bridegroom, accompanied with a number of blessings, and at the same time they tie round her waist a cotton string of the thickness of a goose-quill, which none but married women are permitted to wear. She is now considered as completely his wife; and at this time the dowry is given to the new-married pair, which generally consists of portions of land, slaves and cattle, household goods, and implements of husbandry. These are offered by the friends of both parties: besides which the parents of the bridegroom present gifts to those of the bride, whose property she is looked upon before marriage; but after it she is esteemed the sole property of the husband. The ceremony being now ended, the festival begins, which is celebrated with bonfires, and loud acclamations of joy, accompanied with music and dancing.

III.

We are almost a nation of dancers, musicians, and poets. Every great event, such as a triumphant return from battle, or other cause of public rejoicing, is celebrated in public dances, which are accompanied with songs and music suited to the occasion. The assembly is separated into four divisions, which dance either apart or in succession, and each with a character peculiar to itself. The first division contains the married men, who in their dances frequently exhibit feats of arms, and the representation of a battle. To these succeed the married women, who dance in the second division. The young men occupy the third; and the maidens the fourth. Each represents some interesting scene of real life, such as a great achievement, domestic employment, a pathetic story, or some rural sport. And as the subject is generally founded on some recent event, it is therefore ever new. This gives our dances a spirit and variety which I have scarcely seen elsewhere.* We have many musical instruments, particularly drums of different kinds, a piece of music which resembles a guitar, and another much like a sticcado. These last are chiefly used by betrothed virgins, who play on them on all grand festivals.

As our manners are simple, our luxuries are few. The dress of both sexes is nearly the same. It generally consists of a long piece of calico or muslin, wrapped loosely round the body, somewhat in the form of a Highland plaid. This is usually dyed blue, which is our favorite colour. It is extracted from a berry, and is brighter and richer than any I have seen in Europe. Besides this, our women of distinction wear golden ornaments, which they dispose with some profusion on their arms and legs. When our women are not employed

*When I was in Smyrna I frequently saw the Greeks dance after this manner.

with the men in tillage, their usual occupation is spinning and weaving cotton, which they afterward dye, and make into garments. They also manufacture earthen vessels of which we have many kinds; among the rest, tobacco pipes, made after the same fashion, and used in the same manner, as those in Turkey.*

Our manner of living is entirely plain; for as yet the natives are unacquainted with those refinements in cookery which debauch the taste. Bullocks, goats, and poultry, supply the greatest part of their food. These constitute likewise the principal wealth of the country, and the chief articles of its commerce. The flesh is usually stewed in a pan; to make it savory we sometimes use also pepper, and other spices, and we have salt made of wood ashes. Our vegetables are mostly plantains, eadas, yams, beans, and Indian corn. The head of the family usually eats alone; his wives and slaves have also their separate tables. Before we taste food we always wash our hands: indeed our cleanliness on all occasions is extreme; but on this it is an indispensable ceremony. After washing, libation is made, by pouring out a small portion of the drink on the floor, and by tossing a small quantity of the food in a certain place, for the spirits of departed relations, which the natives suppose to preside over their conduct, and to guard them from evil. They are totally unacquainted with strong or spirituous liquors; and their principal beverage is palm wine. This is got from a tree of that name, by tapping it at the top, and fastening a large gourd to it; and sometimes one tree will yield three or four gallons in a night. When just drawn it is of a delicious sweetness; but in a few days it acquires a spirituous flavour: though I never saw any one intoxicated by it. The same tree also produces nuts and oil. Our principal luxury is in perfumes; one sort of these is an odoriferous wood of delicious fragrance: the other a kind of earth, a small portion of which thrown into the fire diffuses a most powerful odour.** We beat this wood into powder, and mix it with palm oil; with which both men and women perfume themselves.

IV.

In our buildings we study convenience rather than ornament. Each master of a family has a large square piece of ground, surrounded with a moat or

*The bowl is earthen, curiously figured, to which a long reed is fixed as a tube. This tube is sometimes so long as to be borne by one, and frequently, out of grandeur, by two boys.)
**When I was in Smyrna I saw the same kind of earth, and brought some of it with me to England; it resembles musk in strength, but is more delicious in scent and is not unlike the smell of a rose.

fence, or enclosed with a wall, made of red earth tempered: which, when dry, is as hard as brick. Within this are his houses to accommodate his family and slaves; which, if numerous, frequently cause these tenements to present the appearance of a village. In the middle stands the principal building, appropriated to the sole use of the master, and consisting of two apartments; in one of which he sits in the day with his family, the other is left apart for the reception of his friends. He has besides these a distinct apartment in which he sleeps together with his male children. On each side are the apartments of his wives, who have also their separate day and night houses. The habitations of the slaves and their families are distributed throughout the rest of the enclosure. These houses never exceed one story in height: they are always built of wood, or stakes driven into the ground, crossed with wattles, and neatly plastered within and without. The roof is thatched with reeds. Our day houses are left open at the sides; but those in which we sleep are always covered, and plastered in the inside with a composition mixed with cow dung, to keep off the different insects, which annoy us during the night. The walls and floors also of these are generally covered with mats. Our beds consist of a platform, raised three or four feet from the ground, on which are laid skins, and different parts of a spungy tree called plantain. Our covering is calico, or muslin, the same as our dress. The usual seats are a few logs of wood; but we have benches, which are generally perfumed, to accommodate strangers: these compose the greater part of our household furniture. Houses so constructed and furnished require but little skill to erect them. Every man is a sufficient architect for the purpose. The whole neighbourhood afford their unanimous assistance in building them, and in return receive, and expect no other recompense than a feast.

As we live in a country where nature is prodigal of her favours, our wants are few, and easily supplied; of course we have few manufactures. They consist, for the most part, of calicoes, earthenware, ornaments, and instruments of war and husbandry. But these make no part of our commerce, the principal articles of which, as I have observed, are provisions. In such a state money is of little use; however we have some small pieces of coin, if I may call them such. They are made something like an anchor; but I do not remember either their value or denomination. We have also markets, at which I have been frequently with my mother. These are sometimes visited by stout mahogany-coloured men from the south-west of us. We call them Oye-Eboe, which term signifies "red men living at a distance." They generally bring us fire-arms, gunpowder, hats, beads, and dried fish. The last we esteemed a great

rarity, as our waters were only brooks and springs. These articles they barter with us for odoriferous woods and earth, and our salt of wood ashes. They always carry slaves through our land; but the strictest account is exacted of their manner of procuring them, before they are suffered to pass. Sometimes, indeed, we sold slaves to them, but they were only prisoners of war, or such among us as had been convicted of kidnapping, or adultery, and some other crimes, which we esteemed heinous. This practice of kidnapping induces me to think, that, notwithstanding all our strictness, their principal business among us was to trepan our people. I remember, too, they carried great sacks along with them, which not long after, I had an opportunity of fatally seeing applied to that infamous purpose.

V.

Our land is uncommonly rich and fruitful, and produces all kinds of vegetables in great abundance. We have plenty of Indian corn, and vast quantities of cotton and tobacco. Pineapples grow without culture; they are about the size of the largest sugar loaf, and finely flavoured. We have also spices of different kinds, particularly pepper; and a variety of delicious fruits which I have never seen in Europe; together with gums of various kinds, and honey in abundance. All our industry is exerted to improve those blessings of nature. Agriculture is our chief employment; and every one, even to children and women, is engaged in it. Thus we are habituated to labour from our earliest years. Every one contributes something to the common stock: and as we are unacquainted with idleness, we have no beggars. The benefits of such a mode of living are obvious.—The West India planters prefer the slaves of Benin or Eboe, to those of any part of Guinea, for their hardiness, intelligence, integrity and zeal.—Those benefits are felt by us in the general healthiness of the people, and in their vigour and activity; I might have added, too, to their comeliness. Deformity is indeed unknown amongst us. I mean that of shape. Numbers of the natives of Eboe, now in London, might be brought in support of this assertion: for, in regard to complexion, ideas of beauty are wholly relative. I remember while in Africa to have seen three negro children, who were tawny, and another quite white, who were universally regarded as deformed by myself and the natives in general, as far as related to their complexions. Our women too, were, in my eyes at least, uncommonly graceful, alert, and modest to a degree of bashfulness; nor do I remember to have ever heard of an instance of incontinence amongst them before marriage. They

are also remarkably cheerful. Indeed cheerfulness and affability are two of the leading characteristics of our nation.

Out tillage is exercised in a large plain or common, some hours' walk from our dwellings, and all the neighbours resort thither in a body. They use no beasts of husbandry; and their only instruments are hoes, axes, shovels, and beaks, or pointed iron to dig with. Sometimes we are visited by locusts, which come in large clouds, so as to darken the air and destroy our harvest. This, however, happens rarely, but when it does, a famine is produced by it. I remember an instance or two of this happening. This common is often the theatre of war; and therefore when our people go out to till their land, they not only go in a body, but generally take their arms with them for fear of a surprise: and when they apprehend an invasion, they guard the avenues to their dwellings by striking sticks into the ground, which are so sharp at one end as to pierce the foot, and are generally dipped in poison. From what I can recollect of these battles, they appear to have been irruptions of one little state or district into another, to obtain prisoners or booty. Perhaps they were incited to this by those traders, who brought amongst us the European goods which I mentioned. Such a mode of obtaining slaves in Africa is common; and I believe more are procured in this way, and by kidnapping, than in any other.* When a trader wants slaves, he applies to a chief for them, and tempts him with his wares. It is not extraordinary, if on this occasion he yields to the temptation with as little firmness, and accepts the price of his fellow-creature's liberty with as little reluctance as the enlightened merchant. Accordingly he falls on his neighbours, and a desperate battle ensues. If he prevails and takes prisoners, he gratifies his avarice by selling them, but if his party be vanquished, and he falls into the hands of the enemy, he is put to death: for, as he has been known to foment their quarrels, it is thought dangerous to let him survive, and no ransom can save him, though all other prisoners may be redeemed. We have fire-arms, bows and arrows, broad two-edged swords, and javelins, also shields which will cover a man from head to foot. All are taught the use of these weapons; even our women are warriors, and march boldly out to fight along with the men. Our whole district is a kind of militia: on a certain signal given, such as the firing of a gun at night, they all rise in arms and rush upon their enemy. It is, perhaps, sometimes remarkable, that when our people march to the field, a red flag or banner is borne before them. I was once a witness to a battle on our common. We had

*See Anthony Benezet's "Account of that Part of Africa inhabited by the Negroes" (1762) throughout.

all been at work in it one day, as usual, when our people were suddenly attacked. I climbed a tree at some distance, from which I beheld the fight. There were many women, as well as men, on both sides; among others my mother was there, and armed with a broad sword. After fighting for a considerable time with great fury, when many had been killed, our people obtained the victory, and took their enemy's chief prisoner. He was carried off in great triumph, and though he offered a large ransom for his life, he was put to death. A virgin of note among our enemies had been slain in the battle, and her arm was exposed in our marketplace, where our trophies were always exhibited. The spoils were divided according to the merit of the warriors. Those prisoners which were not sold or redeemed we kept as slaves: but how different was their condition from that of the slaves in the West Indies! With us they do no more work than other members of the community, than even their master; their food, clothing, and lodging, were nearly the same as theirs, except that they were not permitted to eat with those who were freeborn; and there was scarcely any other difference between them than a superior degree of importance, which the head of a family possesses in our state, and that authority which, as such, he exercises over every part of his household. Some of these slaves have even slaves under them, as their own property, and for their own use.

VI.

A s to religion, the natives believe that there is one Creator of all things, and that he lives in the sun, and is girded round with a belt that he may never eat or drink; but, according to some, he smokes a pipe, which is our own favourite luxury They believe he governs events, especially our deaths or captivity; but as for the doctrine of eternity, I don't remember to have ever heard of it: some, however, believe in the transmigration of souls in a certain degree.—Those spirits, which are not transmigrated, such as their dear friends or relations, they believe always attend them, and guard them from the bad spirits, or their foes. For this reason they always before eating, as I have observed, put some small portion of the meat, and pour some of the drink, on the ground for them; and they often make oblations of the blood of beasts, or of fowls at their graves. I was very fond of my mother, and was almost constantly with her. When she went to make these oblations at her mother's tomb, which was a kind of small solitary thatched house, I sometimes attended her. There she made her libations, and spent most of the

night in cries and lamentations. I have been often extremely terrified on these occasions. The loneliness of the place, the darkness of the night, and ceremony of libation, naturally awful and gloomy, were heightened by my mother's lamentations; and these concurring with the doleful cries of birds, by which these places were frequented, gave an inexpressible terror to the scene.

We compute the year from the day on which the sun crosses the line, and, on its setting that evening, there is a general shout throughout the land; at least I can speak from my own knowledge, throughout our vicinity. The people, at the same time, make a great noise with rattles, not unlike the basket rattles used by children here, though much larger, and hold up their hands to heaven for a blessing. It is then the greatest offerings are made, and those children who, our wise men foretel, will be fortunate, are then presented to different people. I remember many used to come to see me, and I was carried about to others for that purpose. They have many offerings, particularly at full moons; generally two at harvest, before the fruits are taken out of the ground: and when any young animals are killed, they sometimes offer up a part of them as a sacrifice. These offerings, when made by one of the heads of a family, serve for the whole. I remember we often had them at my father's and my uncle's, and their families have been present. Some of our offerings are eaten with bitter herbs. We had a saying among us to any one of a cross temper, "that if they were to be eaten, they should be eaten with bitter herbs."

We practiced circumcision like the Jews, and made offerings and feasts on that occasion in the same manner as they did. Like them also, our children were named from some event, some circumstance, or fancied foreboding at the time of their birth. I was named Olaudah, which, in our language, signifies "vicissitude or fortunate," also, "one favoured, and having a loud voice and well spoken." I remember we never polluted the name of the object of our adoration; on the contrary, it was always mentioned with the greatest reverence; and we are totally unacquainted with swearing, and all those terms of abuse and reproach which find their way so readily and copiously into the language of more civilized people. The only expressions of that kind I remember were "May you rot!" or "may you swell!" or "may a beast take you!"

I have before remarked that the natives of this part of Africa are extremely cleanly. This necessary habit of decency was with us a part of religion, and therefore we had many purifications and washings; indeed almost as many, and used on the same occasions, if my recollection does not fail me, as the Jews. Those that touched the dead, at anytime, were obliged to wash and

purify themselves before they could enter a dwelling-house, or touch any person or any thing we eat. I was so fond of my mother I could not keep from her, or avoid touching her at some of those periods, in consequence of which I was obliged to be kept out with her, in a little house made for that purpose, till offering was made, and then we were purified.

Though we had no places of public worship, we had priests and magicians, or wise men. I do not remember whether they had different offices, or whether they were united in the same persons, but they were held in great reverence by the people. They calculated our time, and foretold events, as their name imported, for we called them Ah-affoe-way-cah, which signifies "calculators or yearly men," our year being called Ah-affoe. They wore their beards; and when they died they were succeeded by their sons. Most of their implements and things of value were interred with them. Pipes and tobacco were also put into the graves with the corpse, which was always perfumed and ornamented, and animals were offered in sacrifice to them. None accompanied their funerals but those of the same profession or tribe. These buried them after sunset, and always returned from the grave by a different way from that by which they went.

These magicians were also our doctors or physicians. They practiced bleeding by cupping: and were very successful in healing wounds and expelling poisons. They had likewise some extraordinary method of discovering jealousy, theft, and poisoning; the success of which, no doubt, they derived from their unbounded influence over the credulity and superstition of the people. I do not remember what those methods were, except that, as to poisoning, I recollect an instance or two, which I hope it will not be deemed impertinent here to insert, as it may serve as a kind of specimen of the rest, and is still used by the negroes in the West Indies. A young woman had been poisoned, but it was not known by whom. The doctors ordered the corpse to be taken up by some persons and carried to the grave. As soon as the bearers had raised it on their shoulders, they seemed seized with some* sudden impulse, and ran to and fro unable to stop themselves. At last, after having passed through a number of thorns and prickly bushes unhurt, the corpse fell from them close to a house, and defaced it in the fall; and the owner being taken Up, he immediately confessed to the poisoning.**

*See also Lieutenant Matthew's "Voyage," p. 123 [of that volume].
**An instance of this kind happened at Montserrat in the West Indies, in the year 1763. I then belonged to the Charming Sally, Capt. Doran.—The chief mate, Mr. Mansfield, and some of the crew being one day on shore, were present at the burying

The natives are extremely cautious about poison. When they buy any eatable, the seller kisses it all round before the buyer, to shew him it is not poisoned; and the same is done when meat and drink are presented particularly to a stranger. We have serpents of different kinds, some of which are esteemed ominous when they appear in our houses, and these we never molest. I remember two of those ominous snakes, each of which was as thick as the calf of a man's leg, and in colour resembling a dolphin in the water, crept into my mother's night house, where I always lay with her, and coiled themselves into folds, and each time they crowed like a cock. I was desired by some of our wise men to touch these, that I might be interested in the good omens, which I did, for they were quite harmless, and would tamely suffer themselves to be handled; and then were put into a large open earthen pan, and set on one side of the highway. Some of our snakes, however, were poisonous: one of them crossed the road one day, as I was standing on it, and passed between my feet without offering to touch me, to the great surprise of many who saw it; and these incidents were accounted by the wise men, and likewise by my mother and the rest of the people, as remarkable omens in my favour.

VII.

Such is the imperfect sketch, with which my memory has furnished me, of the manners and customs of a people among whom I first drew my breath. And here I cannot forbear suggesting what has long struck me very forcibly, namely, the strong analogy, which, even by this sketch, imperfect as it is, appears to prevail in the manners and customs of my countrymen and those of the Jews, before they reached the Land of Promise, and particularly the Patriarchs, while they were yet in that pastoral state which is described in

of a poisoned negro girl. Though they had often heard of the circumstance of the running in such cases, and had even seen it they imagined it to be a trick of the corpse bearers. The mate therefore desired two of the sailors to take up the coffin, and carry it to the grave. The sailors, who were all of the same opinion, readily obeyed; but they had scarcely raised it to their shoulders, before they began to run furiously about, quite unable to direct themselves, till, at last, without intention, they came to the hut of him who had poisoned the girl. The coffin then immediately fell from their shoulders against the hut, and damaged part of the wall. The owner of the hut was taken into custody on this, and confessed the poisoning. I give this story as it was related by the mate and crew on their return to the ship. The credit which is due to it, I leave with the reader.

Genesis—an analogy which alone would induce me to think that the one people had sprung from the other. Indeed this is the opinion of Dr. Gill, who, in his commentary on Genesis, very ably deduces the pedigree of the Africans from Afer and Afra, the descendants of Abraham by Keturah his wife and concubine (for both these titles are applied to her). It is also conformable to the sentiments of Dr. John Clarke, formerly Dean of Sarum, in his "Truth of the Christian Religion." Both these authors concur in ascribing to us this original. The reasonings of those gentlemen are still further confirmed by the scripture chronology of the Rev. Arthur Bedford; and if any further corroboration were required, this resemblance in so many respects is a strong evidence in support of the opinion.—Like the Israelites in their primitive state, our government was conducted by our chiefs or judges, our wisemen, and elders; and the head of a family, with us, enjoyed a similar authority over his household with that which is ascribed to Abraham and the other Patriarchs. The law of retaliation prevailed almost universally with us as with them: and even their religion appeared to have shed upon us a ray of its glory, though broken and spent in its passage, or eclipsed by the cloud with which time, tradition, and ignorance might have enveloped it. For we had our circumcision (a rite, I believe, peculiar to that people): we had also our sacrifices and burnt-offerings, our washings and purifications, on the same occasions as they had.

As to the difference of colour between the Eboan Africans and the modern Jews, I shall not presume to account for it. It is a subject which has engaged the pens of men both of genius and learning, and is far above my strength. The most able and Rev. Mr. T. Clarkson, however, in his much admired "Essay on the Slavery and Commerce of the Human Species" has ascertained the cause in a manner that at once solves every objection on that account, and, on my mind at least, has produced the fullest conviction. I shall therefore refer to that performance for the theory,* contenting myself with extracting a fact as related by Dr. Mitchell.** "The Spaniards, who have inhabited America under the torrid zone, for any time, are become as dark coloured as our native Indians of Virginia; of which I myself have been a witness." There is also another instance*** of a Portuguese settlement at Mitomba, a river in Sierra Leona, where the inhabitants are bred from a mixture of the first Portuguese discoverers with the natives, and are now become

*Page 178 to 216 [of Clarkson's "Essay" cited above].
**Philos. Trans. No. 476, Sect. 4, cited by the Rev. Mr. Clarkson, p. 205.
***Same page.

in their complexion, and in the woolly quality for their hair, perfect negroes, retaining, however, a smattering of the Portuguese language.

These instances, and a great many more which might be adduced, while they shew how the complexions of the same persons vary in different climates, it is hoped may tend also to remove the prejudice that some conceive against the natives of Africa on account of their colour. Surely the minds of the Spaniards did not change with their complexions! Are there not causes enough to which the apparent inferiority of an African may be ascribed, without limiting the goodness of God, and supposing He forebore to stamp understanding on what is certainly his own image, because "carved in ebony?" Might it not naturally be ascribed to their situation? When they come among Europeans, they are ignorant of their language, religion, manners, and customs. Are any pains taken to teach them these? Are they treated as men? Does not slavery itself depress the mind, and extinguish all its fire, and every noble sentiment? But above all, what advantages do not a refined people possess over those who are rude and uncultivated! Let the polished and haughty European recollect that his ancestors were once like the Africans, uncivilized and even barbarous. Did Nature make them inferior to their sons? And should they too have been made slaves? Every rational mind answers, "No." Let such reflections as these melt the pride of their superiority into sympathy for the wants and miseries of their sable brethren, and compel them to acknowledge, that understanding is not confined to feature or color. If, when they look round the world, they feel exultation, let it be tempered with benevolence to others and gratitude to God, "who hath made of one blood all nations of men for to dwell on all the face of the earth;" (Acts xvii. 26.) and whose wisdom is not our wisdom, neither are our ways his ways.

CHAPTER II

The author's birth and parentage—His being kidnapped with his sister—Their separation—Surprise at meeting again—Are finally separated—Account of the different places and incidents the author met with till his arrival on the coast—The effect the sight of a slave ship had on him—He sails for the West Indies—Horrors of a slave ship—Arrives at Barbadoes, where the cargo is sold and dispersed.

I.

I HOPE the reader will not think I have trespassed on his patience, in intro-
ducing myself to him with some account of the manners and customs of
my country. They had been implanted in me with great care, and made an
impression on my mind, which time could not erase, and which all the
adversity and variety of fortune I have since experienced, served only to rivet
and record; for, whether the love of one's country be real or imaginary, a les-
son of reason or an instinct of nature, I still look back with pleasure on the
first scenes of my life, though that pleasure has been for the most part min-
gled with sorrow.

I have already acquainted the reader with the time and place of my birth.
My father, besides many slaves, had a numerous family, of which seven lived
to grow up, including myself and a sister, who was the only daughter. As I
was the youngest of the sons, I became, of course, the greatest favourite with
my mother, and was always with her, and she used to take particular pains to
form my mind. I was trained up from my earliest years in the art of war: my
daily exercise was shooting and throwing javelins; and my mother adorned
me with emblems, after the manner of our greatest warriors. In this way I
grew up till I was turned the age of eleven, when an end was put to my hap-
piness in the following manner:—When the grown people in the neigh-
bourhood were gone far in the fields to labour, the children generally assem-
bled together in some of the neighbours' premises to play; and some of us
often used to get up into a tree to look out for any assailant, or kidnapper,
that might come upon us. For they sometimes took those opportunities of
our parents' absence, to attack and carry off as many as they could seize. One
day, as I was watching at the top of a tree in our yard, I saw one of those peo-
ple come into the yard of our next neighbour but one, to kidnap, there being
many stout young people in it. Immediately on this I gave the alarm of the
rogue, and he was surrounded by the stoutest of them, who entangled him
with cords, so that he could not escape till some of the grown people came
and secured him.

II.

B ut alas! ere long it was my fate to be thus attacked, and to be carried off,
when none of the grown people were nigh. One day, when all our peo-

ple were gone out to their work as usual, and only I and my sister were left to mind the house, two men and a woman got over our walls, and in a moment seized us both; and without giving us time to cry out, or to make any resistance, they stopped our mouths and ran off with us into the nearest wood. Here they tied our hands, and continued to carry us as far as they could, till night came on, when we reached a small house, where the robbers halted for refreshment and spent the night. We were then unbound, but were unable to take any food; and being quite overpowered by fatigue and grief, our only relief was some sleep, which allayed our misfortune for a short time. The next morning we left the house, and continued travelling all the day. For a long time we had kept the woods, but at last we came into a road which I believed I knew. I had now some hopes of being delivered; for we had advanced but a little way before I discovered some people at a distance, on which I began to cry out for their assistance; but my cries had no other effect than to make them tie me faster and stop my mouth; they then put me into a large sack. They also stopped my sister's mouth, and tied her hands; and in this manner we proceeded till we were out of sight of these people.

When we went to rest the following night, they offered us some victuals; but we refused it; and the only comfort we had was in being in one anoth-er's arms all that night, and bathing each other with tears. But alas! we were soon deprived of even the small comfort of weeping together. The next day proved one of greater sorrow than I had yet experienced; for my sister and I were then separated, while we lay clasped in each other's arms. It was in vain that we besought them not to part us; she was torn from me, and immedi-ately carried away, while I was left in a state of distraction not to be described. I cried and grieved continually; and for several days did not eat any thing but what they forced into my mouth. At length, after many days' travelling, dur-ing which I had often changed masters, I got into the hands of a chieftain, in a pleasant country. This man had two wives and some children, and they all used me extremely well, and did all they could to comfort me; particular-ly the first wife, who was something like my mother. Although I was a great many days' journey from my father's house, yet these people spoke exactly the same language with us. This first master of mine, as I may call him, was a smith, and my principal employment was working his bellows, which were the same kind as I had seen in my vicinity. They were in some respects not unlike the stoves here in gentlemen's kitchens; and were covered over with leather, and in the middle of that leather a stick was fixed, and a person stood up and worked it, in the same manner as is done to pump water out of a cask

with a hand pump. I believe it was gold he worked, for it was of a lovely bright yellow colour, and was worn by the women on their wrists and ankles.

I was there, I suppose, about a month, and they at length used to trust me some little distance from the house. I employed this liberty in embracing every opportunity to inquire the way to my own home: and I also sometimes, for the same purpose, went with the maidens, in the cool of the evenings, to bring pitchers of water from the springs for the use of the house. I had also remarked where the sun rose in the morning, and set in the evening, as I had travelled along: and had observed that my father's house was towards the rising of the sun. I therefore determined to seize the first opportunity of making my escape, and to shape my course for that quarter; for I was quite oppressed and weighed down by grief after my mother and friends; and my love of liberty, ever great, was strengthened by the mortifying circumstance of not daring to eat with the free-born children, although I was mostly their companion.

III.

While I was projecting my escape, one day an unlucky event happened, which quite disconcerted my plan, and put an end to my hopes. I used to be sometimes employed in assisting an elderly woman slave to cook and take care of the poultry: and one morning, while I was feeding some chickens, I happened to toss a small pebble at one of them, which hit it on the middle, and directly killed it. The old slave having soon after missed the chicken, inquired after it; and on my relating the accident (for I told her the truth, because my mother would never suffer me to tell a lie) she flew into a violent passion, threatened that I should suffer for it; and, my master being out, she immediately went and told her mistress what I had done. This alarmed me very much, and I expected an instant flogging, which to me was uncommonly dreadful; for I had seldom been beaten at home. I therefore resolved to fly; and accordingly I ran into a thicket that was hard by, and hid myself in the bushes. Soon afterwards my mistress and the slave returned, and, not seeing me, they searched all the house, but not finding me, and I not making answer when they called me, they thought I had run away, and the whole neighbourhood was raised in the pursuit of me.

In that part of the country, as well as in ours, the houses and villages were skirted with woods, or shrubberies, and the bushes were so thick that a man could readily conceal himself in them, so as to elude the strictest search. The

neighbours continued the whole day looking for me, and several times many of them came within a few yards of the place where I lay hid. I expected every moment, when I heard a rustling among the trees, to be found out, and punished by my master. But they never discovered me, though they often were so near that I even heard their conjectures, as they were looking about for me; and I now learned from them, that any attempt to return home would be hopeless. Most of them supposed I had fled towards home; but the distance was so great, and the way so intricate, that they thought I could never reach it, and that I should be lost in the woods. When I heard this I was seized with a violent panic, and abandoned myself to despair. Night too began to approach, and aggravated all my fears. I had before entertained hopes of getting home and had determined when it should be dark to make the attempt; but I was now convinced it was fruitless, and began to consider that, if possibly I could escape all other animals, I could not those of the human kind; and that, not knowing the way, I must perish in the woods. Thus was I like the hunted deer:

> Ev'ry leaf, and ev'ry whisp'ring breath
> Convey'd a foe, and ev'ry foe a death.

I heard frequent rustlings among the leaves, and being pretty sure they were snakes, I expected every instant to be stung by them. This increased my anguish, and the horror of my situation became now quite insupportable. I at length quitted the thicket, very faint and hungry, for I had not eaten nor drunk any thing all the day. I crept to my master's kitchen, from whence I set out at first, which was an open shed, and laid myself down in the ashes with an anxious wish for death to relieve me from all my pains. I was scarcely awake in the morning, when the old woman slave, who was the first up, came to light the fire, and saw me in the fire place. She was very much surprised to see me, and could scarcely believe her own eyes. She now promised to intercede for me, and went for her master, who soon after came, and, having slightly reprimanded me, ordered me to be taken care of, and not ill treated.

IV.

Soon after this my master's only daughter and child by his first wife, sickened and died, which affected him so much that for some time he was almost frantic, and really would have killed himself, had he not been watched

and prevented. However, in a small time afterwards he recovered, and I was again sold. I was now carried to the left of the sun's rising, through many dreary wastes and dismal woods, amidst the hideous roaring of wild beasts. The people I was sold to used to carry me very often, when I was tired, either on their shoulders or on their backs. I saw many convenient well-built sheds along the road, at proper distances, to accommodate the merchants and travellers. They lie in those buildings along with their wives, who often accompany them: and they always go well armed.

From the time I left my own nation I always found somebody that understood me till I came to the sea coast. The languages of different nations did not totally differ, nor were they so copious as those of the Europeans, particularly the English. They were therefore easily learned; and, while I was journeying thus through Africa, I acquired two or three different tongues. In this manner I had been travelling for a considerable time, when one evening, to my great surprise, whom should I see brought to the house where I was, but my dear sister? As soon as she saw me she gave a loud shriek, and ran into my arms. I was quite overpowered: neither of us could speak; but for a considerable time, clung to each other in mutual embraces, unable to do any thing but weep. Our meeting affected all who saw us; and indeed I must acknowledge, in honour of those sable destroyers of human rights, that I never met with any ill treatment, or saw any offered to their slaves, except tying them, when necessary, to keep them running away.

When these people knew we were brother and sister, they indulged us to be together; and the man, to whom I supposed we belonged, lay with us, he in the middle, while she and I held one another by the hands across his breast all night; and thus for a while we forgot our misfortunes in the joy of being together. But even this small comfort was soon to have an end, for scarcely had the fatal morning appeared, when she was again torn from me for ever! I was now more miserable, if possible, than before. The small relief which her presence gave me from pain was gone, and the wretchedness of my situation was redoubled by my anxiety after her fate, and my apprehensions lest her sufferings should be greater than mine, when I could not be with her to alleviate them.

Yes, dear partner of all my childish sports! Sharer of my joys and sorrows; happy should I have ever esteemed myself to encounter every misery for you, and to procure your freedom by the sacrifice of my own! Though you were early forced from my arms, your image has been always rivetted in my heart, from which neither time nor fortune has been able to remove it: so that, while the thoughts of your sufferings have damped my prosperity, they have

mingled with adversity and increased its bitterness. To that Heaven, which protects the weak from the strong, I commit the care of your innocence and virtues, if they have not already received their full reward, and if your youth and delicacy have not long since fallen victims to the violence of the African trader, the pestilential stench of a Guinea ship, the seasoning in the European colonies, or the lash and lust of a brutal and unrelenting overseer.

I did not long remain after my sister. I was again sold, and carried through a number of places, till, after travelling a considerable time, I came to a town called Tinmah, in the most beautiful country I had yet seen in Africa. It was extremely rich, and there were many rivulets which flowed through it, and supplied a large pond in the centre of the town, where the people washed. Here I first saw and tasted cocoa nuts, which I thought superior to any nuts I had ever tasted before; and the trees which were loaded, were also interspersed among the houses, which had commodious shades adjoining, and were in the same manner as ours, the insides being neatly plastered and whitewashed. Here I also saw and tasted, for the first time, sugar-cane. Their money consisted of little white shells, the size of the fingernail. I was sold for one hundred and seventy-two of these, by a merchant who lived at this place. I had been about two or three days at his house, when a wealthy widow, a neighbour of his came there one evening, and brought with her an only son, a young gentleman about my own age and size. Here they saw me; and, having taken a fancy to me, I was bought of the merchant, and went home with them. Her house and premises were situated close to one of those rivulets I have mentioned, and were the finest I ever saw in Africa: they were very extensive, and she had a number of slaves to attend her. The next day I was washed and perfumed, and when mealtime came, I was led into the presence of my mistress, and ate and drank before her with her son. This filled me with astonishment; and I could scarcely avoid expressing my surprise that the young gentleman should suffer me, who was bound, to eat with him who was free; and not only so, but that he would not at any time either eat or drink till I had taken first, because I was the eldest, which was agreeable to our custom. Indeed every thing here, and their treatment of me, made me forget that I was a slave. The language of these people resembled ours so nearly, that we understood each other perfectly. They had also the very same customs as we. There were likewise slaves daily to attend us, while my young master and I, with other boys, sported with our darts, and bows and arrows, as I had been used to do at home. In this resemblance to my former happy state, I passed about two months; and now I began to think I

was to be adopted into the family, and was beginning to be reconciled to my situation, and to forget by degrees my misfortunes, when all at once the delusion vanished; for, without the least previous knowledge, one morning, early, while my dear master and companion was still asleep, I was awakened out of my reverie to fresh sorrow, and hurried away even amongst the uncircumcised.

Thus, at the very moment I dreamed of the greatest happiness, I found myself most miserable; and it seemed as if fortune* wished to give me this taste of joy, only to render the reverse more poignant. The change I now experienced was as painful as it was sudden and unexpected. It was a change indeed from a state of bliss to a scene which is inexpressible by me, as it discovered to me an element I had never before beheld, and of which till then had no idea; and wherein such instances of hardship and cruelty continually occurred, as I can never reflect on but with horror.

v.

A ll the nations and people I had hitherto passed through resembled our own in their manners, customs, and language: but I came at length to

*This indiscreet mode of calling the providence of God, in his particular dealings with the children of men, by the name of fortune is exceedingly blameworthy. It is a conformity to the expressions of a vain world not to be expected from Gustavus, who generally manifests a becoming sense of the benefits which he received, and a knowledge of the Blessed Fountain from whence they issued. After censuring it as a slip of his pen, let none venture to attribute it to atheistical motives. The tenor of his conduct and of his words belies such an insinuation. He had heard the term thus misapplied by others, and from an imitative habit, he thoughtlessly gave it the same appellation.

What can be thought by short sighted mortals, to have been the designs of a gracious God in permitting such complicated evils to hover around and to oppress this youthful African? The purposes of Him, who afflicts not willingly any of the children of men, cannot but be merciful. Every stripe which He suffers to be inflicted, will hereafter be interpreted into so many varied tokens of His paternal affection towards his redeemed creatures, for "whom He loveth He chasteneth, and scourgeth every son whom He receiveth." While there is an aptitude in human nature to call Divine good "evil," a righteous man is greatly benefited by the cure of this propensity and in committing all things to the complete disposal of "One supremely good and wise," he has the best possible security and assurance of all things working together for his good. Let the pious reader say, after rising up from the perusal of this narrative, if it is not his firm persuasion, that in all these "hidden dangers, toils, and deaths," is evinced the intention of Divine Wisdom to bring the mall, who was exercised with them, to partake of the purchased blessings of salvation. Who, that knows the value of it, would desist from praising God "for his unspeakable gift," or would slightingly speak of the almost imperceptible means by which he was led to the enjoyment of religion?

a country, the inhabitants of which differed from us in all these particulars. I was very much struck with this difference, especially when I came among a people who did not circumcise, and who ate without washing their hands. They cooked their provisions also in iron pots, and had European cutlasses and cross bows, which were unknown to us; and fought with their fists among themselves. Their women were not so modest as ours, for they ate, drank, and slept with their men. But, above all, I was amazed to see no sacrifices or offerings among them. In some of those places the people ornamented themselves with scars, and likewise filed their teeth very sharp. They sometimes wanted to ornament me in the same manner, but I would not suffer them; hoping that I might sometime be among a people who did not thus disfigure themselves, as I thought they did. At last I came to the banks of a large river covered with canoes, in which the people appeared to live, with their household utensils, and provisions of all kinds. I was beyond measure astonished at this, as I had never before seen any water larger than a pond or a rivulet: and my surprise was mingled with no small fear when I was put into one of these canoes, and we began to paddle and move along the river. We continued going on thus till night; and when we came to land, and made fires on the banks, each family by themselves, some dragged their canoes on shore, others cooked in theirs, and laid in them all night. Those on the land had mats, of which they made tents, some in the shape of little houses: in these we slept: and after the morning meal, we embarked again, and proceeded as before. I was often very much astonished to see some of the women as well as the men, jump into the water, dive to the bottom, come up again, and swim about. Thus I continued to travel, both by land and by water, through different countries and various nations, till at the end of six or seven months after I had been kidnapped, I arrived at the sea coast.

It would be tedious and uninteresting to relate all the incidents which befell me during this journey, and which I have not yet forgotten, or to mention the various lands I passed through, and the manners and customs of the different people among whom I lived: I shall therefore only observe, that in all the places where I was, the soil was exceedingly rich; the pomkins, aedas, plantains, yams, &c. &c. were in great abundance, and of incredible size. There were also large quantities of different gums, though not used for any purpose; and every where a great deal of tobacco. The cotton even grew quite wild; and there was plenty of red wood. I saw no mechanics whatever in all the way, except such as I have mentioned. The chief employment in all these countries was agriculture, and both the males and females, as with us, were

brought up to it, and trained in the arts of war.

The first object that saluted my eyes when I arrived on the coast was the sea, and a slave ship, which was then riding at anchor, and waiting for its cargo. These filled me with astonishment, that was soon converted into terror, which I am yet at a loss to describe, and much more the then feelings of my mind when I was carried on board. I was immediately handled and tossed up to see if I was sound, by some of the crew; and I was now persuaded that I had got into a world of bad spirits, and that they were going to kill me. Their complexions too, differing so much from ours, their long hair, and the language they spoke, which was very different from any I had ever heard, united to confirm me in this belief. Indeed such were the horrors of my views and fears at the moment, that if ten thousand worlds had been my own, I would have freely parted with them all to have exchanged my condition with the meanest slave in my own country. When I looked round the ship too, and saw a large furnace or copper boiling and a multitude of black people, of every description, chained together, every one of their countenances expressing dejection and sorrow, I no longer doubted of my fate; and, quite overpowered with horror and anguish, I fell motionless on the deck, and fainted. When I recovered a little, I found some black people about me, who I believed were some of those who brought me on board, and had been receiving their pay; they talked to me in order to cheer me, but all in vain. I asked them if we were not to be eaten by those white men with horrible looks red faces, and long hair. They told me I was not: and one of the crew brought me a small portion of spirituous liquor in a wine glass, but, being afraid of him, I would not take it out of his hand. One of the blacks therefore took it from him and gave it to me, and I took a little down my palate which, instead of reviving me, as they thought it would, threw me into the greatest consternation at the strange feeling it produced, having never tasted any such liquor before.

Soon after this the blacks who brought me on board went off, and left me abandoned to despair. I now saw myself deprived of all chance of returning to my native country, or even the least glimpse of gaining the shore, which I now considered as friendly; and I even wished for my former slavery, in preference to my present situation, which was filled with horrors of every kind, still heightened by my ignorance of what I was to undergo. I was not long suffered to indulge my grief. I was soon put down under the decks, and there I received such a salutation in my nostrils as I had never experienced in my life: so that, with the loathsomeness of the stench, and with my crying

together, I became so sick and low that I was not able to eat, nor had I the least desire to taste any thing. I now wished for the last friend, death, to relieve me; but soon, to my grief, two of the white men offered me eatables; and, on my refusing to eat, one of them held me fast by the hands, and laid me across, I think, the windlass, and tied my feet, while the other flogged me severely. I had never experienced any thing of this kind before, and although, not being used to the water, I naturally feared that element the first time I saw it, yet nevertheless, could I have got over the nettings, I would have jumped over the side, but I could not; and besides the crew used to watch us very closely, who were not chained down to the decks, lest we should leap into the water. I have seen some of these poor African prisoners most severely cut for attempting to do so, and hourly whipped for not eating. This indeed was often the case with myself. In a little time after, amongst the poor chained men, I found some of my own nation, which in a small degree gave ease to my mind. I inquired of these what was to be done with us. They gave me to understand we were to be carried to these white people's country to work for them. I was then a little revived, and thought if it were no worse than working, my situation was not so desperate. But still I feared I should be put to death, the white people looked and acted, as I thought, in so savage a manner; for I had never seen among any people such instances of brutal cruelty: and this is not only strewn towards us blacks, but also to some of the whites themselves. One white man in particular I saw, when we were permitted to be on deck, flogged so unmercifully with a large rope near the foremast, that he died in consequence of it; and they tossed him over the side as they would have done a brute. This made me fear these people the more; and I expected nothing less than to be treated in the same manner. I could not help expressing my fearful apprehensions to some of my countrymen; I asked them if these people had no country, but lived in this hollow place, the ship. They told me they did not, but came from a distant one. 'Then,' said I, 'how comes it, that in all our country we never heard of them?' They told me, because they lived so very far off. I then asked, where their women were: had they any like themselves. I was told they had. 'And why,' said I, 'do we not see them?' they answered, because they were left behind. I asked how the vessel could go. They told me they could not tell; but that there was cloth put upon the masts by the help of the ropes I saw, and then the vessel went on; and the white men had some spell or magic they put in the water, when they liked, in order to stop the vessel. I was exceedingly amazed at this account, and really thought they were spirits. I therefore wished much to be from

amongst them, for I expected they would sacrifice me; but my wishes were in vain, for we were so quartered that it was impossible for any of us to make our escape.

VI.

While we stayed on the coast I was mostly on deck; and one day, to my great astonishment, I saw one of these vessels coming in with the sails up. As soon as the whites saw it, they gave a great shout, at which we were amazed; and the more so as the vessel appeared larger by approaching nearer. At last she came to an anchor in my sight, and when the anchor was let go, I and my countrymen who saw it, were lost in astonishment to observe the vessel stop, and were now convinced it was done by magic. Soon after this the other ship got her boats out, and they came on board of us, and the people of both ships seemed very glad to see each other. Several of the strangers also shook hands with us black people, and made motions with their hands, signifying, I suppose, we were to go to their country; but we did not understand them. At last, when the ship, in which we were, had got in all her cargo, they 'mace ready with many fearful noises, and we were all put under deck, so that we could not see how they managed the vessel.

But this disappointment was the least of my grief. The stench of the hold, while we were on the coast, was so intolerably loathsome, that it was dangerous to remain there for any time, and some of us had been permitted to stay on the deck for the fresh air; but now that the whole ship's cargo were confined together, it became absolutely pestilential. The closeness of the place, and the heat of the climate, added to the number in the ship, being so crowded that each had scarcely room to turn himself, almost suffocated us. This produced copious perspirations, so that the air soon became unfit for respiration, from a variety of loathsome smells, and brought on a sickness among the slaves, of which many died, thus falling victims to the improvident avarice, as I may call it, of their purchasers. This deplorable situation was again aggravated by the galling of the chains, now become insupportable; and the filth of necessary tubs, into which the children often fell, and were almost suffocated. The shrieks of the women, and the groans of the dying, rendered it a scene of horror almost inconceivable. Happily, perhaps, for myself, I was soon reduced so low here that it was thought necessary to keep me almost continually on deck; and from my extreme youth, I was not put in fetters. In this situation I expected every hour to share the fate of my com-

panions, some of whom were almost daily brought upon deck at thé point of death, and I began to hope that death would soon put an end to my miseries. Often did I think many of the inhabitants of the deep much more happy than myself; I envied them the freedom they enjoyed, and as often wished I could change my condition for theirs. Every circumstance I met with served only to render my state more painful, and heighten my apprehensions and my opinion of the cruelty of the whites. One day they had taken a number of fishes; and when they had killed and satisfied themselves with as many as they thought fit, to our astonishment who were on the deck, rather than give any of them to us to eat, as we expected, they tossed the remaining fish into the sea again, although we begged and prayed for some as well as we could, but in vain; and some of my countrymen, being pressed by hunger, took an opportunity, when they thought no one saw them, of trying to get a little privately; but were discovered, and the attempt procured for them some very severe floggings.

One day, when we had a smooth sea and moderate wind, two of my wearied countrymen, who were chained together (I was near them at the time), preferring death to such a life of misery, somehow made through the nettings and jumped into the sea: immediately another quite dejected fellow, who on account of his illness was suffered to be out of irons also followed their example; and I believe many more would very soon have done the same, if they had not been prevented by the ship's crew, who were instantly alarmed. Those of us who were the most active were in a moment put down under the deck; and there was such a noise and confusion amongst the people of the ship as I never heard before, to stop her and get the boat out to go after the slaves. However, two of the wretches were drowned; but they got the other, and afterward flogged him unmercifully, for thus attempting to prefer death to slavery. In this manner we continued to undergo more hardships than I can now relate, hardships which are inseparable from this accursed trade. Many a time we were near suffocation from the want of fresh air, being deprived thereof for days together. This, and the stench of the necessary tubs, carried off many.

VII.

During our passage I first saw flying fishes, which surprised me very much: they used frequently to fly across the ship, and many of them fell on deck. I also now first saw the use of the quadrant. I had often with

astonishment seen the mariners make observations with it, and I could not think what it meant. They at last took notice of my surprise: and one of them, willing to increase it, as well as to gratify my curiosity, made me one day look through it. The clouds appeared to me to be land, which disappeared as they passed along. This heightened my wonder; and I was now more persuaded than ever that I was in another world and that every thing about me was magic At last we came in sight of the island of Barbadoes, at which the whites on board gave a great shout and made many signs of joy to us. We did not know what to think of this, but as the vessel drew nearer we plainly saw the harbour, and other ships of different kinds and sizes; and we soon anchored amongst them off Bridge Town. Many merchants and planters now came on board, though it was in the evening. They put us in separate parcels, and examined us attentively. They also made us jump, and pointed to the land, signifying we were to go there. We thought by this we should be beaten by these ugly men, as they appeared to us; and, when soon after we were all put down under the deck again, there was much dread and trembling among us, and nothing but bitter cries to be heard all the night from these apprehensions, insomuch that at last the white people got some old slaves from the land to pacify us. They told us we were not to be eaten, but to work, and were soon to go on land, where we should see many of our country people. This report eased us much; and, sure enough, soon after we landed, there came to us Africans of all languages.

We were conducted immediately to the merchant's yard, where we were all pent up together like so many sheep in a fold, without regard to sex or age. As every object was new to me, every thing I saw filled me with surprise. What struck me first was that the houses were built with bricks in stories, and were in every other respect different from those I had seen in Africa; but I was still more astonished at seeing people on horseback. I did not know what this could mean; and indeed I thought these people full of nothing but magical arts. While I was in this astonishment one of my fellow prisoners spoke to a countryman of his about the horses, who said they were the same kind they had in their country. I understood them, though they were from a distant part of Africa, and I thought it odd I had not seen any horses there; but afterwards, when I came to converse with different Africans, I found they had many horses amongst them, and much larger than those I then saw.

We were not many days in the merchants' custody before we were sold after the usual manner, which is this:—On a signal given, such as the beat of a drum, the buyers rush at once into the yard where the slaves are confined,

and make choice of that parcel they like best. The noise and clamour with which this is attended, and the eagerness visible in the countenances of the buyers, serve not a little to increase the apprehensions of the terrified Africans, who may well be supposed to consider them the ministers of that destruction to which they think themselves devoted. In this manner, without scruple, are relations and friends separated, most of them never to see each other again. I remember in the vessel in which I was brought over in, in the man's apartment, there were several brothers, who, in the sale, were sold in different lots; and it was very moving on this occasion to see their distress and hear their cries at parting. O, ye nominal Christians! might not an African ask you, "learned you this from your God, who says unto you, Do unto all men as you would men should do unto you? Is it not enough that we are torn from our country and friends, to toil for your luxury and lust of gain? Must every tender feeling be likewise sacrificed to your avarice? Are the dearest friends and relations now rendered more dear by their separation from the rest of their kindred, still to be parted from each other, and thus prevented from cheering the gloom of slavery, with the small comfort of being together, and mingling their sufferings and sorrows? Why are parents to lose their children, brothers their sisters, or husbands their wives? Surely this is a new refinement in cruelty, which, while it has no advantage to atone for it, thus aggravates distress, and adds fresh horrors even to the wretchedness of slavery."

CHAPTER III

The author is carried to Virginia—His distress—Surprise at seeing a picture and a watch—Is bought by Captain Pascal, and sets out for England—His terror during the voyage—Arrives in England—His wonder at a fall of snow—Is sent to Guernsey, and in some time goes on board a ship of war with his master— Some account of the expedition against Louisbourg, under the command of Admiral Boscawen in 1758.

I.

I NOW totally lost the small remains of comfort I had enjoyed in conversing with my countrymen; the women, too, who used to wash and take care of me, were all gone different ways, and I never saw one of them afterwards.

I stayed in this island for a few days; I believe it could not be above a fortnight; when I and some few more slaves, who from very much fretting were not saleable among the rest, were shipped off in a sloop for North America. On the passage we were better treated than when coming from Africa, and we had plenty of rice and fat pork. We were landed up a river a good way from the sea, about Virginia county, where we saw few of our native Africans, and not one soul who could talk to me. I was a few weeks weeding grass and gathering stones in a plantation; and at last all my companions were distributed different ways, and only myself was left. I was now exceedingly miserable, and thought myself worse off than any of the rest of my companions; for they could talk to each other, but I had no person to speak to that I could understand. In this state I was constantly grieving and pining, and wishing for death rather than any thing else. While I was in this plantation the gentleman to whom I supposed the estate belonged being unwell, I was one day sent for to his dwelling house to fan him. When I came into the room where he was, I was very much affrighted at some things I saw, and the more so, as I had seen a black woman slave as I came through the house, who was cooking the dinner, and the poor creature was cruelly loaded with various kinds of iron machines; she had one particularly on her head, which locked her mouth so fast that she could scarcely speak, and could not eat or drink. I much astonished and shocked at this contrivance, which I afterwards learned was called the iron muzzle. Soon after I had a fan put into my hand, to fan the gentleman while he slept; and so I did indeed with great fear. While he was fast asleep I indulged myself a great deal in looking about the room, which to me appeared very fine and curious. The first object that engaged my attention was a watch, which hung on the chimney, and was going. I was quite surprised at the noise it made, and was afraid it would tell the gentleman any thing I might do amiss: and when I immediately after observed a picture hanging in the room, which appeared constantly to look at me, I was still more affrighted, having never seen such things as these before. At one time I thought it was something relative to magic; and not seeing it move, I thought it might be some way the whites had to keep their great men when they died, and offer them libations, as we used to do to our friendly spirits. In this state of anxiety I remained till my master awoke, when I was dismissed out of the room, to my no small satisfaction and relief; for I thought that these people were all made up of wonders. In this place I was called JACOB; but on board the African Snow* I was called MICHAEL.

*A large two-masted Ship.

II.

I had been some time in this miserable, forlorn, and much dejected state, without any one to talk to, which made my life a burden, when the kind and unknown hand of the Creator, who in every deed leads the blind in a way they know not, now began to appear to my comfort; for one day the captain of a merchant ship, called the "Industrious Bee," came on some business to my master's house. This gentleman, whose name was Michael Henry Pascal, was a lieutenant in the royal navy, but now commanded this trading ship, which was somewhere in the confines of the county many miles off. While he was at my master's house it happened that he saw me, and liked me so well that he made a purchase of me. I think I have often heard him say he gave thirty or forty pounds sterling for me; the exact sum I do not now remember. However he meant me for a present to some of his friends in England: and I was sent accordingly from the house of my then master, one Mr. Campbell, to the place where the ship lay. I was conducted on horseback by an elderly black man, a mode of travelling which appeared very odd to me. When I arrived, I was carried on board a fine large ship, loaded with tobacco, &c. and just ready to sail for England. I now thought my condition much mended; having sails to lie on, and plenty of good victuals to eat; and every body on board used me very kindly, quite contrary to what I had seen of any white people before; I therefore began to think that they were not all of the same disposition. A few days after I was on board we sailed for England. I was still at a loss to conjecture my destiny. By this time, however I could smatter a little imperfect English, and I wanted to know as well I could where we were going. Some of the people of the ship used to tell me they were going to carry me back to my own country, and this made me very happy. I was quite rejoiced at the idea of going back; and thought if I should get home what wonders I should have to tell. But I was reserved for another fate, and was soon undeceived when we came within sight of the English coast.

While I was on board of this ship my captain and master named me Gustavus Vassa. I at that time began to understand him a little, and refused to be called so, and told him, as well as I could, that I would be called Jacob; but he said I should not, and still called me Gustavus. And when I refused to answer to my new name, which at first I did, it gained me many a cuff; so at length I submitted, and by it I have been known ever since. The ship had a very long passage; and on that account we had very short allowance of provisions; having towards the last only one pound and a half of bread per week,

and about the same quantity of meat, and one quart of water a-day. We spoke with only one vessel during the voyage, and but once caught a few fishes. In our extremity the captain and people told me in jest they would kill and eat me, but I thought them in earnest, and was depressed beyond measure, expecting every moment to be my last. While I was in this situation one evening they caught a large shark, and got it on board. This rejoiced my heart exceedingly, as I thought it would serve the people to eat instead of their eating me; but very soon, to my astonishment, they cut off a small part of the tail, and tossed the rest over the side. This increased my consternation; and I did not know what to think of these white people, though I very much feared they intended to kill and eat me.

III.

There was on board the ship a young lad, who had never been at sea before, about four or five years older than myself; his name was Richard Baker. He was a native of America, had received an excellent education, and was of a most amiable temper. Soon after I went on board he shewed me a great deal of partiality and attention, and in return I grew very fond of him. We at length became inseparable; and, for the space of two years, he was of great use to me, and was my constant companion and instructor. Although this dear youth had many slaves of his own, yet he and I have gone through many sufferings together on shipboard; and have many nights lain in each other's bosoms, when in great distress. Thus such a friendship was cemented between us, as we cherished till his death, which, to my very grief, happened in the year 1759, when he was up the Archipelago, on board his Majesty's ship the Preston: an event which I never ceased to regret, as I lost at once a kind interpreter, an agreeable companion, and a faithful friend; who at the age of fifteen, discovered a mind superior to prejudice, being not ashamed to notice, to associate with, and to be the friend and instructor of one who was ignorant, a stranger, and a slave! My master had lodged in his mother's house in America: he respected him very much, and made him always eat with him in the cabin. He used often to tell him jocularly that he would kill and eat me. Sometimes he used to say to me—the black people were not good to eat, and ask me if we did not eat people in my country. I said "No:" then he said he would first kill Dick, as he always called him, and afterwards me. Though this hearing relieved my mind a little as to myself, I was alarmed for Dick, and whenever he was called I used to be very much afraid he was to be killed;

and I would peep and watch to see if they were going to kill him; nor was I free from this consternation till we made the land.

One night we lost a man overboard; and the cries and noise were so great and confused, in stopping the ship, that I, who did not know what was the matter, began, as usual, to be very much afraid, and to think they were going to make an offering with me, and perform some magic; in which I still believed that they dealt. As the waves were very high, I thought the Ruler of the seas was angry, and I expected to be offered up to appease him. This filled my mind with agony, and I could not any more, that night, close my eyes again to rest. However, when daylight appeared, I was a little eased in my mind; but still, when called, I thought it was that I might be killed. Some time after this we saw some very large fishes, which I afterwards found were called grampusses. They looked to me extremely terrible, and made their appearance just at dusk. They were so near as to blow the water on the ship's deck. I believed them to be the rulers of the sea: and as the white people did not make any offerings at any time, I thought they were angry at them: and, at last, what confirmed my belief, the wind just then died away, and a calm ensued, and in consequence of it the ship ceased from going. I supposed that the fishes had performed this, and hid myself in the forepart of the ship, through fear of being offered up to appease them, every minute peeping and quaking; but my good friend Dick came shortly to me, and I took an opportunity to ask him, as well as I could, what these fishes were. Not being able to talk much English, I could but just make him understand my question; and not at all, when I asked him if any offerings were to be made to them: however he told me these fishes would devour any body, which sufficiently alarmed me. Here he was called away by the captain, who was leaning over the quarter-deck railing, and looking at the fishes; and most of the people were busied in getting a barrel of pitch to light, for them to play with. The Captain now called me, having learned some of my apprehensions from Dick; and having diverted himself and others, for some time, with my fears, which appeared ludicrous enough in my crying and trembling, he dismissed me. The barrel of pitch was then lighted and put over the side into the water: by this time it was just dark, and the fishes went after it; and to my great joy, I saw them no more.

IV.

However, all my alarms began to subside when we got sight of land; and at last the ship reached Falmouth, after a passage of thirteen weeks.

Every heart on board seemed gladdened on our reaching the shore, and none more than mine. The captain immediately went on shore, and sent on board some fresh provisions, which we wanted very much: we made good use of them, and our famine was soon turned into feasting, almost without ending. It was about the beginning of spring 1757, when I arrived in England, and I was nearly twelve years of age at that time. I was very much struck with the buildings and the pavement of the streets in Falmouth; and, indeed, every object I saw filled me with fresh surprise.

One morning, when I got upon deck, I perceived it covered all over with the snow that fell over-night. As I had never seen any thing of the kind before, I thought it was salt; so I immediately ran down to the mate and desired him, as well as I could, to come and see how somebody in the night had thrown salt all over the deck. He, knowing what it was, desired me to bring some of it down to him: accordingly I took up a handful of it, which I found very cold indeed; and when I brought it to him he desired me to taste it. I did so, and was surprised above measure. I then asked him what it was; he told me it was snow; but I could not by any means understand him. He asked me if we had no such thing in our country; I told him "No." I then asked him the use of it, and who made it: he told me a great man in the heavens, called God: but here again I was to all intents and purposes at a loss to understand him; and the more so, when a little after I saw the air filled with it, in a heavy shower, which fell down on the same day.

After this I went to church; and having never been at such a place before, I was again amazed at seeing and hearing the service. I asked all I could about it; and they gave me to understand it was "worshiping God, who made us and all things." I was still at a loss, and soon got into an endless field of inquiries as well as I was able to speak and ask about things. However, my dear little friend Dick used to be my best interpreter; for I could make free with him and he always instructed me with pleasure. And from what I could understand by him of this God, and in seeing that these white people did not sell one another as we did, I was much pleased: and in this I thought they were much happier than we Africans. I was astonished at the wisdom of the white people in all things which I beheld; but I was greatly amazed at their not sacrificing, nor making any offerings, and at their eating with unwashen hands, and touching the dead. I also could not help remarking the particular slenderness of their women, which I did not at first like, and I thought them not so modest and shamefaced as the African women.

I had often seen my master and Dick employed in reading; and I had a

great curiosity to talk to the books, as I thought they did; and so to learn how all things had a beginning. For that purpose I have often taken up a book, and talked to it, and then put my ears to it, when alone, in hopes it would answer me; and I have been very much concerned when I found it remained silent.

<div align="center">

V.

</div>

My master lodged at the house of a gentleman in Falmouth, who had a fine little daughter, about six or seven years of age, and she grew prodigiously fond of me; insomuch that we used to eat together, and had servants to wait on us. I was so much caressed by this family, that it often reminded me of the treatment I had received from my little noble African master. After I had been here a few days, I was sent on board of the ship; but the child cried so much after me, that nothing could pacify her till I was sent for again. It is ludicrous enough, that I began to fear I should be betrothed to this young lady; and when my master asked me if I would stay there with her behind him, as he was going away with the ship, having taken in the tobacco again, I cried immediately, and said I would not leave him. At last, by stealth, one night I was sent on board the ship again; and in a little time sailed for Guernsey, where she was in part owned by a merchant, one Nicholas Doberry.

As I was now amongst a people who had not their faces scarred, like some of the African nations where I had been, I was very glad at my not having permitted them to ornament me in that manner. When we arrived at Guernsey, my master placed me to board and lodge with one of his mates, who had a wife and family there; and some months afterwards he returned to England, and left me in care of this mate, together with my friend Dick. This mate had a little daughter, aged about five or six years, with her I used to be much delighted. I had often observed that when her mother washed her face it looked very rosy; but when she washed mine it did not look so: I therefore tried oftentimes myself if I could not by washing make my face of the same colour as my little playmate, Mary, but it was all in vain; and I then began to be mortified at the difference in our complexions. This woman behaved to me with great kindness and attention. She taught me every thing in the same manner as she did her own child, and indeed in every respect treated me as such. I remained here till the summer of the year 1757; when my master, being appointed first lieutenant of his majesty's ship the Roebuck, sent for Dick and me, and his old mate: on this we all left Guernsey, and set

out for England in a sloop bound for London. As we were coming up towards the Nore, where the Roebuck lay, a man of war's boat came alongside to press our people: on which each man ran to hide himself. I was very much frightened at this, though I did not understand the meaning thereof, or what to think or do. However I went and hid myself also under a hencoop. Immediately the press-gang came on board, with their swords drawn, and searched all about, pulled the people out by force, and put them into the boat. At last I was found out also, and the man that discovered me held me up by the heels, while they all made their sport of me, I roaring and crying out all the time most lustily; but at last the mate, my conductor, seeing this, came to my assistance, and did all he could to pacify me; but all to very little purpose, till I had seen the boat go off. Soon afterwards we came to the Nore, where the Roebuck lay; and, to our great joy, my master came on board to us, and brought us to the ship.

VI.

When I got on board this large ship, I was indeed amazed to see the quantity of men and the guns. However my surprise began to diminish, as my knowledge increased; and I ceased to feel those apprehensions and alarms which took such strong possession on me when I came first among the Europeans, and for some time after. I began now to pass to an opposite extreme; and was so far from being afraid of any thing new which I saw, that after I had been some time in this ship, I even began to long for an engagement. My griefs too, which in young minds are not perpetual, were now wearing away; and I soon enjoyed myself pretty well, and felt tolerably easy in my situation. There was a number of boys on board, and this made it still more agreeable; being constantly together, and spending a great part of our time in play.

I remained in this ship a considerable time, during which we made several cruises, and visited a variety of places: among others we were twice in Holland, and brought over several persons of distinction from it, but their names have escaped my memory. On the passage one day, for the diversion of those gentlemen, all the boys were called on the quarter-deck, and were paired proportionately, and then made to fight; after which the gentlemen gave the combatants from five to nine shillings each. This was the first time I ever fought with a white boy; and I never had a bloody nose before. This made me fight most desperately; I suppose considerably more than a hour,

and at last, both of us being tired, we were parted. I had a great deal of this kind of sport afterwards, in which the captain and the ship's company used very much to encourage me. Some time afterwards the ship went to Leith, in Scotland, and from thence to the Orkneys, where I was surprised at seeing scarcely any night; and from thence we sailed with a great fleet, full of soldiers, for England. All this time we had never come to an engagement, though frequently cruising off the coast of France, during which we chased many vessels, and took in all seventeen prizes. I had been learning many of the manœuvres of the ship during our cruise; and I was several times made to fire the guns.

One evening, off Havre de Grace, just as it was growing dark, we were standing off shore, and met with a fine large French-built frigate. We immediately got all things ready for fighting: and I now expected I should be gratified in seeing an engagement, which I had so long wished for in vain. But the very moment the word of command was given to fire, we heard those on board the other ship cry, 'Haul down the jib!' and in that instant she hoisted English colours. There was instantly with us an amazing cry of—'Avast!' or 'stop firing!' and I think one or two guns had been let off, but happily they did no mischief. We had hailed them several times; but they not hearing, we received no answer, and that caused us to fire. The boat was then sent on board of her, and she proved to be the Ambuscade man of war, to my no small disappointment.

We returned to Portsmouth, without having been in any action, just at the trial of Admiral Byng, whom I saw several times during it: and my master having left the ship, and gone to London for promotion, Dick and I were put on board the Savage sloop of war, to assist in bringing off the St. George man of war, that had run ashore somewhere on the coast. After staying a few weeks on board the Savage, Dick and I were sent on shore at Deal, and remained there till my master sent for us to London, the place I had long desired exceedingly to see. We therefore both with great pleasure got into a wagon and came to London, where we were received by a Mr. Guerin, a relation of my master. This gentleman had two sisters, very amiable ladies. They took much notice and great care of me.

VII.

Though I had desired so much to see London, when I arrived in it I was unfortunately unable to gratify my curiosity; for I had at this time the

chilblains to such a degree, that I could not stand for several months, and was obliged to be sent to St. George's hospital. There I grew so ill, that the doctors wanted to cut my leg off at different times, apprehending a mortification; but I always said I would rather die than suffer it: and, I thank God, I happily recovered without the operation. After being there several weeks, and just as I had recovered, the small pox broke out on me, so that I was again confined; and I thought myself now particularly unfortunate. However I soon recovered again; and by this time my master having been promoted to be first lieutenant of the Preston man of war, of fifty guns, then new at Deptford, Dick and I went on board her, and soon after sailed for Holland to bring over the late Duke of Cumberland to England.

While I was in this ship an incident happened, which, though trifling, I beg leave to relate, as I could not help taking particular notice of it, and considering it then as a judgment of God. One morning a young man was looking up to the fore-top, and in a wicked tone, common on shipboard, d—d his eyes about something. Just at the moment some small particles of dirt fell into his left eye, and by the evening it was very much inflamed. The next day it grew worse, and within six or seven days he lost it. From this ship my master was appointed a lieutenant on board the Royal George. When he was going he wished me to stay on board the Preston, to learn the French horn, but the ship being ordered for Turkey I could not think of leaving my master, to whom I was very warmly attached; and I told him if he left me behind, it would break my heart. This prevailed with him to take me with him, but he left Dick on board: whom I embraced at parting for the last time.

The Royal George was the largest ship I had ever seen, so that when I came on board of her I was surprised at the number of people, men, women, and children, of every denomination and description, and the largeness of the guns, many of them also of brass, which I had never seen before. Here were also shops or stalls for every kind of goods, and people crying their different commodities about the ship, as in a town. To me it appeared a little world, into which I was again cast without a friend, for I had no longer my dear companion Dick.

We did not stay long here. My master was not many weeks on board before he got an appointment to be sixth lieutenant of the Namur, then at Spithead, fitting up for Vice-admiral Boscawen, who was going, with a large fleet, on an expedition against Louisbourgh. The crew of the Royal George were turned over to her, and the flag of that gallant admiral was hoisted on board, the blue at the main-top-gallant-mast head. There was a very great

fleet of men of war of every description assembled together for this expedition, and I was in hopes soon to be gratified with a sea-fight. All things being now in readiness, this mighty fleet, for there was also Admiral Cormsh's fleet in company, destined for the East Indies, at last weighed anchor, and sailed. The two fleets continued in company for several days, and then parted; Admiral Cormsh, in the Lenox, having first saluted our admiral in the Namur, which he returned. We then steered for America; but, by contrary winds, were driven to Teneriffe, where I was struck with its noted peak. Its prodigious height and its form, resembling a sugar-loaf, filled me with wonder. We remained in sight of this island some days, and then proceeded for America, which we soon made, and got into a commodious harbour called St. George, in Halifax. Here we had fish in abundance, and all other fresh provisions. We were here joined by different men of war, and transport ships with soldiers; after which, our fleet being increased to a prodigious number of ships of all kinds, we sailed for Cape Breton in Nova Scotia. We had the good and gallant General Wolfe on board our ship, whose affability made him highly esteemed and beloved by all the men. He often honoured me, as well as other boys, with marks of his notice; and saved me once a flogging for fighting with a young gentleman.

VIII.

We arrived at Cape Breton in the summer of 1758: and here the soldiers were to be landed, in order to make an attack upon Louisbourgh. My master had some part in superintending the landing; and here I was in a small degree gratified in seeing an encounter between our men and the enemy. The French were posted on the shore to receive us, and disputed our landing for a long time: but at last they were driven from their trenches, and a complete landing was effected. Our troops pursued them as far as the town of Louisbourgh. In this action many were killed on both sides. One thing remarkable I saw this day:—A lieutenant of the Princess Amelia, who, as well as my master, superintended the landing, was giving the word of command, and while his mouth was open a musket ball went through it, and passed out at his cheek. I had that day in my hand the scalp of an Indian king, killed in the engagement: the scalp was taken off by an Highlander. I saw the king's ornaments too, which were very curious, and made of feathers.

Our land forces laid sedge to the town of Louisbourgh, while the French

men of war were blocked up in the harbour by the fleet, the batteries at the same time playing upon them from the land. This they did with such effect, that one day I saw some of the ships set on fire by the shells from the batteries, and I believe two or three of them were quite burnt. At another time, about fifty boats belonging to the English men of war, commanded by Captain George Belfour, of the Ætna fire-ship, and Mr. Laforey, another junior captain, attacked and boarded the only two remaining French men of war in the harbour. They also set fire to a seventy gun ship: but a sixty-four, called the Bienfaisant, they brought off. Whilst here I had often an opportunity of being near captain Belfour, who was pleased to notice me, and liked me so much that he often asked my master to let him have me, but he would not part with me; and no consideration could have induced me to leave him.

At last Louisbourgh was taken, and the English men of war came into the harbour before it, to my very great joy; for I had now liberty of indulging myself, and I went often on shore. When the ships were in harbour we had the most beautiful procession on the water I ever beheld. All the admirals and captains full dressed, and in their barges, ornamented with pendants, came alongside of the Namur. The vice-admiral then went on shore in his barge, followed by the other officers in order of seniority, to take possession of the town and fort. Some time after this the French governor, his lady, and other persons of note, came on board our ship to dine. On this occasion our ships were dressed with colours of all kinds, from the top-gallant-mast head to the deck; and this, with the firing of guns, formed a most grand and magnificent spectacle.

IX.

A s soon as every thing here was settled, Admiral Boscawen sailed with part of the fleet for England, leaving some ships behind with rear Admirals Sir Charles Hardy and Durell. It was now winter; and one evening, during our passage home, about dusk, being in the channel, or near soundings, and beginning to look for land, we described seven sail of large men of war standing off shore. Several people on board of our ship said, as the two fleets were, in forty minutes from the first sight, within hail of each other, that they were English men of war; and some of our people even began to name some of the ships. By this time both fleets began to mingle, and our admiral ordered his flag to be hoisted. At that instant the other fleet, which were French, hoisted their ensigns, and gave us a broadside as they passed. Nothing could create greater surprise and confusion among us than this: the

wind was high, the sea rough, and we had our lower and middle deck guns housed in, so that not a single gun on board was ready to be fired at any of the French ships. However, the Royal William and the Somerset, being our stern-most ships, became a little prepared; and each gave the French ships a broadside as they passed by.

I afterwards heard this was a French squadron, commanded by Mons. Conflans; and certainly had the Frenchmen known our condition, and had a mind to fight us, they might have done us great mischief. But we were not long before we were prepared for an engagement. Immediately many things were tossed overboard; the ships made ready for fighting, and about ten at night we had bent a new mainsail, the old one being split. We now wore ship, and stood after the French fleet, which were one or two ships more than we. However we gave them chase, and continued the pursuit all night; and at day-light we saw six of them, all large ships of the line, and an English East Indiaman, a prize they had taken. We chased them all day till between three and four o'clock in the evening, when we came up with, and passed within a musket shot of one seventy-four gun ship, and the Indiaman also, who now hoisted her colours, but immediately hauled them down again. On this we made a signal for the other ships to take possession of her; and, supposing the man of war would likewise strike, we cheered, but she did not; tho' if we had fired into her, from being so near, we must have taken her. To my utter surprise, the Somerset, who was the next ship a-stern of the Namur, made way likewise; and, thinking they were sure of this French ship, they cheered in the same manner, but still continued to follow us. The French Commodore was about a gun-shot a-head of all, running from us with all speed; and about four o'clock he carried his fore-topmast overboard. This caused another loud cheer with us; and a little after the top-mast came close by us; but, to our great surprise, instead of coming up with her, we found she went as fast as ever, if not faster.

The sea grew now much smoother; and the wind lulling, the seventy-four gun ship we had passed came again by us in the very same direction, and so near, that we heard the people talk as she passed by; yet not a shot was fired on either side; and about five or six o'clock, just as it grew dark, she joined her commodore. We chased all night; but the next day we were out of sight, so that we saw no more of them, and we only had the old Indiaman, called Carnarvon, I think, for our trouble. After this we stood in for the channel, and soon made the land; and, about the close of the year 1758-9, we got safe to St. Helen's. Here the Namur ran aground; and also another large ship a-

stern of us; but, by starting our water, and tossing many things overboard to lighten her, we got the ships off without any damage. We stayed for a short time at Spithead, and then went into Portsmouth harbour to refit, from whence the admiral went to London, and my master and I soon followed, with a pressgang, as we wanted some hands to complete our complement.

CHAPTER IV.

The author is baptized—Narrowly escapes drowning—Goes on an expedition to the Mediterranean—Incidents he met with there—Is witness of an engagement between some English and French ships—A particular account of the celebrated Engagement between Admiral Boscawen and Mons. Le Clue, off Cape Logas, in August 1759—Dreadful explosion or a French ship—The author sails for England—His master appointed to the command of a fire ship—Meets a negro boy, from whom he experiences much benevolence—Prepares for an expedition against Belleisle—A remarkable story of a disaster which befel his ship—Arrives at Belleisle—Operations of the landing and siege—The author's danger and distress, with his manner of extricating himself—Surrender of Belleisle— Transactions afterwards on the coast of France—Remarkable instance of kidnapping—The author returns to England—Hears a talk of peace, and expects his freedom—His ship sails for Deptford to be paid off and when he arrives there he is suddenly seized by his master, and carried forcibly on board a West-India ship, and sold.

I.

I T WAS now between two and three years since I first came to England, a great part of which I had spent at sea; so that I became mured to that service, and began to consider myself as happily situated; for my master treated me always extremely well; and my attachment and gratitude to him were very great. From the various scenes I had beheld on ship-board, I soon grew a stranger to terror of every kind, and was, in that respect at least, almost an Englishman. I have often reflected with surprise that I never felt half the alarm, at any of the numerous dangers in which I have been, that I was filled with at the first sight of the Europeans, and at every act of theirs, even the most trifling, when I first came among them, and for some time afterwards.

That fear, however, the effect of my ignorance, wore away as I began to know them.

I could now speak English tolerably well, and perfectly understood every thing that was said. I not only felt myself quite easy with these new countrymen, but relished their society and manners. I no longer looked upon them as spirits, but as men superior to us, and therefore I had the stronger desire to resemble them, to imbibe their spirit, and imitate their manners. I therefore embraced every occasion of improvement; and every new thing that I observed I treasured up in my memory. I had long wished to be able to read and write; and for this purpose I took every opportunity to gain instruction, but had made as yet but very little progress. However, when I went to London with my master, I had soon an opportunity of improving myself, which I gladly embraced. Shortly after my arrival, he sent me to wait upon the Miss Guerins, who had treated me with so much kindness when I was there before, and they sent me to school.

While I was attending these ladies, their servants told me I could not go to Heaven, unless I was baptized. This made me very uneasy; for I had now some faint idea of a future state: accordingly I communicated my anxiety to the eldest Miss Guerin, with whom I was become a favourite, and pressed her to have me baptized; when, to my great joy, she told me I should. She had formerly asked my master to let me be baptized, but he had refused; however er she now insisted on it; and he, being under some obligation to her brother, complied with her request; so I was baptized at St. Margaret's church, Westminster, in February 1759, by my present name. The clergyman, at the same time, gave me a book, called "a Guide to the Indians," written by the Bishop of Sodor and Man. On this occasion, Miss Guerin did me the honour to stand as godmother, and afterwards gave me a treat.

I used to attend these ladies about the town, in which service I was extremely happy, as I had thus very many opportunities of seeing London, which I desired of all things. I was sometimes, however, with my master at his rendezvous-house, at the foot of Westminster-bridge. Here I used to enjoy myself in playing about the bridge stairs, and often in the watermen's wherries, with other boys. On one of these occasions there was another boy with me in a wherry, and we went out into the current of the river; while there, two more stout boys came to us in another wherry, and, abusing us for taking the boat, desired me to get into the other wherry-boat. Accordingly I went to get out of the wherry I was in, but just as I had got one of my feet into the other boat, the boys shoved it off, so that I fell into the Thames, and

not being able to swim, I should unavoidably have been drowned, but for the assistance of some watermen, who providentially came to my relief.

II.

The Namur being again got ready for sea, my master, with his gang, was ordered on board; and, to my no small grief, I was obliged to leave my school-master, whom I liked very much and always attended while I stayed in London, to repair on board with my master. Nor did I leave my kind patronesses, the Miss Guerins, without uneasiness and regret. They often used to teach me to read, and took great pains to instruct me in the principles of religion and the knowledge of God. I therefore parted from those amiable ladies with reluctance; after receiving from them many friendly cautions how to conduct myself, and some valuable presents.

When I came to Spithead, I found we were destined for the Mediterranean, with a large fleet ready to put to sea. We only waited for the arrival of the admiral, who soon came on board; and about the beginning of the spring, 1759, we sailed; and in eleven days from the Land's End, got to Gibraltar. While we were here I used to be often on shore, and got various fruits in great plenty, and very cheap.

I had frequently told several people, in my excursions on shore, the story of my being kidnapped with my sister, and of our being separated, as before related; and I had as often expressed my anxiety for her fate, and my sorrow at having never met her again. One day, when I was on shore, and mentioning these circumstances to some persons, one of them told me he knew where my sister was, and if I would accompany him, he would conduct me to her. Improbable as this story was, I believed it immediately, and agreed to go with him, while my heart leaped for joy; and, indeed, he conducted me to a black young woman, who was so like my sister that, at first sight, I really thought it was she; but I was quickly undeceived; and, on talking to her, I found her to be of another nation.

While laying here the Preston came in from the Levant. As soon as she arrived, my master told me I should now see my old companion Dick, who was gone in her when she sailed for Turkey. I was much rejoiced at this information, and expected every minute to embrace him; and when the captain came on board, of our ship, which he did immediately after, I ran to inquire about my friend; but with inexpressible sorrow, I learned from the boat's crew that the dear youth was dead, and that they had brought his chest, and

all his other things to my master: these he afterwards gave to me, and I regarded them as a memorial of my friend, whom I loved and grieved for as a brother.

While we were at Gibraltar I saw a soldier hanging by the heels at one of the moles:* I thought this a strange sight, as I had seen a man hanged in London by his neck. At another time I saw the master of a frigate towed to shore on a grating, by several of the men of war's boats, and discharged the fleet, which I understand was a mark of disgrace for cowardice. On board the same ship a sailor was also hung up at the yard-arm.

III.

After lying at Gibraltar for some time, we sailed up the Mediterranean, a considerable way above the Gulph of Lyons, where we were one night overtaken by a terrible gale of wind, much greater than any I had yet experienced. The sea ran so high that, though all the guns were well housed, there was great reason to fear their getting loose, the ship rolled so much; and if they had, it must have proved our destruction. After cruising here for a short time, we came to Barcelona, a Spanish sea-port, remarkable for its silk manufacturers. Here the ships were all to be watered; and my master, who spoke different languages, and used often to interpret for the admiral, superintended the watering of ours. For that purpose he, and the officers of the other ships who were on the same service, had tents pitched in the bay; and the Spanish soldiers were stationed along the shore,—I suppose to see that no depredations were committed by our men.

I constantly attended my master, and was charmed with this place. All the time of our stay it was like a fair with the natives, who brought us fruits of all kinds, and sold them to us much cheaper than I had got them in England. They used also to bring wine down to us in hog and sheep-skins, to my great diversion. The Spanish officers here treated our officers with great politeness and attention; and some of them, in particular, used to come often to my master's tent to visit him; where they did sometimes divert themselves by mounting me on the horses or mules, so that I could not fall, and setting them off at full gallop, my imperfect skill in horsemanship affording them no small entertainment. After the ships were watered, we returned to our old station of cruising off Toulon, for the purpose of intercepting a fleet of French men of war that lay there. One Sunday in our cruise, we came off a

*He had drowned himself in endeavouring to desert.

place where there were two small French frigates lying in shore; and our admiral thinking to take or destroy them, sent two ships in after them—the Culloden and the Conqueror. They soon came up to the Frenchmen; and I saw a smart fight here, both by sea and land: for the frigates were covered by batteries, and they played upon our ships most furiously, which they as furiously returned, and for a long time a constant firing was kept up, on all sides, at an amazing rate. At last one frigate sunk, but the people escaped, though not without much difficulty: and a little after some of the people left the other frigate also, which was a mere wreck. However, our ships did not venture to bring her away, they were so much annoyed from the batteries, which raked them both in going and coming; their top-masts were shot away, and they were otherwise so much shattered, that the admiral was obliged to send in many boats to tow them back to the fleet. I afterwards sailed with a man who fought in one of the French batteries during the engagement, and he told me our ships had done considerable mischief that day on shore and in the batteries.

IV.

After this we sailed for Gibraltar, and arrived there about August, 1759. We remained here with all our sails unbent, while the fleet was watering and doing other necessary things. While we were in this situation, one day the admiral, together with most of the principal officers, and many people of all stations, being on shore, about seven o'clock in the evening we were alarmed by signals from the frigates stationed for that purpose, and in an instant there was a general cry that the French fleet was out, and just passing through the straights. The admiral immediately came on board with some other officers; and it is impossible to describe the noise, hurry, and confusion, throughout the fleet, in bending their sails and slipping their cables; many people and ship's boats were left on shore in the bustle. We had two captains on board of our ship, who came away in the hurry and left their ships to follow. We shewed lights from the gunwales to the main-top-masthead; and all our lieutenants were employed amongst the fleet to tell the ships not to wait for their captains, but to put the sails to the yards, slip their cables, and follow us; and, in this confusion of making ready for fighting, we set out for sea in the dark after the French fleet. Here I could have exclaimed with Ajax,

> O Jove! O father! if it be thy will
> That we must perish, we thy will obey,
> But let us perish by the light of day.

They had got the start of us so far that we were not able to come up with them that night; but at day-light we saw seven sail of the line some miles ahead. We immediately chased them till four o'clock in the evening, our ships then came up with them; and though we were about fifteen large ships, our gallant admiral only fought them with his own division, consisting of seven, so that we were just ship for ship. We passed by the whole of the enemy's fleet in order to come at their commander, Mon. Le Clue, who was in the Ocean, an eighty-four gun ship. As we passed they all fired at us; and at one time three of them fired together, continuing to do so for some time. Notwithstanding which our admiral, to my astonishment, would not suffer a gun to be fired at any of them, but made us lie on our bellies on the deck till we came quite close to the Ocean, which was ahead of them all, when we had orders to pour the whole three tiers into her at once.

The engagement now commenced with great fury on both sides: the Ocean immediately returned our fire, and we continued engaged with each other for some time; during which I was frequently stunned with the thundering of the great guns, whose dreadful contents burned many of my companions into eternity. At last the French line was entirely broken, and we obtained the victory, which was immediately proclaimed with loud huzzas and acclamations. We took three prizes, La Modeste, of sixty-four guns, and Le Temeraire and Centaur, of seventy-four guns each. The rest of the French ships took to flight, with all the sail they could crowd. Our ship being very much damaged, and quite disabled from pursuing the enemy, the admiral immediately quitted her, and went in a broken boat, the only one we had left, on board the Newark, with which, and some other ships, he went after the French. The Ocean, and another large French ship, called the Redoubtable, endeavouring to escape, ran ashore at Cape Logas, on the coast of Portugal, and the French admiral and some of the crew got ashore; but we, finding it impossible to get the ships off, set fire to them both. About midnight I saw the Ocean blew up with a most dreadful explosion. I never beheld a more awful scene. About the space of a minute, the midnight seemed turned into day by the blaze, attended with a noise louder and more terrible than thunder, that seemed to rend every element around us.

My station during the engagement was on the middle deck, where I was

quartered with another boy, to bring powder to the aftermost Gun. And here I was witness to the dreadful fate of many of my companions, who, in the twinkling of an eye, were dashed to pieces, and launched into eternity. Happily I escaped unhurt, though the shot and splinters flew thick about me during the night. Towards the latter part of it my master was wounded, and I saw him carried down to the surgeon; but though I was much alarmed for him, and longed to assist him, I durst not quit my post.

At this station my gun-mate* and I ran a very great risk, for more than half an hour, of blowing up the ship. For when we had taken the cartridges out of the boxes, the bottoms of many of them proving rotten, the powder ran all about the deck, near the match tub: we scarcely had water enough at the last to throw on it. We were also, from our employment, very much exposed to the enemy's shots; for we had to go through nearly the whole length of the ship to bring the powder. I expected therefore every minute to be my last; especially when I saw our men fall so thick about me. But, wishing to guard as much against the dangers as possible, at first I thought it would be the safest not to go for the powder till the Frenchmen had fired their broadside; and then, while they were charging, I could go and come with my powder. But immediately afterwards I thought this caution was fruitless; and, cheering myself with the reflection that there was a time allotted for me to die as well as to be born, I instantly cast off all fear or thought whatever of death, and went through the whole of my duty with alacrity; pleasing myself with the hope, if I survived the battle, of relating it and the dangers I had escaped, to the Miss Guerins, and others, when I should return to London.

V.

O ur ship suffered very much in this engagement; for, besides the number of our killed and wounded, she was almost torn to pieces, and our rigging so much shattered, that our mizen-mast, main-yard, &c. hung over the side of the ship; so that we were obliged to get many carpenters and others, from some of the ships of the fleet, to assist in setting us in some tolerable order. Notwithstanding which, it took us some time before we were completely refitted; after which we left Admiral Broderick to command, and we, with the prizes, steered for England.

On the passage, and as soon as my master recovered of his wounds, the admiral appointed him captain of the Ætna fire-ship, on which he and I left

*A Partner in bringing powder to the same gun.

the Namur, and went on board of her at sea. I liked this small ship very much. I now became the captain's steward, in which situation I was very happy: for I was extremely well treated by all on board; and had leisure to improve myself in reading and writing. Of the latter I had learned a little before I left the Namur, there being a school on board. When we arrived at Spithead, the Ætna went into Portsmouth harbour to refit, which being done, we returned to Spithead, and joined a large fleet that was thought to be intended against Havannah. But about that time the king died; whether that prevented the expedition I know not; but it caused our ship to be stationed at Cowes, in the isle of Wight, till the beginning of the year 1761. Here I spent my time very pleasantly: I was much on shore all about this delightful island, and found the inhabitants very civil.

While I was here, I met with a trifling incident, which surprised me agreeably. I was one day in a field belonging to a gentleman, who had a black boy about my own size, this boy having observed me from his master's house, was transported at the sight of one of his own countrymen, and ran to meet me with the utmost haste. I, not knowing what he was about, turned a little out of his way at first, but to no purpose: he soon came close to me, and caught me in his arms as if I had been his brother, though we had never seen each other before. After we had talked together for some time, he took me to his master's house, where I was treated very kindly. This benevolent boy and I were very happy in frequently seeing each other, till about the month of March 1761, when our ship had orders to fit out again for another expedition. When we got ready, we joined a very large fleet at Spithead, commanded by Commodore Keppel, destined against Belleisle; and having a number of transport ships in company, with troops on board, to make a descent on the place, we sailed once more in quest of fame. I longed to engage in new adventures, and to see fresh wonders.

I had a mind, on which every thing uncommon, and every thing which I considered marvellous, made their full impression. Every extraordinary escape, or signal deliverance, either of myself or others, I looked upon to be effected by the interposition of Providence. We had not been above ten days at sea before an incident of this kind happened, which, whatever credit it may obtain from the reader, made no small impression upon my mind.

VI.

We had on board a gunner, whose name was John Mondle, a man of very indifferent morals. This man's cabin was between the decks, exactly over where I lay, a-breast of the quarter-deck ladder. One night, the 5th of April, being terrified in a dream, he awoke in so great a fright that he could not rest in his bed any longer, nor even remain in his cabin; and he went upon deck about four o'clock in the morning extremely agitated. He immediately told those upon the deck of the agonies of his mind, and the dream which occasioned them: in which he said he had seen many things very awful, and had been warned by St. Peter to repent, who told him time was short. This he said had greatly alarmed him, and he was determined to alter his life. People generally mock the fears of others when they are themselves in safety; and some of his shipmates, who heard him, only laughed at him. However, he made a vow that he never would drink strong liquors again; and he immediately got a light, and gave away his sea-store of liquor. After which his agitation still continuing, he began to read the Scriptures, hoping to find some relief; and soon afterwards he laid himself down again on his bed, and endeavoured to compose himself to sleep, but to no purpose; his mind still continuing in a state of agony. By this time it was exactly half after seven in the morning: I was then under the half deck at the great cabin door; and all at once I heard the people in the waist cry out most fearfully—"The Lord have mercy upon us! We are all lost! The Lord have mercy upon us!"—Mr. Mondle, hearing the cries, immediately ran out of his cabin; and we were instantly struck by the Lynne, a forty gun ship, Captain Clark, which nearly ran us down. This ship had just put about and was by the wind, but had not got full head way, or we must all have perished: for the wind was brisk. However, before Mr. Mondle had got four steps from his cabin door, she struck our ship, and her cutwater right in the middle of his bed and cabin, and ran it up to the combings of the quarter-deck-hatchway, and above three feet below water, and in a minute there was not a bit of wood to be seen where Mr. Mondle's cabin stood, and he was so near being killed that some of the splinters tore his face. As Mr. Mondle must inevitably have perished from this accident, had he not been alarmed in the very extraordinary way I have related, I could not help regarding this as an awful interposition of Providence for his preservation.

The two ships for some time swinged alongside of each other; for ours

being a fire-ship, our grappling-irons caught the Lynne every way, and the yards and rigging went at an astonishing rate. Our ship was in such a shocking condition that we all thought she would instantly go down, and every one ran for their lives, and got as well as they could on board the Lynne; but our lieutenant being the aggressor, he never quitted the ship. However, on finding she did not sink immediately the captain came on board again, and encouraged our people to return and try to save her. Many of them came back, but some would not venture. Some of the ships in the fleet, seeing our situation, immediately sent their boats to our assistance; but it took us the whole day to save the ship with all their help. And by using every possible means, particularly frapping* her together with many hawsers, and putting a great quantity of tallow below water where she was damaged, she was kept together but had we met with any gale of wind she must have gone to pieces, being in such a crazy condition that we had ships to attend us till we arrived at Belleisle, the place of our destination; and then we had all things taken out of the ship, and she was properly repaired. This escape of Mr. Mondle, which he, as well as myself, always considered as a singular act of Providence, I believe had a great influence on his life and conduct ever afterwards.

Now that I am on this subject, I beg leave to relate another instance or two which strongly raised my belief of the particular interposition of Heaven, and which might not otherwise have found a place here, from their insignificance. I belonged for a few days, in the year 1758, to the Jason, of fifty-four guns, at Plymouth. One night, when I was on board, a woman, with a child at her breast, fell from the upper-deck down into the hold, near the keel. Every one thought that the mother and child must be both dashed to pieces; but, to our great surprise, neither of them was hurt. I myself one day fell headlong from the upper-deck of the Ætna down the after-hold, when the ballast was out; and all who saw me fall called out I was killed; but I received not the least injury. And in the same ship a man fell from the mast-head on the deck without being hurt. In these, and in many more instances, I thought I could very plainly trace the hand of God; without whose permission a sparrow cannot fall. I began to raise my fear from man to Him alone, and to call daily on his holy name, with fear and reverence: and I trust He heard my supplications, and graciously condescended to answer me according to his holy word; and to implant the seeds of piety in me, even one of the meanest of his creatures.

*Giving a brace or tightening to the tackle, by a complication of ropes.

VII.

When we had refitted our ship, and all things were in readiness for attacking the place, the troops were in readiness for attacking the place, the troops on board the transports were ordered to disembark; and my master, as a junior captain, had a share in the command of the landing. This was on the 12th of April. The French were drawn up on the shore, and had made every disposition to oppose the landing of our men, only a small part of them this day being able to effect it; most of them, after fighting with great bravery, were cut off, and General Crawford, with a number of others, taken prisoners. In this day's engagement we had also our lieutenant killed.

On the 21st of April we renewed our efforts to land the men, all the men of war being stationed along the shore to cover it, and fired at the French batteries and breastworks from early in the morning till about four o'clock in the evening, when our soldiers effected a safe landing. They immediately attacked the French, and, after a sharp encounter, forced them from the batteries. Before the enemy retreated they blew up several of them, lest they should fall into our hands. Our men then proceeded to besiege the citadel, and my master was ordered on shore to superintend the landing of all the materials necessary for carrying on the siege; in this service I mostly attended him. While I was there I visited different parts of the island; and one day, particularly, my curiosity almost cost me my life. I wanted very much to see the mode of charging the mortars and letting off the shells; and for that purpose I went to an English battery, but very few yards from the walls of the citadel. There, indeed, I had an opportunity of completely gratifying myself in seeing the whole operation; but not without running a very great risk, both from the English shells that burst while I was there, and likewise from those of the French. One of the largest of their shells burst within nine or ten yards of me: there was a single rock close by, about the size of a butt; and I got instant shelter under it in time to avoid the fury of the shell. Where it burst the earth was torn in such a manner that two or three butts might easily have gone into the hole it made, and it threw great quantities of stones and dirt to a considerable distance. Three shots were also fired at me and another boy who was along with me; one of them in particular seemed

Wing'd with red lightning and impetuous rage;

for, with a most dreadful sound, it hissed close by me, and struck a rock at a little distance, which it shattered to pieces. When I saw in what perilous circumstances I was, I attempted to return the nearest way I could find and thereby I got between the English and the French centinels. An English sergeant, who commanded the out-posts, seeing me, and surprised how I came there (which was by stealth along the sea-shore), reprimanded me severely for it, and instantly took the centinel off his post into custody, for his negligence in suffering me to pass the lines.

While I was in this situation I observed, at a little distance, a French horse, belonging to some islanders, and I determined to mount him for the greater expedition in getting off. Accordingly I took some cord, which I had about me, and making a kind of bridle, I put it round the horse's head, and the tame beast very quietly suffered me to tie him thus and mount him. As soon as I was on his back, I began to kick and beat him, and try every means to make him move quickly, but all to very little purpose: I could not drive him out of a slow pace. While I was creeping along, still within reach of the enemy's shot, I met a servant well mounted on an English horse. I immediately stopped; and, crying told him my case, and begged of him to help me, and this he effectually did; for, having a fine large whip, he began to lash my horse so severely, that he set off full speed with me towards the sea, while I was quite unable to hold or manage him. In this manner I went along till I came to a craggy precipice. I could not stop my horse; and my mind was filled with apprehensions of my deplorable fate should he go down the precipice, which he appeared fully disposed to do: I therefore thought I had better throw myself off him at once, which I did immediately with great dexterity, and fortunately escaped unhurt. As soon as I found myself at liberty I made the best of my way to the ship, determined not to be so fool-hardy in future.

VIII.

We continued to besiege the citadel till June, when it surrendered. During the siege I have counted above sixty shells and carcases in the air at once. When this place was taken I went through the citadel, and into the bomb-proofs under it, cut in the solid rock; and I thought it a surprising place, both for strength and building; notwithstanding, our shots and shells had made amazing devastation, and ruinous heaps all around it.

After the taking of this Island, our ships with some others, commanded by Commodore Stanhope, in the Swiftsure, went to Basse-road, where we

blocked up a French fleet. Our ships were there from June till February following; and in that time I saw great many scenes of war, and stratagems, on both sides, to destroy each other's fleet. Sometimes we would attack the French with some ships of the line; at other times with boats; and frequently we made prizes. Once or twice the French attacked us, by throwing shells with their bomb-vessels; one day as a French vessel was throwing shells at our ships, she broke from her springs, behind the isle of I de Re: the tide being complicated, she came within a gunshot of the Nassau; but the Nassau could not bring a gun to bear upon her, and thereby the Frenchman got off. We were twice attacked by their fire-floats, which they chained together, and then let them float down with the tide; but each time we sent boats with grapplings, and towed them safe out of the fleet.

We had different commanders at this place: Commodores Stanhope, Dennis, Lord Howe, &c. From hence, before the Spanish war began, our ship and the Wasp sloop were sent to St. Sebastian, in Spain, by Commodore Stanhope; and Commodore Dennis afterwards sent us as a cartel to Bayonne, in France,* after which** we went, in February 1762, to Belleisle, and there stayed till the summer, when we left it, and returned to Portsmouth.

After our ship was fitted out again for service, in September she went to Guernsey, where I was very glad to see my old hostess, now a widow, and my former little charming companion, her daughter. I spent some time here very happily with them till October, when we had orders to repair to Portsmouth. We parted from each other with a great deal of affection, and I promised to return soon, and see them again; not knowing what all powerful fate had determined for me.

Our ship having arrived at Portsmouth, we went into the harbour and remained there till the end of November, when we heard great talk about a peace; and, to our very great joy, in the beginning of December, we had

*Among others, whom we brought from Bayonne, were two gentlemen, who had been in the West-Indies, where they sold slaves; and they confessed they had made, at one time, a false bill of sale, and sold two Portuguese white men among a lot of slaves.

**Some people have it, that sometimes shortly before persons die, their ward has been seen:—that is, some spirit exactly in their likeness, though they are themselves at other places at the same time. One day while we were at Bayonne, Mr. Mondle saw one of our men, as he thought, in the gun-room; and, a little after, coming on the quarter-deck, he spoke of the circumstance of this man, to some of the officers. They told him that the man was then out of the ship, in one of the boats with the Lieutenant; but Mr. Mondle would not believe it and we searched the ship, when we found that the man was actually out of her; and when the boat resumed some time afterwards, we found the man had been drowned at the very time Mr. Mondle thought he saw him.

orders to go up to London with our ship, to be paid off. We received this news with loud huzzas, and every other demonstration of gladness: and nothing but mirth was to be seen through every part of the ship. I too was not without my share of the general joy on this occasion. I thought now of nothing but being freed, and working for myself, and thereby getting money to enable me to get a good education. For I always had a great desire to be able at least to read and write, and while I was on shipboard I had endeavoured to improve myself in both. While in the Ætna, particularly, the captains' clerk taught me to write, and gave me a smattering of arithmetic, as far as the Rule of Three.

There was also one Daniel Queen, about forty years of age, a man very well educated, who messed with me on board this ship, and he likewise dressed and attended the captain. Fortunately this man soon became very much attached to me, and took great pains to instruct me in many things. He taught me to shave, and dress hair a little, and also to read in the Bible, explaining many passages to me, which I did not comprehend. I was wonderfully surprised to see the laws and rules of my own country written almost exactly here; a circumstance which, I believe, tended to impress our manners and customs more deeply on my memory. I used to tell him of this resemblance; and many a time we have sat up the whole night together at this employment. In short, he was like a father to me; and some used even to call me after his name: they also styled me "the black Christian." Indeed I almost loved him with the affection of a son. Many things I have denied myself, that he might have them; and when I used to play at marbles or any other game, and won a few halfpence, or got some money for shaving any one, I used to buy him a little sugar or tobacco, as far as my stock of money would go. He used to say that he and I never should part, and that when our ship was paid off, as I was as free as himself or any other man on board, he would instruct me in his business, by which I might gain a good livelihood. This gave me new life and spirits; and my heart burned within me, while I thought the time long till I obtained my freedom. For though my master had not promised it to me, yet, besides the assurances I had often received that he had no right to detain me, he always treated me with the greatest kindness, and reposed in me an unbounded confidence. He even paid attention to my morals; and would never suffer me to deceive him, or tell lies, of which he used to tell me the consequences; and that if I did so, God would not love me. So that from all this tenderness I had never once supposed, in all my dreams of freedom, that he would think of detaining me any longer than I wished.

IX.

In pursuance of our orders we sailed from Portsmouth for the Thames, and arrived at Deptford the 10th of December, where we cast anchor just as it was high water. The ship was up about half an hour, when my master ordered the barge to be manned; and, all in an instant, without having before given me the least reason to suspect any thing of the matter, he forced me into the barge, saying, I was going to leave him, but he would take care that I did not. I was so struck with the unexpectedness of this proceeding, that for some time I did not make a reply; only I made an offer to go for my books and chest of clothes, but he swore I should not move out of his sight; and if I did, he would cut my throat, at the same time taking out his hanger. I began, however, to collect myself; and, plucking up courage, I told him that I was free, and he could not by law serve me so. But this only enraged him the more; and he continued to swear, and said he would soon let me know whether he would or not; and at that instant sprung himself into the barge, from the ship, to the astonishment and sorrow of all on board.

The tide, rather unluckily for me, had just turned downward, so that we quickly fell down the river along with it, till we came among some outward-bound West Indiamen; for he was resolved to put me on board the first vessel he could get to receive me. The boat's crew, who pulled against their will, became quite faint at different times, and would have gone ashore, but he would not let them. Some of them strove then to cheer me, and told me he could not sell me, and that they would stand by me, which revived me a little, and I still entertained hopes; for as they pulled me along he asked some vessels to receive me, and they refused.

But, just as we had got a little below Gravesend, we came alongside of a ship going away the next tide for the West-Indies; her name was the Charming Sally, Captain James Doran. My master went on board and agreed with him for me; and in little time I was sent for into the cabin. When I came there Captain Doran asked me if I knew him: I answered I did not; 'Then,' said he, 'You are now my slave.' I told him my master could not sell me to him nor to any one else. 'Why,' said he, 'did not your master buy you?' I confessed he did. 'But I have served him,' said I, 'many years, and he has taken all my wages and prize-money, for I only got one sixpence during the war. Besides this I have been baptized; and, by the laws of the land, no man has a right to sell me:' And I added, that I had heard a lawyer, and others, at different times tell my master so. They both then said, that those people who

told me so, were not my friends: but I replied-it was very extraordinary that the other people did not know the law as well as they. Upon this, Captain Doran said I talked too much English, and if I did not behave myself well and be quiet, he had a method on board to make me. I was too well convinced of his power over me to doubt what he said; and my former sufferings in the slave-ship presenting themselves to my mind, the recollection of them made me shudder. However, before I retired I told them, that as I could not get any right among men here, I hoped I should hereafter in Heaven, and I immediately left the cabin, filled with resentment and sorrow.

The only coat I had with me my master took away with him, and said, 'If your prize-money had been £10,000, I had a right to it all, and would have taken it.' I had about nine guineas, which, during my long sea-faring life, I had scraped together from trifling perquisites and little ventures; and I hid it that instant, lest my master should take that from me likewise, still hoping that, by some means or other, I should make my escape to the shore. Indeed some of my old shipmates told me not to despair, for they would get me back again; and that, as soon as they could get their pay, they would immediately come to Portsmouth to me where this ship was going. But, alas! all my hopes were baffled, and the hour of my deliverance was, as yet, far off. My master, having soon concluded his bargain with the captain, came out of the cabin, and he and his people got into the boat and put off. I followed them with aching eyes as long as I could, and when they were out of sight I threw myself on the deck, with a heart ready to burst with sorrow and anguish.

CHAPTER V.

The author's reflections on his situation—Is deceived by a promise of being delivered—His despair at sailing for the West-Indies—Arrives at Montserrat, where he is sold to Mr. King—Various interesting instances of oppression, cruelty, and extortion, which the author saw practiced upon the slaves in the West-Indies during his captivity, from the year 1763 to 1766—Address on it to the Planters.

I.

THUS, AT the moment I expected all my toils to end, was I plunged, as I supposed, in a new slavery; in comparison of which all my service

hitherto had been perfect freedom; and whose horrors, always present to my mind, now rushed on it with tenfold aggravation. I wept very bitterly for some time; and began to think that I must have done something to displease the Lord, that he thus punished me so severely. This filled me with painful reflections on my past conduct. I recollected that, on the morning of our arrival at Deptford, I had very rashly sworn that as soon as we reached London, I would spend the day in rambling and sport. My conscience smote me for this unguarded expression: I felt that the Lord was able to disappoint me in all things, and immediately considered my present situation as a judgment of Heaven, on account of my presumption in swearing. I therefore, with contrition of heart, acknowledged my transgression to God, and poured out my soul before Him with unfeigned repentance, and with earnest supplications I besought Him not to abandon me in my distress, nor cast me from his mercy for ever. In a little time my grief, spent with its own violence, began to subside; and after the first confusion of my thoughts was over, I reflected with more calmness on my present condition. I considered that trials and disappointments are sometimes for our good; and I thought God might perhaps have permitted this, in order to teach me wisdom and resignation. For he had hitherto shadowed me with the wings of his mercy and by his invisible, but powerful hand, had brought me the way I knew not. These reflections gave me a little comfort, and I arose at last from the deck with dejection and sorrow in my countenance, yet mixed with some faint hope that the Lord would appear for my deliverance.

II.

S oon afterwards, as my new master was going on shore, he called me to him, and told me to behave myself well, and do the business of the ship the same as any of the rest of the boys, and that I should fare the better for it; but I made him no answer. I was then asked if I could swim, and I said, "No." However, I was made to go under the deck, and was carefully watched. The next tide the ship got under way, and soon arrived at the Mother Bank, Portsmouth; where she waited few days for some of the West-India convoy. While here I tried every means I could devise amongst the people of the ship to get me a boat from the shore, as there was none suffered to come alongside of the ship; and their own, whenever it was used, was hoisted in again immediately. A sailor on board took a guinea from me, on presence of getting me a boat; and promised me, time after time, that it was hourly to come

off. When he had the watch upon deck I watched also, and looked long enough, but all in vain; I could never see either the boat or my guinea again. And, what I thought was still the worst of all, the fellow gave information, as I afterwards found, all the while to the mates of my intention to go off if possible; but, rogue-like, he never told them he had got a guinea from me to procure my escape. However, after we had sailed, and his trick was made known to the ship's crew, I had some satisfaction in seeing him detested and despised by them all for his behaviour to me.

I was still in hopes that my old shipmates would not forget their promise to come for me to Portsmouth; and, indeed, at last, but not till the day before we sailed, some of them did come there, and sent me off some oranges, and other tokens of their regard. They also sent me word they would come off to me themselves the next day, or the day after: and a lady also who lived in Gosport, wrote to me that she would come and take me out of the ship at the same time. This lady had been once very intimate with my former master. I used to sell and take care of a great deal of property for her, in different ships; and in return she always shewed great friendship for me, and used to tell my master she would take me away to live with her. But, unfortunately for me, a disagreement soon afterwards took place between them; and she was succeeded in my master's good graces by another lady, who appeared sole mistress of the Ætna, and mostly lodged on board. I was not so great a favourite with this lady as with the former; she had conceived a pique against me, on some occasion when she was on board, and she did not fail to instigate my master to treat me in the manner he did.*

III.

However, the next morning, the 30th of December, the wind being brisk and easterly, the Æolus frigate, which was to escort the convoy made a signal for sailing. All the ships then got up their anchors; and before any of my friends had an opportunity to come off to my relief, to my inexpressible anguish, our ship had got under way. What tumultuous emotions agitated my soul when the convoy got under sail, and I a prisoner on board, now

*Thus was I sacrificed to the envy and resentment of this woman, for knowing that the other lady designed to tale me into her service; which, had I got once on shore, she would not have been able to prevent. She felt her pride alarmed at the superiority of her rival in being attended by a black servant: it was not less to prevent this, than to be revenged on me, that she caused the captain to treat me thus cruelly.

without hope! I kept my swimming eyes upon the land in a state of unutterable grief; not knowing what to do, and despairing how to help myself. While my mind was in this situation, the fleet sailed on, and in one day's time I lost sight of the wished-for land. In the first expressions of my grief, I reproached my fate, and wished I had never been born. I was ready to curse the tide that bore us; the gale that wafted my prison, and even the ship that conducted us; and, in the despair of the moment, I called on death to relieve me from the horrors I felt and dreaded, that I might be in that place.

> Where slaves are free, and men oppress no more.
> Fool that I was, inur'd so long to pain,
> To trust to hope, or dream of joy again!
> * * * * * * * * * *
> Now dragg'd once more beyond the western main,
> To groan beneath some dastard planter's chain;
> Where my poor countrymen in bondage wait
> The long enfranchisement of ling'ring fate:
> Hard ling'ring fate! while, ere the dawn of day,
> Rous'd by the lash they go their cheerless way;
> And as their souls with shame and anguish burn,
> Salute with groans unwelcome morns return
> And, chiding ev'ry hour the slow-pac'd sun,
> Pursue their toils till all his race is run.
> No eye to mark their suff'rings with a tear;
> No friend to comfort, and no hope to cheer
> Then, like the dull unpity'd brutes, repair
> To stalls as wretched, and as coarse a fare;
> Thank heaven one day of mis'ry was o'er,
> Then sink to sleep, and wish to wake no more.*

The turbulence of my emotions, however, naturally gave way to calmer thoughts, and I soon perceived what fate had decreed no mortal on earth

*"The Dying Negro," a poem originally published in 1773. Perhaps it may not be deemed impertinent here to add, that this elegant and pathetic little poem, was occasioned by the following incident, as appears from the advertisement prefixed to it:—'A black who, a few days before, had run away from his master, and got himself christened, with intent to marry a white woman, his fellow-servant, being taken and sent on board a ship in the Thames, took an opportunity of shooting himself through the head.'

could prevent. The convoy sailed on without any accident, with a pleasant gale and smooth sea, for six weeks, till February, when one morning the Æolus ran down a brig, one of the convoy, and she instantly went down and was engulfed in the dark recess of the ocean. The convoy was immediately thrown into great confusion till it was daylight; and the Æolus illuminated with lights to prevent farther mischief. On the 13th of February 1763, from the mast-head, we descried our destined island, Montserrat, and soon after I beheld those

> Regions of sorrow, doleful shades, where peace
> And rest can rarely dwell. Hope never comes
> That comes to all, but torture without end
> Still urges.

At the sight of this land of bondage, a fresh horror ran through all my frame, and chilled me to the heart. My former slavery now rose in dreadful review to my mind, and displayed nothing but misery, stripes, and chains; and in the first paroxysm of my grief, I called upon God's thunder, and his avenging power, to direct the stroke of death to me, rather than permit me to become a slave, and to be sold from lord to lord.

In this state of my mind our ship came to an anchor, and soon after discharged her cargo. I now knew what it was to work hard; I was made to help to unload the ship. And to comfort me in my distress, at that time two of the sailors robbed me of all my money, and ran away from the ship. I had been so long used to an European climate, that at first I felt the scorching West-India sun very painful, while the dashing surf would toss the boat and the people in it, frequently above high-watermark. Sometimes our limbs were broken with this, or even attended with instant death, and I was day by day mangled and torn.

IV.

About the middle of May, when the ship was got ready to sail for England, I all the time believing that fate's blackest clouds were gathering over my head, and expecting that their bursting would mix me with the dead, Captain Doran sent for me on shore one morning; and I was told by the messenger that my fate was determined. With trembling steps and a fluttering heart I came to the captain, and found with him one Mr. Robert King,

a quaker, and the first merchant in the place. The captain then told me my former master had sent me there to be sold; but that he had desired him to get me the best master he could, as he told him I was a very deserving boy, which Captain Doran said he found to be true, and if he were to stay in the West-Indies he would be glad to keep me himself; but he could not venture to take me to London, for he was very sure that when I came there, I would leave him. I at that instant burst out a crying, and begged much of him to take me with him to England, but all to no purpose. He told me he had got me the very best master in the whole island, with whom I should be as happy as if I were in England, and for that reason he chose to let him have me, though he could sell me to his own brother-in-law for a great deal more money than what he got from that gentleman. My new master, Mr. King, then made a reply, and said the reason he had bought me was on account of my good character; and, as he had not the least doubt of my good behaviour, I should be very well off with him. He also told me he did not live in the West-Indies, but at Philadelphia, where he was soon going; and, as I understood something of the rules of arithmetic, when we got there he would put me to school, and fit me for a clerk. This conversation relieved my mind a little, and I left those gentlemen considerably more at ease in myself than when I came to them; and I was very thankful to Captain Doran, and even to my old master, for the character they had given me; a character which I afterwards found of infinite service to me.

I went on board again, and took leave of all my shipmates, and the next day the ship sailed. When she weighed anchor I went to the waterside, and looked at her with a very wishful and aching heart, following her with my eyes until she was totally out of sight. I was so bowed down with grief, that I could not hold up my head for many months; and if my new master had not been kind to me, I believe I should have died under it at last. And indeed I soon found that he fully deserved the good character which Capt. Doran had given me of him; for he possessed a most amiable disposition and temper, and was very charitable and humane. If any of his slaves behaved amiss, he did not beat or use them ill, but parted with them. This made them afraid of disobliging him; and as he treated his slaves better than any other man on the island, so he was better and more faithfully served by them in return. By this kind treatment I did at last endeavour to compose myself; and with fortitude, though moneyless, determined to face whatever fate had decreed for me. Mr. King soon asked me what I could do, and at the same time said he did not mean to treat me as a common slave. I told him I knew something

of seamanship, and could shave and dress hair pretty well; I could refine wines, which I had learned on shipboard, where I had often done it; and that I could write, and understood arithmetic tolerably well as far as the Rule of Three. He then asked me if I knew any thing of gauging; and, on my answering that I did not, he said one of his clerks should teach me to gauge.

V.

Mr. King dealt in all manner of merchandize, and kept from one to six clerks. He loaded many vessels in a year; particularly to Philadelphia, where he was born, and was connected with a great mercantile house in that city. He had besides many vessels and doggers, of different sizes, which used to go about the island; and others to collect rum, sugar, and other goods. I understood pulling and managing those boats very well; and this hard work, which was the first that he set me to, in the sugar seasons used to be my constant employment. I have rowed the boat and slaved at the oars, from one hour to sixteen in the twenty-four; during which I had fifteen pence sterling per day to live on, though sometimes only ten pence. However, this was much more than was allowed to other slaves that used to work often with me, and belonged to other gentlemen on the island: these poor souls had never more than nine pence a day, and seldom more than six pence, from their masters or owners, though they earned them three or four pisterines.* For it is a common practice in the West-Indies for men to purchase slaves, though they have not plantations themselves, in order to let them out to planters and merchants, at so much a piece by the day, and they give what they choose, out of this produce of their daily work; to their slaves for subsistence. This allowance is often very scanty.

My master often gave the owners of these slaves two and a half of these pieces per day, and found the poor fellows in victuals himself, because he thought their owners did not feed them well enough, according to the work they did. The slaves used to like this very well; and, as they knew my master to be a man of feeling, they were always glad to work for him in preference to any other gentleman; some of whom, after they had been paid for their poor people's labours, would not give them their allowance out of it. Many times have I seen these unfortunate wretches beaten for asking for their pay; and often severely flogged by their owners, if they did not bring them their daily or weekly money exactly to the time; though the poor creatures were

*These pisterines are of the value of a shilling.

obliged to wait on the gentlemen they had worked for, sometimes more than half the day before they could get their pay, and this generally on Sundays, when they wanted the time for themselves. In particular, I knew a country-man of mine, who once did not bring the weekly money directly that it was earned; and though he brought it the same day to his master, yet he was staked to the ground for his pretended negligence, and was just going to receive a hundred lashes, but for a gentleman who begged him off fifty.

This poor man was very industrious, and by his frugality had saved so much money, by working on shipboard, that he had got a white man to buy him a boat, unknown to his master. Some time after he had this little estate, the governor wanted a boat to bring his sugar from different parts of the island, and, knowing this to be a negro-man's boat, he seized upon it for himself, and would not pay the owner a farthing. The man on this went to his master, and complained to him of this act of the governor; but the only satisfaction he received was to be damned very heartily by his master, who asked him how dared any of his negroes to have a boat. If the justly-merited ruin of the governor's fortune could be any gratification to the poor man he had thus robbed, he was not without consolation. Extortion and rapine are poor providers, and some time after this, the governor died in the King's Bench, in England, as I was told, in great poverty. The last war favoured this poor negro-man, and he found some means to escape from his christian master: he came to England, where I saw him afterwards several times. Such treatment as this often drives these miserable wretches to despair, and they run away from their masters at the hazard of their lives. Many of them, in this place, unable to get their pay when they have earned it, and fearing to be flogged, as usual, if they return home without it, run away where they can for shelter, and a reward is often offered to bring them in dead or alive. My master used sometimes, in these cases, to agree with their owners, and to settle with them himself; and thereby he saved many of them a flogging.

VI.

Once, for a few days, I was let out to fit a vessel, and I had no victuals allowed me by either party; at last I told my master of this treatment, and he took me away from it. In many of the estates, on the different islands where I used to be sent for rum or sugar, they would not deliver it to me, or to any other negro; he was therefore obliged to send a white man along with me to those places; and then he used to pay him from six to ten pisterines a

day. From being thus employed, during the time I served Mr. King, in going about the different estates on the island, I had all the opportunity I could wish for to see the dreadful usage of the poor men—usage that reconciled me to my situation, and made me bless God for the hands into which I had fallen.

I had the good fortune to please my master in every department in which he employed me; and there was scarcely any part of his business, or household affairs, in which I was not occasionally engaged. I often supplied the place of a clerk, in receiving and delivering cargoes to the ships, in tending stores, and delivering goods; and, besides this, I used to shave and dress my master, when convenient, and take care of his horse; and when it was necessary, which was very often, I worked likewise on board of his different vessels. By these means I became very useful to my master, and saved him, as he used to acknowledge, above a hundred pounds a year. Nor did he scruple to say I was of more advantage to him than any of his clerks; tho' their usual wages in the West-Indies are from sixty to a hundred pounds current a year.

I have sometimes heard it asserted that a negro cannot earn his master the first cost; but nothing can be further from the truth. I suppose nine tenths of the mechanics throughout the West-Indies are negro slaves; and I well know the coopers among them earn two dollars a-day; the carpenters the same, and oftentimes more; also the masons, smiths, and fishermen, &c. and I have known many slaves whose masters would not take a thousand pounds current for them. But surely this assertion refutes itself: for, if it be true, why do the planters and merchants pay such a price for slaves? And, above all, why do those, who make this assertion, exclaim the most loudly against the abolition of the slave trade? So much are men blinded, and to such inconsistent arguments are they driven by mistaken interest! I grant, indeed, that slaves are sometimes, by half-feeding, half-clothing, over-working, and stripes, reduced so low, that they are turned out as unfit for service, and left to perish in the woods, or to expire on a dunghill.

My master was several times offered by different gentlemen one hundred guineas for me, but he always told them he would not sell me, to my great joy: and I used to double my diligence and care for fear of getting into the hands of these men, who did not allow a valuable slave the common support of life. Many of them used to find fault with my master for feeding his slaves so well as he did; although I often went hungry, and an Englishman might think my fare very indifferent: but he used to tell them he always would do it, because the slaves thereby looked better and did more work.

While I was thus employed by my master, I was often a witness to cruel-

ties of every kind, which were exercised on my unhappy fellowslaves. I used frequently to have different cargoes of new negroes in my care for sale; and it was almost a constant practice with our clerks, and other whites, to commit violent depredations on the chastity of the female slaves; and to these atrocities I was, though with reluctance, obliged to submit at all times, being unable to help them. When we have had some of these slaves on board my master's vessels to carry them to other islands, or to America, I have known our mates commit these acts most shamefully, to the disgrace not of christians only, but of men. I have even known them gratify their brutal passion with females not ten years old; and these abominations some of them practiced to such a scandalous excess, that one of our captains discharged the mate and others on that account. And yet in Montserrat I have seen a negroman staked to the ground, and cut most shockingly, and then his ears cut off, bit by bit, because he had been connected with a white woman, who was a common prostitute! As if it were no crime in the whites to rob an innocent African girl of her virtue; but most heinous in a black man only to gratify a passion of nature, where the temptation was offered by one of a different color, though the most abandoned woman of her species.

VII.

One Mr. D— told me he had sold 41,000 negroes, and he once cut off a negro-man's leg for running away. I asked him if the man had died in the operation, how he, as a christian, could answer, for the horrid act, before God. And he told me, answering was a thing of another world; what he thought and did were policy. I told him that the christian doctrine taught us "to do unto others as we would that others should do unto us." He then said that his scheme had the desired effect-it cured that man and some others of running away.

Another negro-man was half hanged, and then burnt, for attempting to poison a cruel overseer. Thus, by repeated cruelties, are the wretched first urged to despair, and then murdered, because they still retain so much of human nature about them as to wish to put an end to their misery, and to retaliate on their tyrants! These overseers are, indeed, for the most part, persons of the worst character of any denomination of men in the West-Indies. Unfortunately, many humane gentlemen, by not residing on their estates, are obliged to leave the management of them in the hands of these human butchers, who cut and mangle the slaves in a shocking manner, on the most

trivial occasions, and altogether treat them, in every respect, like brutes. They pay no regard to the situation of pregnant women, nor the least attention to the lodging of the field negroes. Their huts, which ought to be well covered, and the place dry where they take their short repose, are often open sheds, built in damp places; so that, when the poor creatures return tired from the toils of the field, they contract many disorders, from being exposed to the damp air in this uncomfortable state, while they are heated, and their pores are open.

The neglect certainly conspires with many others to cause a decrease in the births, as well as in the lives of the grown negroes. I can quote many instances of gentlemen who reside on their own estates in the West-Indies, and then the scene is quite changed; the negroes are treated with lenity and proper care, by which their lives are prolonged, and their masters profited. To the honour of humanity, I know several gentlemen who managed their estates in this manner, and found that benevolence was their true interest. And, among many I could mention in Montserrat,* whose slaves looked remarkably well, and never needed any fresh supplies of negroes (and there are many other estates, especially in Barbadoes, which, from such judicious treatment, need no fresh stock of negroes at any time), I have the honour of knowing a most worthy and humane gentleman, who is a native of Barbadoes, and has estates there.** This gentleman has written a treatise on the usage of his own slaves. He allows them two hours for refreshment at mid-day, and many other indulgences and comforts, particularly in their lying; and, besides this, he raises more provisions on his estate than they can destroy; so that by these attentions he saves the lives of his negroes, and keeps them healthy, and as happy as the condition of slavery can admit. I myself, as shall appear in the sequel, managed an estate, where, by such attentions, the negroes were uncommonly cheerful and healthy, and did more work by half than by the common mode of treatment they usually do. For want, therefore, of such care and attention to the poor negroes, and otherwise oppressed as they are, it is no wonder that the decrease should require 20,000 new negroes annually to fill up the vacant places of the dead.

Even in Barbadoes, notwithstanding those humane exceptions which I have mentioned and others with which I am acquainted that justly make it quoted as a place where slaves meet with the best treatment and need fewest recruits of any in the West-Indies; yet this island requires 1,000 negroes

*Mr. Dubury, and many others, in Montserrat.
**Sir Philip Gibbes, Bart. Barbadoes.

annually to keep up the original stock, which is only 80,000. So that the whole term of a negro's life may be said to be there, but sixteen years!* And yet the climate here is in every respect the same as that from which they are taken, except in being more wholesome. Do the British colonies decrease in this manner? And yet what a prodigious difference is there between an English and West-India climate?

VIII.

While I was in Montserrat I knew a negro-man, one Emanuel Sankey, who endeavoured to escape from his miserable bondage, by concealing himself on board of a London ship. But fate did not favour the poor oppressed man; for, being discovered when the vessel was under sail, he was delivered up again to his master. This christian master immediately pinned the wretch to the ground, at each wrist and ancle and then took some sticks of sealing wax, lighted them, and dropped it all over his back. There was another master noted for cruelty:—I believe he had not a slave but had been cut, and pieces fairly taken out of the flesh: and after they had been punished thus, he used to make them get into a long wooden box, or case, he had for that purpose, and shut them up during pleasure. It was just about the height and breadth of man; and the poor wretches had no room when in the case to move.

It was very common in several of the islands, particularly in St. Kitt's, for the slaves to be branded with the initial letters of their master's name, and a load of heavy iron hooks hung about their necks. Indeed on the most trivial occasions they were loaded with chains, and often instruments of torture were added. The iron muzzle, thumb-screws, &c. are so well known as not to need a description, and were sometimes applied for the slightest faults. I have seen a negro beaten till some of his bones were broken, for only letting a pot boil over. It is not uncommon, after a flogging, to make slaves go on their knees and thank their owners, and pray, or rather say, "God bless you." I have often asked many of the men slaves (who used to go several miles to their wives, and late in the night, after having been wearied with a hard day's labour) why they went so far for wives, and did not take them of their own master's negro-women, and particularly those who lived together as household slaves. Their answers have ever been—"Because when the master or

*See Anthony Benezet's "Some Account of Guinea, With an Inquiry into the Slave Trade," p. 16.

mistress choose to punish the women, they make the husbands flog their own wives, and that we could not bear to do." Is it surprising such usage should drive the poor creatures to despair, and make them seek a refuge in death, from those evils which render their lives intolerable—while

> With shudd'ring horror pale, and eyes aghast,
> They view their lamentable lot, and find
> No rest?

This they frequently do. A negro-man, on board a vessel of my master's, while I belonged to her, having been put in irons for some trifling misdemeanour, and kept in that state some days, being weary of life, took an opportunity of jumping over-board into the sea; however he was picked up without being drowned. Another, whose life was also a burden to him, resolved to starve himself to death, and refused to eat any victuals: this procured him a severe flogging; and he also on the first occasion that offered, jumped overboard at Charles Town, but was saved.

Nor is there any greater reward strewn to the little property than there is to the persons and lives of the negroes. I have already related an instance or two of particular oppression, out of many which I have witnessed; but the following is frequent in all the islands:—The wretched field-slaves, after toiling all the day for an unfeeling owner, who gives them but little victuals, steal sometimes a few moments from rest or refreshment to gather some small portion of grass, according as their time will admit. This they commonly tie up in a parcel, either a bits worth (sixpence) or half a bit's worth, and bring it to town, or to the market to sell. Nothing is more common than for the white people, on this occasion, to take the grass from them without paying for it; and not only so, but too often also, to my knowledge, our clerks and many others, at the same time have committed acts of violence on the poor, wretched and helpless females; whom I have seen for hours stand crying to no purpose, and get no redress or pay of any kind. Is not this one common and crying sin enough to bring down God's judgment on the islands? He tells us the oppressor and the oppressed are both in his hands; and if these are not the poor, the broken-hearted, the blind, the captive, the bruised, of which our Saviour speaks, who are they?

One of these depredators once, in St. Eustatia, came on board of our vessel, and bought some fowls and pigs of me, and a whole day after his departure with the things, he returned and wanted his money back:—I refused to give it;

and, he not seeing my captain on board, began the common pranks with me; and swore he would even break open my chest and take my money. I therefore expected, as my captain was absent, that he would be as good as his word: and he was just proceeding to strike me, when fortunately a British seaman on board, whose heart had not been debauched by a West-India climate, interposed and prevented him. But had the cruel man struck me, I certainly should have defended myself, at the hazard of my life. For what is life to a man thus oppressed? He went away, however, swearing; and threatened that whenever he caught me a-shore he would shoot me, and pay for me afterwards.

IX.

The small account, in which the life of a negro is held in the West-Indies, is so universally known, that it might seem impertinent to quote the following extract, if some people had not been hardly enough of late to assert, that negroes are on the same footing in that respect as Europeans. By the 329th Act, page 125, of the Assembly of Barbadoes, it is enacted 'That if any negro, or other slave, under punishment by his master, or his order, for running away, or any other crime or misdemeanour towards his said master, unfortunately shall suffer in life or member, no person whatsoever shall be liable to a fine; but if any man shall out of wantonness, or only of bloody-mindedness, or cruel intention, wilfully kill a negro, or other slave, of his own, he shall pay into the public treasury £15. sterling.' And it is the same in most, if not all, of the West-India islands. Is not this one of the many acts of the islands which call loudly for redress? And do not the Assembly, which enacted it, deserve the appellation of savages and brutes rather than of christians and men? It is an act at once unmerciful, unjust and unwise; which for cruelty would disgrace an assembly of those who are called barbarians; and for its injustice and insanity would shock the morality and common sense of a Samaide or Hottentot.

Shocking as this and many other acts of the bloody West-India code at first view appear, how is the iniquity of it heightened when we consider to whom it may be extended! Mr. James Tobin, a zealous labourer in the vineyard of slavery, gives an account* of a French planter, of his acquaintance, in the island of Martinico, who shewed him many mulattoes working in the fields like beasts of burden; and he told Mr. Tobin these were all the produce of his own loins! And I myself have known similar instances. Pray, reader, are

*In his "Cursory Remarks."

these sons and daughters of the French planter less his children by being begotten on black women? And what must be the virtue of those legislators, and the feelings of those fathers, who estimate the lives of their sons, however begotten, at no more than fifteen pounds; though they should be murdered, as the act says, out of wantonness and bloody-mindedness? But is not the slave-trade entirely a war with the heart of man? And surely that which is begun by breaking down the barriers of virtue, involves in its continuance destruction to every principle, and buries all sentiments in ruin!

I have often seen slaves, particularly those who were meager, in different islands, put into scales and weighed; and then sold from three-pence to six-pence or nine-pence a pound. My master, however, whose humanity was shocked at this mode, used to sell such by the lump. And at or after a sale, even those negroes born in the islands it is not uncommon to see taken from their wives, wives from their husbands, and children from their parents, and sent off to other islands, and wherever else their merciless lords choose; and, probably, never more, during life, see each other! Oftentimes my heart has bled at these partings; when the friends of the departed have been at the water-side, and, with sighs and tears, have kept their eyes fixed on the vessel till it went out of sight.

A poor Creole negro I know well, who, after having been often thus transported from island to island, at last resided in Montserrat. This man used to tell me many melancholy tales of himself. Generally, after he had done working for his master, he used to employ his few leisure moments to go a fishing. When he had caught any fish, his master would frequently take them from him without paying him; and at other times some other white people would serve him in the same manner. One day he said to me very movingly, 'Sometimes when a white man take away my fish I go to my maser, and he get me my right; and when my maser, by strength, take away my fishes, what me must do? I can't go to any body to be righted; then,' said the poor man, looking up above, 'I must look up to God Mighty in the top for right,' this artless tale moved me much, and I could not help feeling the just cause Moses had in redressing his brother against the Egyptian. I exhorted the man to look up still to the God in the top, since there was no redress below. Though I little thought then that I myself should more than once experience such imposition, and need the same exhortation hereafter, in my own transactions in the islands; and that even this poor man and I should some time after, suffer together in the same manner, as shall be related hereafter.

X.

Nor was such usage as this confined to particular places or individuals; for, in all the different islands in which I have been (and I have visited no less than fifteen) the treatment of the slaves was nearly the same, so nearly, indeed, that the history of an island, or even a plantation, with a few such exceptions as I have mentioned, might serve for a history of the whole. Such a tendency has the slave-trade to debauch men's minds, and harden them to every feeling of humanity! For I will not suppose that the dealers in slaves are born worse than other men. No; it is the fatality of this mistaken avarice, that it corrupts the milk of human kindness and turns it into gall. And, had the pursuits of those men been different, they might have been as generous, as tender-hearted, and just, as they are unfeeling, rapacious and cruel. Surely this traffic cannot be good, which spreads like a pestilence, and taints what it touches! Which violates that first natural right of mankind, equality, and independency; and gives one man a dominion over his fellows which God could never intend! For it raises the owner to a state as far above man as it depresses the slave below it; and, with the presumption of human pride, sets distinction between them, immeasurable in extent, and endless in duration! Yet how mistaken is the avarice even of the planters. Are slaves more useful by being thus humbled to the condition of brutes, than they would be if suffered to enjoy the privileges of men? The freedom which diffuses health and prosperity throughout Britain answers you—"No." When you make men slaves, you deprive them of half their virtue, you set them, in your own conduct, an example of fraud, rapine, and cruelty, and compel them to live with you in a state of war; and yet you complain that they are not honest or faithful! You stupefy them with stripes, and think it necessary to keep them in a state of ignorance; and yet you assert that they are incapable of learning, that their minds are such a barren soil or moor that culture would be lost on them, and that they came from a climate, where nature though prodigal of her bounties in a degree unknown to yourselves, has left man alone scant and unfinished, and incapable of enjoying the treasures she has poured out for him!—An assertion at once impious and absurd. Why do you use those instruments of torture? Are they fit to be applied by one rational being to another? And are ye not struck with shame and mortification, to see the partakers of your nature reduced so low? But, above all, are there no dangers attending this mode of treatment? Are you not hourly in dread of an insur-

rection? Nor would it be surprising: for when

> No peace is given
> To us enslav'd, but custody severe;
> And stripes and arbitrary punishment
> Inflicted—What peace can we return?
> But to our power, hostility and hate,
> Untam'd reluctance, and revenge, tho' slow,
> Yet ever plotting how the conqueror least
> May reap his conquest, and may least rejoice
> In doing what we most in suff'ring feel?
>
> <div align="right">Mɪʟᴛᴏɴ.</div>

But by changing your conduct, and treating your slaves as men, every cause of fear would be banished. They would be faithful, honest, intelligent and vigorous; and peace, prosperity, and happiness, would attend you.

CHAPTER VI

Some account of Brimstone-hill in Montserrat—The author surprised by two earthquakes—Favourable change in the author's situation—He commences merchant with three-pence—His various success in dealing in the different islands, and America, and the impositions he meets with in his transactions with white people—A curious imposition on human nature—Danger of the surfs in the West-Indies—Remarkable instance of kidnapping a free mulatto—The author is nearly murdered by Dr. Perkins, in Savannah.

I.

IN THE preceding chapter I have set before the reader a few of those many instances of oppression, extortion, and cruelty, to which I have been a witness in the West-Indies; but were I to enumerate them all, the catalogue would be tedious and disgusting. The punishments of the slaves on every trifling occasion are so frequent, and so well known, together with the different instruments with which they are tortured, that it cannot any longer afford novelty to recite them; and they are too shocking to yield delight

either to the writer or the reader. I shall therefore hereafter only mention such as incidentally befel myself in the course of my adventures.

In the variety of departments in which I was employed by my master, I had an opportunity of seeing many curious scenes in different islands; but, above all, I was struck with a celebrated curiosity called Brimstonehill, which is a high and steep mountain, some few miles from the town of Plymouth, in Montserrat. I had often heard of some wonders that were to be seen on this hill, and I went once with some white and black people to visit it. When we arrived at the top, I saw under different cliffs great flakes of brimstone, occasioned by the steams of various little ponds, which were then boiling naturally in the earth. Some of these ponds were as white as milk, some quite blue, and many others of different colours. I had taken some potatoes with me, and I put them into different ponds, and in a few minutes they were well boiled. I tasted some of them, but they were very sulphurous; and the silver shoe-buckles, and all the other things we had among us of that metal, were, in a little time, turned as black as lead.

Whilst I was in the island, one night I felt a strange sensation, on being told that the house where I lived was haunted by spirits! And once, at midnight, as I was sleeping on a large chest, I felt the whole building shake in an uncommon and astonishing manner; so much so, that it shook me off the chest where I then lay. I was exceedingly frightened, and thought it was the visitation of the spirits. It threw me into such a tremor as is not to be described. I instantly covered my head all over as I lay, and did not know what to think or do; and in this consternation, a gentleman, who lay in the next room just by me, came out, and I was glad to hear him, and made a sham cough, and he asked me if I felt the earthquake, I told him I was shaken off the chest where I lay, but did not know what occasioned it; and he told me it was an earthquake, and that it shook him out of his bed. On hearing this I became easy in my mind.

At another time a circumstance of this kind happened, when I was on board of a vessel in Montserrat-Road, at midnight, as we were asleep, and it shook the vessel in the most unaccountable manner imaginable, and to me it seemed as when a vessel or a boat runs on gravel, as near as I can describe it. Many things on board were moved out of their places, but happily no damage was done.

II.

About the end of the year 1763, kind Providence seemed to be rather
more favourable to me. One of my master's vessels, a Bermudas sloop,
about sixty tons burden, was commanded by one Capt. Thomas Farmer, an
Englishman, a very alert and active man, who gained my master a great deal
of money, by his good management in carrying passengers from one island
to another. But very often his sailors used to get drunk and run away from
the vessel, which hindered him in his business very much. This man had
taken a liking to me; and many different times begged of my master to let
me go a trip with him as a sailor; but he would tell him he could not spare
me though the vessel sometimes could not go for want of hands; for sailors
were generally very scarce in the island. However, at last, from necessity or
force, my master was prevailed on, though very reluctantly, to let me go with
this captain; but he gave him great charge to take care that I did not run
away, for if I did he would make him pay for me. This being the case, the
captain had for some time a sharp eye upon me whenever the vessel
anchored; and as soon as she returned I was sent for on shore again. Thus was
I slaving as it were for life, sometimes at one thing, and sometimes at anoth-
er; so that the captain and I were nearly the most useful men in my master's
employment. I also became so useful to the captain on shipboard, that, many
times, when he used to ask for me to go with him, though it should be but
for twenty-four hours, to some of the islands near us, my master would
answer he could not spare me; at which the captain would swear, and would
not go the trip, and tell my master that I was better to him on board than
any three white men he had. For they used to behave ill in many respects,
particularly in getting drunk, and then they frequently got the boat stove, so
as to hinder the vessel from coming back so soon as she might have done.
This my master knew very well; and at last, by the captain's constant
entreaties, after I had been several times with him, one day, to my great joy,
told me the captain would not let him rest, and asked whether I would go
aboard as a sailor, or stay on shore and mind the stores, for he could not bear
any longer to be plagued in this manner. I was very happy at this proposal,
for I immediately thought I might in time stand a chance, by being on board,
to get a little money, or possibly make my escape if I should be used ill. I also
expected to get better food, and in a greater abundance; for I had oftentimes
felt much hunger, though my master treated his slaves, as I have observed,
uncommonly well. I therefore, without hesitation, answered him, that I

would go and be a sailor, if he pleased. Accordingly I was ordered on board directly. Nevertheless, between the vessel and the shore, when she was in port, I had little or no rest, as my master always wished to have me along with him. Indeed he was a very pleasant gentleman, and but for my expectations on shipboard, I should not have thought of leaving him. But the captain liked me also very much, and I was entirely his right-hand man. I did all I could to deserve his favour, and in return I received better treatment from him, than I believe, any other, in my situation, ever met with in the West-Indies.

III.

After I had been sailing for some time with this captain, at length I endeavoured to try my luck and commence merchant. I had but a very small capital to begin with; for one single half bit, which is equal to three-pence in England, made up my whole stock. However I trusted to the Lord to be with me; and at one of our trips to St. Eustatia, a Dutch island, I bought a glass tumbler with my half bit, and when I came to Montserrat I sold it for a bit, or six-pence. Luckily we made several successive trips to St. Eustatia, which was a general mart for the West-Indies, about twenty leagues from Montserrat; and in our next, finding my tumbler so profitable, with this one bit I bought two tumblers more; and when I came back I sold them for two bits, equal to a shilling sterling. When we went again I bought with these two bits four more of these glasses, which I sold for four bits of our return to Montserrat; and in our next voyage to St. Eustatia, I bought two glasses with one bit, and with the other three I bought a jug of Geneva, nearly three pints in measure. When we came to Montserrat, I sold the gin for eight bits, and the tumblers for two, so that my capital now amounted in all to a dollar, well husbanded, and acquired in the space of a month or six weeks, when I blessed the Lord that I was so rich.

As we sailed to different islands, I laid this money out in various things occasionally, and it used to turn to very good account, especially when we went to Guadaloupe, Grenada, and the rest of the French islands. Thus was I going all about the islands upwards of four years, and ever trading as I went, during which I experienced many instances of ill-usage, and have seen many injuries done to other negroes in our dealings with whites. Amidst our recreations, when we have been dancing and merry-making, they without cause, have molested and insulted us. Indeed I was more than once obliged to look

up to God on high, as I had advised the poor fisherman some time before.

And I had not been long trading for myself in the manner above related, when I experienced the like trial in company with him as follows: This man being used to the water, was, upon an emergency, put on board of us by his master to work as another hand, on a voyage to Santa Cruz; and at our sailing he had brought his little all for a venture, which consisted of six bits' worth of limes and oranges in a bag; I had also my whole stock, about twelve bits' worth of the same kind of goods, separate in two bags; for we had heard that these fruits sold well in that island. When we came there, in some little convenient time, he and I went on shore with our fruits to sell them; but we had scarcely landed when we were met by two white men, who presently took our three bags from us. We could not at first guess what they meant to do; and for some time we thought they were jesting with us; but they soon let us know otherwise, for they took our ventures immediately to a house hard by, and adjoining the fort, while we followed all the way begging of them to give us our fruits, but in vain. They not only refused to return them, but they swore at us, and threatened if we did not immediately depart they would flog us well. We told them those three bags were our all, that we brought them with us to sell, and that we came from Montserrat, and shewed them the vessel. But this was rather against us, as they now saw we were strangers as well as slaves. They still therefore swore, and desired us to be gone, and even took sticks to beat us; while we, seeing that they meant what they said, went off in the greatest confusion and despair. Thus, in the very minute of gaining more by three times than I ever did by any venture in my life before, was I deprived of every farthing I was worth. An insupportable misfortune! But how to help ourselves we knew not. In our consternation we went to the commanding officer of the fort, and told him how we had been served by some of his people; but we obtained not the least redress. He answered our complaints only by a volley of imprecations against us, and immediately took a horse-whip, in order to chastise us; so that we were obliged to turn out much faster than we came in. I then, in the agony of distress and indignation, wished that the ire of God, in his forked lightning, might transfix these cruel oppressors among the dead. We however returned to the house, and begged and besought them again and again for our fruits, till at last some other people being in the house, asked, if we would be contented if they kept one bag and gave us the other two. We, seeing no remedy whatever, consented to this; and they, observing one bag to have both kinds of fruit in it, which belonged to my companion, kept that; and the

other two, being mine, they gave us back. As soon as I got them, I ran as fast as I could, and got the first negro-man I could to help me off. My companion stayed a little longer to plead; he told them that the bag they had was his, and that it was all he was worth in the world. But this was of no avail, and he was obliged to return without it. The poor old man wringing his hands cried bitterly for his loss; and, indeed, he then did look up to God on high, which so moved me with pity for him, that I gave him nearly one third of my fruits. We then proceeded to the markets to sell them; and Providence was more favourable than we could have expected, for we sold our fruits uncommonly well; I got for mine about thirty-seven bits. Such a surprising reverse of fortune, in so short a time, seemed like a dream, and proved no small encouragement for me to trust the Lord in any situation. My captain afterwards frequently used to take my part, and get me my right, when I had been plundered or used ill by these tender christian depredators; among whom I have shuddered to observe the unceasing blasphemous execrations which are wantonly thrown out by persons of all ages and conditions, not only without occasion, but even as if they were indulgences and pleasures.

IV.

At one of our trips to St. Kitt's, I had eleven bits of my own; and my friendly captain lent me five more, with which I bought a Bible. I was very glad to get this book, which I could scarcely meet with any where. I think there were none sold in Montserrat; and, much to my grief, from being forced out of the Ætna, in the manner I have related, my Bible, and the "Guide to the Indians," the two books I loved above all others, were left behind.

While I was in St. Kitt's, a very curious imposition on human nature took place:—A white man wanted to marry, in the church, a free black woman that had land and slaves in Montserrat: but the clergyman told him it was against the law of the place to marry a white and a black in the church. The man then asked to be married on the water, to which the parson consented, and the lovers went in one boat, and the parson and clerk in another, and thus the ceremony was performed. After this the loving pair came on board our vessel, and my captain treated them extremely well, and brought them safe to Montserrat.

The reader cannot but judge of the irksomeness of this situation to a mind like mine, in being daily exposed to new hardships and impositions,

after having seen many better days, and been, as it were, in a state of freedom and plenty; added to which, every part of the world in which I had hitherto been, seemed to me a paradise in comparison of the West-Indies. My mind was therefore hourly replete with inventions and thoughts of being freed, and, if possible, by honest and honourable means; for I always remembered the old adage, and I trust that it has ever been my ruling principle, that Honesty is the best policy; and likewise that other golden precept—To do unto all men as I would they should do unto me. However, as I was from early years a predestinarian, I thought whatever fate had determined must ever come to pass; and therefore, if ever it were my lot to be freed, nothing could prevent me, although I should at present see no means or hope to obtain my freedom; on the other hand, if it were my fate not to be freed, I never should be so; and all my endeavours for that purpose would be fruitless. In the midst of these thoughts I therefore looked up with prayers anxiously to God for my liberty; and at the same time used every honest means, and did all that was possible on my part, to obtain it.

In process of time I became master of a few pounds, and in a fair way of making more, which my friendly captain knew very well: this occasioned him sometimes to take liberties with me; but whenever he treated me waspishly I used plainly to tell him my mind, and that I would die before I would be imposed upon as other negroes were; and that to me life had lost its relish when liberty was gone. This I said, although I foresaw my then well-being, or future hopes of freedom (humanly speaking) depended on this man. However, as he could not bear the thoughts of my not sailing with him, he always became mild on my threats. I therefore continued with him; and, from my great attention to his orders and his business, I gained him credit, and through his kindness to me I at last procured my liberty.

While I thus went on, filled with the thoughts of freedom, and resisting oppression as well as I was able, my life hung daily in suspense, particularly in the surfs I have formerly mentioned, as I could not swim. These are extremely violent throughout the West-Indies, and I was ever exposed to their howling rage and devouring fury in all the islands. I have seen them strike and toss a boat right up an end, and maim several on board. Once in the Grenada islands, when I and about eight others were pulling a large boat with two puncheons of water in it, a surf struck us, and drove the boat and all in it about half a stone's throw, among some trees, and above the highwater mark. We were obliged to get all the assistance we could, from the nearest estate, to mend the boat, and launch it into the water again. At

Montserrat one night, in pressing hard to get off the shore on board, the punt was overset with us four times; the first time I was very near being drowned; however the jacket I had on kept me up above water a little time, while I called on a man near me, who was a good swimmer, and told him I could not swim. He then made haste to me, and, just as I was sinking, he caught hold of me, and brought me to sounding, and then he went and brought the punt also. As soon as we had turned the water out of her, least we should be used ill for being absent, we attempted again three times more, and as often the horrid surfs served us as at first; but at last, the fifth time we attempted, we gained our point, at the imminent hazard of our lives.

One day also, at Old Road, in Montserrat, our captain, and three men besides myself, were going in a large canoe, in quest of rum and sugar, when a single surf tossed the canoe an amazing distance from the water, and some of us near a stone's throw from each other: most of us were very much bruised; so that I and many more often said, and really thought, that there was not such another place under the heavens as this. I longed therefore much to leave it, and daily wished to see my master's promise performed of going to Philadelphia.

V.

While we lay in this place, a very cruel thing happened on board of our sloop, which filled me with horror; though I found afterwards such practices were frequent. There was a very clever and decent free young mulatto-man who sailed a long time with us: he had a free woman for his wife, by whom he had a child; and she was then living on shore, and all very happy. Our captain and mate, and other people on board, and several elsewhere, even the natives of Bermudas, then with us, all knew this young man from a child that he was always free, and no one had ever claimed him as their property. However, as might too often overcomes right in these parts, it happened that a Bermudas captain, whose vessel lay there for a few days in the road, came on board of us and seeing the mulatto-man, whose name was Joseph Clipson, he told him he was not free, and that he had orders from his master to bring him to Bermudas. The poor man could not believe the captain to be in earnest, but he was very soon undeceived, his men laying violent hands on him; and although he shewed a certificate of his being born free in St. Kitt's, and most people on board knew that he served his time to boat-building and always passed for a free man, yet he was forcibly taken out of

our vessel. He then asked to be carried ashore, before the secretary or magistrates, and these infernal invaders of human rights promised him he should; but, instead of that, they carried him on board of the other vessel; and the next day, without giving the poor man any hearing ashore, or suffering him even to see his wife or child, he was carried away, and probably doomed never more in this world to see them again.

Nor was this the only instance of this kind of barbarity to which I was a witness. I have since often seen in Jamaica and other islands, free men, whom I have known in America, thus villainously trepanned and kept in bondage. I have heard of two similar practices even in Philadelphia: and were it not for the benevolence of the Quakers in that city, many of the sable race, who now breathe the air of liberty, would, I believe, be groaning under some planter's chains. These things opened my mind to a new scene of horror, to which I had been before a stranger. Hitherto I had thought only slavery dreadful; but the state of a free negro appeared to me now equally so at least, and in some respects even worse; for they live in constant alarm for their liberty, which is but nominal; and they are universally insulted and plundered without the possibility of redress; such being the equity of the West-Indian laws, that no free negro's evidence will be admitted in their courts of justice. In this situation is it surprising that slaves, when mildly treated, should prefer even the misery of slavery to such a mockery of freedom? I was now completely disgusted with the West-Indies, and thought I never should be entirely free till I had left them.

> With thoughts like these my anxious boding mind,
> Recall'd those pleasing scenes I left behind;
> Scenes where fair Liberty in bright array
> Makes darkness bright, and e'en illumines day;
> Where nor complexion, wealth, nor station can
> Protect the wretch who makes a slave of man.

I determined to make every exertion to obtain my freedom, and to return to Old England. For this purpose I thought a knowledge of Navigation might be of use to me; for, though I did not intend to run away unless I should be ill used, yet, in such a case, if I understood navigation, I might attempt my escape in our sloop, which was one of the swiftest sailing vessels in the West-Indies, and I could be at no loss for hands to join me. Had I made this attempt, I had intended to go in her to England; but this, as I said,

was only to be in the event of my meeting with any ill usage. I therefore employed the mate of our vessel to teach me Navigation, for which I agreed to give him twenty-four dollars, and actually paid him part of the money down; though when the captain, some time after, came to know that the mate was to have such a sum for teaching me, he rebuked him, and said it was a shame for him to take any money from me. However, my progress in this useful art was much retarded by the constancy of our work.

VI.

Had I wished to run away I did not want opportunities, which frequently presented themselves; and particularly at one time, soon after this. When we were at the island of Guadaloupe there was a large fleet of merchantmen bound for Old France; and seamen then being very scarce, they gave from fifteen to twenty pounds a man for the run. Our mate and all the white sailors left our vessel on this account, and went aboard of the French ships. They would have had me also to go with them, for they regarded me, and swore to protect me, if I would go: and, as the fleet was to sail the next day, I really believe I could have got safe to Europe at that time. However, as my master was kind, I would not attempt to leave him; still remembering the old maxim, that honesty is the best policy, I suffered them to go without me. Indeed my captain was much afraid of my leaving him and the vessel at that time, as I had so fair an opportunity: but, I thank God, this fidelity of mine turned out much to my advantage hereafter, when I did not in the least think of it; and made me so much in favour with the captain, that he used now and then to teach me some parts of Navigation himself. But some of our passengers, and others, seeing this, found much fault with him for it, saying it was a very dangerous thing to let a negro know Navigation; and thus I was hindered again in my pursuits.

About the latter end of the year 1764, my master bought a larger sloop, called the Prudence, about seventy or eighty tons, of which my captain had the command. I went with him into this vessel, and we took a load of new slaves for Georgia and Charles Town. My master now left me entirely to the captain, though he still wished me to be with him; but I, who always much wished to lose sight of the West-Indies, was not a little rejoiced at the thoughts of seeing any other country. Therefore, relying on the goodness of my captain, I got ready all the little venture I could; and, when the vessel was ready, we sailed to my great joy. When we got to our destined places, Georgia

and Charles Town, I expected I should have an opportunity of selling my lit-
tle property to advantage; but here, particularly in Charles Town, I met with
buyers, white men, who imposed on me as in other places. Notwithstanding,
I was resolved to have fortitude: thinking no lot or trial too hard when kind
Heaven is the rewarder.

We soon got loaded again, and returned to Montserrat; and there,
amongst the rest of the islands, I sold my goods well; and in this manner I
continued trading during the year 1764; meeting with various scenes of
imposition, as usual. After this, my master fitted out his vessel for
Philadelphia, in the year 1765; and during the time of loading her, and get-
ting ready for the voyage, I worked with double alacrity, from the hope of
getting money enough by these voyages to buy my freedom, in time, if it
should please God; and also to see the city of Philadelphia, having heard a
great deal about it for some years past; besides which I had always longed to
prove my master's promise the first day I came to him. In the midst of these
elevated ideas, and while I was about getting my little merchandise in readi-
ness, one Sunday my master sent for me to his house. When I came there I
found him and the captain together; and, on my going in, I was struck with
astonishment at his telling me, he heard that I meant to run away from him
when I got to Philadelphia;—"And therefore," said he, "I must sell you again:
you cost me a great deal of money, no less than forty pounds sterling; and it
will not do to lose so much. You are a valuable fellow," continued he, "and I
can any day get for you one hundred guineas, from many gentlemen in this
island." And then he told me of Captain Doran's brother-in-law, a severe
master, who ever wanted to buy me to make me his overseer.

My captain also said, he could get much more than a hundred guineas for
me in Carolina. This I knew to be a fact; for the gentleman that wanted to
buy me, came off several times on board of us, and spoke to me to live with
him, and said he would use me well. When I asked to what work he would
put me, he said, as I was a sailor, he would make me a captain of one of his
rice vessels. But I refused: and fearing at the same time, by a sudden turn I
saw in the captain's temper, he might mean to sell me, I told the gentleman
I would not live with him on any condition, and that I certainly would run
away with his vessel: but he said, he did not fear that, as he would catch me
again: and then he told me how cruelly he would serve me if I should do so.
My captain, however, gave him to understand that I knew something of
Navigation: so he thought better of it; and, to my great joy, he went away. I
now told my master, I did not say I would run away in Philadelphia, neither

did I mean it, as he did not use me ill, nor yet the captain; for if they did, I certainly would have made some attempts before now; but as I thought that if it were God's will I ever should be freed it would be so, and, on the contrary, if it was not his will it would not happen; so I hoped if ever I were freed, whilst I was used well, it should be by honest means; but as I could not help myself, he must do as he pleased; I could only hope and trust in the God of Heaven; and at that instant my mind was big with inventions, and full of schemes to escape.

I then appealed to the captain whether he ever saw any sign of my making the least attempt to run away; and asked him if I did not always come on board according to the time for which he gave me liberty; and more particularly, when all our men left us at Guadaloupe, and went on board the French fleet, and advised me to go with them, whether I might not, and that he could not have got me again. To my no small surprise, and very great joy, the captain confirmed every syllable I said, and even more; for he said he had tried different times to see if I would make any attempt of this kind, both at St. Eustatia and in America, and he never found that I made the smallest; but, on the contrary, I always came on board according to his orders;—and he did really believe, if ever I meant to run away, that, as I could never have had a better opportunity, I would have done it the night the mate and all the people left our vessel at Guadaloupe. The captain then informed my master, who had been thus imposed on by our mate (though I did not know who was my enemy), the reason the mate had for imposing this lie upon him; which was, because I had acquainted the captain with the provisions the mate had given away or taken out of the vessel.

This speech of the captain was like life to the dead to me, and instantly my soul glorified God: and still more so on hearing my master immediately say that I was a sensible fellow, and he never did intend to use me as a common slave; and that, but for the entreaties of the captain, and his character of me, he would not have let me go from the stores about as I had done: that also, in so doing, he thought by carrying one little thing or other to different places to sell I might make money: that he intended to encourage me in this, by crediting me with half a puncheon of rum and half a hogshead of sugar at a time: so that, from being careful, I might have money enough, in some time, to purchase my freedom: and, when that was the case, I might depend upon it he would let me have it for forty pounds sterling money, which was only the same price he gave for me. This soon gladdened my poor heart beyond measure; though indeed it was no more than the idea I had formed

in my mind of my master long before, and I immediately made him this reply: 'Sir, I always had that very thought of you; indeed I had; and that made me so diligent in serving you.' He then gave me a large piece of silver coin, such as I had never seen or had before, and told me to get ready for the voyage, and he would credit me with a fierce of sugar and another of rum; he also said that he had two amiable sisters in Philadelphia, from whom I might get some necessary things. Upon this my noble captain desired me to go a board: and, knowing the African Metal, he charged me not to say any thing of this matter to any body; and he promised that the lying mate should not go with him any more.

VII.

This was a change indeed; in the same hour to feel the most exquisite pain, and, in the turn of a moment, the fullest joy. It caused in me such sensations as I was only able to express in my looks; my heart was so over-powered with gratitude that I could have kissed both of their feet. When I left the room I immediately went, or rather flew, to the vessel, which being loaded, my master, as good as his word, trusted me with a fierce of rum and another of sugar, when we sailed, and arrived safe at the elegant town of Philadelphia. I soon sold my goods here pretty well and in this charming town I found every thing plentiful and cheap.

While I was in this place a very extraordinary occurrence befel me. I had been told one evening of a WISE WOMAN, a Mrs. Davis, who revealed secrets, foretold events, &c. I put little faith in this story at first as I could not con-ceive that any mortal could foresee the future disposals of Providence, nor did I believe in any other revelation than that of the Holy Scriptures. However, I was greatly astonished at seeing this woman in a dream that night, though a person I never before beheld in my life. This made such an impression on me, that I could not get the idea next day out of my mind, and I then became as anxious to see her as I was before indifferent. Accordingly in the evening, after we left off working, I inquired where she lived, and being directed to her, to my inexpressible surprise, beheld the very woman in the very same dress she appeared to me to wear in the vision. She immediately told me I had dreamed of her the preceding night; related to me many things that had happened with a correctness that astonished me; and finally told me I should not be long a slave. This was the more agreeable news, as I believed it the more readily than her having so faithfully related

the past incidents of my life. She said I should be twice in very great danger of my life within eighteen months, which if I escaped, I should afterwards go on well; so, giving me her blessing, we parted. After staying here some time till our vessel was loaded and I had bought in my little traffic, we sailed from this agreeable spot for Montserrat, once more to encounter the raging surfs.

We arrived safe at Montserrat, where we discharged our cargo, and soon after that we took slaves on board for St. Eustatia, and from thence to Georgia. I had always exerted myself, and did double work, in order to make our voyages as short as possible; and from thus over-working myself while we were at Georgia I caught a fever and ague. I was very ill for eleven days, and near dying; eternity was now exceedingly impressed on my mind, and I feared very much that awful event. I prayed the Lord therefore to spare me; and I made a promise in my mind to God, that I would be good if ever I should recover. At length, from having an eminent doctor to attend me, I was restored again to health; soon after we got the vessel loaded, and set off for Montserrat. During the passage, as I was perfectly restored, and had much business of the vessel to mind, all my endeavours to keep up my integrity, and perform my promise to God, began to fail; and, in spite of all I could do, as we drew nearer and nearer to the islands, my resolutions more and more declined, as if the very air of that country or climate seemed fatal to piety. When we were safe arrived at Montserrat, and I had got ashore, I forgot my former resolutions. Alas! how prone is the heart to leave that God it wishes to love! And how strongly do the things of this world strike the senses and captivate the soul!

After our vessel was discharged, we soon got her ready, and took in, as usual, some of the poor oppressed natives of Africa, and other negroes; we then set off again for Georgia and Charlestown. We arrived at Georgia, and having landed part of our cargo, proceeded to Charlestown with the remainder. While we were there I saw the town illuminated; the guns were fired, and bonfires and other demonstrations of joy strewn, on account of the repeal of the stamp-act. Here I disposed of some goods on my own account; the white men buying them with smooth promises, and fair words, giving me, however, but very indifferent payment.

There was one gentleman particularly who bought a puncheon of rum of me, and gave me a great deal of trouble. Although I used the interest of my friendly captain, I could obtain nothing for it, and could not oblige him to pay me. This vexed me much, not knowing how to act. I lost some time in seeking after this Christian; and though, when the Sabbath came, which the

negroes usually make their holiday, I was inclined to go to public worship yet I was obliged to hire some black men to help to pull a boat across the water to go in quest of this gentleman. When I found him, after much entreaty both from myself and my worthy captain, he at last paid me in dollars, some of them, however, were copper, and of consequence of no value. But he took advantage of my being a negro-man, and obliged me to put up with those or none, although I objected to them. Immediately after, as I was trying to pass them in the market amongst other white men, I was abused for offering to pass bad coin, and though I shewed them the man I had got them from, I was within one minute of being tied up and flogged without either judge or jury. However, by the help of a good pair of heels, I ran off and so escaped the bastinadoes I should have received. I got on board as fast as I could, but still continued in fear of them until we sailed, which, I thank God, we did, not long after; and I have never been amongst them since.

VIII.

We soon came to Georgia, where we were to complete our lading; and here worse fate than ever attended me: for one Sunday night, as I was with some negroes, in their master's yard, in the town of Savannah, it happened that their master, one Doctor Perkins, who was a very severe and cruel man, came in, drunk; and not liking to see any strange negroes in his yard, he and a ruffian of a white man he had in his service, beset me in an instant, and both of them struck me with the first weapons they could get hold of. I cried out as long as I could for help and mercy; but though I gave a good account of myself, and he knew my captain, who lodged hard by him, it was to no purpose. They beat and mangled me in a shameful manner, leaving me nearly dead. I lost so much blood from the wounds I received that I lay quite motionless, and was so benumbed that I could not feel any thing for many hours. Early in the morning they took me away to the jail.

As I did not return to the ship all night, my captain not knowing where I was, and being uneasy that I did not then make my appearance, made inquiry after me; and having found where I was, he immediately came to me. As soon as the good man saw me so cut and mangled, he could not forbear weeping. He soon got me out of jail to his lodgings, and immediately sent for the best doctors in the place, who at first declared it as their opinion that I could not recover. My captain on this went to all the lawyers in the town for their advice, but they told him they could do nothing for me as I was a

negro. He then went to Doctor Perkins, the hero who had vanquished me, and menaced him, swearing he would be revenged of him, and challenged him to fight. But cowardice is ever the companion of cruelty—and the doctor refused.

However by the skilfulness of one Dr. Brady of that place, I began at last to amend. But although I was so sore and bad, with the wounds I had all over me, that I could not rest in any posture; yet I was in more pain on account of the captain's uneasiness about me than I otherwise should have been. The worthy man nursed and watched me all the hours of the night; and I was, through his attention and that of the doctor, able to get out of bed in about sixteen or eighteen days. All this time I was very much wanted on board, as I used frequently to go up and down the river for rafts, and other parts of our cargo, and stow them, when the mate was sick or absent. In about four weeks I was able to go on duty; and in a fortnight after, having got in all our lading, our vessel set sail for Montserrat, and in less than three weeks we arrived there safe, towards the end of the year. This ended my adventures in 1765; for I did not leave Montserrat again till the beginning of the following year.

CHAPTER VII.

The author's disgust at the West-Indies—Forms schemes to obtain his free-dom—Ludicrous disappointment he and his captain meet with in Georgia—At last, by several successful voyages he acquires a sum of money sufficient to purchase it—Applies to his master, who accepts it, and grants his manumission, to his great joy—He afterwards enters as a freeman on board one of Mr. King's ships, and sails for Georgia—Impositions on free negroes as usual—His venture of turkies—Sails for Montserrat, and on his passage, his friend, the Captain, falls in and dies.

I.

EVERY DAY now brought me nearer my freedom, and I was impatient till we proceeded again to sea, that I might have an opportunity of getting a sum large enough to purchase it. I was not long ungratified; for in the beginning of the year 1766, my master bought another sloop, named the Nancy, the largest I had ever seen. She was partly laden, and was to proceed to Philadelphia. Our captain had his choice of three, and I was well pleased he chose this, which was the largest; for, from his having a large vessel, I had

more room, and could carry a larger quantity of goods with me. Accordingly, when we had delivered our old vessel, the Prudence, and completed the lading of the Nancy, having made near three hundred per cent. by four barrels of pork I brought from Charlestown, I laid in as large a cargo as I could, trusting to God's Providence to prosper my undertaking. With these views I sailed for Philadelphia. On our passage, when we drew near the land, I was for the first time surprised at the sight of some whales, having never seen any such large sea-monsters before; and, as we sailed by the land, one morning I saw a puppy whale close by the vessel; it was about the length of a wherry-boat, and it followed us all the day until we got within the Capes. We arrived safe and in good time at Philadelphia, and I sold my goods there chiefly to the Quakers. They always appeared to be a very honest and discreet sort of people, and never attempted to impose on me; I therefore liked them, and ever after chose to deal with them in preference to any others.

One Sunday morning while I was here, as I was going to church, I chanced to pass a meeting-house. The doors being open, and the house full of people, it excited my curiosity to go in. When I entered the house, to my great surprise, I saw a very tall woman standing in the midst of them, speaking in an audible voice something which I could not understand. Having never seen any thing of this kind before, I stood and stared about me for some time, wondering at this odd scene. As soon as it was over, I took an opportunity to make enquiry about the place and people, when I was informed they were called Quakers. I particularly asked what that woman I saw in the midst of them had said, but none of them were pleased to satisfy me; so I quitted them, and soon after, as I was returning, I came to a church crowded with people; the church-yard was full likewise, and a number of people were even mounted on ladders, looking in at the windows. I thought this a strange sight, as I had never seen churches, either in England or the West-Indies, crowded in this manner before. I therefore made bold to ask some people the meaning of all this, and they told me the Rev. George Whitfield was preaching. I had often heard of this gentleman, and had wished to see and hear him; but I had never before had an opportunity. I now therefore resolved to gratify myself with the sight, and pressed in amidst the multitude. When I got into the church I saw this pious man exhorting the people with the greatest fervour and earnestness, and sweating as much as ever I did while in slavery on Montserrat beach. I was very much struck and impressed with this; I thought it strange I had never seen divines exert themselves in this manner before; and was no longer at a loss to account for the thin congregations they preached to.

II.

When we had discharged our cargo here, and were loaded again, we left this fruitful land once more, and set sail for Montserrat. My traffic had hitherto succeeded so well with me, that I thought, by selling my goods when we arrived at Montserrat, I should have enough to purchase my freedom. But as soon as our vessel arrived there, my master came on board, and gave orders for us to go to St. Eustatia, and discharge our cargo there, and from thence to proceed for Georgia. I was much disappointed at this; but thinking, as usual, it was of no use to murmur at the decrees of fate, I submitted without repining, and we went to St. Eustatia.

After we had discharged our cargo there, we took in a live cargo, as we call a cargo of slaves. Here I sold my goods tolerably well; but not being able to lay out all my money in this small island to as much advantage as in many other places, I laid out only part, and the remainder I brought away with me neat. We sailed from hence for Georgia and I was glad when we got there, though I had not much reason to like the place from my last adventure in Savannah, but I longed to get back to Montserrat and procure my freedom, which I expected to be able to purchase when I returned. As soon as we had arrived here I waited on my careful doctor, Mr. Brady, to whom I made the most-grateful acknowledgments in my power, for his former kindness and attention during my illness.

While we remained here, an odd circumstance happened to the Captain and me, which disappointed us both a great deal. A silversmith, whom we had brought to this place some voyages before, agreed with the Captain to return to the West-Indies, and promised at the same time to give the Captain a great deal of money, having pretended to take a liking to him, and being, as we thought, very rich. But while we stayed to load our vessel this man was taken ill, in a house where he worked, and in a week's time became very bad. The worse he grew the more he used to speak of giving the Captain what he had promised him, so that he expected something considerable from the death of this man, who had no wife or child, and he attended him day and night.

I used also to go with the Captain, at his own desire, to attend him; especially when we saw there was no appearance of his recovery: and in order to recompence me for my trouble, the Captain promised me ten pounds, when he should get the man's property. I thought this would be of great service to me, although I had nearly money enough to purchase my freedom, if I should get safe this voyage to Montserrat. In this expectation I laid out above

eight pounds of my money for a suit of superfine clothes to dance in at my freedom, which I hoped was then at hand. We still continued to attend this man, and were with him even on the last day he lived, till very late at night when we went on board. After we were got to bed, about one or two o'clock in the morning, the Captain was sent for, and was informed the man was dead. On this he came to my bed, and, waking me, informed me of it, and desired me to get up, procure a light, and to go immediately with him. I told him I was very sleepy, and wished he would take somebody else with him; or else, as the man was dead, and could want no further attendance, to let all things remain as they were till the next morning. 'No, no,' said he, 'we will have the money to-night. I cannot wait till to-morrow, so let us got' accordingly I got up and struck a light, and away we both went, and saw the man as dead as we could wish. The Captain said he would give him a grand burial, in gratitude for the promised treasure; and desired that all the things belonging to the deceased might be brought forth. Amongst others there was a nest of trunks, of which he had kept the keys whilst the man was ill; and when they were produced, we opened them with no small eagerness and expectation;-as there were a great number within one another, with much impatience we took them out of each other. At last, when we came to the smallest, and had opened it, we saw it was full of papers, which we supposed to be notes; at the sight of which our hearts leapt for joy; and that instant the Captain, clapping his hands, cried out—'Thank God! here it is!'

But when we began to examine the supposed treasure and long-looked-for bounty, alas! alas! how uncertain and deceitful are all human affairs! what had we found? While we thought we were embracing a substance, we grasped an empty nothing. The whole amount in the nest of trunks was only a dollar and a half; and all that the man possessed would not pay for his coffin! Our sudden and exquisite joy was now succeeded by as sudden and exquisite pain; and my captain and I exhibited, for some time, most ridiculous figures-pictures of chagrin and disappointment! We went away greatly mortified, and left the deceased to do as well as he could for himself, as we had taken so good care of him when alive for nothing.

III.

We set sail once more for Montserrat, and arrived there safe; but much out of humour with our friend, the silversmith. When we had unladen the vessel, and I had sold my venture, finding myself master of about

forty-seven pounds, I consulted my true friend, the Captain, how I should proceed in offering my master the money for my freedom. He told me to come on a certain morning, when he and my master would be at breakfast together. Accordingly, on that morning I went, and met the Captain there, as he had appointed. When I went in I made my obeisance to my master, and with my money in my hand, and many fears in my heart, I prayed him to be as good as his offer to me, when he was pleased to promise me my freedom as soon as I could purchase it. This speech seemed to confound him; he began to recoil; and my heart that instant sunk within me. 'What,' said he, 'give you your freedom? Why, where did you get the money? Have you got forty pounds sterling?' 'Yes, sir,' I answered. 'How did you get it?' replied he. I told him, 'very honestly.' The Captain then said he knew I got the money very honestly and with much industry, and that I was particularly careful. On which my master replied, I got money much faster than he did; and said he would not have made me the promise which he did, had he thought I should have got the money so soon. 'Come, come,' said my worthy Captain, clapping my master on the back, 'Come Robert (which was his name), I think you must let him have his freedom. You have laid your money out very well; you have received good interest for it all this time, and here is now the principal at last. I know GUSTAVUS has earned you more than a hundred a year, and he will still save you money, as he will not leave you. Come, Robert, take the money.' My master then said, he would not be worse than his promise; and, taking the money, told me to go to the Secretary at the Register Office, and get my manumission drawn up.

These words of my master were like a voice from heaven to me: in an instant all my trepidation was turned into unutterable bliss, and I most reverently bowed myself with gratitude, unable to express my feelings, but by the overflowing of my eyes, and a heart replete with thanks to God; while my true and worthy friend, the Captain, congratulated us both with a peculiar degree of heartfelt pleasure. As soon as the first transports of my joy were over, and that I had expressed my thanks to these my worthy friends in the best manner I was able, I rose with a heart full of affection and reverence, and left the room, in order to obey my master's joyful mandate of going to the Register Office. As I was leaving the house I called to mind the words of the Psalmist, in the 126th Psalm, and like him, 'I glorified God in my heart, in whom I trusted.' These words had been impressed on my mind from the very day I was forced from Deptford to the present hour, and I now saw them, as I thought, fulfilled and verified.

My imagination was all rapture as I flew to the Register Office; and in this respect, like the apostle Peter* (whose deliverance from prison was so sudden and extraordinary, that he thought he was in a vision) I could scarcely believe I was awake. Heavens! who could do justice to my feelings at this moment? Not conquering heroes themselves, in the midst of a triumph—Not the tender mother who has just regained her long-lost infant, and presses it to her heart—Not the weary, hungry mariner, at the sight of the desired friendly port—Not the lover, when he once more embraces his beloved mistress, after she has been ravished from his arms!—All within my breast was tumult, wildness, and delirium! My feet scarcely touched the ground; for they were winged with joy, and, like Elijah, as he rose to Heaven, they 'were with lightning sped as I went on.' Every one I met I told of my happiness, and blazed about the virtue of my amiable master and Captain.

When I got to the office and acquainted the Register with my errand, he congratulated me on the occasion, and told me he would draw up my manumission for half-price, which was a guinea. I thanked him for his kindness; and, having received it and paid him, I hastened to my master to get him to sign it, that I might be fully released. Accordingly he signed the manumission that day; so that, before night, I, who had been a slave in the morning, trembling at the will of another, was become my own master, and completely free. I thought this was the happiest day I had ever experienced; and my joy was still heightened by the blessings and prayers of many of the sable race, particularly the aged, to whom my heart had ever been attached with reverence.

As the form of my manumission has something peculiar in it, and expresses the absolute power and dominion one man claims over his fellow, I shall beg leave to present it before my readers at full length.**

IV.

In short, the fair as well as black people immediately styled me by a new appellation,—to me the most desirable in the world,—which was "Freeman," and, at the dances I gave, my Georgia superfine blue clothes made no indifferent appearance, as I thought. Some of the sable females, who formerly stood aloof, now began to relax and appear less coy; but my heart was still fixed on London, where I hoped to be ere long. So that my worthy Captain and his owner, my late master, finding that the bent of my mind

*Acts xii. 9.
**See Appendix A.

was towards London, said to me, 'We hope you won't leave us, but that you will still be with the vessels.' Here gratitude bowed me down; and none but the generous mind can judge of my feelings, struggling between inclination and duty. However notwithstanding my wish to be in London, I obediently answered my benefactors that I would go in the vessel, and not leave them; and from that day I was entered on board as an able-bodied seaman, at thirty-six shillings per month, besides what perquisites I could make. My intention was to make a voyage or two, entirely to please these my honoured patrons; but I determined that the year following, if it pleased God, I would see Old England once more, and surprise my old master, Captain Pascal, who was hourly in my mind; for I still loved him, notwithstanding his usage to me, and I pleased myself with thinking of what he would say when he saw what the Lord had done for me in so short a time, instead of being, as he might perhaps suppose, under the cruel yoke of some planter.

With such reveries I used often to entertain myself, and shorten the time till my return; and now, being as in my original free African style, I embarked on board the Nancy, after having got all things ready for our voyage. In this state of serenity we sailed for St. Eustatia; and having smooth seas and calm weather, we soon arrived there; after taking our cargo on board, we proceeded to Savannah in Georgia, in August, 1766. While we were there, as usual, I used to go for the cargo up the rivers in boats; and, when on this business, I have been frequently beset by Alligators, which were very numerous on that coast and river. I have shot many of them when they have been near getting into our boats; which we have with great difficulty sometimes prevented, and have been very much frightened at them. I have seen a young one sold in Georgia alive for sixpence.

During our stay at this place, one evening a slave belonging to Mr. Read, a merchant of Savannah, came near our vessel, and began to use me very ill. I entreated him, with all the patience of which I was master, to desist, as I knew there was little or no law for a free negro here. But the fellow, instead of taking my advice, persevered in his insults, and even struck me. At this I lost all temper, and fell on him, and beat him soundly. The next morning his master came to our vessel, as we lay alongside the wharf, and desired me to come ashore that he might have me flogged all round the town, for beating his negro slave! I told him he had insulted me, and had given the provocation by first striking me. I had also told my Captain the whole affair that morning, and desired him to go along with me to Mr. Read, to prevent bad consequences; but he said that it did not signify, and if Mr. Read said any

thing he would make matters up, and desired me to go to work, which I accordingly did.

The Captain being on board when Mr. Read came and applied to him to deliver me up, he said he knew nothing of the matter, I was a free man. I was astonished and frightened at this, and thought I had better keep where I was, than go ashore and be flogged round the town, without judge or jury. I therefore refused to stir; and Mr. Read went away, swearing he would bring all the constables in the town, for he would have me out of the vessel. When he was gone, I thought his threat might prove too true to my sorrow; and I was confirmed in this belief, as well by the many instances I had seen of the treatment of free negroes, as from a fact that had happened within my own knowledge here a short time before.

There was a free black man, a carpenter, that I knew, who for asking a gentleman that he had worked for, for the money he had earned, was put into gaol; and afterwards this oppressed man was sent from Georgia, with false accusations, of an intention to set the gentleman's house on fire, and run away with his slaves. I was therefore much embarrassed, and very apprehensive of a flogging at least. I dreaded, of all things, the thoughts of being stripped, as I never in my life had the marks of any violence of that kind. At that instant a rage seized my soul, and for a little I determined to resist the first man that should attempt to lay violent hands on me, or basely use me without a trial; for I would sooner die like a free man, than suffer myself to be scourged, by the hands of ruffians, and my blood drawn like a slave.

The Captain and others, more cautious, advised me to make haste and conceal myself; for they said Mr. Read was a very spiteful man, and he would soon come on board with constables and take me. At first I refused this counsel, being determined to stand my ground; but at length, by the prevailing entreaties of the Captain and Mr. Dixon, with whom we lodged, I went to Mr. Dixon's house, which was a little out of the town, at a place called Yeama-chra. I was but just gone when Mr. Read, and the constables, came for me, and searched the vessel; but, not finding me there, he swore he would have me dead or alive. I was secreted about five days; however the good character which my Captain always gave me, as well as some other gentlemen, who also knew me, procured me some friends. At last some of them told my Captain that he did not use me well, in suffering me thus to be imposed upon, and said they would see me redressed, and get me on board some other vessel. My Captain, on this, immediately went to Mr. Read, and told him, that ever since I eloped from the vessel his work had been neglected, and he

could not go on with her loading, himself and mate not being well; and as I had managed things on board for them, my absence must have retarded his voyage, and consequently hurt the owner. He therefore begged of him to forgive me, as he said he never heard any complaint of me before, during the several years I had been with him. After repeated entreaties, Mr. Read said I might go to hell; and that he would not meddle with me; on which my Captain came immediately to me at his lodging, and telling me how pleasantly matters had gone on, desired me to go on board.

Some of my other friends then asked him if he had got the constable's warrant from them; the Captain said, "No." On this I was desired by them to stay in the house; and they said they would get me on board of some other vessel before the evening. When the Captain heard this he became almost distracted. He went immediately for the warrant, and, after using every exertion in his power, he at last got it from my hunters; but I had all the expenses to pay.

V.

After I had thanked all my friends for their kindness, I went on board again to my work, of which I had always plenty. We were in haste to complete our lading, and were to carry twenty head of cattle with us to the West-Indies, where they are a very profitable article. In order to encourage me in working, and to make up for the time I had lost, my Captain promised me the privilege of carrying two bullocks of my own with me, this made me work with redoubled ardour. As soon as I had got the vessel loaded, in doing which I was obliged to perform the duty of the mate as well as my own work, and when the bullocks were near coming on board, I asked the Captain leave to bring my two, according to his promise; but, to my great surprise, he told me there was no room for them. I then asked him to permit me to take one; but he said he could not. I was a good deal mortified at this usage, and told him I had no notion that he intended thus to impose on me; nor could I think well of any man that was so much worse than his word. On this we had some disagreement, and I gave him to understand that I intended to leave the vessel. At this he appeared to be very much dejected, and our mate, who had been very sickly, and whose duty had long devolved upon me, advised him to persuade me to stay. In consequence of which he spoke very kindly to me, making many fair promises, telling me that, as the mate was so sickly, he could not do without me, and that, as the safety of the

vessel and cargo depended greatly upon me, he therefore hoped that I would not be offended at what had passed between us, and swore he would make up all matters when we arrived in the West-Indies; so I consented to slave on as before.

Soon after this, as the bullocks were coming on board, one of them ran at the Captain, and butted him so furiously in the breast, that he never recovered of the blow. In order to make me some amends for his treatment about the bullocks, the Captain now pressed me very much to take some turkeys, and other fowls, with me, and gave me liberty to take as many as I could find room for, but I told him he knew very well I had never carried any turkeys before, as I always thought they were such tender birds as were not fit to cross the seas. However, he continued to press me to buy them for once; and, what seemed very surprising to me, the more I was against it, the more he urged my taking them, insomuch that he insured me from all losses that might happen by them, and I was prevailed on to take them. But I thought this very strange, as he had never acted so with me before. This, and not being able to dispose of my paper-money in any other way, induced me at length to take four dozen. The turkeys, however, I was so dissatisfied about that I determined to make no more voyages to this quarter, nor with this Captain; and was very apprehensive that my free voyage would be the worst I had ever made.

We set sail for Montserrat. The Captain and mate had been both complaining of sickness when we sailed, and as we proceeded on our voyage they grew worse. This was about November, and we had not been long at sea before we began to meet with strong northerly gales and rough seas; and in about seven or eight days all the bullocks were near being drowned, and four or five of them died. Our vessel, which had not been tight at first, was much less so now: and, though we were but nine in the whole, including five sailors and myself, yet we were obliged to attend to the pumps, every half or three quarters of an hour. The Captain and mate came on deck as often as they were able, which was now but seldom; for they declined so fast, that they were not well enough to make observations above four or five times the whole passage. The whole care of the vessel rested therefore upon me, and I was obliged to direct her by mere dint of reason, not being able to work a traverse.

The Captain was now very sorry he had not taught me navigation, and protested, if ever he should get well again, he would not fail to do so. But in about seventeen days his illness increased so much, that he was obliged to keep his bed, continuing sensible, however, until the last, constantly having the owner's interest at heart; for this just and benevolent man ever appeared

much concerned about the welfare of what he was intrusted with. When this dear friend found the symptoms of death approaching, he called me by my name; and, when I came to him, he asked (with almost his last breath) if he had ever done me any harm. 'God forbid I should think so!' I replied, 'I should then be the most ungrateful of wretches to the best of benefactors.' While I was thus expressing my affection and sorrow by his bedside, he expired without saying another word, and the day following we committed his body to the deep. Every man on board loved him, and regretted his death; but I was exceedingly affected at it, and found that I did not know, till he was gone, the strength of my regard for him. Indeed I had every reason in the world to be attached to him; for, besides that he was in general mild, affable, generous, faithful, benevolent, and just, he was to me a friend and father; and had it pleased Providence that he had died but five months before, I verily believe I should not have obtained my freedom when I did; and it is not improbable that I might not have been able to get it at any rate afterwards.

VI.

The Captain being dead, the mate came on the deck, and made such observations as he was able, but to no purpose. In the course of a few days more, the few bullocks that remained were found dead; but the turkeys I had, though on the deck, and exposed to so much wet and bad weather, did well, and I afterwards gained near three hundred per cent. on the sale of them. So that in the event it proved a happy circumstance for me that I had not bought the bullocks I intended, for they must have perished with the rest. I could not help looking upon this, otherwise trifling, circumstance, as a particular providence of God; and was accordingly thankful. The care of the vessel took up all my time, and engaged my attention entirely. As we were now out of the variable winds, I thought I should not be much puzzled to hit the islands. I was persuaded I steered right for Antigua, which I wished to reach, as the nearest to us; and in the course of nine or ten days we made that island to our great joy, and the day after we came safe to Montserrat.

Many were surprised when they heard of my conducting the sloop into the port; and I now obtained a new appellation, and was called "Captain." This elated me not a little, and it was quite flattering to my vanity to be thus styled by as high a title as any sable freeman in this place possessed. When the death of the Captain became known, he was much regretted by all who knew him; for he was a man universally respected. At the same time the sable

Captain lost no fame; for the success I had met with increased the affection of my friends in no small measure; and I was offered, by a gentleman of the place, the command of his sloop, to go amongst the islands, but I refused.

CHAPTER VIII.

The author, to oblige Mr. King, once more embarks for Georgia, in the Nancy—A new Captain is appointed—They sail, and steer a new course—Three remarkable dreams—The vessel is wrecked on Bahama Banks; but the crew are preserved, principally by means of the author—He sets out from an island with the Captain, in a small boat, in quest of a ship—Their distress—Meet with a wrecker—Sail for Providence—Are overtaken again by a terrible storm, and are all near perishing—Arrive at New Providence—The author, after some time, sails from thence to Georgia—Meets with another storm, and is obliged to put back and refit-Arrives at Georgia—Meets new impositions—Two white men attempt to kidnap him—Officiates as a parson at a funeral ceremony—Bids adieu to Georgia, and sails for Martinico.

I.

A S I HAD NOW, by the death of my Captain, lost my great benefactor and friend, I had little inducement to remain longer in the West-Indies, except my gratitude to Mr. King, which I thought I had pretty well discharged in bringing back his vessel safe, and delivering his cargo to his satisfaction. I began to think of leaving this part of the world, of which I had been long tired, and of returning to England, where my heart had always been; but Mr. King still pressed me very much to stay with his vessel: and he had done so much for me, that I found myself unable to refuse his requests, and consented to go another voyage to Georgia, as the mate, from his ill state of health, was quite useless in the vessel. Accordingly a new Captain was appointed, whose name was William Phillips, an old acquaintance of mine; and, having refitted our vessel, and taken several slaves on board, we set sail for St. Eustatia, where we stayed but a few days: and on the 30th of January, 1767, we steered for Georgia. Our new Captain boasted strangely of his skill in navigating and conducting a vessel; and in consequence of this he steered a new course, several points more to the westward than we ever did before;—

this appeared to me very extraordinary.

On the 4th of February, which was soon after we had got into our new course, I dreamed the ship was wrecked amidst the surfs and rocks, and that I was the means of saving every one on board, and on the night following I dreamed the very same dream. These dreams, however, made no impression on my mind; and the next evening, it being my watch below, I was pumping the vessel a little after eight o'clock, just before I went off the deck, as is the custom, and being weary with the duty of the day, and tired at the pump (for we made a good deal of water), I began to express my impatience, and uttered with an oath, 'Damn the vessel's bottom out!' But my conscience instantly smote me for the expression. When I left the deck I went to bed, and had scarcely fallen asleep when I dreamed the same dream again about the ship as I had dreamed the two preceding nights.

At twelve o'clock the watch was changed; and, as I had always the charge of the captain's watch, I then went upon deck. At half after one in the morning, the man at the helm saw something under the lee-beam that the sea washed against, and he immediately called to me that there was a grampus, and desired me to look at it. Accordingly I stood up, and observed it for some time; but, when I saw the sea wash against it again and again, I said it was not a fish but a rock. Being soon certain of this, I went down to the Captain, and with some confusion told him the danger we were in, and desired him to come upon deck immediately. He said it was very well, and I went up again. As soon as I was upon deck, the wind, which had been pretty high, having abated a little, the vessel began to be carried sideways towards the rock, by means of the current. Still the Captain did not appear. I therefore went to him again and told him the vessel was then near a large rock, and desired he would come up with all speed. He said he would, and I returned on the deck. When I was upon the deck again, I saw we were not above a pistol-shot from the rock, and I heard the noise of the breakers all around us. I was exceedingly alarmed at this; and the Captain having not yet come on the deck, I lost all patience; and, growing quite enraged, I ran down to him again, and asked him why he did not come up, and what he could mean by all this? 'The breakers,' said I, 'are around us, and the vessel is almost on the rock.' With that he came on the deck with me, and tried to put the vessel about, and get her out of the current; but all to no purpose, the wind being very small. We then called all hands up immediately; and after a little we got up one end of a cable, and fastened it to the anchor. By this time the surf was foaming round us, and made a dreadful noise on the breakers, and the very

moment we let the anchor go, the vessel struck against the rocks.

II.

O ne swell now succeeded another, as if it were one wave calling on its fellow. The roaring of the billows increased, and, with one single heave of the swells, the sloop was pierced and transfixed among the rocks!* In a moment a scene of horror presented itself to my mind, such as I never had conceived or experienced before. All my sins stared me in the face; and especially I thought that God had hurled his direful vengeance on my guilty head, for cursing the vessel on which my life depended. My spirits at this forsook me, and I expected every moment to go to the bottom; I determined, if I should still be saved, that I would never swear again. And in the midst of my distress, while the dreadful surfs were dashing with unremitting fury among the rocks, I remembered the Lord, though fearful that I was undeserving of forgiveness, and I thought that as he had often delivered, he might yet deliver; and, calling to mind the many mercies he had strewn me in times past, they gave me some small hope that he might still help me. I then began to think how we might be saved; and, I believe no mind was ever like mine, so replete with inventions and confused with schemes; though how to escape death I knew not.

The captain immediately ordered the hatches to be nailed down on the slaves in the hold, where above twenty of them were, all of whom must unavoidably have perished if he had been obeyed. When he desired the men to nail down the hatches, I thought that my sin was the cause of this, and that God would charge me with these people's blood. This thought rushed

*In his Edition of 1792, the author had inserted, in addition to the plate of *The Nancy foundering on the Bahamas Banks*, 1767, the following quotations from Scripture, which are very applicable to his prophetic dream and his subsequent shipwreck:

Now a thing was secretly brought to me, and mine ear received a little thereof—In thoughts from the visions of the night, when deep sleep falleth on men. JOB iv. 12, 13.

For God speaketh once, yea, twice, yet man perceiveth it not. In a dream, in a vision of the night, when deep sleep falleth upon men, in slumberings upon the bed; then He openeth the ears of men and sealeth their instruction—Lo, all these things worketh God oftentimes with man, to bring back his soul from the pit, to be enlightened with the light of the living. JOB xxxiii. 14-16. 29, 30. *They ran the ship aground; and the fore part struck fast and remained unmovable, but the hinder part was broken by the violence of the waves.— Howbeit we must be cast upon a certain island; wherefore, sirs, be of good cheer; for I believe God, that it shall be even as it was told me,—And so it came to pass that they escaped all safe to land.* ACTS xxvii. 41, 26, 25, 44.

upon my mind that instant with such violence, that it quite overpowered me, and I fainted. I recovered just as the people were about to nail down the hatches; perceiving which, I desired them to stop. The Captain then said, "it must be done;" I asked him "why?" He said that every one would endeavour to get into the boat, which was but small, and thereby we should be drowned; for it would not have carried above ten at the most. I could no longer restrain my emotion, and I told him he deserved drowning for not knowing how to navigate the vessel; and I believe the people would have tossed him overboard if I had given them the least hint of it. However the hatches were not nailed down; and, as none of us could leave the vessel then, on account of the darkness, and as we knew not where to go, and were convinced besides that the boat could not survive the surfs, we all said we would remain on the dry part of the vessel, and trust to God till day-light appeared, when we should know better what to do.

I then advised to get the boat prepared against morning, and some of us began to set about it; but others abandoned all care of the ship and themselves, and fell to drinking. Our boat had a piece out of her bottom near two feet long, and we had no materials to mend her; however, necessity being the mother of invention, I took some pump leather and nailed it to the broken part, and plastered it over with tallow-grease. And, thus prepared, with the utmost anxiety of mind we watched for day-light, and thought every minute an hour till it appeared. At last it saluted our longing eyes, and kind Providence accompanied its approach with what was no small comfort to us- for the dreadful swells began to subside; and the next thing that we discovered to raise our dropping spirits, was a small key or desolate island, about five or six miles off; but a barrier soon presented itself; for there was not water enough for our boat to go over the reefs, and this threw us again into a sad consternation. But there was no alternative, we were therefore obliged to put but few things in the boat at once; and, what was still worse, all of us were frequently under the necessity of getting out to drag and lift it over the reefs. This cost us much labour and fatigue; and what was yet more distressing, we could not avoid having our legs cut and torn very much with the rocks.

There were only four people that would work with me at the oars; and they consisted of three black men, and a Dutch Creole sailor; and though we went with the boat fives times that day, we had no others to assist us. But had we not worked in this manner, I really believe the people could not have been saved; for not one of the white men did any thing to preserve their lives. Indeed they soon got so drunk that they were not able; but lay about the

deck like swine, so that we were at last obliged to lift them into the boat and carry them on shore by force. This want of assistance made our labour intolerably severe; insomuch that, by going on shore so often that day, the skin was partly stripped off my hands. We continued, however, all the day to toil and strain our exertions, till we had brought all on board safe to the shore; so that out of thirty-two people we lost not one.

III.

My dream now resumed upon my mind with all its force; it was fulfilled in every part; for our danger was the same I had dreamed of; and I could not help looking on myself as the principal instrument in effecting our deliverance. For, owing to some of our people getting drunk, the rest of us were obliged to double our exertions; and it was fortunate we did, for in a very little time longer the patch of leather on the boat would have been worn out, and she would have been no longer fit for service. Situated as we were, who could think that men should be so careless of the danger they were in? For, if the wind had but raised the swell, as it was when the vessel struck, we must have bid a final farewell to all hopes of deliverance; and though I warned the people who were drinking, and entreated them to embrace the moment of deliverance, nevertheless they persisted, as if not possessed of the least spark of reason. I could not help thinking, that, if any of these people had been lost, God would charge me with their lives; which, perhaps, was one cause of my labouring so hard for their preservation; and indeed every one of them afterwards seemed so sensible of the service I had rendered them, that while we were on the key I was a kind of chieftain amongst them.

I brought some limes, oranges, and lemons on shore; and finding it to be a good soil where we were, I planted several of them as a token to any one that might be cast away hereafter. This key, as we afterwards found, was one of the Bahama islands, which consist of a cluster of large islands, with smaller ones, or keys, as they are called, interspersed among them. It was about a mile in circumference, with a white sandy beach running in a regular order along it. On that part of it where we first attempted to land, there stood some very large birds, called flamingoes: these, from the reflection of the sun, appeared to us at a little distance as large as men; and when they walked backwards and forwards, we could not conceive what they were: our Captain swore they were cannibals. This created a great panic among us, and we held a consultation how to act. The Captain wanted to go to a key that was with-

in sight, but a great way off; but I was against it, as in so doing we should not be able to save all the people. 'And therefore,' said I, 'let us go on shore here, and perhaps these cannibals may take to the water.' Accordingly we steered towards them, and when we approached them, to our very great joy and no less wonder, they walked off, one after the other, very deliberately; and at last they took to flight, and relieved us entirely from our fears. About the key there were turtles, and several sorts of fish, in such abundance that we caught them without bait which was a great relief to us after the salt provisions on board. There was also a large rock on the beach about ten feet high, which was in the form of a punch-bowl at the top: this we could not help thinking Providence had ordained to supply us with rain-water; and it was something singular that, if we did not take it when it rained, in some little time after it would turn as salt as sea-water.

IV.

Our first care, after refreshment, was to make ourselves tents to lodge in, which we did as well as we could with some sails we had brought from the ship. We then began to think how we might get from this uninhabited place; and we determined to repair our boat, which was very much shattered, and to put to sea in quest of a ship, or some inhabited island. It took us up eleven days before we could get the boat ready for sea, in the manner we wanted it, with a sail and other necessaries. Having got all things prepared, the Captain wanted me to stay on shore, while he went to sea in quest of a vessel to take all the people off the key. But this I refused; and the Captain, and myself, with five more, set off in the boat towards New Providence. We had no more than two musketload of gunpowder with us, if any thing should happen; and our stock of provisions consisted of three gallons of rum, four of water, some salt beef, some biscuit; and in this manner we proceeded to sea.

On the second day of our voyage, we came to an island called Abbico, the largest of the Bahama islands. We were much in want of water; for by this time our water was expended, and we were exceedingly fatigued; in pulling two days in the heat of the sun; and it being late in the evening, we hauled the boat ashore to try for water, and to remain during the night: when we came ashore we searched for water, but could find none. When it was dark, we made a fire around us for fear of the wild beasts, as the place was an entire thick wood, and we took it by turns to watch. In this situation we found very little rest, and waited with impatience for the morning. As soon as the light

appeared, we set off again with our boat, in hopes of finding assistance dur-
ing the day. We were now much dejected and weakened by pulling the boat;
for our sail was of no use, and we were almost famished for want of fresh
water to drink. We had nothing left to eat but salt beef, and that we could
not use without water.

In this situation we toiled all day in sight of the island, which was very
long; in the evening, seeing no relief, we made shore again, and fastened our
boat. We then went to look for fresh water, being quite faint for the want of
it; and we dug and searched about for some all the remainder of the evening,
but could not find one drop; so that our dejection at this period became
excessive, and our terror so great, that we expected nothing but death to
deliver us. We could not touch our beef, which was salt as brine, without
fresh water; and we were in the greatest terror from the apprehension of wild
beasts. When unwelcome night came, we acted as on the night before; and
the next morning we set off again from the island in hopes of seeing some
vessel. In this manner we toiled, as well as we were able, till four o'clock, dur-
ing which we passed several keys, but could not meet with a ship; and, still
famishing with thirst, went ashore on one of those keys again, in hopes of
finding some water. Here we found some leaves with a few drops of water on
them, which we lapped with much eagerness; we then dug in several places,
but without success.

As we were digging holes in search of water, there came forth some very
thick and black stuff; but none of us could touch it, except the poor Dutch
creole, who drank about a quart of it as eagerly as if it had been wine. We
tried to catch fish, but could not; and we now began to repine at our fate,
and abandon ourselves to despair; when, in the midst of our murmuring, the
captain all at once cried out, 'A sail! a sail! a sail!' This gladdening sound was
like a reprieve to a convict, and we all instantly turned to look at it;—but in
a little time some of us began to be afraid it was not a sail. However at a ven-
ture we embarked, and steered after it; and, in half an hour, to our unspeak-
able joy, we plainly saw that it was a vessel. At this our drooping spirits
revived, and we made towards her with all the speed imaginable. When we
came near to her we found she was a little sloop, about the size of a
Gravesend troy, and quite full of people;—a circumstance of which we could
not make out the meaning. Our Captain, who was a Welchman, swore that
they were pirates and would kill us. I said "be that as it might, we must board
her, if we were to die by it; and, if they should not receive us kindly, we must
oppose them, as well as we could; for there was no alternative between their

perishing and ours." This counsel was immediately taken and I really believe that the Captain, myself, and the Dutchman would then have faced twenty men. We had two cutlasses and a musket, that I brought in the boat, and in this situation we rowed alongside and immediately boarded her. I believe there were about forty hands on board; but how great our surprise, as soon we got on board, to find that the major part of them were in the same predicament as ourselves!

They belonged to a whaling schooner, that was wrecked, two days before us, about nine miles to the north of our vessel. When she was wrecked, some of them had taken to their boats, and had left some of their people and property on a key as we had done, and were going, like us, to New Providence in quest of a ship, when they met with this little sloop, called a wrecker; whose employment in those seas is to look after wrecks. They were then going to take the remainder of the people belonging to the schooner; for which the wrecker was to have all things belonging to the vessel, and likewise their people's help to get all they could out of her, and were then to carry the crew to New Providence.

V.

We told the people of the wrecker the condition of our vessel; and we made the same agreement with them as the schooner's people had done; and, on their complying, we begged of them to go to our key directly, because our people were in want of water. They agreed, therefore, to go along with us first; and in two days we arrived at the key, to the inexpressible joy of the people that we had left behind, as they had been reduced to great extremities for want of water in our absence. Luckily for us, the wrecker had now more people on board than she could carry or victual for any moderate length of time; they therefore hired the schooner's people to work on the wreck, and we left them our boat, and embarked for New Providence.

Nothing could have been more fortunate than our meeting with this wrecker, for New Providence was at such a distance, we never could have reached it in our boat. The island of Abbico was much longer than we expected; and it was not till after sailing for three or four days, that we got safe to the farther end of it, towards New Providence. When arrived there we watered, and got a good many lobsters and other shell-fish; which proved a great relief to us, as our provisions and water were almost exhausted. We then proceeded on our voyage, but the day after we left the island, and late in the evening, while we were yet amongst the Bahama keys, we were overtaken by

a violent gale of wind which obliged us to cut away the mast. The vessel was very near foundering; for she parted from her anchors and struck several times on the shoals. We here expected her every minute to go to pieces, and each moment to be our last: so much so, that my old captain, and sickly useless mate, and several others, fainted; and death stared us in the face on every side.

All the swearers on board now began to call on the God of Heaven to assist them: and, sure enough, beyond our comprehension, He did assist us, and in a miraculous manner delivered us! In the very height of our extremity the wind lulled for a few minutes, and although the swell was high, beyond expression, two men, who were expert swimmers, attempted to go to the buoy of the anchor, which we still saw in the water at some distance, in a little punt that belonged to the wrecker, which was not large enough to carry more than two. She filled at different times in their endeavours to get into her, alongside of our vessel; and nothing but death appeared before them and us; but, however, they said they might as well die that way as any other. A coil of very small rope, with a little buoy, was put in along with them; and, at last, they got the punt clear from the vessel, and these two intrepid water heroes paddled away for life towards the buoy of the anchor.

Our eyes were fixed on them all the time, expecting every minute to be their last: and the prayers of all those that remained in their senses, were offered up to God, on their behalf, for a speedy deliverance, and for our own, which depended on them; and He heard and answered us! These two men at last reached the buoy; and, having fastened the punt to it, they tied one end of their rope to the small buoy that they had in the punt, and sent it adrift towards the vessel. We on board, observing this, threw out boat-hooks and leads fastened to lines, in order to catch the buoy: at last we caught it, and fastened a hawser to the end of the small rope. We then gave them a sign to pull, and they pulled the hawser to them and fastened it to the buoy; which being done, we hauled for our lives; and, through the mercy of God, we got again from the shoals into deep water, and the punt got safe to the vessel.

It is impossible for any to conceive our heart-felt joy, at this second deliverance from ruin, but those who have suffered the same hardships. Those whose strength and senses were gone, came to themselves, and were now as elated as they were before depressed. Two days after this the wind ceased, and the water became smooth. The punt then went on shore, and we cut down some trees; and having found our mast and mended it, we brought it on board, and fixed it up. As soon as we had done this we got up the anchor, and away we went once more for New Providence, which in three days more

we reached safe, after having been above three weeks in a situation from which we did not expect to escape with life.

VI.

The inhabitants here were very kind to us; and having learned our situation, they shewed us a great deal of hospitality and friendship. Soon after this, every one of my old fellow-sufferers, that were free, parted from us, and shaped their course as inclination led them. One merchant, who had a large sloop, seeing our condition, and knowing we wanted to go to Georgia, told four of us that his vessel was going there; and offered us our passage free, on condition of our helping to load and work the vessel. As we could not get any wages, and found it very hard to get off the place, we consented to his proposal; and went on board and helped to load the sloop, though we had only our victuals allowed us. When entirely loaded, he told us she was going to Jamaica first, where we must go if we went in her. This, however, I refused; but my fellow-sufferers, not having any money to help themselves with, were obliged by necessity to accept of the offer, and to steer the course, though they did not like it.

We stayed in New Providence about seventeen or eighteen days; during which time I met with many friends, who gave me encouragement to stay there with them, but I declined it; though, had not my heart been fixed on England, I should have stayed, as I liked the place extremely, and there were some free black people here who were very happy, and we passed our time pleasantly together, with the melodious sound of the catguts, under the lime and lemon trees. At length Captain Phillips hired a sloop to carry him and some of the slaves, that he could not sell here, to Georgia; and I agreed to go with him in the vessel, meaning now to take my farewell of that place. When the vessel was ready, we all embarked; and I took my leave of New Providence, not without regret.

We sailed about four o'clock in the morning, with a fair wind, for Georgia; and, about eleven o'clock the same morning, a sudden and short gale sprung up and blew away most of our sails; and, as we were still among the keys, in a very few minutes it dashed the sloop against the rocks. Luckily for us the water was deep; and the sea was not so angry, but that, after having for sometime laboured hard, and being many in number, we were saved through God's mercy: and, by using our greatest exertions, we got the vessel off. The next day we returned to Providence where we soon got her again

refitted. Some of the people swore that we had spells set upon us, by some-body in Montserrat; and others said that we had witches and wizards amongst the poor helpless slaves; and that we never should arrive safe at Georgia. But these things did not deter me; I said, 'Let us again face the winds and seas, and swear not, but trust to God, and he will deliver us.' We therefore once more set sail: and with hard labour, in seven days' time, arrived safe at Georgia.

After our arrival we went up to the town of Savannah; and the same evening I went to a friend's house to lodge, whose name was Mosa, a black man. We were very happy at meeting each other; and, after supper, we had a light, until between nine and ten o'clock at night. About that time the watch or patrol came by, and, discerning a light in the house, they knocked at the door; we opened it, and they came in and sat down, and drank some punch with us; they also begged some limes of me, as they understood I had some, which I readily gave them. A little after this, they told me I must go to the watch-house with them; this surprised me a good deal after our kindness to them, and I asked them, 'Why so?' They said, that all negroes, who had a light in their houses after nine o'clock were to be taken into custody, and either pay some dollars or be flogged. Some of these people knew that I was a free man; but, as the man of the house was not free, and had his master to protect him, they did not take the same liberty with him they did with me. I told them that I was a free man, and just arrived from Providence; that we were not making any noise, and that I was not a stranger in that place, but was very well known there; 'Besides,' said I, 'what will you do with me?'—'That you shall see,' replied they; 'but you must go to the watch-house with us.'

Now, whether they meant to get money from me or not, I was at a loss to know, but I thought immediately of the oranges and limes at Santa Cruz; and seeing that nothing would pacify them, I went with them to the watch-house, where I remained during the night. Early the next morning these imposing ruffians flogged a negro-man and woman that they had in the watch-house, and then they told me that I must be flogged too. I asked why; and if there was no law for free men; and told them if there was, I would have it put in force against them. But this only exasperated them the more, and they instantly swore they would serve me as Dr. Perkins had done; and were going to lay violent hands on me; when one of them, more humane than the rest, said, that as I was a free man they could not justify stripping me by law. I then immediately sent for Dr. Brady, who was known to be a honest and worthy man; and, on his coming to my assistance, they let me go.

VIII.

T his was not the only disagreeable incident I met with while I was in this place; for, one day, being a little way out of the town of Savannah, I was beset by two white men, who meant to play their usual tricks with me in the way of kidnapping. As soon as these men accosted me, one of them said to the other, 'This is the very fellow we are looking for, that you loss:' end the other swore immediately that I was the identical person. On this they made up to me, and were about to handle me, but I told them to be still and keep off, for I had seen those tricks played upon other free blacks, and they must not think to serve me so. At this they paused a little, and one said to the other, "It will not do;" and the other answered that I talked too good English. I replied I believed I did; and I had also with me a revengeful stick equal to the occasion; and my mind was likewise good. Happily, however it was not used: and, after we had talked together a little in this manner, the rogues left me.

I stayed in Savannah some time, anxiously trying to get to Montserrat, once more to see Mr. King, my old master; and then to take a final farewell of the American quarter of the globe. At last I met with a sloop called the Speedwell, Captain John Bunton, which belonged to Grenada, and was bound to Martinico, a French island, with a cargo of rice, and I shipped myself on board of her.

Before I left Georgia, a black woman, who had a child lying dead, being very tenacious of the church burial-service, and not able to get any white person to perform it, applied to me for that purpose. I told her I was no parson; and besides, that the service over the dead did not affect the soul. This however did not satisfy her; she still urged me very hard. I therefore complied with her entreaties, and at last consented to act the parson for the first time in my life. As she was much respected, there was a great company both of white and black people at the grave. I then, accordingly, assumed my new vocation, and performed the funeral ceremony to the satisfaction of all present; after which I bade adieu to Georgia, and sailed for Martinico.

CHAPTER IX.

The author arrives at Martinico—Meets with new difficulties—Gets to Montserrat, where he takes leave of his old master, and sails for England—Meets

Capt. Pascal—Learns the French horn—Hires himself with Dr. Irving, where he reams to freshen sea water—Leaves the Dr. and goes a voyage to Turkey and Portugal: and afterwards goes a voyage to Grenada, and another to Jamaica— Returns to the Dr. and they embark together on a voyage to the North Pole, with the Hon. Captain Phipps—Some account of that voyage, and the dangers the author was in—He returns to England.

I.

I THUS took a final leave of Georgia; for the treatment I had received in it disgusted me very much against the place; and when I left it and sailed for Martinico, I determined never more to revisit it. My new Captain conducted his vessel safer than my former one; and after an agreeable voyage, we got safe to our intended port. While I was on this island I went about a good deal, and found it very pleasant; in particular, I admired the town of St. Pierre, which is the principal one in the island, and built more like an European town than any I had seen in the West-Indies. In general also, slaves were better treated, had more holidays, and looked better than those in the English islands. After we had done our business here, I wanted my discharge, which was necessary; for it was then the month of May, and I wished much to be at Montserrat to bid farewell to Mr. King, and all my other friends there in time to sail for old England in the July fleet. But, alas! I had put a great stumbling block in my own way, by which I was near losing my passage that season to England. I had lent my Captain some money which I now wanted, to enable me to prosecute my intentions. This I told him; but when I applied for it, though I urged the necessity of my occasion I met with so much shuffling from him, that I began at last to be afraid of losing my money, as I could not recover it by law. For I have already mentioned, that throughout the West Indies no black man's testimony is admitted, on any occasion, against any white person whatever, and therefore my own oath would have been of no use. I was obliged, therefore, to remain with him till he might be disposed to return it to me.

Thus we sailed from Martinico for the Grenades. I frequently pressed the Captain for my money, to no purpose; and, to render my condition worse, when we got there, the Captain and his owners quarrelled. So that my situation became daily more irksome; for besides that we on board had little or no victuals allowed us, and I could not get my money nor wages, I could then have gotten my passage free to Montserrat had I been able to accept it. The

worst of all was, that it was growing late in July, and the ships in the islands must sail by the 26th of that month. At last, however, with a great many entreaties, I got my money from the Captain, and took the first vessel I could meet with for St. Eustatia. From thence I went in another to Basseterre in St. Kitt's where I arrived on the 19th of July.

On the 22nd, having met with a vessel bound to Montserrat, I wanted to go in her, but the Captain and others would not take me on board until I should advertise myself, and give notice of my going off the island. I told them of my haste to be in Montserrat, and that the time then would not admit of advertising, it being late in the evening, and the vessel about to sail; but he insisted it was necessary, and otherwise he said he would not take me. This reduced me to great perplexity, for if I should be compelled to submit to this degrading necessity, which every black freeman is under, of advertising himself like a slave, when he leaves an island, and which I thought a gross imposition upon any freeman, I feared I should miss that opportunity of going to Montserrat, and then I could not get to England that year. The vessel was just going off, and no time could be lost; I immediately therefore set about it, with a heavy heart, to try whom I could get to befriend me in complying with the demands of the Captain. Luckily I found, in a few minutes, some gentlemen of Montserrat whom I knew; and having told them my situation, I requested their friendly assistance in helping me off the island. Some of them, on this, went with me to the Captain and satisfied him of my freedom; and, to my very great joy, he desired me to go on board.

II.

We then set sail, and the next day, the 23rd, I arrived at the wished-for place, after an absence of six months, in which I had more than once experienced the delivering hand of Providence, when all human means of escaping destruction seemed hopeless. I saw my friends with a gladness of heart which was increased by my absence and the dangers I had escaped; and I was received with great friendship by them all, but particularly by Mr. King, to whom I related the fate of his sloop, the Nancy, and the causes of her being wrecked. I now learned with extreme sorrow, that his house was washed away during my absence, by the bursting of a pond at the top of a mountain that was opposite the town of Plymouth. It swept great part of the town away, and Mr. King lost a great deal of property from the inundation, and nearly his life. When I told him I intended to go to London that season,

and that I had come to visit him before my departure, the good man expressed a great deal of affection for me and sorrow that I should leave him, and warmly advised me to stay there; insisting, as I was much respected by all the gentlemen in the place, that I might do very well, and in a short time have land and slaves of my own. I thanked him for this instance of his friendship; but, as I wished very much to be in London, I declined remaining any longer there, and begged he would excuse me. I then requested he would be kind enough to give me a certificate of my behaviour while in his service, with which he very readily complied, and gave me the following:

Montserrat, 26th of the Seventh Month, 1767.
The bearer hereof, GUSTAVUS VASSA, was my slave for upwards
of three years, during which he has always behaved himself
well, and discharged his duty with honesty and assiduity.
ROBERT KING.

> To all whom this may concern.

Having obtained this, I parted from my kind master, after many sincere professions of gratitude and regard, and prepared for my departure for London. I immediately agreed to go with one Capt. John Hamer, for seven guineas (the passage to London), on board a ship called the Andromache; and on the 24th and 25th, I had free dances, as they are called, with some of my friends and countrymen, previous to my setting off; after which I took leave of all my friends, and on the 26th I embarked for London, exceedingly glad to see myself once more on board of a ship; and still more so, in steering the course I had long wished for. With a light heart I bade Montserrat farewell, and never had my feet on it since: and with it I bade adieu to the sound of the cruel whip, and all other dreadful instruments of torture; adieu to the offensive sight of the violated chastity of the sable females, which has too often accosted my eyes; adieu to oppressions; (although to me less severe than most of my countrymen) and adieu to the angry, howling dashing surfs. I wished for a grateful and thankful heart to praise the Lord God on high for all his mercies! In this ecstacy I steered the ship all night.

III.

We had a most prosperous voyage, and, at the end of seven weeks, arrived at Cherry Garden stairs. Thus were my longing eyes once

more gratified with a sight of London, after having been absent from it above four years. I immediately received my wages, and I never had earned seven guineas so quickly in my life before; I had thirty-seven guineas in all, when I got cleared of the ship. I now entered upon a scene quite new to me, but full of hope. In this situation my first thoughts were to look out for some of my former friends, and amongst the first of those were the Miss Guerins. As soon as I had regaled myself I went in quest of those kind ladies, whom I was very impatient to see, and, with some difficulty and perseverance, I found them at May's-hill, Greenwich. They were most agreeably surprised to see me, and I quite overjoyed at meeting with them. I told them my history, at which they expressed great wonder, and freely acknowledged it did their cousin, Captain Pascal, no honour. He then visited there frequently; and I met him, four or five days after, in Greenwich park. When he saw me, he appeared a good deal surprised, and asked me how I came back. I answered, "In a ship." To which he replied dryly, 'I suppose you did not walk back to London on the water.' As I saw, by his manner, that he did not seem to be sorry for his behaviour to me, and that I had not much reason to expect any favour from him, I told him that he had used me very ill, after I had been such a faithful servant to him for so many years, on which, without saying any more, he turned about and went away. A few days after this I met Captain Pascal at Miss Guerin's house, and asked him for my prize-money. He said there was none due to me, for, if my prize-money had been £10,000, he had a right to it all. I told him I was informed otherwise: on which he bade me defiance, and, in a bantering tone, desired me to commence a law-suit against him for it; 'There are lawyers enough,' said he, 'that will take the cause in hand, and you had better try it.' I told him then that I would try it, which enraged him very much; however, out of regard to the ladies I remained still, and never made any farther demand of my right.

Some time afterwards, these friendly ladies asked me what I meant to do with myself, and how they could assist me. I thanked them, and said, if they pleased, I would be their servant; but if not, I had thirty-seven guineas, which would support me for some time, and I would be much obliged to them to recommend me to some person who would teach me a trade whereby I might earn my living. They answered me very politely, that they were sorry it did not suit them to take me as their servant, and asked me what business I should like to learn. I said "hair dressing." They then promised to assist me in this; and soon after they recommended me to a gentleman, whom I had known before, one Captain O'Hara, who treated me with much

kindness, and procured me a master, a hair dresser, in Coventry Court, Haymarket, with whom he placed me.

I was with this man from September till the February following. In that time we had a neighbour in the same Court, who taught the French-horn. He used to blow it so well that I was charmed with it, and agreed with him to teach me to blow it. Accordingly he took me in hand, and began to instruct me, and I soon learned all the three parts. I took great delight in blowing on this instrument, the evenings being long, and besides that I was fond of it, I did not like to be idle, and it filled up my vacant hours innocently. At this time also I agreed with the Rev. Mr. Gregory, who lived in the same court, where he kept an academy and an evening school, to improve me in Arithmetic. This he did as far as Barter and Alligation; so that all the time I was here I was entirely employed.

In February 1768, I hired myself to Dr. Charles Irving, in Pall-mall, so celebrated for his successful experiments in making sea water fresh; and here I had plenty of hair-dressing to improve my hand. This gentleman was an excellent master; he was exceedingly kind and good-tempered; and allowed me in the evenings to attend my schools, which I esteemed a great blessing; therefore I thanked God and him for it, and used all diligence to improve the opportunity. This diligence and attention recommended me to the notice and care of my three preceptors, who, on their parts, bestowed a great deal of pains in my instruction, and besides were all very kind to me. My wages, however, which were by two thirds less than ever I had in my life (for I had only £12 per annum), I soon found would not be sufficient to defray this extraordinary expence of masters and my own necessary expences. My old thirty-seven guineas had by this time worn all away to one. I thought it best therefore to try the sea again in quest of more money, as I had been bred to it, and had hitherto found the profession of it successful. I had also, a very great desire to see Turkey, and I now determined to gratify it.

Accordingly, in the month of May, 1768, I told the doctor of my wish to go to sea again, to which he made no opposition; and we parted on friendly terms. The same day I went into the city in quest of a master. I was extremely fortunate in my enquiry; for I soon heard of a gentleman who had a ship going to Italy and Turkey, and he wanted a man who could dress hair well. I was overjoyed at this, and went immediately on board of his ship, as I had been directed, which I found to be fitted up with great taste, and I already foreboded no small pleasure in sailing in her. Not finding the gentleman on board, I was directed to his lodgings, where I met with him the next day, and

gave him a specimen of my dressing. He liked it so well that he hired me immediately, so that I was perfectly happy; for the ship, master, and voyage, were entirely to my mind.

IV.

T he ship was called the Delaware, and my master's name was John Jolly, a neat, smart, good-humoured man, just such a one as I wished to serve. We sailed from England in July following, and our voyage was extremely pleasant. We went to Villa Franca, Nice, and Leghorn; and in all these places I was charmed with the richness and beauty of the countries, and struck with the elegant buildings with which they abound. We had always in them plenty of extraordinary good wines and rich fruits, of which I was very fond; and I had frequent occasions of gratifying both my taste and curiosity; for my Captain always lodged on shore in those places, which afforded me opportunities to see the country around. I also learned navigation of the mate, of which I was very fond.

When we left Italy we had delightful sailing among the Archipelago islands, and from thence to Smyrna in Turkey. This is a very ancient city, the houses are built of stone, and most of them have graves adjoining to them, so that they sometimes present the appearance of churchyards. Provisions are very plentiful in this city, and good wine less than a penny a pint. The grapes, pomegranates, and many other fruits, were also the richest and largest I ever saw or tasted. The natives are good-looking and strong made, and always treated me with great civility. In general, I believe, they are fond of black people; and several of them gave me pressing invitations to stay amongst them, although they keep the Franks, or Christians, separate, and do not suffer them to dwell immediately amongst them. I was astonished at not seeing women in any of their shops, and very rarely any in the streets; and whenever I did, they were covered with a veil from head to foot, so that I could not see their faces, except when any of them, out of curiosity, uncovered them to look at me, which they sometimes did. I was surprised to see how the Greeks are, in some measure, kept under by the Turks, as the negroes are in the West Indies by the white people. The less refined Greeks, as I have already hinted, dance here in the same manner as we do in our nation.

On the whole, during our stay here, which was about five months, I liked the place and the Turks extremely well. I could not help observing one remarkable circumstance there:—the tails of the sheep are flat, and so very

large, that I have known the tail even of a lamb to weigh from eleven to thirteen pounds. The fat of them is very white and rich, and is excellent in puddings, for which it is much used. Our ship being at length richly loaded with silk and other articles, we sailed for England.

In May 1769, soon after our return from Turkey, our ship made a delightful voyage to Oporto in Portugal, where we arrived at the time of the carnival. On our arrival, there were sent on board of us thirty-six articles to be observed, with very heavy penalties if we should break any of them: and none of us even dared to go on board any other vessel or on shore, till the Inquisition had sent on board and searched for every thing illegal, especially Bibles. All we had were produced, and certain other things were sent on shore till the ships were going away: and any person, in whose custody a Bible was found concealed, was to be imprisoned and flogged, and sent into slavery for ten years.

I saw here many magnificent sights, particularly the garden of Eden, where many of the clergy and laity went in procession in their several orders with the host, and sung Te Deum. I had a great curiosity to go into some of their churches, but could not gain admittance without using the necessary sprinkling of holy water at my entrance. From curiosity, and a wish to be holy, I therefore complied with this ceremony; but its virtues were lost upon me, for I found myself nothing the better for it. This place abounds with plenty of all kinds of provisions. The town is well built and pretty, and commands a fine prospect. Our ship having taken in a load of wine and other commodities, we sailed for London, and arrived there in July following.

V.

Our next voyage was to the Mediterranean. The ship was again got ready, and we sailed in September for Genoa. This is one of the finest cities I ever saw; some of the edifices were of beautiful marble, and made a most notable appearance; and many had very curious fountains before them. The churches were rich and magnificent, and curiously adorned both in the inside and out. But all this grandeur was, in my eyes, disgraced by the galley-slaves, whose condition, both there and in other parts of Italy, is truly piteous and wretched. After we had staid there some weeks, during which we bought many different things we wanted, and got them very cheap, we sailed to Naples, a charming city and remarkably clean. The bay is the most beautiful I ever saw; the moles for shipping are excellent. I thought it extraordinary to

see grand operas acted here on Sunday nights, and even attended by their Majesties. I too, like these great ones, went to those sights, and vainly served God in the day while I thus served mammon effectually at night.

While we remained here, there happened an eruption of Mount Vesuvius, of which I had a perfect view. It was extremely awful; and we were so near that the ashes from it used to be thick on our deck. After we had transacted our business at Naples, we sailed with a fair wind once more for Smyrna, and arrived there in December. A seraskier, or officer, took a liking to me here, and wanted me to stay, offering me two wives. But I refused the temptation, thinking one was as much as some could manage, and more than others would venture on. The merchants here travel in caravans or large companies. I have seen many caravans from India, with some hundreds of camels, laden with different goods. The people of these caravans are quite brown. Among other articles, they brought with them a great quantity of locusts, which are a kind of pulse, sweet and pleasant to the palate, and in shape resembling French beans, but longer. Each kind of goods is sold in a street by itself, and I always found the Turks very honest in their dealings. They let no Christians into their mosques, or churches; for which I was very sorry, being always fond of going to see the different modes of worship of the people wherever I went.

The plague broke out while we were in Smyrna; and we stopped taking goods into the ship till it was over. She was then richly laden, and we sailed, in March 1770, for England. One day, on our passage, we met with an accident, which was near burning the ship: A black cook, in melting some fat, overset the pan into the fire under the deck, which immediately began to blaze, and the flame went up very high under the fore-top. With the fright the poor cook became almost white, and altogether speechless. Happily, however, we got the fire out without doing much mischief. After various delays in this passage, we arrived in Sandgate creek in July; and, at the latter end of the year, some new event occurred, so that my noble Captain, the ship, and I, all separated.

In April 1771, I shipped myself as a steward with Captain William Robertson, of the ship Grenada Planter, once more to try my fortune in the West Indies; and we sailed from London for Madeira, Barbadoes, and the Grenades. When we were at this last place, having some goods to sell, I met once more with my former kind of West-India customers. A white man, an islander, bought some goods of me to the amount of some pounds, and made me many fair promises, as usual, but without any intention of paying me. He had likewise bought goods from some more of our people, whom he intend-

ed to serve in the same manner; but still he amused us with promises. However, when our ship was loaded and near sailing, this honest buyer discovered no intention or sign of paying for any thing he had bought of us; but, on the contrary, when I asked him for my money, he threatened me and another black man he had bought goods of, so that we found we were like to get more blows than payment. On this we went to complain to one Mr. Mac Intosh, a justice of the peace; we told his worship of the man's villainous tricks, and begged that he would be kind enough to see us redressed. But being negroes, although free, we could not get any remedy; and our ship being then just upon the point of sailing, we knew not how to help ourselves, though we thought it hard to lose our property in this manner. Luckily for us, however, this man was also indebted to three white sailors, who could not get a farthing from him; they therefore readily joined us, and we all went together in search of him. When we found where he was, I took him out of a house and threatened him with vengeance; on which, finding he was likely to be handled roughly, the rogue offered each of us some small allowance, but nothing near our demands. This exasperated us much more; and some were for cutting his ears off; but he begged hard for mercy, which was at last granted him, after we had entirely stripped him. We then let him go, for which he thanked us, glad to get off so easily, and ran into the bushes, after having wished us a good voyage. We then repaired on board, and shortly after set sail for England.

VI.

I cannot help remarking here a very narrow escape we had from being blown up, owing to a piece of negligence of mine. Just as our ship was under sail, I went down under the cabin, to do some business, and had a lighted candle in my hand, which, in my hurry, without thinking, I held in a barrel of gunpowder. It remained in the powder, until it was near catching fire, when, fortunately, I observed it, and snatched it out in time, and providentially no harm happened; but I was so overcome with terror, that I immediately fainted at this deliverance.

In twenty-eight days' time we arrived in England, and I got clear of the ship. But being still of a roving disposition, and desirous of seeing as many different parts of the world as I could, I shipped myself soon after, in the same year, as steward, on board of a fine large ship, called the Jamaica, Captain David Watt, and we sailed from England in December 1771, for

Nevis and Jamaica. I found Jamaica to be a very fine large island, well-peopled, and the most considerable of the West-India islands. There was a vast number of negroes here, whom I found, as usual, exceedingly imposed upon by the white people, and the slaves punished as in the other islands. There are negroes whose business it is to flog slaves; they go about to different people for employment, and the usual pay is from one to four bits. I saw many cruel punishments inflicted on the slaves in the short time I stayed here. In particular I was present when a poor fellow was tied up, and kept hanging by the wrists at some distance from the ground, and then some half-hundred weights were fixed to his ancles, in which posture he was flogged most unmercifully.—There were also, as I heard, two different masters noted for cruelty on the island, who had staked up two negroes naked, and in two hours the vermin stung them to death. I heard gentleman, whom I knew, tell my Captain, that he passed sentence on a negroe man to be burnt alive for attempting to poison an overseer.

I pass over numerous instances, in order to relieve the reader by a milder scene of roguery. Before I had been long on the island, one Mr. Smith, at Port Morant, bought goods of me to the amount of £25 sterling: but when I demanded payment from him, he was each time going to beat me, and threatened to put me in gaol. One time he would say I was going to set his house on fire; at another he would swear I was going to run away with his slaves. I was astonished at this usage from a person who was in the situation of a gentleman; but I had no alternative, and was therefore obliged to submit. When I came to Kingston, I was surprised to see the number of Africans who were assembled together on Sundays; particularly at a large commodious place, called Spring Bath. Here each different nation of Africa meets and dances after the manner of their own country. They still retain most of their native customs: they bury their dead, and put victuals, pipes, and tobacco, and other things in the grave with the corpse, in the same manner as in Africa.

Our ship having got her loading, we sailed for London, where we arrived in the August following. On my return to London, I waited on my old and good master, Dr. Irving, who made me an offer of his service again. Being now tired of the sea, I gladly accepted it. I was very happy in living with this gentleman once more; during which time we were daily employed in reducing old Neptune's dominions, by purifying the briny element, and making it fresh. Thus I went on till May 1773, when I was roused by the sound of fame to seek new adventures, and find, towards the North Pole, what our Creator

never intended we should, a passage to India. An expedition was fitting out to explore a north-east passage, conducted by the Hon. Constantine John Phipps, since Lord Mulgrave, in his Majesty's sloop of war the Race Horse.

VII.

M y master being anxious for the reputation of this adventure, we therefore prepared every thing for our voyage, and I attended him on board the Race Horse, the 24th day of May, 1773. We proceeded to Sheerness where we were joined by his Majesty's sloop the Carcass, commanded by Captain Lutwidge. On the 4th of June we sailed towards our destined place, the Pole; and on the 15th of the same month we were off Shetland. On this day I had a great and unexpected deliverance from an accident which was near blowing up the ship, and destroying the crew, which made me ever after, during the voyage, uncommonly cautious. The ship was so filled that there was very little room for any one on board; which placed me in a very awkward situation. I had resolved to keep a journal of this singular and interesting voyage; and I had no other place for this purpose but a little cabin, or the doctor's store-room, where I slept. This little place was stuffed with all manner of combustibles, particularly with tow and aquafortis, and many other dangerous things. Unfortunately it happened in the evening, as I was writing my journal, that I had occasion to take the candle out of the lanthorn, and a spark having touched a single thread of the tow, all the rest caught the flame, and immediately the whole was in a blaze. I beheld nothing but present death before me, and expected to be the first to perish in the flames. In a moment the alarm was spread, and many people who were near, ran to assist in putting out the fire.

All this time I was in the very midst of the flames; my shirt, and the handkerchief on my neck, were burnt, and I was almost smothered with the smoke. But through God's mercy, as I was nearly giving up all hopes, some people brought blankets and mattresses and threw them on the flames: by which means, in a short time, the fire was put out. I was severely reprimanded and menaced by such of the officers as knew it; and strictly charged never more to go there with a light; and, indeed, my fears made me give heed to this command for a little time; but at last, not being able to write my journal in any other part of the ship, I was tempted again to venture, by stealth, with a light in the same cabin, though not without considerable fear and dread on my mind.

On the 20th of June we began to use Dr. Irving's apparatus for making salt water fresh. I used to attend the distillery; I frequently purified from twenty-six to forty gallons a day. The water thus distilled was perfectly pure, well tasted, and free from salt; and was used on various occasions on board the ship. On the 28th of June, being in lat. 78° we made Greenland, where I was surprised to see the sun did not set. The weather now became extremely cold; and as we sailed between north and east, which was our course, we saw many very high and curious mountains of ice; and also a great number of very large whales, which used to come close to our ship, and blow the water up to a very great height in the air. One morning we had vast quantities of sea-horses about the ship, which neighed exactly like any other horses. We fired some harpoon guns amongst them in order to take some, but we could not get any.

On the 30th, the Captain of a Greenland ship came on board, and told us of three ships that were lost in the ice; however, we still held on our course till July the 11th, when we were stopped by one compact impenetrable body of ice. We ran along it from east to west above ten degrees; and on the 27th we got as far north as 80°, 37'; and in 19 or 20 degrees east longitude from London. On the 29th and 30th of July, we saw one continued plain of smooth unbroken ice bounded only by the horizon, and we fastened to a piece of ice that was eight yards eleven inches thick. We had generally sunshine, and constant day-light; which gave cheerfulness and novelty to the whole of this striking, grand, and uncommon scene; and, to heighten it still more, the reflection of the sun from the ice gave the clouds a most beautiful appearance.

We killed many different animals at this time, and, among the rest, nine bears. Though they had nothing in their paunches but water, yet they were all very fat. We used to decoy them to the ship sometimes by burning feathers or skins. I thought them coarse eating, but some of the ship's company relished them very much. Some of our people once, in a boat, fired at and wounded a sea-horse, which dived immediately; and in a little time after brought up with it a number of others. They all joined in an attack upon the boat, and were with difficulty prevented from staving or oversetting her; but a boat from the Carcass having come to assist ours, and joined it, they dispersed after having wrested an oar from one of the men. One of the ship's boats had before been attacked in the same manner, but happily no harm was done. Though we wounded several of these animals we got but one.

VII.

We remained hereabouts until the 1st of August, when the two ships got completely fastened in the ice occasioned by the loose ice that set in from the sea. This made our situation very dreadful and alarming; so that on the 7th day we were in very great apprehension of having the ship squeezed to pieces. The officers held a council to know what was best to do in order to save our lives, and it was determined that we should endeavour to escape by dragging our boats along the ice towards the sea; which, however, was farther off than any of us thought. This determination filled us with extreme dejection, and confounded us with despair; for we had very little prospect of escaping with life. However, we sawed some of the ice about the ships, to keep it from hurting them, and thus kept them in a kind of pond. We then began to drag the boats, as well as we could, towards the sea; but, after two or three days' labour we made very little progress; so that some of our hearts totally failed us, and I really began to give up myself for lost, when I saw our surrounding calamities.

While we were at this hard labour, I once fell into a pond we had made amongst some loose ice, and was very near being drowned; but providentially some people were near who gave me immediate assistance, and thereby I escaped drowning. Our deplorable condition, which kept up the constant apprehension of our perishing in the ice brought me gradually to think of eternity in such a manner as I had never done before. I had the fears of death hourly upon me, and shuddered at the thoughts of meeting the grim king of terrors in the natural state I then was in, and was exceedingly doubtful of a happy eternity, if I should die in it. I had no hopes of my life being prolonged for any time, for we saw that our existence could not be long on the ice after leaving the ships, which were now out of sight, and some miles from the boats. Our appearance now became truly lamentable; pale dejection seized every countenance; many, who had been before blasphemers, in this our distress began to call on the good God of heaven for his help; and, in the time of our utter need He heard us, and, against hope or human probability, He delivered us!

It was the eleventh day of the ships being thus fastened, and the fourth of our drawing the boats in this manner, that the wind changed to the E. N. E. The weather immediately became mild and the ice broke towards the sea, which was to the S. W. of us. Many of us, on this, got on board again, and with all our might we hove the ships into every open water we could find and

made all the sail on them in our power; and now, having a prospect of success, we made signals for the boats and the remainder of the people. This seemed to us like a reprieve from death; and happy was the man who could first get on board of any ship, or the first boat he could meet. We proceeded in this manner till we got into open water again, which we accomplished in about thirty hours, to our infinite joy and gladness of heart. As soon as we were out of danger, we came to anchor and refitted; and on the 19th of August we sailed from this uninhabited extremity of the world, where the inhospitable climate affords neither food nor shelter, and not a tree or shrub of any kind grows amongst its barren rocks; but where all is one desolate and expanded waste of ice, which even the constant beams of the sun, for six months in the year, cannot penetrate or dissolve. The sun now being on the decline, the days shortened as we sailed to the southward: and, on the 28th, in lat. 73°, it was dark by ten o'clock at night. September the 10th, in latitude 58°, 59', we met a very severe gale of wind and high seas, and shipped a great deal of water in the space of ten hours. This made us labour exceedingly hard at all our pumps a whole day, and one sea, which struck the ship with more force than any thing I ever met with of the kind before, laid her under water for some time, so that we thought she would have gone down. Two boats were washed from the booms, and the long boat from the chucks: all other movable things on the decks were also washed away; among which were many curious things of different kinds which we had brought from Greenland; and in order to lighten the ship we were obliged to toss some of our guns overboard. We saw a ship, at the same time, in very great distress, and her masts gone; but we were unable to assist her. We now lost sight of the Carcass till the 26th, when we saw land about Orfordness, off which place she joined us. From thence we sailed for London, and on the 30th came up to Deptford. And thus ended our Arctic voyage, to the no small joy of all on board, after having been absent four months, in which time, at the imminent hazard of our lives, we explored nearly as far towards the Pole as 81 degrees north, and 20 degrees east longitude; being much farther, by all accounts, than any navigator had ever ventured before; in which we fully proved the impracticability of finding a passage that way to India.

CHAPTER X.

The author leaves Dr. Irving, and engages on board a Turkey ship—Account of a black man's being kidnapped on board, and sent to the West-Indies, and the author's fruitless endeavours to procure his freedom—Some account of the manner of the author's conversion to the faith of Jesus Christ.

I.

O UR VOYAGE to the North Pole being ended, I returned to London with Dr. Irving; with whom I continued for some time, during which I began seriously to reflect on the dangers I had escaped, particularly those of my last voyage, which made a lasting impression on my mind, and, by the grace of God, proved afterwards a mercy to me; it caused me to reflect deeply on my eternal state, and to seek the Lord with full purpose of heart ere it was too late. I rejoiced greatly; and heartily thanked the Lord for directing me to London, where I was determined to work out my own salvation, and, in so doing, procure a title to heaven; this being the result of a mind blinded by ignorance and sin.

In process of time I left my master, Dr. Irving, the purifier of waters. I lodged in Coventry Court, Haymarket, where I was continually oppressed and much concerned about the salvation of my soul, and was determined in my own strength to be a first-rate Christian. I used every means for this purpose; and not being able to find any person amongst those with whom I was then acquainted, that acquiesced with me in point of religion, or, in scripture language, that would shew me any good, I was much dejected, and knew not where to seek relief; however, I first frequented the neighbouring churches, St. James's and others, two or three times a day for many weeks. Still I came away dissatisfied; something was wanting that I could not obtain, and I really found more heart-felt relief in reading my Bible at home than in attending the church, and being resolved to be saved, I pursued other methods. First I went among the people called Quakers, whose meeting at times was held in silence, and I remained as much in the dark as ever. I then searched into the Roman Catholic principles; but was not in the least edified. I at length had recourse to the Jews, which availed me nothing, as the fear of eternity daily harassed my mind, and I knew not where to seek shelter from the wrath to come.

II.

However, this was my conclusion, at all events, to read the Four Evangelists, and whatever sect or party I found adhering thereto, such I would join. Thus I went on heavily without any guide to direct me the way that leadeth to eternal life. I asked different people questions about the manner of going to heaven, and was told different ways. Here I was much staggered, and could not find any at that time more righteous than myself, or indeed so much inclined to devotion. I thought we should not all be saved (this is agreeable to the scriptures), nor would all be damned. I found none among the circle of my acquaintance that kept wholly the Ten Commandments. So righteous was I in my own eyes, that I was convinced I excelled many of them in that point, by keeping eight out of ten; and finding those, who in general termed themselves Christians, not so honest nor so good in their morals as the Turks, I really thought the Turks were in a safer way of salvation than my neighbours; so that between hopes and fears I went on, and the chief comforts I enjoyed were in the musical French-horn, which I then practiced, and also dressing of hair. Such was my situation some months, experiencing the dishonesty of many people here. I determined at last to set out for Turkey and there to end my days.

It was now early in the spring 1874. I sought for a master, and found a captain John Hughes, commander of a ship called the Anglicania, fitting out in the river Thames, and bound to Smyrna in Turkey. I shipped myself with him as steward; at the same time I recommended to him a very clever black man, John Annis, as a cook. This man was on board the ship near two months doing his duty: he had formerly lived many years with Mr. William Kirkpatrick, a gentleman of the island of St. Kitt's, from whom he parted by consent, though he afterwards tried many schemes to inveigle the poor man. He had applied to many Captains, who traded to St. Kitt's, to trepan him; and when all their attempts and schemes of kidnapping proved abortive, Mr. Kirkpatrick came to our ship at Union Stairs, on Easter Monday, April the 4th, with two wherry-boats and six men, having learned that the man was on board; and tied, and forcibly took him away from the ship, in the presence of the crew and the chief mate, who had detained him after he had information to come away. I believe this was a combined piece of business: but be that as it may, it certainly reflected great disgrace on the mate and Captain also; who, although they had desired the oppressed man to stay on board, yet

notwithstanding this vile act on the man who had served him, he did not in the least assist to recover him, or pay me a farthing of his wages, which was about Five Pounds. I proved the only friend he had who attempted to regain him his liberty, if possible, having known the want of liberty myself. I sent, as soon as I could, to Gravesend, and got knowledge of the ship in which he was; but, unluckily, she had sailed the first tide after he was put on board. My intention was then immediately to apprehend Mr. Kirkpatrick, who was about setting off for Scotland; and having obtained a habeas corpus for him, and got a tipstaff to go with me to St. Paul's church-yard, where he lived, he, suspecting something of this kind, set a watch to look out. My being known to them obliged me to use the following deception: I whitened my face, that they might not know me; and this had the desired effect. He did not go out of his house that night, and next morning I contrived a well plotted stratagem, notwithstanding he had a gentleman in his house to personate him. My direction to the tipstaff had the desired effect; he got admittance into the house, and conducted him to a judge, according to the writ. When he came there, his plea was, that he had not the body in custody, on which he was admitted to bail. I proceeded immediately to that well-known philanthropist Granville Sharp, Esq. who received me with the utmost kindness, and gave me every instruction that was needful on the occasion. I left him in full hope that I should gain the unhappy man his liberty, with the warmest sense of gratitude towards Mr. Sharp for his kindness. But, alas! my attorney proved unfaithful: he took my money, lost me many months' employ, and did not the least good in the cause. When the poor man arrived at St. Kitt's, he was, according to custom, staked to the ground with four pins through a cord, two on his wrists, and two on his ancles; was cut and flogged most unmercifully, and afterwards loaded cruelly with irons about his neck. I had two very moving letters from him, while he was in this situation; and I made attempts to go after him at a great hazard, but was sadly disappointed: I also was told of it by some very respectable families, now in London, who saw him in St. Kitt's, in the same state, in which he remained till kind death released him out of the hands of his tyrants.

III.

During this disagreeable business I was under strong convictions of sin, and thought that my state was worse than any man's, my mind was unaccountably disturbed; I often wished for death, though at the same time

convinced that I was altogether unprepared for that awful summons. Suffering much by villains in the late cause, and being much concerned about the state of my soul, these things (but particularly the latter) brought me very low; so that I became a burden to myself, and viewed all things around me as emptiness and vanity, which could give no satisfaction to a troubled conscience. I was again determined to go to Turkey, and resolved, at that time, never more to return to England. I engaged as steward on board a Turkeyman, the Wester Hall, Captain Lina; but was prevented by means of my late Captain, Mr. Hughes, and others. All this appeared to be against me, and the only comfort I then experienced was in reading the holy scriptures, where I saw that 'there is no new thing under the sun.' (Eccles. i. 9.) And what was appointed for me I must submit to. Thus I continued to travel in much heaviness, and frequently murmured against the Almighty, particularly in his providential dealings; and, awful to think! I began to blaspheme, and wished often to be any thing but a human being.

In these severe conflicts the Lord answered me by awful 'visions of the night, when deep sleep falleth upon men, in slumbering upon the bed.' (Job xxxiii. 15.) He was pleased, in much mercy, to give me to see, and in some measure understand, the great and awful scene of the judgment-day that 'no unclean person, no unholy thing, can enter into the kingdom of God.' (Eph. v. 5.) I would then, if it had been possible, have changed my nature with the meanest worm on the earth; and was ready to say to the mountains and rocks, 'fall on me.' (Rev. vi. 16.) But all in vain! I then in the greatest agony requested the Divine Creator, that he would grant me a small space of time to repent of my follies and vile iniquities, which I felt to be grievous. The Lord, in his manifold mercies, was pleased to grant my request; and being yet in a state of time, the sense of God's mercies was so great on my mind when I awoke, that my strength entirely failed me for many minutes, and I was exceedingly weak. This was the first spiritual mercy I ever was sensible of; and being on praying ground, as soon as I recovered a little strength, and got out of bed and dressed myself, I invoked Heaven from my inmost soul, and fervently begged that God would never again permit me to blaspheme his most holy name. The Lord, who is long-suffering, and full of compassion to such poor rebels as we are, condescended to hear and answer. I felt that I was altogether unholy, and saw clearly what a bad use I had made of the faculties I was endowed with; they were given me to glorify God with; I thought, therefore, I had better want them here, and enter into life eternal, than abuse them and be cast into hell-fire.

I prayed to be directed, if there were any holier persons than those with whom I was acquainted, that the Lord would point them out to me. I appealed to the Searcher of hearts, whether I did not wish to love him more, and serve him better. Notwithstanding all this, the reader may easily discern, if a believer, that I was still in nature's darkness. At length I hated the house in which I lodged, because God's most holy name was blasphemed in it; then I saw the word of God verified, viz. 'Before they call, I will answer; and while they are yet speaking, I will hear.'

I had a great desire to read the Bible the whole day at home; but not having a convenient place for retirement, I left the house in the day, rather than stay amongst the wicked ones; and that day, as I was walking, it pleased God to direct me to a house where there was an old sea-faring man, who experienced much of the love of God shed abroad in his heart. He began to discourse with me, and, as I desired to love the Lord, his conversation rejoiced me greatly; and indeed I had never heard before the love of Christ to believers set forth in such a manner, and in so clear a point of view. Here I had more questions to put to the man, than his time would permit him to answer; and in that memorable hour there came in a dissenting minister; he joined our discourse, and asked me some few questions; among others, where I heard the gospel preached. I knew not what he meant by "hearing the gospel;" I told him I had read the gospel; and he asked me, where I went to church, or whether I went at all or not. To which I replied 'I attend St. James's, St. Martin's, and St. Ann's Soho.'—'So,' said he, 'you are a church-man?' I answered, I was. He then invited me to a love-feast at his chapel that evening. I accepted the offer, and thanked him; and soon after he went away, I had some further discourse with the old Christian, added to some profitable reading, which made me exceedingly happy. When I left him he reminded me of coming to the feast; I assured him I would be there. Thus we parted, and I weighed over the heavenly conversation that had passed between these two men, which cheered my then heavy and drooping spirit more than any thing I had met with for many months.

However, I thought the time long in going to my supposed banquet. I also wished much for the company of these friendly men, their company pleased me much: and I thought the gentleman very kind in asking me, a stranger, to a feast; but how singular did it appear to me, to have it in a chapel! When the wished-for hour came I went, and happily the old man was there, who kindly seated me, as he belonged to the place. I was much astonished to see the place filled with people, and no signs of eating and drinking.

There were many ministers in the company. At last they began by giving out hymns, and, between the singing, the ministers engaged in prayer: in short, I knew not what to make of this sight, having never seen any thing of the kind in my life before now. Some of the guests began to speak their experience, agreeably to what I read in the Scriptures: much was said by every speaker of the providence of God, and his unspeakable mercies to each of them. This I knew in a great measure, and could most heartily join them. But when they spoke of a future state, they seemed to be altogether certain of their calling and election of God; and that no one could ever separate them from the love of Christ, or pluck them out of his hands. This filled me with utter consternation, intermingled with admiration. I was so amazed as not to know what to think of the company; my heart was attracted, and my affections were enlarged; I wished to be as happy as they, and was persuaded in my mind that they were different from the world, that lieth in wickedness. (I John v. 19.) Their language and singing, &c. did well harmonize; I was entirely overcome, and wished to live and die thus. Lastly, some persons produced some neat baskets full of buns, which they distributed about; and each person communicated with his neighbour, and sipped water out of different mugs, which they handed about to all who were present.

This kind of Christian fellowship I had never seen, nor ever thought of seeing on earth. It fully reminded me of what I had read in the holy Scriptures, of the primitive Christians, who loved each other and broke bread, in partaking of it, even from house to house. This entertainment (which lasted about four hours) ended in singing and prayer. It was the first soul-feast I ever was present at. These last twenty-four hours produced me things spiritual and temporal, sleeping and waking, judgment and mercy, that I could not but admire the goodness of God, in directing the blind, blasphemous sinner in the path that he knew not of, even among the just, and instead of judgment he hath shewed mercy, and will hear and answer the prayers and supplications of every returning prodigal.

> O! to grace how great a debtor
> Daily I'm constrain'd to be!

IV.

After this I was resolved to win heaven, if possible; and if I perished I thought it should be at the feet of Jesus, in praying to him for salvation.

After having been an eye-witness to some of the happiness which attended those who feared God, I knew not how, with any propriety, to return to my lodgings, where the name of God was continually profaned, at which I felt the greatest horror; I paused in my mind for some time, not knowing what to do; whether to hire a bed elsewhere, or go home again. At last, fearing an evil report might arise, I went home, with a farewell to card-playing and vain jesting, &c. I saw that time was very short, eternity long, and very near; and I viewed those persons alone blessed, who were found ready at midnight call, or when the judge of all, both quick and dead, cometh.

The next day I took courage, and went to Holborn, to see my new and worthy acquaintance, the old man, Mr. C—. He and his wife, a gracious woman, were at work in silk-weaving; they seemed mutually happy, and both quite glad to see me, and I more to see them. I sat down and we conversed much about soul matters, &c. Their discourse was amazingly delightful, edifying, and pleasant. I knew not at last how to leave this agreeable pair, till time summoned me away. As I was departing, they lent me a little book, entitled "The Conversion of an Indian." It was in questions and answers. The poor man came over the sea to London, to enquire after the Christian's God whom, through rich mercy, he found, and had not his journey in vain. The above book was of great use to me, and at that time was a means of strengthening my faith; in parting, they both invited me to call on them when I pleased. This delighted me, and I took care to make all the improvement from it I could; and so far I thanked God for such company and desires. I prayed that the many evils I felt within might be done away, and that I might be weaned from my former carnal acquaintances. This was quickly heard and answered, and I was soon connected with those who the scripture calls "the excellent of the earth." I heard the gospel preached, and the thoughts of my heart and actions were laid open by the preachers, and the way of salvation by Christ alone was evidently set forth.

Thus I went on happily for near two months: and I once heard, during this period, a reverend gentleman, Mr. G—, speak of a man who had departed this life in full assurance of his going to glory. I was much astonished at the assertion; and did very deliberately inquire how he could get at this knowledge. I was answered fully, agreeably to what I read in the oracles of truth: and was told also, that if I did not experience the new birth, and the pardon of my sins, through the blood of Christ, before I died, I could not enter the kingdom of heaven.

I knew not what to think of this report, as I thought I kept eight com-

mandments out of ten: then my worthy interpreter told me I did not do it, nor could I; and he added, that no man ever did or could keep the commandments, without offending in one point. I thought this sounded very strangely; it puzzled me much for many weeks; for I thought it a hard saying. I then asked my friend Mr. L——d, who was clerk in a chapel, why the commandments of God were given, if we could not be saved by them. To which he replied, 'The law is a school-master to bring us to Christ,' who alone could, and did keep the commandments, and fulfilled all their requirements for his elect people, even those to whom he had given a living faith, and the sins of those chosen vessels were already atoned for, and forgiven them whilst living; and if I did not experience the same before my exit, the Lord would say at that great day to me, "Go, ye cursed," &c. &c. for God would appear faithful in his judgments to the wicked, as he would be faithful in strewing mercy to those who were ordained to it before the world was; therefore Christ Jesus seemed to be all in all to that man's soul.

V.

I was much wounded at this discourse, and brought into such a dilemma as I never expected. I asked him, if he was to die that moment, whether he was sure to enter the kingdom of God: and added, 'Do you know that your sins are forgiven you?' He answered in the affirmative. Then confusion, anger, and discontent seized me, and I staggered much at this sort of doctrine: it brought me to a stand, not knowing what to believe, whether salvation by works, or by faith only in Christ. I requested him to tell me how I might know when my sins were forgiven me. He assured me he could not, and that none but God alone could do this. I told him it was very mysterious; but he said it was really matter of fact, and quoted many portions of a scripture immediately to the point, to which I could make no reply. He then desired me to pray to God to shew me these things. I answered I prayed to God every day. He said, 'I perceive you are a church-man.' I answered I was. He then entreated me to beg of God to shew me what I was, and the true state of my soul. I thought the prayer very short and odd; so we parted for that time.

I weighed all these things over, and could not help thinking how it was possible for a man to know his sins were forgiven him in this life. I wished that God would reveal this self-same thing to me. In a short time after this, I went to Westminster chapel: The Rev. Mr. P— preached from Lam. iii 39. It was a wonderful sermon; he clearly shewed that a living man had no cause

to complain for the punishments of his sins he evidently justified the Lord in all his dealings with the sons of men he also shewed the justice of God in the eternal punishment of the wicked and impenitent. The discourse seemed to me like a two-edged sword cutting all ways. It afforded me much joy, intermingled with many fears about my soul; and when it was ended he gave it out that he intended, the ensuing week, to examine all those who meant to attend the Lord's table. Now I thought much of my good works, and at the same time was doubtful of my being a proper object to receive the sacrament; I was full of meditation till the day of examining.

However I went to the chapel; and, though much distressed, I addressed the reverend gentleman, thinking if I was not right, he would endeavour to convince me of it. When I conversed with him, the first thing he asked me was, What I knew of Christ. I told him I believed in him, and had been baptized in his name. 'Then,' said he, 'when were you brought to the knowledge of God? and how were you convinced of sin?' I knew not what he meant by these questions. I told him I kept eight commandments out of ten; but that I sometimes swore on board of ship, and sometimes when on shore, and broke the sabbath. He then asked me if I could read. I answered 'Yes.' 'Then,' said he, 'do you read in the Bible, He that offends in one point is guilty of all?' I said, 'Yes.' Then he assured me, that one sin, unatoned for, was as sufficient to damn a soul, as one leak was to sink a ship. Here I was struck with awe; for the minister exhorted me much, and reminded me of the shortness of time, and the length of eternity; and that no unregenerate soul, or any thing unclean, could enter the kingdom of Heaven.

He did not admit me as a communicant; but recommended me to read the scriptures, and hear the word preached; not to neglect fervent prayer to God, who has promised to hear the supplications of those who seek him in godly sincerity; so I took my leave of him with many thanks, and resolved to follow his advice, so far as the Lord would condescend to enable me.

VI.

During this time I was out of employ; nor was likely to get a situation suitable for me: which obliged me to go once more to sea. I engaged as steward of a ship called the Hope, Captain Richard Strange, bound from London to Cadiz in Spain. In a short time after I was on board I heard the name of God much blasphemed, and I feared greatly least I should catch the horrible infection. I thought if I sinned again, after having life and death set

evidently before me, I should certainly go to hell. My mind was uncommonly chagrined, and I murmured much at God's providential dealings with me, and was discontented with the commandments, that I could not be saved by what I had done. I hated all things, and wished I had never been born: confusion seized me, and I wished to be annihilated.

One day I was standing on the very edge of the stern of the ship, thinking to drown myself, but this scripture was instantaneously impressed on my mind—'That no murderer hath eternal life abiding in him.' (I John iii. 15.) Then I paused, and thought myself the unhappiest man living. Again I was convinced that the Lord was better to me than I deserved, and I was better off in the world than many. After this I began to fear death; I fretted, mourned, and prayed, till I became a burthen to others but more so to myself. At length I concluded to beg my bread on shore, rather than go again to sea amongst a people who feared not God, and I entreated the Captain three different times to discharge me he would not, but each time gave me greater and greater encouragement to continue with him, and all on board shewed me very great civility: notwithstanding all this, I was unwilling to embark again. At last some of my religious friends advised me, by saying it was my lawful calling, consequently it was my duty to obey, and that God was not confined to place, &c. &c. particularly Mr. G. the governor of Tothillfields Bridewell, who pitied my case, and read the eleventh chapter of the Hebrews to me, with exhortations. He prayed for me, and I believe that he prevailed on my behalf, as my burden was then greatly removed, and I found a heart-felt resignation to the will of God.

The good man gave me a pocket Bible, and Alleine's "Alarm to the unconverted." We parted, and the next day I went on board again. We sailed for Spain, and I found favour with the Captain. It was the fourth of September when we sailed from London, and we had a delightful voyage to Cadiz, where we arrived the twenty-third of the same month. The place is strong, commands a fine prospect, and is very rich. The Spanish galleons frequent that port, and some arrived whist we were there. I had many opportunities of reading the scriptures. I wrestled hard with God in fervent prayers, who had declared in his word that he would hear the groanings and deep sighs of the poor in spirit. This I found verified, to my utter astonishment and comfort, in the following manner:—On the morning of the sixth of October (I pray you to attend), all that day, I thought I should see or hear something supernatural. I had a secret impulse on my mind of something that was to take place, which drove me, for all that time, to a throne of grace.

It pleased God to enable me to wrestle with him as Jacob did: I prayed that if sudden death were to happen, and I perished, it might be at Christ's feet.

In the evening of the same day, as I was reading and meditating on the fourth chapter of the Acts, twelfth verse, under the solemn apprehensions of eternity, and reflecting on my past actions, I began to think I had lived a moral life, and that I had a proper ground to believe I had an interest in the divine favour; but still meditating on the subject, not knowing whether salvation was to be had partly for our own good deeds, or solely as the sovereign gift of God. In this deep consternation the Lord was pleased to break in upon my soul with his bright beams of heavenly light; and in an instant, as it were, removing the veil, and letting light into a dark place. (Isa. xxv. 7.) I saw clearly, with the eye of faith, the crucified Saviour bleeding on the cross on Mount Calvary: the Scriptures became an unsealed book; I saw myself a condemned criminal under the law, which came with its full force to my conscience and when 'the commandment came, sin revived, and I died.' I saw the Lord Jesus Christ in his humiliation, loaded, and bearing my reproach, sin, and shame.

I then clearly perceived, that by the deeds of the law no flesh living could be justified. I was then convinced, that by the first Adam sin came, and by the second Adam, the Lord Jesus Christ, all that are saved must be made alive. It was given me at that time to know what it was to be born again. (John iii. 5.) I saw the eighth chapter to the Romans, and the doctrines of God's decrees verified, agreeably to his eternal, everlasting, and unchangeable purposes. The word of God was sweet to my taste, yea, sweeter than honey and the honey-comb. Christ was revealed to my soul as the chiefest among ten thousand.—These heavenly moments were really as life to the dead, and what John calls an earnest of the Spirit. (John xvi. 13, 14, &c.) This was indeed unspeakable, and I firmly believe, undeniable to many.

VII.

Now every leading providential circumstance that happened to me, from the day I was taken from my parents to that hour, was then, in my view, as if it had but just then occurred. I was sensible of the invisible hand of God, which guided and protected me, when in truth I knew it not: still the Lord pursued me, although I slighted and disregarded it; this mercy melted me down. When I considered my poor wretched state, I wept, seeing what a great debtor I was to sovereign free grace. Now the Ethiopian was willing

to be saved by Jesus Christ, the sinner's only surety, and also to rely on none other person or thing for salvation. Self was obnoxious, and good works I had none; for it is God that worketh in us both to will and to do. Oh! the amazing things of that hour can never be told! It was joy in the Holy Ghost! I felt an astonishing change; the burden of sin, the gaping jaws of hell, and the fears of death, that weighed me down before, now lost their horror; indeed I thought death would now be the best earthly friend I ever had. Such were my grief and joy as I believe are seldom experienced. I was bathed in tears, and said, "What am I, that God should thus look on me, the vilest of sinners?" I felt a deep concern for my mother and friends, which occasioned me to pray with fresh ardour; and in the abyss of thought, I viewed the unconverted people of the world in a very awful state, being without God and without hope.

It pleased God to pour out on me the spirit of prayer and the grace of supplication, so that in loud acclamations I was enabled to praise and glorify his most holy name. When I got out of the cabin, and told some of the people what the Lord had done for me, alas! who could understand me or believe my report!—None but to whom the arm of the Lord was revealed. I became a barbarian to them in talking of the love of Christ: his name was to me as ointment poured forth; indeed it was sweet to my soul, but to them a rock of offence. I thought my case singular, and every hour a day until I came to London; for I much longed to be with some to whom I could tell of the wonders of God's love towards me, and join in prayer to him whom my soul loved and thirsted after. I had uncommon commotions within, such as few can tell aught about. Now the Bible was my only companion and comfort; I prized it much, with many thanks to God that I could read it for myself, and was not left to be tossed about or led by man's devices and notions. The worth of a soul cannot be told.—May the Lord give the reader an under standing in this!

Whenever I looked in the Bible I saw things new, and many texts were immediately applied to me with great comfort, for I knew that to me was the word of salvation sent. Sure I was, that the Spirit, which indited the word, opened my heart to receive the truth of it as it is in Jesus, that the same Spirit enabled me to act with faith upon the promises which were precious to me, and enable me to believe, to the salvation of my soul. By free grace I was persuaded that I had a part in the first resurrection, and was enlightened with the "light of the living." (Job xxxiii. 30.) I wished for a man of God, with whom I might converse: my soul was like the chariots of Aminadab. (Canticles vi. 12.) These, among others, were the precious promises that were

so powerfully applied to me: "All things whatsoever ye shall ask in prayer, believing, ye shall receive." (Matt. xxi. 22.) "Peace I leave with you, my peace I give unto you." (John xiv. 27.) I saw the blessed Redeemer to be the fountain of life, and the well of salvation. I experienced him to be all in all. He had brought me by a way that I knew not, and he had made crooked paths straight. Then in his name I set up my Ebenezer, saying, "Hitherto He hath helped me:" and could say to the sinners about me, "Behold what a Saviour I have!" Thus I was, by the teaching of that all-glorious Deity, the great One in Three and Three in One, confirmed in the truths of the Bible, those oracles of everlasting truth, on which every soul living must stand or fall eternally, agreeably to Acts iv. 12: "Neither is there salvation in any other: for there is none other name under heaven given among men whereby we must be saved, but only Jesus Christ." May God give the reader a right understanding in these facts! "To him that believeth all things are possible, but to them that are unbelieving nothing is pure." (Titus i. 15.)

During this period we remained at Cadiz until our ship got laden. We sailed about the fourth of November; and, having a good passage, we arrived in London the month following, to my comfort, with heartfelt gratitude to God for his rich and unspeakable mercies.

VIII.

On my return I had but one text which puzzled me, or that the devil endeavoured, to buffet me with, viz. Rom. xi. 6. and, as I had heard of the Rev. Mr. Romaine, and his great knowledge in the scriptures, I wished much to hear him preach. One day I went to Blackfriars church, and, to my great satisfaction and surprise, he preached from that very text. He very clearly shewed the difference between human works and free election, which is according to God's sovereign will and pleasure. These glad tidings set me entirely at liberty, and I went out of the church rejoicing, seeing my spots were those of God's children. I went to Westminster chapel, and saw some of my old friends, who were glad when they perceived the wonderful change that the Lord had wrought in me, particularly Mr. G. Smith, my worthy acquaintance, who was a man of a choice spirit, and had great zeal for the Lord's service. I enjoyed his correspondence till he died in the year 1784. I was again examined in that same chapel, and was received into church-fellowship amongst them; I rejoiced in spirit, making melody in my heart to the God of all my mercies. Now my whole wish was to be dissolved, and to

be with Christ. But, alas! I must wait my appointed time.

Miscellaneous Verses; Or, Reflections On The State Of My Mind.

*During my first Convictions of the Necessity
of believing the Truth, and of experiencing
the inestimable benefits of Christianity.*

Well may I say my life has been
One scene of sorrow and of pain;
From early days I griefs have known,
And as I grew my griefs have grown.

Dangers were always in my path,
And fear of wrath and sometimes death;
While pale dejection in me reign'd,
I often wept, by grief constrain'd.

When taken from my native land,
By an unjust and cruel band,
How did uncommon dread prevail!
My sighs no more I could conceal.

To ease my mind I often strove,
And tried my trouble to remove;
I sung and utter'd sighs between,
Assay'd to stifle guilt with sin.

But O! not all that I could do
Would stop the current of my woe,
Conviction still my vileness shew'd;
How great my guilt; how lost to good!

'Prevented, that I could not die,
Nor could to one sure refuge fly,

An orphan state I had to mourn,
Forsook by all, and left forlorn.'

Those who beheld my downcast mien,
Could never guess by woes unseen;
They by appearance could not know
The troubles that I waded through.

Lust, anger, blasphemy, and pride,
With legions of such ills beside,
Troubled my thoughts, while doubts and fears
Clouded and darken'd most my years.

'Sighs now no more would be confin'd;
They breath'd the trouble of my mind;'
I wish'd for death, but check'd the word,
And often pray'd unto the Lord.

Unhappy, more than some on earth,
I thought the place that gave me birth;
Strange thoughts oppress'd, while I replied,
"Why not in Ethiopia died?

And why thus spar'd, when nigh to hell?"
God only knew—I could not tell!
'A tott'ring fence, a bowing wall,
I thought myself e'er since the fall.'

Oft times I mus'd, and nigh despair,
While birds melodious fill'd the air.
'Thrice happy songsters, ever free!'
How blest were they compar'd to me!

Thus all things added to my pain,
While grief compell'd me to complain;
When sable clouds began to rise,
My mind grew darker than the skies.

The English nation call'd to leave,
How did my breast with sorrow heave!
I long'd for rest—cried "Help me, Lord!
Some mitigation, Lord, afford!"

Yet on, dejected, still I went,
Heart-throbbing woes within me pent;
Nor land, nor sea, could comfort give,
Nor aught my anxious mind relieve.

Weary with troubles, yet unknown
To all but God and self alone,
Numerous months for peace I strove,
Numerous foes I had to prove.

Inur'd to dangers, grief, and woes,
Train'd up 'midst perils, death, and foes,
I said, "Must it thus ever be?
No quiet is permitted me."

Hard hap, and more than heavy lot!
I pray'd to God, "Forget me not:
What thou ordain'st help me to bear;
But, O! deliver from despair!"

Strivings and wrestling seem'd in vain;
Nothing I did could ease my pain:
Then gave I up my work and will,
Confess'd and own'd my doom was hell!

Like some poor pris'ner at the bar,
Conscious of guilt, of sin, and fear,
Arraign'd and self-condemn'd I stood,
'Lost in the world and in my blood!'

Yet here, 'midst blackest clouds confin'd,
A beam from Christ, the day-star, shin'd;

"Surely, thought I, if Jesus please,
He can at once sign my release."

I, ign'rant of his righteousness,
Set up my labours in its place;
'Forgot for why his blood was shed,
And pray'd and fasted in his stead.'

He died for sinners—I am one;
Might not his blood for me atone?
Though I am nothing else but sin,
Yet surely he can make me clean!

Thus light came in, and I believ'd;
Myself forgot, and help receiv'd!
My Saviour then, I know, I found,
For, eas'd from guilt, no more I groan'd.

O, happy hour, in which I ceas'd
To mourn, for then I found a rest!
My soul and Christ were now as one:
Thy light, O Jesus, in me shone.

Bless'd be thy name; for now I know
I and my works can nothing do;
"The Lord alone can ransom man—
For this the spotless Lamb was slain."

When sacrifices, works, and pray'r,
Prov'd vain, and ineffectual were,
"Lo then I come!" the Saviour cried,
And, bleeding, bow'd his head and died.

He died for all who ever saw
No help in them, nor by the law;
I this have seen and gladly own
"Salvation is by Christ alone!"*

*Acts vi. 12.

CHAPTER XI.

The author embarks on board a ship bound to Cadiz. Is near being ship-wrecked—Goes to Malaga—Remarkably fine Cathedral there—The author disputes with a Popish priest—Picks up eleven miserable men at sea in returning to England—Engages again with Dr. Irving to accompany him to Jamaica and the Musquito shore—Meets with an Indian Prince on board—The author attempts to instruct him in the truths of the Gospel—Frustrated by the bad example of some in the ship—They arrive on the Musquito shore with some slaves they purchased at Jamaica, and begin to cultivate a Plantation—Some account of the manners and customs of the Musquito Indians—Successful device of the author's to quell a riot among them—Curious entertainment given by them to Dr. Irving and the author, who leaves the shore and goes for Jamaica—Is barbarously treated by a man with whom he engaged for his passage—Escapes, and goes to the Musquito Admiral, who treats him kindly—He gets another vessel, and goes on board—Instances of bad treatment—Meets Dr. Irving—Gets to Jamaica—Is cheated by his Captain—Leaves the Doctor, and sails for England.

I.

WHEN OUR ship was got ready for sea again, I was intreated by the Captain to go in her once more; but, as I felt myself as happy as I could wish to be in this life, I for some time refused; however, the advice of my friends at last prevailed, and, in full resignation to the will of God, I again embarked for Cadiz in March 1775. We had a very good passage, without any material accident, until we arrived off the Bay of Cadiz; when one Sunday, just as we were going into the harbour, the ship struck against a rock, and knocked off a garboard plank, which is the next to the keel. In an instant all hands were in the greatest confusion, and began with loud cries to call on God to have mercy on them. Although I could not swim, and saw no way of escaping death, I felt no dread in my then situation, having no desire to live. I even rejoiced in spirit, thinking this death would be sudden glory. But the fulness of time was not yet come. The people near to me were very much astonished in seeing me thus calm and resigned; but I told them of the peace of God, which, through sovereign grace I enjoyed, and these words were that instant in my mind:

Christ is my pilot wise, my compass is his word;
My soul each storm defies, while I have such a Lord.
 I trust his faithfulness and power,
 To save me in the trying hour.

Though rocks and quicksands deep thro' all my passage lie,
Yet Christ shall safely keep and guide me with his eye.
 How can I sink with such a prop,
 That bears the world and all things up.

At this time there were many large Spanish flukers, or passage-vessels, full of people crossing the channel; a number of them, seeing our condition, came along-side of us. As many hands, as could be employed, began to work; some at our three pumps, and the rest unloading the ship as fast as possible. There being only a single rock called the Porpus on which we struck, we soon got off it, and providentially it was then high water; we therefore run the ship ashore at the nearest place to keep her from sinking. After many tides, with a great deal of care and industry, we got her repaired again. When we had dispatched our business at Cadiz, we went to Gibraltar, and from thence to Malaga, a very pleasant and rich city, where there is one of the finest cathedrals I had ever seen. It had been above fifty years in building, as I had heard, though it was not then quite finished; great part of the inside, however, was completed and highly decorated with the richest marble columns, and many superb paintings; it was lighted occasionally by an amazing number of wax tapers of different sizes, some of which were as thick as a man's thigh; these, however, were only used on some of their grand festivals.

I was very much shocked at the custom of bullbaiting, and other diversions which prevailed here on Sunday evenings, to the great scandal of Christianity and morals. I used to express my abhorrence of it to a priest whom I met with. I had frequent contests about religion with the reverend father, in which he took great pains to make a proselyte of me to his church; and I no less to convert him to mine. On these occasions I used to produce my Bible, and shew him in what points his church erred. He then said he had been in England, and that every person there read the Bible, which was very wrong; but I answered him, that Christ desired us to search the Scriptures. In his zeal for my conversion, he solicited me to go to one of the universities in Spain, and declared that I should have my education free; and told me, if I got myself made a priest, I might in time become even Pope; and that Pope

Benedict was a black man. As I was ever desirous of learning, I paused some time upon this temptation, and thought by being crafty, I might catch some with guile; but I began to think it would only be hypocrisy in me to embrace his offer, as I could not in conscience conform to the opinions of his church. I was therefore enabled to regard the word of God, which says, 'Come out from amongst them;' and I refused Father Vincent's offer. So we parted without conviction on either side.

II.

Having taken at this place some fine wines, fruits, and money, we proceeded to Cadiz, where we took about two tons more of money, &c. and then sailed for England in the month of June. When we were about the north latitude 42°, we had contrary winds for several days, and the ship did not make in that time above six or seven miles straight course. This made the Captain exceedingly fretful and peevish: and I was very sorry to hear God's most holy name often blasphemed by him. One day, as he was in that impious mood, a young gentleman on board, who was a passenger, reproached him, and said he acted wrong; for we ought to be thankful to God for all things, as we were not in want of any thing on board; and though the wind was contrary for us, yet it was fair for some others, who, perhaps, stood in more need of it than we. I immediately seconded this young gentleman with some boldness, and said we had not the least cause to murmur, for that the Lord was better to us than we deserved, and that he had done all things well.

I expected that the Captain would be very angry with me for speaking, but he replied not a word. However before that time on the following day, being the 21st, of June, much to our great joy and astonishment, we saw the providential hand of our benign Creator, whose ways with his blind creatures are past finding out. The preceding night I dreamed that I saw a boat immediately off the starboard main shrouds; and exactly at half-past one o'clock, the following day, at noon while I was below, just as we had dined in the cabin, the man at the helm cried out, "A boat!" which brought my dream that instant into my mind. I was the first man that jumped on the deck; and looking from the shrouds onward, according to my dream, I descried a little boat at some distance: but as the waves were high, it was as much as we could do sometimes to discern her. We however stopped the ship's way, and the boat, which was extremely small, came alongside with eleven miserable men, whom we took on board immediately. To all human appearance, these peo-

ple must have perished in the course of an hour or less; the boat being small, it barely contained them. When we took them up they were half drowned, and had no victuals, compass, water, or any other necessary; and had only one bit of an oar to steer with, and that right before the wind, so that they were obliged to trust entirely to the mercy of the waves. As soon as we got them all on board, they bowed themselves on their knees, and with hands and voices lifted up to Heaven, thanked God for their deliverance; and I trust that my prayers were not wanting amongst them at the same time. This mercy of the Lord quite melted me, and I recollected his words, which I saw thus verified, in the 107th Psalm:—"O give thanks unto the Lord, for he is good, for his mercy endureth for ever.—Hungry and thirsty, their souls fainted in them. They cried unto the Lord in their trouble, and he delivered them out of their distresses. And he led them forth by the right way, that they might go to a city of habitation. O that men would praise the Lord for his goodness, and for his wonderful works to the children of men. For he satisfieth the longing soul, and filleth the hungry soul with goodness.

"Such as sit in darkness and in the shadow of death: then they cried unto the Lord in their trouble, and he saved them out of their distresses. They that go down to the sea in ships; that do business in great waters; these see the works of the Lord, and his wonders in the deep.—Whoso is wise and will observe these things, even they shall understand the loving-kindness of the Lord."

The poor distressed Captain said, "The Lord is good; for seeing that I am not fit to die, he therefore gave me a space of time to repent." I was very glad to hear this expression, and took an opportunity, when convenient, of talking to him on the providence of God. They told us they were Portuguese, and were in a brig loaded with corn, which shifted that morning at five o'clock, owing to which the vessel sunk that instant with two of the crew; and how these eleven got into the boat, which was lashed to the deck, not one of them could tell. We provided them with every necessary, and brought them all safe to London; and I hope the Lord gave them repentance unto eternal life.

III.

I was happy once more amongst my friends and brethren, till November, when my old friend, the celebrated Dr. Irving, bought a remarkably fine sloop, about 150 tons. He had a mind for a new adventure in cultivating a plantation at Jamaica and the Musquito Shore; he asked me to go with him, and said that he would trust me with his estate in preference to any one. By

the advice, therefore, of my friends, I accepted of the offer, knowing that the harvest was fully ripe in those parts, and I hoped to be an instrument under God, of bringing some poor sinner to my well-beloved master, Jesus Christ. Before I embarked, I found with the Dr. four Musquito Indians, who were chiefs in their own country, and were brought here by some English traders for some selfish ends. One of them was the Musquito king's son, a youth of about eighteen years of age; and whilst he was here he was baptized by the name of George. They were going back at the government's expence, after having been in England about a year, during which they learned to speak pretty good English. When I came to talk to them, about eight days before we sailed, I was very much mortified in finding that they had not frequented any churches since they were there to be baptized, nor was any attention paid to their morals. I was very sorry for this mock christianity, and had just an opportunity to take some of them once to church before we sailed.

We embarked in the month of November 1775, on board of the sloop, the Morning Star, Captain David Miller, and sailed for Jamaica. In our passage I took all the pains that I could to instruct the Indian prince in the doctrines of Christianity, of which he was entirely ignorant; and, to my great joy, he was quite attentive, and received with gladness the truths that the Lord enabled me to set forth to him. I taught him, in the compass of eleven days, all the letters; and he could put even two or three of them together, and spell them. I had Fox's Martyrology with cuts, and he used to be very fond of looking into it, and would ask many questions about the Papal cruelties he saw depicted there, which I explained to him. I made such progress with this youth, especially in religion, that when I used to go to bed at different hours of the night, if he was in his bed he would get up on purpose to go to prayer with me, without any other clothes than his shirt; and before he would eat any of his meals amongst the gentlemen in the cabin, he would first come to me to pray, as he called it. I was well pleased at this, and took great delight in him and used much supplication to God for his conversion. I was in full hope of seeing daily every appearance of that change which I could wish; not knowing the devices of Satan, who had many of his emissaries to sow his tares as fast as I sowed the good seed, and pull down as fast as I built up.

Thus we went on nearly four-fifths of our passage, when Satan at last got the upper hand. Some of his messengers, seeing this poor heathen much advanced in piety, began to ask him whether I had converted him to Christianity; laughed and made their jest at him, for which I rebuked them as much as I could. But this treatment caused the prince to halt between two

opinions. Some of the true sons of Belial, who did not believe that there was any hereafter, told him never to fear the devil, for there was none existing; and if ever he came to the prince, they desired he might be sent to them. Thus they teazed the poor innocent youth, so that he would not learn his book any more! He would not drink nor carouse with these ungodly actors, nor would he be with me even at prayers. This grieved me very much. I endeavoured to persuade him as well as I could, but he would not come; and entreated him very much to tell me his reasons for acting thus. At last he asked me,—"How comes it that all the white men on board, who can read and write, observe the sun and know all things, yet swear, lie, and get drunk, only excepting yourself?" I answered him, the reason was that they did not fear God; and that if any one of them died so, they could not go to, or be happy with, God. He replied that if a certain person went to hell, he would go to hell too. I was sorry to hear this; and as he sometimes had the toothache, and also some other persons in the ship at the same time, I asked him, if their tooth-ache made his easy. He said, "No." Then I told him if he and these people went to hell together, their pains would not make his any lighter. This had great weight with him; it depressed his spirits much; and he became ever after, during the passage, fond of being alone.

IV.

When we came into the latitude of Martinico and near making the land, one morning we had a brisk gale of wind, and, carrying too much sail, the main mast went over the side. Many people were then all about the deck, and the yards, masts, and rigging, came tumbling all about us, yet there was not one of us in the least hurt; although some were within a hair's breadth of being killed: and particularly, I saw two men, who, by the providential hand of God, were most miraculously preserved from being smashed to pieces. On the 5th of January we made Antigua and Montserrat, and ran along the rest of the islands; and on the 14th we arrived at Jamaica. One Sunday, while we were there, I took the Musquito Prince George to church where he saw the sacrament administered. When we came out we saw all kinds of people, almost from the church door for the space of half a mile down to the waterside, buying and selling all kinds of commodities: and these acts afforded me greater matter of exhortation to this youth who was much astonished.

Our vessel being ready to sail for the Musquito shore, I went with the

Doctor on board a Guineaman, to purchase some slaves to carry with us, and cultivate a plantation; and I chose them all of my own countrymen, some of whom came from Lybia. On the 12th of February we sailed from Jamaica, and on the 18th arrived at the Musquito shore, at a place called Dupeupy. All our Indian guests now, after I had admonished them, and a few cases of liquor given them by the Doctor, took an affectionate leave of us, and went ashore, where they were met by the Musquito king, and we never saw one of them afterwards. We then sailed to the southward of the shore, to a place called Cape Gracias a Dios, where there was a large lagoon or lake, which received the emptying of two or three very fine large rivers, and abounded much in fish and land tortoise. Some of the native Indians came on board of us here; we used them well and told them that we were come to dwell amongst them, at which they seemed pleased. So the Doctor and I, with some others, went with them ashore; and they took us to different places to view the land, in order to choose a place to make a plantation of.

We fixed on a spot near a river's bank, in a rich soil; and having got our necessaries out of the sloop, we began to clear away the woods, and to plant different kinds of vegetables which had a quick growth. While we were employed in this manner, our vessel went northward to Black River to trade. While she was there, a Spanish guarda costa met with and took her.-This proved very hurtful, and a great embarrassment to us. However we went on with the culture of the land. We used to make fires every night all around us, to keep off wild beasts, which, as soon as it was dark, set up a most hideous roaring. Our habitation being far up in the woods, we frequently saw different kinds of animals; but none of them ever hurt us, except poisonous snakes, the bite of which the Doctor used to cure by giving to the patient, as soon as possible, about half a tumbler of strong rum, with a good deal of Cayenne pepper in it. In this manner he cured two natives and one of his own slaves.

V.

The Indians were exceedingly fond of the Doctor, and they had good reason for it; for I believe they never had such an useful man amongst them. They came from all quarters to our dwelling; and some Woolwow, or flat-headed Indians, who lived fifty or sixty miles above our river and this side of the South Sea, brought us a good deal of silver in exchange for our goods. The principal articles we could get from our neighbouring Indians

were turtle oil, and shells, a little silk-grass, and some provisions; but they would not work at any thing for us, except fishing; and a few times they assisted to cut down some trees, in order to build houses, which they did exactly like the Africans, by the joint labour of men, women, and children.

I do not recollect any of them to have had more than two wives. These always accompanied their husbands when they came to our dwelling, and then they generally carried whatever was brought to us, and always squatted down behind their husbands. Whenever we gave them any thing to eat, the men and their wives ate separate. I never saw the least sign of incontinence among them. The women are ornamented with beads, and fond of painting themselves; the men also paint, even to excess, both their faces and shirts: their favourite colour is red. The women generally cultivate the ground, and the men are all fishermen and canoe makers. Upon the whole, I never met any nation that were so simple in their manners as these people, or had so little ornament in their houses. Neither had they, as I ever could learn, one word expressive of an oath. The worst word I ever heard amongst them, when they were quarrelling, was one, that they had got from the English, which was "you rascal." I never saw any mode of worship among them; but in this they were not worse than their European brethren or neighbours; for I am sorry to say that there was not one white person in our dwelling, nor any where else, that I saw in different places I was at on the shore, that was better or more pious than those unenlightened Indians; but they either worked or slept in Sundays: and, to my sorrow, working was too much Sunday's employment with ourselves; so much so, that, in some length of time, we really did not know one day from another. This mode of living laid the foundation of my decamping at last. The natives are well made and war-like; and they particularly boast of having never been conquered by the Spaniards. They are great drinkers of strong liquors, when they can get them. We used to distil rum from pineapples, which were plentiful here; and then we could not get them away from our place. Yet they seemed to be singular, in point of honesty, above any other nation I was ever amongst. The country being hot, we lived under an open shed, where we had all kinds of goods, without a door or lock to any one article; yet we slept in safety, and never lost any thing, or were disturbed. This surprised us a good deal; and the Doctor, myself, and others, used to say if we were to lie in that manner in Europe we should have our throats cut the first night.

The Indian Governor goes once in a certain time all about the province or district, and has a number of men with him as attendants and assistants.

He settles all the differences among the people, like the judge here, and is treated with very great respect. He took care to give us timely notice before he came to our habitation, by sending his stick as a token, for rum, sugar, and gunpowder, which we did not refuse sending; and at the same time we made the utmost preparations to receive his honour and his train.

When he came, with his tribe and all our neighbouring chieftains, we expected to find him a grave reverend judge, solid, and sagacious; but instead of that, before he and his gang came in sight, we heard them very clamorous; and they even had plundered some of our good neighbouring Indians, having intoxicated themselves with our liquor. When they arrived, we did not know what to make of our new guests, and would gladly have dispensed with the honour of their company. However, having no alternative, we feasted them plentifully all the day till the evening; when the Governor, getting quite drunk, grew very unruly, and struck one of our most friendly chiefs, who was our nearest neighbour, and also took his gold-laced hat from him. At this a great commotion took place; and the Doctor interfered to make peace, as we could all understand one another, but to no purpose; and at last they became so outrageous, that the Doctor, fearing he might get into trouble, left the house and made the best of his way to the nearest wood, leaving me to do as well as I could among them.

I was so enraged with the governor, that I could have wished to have seen him tied fast to a tree, and flogged for his behaviour, but I had not people enough to cope with his party. I therefore thought of a stratagem to appease the riot. Recollecting a passage I had read in the life of Columbus, when he was among the Indians in Mexico, or Peru, where, on some occasion, he frightened them, by telling them of certain events in the heavens, I had recourse to the same expedient, and it succeeded beyond my most sanguine expectations. When I had formed my determination, I went in the midst of them, and taking hold of the governor, I pointed up to the heavens. I menaced him and the rest: I told them God lived there, and that he was angry with them, and they must not quarrel so; that they were all brothers, and if they did not leave off and go away quietly, I would take the book (pointing to the Bible), read, and tell God to make them dead. This operated on them like magic. The clamour immediately ceased, and I gave them some rum and a few other things; after which they went away peaceably; and the governor afterwards gave our neighbour, who was called Captain Plasmyah, his hat again. When the Doctor returned, he was exceedingly glad at my success in thus getting rid of our troublesome guest.

VI.

The Musquito people within our vicinity, out of respect to the Doctor, myself, and his people, made entertainments of the grand kind, called in their tongue "tourrie" or "dryckbot." The English of this expression is, "a feast of drinking about," of which it seems a corruption of language. The drink consisted of pine-apples roasted, and casades chewed or beaten in mortars; which, after lying some time, ferments, and becomes so strong as to intoxicate when drank in any quantity. We had timely notice given to us of the entertainment. A white family within five miles of us, told us how the drink was made; I and two others went before the time to the village where the mirth was appointed to be held, and there we saw the whole art of making the drink, and also the kind of animals that were to be eaten there. I cannot say the sight of either the drink or the meat was enticing to me. They had some thousands of pine-apples roasting, which they squeezed, dirt and all, into a canoe they had there for the purpose. The casade-drink, was in beef barrels and other vessels, and looked exactly like hogwash. Men, women, and children were thus employed in roasting the pine-apples and squeezing them with their hands. For food they had many land torpins or tortoises, some dried turtle, and three large alligators alive, and tied fast to the trees. I asked the people what they were going to do with these alligators; and I was told they were to he eaten. I was much surprised at this, and went home not a little disgusted at the preparations.

When the day of the feast was come, we took some rum with us, and went to the appointed place, where we found a great assemblage of those people, who received us very kindly. The mirth had begun before we came: and they were dancing with music: and the musical instruments were nearly the same as those of any other sable people, but, as I thought, much less melodious than those of any other nation I ever knew. They had many curious gestures in dancing, and a variety of motions and postures of their bodies, which to me were in no wise attracting. The males danced by themselves, and the females also by themselves, as with us. The Doctor shewed his people the example by immediately joining the women's party, though not by their choice. On perceiving the women disgusted, he joined the males.

At night there were great illuminations, by setting fire to many pine-trees, while the dryckbot went round merrily, by calabashes or gourds; but the liquor might more justly be called eating than drinking. One Owden, the oldest father in the vicinity, was dressed in a strange and terrifying form.

Around his body were skins adorned with different kinds of feathers, and he had on his head a very large and high headpiece in the form of a Grenadier's cap, with prickles like a porcupine: and he made a certain noise which resembled the cry of an alligator. Our people skipped amongst them out of complaisance, though some could not drink of their tourrie; but our rum met with customers enough, and was soon gone. The alligators were killed, and some of them roasted. Their manner of roasting is by digging a hole in the earth, and filling it with wood, which they burn to coal, and then they lay sticks across, on which they lay the meat. I had a raw piece of the alligator in my hand: it was very rich: I thought it looked like fresh salmon and it had a most fragrant smell, but I could not eat any of it. This merry-making at last ended without the least discord in any person in the company, although it was made up of different nations and complexions.

VII.

The rainy season came on here about the latter end of May, and continued till August very heavily; so that the rivers overflowed, and our provisions, then in the ground, were washed away.—I thought this was, in some measure, a judgment upon us for working on Sundays, and it hurt my mind very much. I often wished to leave this place and sail for Europe; for our mode of procedure and living, in this heathenish form, was very irksome to me. The word of God saith "What does it avail a man if he gain the whole world, and lose his own soul?" This was much and heavily impressed on my mind; and though I did not know how to speak to the Doctor for my discharge, it was disagreeable for me to stay any longer. But about the middle of June, I took courage enough to ask him for it. He was very unwilling at first to grant me my request; but I gave him so many reasons for it, that at last he consented to my going, and gave me the following certificate of my good behaviour:

> The bearer, Gustavus Vassa, has served me several years with strict honesty, sobriety, and fidelity. I can therefore, with justice recommend him for these qualifications, and indeed in every respect I consider him as an excellent servant. I do hereby certify that he always behaved well, and that he is perfectly trust-worthy.
>
> Charles Irving.

Musquito Shore, June 15, 1776.

Though I was much attached to the Doctor, I was happy when he consented. I got every thing ready for my departure, and hired some Indians, with a large canoe, to carry me off. All my poor countrymen, the slaves, when they heard of my leaving them, were very sorry, as I had always treated them with care and affection, and did every thing I could to comfort the poor creatures, and render their condition easy. Having taken leave of my old friends and companions, on the 18th of June, accompanied by the Doctor, I left that spot of the world, and went southward above 20 miles along the river. There I found a sloop, the Captain of which told me he was going to Jamaica. Having agreed for my passage with him and one of the owners' who was also on board, named Hughes, the Doctor and I parted, not without shedding tears on both sides.

The vessel then sailed along the river till night, when she stopped in a lagoon within the same river. During the night a schooner belonging to the same owners came in, and as she was in want of hands, Hughes, the owner of the sloop, asked me to go in the schooner as a sailor, and said he would give me wages. I thanked him; but I said I wanted to go to Jamaica. He then immediately changed his tone, and swore and abused me very much, and asked how I came to be freed. I told him, and said that I came into that vicinity with Dr. Irving whom he had seen that day. This account was of no use; he still swore exceedingly at me, and cursed the master for a fool that sold me my freedom, and the Doctor for another in letting me go from him. Then he desired me to go in the schooner, or else I should not go out of the sloop as a free man. I said this was very hard, and begged to be put on shore again; but he swore that I should not. I said that I had been twice amongst the Turks, yet had never seen any such usage with them, and much less could I have expected any thing of this kind among the Christians. This incensed him exceedingly; and with a volley of oaths and imprecations, he replied, "Christians! damn you, you are one of St. Paul's men; but, by G—d, except you have St. Paul's or St. Peter's faith, and walk upon the water to the shore, you shall not go out of the vessel;" which I now learnt was going amongst the Spaniards towards Carthagena, where he swore he would sell me. I simply asked him what right he had to sell me? but, without another word, he made some of his people tie ropes round each of my ancles, and also to each wrist, and another rope round my body, and hoisted me up, without letting my feet touch or rest upon any thing.

Thus I hung, without any crime committed, and without judge or jury, merely because I was a freeman, and could not, by the law, get any redress

from a white person in those parts of the world. I was in great pain from my situation, and cried and begged very hard for some mercy, but all in vain. My tyrant, in a rage, brought a musket out of the cabin, and loaded it before me and the crew, and swore that he would shoot me if I cried any more. I had now no alternative; I therefore remained silent, seeing not one white man on board who said a word in my behalf. I hung in that manner from between ten and eleven o'clock at night till about one in the morning: when, finding my cruel abuser fast asleep, I begged some of his slaves to slacken the rope that was round my body, that my feet might rest on something. This they did at the risk of being cruelly used by their master, who beat some of them severely at first for not tying me when he commanded them.

VIII.

Whilst I remained in this condition, till between five and six o'clock in the morning, I trust I prayed to God to forgive this blasphemer, who cared not what he did, but, when he got up out of his sleep in the morning, was of the very same temper and disposition as when he left me at night. When they got up the anchor, and the vessel was getting under way I once more cried and begged to be released; and now, being fortunately in the way of their hoisting the sails, they released me. When I was let down I spoke to one Mr. Cox, a carpenter, whom I knew on board, on the impropriety of this conduct. He also knew the Doctor, and the good opinion he ever had of me. This man went to the Captain, and told him not to carry me away in that manner; that I was the Doctor's steward, who regarded me very highly, and would resent this usage when he should come to know it. On which he desired a young man to put me ashore in a small canoe I brought with me. This sound gladdened my heart, and I got hastily into the canoe, and set off whilst my tyrant was down in the cabin; but he soon I spied me out when I was not above thirty or forty yards from the vessel, and, running upon the deck with a loaded musket in his hand, he presented it at me and swore heavily and dreadfully that he would shoot me that instant, if I did not come back on board. As I knew the wretch would have done as he said, without hesitation, I put back to the vessel again; but, as the good Lord would have it, just as I was alongside, he was abusing the Captain for letting me go from the vessel; which the Captain returned, and both of them soon got into a very great heat.

The young man, that was with me, now got out of the canoe, the vessel was sailing on fast with a smooth sea: and I then thought it was neck or noth-

ing, so at that instant I set off again for my life, in the canoe, towards the shore; and fortunately the confusion was so great amongst them on board, that I got out of the reach of the musket shot, unnoticed, while the vessel sailed on with a fair wind a different way so that they could not overtake me without tacking: but, even before that could be done, I should have been on shore, which I soon reached, with many thanks to God for this unexpected deliverance.

I then went and told the other owner, who lived near the shore (with whom I had agreed for my passage) of the usage I had met with. He was very much astonished, and appeared very sorry for it. After treating me with kindness, he gave me some refreshment, and three heads of roasted Indian corn, for a voyage of about eighteen miles south, to look for another vessel.—He then directed me to an Indian chief of a district, who was also the Musquito admiral, and had once been at our dwelling; after which I set off with the canoe across a large lagoon alone (for I could not get any one to assist me) though I was much jaded, and had pains in my bowels, by means of the rope I hung by the night before. I was therefore at different times unable to manage the canoe, for the paddling was very laborious. However, a little before dark, I got to my destined place, where some of the Indians knew me, and received me kindly. I asked for the admiral; and they conducted me to his dwelling. He was glad to see me, and refreshed me with such things as the place afforded: and I had a hammock to sleep in. They acted towards me more like Christians than those whites I was among the last night, though they had been baptized. I told the admiral I wanted to go to the next port to get a vessel to carry me to Jamaica, and requested him to send the canoe back which I then had, for which I was to pay him. He agreed with me, and sent five able Indians with a large canoe to carry my things to my intended place, about fifty miles; and we set off the next morning. When we got out of the lagoon and went along shore, the sea was so high that the canoe was oftentimes very near being filled with water. We were obliged to go ashore and drag her across different necks of land; we were also two nights in the swamps, which swarmed with musquito flies, and they proved troublesome to us. This tiresome journey of land and water ended, however, on the third day, to my great joy; and I got on board of a sloop commanded by one Captain Jenning. She was then partly loaded, and he told me he was expecting daily to sail for Jamaica; and having agreed with me to work my passage, I went to work accordingly.

I was not many days on board before we sailed; but, to my sorrow and

disappointment, though used to such tricks, we went to the southward along the Musquito shore, instead of steering for Jamaica. I was compelled to assist in cutting a great deal of mahogany wood on the shore as we coasted along it, and load the vessel with it, before she sailed. This fretted me much; but, as I did not know how to help myself among these deceivers, I thought patience was the only remedy I had lest, and even that was forced. There was much hard work and little victuals on board, except by good luck we happened to catch turtles. On this coast there was also a particular kind of fish called manatee, which is most excellent eating, and the flesh is more like beef than fish; the scales are as large as a shilling, and the skin thicker than I ever saw that of any other fish. Within the brackish waters along shore there were likewise vast numbers of alligators, which made the fish scarce. I was on board this sloop sixteen days, during which, in our coasting, we came to another place, where there was a smaller sloop called the Indian Queen, commanded by one John Baker. He also was an Englishman, and had been a long time along the shore trading for turtle-shells and silver, and had got a good quantity of each on board. He wanted some hands very much; and, understanding I was a free-man, and wanted to go to Jamaica, he told me if he could get one or two, that he would sail immediately for that island; he also pretended to shew me some marks of attention and respect, and promised to give me forty-five shillings sterling a month if I would go with him. I thought this much better than cutting wood for nothing. I therefore told the other Captain that I wanted to go to Jamaica in the other vessel, but he would not listen to me, and, seeing me resolved to go in a day or two, he got the vessel under sail, intending to carry me away against my will. This treatment mortified me exceedingly. I immediately, according to an agreement I had made with the Captain of the Indian Queen, called for her boat which was lying near us, and it came alongside; and, by the means of a north-pole shipmate whom I met with in the sloop I was in, I got my things into the boat, and went on board of the Indian Queen, July the 10th. A few days after I was there, we got all things ready and sailed; but again, to my great mortification, this vessel still went to the south, nearly as far as Carthagena, trading along the coast, instead of going to Jamaica, as the Captain had promised me: and what was worst of all, he was a very cruel and bloody-minded man, and was a horrid blasphemer. Among others, he had a white pilot, one Stoker, whom he beat often as severely as he did some negroes he had on board. One night in particular, aster he had beaten this man most cruelly, he put him into the boat, and made two negroes row him to a desolate key, or

small island; and he loaded two pistols, and swore bitterly that he would shoot the negroes if they brought Stoker on board again. There was not the least doubt but that he would do as he said, and the two poor fellows were obliged to obey the cruel mandate; but when the Captain was asleep, the two negroes took a blanket and carried it to the unfortunate Stoker, which I believe was the means of saving his life from the annoyance of insects. A great deal of entreaty was used with the Captain the next day, before he would consent to let Stoker come on board; and when the poor man was brought on board, he was very ill, from his situation during the night, and he remained so till he was drowned a little time after.

IX.

As we sailed southward we came to many uninhabited islands, overgrown with fine large cocoa-nut trees. As I was very much in want of provisions, I brought a boat-load of the nuts on board, which lasted me and others for several weeks, and afforded us many a delicious repast in our scarcity.

One day, before this, I could not help observing the providential hand of God, that ever supplies all our wants, though in the ways and manner we know not. I had been a whole day without food, and made signals for boats to come off, but in vain. I therefore earnestly prayed to God for relief in my need; and at the close of the evening I went off the deck. Just as I had laid down, I heard a noise on the deck; and not knowing what it meant, I went directly on the deck again, when what should I see, but a fine large fish about seven or eight pounds, which had jumped on board! I took it, and admired, with thanks, the good hand of God; and, what I considered as not less extraordinary, the Captain, who was very avaricious, did not attempt to take it from me, there being only he and I on board; for the rest were all gone ashore trading.

Sometimes the people did not come off for some days: this used to fret the Captain, and then he would vent his fury on me by beating me or making me feel in other cruel ways. One day especially, in his wild wicked, and mad career, after striking me several times with different things, and once across my mouth, even with a red burning stick out of the fire, he got a barrel of gunpowder on the deck, and swore that he would blow up the vessel. I was then at my wit's end, and earnestly prayed to God to direct me. The head was out of the barrel; and the Captain took a lighted stick out of the fire to blow himself and me up, because there was a vessel, then in sight,

coming in, which he supposed was a Spaniard, and he was afraid of falling
into their hands. Seeing this, I got an axe, unnoticed by him, and placed
myself between him and the powder, having resolved in myself, as soon as he
attempted to put the fire in the barrel, to chop him down at that instant. I
was more than an hour in this situation, during which he struck me often,
still keeping the fire in his hand for this wicked purpose. I really should have
thought myself justifiable, in any other part of the world, if I had killed him,
and prayed to God, who gave me a mind that rested solely on himself. I
prayed for resignation, that his will might be done: and the following two
portions of his holy word, which occurred to my mind, buoyed up my hope,
and kept me from taking the life of this wicked man. "He hath determined
the times before appointed, and set bounds to our habitations." (Acts xvii.
26.) And, "Who is there among you that feareth the Lord, that obeyeth the
voice of his servant, that walketh in darkness, and hath no light? Let him
trust in the name of the Lord, and stay upon his God." (Isaiah i. 10.) And
this, by the grace of God, I was enabled to do. I found Him a present help
in the time of need, and the Captain's fury began to subside as the night
approached; but I found

> That he, who cannot stem his anger's tide,
> Doth a wild horse, without a bridle, ride.

The next morning we discovered that the vessel, which had caused such
a fury in the Captain, was an English sloop. They soon came to an anchor
where we were, and, to my no small surprise, I learned that Dr. Irving was
on board of her, on his way from the Musquito shore to Jamaica. I was for
going immediately to see this old master and friend, but the Captain would
not suffer me to leave the vessel. I then informed the Doctor, by letter, how
I was treated, and begged that he would take me out of the sloop: but he
informed me that it was not in his power, as he was a passenger himself; but
he sent me some rum and sugar for my own use. I now learned that after I
had left the estate which I managed for this gentleman on the Musquito
shore, during which the slaves were well fed and comfortable, a white over-
seer had supplied my place: this man, through inhumanity and ill-judged
avarice, beat and cut the poor slaves most unmercifully; and the consequence
was, that every one got into a large Puriogua canoe, and endeavoured to
escape; but, not knowing where to go, or how to manage the canoe, they
were all drowned: in consequence of which the Doctor's plantation was left

uncultivated, and he was now returning to Jamaica to purchase more slaves and stock it again.

On the 14th of October, the Indian Queen arrived at Kingston in Jamaica. When we were unloaded I demanded my wages, which amounted to eight pounds five shillings sterling; but Captain Baker refused to give me one farthing, although it was the hardest earned money I have worked for in my life. I found out Dr. Irving on this, and acquainted him with the Captain's knavery. He did all he could to help me to get my money; and we went to every magistrate in Kingston (and there were nine), but they all refused to do any thing for me, and said my oath could not be admitted against a white man. Nor was this all for Baker threatened that he would beat me severely if he could catch me, for attempting to demand my money; and this he would have done but I got, by means of Dr. Irving, under the protection of Captain Douglas, of the Squirrel man of war. I thought this exceedingly hard usage; though indeed I found it to be too much the practice there to pay free negro men for their labour in this manner.

One day I went with a free negro tailer, named Joe Diamond, to one Mr. Cochran, who was indebted to him some trifling sum; and the man, not being able to get his money, began to murmur. The other immediately took a horse-whip to pay him with it: but by the help of a good pair of heels, the tailor got off. Such oppressions as these made me seek for a vessel to get off the islands as fast as I could: and by the mercy of God, I found a ship in November bound for England, when I embarked with a convoy, after having taken a last farewell of Dr. Irving.—When I left Jamaica he was employed in refining sugars, and offered me a place, but I refused. And some months after my arrival in England I learned, with much sorrow, that this my amiable friend was dead owing to his having eaten some poisoned fish.

We had many heavy gales of wind in our passage: in the course of which no material accident occurred, except that an American privateer, falling in with the fleet, was captured and set fire to by his Majesty's ship the Squirrel.

On January the seventh 1777, we arrived at Plymouth. I was happy once more to tread upon English ground: and, after passing some little time at Plymouth and Exeter, among some pious friends, whom I was happy to see, I went to London, with a heart replete with thanks to God for past mercies.

CHAPTER XII.

Different transactions of the author's life till the present time—His applica-
tion to the late Bishop of London to be appointed a Missionary to Africa—Some
account of his share in the conduct of the late expedition to Sierra Leona—
Petition to the Queen—Conclusion.

I.

S UCH WERE the various scenes to which I was a witness, and the fortune
I experienced until the year 1777. Since that period my life has been
more uniform, and the incidents of it fewer, than in any other equal number
of years preceding; I therefore hasten to the conclusion of a narrative, which
I fear the reader may think already sufficiently tedious.

I had suffered so many impositions in my commercial transactions in dif-
ferent parts of the world, that I became heartily disgusted with the seafaring
life, and was determined not to return to it, at least for some time. I there-
fore once more engaged in service shortly after my return and continued, for
the most part, in this situation until 1784.

Soon after my arrival in London, I saw a remarkable circumstance rela-
tive to African complexion, which I thought so extraordinary that I shall beg
leave just to mention it:—A white negro woman, that I had formerly seen in
London and other parts, had married a white man, by whom she had three
boys, and they were every one mulattoes, and yet they had fine light hair.

In 1779, I served Governor Macnamara, who had been a considerable
time on the coast of Africa. In the time of my service I used to ask frequent-
ly other servants to join me in family prayer, but this only excited their mock-
ery. However, the Governor, understanding that I was of a religious turn,
wished to know what religion I was of; I told him I was a protestant of the
church of England, agreeable to the thirty-nine articles of that church; and
that whomsoever I found to preach according to that doctrine, those I would
hear. A few days after this, we had some more discourse on the same subject;
when he said he would, if I chose, as he thought I might be of service in con-
verting my countrymen to the Gospel-faith, get me sent out as a missionary
to Africa. I at first refused going, and told him how I had been served on a
like occasion by some white people, the last voyage I went to Jamaica, when
I attempted (if it were the will of God), to be the means of converting the

Indian prince; and said I supposed they would serve me worse than Alexander the coppersmith did St. Paul, if I should attempt to go amongst them in Africa. He told me not to fear, for he would apply to the Bishop of London to get me ordained. On these terms I consented to the Governor's proposal to go to Africa, in hope of doing good, if possible, amongst my countrymen; so, in order to have me sent out properly, we immediately wrote the following letters to the late Bishop of London:

To The Right Reverend Father in God, ROBERT,
Lord Bishop of London.
THE MEMORIAL OF GUSTAVUS VASSA

SHEWETH,

THAT your memorialist is a native of Africa, and has a knowledge of the manners and customs of the inhabitants of that country.

That your memorialist has resided in different parts of Europe for twenty-two years last past, and embraced the Christian faith in the year 1759.

That your memorialist is desirous of returning to Africa as a missionary, if encouraged by your Lordship, in hopes of being able to prevail upon his countrymen to become Christians; and your memorialist is the more induced to undertake the same, from the success that has attended the like undertakings when encouraged by the Portuguese through their different settlements on the coast of Africa, and also by the Dutch; both governments encouraged the blacks, who by their education are qualified to undertake the same, and are found more proper than European clergymen, unacquainted with the language and customs of the country.

Your memorialist's only motive for soliciting the office of a missionary is, that he may be a means, under God, of reforming his countrymen and persuading them to embrace the Christian religion. Therefore your memorialist humbly prays your Lordship's encouragement and support in the undertaking.

GUSTAVUS VASSA.

At Mr. Guthrie's, Taylor,
 No. 17, Hedge-lane.
 My Lord,

 I HAVE resided near seven years on the coast of Africa, for most part of the time as commanding officer. From the knowledge I have of the country and its inhabitants, I am inclined to think that the within plan will be attended with great success, if countenanced by your Lordship. I beg further to represent to your Lordship, that the like attempts, when encouraged by other governments, have met with uncommon success; and at this very time I know a very respectable character, a black priest, at Cape Coast Castle, I know the within named GUSTAVUS VASSA, and believe him a moral good man.

 I have the honour to be,
 My Lord,
 Your Lordship's
 Humble and obedient Servant,
 MATT. MACNAMARA.
Grove, 11th March, 1779.

This letter was also accompanied by the following from Doctor Wallace, who had resided in Africa for many years, and whose sentiments on the subject of the African mission were the same with Governor Macnamara's.

 My Lord, March 13, 1779.
 I have resided near five years on Senegambia on the coast of Africa, and have had the honour of filling very considerable employments in that province. I do approve of the within plan, and think the undertaking very laudable and proper, and that it deserves your Lordship's protection and encouragement, in which case it must be attended with the intended success.

 I am, my Lord,
 Your Lordship's
 Humble and obedient Servant,
 THOMAS WALLACE.

With these letters I waited on the Bishop, by the Governor's desire, and presented them to his Lordship. He received me with much condescension and politeness; but, from some certain scruples of delicacy, and saying the Bishops were not of opinion in sending a new missionary to Africa, he declined to ordain me.

My sole motive for thus dwelling on this transaction, or inserting these papers, is the opinion which gentlemen of sense and education, who are acquainted with Africa, entertain of the probability of converting the inhabitants of it to the faith of Jesus Christ, if the attempt were countenanced by the legislature.

II.

Shortly after this I left the Governor, and served a nobleman in the Dorsetshire militia, with whom I was encamped at Coxheath for some time; but the operations there were too minute and uninteresting to make detail of.

In the year 1783, I visited eight counties in Wales, from motives of curiosity. While I was in that part of the country I was led to go down into a coal-pit in Shropshire, but my curiosity nearly cost me my life; for while I was in the pit the coals fell in, and buried one poor man, who was not far from me: upon this I got out as fast as I could, thinking the surface of the earth the safest part of it.

In the spring of 1784, I thought of visiting old ocean again. In consequence of this I embarked as steward on board a fine new ship called the London, commanded by Martin Hopkins, and sailed for New York. I admired this city very much; it is large and well-built, and abounds with provisions of all kinds. While we lay here, a circumstance happened which I thought extremely singular:—One day a malefactor was to be executed on a gallows; but with condition that if any woman, having nothing on but her shift, married the man under the gallows, his life was to be saved. This extraordinary privilege was claimed; a woman presented herself; and the marriage ceremony was performed.

Our ship having got laden, we returned to London in January 1785. When she was again ready for another voyage, the Captain being an agreeable man, I sailed with him from hence in the spring, March 1785, for Philadelphia. On the 5th of April we took our departure from the Land's end, with a pleasant gale; and about nine that night the moon shone bright,

and the sea was smooth, while our ship was going free by the wind, at the rate of about four or five miles an hour.—At this time another ship was going nearly as fast as we on the opposite point, meeting us right in the teeth, yet none on board observed either ship until we struck each other forcibly head to head, to the astonishment and consternation of both crews. She did us much damage, but I believe we did her more; for, when we passed by each other, which we did very quickly, they called to us to bring to, and hoist out our boats, but we had enough to do to mind ourselves; and in about eight minutes we saw no more of her. We refitted as well as we could the next day, and proceeded on our voyage, and in May arrived at Philadelphia.

I was very glad to see this favourite old town once more; and my pleasure was much increased in seeing the worthy Quakers, freeing and easing the burthens of many of my oppressed African brethren. It rejoiced my heart when one of these friendly people took me to see a free-school they had erected for every denomination of black people, whose minds are cultivated here, and forwarded to virtue; and thus they are made useful members of the community. Does not the success of this practice say loudly to the planters, in the language of scripture—"Go ye, and do likewise!"

In October 1785, I was accompanied by some of the Africans, and presented an address of thanks to the gentlemen called friends or Quakers, in the Whitehart-court, Lombard-street.* These gentlemen received us very kindly, with a promise to exert themselves on behalf of the oppressed Africans, and we parted.

III.

W hile in town, I chanced once to be invited to a Quaker's wedding. The simple and yet expressive mode used at their solemnizations is worthy of note. The following is the true form of it:

After the company have met, they have seasonable exhortations by several of the members, the bride and bridegroom stand up, and, taking each other by the hand, in a solemn manner, the man audibly declares to this purpose:

> Friends, in the fear of the Lord, and in the presence of this
> assembly, whom I desire to be my witnesses, I take this my friend, M.
> N. to be my wife; promising, through divine assistance, to be unto her a
> loving and faithful husband till death separate us.

*See Appendix B.

And the woman makes the like declaration.—Then the two first sign their names to the record, and as many more witnesses as have a mind. I had the honour to subscribe mine to a register in Whitehart-court, Lombard-street. This mode I highly recommend.

We returned to London in August, and our ship not going immediately to sea, I shipped as a steward in an American ship called the Harmony, Captain John Willett, and left London in March 1786, bound to Philadelphia. Eleven days after sailing, we carried our foremast away. We had a nine weeks passage, which caused our trip not to succeed well, the market for our goods proving bad; and, to make it worse, my commander began to play me the like tricks as others too often practice on free negroes in the West Indies. But I thank God, I found many friends here who in some measure prevented him. On my return to London in August, I was very agreeably surprised to find, that the benevolence of government adopted the plan of some philanthropic individuals, to send the Africans from hence to their native quarter; and that some vessels were then engaged to carry them to Sierra Leona; an act which redounded to the honour of all concerned in its promotion, and filled me with prayers and much rejoicing.

There was then in the city a select committee of gentlemen for the black poor, to some of whom I had the honour of being known; and as soon as they heard of my arrival, they sent for me to the committee. When I came there, they informed me of the intention of government; and as they seemed to think me qualified to superintend part of the undertaking, they asked me to go with the black poor to Africa. I pointed out to them many objections to my going; and particularly I expressed some difficulties on the account of the slave dealers, as I would certainly oppose their traffic in the human species by every means in my power. However, these objections were overruled by the gentlemen of the committee, who prevailed on me to consent to go; and recommended me to the honourable Commissioners of his Majesty's Navy, as a proper person to act as commissary for government in the intended expedition; and they accordingly appointed me in November 1786, to that office, and gave me sufficient power to act for the government in the capacity of commissary, having received my warrant and the following order:

By the principal Officers and Commissioners of his Majesty's Navy.

WHEREAS you are directed, by our warrant of the 4th of last month, to receive into your charge, from Mr. Joseph Irwin, the surplus provisions remaining of what was provided for the voyage, as well as the provisions for the support of the black poor, after the landing at Sierra Leona, with the cloathing, tools, and all other articles provided at government's expence; and as the provisions were laid in at the rate of two months for the voyage, and for four months after landing, but the number embarked being so much less than we expected, whereby there may be a considerable surplus of provisions, cloathing, &c. these are, in addition to former orders, to direct and require you to appropriate or dispose of such surplus to the best advantage you can for the benefit of government, keeping and rendering to us a faithful account of what you do herein. And for your guidance in preventing any white persons going, who are not intended to have the indulgence of being carried thither, we send you herewith a list of those recommended by the committee for the black poor, as proper persons to be permitted to embark, and acquaint you that you are not to suffer any others to go who do not produce a certificate from the committee for the black poor, of their having their permission for it. For which this shall be your warrant. Dated at the Navy-Office, January 16, 1787.

> J. HINSLOW,
> GEO. MARSH,
> W. PALMER

To Mr. Gustavus Vassa, Commissary
 of Provisions and Stores for the
 Black Poor to Sierra Leona.
 }

I proceeded immediately to the executing of my duty on board the vessels destined for the voyage, where I continued till the March following.

IV.

D uring my continuance in the employment of government I was struck
with the flagrant abuses committed by the agent, and endeavoured to
remedy them, but without any effect. One instance, among many which I
could produce, may serve as a specimen. Government had ordered to be pro-
vided all necessaries (slops, as they are called, included) for 750 persons;
however, not being able to muster more than 426, I was ordered to send the
superfluous slops, &c. to the king's stores at Portsmouth; but, when I
demanded them for that purpose from the agent, it appeared they had never
been bought, though paid for by government. But that was not all, govern-
ment were not the only objects of peculation; these poor people suffered
infinitely more; their accommodations were most wretched; many of them
wanted beds, and many more clothing and other necessaries.

For the truth of this, and much more, I do not seek credit from my own
assertion. I appeal to the testimony of Captain Thompson, of the Nautilus,
who convoyed us; to whom I applied in February 1787 for a remedy, when
I had remonstrated to the agent in vain, and even brought him to be a wit-
ness of the in justice and oppression I had complained of.* I appeal also to a
letter written by these wretched people, so early as the beginning of the pre-
ceding January, and published in the Morning Herald, on the fourth of that
month, signed by twenty of their chiefs.

I could not silently suffer government to be thus cheated, and my
countrymen plundered and oppressed, and even left destitute of the neces-
saries for almost their existence. I therefore informed the Commissioners of
the Navy of the agent's proceeding; but my dismission was soon after pro-
cured by the means of a gentleman** in the city, whom the agent, conscious
of his peculation, had deceived by letters, and who, moreover, empowered
the same agent to receive on board, at the government's expence, a number
of persons as passengers, contrary to the orders I received. By this I suffered a
considerable loss in my property: however, the commissioners were satisfied
with my conduct, and wrote to Captain Thompson, expressing their
approbation of it.

*He then told the agent before me, he was informed by Mr. Steel, M. P. that the said
expedition had cost 33,000 and he desired that the things might be had.
** Witness Thomas Steele, Esq. M. P. of the Treasury, and Sir, Charles Middleton, Bart.
&c. I should have publicly exposed him (even in writing falsely of me last March), were
it not out of respect to the worthy Quakers and others.

Thus provided, they proceeded on their voyage; and at last, worn out by treatment, perhaps not the most mild, and wasted by sickness, brought on by want of medicine, clothes, bedding, &c. they reached Sierra Leona just at the commencement of the rains. At that season of the year it is impossible to cultivate the lands, their provisions therefore were exhausted before they could derive any benefit from agriculture; and it is not surprising that many, especially the Lascars, whose constitutions are very tender, and who had been cooped up in ships from October to June, and accommodated in the manner I have mentioned, should be so wasted by their confinement as not long to survive it.

Thus ended my part of the long-talked-of expedition to Sierra Leona; an expedition, which, however unfortunate in the event, was humane and politic in its design; nor was its failure owing to government; every thing was done on their part; but there was evidently sufficient mismanagement, attending the conduct and execution of it, to defeat its success.

I should not have been so ample in my account of this transaction, had not the share I bore in it been made the subject of partial animadversion, and even my dismission from my employment thought worthy of being made, by Hoare and others, matter of public triumph. The motive which might influence any person to descend to a petty contest with an obscure African, and to seek gratification by his depression, perhaps it is not proper here to enquire into or relate, even if its detection were necessary to my vindication;* but I thank Heaven it is not. I wish to stand by my own integrity, and not to shelter myself under the impropriety of another; and I trust the behaviour of the Commissioners of the Navy to me entitle me to make this assertion; for after I had been dismissed, March 24, I drew up a memorial.**

The above petition was delivered into the hands of their Lordships who were kind enough, in the space of some few months afterwards, without hearing, to order me £50. sterling—that is £18. wages for the time (upwards of four months) I acted a faithful part in their service. Certainly the sum is more than a free negro would have had in the western colonies!!!

V.

From that period to the present, my life has passed in an even tenour, and great part of my study and attention has been to assist in the cause of my

*See the Public Advertiser, July 4, 1787
**See Appendix C.

much injured countrymen.

March the 21st, 1788, I had the honour of presenting the Queen with a petition on behalf of my African brethren, which was received most graciously by her Majesty.*

The negro consolidated act, made by the assembly of Jamaica last year, and the new act of amendment now in agitation there, contain a proof of the existence of those charges that have been made against the planters relative to the treatment of their slaves.

I hope to have the satisfaction of seeing the renovation of liberty and justice, resting on the British government, to vindicate the honour of our common nature. These are concerns which do not, perhaps, belong to any particular office: but to speak more seriously, to every man of sentiment actions like these are the just and sure foundation of future fame, a reversion, though remote, is coveted by some noble minds as a substantial good. It is upon these grounds that I hope and expect the attention of gentlemen in power. These are designs consonant to the elevation of their rank, and the dignity of their stations; they are ends suitable to the nature of a free and generous government; and connected with views of empire and dominion, suited to the benevolence and solid merit of the legislature. It is a pursuit of substantial greatness. May the time come-at least the speculation to me is pleasing-when the sable people shall gratefully commemorate the auspicious æra of extensive freedom! Then shall those persons** particularly be named with praise and honour who generously proposed, and stood forth in the cause of humanity, liberty, and good policy, and brought to the ear of the legislature designs worthy of a royal patronage and adoption. May Heaven make the British senators the dispersers of light, liberty, and science, to the uttermost parts of the earth! Then will be Glory to God in the highest; on earth peace and good-will to men.—Glory, honour, peace, to every soul of man that worketh good: to the Britons first (because to them the gospel is preached), and also to the nations. Those that honour their Maker have mercy on the poor. It is righteousness exalteth a nation, but sin is a reproach to any people, destruction shall be to the workers of iniquity, and the wicked shall fall by their own wickedness. May the blessings of the Lord be upon the

*At the request of some of my most particular friends I take the liberty of inserting it. See Appendix D.
**Granville Sharp, Esq. the Rev. Thomas Clarkson the Rev. James Ramsay, our approved friends, men of virtue, are an honour to their country, ornamental to human nature, happy in themselves, and benefactors to mankind!

heads of all those who commiserated the cases of the oppressed negroes, and the fear of God prolong their days; and may their expectations be filled with gladness! "The liberal devise liberal things, and by liberal things shall stand." Isaiah xxxii. 8. They can say with pious Job, "Did not I weep for him that was in trouble? Was not my soul grieved for the poor?" Job xxx. 25.

VI.

A s the inhuman traffic of slavery is to be taken into the consideration of the British legislature, I doubt not, if a system of commerce was established in Africa, the demand for manufactures will most rapidly augment, as the native inhabitants will insensibly adopt the British fashions, manners, customs, &c. In proportion to the civilization, so will be the consumption of British manufactures.

The wear and tear of a continent, nearly twice as large as Europe, and rich in vegetable and mineral productions, is much easier conceived than calculated.

A case in point. It cost the Aborigines of Britain little or nothing in clothing, &c. The difference between their forefathers and the present generation, in point of consumption, is literally infinite. The supposition is most obvious.—It will be equally immense in Africa.—The same cause, viz. civilization, will ever have the same effect.

It is trading upon safe grounds. A commercial intercourse with Africa opens an inexhaustible source of wealth to the manufacturing interests of Great Britain;* and to all which the slave-trade is an objection.

If I am not misinformed, the manufacturing interest is equal, if not superior, to the landed interest, as to the value, for reasons which will soon appear. The abolition of slavery, so diabolical, will give a most rapid

*In the ship Trusty, lately for the new Settlement of Sierra Leona, in Africa, where 1,300 pair of shoes (an article hitherto scarcely known to be exported to that country) with several others equally new, as articles of export. Thus will it not become the interest, as well as the duty, of every artificer, mechanic, and tradesman, publicly to enter their protest against this traffic of the human species?—What a striking, what a beautiful contrast is here presented to view, when compared with the cargo of a slave ship! Every feeling heart, indeed, sensibly participates of the joy, and with a degree of rapture reads of barrels of flour instead of gunpowder—biscuits and bread instead of horse beans—implements of husbandry instead of guns for destruction, rapine, and murder—and various articles of usefulness are the pleasing substitutes for the torturing thumbscrew, and the galling chain, &c.

extension of manufactures, which is totally and diametrically opposite to what some interested people assert.

The manufactures of this country must and will, in the nature and reason of things, have a full and constant employ, by supplying the African markets.

Population, the bowels, and surface of Africa, abound in valuable and useful returns; the hidden treasures of centuries will be brought to light and into circulation. Industry, enterprise, and mining, will have their final scope, proportionately as they civilize. In a word, it lays open an endless field of commerce to the British manufacturers and merchant adventurers. The manufacturing interest and the general interests are synonimous. The abolition of slavery would be in reality an universal good.

Tortures, murder, and every other imaginable barbarity and iniquity, are practiced upon the poor slaves with impunity. I hope the slave trade will be abolished. I pray it may be an event at hand. The great body of manufacturers, uniting in the cause, will considerably facilitate and expedite it; and as I have already stated, it is most substantially their interest and advantage, and as such the nation's at large, except those persons conceded in manufacturing neck-yokes, collars, chains, hand-cuffs, leg-bolts, drags, thumbscrews, iron muzzles, and coffins; cats, scourges, and other instruments of torture used in the slave-trade. In a short time one sentiment will alone prevail, from motives of interest as well as justice and humanity. Europe contains one hundred and twenty millions of inhabitants. Query—How many millions cloth Africa contain? Supposing the Africans, collectively and individually, to expend £5. a head in raiment and furniture yearly, when civilized, &c. an immensity beyond the reach of imagination!

This I conceive to be a theory founded upon facts, and therefore an infallible one. If the blacks were permitted to remain in their own country, they would double themselves every fifteen years. In proportion to such increase will be the demand for manufactures. Cotton and indigo grow spontaneously in most parts of Africa; a consideration this of no small consequence to the manufacturing towns of Great Britain. It opens a most immense, glorious, and happy prospect; the clothing, &c. of a continent ten thousand miles in circumference, and immensely rich in productions of every denomination in return for manufactures.

VII.

S ince the first publication of my narrative, I have been in a great variety of scenes* in many parts of Great-Britain, Ireland, and Scotland, an account of which might well be added here; but as this would swell the volume too much, I shall only observe in general, that in May 1791, I sailed from Liverpool to Dublin, where I was very kindly received, and from thence to Cork, and then travelled over many counties in Ireland. I was every where exceedingly well treated, by persons of all ranks. I found the people extremely hospitable, particularly in Belfast, where I took my passage on board of a vessel for Clyde, on the 29th of January, and arrived at Greenock on the 30th.—Soon after I resumed to London, where I found persons of note from Holland and Germany, who requested me to go there; and I was glad to hear that an edition of my Narrative had been printed in both places, also in New York. I remained in London till I heard the debate in the house of Commons on the slave-trade, April the 2d and 3d. I then went to Soham in Cambridgeshire, and was married on the 7th of April to Miss Cullen, daughter of James and Ann Cullen, late of Ely.**

I have only therefore to request the reader's indulgence, and conclude. I am far from the vanity of thinking there is any merit in this narrative: I hope censure will be suspended, when it is considered that it was written by one who was as unwilling as unable to adorn the plainness of truth by the colouring of imagination. My life and fortune have been extremely chequered, and my adventures various. Even those I have related are considerably abridged. If any incident in this little work should appear uninteresting and trifling to most readers, I can only say, as my excuse for mentioning it, that almost every event of my life made an impression on my mind, and influenced my conduct. I early accustomed myself to look at the hand of God in the minutest occurrence, and to learn from it a lesson of morality and religion; and in this light every circumstance I have related was, to me, of importance. After all, what makes any event important, unless by its observation we become better

*Viz. Some curious adventures beneath the earth, in a river in Manchester,—and a most astonishing one under the Peak of Derbyshire—and in September 1792, I went 90 fathoms down St. Anthony's Colliery, at Newcastle, under the river Tyne, some hundreds of yards on the Durham side.

**See Gentleman's Magazine for April 1792, Literary and Biographical Magazine and British Review for May 1792, and the Edinburgh Historical Register or Monthly Intelligencer for April 1792.

and wiser, and learn *to do justly, to love mercy, and to walk humbly before God?* To those who are possessed of this spirit, there is scarcely any book or incident so trifling that does not afford some profit, while to others the experience of ages seems of no use; and even to pour out to them the treasures of wisdom is throwing the jewels of instruction away.

APPENDIX.

A.

Montserrat.—To all men unto whom these presents shall come:

I, Robert King, of the parish of St. Anthony in the said island, merchant, send greeting: Know ye, that I, the aforesaid Robert King, for, and in consideration of the sum of seventy pounds current money of the said island, to me in hand paid, and to the intent that a negro man-slave, named Gustavus Vassa, shall and may become free, have manumitted, emancipated, enfranchised, and set free, and by these presents do manumit, emancipate, enfranchise, and set free, the aforesaid negro man-slave, named Gustavus Vassa, for ever; hereby giving, granting, and releasing unto him, the said Gustavus Vassa, all right, title, dominion, sovereignty, and property, which, as lord and master over the aforesaid Gustavus Vassa, I had, or now have, or by any means whatsoever I may or can hereafter possibly have over him, the aforesaid negro, for ever. In witness whereof I, the abovesaid Robert King, have unto these presents set my hand and seal, this tenth day of the seventh month, in the year of our Lord one thousand seven hundred and sixty-six.

ROBERT KING.

Signed, sealed, and delivered in the presence of Terry Legay, Montserrat.

Registered the within manumission, at full length, this eleventh day of July, 1766, in liber D.

TERRY LEGAY, Register.

B.

Gentlemen,

By reading your book intitled, "A Caution to Great Britain and her Colonies, concerning the calamitous state of the enslaved negroes," We, part of the poor, oppressed, needy, and much degraded negroes, desire to approach you, with this address of thanks, with our inmost love and warmest acknowledgment, and with the deepest sense of your benevolence, unwearied labour, and kind interposition, towards breaking the yoke of slavery, and to administer a little comfort and ease to thousands and tens of thousands of very grievously afflicted and too heavy burthened negroes.

 Gentlemen, could you, by perseverance, at last be enabled, under God, to lighten in any degree the heavy burthen of the afflicted, no doubt it would, in some measure, be the possible means under God of saving the souls of many of the oppressors; and if so, sure we are that the God, whose eyes are ever upon all his creatures, and always rewards every true act of virtue, and regards the prayers of the oppressed, will give to you and yours those blessings which it is not in our power to express or conceive, but which we, as a part of those captivated, oppressed, and afflicted people, most earnestly wish and pray for.

C.

To the Right Hon. the Lords Commissioners of his Majesty's Treasury.

The Memorial and Petition of GUSTAVUS VASSA, a black Man, late Commissary to the black Poor, going to Africa,

HUMBLY SHEWETH,

THAT your Lordships' memoralist was, by the hon. the commissioners of his majesty's navy, on the 4th of December last, appointed to the above employment by warrant from that board.

That he accordingly proceeded to the execution of his duty on board of the Vernon, being one of the ships appointed to proceed to Africa with the above poor.

That your memorialist, to his great grief and astonishment, received a letter of dismission, from the hon. commissioners of the navy, by your Lordships' orders.

That conscious of having acted with the most perfect fidelity and the greatest assiduity, in discharging the trust reposed in him, he is altogether at a loss to conceive the reasons of your lordships having altered the favourable opinion you were pleased to conceive of him, sensible that your Lordships would not proceed to so severe a measure without some apparent good cause; he therefore has every reason to believe that his conduct has been grossly misrepresented to your Lordships, and he is the more confirmed in his opinion, because by opposing measures of others concerned in the same expedition, which tended to defeat your Lordships' humane intentions, and to put the government to a very considerable additional expence, he created a number of enemies, whose misrepresentations, he has too much reason to believe, laid the foundation of his dismission. Unsupported by friends, and unaided by the advantages of a liberal education, he can only hope for redress from the justice of his cause, in addition to the mortification of having been removed from his employment, and the advantage which he reasonably might have expected to have derived therefrom. He has had the misfortune to have sunk a considerable part of his little property in fitting himself, out, and in other expences arising out of his situation, an account of which he here annexes. Your memorialist will not trouble your Lordships with a vindication of any part of his conduct, because he knows not of what crimes he is accused; he, however, earnestly entreats that you will be acted in the public service; and if it be found that his dismission arose from false representations, he is confident that in your Lordships' justice he shall find redress.

Your petitioner therefore humbly prays that your Lordships will take his case into consideration, and that you will be pleased to order payment of the above-referred-to

account, amounting to 321.4s. and also the wages intended, which is most humbly submitted.

London, May 12th, 1787.

D.

To the QUEEN's most excellent Majesty:

MADAM,

Your Majesty's well known benevolence and humanity embolden me to approach your royal presence, trusting that the obscurity of my situation will not prevent your Majesty from attending to the sufferings for which I plead.

Yet I do not solicit your royal pity for my own distress; my sufferings, although numerous, are, in a measure, forgotten. I supplicate your Majesty's compassion for millions of my African countrymen, who groan under the lash of tyranny in the West-Indies.

The oppression and cruelty exercised to the unhappy negroes there, have at length reached the British legislature, and they are now deliberating on its redress; even several persons of property in slaves in the West-Indies, have petitioned parliament against its continuance, sensible that it is as impolite as it is unjust-and what is inhuman must ever be unwise.

Your Majesty's reign has hitherto been distinguished by private acts of benevolence and bounty; surely the more extended the misery is, the greater claim it has to your Majesty's compassion, and the greater must be your Majesty's pleasure in administering to its relief.

I presume, therefore, gracious Queen, to implore your interposition with your royal consort, in favour of the wretched Africans; that by your Majesty's benevolent influence, a period may now be put to their misery; and that they may be raised from the condition of brutes, to which they are at present degraded, to the rights and situation of freemen, and admitted to partake of the blessings of your Majesty's happy government; so shall your Majesty enjoy the heart-felt pleasure

of procuring happiness to millions, and be rewarded in the grateful prayers of themselves and of their posterity.

And may the All-bountiful Creator shower on your Majesty, and the Royal Family, every blessing that this world can afford, and every fulness of joy which divine revelation has promised us in the next.

I am, your Majesty's
Most dutiful and devoted Servant to command,
GUSTAVUS VASSA,

The Oppressed Ethiopian.
Nc. 53, Baldwin's Gardens:

FINIS.

SOJOURNER TRUTH

(1797-1883)

Sojourner Truth was born a slave named Isabella Baumfree around 1797 in Hurley, Ulster County, New York on the estate of a Dutch family, the Hardenberghs. She grew up speaking no English, just the Dutch she acquired from her masters, and when Colonel Hardenbergh died a few years after Belle was born, she and her family moved into the cellar of Hardenbergh's son, Charles. There, "Belle," as she was known, lived with her parents James and Betsy and 12 siblings in deplorable conditions, though Charles was considered a fairly decent slave owner, since he did not separate families or inflict corporal punishment.

Still, the second youngest of 13 children, Belle never developed much of a relationship with any of her brothers or sisters because she was bought and sold several times in the years that followed and she separated from them. Despite this severance from her family roots, Belle did acquire a religious reverence from her mother at an early age, which inspired a lifelong devotion to God.

When Charles Hardenbergh died in 1808, Belle and her younger brother were sold as chattel to John Neely, who beat her because of his dislike of the Dutch community and Belle's inability to understand his English commands. However, her prayers were answered and she was again sold, this time back to a Dutch tavern owner named Martin Scriver. In 1810, she was sold once again for seventy pounds to John I. Dumont and spent the next 16 years of her life on his estate, cooking, cleaning and working the fields.

As a teenager, Belle proved herself a tireless worker, extraordinarily strong, both physically and spiritually. Dumont once commented that she was "better to me than a man—for she will do a good family's washing in the night, and be ready in the morning to go into the field, where she will do as much raking and binding as my best hands."

When she was around 14 years old, Belle was forced to marry an older

slave named Thomas, also owned by Dumont, and over the next eleven years, the couple had five children, most of them taken from her and sold. The year 1826 was a momentous one in her life, as the state of New York passed a law emancipating all slaves in the state beginning in 1827. Dumont promised he'd free Belle one year early, but reneged on that promise, prompting her to flee his estate with an infant daughter in her arms. She escaped at dawn and took up refuge and employment in a Quaker household, the Van Wagenens, who purchased the remainder of her time from Dumont.

In the summer of 1827, Isabella took the name Van Wagenen because she did not want to bear the name of her previous owner. It was here with the Van Wagenens where Belle found some peace and believed she received a message from God. This epiphany set her on an evangelical path, and she admittedly got caught up in the atmosphere of excitement that was sweeping American Protestantism. She ended up joining the Methodist Church and the Zion African Church and began preaching at local congregations against oppression.

HER SON, Peter had been illegally sold across state lines and taken to Alabama, and with the help of the local Quakers, Belle waged a court battle, successfully suing and recovering her young son. Around 1829, she moved to New York City with her two youngest children and supported herself with domestic work, all the while continuing her activity with various self-proclaimed prophets such as Matthias (Robert Matthews) and later, the Millerites. Belle often preached at these gatherings and developed a presence and oratorical manner which left her audiences captivated and spellbound.

Eventually, she would meet Elijah Pierson, a zealous religious missionary, and Belle preached in the streets, becoming an advocate for the poor and displaced. But in 1843, after her son Peter's death, Isabella Wagenen renewed her commitment to spreading the word of God across the land. She changed her name to "Sojourner Truth," and claimed to be obeying a supernatural call to "travel up and down the land." She sang, preached, and engaged in lively debates in churches, meeting halls and on village streets, exhorting those in attendance to accept and embrace the messages of the Bible.

In that same year, Truth left New York City, which she considered "the second Sodom," and she became involved with the Northampton Association, a white utopian community in Florence, Massachusetts, where she was introduced to abolitionism and the more advanced ideas of social reform. Here, Truth first met Frederick Douglass and William Lloyd

Garrison and decided to embark on an abolitionist lecture circuit with them. She demonstrated a great deal of power from the podium, seizing audiences from her opening line, "Children, I talk to God and God talks to me," and her passionate calls for black freedom and women's rights made her a major attraction and earned her much renown.

Although she had been somewhat educated by the Van Wagenens, Truth was still illiterate when Olive Gilbert, a feminist and member of the Northampton Association, helped her record her remarkable and tragic life in the *Narrative of Sojourner Truth*, which initially appeared in 1850. She began to travel about the Midwest, drawing huge crowds at suffrage gatherings and abolitionist meetings, selling copies of her narrative along the way. Before the Civil War began, she was at one fiery meeting where Frederick Douglass was in the process of suggesting that blacks might consider violence as an anti-slavery tactic. Sojourner Truth then took the podium and responded, "Frederick, is God dead?" According to observers, the force and impact of her succinct phrase was electrifying, and changed the entire mood of the house.

Truth was not above using her words, nor her body to make a point. At an 1851 woman's rights convention in Akron, Ohio, she spoke proudly of her strength and determination, and by implication, the strengths of all woman. She was a large woman, nearly six feet tall, but lean and muscular, and her eyes were piercing and commanded attention. Mrs. Frances Dana Gage, a white reformer who chaired the meeting, retold the story of Truth's dramatic speech in the 1851 convention, though some scholars have doubt-ed the accuracy, as well as the dialect, which was more in tune with contemporary conventions about black speech than Truth's true voice. The speech became known as Truth's "Ain't I a Woman" address, which became the motto of her historical image, whether it was entirely accurate or not. According to Gage, this is some of what transpired:

> Nobody eber help me into carriages, or ober mud puddles, or gives me any best place and ar'n't I a woman? Look at me! Look at my arm! I have plowed, and planted, and gathered into barns, and no man could head me—and ar'n't I a woman?
>
> I could work as much and eat as much as a man . . . and bear de lash as well, and ar'n't I a woman?

Whatever the exact words were, it's clear from newspaper accounts of the convention that Truth's dynamic appearance was not exaggerated. There were

a large percentage of women who did not want Truth to speak that day, fearing the women's cause would be diluted with a message of abolition. According to Gage, the hecklers were completely disarmed. "She had taken us up in her strong arms and carried us safely over the slough of difficulty, turning the whole tide in our favor. I have never in my life seen anything like the magical influence that subdued the mobbish spirit of the day and turned the jibes and sneers of an excited crowd into notes of respect and admiration."

When hecklers at another meeting attempted to shout her down with claims that she was far too forceful to be a woman, Truth bore her breasts. Her notoriety grew in leaps and bounds and when Harriet Beecher Stowe, whose *Uncle Tom's Cabin* had made her one of America's favorite writers, profiled Truth in *Atlantic Monthly* in 1863, it boosted her reputation nationally, and Truth was invited to the White House by Abraham Lincoln the following year.

The article was meant partially as an obituary for Sojourner Truth, since there were rumors at the time that she had been killed. In fact, she had been hurt and arrested in Indiana by pro-slavery forces. She would later become one of America's first "freedom riders," during the Civil War, when she demanded to ride aboard a streetcar in Washington D.C., then mounted a successful legal challenge to segregated streetcars.

In the years that followed the Civil War, Truth gave aid to freed people and became a voice against black poverty, white racism and violence. One focus of her later years saw her guiding Southern blacks to the west, in effect attempting to create a domain of black independence. She herself eventually moved to Battle Creek, Michigan and in the 1870s, Truth was an active supporter of the American Woman Suffrage Association. She continued to engage in attempts to secure land in Kansas from the U.S. government for former slaves. Her last major speaking tour was also an effort to rally this move, and when thousands of southern blacks, known as "Exodusters" actually heeded her call, Truth was there to assist in the move. She returned to Battle Creek, where she remained until her death in 1883.

Sojourner Truth's narrative gathered a great deal of force for both the abolition movement and the women's rights movement by presenting a powerful picture of Northern slavery. Truth's narrative also became a central document in a life where she established herself as one of the earliest women freedom fighters and inspired people of all races and sexes in the reshaping of American society.

Narrative of Sojourner Truth: A Northern Slave

HER BIRTH AND PARENTAGE

The subject of this biography, Sojourner Truth, as she now calls herself, but whose name originally was Isabella, was the daughter of James and Betsey, slaves of one Col. Ardinburgh, Hurley, Ulster County, N.Y. Sojourner does not know in what year she was born, but knows she was liberated under the act of 1817, which freed all slaves who were forty years old and upward. Ten thousand slaves were then set at liberty. Those under forty years of age were retained in servitude ten years longer, when all were emancipated.

Col. Ardinburgh belonged to that class of people called Low Dutch.

Of her first master, she can give no account, as she must have been a mere infant when he died; and she with her parents and some ten or twelve other fellow human chattels, became the legal property of his son, Charles Ardinburgh. She distinctly remembers hearing her father and mother say that their lot was a fortunate one, as Master Charles was the best of the family,—being, comparatively speaking, a kind master to his slaves.

James and Betsey having, by their faithfulness, docility, and respectful behavior, won his particular regard, received from him particular favors— among which was a lot of land, lying back on the slope of a mountain, where, by improving the pleasant evenings and Sundays, they managed to raise a little tobacco, corn, or flax; which they exchanged for extras, in the articles of food or clothing for themselves and children. She has no remembrance that Saturday afternoon was ever added to their own time, as it is by *some* masters in the Southern States.

ACCOMMODATIONS.

Among Isabella's earliest recollections was the removal of her master, Charles Ardinburgh, into his new house, which he had built for a hotel, soon after the decease of his father. A cellar, under this hotel, was assigned to his slaves, as their sleeping apartment,—all the slaves he possessed, of both sexes, sleeping (as is quite common in a state of slavery) in the same room. She carries in her mind, to this day, a vivid picture of this dismal chamber; its only lights consisting of a few panes of glass, through which she thinks the sun never shone, but with thrice reflected rays; and the space between the loose boards of the floor, and the uneven earth below, was often filled with mud and water, the uncomfortable splashings of which were as annoying as its noxious vapors must have been chilling and fatal to health. She shudders, even now, as she goes back in memory, and revisits this cellar, and sees its inmates, of both sexes and all ages, sleeping on those damp boards, like the horse, with a little straw and a blanket; and she wonders not at the rheumatisms, and fever-sores, and palsies, that distorted the limbs and racked the bodies of those fellow-slaves in after-life. Still, she does not attribute this cruelty—for cruelty it certainly is, to be so unmindful of the health and comfort of any being, leaving entirely out of sight his more important part, his everlasting interests,—so much to any innate or constitutional cruelty of the master, as to that gigantic inconsistency, that inherited habit among slaveholders, of expecting a willing and intelligent obedience from the slave, because he is a MAN—at the same time every thing belonging to the soul-harrowing system does its best to crush the last vestige of a man within him; and when it is crushed, and often before, he is denied the comforts of life, on the plea that he knows neither the want nor the use of them, and because he is considered to be little more or little *less* than a beast.

HER BROTHERS AND SISTERS.

Isabella's father was very tall and straight, when young, which gave him the name of 'Bomefree'—low Dutch for tree—at least, this is SOJOURNER's pronunciation of it—and by this name he usually went. The most familiar appellation of her mother was 'Mau-mau Bett.' She was the mother of some ten or twelve children; though Sojourner is far from knowing the exact num-

ber of her brothers and sisters; she being the youngest, save one, and all older than herself having been sold before her remembrance. She was privileged to behold six of them while she remained a slave.

Of the two that immediately preceded her in age, a boy of five years, and a girl of three, who were sold when she was an infant, she heard much; and she wishes that all who would fain believe that slave parents have not natural affection for their offspring could have listened as she did, while Bomefree and Mau-mau Bett,—their dark cellar lighted by a blazing pine-knot,— would sit for hours, recalling and recounting every endearing, as well as harrowing circumstance that taxed memory could supply; from the histories of those dear departed ones, of whom they had been robbed, and for whom their hearts still bled. Among the rest, they would relate how the little boy, on the last morning he was with them, arose with the birds, kindled a fire, calling for his Mau-mau to 'come, for all was now ready for her'—little dreaming of the dreadful separation which was so near at hand, but of which his parents had an uncertain, but all the more cruel foreboding. There was snow on the ground, at the time of which we are speaking; and a large old-fashioned sleigh was seen to drive up to the door of the late Col. Ardinburgh. This event was noticed with childish pleasure by the unsuspicious boy; but when he was taken and put into the sleigh, and saw his little sister actually shut and locked into the sleigh box, his eyes were at once opened to their intentions; and, like a frightened deer he sprang from the sleigh, and running into the house, concealed himself under a bed. But this availed him little. He was re-conveyed to the sleigh, and separated for ever from those whom God had constituted his natural guardians and protectors, and who should have found him, in return, a stay and a staff to them in their declining years. But I make no comments on facts like these, knowing that the heart of every slave parent will make its own comments, involuntarily and correctly, as soon as each heart shall make the case its own. Those who are not parents will draw their conclusions from the promptings of humanity and philanthropy:— these, enlightened by reason and revelation, are also unerring.

HER RELIGIOUS INSTRUCTION.

Isabella and Peter, her youngest brother, remained, with their parents, the legal property of Charles Ardinburgh till his decease, which took place

when Isabella was near nine years old.

After this event, she was often surprised to find her mother in tears; and when, in her simplicity, she inquired, 'Mau-mau, what makes you cry?' she would answer, 'Oh, my child, I am thinking of your brothers and sisters that have been sold away from me.' And she would proceed to detail many circumstances respecting them. But Isabella long since concluded that it was the impending fate of her only remaining children, which her mother but too well understood, even then, that called up those memories from the past, and made them crucify her heart afresh.

In the evening, when her mother's work was done, she would sit down under the sparkling vault of heaven, and calling her children to her, would talk to them of the only Being that could effectually aid or protect them. Her teachings were delivered in Low Dutch, her only language, and, translated into English, ran nearly as follows:—

'My children, there is a God, who hears and sees you.' 'A *God*, mau-mau! Where does he live?' asked the children. 'He lives in the sky,' she replied; 'and when you are beaten, or cruelly treated, or fall into any trouble, you must ask help of him, and he will always hear and help you.' She taught them to kneel and say the Lord's Prayer. She entreated them to refrain from lying and stealing, and to strive to obey their masters.

At times, a groan would escape her, and she would break out in the language of the Psalmist—'Oh Lord, how long?' 'Oh Lord, how long?' And in reply to Isabella's question—'What ails you, mau-mau?' her only answer was, 'Oh, a good deal ails me'—'Enough ails me.' Then again, she would point them to the stars, and say, in her peculiar language, 'Those are the same stars, and that is the same moon, that look down upon your brothers and sisters, and which they see as they look up to them, though they are ever so far away from us, and each other.'

Thus, in her humble way, did she endeavor to show them their Heavenly Father, as the only being who could protect them in their perilous condition; at the same time, she would strengthen and brighten the chain of family affection, which she trusted extended itself sufficiently to connect the widely scattered members of her precious flock. These instructions of the mother were treasured up and held sacred by Isabella, as our future narrative will show.

THE AUCTION.

At length, the never-to-be-forgotten day of the terrible auction arrived, when the 'slaves, horses, and other cattle' of Charles Ardinburgh, deceased, were to be put under the hammer, and again change masters. Not only Isabella and Peter, but their mother, were now destined to the auction block, and would have been struck off with the rest to the highest bidder, but for the following circumstance: A question arose among the heirs, 'Who shall be burdened with Bomefree, when we have sent away his faithful Mau-mau Bett?' He was becoming weak and infirm; his limbs were painfully rheumatic and distorted—more from exposure and hardship than from old age, though he was several years older than Mau-mau Bett: he was no longer considered of value, but must soon be a burden and care to some one. After some contention on the point at issue, none being willing to be burdened with him, it was finally agreed, as most expedient for the heirs, that the price of Mau-mau Bett should be sacrificed, and she receive her freedom, on condition that she take care of and support her faithful James,—faithful, not only to her as a husband, but proverbially faithful as a slave to those who would not willingly sacrifice a dollar for his comfort, now that he had commenced his descent into the dark vale of decrepitude and suffering. This important decision was received as joyful news indeed to our ancient couple, who were the objects of it, and who were trying to prepare their hearts for a severe struggle, and one altogether new to them, as they had never before been separated; for, though ignorant, helpless, crushed in spirit, and weighed down with hardship and cruel bereavement, they were still human, and their human hearts beat within them with as true an affection as ever caused a human heart to beat. And their anticipated separation now, in the decline of life, after the last child had been torn from them, must have been truly appalling. Another privilege was granted them—that of remaining occupants of the same dark, humid cellar I have before described: otherwise, they were to support themselves as they best could. And as her mother was still able to do considerable work, and her father a little, they got on for some time very comfortably. The strangers who rented the house were humane people, and very kind to them; they were not rich, and owned no slaves. How long this state of things continued, we are unable to say, as Isabella had not then sufficiently cultivated her organ of time to calculate years, or even weeks or hours. But she thinks her mother must have lived several years after the death of Master Charles. She remembers going to visit her parents some three or

four times before the death of her mother, and a good deal of time seemed to her to intervene between each visit.

At length her mother's health began to decline—a fever-sore made its ravages on one of her limbs, and the palsy began to shake her frame; still, she and James tottered about, picking up a little here and there, which, added to the mites contributed by their kind neighbors, sufficed to sustain life, and drive famine from the door.

DEATH OF MAU-MAU BETT.

One morning, in early autumn (from the reason above mentioned, we cannot tell what year), Mau-mau Bett told James she would make him a loaf of rye-bread, and get Mrs. Simmons, their kind neighbor, to bake it for them, as she would bake that forenoon. James told her he had engaged to rake after the cart for his neighbors that morning; but before he commenced, he would pole off some apples from a tree near, which they were allowed to gather; and if she could get some of them baked with the bread, it would give it a nice relish for their dinner. He beat off the apples, and soon after, saw Mau-mau Bett come out and gather them up.

At the blowing of the horn for dinner, he groped his way into his cellar, anticipating his humble, but warm and nourishing meal; when, lo! instead of being cheered by the sight and odor of fresh-baked bread and the savory apples, his cellar seemed more cheerless than usual, and at first neither sight nor sound met eye or ear. But, on groping his way through the room, his staff, which he used as a pioneer to go before, and warn him of danger, seemed to be impeded in its progress, and a low, gurgling, choking sound proceeded from the object before him, giving him the first intimation of the truth as it was, that Mau-mau Bett, his bosom companion, the only remaining member of his large family, had fallen in a fit of the palsy, and lay helpless and senseless on the earth! Who among us, located in pleasant homes, surrounded with every comfort, and so many kind and sympathizing friends, can picture to ourselves the dark and desolate state of poor old James—penniless, weak, lame, and nearly blind, as he was at the moment he found his companion was removed from him, and he was left alone in the world, with no one to aid, comfort, or console him? for she never revived again, and lived only a few hours after being discovered senseless by her poor bereaved James.

LAST DAYS OF BOMEFREE.

Isabella and Peter were permitted to see the remains of their mother laid in their last narrow dwelling, and to make their bereaved father a little visit, ere they returned to their servitude. And most piteous were the lamentations of the poor old man, when, at last, *they* also were obliged to bid him "Farewell!" Juan Fernandes, on his desolate island, was not so pitiable an object as this poor lame mall. Blind and crippled, he was too superannuated to think for a moment of taking care of himself, and he greatly feared no persons would interest themselves in his behalf. 'Oh,' he would exclaim, 'I had thought God would take me first,—Mau-mau was so much smarter than I, and could get about and take care of herself;—and I am *so old*, and *so helpless*. What *is* to become of me? I can't do any thing more—my children arc all gone, and here I am left helpless and alone.' 'And then, as I was taking leave of him,' said his daughter, in relating it, 'he raised his voice, and cried aloud like a child—Oh, *how he* DID *cry!* I HEAR it *now*—and remember it as well as if it were but yesterday—*poor old man!!!* He thought God had done it all—and my heart bled within me at the sight of his misery. He begged me to get permission to come and see him sometimes, which I readily and heartily promised him.' But when all had left him, the Ardinburghs, having some feeling left for their faithful and favorite slave, 'took turns about' in keeping him—permitting him to stay a few weeks at one house, and then a while at another, and so around. If, when he made a removal, the place where he was going was not too far off, he took up his line of march, staff in hand, and asked for no assistance. If it was twelve or twenty miles, they gave him a ride. While he was living in this way, Isabella was twice permitted to visit him. Another time she walked twelve miles, and carried her infant in her arms to see him, but when she reached the place where she hoped to find him, he had just left for a place some twenty miles distant, and she never saw him more. The last time she *did* see him, she found him seated on a rock, by the road side, alone, and far from any house. He was then migrating from the house of one Ardinburgh to that of another, several miles distant. His hair was white like wool—he was almost blind—and his gait was more a creep than a walk—but the weather was warm and pleasant, and he did not dislike the journey. When Isabella addressed him, he recognized her voice, and was exceeding glad to see her. He was assisted to mount the wagon, was carried back to the famous cellar of which we have spoken, and there they held their last earthly conversation. He again, as usual, bewailed his loneliness,—spoke

in tones of anguish of his many children, saying, 'They are all taken away from me! I have now not one to give me a cup of cold water—why should I live and not die?' Isabella, whose heart yearned over her father, and who would have made any sacrifice to have been able to be with, and take care of him, tried to comfort, by telling him that 'she had heard the white folks say, that all the slaves in the State would be freed in ten years, and that then she would come and take care of him.' 'I would take just as good care of you as Mau-mau would, if she was here'—continued Isabel. 'Oh, my child,' replied he, 'I cannot *live* that long.' 'Oh *do,* daddy, do live, and I will take such *good* care of you,' was her rejoinder. She now says, 'Why, I thought then, in my ignorance, that he *could* live, if he *would.* I just as much thought so, as I ever thought any thing in my life—and I *insisted* on his living: but he shook his head, and insisted he could not.'

But before Bomefree's good constitution would yield either to age, expo-sure, or a strong desire to die, the Ardinburghs again tired of him, and offered freedom to two old slaves—Cæsar, brother of Mau-mau Bett, and his wife Betsey—on condition that they should take care of James. (I was about to say, 'their brother-in-law'—but as slaves are neither *husbands* nor *wives* in law, the idea of their being brothers-in-law is truly ludicrous.) And although they were too old and infirm to take care of themselves, (Cæsar having been afflicted for a long time with fever-sores, and his wife with the jaundice), they eagerly accepted the boon of freedom, which had been the life-long desire of their souls—though at a time when emancipation was to them little more than destitution, and was a freedom more to be desired by the master than the slave. Sojourner declares of the slaves in their ignorance, that 'their thoughts are no longer than her finger.'

DEATH OF BOMEFREE.

A rude cabin, in a lone wood, far from any neighbors, was granted to our freed friends, as the only assistance they were now to expect. Bomefree, from this time, found his poor needs hardly supplied, as his new providers were scarce able to administer to their own wants. However, the time drew near when things were to be decidedly worse rather than better; for they had not been together long, before Betsey died, and shortly after, Cæsar followed her to 'that bourne from whence no traveller returns'—leaving poor James

again desolate, and more helpless than ever before; as, this time, there was no kind family in the house, and the Ardinburghs no longer invited him to their homes. Yet, lone, blind and helpless as he was, James for a time lived on. One day, an aged colored woman, named Soan, called at his shanty, and James besought her, in the most moving manner, even with tears, to tarry awhile and wash and mend him up, so that he might once more be decent and comfortable; for he was suffering dreadfully with the filth and vermin that had collected upon him.

Soan was herself an emancipated slave, old and weak, with no one to care for her; and she lacked the courage to undertake a job of such seeming magnitude, fearing she might herself get sick, and perish there without assistance; and with great reluctance, and a heart swelling with pity, as she afterwards declared, she felt obliged to leave him in his wretchedness and filth. And shortly after her visit, this faithful slave, this deserted wreck of humanity, was found on his miserable pallet, frozen and stiff in death. The kind angel had come at last, and relieved him of the many miseries that his fellow-man had heaped upon him. Yes, he had died, chilled and starved, with none to speak a kindly word, or do a kindly deed for him, in that last dread hour of need!

The news of his death reached the ears of John Ardinburgh, a grandson of the old Colonel; and he declared that 'Bomefree, who had ever been a kind and faithful slave, should now have a *good* funeral.' And now, gentle reader, what think you constituted a good funeral? Answer—some black paint for the coffin, and—a jug of ardent spirits! What a compensation for a life of toil, of patient submission to repeated robberies of the most aggravated kind, and, also, far more than murderous neglect!! Mankind often vainly attempt to atone for unkindness or cruelty to the living, by honoring the same after death; but John Ardinburgh undoubtedly meant his pot of paint and jug of whisky should act as an opiate on his slaves, rather than on his own seared conscience.

COMMENCEMENT OF ISABELLA'S TRIALS IN LIFE.

H aving seen the sad end of her parents, so far as it relates to this earthly life, we will return with Isabella to that memorable auction which threatened to separate her father and mother. A slave auction is a terrible affair to its victims, and its incidents and consequences are graven on their hearts as with a pen of burning steel.

At this memorable time, Isabella was struck off, for the sum of one hundred dollars, to one John Nealy, of Ulster County, New York; and she has an impression that in this sale she was connected with a lot of sheep. She was now nine years of age, and her trials in life may be dated from this period. She says, with emphasis, *'Now the war begun.'* She could only talk Dutch—and the Nealys could only talk English. Mr. Nealy could *understand* Dutch, but Isabel and her mistress could neither of them understand the language of the other—and this, of itself, was a formidable obstacle in the way of a *good* understanding between them, and for some time was a fruitful source of dissatisfaction to the mistress, and of punishment and suffering to Isabella. She says, 'If they sent me for a frying-pall, not knowing what they meant, perhaps I carried them the pot-hooks and trammels. Then, oh! how angry mistress would be with me!' Then she suffered *'terribly—terribly,'* with the cold. During the winter her feet were badly frozen, for want of proper covering. They gave her a plenty to eat, and also a plenty of whippings. One Sunday morning, in particular, she was told to go to the team; on going there, she found her master with a bundle of rods, prepared in the embers, and bound together with cords. When he had tied her hands together before her, he gave her the most cruel whipping she was ever tortured with. He whipped her till the flesh was deeply lacerated, and the blood streamed from her wounds—and the scars remain to the present day, to testify to the fact. 'And now,' she says, 'when I hear 'em tell of whipping women on the bare flesh, it makes *my* flesh crawl, and my very hair rise on my head! Oh! my God!' she continues, 'what a way is this of treating human beings?' In these hours of her extremity, she did not forget the instructions of her mother, to go to God in all her trials, and every affliction; and she not only remembered, but obeyed: going to Him, 'and telling Him all—and asking Him if He thought it was right,' and begging Him to protect and shield her from her persecutors.

She always asked with an unwavering faith that she should receive just what she pleaded for—'And now,' she says, 'though it seems *curious,* I do not remember ever asking for any thing but what I got it. And I always received it as an answer to my prayers. When I got beaten, I never knew it long enough beforehand to pray; and I always thought if I only had *had* time to pray to God for help, I should have escaped the beating.' She had no idea God had any knowledge of her thoughts, save what she told him; or heard her prayers, unless they were spoken audibly. And consequently, she could not pray unless she had time and opportunity to go by herself, where she could talk to God without being overheard.

TRIALS CONTINUED.

W hen she had been at Mr. Nealy's several months, she began to beg God most earnestly to send her father to her, and as soon as she commenced to pray, she began as confidently to look for his coming, and, ere it was long, to her great joy, he came. She had no opportunity to speak to him of the troubles that weighed so heavily on her spirit, while he remained; but when he left, she followed him to the gate, and unburdened her heart to him, inquiring if he could not do something to get her a new and better place. In this way the slaves often assist each other, by ascertaining who are kind to their slaves, comparatively; and then using their influence to get such an one to hire or buy their friends; and masters, often from policy, as well as from latent humanity, allow those they are about to sell or let, to choose their own places, if the persons they happen to select for masters are considered safe *pay.* He promised to do all he could, and they parted. But, every day, as long as the snow lasted, (for there was snow on the ground at the time,) she returned to the spot where they separated, and walking in the tracks her father had made in the snow, repeated her prayer that 'God would help her father get her a new and better place.'

A long time had not elapsed, when a fisherman by the name of Scriver appeared at Mr. Nealy's, and inquired of Isabel 'if she would like to go and live with him.' She eagerly answered 'Yes,' nothing doubting but he was sent in answer to her prayer; and she soon started off with him, walking while he rode; for he had bought her at the suggestion of her father, paying one hundred and five dollars for her. He also lived in Ulster County but some five or six miles from Mr. Nealy's.

Scriver, besides being a fisherman, kept a tavern for the accommodation of people of his own class—for his was a rude, uneducated family, exceedingly profane in their language, but, on the whole, an honest, kind and well-disposed people.

They owned a large farm, but left it wholly unimproved; attending mainly to their vocations of fishing and inn-keeping. Isabella declares she can ill describe the life she led with them. It was a wild, out-of-door kind of life. She was expected to carry fish, to hoe corn, to bring roots and herbs from the wood for beers, go to the Strand for a gallon of molasses or liquor as the case might require, and 'browse around,' as she expresses it. It was a life that suited her well for the time—being as devoid of hardship or terror as it was of improvement; a need which had not yet become a want.

Instead of improving at this place, morally, she retrograded, as their example taught her to curse; and it was here that she took her first oath. After living with them about a year and a half, she was sold to one John J. Dumont, for the sum of seventy pounds. This was in 1810. Mr. Dumont lived in the same county as her former masters, in the town of New Paltz, and she remained with him till a short time previous to her emancipation by the State, in 1828.

HER STANDING WITH HER
NEW MASTER AND MISTRESS.

Had Mrs. Dumont possessed that vein of kindness and consideration for the slaves, so perceptible in her husband's character, Isabella would have been as comfortable here, as one had *best* be, if one *must* be a slave. Mr. Dumont had been nursed in the very lap of slavery, and being naturally a man of kind feelings, treated his slaves with all the consideration he did his *other* animals, and *more,* perhaps. But Mrs. Dumont, who had been born and educated in a non-slaveholding family, and, like many others, used only to work-people, who, under the most stimulating of human motives, were willing to put forth their every energy, could not have patience with the creeping gait, the dull understanding, or see any cause for the listless manners and careless, slovenly habits of the poor down-trodden outcast—entirely forgetting that every high and efficient motive had been removed far from him; and that, had not his very intellect been crushed out of him, the slave would find little ground for aught but hopeless despondency. From this source arose a long series of trials in the life of our heroine, which we must pass over in silence; some from motives of delicacy, and others, because the relation of them might inflict undeserved pain on some now living, whom Isabel remembers only with esteem and love; therefore, the reader will not be surprised if our narrative appears somewhat tame at this point, and may rest assured that it is not for want of facts, as the most thrilling incidents of this portion of her life are from various motives suppressed.

One comparatively trifling incident she wishes related, as it made a deep impression on her mind at the time—showing, as she thinks, how God shields the innocent, and causes them to triumph over their enemies, and

also how she stood between master and mistress. In her family, Mrs. Dumont employed two white girls, one of whom, named Kate, evinced a disposition to 'lord it over' Isabel, and, in her emphatic language, 'to grind her down.' Her master often shielded her from the attacks and accusations of others, praising her for her readiness and ability to work, and these praises seemed to foster a spirit of hostility to her, in the minds of Mrs. Dumont and her white servant, the latter of whom took every opportunity to cry up her faults, lessen her in the esteem of her master and increase against her the displeasure of her mistress, which was already more than sufficient for Isabel's comfort. Her master insisted that she could do as much work as half a dozen common people, and do it well, too; whilst her mistress insisted that the first was true, only because it ever came from her hand but half performed. A good deal of feeling arose from this difference of opinion, which was getting to rather an uncomfortable height, when, all at once, the potatoes that Isabel cooked for breakfast assumed a dingy, dirty look. Her mistress blamed her severely, asking her master to observe 'a fine specimen of Bell's work!'— adding, 'it is the way all her work is done.' Her master scolded also this time, and commanded her to be more careful in future. Kate joined with zest in the censures, and was very hard upon her. Isabella thought that she had done all she well could to have them nice; and became quite distressed at these appearances, and wondered what she should do to avoid them. In this dilemma, Gertrude Dumont (Mr. D.'s eldest child, a good, kind-hearted girl of ten years, who pitied Isabel sincerely), when she heard them all blame her so unsparingly, came forward, offering her sympathy and assistance, and when about to retire to bed, on the night of Isabella's humiliation, she advanced to Isabel, and told her, if she would wake her early next morning, she would get up and attend to her potatoes for her, while she (Isabella) went to milking, and they would see if they could not have them nice, and not have 'Poppee,' her word for father and 'Matty,' her word for mother, and all of 'em, scolding so terribly.

Isabella gladly availed herself of this kindness, which touched her to the heart, amid so much of an opposite spirit. When Isabella had put the potatoes over to boil Getty told her she would herself tend the fire, while Isabel milked. She had not long been seated by the fire, in performance of her promise, when Kate entered, and requested Gertrude to go out of the room and do something for her, which she refused, still keeping her place in the corner. While there, Kate came sweeping about the fire, caught up a chip, lifted some ashes with it, and dashed them into the kettle. Now the mystery

was solved, the plot discovered! Kate was working a little too fast at making her mistress's words good, at showing that Mrs. Dumont and herself were on the right side of the dispute, and consequently at gaining power over Isabella. Yes, she was quite too fast, inasmuch as she had overlooked the little figure of justice, which sat in the corner, with scales nicely balanced, waiting to give all their dues.

But the time had come when she was to be overlooked no longer. It was Getty's turn to speak now. 'Oh, Poppee! oh, Poppee!' said she, 'Kate has been putting ashes in among the potatoes! I saw her do it! Look at those that fell on the outside of the kettle! You can now see what made the potatoes so dingy every morning, though Bell washed them clean!' And she repeated her story to every new comer, till the fraud was made as public as the censure of Isabella had been. Her mistress looked blank, and remained dumb—her master muttered something which sounded very like an oath—and poor Kate was so chop-fallen, she looked like a convicted criminal, who would gladly have hid herself (now that the baseness was out), to conceal her mortified pride and deep chagrin.

It was a fine triumph for Isabella and her master, and she became more ambitious than ever to please him; and he stimulated her ambition by his commendation, and by boasting of her to his friends, telling them that '*that* wench' (pointing to Isabel) 'is better to me than a *man*—for she will do a good family's washing in the night, and be ready in the morning to go into the field, where she will do as much at raking and binding—as my best hands.' Her ambition and desire to please were so great, that she often worked several nights in succession, sleeping only short snatches, as she sat in her chair, and some nights she would not allow herself to take any sleep, save what she could get resting herself against the wall, fearing that if she sat down, she would sleep too long. These extra exertions to please, and the praises consequent upon them, brought upon her head the envy of her fellow-slaves, and they taunted her with being the *'white folks' nigger.'* On the other hand, she received a larger share of the confidence of her master, and many small favors that were by them unattainable. I asked her if her master, Dumont, ever whipped her? She answered, 'Oh yes, he sometimes whipped me soundly, though never cruelly. And the most severe whipping he ever give me was because *I* was cruel to a cat.' At this time she looked upon her master as a *God,* and believed that he knew of and could see her at all times, even as God himself. And she used sometimes to confess her delinquencies, from the conviction that he already knew them, and that she should fare better if

she confessed voluntarily: and if any one talked to her of the injustice of her being a slave, she answered them with contempt and immediately told her master. She then firmly believed that slavery was right and honorable. Yet she now sees very clearly the false position they were all in, both masters and slaves; and she looks back, with utter astonishment, at the absurdity of the claims so arrogantly set up by the masters, over beings designed by God to be as free as kings; and at the perfect stupidity of the slave, in admitting for one moment the validity of these claims.

In obedience to her mother's instructions, she had educated herself to such a sense of honesty, that, when she had become a mother, she would sometimes whip her child when it cried to her for bread, rather than give it a piece secretly, lest it should learn to take what was not its own! And the writer of this knows, from personal observation, that the slaveholders of the South feel it to be a religious duty to teach their slaves to be honest, and never to take what is not their own! Oh consistency, art thou not a jewel? Yet Isabella glories in the fact that she was faithful and true to her master; she says, 'It made me true to my God'—meaning, that it helped to form in her a character that loved truth, and hated a lie, and had saved her from the bitter pains and fears that are sure to follow in the wake of insincerity and hypocrisy.

As she advanced in years, an attachment sprung up between herself and a slave named Robert. But his master, an Englishman by the name of Catlin, anxious that no one's property but his own should be enhanced by the increase of his slaves, forbade Robert's visits to Isabella, and commanded him to take a wife among his fellow-servants. Notwithstanding this interdiction, Robert, following the bent of his inclinations, continued his visits to Isabel, though very stealthily, and, as he believed, without exciting the suspicion of his master; but one Saturday afternoon, hearing that Bell was ill, he took the liberty to go and see her. The first intimation *she* had of his visit was the appearance of her master, inquiring 'if she had seen Bob.' On her answering in the negative, he said to her, 'If you see him, tell him to take care of himself, for the Catlins are after him.' Almost at that instant, Bob made his appearance; and the first people he met were his old and his young masters. They were terribly enraged at finding him there, and the eldest began cursing, and calling upon his son to '*Knock down* the d—d black rascal;' at the same time, they both fell upon him like tigers, beating him with the heavy ends of their canes, bruising and mangling his head and face in the most awful manner, and causing the blood, which streamed from his wounds, to

cover him like a slaughtered beast, constituting him a most shocking specta-cle. Mr. Dumont interposed at this point, telling the ruffians they could no longer thus spill human blood on *his* premises—he would have 'no niggers killed there.' The Catlins then took a rope they had taken with them for the purpose, and tied Bob's hands behind him in such a manner, that Mr. Dumont insisted on loosening the cord, declaring that no brute should be tied in *that* manner, where *he* was. And as they led him away, like the great-est of criminals, the more humane Dumont followed them to their homes, as Robert's protector; and when he returned, he kindly went to Bell, as he called her, telling her he did not think they would strike him any more, as their wrath had greatly cooled before he left them. Isabella had witnessed this scene from her window, and was greatly shocked at the murderous treatment of poor Robert, whom she truly loved, and whose only crime, in the eye of his persecutors, was his affection for her. This beating, and we know not what after treatment, completely subdued the spirit of its victim, for Robert ven-tured no more to visit Isabella, but like an obedient and faithful chattel, took himself a wife from the house of his master. Robert did not live many years after his last visit to Isabel, but took his departure to that country, where 'they neither marry nor are given in marriage,' and where the oppressor cannot molest.

ISABELLA'S MARRIAGE.

S ubsequently, Isabella was married to a fellow-slave, named Thomas, who had previously had two wives, one of whom, if not both, had been torn from him and sold far away. And it is more than probable, that he was not only allowed but encouraged to take another at each successive sale. I say it is probable, because the writer of this knows from personal observation, that such is the custom among slaveholders at the present day; and that in a twen-ty months' residence among them, we never knew any one to open the lip against the practice; and when we severely censured it, the slaveholder had nothing to say; and the slave pleaded that, under existing circumstances, he could do no better.

Such an abominable state of things is silently tolerated, to say the least, by slaveholders—deny it who may. And what is that religion that sanctions,

even by its silence, all that is embraced in the '*Peculiar Institution*'? If there *can* be any thing more diametrically opposed to the religion of Jesus, than the working of this soul-killing system—which is as truly sanctioned by the religion of America as are her ministers and churches—we wish to be shown where it can be found.

We have said, Isabella was married to Thomas—she was, after the fashion of slavery, one of the slaves performing the ceremony for them; as no true minister of Christ *can* perform, as in the presence of God, what he knows to be a mere *farce,* a *mock* marriage, unrecognized by any civil law, and liable to be annulled any moment, when the interest or caprice of the master should dictate.

With what feelings must slaveholders expect us to listen to their horror of amalgamation in prospect, while they are well aware that we know how calmly and quietly they contemplate the present state of licentiousness their own wicked laws have created, not only as it regards the slave, but as it regards the more privileged portion of the population of the South?

Slaveholders appear to me to take the same notice of the vices of the slave, as one does of the vicious disposition of his horse. They are often an inconvenience; further than that, they care not to trouble themselves about the matter.

ISABELLA AS A MOTHER.

In process of time, Isabella found herself the mother of five children, and she rejoiced in being permitted to be the instrument of increasing the property of her oppressors! Think, dear reader, without a blush, if you can, for one moment, of a *mother* thus willingly, and with *pride,* laying her own children, the 'flesh of her flesh,' on the altar of slavery—a sacrifice to the bloody Moloch! But we must remember that beings capable of such sacrifices are not mothers; they are only 'things,' 'chattels,' 'property.'

But since that time, the subject of this narrative has made some advances from a state of chattelism towards that of a woman and a mother; and she now looks back upon her thoughts and feelings there, in her state of ignorance and degradation, as one does on the dark imagery of a fitful dream. One moment it seems but a frightful illusion; again it appears a terrible real-

ity. I would to God it were but a dreamy myth, and not, as it now stands, a horrid reality to some three millions of chattelized human beings.

I have already alluded to her care not to teach her children to steal, by her example; and she says, with groanings that cannot be written, 'The Lord only knows how many times I let my children go hungry, rather than take secretly the bread I liked not to ask for.' All parents who annul their preceptive teachings by their daily practices would do well to profit by her example.

Another proof of her master's kindness of heart is found in the following fact. If her master came into the house and found her infant crying (as she could not always attend to its wants and the commands of her mistress at the same time), he would turn to his wife with a look of reproof, and ask her why she did not see the child taken care of, saying, most earnestly, 'I will not hear this crying; I can't bear it, and I will not hear any child cry so. Here, Bell, take care of this child, if no more work is done for a week.' And he would linger to see if his orders were obeyed, and not countermanded.

When Isabella went to the field to work, she used to put her infant in a basket, tying a rope to each handle, and suspending the basket to a branch of a tree, set another small child to swing it. It was thus secure from reptiles, and was easily administered to, and even lulled to sleep, by a child, too young for other labors. I was quite struck with the ingenuity of such a baby—tender, as I have sometimes been with the swinging hammock the native mother prepares for her sick infant—apparently so much easier than aught we have in our more civilized homes; easier for the child, because it gets the motion without the least jar; and easier for the nurse, because the hammock is strung so high as to supersede the necessity of stooping.

SLAVEHOLDER'S PROMISES.

After emancipation had been decreed by the State, some years before the time fixed for its consummation, Isabella's master told her if she would do well, and be faithful, he would give her free papers,' one year before she was legally free by statute. In the year 1826, she had a badly diseased hand, which greatly diminished her usefulness; but on the arrival of July 4, 1827, the time specified for her receiving her 'free papers,' she claimed the fulfillment of her master's promise; but he refused granting it, on account (as he alleged) of the loss he had sustained by her hand. She plead that she had

worked all the time, and done many things she was not wholly able to do, although she knew she had been less useful than formerly; but her master remained inflexible. Her very faithfulness probably operated against her now, and he found it less easy than he thought to give up the profits of his faithful Bell, who had so long done him efficient service.

But Isabella inwardly determined that she would remain quietly with him only until she had spun his wool—about one hundred pounds—and then she would leave him, taking the rest of the time to herself. 'Ah!' she says, with emphasis that cannot be written, 'the slaveholders are TERRIBLE for promising to give you this or that, or such and such a privilege, if you will do thus and so; and when the time of fulfillment comes, and one claims the promise, they, forsooth, recollect nothing of the kind; and you are, like—as not, taunted with being a LIAR; or, at best, the slave is accused of not having performed *his* part or condition of the contract.' 'Oh!' said she, 'I have felt as if I could not live through the *operation* sometimes. Just think of us! so eager for our pleasures, and just foolish enough to keep feeding and feeding ourselves up with the idea that we should get what had been thus fairly promised; and when we think it is almost in our hands, find ourselves flatly denied! Just think! how *could* we bear it? Why, there was Charles Brodhead promised his slave Ned, that when harvesting was over, he might go and see his wife, who lived some twenty or thirty miles off. So Ned worked early and late, and as soon as the harvest was all in, he claimed the promised boon. His master said, he had merely told him he 'would *see* if he could go, when the harvest was over; but now he saw that he *could not go.*' But Ned, who still claimed a positive promise, on which he had fully depended, went on cleaning his shoes. His master asked him if he intended going, and on his replying 'yes,' took up a sled-stick that lay near him, and gave him such a blow on the head as broke his skull, killing him dead on the spot. The poor colored people all felt struck down by the blow.' Ah! and well they might. Yet it was but one of a long series of bloody, and other most effectual blows, struck against their liberty and their lives.* But to return from our digression.

The subject of this narrative was to have been free July 4, 1827, but she continued with her master till the wool was spun, and the heaviest of the 'fall's work' closed up, when she concluded to take her freedom into her own hands, and seek her fortune in some other place.

*Yet no official notice was taken of his more than brutal murder.

HER ESCAPE.

The question in her mind, and one not easily solved, now was, 'How can I get away?' So, as was her usual custom, she 'told God she was afraid to go in the night, and in the day every body would see her.' At length, the thought came to her that she could leave just before the day dawned, and get out of the neighborhood where she was known before the people were much astir. 'Yes,' said she, fervently, 'that's a good thought! Thank you, God, for that thought!' So, receiving it as coming direct from God, she acted upon it, and one fine morning, a little before day-break, she might have been seen stepping stealthily away from the rear of Master Dumont's house, her infant on one arm and her wardrobe on the other; the bulk and weight of which, probably, she never found so convenient as on the present occasion, a cotton handkerchief containing both her clothes and her provisions.

As she gained the summit of a high hill, a considerable distance from her master's, the sun offended her by coming forth in all his pristine splendor. She thought it never was so light before; indeed, she thought it much too light. She stopped to look about her, and ascertain if her pursuers were yet in sight. No one appeared, and, for the first time, the question came up for settlement, 'Where, and to whom, shall I go?' In all her thoughts of getting away, she had not once asked herself whither she should direct her steps. She sat down, fed her infant, and again turning her thoughts to God, her only help, she prayed him to direct her to some safe asylum. And soon it occurred to her, that there was a man living somewhere in the direction she had been pursuing, by the name of Levi Rowe, whom she had known, and who, she thought, would be likely to befriend her. She accordingly pursued her way to his house, where she found him ready to entertain and assist her, though he was then on his death-bed. He bade her partake of the hospitalities of his house, said he knew of two good places where she might get in, and requested his wife to show her where they were to be found. As soon as she came in sight of the first house, she recollected having seen it and its inhabitants before, and instantly exclaimed, 'That's the place for me; I shall stop there.' She went there, and found the good people of the house, Mr. and Mrs. Van Wagener, absent, but was kindly received and hospitably entertained by their excellent mother, till the return of her children. When they arrived, she made her case known to them. They listened to her story, assuring her they never turned the needy away, and willingly gave her employment.

She had not been there long before her old master, Dumont, appeared, as

she had anticipated; for when she took French leave of him, she resolved not to go too far from him, and not put him to as much trouble in looking her up—for the latter he was sure to do—as Tom and Jack had done when they ran away from him, a short time before. This was very considerate in her, to say the least, and a proof that 'like begets like.' He had often considered *her* feelings, though not always, and she was equally considerate.

When her master saw her, he said, 'Well, Bell, so you've run away from me.' 'No, I did not run away; I walked away by day-light, and all because you had promised me a year of my time.' His reply was, 'You must go back with me.' Her decisive answer was, 'No, I won't go back with you.' He said, 'Well, I shall take the *child.' This* also was as stoutly negatived.

Mr. Isaac S. Van Wagener then interposed, saying, he had never been in the practice of buying and selling slaves; he did not believe in slavery; but, rather than have Isabella taken back by force, he would buy her services for the balance of the year—for which her master charged twenty dollars; and five in addition for the child. The sum was paid, and her master Dumont departed; but not till he had heard Mr. Van Wagener tell her not to call him master,—adding, 'There is but *one* master; and he who is *your* master is *my* master.' Isabella inquired what she *should* call him? He answered, 'Call me Isaac Van Wagener, and my wife is Maria Van Wagener.' Isabella could not understand this, and thought it a *mighty change,* as it most truly was from a master whose' word was law, to simple Isaac S. Van Wagener, who was master to *no* one. With these noble people, who, though they could not be the masters of slaves, were undoubtedly a portion of God's nobility, she resided one year, and from them she derived the name of Van Wagener; he being her last master in the eye of the law, and a slave's surname is ever the same as his master; that is, if he is allowed to have any other name than Tom, Jack, or Guffin. Slaves have sometimes been severely punished for adding their master's name to their own. But when they have no particular title to it, it is no particular offence.

ILLEGAL SALE OF HER SON.

A little previous to Isabel's leaving her old master, he had sold her child, a boy of five years, to a Dr. Gedney, who took him with him as far as New York City, on his way to England; but finding the boy too small for his

service, he sent him back to his brother, Solomon Gedney. This man disposed of him to his sister's husband, a wealthy planter, by the name of Fowler, who took him to his own home in Alabama.

This illegal and fraudulent transaction had been perpetrated some months before Isabella knew of it, as she was now living at Mr. Van Wagener's. The law expressly prohibited the sale of any slave out of the State,—and all minors were to be free at twenty-one years of age; and Mr. Dumont had sold Peter with the express understanding, that he was soon to return to the State of New York, and be emancipated at the specified time.

When Isabel heard that her son had been sold South, she immediately started on foot and alone, to find the man who had thus dared, in the face of all law, human and divine, to sell her child out of the State; and if possible, to bring him to account for the deed.

Arriving at New Paltz, she went directly to her former mistress, Dumont, complaining bitterly of the removal of her son. Her mistress heard her through, and then replied—'*Ugh!* a *fine* fuss to make about a little nigger! Why, haven't you as many of 'em left as you can see to and take care of? A pity 'tis, the niggers are not all in Guinea!! Making such a halloo-balloo about the neighborhood; and all for a paltry nigger!!!' Isabella heard her through, and after a moment's hesitation, answered, in tones of deep determination— '*I'll have my child again.*' 'Have *your child* again!' repeated her mistress—her tones big with contempt, and scorning the absurd idea of her getting him. 'How can you get him? And what have you to support him with, if you could? Have you any money?' 'No,' answered Bell, 'I have no money, but God has enough, or what's better! And I'll have my child again.' These words were pronounced in the most slow, solemn and determined measure and manner. And in speaking of it, she says, 'Oh, my God! I know'd I'd have him agin. I was sure God would help me to get him. Why, I felt so *tall within*— I felt as if the *power of a nation* was with me!'

The impressions made by Isabella on her auditors, when moved by lofty or deep feeling, can never be transmitted to paper (to use the words of another), till by some Daguerrian art, we are enabled to transfer the look, the gesture, the tones of voice in connection with the quaint, yet fit expressions used, and the spirit-stirring animation that, at such a time, pervades all she says.

After leaving her mistress, she called on Mrs. Gedney, mother of him who had sold her boy; who, after listening to her lamentations, her grief being mingled—with indignation at the sale of her son, and her declaration that she would have him again—said, 'Dear me! What a disturbance to make

about your child! What, is *your* child better than *my* child? My child is gone out there, and yours is gone to live with her, to have enough of everything, and to be treated like a gentleman!' And here she laughed at Isabel's absurd fears, as she would represent them to be. 'Yes,' said Isabel, '*your* child has gone there, but she is *married* and my boy has gone as a *slave,* and he is too little to go so far from his mother. Oh, I must have my child.' And here the continued laugh of Mrs. G. seemed to Isabel, in this time of anguish and distress, almost demoniacal. And well it was for Mrs. Gedney, that, at that time, she could not even dream of the awful fate awaiting her own beloved daughter, at the hands of him whom she had chosen as worthy the wealth of her love and confidence, and in whose society her young heart had calculated on a happiness, purer and more elevated than was ever conferred by a kingly crown. But, alas! she was doomed to disappointment, as we shall relate by and by. At this point, Isabella earnestly begged of God that He would show to those about her that He was her helper; and she adds, in narrating, 'And He did; or, if He did not show them, He did me.'

IT IS OFTEN DARKEST JUST BEFORE DAWN.

This homely proverb was illustrated in the case of our sufferer; for, at the period at which we have arrived in our narrative, to her the darkness seemed palpable, and the waters of affliction covered her soul; yet light was about to break in upon her.

Soon after the scenes related in our last chapter, which had harrowed up her very soul to agony, she met a man (we would like to tell you *who,* dear reader, but it would be doing him no kindness, even to the present day, to do so), who evidently sympathized with her, and counselled her to go to the Quakers, telling her they were already feeling very indignant at the fraudulent sale of her son, and assuring her that they would readily assist her, and direct her what to do. He pointed out to her two houses, where lived some of those people, who formerly, more than any other sect, perhaps, lived out the principles of the gospel of Christ. She wended her way to their dwellings, was listened to, unknown as she personally was to them, with patience, and soon gained their sympathies and active co-operation.

The gave her lodgings for the night; and it is very amusing to hear her tell of the 'nice, high, clean, white, *beautiful* bed' assigned her to sleep in, which

contrasted so strangely with her former pallets, that she sat down and contemplated it, perfectly absorbed in wonder that *such* a bed should have been appropriated to one like herself. For some time she thought that she would lie down beneath it, on her usual bedstead, the floor. 'I did, indeed,' says she, laughing heartily at her former self. However, she finally concluded to make use of the bed, for fear that not to do so might injure the feelings of her good hostess. In the morning, the Quaker saw that she was taken and set down near Kingston, with directions to go to the Court House, and enter complaint to the Grand Jury.

By a little inquiry, she found which was the building she sought, went into the door, and taking the first man she saw of imposing appearance for the *grand* jury, she commenced her complaint. But he very civilly informed her there was no Grand Jury there; she must go up stairs. When she had with some difficulty ascended the flight through the crowd that filled them, she again turned to the *'grandest'* looking mall she could select, telling him she had come to enter a complaint to the Grand Jury. For his own amusement, he inquired what her complaint was; but, when he saw it was a serious matter, he said to her, 'This is no place to enter a complaint—go in there,' pointing in a particular direction.

She then went in, where she found the Grand Jurors indeed sitting, and again commenced to relate her injuries. After holding some conversation among themselves, one of them rose, and bidding her follow him, led the way to a side office, where he heard her story, and asked her 'if she could *swear* that the child she spoke of was her son?' 'Yes,' she answered, 'I *swear* it's my son.' 'Stop, stop!' said the lawyer, 'you must swear by this book'—giving her a book, which she thinks must have been the Bible. She took it, and putting it to her lips, began again to swear it was her child. The clerks, unable to preserve their gravity any longer, burst into an uproarious laugh; and one of them inquired of lawyer Chip of what use it could be to make *her* swear. 'It will answer the law,' replied the officer. He then made her comprehend just what he wished her to do, and she took a lawful oath, as far as the outward ceremony could make it one. All can judge how far she understood its spirit and meaning.

He now gave her a writ, directing her to take it to the constable of New Paltz, and have him serve it on Solomon Gedney. She obeyed, walking, or rather *trotting*, in her haste, some eight or nine miles.

But while the constable, through mistake, served the writ on a brother of the real culprit, Solomon Gedney slipped into a boat, and was nearly across

the North River, on whose banks they were standing, before the dull Dutch constable was aware of his mistake. Solomon Gedney, meanwhile, consulted a lawyer, who advised him to go to Alabama and bring back the boy, otherwise it might cost him fourteen years' imprisonment, and a thousand dollars in cash. By this time, it is hoped, he began to feel that selling slaves unlawfully was not so good a business as he had wished to find it. He secreted himself till due preparations could be made, and soon set sail for Alabama. Steamboats and railroads had not then annihilated distance to the extent they now have, and although he left in the fall of the year, spring came ere he returned, bringing the boy with him—but holding on to him as his property. It had ever been Isabella's prayer, not only that her son might be returned, but that he should be delivered from bondage, and into her own hands, lest he should be punished out of mere spite to her, who was so greatly annoying and irritating to her oppressors; and if her suit was gained, her very triumph would add vastly to their irritation.

She again sought advice of Esquire Chip, whose counsel was, that the aforesaid constable serve the before-mentioned writ upon the right person. This being done, soon brought Solomon Gedney up to Kingston, where he gave bonds for his appearance at court, in the sum of $600.

Esquire Chip next informed his client, that her case must now lie over till the next session of the court, some months in the future. 'The law must take its course,' said he.

'What! wait another court! wait *months?*' said the persevering mother. 'Why, long before that time, he can go clear off, and take my child with him—no one knows where. I *cannot* wait; I *must* have him *now,* whilst he is to be had.' 'Well,' said the lawyer, very coolly, 'if he puts the boy out of the way, he must pay the $600—one half of which will be yours;' supposing, perhaps, that $300 would pay for a 'heap of children,' in the eye of a slave who never, in all her life, called a dollar her own. But in this instance, he was mistaken in his reckoning. She assured him, that she had not been seeking money, neither would money satisfy her; it was her son, and her son alone she wanted, and her son she must have. Neither could she wait court, not she. The lawyer used his every argument to convince her, that she ought to be very thankful for what they had done for her; that it was a great deal, and it was but reasonable that she should now wait patiently the time of the court.

Yet she never felt, for a moment, like being influenced by these suggestions. She felt confident she was to receive a full and literal answer to her

prayer, the burden of which had been—'O Lord, give my son into my hands, and that speedily! Let not the spoilers have him any longer.' Notwithstanding, she very distinctly saw that those who had thus far helped her on so kindly were *wearied* of her, and she feared God was wearied also. She had a short time previous learned that Jesus was a Saviour, and an intercessor; and she thought that if Jesus could but be induced to plead for her in the present trial, God would listen to *him*, though he were wearied of *her* importunities. To him, of course, she applied. As she was walking about, scarcely knowing whither she went, asking within herself, 'Who will show me any good, and lend a helping hand in this matter,' she was accosted by a perfect stranger, and one whose name she has never learned, in the following terms: 'Halloo, there; how do you get along with your boy? do they give him up to you?' She told him all, adding that now every body was tired, and she had none to help her. He said, 'Look here! I'll tell you what you'd better do. Do you see that stone house yonder?' pointing, in a particular direction. 'Well, lawyer Demain lives there, and do you go to him, and lay your case before him; I think he'll help you. *Stick to him.* Don't give him peace till he does. I feel sure if you press him, he'll do it for you.' She needed no further urging, but trotted off at her peculiar gait in the direction of his house, as fast as possible,—and she was not encumbered with stockings, shoes, or any other heavy article of dress. When she had told him her story, in her impassioned manner, he looked at her a few moments, as if to ascertain if he were contemplating a new variety of the genus Homo, and then told her, if she would give him five dollars, he would get her son for her, in twenty-four hours. 'Why,' she replied, '*I* have no *money*, and never had a dollar in my life!' Said he, 'If you will go to those Quakers in Poppletown, who carried you to court, they will help you to five dollars in cash, I have no doubt, and you shall have your son in twenty-four hours, from the time you bring me that sum.' She performed the journey to Poppletown, a distance of some ten miles, very expeditiously; collected considerably more than the sum specified by the barrister; then, shutting the money tightly in her hand, she trotted back, and paid the lawyer a larger fee than he had demanded. When inquired of by people what she had done with the overplus, she answered, 'Oh, I got it for lawyer Demain, and I gave it to him.' They assured her she was a *fool* to do so, that she should have kept all over five dollars, and purchased herself shoes with it. 'Oh, I do not want money or clothes now, I only want my son; and if five dollars will get him, more will *surely* get him.' And if the lawyer had returned it to her, she avers, she would not have accepted it. She

was perfectly willing he should have every coin she could raise, if he would but restore her lost son to her. Moreover, the five dollars he required were for the remuneration of him who should go after her son and his master, and not for his own services.

The lawyer now renewed his promise, that she should have her son in twenty-four hours. But Isabella, having no idea of this space of time, went several times in a day, to ascertain if her son had come. Once when the servant opened the door and saw her, she said, in a tone expressive of much surprise, 'Why, this woman's come again!' She then wondered if she went too often. When the lawyer appeared, he told her the twenty-four hours would not expire till the next morning, if she would call then, she would see her son. The next morning saw Isabel at the lawyer's door, while he was yet in his bed. He now assured her it was morning till noon; and that before noon her son would be there, for he had sent the famous 'Matty Styles' after him, who would not fail to have the boy and his master on hand in due season, either dead or alive; of that he was sure. Telling her she need not come again; he would himself inform her of their arrival.

After dinner, he appeared at Mr. Rutzer's (a place the lawyer had procured for her, while she awaited the arrival of her boy), assuring her her son had come; but that he stoutly denied having any mother, or any relatives in that place; and said, 'she must go over and identify him.' She went to the office, but at sight of her the boy cried aloud, and regarded her as some terrible being, who was about to take him away from a kind and loving friend. He knelt, even, and begged them, with tears, not to take him away from his dear master, who had brought him from the dreadful South, and been so kind to him.

When he was questioned relative to the bad scar on his forehead, he said, 'Fowler's horse hove him.' And of the one on his cheek, 'That was done by running against the carriage.' In answering these questions he looked imploringly at his master, as much as to say, 'If they are falsehoods, you bade me say them; may they be satisfactory to you, at least.'

The justice, noting his appearance, bade him forget his master and attend only to him. But the boy persisted in denying his mother, and clinging to his master, saying his mother did not live in such a place as that. However, they allowed the mother to identify her son; and Esquire Demain pleaded that he claimed the boy for her, on the ground that he had been sold out of the State, contrary to the laws in such cases made and provided—spoke of the penalties annexed to said crime, and of the sum of money the delinquent was to

pay, in case any one chose to prosecute him for the offence he had commit-
ted. Isabella, who was sitting in a corner, scarcely daring to breathe, thought
within herself, 'If I can but get the boy, the $200 may remain for whoever
else chooses to prosecute—*I* have done enough to make myself enemies
already'—and she trembled at the thought of the formidable enemies she had
probably arrayed against herself—helpless and despised as she was. When the
pleading was at an end, Isabella understood the Judge to declare, as the sen-
tence of the Court, that the 'boy be delivered into the hands of the mother—
having no other master, no other controller, no other conductor, but his
mother.' This sentence was obeyed; he was delivered into her hands, the boy
meanwhile begging, most piteously, not to be taken from his dear master,
saying she was not his mother, and that his mother did not live in such a
place as that. And it was some time before lawyer Demain, the clerks, and
Isabella, could collectively succeed in calming the child's fears, and in
convincing him that Isabella was not some terrible monster, as he had for the
last months, probably, been trained to believe; and who, in taking him away
from his master, was taking him from all good, and consigning him to all evil.

When at last kind words and *bon bons* had quieted his fears, and he could
listen to their explanations, he said to Isabella—'Well, you *do* look like my
mother *used* to;' and she was soon able to make him comprehend some of
the obligations he was under, and the relation he stood in, both to herself and
his master. She commenced as soon as practicable to examine the boy, and
found, to her utter astonishment, that from the crown of his head to the sole
of his foot, the callosities and indurations on his entire body were most
frightful to behold. His back she described as being like her fingers, as she
laid them side by side.

'Heavens! what is all *this?*' said Isabel. He answered, 'It is where Fowler
whipped, kicked, and beat me.' She exclaimed, 'Oh, Lord Jesus, look! see my
poor child! Oh Lord, "render unto them double" for all this! Oh my God!
Pete, how *did* you bear it?'

'Oh, this is nothing, mammy—if you should see Phillis, I guess you'd
scare! She had a little baby, and Fowler cut her till the milk as well as blood
ran down *her* body. You would *scare* to see Phillis, mammy.'

When Isabella inquired, 'What did Miss Eliza* say, Pete, when you were
treated so badly?' he replied, 'Oh, mammy, she said she wished I was with
Bell. Sometimes I crawled under the stoop, mammy, the blood running all

*Meaning Mrs. Eliza Fowler.

about me, and my back would stick to the boards; and sometimes Miss Eliza would come and grease my sores, when all were abed and asleep.'

DEATH OF MRS. ELIZA FOWLER.

As soon as possible she procured a place for Peter, as tender of locks, at a place called Wahkendall, near Greenkills. After he was thus disposed of, she visited her sister Sophia, who resided at Newburg, and spent the winter in several different families where she was acquainted. She remained some time in the family of a Mr. Latin, who was a visiting relative of Solomon Gedney, and the latter, when he found Isabel with his cousin, used all his influence to persuade him she was a great mischief-maker and a very troublesome person,—that she had put him to some hundreds of dollars expense, by fabricating lies about him and especially his sister and her family, concerning her boy, when the latter was living so like a gentleman with them; and, for his part, he would not advise his friends to harbor or encourage her. However, his cousins the Latins, could not see with the eyes of *his* feelings, and consequently his words fell powerless on them, and they retained her in their service as long as they had aught for her to do.

She then went to visit her former master, Dumont. She had scarcely arrived there, when Mr. Fred Waring entered, and seeing Isabel, pleasantly accosted her, and asked her 'whet she was driving at now-a-days.' On her answering 'nothing particular,' he requested her to go over to his place, and assist his folks, as some of them were sick, and they needed an extra hand. She very gladly assented. When Mr. W. retired her master wanted to know why she wished to help people, that called her the 'worst of devils,' as Mr. Waring had done in the courthouse—for he was the uncle of Solomon Gedney, and attended the trial we have described—and declared 'that she was a *fool* to; *he* wouldn't do it.' 'Oh,' she told him, 'she would not mind that, but was very glad to have people forget their anger towards her.' She went over, but too happy to feel that their resentment was passed, and commenced her work with a light heart and a strong will. She had not worked long in this frame of mind, before a young daughter of Mr. Waring rushed into the room, exclaiming, with uplifted hands—'Heavens and earth, Isabella! Fowler's murdered Cousin Eliza!' 'Ho,' said Isabella, *'that's* nothing—he liked

to have killed *my* child; nothing saved him but God.' Meaning, that she was not at all surprised at it, for a man whose heart was sufficiently hardened to treat a mere child as hers had been treated, was, in her opinion, more fiend than human, and prepared for the commission of any crime that his passions might prompt him to. The child further informed her, that a letter had arrived by mail bringing the news.

Immediately after this announcement, Solomon Gedney and his mother came in, going direct to Mrs. Waring's room, where she soon heard tones as of some one reading. She thought something said to her inwardly, 'Go up stairs and hear.' At first she hesitated, but it seemed to press her the more—'Go up and hear!' She went up, unusual as it is for slaves to leave their work and enter unbidden their mistress's room, for the sole purpose of seeing or hearing what may be seen or heard there. But on this occasion, Isabella says, she walked in at the door, shut it, placed her back against it, and listened. She saw them and heard them read—'He knocked her down with his fist, jumped on her with his knees, broke her collar bone, and tore out her windpipe! He then attempted his escape, but was pursued and arrested, and put in an iron bank for safe-keeping!' And the friends were requested to go down and take away the poor innocent children who had thus been made in one short day more than orphans.

If this narrative should ever meet the eye of those innocent sufferers for another's guilt, let them not be too deeply affected by the relation; but, placing their confidence in Him who sees the end from the beginning, and controls the results, rest secure in the faith, that, although they may physically suffer for the sins of others, if they remain but true to themselves, their highest and more enduring interests can never suffer from such a cause. This relation should be suppressed for their sakes, were it not even now so often denied, that slavery is fast undermining all true regard for human life. We know this one instance is not a demonstration to the contrary; but, adding this to the lists of tragedies that weekly come up to us through the Southern mails, may we not admit them as proofs irrefragable? The newspapers confirm this account of the terrible affair.

When Isabella had heard the letter, all being too much absorbed in their own feelings to take note of her, she returned to her work, her heart swelling with conflicting emotions. She was awed at the dreadful deed; she mourned the fate of the loved Eliza, who had in such an undeserved and barbarous manner been put away from her labors and watchings as a tender mother; and, 'last though not least,' in the development of her character and spirit,

her heart bled for the afflicted relatives; even those of them who 'laughed at her calamity, and mocked when her fear came.' Her thoughts dwelt long and intently on the subject, and the wonderful chain of events that had conspired to bring her that day to that house, to listen to that piece of intelligence—to that house, where she never was before or afterwards in her life, and invited there by people who had so lately been hotly incensed against her. It all seemed very remarkable to her, and she viewed it as flowing from a special providence of God. She thought she saw clearly, that their unnatural bereavement was a blow dealt in retributive justice: but she found it not in her heart to exult or rejoice over them. She felt as if God had more than answered her petition, when she ejaculated, in her anguish of mind, 'Oh, Lord, render unto them double!' She said, 'I dared not find fault with God, exactly; but the language of my heart was, 'Oh, my God! that's too much—I did not mean quite so much, God!' It was a terrible blow to the friends of the deceased; and her selfish mother (who, said Isabella, made such a 'to-do about *her* boy, not from affection, 'but to have her own will and way') went deranged, and walking to and fro in her delirium, called aloud for her poor murdered daughter—'*Eliza! Eliza!*'

The derangement of Mrs. G. was a matter of hearsay, as Isabella saw her not after the trial, but she has no reason to doubt the truth of what she heard. Isabel could never learn the subsequent fate of Fowler, but heard in the spring of '49 that his children had been seen in Kingston—one of whom was spoken of as a fine, interesting girl, albeit a halo of sadness fell like a veil about her.

ISABELLA'S RELIGIOUS EXPERIENCE.

We will now turn from the outward and temporal to the inward and spiritual life of our subject. It is ever both interesting and instructive to trace the exercises of a human mind, through the trials and mysteries of life and especially a naturally powerful mind, left as hers was almost entirely to its own workings, and the chance influences it met on its way; and especially to note its reception of that divine 'light, that lighteth every man that cometh into the world.'

We see, as knowledge dawns upon it, truth and error strangely commingled; here, a bright spot illuminated by truth—and there, one darkened and distorted by error; and the state of such a soul may be compared to a land-

scape at early dawn, where the sun is seen superbly gilding some objects, and causing others to send forth their lengthened, distorted, and sometimes hideous shadows.

Her mother, as we have already said, talked to her of God. From these conversations, her incipient mind drew the conclusion, that God was 'a great man'; greatly superior to other men in power; and being located 'high in the sky,' could see all that transpired on the earth. She believed he not only saw, but noted down all her actions in a great book, even as her master kept a record of whatever he wished not to forget. But she had no idea that God knew a thought of hers till she had uttered it aloud.

As we have before mentioned, she had ever been mindful of her mother's injunctions, spreading out in detail all her troubles before God, imploring and firmly trusting him to send her deliverance from them. Whilst yet a child, she listened to a story of a wounded soldier, left alone in the trail of a flying army, helpless and starving, who hardened the very ground about him with kneeling in his supplications to God for relief, until it arrived. From this narrative, she was deeply impressed with the idea, that if *she* also were to present her petitions under the open canopy of heaven, speaking very loud, she should the more readily be heard; consequently, she sought a fitting spot for this, her rural sanctuary. The place she selected, in which to offer up her daily orisons, was a small island in a small stream, covered with large willow shrubbery, beneath which the sheep had made their pleasant winding paths; and sheltering themselves from the scorching rays of a noon-tide sun, luxuriated in the cool shadows of the graceful willows, as they listened to the tiny falls of the silver waters. It was a lonely spot, and chosen by her for its beauty, its retirement, and because she thought that there, in the noise of those waters, she could speak louder to God, without being overheard by any who might pass that way. When she had made choice of her sanctum, at a point of the island where the stream met, after having been separated, she improved it by pulling away the branches of the shrubs from the centre, and weaving them together for a wall on the outside, forming a circular arched alcove, made entirely of the graceful willow. To this place she resorted daily, and in pressing times much more frequently.

At this time, her prayers, or, more appropriately, 'talks with God,' were perfectly original and unique, and would be well worth preserving, were it possible to give the tones and manner with the words; but no adequate idea of them can be written while the tones and manner remain inexpressible.

She would sometimes repeat, 'Our Father in heaven,' in her Low Dutch,

as taught her by her mother; after that, all was from the suggestions of her own rude mind. She related to God, in minute detail, all her troubles and sufferings, inquiring, as she proceeded, 'Do you think that's right, God?' and closed by begging to be delivered from the evil, whatever it might be.

She talked to God as familiarly as if he had been a creature like herself; and a thousand times more so, than if she had been in the presence of some earthly potentate. She demanded, with little expenditure of reverence or fear, a supply of all her more pressing wants, and at times her demands approached very near to commands. She felt as if God was under obligation to her, much more than she was to him. He seemed to her benighted vision in some manner bound to do her bidding.

Her heart recoils now, with very dread, when she recalls these shocking, almost blasphemous conversations with the great Jehovah. And well for her self did she deem it, that, unlike earthly potentates, his infinite character combined the tender father with the omniscient and omnipotent Creator of the universe.

She at first commenced promising God, that if he would help her out of all her difficulties, she would pay him by being very good; and this goodness she intended as a remuneration to God. She could think of no benefit that was to accrue to herself or her fellow-creatures, from her leading a life of purity and generous self-sacrifice for the good of others; as far as any but God was concerned, she saw nothing in it but heart-trying penance, sustained by the sternest exertion; and this she soon found much more easily promised than performed.

Days wore away—new trials came—God's aid was invoked, and the same promises repeated; and every successive night found her part of the contract unfulfilled. She now began to excuse herself, by telling God she could not be good in her present circumstances; but if he would give her a new place, and a good master and mistress, she could and would be good; and she expressly stipulated, that she would be good one day to show God how good she would be all of the time when he should surround her with the right influences, and she should be delivered from the temptations that then so sorely beset her. But, alas! when night came, and she became conscious that she had yielded to *all* her temptations, and entirely failed of keeping her word with God, having prayed and promised one hour, and fallen into the sins of anger and profanity the next, the mortifying reflection weighed on her mind, and blunted her enjoyment. Still, she did not lay it deeply to heart, but continued to repeat her demands for aid, and her promises of pay, with full purpose

of heart, at each particular time, that that day she would not fail to keep her plighted word.

Thus perished the inward spark, like a flame just igniting, when one waits to see whether it will burn on or die out, till the long-desired change came, and she found herself in a new place, with a good mistress, and one who never instigated an otherwise kind master to be unkind to her; in short, a place where she had literally nothing to complain of, and where, for a time, she was more happy than she could well express. 'Oh, every thing there was so pleasant, and kind, and good, and all so comfortable; enough of everything; indeed, it was beautiful!' she exclaimed.

Here, at Mr. Van Wagener's,—as the reader will readily perceive she must have been,—she was so happy and satisfied, that God was entirely forgotten. Why should her thoughts turn to him, who was only known to her as a help in trouble? She had no trouble now; her every prayer had been answered in every minute particular. She had been delivered from her persecutors and temptations, her youngest child had been given her, and the others she knew she had no means of sustaining if she had them with her, and was content to leave them behind. Their father, who was much older than Isabel, and who preferred serving his time out in slavery, to the trouble and dangers of the course she pursued, remained with and could keep an eye on them—though it is comparatively little that they can do for each other while they remain in slavery, and this little the slave, like persons in every other situation of life, is not always disposed to perform. There *are* slaves, who, copying the selfishness of their superiors in power, in their conduct towards their fellows who may be thrown upon their mercy, by infirmity or illness, allow them to suffer for want of that kindness and care which it is fully in their power to render them.

The slaves in this country have ever been allowed to celebrate the principal, if not some of the lesser festivals observed by the Catholics and Church of England; many of them not being required to do the least service for several days, and at Christmas they have almost universally an entire week to themselves, except, perhaps, the attending to a few duties, which are absolutely required for the comfort of the families they belong to. If much service is desired, they are hired to do it, and paid for it as if they were free. The more sober portion of them spend these holidays in earning a little money. Most of them visit and attend parties and balls, and not a few of them spend it in the lowest dissipation. This respite from toil is granted them by all religionists, of whatever persuasion, and probably originated from the

fact that many of the first slaveholders were members of the Church of England.

Frederick Douglass, who has devoted his great heart and noble talents entirely to the furtherance of the cause of his down-trodden race, has said— 'From what I know of the effect of their holidays upon the slave, I believe them to be among the most effective means, in the hands of the slaveholder, in keeping down the spirit of insurrection. Were the slaveholders at once to abandon this practice, I have not the slightest doubt it would lead to an immediate insurrection among the slaves. These holidays serve as conductors, or safety-valves, to carry off the rebellious spirit of enslaved humanity. But for these, the slave would be forced up to the wildest desperation; and woe betide the slaveholder, the day he ventures to remove or hinder the operation of those conductors! I warn him that, in such an event, a spirit will go forth in their midst, more to be dreaded than the most appalling earthquake.'

When Isabella had been at Mr. Van Wagener's a few months, she saw in prospect one of the festivals approaching. She knows it by none but the Dutch name, Pingster, as she calls it—but I think it must have been Whitsuntide, in English. She says she 'looked back into Egypt,' and everything looked 'so pleasant there,' as she saw retrospectively all her former companions enjoying their freedom for at least a little space, as well as their wonted convivialities, and in her heart she longed to be with them. With this picture before her mind's eye, she contrasted the quiet, peaceful life she was living with the excellent people of Wahkendall, and it seemed so dull and void of incident, that the very contrast served but to heighten her desire to return, that, at least, she might enjoy with them, once more, the coming festivities. These feelings had occupied a secret corner of her breast for some time, when, one morning, she told Mrs. Van Wagener that her old master Dumont would come that day, and that she should go home with him on his return. They expressed some surprise, and asked her where she obtained her information. She replied, that no one had told her, but she felt that he would come.

It seemed to have been one of those 'events that cast their shadows before'; for, before night, Mr. Dumont made his appearance. She informed him of her intention to accompany him home. He answered with a smile, 'I shall not take you back again; you ran away from me.' Thinking his manner contradicted his words, she did not feel repulsed, but made herself and child ready; and when her former master had seated himself in the open dearborn, she walked towards it, intending to place herself and child in the rear, and go

with him. But, ere she reached the vehicle, she says that God revealed him-
self to her, with all the suddenness of a flash of lightning, showing her, 'in the
twinkling of an eye, that he was *all over*'—that he pervaded the universe—
'and that there was no place where God was not.' She became instantly con-
scious of her great sin in forgetting her almighty Friend and 'ever-present
help in time of trouble.' All her unfulfilled promises arose before her, like a
vexed sea whose waves run mountains high; and her soul, which seemed but
one mass of lies, shrunk back aghast from the 'awful look' of him whom she
had formerly talked to, as if he had been a being like herself; and she would
now fain have hid herself in the bowels of the earth, to have escaped his dread
presence. But she plainly saw there was no place, not even in hell, where he
was not: and where could she flee? Another such 'a look,' as she expressed it,
and she felt that she must be extinguished forever, even as one, with the
breath of his mouth, 'blows out a lamp,' so that spark remains.

A dire dread of annihilation now seized her, and she waited to see if by
'another look,' she was to be stricken from existence,—swallowed up, even as
the fire licketh up the oil with which it comes in contact.

When at last the second look came not, and her attention was once more
called to outward things, she observed her master had left, and exclaiming
aloud, 'Oh, God, I did not know you were so big,' walked into the house,
and made an effort to resume her work. But the workings of the inward man
were too absorbing to admit of much attention to her avocations. She desired
to talk to God, but her vileness utterly forbade it, and she was not able to
prefer a petition. 'What!' said she, 'shall I lie again to God? I have told him
nothing but lies, and shall I speak again, and tell another lie to God?' She
could not, and now she began to wish for some one to speak to God for her.
Then a space seemed opening between her and God, and she felt that if some
one who was worthy in the sight of heaven, would but plead *for* her in their
own name, and not let God know it came *from* her, who was so unworthy,
God might grant it. At length a friend appeared to stand between herself and
an insulted Deity; and she felt as sensibly refreshed as when, on a hot day, an
umbrella had been interposed between her scorching head and a burning
sun. But who was this friend? became the next inquiry. Was it Deencia, who
had so often befriended her? She looked at her with her new power of sight—
and, lo! she, too, seemed all 'bruises and putrefying sores,' like herself. No, it
was some one very different from Deencia.

'Who *are* you?' she exclaimed, as the vision brightened into a form dis-
tinct, beaming with the beauty of holiness, and radiant with love. She then

said, audibly addressing the mysterious visitant—'I *know* you and I *don't* know you.' Meaning, 'You seem perfectly familiar; I feel that you not only love me, but that you always *have* loved me—yet I know you not—I cannot call you by name.' When she said, 'I know you,' the subject of the vision remained distinct and quiet. When she said, 'I don't know you,' it moved restlessly about, like agitated waters. So while she repeated, without inter-mission, 'I know you, I know you,' that the vision might remain—'Who are you?' was the cry of her heart, and her whole soul was in one deep prayer that this heavenly personage might be revealed to her, and remain with her. At length, after bending both soul and body with the intensity of this desire, till breath and strength seemed failing, and she could maintain her position no longer, an answer came to her, saying distinctly, 'It is Jesus.' 'Yes,' she responded, 'it is *Jesus.'*

Previous to these exercises of mind, she heard Jesus mentioned in reading or speaking, but had received from what she heard no impression that he was any other than an eminent man, like a Washington or a Lafayette. Now he appeared to her delighted mental vision as so mild so good, and so every way lovely, and he loved her so much! And, how strange that he had always loved her, and she had never known it! And how great a blessing he conferred, in that he should stand between her and God! And God was no longer a terror and a dread to her.

She stopped not to argue the point, even in her own mind, whether he had reconciled her to God, or God to herself (though she thinks the former now), being but too happy that God was no longer to her as a consuming fire, and Jesus was 'altogether lovely.' Her heart was now full of joy and glad-ness, as it had been of terror, and at one time of despair. In the light of her great happiness, the world was clad in new beauty, the very air sparkled as with diamonds, and was redolent of heaven. She contemplated the unap-proachable barriers that existed between herself and the great of this world, as the world calls greatness, and made surprising comparisons between them, and the union existing between herself and Jesus,—Jesus, the transcendently lovely as well as great and powerful; for so he appeared to her, though he seemed but human; and she watched for his bodily appearance, feeling that she should know him, if she saw him; and when he came, she should go and dwell with him, as with a dear friend.

It was not given her to see that he loved any other; and she thought if oth-ers came to know and love him, as she did, she should be thrust aside and forgotten, being herself but a poor ignorant slave, with little to recommend

her to his notice. And when she heard him spoken of, she said mentally—'What! others know Jesus! I thought no one knew Jesus but me!' and she felt a sort of jealousy, lest she should be robbed of her newly found treasure.

She conceived, one day, as she listened to reading, that she heard an intimation that Jesus was married, and hastily inquired if Jesus had a wife. 'What!' said the reader, *'God* have a wife?' 'Is Jesus *God?'* inquired Isabella. 'Yes, to be sure he is,' was the answer returned. From this time, her conceptions of Jesus became more elevated and spiritual; and she sometimes spoke of him as God, in accordance with the teaching she had received.

But when she was simply told, that the Christian world was much divided on the subject of Christ's nature—some believing him to be coequal with the Father—to be God in and of himself, 'very God, of very God';—some, that he is the 'well-beloved,' 'only begotten Son of God';—and others, that he is, or was, rather, but a mere man—she said, 'Of that I only know as I saw. I did not see him to be God; else, how could he stand between me and God? I saw him as a friend, standing between me and God, through whom, love flowed as from a fountain.' Now, so far from expressing her views of Christ's character and office in accordance with any system of theology extant, she says she believes Jesus is the same spirit that was in our first parents, Adam and Eve, in the beginning, when they came from the hand of their Creator. When they sinned through disobedience, this pure spirit forsook them, and fled to heaven; that there it remained, until it returned again in the person of Jesus; and that, previous to a personal union with him, man is but a brute, possessing only the spirit of an animal.

She avers that, in her darkest hours, she had no fear of any worse hell than the one she then carried in her bosom; though it had ever been pictured to her in its deepest colors, and threatened her as a reward for all her misdemeanors. Her vileness and God's holiness and all-pervading presence, which filled immensity, and threatened her with instant annihilation, composed the burden of her vision of terror. Her faith in prayer is equal to her faith in the love of Jesus. Her language is, 'Let others say what they will of the efficacy of prayer, *I* believe in it, and *I* shall pray. Thank God! Yes, *I shall always pray,'* she exclaims, putting her hands together with the greatest enthusiasm.

For some time subsequent to the happy change we have spoken of, Isabella's prayers partook largely of their former character; and while, in deep affliction, she labored for the recovery of her son, she prayed with constancy

and fervor; and the following may be taken as a specimen:—'Oh, God, you know how much I am distressed, for I have told you again and again. Now, God, help me get my son. If you were in trouble, as I am, and I could help you, as you can me, think I wouldn't do it? Yes, God, you *know* I would do it.' 'Oh, God, you know I have no money, but you can make the people do for me, and you must make the people do for me. I will never give you peace till you do, God.' 'Oh, God, make the people hear me—don't let them turn me off, without hearing and helping me.' And she has not a particle of doubt, that God heard her, and especially disposed the hearts of thoughtless clerks, eminent lawyers, and grave judges and others—between whom and herself there seemed to her almost an infinite remove—to listen to her suit with patient and respectful attention, backing it up with all needed aid. The sense of her nothingness, in the eyes of those with whom she contended for her rights, sometimes fell on her like a heavy weight, which nothing but her unwavering confidence in an arm which she believed to be stronger than all others combined could have raised from her sinking spirit. 'Oh! how little I did feel,' she repeated, with a powerful emphasis. 'Neither would you wonder, if you could have seen me, in my ignorance and destitution, trotting about the streets, meanly clad, bare-headed, and bare-footed! Oh, God only could have made such people hear me; and he did it in answer to my prayers.' And this perfect trust, based on the rock of Deity, was a soul-protecting fortress, which, raising her above the battlements of fear, and shielding her from the machinations of the enemy, impelled her onward in the struggle, till the foe was vanquished, and the victory gained.

We have now seen Isabella, her youngest daughter, and her only son, in possession of, at least, their nominal freedom. It has been said that the freedom of the most free of the colored people of this country is but nominal; but stinted and limited as it is, at best, it is an *immense* remove from chattel slavery. This fact is disputed, I know; but I have no confidence in the honesty of such questionings. If they are made in sincerity, I honor not the judgment that thus decides.

Her husband, quite advanced in age, and infirm of health, was emancipated, with the balance of the adult slaves of the State, according to law, the following summer, July 4, 1828.

For a few years after this event, he was able to earn a scanty living, and when he failed to do that, he was dependent on the 'world's cold charity,' and died in a poor-house. Isabella had herself and two children to provide for; her wages were trifling, for at that time the wages of females were at a small

advance from nothing, and she doubtless had to learn the first elements of economy—for what slaves, that were never allowed to make any stipulations or calculations for themselves, ever possessed an adequate idea of the true value of time, or, in fact, of any material thing in the universe? To such, 'prudent using' is meanness—and 'saving' is a word to be sneered at. Of course, it was not in her power to make to herself a home, around whose sacred hearth-stone she could collect her family, as they gradually emerged from their prison-house of bondage; a home, where she could cultivate their affection, administer to their wants, and instill into the opening minds of her children those principles of virtue, and that love of purity, truth and benevolence, which must ever form the foundation of a life of usefulness and happiness. No—all this was far beyond her power or means, in more senses than one; and it should be taken into the account, whenever a comparison is instituted between the progress made by her children in virtue and goodness, and the progress of those who have been nurtured in the genial warmth of a sunny home, where good influences cluster, and bad ones are carefully excluded—where 'line upon line, and precept upon precept,' are daily brought to their quotidian tasks—and where, in short, every appliance is brought in requisition, that self-denying parents *can* bring to bear on one of the dearest objects of a parent's life, the promotion of the welfare of their children. But God forbid that this suggestion should be wrested from its original intent, and made to shield any one from merited rebuke! Isabella's children are now of an age to know good from evil, and may easily inform themselves on any point where they may yet be in doubt; and if they now suffer themselves to be drawn by temptation into the paths of the destroyer, or forget what is due to the mother who has done and suffered so much for them, and who, now that she is descending into the vale of years, and feels her health and strength declining, will turn her expecting eyes to them for aid and comfort, just as instinctively as the child turns its confiding eye to its fond parent, when it seeks for succor or for sympathy—(for it is now their turn to do the work, and hear the burdens of life, as all must bear them in turn, as the wheel of life rolls on)—if, I say, they forget this, their duty and their happiness, and pursue an opposite course of sin and folly, they must lose the respect of the wise and good, and find, when too late, that 'the way of the transgressor is hard.'

NEW TRIALS.

The reader will pardon this passing homily, while we return to our narrative.

We were saying that the day-dreams of Isabella and her husband—the plan they drew of what they would do, and the comforts they thought to have, when they should obtain their freedom, and a little home of their own—had all turned to 'thin air,' by the postponement of their freedom to so late a day. These delusive hopes were never to be realized, and a new set of trials was gradually to open before her. These were the heart-wasting trials of watching over her children, scattered, and imminently exposed to the temptations of the adversary, with few, if any, fixed principles to sustain them.

'Oh,' she says, 'how little did I know myself of the best way to instruct and counsel them! Yet I did the best I then knew, when with them. I took them to the religious meetings; I talked to, and prayed for and with them; when they did wrong, I scolded at and whipped them.'

Isabella and her son had been free about a year, when they went to reside in the city of New York; a place which she would doubtless have avoided, could she have seen what was there in store for her; for this view into the future would have taught her what she only learned by bitter experience, that the baneful influences going up from such a city were not the best helps to education, commenced as the education of *her* children had been.

Her son Peter was, at the time of which we are speaking, just at that age when no lad should be subjected to the temptations of such a place, unprotected as he was, save by the feeble arm of a mother, herself a servant there. He was growing up to be a tall, well-formed, active lad, of quick perceptions, mild and cheerful in his disposition, with much that was open, generous and winning about him, but with little power to withstand temptation, and a ready ingenuity to provide himself with ways and means to carry out his plans, and conceal from his mother and her friends, all such as he knew would not meet their approbation. As will be readily believed, he was soon drawn into a circle of associates who did not improve either his habits or his morals.

Two years passed before Isabella knew what character Peter was establishing for himself among his low and worthless comrades—passing under the assumed name of Peter Williams, and she began to feel a parent's pride in the promising appearance of her only son. But, alas! this pride and pleasure were

shortly dissipated, as distressing facts relative to him came one by one to her astonished ear. A friend of Isabella's, a lady, who was much pleased with the good humor, ingenuity, and open confessions of Peter, when driven into a corner, and who, she said, 'was so smart, he ought to have an education, if any one ought,'—paid ten dollars, as tuition fee, for him to attend a navigation school. But Peter, little inclined to spend his leisure hours in study, when he might be enjoying himself in the dance, or otherwise, with his boon companions, went regularly and made some plausible excuses to the teacher, who received them as genuine, along with the ten dollars of Mrs. ———, and while his mother and her friend believed him improving at school, he was, to their latent sorrow, improving in a very different place or places, and on entirely opposite principles. They also procured him an excellent place as a coachman. But, wanting money, he sold his livery, and other things belonging to his master; who, having conceived a kind regard for him, considered his youth, and prevented the law from falling, with all its rigor, upon his head. Still he continued to abuse his privileges, and to involve himself in repeated difficulties, from which his mother as often extricated him. At each time, she talked much, and reasoned and remonstrated with him; and he would, with such perfect frankness, lay open his whole soul to her, telling her he had never intended doing harm,—how he had been led along, little by little, till, before he was aware, he found himself in trouble—how he had *tried* to be good—and how, when he would have been so, 'evil was present with him,'— indeed he knew not *how* it was.

His mother, beginning to feel that the city was no place for him, urged his going to sea, and would have shipped him on board a man-of-war; but Peter was not disposed to consent to that proposition, while the city and its pleasures were accessible to him. Isabella now became a prey to distressing fears, dreading lest the next day or hour come fraught with the report of some dreadful crime, committed or abetted by her son. She thanks the Lord for sparing her that giant sorrow, as all his wrong doings never ranked higher, in the eye of the law, than misdemeanors. But as she could see no improvement in Peter, as a last resort, she resolved to leave him, for a time, unassisted, to bear the penalty of his conduct, and see what effect that would have on him. In the trial hour, she remained firm in her resolution. Peter again fell into the hands of the police, and sent for his mother, as usual; but she went not to his relief. In his extremity, he sent for Peter Williams, a respectable colored barber, whose name he had been wearing, and who sometimes helped young culprits out of their troubles, and sent them from city

dangers, by shipping them on board of whaling vessels.

The curiosity of this man was awakened by the culprit's bearing his own name. He went to the Tombs and inquired into his case, but could not believe what Peter told him respecting his mother and family. Yet he redeemed him, and Peter promised to leave New York in a vessel that was to sail in the course of a week. He went to see his mother, and informed her of what had happened to him. She listened incredulously, as to an idle tale. He asked her to go with him and see for herself. She went, giving no credence to his story till she found herself in the presence of Mr. Williams, and heard him saying to her, 'I am very glad I have assisted your son; he stood in great need of sympathy and assistance; but I could not think he had such a mother here, although he assured me he had.'

Isabella's great trouble now was, a fear lest her son should deceive his benefactor, and be missing when the vessel sailed; but he begged her earnestly to trust him, for he said he had resolved to do better, and meant to abide by the resolve. Isabella's heart gave her no peace till the time of sailing, when Peter sent Mr. Williams and another messenger whom she knew, to tell her he had sailed. But for a month afterwards she looked to see him emerging from some by-place in the city, and appearing before her; so afraid was she that he was still unfaithful, and doing wrong. But he did not appear, and at length she believed him really gone. He left in the summer of 1839, and his friends heard nothing further from him till his mother received the following letter, dated 'October 17, 1840':—

> 'My Dear And Beloved Mother:
>
> 'I take this opportunity to write to you and inform you that I am well and in hopes for to find you the same. I am got on board the same unlucky ship Done, of Nantucket. I am sorry for to say, that I have been punished once severely, by shoving my head in the fire for other folks. We have had bad luck, but in hopes to have better. We have about 230 on board, but in hopes, if don't have good luck, that my parents will receive me with thanks. I would like to know how my sisters are. Does my cousins live in New York yet? Have you got my letter? If not, inquire to Mr. Pierce Whiting's. I wish you would write me an answer as soon as possible. I am your only son, that is so far from your home, in the wide, briny ocean. I have seen more of the world than ever I expected and if I ever should

return home safe, I will tell you all my troubles and hardships. Mother, I hope you do not forget me, your dear and only son. I should like to know how Sophia, and Betsey, and Hannah, come on. I hope you all will forgive me for all that I have done.

'Your son,

PETER VAN WAGENER.'

Another letter reads as follows, dated 'March 22, 1841':—

'MY DEAR MOTHER:

'I take this opportunity to write to you, and inform you that I have been well and in good health. I have wrote you a letter before, but have received no answer from you, and was very anxious to see you. I hope to see you in a short time. I have had very hard luck, but are in hopes to have better in time to come. I should like if my sisters are well, and all the people round the neighborhood. I expect to be home in twenty-two months or thereabouts. I have seen Samuel Laterett. Beware! There has happened very bad news to tell you, that Peter Jackson is dead. He died within two days' sail of Otaheite, one of the Society Islands. The Peter Jackson that used to live at Laterett's; he died on board the ship Done, of Nantucket, Captain Miller, in the latitude 15 53, and longitude 148 30 W. I have no more to say at present, but write as soon as possible.

'Your only son,

PETER VAN WAGENER.'

Another, containing the last intelligence she has had from her son, reads as follows, and was dated 'Sept. 19, 1841':—

'DEAR MOTHER:

'I take this opportunity to write to you and inform you that I am well and in good health, and in hopes to find you in the same. This is the fifth letter that I have wrote to you, and have received no answer, and it makes me very uneasy. So pray write as quick as you can, and tell me how all the people is about the neighborhood. We are out from home twenty-three months, and in hopes to be home in fifteen months. I have not

much to say; but tell me if you have been up home since I left
or not. I want to know what sort of a time is at home. We had
very bad luck when we first came out, but since we have had
very good; so I am in hopes to do well yet; but if I don't do
well, you need not expect me home these five years. So write as
quick as you can, won't you? So now I am going to put an end
to my writing, at present. Notice—when this you see, remem-
ber me, and place me in your mind.

> Get me to my home, that's in the far distant west,
> To the scenes of my childhood, that I like the best;
> There the tall cedars grow, and the bright waters flow,
> Where my parents will greet me, white man, let me go!
> Let me go to the spot where the cateract plays,
> Where oft I have sported in my boyish days;
> And there is my poor mother, whose heart ever flows,
> At the sight of her poor child, to her let me go, let me go!

> 'Your only son,
>
> PETER VAN WAGENER.'

Since the date of the last letter, Isabella has heard no tidings from her
long-absent son, though ardently does her mother's heart long for such tid-
ings, as her thoughts follow him around the world, in his perilous vocation,
saying within herself—'He is good now, I have no doubt; I feel sure that he
has persevered, and kept the resolve he made before he left home;—he
seemed so different before he went, so determined to do better.' His letters
are inserted here for preservation, in case they prove the last she ever hears
from him in this world.

FINDING A BROTHER AND SISTER.

When Isabella had obtained the freedom of her son, she remained in
Kingston, where she had been drawn by the judicial process, about a
year, during which time she became a member of the Methodist Church
there: and when she went to New York, she took a letter missive from that

church to the Methodist Church in John street. Afterwards, she withdrew her connection with that church, and joined Zion's Church, in Church street, composed entirely of colored people. With the latter church she remained until she went to reside with Mr. Pierson, after which she was gradually drawn into the 'kingdom' set up by the prophet Matthias, in the name of God the Father; for he said the spirit of God the Father dwelt in him.

While Isabella was in New York, her sister Sophia came from Newburg to reside in the former place. Isabel had been favored with occasional interviews with this sister, although at one time she lost sight of her for the space of seventeen years—almost the entire period of her being at Mr. Dumont's—and when she appeared before her again, handsomely dressed, she did not recognize her, till informed who she was. Sophia informed her that her brother Michael—a brother she had never seen—was in the city; and when she introduced him to Isabella, he informed her that their sister Nancy had been living in the city, and had deceased a few months before. He described her features, her dress, her manner, and said she had for some time been a member in Zion's Church, naming the class she belonged to. Isabella almost instantly recognized her as a sister in the church, with whom she had knelt at the altar, and with whom she had exchanged the speaking pressure of the hand, in recognition of their spiritual sisterhood; little thinking, at the time, that they were also children of the same earthly parents—even Bomefree and Mau-mau Bett. As inquiries and answers rapidly passed, and the conviction deepened that this was their sister, the very sister they had heard so much of but had never seen (for she was the self-same sister that had been locked in the great old-fashioned sleigh-box, when she was taken away, never to behold her mother's face again this side the spirit-land, and Michael, the narrator, was the brother who had shared her fate), Isabella thought, 'D——n! here she was; we met; and was I not, at the time, struck with the peculiar feeling of her hand—the bony hardness so just like mine? and yet I could not know she was my sister; and now I see she looked so like my mother!' And Isabella wept, and not alone; Sophia wept, and the strong man, Michael, mingled his tears with theirs. 'Oh Lord,' inquired Isabella, 'what is this slavery, that it can do such dreadful things? what evil can it not do?' Well may she ask; for surely the evils it can and does do, daily and hourly, can never be summed up, till we can see them as they are recorded by him who writes no errors, and reckons without mistake. This account, which now varies so widely in the estimate of different minds, will be viewed alike by all.

Think you, dear reader, when that day comes, the most 'rabid abolition-

ist' will say—'Behold, I saw all this while on the Barth?' Will he not rather say, 'Oh, who has conceived the breadth and depth of this moral malaria, this putrescent plague-spot?' Perhaps the pioneers in the slave's cause will be as much surprised as any to find that with all *their* looking, there remained so much unseen.

GLEANINGS.

There are some hard things that crossed Isabella's life while in slavery, that she has no desire to publish, for various reasons. First, because the parties from whose hands she suffered them have rendered up their account to a higher tribunal, and their innocent friends alone are living, to have their feelings injured by the recital; secondly, because they are not all for the public ear, from their very nature; thirdly, and not least, because, she says, were she to tell all that happened to her as a slave—all that she knows is 'God's truth'—it would seem to others, especially the uninitiated, so unaccountable, so unreasonable, and what is usually called so unnatural (though it may be questioned whether people do not always act naturally), they would not easily believe it. 'Why, no!' she says, 'they'd call me a liar! they would, indeed! and I do not wish to say anything to destroy my own character for veracity, though what I say is strictly true.' Some things have been omitted through forgetfulness, which not having been mentioned in their places, can only be briefly spoken of here;—such as, that her father Bomefree had had two wives before he took Mau-mau Bett; one of whom, if not both, were torn from him by the iron hand of the ruthless trafficker in human flesh;—that her husband, Thomas, after one of *his* wives had been sold away from him, ran away to New York City, where he remained a year or two, before he was discovered and taken back to the prison-house of slavery;—that her master Dumont, when he promised Isabella one year of her time, before the State should make her free, made the same promise to her husband, and in addition to freedom, they were promised a log cabin for a home of their own; all of which, with the one-thousand-and-one day-dreams resulting therefrom, went into the repository of unfulfilled promises and unrealized hopes,—that she had often heard her father repeat a thrilling story of a little slave-child, which, because it annoyed the family with its cries, was caught up by a white man, who dashed its brains out against the wall. An Indian (for Indians were plenty in

that region then) passed along as the bereaved mother washed the bloody corpse of her murdered child, and learning the cause of its death, said, with characteristic vehemence, 'If I had been here, I would have put my toma-hawk in his head!' meaning the murderer's.

Of the cruelty of one Hasbrouck.—He had a sick slave-woman, who was lingering with a slow consumption, whom he made to spin, regardless of her weakness and suffering; and this woman had a child, that was unable to walk or talk, at the age of five years, neither could it cry like other children, but made a constant, piteous, moaning sound. This exhibition of helplessness and imbecility, instead of exciting the master's pity, stung his cupidity, and so enraged him, that he would kick the poor thing about like a foot-ball.

Isabella's informant had seen this brute of a man, when the child was curled up under a chair, innocently amusing itself with a few sticks, drag it thence, that he might have the pleasure of tormenting it. She had seen him, with one blow of his foot, send it rolling quite across the room, and down the steps at the door. Oh, how she wished it might instantly die! 'But,' she said, 'it seemed as tough as a moccasin.' Though it *did* die at last, and made glad the heart of its friends; and its persecutor, no doubt, rejoiced with them, but from very different motives. But the day of his retribution was not far off—for he sickened, and his reason fled. It was fearful to hear his old slave soon tell how, in the day of his calamity, she treated *him*.

She was very strong, and was therefore selected to support her master, as he sat up in bed, by putting her arms around, while she stood behind him. It was then that she did her best to wreak her vengeance on him. She would clutch his feeble frame in her iron grasp, as in a vice; and, when her mistress did not see, would give him a squeeze, a shake, and lifting him tip, set him down again, as *hard as possible*. If his breathing betrayed too tight a grasp, and her mistress said, 'Be careful, don't hurt him, Soan!' her ever-ready answer was, 'Oh no, Missus, no,' in her most pleasant tone—and then, as soon as Missus's eyes and ears were engaged away, another grasp—another shake—another bounce. She was afraid the disease alone would let him recover,—an event she dreaded more than to do wrong herself. Isabella asked her, if she were not afraid his spirit would haunt her. 'Oh, no,' says Soan, 'he was so wicked, the devil will never let him out of hell long enough for that.'

Many slaveholders boast of the love of their slaves. How would it freeze the blood of some of them to know what kind of love rankles in the bosoms of slaves for them! Witness the attempts to poison Mrs. Calhoun, and hun-dreds of similar cases. Most 'surprising' to every body, because committed by

slaves supposed to be so *grateful* for their chains.

These reflections bring to mind a discussion on this point, between the writer and a slaveholding friend in Kentucky, on Christmas morning, 1846. We had asserted, that until mankind were far in advance of what they now are, irresponsible power over our fellow-beings would be, as it is, abused. Our friend declared it *his* conviction, that the cruelties of slavery existed chiefly in imagination, and that no person in D—— County, where we then were, but would be above ill-treating a helpless slave. We answered, that if his belief was well-founded, the people in Kentucky were greatly in advance of the people of New England—for we would not dare say as much as that of any school-district there, letting alone counties. No, we would not answer for our own conduct even on so delicate a point.

The next evening, he very magnanimously overthrew his own position and established ours, by informing us that, on the morning previous, and as near as we could learn, at the very hour in which we were earnestly discussing the probabilities of the case, a young woman of fine appearance, and high standing in society, the pride of her husband, and the mother of an infant daughter, only a few miles from us, ay, in D—— County, too, was actually beating in the skull of a slave-woman called Tabby, and not content with that, had her tied up and whipped, after her skull was broken, and she died hanging to the bedstead, to which she had been fastened. When informed that Tabby was dead, she answered, 'I am *glad of it,* for she has worried my life out of me.' But Tabby's highest good was probably not the end proposed by Mrs. M—— , for no one supposed she meant to kill her. Tabby was considered quite lacking in good sense, and no doubt belonged to that class at the South, that are silly enough to 'die of moderate correction.'

A mob collected around the house for an hour or two, in that manner expressing a momentary indignation. But was she treated as a murderess? Not at all! She was allowed to take boat (for her residence was near the beautiful Ohio) that evening, to spend a few months with her absent friends, after which she returned and remained with her husband, no one to 'molest or make her afraid.'

Had she been left to the punishment of an outraged conscience from right motives, I would have 'rejoiced with exceeding joy.' But to see the life of one woman, and she a murderess, put in the balance against the lives of three millions of innocent slaves, and to contrast her punishment with what I felt would be the punishment of one who was merely suspected of being an equal friend of all mankind, regardless of color or condition, caused my

blood to stir within me, and my heart to sicken at the thought. The husband of Mrs. M—— was absent from home, at the time alluded to; and when he arrived, some weeks afterwards, bringing beautiful presents to his cherished companion, he beheld his once happy hope deserted, Tabby murdered and buried in the garden, and the wife of his bosom, and the mother of his child, the doer of the dreadful deed, a *murderess!*

When Isabella went to New York City, she went in company with a Miss Grear, who introduced her to the family of Mr. James Latourette, a wealthy merchant, and a Methodist in religion; but who, the latter part of his life, felt that he had outgrown ordinances, and advocated free meetings, holding them at his own dwelling-house for several years previous to his death. She worked for them, and they generously gave her a home while she labored for others, and in their kindness made her as one of their own.

At that time, the 'moral reform' movement was awakening the attention of the benevolent in that city. Many women, among whom were Mrs. Latourette and Miss Grear, became deeply interested in making an attempt to reform their fallen sisters, even the most degraded of them; and in this enterprise of labor and danger, they enlisted Isabella and others, who for a time put forth their most zealous efforts, and performed the work of missionaries with much apparent success. Isabella accompanied those ladies to the most wretched abodes of vice and misery, and sometimes she went where they dared not follow. They even succeeded in establishing prayer-meetings in several places, where such a thing might least have been expected.

But these meetings soon became the most noisy, shouting, ranting, and boisterous of gatherings; where they became delirious with excitement, and then exhausted from over-action. Such meetings Isabel had not much sympathy with, at best. But one evening she attended one of them, where the members of it, in a fit of ecstasy, jumped upon her cloak in such a manner as to drag her to the floor—and then, thinking she had fallen in a spiritual trance, they increased their glorifications on her account,—jumping, shouting, stamping, and clapping of hands; rejoicing so much over her spirit, and so entirely overlooking her body, that she suffered much, both from fear and bruises; and ever after refused to attend any more such meetings, doubting much whether God had any thing to do with such worship.

THE MATTHIAS DELUSION.

W e now come to an eventful period in the life of Isabella, as identified with one of the most extraordinary religious delusions of modern times; but the limits prescribed for the present work forbid a minute narration of all the occurrences that transpired in relation to it.

After she had joined the African Church in Church street, and during her membership there, she frequently attended Mr. Latourette's meetings, at one of which, Mr. Smith invited her to go to a prayer-meeting, or to instruct the girls at the Magdalene Asylum, Bowery Hill, then under the protection of Mr. Pierson, and some other persons, chiefly respectable females. To reach the Asylum, Isabella called on Katy, Mr. Pierson's colored servant, of whom she had some knowledge. Mr. Pierson saw her there, conversed with her, asked her if she had been baptized, and was answered, characteristically, 'By the Holy Ghost.' After this, Isabella saw Katy several times, and occasionally Mr. Pierson, who engaged her to keep his house while Katy went to Virginia to see her children. This engagement was considered an answer to prayer by Mr. Pierson, who had both fasted and prayed on the subject, while Katy and Isabella appeared to see in it the hand of God.

Mr. Pierson was characterized by a strong devotional spirit, which finally became highly fanatical. He assumed the title of Prophet, asserting that God had called him in an omnibus, in these words:—'Thou are Elijah, the Tishbite. Gather unto me all the members of Israel at the foot of Mount Carmel'; which he understood as meaning the gathering of his friends at Bowery Hill. Not long afterward, he became acquainted with the notorious Matthias, whose career was as extraordinary as it was brief. Robert Matthews, or Matthias (as he was usually called), was of Scotch extraction, but a native of Washington County, New York, and at that time about forty-seven years of age. He was religiously brought up, among the Anti-Burghers, a sect of Presbyterians; the clergyman, the Rev. Mr. Bevridge, visiting the family after the manner of the church, and being pleased with Robert, put his hand on his head, when a boy, and pronounced a blessing, and this blessing, with his natural qualities, determined his character; for he ever after thought he should be a distinguished man. Matthias was brought up a farmer till nearly eighteen years of age, but acquired indirectly the art of a carpenter, without any regular apprenticeship, and showed considerable mechanical skill. He obtained property from his uncle, Robert Thompson, and then he went into business as a store-keeper, was considered respectable, and became a member

of the Scotch Presbyterian Church. He married in 1813, and continued in business in Cambridge. In 1816, he ruined himself by a building speculation, and the derangement of the currency which denied bank facilities, and soon after he came to New York with his family, and worked at his trade. He afterwards removed to Albany, and became a hearer at the Dutch Reformed Church, then under Dr. Ludlow's charge. He was frequently much excited on religious subjects.

In 1829, he was well known, if not for street preaching, for loud discussions and pavement exhortations, but he did not make set sermons. In the beginning of 1830, he was only considered zealous; but in the same year he prophesied the destruction of the Albanians and their capital, and while preparing to shave, with the Bible before him, he suddenly put down the soap and exclaimed, 'I have found it! I have found a text which proves that no man who shaves his beard can be a true Christian'; and shortly afterwards, without shaving, he went to the Mission House to deliver an address which he had promised, and in this address he proclaimed his new character, pronounced vengeance on the land, and that the law of God was the only rule of government, and that he was commanded to take possession of the world in the name of the King of kings. His harangue was cut short by the trustees putting out the lights. About this time, Matthias laid by his implements of industry, and in June, he advised his wife to fly with him from the destruction which awaited them in the city; and on her refusal, partly on account of Matthias calling himself a Jew, whom she was unwilling to retain as a husband, he left her, taking some of the children to his sister in Argyle forty miles from Albany. At Argyle he entered the church and interrupted the minister, declaring the congregation in darkness, and warning them to repentance. He was, of course, taken out of the church, and as he was advertised in the Albany papers, he was sent back to his family. His beard had now obtained a respectable length, and thus he attracted attention, and easily obtained an audience in the streets. For this he was sometimes arrested, once by mistake for Adam Paine, who collected the crowd, and then left Matthias with it on the approach of the officers. He repeatedly urged his wife to accompany him on a mission to convert the world, declaring that food could be obtained from the roots of the forest, if not administered otherwise. At this time he assumed the name of Matthias, called himself a Jew, and set out on a mission, taking a western course, and visiting a brother at Rochester, a skilful mechanic, since dead. Leaving his brother, he proceeded on his mission over the Northern States, occasionally returning to Albany.

After visiting Washington, and passing through Pennsylvania, he came to New York. His appearance at that time was mean, but grotesque, and his sentiments were but little known.

On May the 5th, 1832, he first called on Mr. Pierson, in Fourth street, in his absence. Isabella was alone in the house, in which she had lived since the previous autumn. On opening the door, she, for the first time, beheld Matthias, and her early impression of seeing Jesus in the flesh rushed into her mind. She heard his inquiry, and invited him into the parlor; and being naturally curious, and much excited, and possessing a good deal of tact, she drew him into conversation, stated her own opinions, and heard his replies and explanations. Her faith was at first staggered by his declaring himself a Jew; but on this point she was relieved by his saying, 'Do you not remember how Jesus prayed?' and repeated part of the Lord's Prayer, in proof that the Father's kingdom was to come, and not the Son's. She then understood him to be a converted Jew, and in the conclusion she says she *felt* as if God had sent him to set up the kingdom.' Thus Matthias at once secured the good will of Isabella, and we may suppose obtained from her some information in relation to Mr. Pierson, especially that Mrs. Pierson declared there was no true church, and approved of Mr. Pierson's preaching. Matthias left the house, promising to return on Saturday evening. Mr. P. at this time had not seen Matthias.

Isabella, desirous of hearing the expected conversation between Matthias and Mr. Pierson on Saturday, hurried her work, got it finished, and was permitted to be present. Indeed, the sameness of belief made her familiar with her employer, while her attention to her work, and characteristic faithfulness increased his confidence. This intimacy, the result of holding the same faith, and the principle afterwards adopted of having but one table, and all things in common, made her at once the domestic and the equal, and the depositary of very curious, if not valuable information. To this object, even her color assisted. Persons who have travelled in the South know the manner in which the colored people, and especially slaves, are treated; they are scarcely regarded as being present. This trait in our American character has been frequently noticed by foreign travellers. One English lady remarks that she discovered, in course of conversation with a Southern married gentleman, that a colored girl slept in his bedroom, in which also was his wife; and when he saw that it occasioned some surprise, he remarked, 'What would he do if he wanted a glass of water in the night?' Other travellers have remarked that the presence of colored people never seemed to interrupt conversation of any

kind for one moment. Isabella, then, was present at the first interview between Matthias and Pierson. At this interview, Mr. Pierson asked Matthias if he had a family, to which he replied in the affirmative; he asked him about his beard, and he gave a scriptural reason, asserting also that the Jews did not shave, and that Adam had a beard. Mr. Pierson detailed to Matthias his experience, and Matthias gave his, and they mutually discovered that they held the same sentiments, both admitting the direct influence of the Spirit, and the transmission of spirits from one body to another. Matthias admitted the call of Mr. Pierson, in the omnibus in Wall street, which, on this occasion, he gave in these words:—'Thou art Elijah the Tishbite, and thou shalt go before me in the spirit and power of Elias, to prepare my way before me.' And Mr. Pierson admitted Matthias's call, who *completed* his declaration on the 20th of June, in Argyle, which, by a curious coincidence, was the very day on which Pierson had received his call in the omnibus. Such singular coincidences have a powerful effect on excited minds. From that discovery, Pierson and Matthias rejoiced in each other, and became kindred spirits— Matthias, however, claiming to be the Father, or to possess the spirit of the Father—he was God upon earth, because the spirit of God dwelt in him, while Pierson then understood that his mission was like that of John the Baptist, which the name Elias meant. This conference ended with an invitation to supper, and Matthias and Pierson washing each other's feet. Mr. Pierson preached on the following Sunday, but after which, he declined in favor of Matthias, and some of the party believed that the 'kingdom had then come.'

As a specimen of Matthias's preaching and sentiments, the following is said to be reliable:

'The spirit that built the Tower of Babel is now in the world—it is the spirit of the devil. The spirit of man never goes upon the clouds; all who think so are Babylonians. The only heaven is on the earth. All who are ignorant of truth are Ninevites. The Jews did not crucify Christ—it was the Gentiles. Every Jew has his guardian angel attending him in this world. God don't speak through preachers; he speaks through me, his prophet.

"'John the Baptist,'" (addressing Mr. Pierson), "'read the tenth chapter of Revelations.'" After the reading of the chapter, the prophet resumed speaking, as follows:—

'Ours is the mustard-seed kingdom which is to spread all over the earth. Our creed is truth, and no man can find truth unless he obeys John the Baptist, and comes clean into the church.

'All *real* men will be saved; all *mock* men will be damned. When a person has the Holy Ghost, then he is a man, and not till then. They who teach women are of the wicked. The communion is all nonsense; so is prayer. Eating a nip of bread and drinking a little wine won't do any good. All who admit members into their church, and suffer them to hold their lands and houses, their sentence is, "Depart, ye wicked, I know you not." All females who lecture their husbands, their sentence is the same. The sons of truth are to enjoy all the good things of this world, and must use their means to bring it about. Every thing that has the smell of woman will be destroyed. Woman is the capsheaf of the abomination of desolation—full of all deviltry. In a short time, the world will take fire and dissolve; it is combustible already. All women, not obedient, had better become so as soon as possible, and let the wicked spirit depart, and become temples of truth. Praying is all mocking. When you see any one wring the neck of a fowl, instead of cutting off its head, he has not got the Holy Ghost. (Cutting gives the least pain.)

'All who eat swine's flesh are of the devil; and just as certain as he eats it, he will tell a lie in less than half an hour. If you eat a piece of pork, it will go crooked through you, and the Holy Ghost will not stay in you, but one or the other must leave the house pretty soon. The pork will be as crooked in you as rams' horns, and as great a nuisance as the hogs in the street.

'The cholera is not the right word; it is choler, which means God's wrath. Abraham, Isaac, and Jacob are now in this world; they did not go up in the clouds, as some believe—why should they go there? They don't want to go there to box the compass from one place to another. The Christians now-a-days are for setting up the *Son's* kingdom. It is not his, it is the *Father's* kingdom. It puts me in mind of the man in the country, who took his son in business, and had his sign made, "Hitchcock & Son"; but the son wanted it "Hitchcock & Father"—and that is the way with your Christians. They talk of the Son's kingdom first, and not the Father's kingdom.'

Matthias and his disciples at this time did not believe in a resurrection of the body, but that the spirits of the former saints would enter the bodies of the present generation, and thus begin heaven upon earth, of which he and Mr. Pierson were the first fruits.

Matthias made the residence of Mr. Pierson his own; but the latter, being apprehensive of popular violence in his house, if Matthias remained there, proposed a monthly allowance to him, and advised him to occupy another dwelling. Matthias accordingly took a house in Clarkson street, and then sent for his family at Albany, but they declined coming to the city. However, his

brother George complied with a similar offer, bringing his family with him, where they found very comfortable quarters. Isabella was employed to do the housework. In May, 1833, Matthias left his house, and placed the furniture, part of which was Isabella's, elsewhere, living himself at the hotel corner of Marketfield and West streets. Isabella found employment at Mr. Whiting's, Canal street, and did the washing for Matthias by Mrs. Whiting's permission.

Of the subsequent removal of Matthias to the farm and residence of Mr. B. Folger, at Sing Sing, where he was joined by Mr. Pierson, and others laboring under a similar religious delusion—the sudden, melancholy and somewhat suspicious death of Mr. Pierson, and the arrest of Matthias on the charge of his murder, ending in a verdict of not guilty—the criminal connection that subsisted between Matthias, Mrs. Folger, and other members of the 'Kingdom,' as 'match-spirits'—the final dispersion of this deluded company, and the voluntary exilement of Matthias in the far West, after his release—&c. &c., we do not deem it useful or necessary to give any particulars. Those who are curious to know what there transpired are referred to a work published in New York in 1835, entitled 'Fanaticism; its Sources and Influence; illustrated by the simple Narrative of Isabella, in the case of Matthias, Mr. and Mrs. B. Folger, Mr. Pierson, Mr. Mills, Catharine, Isabella, &c. &c. By G. Vale, 84 Roosevelt street.' Suffice it to say, that while Isabella was a member of the household at Sing Sing, doing much laborious service in the spirit of religious disinterestedness, and gradually getting her vision purged and her mind cured of its illusions, she happily escaped the contamination that surrounded her,—assiduously endeavoring to discharge all her duties in a becoming manner.

FASTING.

When Isabella resided with Mr. Pierson, he was in the habit of fasting every Friday; not eating or drinking anything from Thursday evening to six o'clock on Friday evening.

Then, again, he would fast two nights and three days, neither eating nor drinking; refusing himself even a cup of cold water till the third day at night, when he took supper again, as usual.

Isabella asked him why he fasted. He answered, that fasting gave him great light in the things of God; which answer gave birth to the following

train of thought in the mind of his auditor:—'Well, if fasting will give light inwardly and spiritually, I need it as much as any body,—and I'll fast too. If Mr. Pierson needs to fast two nights and three days, then I, who need light more than he does, ought to fast more, and I will fast three nights and three days.'

This resolution she carried out to the letter, putting not so much as a drop of water in her mouth for three whole days and nights. The fourth morning, as she arose to her feet, not having power to stand, she fell to the floor; but recovering herself sufficiently, she made her way to the pantry, and feeling herself quite voracious, and fearing that she might now offend God by her voracity, compelled herself to breakfast on dry bread and water-eating a large six-penny loaf before she felt at all stayed or satisfied. She says she did get light, but it was all in her body and none in her mind—and this lightness of body lasted a long time. Oh! she was so light, and felt so well, she could 'skim around like a gull.'

THE CAUSE OF HER LEAVING THE CITY.

The first years spent by Isabella in the city, she accumulated more than enough to supply all her wants, and she placed all the overplus in the Savings Bank. Afterwards, while living with Mr. Pierson, he prevailed on her to take it thence, and invest it in a common fund which he was about establishing, as a fund to be drawn from by all the faithful; the faithful, of course, were the handful that should subscribe to his peculiar creed. This fund, commenced by Mr. Pierson, afterwards became part and parcel of the kingdom of which Matthias assumed to be head; and at the breaking up of the kingdom, her little property was merged in the general ruin—or went to enrich those who profited by the loss of others, if any such there were. Mr. Pierson and others had so assured her, that the fund would supply all her wants, at all times, and in all emergencies, and to the end of life, that she became perfectly careless on the subject—asking for no interest when she drew her money from the bank, and taking no account of the sum she placed in the fund. She recovered a few articles of furniture from the wreck of the kingdom, and received a small sum of money from Mr. B. Folger, as the price of Mrs. Folger's attempt to convict her of murder. With this to start upon, she commenced anew her labors, in the hope of yet being able to accumulate a

sufficiency to make a little home for herself, in her advancing age. With this stimulus before her, she toiled hard, working early and late, doing a great deal for a little money, and turning her hand to almost any thing that promised good pay. Still, she did not prosper; and somehow, could not contrive to lay by a single dollar for a 'rainy day.'

When this had been the state of her affairs some time, she suddenly paused, and taking a retrospective view of what had passed, inquired within herself, why it was that, for all her unwearied labors, she had nothing to show; why it was that others, with much less care and labor could hoard up treasures for themselves and children? She became more and more convinced, as she reasoned, that every thing she had undertaken in the city of New York had finally proved a failure, and where her hopes had been raised the highest, there she felt the failure had been the greatest, and the disappointment most severe.

After turning it in her mind for some time, she came to the conclusion, that she had been taking part in a great drama, which was, in itself, but one great system of robbery and wrong. 'Yes,' she said, 'the rich rob the poor, and the poor rob one another.' True, she had not received labor from others, and stinted their pay, as she felt had been practiced against her; but she had taken their work from them, which was their only means to get money, and was the same to them in the end. For instance—a gentleman where she lived would give her a half dollar to hire a poor man to clear the new-fallen snow from the steps and side-walks. She would arise early, and perform the labor herself, putting the money into her own pocket. A poor man would come along, saying she ought to have let him have the job; he was poor, and needed the pay for his family. She would harden her heart against him, and answer—'I am poor too, and I need it for mine.' But, in her retrospection, she thought of all the misery she might have been adding to, in her selfish grasping, and it troubled her conscience sorely; and this insensibility to the claims of human brotherhood, and the wants of the destitute and wretched poor, she now saw, as she never had done before, to be unfeeling, selfish and wicked. These reflections and convictions gave rise to a sudden revulsion of feeling in the heart of Isabella, and she began to look upon money and property with great indifference, if not contempt—being at that time unable, probably, to discern any difference between a miserly grasping at and hoarding of money and means, and a true use of the good things of this life for one's own comfort, and the relief of such as she might be enabled to befriend and assist. One thing she was sure of—that the precepts, 'Do unto others as

ye would that others should do unto you,' 'Love your neighbor as yourself,' and so forth, were maxims that had been but little thought of by herself, or practiced by those about her.

Her next decision was, that she must leave the city; it was no place for her; yea, she felt called in spirit to leave it, and to travel east and lecture. She had never been further east than the city, neither had she any friends there of whom she had particular reason to expect any thing; yet to her it was plain that her mission lay in the east, and that she would find friends there. She determined on leaving; but these determinations and convictions she kept close locked in her own breast, knowing that if her children and friends were aware of it, they would make such an ado about it as would render it very unpleasant, if not distressing to all parties. Having made what preparations for leaving she deemed necessary,—which was, to put up a few articles of clothing in a pillow-case, all else being deemed an unnecessary incumbrance,—about an hour before she left, she informed Mrs. Whiting, the woman of the house where she was stopping, that her name was no longer Isabella, but SOJOURNER; and that she was going east. And to her inquiry, 'What are you going east for?' her answer was, 'The Spirit calls me there, and I must go.'

She left the city on the morning of the 1st of June, 1843, crossing over to Brooklyn, L.I.; and taking the rising sun for her only compass and guide, she 'remembered Lot's wife,' and hoping to avoid her fate, she resolved not to look back till she felt sure the wicked city from which she was fleeing was left too far behind to be visible in the distance; and when she first ventured to look back, she could just discern the blue cloud of smoke that hung over it, and she thanked the Lord that she was thus far removed from what seemed to her a second Sodom.

She was now fairly started on her pilgrimage; her bundle in one hand, and a little basket of provisions in the other, and two York shillings in her purse—her heart strong in the faith that her true work lay before her, and that the Lord was her director; and she doubted not he would provide for and protect her, and that it would be very censurable in her to burden herself with any thing more than a moderate supply for her then present needs. Her mission was not merely to travel east, but to 'lecture,' as she designated it; 'testifying of the hope that was in her'—exhorting the people to embrace Jesus, and refrain from sin, the nature and origin of which she explained to them in accordance with her own most curious and original views. Through her life, and all its chequered changes, she has ever clung fast to her first perma-

nent impressions on religious subjects.

Wherever night overtook her, there she sought for lodgings—free if she might—if not, she paid; at a tavern, if she chanced to be at one—if not, at a private dwelling; with the rich, if they would receive her—if not, with the poor.

But she soon discovered that the largest houses were nearly always full; if not quite full, company was soon expected; and that it was much easier to find an unoccupied corner in a small house than in a large one; and if a person possessed but a miserable roof over his head, you might be sure of a welcome to part of it.

But this, she had penetration enough to see, was quite as much the effect of a want of sympathy as of benevolence; and this was also very apparent in her religious conversations with people who were strangers to her. She said, 'she never could find out that the rich had any religion. If *I* had been rich and accomplished, I could; for the rich could always find religion in the rich, and I could find it among the poor.'

At first, she attended such meetings as she heard of, in the vicinity of her travels, and spoke to the people as she found them assembled. Afterwards, she advertised meetings of her own, and held forth to large audiences, having, as she said, 'a good time.'

When she became weary of travelling, and wished a place to stop a while and rest herself, she said, some opening for her was always near at hand; and the first time she needed rest, a man accosted her as she was walking, inquiring if she was looking for work. She told him that was not the object of her travels, but that she would willingly work a few days, if any one wanted. He requested her to go to his family, who were sadly in want of assistance, which he had been thus far unable to supply. She went to the house where she was directed and was received by his family, one of whom was ill, as a 'Godsend', and when she felt constrained to resume her journey, they were very sorry, and would fain have detained her longer; but as she urged the necessity of leaving, they offered her what seemed in her eyes a great deal of money as a remuneration for her labor, and an expression of their gratitude for her opportune assistance; but she would only receive a very little of it; enough, as she says, to enable her to pay tribute to Caesar, if it was demanded of her, and two or three York shillings at a time were all she allowed herself to take; and then, with purse replenished, and strength renewed, she would once more set out to perform her mission.

THE CONSEQUENCES OF REFUSING
A TRAVELLER A NIGHT'S LODGING.

As she drew near the centre of the Island, she commenced, one evening at nightfall, to solicit the favor of a night's lodging. She had repeated her request a great many, it seemed to her some twenty times, and as many times she received a negative answer. She walked on, the stars and the tiny horns of the new moon shed but a dim light on her lonely way, when she was familiarly accosted by two Indians, who took her for an acquaintance. She told them they were mistaken in the person; she was a stranger there, and asked them the direction to a tavern. They informed her it was yet a long way—some two miles or so; and inquired if she were alone. Not wishing for their protection, or knowing what might be the character of their kindness, she answered, 'No, not exactly,' and passed on. At the end of a weary way, she came to the tavern,—or, rather, to a large building, which was occupied as courthouse, tavern, and jail,—and on asking for a night's lodging, was informed she could stay, if she would consent to be locked in. This to her mind was an insuperable objection. To have a key turned on her was a thing not to be thought of, at least not to be endured, and she again took up her line of march, preferring to walk beneath the open sky, to being locked up by a stranger in such a place. She had not walked far, before she heard the voice of a woman under an open shed; she ventured to accost her, and inquired if she knew where she could get in for the night. The woman answered, that she did not, unless she went home with them; and turning to her 'good man,' asked him if the stranger could not share their home for the night, to which he cheerfully assented, Sojourner thought it evident he had been taking a drop too much, but as he was civil and good-natured, and she did not feel inclined to spend the night alone in the open air, she felt driven to the necessity of accepting their hospitality, whatever it might prove to be. The woman soon informed her that there was a ball in the place, at which they would like to drop in a while, before they went to their home.

Balls being no part of Sojourner's mission, she was not desirous of attending; but her hostess could be satisfied with nothing short of a taste of it, and she was forced to go with her, or relinquish their company at once, in which move there might be more exposure than in accompanying her. She went, and soon found herself surrounded by an assemblage of people, collected from the very dregs of society, too ignorant and degraded to understand,

much less entertain, a high or bright idea,—in a dirty hovel, destitute of every comfort, and where the fumes of whisky were abundant and powerful.

Sojourner's guide there was too much charmed with the combined entertainments of the place to be able to tear herself away, till she found her faculties for enjoyment failing her, from a too free use of liquor; and she betook herself to bed till she could recover them. Sojourner, seated in a corner, had time for many reflections, and refrained from lecturing them in obedience to the recommendation 'Cast not your pearls,' &c. When the night was far spent, the husband of the sleeping woman aroused the sleeper, and reminded her that she was not very polite to the woman she had invited to sleep at her house and of the propriety of returning home. They once more emerged into the pure air, which to our friend Sojourner, after so long breathing the noisome air of the ball-room, was most refreshing and grateful. Just as day dawned, they reached the place they called their home. Sojourner now saw that she had lost nothing in the shape of rest by remaining so long at the ball, as their miserable cabin afforded but one bunk or pallet for sleeping; and had there been many such, she would have preferred sitting up all night to occupying one like it. They very politely offered her the bed, if she would use it, but civilly declining, she waited for morning with an eagerness of desire she never felt before on the subject, and was never more happy than when the eye of day shed its golden light once more over the earth. She was once more free, and while day-light should last, independent, and needed no invitation to pursue her journey. Let these facts teach us, that every pedestrian in the world is not a vagabond, and that it is a dangerous thing to compel any one to receive that hospitality from the vicious and abandoned which they should have received from us,—as thousands can testify, who have thus been caught in the snares of the wicked.

The fourth of July, Isabella arrived at Huntingdon; from thence she went to Cold Springs, where she found the people making preparations for a mass temperance-meeting. With her usual alacrity, she entered into their labors, getting up dishes *a la New York,* greatly to the satisfaction of those she assisted. After remaining at Cold Springs some three weeks, she returned to Huntingdon, where she took boat for Connecticut. Landing at Bridgeport, she again resumed her travels towards the north-east, lecturing some, and working some, to get wherewith to pay tribute to Cæsar, as she called it; and in this manner she presently came to the city of New Haven, where she found many meetings, which she attended—at some of which she was allowed to express her views freely, and without reservation. She also called

meetings expressly to give herself an opportunity to be heard; and found in the city many true friends of Jesus, as she judged, with whom she held communion of spirit, having no preference for one sect more than another, but being well satisfied with all who gave her evidence of having known or loved the Saviour.

After thus delivering her testimony in this pleasant city, feeling she had not as yet found an abiding place, she went from thence to Bristol, at the request of a zealous sister, who desired her to go to the latter place, and hold a religious conversation with some friends of hers there. She went as requested, found the people kindly and religiously disposed, and through them she became acquainted with several very interesting persons.

A spiritually minded brother in Bristol, becoming interested in her new views and original opinions, requested as a favor that she would go to Hartford, to see and converse with friends of his there. Standing ready to perform any service in the Lord, she went to Hartford as desired, bearing in her hand the following note from this brother:—

> 'SISTER,—I send you this living messenger, as I believe her to be one that God loves. Ethiopia is stretching forth her hands unto God. You can see by this sister, that God does by his Spirit alone teach his own children things to come. Please receive her, and she will tell you some new things. Let her tell her story without interrupting her, and give close attention, and you will see she has got the lever of truth, that God helps her to pry where but few can. She cannot read or write, but the law is in her heart.
>
> 'Send her to brother —— brother ——, and where she can do the most good.
>
> 'From your brother,　　　　H. L. B.'

SOME OF HER VIEWS AND REASONINGS.

As soon as Isabella saw God as an all-powerful, all-pervading spirit she became desirous of hearing all that had been written of him, and listened to the account of the creation of the world and its first inhabitants, as

contained in the first chapters of Genesis, with peculiar interest. For some time she received it all literally, though it appeared strange to her that 'God worked by the day, got tired, and stopped to rest,' &c. But after a little time, she began to reason upon it, thus—'Why, if God works by the day, and one day's work tires him, and he is obliged to rest, either from weariness or on account of darkness, or if he waited for the "cool of the day to walk in the garden," because he was inconvenienced by the heat of the sun, why then it seems that God cannot do as much as *I* can; for *I* can bear the sun at noon, and work several days and nights in succession without being much tired. Or, if he rested nights because of the darkness, it is very queer that he should make the night so dark that he could not see himself. If *I* had been God, I would have made the night light enough for my own convenience, surely.' But the moment she placed this idea of God by the side of the impression she had once so suddenly received of his inconceivable greatness and entire spirituality, that moment she exclaimed mentally, 'No, God does not stop to rest, for he is a spirit, and cannot tire; he cannot want for light, for he hath all light in himself. And if "God is all in all," and "worketh all in all," as I have heard them read, then it is impossible he should rest at all; for if he did, every other thing would stop and rest too; the waters would not flow, and the fishes could not swim; and all motion must cease. God could have no pauses in his work, and he needed no Sabbaths of rest. Man might need them, and he should take them when he needed them, whenever he required rest. As it regarded the worship of God, he was to be worshipped at all times and in all places; and one portion of time never seemed to her more holy than another.'

These views which were the result of the workings of her own mind, assisted solely by the light of her own experience and very limited knowledge, were, for a long time after their adoption, closely locked in her own breast, fearing lest their avowal might bring upon her the imputation of 'infidelity'—the usual charge preferred by all religionists, against those who entertain religious views and feelings differing materially from their own. If, from their own sad experience, they are withheld from shouting the cry of 'infidel,' they fail not to see and to feel, ay, and to say, that the dissenters are not of the right spirit, and that their spiritual eyes have never been unsealed.

While travelling in Connecticut, she met a minister with whom she held a long discussion on these points, as well as on various other topics, such as the origin of all things, especially the origin of evil, at the same time bearing her testimony strongly against a paid ministry. He belonged to that class,

and, as a matter of course, as strongly advocated his own side of the question.

I had forgotten to mention, in its proper place, a very important fact, that when she was examining the Scriptures, she wished to hear them without comment; but if she employed adult persons to read them to fuel, and she asked them to read a passage over again, they invariably commenced to explain, by giving her their version of it; and in this way, they tried her feelings exceedingly. In consequence of this, she ceased to ask adult persons to read the Bible to her, and substituted children in their stead. Children, as soon as they could read distinctly, would reread the same sentence to her, as often as she wished, and without comment; and in that way she was enabled to see what her own mind could make out of the record, and that, she said, was what she wanted, and not what others thought it to mean. She wished to compare the teachings of the Bible with the witness within her; and she came to the conclusion, that the spirit of truth spoke in those records, but that the recorders of those truths had intermingled with them ideas and suppositions of their own. This is one among the many proofs of her energy and independence of character.

When it became known to her children, that Sojourner had left New York, they were filled with wonder and alarm. Where could she have gone, and why had she left? were questions no one could answer satisfactorily. Now, their imaginations painted her as a wandering maniac—and again they feared she had been left to commit suicide, and many were the tears they shed at the loss of her.

But when she reached Berlin, Conn., she wrote to them by amanuensis, informing them of her whereabouts, and waiting an answer to her letter; thus quieting their fears, and gladdening their hearts once more with assurances of her continued life and her love.

THE SECOND ADVENT DOCTRINES.

In Hartford and vicinity, she met with several persons who believed in the 'Second Advent' doctrines; or, the immediate personal appearance of Jesus Christ. At first she thought she had never heard of 'Second Advent.' But when it was explained to her, she recollected having once attended Mr. Miller's meeting in New York, where she saw a great many enigmatical pictures hanging on the wall, which she could not understand, and which, being

out of the reach of her understanding, failed to interest her. In this section of country, she attended two camp-meetings of the believers in these doctrines—the 'second advent' excitement being then at its greatest height. The last meeting was at Windsor Lock. The people, as a matter of course, eagerly inquired of her concerning her belief, as it regarded their most important tenet. She told them it had not been revealed to her; perhaps, if she could read, she might see it differently. Sometimes, to their eager inquiry, 'Oh, don't you believe the Lord is coming?' she answered, 'I believe the Lord is as near as he can be, and not be it.' With these evasive and non-exciting answers, she kept their minds calm as it respected her unbelief, till she could have an opportunity to hear their views fairly stated, in order to judge more understandingly of this matter, and see if, in her estimation, there was any good ground for expecting an event which was, in the minds of so many, as it were, shaking the very foundations of the universe. She was invited to join them in their religious exercises, and accepted the invitation—praying, and talking in her own peculiar style, and attracting many about her by her singing.

When she had convinced the people that she was a lover of God and his cause, and had gained a good standing with them, so that she could get a hearing among them, she had become quite sure in her own mind that they were laboring under a delusion, and she commenced to use her influence to calm the fears of the people, and pour oil upon the troubled waters. In one part of the grounds, she found a knot of people greatly excited: she mounted a stump and called out, 'Hear! hear!' When the people had gathered around her, as they were in a state to listen to any thing new, she addressed them as 'children,' and asked them why they made such a 'To-do;—are you not commanded to "watch and pray?" You are neither watching nor praying.' And she bade them, with the tones of a kind mother, retire to their tents, and there watch and pray, without noise or tumult, for the Lord would not come to such a scene of confusion; 'the Lord came still and quiet.' She assured them, 'the Lord might come, move all through the camp, and go away again, and they never know it,' in the state they then were.

They seemed glad to seize upon any reason for being less agitated and distressed, and many of them suppressed their noisy terror, and retired to their tents to 'watch and pray'; begging others to do the same, and listen to the advice of the good sister. She felt she had done some good, and then went to listen further to the preachers. They appeared to her to be doing their utmost to agitate and excite the people, who were already too much excited; and

when she had listened till her feelings would let her listen silently no longer, she arose and addressed the preachers. The following are specimens of her speech:—

'Here you are talking about being "changed in the twinkling of an eye." If the Lord should come, he'd change you to *nothing!* for there is nothing to you.

'You seem to be expecting to go to some parlor *away up* somewhere, and when the wicked have been burnt, you are coming back to walk in triumph over their ashes—this is to be your New Jerusalem!! Now I can't see any thing so very *nice* in that, coming back to such a *muss* as that will be, a world covered with the ashes of the wicked! Besides, if the Lord comes and burns—as you say he will—I am not going away; *I* am going to stay here and *stand the fire*, like Shadrach, Meshach, and Abednego! And Jesus will walk with me through the fire, and keep me from harm. Nothing belonging to God can burn, any more than God himself; such shall have no need to go away to escape the fire! No, I shall remain. Do you tell me that God's children *can't stand fire?'* And her manner and tone spoke louder than words, saying, 'It is *absurd* to think so!'

The ministers were taken quite aback at so unexpected an opposer, and one of them, in the kindest possible manner, commenced a discussion with her, by asking her questions, and quoting Scripture to her; concluding finally, that although she had learned nothing of the great doctrine which was so exclusively occupying their minds at the time, she had learned much that man had never taught her.

At this meeting, she received the address of different persons, residing in various places, with an invitation to visit them. She promised to go soon to Cabotville, and started shaping her course for that place. She arrived at Springfield one evening at six o'clock, and immediately began to search for a lodging for the night. She walked from six till past nine, and was then on the road from Springfield to Cabotville, before she found any one sufficiently hospitable to give her a night's shelter under their roof. Then a man gave her twenty-five cents, and bade her go to a tavern and stay all night. She did so, returning in the morning to thank him, assuring him she had put his money to its legitimate use. She found a number of the friends she had seen at Windsor when she reached the manufacturing town of Cabotville (which has lately taken the name of Chicopee), and with them she spent a pleasant week or more; after which, she left them to visit the Shaker village in Enfield. She now began to think of finding a resting place, at least, for a season; for she had performed quite a long journey, considering she had walked most of the

way; and she had a mind to look in upon the Shakers, and see how things were there, and whether there was any opening there for her. But on her way back to Springfield, she called at a house and asked for a piece of bread; her request was granted, and she was kindly invited to tarry all night, as it was getting late, and she would not be able to stay at every house in that vicinity, which invitation she cheerfully accepted. When the man of the house came in, he recollected having seen her at the camp-meeting, and repeated some conversations, by which she recognized him again. He soon proposed having a meeting that evening, went out and notified his friends and neighbors, who came together, and she once more held forth to them in her peculiar style. Through the agency of this meeting, she became acquainted with several people residing in Springfield, to whose houses she was cordially invited, and with whom she spent some pleasant time.

One of these friends, writing of her arrival there, speaks as follows. After saying that she and her people belonged to that class of persons who believed in the second advent doctrines, and that this class, believing also in freedom of speech and action, often found at their meetings many singular people, who did not agree with them in their principal doctrine; and that, being thus prepared to hear new and strange things, 'They listened eagerly to Sojourner, and drank in all she said';—and also, that she 'soon became a favorite among them, that when she arose to speak in their assemblies, her commanding figure and dignified manner hushed every trifler into silence, and her singular and sometimes uncouth modes of expression never provoked a laugh, but often were the whole audience melted into tears by her touching stories.' She also adds, 'Many were the lessons of wisdom and faith I have delighted to learn from her.' . . . 'She continued a great favorite in our meetings, both on account of her remarkable gift in prayer, and still more remarkable talent for singing, . . . and the aptness and point of her remarks, frequently illustrated by figures the most original and expressive.

'As we were walking the other day, she said she had often thought what a beautiful world this would be, when we should see every thing right side up. Now, we see every thing topsy-turvy, and all is confusion.' For a person who knows nothing of this fact in the science of optics, this seemed quite a remarkable idea.

'We also loved her for her sincere and ardent piety, her unwavering faith in God, and her contempt of what the world calls fashion, and what we call folly.

'She was in search of a quiet place, where a way-worn traveller might rest.

She had heard of Fruitlands, and was inclined to go there; but the friends she found here thought it best for her to visit Northampton. She passed her time, while with us, working wherever her work was needed, and talking where work was not needed.

'She would not receive money for her work, saying she worked for the Lord; and if her wants were supplied, she received it as from the Lord.

'She remained with us till far into winter, when we introduced her at the Northampton Association.' . . . 'She wrote to me from thence, that she had found the quiet resting place she had so long desired. And she has remained there ever since.'

ANOTHER CAMP-MEETING.

W hen Sojourner had been at Northampton a few months, she attended another camp-meeting, at which she performed a very important part.

A party of wild young men, with no motive but that of entertaining themselves by annoying and injuring the feelings of others, had assembled at the meeting, hooting and yelling, and in various ways interrupting the services, and causing much disturbance. Those who had the charge of the meeting, having tried their persuasive powers in vain, grew impatient and tried threatening.

The young men, considering themselves insulted, collected their friends, to the number of a hundred or more, dispersed themselves through the grounds, making the most frightful noises, and threatening to fire the tents. It was said the authorities of the meeting sat in grave consternation, decided to have the ring-leaders arrested, and sent for the constable, to the great displeasure of some of the company, which were opposed to such an appeal to force and arms. Be that as it may, Sojourner, seeing great consternation depicted in every countenance, caught the contagion and, ere she was aware, found herself quaking with fear.

Under the impulse of this sudden emotion, she fled to the most retired corner of a tent, and secreted herself behind a trunk, saying to herself, 'I am the only colored person here, and on me, probably, their wicked mischief will fall first, and perhaps fatally.' But feeling how great was her insecurity even there, as the very tent began to shake from its foundations, she began to soliloquize as follows:—

'Shall I run away and hide from the Devil? Me, a servant of the living God? Have I not faith enough to go out and quell that mob, when I know it is written—"One shall chase a thousand, and two put ten thousand to flight"? I know there are not a thousand here; and I know I am a servant of the living God. I'll go to the rescue, and the Lord shall go with and protect me.

'Oh,' said she, 'I felt as if I had *three hearts!* and that they were so large, my body could hardly hold them!'

She now came forth from her hiding-place, and invited several to go with her and see what they could do to still the raging of the moral elements. They declined, and considered her wild to think of it.

The meeting was in the open fields—the full moon shed its saddened light over all—and the woman who was that evening to address them was trembling on the preachers' stand. The noise and confusion were now terrific. Sojourner left the tent alone and unaided, and walking some thirty rods to the top of a small rise of ground, commenced to sing, in her most fervid manner, with all the strength of her most powerful voice, the hymn on the resurrection of Christ—

> It was early in the morning—it was early in the morning,
> Just at the break of day—
> When he rose—when he rose—when he rose,
> And went to heaven on a cloud.

All who have ever heard her sing this hymn will probably remember it as long as they remember her. The hymn, the tune, the style, are each too closely associated with to be easily separated from herself, and when sung in one of her most animated moods, in the open air, with the utmost strength of her most powerful voice, must have been truly thrilling.

As she commenced to sing, the young men made a rush towards her, and she was immediately encircled by a dense body of the rioters, many of them armed with sticks or clubs as their weapons of defence, if not of attack. As the circle narrowed around her, she ceased singing, and after a short pause, inquired, in a gentle but firm tone, 'Why do you come about me with clubs and sticks? I am not doing harm to any one.' 'We ar'n't a going to hurt you, old woman; we came to hear you sing,' cried many voices, simultaneously. 'Sing to us, old woman,' cries one. 'Talk to us, old woman,' says another. 'Pray, old woman,' says a third. 'Tell us your experience,' says a fourth. 'You stand and smoke so near me, I cannot sing or talk,' she answered.

'Stand back,' said several authoritative voices, with not the most gentle or courteous accompaniments, raising their rude weapons in the air. The crowd suddenly gave back, the circle became larger, as many voices again called for singing, talking, or praying, backed by assurances that no one should be allowed to hurt her—the speakers declaring with an oath, that they would '*knock down*' any person who should offer her the least indignity.

She looked about her, and with her usual discrimination, said inwardly— 'Here must be many young men in all this assemblage, bearing within them hearts susceptible of good impressions. I will speak to them.' She did speak; they silently heard, and civilly asked her many questions. It seemed to her to be given her at the time to answer them with truth and wisdom beyond herself. Her speech had operated on the roused passions of the mob like oil on agitated waters, they were, as a whole, entirely subdued, and only clamored when she ceased to speak or sing. Those who stood in the background, after the circle was enlarged, cried out, 'Sing aloud, old woman, we can't hear.' Those who held the sceptre of power among them requested that she should make a pulpit of a neighboring wagon. She said, 'If I do, they'll overthrow it.' 'No, they sha'n't—he who dares hurt you, we'll knock him down instantly, d—n him,' cried the chiefs. 'No we won't, no we won't, nobody shall hurt you,' answered the many voices of the mob. They kindly assisted her to mount the wagon, from which she spoke and sung to them about an hour. Of all she said to them on the occasion she remembers only the following:—

'Well, there are two congregations on this ground. It is written that there shall be a separation, and the sheep shall be separated from the goats. The other preachers have the sheep, *I* have the goats. And I have a few sheep among my goats, but they are *very* ragged.' This exordium produced great laughter. When she became wearied with talking, she began to cast about her to contrive some way to induce them to disperse. While she paused, they loudly clamored for 'more,' 'more,'—'sing,' 'sing more.' She motioned them to be quiet, and called out to them: 'Children, I have talked and sung to you, as you asked me; and now I have a request to make of you: will you grant it?' 'Yes, yes, yes,' resounded from every quarter. 'Well, it is this,' she answered: 'if I will sing one more hymn for you, will you then go away, and leave us this night in peace?' 'Yes, yes,' came faintly, feebly from a few. 'I repeat it,' said Sojourner, 'and I want an answer from you all, as of one accord. If I will sing you one more, you will go away, and leave us this night in peace?' 'Yes, yes, yes,' shouted many voices, with hearty emphasis. 'I repeat my request once more,' said she, 'and I want you all to answer.' And she reiterated the

words again. This time a long, loud 'Yes-yes-yes,' came up, as from the mul-
titudinous mouth of the entire mob. 'AMEN! it is SEALED,' repeated
Sojourner, in the deepest and most solemn tones of her powerful and
sonorous voice. Its effect ran through the multitude, like an electric shock;
and the most of them considered themselves bound by their promise, as they
might have failed to do under less imposing circumstances. Some of them
began instantly to leave; others said, 'Are we not to have one more hymn?'
'Yes,' answered their entertainer, and she commenced to sing:

> 'I bless the Lord I've got my seal—to-day and to-day—
> To slay Goliath in the field—to-day and to-day;
> The good old way is a righteous way,
> I mean to take the kingdom in the good old way.'

While singing, she heard some enforcing obedience to their promise while a
few seemed refusing to abide by it. But before she had quite concluded, she
saw them turn from her, and in the course of a few minutes, they were run-
ning as fast as they well could in a solid body; and she says she can compare
them to nothing but a swarm of bees, so dense was their phalanx, so straight
their course, so hurried their march. As they passed with a rush very near the
stand of the other preachers, the hearts of the people were smitten with fear,
thinking that their entertainer had failed to enchain them longer with her
spell, and that they were coming upon them with redoubled and remorseless
fury. But they found they were mistaken, and that their fears were ground-
less; for, before they could well recover from their surprise, every rioter was
gone, and not one was left on the grounds, or seen there again during the
meeting. Sojourner was informed that as her audience reached the main
road, some distance from the tents, a few of the rebellious spirits refused to
go on, and proposed returning; but their leaders said, 'No—we have prom-
ised to leave—all promised, and we must go, all go, and you shall none of
you return again.'

She did not fall in love at first sight with the Northampton Association,
for she arrived there at a time when appearances did not correspond with the
ideas of Associationists, as they had been spread out in their writings; for
their phalanx was a factory, and they were wanting in means to carry out
their ideas of beauty and elegance, as they would have done in different cir-
cumstances. But she thought she would make an effort to tarry with them
one night, though that seemed to her no desirable affair. But as soon as she

saw that accomplished, literary, and refined persons were living in that plain and simple manner, and submitting to the labors and privations incident to such an infant institution, she said, "Well, if these can live here, *I* can." Afterwards, she gradually became pleased with, and attached to, the place and the people, as well she might; for it must have been no small thing to have found a home in a 'Community composed of some of the choicest spirits of the age,' where all was characterized by an equality of feeling, a liberty of thought and speech, and a largeness of soul, she could not have before met with, to the same extent, in any of her wanderings.

Our first knowledge of her was derived from a friend who had resided for a time in the 'Community,' and who, after describing her, and singing one of her hymns, wished that we might see her. But we little thought, at that time, that we should ever pen these 'simple annals' of this child of nature.

When we first saw her, she was working with a hearty good will; saying she would not be induced to take regular wages, believing, as once before, that now Providence had provided her with a never-failing fount, from which her every want might be perpetually supplied through her mortal life. In this, she had calculated too fast. For the Associationists found, that, taking every thing into consideration, they would find it most expedient to act individually; and again, the subject of this sketch found her dreams unreal, and herself flung back upon her own resources for the supply of her needs. This she might have found more inconvenient at her time of life—for labor, exposure, and hardship had made sad inroads upon her iron constitution, by inducing chronic disease and premature old age—had she not remained under the shadow of one,* who never wearies in doing good, giving to the needy, and supplying the wants of the destitute. She has now set her heart upon having a little home of her own, even at this late hour of life, where she may feel a greater freedom than she can in the house of another, and where she can repose a little, after her day of action has passed by. And for such a 'home' she is now dependent on the charities of the benevolent, and to them we appeal with confidence.

Through all the scenes of her eventful life may be traced the energy of a naturally powerful mind—the fearlessness and child-like simplicity of one untrammeled by education or conventional customs—purity of character—an unflinching adherence to principle—and a native enthusiasm, which, under different circumstances, might easily have produced another Joan of Arc.

*George W. Benson.

With all her fervor, and enthusiasm, and speculation, her religion is not tinctured in the least with gloom. No doubt, no hesitation, no despondency, spreads a cloud over her soul; but all is bright, clear, positive, and at times ecstatic. Her trust is in God, and from him she looks for good, and not evil. She feels that 'perfect love casteth out fear.'

Having more than once found herself awaking from a mortifying delusion,—as in the case of the Sing Sing kingdom—and resolving not to be thus deluded again, she has set suspicion to guard the door of her heart, and allows it perhaps to be aroused by too slight causes, on certain subjects—her vivid imagination assisting to magnify the phantoms of her fears into gigantic proportions, much beyond their real size; instead of resolutely adhering to the rule we all like best, when it is to be applied to ourselves—that of placing every thing we see to the account of the best possible motive, until time and circumstance prove that we were wrong. Where no good motive can be assigned, it may become our duty to suspend our judgment till evidence can be had.

In the application of this rule, it is an undoubted duty to exercise a commendable prudence, by refusing to repose any important trust to the keeping of persons who may be strangers to us, and whose trustworthiness we have never seen tried. But no possible good, but incalculable evil may and does arise from the too common practice of placing all conduct, the source of which we do not fully understand, to the worst of intentions. How often is the gentle, timid soul discouraged, and driven perhaps to despondency, by finding its 'good evil spoken of'; and a well-meant but mistaken action loaded with an evil design!

If the world would but sedulously set about reforming itself on this one point, who can calculate the change it would produce—the evil it would annihilate, and the happiness it would confer! None but an all-seeing eye could at once embrace so vast a result. A result, how desirable! and one that can be brought about only by the most simple process—that of every individual seeing to it that he commit not this sin himself. For why should we allow in ourselves, the very fault we most dislike, when committed against us? Shall we not at least aim at consistency?

Had she possessed less generous self-sacrifice, more knowledge of the world and of business matters in general and had she failed to take it for granted that others were like herself, and would, when her turn came to need, do as she had done, and find it 'more blessed to give than to receive,' she might have laid by something for the future. For few, perhaps, have ever

possessed the power and inclination, in the same degree, at one and the same time, to labor as she has done, both day and night, for so long a period of time. And had these energies been well-directed, and the proceeds well husbanded, since she has been her own mistress, they would have given her an independence during her natural life. But her constitutional biases, and her early training, or rather want of training, prevented this result; and it is too late now to remedy the great mistake. Shall she then be left to want? Who will not answer, 'No!'

FREDERICK DOUGLASS

(1818-1895)

rederick Augustus Washington Bailey was born into slavery and by the end of the 19th century, he had gone on to become a writer, newspaper editor, and adviser to several presidents. In every sense, he led a remarkable life, rising from the depths of human cruelty to the prestige and honor that was his due. He devoted his entire life to abolishing slavery, as well as advocating the rights of women, and his sermons, narratives and autobiographies were among the strongest voices for social equality in American history.

Douglass was born in a slave cabin in February of 1818 on the Eastern shore of Maryland, the son of a slave, Harriet Bailey and an unknown white father. He was taken from his mother at just a few weeks old to be raised by his grandparents. At around the age of six, he was taken by his grandmother to the Lloyd plantation and left there, where he stayed for two years and never recovered from the betrayal and abandonment he felt from the separation. His situation was so bleak that he remembered having to fight with his master's dogs for food and sleeping on the floor of the kitchen in the winter with other slave children because there were no beds or blankets.

When he was about eight years old, he was sent to Baltimore to serve as a house boy to Hugh and Sophia Auld, relatives of his master. Mrs. Auld apparently took a liking to the young Frederick, making repeated attempts to teach him to read and write, despite her husband's disapproval, since slaves were forbidden literacy instruction by law. However, Douglass was so inspired, he soon began to trade food for more advanced reading and writing lessons from the older boys in the neighborhood, since Mr. Auld had now forbidden his wife from continuing to educate him.

Douglass learned at an early age that knowledge was a pathway to freedom. It was a "special revelation," Douglass writes in his *Narrative of the Life of Frederick Douglass*. He had heard firsthand, when Mr. Auld scolded Mrs.

Auld for teaching Douglass to read, the fear many owners had about a slave who was educated. "A nigger should know nothing but to obey his master—to do as he is told to do. Learning would spoil the best nigger in the world. "Now," said he, "if you teach that nigger (speaking of myself) how to read, there would be no keeping him. It would forever unfit him to be a slave. He would at once become unmanageable, and of no value to his master. As to himself, it could do him no good, but a great deal of harm. It would make him discontented and unhappy."

Mr. Auld's stern warning to his wife served as a lifelong lesson to Douglass, who never forgot what he heard. In his narrative, he remembered the revelation this way:

> The very decided manner with which he spoke, and strove to impress his wife with the evil consequences of giving me instruction, served to convince me that he was deeply sensible of the truths he was uttering. It gave me the best assurance that I might rely with the utmost confidence on the results which, he said, would flow from teaching me to read. What he most dreaded, that I most desired. What he most loved, that I most hated. That which to him was a great evil, to be carefully shunned, was to me a great good, to be diligently sought; and the argument which he so warmly urged, against my learning to read, only served to inspire me with a desire and determination to learn. In learning to read, I owe almost as much to the bitter opposition of my master, as to the kindly aid of my mistress. I acknowledge the benefit of both.

Shortly afterward, when he was just twelve or thirteen years old, Douglass purchased a copy of *The Columbian Orator*, an immensely popular schoolbook of the time which enabled him to acquire an understanding of the written and spoken word, and how they could be effective tools for delivering a message. The speeches greatly affected him, and he began reading local newspapers, hungry to learn more about the growing movement against slavery.

Douglass established himself as a bright and curious young man in Baltimore, but any respect he had earned in the community came to an abrupt end in 1833, when an Auld family dispute led to Douglass's return to another of Auld's plantations in Saint Michaels, Maryland. Here, the 15 year old Douglass was sent back into the fields and was miserable about his

predicament. He received constant beatings, had to steal food from neighboring farms, and when he organized a Sunday religious service for slaves, Thomas Auld sent him to Edward Covey, a farmer with a notorious reputation for "breaking" slaves who had become independent or difficult to control.

Covey was successful in breaking Douglass as well, mostly through beatings and never ending work in the fields. "I was broken in body, soul, and spirit," he wrote. "My natural elasticity was crushed, my intellect languished, the disposition to read departed, the cheerful spark that lingered about my eye died. The dark night of slavery closed in upon me; and behold a man transformed into a brute!"

However, after six months of beatings and abuse, Douglass managed the courage and conviction one day of rising against Covey and physically fighting back in a manner which risked his life. For over two hours, the two fought, and Douglass claims to have gotten the best of Covey.

Curiously, Covey never had Douglass beaten for the incident, and never laid a finger on him for the remaining six months of his service to Covey, mainly because he would risk his reputation as a "slavebreaker," if word got out that he could not control a 16 year old slave.

At the end of his contract with Covey, Douglass was sent to work for a new farmer named William Freeland, who was, in comparison, a relatively kind master. But by this point, Douglass was more interested in freedom, and his passion to rebel firmly took root. He quickly started an illegal school for blacks in the area, holding secret classes at night and on Sundays. Soon afterwards, Douglass and five other slaves in his group began to plot their escape to the North.

Their attempt was foiled when one of Douglass's associates exposed the plot, and the slaves were thrown in jail. While imprisoned, he expected to be sold to "a life of living hell," but to his surprise, he was retrieved by one of the Auld family members and sent back to Baltimore. There, Douglass was trained as a caulker and hired out to shipbuilders where he became a highly skilled craftsman, but also the recipient of racist beatings. As time passed, Douglass became resentful of handing over his wages to the Aulds, even when he was permitted more and more freedoms.

In his spare time, Douglass pursued his studies again, and joined the East Baltimore Mental Improvement Society, where he honed his debating skills. This was also the place Douglass met a free black woman named Anna Murray, and the two were engaged in 1836. However, in two years' time, Douglass could no longer tolerate having to hand over money to Hugh Auld.

He resolved that he would rather escape on a northbound train and risk capture as well as perhaps never seeing his fiancee again than to continue a life in bondage.

On September 3, 1838, with money he borrowed from Anna, and false documents indicating he was a free seaman, Douglass boarded a train headed north, dressed as a sailor. Soon he arrived in New York City, and was at a loss for words at the joy of being free, as well as the anguish, loneliness and fear of being kidnapped while in this strange new world. He ultimately met David Ruggles, an officer in the New York Vigilance Committee who was part of a network of sympathizers who harbored runaway slaves and helped to transport them on the underground railroad. When he began to feel safe in New York, Douglass sent for his fiancee, Anna Murray, and the two were married on September 15, 1838. In order to steer clear from slave catchers, he changed his name from Frederick Bailey to Frederick Douglass, and the two of them headed to New Bedford, Massachusetts, with Douglass hoping to find work as a caulker.

It was in New Bedford that Douglass became involved in both the abolitionist movement and the church. At just 23 years of age, he met one of his heroes, William Lloyd Garrison, a pacifist who believed that slavery could end through moral persuasion. But Garrison's persistence and unbending position was controversial, especially to those in the North who preferred a more moderate, tempered campaign toward abolition. His passion and sincerity had a strong effect on Douglass, and when Garrison heard Douglass speak, he offered him a job on the lecture circuit, to talk about his life and to sell subscriptions to two newspapers Garrison was involved with—the *Liberator* and the *Anti-Slavery Standard*.

As a speaker, Douglass was an immediate sensation. He was dynamic, witty, sarcastic and elegant, and his speeches often went beyond his experiences as a slave. Douglass was not afraid to be political, talking not only of the lashes he received, but of the racism and inequalities that free blacks experienced in the north. His speeches had become so unnerving and polished that many people in the audience began to doubt him after time.

They were convinced an uneducated man just six years out of bondage would be incapable of such eloquence and ability. With his reputation on the line, Douglass published the story of his life in 1845, the *Narrative of the Life of Frederick Douglass*, and he decided to give the actual names, places and activities of the people connected with his Maryland slave period. When he finished his manuscript, he showed it to abolitionist leader Wendell Phillips,

he was advised to burn it before he was tracked down and returned to Maryland. But Douglass was adamant about having his story read and his book became a best–seller.

With the success of the book, however, came a great deal of attention, and since the Auld family was legally entitled to retrieve the fugitive Douglass, he decided to leave America for England, which was free from slave catchers. Douglass now had four children with Anna, but he was bound for England and would ultimately travel the British Isles for two years, speaking against slavery in America.

In 1846, Douglass stepped onstage to deliver what would become known as his most controversial speech at the World Temperance Convention in London. He attacked the American temperance movement because it failed to criticize slave owners who used alcohol to pacify slaves. When he was accused by Reverend Samuel Cox, a member of the American delegation, of attempting to destroy the unity of the movement, Douglass called Cox a bigot and accused him of being a clandestine supporter of slavery.

By the end of 1846, some of his English friends collected enough money to buy Douglass his outright freedom from the Auld family, and Douglass returned to America a prestigious author, lecturer, and above all, a free man. He immediately began work on an abolitionist newspaper, moving his family to Rochester, New York and founding the four page weekly, *North Star*. Douglass was equally vigilant in fighting for women's rights, and established close relationships with prominent activists of the time, such as Susan B. Anthony and Elizabeth Cady Stanton.

The paper, though not a great financial success, lifted Douglass to prominence, made him one of the most respected black leaders in the country, and created a great demand for him as a speaker and writer. By 1847, however, Douglass met with white militant and abolitionist John Brown, who persuaded Douglass that his pacifistic approach toward ending slavery was not the most effective tactic. Douglass began telling audiences that he believed southern slaves should revolt and spread "death and destruction" and questioned Garrison's antislavery reformation proposals. He urged readers of the *North Star* to engage in politics, and he became more active in the underground railroad.

In 1855, Douglass published the second of his autobiographies, *My Bondage and My Freedom*, and his notoriety continued to grow. John Brown wanted Douglass to join in the infamous attack on Harper's Ferry in 1859, but Douglass felt strongly that Americans would not tolerate such an attack,

and refused to join. However, after the attack, where Brown was ultimately tried and hanged, Douglass's name surfaced as a possible co-conspirator, and Douglass fled to Canada, despite insisting he was not involved. He sailed to England again to resume a lecture tour, where he was more popular than ever, but when news reached him that his youngest child Annie had died, he returned home, heartbroken, and about to witness his country in the turmoil of the Civil War.

As the war between the states developed, Douglass set two goals which he would champion—the emancipation of all slaves, and the right of blacks to enlist in the armies of the North. In time, the North would agree with Douglass, who lectured constantly, imploring President Abraham Lincoln to grant slaves their freedom. As the war dragged on, Lincoln ultimately believed that stronger policies needed to be taken against the Confederate States of America, and in December of 1862, Lincoln delivered the Emancipation Proclamation just months after the battle of Antietam in Maryland, where Union troops pushed back the Confederate army. The following year, Congress authorized the enlistment of blacks to fight in the Union army.

With two of Douglass's goals met, he continued to fight for equality, since black soldiers were paid about half of what white soldiers were paid, and Confederate soldiers often executed captured black troops. After the war, the Thirteenth Amendment to the U.S. Constitution was ratified and slavery was officially abolished in the United States, and Douglass turned his attention to black rights, fighting for the right to vote. In 1867, Douglass was asked by President Andrew Johnson to take charge of the Freedman's Bureau, which would have given him the position of overseeing government programs to aid the needs of southern blacks. But Douglass refused because he disagreed with Johnson's policies and saw the olive branch Johnson offered as a self-preserving appeasement, since Johnson's days in office appeared to be numbered.

Douglass later aligned himself with Ulysses S. Grant, who won the presidency in 1868 and managed to pass the Fifteenth Amendment guaranteeing all citizens the right to vote, regardless of race. Douglass would go on to lecture throughout the country, solidifying his stature as one of the world's greatest orators. In 1877, President Rutherford B. Hayes appointed him a marshall for Washington, D.C., overseeing the criminal justice system in the nation's capital.

In 1881, Douglass published the third of his autobiographical volumes,

The Life and Times of Frederick Douglass, and the following year, his wife Anna passed away after a long illness. Though he remarried a few years later to Helen Pitts and spent nine years with her, Douglass died of a massive heart attack in 1895 at the age of 77. Crowds gathered at the Washington church where he lay in state, and his body was taken to Rochester for burial.

Frederick Douglass's entire life was a struggle for the rights of his people, and for humanity. His was a voice that could not be silenced, no matter how much cruelty he faced, and his power and determination were among the most important building blocks in American society and law.

disposed to find fault with them; they can seldom do any thing to please her; she is never better pleased than when she sees them under the lash, especially when she suspects her husband of showing to his mulatto children favors which he withholds from his black slaves. The master is frequently compelled to sell this class of his slaves, out of deference to the feelings of his white wife; and, cruel as the deed may strike any one to be, for a man to sell his own children to human flesh-mongers, it is often the dictate of humanity for him to do so; for, unless he does this, he must not only whip them himself, but must stand by and see one white son tie up his brother, of but few shades darker complexion than himself, and ply the gory lash to his naked back; and if he lisp one word of disapproval, it is set down to his parental partiality, and only makes a bad matter worse, both for himself and the slave whom he would protect and defend.

Every year brings with it multitudes of this class of slaves. It was doubtless in consequence of a knowledge of this fact, that one great statesman of the south predicted the downfall of slavery by the inevitable laws of population. Whether this prophecy is ever fulfilled or not, it is nevertheless plain that a very different-looking class of people are springing up at the south, and are now held in slavery, from those originally brought to this country from Africa; and if their increase do no other good, it will do away the force of the argument, that God cursed Ham, and therefore American slavery is right. If the lineal descendants of Ham are alone to be scripturally enslaved, it is certain that slavery at the south must soon become unscriptural; for thousands are ushered into the world, annually, who, like myself, owe their existence to white fathers, and those fathers most frequently their own masters.

I have had two masters. My first master's name was Anthony. I do not remember his first name. He was generally called Captain Anthony—a title which, I presume, he acquired by sailing a craft on the Chesapeake Bay. He was not considered a rich slaveholder. He owned two or three farms, and about thirty slaves. His farms and slaves were under the care of an overseer. The overseer's name was Plummer. Mr. Plummer was a miserable drunkard, a profane swearer, and a savage monster. He always went armed with a cowskin and a heavy cudgel. I have known him to cut and slash the women's heads so horribly, that even master would be enraged at his cruelty, and would threaten to whip him if he did not mind himself. Master, however, was not a humane slaveholder. It required extraordinary barbarity on the part of an overseer to affect him. He was a cruel man, hardened by a long life of slave-holding. He would at times seem to take great pleasure in whipping a

slave. I have often been awakened at the dawn of day by the most heart-rend-ing shrieks of an own aunt of mine, whom he used to tie up to a joist, and whip upon her naked back till she was literally covered with blood. No words, no tears, no prayers, from his gory victim, seemed to move his iron heart from its bloody purpose. The louder she screamed, the harder he whipped; and where the blood ran fastest, there he whipped longest. He would whip her to make her scream, and whip her to make her hush; and not until overcome by fatigue, would he cease to swing the blood-clotted cowskin. I remember the first time I ever witnessed this horrible exhibition. I was quite a child, but I well remember it. I never shall forget it whilst I remember any thing. It was the first of a long series of such outrages, of which I was doomed to be a witness and a participant. It struck me with awful force. It was the blood-stained gate, the entrance to the hell of slavery, through which I was about to pass. It was a most terrible spectacle. I wish I could commit to paper the feelings with which I beheld it.

This occurrence took place very soon after I went to live with my old master, and under the following circumstances. Aunt Hester went out one night,—where or for what I do not know,—and happened to be absent when my master desired her presence. He had ordered her not to go out evenings, and warned her that she must never let him catch her in company with a young man, who was paying attention to her belonging to Colonel Lloyd. The young man's name was Ned Roberts, generally called Lloyd's Ned. Why master was so careful of her, may be safely left to conjecture. She was a woman of noble form, and of graceful proportions, having very few equals, and fewer superiors, in personal appearance, among the colored or white women of our neighborhood.

Aunt Hester had not only disobeyed his orders in going out, but had been found in company with Lloyd's Ned; which circumstance, I found, from what he said while whipping her, was the chief offence. Had he been a man of pure morals himself, he might have been thought interested in protecting the innocence of my aunt; but those who knew him will not suspect him of any such virtue. Before he commenced whipping Aunt Hester, he took her into the kitchen, and stripped her from neck to waist, leaving her neck, shoulders, and back, entirely naked. He then told her to cross her hands, call-ing her at the same time a d—d b—h. After crossing her hands, he tied them with a strong rope, and led her to a stool under a large hook in the joist, put in for the purpose. He made her get upon the stool, and tied her hands to the hook. She now stood fair for his infernal purpose. Her arms were

stretched up at their full length, so that she stood upon the ends of her toes. He then said to her, "Now, you d—d b—h, I'll learn you how to disobey my orders!" and after rolling up his sleeves, he commenced to lay on the heavy cowskin, and soon the warm, red blood (amid heart-rending shrieks from her, and horrid oaths from him) came dripping to the floor. I was so terrified and horror-stricken at the sight, that I hid myself in a closet, and dared not venture out till long after the bloody transaction was over. I expected it would be my turn next. It was all new to me. I had never seen any thing like it before. I had always lived with my grandmother on the outskirts of the plantation, where she was put to raise the children of the younger women. I had therefore been, until now, out of the way of the bloody scenes that often occurred on the plantation.

CHAPTER II

M Y MASTER's family consisted of two sons, Andrew and Richard; one daughter, Lucretia, and her husband, Captain Thomas Auld. They lived in one house, upon the home plantation of Colonel Edward Lloyd. My master was Colonel Lloyd's clerk and superintendent. He was what might be called the overseer of the overseers. I spent two years of childhood on this plantation in my old master's family. It was here that I witnessed the bloody transaction recorded in the first chapter; and as I received my first impressions of slavery on this plantation, I will give some description of it, and of slavery as it there existed. The plantation is about twelve miles north of Easton, in Talbot county, and is situated on the border of Miles River. The principal products raised upon it were tobacco, corn, and wheat. These were raised in great abundance; so that, with the products of this and the other farms belonging to him, he was able to keep in almost constant employment a large sloop, in carrying them to market at Baltimore. This sloop was named Sally Lloyd, in honor of one of the colonel's daughters. My master's son-in-law, Captain Auld, was master of the vessel; she was otherwise manned by the colonel's own slaves. Their names were Peter, Isaac, Rich, and Jake. These were esteemed very highly by the other slaves, and looked upon as the privileged ones of the plantation; for it was no small affair, in the eyes of the slaves, to be allowed to see Baltimore.

Colonel Lloyd kept from three to four hundred slaves on his home plan-

summer, but that some slave had to take the lash for stealing fruit. The colonel had to resort to all kinds of stratagems to keep his slaves out of the garden. The last and most successful one was that of tarring his fence all around; after which, if a slave was caught with any tar upon his person, it was deemed sufficient proof that he had either been into the garden, or had tried to get in. In either case, he was severely whipped by the chief gardener. This plan worked well; the slaves became as fearful of tar as of the lash. They seemed to realize the impossibility of touching *tar* without being defiled.

The colonel also kept a splendid riding equipage. His stable and carriage-house presented the appearance of some of our large city livery establishments. His horses were of the finest form and noblest blood. His carriage-house contained three splendid coaches, three or four gigs, besides dearborns and barouches of the most fashionable style.

This establishment was under the care of two slaves—old Barney and young Barney—father and son. To attend to this establishment was their sole work. But it was by no means an easy employment; for in nothing was Colonel Lloyd more particular than in the management of his horses. The slightest inattention to these was unpardonable, and was visited upon those, under whose care they were placed, with the severest punishment; no excuse could shield them, if the colonel only suspected any want of attention to his horses—a supposition which he frequently indulged, and one which, of course, made the office of old and young Barney a very trying one. They never knew when they were safe from punishment. They were frequently whipped when least deserving, and escaped whipping when most deserving it. Every thing depended upon the looks of the horses, and the state of Colonel Lloyd's own mind when his horses were brought to him for use. If a horse did not move fast enough, or hold his head high enough, it was owing to some fault of his keepers. It was painful to stand near the stable-door, and hear the various complaints against the keepers when a horse was taken out for use. "This horse has not had proper attention. He has not been suffi-ciently rubbed and curried, or he has not been properly fed; his food was too wet or too dry; he got it too soon or too late; he was too hot or too cold; he had too much hay, and not enough of grain; or he had too much grain, and not enough of hay; instead of old Barney's attending to the horse, he had very improperly left it to his son." To all these complaints, no matter how unjust, the slave must answer never a word. Colonel Lloyd could not brook any con-tradiction from a slave. When he spoke, a slave must stand, listen, and trem-ble; and such was literally the case. I have seen Colonel Lloyd make old

Barney, a man between fifty and sixty years of age, uncover his bald head, kneel down upon the cold, damp ground, and receive upon his naked and toil-worn shoulders more than thirty lashes at the time. Colonel Lloyd had three sons—Edward, Murray, and Daniel,—and three sons-in-law, Mr. Winder, Mr. Nicholson, and Mr. Lowndes. All of these lived at the Great House Farm, and enjoyed the luxury of whipping the servants when they pleased, from old Barney down to William Wilkes, the coach-driver. I have seen Winder make one of the house-servants stand off from him a suitable distance to be touched with the end of his whip, and at every stroke raise great ridges upon his back.

To describe the wealth of Colonel Lloyd would be almost equal to describing the riches of Job. He kept from ten to fifteen house-servants. He was said to own a thousand slaves, and I think this estimate quite within the truth. Colonel Lloyd owned so many that he did not know them when he saw them; nor did all the slaves of the out-farms know him. It is reported of him, that, while riding along the road one day, he met a colored man, and addressed him in the usual manner of speaking to colored people on the public highways of the south: "Well, boy, whom do you belong to?" "To Colonel Lloyd," replied the slave. "Well, does the colonel treat you well?" "No, sir," was the ready reply. "What, does he work you too hard?" "Yes, sir." "Well, don't he give you enough to eat?" "Yes, sir, he gives me enough, such as it is."

The colonel, after ascertaining where the slave belonged, rode on; the man also went on about his business, not dreaming that he had been conversing with his master. He thought, said, and heard nothing more of the matter, until two or three weeks afterwards. The poor man was then informed by his overseer that, for having found fault with his master, he was now to be sold to a Georgia trader. He was immediately chained and handcuffed; and thus, without a moment's warning, he was snatched away, and forever sundered, from his family and friends, by a hand more unrelenting than death. This is the penalty of telling the truth, of telling the simple truth, in answer to a series of plain questions.

It is partly in consequence of such facts, that slaves, when inquired of as to their condition and the character of their masters, almost universally say they are contented, and that their masters are kind. The slaveholders have been known to send in spies among their slaves, to ascertain their views and feelings in regard to their condition. The frequency of this has had the effect to establish among the slaves the maxim, that a still tongue makes a wise head. They suppress the truth rather than take the consequences of telling it,

and in so doing prove themselves a part of the human family. If they have any thing to say of their masters, it is generally in their masters' favor, especially when speaking to an untried man. I have been frequently asked, when a slave, if I had a kind master, and do not remember ever to have given a negative answer; nor did I, in pursuing this course, consider myself as uttering what was absolutely false; for I always measured the kindness of my master by the standard of kindness set up among slaveholders around us. Moreover, slaves are like other people, and imbibe prejudices quite common to others. They think their own better than that of others. Many, under the influence of this prejudice, think their own masters are better than the masters of other slaves; and this, too, in some cases, when the very reverse is true. Indeed, it is not uncommon for slaves even to fall out and quarrel among themselves about the relative goodness of their masters, each contending for the superior goodness of his own over that of the others. At the very same time, they mutually execrate their masters when viewed separately. It was so on our plantation. When Colonel Lloyd's slaves met the slaves of Jacob Jepson, they seldom parted without a quarrel about their masters; Colonel Lloyd's slaves contending that he was the richest, and Mr. Jepson's slaves that he was the smartest, and most of a man. Colonel Lloyd's slaves would boast his ability to buy and sell Jacob Jepson. Mr. Jepson's slaves would boast his ability to whip Colonel Lloyd. These quarrels would almost always end in a fight between the parties, and those that whipped were supposed to have gained the point at issue. They seemed to think that the greatness of their masters was transferable to themselves. It was considered as being bad enough to be a slave; but to be a poor man's slave was deemed a disgrace indeed!

CHAPTER IV

Mʀ. Hᴏᴘᴋɪɴs remained but a short time in the office of overseer. Why his career was so short, I do not know, but suppose he lacked the necessary severity to suit Colonel Lloyd. Mr. Hopkins was succeeded by Mr. Austin Gore, a man possessing, in an eminent degree, all those traits of character indispensable to what is called a first-rate overseer. Mr. Gore had served Colonel Lloyd, in the capacity of overseer, upon one of the out-farms, and had shown himself worthy of the high station of overseer upon the home or Great House Farm.

Mr. Gore was proud, ambitious, and persevering. He was artful, cruel, and obdurate. He was just the man for such a place, and it was just the place for such a man. It afforded scope for the full exercise of all his powers, and he seemed to be perfectly at home in it. He was one of those who could torture the slightest look, word, or gesture, on the part of the slave, into impudence, and would treat it accordingly. There must be no answering back to him; no explanation was allowed a slave, showing himself to have been wrongfully accused. Mr. Gore acted fully up to the maxim laid down by slaveholders,—"It is better that a dozen slaves should suffer under the lash, than that the overseer should be convicted, in the presence of the slaves, of having been at fault." No matter how innocent a slave might be—it availed him nothing, when accused by Mr. Gore of any misdemeanor. To be accused was to be convicted, and to be convicted was to be punished; the one always following the other with immutable certainty. To escape punishment was to escape accusation; and few slaves had the fortune to do either, under the overseership of Mr. Gore. He was just proud enough to demand the most debasing homage of the slave, and quite servile enough to crouch, himself, at the feet of the master. He was ambitious enough to be contented with nothing short of the highest rank of overseers, and persevering enough to reach the height of his ambition. He was cruel enough to inflict the severest punishment, artful enough to descend to the lowest trickery, and obdurate enough to be insensible to the voice of a reproving conscience. He was, of all the overseers, the most dreaded by the slaves. His presence was painful; his eye flashed confusion; and seldom was his sharp, shrill voice heard, without producing horror and trembling in their ranks.

Mr. Gore was a grave man, and, though a young man, he indulged in no jokes, said no funny words, seldom smiled. His words were in perfect keeping with his looks, and his looks were in perfect keeping with his words. Overseers will sometimes indulge in a witty word, even with the slaves; not so with Mr. Gore. He spoke but to command, and commanded but to be obeyed; he dealt sparingly with his words, and bountifully with his whip, never using the former where the latter would answer as well. When he whipped, he seemed to do so from a sense of duty, and feared no consequences. He did nothing reluctantly, no matter how disagreeable; always at his post, never inconsistent. He never promised but to fulfil. He was, in a word, a man of the most inflexible firmness and stone-like coolness.

His savage barbarity was equalled only by the consummate coolness with which he committed the grossest and most savage deeds upon the slaves

under his charge. Mr. Gore once undertook to whip one of Colonel Lloyd's slaves, by the name of Demby. He had given Demby but few stripes, when, to get rid of the scourging, he ran and plunged himself into a creek, and stood there at the depth of his shoulders, refusing to come out. Mr. Gore told him that he would give him three calls, and that, if he did not come out at the third call, he would shoot him. The first call was given. Demby made no response, but stood his ground. The second and third calls were given with the same result. Mr. Gore then, without consultation or deliberation with any one, not even giving Demby an additional call, raised his musket to his face, taking deadly aim at his standing victim, and in an instant poor Demby was no more. His mangled body sank out of sight, and blood and brains marked the water where he had stood.

A thrill of horror flashed through every soul upon the plantation, excepting Mr. Gore. He alone seemed cool and collected. He was asked by Colonel Lloyd and my old master, why he resorted to this extraordinary expedient. His reply was, (as well as I can remember,) that Demby had become unmanageable. He was setting a dangerous example to the other slaves,—one which, if suffered to pass without some such demonstration on his part, would finally lead to the total subversion of all rule and order upon the plantation. He argued that if one slave refused to be corrected, and escaped with his life, the other slaves would soon copy the example; the result of which would be, the freedom of the slaves, and the enslavement of the whites. Mr. Gore's defence was satisfactory. He was continued in his station as overseer upon the home plantation. His fame as an overseer went abroad. His horrid crime was not even submitted to judicial investigation. It was committed in the presence of slaves, and they of course could neither institute a suit, nor testify against him; and thus the guilty perpetrator of one of the bloodiest and most foul murders goes unwhipped of justice, and uncensured by the community in which he lives. Mr. Gore lived in St. Michael's, Talbot county, Maryland, when I left there; and if he is still alive, he very probably lives there now; and if so, he is now, as he was then, as highly esteemed and as much respected as though his guilty soul had not been stained with his brother's blood.

I speak advisedly when I say this,—that killing a slave, or any colored person, in Talbot county, Maryland, is not treated as a crime, either by the courts or the community. Mr. Thomas Lanman, of St. Michael's, killed two slaves, one of whom he killed with a hatchet, by knocking his brains out. He used to boast of the commission of the awful and bloody deed. I have heard

him do so laughingly, saying, among other things, that he was the only benefactor of his country in the company, and that when others would do as much as he had done, we should be relieved of "the d—d niggers."

The wife of Mr. Giles Hicks, living but a short distance from where I used to live, murdered my wife's cousin, a young girl between fifteen and sixteen years of age, mangling her person in the most horrible manner, breaking her nose and breastbone with a stick, so that the poor girl expired in a few hours afterward. She was immediately buried, but had not been in her untimely grave but a few hours before she was taken up and examined by the coroner, who decided that she had come to her death by severe beating. The offence for which this girl was thus murdered was this:—She had been set that night to mind Mrs. Hicks's baby, and during the night she fell asleep, and the baby cried. She, having lost her rest for several nights previous, did not hear the crying. They were both in the room with Mrs. Hicks. Mrs. Hicks, finding the girl slow to move, jumped from her bed, seized an oak stick of wood by the fireplace, and with it broke the girl's nose and breastbone, and thus ended her life. I will not say that this most horrid murder produced no sensation in the community. It did produce sensation, but not enough to bring the murderess to punishment. There was a warrant issued for her arrest, but it was never served. Thus she escaped not only punishment, but even the pain of being arraigned before a court for her horrid crime.

Whilst I am detailing bloody deeds which took place during my stay on Colonel Lloyd's plantation, I will briefly narrate another, which occurred about the same time as the murder of Demby by Mr. Gore.

Colonel Lloyd's slaves were in the habit of spending a part of their nights and Sundays in fishing for oysters, and in this way made up the deficiency of their scanty allowance. An old man belonging to Colonel Lloyd, while thus engaged, happened to get beyond the limits of Colonel Lloyd's, and on the premises of Mr. Beal Bondly. At this trespass, Mr. Bondly took offence, and with his musket came down to the shore, and blew its deadly contents into the poor old man.

Mr. Bondly came over to see Colonel Lloyd the next day, whether to pay him for his property, or to justify himself in what he had done, I know not. At any rate, this whole fiendish transaction was soon hushed up. There was very little said about it at all, and nothing done. It was a common saying, even among little white boys, that it was worth a half-cent to kill a "nigger," and a half-cent to bury one.

the days of the month, nor the months of the year. On setting sail, I walked aft, and gave to Colonel Lloyd's plantation what I hoped would be the last look. I then placed myself in the bows of the sloop, and there spent the remainder of the day in looking ahead, interesting myself in what was in the distance rather than in things near by or behind.

In the afternoon of that day, we reached Annapolis, the capital of the State. We stopped but a few moments, so that I had no time to go on shore. It was the first large town that I had ever seen, and though it would look small compared with some of our New England factory villages, I thought it a wonderful place for its size—more imposing even than the Great House Farm!

We arrived at Baltimore early on Sunday morning, landing at Smith's Wharf, not far from Bowley's Wharf. We had on board the sloop a large flock of sheep; and after aiding in driving them to the slaughterhouse of Mr. Curtis on Louden Slater's Hill, I was conducted by Rich, one of the hands belonging on board of the sloop, to my new home in Alliciana Street, near Mr. Gardner's ship-yard, on Fells Point.

Mr. and Mrs. Auld were both at home, and met me at the door with their little son Thomas, to take care of whom I had been given. And here I saw what I had never seen before; it was a white face beaming with the most kindly emotions; it was the face of my new mistress, Sophia Auld. I wish I could describe the rapture that flashed through my soul as I beheld it. It was a new and strange sight to me, brightening up my pathway with the light of happiness. Little Thomas was told, there was his Freddy,—and I was told to take care of little Thomas; and thus I entered upon the duties of my new home with the most cheering prospect ahead.

I look upon my departure from Colonel Lloyd's plantation as one of the most interesting events of my life. It is possible, and even quite probable, that but for the mere circumstance of being removed from that plantation to Baltimore, I should have to-day, instead of being here seated by my own table, in the enjoyment of freedom and the happiness of home, writing this Narrative, been confined in the galling chains of slavery. Going to live at Baltimore laid the foundation, and opened the gateway, to all my subsequent prosperity. I have ever regarded it as the first plain manifestation of that kind providence which has ever since attended me, and marked my life with so many favors. I regarded the selection of myself as being somewhat remarkable. There were a number of slave children that might have been sent from the plantation to Baltimore. There were those younger, those older, and those

The Narrative of the Life of Frederick Douglass, An American Slave.

CHAPTER I

I WAS BORN in Tuckahoe, near Hillsborough, and about twelve miles from Easton, in Talbot county, Maryland. I have no accurate knowledge of my age, never having seen any authentic record containing it. By far the larger part of the slaves know as little of their ages as horses know of theirs, and it is the wish of most masters within my knowledge to keep their slaves thus ignorant. I do not remember to have ever met a slave who could tell of his birthday. They seldom come nearer to it than planting-time, harvest-time, cherry-time, spring-time, or fall-time. A want of information concerning my own was a source of unhappiness to me even during childhood. The white children could tell their ages. I could not tell why I ought to be deprived of the same privilege. I was not allowed to make any inquiries of my master concerning it. He deemed all such inquiries on the part of a slave improper and impertinent, and evidence of a restless spirit. The nearest estimate I can give makes me now between twenty-seven and twenty-eight years of age. I come to this, from hearing my master say, some time during 1835, I was about seventeen years old.

My mother was named Harriet Bailey. She was the daughter of Isaac and Betsey Bailey, both colored, and quite dark. My mother was of a darker complexion than either my grandmother or grand-father.

My father was a white man. He was admitted to be such by all I ever heard speak of my parentage. The opinion was also whispered that my master was my father; but of the correctness of this opinion, I know nothing; the means of knowing was withheld from me. My mother and I were separated when I was but an infant—before I knew her as my mother. It is a common custom, in the part of Maryland from which I ran away, to part children from their mothers at a very early age. Frequently, before the child has

reached its twelfth month, its mother is taken from it, and hired out on some farm a considerable distance off, and the child is placed under the care of an old woman, too old for field labor. For what this separation is done, I do not know, unless it be to hinder the development of the child's affection toward its mother, and to blunt and destroy the natural affection of the mother for the child. This is the inevitable result.

I never saw my mother, to know her as such, more than four or five times in my life; and each of these times was very short in duration, and at night. She was hired by a Mr. Stewart, who lived about twelve miles from my home. She made her journeys to see me in the night, travelling the whole distance on foot, after the performance of her day's work. She was a field hand, and a whipping is the penalty of not being in the field at sunrise, unless a slave has special permission from his or her master to the contrary—a permission which they seldom get, and one that gives to him that gives it the proud name of being a kind master. I do not recollect of ever seeing my mother by the light of day. She was with me in the night. She would lie down with me, and get me to sleep, but long before I waked she was gone. Very little communication ever took place between us. Death soon ended what little we could have while she lived, and with it her hardships and suffering. She died when I was about seven years old, on one of my master's farms, near Lee's Mill. I was not allowed to be present during her illness, at her death, or burial. She was gone long before I knew any thing about it. Never having enjoyed, to any considerable extent, her soothing presence, her tender and watchful care, I received the tidings of her death with much the same emotions I should have probably felt at the death of a stranger.

Called thus suddenly away, she left me without the slightest intimation of who my father was. The whisper that my master was my father, may or may not be true; and, true or false, it is of but little consequence to my purpose whilst the fact remains, in all its glaring odiousness, that slaveholders have ordained, and by law established, that the children of slave women shall in all cases follow the condition of their mothers; and this is done too obviously to administer to their own lusts, and make a gratification of their wicked desires profitable as well as pleasurable; for by this cunning arrangement, the slaveholder, in cases not a few, sustains to his slaves the double relation of master and father.

I know of such cases; and it is worthy of remark that such slaves invariably suffer greater hardships, and have more to contend with, than others. They are, in the first place, a constant offence to their mistress. She is ever

of the same age. I was chosen from among them all, and was the first, last, and only choice.

I may be deemed superstitious, and even egotistical, in regarding this event as a special interposition of divine Providence in my favor. But I should be false to the earliest sentiments of my soul, if I suppressed the opinion. I prefer to be true to myself, even at the hazard of incurring the ridicule of others, rather than to be false, and incur my own abhorrence. From my earliest recollection, I date the entertainment of a deep conviction that slavery would not always be able to hold me within its foul embrace; and in the darkest hours of my career in slavery, this living word of faith and spirit of hope departed not from me, but remained like ministering angels to cheer me through the gloom. This good spirit was from God, and to him I offer thanksgiving and praise.

CHAPTER VI

A NEW mistress proved to be all she appeared when I first met her at the door,—a woman of the kindest heart and finest feelings. She had never had a slave under her control previously to myself, and prior to her marriage she had been dependent upon her own industry for a living. She was by trade a weaver; and by constant application to her business, she had been in a good degree preserved from the blighting and dehumanizing effects of slavery. I was utterly astonished at her goodness. I scarcely knew how to behave towards her. She was entirely unlike any other white woman I had ever seen. I could not approach her as I was accustomed to approach other white ladies. My early instruction was all out of place. The crouching servility, usually so acceptable a quality in a slave, did not answer when manifested toward her. Her favor was not gained by it; she seemed to be disturbed by it. She did not deem it impudent or unmannerly for a slave to look her in the face. The meanest slave was put fully at ease in her presence, and none left without feeling better for having seen her. Her face was made of heavenly smiles, and her voice of tranquil music.

But, alas! this kind heart had but a short time to remain such. The fatal poison of irresponsible power was already in her hands, and soon commenced its infernal work. That cheerful eye, under the influence of slavery, soon became red with rage; that voice, made all of sweet accord, changed to

CHAPTER VII

I LIVED IN Master Hugh's family about seven years. During this time, I suc-
ceeded in learning to read and write. In accomplishing this, I was com-
pelled to resort to various stratagems. I had no regular teacher. My mistress,
who had kindly commenced to instruct me, had, in compliance with the
advice and direction of her husband, not only ceased to instruct, but had set
her face against my being instructed by any one else. It is due, however, to
my mistress to say of her, that she did not adopt this course of treatment
immediately. She at first lacked the depravity indispensable to shutting me
up in mental darkness. It was at least necessary for her to have some training
in the exercise of irresponsible power, to make her equal to the task of treat-
ing me as though I were a brute.

My mistress was, as I have said, a kind and tender-hearted woman; and
in the simplicity of her soul she commenced, when I first went to live with
her, to treat me as she supposed one human being ought to treat another. In
entering upon the duties of a slaveholder, she did not seem to perceive that I
sustained to her the relation of a mere chattel, and that for her to treat me as
a human being was not only wrong, but dangerously so. Slavery proved as
injurious to her as it did to me. When I went there, she was a pious, warm,
and tender-hearted woman. There was no sorrow or suffering for which she
had not a tear. She had bread for the hungry, clothes for the naked, and com-
fort for every mourner that came within her reach. Slavery soon proved its
ability to divest her of these heavenly qualities. Under its influence, the ten-
der heart became stone, and the lamblike disposition gave way to one of
tiger-like fierceness. The first step in her downward course was in her ceas-
ing to instruct me. She now commenced to practise her husband's precepts.
She finally became even more violent in her opposition than her husband
himself. She was not satisfied with simply doing as well as he had com-
manded; she seemed anxious to do better. Nothing seemed to make her more
angry than to see me with a newspaper. She seemed to think that here lay the
danger. I have had her rush at me with a face made all up of fury, and snatch
from me a newspaper, in a manner that fully revealed her apprehension. She
was an apt woman; and a little experience soon demonstrated, to her satis-
faction, that education and slavery were incompatible with each other.

From this time I was most narrowly watched. If I was in a separate room
any considerable length of time, I was sure to be suspected of having a book,
and was at once called to give an account of myself. All this, however, was

too late. The first step had been taken. Mistress, in teaching me the alphabet, had given me the *inch,* and no precaution could prevent me from taking the *ell.* The plan which I adopted, and the one by which I was most successful, was that of making friends of all the little white boys whom I met in the street. As many of these as I could, I converted into teachers. With their kindly aid, obtained at different times and in different places, I finally succeeded in learning to read. When I was sent of errands, I always took my book with me, and by going one part of my errand quickly, I found time to get a lesson before my return. I used also to carry bread with me, enough of which was always in the house, and to which I was always welcome; for I was much better off in this regard than many of the poor white children in our neighborhood. This bread I used to bestow upon the hungry little urchins, who, in return, would give me that more valuable bread of knowledge. I am strongly tempted to give the names of two or three of those little boys, as a testimonial of the gratitude and affection I bear them; but prudence forbids;—not that it would injure me, but it might embarrass them; for it is almost an unpardonable offence to teach slaves to read in this Christian country. It is enough to say of the dear little fellows, that they lived on Philpot Street, very near Durgin and Bailey's ship-yard. I used to talk this matter of slavery over with them. I would sometimes say to them, I wished I could be as free as they would be when they got to be men. "You will be free as soon as you are twenty-one, *but I am a slave for life!* Have not I as good a right to be free as you have?" These words used to trouble them; they would express for me the liveliest sympathy, and console me with the hope that something would occur by which I might be free.

I was now about twelve years old, and the thought of being *a slave for life* began to bear heavily upon my heart. Just about this time, I got hold of a book entitled "The Columbian Orator." Every opportunity I got, I used to read this book. Among much of other interesting matter, I found in it a dialogue between a master and his slave. The slave was represented as having run away from his master three times. The dialogue represented the conversation which took place between them, when the slave was retaken the third time. In this dialogue, the whole argument in behalf of slavery was brought forward by the master, all of which was disposed of by the slave. The slave was made to say some very smart as well as impressive things in reply to his master—things which had the desired though unexpected effect; for the conversation resulted in the voluntary emancipation of the slave on the part of the master.

In the same book, I met with one of Sheridan's mighty speeches on and in behalf of Catholic emancipation. These were choice documents to me. I read them over and over again with unabated interest. They gave tongue to interesting thoughts of my own soul, which had frequently flashed through my mind, and died away for want of utterance. The moral which I gained from the dialogue was the power of truth over the conscience of even a slave-holder. What I got from Sheridan was a bold denunciation of slavery, and a powerful vindication of human rights. The reading of these documents enabled me to utter my thoughts, and to meet the arguments brought forward to sustain slavery; but while they relieved me of one difficulty, they brought on another even more painful than the one of which I was relieved. The more I read, the more I was led to abhor and detest my enslavers. I could regard them in no other light than a band of successful robbers, who had left their homes, and gone to Africa, and stolen us from our homes, and in a strange land reduced us to slavery. I loathed them as being the meanest as well as the most wicked of men. As I read and contemplated the subject, behold! that very discontentment which Master Hugh had predicted would follow my learning to read had already come, to torment and sting my soul to unutterable anguish. As I writhed under it, I would at times feel that learning to read had been a curse rather than a blessing. It had given me a view of my wretched condition, without the remedy. It opened my eyes to the horrible pit, but to no ladder upon which to get out. In moments of agony, I envied my fellow-slaves for their stupidity. I have often wished myself a beast. I preferred the condition of the meanest reptile to my own. Any thing, no matter what, to get rid of thinking! It was this everlasting thinking of my condition that tormented me. There was no getting rid of it. It was pressed upon me by every object within sight or hearing, animate or inanimate. The silver trump of freedom had roused my soul to eternal wakefulness. Freedom now appeared, to disappear no more forever. It was heard in every sound, and seen in every thing. It was ever present to torment me with a sense of my wretched condition. I saw nothing without seeing it, I heard nothing without hearing it, and felt nothing without feeling it. It looked from every star, it smiled in every calm, breathed in every wind, and moved in every storm.

I often found myself regretting my own existence, and wishing myself dead; and but for the hope of being free, I have no doubt but that I should have killed myself, or done something for which I should have been killed. While in this state of mind, I was eager to hear any one speak of slavery. I was a ready listener. Every little while, I could hear something about the abo-

litionists. It was some time before I found what the word meant. It was always used in such connections as to make it an interesting word to me. If a slave ran away and succeeded in getting clear, or if a slave killed his master, set fire to a barn, or did any thing very wrong in the mind of a slaveholder, it was spoken of as the fruit of *abolition*. Hearing the word in this connection very often, I set about learning what it meant. The dictionary afforded me little or no help. I found it was "the act of abolishing;" but then I did not know what was to be abolished. Here I was perplexed. I did not dare to ask any one about its meaning, for I was satisfied that it was something they wanted me to know very little about. After a patient waiting, I got one of our city papers, containing an account of the number of petitions from the north, praying for the abolition of slavery in the District of Columbia, and of the slave trade between the States. From this time I understood the words *abolition* and *abolitionist*, and always drew near when that word was spoken, expecting to hear something of importance to myself and fellow-slaves. The light broke in upon me by degrees. I went one day down on the wharf of Mr. Waters; and seeing two Irishmen unloading a scow of stone, I went, unasked, and helped them. When we had finished, one of them came to me and asked me if I were a slave. I told him I was. He asked, "Are ye a slave for life?" I told him that I was. The good Irishman seemed to be deeply affected by the statement. He said to the other that it was a pity so fine a little fellow as myself should be a slave for life. He said it was a shame to hold me. They both advised me to run away to the north; that I should find friends there, and that I should be free. I pretended not to be interested in what they said, and treated them as if I did not understand them; for I feared they might be treacherous. White men have been known to encourage slaves to escape, and then, to get the reward, catch them and return them to their masters. I was afraid that these seemingly good men might use me so; but I nevertheless remembered their advice, and from that time I resolved to run away. I looked forward to a time at which it would be safe for me to escape. I was too young to think of doing so immediately; besides, I wished to learn how to write, as I might have oc-casion to write my own pass. I consoled myself with the hope that I should one day find a good chance. Meanwhile, I would learn to write.

The idea as to how I might learn to write was suggested to me by being in Durgin and Bailey's ship-yard, and frequently seeing the ship carpenters, after hewing, and getting a piece of timber ready for use, write on the timber the name of that part of the ship for which it was intended. When a piece of timber was intended for the larboard side, it would be marked thus—"L."

When a piece was for the starboard side, it would be marked thus—"S." A piece for the larboard side forward, would be marked thus—"L. F." When a piece was for starboard side forward, it would be marked thus—"S. F." For larboard aft, it would be marked thus— "L. A." For star-board aft, it would be marked thus—"S. A." I soon learned the names of these letters, and for what they were intended when placed upon a piece of timber in the ship-yard. I immediately commenced copying them, and in a short time was able to make the four letters named. After that, when I met with any boy who I knew could write, I would tell him I could write as well as he. The next word would be, "I don't believe you. Let me see you try it." I would then make the letters which I had been so fortunate as to learn, and ask him to beat that. In this way I got a good many lessons in writing, which it is quite possible I should never have gotten in any other way. During this time, my copy-book was the board fence, brick wall, and pavement; my pen and ink was a lump of chalk. With these, I learned mainly how to write. I then commenced and continued copying the Italics in Webster's Spelling Book, until I could make them all without looking on the book. By this time, my little Master Thomas had gone to school, and learned how to write, and had written over a number of copy-books. These had been brought home, and shown to some of our near neighbors, and then laid aside. My mistress used to go to class meeting at the Wilk Street meetinghouse every Monday afternoon, and leave me to take care of the house. When left thus, I used to spend the time in writing in the spaces left in Master Thomas's copy-book, copying what he had written. I continued to do this until I could write a hand very similar to that of Master Thomas. Thus, after a long, tedious effort for years, I finally succeeded in learning how to write.

CHAPTER VIII

IN A VERY short time after I went to live at Baltimore, my old master's youngest son Richard died; and in about three years and six months after his death, my old master, Captain Anthony, died, leaving only his son, Andrew, and daughter, Lucretia, to share his estate. He died while on a visit to see his daughter at Hillsborough. Cut off thus unexpectedly, he left no will as to the disposal of his property. It was therefore necessary to have a valuation of the property, that it might be equally divided between Mrs. Lucretia

and Master Andrew. I was immediately sent for, to be valued with the other property. Here again my feelings rose up in detestation of slavery. I had now a new conception of my degraded condition. Prior to this, I had become, if not insensible to my lot, at least partly so. I left Baltimore with a young heart overborne with sadness, and a soul full of apprehension. I took passage with Captain Rowe, in the schooner Wild Cat, and, after a sail of about twenty-four hours, I found myself near the place of my birth. I had now been absent from it almost, if not quite, five years. I, however, remembered the place very well. I was only about five years old when I left it, to go and live with my old master on Colonel Lloyd's plantation; so that I was now between ten and eleven years old.

We were all ranked together at the valuation. Men and women, old and young, married and single, were ranked with horses, sheep, and swine. There were horses and men, cattle and women, pigs and children, all holding the same rank in the scale of being, and were all subjected to the same narrow examination. Silvery-headed age and sprightly youth, maids and matrons, had to undergo the same indelicate inspection. At this moment, I saw more clearly than ever the brutalizing effects of slavery upon both slave and slave-holder.

After the valuation, then came the division. I have no language to express the high excitement and deep anxiety which were felt among us poor slaves during this time. Our fate for life was now to be decided. We had no more voice in that decision than the brutes among whom we were ranked. A single word from the white men was enough—against all our wishes, prayers, and entreaties—to sunder forever the dearest friends, dearest kindred, and strongest ties known to human beings. In addition to the pain of separation, there was the horrid dread of falling into the hands of Master Andrew. He was known to us all as being a most cruel wretch,—a common drunkard, who had, by his reckless mismanagement and profligate dissipation, already wasted a large portion of his father's property. We all felt that we might as well be sold at once to the Georgia traders, as to pass into his hands; for we knew that that would be our inevitable condition,—a condition held by us all in the utmost horror and dread.

I suffered more anxiety than most of my fellow-slaves. I had known what it was to be kindly treated; they had known nothing of the kind. They had seen little or nothing of the world. They were in very deed men and women of sorrow, and acquainted with grief. Their backs had been made familiar with the bloody lash, so that they had become callous; mine was yet tender;

of property; for, during this interval, a great change had taken place in Master Hugh and his once kind and affectionate wife. The influence of brandy upon him, and of slavery upon her, had effected a disastrous change in the characters of both; so that, as far as they were concerned, I thought I had little to lose by the change. But it was not to them that I was attached. It was to those little Baltimore boys that I felt the strongest attachment. I had received many good lessons from them, and was still receiving them, and the thought of leaving them was painful indeed. I was leaving, too, without the hope of ever being allowed to return. Master Thomas had said he would never let me return again. The barrier betwixt himself and brother he considered impassable.

I then had to regret that I did not at least make the attempt to carry out my resolution to run away; for the chances of success are tenfold greater from the city than from the country.

I sailed from Baltimore for St. Michael's in the sloop Amanda, Captain Edward Dodson. On my passage, I paid particular attention to the direction which the steamboats took to go to Philadelphia. I found, instead of going down, on reaching North Point they went up the bay, in a north-easterly direction. I deemed this knowledge of the utmost importance. My determination to run away was again revived. I resolved to wait only so long as the offering of a favorable opportunity. When that came, I was determined to be off.

CHAPTER IX

I HAVE NOW reached a period of my life when I can give dates. I left Baltimore, and went to live with Master Thomas Auld, at St. Michael's, in March, 1832. It was now more than seven years since I lived with him in the family of my old master, on Colonel Lloyd's plantation. We of course were now almost entire strangers to each other. He was to me a new master, and I to him a new slave. I was ignorant of his temper and disposition; he was equally so of mine. A very short time, however, brought us into full acquaintance with each other. I was made acquainted with his wife not less than with himself. They were well matched, being equally mean and cruel. I was now, for the first time during a space of more than seven years, made to feel the painful gnawings of hunger—a something which I had not experienced before since I left Colonel Lloyd's plantation. It went hard enough with me

then, when I could look back to no period at which I had enjoyed a suffi-
ciency. It was tenfold harder after living in Master Hugh's family, where I had
always had enough to eat, and of that which was good. I have said Master
Thomas was a mean man. He was so. Not to give a slave enough to eat, is
regarded as the most aggravated development of meanness even among slave-
holders. The rule is, no matter how coarse the food, only let there be enough
of it. This is the theory; and in the part of Maryland from which I came, it
is the general practice,—though there are many exceptions. Master Thomas
gave us enough of neither coarse nor fine food. There were four slaves of us
in the kitchen—my sister Eliza, my aunt Priscilla, Henny, and myself; and
we were allowed less than a half of a bushel of corn-meal per week, and very
little else, either in the shape of meat or vegetables. It was not enough for us
to subsist upon. We were therefore reduced to the wretched necessity of liv-
ing at the expense of our neighbors. This we did by begging and stealing,
whichever came handy in the time of need, the one being considered as legit-
imate as the other. A great many times have we poor creatures been nearly
perishing with hunger, when food in abundance lay mouldering in the safe
and smoke-house, and our pious mistress was aware of the fact; and yet that
mistress and her husband would kneel every morning, and pray that God
would bless them in basket and store!

Bad as all slaveholders are, we seldom meet one destitute of every element
of character commanding respect. My master was one of this rare sort. I do
not know of one single noble act ever performed by him. The leading trait
in his character was meanness; and if there were any other element in his
nature, it was made subject to this. He was mean; and, like most other mean
men, he lacked the ability to conceal his meanness. Captain Auld was not
born a slaveholder. He had been a poor man, master only of a Bay craft. He
came into possession of all his slaves by marriage; and of all men, adopted
slaveholders are the worst. He was cruel, but cowardly. He commanded with-
out firmness. In the enforcement of his rules, he was at times rigid, and at
times lax. At times, he spoke to his slaves with the firmness of Napoleon and
the fury of a demon; at other times, he might well be mistaken for an inquir-
er who had lost his way. He did nothing of himself. He might have passed
for a lion, but for his ears. In all things noble which he attempted, his own
meanness shone most conspicuous. His airs, words, and actions, were the
airs, words, and actions of born slaveholders, and, being assumed, were awk-
ward enough. He was not even a good imitator. He possessed all the dispo-
sition to deceive, but wanted the power. Having no resources within himself,

he was compelled to be the copyist of many, and being such, he was forever the victim of inconsistency; and of consequence he was an object of contempt, and was held as such even by his slaves. The luxury of having slaves of his own to wait upon him was something new and unprepared for. He was a slaveholder without the ability to hold slaves. He found himself incapable of managing his slaves either by force, fear, or fraud. We seldom called him "master;" we generally called him "Captain Auld," and were hardly disposed to title him at all. I doubt not that our conduct had much to do with making him appear awkward, and of consequence fretful. Our want of reverence for him must have perplexed him greatly. He wished to have us call him master, but lacked the firmness necessary to command us to do so. His wife used to insist upon our calling him so, but to no purpose. In August, 1832, my master attended a Methodist camp-meeting held in the Bay-side, Talbot county, and there experienced religion. I indulged a faint hope that his conversion would lead him to emancipate his slaves, and that, if he did not do this, it would, at any rate, make him more kind and humane. I was disappointed in both these respects. It neither made him to be humane to his slaves, nor to emancipate them. If it had any effect on his character, it made him more cruel and hateful in all his ways; for I believe him to have been a much worse man after his conversion than before. Prior to his conversion, he relied upon his own depravity to shield and sustain him in his savage barbarity; but after his conversion, he found religious sanction and support for his slaveholding cruelty. He made the greatest pretensions to piety. His house was the house of prayer. He prayed morning, noon, and night. He very soon distinguished himself among his brethren, and was soon made a class-leader and exhorter. His activity in revivals was great, and he proved himself an instrument in the hands of the church in converting many souls. His house was the preachers' home. They used to take great pleasure in coming there to put up; for while he starved us, he stuffed them. We have had three or four preachers there at a time. The names of those who used to come most frequently while I lived there, were Mr. Storks, Mr. Ewery, Mr. Humphry, and Mr. Hickey. I have also seen Mr. George Cookman at our house. We slaves loved Mr. Cookman. We believed him to be a good man. We thought him instrumental in getting Mr. Samuel Harrison, a very rich slaveholder, to emancipate his slaves; and by some means got the impression that he was laboring to effect the emancipation of all the slaves. When he was at our house, we were sure to be called in to prayers. When the others were there, we were sometimes called in and sometimes not. Mr. Cookman took more

notice of us than either of the other ministers. He could not come among us without betraying his sympathy for us, and, stupid as we were, we had the sagacity to see it.

While I lived with my master in St. Michael's, there was a white young man, a Mr. Wilson, who proposed to keep a Sabbath school for the instruction of such slaves as might be disposed to learn to read the New Testament. We met but three times, when Mr. West and Mr. Fairbanks, both class-leaders, with many others, came upon us with sticks and other missiles, drove us off, and forbade us to meet again. Thus ended our little Sabbath school in the pious town of St. Michael's.

I have said my master found religious sanction for his cruelty. As an example, I will state one of many facts going to prove the charge. I have seen him tie up a lame young woman, and whip her with a heavy cowskin upon her naked shoulders, causing the warm red blood to drip; and, in justification of the bloody deed, he would quote this passage of Scripture—"He that knoweth his master's will, and doeth it not, shall be beaten with many stripes."

Master would keep this lacerated young woman tied up in this horrid situation four or five hours at a time. I have known him to tie her up early in the morning, and whip her before breakfast; leave her, go to his store, return at dinner, and whip her again, cutting her in the places already made raw with his cruel lash. The secret of master's cruelty toward "Henny" is found in the fact of her being almost helpless. When quite a child, she fell into the fire, and burned herself horribly. Her hands were so burnt that she never got the use of them. She could do very little but bear heavy burdens. She was to master a bill of expense; and as he was a mean man, she was a constant offence to him. He seemed desirous of getting the poor girl out of existence. He gave her away once to his sister; but, being a poor gift, she was not disposed to keep her. Finally, my benevolent master, to use his own words, "set her adrift to take care of herself." Here was a recently-converted man, holding on upon the mother, and at the same time turning out her helpless child, to starve and die! Master Thomas was one of the many pious slaveholders who hold slaves for the very charitable purpose of taking care of them.

My master and myself had quite a number of differences. He found me unsuitable to his purpose. My city life, he said, had had a very pernicious effect upon me. It had almost ruined me for every good purpose, and fitted me for every thing which was bad. One of my greatest faults was that of letting his horse run away, and go down to his father-in-law's farm, which was

about five miles from St. Michael's. I would then have to go after it. My reason for this kind of carelessness, or carefulness, was, that I could always get something to eat when I went there. Master William Hamilton, my master's father-in-law, always gave his slaves enough to eat. I never left there hungry, no matter how great the need of my speedy return. Master Thomas at length said he would stand it no longer. I had lived with him nine months, during which time he had given me a number of severe whippings, all to no good purpose. He resolved to put me out, as he said, to be broken; and, for this purpose, he let me for one year to a man named Edward Covey. Mr. Covey was a poor man, a farm-renter. He rented the place upon which he lived, as also the hands with which he tilled it. Mr. Covey had acquired a very high reputation for breaking young slaves, and this reputation was of immense value to him. It enabled him to get his farm tilled with much less expense to himself than he could have had it done without such a reputation. Some slaveholders thought it not much loss to allow Mr. Covey to have their slaves one year, for the sake of the training to which they were subjected, without any other compensation. He could hire young help with great ease, in consequence of this reputation. Added to the natural good qualities of Mr. Covey, he was a professor of religion—a pious soul—a member and a class-leader in the Methodist church. All of this added weight to his reputation as a "nigger-breaker." I was aware of all the facts, having been made acquainted with them by a young man who had lived there. I nevertheless made the change gladly; for I was sure of getting enough to eat, which is not the smallest consideration to a hungry man.

CHAPTER X

I HAD LEFT Master Thomas's house, and went to live with Mr. Covey, on the 1st of January, 1833. I was now, for the first time in my life, a field hand. In my new employment, I found myself even more awkward than a country boy appeared to be in a large city. I had been at my new home but one week before Mr. Covey gave me a very severe whipping, cutting my back, causing the blood to run, and raising ridges on my flesh as large as my little finger. The details of this affair are as follows: Mr. Covey sent me, very early in the morning of one of our coldest days in the month of January, to the woods, to get a load of wood. He gave me a team of unbroken oxen. He told

me which was the in-hand ox, and which the off-hand one. He then tied the
end of a large rope around the horns of the in-hand ox, and gave me the
other end of it, and told me, if the oxen started to run, that I must hold on
upon the rope. I had never driven oxen before, and of course I was very awk-
ward. I, however, succeeded in getting to the edge of the woods with little
diffi- culty; but I had got a very few rods into the woods, when the oxen took
fright, and started full tilt, carrying the cart against trees, and over stumps,
in the most frightful manner. I expected every moment that my brains would
be dashed out against the trees. After running thus for a considerable dis-
tance, they finally upset the cart, dashing it with great force against a tree,
and threw themselves into a dense thicket. How I escaped death, I do not
know. There I was, entirely alone, in a thick wood, in a place new to me. My
cart was upset and shattered, my oxen were entangled among the young
trees, and there was none to help me. After a long spell of effort, I succeed-
ed in getting my cart righted, my oxen disentangled, and again yoked to the
cart. I now proceeded with my team to the place where I had, the day before,
been chopping wood, and loaded my cart pretty heavily, thinking in this way
to tame my oxen. I then proceeded on my way home. I had now consumed
one half of the day. I got out of the woods safely, and now felt out of danger.
I stopped my oxen to open the woods gate; and just as I did so, before I could
get hold of my ox-rope, the oxen again started, rushed through the gate,
catching it between the wheel and the body of the cart, tearing it to pieces,
and coming within a few inches of crushing me against the gate-post. Thus
twice, in one short day, I escaped death by the merest chance. On my return,
I told Mr. Covey what had happened, and how it happened. He ordered me
to return to the woods again immediately. I did so, and he followed on after
me. Just as I got into the woods, he came up and told me to stop my cart,
and that he would teach me how to trifle away my time, and break gates. He
then went to a large gum-tree, and with his axe cut three large switches, and,
after trimming them up neatly with his pocket-knife, he ordered me to take
off my clothes. I made him no answer, but stood with my clothes on. He
repeated his order. I still made him no answer, nor did I move to strip myself.
Upon this he rushed at me with the fierceness of a tiger, tore off my clothes,
and lashed me till he had worn out his switches, cutting me so savagely as to
leave the marks visible for a long time after. This whipping was the first of a
number just like it, and for similar offences.

I lived with Mr. Covey one year. During the first six months, of that year,
scarce a week passed without his whipping me. I was seldom free from a sore

fered me to go unpunished.

My term of actual service to Mr. Edward Covey ended on Christmas day, 1833. The days between Christmas and New Year's day are allowed as holi days; and, accordingly, we were not required to perform any labor, more than to feed and take care of the stock. This time we regarded as our own, by the grace of our masters; and we therefore used or abused it nearly as we pleased. Those of us who had families at a distance, were generally allowed to spend the whole six days in their society. This time, however, was spent in various ways. The staid, sober, thinking and industrious ones of our number would employ themselves in making corn-brooms, mats, horse-collars, and baskets; and another class of us would spend the time in hunting opossums, hares, and coons. But by far the larger part engaged in such sports and merriments as playing ball, wrestling, running foot-races, fiddling, dancing, and drinking whisky; and this latter mode of spending the time was by far the most agreeable to the feelings of our masters. A slave who would work during the holidays was considered by our masters as scarcely deserving them. He was regarded as one who rejected the favor of his master. It was deemed a disgrace not to get drunk at Christmas; and he was regarded as lazy indeed, who had not provided himself with the necessary means, during the year, to get whisky enough to last him through Christmas.

From what I know of the effect of these holidays upon the slave, I believe them to be among the most effective means in the hands of the slaveholder in keeping down the spirit of insurrection. Were the slaveholders at once to abandon this practice, I have not the slightest doubt it would lead to an immediate insurrection among the slaves. These holidays serve as conductors, or safety-valves, to carry off the rebellious spirit of enslaved humanity. But for these, the slave would be forced up to the wildest desperation; and woe betide the slaveholder, the day he ventures to remove or hinder the operation of those conductors! I warn him that, in such an event, a spirit will go forth in their midst, more to be dreaded than the most appalling earthquake.

The holidays are part and parcel of the gross fraud, wrong, and inhumanity of slavery. They are professedly a custom established by the benevolence of the slaveholders; but I undertake to say, it is the result of selfishness, and one of the grossest frauds committed upon the down-trodden slave. They do not give the slaves this time because they would not like to have their work during its continuance, but because they know it would be unsafe to deprive them of it. This will be seen by the fact, that the slaveholders like to have their slaves spend those days just in such a manner as to make them

as glad of their ending as of their beginning. Their object seems to be, to disgust their slaves with freedom, by plunging them into the lowest depths of dissipation. For instance, the slaveholders not only like to see the slave drink of his own accord, but will adopt various plans to make him drunk. One plan is, to make bets on their slaves, as to who can drink the most whisky without getting drunk; and in this way they succeed in getting whole multitudes to drink to excess. Thus, when the slave asks for virtuous freedom, the cunning slaveholder, knowing his ignorance, cheats him with a dose of vicious dissipation, artfully labelled with the name of liberty. The most of us used to drink it down, and the result was just what might be supposed; many of us were led to think that there was little to choose between liberty and slavery. We felt, and very properly too, that we had almost as well be slaves to man as to rum. So, when the holidays ended, we staggered up from the filth of our wallowing, took a long breath, and marched to the field,—feeling, upon the whole, rather glad to go, from what our master had deceived us into a belief was freedom, back to the arms of slavery.

I have said that this mode of treatment is a part of the whole system of fraud and inhumanity of slavery. It is so. The mode here adopted to disgust the slave with freedom, by allowing him to see only the abuse of it, is carried out in other things. For instance, a slave loves molasses; he steals some. His master, in many cases, goes off to town, and buys a large quantity; he returns, takes his whip, and commands the slave to eat the molasses, until the poor fellow is made sick at the very mention of it. The same mode is sometimes adopted to make the slaves refrain from asking for more food than their regular allowance. A slave runs through his allowance, and applies for more. His master is enraged at him; but, not willing to send him off without food, gives him more than is necessary, and compels him to eat it within a given time. Then, if he complains that he cannot eat it, he is said to be satisfied neither full nor fasting, and is whipped for being hard to please! I have an abundance of such illustrations of the same principle, drawn from my own observation, but think the cases I have cited sufficient. The practice is a very common one.

On the first of January, 1834, I left Mr. Covey, and went to live with Mr. William Freeland, who lived about three miles from St. Michael's. I soon found Mr. Freeland a very different man from Mr. Covey. Though not rich, he was what would be called an educated southern gentleman. Mr. Covey, as I have shown, was a well-trained negro-breaker and slave-driver. The former (slaveholder though he was) seemed to possess some regard for honor, some reverence for justice, and some respect for humanity. The latter seemed total-

want of manhood, if we submitted to our enslavement without at least one noble effort to be free. We met often, and consulted frequently, and told our hopes and fears, recounted the difficulties, real and imagined, which we should be called on to meet. At times we were almost disposed to give up, and try to content ourselves with our wretched lot; at others, we were firm and unbending in our determination to go. Whenever we suggested any plan, there was shrinking—the odds were fearful. Our path was beset with the greatest obstacles; and if we succeeded in gaining the end of it, our right to be free was yet questionable—we were yet liable to be returned to bondage. We could see no spot, this side of the ocean, where we could be free. We knew nothing about Canada. Our knowledge of the north did not extend farther than New York; and to go there, and be forever harassed with the frightful liability of being returned to slavery—with the certainty of being treated tenfold worse than before—the thought was truly a horrible one, and one which it was not easy to overcome. The case sometimes stood thus: At every gate through which we were to pass, we saw a watchman—at every ferry a guard—on every bridge a sentinel—and in every wood a patrol. We were hemmed in upon every side. Here were the difficulties, real or imagined—the good to be sought, and the evil to be shunned. On the one hand, there stood slavery, a stern reality, glaring frightfully upon us,—its robes already crimsoned with the blood of millions, and even now feasting itself greedily upon our own flesh. On the other hand, away back in the dim distance, under the flickering light of the north star, behind some craggy hill or snow-covered mountain, stood a doubtful freedom—half frozen—beckoning us to come and share its hospitality. This in itself was sometimes enough to stagger us; but when we permitted ourselves to survey the road, we were frequently appalled. Upon either side we saw grim death, assuming the most horrid shapes. Now it was starvation, causing us to eat our own flesh;—now we were contending with the waves, and were drowned;—now we were overtaken, and torn to pieces by the fangs of the terrible bloodhound. We were stung by scorpions, chased by wild beasts, bitten by snakes, and finally, after having nearly reached the desired spot,—after swimming rivers, encountering wild beasts, sleeping in the woods, suffering hunger and nakedness,—we were overtaken by our pursuers, and, in our resistance, we were shot dead upon the spot! I say, this picture sometimes appalled us, and made us

> "rather bear those ills we had,
> Than fly to others, that we knew not of."

In coming to a fixed determination to run away, we did more than Patrick Henry, when he resolved upon liberty or death. With us it was a doubtful liberty at most, and almost certain death if we failed. For my part, I should prefer death to hopeless bondage.

Sandy, one of our number, gave up the notion, but still encouraged us. Our company then consisted of Henry Harris, John Harris, Henry Bailey, Charles Roberts, and myself. Henry Bailey was my uncle, and belonged to my master. Charles married my aunt: he belonged to my master's father-in-law, Mr. William Hamilton.

The plan we finally concluded upon was, to get a large canoe belonging to Mr. Hamilton, and upon the Saturday night previous to Easter holidays, paddle directly up the Chesapeake Bay. On our arrival at the head of the bay, a distance of seventy or eighty miles from where we lived, it was our purpose to turn our canoe adrift, and follow the guidance of the north star till we got beyond the limits of Maryland. Our reason for taking the water route was, that we were less liable to be suspected as runaways; we hoped to be regarded as fishermen; whereas, if we should take the land route, we should be subjected to interruptions of almost every kind. Any one having a white face, and being so disposed, could stop us, and subject us to examination.

The week before our intended start, I wrote several protections, one for each of us. As well as I can remember, they were in the following words, to wit:—

"This is to certify that I, the undersigned, have given the bearer, my servant, full liberty to go to Baltimore, and spend the Easter holidays. Written with mine own hand, &c., 1835.

"WILLIAM HAMILTON,
"Near St. Michael's, in Talbot county, Maryland."

We were not going to Baltimore; but, in going up the bay, we went toward Baltimore, and these protections were only intended to protect us while on the bay.

As the time drew near for our departure, our anxiety became more and more intense. It was truly a matter of life and death with us. The strength of our determination was about to be fully tested. At this time, I was very active in explaining every difficulty, removing every doubt, dispelling every fear, and inspiring all with the firmness indispensable to success in our undertak-

ing; assuring them that half was gained the instant we made the move; we had talked long enough; we were now ready to move; if not now, we never should be; and if we did not intend to move now, we had as well fold our arms, sit down, and acknowledge ourselves fit only to be slaves. This, none of us were prepared to acknowledge. Every man stood firm; and at our last meeting, we pledged ourselves afresh, in the most solemn manner, that, at the time appointed, we would certainly start in pursuit of freedom. This was in the middle of the week, at the end of which we were to be off. We went, as usual, to our several fields of labor, but with bosoms highly agitated with thoughts of our truly hazardous undertaking. We tried to conceal our feelings as much as possible; and I think we succeeded very well.

After a painful waiting, the Saturday morning, whose night was to witness our departure, came. I hailed it with joy, bring what of sadness it might. Friday night was a sleepless one for me. I probably felt more anxious than the rest, because I was, by common consent, at the head of the whole affair. The responsibility of success or failure lay heavily upon me. The glory of the one, and the confusion of the other, were alike mine. The first two hours of that morning were such as I never experienced before, and hope never to again. Early in the morning, we went, as usual, to the field. We were spreading manure; and all at once, while thus engaged, I was overwhelmed with an indescribable feeling, in the fulness of which I turned to Sandy, who was near by, and said, "We are betrayed!" "Well," said he, "that thought has this moment struck me." We said no more. I was never more certain of any thing.

The horn was blown as usual, and we went up from the field to the house for breakfast. I went for the form, more than for want of any thing to eat that morning. Just as I got to the house, in looking out at the lane gate, I saw four white men, with two colored men. The white men were on horseback, and the colored ones were walking behind, as if tied. I watched them a few moments till they got up to our lane gate. Here they halted, and tied the colored men to the gate-post. I was not yet certain as to what the matter was. In a few moments, in rode Mr. Hamilton, with a speed betokening great excitement. He came to the door, and inquired if Master William was in. He was told he was at the barn. Mr. Hamilton, without dismounting, rode up to the barn with extraordinary speed. In a few moments, he and Mr. Freeland returned to the house. By this time, the three constables rode up, and in great haste dismounted, tied their horses, and met Master William and Mr. Hamilton returning from the barn; and after talking awhile, they all walked up to the kitchen door. There was no one in the kitchen but myself and John.

Henry and Sandy were up at the barn. Mr. Freeland put his head in at the door, and called me by name, saying, there were some gentlemen at the door who wished to see me. I stepped to the door, and inquired what they wanted. They at once seized me, and, without giving me any satisfaction, tied me—lashing my hands closely together. I insisted upon knowing what the matter was. They at length said, that they had learned I had been in a "scrape," and that I was to be examined before my master; and if their information proved false, I should not be hurt.

In a few moments, they succeeded in tying John. They then turned to Henry, who had by this time returned, and commanded him to cross his hands. "I won't!" said Henry, in a firm tone, indicating his readiness to meet the consequences of his refusal. "Won't you?" said Tom Graham, the constable. "No, I won't!" said Henry, in a still stronger tone. With this, two of the constables pulled out their shining pistols, and swore, by their Creator, that they would make him cross his hands or kill him. Each cocked his pistol, and, with fingers on the trigger, walked up to Henry, saying, at the same time, if he did not cross his hands, they would blow his damned heart out. "Shoot me, shoot me!" said Henry; "you can't kill me but once. Shoot, shoot,—and be damned! *I won't be tied!*" This he said in a tone of loud defiance; and at the same time, with a motion as quick as lightning, he with one single stroke dashed the pistols from the hand of each constable. As he did this, all hands fell upon him, and, after beating him some time, they finally overpowered him, and got him tied.

During the scuffle, I managed, I know not how, to get my pass out, and, without being discovered, put it into the fire. We were all now tied; and just as we were to leave for Easton jail, Betsy Freeland, mother of William Freeland, came to the door with her hands full of biscuits, and divided them between Henry and John. She then delivered herself of a speech, to the following effect:—addressing herself to me, she said, "*You devil! You yellow devil!* it was you that put it into the heads of Henry and John to run away. But for you, you long-legged mulatto devil! Henry nor John would never have thought of such a thing." I made no reply, and was immediately hurried off towards St. Michael's. Just a moment previous to the scuffle with Henry, Mr. Hamilton suggested the propriety of making a search for the protections which he had understood Frederick had written for himself and the rest. But, just at the moment he was about carrying his proposal into effect, his aid was needed in helping to tie Henry; and the excitement attending the scuffle caused them either to forget, or to deem it unsafe, under the circumstances,

Mr. Gardner were, to do whatever the carpenters commanded me to do. This was placing me at the beck and call of about seventy-five men. I was to regard all these as masters. Their word was to be my law. My situation was a most trying one. At times I needed a dozen pair of hands. I was called a dozen ways in the space of a single minute. Three or four voices would strike my ear at the same moment. It was—"Fred., come help me to cant this timber here."—"Fred., come carry this timber yonder."—"Fred., bring that roller here."—"Fred., go get a fresh can of water."—"Fred., come help saw off the end of this timber."—"Fred., go quick, and get the crowbar."—"Fred., hold on the end of this fall."—"Fred., go to the blacksmith's shop, and get a new punch."—"Hurra, Fred.! run and bring me a cold chisel."—"I say, Fred., bear a hand, and get up a fire as quick as lightning under that steam-box."—"Halloo, nigger! come, turn this grindstone."—"Come, come! move, move! and *bowse* this timber forward."—"I say, darky, blast your eyes, why don't you heat up some pitch?"—"Halloo! halloo! halloo!" (Three voices at the same time.) "Come here!—Go there!—Hold on where you are! Damn you, if you move, I'll knock your brains out!"

This was my school for eight months; and I might have remained there longer, but for a most horrid fight I had with four of the white apprentices, in which my left eye was nearly knocked out, and I was horribly mangled in other respects. The facts in the case were these: Until a very little while after I went there, white and black ship-carpenters worked side by side, and no one seemed to see any impropriety in it. All hands seemed to be very well satisfied. Many of the black carpenters were freemen. Things seemed to be going on very well. All at once, the white carpenters knocked off, and said they would not work with free colored workmen. Their reason for this, as alleged, was, that if free colored carpenters were encouraged, they would soon take the trade into their own hands, and poor white men would be thrown out of employment. They therefore felt called upon at once to put a stop to it. And, taking advantage of Mr. Gardner's necessities, they broke off, swearing they would work no longer, unless he would discharge his black carpenters. Now, though this did not extend to me in form, it did reach me in fact. My fellow-apprentices very soon began to feel it degrading to them to work with me. They began to put on airs, and talk about the "niggers" taking the country, saying we all ought to be killed; and, being encouraged by the journey-men, they commenced making my condition as hard as they could, by hectoring me around, and sometimes striking me. I, of course, kept the vow I made after the fight with Mr. Covey, and struck back again, regard-

less of consequences; and while I kept them from combining, I succeeded very well; for I could whip the whole of them, taking them separately. They, however, at length combined, and came upon me, armed with sticks, stones, and heavy handspikes. One came in front with a half brick. There was one at each side of me, and one behind me. While I was attending to those in front, and on either side, the one behind ran up with the hand-spike, and struck me a heavy blow upon the head. It stunned me. I fell, and with this they all ran upon me, and fell to beating me with their fists. I let them lay on for a while, gathering strength. In an instant, I gave a sudden surge, and rose to my hands and knees. Just as I did that, one of their number gave me, with his heavy boot, a powerful kick in the left eye. My eyeball seemed to have burst. When they saw my eye closed, and badly swollen, they left me. With this I seized the hand-spike, and for a time pursued them. But here the carpenters interfered, and I thought I might as well give it up. It was impossible to stand my hand against so many. All this took place in sight of not less than fifty white ship-carpenters, and not one interposed a friendly word; but some cried, "Kill the damned nigger! Kill him! kill him! He struck a white person." I found my only chance for life was in flight. I succeeded in getting away without an additional blow, and barely so; for to strike a white man is death by Lynch law,—and that was the law in Mr. Gardner's ship-yard; nor is there much of any other out of Mr. Gardner's ship-yard.

I went directly home, and told the story of my wrongs to Master Hugh; and I am happy to say of him, irreligious as he was, his conduct was heavenly, compared with that of his brother Thomas under similar circumstances. He listened attentively to my narration of the circumstances leading to the savage outrage, and gave many proofs of his strong indignation at it. The heart of my once overkind mistress was again melted into pity. My puffed-out eye and blood-covered face moved her to tears. She took a chair by me, washed the blood from my face, and, with a mother's tenderness, bound up my head, covering the wounded eye with a lean piece of fresh beef. It was almost compensation for my suffering to witness, once more, a manifestation of kindness from this, my once affectionate old mistress. Master Hugh was very much enraged. He gave expression to his feelings by pouring out curses upon the heads of those who did the deed. As soon as I got a little the better of my bruises, he took me with him to Esquire Watson's, on Bond Street, to see what could be done about the matter. Mr. Watson inquired who saw the assault committed. Master Hugh told him it was done in Mr. Gardner's ship-yard at midday, where there were a large company of men at work. "As to

western friends have conducted what they call the *underground railroad*, but which I think, by their open declarations, has been made most emphatically the *upperground railroad*. I honor those good men and women for their noble daring, and applaud them for willingly subjecting themselves to bloody persecution, by openly avowing their participation in the escape of slaves. I, however, can see very little good resulting from such a course, either to themselves or the slaves escaping; while, upon the other hand, I see and feel assured that those open declarations are a positive evil to the slaves remaining, who are seeking to escape. They do nothing towards enlightening the slave, whilst they do much towards enlightening the master. They stimulate him to greater watchfulness, and enhance his power to capture his slave. We owe something to the slave south of the line as well as to those north of it; and in aiding the latter on their way to freedom, we should be careful to do nothing which would be likely to hinder the former from escaping from slavery. I would keep the merciless slaveholder profoundly ignorant of the means of flight adopted by the slave. I would leave him to imagine himself surrounded by myriads of invisible tormentors, ever ready to snatch from his infernal grasp his trembling prey. Let him be left to feel his way in the dark; let darkness commensurate with his crime hover over him; and let him feel that at every step he takes, in pursuit of the flying bondman, he is running the frightful risk of having his hot brains dashed out by an invisible agency. Let us render the tyrant no aid; let us not hold the light by which he can trace the footprints of our flying brother. But enough of this. I will now proceed to the statement of those facts, connected with my escape, for which I am alone responsible, and for which no one can be made to suffer but myself.

In the early part of the year 1838, I became quite restless. I could see no reason why I should, at the end of each week, pour the reward of my toil into the purse of my master. When I carried to him my weekly wages, he would, after counting the money, look me in the face with a robber-like fierceness, and ask, "Is this all?" He was satisfied with nothing less than the last cent. He would, however, when I made him six dollars, sometimes give me six cents, to encourage me. It had the opposite effect. I regarded it as a sort of admission of my right to the whole. The fact that he gave me any part of my wages was proof, to my mind, that he believed me entitled to the whole of them. I always felt worse for having received any thing; for I feared that the giving me a few cents would ease his conscience, and make him feel himself to be a pretty honorable sort of robber. My discontent grew upon me. I was ever on the look-out for means of escape; and, finding no direct means, I determined

to try to hire my time, with a view of getting money with which to make my escape. In the spring of 1838, when Master Thomas came to Baltimore to purchase his spring goods, I got an opportunity, and applied to him to allow me to hire my time. He unhesitatingly refused my request, and told me this was another stratagem by which to escape. He told me I could go nowhere but that he could get me; and that, in the event of my running away, he should spare no pains in his efforts to catch me. He exhorted me to content myself, and be obedient. He told me, if I would be happy, I must lay out no plans for the future. He said, if I behaved myself properly, he would take care of me. Indeed, he advised me to complete thoughtlessness of the future, and taught me to depend solely upon him for happiness. He seemed to see fully the pressing necessity of setting aside my intellectual nature, in order to contentment in slavery. But in spite of him, and even in spite of myself, I continued to think, and to think about the injustice of my enslavement, and the means of escape.

About two months after this, I applied to Master Hugh for the privilege of hiring my time. He was not acquainted with the fact that I had applied to Master Thomas, and had been refused. He too, at first, seemed disposed to refuse; but, after some reflection, he granted me the privilege, and proposed the following terms: I was to be allowed all my time, make all contracts with those for whom I worked, and find my own employment; and, in return for this liberty, I was to pay him three dollars at the end of each week; find myself in calking tools, and in board and clothing. My board was two dollars and a half per week. This, with the wear and tear of clothing and calking tools, made my regular expenses about six dollars per week. This amount I was compelled to make up, or relinquish the privilege of hiring my time. Rain or shine, work or no work, at the end of each week the money must be forthcoming, or I must give up my privilege. This arrangement, it will be perceived, was decidedly in my master's favor. It relieved him of all need of looking after me. His money was sure. He received all the benefits of slave-holding without its evils; while I endured all the evils of a slave, and suffered all the care and anxiety of a freeman. I found it a hard bargain. But, hard as it was, I thought it better than the old mode of getting along. It was a step towards freedom to be allowed to bear the responsibilities of a freeman, and I was determined to hold on upon it. I bent myself to the work of making money. I was ready to work at night as well as day, and by the most untiring perseverance and industry, I made enough to meet my expenses, and lay up a little money every week. I went on thus from May till August. Master Hugh

then refused to allow me to hire my time longer. The ground for his refusal was a failure on my part, one Saturday night, to pay him for my week's time. This failure was occasioned by my attending a camp meeting about ten miles from Baltimore. During the week, I had entered into an engagement with a number of young friends to start from Baltimore to the camp ground early Saturday evening; and being detained by my employer, I was unable to get down to Master Hugh's without disappointing the company. I knew that Master Hugh was in no special need of the money that night. I therefore decided to go to camp meeting, and upon my return pay him the three dollars. I staid at the camp meeting one day longer than I intended when I left. But as soon as I returned, I called upon him to pay him what he considered his due. I found him very angry; he could scarce restrain his wrath. He said he had a great mind to give me a severe whipping. He wished to know how I dared go out of the city without asking his permission. I told him I hired my time and while I paid him the price which he asked for it, I did not know that I was bound to ask him when and where I should go. This reply troubled him; and, after reflecting a few moments, he turned to me, and said I should hire my time no longer; that the next thing he should know of, I would be running away. Upon the same plea, he told me to bring my tools and clothing home forthwith. I did so; but instead of seeking work, as I had been accustomed to do previously to hiring my time, I spent the whole week without the performance of a single stroke of work. I did this in retaliation. Saturday night, he called upon me as usual for my week's wages. I told him I had no wages; I had done no work that week. Here we were upon the point of coming to blows. He raved, and swore his determination to get hold of me. I did not allow myself a single word; but was resolved, if he laid the weight of his hand upon me, it should be blow for blow. He did not strike me, but told me that he would find me in constant employment in future. I thought the matter over during the next day, Sunday, and finally resolved upon the third day of September, as the day upon which I would make a second attempt to secure my freedom. I now had three weeks during which to prepare for my journey. Early on Monday morning, before Master Hugh had time to make any engagement for me, I went out and got employment of Mr. Butler, at his ship-yard near the drawbridge, upon what is called the City Block, thus making it unnecessary for him to seek employment for me. At the end of the week, I brought him between eight and nine dollars. He seemed very well pleased, and asked why I did not do the same the week before. He little knew what my plans were. My object in working steadily

was to remove any suspicion he might entertain of my intent to run away; and in this I succeeded admirably. I suppose he thought I was never better satisfied with my condition than at the very time during which I was planning my escape. The second week passed, and again I carried him my full wages; and so well pleased was he, that he gave me twenty-five cents, (quite a large sum for a slaveholder to give a slave,) and bade me to make a good use of it. I told him I would.

Things went on without very smoothly indeed, but within there was trouble. It is impossible for me to describe my feelings as the time of my contemplated start drew near. I had a number of warm-hearted friends in Baltimore,—friends that I loved almost as I did my life,—and the thought of being separated from them forever was painful beyond expression. It is my opinion that thousands would escape from slavery, who now remain, but for the strong cords of affection that bind them to their friends. The thought of leaving my friends was decidedly the most painful thought with which I had to contend. The love of them was my tender point, and shook my decision more than all things else. Besides the pain of separation, the dread and apprehension of a failure exceeded what I had experienced at my first attempt. The appalling defeat I then sustained returned to torment me. I felt assured that, if I failed in this attempt, my case would be a hopeless one—it would seal my fate as a slave forever. I could not hope to get off with any thing less than the severest punishment, and being placed beyond the means of escape. It required no very vivid imagination to depict the most frightful scenes through which I should have to pass, in case I failed. The wretchedness of slavery, and the blessedness of freedom, were perpetually before me. It was life and death with me. But I remained firm, and, according to my resolution, on the third day of September, 1838, I left my chains, and succeeded in reaching New York without the slightest interruption of any kind. How I did so,—what means I adopted,—what direction I travelled, and by what mode of conveyance,—I must leave unexplained, for the reasons before mentioned.

I have been frequently asked how I felt when I found myself in a free State. I have never been able to answer the question with any satisfaction to myself. It was a moment of the highest excitement I ever experienced. I suppose I felt as one may imagine the unarmed mariner to feel when he is rescued by a friendly man-of-war from the pursuit of a pirate. In writing to a dear friend, immediately after my arrival at New York, I said I felt like one who had escaped a den of hungry lions. This state of mind, however, very

soon subsided; and I was again seized with a feeling of great insecurity and loneliness. I was yet liable to be taken back, and subjected to all the tortures of slavery. This in itself was enough to damp the ardor of my enthusiasm. But the loneliness overcame me. There I was in the midst of thousands, and yet a perfect stranger; without home and without friends, in the midst of thousands of my own brethren—children of a common Father, and yet I dared not to unfold to any one of them my sad condition. I was afraid to speak to any one for fear of speaking to the wrong one, and thereby falling into the hands of money-loving kidnappers, whose business it was to lie in wait for the panting fugitive, as the ferocious beasts of the forest lie in wait for their prey. The motto which I adopted when I started from slavery was this— "Trust no man!" I saw in every white man an enemy, and in almost every colored man cause for distrust. It was a most painful situation; and, to understand it, one must needs experience it, or imagine himself in similar circumstances. Let him be a fugitive slave in a strange land—a land given up to be the hunting- ground for slaveholders—whose inhabitants are legalized kidnappers—where he is every moment subjected to the terrible liability of being seized upon by his fellowmen, as the hideous crocodile seizes upon his prey!—I say, let him place himself in my situation—without home or friends—without money or credit—wanting shelter, and no one to give it— wanting bread, and no money to buy it,—and at the same time let him feel that he is pursued by merciless men-hunters, and in total darkness as to what to do, where to go, or where to stay,—perfectly helpless both as to the means of defence and means of escape,—in the midst of plenty, yet suffering the terrible gnawings of hunger,—in the midst of houses, yet having no home,— among fellow-men, yet feeling as if in the midst of wild beasts, whose greediness to swallow up the trembling and half-famished fugitive is only equalled by that with which the monsters of the deep swallow up the helpless fish upon which they subsist,—I say, let him be placed in this most trying situation,—the situation in which I was placed,—then, and not till then, will he fully appreciate the hardships of, and know how to sympathize with, the toil-worn and whip-scarred fugitive slave.

Thank Heaven, I remained but a short time in this distressed situation. I was relieved from it by the humane hand of Mr. DAVID RUGGLES, whose vigilance, kindness, and perseverance, I shall never forget. I am glad of an opportunity to express, as far as words can, the love and gratitude I bear him. Mr. Ruggles is now afflicted with blindness, and is himself in need of the same kind offices which he was once so forward in the performance of

toward others. I had been in New York but a few days, when Mr. Ruggles sought me out, and very kindly took me to his boarding-house at the corner of Church and Lespenard Streets. Mr. Ruggles was then very deeply engaged in the memorable *Darg* case, as well as attending to a number of other fugitive slaves, devising ways and means for their successful escape; and, though watched and hemmed in on almost every side, he seemed to be more than a match for his enemies.

Very soon after I went to Mr. Ruggles, he wished to know of me where I wanted to go; as he deemed it unsafe for me to remain in New York. I told him I was a calker, and should like to go where I could get work. I thought of going to Canada; but he decided against it, and in favor of my going to New Bedford, thinking I should be able to get work there at my trade. At this time, Anna,* my intended wife, came on; for I wrote to her immediately after my arrival at New York, (notwithstanding my homeless, houseless, and helpless condition,) informing her of my successful flight, and wishing her to come on forthwith. In a few days after her arrival, Mr. Ruggles called in the Rev. J. W. C. Pennington, who, in the presence of Mr. Ruggles, Mrs. Michaels, and two or three others, performed the marriage ceremony, and gave us a certificate, of which the following is an exact copy:—

"This may certify, that I joined together in holy matrimony Frederick Johnson** and Anna Murray, as man and wife, in the presence of Mr. David Ruggles and Mrs. Michaels.
 "JAMES W. C. PENNINGTON.
"New York, Sept. 15, 1838"

Upon receiving this certificate, and a five-dollar bill from Mr. Ruggles, I shouldered one part of our baggage, and Anna took up the other, and we set out forthwith to take passage on board of the steamboat John W. Richmond for Newport, on our way to New Bedford. Mr. Ruggles gave me a letter to a Mr. Shaw in Newport, and told me, in case my money did not serve me to New Bedford, to stop in Newport and obtain further assistance; but upon our arrival at Newport, we were so anxious to get to a place of safety, that, notwithstanding we lacked the necessary money to pay our fare, we decided to take seats in the stage, and promise to pay when we got to New Bedford. We were encouraged to do this by two excellent gentlemen, residents of New

*She was free.
**I had changed my name from Frederick *Bailey* to that of *Johnson*.

Bedford, whose names I afterward ascertained to be Joseph Ricketson and William C. Taber. They seemed at once to understand our circumstances, and gave us such assurance of their friendliness as put us fully at ease in their presence. It was good indeed to meet with such friends, at such a time. Upon reaching New Bedford, we were directed to the house of Mr. Nathan Johnson, by whom we were kindly received, and hospitably provided for. Both Mr. and Mrs. Johnson took a deep and lively interest in our welfare. They proved themselves quite worthy of the name of abolitionists. When the stage-driver found us unable to pay our fare, he held on upon our baggage as security for the debt. I had but to mention the fact to Mr. Johnson, and he forthwith advanced the money.

We now began to feel a degree of safety, and to prepare ourselves for the duties and responsibilities of a life of freedom. On the morning after our arrival at New Bedford, while at the breakfast-table, the question arose as to what name I should be called by. The name given me by my mother was, "Frederick Augustus Washington Bailey." I, however, had dispensed with the two middle names long before I left Maryland so that I was generally known by the name of "Frederick Bailey." I started from Baltimore bearing the name of "Stanley." When I got to New York, I again changed my name to "Frederick Johnson," and thought that would be the last change. But when I got to New Bedford, I found it necessary again to change my name. The reason of this necessity was, that there were so many Johnsons in New Bedford, it was already quite difficult to distinguish between them. I gave Mr. Johnson the privilege of choosing me a name, but told him he must not take from me the name of "Frederick." I must hold on to that, to preserve a sense of my identity. Mr. Johnson had just been reading the "Lady of the Lake," and at once suggested that my name be "Douglass." From that time until now I have been called "Frederick Douglass;" and as I am more widely known by that name than by either of the others, I shall continue to use it as my own.

I was quite disappointed at the general appearance of things in New Bedford. The impression which I had received respecting the character and condition of the people of the north, I found to be singularly erroneous. I had very strangely supposed, while in slavery, that few of the comforts, and scarcely any of the luxuries, of life were enjoyed at the north, compared with what were enjoyed by the slaveholders of the south. I probably came to this conclusion from the fact that northern people owned no slaves. I supposed that they were about upon a level with the non-slaveholding population of the south. I knew *they* were exceedingly poor, and I had been accustomed to

regard their poverty as the necessary consequence of their being non-slave-holders. I had somehow imbibed the opinion that, in the absence of slaves, there could be no wealth, and very little refinement. And upon coming to the north, I expected to meet with a rough, hard-handed, and uncultivated population, living in the most Spartan-like simplicity, knowing nothing of the ease, luxury, pomp, and grandeur of southern slaveholders. Such being my conjectures, any one acquainted with the appearance of New Bedford may very readily infer how palpably I must have seen my mistake.

In the afternoon of the day when I reached New Bedford, I visited the wharves, to take a view of the shipping. Here I found myself surrounded with the strongest proofs of wealth. Lying at the wharves, and riding in the stream, I saw many ships of the finest model, in the best order, and of the largest size. Upon the right and left, I was walled in by granite warehouses of the widest dimensions, stowed to their utmost capacity with the necessaries and comforts of life. Added to this, almost every body seemed to be at work, but noiselessly so, compared with what I had been accustomed to in Baltimore. There were no loud songs heard from those engaged in loading and unloading ships. I heard no deep oaths or horrid curses on the laborer. I saw no whipping of men; but all seemed to go smoothly on. Every man appeared to understand his work, and went at it with a sober, yet cheerful earnestness, which betokened the deep interest which he felt in what he was doing, as well as a sense of his own dignity as a man. To me this looked exceedingly strange. From the wharves I strolled around and over the town, gazing with wonder and admiration at the splendid churches, beautiful dwellings, and finely-cultivated gardens; evincing an amount of wealth, comfort, taste, and refinement, such as I had never seen in any part of slaveholding Maryland.

Every thing looked clean, new, and beautiful. I saw few or no dilapidated houses, with poverty-stricken inmates; no half-naked children and bare-footed women, such as I had been accustomed to see in Hillsborough, Easton, St. Michael's, and Baltimore. The people looked more able, stronger, healthier, and happier, than those of Maryland. I was for once made glad by a view of extreme wealth, without being saddened by seeing extreme poverty. But the most astonishing as well as the most interesting thing to me was the condition of the colored people, a great many of whom, like myself, had escaped thither as a refuge from the hunters of men. I found many, who had not been seven years out of their chains, living in finer houses, and evidently enjoying more of the comforts of life, than the average of slaveholders in Maryland. I will venture to assert, that my friend Mr. Nathan Johnson (of

whom I can say with a grateful heart, "I was hungry, and he gave me meat; I was thirsty, and he gave me drink; I was a stranger, and he took me in") lived in a neater house; dined at a better table; took, paid for, and read, more newspapers; better understood the moral, religious, and political character of the nation,—than nine tenths of the slaveholders in Talbot county Maryland. Yet Mr. Johnson was a working man. His hands were hardened by toil, and not his alone, but those also of Mrs. Johnson. I found the colored people much more spirited than I had supposed they would be. I found among them a determination to protect each other from the blood-thirsty kidnapper, at all hazards. Soon after my arrival, I was told of a circumstance which illustrated their spirit. A colored man and a fugitive slave were on unfriendly terms. The former was heard to threaten the latter with informing his master of his whereabouts. Straightway a meeting was called among the colored people, under the stereotyped notice, "Business of importance!" The betrayer was invited to attend. The people came at the appointed hour, and organized the meeting by appointing a very religious old gentleman as president, who, I believe, made a prayer, after which he addressed the meeting as follows: *"Friends, we have got him here, and I would recommend that you young men just take him outside the door, and kill him!"* With this, a number of them bolted at him; but they were intercepted by some more timid than themselves, and the betrayer escaped their vengeance, and has not been seen in New Bedford since. I believe there have been no more such threats, and should there be here-after, I doubt not that death would be the consequence.

I found employment, the third day after my arrival, in stowing a sloop with a load of oil. It was new, dirty, and hard work for me; but I went at it with a glad heart and a willing hand. I was now my own master. It was a happy moment, the rapture of which can be understood only by those who have been slaves. It was the first work, the reward of which was to be entirely my own. There was no Master Hugh standing ready, the moment I earned the money, to rob me of it. I worked that day with a pleasure I had never before experienced. I was at work for myself and newly-married wife. It was to me the starting-point of a new existence. When I got through with that job, I went in pursuit of a job of calking; but such was the strength of prejudice against color, among the white calkers, that they refused to work with me, and of course I could get no employment.* Finding my trade of no immediate benefit, I threw off my

* I am told that colored persons can now get employment at calking in New Bedford—a result of anti-slavery effort.

calking habiliments, and prepared myself to do any kind of work I could get to do. Mr. Johnson kindly let me have his wood-horse and saw, and I very soon found myself a plenty of work. There was no work too hard—none too dirty. I was ready to saw wood, shovel coal, carry wood, sweep the chimney, or roll oil casks,—all of which I did for nearly three years in New Bedford, before I became known to the anti-slavery world.

In about four months after I went to New Bedford, there came a young man to me, and inquired if I did not wish to take the "Liberator." I told him I did; but, just having made my escape from slavery, I remarked that I was unable to pay for it then. I, however, finally became a subscriber to it. The paper came, and I read it from week to week with such feelings as it would be quite idle for me to attempt to describe. The paper became my meat and my drink. My soul was set all on fire. Its sympathy for my brethren in bonds—its scathing denunciations of slaveholders—its faithful exposures of slavery—and its powerful attacks upon the upholders of the institution— sent a thrill of joy through my soul, such as I had never felt before!

I had not long been a reader of the "Liberator," before I got a pretty correct idea of the principles, measures and spirit of the anti-slavery reform. I took right hold of the cause. I could do but little; but what I could, I did with a joyful heart, and never felt happier than when in an anti-slavery meeting. I seldom had much to say at the meetings, because what I wanted to say was said so much better by others. But, while attending an anti-slavery convention at Nantucket, on the 11th of August, 1841, I felt strongly moved to speak, and was at the same time much urged to do so by Mr. William C. Coffin, a gentleman who had heard me speak in the colored people's meeting at New Bedford. It was a severe cross, and I took it up reluctantly. The truth was, I felt myself a slave, and the idea of speaking to white people weighed me down. I spoke but a few moments, when I felt a degree of freedom, and said what I desired with considerable ease. From that time until now, I have been engaged in pleading the cause of my brethren—with what success, and with what devotion, I leave those acquainted with my labors to decide.

APPENDIX

I FIND, since reading over the foregoing Narrative, that I have, in several instances, spoken in such a tone and manner, respecting religion, as may possibly lead those unacquainted with my religious views to suppose me an opponent of all religion. To remove the liability of such misapprehension, I deem it proper to append the following brief explanation. What I have said respecting and against religion, I mean strictly to apply to the *slaveholding religion* of this land, and with no possible reference to Christianity proper; for, between the Christianity of this land, and the Christianity of Christ, I recognize the widest possible difference—so wide, that to receive the one as good, pure, and holy, is of necessity to reject the other as bad, corrupt, and wicked. To be the friend of the one, is of necessity to be the enemy of the other. I love the pure, peaceable, and impartial Christianity of Christ: I therefore hate the corrupt, slaveholding, women-whipping, cradle-plundering, partial and hypocritical Christianity of this land. Indeed, I can see no reason, but the most deceitful one, for calling the religion of this land Christianity. I look upon it as the climax of all misnomers, the boldest of all frauds, and the grossest of all libels. Never was there a clearer case of "stealing the livery of the court of heaven to serve the devil in." I am filled with unutterable loathing when I contemplate the religious pomp and show, together with the horrible inconsistencies, which every where surround me. We have men-stealers for ministers, women-whippers for missionaries, and cradle-plunderers for church members. The man who wields the blood-clotted cowskin during the week fills the pulpit on Sunday, and claims to be a minister of the meek and lowly Jesus. The man who robs me of my earnings at the end of each week meets me as a class-leader on Sunday morning, to show me the way of life, and the path of salvation. He who sells my sister, for purposes of prostitution, stands forth as the pious advocate of purity. He who proclaims it a religious duty to read the Bible denies me the right of learning to read the name of the God who made me. He who is the religious advocate of marriage robs whole millions of its sacred influence, and leaves them to the ravages of wholesale pollution. The warm defender of the sacredness of the family relation is the same that scatters whole families,—sundering husbands and wives, parents and children, sisters and brothers,—leaving the hut vacant, and the hearth desolate. We see the thief preaching against theft, and the adulterer against adultery. We have men sold to build churches, women

sold to support the gospel, and babes sold to purchase Bibles for the *poor hea-*
then! All for the glory of God and the good of souls! The slave auctioneer's bell
and the church-going bell chime in with each other, and the bitter cries of
the heart-broken slave are drowned in the religious shouts of his pious mas-
ter. Revivals of religion and revivals in the slave-trade go hand in hand
together. The slave prison and the church stand near each other. The clank-
ing of fetters and the rattling of chains in the prison, and the pious psalm and
solemn prayer in the church, may be heard at the same time. The dealers in
the bodies and souls of men erect their stand in the presence of the pulpit,
and they mutually help each other. The dealer gives his blood-stained gold to
support the pulpit, and the pulpit, in return, covers his infernal business with
the garb of Christianity. Here we have religion and robbery the allies of each
other—devils dressed in angels' robes, and hell presenting the semblance of
paradise.

> "Just God! and these are they,
> Who minister at thine altar, God of right!
> Men who their hands, with prayer and blessing, lay
> On Israel's ark of light.
>
> "What! preach, and kidnap men?
> Give thanks, and rob thy own afflicted poor?
> Talk of thy glorious liberty, and then
> Bolt hard the captive's door?
>
> "What! servants of thy own
> Merciful Son, who came to seek and save
> The homeless and the outcast, fettering down
> The tasked and plundered slave!
>
> "Pilate and Herod friends!
> Chief priests and rulers, as of old, combine!
> Just God and holy! is that church which lends
> Strength to the spoiler thine?"

The Christianity of America is a Christianity, of whose votaries it may be
as truly said, as it was of the ancient scribes and Pharisees, "They bind heavy
burdens, and grievous to be borne, and lay them on men's shoulders, but they

themselves will not move them with one of their fingers. All their works they do for to be seen of men.—synagogues, . . . and to be called of men, Rabbi, Rabbi.—But woe unto you, scribes and Pharisees, hypocrites! for ye shut up the kingdom of heaven against men; for ye neither go in yourselves, neither suffer ye them that are entering to go in. Ye devour widows' houses, and for a pretence make long prayers; therefore ye shall receive the greater damnation. Ye compass sea and land to make one proselyte, and when he is made, ye make him twofold more the child of hell than yourselves.—Woe unto you, scribes and Pharisees, hypocrites! for ye pay tithe of mint, and anise, and cumin, and have omitted the weightier matters of the law, judgment, mercy, and faith; these ought ye to have done, and not to leave the other undone. Ye blind guides! which strain at a gnat, and swallow a camel. Woe unto you, scribes and Pharisees, hypocrites! for ye make clean the outside of the cup and of the platter; but within, they are full of extortion and excess.—Woe unto you, scribes and Pharisees, hypocrites! for ye are like unto whited sepulchres, which indeed appear beautiful outward, but are within full of dead men's bones, and of all uncleanness. Even so ye also outwardly appear righteous unto men, but within ye are full of hypocrisy and iniquity."

Dark and terrible as is this picture, I hold it to be strictly true of the overwhelming mass of professed Christians in America. They strain at a gnat, and swallow a camel. Could any thing be more true of our churches? They would be shocked at the proposition of fellowshipping a *sheep*-stealer; and at the same time they hug to their communion a *man*-stealer, and brand me with being an infidel, if I find fault with them for it. They attend with Pharisaical strictness to the outward forms of religion, and at the same time neglect the weightier matters of the law, judgment, mercy, and faith. They are always ready to sacrifice, but seldom to show mercy. They are they who are represented as professing to love God whom they have not seen, whilst they hate their brother whom they have seen. They love the heathen on the other side of the globe. They can pray for him, pay money to have the Bible put into his hand, and missionaries to instruct him; while they despise and totally neglect the heathen at their own doors.

Such is, very briefly, my view of the religion of this land; and to avoid any misunderstanding, growing out of the use of general terms, I mean by the religion of this land, that which is revealed in the words, deeds, and actions, of those bodies, north and south, calling themselves Christian churches, and yet in union with slaveholders. It is against religion, as presented by these bodies, that I have felt it my duty to testify.

I conclude these remarks by copying the following portrait of the religion of the south, (which is, by communion and fellowship, the religion of the north,) which I soberly affirm is "true to the life," and without caricature or the slightest exaggeration. It is said to have been drawn, several years before the present anti-slavery agitation began, by a northern Methodist preacher, who, while residing at the south, had an opportunity to see slaveholding morals, manners, and piety, with his own eyes. "Shall I not visit for these things? saith the Lord. Shall not my soul be avenged on such a nation as this?"

A PARODY

"Come, saints and sinners, hear me tell
How pious priests whip Jack and Nell,
And women buy and children sell,
And preach all sinners down to hell,
 And sing of heavenly union.

"They'll bleat and baa, dona like goats,
Gorge down black sheep, and strain at motes,
Array their backs in fine black coats,
Then seize their negroes by their throats,
 And choke, for heavenly union.

"They'll church you if you sip a dram,
And damn you if you steal a lamb;
Yet rob old Tony, Doll, and Sam,
Of human rights, and bread and ham;
 Kidnapper's heavenly union.

"They'll loudly talk of Christ's reward,
And bind his image with a cord,
And scold, and swing the lash abhorred,
And sell their brother in the Lord
 To handcuffed heavenly union.

"They'll read and sing a sacred song,
And make a prayer both loud and long,
And teach the right and do the wrong,
Hailing the brother, sister throng,
 With words of heavenly union.

"We wonder how such saints can sing,
Or praise the Lord upon the wing,
Who roar, and scold, and whip, and sting,
And to their slaves and mammon cling,
 In guilty conscience union.

"They'll raise tobacco, corn, and rye,
And drive, and thieve, and cheat, and lie,
And lay up treasures in the sky,
By making switch and cowskin fly,
 In hope of heavenly union.

"They'll crack old Tony on the skull,
And preach and roar like Bashan bull,
Or braying ass, of mischief full,
Then seize old Jacob by the wool,
 And pull for heavenly union.

"A roaring, ranting, sleek man-thief,
Who lived on mutton, veal, and beef,
Yet never would afford relief
To needy, sable sons of grief,
 Was big with heavenly union.

"'Love not the world,' the preacher said,
And winked his eye, and shook his head;
He seized on Tom, and Dick, and Ned,
Cut short their meat, and clothes, and bread,
 Yet still loved heavenly union.

"Another preacher whining spoke
Of One whose heart for sinners broke:

He tied old Nanny to an oak,
And drew the blood at every stroke,
 And prayed for heavenly union.

"Two others oped their iron jaws,
And waved their children-stealing paws;
There sat their children in gewgaws;
By stinting negroes' backs and maws,
 They kept up heavenly union.

"All good from Jack another takes,
And entertains their flirts and rakes,
Who dress as sleek as glossy snakes,
And cram their mouths with sweetened cakes;
 And this goes down for union."

Sincerely and earnestly hoping that this little book may do something toward throwing light on the American slave system, and hastening the glad day of deliverance to the millions of my brethren in bonds—faithfully relying upon the power of truth, love, and justice, for success in my humble efforts—and solemnly pledging my self anew to the sacred cause,—I subscribe myself, FREDERICK DOUGLASS

LYNN, *Mass., April* 28, 1845.

THE END

NAT LOVE

(1854-1921)

Nat Love was born a slave in June 1854, his mother and father owned by Robert Love, who ran a plantation in Davidson County, Tennessee. It was the beginning of a spectacular and colorful life, as Love would ultimately become known as Deadwood Dick, the most famous black cowboy of all.

Love's depictions of slave life are fairly typical in comparison with many slave narratives. He understood the cruelties his family suffered through slavery, and at a young age, he had an awareness of the implications of the Civil War. He remembers his siblings and friends on the plantation playing an imaginary version of war, where no one wanted to be a rebel soldier, since it was their understanding that the Union soldiers were fighting for the abolition of slavery. Even though Union soldiers under General Ulysses S. Grant's command marched through Tennessee confiscating any food or supplies they could get their hands on, even from slave quarters, Love still looked on them as a source of wonderment.

Despite the North's victory over the South, Love recalls that it took a very long time for news of their freedom to reach the plantation, and with the exception of some prolonged celebrations, Love noted that very little had actually changed for many slaves. They had become so reliant on their masters that most slaves simply stayed on the plantations and continued to work in the same basic conditions as they had prior to emancipation.

Love's father, however, rented twenty acres of land from the estate of his master, and was determined to strike out on his own. The initial going was difficult, as provisions were scarce. The family made brooms, straw mats and chair bottoms from cane and reeds, and Nat and his brother walked over 10 miles into town, loaded up with goods to be exchanged for seed and food. The Love family also farmed as much of the twenty acres as they could, growing corn, tobacco and a few vegetables. But since the land was uncultivated,

it had to be painstakingly plowed and harrowed before planting—work they had to do themselves.

Love writes glowingly of his father, who could read a little and made a determined effort to teach his children to do the same, despite the fact that there was no school for blacks in the area and much work to be done in the fields. Love describes him as "a loving husband and father," and a man not easily discouraged. "Had he lived," Love wrote, "this history would not have been written."

When Love was just fifteen years old, his father died after a brief illness, and the possibility of losing the farm threatened to devastate the family. Young Nat, despite having an older brother, Jordan, claimed the role of head of the family, and took it upon himself to take a job at a nearby farm for $1.50 per month, which would provide food and clothing for the family, which now included the orphaned children of his late sister.

Soon, Love was working on another nearby ranch, when the son of a ranch owner, seeking to make his own chores less dangerous, agreed to pay Love ten cents for every colt he could break. Love displayed a remarkable talent for holding onto the unbridled wild colts, and before long, other boys on the ranch were paying him to break more horses. Love was making what he considered good money, doing work he considered far more exciting than laborious. After demonstrating considerable skill and nerve by breaking a notoriously wild horse for twenty-five cents (which Love lost in the wild jumping and bucking), his reputation was cemented, and he was able to keep his family in shoes and food for a while. Still, there was considerable work to be done to keep the family farm, and the Love family picked nuts and berries and sold them in town to supplement whatever food supply they could take from the crops.

It was around this time that Love began to feel what he described as a "selfish" desire to go west and see more of the world. "It was hard to think of leaving mother and the children," he wrote, "but freedom is sweet and I wanted to make more of the opportunity and my life than I could see possible around home."

He admits that he even saw the outlook as discouraging, since he didn't have the clothing or the money, but an opportunity presented itself unexpectedly. A man by the name of Johnson was going to raffle a horse for fifty cents a chance, and Love sold two chickens for the price of a chance. Winning the horse, Love then resold it to Johnson for fifty dollars, who raffled it again, and again, Love won the horse, which he promptly resold.

With one hundred dollars now, Love returned home and gave his mother half of the money, telling her he was taking the other half to head west. She begged him to stay, which he did for another month, and Love was content that the farm was now operating fairly well. The children were older now and were more helpful in the fields, and Jordan and an uncle agreed to run the farm.

In February 1869, at just fifteen years of age, Nat Love left home, striking out for Kansas where he'd heard there was work. He stumbled across what he described as some "wild cow boys," and followed them back to their camp. He was invited to sit down with them for breakfast, where he noticed there were a few colored cowboys. After asking many questions, he told them he had experience breaking horses, and after a successful "test" aboard what proved to be Love's most difficult ride, he was offered a job at thirty dollars a month, with the possibility of more later. It was then that Love received his first nickname, "Red River Dick."

The boss took him into town and outfitted him with chaps, a new saddle, some blankets and a 45. Colt revolver. He was now a member of the Duval outfit, and Love stayed with them for over three years. The crew, finishing up their work in Dodge City, decided to hit the trails, and what followed was a series of adventures for which Love became renowned.

A few miles out of Dodge, Love described weathering the hardest hailstorm he'd ever seen, hindering both the men and the horses and giving him a taste of the harsh life he'd signed on for. But hail was the least of his worries. Near Dodge City, the outfit encountered a band of the old Victoria tribe of Indians, and a ferocious fight ensued. With only fifteen men in his outfit, they were easily outnumbered by what Love estimated to be "about a hundred painted bucks all well mounted." The Indians charged, "yelling like demons" and taking the Duval crew by surprise. They stood their ground and fought the Indians off, but not before having one of their men killed and losing all but six of their horses.

Love thought he was about to die in the battle and admits to doubting his courage. But too scared to run, he began firing and claims he lost all his fear forever after this encounter. For the next three years, he traveled all over Texas, Wyoming and the Dakotas, earning a reputation as a "good all around cow boy." In 1872, he took work with the Peter Gallinger company who worked along the Gila River in southern Arizona, but not without a touch of regret for leaving the Duval outfit, whom he described as "true and tried companions." With the Gallinger company, Love earned more money and

soon became one of their most trusted men, rounding up herds and riding up to 80 miles a day for days on end. It was a sense of worth and freedom that propelled Love to write:

> . . . my only ambition was to learn the business and excel in all things connected with the cow boy life that I was leading and for which I had genuine liking. Mounted on my favorite horse, my long horsehide lariat near my hand, and my trusty guns in my belt and the broad plains stretching away for miles and miles, every foot of which I was familiar with, I felt I could defy the world. What man with the fire of life and youth and health in his veins could not rejoice in such a life?

Indians and "white outlaws" created no end of trouble for the herders, running off the choicest part of a herd or the best horses, and Love and his company often rode over a hundred miles chasing down the thieves and administering the only law of the land at the end of a 45. Colt Pistol. Love became fairly proficient with his gun, and the element of danger in his work was something he gloried in. He was learning the ins and outs of the cattle business, and he became a valued range rider and brand reader. Love learned Spanish, which he could "speak like a native," and his knowledge of trails out west ultimately earned him more responsibilities with the Gallinger company. In time, he became "head brand reader" and his expertise put him in high demand.

A $200 contest in Deadwood City, South Dakota, where Love bested the best cowboys in the west at roping, riding and shooting, earned him the prize and the nickname "Deadwood Dick," which would become his moniker for the rest of his life, inspiring countless dime novels at the time. Though it is important to understand that many books about the west are filled with exaggerations and tall tales, and Love's accounts of some adventures are difficult to verify, his autobiography gives a detailed account of what life was like on the trails. He describes the monotony of riding day after day, hoping for something to happen, even something dangerous, just to add some excitement to the job. Skirmishes with Indians were frequent occurrences, so frequent that Love admits to writing about them only when a man was killed. He even demonstrates a sense of humor about the danger of life on the range when describing one particular Indian fight where his men were vastly outnumbered:

. . . it became evident that the Indians were too much for us. Then it became a question of running or being scalped. We thought it best to run as we did not think we could very well spare any hair at that par-ticular time, any way we mostly preferred to have our hair cut in the regular way by a competent barber, not that the Indians would charge us too much, they would probably have done the job for nothing, but we didn't want to trouble them, and we did not grudge the price of a hair cut any way, so we put spurs to our horses and they soon carried us out of danger.

Not long after that, in 1876, Love found himself ambushed by Yellow Dog's tribe of Indians near Yellow Horse Canyon. Shot through the chest and thigh, he put up a brave fight, managed to shoot back at them before running out of ammunition and was captured. Because he continued to fight so gamely with his bare hands before capture, he believes the Indians respect-ed his bravery enough to spare him his life. He also notes that Yellow Dog's tribe was composed largely of half-breeds, with a "large percentage of colored blood in the tribe," and that he felt he was too good a man to die. They nursed his wounds and Love was soon adopted by the tribe and selected to marry the chief's daughter, but he was carefully biding his time for an escape attempt, as he "did not want to get married under such circumstances."

After about a month in captivity, he snuck out of his camp, stole a pony and rode him for twelve hours straight without a saddle, returning to his home ranch in Texas, where he was greeted by a very warm reception from the boys, who told Love that his legend was so great, they all knew he'd find a way to escape if he wasn't killed. They marveled at the way Love managed to recover from the injuries he received, and Love credits the Indian doctors for saving his life. While in captivity, he learned a great deal about Indian cul-ture, which he describes with admiration. He also learned that in the fight leading up to his capture, he had killed five Indians and wounded three, and he writes: "It is a terrible thing to kill a man no matter what the cause. But as I am writing a true history of my life, I cannot leave these facts out. But every man who died at my hands was either seeking my life or died in open warfare, when it was a case of killing or being killed."

In the early 1880s, Love writes about falling in love with a Spanish girl in the city of Old Mexico. The girl's mother will not let her go north with Love, and Love is somewhat heartbroken, but many months later, he returns to Old Mexico, hiding in the mess wagon. The girl appears on the streets, ask-

ing about Love's whereabouts, and the boss, playing along with the joke, tells her he hasn't been seen in some time. Crestfallen, the girl walks away when Love emerges from the wagon, announcing his presence, and the two begin to kiss and embrace in front of everyone. They become engaged and agree to marry in the fall, but the girl gets very sick and dies that spring.

The loss has a profound effect on Love, who admits to becoming even more wild and reckless following the death of his fiancee. He engages in more fights with Indians and Mexicans, but while his horses are shot out from under him on a frequent basis, and men are killed all around him, Love always manages to escape "with a trifling wound at best."

Love writes about the great buffalo slaughters that changed the landscape of the west, along with the development of the railroads and cities and towns. The boundless plains are no longer boundless to many of the cowboys, and many quit the life "for pursuits of our more civilized brother."

In 1889, Love did the same, and moved to Denver, where he married a woman and accepted a porter's position in the Pullman service on the Denver and Rio Grande Railroad. The last part of Love's autobiography is something of a Paean to America, as his travels around the country by rail give him the opportunity to speak about the beauty of his country, about which he writes passionately.

Early in the book, Love writes strongly about the indignity and injustice of slavery in America. But while Love's description of slave life in the beginning of his book may be typical of many slave narratives, it only underscores how scarce racial matters have become in the rest of his autobiography. As soon as Love proved himself a worthy cowboy in Dodge City, he was quickly accepted by the men he worked with. Out west, he noted, blacks were treated no different from whites "as long as our money held out," and his book seems to bear that out. His competence and expertise allowed him to rise in the ranks of the companies he worked in, and he appeared to be respected and adored by his fellow cowboys. Bat Masterson bailed him out of jail after an alcohol-induced attempt to rope and drag a cannon out of Fort Dodge to fight Indians with because Love was "the only cowboy he likes." He has nothing but kind words about Buffalo Bill and other scouts, whom he describes as among the finest men he's ever met. And Love also writes about his acquaintance with Billy the Kid, who once gave him a tour of the cabin he grew up in. Though he admits a fondness for "the Kid," he acknowledges that the world is probably a better place with him gone, and expresses admiration for Pat Garrett, the man who finally brought Billy the Kid down.

Nat Love published his autobiography in 1907 to critical and commercial success, and died in 1925 at the age of 71, and in a completely different world from the one into which he was born.

Life and Adventures of Nat Love
Better Known in the
Cattle Country as Deadwood Dick

PREFACE

Having passed the half century mark in life's journey, and yielding to persistent requests of many old and valued friends of the past and present, I have decided to write the record of slave, cow-boy and pullman porter will prove of interest to the reading public generally and particularly to those who prefer facts to fiction, (and in this case again facts will prove stranger than fiction). I assure my readers that every event chronicled in this history is based on facts, and my personal experiences, of more than fifty years of an unusually adventurous life.

While many things contained in this record happened many years ago, they are as fresh in my memory as if they happened but yesterday. I have tried to record events simply as they are, without attempting to varnish over the bad spots or draw on my imagination to fill out a chapter at the cost of the truth. It has been my aim to record things just as they happened, believing they will prove of greater interest thereby; and if I am able to add to the interest and enjoyment of a single reader I will consider myself well repaid for the time and labor of preparing this history.

To my playmates of my boyhood, who may chance to read this I send greetings and wish them well. To the few friends, who assisted myself and widowed mother in our early struggles, I tender my sincerest thanks, and hope they have prospered as they deserve. For those who proved our enemies, I have no word of censure. They have reaped their reward.

To that noble but ever decreasing band of men under whose blue and buckskin shirts there lives a soul as great and beats a heart as true as ever human breast contained—to the cow-boys, rangers, scouts, hunters and trappers and cattle—men of the "GREAT WESTERN PLAINS," I extend the hand of greeting acknowledging the FATHER-HOOD of GOD and the

BROTHERHOOD of men; and to my mother's Sainted name this book is reverently dedicated.

THE AUTHOR.

CHAPTER I.

SLAVERY DAYS. THE OLD PLANTATION. MY EARLY FORAG-ING. THE STOLEN DEMIJOHN. MY FIRST DRINK. THE CURSE OF SLAVERY.

In an old log cabin, on my Master's plantation in Davidson County in Tennessee in June, 1854, I first saw the light of day. The exact date of my birth I never knew, because in those days no count was kept of such trival matters as the birth of a slave baby. They were born and died and the account was balanced in the gains and losses of the Master's chattels, and one more or less did not matter much one way or another. My father and mother were owned by Robert Love, an extensive planter and the owner of many slaves. He was in his way and in comparison with many other slave owners of those days a kind and indulgent Master.

My father was a sort of foreman of the slaves on the plantation, and my mother presided over the kitchen at the big house and my Master's table, and among her other duties were to milk the cows and run the loom, weaving clothing for the other slaves. This left her scant time to look after me, so I early acquired the habit of looking out for myself. The other members of father's family were my sister Sally, about eight years old, and my brother Jordan, about five. My sister Sally was supposed to look after me when my mother was otherwise occupied; but between my sister's duties of helping mother and chasing the flies from Master's table, I received very little look-ing after from any of the family, therefore necessity compelled me at an early age to look after myself and rustle my own grub. My earliest recollections are of pushing a chair in front of me and toddling from one to the other of my Master's family to get a mouthful to eat like a pet dog, and later on as I became older, making raids on the garden to satisfy my hunger, much to the damage of the young onions, watermelons, turnips, sweet potatoes, and other things I could find to eat. We had to use much caution during these raids on the garden, because we well knew what we would catch if someone

caught us, but much practice made us experts in escaping undetected.

One day when Master and the family went to town mother decided to make some wine of which she was very fond, accordingly she gathered some grapes and after pressing them she made some fairly good wine. This she placed in a demijohn, and this for better security she hid in the garden, as she thought unknown to anyone, but my brother, sister and myself had been watching the process with considerable curiosity, which finally reached such a pitch that there was nothing to it; we must sample a liquid that looked so good. So Jordan went to the hay loft from where a good view could be obtained all around, while myself and Sally busied ourselves in the vineyard. Presently Mother thinking all secure left the house with the demijohn and proceeded to hide it. Jordan, from the hay loft, noted that mother never left the garden until she returned to the house, empty handed, but he was unable to see the exact hiding place.

It was several days later while passing through the garden that we ran across the lost demijohn. It did not take us long to discover that its contents suited our tastes. Sally and Jordan dragged it into a sweet corn patch, where we were safe from observation. An oyster can was secured to serve as a glass and the way we attacked that wine was a caution to the Temperance Workers. And I can assure you we enjoyed ourselves for a while, but for how long I am unable to tell exactly. Mother soon missed us but being very busy she could not look for us until evening, when she started out to look us up, after searching and calling in vain. She decided to take the dogs to help find us. With their aid we were soon located, lying in the sweet corn, "dead drunk," while the demijohn quite empty, bottom side up, stared at mother with a reproachful stare, and the oyster can which had served up and took me to the house, and let Sally and Jordan lie in near by, bearing mute witness against us. Mother picked me up and took me to the house, and let Sally and Jordan lie in the sweet corn all night, to dwell on the events. Immediately preceding our return to consciousness is a painful subject to me as it was exceedingly painful then. I was most feverish the next day with a head on my shoulders several sizes larger than the one I was used to wearing. Sally and Jordan were enjoying about the same health as myself, but the state of our health did not exempt us from mother's wrath. We all received a good sound old-fashioned thrashing. A fitting prelude to my first "drunk."

I suppose I acquired the taste for strong drink on this occasion; be that as it may, the fact remains that I could out-drink any man I ever met in the cattle country. I could drink large quantities of the fiery stuff they called

whiskey on the range without it affecting me in any way, but I have never been downright drunk since that time in the sweet corn patch. Our plantation was situated in the heart of the black belt of the south, and on the plantations all around us were thousands of slaves, all engaged in garnering the dollars that kept up the so-called aristocracy of the south, and many of the proud old families owe their standing and wealth to the toil and sweat of the black man's brow, where if they had to pay the regular rate of wages to hire laborers to cultivate their large estates, their wealth would not have amounted to a third of what it was. Wealth was created, commerce carried on, cities built, and the new world well started on the career that has led to its present greatness and standing in the world of nations. All this was accomplished by the sweat of the black man's brow. By black man I do not mean to say only the black men, but the black woman and black child all helped to make the proud south what it was, the boast of every white man and woman, with a drop of southern blood in their veins, and what did the black man get in return? His keep and care you say? Ye gods and little fishes! Is there a man living today who would be willing to do the work performed by the slaves of that time for the same returns, his care and keep? No, my friends, we did it because we were forced to do it by the dominant race. We had as task masters, in many instances, perfect devils in human form, men who delighted in torturing the black human beings, over whom chance and the accident of birth had placed them. I have seen men beaten to the ground with the butts of the long whips carried by these brutal overseers, and for no other reason than that they could not raise to their shoulders a load sufficient for four men to carry. I have seen the long, cruel lash curl around the shoulders of women who refused to comply with the licentious wishes of the men who owned them, body and soul—did I say soul? No, they did not own their soul; that belonged to God alone, and many are the souls that have returned to him who gave them, rather than submit to the desires of their masters, desires to which submission was worse than death. I have seen the snake-like lash draw blood from the tender limbs of mere babies, hardly more than able to toddle, their only offense being that their skin was black. And young as I was my blood often boiled as I witnessed these cruel sights, knowing that they were allowed by the laws of the land in which I was born. I used to think it was not the country's fault, but the fault of the men who made the laws. Of all the curses of this fair land, the greatest curse of all was the slave auction block of the south, where human flesh was bought and sold. Husbands were torn from their wives, the baby from its mother's breast, and the most sacred com-

mands of God were violated under the guise of modern law, or the law of the land, which for more than two hundred years has boasted of its freedom, and the freedom of its people.

Some of the slaves, like us, had kind and indulgent masters. These were lucky indeed, as their lot was somewhat improved over their less fortunate brothers, but even their lot was the same as that of the horse or cow of the present day. They were never allowed to get anything in the nature of education, as smart negroes were not in much demand at that time, and the reason was too apparent, education meant the death of the institution of slavery in this country, and so the slave owners took good care that their slaves got none of it.

Go and see the play of "Uncle Tom's Cabin," and you will see the black man's life as I saw it when a child. And Harriett Beecher Stowe, the black man's Saviour, well deserves the sacred shrine she holds, along with the great Lincoln, in the black man's heart.

CHAPTER II.

WAR. "THE REBELS AND YANKEES." I RAISE A REGIMENT TO FIGHT. DIFFICULTY IN FINDING AN ENEMY. ASH SAKE. FREEDOM.

When I was ten years old the war broke out between the "North and the South." And there was little else talked about, among the slaves as well as the slave owners of the neighborhood. And naturally the many different stories we heard worked us children to a high state of excitement. So much so that we wanted to go to war, and fight for the Union, because among us slave children there was no difference of opinion, as to which side was right.

The Union was "IT," and we were all "Yankees." Not being able to go to war as our masters did, we concluded to play war, accordingly I gathered all the boys of the neighborhood together, into a regiment, which it was my intention to divide into two parties of Rebels and Yankees, but in this I met an insurmountable obstacle. Not one of the boys wanted to be a rebel, consequently we had to look elsewhere for an enemy to give us battle, and serve as a vent for our growing enthusiasm. The next Sunday preceding the organ-

ization of our regiment, we started out over the surrounding country in quest of trouble, which we were not long in finding, as we soon ran across a nest of yellow jackets. These we proceeded to exterminate, in which we were successful after a short but destructive battle. We suffered considerably in wounded but lost none of our soldiers. This engagement we called the capture of fort "Hell." For some time thereafter we made regular raids into the surrounding country in quest of an enemy. We were eventually successful in our quest, as in quick order we ran across and captured a company of bumble bees. This we called the "Battle of the Wilderness." Victory over a nest of hornets we called the capture of "Fort Sumter." A large nest of wasps gave us perhaps the hardest fight of our campaigning. This we ran across in the fields not far from home. There was an unusually large number of them, and as is usually the case with these insects, they proved very ferocious. Nothing loth, however, we attacked with cheers, only to be driven back time and again and finally we were compelled to make a very undignified retreat, at full speed in the direction of home. Not to be beaten, however, we secured reinforcements and more ammunition, in the shape of old rags, brooms and so forth, and returned to the charge, and although we were driven back several times we stayed until we won out, and the last insect lay a quivering mass on the ground. There was not one among us, not wounded in some manner, as for myself I had enough of it. My nose looked like a clutch slipper, and it was several days before my eyes were able to perform the duties for which they were made. However, the Union forces were victorious and we were happy. Our masters told us if the soldiers caught us, they would hang us all, which had the effect of keeping most of us close around home. Master had gone to join Lee's forces, taking with him father, who was engaged in building forts, which work kept him with the Confederate army until General Grant arrived in the country, when he was allowed to come home. From then on Union soldiers passed the neighborhood most every day on their way south, to join the fighting regiments.

We soon found out they would not hurt us and they were the wonderment and pride of our youthful minds. They would take everything they could find to eat for themselves and horses, leaving the plantation stripped clean of provisions and food, which entailed considerable misery and hardships on those left at home, especially the colored people who were not used to such a state of affairs, and were not accustomed to providing for their own wants. Finally Lee surrendered and master returned home. But in common with other masters of those days he did not tell us we were free. And instead

of letting us go he made us work for him the same as before, but in all other respects he was kind. He moved our log cabin on a piece of ground on a hill owned by him, and in most respects things went on the same as before the war. It was quite a while after this that we found out we were free and good news, like bad news, sometimes travels fast. It was not long before all the slaves in the surrounding country were celebrating their freedom. And "Massa Lincoln" was the hero of us all.

While a great many slaves rejoiced at the altered state of affairs; still many were content to remain as before, and work for their old masters in return for their keep. My father, however, decided to start out for himself, to that end he rented twenty acres of land, including that on which our cabin stood, from our late master.

We were at this time in a most destitute condition, and father had a very hard time to get a start, without food or money and almost naked, we existed for a time on the only food procurable, bran and cracklins. The limited supply of provisions made the culinary duties most simple, much to the disgust of mother, who was one of the best cooks in the country, but beggars cannot be choosers, and she very cheerfully proceeded to make the best of what we had. She would make a great fire in the large fire place in the cabin. The fire when hot enough, was raked from the hearth and a small place cleaned away, in the center of this clean space, mother would lay a cabbage leaf, on which she would pour some batter made from bran and water or buttermilk and a little salt. Then on top another cabbage leaf was laid and hot coals raked over the whole, and in a short time it would be baked nicely. This we called ash cake.

This, with occasional cracklins made up our entire bill of fare for many months. Father would make brooms and mats from straw and chair bottoms from cane and reeds, in which my brother and I would help him, after he had taught us how. During the week a large load was made and Friday night father would take the load on his shoulders and walk to town, a dozen miles, where he would sell them and bring seed and food home. When the weather would permit we worked in the field, preparing for our first crop.

The twenty acres, being mostly uncultivated, had to be cleared, plowed and thoroughly harrowed. Our first crop consisted of corn, tobacco and a few vegetables.

Father would lay off the corn rows. Jordan and I would drop the corn while father came behind and covered the rows.

In this manner we soon had in a considerable crop of corn and some veg-

etables for our own use. During the winter which was sometimes severe, during which time nothing, of course, could be done in the farming line, and when not otherwise engaged, we started to try and learn ourselves something in the educational line. Father could read a little, and he helped us all with our A B C's, but it is hard work learning to read and write without a teacher, and there was no school a black child could attend at that time. However, we managed to make some headway, then spring came and with it the routine of farm work. Father was a man of strong determination, not easily discouraged, and always pushing forward and upward, quick to learn things and slow to forget them, a keen observer and a loving husband and father. Had he lived this history would not have been written.

CHAPTER III.

RAISING TOBACCO, OUR FIRST YEAR OF FREEDOM. MORE PRIVATIONS. FATHER DIES. IT NEVER RAINS—BUT IT POURS. I BECOME THE HEAD OF THE FAMILY AND START TO WORK AT $1.50 PER MONTH.

As soon as the corn crop was in the ground we commenced to plant tobacco. Before the seed was sown, it was necessary to gather large piles of brush and wood and burn it to ashes on the ground to destroy the seeds of the weeds. The ground was then spaded and raked thoroughly, and the seed sown. After it had come up and got a fair start, it was transplanted in rows about three feet apart. When the plants become large enough it is necessary to pull the suckers off, also the worms off the leaves. This task fell upon Jordan and myself.

In picking the worms off the plants it is necessary to use the greatest care that the plants are not damaged, but Jordan and I were afraid to touch the worms with our fingers, so we took sticks and knocked them off, also a few leaves with each worm. This fact called forth some rather strong language from father, who said we were doing more harm than good. But our aversion to the worms was so strong that we took several thrashings before we could bring ourselves to use our fingers instead of a stick. When the tobacco was ripe there would be yellow spots on the leaves. It was then cut, let lie for one day, then hung on a scaffold to be sun cured. It was allowed to remain on the

scaffold for perhaps a week, then it was hung up in the barn to be smoked, after which it was made into a big bulk and a weight placed on it to press it out, then it was stripped, and put into hands and then it was ready for the market. Our crop the first year was not large and the most of it went to pay the rent and the following winter proved a hard one, and entailed considerable privation and suffering among the many ex-slaves, who had so recently been thrown on their own resources, without money or clothing or food, and only those who have had the experience can appreciate the condition of things or rather lack of things, at the close of the war, and these conditions did not only affect the ex-slaves and colored people, but covered the entire south, and many former well-to-do slave owners now found themselves without a penny they could call their own, having been stripped of everything and compelled to start all over again. Surely "war is hell"—but slavery is worse. Early in the spring father went to work for a neighboring planter a couple of weeks in order to get his plows and horses again to plow his land. A somewhat larger crop was put in this year, but unfortunately for us when everything was planted father took sick and died shortly after. This was a stunning loss to us just at a time when we most needed a father and husband's help, counsel and protection. But we did not lose courage for long.

The crop must be looked after and the coming winter provided against. My sister Sally had been married about three years at this time and was with her husband and two little girls on a small farm some distance away, which my brother-in-law rented. That left mother, Jordan and I to look after things. Although I was the youngest, I was the most courageous, always leading in mischief, play and work. So I now took the leadership, and became the head of the family. Things were beginning to take on a more hopeful look, when my brother-in-law died, leaving my sister sick with two small children and in about the same circumstances as ourselves. Everything, indeed, looked hopeless now, as our late master and his brother had left the old place and gone north. So remembering I was the only man on the place now, though only fifteen years old, I said to mother and sister who were weeping bitterly, "brace up, and don't lose your heads. I will look after you all." I said this with a bravado I was far from feeling, but I could not see the use of weeping now there was work to be done, if we were to keep from starving the coming winter. We all turned in to help one another and in this manner. The crop was gathered and we were in fairly good condition for the coming winter, but the work was too much for Sally who lingered through the winter and early in the spring we laid her beside her father and husband, and her two little

orphans were left to us. It now became very apparent to me that something must be done, because the crop raised the year before was barely enough to last us through the winter and we would soon be in actual need again. We needed clothing, especially the little girls of my sister, and we had no money to buy seed for this season's crop or food to last us out. So I concluded to go to work for some one if I could find anything to do. With that resolve, I put on my best rags and to mother's inquiry as to where I was going I told her I did not know myself. It fairly made my heart ache to see my little nieces going around almost naked, bare footed, and have them always asking for things I was powerless to give them. I determined to go from place to place until I secured employment of some kind that would in a measure, permit me to feed, and as far as I was able, clothe mother and the children, now dependent on me.

The fact that I was now free, gave me new born courage to face the world and what the future might hold in store for me. After tramping around the country for two days, I finally secured work with a Mr. Brooks, about six miles from home at one dollar and fifty cents a month. Notwithstanding the smallness of my prospective wages, I was happy and returned home in a jubilant frame of mind, to impart the news to mother. I was to commence the next morning. Mother said it was not much, but better than nothing. I told mother that I thought I could bring some food and clothing home for the children before the month was out. The little ones hearing this, were overjoyed and looked on me as a rich man indeed. Jordan was to remain at home and attend to what little there was to do, and the next day I started work for Mr. Brooks. In less than a week I made my first visit home, taking with me some potatoes, bacon, cornmeal, and some molasses, which I had rustled in various ways. I also had a bundle of old clothing given to me by the neighbors, which mother could make over for the children, and to say the children were happy is but a mild expression.

For the second month I received a raise of fifty cents, and the third month of my employment, so good did I work, that I received three dollars. With so many at home to provide for, my wages did not last long, but out of my three dollars I bought each of the children a book. The rest went for provisions and clothing. One day while passing the store of Mr. Graves, near our home I saw a checked sunbonnet and a red calico dress which struck my fancy as just what I wanted for mother. On asking the price Mr. Graves told me I could have the sunbonnet for twenty-five cents and the dress for four bits. That seemed to be within my means, and quite reasonable. I asked him

to keep them for me until I got my wages at the end of the month. This Mr. Graves promised to do if I would pay him something down. I only had fifteen cents of which I paid five cents on the bonnet and ten cents on the dress and went on my way, filled with happy thoughts as the result of my bargain. I resolved to be very saving this month and I became very impatient for my month to end and was continually asking Mr. Brooks if my month was not soon over. He would laugh and say "yes, soon." But it seemed to me that was the longest month I ever knew. When at last the month was over he gave me fifty cents, claiming I had drawn my wages during the month. I knew that was not so. I also knew I had a balance coming to me and told him so. But he denied it and the result was that we had a fight. I hit him in the head with a rock and nearly killed him after which I felt better. Then going to Mr. Graves the storekeeper, I told him the whole trouble. He expressed sympathy for me and said to give him the fifty cents and take the bonnet and dress, and we will call it square. And you can imagine my feelings as I took the things home to mother, and she was more pleased with them than any queen with her silks and satins. There being plenty of work to do at home, I did not again look for other work. The only thing that worried me was that the little ones were still without shoes, but on my promise to soon get them some they were satisfied. It was here I got my first lessons in self-dependence and life's struggles. I learned true usefulness and acquired the habit of helping others which I carried with me all through my after life and that trait perhaps more than any other endeared me to my companions on the range and all with whom I have had dealings.

CHAPTER IV.

BOYHOOD SPORTS. MORE DEVILMENT. THE ROCK BATTLES. I HUNT RABBITS IN MY SHIRT TAIL. MY FIRST EXPERIENCE IN ROUGH RIDING. A QUESTION OF BREAKING THE HORSE OR BREAKING MY NECK.

In those days it was more the custom, than now, to work six days and rest on the seventh, accordingly us boys always had our Sundays free. And we never lost an opportunity to put in motion some devilment to make the time pass in what we thought was the most pleasant way. Anything to have a great

time. Our chief means of having fun for a while was the rock battles. We boys of the entire neighborhood would get together, then divide in equal numbers on a side, then after gathering all the available rocks from the landscape, we would proceed to have a pitched battle, throwing the rocks at each other as hard as we could, and with a grim intent to commit battery. As a rational consequence the bravest would force the weaker side to retreat. It then became a question of running or being rocked to death. After these battles we were all usually in very bad condition, having received very hard knocks on sundry and various parts of our anatomy, but for all that we have never bore malice toward each other. We were careful to keep these escapades from the knowledge of our elders. In this way we were quite successful until one time we had a boy nearly killed, then we thought the old folks would whip us all to death. This incident ended the rock battles. But we soon had something else doing to furnish ourselves fun and excitement.

About this time we planned a rabbit hunt, after the small cotton tail rabbits, which were plentiful in the surrounding country. Getting all the boys together and securing the track hounds of the neighborhood we were off. It was not long before the dogs caught track of something and away they went with all the boys behind. Now at that time it was not customary for us boys of the plantation to wear shoes and pants, the principal reason being that we did not have either shoes or pants to wear. So you can perhaps imagine the sight presented by a score or more of boys of all ages chasing behind the hounds, with our shirt tails flying through bushes, thorns and brambles, up hill and down hill, many of us bleeding like stabbed pigs, but we were too much interested to pay any attention to a little blood. We wanted the rabbits, and everything else was of secondary importance, even the calls of the younger boys who got tired and fell behind. Onward we went over rocks, through fields, over fences, until we could hear the dogs no more, then tired out we had to stop. I told the boys to sit down, that I thought the dogs would come this way again. It was not long before I thought I heard something and told the boys to hush and have their rocks ready to kill the rabbit. It never occurred to me that it would be anything but a rabbit. The bay of the dogs came nearer, then over the fence jumped a big red fox right in front of me. He stopped and we looked in each others eyes. It was hard to tell which of us was the most surprised, however, I was the first to run away, and run I did. I ran like a black tailed deer. Many times I thought I felt him nibble at my shirt tails, and his eyes grew in my imagination as large as wagon wheels and Mr. Fox, himself, seemed to grow as big as an elephant. When at last I

dropped from sheer exhaustion and could summon courage to look behind me, I could see nothing. It was then I realized I was not so game as I thought I was and the knowledge was not pleasant by any means. Not far from our house there was a horse ranch, owned by a Mr. Williams. He had two sons about my own age and I would often go and see them on Sundays. As I was very fond of riding horses most of the horses on the ranch were very wild. So one day the oldest boy and I made a plan to break the young colts. The only chance we had of doing so was on Sunday, when the family went to church, as we did not think Mr. Williams would approve of our plan. Mr. Williams' boy said he would give me ten cents for every colt I broke. That was perfectly satisfactory to me. The money was made of shin plaster those days (paper). The next Sunday I started to break horses. We did not dare to put the bridle on them as we were afraid the boss might surprise us and we would not be quick enough to get it off. Our mode of procedure was to drive one at a time in the barn, get it in a stall, then after much difficulty I would manage to get on its back. Then the door was opened and the pole removed and the horse liberated with me on its back, then the fun would commence. The colt would run, jump, kick and pitch around the barn yard in his efforts to throw me off. But he might as well tried to jump out of his skin because I held on to his mane and stuck to him like a leech. The colt would usually keep up his bucking until he could buck no more, and then I would get my ten cents. Ten cents is a small amount of money these days, but in those days that amount was worth more to me than ten dollars now.

Well, we went on Sunday after Sunday and I broke about a dozen colts in this way, and also managed to do it without the boss discovering the favor I was undoubtedly doing him, in breaking all his wild horses. Only his boys were aware of the doings and they paid me. So I had no scruples about what I was doing, especially as it afforded me great fun. Finally the boys wanted me to break a big handsome black horse called Black Highwayman. Knowing the horse's uncertain temper and wild disposition and taking into consideration its size, I refused to break him for ten cents, as the fact was I was rather scared of him. After considerable bargaining, in which I held out for fifty cents, we finally compromised on twenty-five cents. But I can assure you it was more for the money than the fun of the thing, that I finally consented to ride him. With great difficulty we managed to get him in a stall as we did the others, but I no sooner landed on his back than he jumped in the manger with me hanging to his mane. Finally the door was opened and the pole removed and out of the barn we shot like a black cloud, around the yard we

flew, then over the garden fence. At this juncture the track hounds became interested and promptly followed us. Over the fields we went, the horse clearing the highest fences and other obstacles in his way with the greatest ease. My seat on his back was not the most comfortable place in the world, but as the horse did not evince any disposition to stop and let me get off, I concluded to remain where I was. All the dogs of the neighborhood were fast joining in the race and I had quite a respectable following. After running about two miles we cleared a fence into a pasture where there was a large number of other horses and young colts, who promptly stampeded as we joined them, Highwayman taking the lead with me on his back, looking very much like a toad. And all the dogs in the country strung out in the rear. Naturally we formed a spectacle that could not fail to attract the attention of the neighbors, who soon as possible mounted horses and started in pursuit and vainly tried to catch my black mount but could get nowhere near him, while I without bridle or anything to control him could do nothing but let him run as all the other horses bunched around us and the dogs kept up a continual din. I simply held on and let him go. It was a question of breaking the horse or breaking my neck. We went over everything, through everything, until finally the killing pace told and Black Highwayman fell, a thoroughly exhausted and completely conquered and well broken horse. As for myself, I was none the worse for my exciting ride. But on looking for my twenty-five cents, I found it gone. The boys had paid me in advance, as I insisted, and I had tied the money up in a corner of my shirt tail and during my wild ride it had come untied and worked out. This was a great misfortune to me and for a while I was inconsolable. I asked the boys if they would make it right, but no, they had paid me once and they refused to give me another quarter. This riled me considerable and I told them all right, to come again when they wanted a horse broken. That settled us and the horse breaking. The experiences I gained in riding during these times, often stood me in good stead in after years during my wild life on the western plains. Mr. Williams of course, heard of my last wild ride, but instead of being angry, he seemed to see the funny side of it, which I could not.

The spectators wondered how in the world I ever escaped a broken neck and I have often wondered how I escaped in after years from situations that seemed to be sure death. But escape I did and am now hale and hearty, without pain, with muscles like iron and able at any time to run a hundred yards in eleven seconds or jump a six foot fence.

CHAPTER V.

HOME LIFE. PICKING BERRIES. THE PIGS COMMIT LARCE-
NY. NUTTING. WE GO TO MARKET. MY FIRST DESIRE TO SEE
THE WORLD. I WIN A HORSE IN A RAFFLE. THE LAST OF HOME.

I now settled down to the work around the farm and the problem of mak-
ing a living for those dependent on me. The crop was all in and after
attending to such work around home as had to be done, we found a source
of revenue in gathering berries for market. Large quantities of black berries
and others grew wild in the woods near by. And they always found a ready
market. With small pails and a big basket mother and I would start out after
the work at home was done. Reaching the woods we would sit under the
bushes and fill the pails, then empty them into the big basket until that was
full which usually comprised our day's work.

One day, wishing to secure a large quantity of berries for market, we went
early in the morning and on reaching the woods we placed the big basket in
what we thought a safe place, and after some hours of industrious work, the
big basket was full of nice ripe blackberries. We then proceeded to fill our pails
again which would be sufficient for the day. This accomplished, we prepared
to start for home. But when mother went to take the big basket it was empty.

The stray pigs had found them and committed larceny. Mother felt so
bad she cried. We had put in a hard day's work for nothing. It had been our
intention to take them to town on the morrow and buy something for
Sunday, but now the fruit of our labor was gone and the disappointment was
great. I looked at mother, then at the empty basket and did not know for
which to feel most sorry. So I said, "Well, there is no use grieving over spilt
milk. If we had not had them we could not have lost them, and there are
plenty more of the same kind for the picking." Mother turned toward me, and
said, with a look I will always remember, "My boy, whatever happens, you
never get discouraged." I did not see the use of losing courage and I think the
only time I weakened was when father died, as he could not be replaced.

We went on talking and picking berries, and before we knew it the bas-
ket was full again and the pails. It was now night so mother took the bushel
basket on her head and I took the pails and we were soon home. That night
mother took my clothing, as was customary, and washed and pressed it so I
would look nice and clean to go to market the next day. As I only had one
outfit of clothes I had necessarily to go without them during the washing

process, however, mother always kept me clean, at considerable labor on her part. The next morning, early, mother and I started for town, five miles distant, walking along the hot, dusty road, each of us with a basket of berries on our heads and bunches of cucumbers in our hands, mother having much the larger load, but she was a very strong woman. As it chanced we had a lucky day and sold our stock of berries and cucumbers in a short time. We then bought what we needed and had a little money left but for all that, I was not quite satisfied. I wanted mother to buy something that was not necessary, but she said, "My son, if we don't save a few cents now what will it be later on? We will have to go to the poorhouse." I said, "Dear mother if there is a house poorer than ours I don't want to see it." I will always remember the sight of mother's face as she turned to me, the tears running down her cheeks as she answered, "Yes, my son, you are right there are few houses poorer than ours now." The same year when fall came mother and I thought we had the bull by the horns. There were several fine groves of walnut, hickory nut, chestnut and shirly bark nut trees in the woods and I made a sleigh on which I nailed a big box. I tied a rope for a tongue and with a stick on the end, mother and I working as a sort of double team would draw through the woods among the trees gathering the different kinds of nuts and as the box was big, large quantities could be gathered in this manner. During the nut season we worked every day from morning to night, gathering large quantities of nuts for which we always found a ready market. As we worked we talked of what we would buy with the money and making plans for the future. The nuts we sold usually brought us: chestnuts one dollar a bushel; walnuts fifty cents, and hickory nuts fifty cents a bushel. This money added to the proceeds of the crop netted us quite a nice sum and made our condition much better, but I assure you, dear readers, it took hard work from morning to night to make both ends meet but with the help of God we made them meet, and during this time we were always healthy and the knowledge that we were free and working for ourselves gave us courage to continue the struggle. It was about this time that I commenced thinking about going west.

I wanted to see more of the world and as I began to realize there was so much more of the world than what I had seen, the desire to go grew on me from day to day. It was hard to think of leaving mother and the children, but freedom is sweet and I wanted to make more of the opportunity and my life than I could see possible around home. Besides I suppose, I was a little selfish as mortals are prone to be. Finally the desire to go out in the world grew so strong that I mentioned it to mother, but she did not give me much

encouragement, and I don't think she thought I had the courage to go, and besides I had neither clothing or money and to tell the truth, the outlook was discouraging even to me, but I continued to look for an opportunity which happened in a very unexpected manner shortly after. One day a man by the name of Johnson announced that he would raffle a fine beautiful horse at fifty cents a chance. I heard of it at once, but had no money with which to get a chance. However, when there's a will there's a way, so I went to the barn and caught two chickens which I sold for fifty cents and at once got a chance. My chance won the horse. Mr. Johnson said he would give me fifty dollars for the horse and as I needed the money more than the horse I sold the horse back. Mr. Johnson at once raffled him off again and again I won the horse, which I again sold for fifty dollars. With nearly a hundred dollars I went home and told mother of what I had done and gave her half of the money, telling her I would take the other half and go out in the world and try and better my condition. I then went to town and bought some underwear and other needful articles, intending to leave at once, but mother pleaded with me so hard to stay home, that I finally consented to remain one more month, but at the end of that time she pleaded for one more and I could not refuse her. During this time my uncle came to live with us and I asked him to take my place at home. This he consented to do gladly. Things were going on fairly well at home now. The farm was yielding a fair living and the children having grown much larger they were a source of help instead of an hindrance and now that my uncle and my brother Jordan were home to look after mother, I felt I could better leave them now, because I was not really needed at home. After gathering what few things I wanted to take with me and providing myself with some needed clothes, I bade mother and the old home farewell, and started out for the first time alone in a world I knew very little about.

CHAPTER VI.

THE WORLD IS BEFORE ME. I JOIN THE TEXAS COWBOYS. RED RIVER DICK. MY FIRST OUTFIT. MY FIRST INDIAN FIGHT. I LEARN TO USE MY GUN.

It was on the tenth day of February, 1869, that I left the old home, near Nashville, Tennessee. I was at that time about fifteen years old, and

though while young in years the hard work and farm life had made me strong and hearty, much beyond my years, and I had full confidence in myself as being able to take care of myself and making my way.

I at once struck out for Kansas of which I had heard something. And believing it was a good place in which to seek employment. It was in the west, and it was the great west I wanted to see, and so by walking and occasional lifts from farmers going my way and taking advantage of every thing that promised to assist me on my way, I eventually brought up at Dodge City, Kansas, which at that time was a typical frontier city, with a great many saloons, dance halls, and gambling houses, and very little of anything else. When I arrived the town was full of cow boys from the surrounding ranches, and from Texas and other parts of the west. As Kansas was a great cattle center and market, the wild cow boy, prancing horses of which I was very fond, and the wild life generally, all had their attractions for me, and I decided to try for a place with them. Although it seemed to me I had met with a bad outfit, at least some of them, going around among them I watched my chances to get to speak with them, as I wanted to find some one whom I thought would give me a civil answer to the questions I wanted to ask, but they all seemed too wild around town, so the next day I went out where they were in camp.

Approaching a party who were eating their breakfast, I got to speak with them. They asked me to have some breakfast with them, which invitation I gladly accepted. During the meal I got a chance to ask them many questions. They proved to be a Texas outfit, who had just come up with a herd of cattle and having delivered them they were preparing to return. There were several colored cow boys among them, and good ones too. After breakfast I asked the camp boss for a job as cow boy. He asked me if I could ride a wild horse. I said "yes sir." He said if you can I will give you a job. So he spoke to one of the colored cow boys called Bronko Jim, and told him to go out and rope old Good Eye, saddle him and put me on his back. Bronko Jim gave me a few pointers and told me to look out for the horse was especially bad on pitching. I told Jim I was a good rider and not afraid of him. I thought I had rode pitching horses before, but from the time I mounted old Good Eye I knew I had not learned what pitching was. This proved the worst horse to ride I had ever mounted in my life, but I stayed with him and the cow boys were the most surprised outfit you ever saw, as they had taken me for a tenderfoot, pure and simple. After the horse got tired and I dismounted the boss said he would give me a job and pay me $30.00 per month and more later

on. He asked what my name was and I answered Nat Love, he said to the boys we will call him Red River Dick. I went by this name for a long time.

The boss took me to the city and got my outfit, which consisted of a new saddle, bridle and spurs, chaps, a pair of blankets and a fine 45 Colt revolver. Now that the business which brought them to Dodge City was concluded, preparations were made to start out for the Pan Handle country in Texas to the home ranch. The outfit of which I was now a member was called the Duval outfit, and their brand was known as the Pig Pen brand. I worked with this outfit for over three years. On this trip there were only about fifteen of us riders, all excepting myself were hardy, experienced men, always ready for anything that might turn up, but they were as jolly a set of fellows as one could find in a long journey. There now being nothing to keep us longer in Dodge City, we prepared for the return journey, and left the next day over the old Dodge and Sun City lonesome trail, on a journey which was to prove the most eventful of my life up to now.

A few miles out we encountered some of the hardest hail storms I ever saw, causing discomfort to man and beast, but I had no notion of getting discouraged but I resolved to be always ready for any call that might be made on me, of whatever nature it might be, and those with whom I have lived and worked will tell you I have kept that resolve. Not far from Dodge City on our way home we encountered a band of the old Victoria tribe of Indians and had a sharp fight.

These Indians were nearly always harrassing travelers and traders and the stock men of that part of the country, and were very troublesome. In this band we encountered there were about a hundred painted bucks all well mounted. When we saw the Indians they were coming after us yelling like demons. As we were not expecting Indians at this particular time, we were taken somewhat by surprise.

We only had fifteen men in our outfit, but nothing daunted we stood our ground and fought the Indians to a stand. One of the boys was shot off his horse and killed near me. The Indians got his horse, bridle and saddle. During this fight we lost all but six of our horses, our entire packing outfit and our extra saddle horses, which the Indians stampeded, then rounded them up after the fight and drove them off. And as we only had six horses left us, we were unable to follow them, although we had the satisfaction of knowing we had made several good Indians out of bad ones.

This was my first Indian fight and likewise the first Indians I had ever seen. When I saw them coming after us and heard their blood curdling yell,

I lost all courage and thought my time had come to die. I was too badly scared to run, some of the boys told me to use my gun and shoot for all I was worth. Now I had just got my outfit and had never shot off a gun in my life, but their words brought me back to earth and seeing they were all using their guns in a way that showed they were used to it, I unlimbered my artillery and after the first shot I lost all fear and fought like a veteran.

We soon routed the Indians and they left, taking with them nearly all we had, and we were powerless to pursue them. We were compelled to finish our journey home almost on foot, as there were only six horses left to fourteen of us. Our friend and companion who was shot in the fight, we buried on the plains, wrapped in his blanket with stones piled over his grave. After this engagement with the Indians I seemed to lose all sense as to what fear was and thereafter during my whole life on the range I never experienced the least feeling of fear, no matter how trying the ordeal or how desperate my position.

The home ranch was located on the Palo Duro river in the western part of the Pan Handle, Texas, which we reached in the latter part of May, it taking us considerably over a month to make the return journey home from Dodge City. I remained in the employ of the Duval outfit for three years, making regular trips to Dodge City every season and to many other places in the surrounding states with herds of horses and cattle for market and to be delivered to other ranch owners all over Texas, Wyoming and the Dakotas. By strict attention to business, born of a genuine love of the free and wild life of the range, and absolute fearlessness, I became known throughout the country as a good all around cow boy and a splendid hand in a stampede.

After returning from one of our trips north with a bunch of cattle in the fall of 1872, I received and accepted a better position with the Pete Gallinger company, whose immense range was located on the Gila River in southern Arizona. So after drawing the balance of my pay from the Duval company and bidding good bye to the true and tried companions of the past three years, who had learned me the business and been with me in many a trying situation, it was with genuine regret that I left them for my new position, one that meant more to me in pay and experience. I stayed with Pete Gallinger company for several years and soon became one of their most trusted men, taking an important part in all the big round-ups and cuttings throughout western Texas, Arizona and other states where the company had interests to be looked after, sometimes riding eighty miles a day for days at a time over the trails of Texas and the surrounding country and naturally I soon became well known among the cowboys rangers, scouts and guides it was my pleas-

ure to meet in my wanderings over the country, in the wake of immense herds of the long horned Texas cattle and large bands of range horses. Many of these men who were my companions on the trail and in camp, have since become famous in story and history, and a braver, truer set of men never lived than these wild sons of the plains whose home was in the saddle and their couch, mother earth, with the sky for a covering. They were always ready to share their blanket and their last ration with a less fortunate fellow companion and always assisted each other in the many trying situations that were continually coming up in a cowboy's life.

When we were not on the trail taking large herds of cattle or horses to market or to be delivered to other ranches we were engaged in range riding, moving large numbers of cattle from one grazing range to another, keeping them together, and hunting up strays which, despite the most earnest efforts of the range riders would get away from the main herd and wander for miles over the plains before they could be found, overtaken and returned to the main herd.

Then the Indians and the white outlaws who infested the country gave us no end of trouble, as they lost no opportunity to cut out and run off the choicest part of a herd of long horns, or the best of a band of horses, causing the cowboys a ride of many a long mile over the dusty plains in pursuit, and many are the fierce engagements we had, when after a long chase of perhaps hundreds of miles over the ranges we overtook the thieves. It then became a case of "to the victor belongs the spoils," as there was no law respected in this wild country, except the law of might and the persuasive qualities of the 45 Colt pistol.

Accordingly it became absolutely necessary for a cowboy to understand his gun and know how to place its contents where it would do the most good, therefore I in common with my other companions never lost an opportunity to practice with my 45 Colts and the opportunities were not lacking by any means and so in time I became fairly proficient and able in most cases to hit a barn door providing the door was not too far away, and was steadily improving in this as I was in experience and knowledge of the other branches of the business which I had chosen as my life's work and which I had begun to like so well, because while the life was hard and in some ways exacting, yet it was free and wild and contained the elements of danger which my nature craved and which began to manifest itself when I was a pugnacious youngster on the old plantation in our rock battles and the breaking of the wild horses. I gloried in the danger, and the wild and free life

of the plains, the new country I was continually traversing, and the many new scenes and incidents continually arising in the life of a rough rider.

CHAPTER VII

I LEARN TO SPEAK SPANISH AND AM MADE CHIEF BRAND READER. THE BIG ROUND-UPS. RIDING THE 7-Y-L STEER. LONG RIDES. HUNTING STRAYS.

Having now fairly begun my life as a cowboy, I was fast learning the many ins and outs of the business, while my many roamings over the range country gave me a knowledge of it not possessed by many at that time. Being of a naturally observant disposition, I noticed many things to which others attached no significance. This quality of observance proved of incalculable benefit to me in many ways during my life as a range rider in the western country. My employment with the Pete Gallinger company took me all over the Pan Handle country, Texas, Arizona, and New Mexico with herds of horses and cattle for market and to be delivered to other ranch owners and large cattle breeders. Naturally I became very well acquainted with all the many different trails and grazing ranges located in the stretch of country between the north of Montana and the Gulf of Mexico, and between the Missouri state line and the Pacific ocean. This whole territory I have covered many times in the saddle, sometimes at the rate of eighty or one hundred miles a day. These long rides and much traveling over the country were of great benefit to me, as it enabled me to meet so many different people connected with the cattle business and also to learn the different trails and the lay of the country generally.

Among the other things that I picked up on my wanderings, was a knowledge of the Spanish language, which I learned to speak like a native. I also became very well acquainted with the many different brands scattered over this stretch of country, consequently it was not long before the cattle men began to recognize my worth and the Gallinger company made me their chief brand reader, which duties I performed for several years with honor to myself and satisfaction to my employers. In the cattle country, all the large cattle raisers had their squad of brand readers whose duty it was to attend all the big round-ups and cuttings throughout the country, and to pick out their

own brands and to see that the different brands were not altered or counterfeited. They also had to look to the branding of the young stock.

During the big round-ups it was our duty to pick out our brand, and then send them home under the charge of our cowboys, likewise the newly branded stock. After each brand was cut out and started homeward, we had to stay with the round up to see that strays from the different herds from the surrounding country did not again get mixed up, until the different home ranges were reached. This work employed a large number of cowboys, who lived, ate and often slept in the saddle, as they covered many hundreds of miles in a very short space of time. This was made possible as every large cattleman had relays of horses sent out over the country where we might be expected to touch, and so we could always count on finding a fresh horse awaiting us at the end of a twenty-five or a fifty mile ride. But for us brand readers there was no rest, we merely changed our saddles and outfit to a fresh horse and were again on the go. After the general round up was over, cowboy sports and a good time generally was in order for those engaged in it. The interest of nearly all of us centered in the riding of what was known as the 7 Y-L steer. A big long horn wild steer, generally the worst in the herd, was cut out and turned loose on the open prairie. The cow boy who could rope and ride him would get the steer as his reward, and let me assure you dear reader, that it was not so easy as it sounds, as the steer separated from its fellows would become extremely ferocious and wild, and the man who attempted to rope and ride him would be in momentary danger of losing his life, if he relaxed in the least his vigilance and caution, because a wild steer is naturally ferocious. Even in cutting them out of the round up I have known them to get mad and attack the cowboys who only saved themselves by the quickness of their horses, or the friendly intervention of a comrade who happened to be near to rope the maddened long horn, and thus divert his attention to other things. But in the case of the 7 Y-L steer such intervention is against the rules, and the cowboy who attempts to rope and ride the steer must at all times look out for himself. I have seen two horses and their riders gored to death in this sport, and I have had to shoot more than one steer to save myself and horse after my horse had fallen with me and placed himself as well as me at the maddened beast's mercy. At such times it takes a cool head and a steady hand as no random shot will stop a wild steer. The bullet must be placed in a certain spot, the center of the forehead, to accomplish its mission. The last time I had a horse fall with me in roping the 7 Y-L steer, he fell as the steer was but a few feet away, falling in such a way that my leg caught under

the saddle, holding me fast. Quick as I could I gave the steer a bullet in the head and he stumbled and fell dead on top of my horse and me, so that the boys had to interfere to the extent of dragging the steer and horse off of my leg.

The cowboy who is successful in roping the steer must then mount and ride him. If he does that successfully the steer becomes his personal property to do with as he will, only a slight reward for the risking of his life and the trouble of accomplishing the feat. But it is done more for sport's sake than anything else, and the love of showing off, a weakness of all cow boys more or less. But really it takes a high class of horsemanship to ride a long horn, to get on his back and stay there as he runs, jumps, pitches side ways, backwards, forward, up and down, then over the prairie like a streak of lightning. I have had the experience and I can assure you it is no child's play. More than one 7 Y-L steer has fallen to my lot, but I had to work for it, and work hard. After all it was only part of the general routine of the cow boy's life, in which danger plays so important a part. It is seldom thought of being merely a matter of course, and none of us would have foregone the sport, had we known that sure death awaited us as the result, because above all things, the test of a cow boy's worth is his gameness and his nerve. He is not supposed to know what fear means, and I assure you there are very few who know the meaning of that word.

Most of my readers no doubt have heard of the great round ups and cuttings, connected with the cattle raiser's life. But not one in a hundred has any idea as to how an immense herd of wild cattle are handled in a big round up. My many years of experience has given me unusual knowledge on the subject, and you may bring any cattleman or boss to me, and I will guarantee to answer any question he can ask me about the cattle business. The first general round up occurs about the first of April. This round up is to run in all the near cattle belonging to each man, and head them toward our respective ranges. If we find any other brand mixed up with ours we head them toward their own range, and keep our own together. Every cow boy does the same and in this way every cattleman is enable to get his own brand together on his own range, so that when the next general round up occurs he will have most of his near cattle together on the home range. In order to get the cattle together in the first general round up, we would have to ride for hundreds of miles over the country in search of the long horn steers and old cows that had drifted from the home range during the winter and were now scattered to the four winds of heaven. As soon as they were found they were started off under the care of cow boys for the place agreed upon for the general round up

whether they belonged to us or not, while the rest of us continued the search. All the cow boys from the many different outfits working this way enabled us to soon get all the strays rounded up in one great herd in which the cattle of a dozen different owners were mixed up together. It then became our duty to cut out our different herds and start them homewards. Then we had to brand the young stock that had escaped that ordeal at the hands of the range riders. On finding the strays and starting them homewards, we had to keep up the search, because notwithstanding the fact that we had done range riding or line riding all winter, a large number of cattle would manage to evade the vigilance of the cow boys and get away. These must all be accounted for at the great round up, as they stood for dollars and cents, profit and loss to the great cattle kings of the west. In going after these strayed and perhaps stolen cattle we boys always provided ourselves with everything we needed, including plenty of grub, as sometimes we would be gone for nearly two months and sometimes much longer. It was not an uncommon occurrence for us to have shooting trouble over our different brands. In such disputes the boys would kill each other if others did not interfere in time to prevent it, because in those days on the great cattle ranges there was no law but the law of might, and all disputes were settled with a forty-five Colt pistol. In such cases the man who was quickest on the draw and whose eye was the best, pretty generally got the decision. Therefore it was of the greatest importance that the cow boy should understand his gun, its capabilities and its shooting qualities. A cow boy would never carry anything but the very best gun obtainable, as his life depended on it often. After securing a good gun the cow boy had to learn how to use it, if he did not already know how. In doing so no trouble or expense was spared, and I know there were very few poor shots on the ranges over which we rode and they used the accomplishment to protect themselves and their employer's cattle from the Indian thiefs and the white desperadoes who infested the cattle country, and who lost no opportunity to stampede the herds and run off large numbers of them. Whenever this happened it generally resulted in a long chase and a fierce fight in which someone was sure to get hurt, and hurt badly. But that fact did not bother us in the least. It was all simply our duty and our business for which we were paid and paid good, and so we accepted things as they came, always ready for it whatever it might be, and always taking pride in our work in which we always tried to excel.

Christmas, Dec. 25, 1872, is a day in my memory which time cannot blot out. I and a number of friends were in a place called Holbrook, Ariz. A

dispute started over a saddle horse with the following result. Arizona Bob drew his forty-five Colt revolver, but before he had time to fire he was instantly killed by A. Jack. Then a general fight ensued in which five horses and three men were killed.

It was a sad thing for me to see my friends dead in a corral on a Christmas morning, but I helped bury the dead and took care of the wounded. The names were A. Jack, Wild Horse Pete and Arizona Bill.

CHAPTER VIII.

ON THE TRAIL. A TEXAS STORM. A CATTLE STAMPEDE. BATTLE WITH THE ELEMENTS. AFTER BUSINESS COMES PLEASURE.

After the round ups and on returning from our long rides after strayed cattle we would have to prepare to take the trail with herds of cattle and horses for market and to be delivered to other large ranch owners. The party of cow boys to make these trips were all selected men. We would spend several days at the home ranch resting up and preparing our outfit, in which our guns, saddles, blankets and horses were given a thorough overhauling and placed in first class condition, as they would be called on to do good hard service on these trips on the trail. The nature of our journey would depend very much on the kind of cattle we were called upon to handle. Sometimes it would be all classes together; on other occasions the herd would consist of a certain kind, such as long yearlings, short yearlings, tail end and scabs. The larger demand however, seemed to be for straight three and four year old steers. These latter kind were the easiest to handle on the trail. It is no doubt necessary that I explain the difference between the different kinds I mention here. Short yearlings were those over one year old and short of two years, long yearlings those two years and short of three years, tail end and scabs mean nearly the same thing, and comprise all the very young stock of all classes not yet reached the dignity of yearlings. These latter were in demand from the cattle men, who took them to feed until they got their growth or to raise from, as stock cattle three or four years old were generally the market or beef cattle. These latter were by all odds the easiest to handle on the trail. Sometimes we would have an order for five or six hundred head of all class-

es of cattle, then again we would have to start out with fifteen hundred head of shipping steers, or several hundred head of horses.

Shortly after I entered the employ of the Pete Gallinger company, and after the round-ups of the early season, we received an order for two thousand five hundred head of three year old steers to be delivered at Dodge City, Kansas. This was the largest herd I had up to the present time followed good rest at the home ranch, we strung the large herd out with two months provisions, and the camp wagon. After a and one hundred extra saddle horses and several pack horses, on the trail. Our outfit consisted of forty picked cow boys, along the old Chillers trail en route for Kansas, and we started on what proved to be an eventful journey. The herd behaved splendidly and gave us very little trouble until we crossed the Red river and struck the Old Dog and Sun City trail, here they became restless, and stampeded nearly every night, and whenever they got half a chance. This made it very hard on us cowboys, as it is no easy matter to ride the lines of such a large herd, let alone having to chase them back in line from many miles over the prairie where they had stampeded in their wild career. After crossing the Kansas line at a place known as the South Forks, while making for the head of the Cimarron river on the twenty-seventh of June, we experienced one of the hardest rain and hail storms I had ever seen, in the western country, the rain came down in torrents only to cease and give place to hail stones the size of walnuts. While the thunder and lightning was incessant. It was shortly after dark when the storm commenced. The twenty-five hundred head of cattle strung out along the trail became panic stricken and stampeded, and despite our utmost efforts, we were unable to keep them in line.

Imagine, my dear reader, riding your horse at the top of his speed through torrents of rain and hail, and darkness so black that we could not see our horses heads, chasing an immense herd of maddened cattle which we could hear but could not see, except during the vivid flashes of lightning which furnished our only light. It was the worst night's ride I ever experienced. Late the next morning we had the herd rounded up thirty miles from where they started from the night before. On going back over the country to our camp of the night before, we saw the great danger we had been in during our mad ride. There were holes, cliffs, gulleys and big rocks scattered all around, some of the cliffs going down a sheer fifty feet or more, where if we had fallen over we would have been dashed to pieces on the rocks below, but we never thought of our personal danger that night, and we did not think particularly of it when we saw it further than to make a few joking remarks about what

would have happened if some one of us had gone over. One of the boys offered to bet that a horse and rider going over one of those cliffs would bring up in China, while others thought he would bring up in Utah. It was our duty to save the cattle, and every thing else was of secondary importance. We never lost a single steer during this wild night—something we were justly proud of. This proved the last trouble we were to have with the herd, and we soon reached the five mile divide, five miles from Dodge City without further incident, and with our herd intact. Here we were to hold them until turned over to their new owners. This accomplished, our work was done and done well for this trip. Then we all headed for Dodge City to have a good time, and I assure you we had it. It was our intention and ambition to paint the town a deep red color and drink up all the bad whiskey in the city. Our nearly two months journey over the dusty plains and ranges had made us all inordinately thirsty and wild, and here is where we had our turn, accordingly we started out to do the town in true western style, in which we were perfectly successful until the town had done us, and we were dead broke. This fact slowed us up, because being broke we could not get up any more steam and we had to cool down right there. We then started out to find our boss, but that gentleman being wise in his time and generation, and knowing we would soon all be broke, and would be wanting more money, and that he would let us have it if we asked him for it only to be thrown away, he made himself scarce, and he kept out of our sight until we cooled off. For my part I would not spend all my money. I would draw about fifty dollars, then I would get what things I wanted and then would let the other go free, but while our money lasted we would certainly enjoy ourselves, in dancing, drinking and shooting up the town. It was our delight to give exhibitions of rough riding, roping and everything else we could think of to make things go fast enough' to suit our ideas of speed. After several days spent in this manner we would begin to make ready to start on the return journey home to Texas. We left Dodge City on the first of July and on the fifteenth of August we were back on the old home ranch, where we rested up a few days before again starting out to ride the range after tile long horns again. As I was a brand reader I had little time to rest as my services were in demand from many of the large cattle kings of Texas and Arizona, and when ever a dispute arose over brands, I was generally sent for to straighten matters out. This with the numerous round ups which I had to attend and the many transfers of cattle throughout the pan handle country kept me continually on the go. When my services were not needed as a brand reader I rode the range along

with the other cow boys. This kept us almost continually in the saddle, and away from the home ranch for days at a time; when this was the case our food consisted of biscuit and cakes which we made ourselves from meal which we carried with us, and such meat and game as we could knock over with our guns. We camped wherever it suited and where there was feed for our horses. A cow boy's first care is always after his gun and his horse, that animal often meaning life and liberty to the cow boy in a tight place and the cow boy without a horse is like a chicken without its head, completely lost. My faithful horse has times without number carried me out of danger and preserved my life. We were not destined to have much rest this season as shortly after we returned from the trip to Dodge City, the boss bought a large herd of cattle down on the Rio Grande, just over the line in Mexico, which we had orders for, so we had to start out and round them up. This was no easy matter as they were scattered over a large range of territory and many strays had to be rounded up and got with the main herd. This we finally accomplished, after a great deal of hard riding over the rough Rio Grande country, and both men and horses were completely tired out, so we went into camp, only holding the herd together and getting rested up. This opportunity we improved by getting acquainted and fraternizing with the cow boys of one of the oldest cattle countries this side of the herring pond—Old Mexico. These men were for the most part typical greasers, but they proved to us that they knew a thing or two about the cattle business, and all things considered they were a jolly companionable sort of an outfit. From them we learned a few pointers and also gave them a few very much to our mutual benefit. We remained here a few days before starting northward with our herd, but these few days proved very pleasant ones to us boys who, on account of the monotony of the life we led always welcomed new experiences or events that would give us something to think and talk about while on our long rides behind the slow moving herd of long-horn steers, or around our camp fires when in camp on the plains, and it gave us especial pleasure to meet men of the same calling from other states over the west. It not only gave us pleasure, but it added to our cow knowledge, and of the country over which we might at any time be called on to drive cattle, and in such cases a knowledge of the country was most valuable to us. Then a cow boy's life contains many things in which he is continually trying to improve and excel, such as roping, shooting, riding and branding and many other things connected with the cattle business. We, in common with other trades, did not know it all, and we were always ready to learn anything new when we met any one who was capable of teaching us.

CHAPTER IX.

EN ROUTE TO WYOMING. THE INDIANS DEMAND TOLL.
THE FIGHT. A BUFFALO STAMPEDE. TRAGIC DEATH OF CAL.
SURCEY. AN EVENTFUL TRIP.

After getting the cattle together down on the Rio Grande and both man
and beast had got somewhat rested up, we started the herd north. They
were to be delivered to a man by the name of Mitchell, whose ranch was
located along the Powder river, up in northern Wyoming. It was a long dis-
tance to drive cattle from Old Mexico to northern Wyoming, but to us it was
nothing extraordinary as we were often called on to make even greater dis-
tances, as the railroads were not so common then as now, and transportation
by rail was very little resorted to and except when beef cattle were sent to the
far east, they were always transported on the hoof overland. Our route lay
through southern Texas, Indian Territory, Kansas and Nebraska, to the
Shoshone mountains in northern Wyoming. We had on this trip five hun-
dred head of mostly four year old long horn steers. We did not have much
trouble with them until we struck Indian Territory. On nearing the first
Indian reservation, we were stopped by a large body of Indian bucks who said
we could not pass through their country unless we gave them a steer for the
privilege. Now as we were following the regular government trail which was
a free public highway, it did not strike us as justifiable to pay our way, accord-
ingly our boss flatly refused to give the Indians a steer, remarking that we
needed all the cattle we had and proposed to keep them, but he would not
mind giving them something much warmer if they interfered with us. This
ultimatum of our boss had the effect of starting trouble right there. We went
into camp at the edge of the Indian country. All around us was the tall blue
grass of that region which in places was higher than a horse, affording an
ideal hiding place for the Indians. As we expected an attack from the Indians,
the boss arranged strong watches to keep a keen lookout. We had no sooner
finished making camp when the Indians showed up, and charged us with a
yell or rather a series of yells, I for one had got well used to the blood cur-
dling yells of the Indians and they did not scare us in the least. We were all
ready for them and after a short but sharp fight the Indians withdrew and
every thing became quiet, but us cow boys were not such guys as to be fooled
by the seeming quietness. We knew it was only the calm before the storm,
and we prepared ourselves accordingly, but we were all dead tired and it was

necessary that we secure as much rest as possible, so the low watch turned in to rest until midnight, when they were to relieve the upper watch, in whose hands the safety of the camp was placed till that time. Every man slept with his boots on and his gun near his hand. We had been sleeping several hours, but it seemed to me only a few minutes when the danger signal was given. Immediately every man was on his feet, gun in hand and ready for business. The Indians had secured reinforcements and after dividing in two bands, one band hid in the tall grass in order to pick us off and shoot us as we attempted to hold our cattle, while the other band proceeded to stampede the herd, but fortunately there were enough of us to prevent the herd from stringing out on us, as we gave our first attention to the cattle we got them to merling. Back and forward, through the tall grass, the large herd charged, the Indians being kept too busy keeping out of their way to have much time to bother with us. This kept up until daylight, but long before that time we came to the conclusion that this was the worst herd of cattle to stampede we ever struck, they seemed perfectly crazy even after the last Indian had disappeared. We were unable to account for the strange actions of the cattle until daylight, when the mystery was a mystery no longer. The Indians in large numbers had hid in the tall grass for the purpose of shooting us from ambush and being on foot they were unable to get out of the way of the herd as it stampeded through the grass, the result was that scores of the painted savages were trampled under the hoofs of the maddened cattle, and in the early gray dawn of the approaching day we witnessed a horrible sight, the Indians were all cut to pieces, their heads, limbs, trunk and blankets all being ground up in an inseparable mass, as if they had been through a sausage machine. The sight was all the more horrible as we did not know the Indians were hidden in the grass during the night, but their presence there accounted for the strange actions of the herd during the night. We suffered no loss or damage except the loss of our rest, which we sorely needed as we were all pretty well played out. However, we thought it advisable to move our herd on to a more desirable and safe camping place, not that we greatly feared any more trouble from the Indians, not soon at any rate, but only to be better prepared and in better shape to put up a fight if attacked. The second night we camped on the open plain where the grass was not so high and where the camp could be better guarded. After eating our supper and placing the usual watch the men again turned in, expecting this time to get a good night's rest. It was my turn to take the first watch and with the other boys, who were to watch with me, we took up advantageous positions on the lookout. Everything soon became

still, the night was dark and sultry. It was getting along toward midnight when all at once we became aware of a roaring noise in the north like thunder, slowly growing louder as it approached, and I said to the boys that it must be a buffalo stampede. We immediately gave the alarm and started for our herd to get them out of the way of the buffalo, but we soon found that despite our utmost efforts we would be unable to get them out of the way, so we came to the conclusion to meet them with our guns and try and turn the buffalo from our direction if possible, and prevent them from going through our herd. Accordingly all hands rode to meet the oncoming stampede, pouring volley after volley into the almost solid mass of rushing beasts, but they paid no more attention to us than they would have paid to a lot of boys with pea shooters. On they came, a maddened, plunging, snorting, bellowing mass of horns and hoofs. One of our companions, a young fellow by the name of Cal Surcey, who was riding a young horse, here began to have trouble in controlling his mount and before any of us could reach him his horse bolted right in front of the herd of buffalo and in a trice the horse and rider went down and the whole herd passed over them. After the herd had passed we could only find a few scraps of poor Cal's clothing, and the horse he had been riding was reduced to the size of a jack rabbit. The buffalo went through our herd killing five head and crippling many others, and scattering them all over the plain. This was the year that the great buffalo slaughter commenced and such stampedes were common then. It seemed to me that as soon as we got out of one trouble we got into another on this trip. But we did not get discouraged, but only wondered what would happen next. We did not care much for ourselves, as we were always ready and in most cases anxious for a brush with the Indians, or for the other dangers of the trail, as they only went to relieve the dull monotony of life behind the herd. But these cattle were entrusted to our care and every one represented money, good hard cash. So we did not relish in the least having them stampeded by the Indians or run over by the buffaloes. If casualties kept up at this rate, there would not be very many cattle to deliver in Wyoming by the time we got there. After the buffalo stampede we rounded up our scattered herd and went into camp for a couple of days' rest before proceeding on our journey north. The tragic death of Cal Surcey had a very depressing effect on all of us as he was a boy well liked by us all, and it was hard to think that we could not even give him a Christian burial. We left his remains trampled into the dust of the prairie and his fate caused even the most hardened of us to shudder as we contemplated it. After getting fairly rested we proceeded on our journey north and

were soon out of the Indian Territory, though we often met small bands of roving bucks, but aside from exchanging a few shots at each other they caused us no trouble. We crossed Kansas and Nebraska and reached the end of our long journey without further incident worthy of note, and we delivered our herd only five head short which was not bad considering the distance we had travelled and the events that had happened. It was a wonder that we had been able to get through with half of our herd or men. Consequently it was with genuine relief that we turned the cattle over to their new owners and received our receipt therefor. We remained at the Mitchell ranch in Wyoming several days, fraternizing with our northern brothers, swapping yarns and having a good time generally. On the return journey to Arizona we were of course, able to make better time and we returned more direct by way of Colorado and Utah, taking note of the cattle trails and the country over which we passed. In that way we secured valuable information of the trails and the country that stood us in good stead in future trips north. Arriving home at the Pete Gallinger ranch, in Arizona, we became the heroes of the range, and we received unstinted praise from our boss, but the loss of Cal Surcey was universally regretted.

We were relieved of all duty until we got thoroughly rested up, while our horses had the best the ranch afforded. But at a large cattle ranch there is always something doing and it was not long before we were again in the saddle and preparing for another trip on the trail. To the cow boy accustomed to riding long distances, life in the saddle ceases to be tiresome. It is only the dull monotony of following a large herd of cattle on the trail day after day that tires the rider and makes him long for something to turn up in the way of excitement. It does not matter what it is just so It is excitement of some kind. This the cow boy finds in dare-devil riding, shooting, roping and such sports when he is not engaged in fighting Indians or protecting his herds from the organized bands of white cattle thieves that infested the cattle country in those days. It was about this time that I hired to Bill Montgomery for a time to assist in taking a band of nine hundred head of horses to Dodge City. The journey out was without incident, on arriving at Dodge City we sold the horses for a good price returning to the old ranch in Arizona by the way of the old lone and lonesome Dodge City trail. While en route home on this trail we had a sharp fight with the Indians. When I saw them coming I shouted to my companions, "We will battle them to hell!" Soon we heard their yells as they charged us at full speed. We met them with a hot fire from our Winchesters, but as they were in such large numbers we saw that we

could not stop them that way and it soon developed into a hand to hand fight. My saddle horse was shot from under me; at about the same time my partner James Holley was killed, shot through the heart. I caught Holley's horse and continued the fight until it became evident that the Indians were too much for us, then it became a question of running or being scalped. We thought it best to run as we did not think we could very well spare any hair at that particular time, any way we mostly preferred to have our hair cut in the regular way by a competent barber, not that the Indians would charge us too much, they would have probably done the job for nothing, but we didn't want to trouble them, and we did not grudge the price of a hair cut any way, so we put spurs to our horses and they soon carried us out of danger. Nearly every one of us were wounded in this fight but Holley was the only man killed on our side though a few of the Indians were made better as the result of it. We heard afterwards that Holley was scalped and his body filled with arrows by the red devils. This was only one of the many similar fights we were constantly having with the Indians and the cattle thieves of that part of the country. They were so common that it was not considered worth mentioning except when we lost a man, as on this occasion. This was the only trouble we had on this trip of any importance and we soon arrived at the Montgomery ranch in Texas where after a few days rest with the boys, resting up, I made tracks in the direction of my own crib in Arizona.

CHAPTER X.

WE MAKE A TRIP TO NEBRASKA. THE HOLE IN THE WALL COUNTRY. A LITTLE SHOOTING SCRAPE. CATTLE ON THE TRAIL AND THE WAY TO HANDLE THEM. A BIT OF MORALIZATION.

The ranch boss's voice rang out sharply, but kindly as he entered our quarters where we were engaged in all sorts of occupations, some of the boys playing cards, others smoking and swapping stories, while those more industrious were diligently engaged in cleaning their forty-fives. I glanced up from my long barreled rifle I was just putting the finishing touches to, wondering what was up now. The boss informed us that we were to take another herd of cattle north, away up in the northwestern part of Nebraska, and

that all of us who were on the last trip had been selected for the duty again this trip. This announcement was met with exclamations of approval from the boys who had now got thoroughly rested up and were anxious for regular duty again. Since our return from Wyoming we had not been doing much, but taking it easy with occasional range riding and were becoming rusty in consequence. We were to start on our second journey north this season as soon as possible, so we lost no time in getting ready. We were to take the same size herd as before. It did not take us long to round the herd up and the second day from the time we received the order we were off. Our route was different this time, starting from the home ranch in Arizona we went by way of New Mexico, Colorado and into Nebraska, by way of the Platte river, which we crossed neat where the forks of the North and South Platte unite. It was now late in the season and we had to hurry in order to get through in good weather, therefore we put the cattle to the limit of their traveling powers. Beef cattle, that is, four year old long horns differ greatly from other cattle in their travel. The first day after being put out on the trail they will travel twenty-five miles without any trouble then as the pace begins to tell on them they fall back to fifteen or twenty miles a day, and there also seems to be an understanding among the cattle themselves that each must take a turn at leading the herd, those that start in the lead in the morning will be away back in the center of the herd at noon, and those that started in the center are now leading. This they keep up until all have had their turn at leading and as a rule if they are not scared by something they will stay pretty well bunched. We allowed the herd to graze and rest during the night, only traveling during the day, as a herd of cattle should never be moved off their grazing ground until the dew is off the grass because their feet are made soft by the wet grass and If they are moved onto the hard trail while in that condition sore heels are sure to result, and a steer with sore heels cannot travel and will have to be left behind on the trail or the herd held until those affected have recovered. Our saddle horses travel several times the distance that a herd of cattle does on the trail, as it is necessary to ride from one end of the herd to the other to keep them in line and headed in the right direction. This work is hard on the horses but that is always provided for by having a small herd of horses along under the charge of a horse rustler as we called him and any of the boys could change his tired horse for a fresh one at any time he chose, but he would have no one to help him make the change. He would have to rope, throw, saddle and bridle the horse himself without any assistance whatever from his companions, and this was no easy matter as most of

the horses were wild Texas mustangs and had never had the saddle on more than once or twice and so as often happened the cow boy would be led a hard life before he finally made the change of mounts. On such occasions he always received the unwelcome and unasked advice of the other boys, but as most of the boys were expert at that business there was slight chance for railing and chaff. But if for any reason he should get the laugh from his companions he always took it in the same spirit in which it was given, only waiting his chance to get even, and such a chance was not long in coming. This particular herd acted very well and gave us no trouble to speak of. Our route lay over the old Hays' and Elsworth trail, one of the best known cattle trails in the west, then by way of Olga, Nebraska, at that time a very small and also a very tough place. It was a rendezvous of the tough element and the bad men of the cow country. There were a large number of cow boys there from the surrounding ranges and the place looked very enticing to our tired and thirsty crowd, but we had our herd to look after and deliver so we could not stop, but pushed on north crossing the Platte river, then up the trail that led by the hole in the wall country, near which place we went into camp. Then as now this hole in the wall country was the refuge of the train robbers, cattle thieves and bandits of the western country, and when we arrived the place was unusually full of them, and it was not long before trouble was brewing between our men and the natives which culminated in one of our men shooting and killing one of the bad men of the hole. Fearing more trouble and not being in the best possible shape to meet it, burdened as we were with five hundred head of cattle we broke camp at once and proceeded on our journey north. We arrived at the ranch where our herd were to be delivered without further incident and with all our cattle intact and after turning the herd over to their new owners and spending several days in getting acquainted with our northern neighbors, the Nebraska cowboys whom we found hot numbers and a jolly all round crowd of cattle men, we left for Arizona on the return journey by way of Wyoming, Colorado and New Mexico, arriving home in good shape late in the fall without further incident, and were soon engaged in range riding over our own ranges again, and getting everything in shape for the winter, but we had to be out on the range off and on all winter. Then in the spring came the usual round ups, cuttings and brandings, during which time all our men were needed at the home ranch. I had long since developed into a first class cow boy and besides being chief brand reader in Arizona and the pan handle country. My expertness in riding, roping and in the general routine of the cow boy's life, including my wide knowl-

edge of the surrounding country, gained in many long trips with herds of cat-
tle and horses, made my services in great demand and my wages increased
accordingly. To see me now you would not recognize the bronze hardened
dare devil cow boy, the slave boy who a few years ago hunted rabbits in his
shirt tail on the old plantation in Tennessee, or the tenderfoot who shrank
shaking all over at the sight of a band of painted Indians. I had long since felt
the hot sting of the leaden bullet as it plowed its way through some portion
of my anatomy. Likewise I had lost all sense of fear, and while I was not the
wild blood thirsty savage and all around bad man many writers have pictured
me in their romances, yet I was wild, reckless and free, afraid of nothing, that
is nothing that I ever saw, with a wide knowledge of the cattle country and
the cattle business and of my guns with which I was getting better acquaint-
ed with every day, and not above taking my whiskey straight or returning
bullet for bullet in a scrimmage. I always had been reckless, as evidenced by
my riding of Black Highwayman on the old home plantation and I never lost
courage or my nerve under the most trying circumstances, always cool,
observant and ready for what might turn up, made me liked and respected
by my employers and those of the cattle kings of the western country it was
my good fortune to meet and know. On our own ranch, among my own
companions my position was as high as a king, enjoying the trust and confi-
dence of my employers and the homage of the men many of whom were
indebted to me on occasions when my long rope or ever ready forty-five colt
pistol had saved them from serious injury or death. But I thought nothing of
those things then, my only ambition was to learn the business and excel in
all things connected with the cow boy's life that I was leading and for which
I had genuine liking. Mounted on my favorite horse, my long horsehide lar-
iat near my hand, and my trusty guns in my belt and the broad plains stretch-
ing away for miles and miles, every foot of which I was familiar with, I felt I
could defy the world. What man with the fire of life and youth and health
in his veins could not rejoice in such a life? The fall and winter of 1874
passed on the Arizona ranch without any unusual occurrence, the cattle win-
tered well and prospects were bright for the coming year. In the early spring
we again began preparing for the big round up, the brandings and the cut-
tings. There had been hundreds of calves and colts added to the vast herds,
these all had to be cut out and branded, while all the cattle that had strayed
during the winter had to be rounded up and accounted for. This work kept
us in the saddle the greater part of the time. Sometimes we would be absent
for days and weeks at a time on the trail of a bunch of strayed cattle. On these

trips we often encountered big herds of buffalo and these supplied us with meat, and such meat! A buffalo steak fresh from a still quivering buffalo broiled over coals is a dish fit for the Gods. Coming back from one of these trips after strays early in 1875 we were notified to get ready to take a herd of five hundred head of horses up in South Dakota, the trip was a long one but horses can travel much faster than cattle and on the whole are much easier to handle. On the trails we were all happy at the prospect of the trip and were not long in getting ready and getting the horses started out on the trail, we took them by way of New Mexico, Colorado and Nebraska. They gave us very little trouble on the way up, and we reached our destination and delivered them without incident worthy of note, returning by way of Wyoming, Colorado and New Mexico. On starting out on the return journey we came down Fold creek and stopped at the old log saloon to get a drink, that being the first place where we could get any whiskey. Here in moving around among the large number of cow boys and tough characters, generally, another fuss was started between our men and some cattle rustlers resulting in some shooting, but fortunately without serious consequences. As we were not looking for trouble, and not wishing to kill any one we left at once for home. It was our policy to always avoid trouble if possible while on these trips, but to always defend ourselves and our rights against all comers, be they white men or Indians and then it would look bad for us to have to report the loss of a man or so in a saloon fight when we were sent out to attend to business, for that reason we did not stop to give an exhibition of our fighting qualities, although we were very anxious to have matters out with them. We arrived home safely with all well and in time to assist in the round ups and the other ranch work in which we were needed.

CHAPTER XI.

A BUFFALO HUNT. I LOSE MY LARIAT AND SADDLE. I ORDER A DRINK FOR MYSELF AND MY HORSE. A CLOSE PLACE IN OLD MEXICO.

When there was not much doing around the ranch, we boys would get up a buffalo hunt. Buffaloes were plentiful in those days and one did not have to ride far before striking a herd. Going out on the open plain we were not long in sighting a herd, peacefully grazing on the luxuriant grass,

and it would have been an easy task to shoot them but that was not our idea
of sport. In the first place it was too easy. Then to shoot them would rob the
hunt of all element of danger and excitement, for that reason we prepared to
rope them and then dispatch them with the knife or revolver. As soon as the
herd caught sight of us they promptly proceeded to stampede and were off
like the wind. We all had pretty good mounts and we started in pursuit. It is
a grand sight to see a large herd of several thousand buffalo on a stampede,
all running with their heads down and their tongues hanging out lilac a yard
of red flannel, snorting and bellowing they crowd along, shaking the ground
for yards around. We soon reached the rear of the herd and began operations.
I had roped and dispatched several, when my attention was attracted by a
magnificent bull buffalo, which I made up my mind to get, running free
behind the herd. My buffalo soon came within range and my rope settled
squarely over his horns and my horse braced himself for the strain but the
bull proved too much for us. My horse was knocked down, the saddle
snatched from under me and off my horse's back and my neck nearly broken
as I struck the hardest spot in that part of Texas After I got through count-
ing the stars not to mention the moons that I could see quite plainly, I
jumped to my feet and after assuring myself that I was all there I looked for
my horse, he was close by just getting up while in the distance and fast grow-
ing more distant each moment was my favorite saddle flying in the breeze,
hanging to the head of the infuriated buffalo.

Now I did not think I could very well lose that saddle so I sprang on my
horse's bare back and started in pursuit. My horse could run like a deer and
his hard fall did not seem to affect him much, so it did not take us long to
overtake the plunging herd. Running my horse close up by the side of the
thief who stole my saddle, I placed the muzzle of my forty-five close against
his side and right there I took charge of Mr. Buffalo and my outfit.

It was no trouble to get all the buffalo meat we wanted in those days, all
that was necessary was to ride out on the prairie and knock them over with
a bullet, a feat that any cow boy can accomplish without useless waste of
ammunition, and a running buffalo furnishes perhaps the best kind of a
moving target for practice shooting. And the man that can drop his buffalo
at two hundred yards the first shot can hit pretty much anything he shoots at.

I never missed anything I shot at within this distance and many a time
when I thought the distance of an object was too great, the boys have encour-
aged me by saying, shoot, you never miss, and as much to my surprise as
theirs, my old stand by placed the bullet where I aimed.

I early in my career recognized the fact that a cow boy must know how to use his guns, and therefore I never lost an opportunity to improve my shooting abillties, until I was able to hit anything within range of my forty-five or my Winchester. This ability has tlmes withont number proved of incalculable value to me, when in tight places. It has often saved the life of myself and companions and so by constant practice I soon became known as the best shot in the Arizona and pan handle country.

After the buffalo hunt we were sent down in Old Mexico to get a herd of horses, that our boss had bought from the Mexicans in the southwestern part of Old Mexico. We made the journey out all right without special incident, but after we had got the horses out on the trail, headed north I was possessed with a desire to show off and I thought surprise the staid old greasers on whom we of the northern cattle country looked with contempt. So accordingly I left the boys to continue with the herd, while I made for the nearest saloon, which happened to be located in one of the low mud houses of that country, with a wide door and clay floor. As the door was standing open, and looked so inviting I did not want to go to the trouble of dismounting so urging my horse forward, I rode in the saloon, first however, scattering with a few random shots the respectable sized crowd of dirty Mexicans hanging around as I was in no humor to pay for the drinks for such a motley gathering. Riding up to the bar, I ordered keller for myself and a generous measure of pulky for my horse, both popular Mexican drinks.

The fat wobbling greaser who was behind the bar looked scared, but he proceeded to serve us with as much grace as he could command. My forty-five colt which I proceeded to reload, acting as a persuader. Hearing a commotion outside I realized that I was surrounded. The crowd of Mexican bums had not appreciated my kindly greeting as I rode up and it seems did not take kindly to being scattered by bullets. And not realizing that I could have killed them all, just as easy as I scattered them, and seeing there was but two of us—I and my horse—they had summoned sufficient courage to come back and seek revenge. There was a good sized crowd of them, every one with some kind of shooting iron, and I saw at once that they meant business. I hated to have to hurt some of them but I could see I would have to or be taken myself, and perhaps strung up to ornament a telegraph pole. This pleasant experience I had no especial wish to try, so putting spurs to my horse I dashed out of the saloon, then knocking a man over with every bullet from my Colts I cut for the open country, followed by several volleys from the angry Mexicans' pop guns.

The only harm their bullets did, however, was to wound my horse in the hip, not seriously, however, and he carried me quickly out of range. I expected to be pursued, however, as I had no doubt I had done for some of those whom I knocked over, so made straight for the Rio Grande river riding day and night until I sighted that welcome stream and on the other side I knew I was safe. Crossing the Rio Grande and entering Texas at the Eagle pass, I rode straight to the old home ranch where I stayed resting up until the boys got the horses out of Mexico into Texas, then I joined them and assisted in driving the horses into the ranch. I congratulated myself that I escaped so easily and with such little damage. It was certainly a close place but I have been in even closer places numbers of times and always managed to escape. Either through trick, the fleetness of my horse or my shooting and sometimes through all combined. At this time I was known all over the cattle country as "Red River Dick," the name given to me by the boss of the Duval outfit, when I first joined the cow boys at Dodge City, Kansas.

And many of the cattle kings of the west as well as the Indians and scores of bad men all over the western country have at some time or other had good reason to remember the name of "Red River Dick."

This was in 1875. It was not till the next year that I won the name of "Deadwood Dick," a name I made even better known than "Red River Dick." And a name I was proud to carry and defend, if necessary, with my life. This season we made several trips North. The horses we brought up from Texas now had to be driven to old man Keith's in Nebraska, on the North Platte river. On this trip we had no trouble to speak of. Several bands of Indians showed up at different times but a shot or so from one of the boys would send them scurrying off at full speed, without stopping to sample further our fighting abilities.

This was in some ways disappointing to us as we were spoiling for a fight or excitement of some kind. However, nothing turned up, so after delivering the horses to their new owners, we made tracks for home again. It was the same round of duties, season after season, but all our trips on the trail were not by any means alike, we were continually visiting new country and new scenes, traveling over trails new to us, but old in history. Many of these old trails are now famous in history.

Each trip gave us new experiences, and traveling so much as we were, there were few outfits in the cattle country that knew the trails and the country as we did. And we were continually adding to this knowledge and experience. After returning from old man Keith's in Nebraska we had to take the

trail again with a herd of cattle for the Spencer brothers, whose ranch was located just north of the Red Light about sixty-five miles north of the bad lands in South Dakota. This was one of the largest cattle ranches in the West.

Their brand was known as the R Box Circle Brand. There we remained for some time, adding to our knowledge of the cattle business such things as can only be learned at a large cattle ranch. On our way home we passed through Laramie, Wyoming. As fate would have it, we arrived at Laramie City on July 4, 1875, just as the notorious Jack Watkins escaped from the Albany county jail, and the excitement in the town was at fever heat. Jack Watkins, who was probably the most desperate criminal that was ever placed behind prison bars, had been arrested and placed in close confinement, as the officers of the western states had long tried to effect his capture. And they did not want to take any chances of losing him, now they had him, but for all their caution he had escaped, shooting Deputy Sheriff Lawrence in the leg, crippling him for life.

Ex-Conductor Brophy was at that time sheriff. The officers noting our arrival at such time, at once ordered us out of the city, as they suspected we knew something about the outbreak. We protested our innocence of any knowledge of the trouble. But appearances were against us, so we had to leave, going direct to Cheyenne, Wyoming. Here we disposed of a small band of horses our boss had along, and which we did not wish to take back home with us. They were sold to the Swarn Brothers at a good price.

We remained in Cheyenne until the 18th of July, when we left for Texas, arriving at the old Pall Dora range ranch on the 10th of August. We had no more than got rested up before we were again called out on active duty. The many large cattle owners of the panhandle country had got together and come to the conclusion that the wild mustang horses, large bands of which were running wild over the Arizona and Texas plains, would make good cattle horses, and to that end a plan of campaign was arranged, whereby they could be captured, and broken in and put to some use, instead of causing damage to the range, as at present.

CHAPTER XII.

THE BIG WILD MUSTANG HUNT. WE TIRE THEM OUT. THE INDIANS CAPTURE OUR MESS WAGON AND COOK. OUR BILL

OF FARE BUFFALO MEAT WITHOUT SALT.

It was a bright clear morning in September as we were all gathered at the old home ranch, prepared to start on the great mustang hunt. There was one of the best men from each of the big cattle ranges in the panhandle and Arizona country, making twenty of the best range riders ever assembled together for a single purpose, while we were mounted on the best and fastest horses the Texas and Arizona cattle country could produce, while a horse rustler had left four days before with twenty more equally as good horses, giving each of us two horses apiece. We carried with us four days' rations, consisting of dried beef, crackers, potatoes, coffee—we had no sugar. The mess wagon well stocked with provisions for a two months' trip had also left four days before for a place in the wild horse district, where we knew the mustangs were to be found.

Many of the cattle men of Texas and Arizona were present to see us off, and the boss gave us a little talk on what was expected of us, and said, among other things, we were twenty of the best and gamest cow boys who ever roamed the western plains, and that he knew we would make good on hearing these words—we one and all resolved to do our best.

And swinging into the saddle we emptied our guns as a parting salutation and started on a dead run across the plains towards the scene of our duty. After a hard ride of ten days we sighted a band of about seventy-five mustangs. We at once proceeded to run them down. It was decided that twenty of us should surround the herd in a large circle, ten or fifteen miles across, which would leave a space of several miles between each rider, but not of a greater distance than he could easily cover when he saw the band coming his way or heard our signals.

The horse rustler was to keep the extra horses at a place where they would be safe and at the same time handy to the riders. Our plans completed, each rider made preparations to start for his station. But here another difficulty arose. We had not yet seen anything of our cook and mess wagon. It had not arrived at the place agreed upon, although it had had ample time to do so. Our provisions which we carried were quite low, so after waiting as long as we could, and the mess wagon failing to show up, we decided to start the hunt and take our chances on grub from what we could knock over with our guns.

Accordingly the boys all started out for their several stations. After waiting a reasonable length of time to give them an opportunity to reach their positions, we made for the herd, which as near as we could judge contained

about seventy-five of the prettiest horses it was ever my pleasure to see. The magnificent stallion who happened to be on guard had no sooner seen us than he gave the danger signal to the herd, who were off like the wind, led by a beautiful snow white stallion. To get them going was our only duty at present, and we well knew the importance of saving our saddle horses for the more serious work before us. Therefore we only walked our horses, or went on a dog trot, keeping a sharp lookout for the herd's return.

The band of wild horses would run ten or fifteen miles across the prairie, where they would catch sight of the other boys, then off they would go in another direction, only to repeat the performance, as they struck the other side of the circle. In this way they would make from fifty to sixty miles to our ten, and we were slowly working them down. We kept them going this way day and night, not giving them a moment's rest or time to eat. After keeping them on the go this way for ten days we were able to get within a mile of them and could see some of the stallions taking turns at leading the herd, while other stallions would be in the rear fighting them on. In a few days more we were near enough to begin shooting the stallions out of the herd. Then we could handle them a great deal better. At this time our want of grub began to tell on us. Our cook and mess wagon had not showed up, so we had long since given them up as lost. We believed they had been captured by the Indians and future events proved we were right.

Our only food consisted of buffalo meat of which we were able to secure plenty, but buffalo meat for breakfast, dinner and supper every day without bread or salt is not the most palatable bill of fare, especially when it is all we had day after day, without any prospect of a change until we got home. But we were game and resolved to stay with our work until it was finished, especially as we only had twenty men and everyone was badly needed in the work ahead of us, so we did not think we could spare a man to return home after grub. So we swallowed our buffalo meat day after day and kept the horses moving.

They were now pretty well worked down, and we proceeded to work them toward a place where we could begin to rope them. There were now only a few stallions left in the herd as we had shot nearly all of them, and the others were too tired to cause us any trouble. We had now been out of grub over three weeks except buffalo meat and such other game as we could bring down with our guns. Our fears that the cook and mess wagon had been captured by the Indians proved well founded, as we about this time met an outfit who had seen the place where the cook was killed. They said the surroundings indicated that quite a large band had surprised the cook and driv-

er, but that they had put up a brave fight as evidenced by the large number of empty rifle and revolver shells scattered around. Our first impulse after hearing this was to start in pursuit of the red skins and get revenge, but calmer judgment showed that such a course would be useless, because the Indians had a couple of weeks start of us and we did not know what tribe had committed the offense as there were so many Indians in that part of the country and in the Indian territory, and besides our horses were in no shape to chase Indians, so much to our regret our comrades had to go unrevenged at least for the present, but we all swore to make the Indians pay dearly, especially the guilty ones, if it were possible to discover who they were. We continued to work the mustangs back and forth, and in thirty days from the time we started out we had about sixty head hemmed up in Yellow Fox Canyon and were roping and riding them. They were not hard to handle as they were so poor some of them could hardly walk. This was not to be wondered at, as we had kept them on the go for the past thirty days, never once giving them a moment's rest day or night, and in that time they had very little to eat and no sleep. After roping and riding them all we got them together and headed for home.

Arriving at the ranch the mustangs were allowed to eat all they wanted and were roped and ridden until they were fairly well broken, when they were turned out with the other ranch horses. They proved good saddle horses, but as soon as they were turned out with the ranch horses they would start for their old feeding grounds, leading the other horses with them. We found it impossible to thoroughly domesticate them, so for that reason we gave them up as a bad proposition, and did not attempt to capture any more, though at that time thousands of wild mustangs were on the plains of Texas, Arizona, Wyoming and in fact all over the West. They were large, fine and as pretty a lot of horses as one could wish to see. They were seldom molested, though once in a while the Indians would make a campaign against them and capture a few, but not often, as they were so hard to capture. It was not worth the trouble, as it was almost impossible to approach them nearer than two miles, and there was always some stallions on the lookout while the others grazed over the plains, so it was out of the question to surprise them. At the first sign of danger the stallion sentinel would give his shrill neigh of warning and the herd were off like the wind.

We received unstinted praise from our employers for bringing to a successful conclusion the errand on which we were sent under such trying circumstances. But now that we were where grub was plentiful we looked on

our experience as nothing to make a fuss over.

But we deeply regretted the loss of our cook and mess wagon, and we resolved that if we ever found the guilty parties to make it rather warm for them. This we never did, neither did we ever hear more of the fate of the cook. Our work, so far as trips on the trail were concerned, was over for this season, and we could count on a long rest until spring, as aside from range riding and feeding there was nothing doing around the home ranch. But sometimes the range riding kept us on the go pretty lively, especially during and after a big storm, which sometimes scattered the cattle all over the surrounding country, and it would take some lively riding to get them all together again. Then the Indians and the white cattle thieves would make raids on our herds, running them off in great numbers and stampeding the balance of the herd.

This generally resulted in us chasing them sometimes for miles over the prairies, and we generally were successful in recovering our cattle and punishing the cattle thieves in a manner that they did not soon forget. But then again sometimes they would stampede the herd in the night, and under the cover of darkness and the excitement would manage to make off with some of the best horses or the choicest cattle, and by the time we missed them the thieves would have such a start that it was impossible to overtake them, but if they were overtaken, vengeance was swift and sure.

CHAPTER XIII.

ON THE TRAIL WITH THREE THOUSAND HEAD OF TEXAS STEERS. RUMORS OF TROUBLE WITH THE INDIANS AT DEADWOOD. THE ROPING CONTEST. I WIN THE NAME OF DEADWOOD DICK. THE SHOOTING MATCH. THE CUSTER MASSACRE. THE VIEW OF THE BATTLE FIELD. GOVERNMENT SCOUTS. AT HOME AGAIN.

In the spring of 1876 orders were received at the home ranch for three thousand head of three-year-old steers to be delivered near Deadwood, South Dakota. This being one of the largest orders we had ever received at one time, every man around the ranch was placed on his mettle to execute the order in record time.

Cow boys mounted on swift horses were dispatched to the farthest limits of the ranch with orders to round up and run in all the three-year-olds on the place, and it was not long before the ranch corrals began to fill up with the long horns as they were driven by the several parties of cow boys; as fast as they came in we would cut out, under the bosses' orders such cattle as were to make up our herd.

In the course of three days we had our herd ready for the trail and we made our preparations to start on our long journey north. Our route lay through New Mexico, Colorado and Wyoming, and as we had heard rumors that the Indians were on the war path and were kicking up something of a rumpus in Wyoming, Indian Territory and Kansas, we expected trouble before we again had the pleasure of sitting around our fire at the home ranch. Quite a large party was selected for this trip owing to the size of the herd and the possibility of trouble on the trail from the Indians. We, as usual, were all well armed and had as mounts the best horses our ranch produced, and in taking the trail we were perfectly confident that we could take care of our herd and ourselves through anything we were liable to meet. We had not been on the trail long before we met other outfits, who told us that General Custer was out after the Indians and that a big fight was expected when the Seventh U. S. Cavalry, General Custer's command, met the Crow tribe and other Indians under the leadership of Sitting Bull, Rain-in-the-Face, Old Chief Joseph, and other chiefs of lesser prominence, who had for a long time been terrorizing the settlers of that section and defying the Government.

As we proceeded on our journey it became evident to us that we were only a short distance behind the soldiers. When finally the Indians and soldiers met in the memorable battle or rather massacre in the Little Big Horn Basin on the Little Big Horn River in northern Wyoming, we were only two days behind them, or within 60 miles, but we did not know that at the time or we would have gone to Custer's assistance. We did not know of the fight or the outcome until several days after it was over. It was freely claimed at the time by cattle men who were in a position to know and with whom I talked that if Reno had gone to Custer's aid as he promised to do, Custer would not have lost his entire command and his life.

It was claimed Reno did not obey his orders, however that may be, it was one of the most bloody massacres in the history of this country. We went on our way to Deadwood with our herd, where we arrived on the 3rd of July, 1876, eight days after the Custer massacre took place.

The Custer Battle was June 25, '76, the battle commenced on Sunday

afternoon and lasted about two hours. That was the last of General Custer and his Seventh Cavalry. How I know this so well is because we had orders from one of the Government scouts to go in camp, that if we went any farther North we were liable to be captured by the Indians.

We arrived in Deadwood in good condition without having had any trouble with the Indians on the way up. We turned our cattle over to their new owners at once, then proceeded to take in the town. The next morning, July 4th, the gamblers and mining men made up a purse of $200 for a roping contest between the cow boys that were then in town, and as it was a holiday nearly all the cow boys for miles around were assembled there that day. It did not take long to arrange the details for the contest and contestants, six of them being colored cow boys, including myself. Our trail boss was chosen to pick out the mustangs from a herd of horses just off the range, and he picked out twelve of the most wild and vicious horses that he could find.

The conditions of the contest were that each of us who were mounted was to rope, throw, tie, bridle and saddle and mount the particular horse picked for us in the shortest time possible. The man accomplishing the feat in the quickest time to be declared the winner.

It seems to me that the horse chosen for me was the most vicious of the lot. Everything being in readiness, the "45" cracked and we all sprang forward together, each of us making for our particular mustang.

I roped, threw, tied, bridled, saddled and mounted my mustang in exactly nine minutes from the crack of the gun. The time of the next nearest competitor was twelve minutes and thirty seconds. This gave me the record and championship of the West, which I held up to the time I quit the business in 1890, and my record has never been beaten. It is worthy of passing remark that I never had a horse pitch with me so much as that mustang, but I never stopped sticking my spurs in him and using my quirt on his flanks until I proved his master. Right there the assembled crowd named me Deadwood Dick and proclaimed me champion roper of the western cattle country.

The roping contest over, a dispute arose over the shooting question with the result that a contest was arranged for the afternoon, as there happened to be some of the best shots with rifle and revolver in the West present that day. Among them were Stormy Jim, who claimed the championship; Powder Horn Bill, who had the reputation of never missing what he shot at; also White Head, a half breed, who generally hit what he shot at, and many other men who knew how to handle a rifle or 45-colt.

The range was measured off 100 and 250 yards for the rifle and 150 for

the Colt 45. At this distance a bulls eye about the size of an apple was put up. Each man was to have 14 shots at each range with the rifle and 12 shots with the Colts 45. I placed every one of my 14 shots with the rifle in the bulls eye with ease, all shots being made from the hip; but with the 45 Colts I missed it twice, only placing 10 shots in the small circle, Stormy Jim being my nearest competitor, only placing 8 bullets in the bulls eye clear, the rest being quite close, while with the 45 he placed 5 bullets in the charmed circle. This gave me the championship of rifle and revolver shooting as well as the roping cons test, and for that day I was the hero of Deadwood, and the purse of Woo which I had won on the roping contest went toward keeping things moving, and they did move as only a large crowd of cattle men can move things. This lasted for several days when most of the cattle men had to return to their respective ranches, as it was the busy season, accordingly our outfit began to make preparations to return to Arizona.

In the meantime news had reached us of the Custer massacre, and the indignation and sorrow was universal, as General Custer was personally known to a large number of the cattle men of the West. But we could do nothing now, as the Indians were out in such strong force. There was nothing to do but let Uncle Sam revenge the loss of the General and his brave command, but it is safe to say not one of us would have hesitated a moment in taking the trail in pursuit of the blood thirsty red skins had the opportunity offered.

Everything now being in readiness with us we took the trail homeward bound, and left Deadwood in a blaze of glory. On our way home we visited the Custer battle field in the Little Big Horn Basin.

There was ample evidence of the desperate and bloody fight that had taken place a few days before. We arrived home in Arizona in a short time without further incident, except that on the way back we met and talked with many of the famous Government scouts of that region, among them Buffalo Bill (William F. Cody), Yellow Stone Kelley, and many others of that day, some of whom are now living, while others lost their lives in the line of duty, and a finer or braver body of men never lived than these scouts of the West. It was my pleasure to meet Buffalo Bill often in the early 70s, and he was as fine a man as one could wish to meet, kind, generous, true and brave.

Buffalo Bill got his name from the fact that in the early days he was engaged in hunting buffalo for their hides and furnishing U. P. Railroad graders with meat, hence the name Buffalo Bill. Buffalo Bill, Yellowstone Kelley, with many others were at this time serving under Gen. C. C. Miles.

The name of Deadwood Dick was given to me by the people of Deadwood, South Dakota, July 4, 1876, after I had proven myself worthy to carry it, and after I had defeated all comers in riding, roping, and shooting, and I have always carried the name with honor since that time.

We arrived at the home ranch again on our return from the trip to Deadwood about the middle of September, it taking us a little over two months to make the return journey, as we stopped in Cheyenne for several days and at other places, where we always found a hearty welcome, especially so on this trip, as the news had preceded us, and I received enough attention to have given me the big head, but my head had constantly refused to get enlarged again ever since the time I sampled the demijohn in the sweet corn patch at home.

Arriving at home, we received a send off from our boss and our comrades of the home ranch, every man of whom on hearing the news turned loose his voice and his artillery in a grand demonstration in my honor.

But they said it was no surprise to them, as they had long known of my ability with the rope, rifle and 45 Colt, but just the same it was gratifying to know I had defeated the best men of the West, and brought the record home to the home ranch in Arizona. After a good rest we proceeded to ride the range again, getting our herds in good condition for the winter now at hand.

CHAPTER XIV.

RIDING THE RANGE. THE FIGHT WITH YELLOW DOG'S TRIBE. I AM CAPTURED AND ADOPTED BY THE INDIANS. MY ESCAPE. I RIDE A HUNDRED MILES IN TWELVE HOURS WITHOUT A SADDLE. MY INDIAN PONY. "YELLOW DOG CHIEF." THE BOYS PRESENT ME WITH A NEW OUTFIT. IN THE SADDLE AND ON THE TRAIL AGAIN.

It was a bright, clear fall day, October 4, 1876, that quite a large number of us boys started out over the range hunting strays which had been lost for some time. We had scattered over the range and I was riding along alone when all at once I heard the well known Indian war whoop and noticed not far away a large party of Indians making straight for me. They were all well mounted and they were in full war paint, which showed me that they were

on the war path, and as I was alone and had no wish to be scalped by them I decided to run for it. So I headed for Yellow Horse Canyon and gave my horse the rein, but as I had considerable objection to being chased by a lot of painted savages without some remonstrance, I turned in my saddle every once in a while and gave them a shot by way of greeting, and I had the satisfaction of seeing a painted brave tumble from his horse and go rolling in the dust every time my rifle spoke, and the Indians were by no means idle all this time, as their bullets were singing around me rather lively, one of them passing through my thigh, but it did not amount to much. Reaching Yellow Horse Canyon, I had about decided to stop and make a stand when one of their bullets caught me in the leg, passing clear through it and then through my horse, killing him. Quickly falling behind him I used his dead body for a breast work and stood the Indians off for a long time, as my aim was so deadly and they had lost so many that they were careful to keep out of range.

But finally my ammunition gave out, and the Indians were quick to find this out, and they at once closed in on me, but I was by no means subdued, wounded as I was and almost out of my head, and I fought with my empty gun until finally overpowered. When I came to my senses I was in tile Indians' camp.

My wounds had been dressed with some kind of herbs, the wound in my breast just over the heart was covered thickly with herbs and bound up. My nose had been nearly cut off, also one of my fingers had been nearly cut off. These wounds I received when I was fighting my captors with my empty gun. What caused them to spare my life I cannot tell, but it was I think partly because I had proved myself a brave man, and all savages admire a brave man and when they captured a man whose fighting powers were out of the ordinary they generally kept him if possible as he was needed in the tribe.

Then again Yellow Dog's tribe was composed largely of half breeds, and there was a large percentage of colored blood in the tribe, and as I was a colored man they wanted to keep me, as they thought I was too good a man to die. Be that as it may, they dressed my wounds and gave me plenty to eat, but the only grub they had was buffalo meat which they cooked over a fire of buffalo chips, but of this I had all I wanted to eat. For the first two days after my capture they kept me tied hand and foot. At the end of that time they untied my feet, but kept my hands tied for a couple of days longer, when I was given my freedom, but was always closely watched by members of the tribe. Three days after my capture my ears were pierced and I was adopted into the tribe. The operation of piercing my ears was quite painful, in the

method used, as they had a small bone secured from a deer's leg, a small thin bone, rounded at the end and as sharp as a needle. This they used to make the holes, then strings made from the tendons of a deer were inserted in place of thread, of which the Indians had none. Then horn ear rings were placed in my ears and the same kind of salve made from herbs which they placed on my wounds was placed on my ears and they soon healed.

The bullet holes in my leg and breast also healed in a surprisingly short time. That was good salve all right. As soon as I was well enough I took part in the Indian dances. One kind or another was in progress all the time. The war dance and the medicine dance seemed the most popular. When in the war dance the savages danced around me in a circle, making gestures, chanting, with every now and then a blood curdling yell, always keeping time to a sort of music provided by stretching buffalo skins tightly over a hoop.

When I was well enough I joined the dances, and I think I soon made a good dancer. The medicine dance varies from the war dance only that in the medicine dance the Indians danced around a boiling pot, the pot being filled with roots and water and they dance around it while it boils. The medicine dance occurs about daylight.

I very soon learned their ways and to understand them, though our conversation was mostly carried on by means of signs. They soon gave me to understand that I was to marry the chief's daughter, promising me 100 ponies to do so, and she was literally thrown in my arms; as for the lady she seemed perfectly willing if not anxious to become my bride. She was a beautiful woman, or rather girl; in fact all the squaws of this tribe were good looking, out of the ordinary, but I had other notions just then and did not want to get married under such circumstances, but for prudence sake I seemed to enter into their plans, but at the same time keeping a sharp lookout for a chance to escape. I noted where the Indians kept their horses at night, even picking out the handsome and fleet Indian pony which I meant to use should opportunity occur, and I seemed to fall in with the Indians' plans and seemed to them so contented that they gave me more and more freedom and relaxed the strict watch they had kept on me, and finally in about thirty days from the time of my capture my opportunity arrived.

My wounds were now nearly well, and gave me no trouble. It was a dark, cloudy night, and the Indians, grown careless in their fancied security, had relaxed their watchfulness. After they had all thrown themselves on the ground and the quiet of the camp proclaimed them all asleep I got up and crawling on my hands and knees, using the greatest caution for fear of mak-

ing a noise, I crawled about 250 yards to where the horses were picketed, and going to the Indian pony I had already picked out I slipped the skin thong in his mouth which the Indians use for a bridle, one which I had secured and carried in my shirt for some time for this particular purpose, then springing to his back I made for the open prairie in the direction of the home ranch in Texas, one hundred miles away. All that night I rode as fast as my horse could carry me and the next morning, twelve hours after I left the Indians camp I was safe on the home ranch again. And my joy was without bounds, and such a reception as I received from the boys. They said they were just one day late, and if it hadn't been for a fight they had with some of the same tribe, they would have been to my relief. As it was they did not expect to ever see me again alive. But that they know that if the Indians did not kill me, and gave me only half a chance I would get away from them, but now that I was safe home again, nothing mattered much and nothing was too good for me.

It was a mystery to them how I managed to escape death with such wounds as I had received, the marks of which I will carry to my grave and it is as much a mystery to me as the bullet that struck me in the breast just over the heart passed clear through, coming out my back just below the shoulder. Likewise the bullet in my leg passed clear through, then through my horse, killing him.

Those Indians are certainly wonderful doctors, and then I am naturally tough as I carry the marks of fourteen bullet wounds on different part of my body, most any one of which would be sufficient to kill an ordinary man, but I am not even crippled. It seems to me that if ever a man bore a charm I am the man, as I have had five horses shot from under me and killed, have fought Indians and Mexicans in all sorts of situations, and have been in more tight places than I can number. Yet I have always managed to escape with only the mark of a bullet or knife as a reminder. The fight with the Yellow Dog's tribe is probably the closest call I ever had, and as close a call as I ever want.

The fleet Indian pony which carried me to safety on that memorable hundred mile ride, I kept for about five years. I named him "The Yellow Dog Chief." And he lived on the best the ranch afforded, until his death which occurred in 1881, never having anything to do except an occasional race, as he could run like a deer. I thought too much of him to use him on the trail and he was the especial pet of every one on the home ranch, and for miles around.

I heard afterwards that the Indians pursued me that night for quite a distance, but I had too much the start and besides I had the fastest horse the

Indians owned. I have never since met any of my captors of that time. As they knew better than to venture in our neighborhood again. My wound healed nicely, thanks to the good attention the Indians gave me. My captors took everything of value I had on me when captured. My rifle which I especially prized for old associations salve; also my forty fives, saddle and bridle, in fact my whole outfit leaving me only the few clothes I had on at the time.

My comrades did not propose to let this bother me long, however, because they all chipped in and bought me a new outfit, including the best rifle and revolvers that could be secured, and I had my pick of the ranch horses for another mount. During my short stay with the Indians I learned a great deal about them, their ways of living, sports, dances, and mode of warfare which proved of great benefit to me in after years. The oblong shields they carried were made from tanned buffalo skins and so tough were they made that an arrow would not pierce them although I have seen them shoot an arrow clean through a buffalo. Neither will a bullet pierce them unless the ball hits the shield square on, otherwise it glances off.

All of them were exceedingly expert with the bow and arrow, and they are proud of their skill and are always practicing in an effort to excel each other. This rivalry extends even to the children who are seldom without their bows and arrows.

They named me Buffalo Papoose, and we managed to make our wants known by means of signs. As I was not with them a sufficient length of time to learn their language, I learned from them that I had killed five of their number and wounded three while they were chasing me and in the subsequent fight with my empty gun. The wounded men were hit in many places, but they were brought around all right, the same as I was. After my escape and after I arrived home it was some time before I was again called to active duty, as the boys would not hear of me doing anything resembling work, until I was thoroughly well and rested up. But I soon began to long for my saddle and the range.

And when orders were received at the ranch for 2000 head of cattle, to be delivered at Dodge City, Kansas, I insisted on taking the trail again. It was not with any sense of pride or in bravado that I recount here the fate of the men who have fallen at my hand.

It is a terrible thing to kill a man no matter what the cause. But as I am writing a true history of my life, I cannot leave these facts out. But every man who died at my hands was either seeking my life or died in open warfare, when it was a case of killing of being killed.

CHAPTER XV.

ON A TRIP TO DODGE CITY, KAN. I ROPE ONE OF UNCLE SAM'S CANNON. CAPTURED BY THE SOLDIERS. BAT MASTERSON TO MY RESCUE. LOST ON THE PRAIRIE. THE BUFFALO HUNTER CATER. MY HORSE GETS AWAY AND LEAVES ME ALONE ON THE PRAIRIE. THE BLIZZARD. FROZEN STIFF.

In the spring of 1877, now fully recovered from the effects of the very serious wounds I had received at the hands of the Indians and feeling my old self again, I joined the boys in their first trip of the season, with a herd of cattle for Dodge City. The trip was uneventful until we reached our destination. This was the first time I had been in Dodge City since I had won the name of "DEADWOOD DICK", and many of tine boys, who knew me when I first joined the cow boys there in 1869, were there to greet me now. After our herd had been delivered to their new owners, we started out to properly celebrate the event, and for a space of several days we kept the old town on the jump.

And so when we finally started for home all of us had more or less of the bad whiskey of Dodge City under our belts and were feeling rather spirited and ready for anything.

I probably had more of the bad whiskey of Dodge City than any one and was in consequence feeling very reckless, but we had about exhausted our resources of amusement in the town, and so were looking for trouble on the trail home.

On our way back to Texas, our way led past old Fort Dodge. Seeing the soldiers and the cannon in the fort, a bright idea struck me, but a fool one just the same. It was no less than a desire to rope one of the cannons. It seemed to me that it would be a good thing to rope a cannon and take it back to Texas with us to fight Indians with.

The bad whiskey which I carried under my belt was responsible for the fool idea, and gave me the nerve to attempt to execute the idea. Getting my lariat rope ready I rode to a position just opposite the Fate of the fort, which was standing open. Before the gate paced a sentry with his gun on his shoulder and his white gloves showing up clean and white against the dusty grey surroundings. I waited until the sentry had passed the gate, then putting spurs to my horse I dashed straight for and through the gate into the yard. The surprised sentry called halt, but I paid no attention to him. Making for the cannon at full speed my rope left my hand and settled square over the

cannon, then turning and putting spurs to my horse I tried to drag the cannon after me, but strain as he might my horse was unable to budge it an inch. In the meantime the surprised sentry at the gate had given the alarm and now I heard the bugle sound, boots and saddles, and glancing around I saw the soldiers mounting to come after me, and finding I could not move the cannon, I rode close up to it and got my lariat off then made for the gate again at full speed. The guard jumped in front of me with his gun up, calling halt, but I went by him like a shot, expecting to hear the crack of his musket, but for some reason he failed to fire on me, and I made for the open prairie with the cavalry in hot pursuit.

My horse could run like a wild deer, but he was no match for the big, strong, fresh horses of the soldiers and they soon had me. Relieving me of my arms they placed me in the guard house where the commanding officer came to see me. He asked me who I was and what I was after at the fort. I told him and then he asked me if I knew anyone in the city. I told him I knew Bat Masterson. He ordered two guards to take me to the city to see Masterson. As soon as Masterson saw me he asked me what the trouble was, and before I could answer, the guards told him I rode into the fort and roped one of the cannons and tried to pull it out. Bat asked me what I wanted with a cannon and what I intended doing with it. I told him I wanted to take it back to Texas with me to fight the Indians with; then they all laughed. Then Bat told them that I was all right, the only trouble being that I had too much bad whiskey under my shirt. They said I would have to set the drinks for the house. They came to $15.00, and when I started to pay for them, Bat said for me to keep my money that he would pay for them himself, which he did. Bat said that I was the only cowboy that he liked, and that his brother Jim also thought very much of me. I was then let go and I joined the boys and we continued on our way home, where we arrived safely on the 1st of June, 1877.

We at once began preparing for the coming big round up. As usual this kept us very busy during the months of July and August, and as we received no more orders for cattle this season, we did not have to take the trail again, but after the round up was over, we were kept busy in range riding, and the general all around work of the big cattle ranch. We had at this time on the ranch upwards of 30,000 head of cattle, our own cattle, not to mention the cattle belonging to the many other interests without the Pan Handle country, and as all these immense herds used the range of the country, in common as there was no fences to divide the ranches, consequently the cattle belong-

ing to the different herds often got mixed up and large numbers of them strayed.

At the round ups it was our duty to cut out and brand the young calves, take a census of our stock, and then after the round up was over we would start out to look for possible strays. Over the range we would ride through canyons and gorges, and every place where it was possible for cattle to stray, as it was important to get them with the main herd before winter set in, as if left out in small bunches there was danger of them perishing in the frequent hard storms of the winter. While range riding or hunting for strays, we always carried with us on our saddle the branding irons of our respective ranches, and whenever we ran across a calf that had not been branded we had to rope the calf, tie it, then a fire was made of buffalo chips, the only fuel besides grass to be found on the prairie.

The irons were heated and the calf was branded with the brand of the finder, no matter who it personally belonged to. It now became the property of the finder. The lost cattle were then driven to the main herd. After they were once gotten together it was our duty to keep them together during the winter and early spring. It was while out hunting strays that I, got lost, the first and only time I was ever lost in my life, and for four days I had an experience that few men ever went through and lived, as it was a close pull for me.

I had been out for several days looking for lost cattle and becoming separated from the other boys and being in a part of the country unfamiliar to me. It was stormy when I started out from the home ranch and when I had ridden about a hundred miles from home it began to storm in earnest, rain, hail, sleet, and the clouds seemed to touch the earth and gather in their inpenterable embrace every thing thereon. For a long time I rode on in the direction of home, but as I could not see fifty yards ahead it was a case of going it blind. After riding for many weary hours through the storm I came across a little log cabin on the Palidore river. I rode up to within one hundred yards of it where I was motioned to stop by an old long haired man who stepped out of the cabin door with a long buffalo gun on his arm. It was with this he had motioned me to stop.

I promptly pulled up and raised my hat, which, according to the custom of the cowboy country, gave him to understand I was a cowboy from the western cow ranges. He then motioned me to come on. Riding up to the cabin he asked me to dismount and we shook hands.

He said, when I saw you coming I said to myself that must be a lost cowboy from some of the western cow ranges. I told him I was lost all right, and

I told him who I was and where from. Again we shook hands, he saying as we did so, that we were friends until we met again, and he hoped forever. He then told me to picket out my horse and come in and have some supper, which very welcome invitation I accepted.

His cabin was constructed of rough hewn logs, somewhat after the fashion of a Spanish block house. One part of it was constructed under ground, a sort of dug out, while the upper portion of the cabin proper was provided with many loop holes, commanding every direction.

He later told me these loop holes had stood him in handy many a time when he had been attacked by Indians, in their efforts to capture him. On entering his cabin I was amazed to see the walls covered with all kinds of skins, horns, and antlers. Buffalo skins in great numbers covered the floor and bed, while the walls were completely hidden behind the skins of every animal of that region, including large number of rattle snakes skins and many of their rattles.

His bed, which was in one corner of the dug out, was of skins, and to me, weary from my long ride through the storm, seemed to be the most comfortable place on the globe just then. He soon set before me a bountious supper, consisting of buffalo meat and corn dodgers, and seldom before have I enjoyed a meal as I did that one. During supper he told me many of his experiences in the western country. His name was Cater, and he was one of the oldest buffalo hunters in that Part of Texas, having hunted and trapped over the wild country ever since the early thirties, and during that time he had many a thrilling adventure with Indians and wild animals.

I stayed with him that night and slept soundly on a comfortable bed he made for me. The next morning he gave me a good breakfast and I prepared to take my departure as the storm had somewhat moderated, and I was anxious to get home, as the boys knowing I was out would be looking for me if I did not show up in a reasonable time.

My kind host told me to go directly northwest and I would strike the Calones flats, a place with which I was perfectly familiar. He said it was about 75 miles from his place. Once there I would have no difficulty in finding my way home. Cater put me up a good lunch to last me on my way, and with many expressions of gratitude to him, I left him with his skins and comfortable, though solitary life. All that day and part of the night I rode in the direction he told me, until about 11 o'clock when I became so tired I decided to go into camp and give my tired horse a rest and a chance to eat. Accordingly I dismounted and removed the saddle and bridle from my horse

I hobbled him and turned him loose to graze on the luxuriant grass, while I, tired out, laid down with my head on my saddle fully dressed as I was, not even removing my belt containing my 45 pistol from my waist, laying my Winchester close by. The rain had ceased to fall, but it was still cloudy and threatening. It was my intention to rest a few hours then continue on my way; and as I could not see the stars on account of the clouds and as it was important that I keep my direction northwest in order to strike the Flats, I had carefully taken my direction before sundown, and now on moving my saddle I placed it on the ground pointing in the direction I was going when I stopped so that it would enable me to keep my direction when I again started out. I had been laying there for some time and my horse was quietly grazing about 20 yards off, when I suddenly heard something squeal. It sounded like a woman's voice. It frightened my horse and he ran for me. I jumped to my feet with my Winchester in my hand. This caused my horse to rear and wheel and I heard his hobbles break with a sharp snap. Then I heard the sound of his galloping feet going across the Pan Handle plains until the sound was lost in the distance. Then I slowly began to realize that I was left alone on the plains on foot, how many miles from home I did not know. Remembering I had my guns all right, it was my impulse to go in pursuit of my horse as I thought I could eventually catch him after he had got over his scare, but when I thought of my 40 pound saddle, and I did not want to leave that, so saying to myself that is the second saddle I ever owned, the other having been taken by the Indians when I was captured, and this saddle was part of the outfit presented to me by the boys, and so tired and as hungry as a hawk, I shouldered my saddle and started out in the direction I was going when I went into camp, saying to myself as I did so, if my horse could pack me and my outfit day and night I can at least pack my outfit. Keeping my direction as well as I could I started out over the prairie through the dark, walking all that night and all the next day without anything to eat or drink until just about sundown and when I had begun to think I would have to spend another night on the prairie without food or drink, when I emerged from a little draw on to a raise on the prairie, then looking over on to a small flat I saw a large herd of buffalo. These were the first I had seen since I became lost and the sight of them put renewed life and hope in me as I was then nearly famished, and when I saw them I knew I had something to eat.

Off to one side about 20 yards from the main herd and about 150 yards from me was a young calf. Placing my Winchester to my shoulder I glanced along the shining barrel, but my hands shook so much I lowered it again, not

that I was afraid of missing it as I knew I was a dead shot at that distance, but my weakness caused by my long enforced fast and my great thirst made my eyes dim and my hands shake in a way they had never done before, so waiting a few moments I again placed the gun to my shoulder and this time it spoke and the calf dropped where it had stood. Picking up my outfit I went down to where my supper was laying. I took out my jack knife and commenced on one of his hind quarters. I began to skin and eat to my hearts content, but I was so very thirsty. I had heard of people drinking blood to quench their thirst and that gave me an idea, so cutting the calf's throat with my knife I eagerly drank the fresh warm blood.

It tasted very much like warm sweet milk. It quenched my thirst and made me feel strong, when I had eaten all I could, I cut off two large chunks of the meat and tied them to my saddle, then again shouldering the whole thing I started On my way feeling almost as satisfied as if I had my horse with me. I was lost two days, and two nights, after my horse left me and all that time I kept walking packing my 40 pounds saddle and my Winchester and two cattle pistols.

On the second night about daylight the weather became more threatening and I saw in the distance a long column which looked like smoke. It seemed to be coming towards me at the rate of a mile a minute. It did not take it long to reach me, and when it did I struggled on for a few yards but it was no use, tired as I was from packing my heavy outfit for more than 48 hours and my long tramp, I had not the strength to fight against the storm so I had to come alone. When I again came to myself I was covered up head and foot in the snow, in the camp of some of my comrades from the ranch.

It seemed from what I was told afterwards that the boys knowing I was out in the storm and failing to show up, they had started out to look for me, they had gone in camp during the storm and when the blizzard had passed they noticed an object out on the prairie in the snow, with one hand frozen, clenched around my Winchester and the other around the horn of my saddle, and they had hard work to get my hands loose, they picked me up and placed me on one of the horses and took me to camp where they stripped me of my clothes and wrapped me up in the snow, all the skin came off my nose and mouth and my hands and feet had been so badly frozen that the nails all came off. After had got thawed out in the mess wagon and took me home in 15 days I was again in the saddle ready for business but I will never forget those few days I was lost and the marks of that storm I will carry with me always.

CHAPTER XVI.

THE OLD HAZE AND ELSWORTH TRAIL. OUR TRIP TO CHEYENNE. EX-SHERIFF PAT A. GARRET. THE DEATH OF "BILLY THE KID". THE LINCOLN COUNTY CATTLE WAR.

Early the next spring 1878 we went on a short trip to Junction City, Kan., with a small herd of horses for Hokin and Herst. We started out from the home ranch early in April, stringing the herd out along the old Haze and Elsworth trail. Everything went well until we were several days out and we had went in camp for the night. The herd had been rounded up and were grazing in the open prairie under the usual watch. And all the cowboys except the first watch had turned in for a good night's rest, when it began to storm finally developing into a genuine old fashioned Texas storm, with the usual result that the herd stampeded.

The watch at once gave the alarm and we awoke to find everything in confusion. It was a very dark night and under such circumstances it is hard to control a herd of horses in a stampede. In a few moments every man was in the saddle, as we always kept our saddle horses picketed cut, so they could not join the other horses. And it was our custom when on the trail with a herd of horses on going into camp to leave our saddle horses, saddled and bridled, merely loosing the cinches of the saddles though sometimes we removed the bridles, to enable them to graze better. So when the alarm was given in this instance, it did not take us long to get in the saddle and after the horses who were now going across the prairie as only frightened horses can go in a stampede.

The storm continued with more or less fury all night and it was late the next day before we got the herd rounded up and under any sort of control. The next morning we found that one of the boys, Frank Smith, had lost his horse and outfit during the night. While chasing the horses over the prairie, his horse stepped in a prairie dog's hole and fell. Throwing his rider and snatching the rope out of Smith's hand, the horse made off over the prairie carrying with him bridle, saddle and outfit, and we never saw or heard of him again. After getting our breakfast, we continued north, and all went well with us until we struck the Wakeeny river, near Junction City, when in fording the stream. It was high water and we were forced to swim our horses across. All went well with the herd and the boys were following when one of them came near being drowned, and was only saved by my quick rope.

I had entered the river and my horse was swimming easily, when on glancing around I saw one of the boys, Loyd Hoedin by name, go under the water. Both man and horse completely disappeared. They soon came up only to disappear again. I saw at once something was wrong so when they came up the second time I threw my rope. It fell near Hoedin, who had the presence of mind to grasp it, and hold on while I snaked both man and horse out to safety. After reaching Junction City and turning the herd over to their new owners we started out to have the usual good time. This lasted for several days during which time we cleaned up pretty near all the money there was in the Junction with our horses in a six hundred yard race, between ourselves and cow boys from different outfits who happened to be in the city.

Our horses without exception proved the fastest runners, accordingly we pocketed considerable coin, and in consequence we were feeling first rate when we struck the trail homeward bound. We arrived at the home ranch all right in June. This was the last trip we were called to make this season, and our time for the remainder of the year was taken up with the general routine work of the large cattle ranch.

Late the next season we took the trail en route to Cheyenne, Wyoming, with two thousand head of fine Texas steers for the Swan Brothers, 20 miles northwest of Cheyenne. Nothing of unusual importance happened on this trip aside from the regular incidents pertaining to driving such a large herd of cattle on the trail. We had a few stampedes and lost a few cattle, arriving in Cheyenne we had a royal good time for a few days as usual before starting home. On arriving at the home ranch again we found considerable excitement, owing to the war between the cattle men and cattle rustlers and every man was needed at home and few there were who did not take part in one way or another in the most bitter and furious cattle war of history and I being one of the leading cowboys of the West, necessarily took an active part in the dispute and many were the sharp clashes between the waring factions that I witnessed and fought in and was wounded many times in these engagements. For years the cattle rustlers had been invading the large cattle ranges belonging to the large cattle kings of the West and running off and branding large numbers of choice cattle and horses, this led to many a sharp fight between the cowboys and the rustlers, but of late these thieves had become so bold and the losses of the cattle men had become so great that the latter determined to put a stop to it, and so open war was declared.

On one side was the large ranchmen and cattle men and on the other the Indians, half breeds, Mexicans and white outlaws that made the cattle country

their rendezvous. The cattle men had now organized with the given determination of either killing or running out of the country for good these thieves, who had caused them so much loss. And during the war many of them cashed in and the others for the most part left for pastures new, having been virtually whipped out of the country. It was a desperate and bloody war while it lasted.

But it was satisfactory to the cattle men who could now rest easier in the security of their herds and their grazing grounds. It was at this time that I saw considerable of William H. Bonney alias "Billie the kid", the most noted desperado and all around bad man the world has known.

The first time I met Billie the Kid was in Antonshico, New Mexico, in a saloon, when he asked me to drink with him, that was in 1877. Later he hired to Pete Galligan, the man in whose employ I was. Galligan hired the Kid to drive his buck board between the White Oaks, the nearest town, and Galligan's ranch with provisions for the boys, and the Kid told me himself that one these trips he would drive the team, on a dead run, the whole distance of 30 miles to the Oaks order to get there quick so he would have more time to stay around town before it was time to start back, then when he would arrive home the team was nearly dead from exhaustion. He remained in the employ of Galligan for about eleven months, then he was hired by John Chisholm to rustle cattle for him. Chisholm agreed to pay the Kid so much per head for all the cattle the Kid rustled. When the time came for a settlement, Chisholm failed to settle right or to the Kid's satisfaction, then the Kid told Chisholm he would give him one day to make up his mind to settle right, but before the Kid could see Chisholm again, Chisholm left the country going east where his brother was. The Kid then swore vengence, and said he would take his revenge out of Chisholm's men, and he at once began killing all the employ of John Chisholm. He would ride up to a bunch of cowboys and enquire if they worked for Chisholm. If they replied in the affirmative, he would shoot them dead on the spot, and few men were quicker with a 45 or a deadly shot than "Billie the Kid". The next time I met the Kid was in Holbrook, Arizona, just after a big round up. The Kid, Buck Cannon, and Billie Woods were together. I was on my way to Silver City, New Mexico, in the fall of 1880 when I met them, and as they were going there also, we rode on together The "Kid" showed me the little log cabin where he said he was born. I went in the cabin with him, and he showed me how it was arranged when he lived there, showing me where the bed sat and the stove and table. He then pointed out the old postoffice which he said he had been in lots of times.

He told me he was born and raised in Silver City, New Mexico, which is near the Moggocilion Mountains, and at that time the Kid was badly wanted by the sheriffs of several counties for numerous murders committed by him mostly of John Chisholm's men in Texas and New Mexico.

The Kid bid me good bye. He said he was going to the mountains as he knew them well, and once there he was all right as he could stand off a regiment of soldiers. The three of them departed together. I never saw him again until the spring of 1881. I was in the city of Elmorgo, New Mexico, and saw him the morning he was forced to flee to the mountains to escape arrest. We could see him up there behind the rocks. He was well armed having with him two Winchesters and two 45 Colts revolvers and plenty of ammunition, and although the officers wanted him badly, no one dared go up after him as it was certain death to come with range of the Kid's guns. Later on he escaped and the next time I saw him has in Antonshico, New Mexico. It was in June, and we had come up from Colonas after some saddle horses, and I met and talked with him.

The next time I saw him he was laying dead at Pete Maxwell's ranch in Lincoln county, New Mexico, having been killed by Pat A. Garret at that time sheriff of Lincoln county, New Mexico. We arrived in Lincoln county the very night he was killed at Pete Maxwell's ranch and went into camp a short distance from Maxwell's, and we saw the Kid a short time after he had been killed. The Kid had been arrested by Pat Garret and his posse a short time before at Stinking Springs, New Mexico, along with Tom Pickett, Billy Wilson and Dave Rudebough, after arresting these men which was only effected after a hard fight and after the Kid's ammunition had given out. Garret took the men heavily ironed to Los Vegas. When it became known that Billy the Kid had been captured a mob formed for the purpose of lynching him. But Garret placed his prisoners in a box car over which himself and deputies stood guard until the train pulled out which was nearly two hours. During that time the mob was furious to get at the men, but they well knew the temper of Sheriff Garret so they kept their distance.

The men were tried and convicted. The Kid and Rudbough were sentenced to be hanged. Rudbough for having killed a jailer at Los Vegas in 1880. The judge on passing sentence on the Kid, said you are sentenced to be hanged by the neck until you are dead-dead-dead. The Kid laughed in the judge's face saying, and you can go to Hell, Hell, Hell. After the Kid had been sentenced he was placed in jail at Los Vegas, ironed hand and foot, and under heavy guard, but never lost confidence and was always looking for a

chance to escape. When the day of his execution was not much more than a week off, the Kid saw his chance, while eating his supper both handcuffs had been fastened to one wrist so the Kid could better feed himself. He was only guarded by one deputy Bell. The other deputy, Ollinger, had gone to supper across the street from the jail. Bell turned his head for a moment and the Kid noticing the movement quick as a flash brought the handcuffs down on Bell's head, stunning him. The Kid then snatched Bell's revolver, he shot the deputy through the body. Bell staggered to the steps down which he fell and into the yard below where he died. Ollinger hearing the shot rushed across the street. As he entered the jail yard he looked up and saw the Kid at a window. As he did so the Kid shot Ollinger dead with a shot gun which was loaded with buck shot. The Kid then broke the gun across the window sill, then going to the room where the weapons were kept the Kid picked out what guns he wanted and broke the balance. Then he made the first person he met break the irons from his legs and bring him a horse. The Kid then took four revolvers and two Winchester rifles and rode away. Sheriff Garret was at White Oaks at the time and as soon he as heard of the escape he hurried home and organized a posse to recapture the Kid, but the Kid was at liberty two months before he was finally rounded up and killed at Pete Maxwell's ranch. At the time the Kid escaped at Los Vegas myself and a party of our boys had our horses at Menderhall and Hunter's livery stable, just a few doors from the jail and I was standing on the street talking to a friend when the Kid rode by. From Los Vegas he went to the borders of Lincoln county where his ever ready revolver was always in evidence. Shortly after his escape he shot and killed William Mathews and a companion whom he met on the prairie without apparent cause, and several other murders were attrib uted to him before he was finally located at Maxwell's ranch and killed by Sheriff Garret.

The Kid was only 22 years of age when his wild career was ended by the bullet from the sheriff's pun and it is safe to assert he had at lease one murder to the credit of every year of his life. He was killed by Sheriff Garret in a room of one of the old houses at Fort Sumner, known at that time as Maxwell's ranch, July 12, 1881, about two months after his escape from the Lincoln county jail, and Sheriff Pat A. Garret, one of the nervest men of that country of nervy men and the only man who ever pursued the Kid and lived to tell the tale, is at present at the head of the Customs Service at El Paso, Texas, and to meet him and note his pleasant smile and kindly disposition, one would not believe him the man who sent Billie the Kid to his last

account. But behind the pleasant twinkle in his eye and the warm hand clasp there is a head as cool and a nerve as steady as ever held a 45.

CHAPTER XVII.

ANOTHER TRIP TO OLD MEXICO. I ROPE AN ENGINE. I FALL IN LOVE. MY COURTSHIP. DEATH OF MY SWEETHEART. MY PROMISED WIFE. I MUST BEAR A CHARMED LIFE. THE ADVENT OF PROGRESS. THE LAST OF THE RANGE.

On one of these memorable trips after cattle, and with cattle on the trail, one that I will most likely remember, the longest was a trip to Old Mexico after a herd of horses. It was on this trip that I fell in love, the first time in my life. During my wild career on the western plains I had met many handsome women, and they often made much of me, but somehow I had never experienced the feeling called love, until I met my charming sweetheart in Old Mexico. I had perhaps been too much absorbed in the wild life of the plains, in the horses, and cattle which made up my world, to have the time or inclination to seek or enjoy the company of the gentler sex. But now that I had met my fate, I suppose I became as silly about it as any tenderfoot from the east could possibly be as evidence of how badly I was hit. While on the trail with the herd our route lay along a narrow gauge railroad, and I was feeling up in the air caused no doubt partly from the effects of love and partly from the effects of Mexican whiskey, a generous measure I had under my belt, however I was feeling fine, so when the little engine came puffing along in the distance I said to the boys I have roped nearly everything that could be roped, so now I am going to rope the engine. They tried to persuade me not to make the attempt, but I was in no mood to listen to reason or anything else, so when the engine came along I put my spurs to my horse and when near enough I let fly my lariat. The rope settled gracefully around the smoke stack, and as usual my trained horse set himself back for the shock, but the engine set both myself and my horse in the ditch, and might have continued to set us in places had not something given way, as it was the rope parted, but the boys said afterwards that they thought they would have to send for a wrecking train to clean the track or rather the ditch.

Roping a live engine is by long odds worse than roping wild Buffalo on

the plains or Uncle Sam's cannon at the forts. This incident cleared the atmosphere somewhat, but my love was as strong as ever and I thanked my lucky start she did not see me as they dragged me out of the ditch.

I first saw my sweetheart as we were driving the herd along the dusty road, passing a small adobe house near the city of Old Mexico. I saw a handsome young Spanish girl standing in the yard and I suppose I fell in love with her at first sight, anyway I pretended to be very thirsty and rode up and asked her for a drink. She gave it to me and I exchanged a few words with her before joining the boys and the herds.

After that I saw her quite often during my stay in Old Mexico before we again returned home. One day shortly before I was to leave for the North I went to see her and overheard a conversation between her and her mother, in which her mother said to her: "My daughter will you leave your mother for to go with the wild cowboy?" And she answered no mother I will not leave you to go with any wild cowboy. On hearing this I bid her goodbye and a long farewell, as I told her I did not expect to ever see her again. Then leaping to the back of my faithful horse I rode like mad across the Mexican plains, until I had somewhat cooled down, but it was a hard blow to me, as I truly loved her. After that I joined the boys and returned up the trail with them. Six or seven months later we were again in Old Mexico with a herd of cattle and went in camp some distance out from the city, and as soon as she heard our outfit had returned she rode out to the camp and after looking around and not seeing me, she said to the camp boss, "Where is the wild cowboy that was here with you last time? Did he not come up the trail with you." The boss told her I had come up the trail but that I had not been seen since crossing the last mountains as of course he knew whom she meant as my little love affair was pretty generally known among the boys. When the boss told her that I had not been seen since they had crossed the last mountains, she hung her head and looked completely heart broken. I was lying in the mess wagon at the time an interested spectator of all that took place, and seeing her looking so downhearted I could hardly restrain myself from jumping out of the wagon and taking her in my arms. After a time she slowly raised her head and looked long and wistfully up the trail. Then turning to the camp boss again she said, "Camp boss tell me truly if Nat Love works with you and did he come on this trip with you". The boss answered her as before that I had not been seen since crossing the last mountains, which was true as I had been riding in the mess wagon. On hearing the boss' answer she took it as final and started to ride away.

I thought it high time to make my presence known, as with the sight of her, all my old love returned, and I forgot every thing except that I loved her. So I jumped out of the wagon exclaiming here I am, and in a minute we were locked in each others arms and I believe I kissed her before all the boys, but I didn't care, she was mine now. We became engaged and were to be married in the fall and were to make our home in the city of Mexico, but in the spring she took sick and died. Her death broke me all up and after I buried her I became very wild and reckless, not caring what happened to me and when you saw me in the saddle you saw me at home, and while I saw many women since I could never care for any as I did for her. And I vainly tried to forget her and my sorrow in the wild life of the plains and every danger I could find courting death in fights with Indians and Mexicans and dare devil riding on the range, but it seemed to me that I bore a charmed life. Horses were shot from under me, men were killed around me, but always I escaped with a trifling wound at the worst. As time passed I began to recover from my disappointment and to take my old interest in the work of the ranch, and as my reputation had spread over the country I did not lack work, but was kept on the go all the time, first with one large cattle owner, then with another. Most of my working being in the round ups and brandings, brand reading, and with large herds on the trail, as during my long experience in the cattle country I had traveled every known trail, and over immense stretches of country where there was no sign of a trail, nothing but the wide expanse of prairie; bare except for the buffalo grass, with here and there a lone tree or a giant cactus standing as a lone sentinel in the wildest of long stretches of grazing land rolling away in billows of hill and gully, like the waves of the ocean. Likewise I could read, identify and place every brand or mark placed on a horse or steer between the Gulf of Mexico and the borders of Canada, on the North and from Missouri to California. Over this stretch of country I have often traveled with herds of horses or cattle or in searching for strays or hunting the noble buffalo on his own native feeding grounds. The great buffalo slaughter commenced in the west in 1874, and in 1877 they had become so scarce that it was a rare occasion when you came across a herd containing more than fifty animals where before you could find thousands in a herd. Many things were responsible for the slaughter, but the principal reason that they had now become so scarce was that in 1875 and 1876 the Indians started to kill them in large numbers for their skins. Thousands were killed by them, skinned and the carcasses left as food for the wolves and vultures of the prairie. Many were killed by the white hunters to furnish meat for the railroad graders and the troupe at the frontier forts.

While the big cattle ranches were always kept well supplied with buffalo meat, on the stock of my rifle is one hundred and twenty-six notches, each one representing a fine buffalo that has fallen to my own hand, while some I have killed with the knife and 45 colts, I forgot to cut a notch for. Buffalo hunting, a sport for kings, thy time has passed. Where once they roamed by the thousands now rises the chimney and the spire, while across their once peaceful path now thunders the iron horse, awakening the echoes far and near with bell and whistle, where once could only be heard the sharp crack of the rifle or the long doleful yelp of the coyote. At the present time the only buffalo to be found are in the private parks of a few men who are preserving them for pleasure or profit.

With the march of progress came the railroad and no longer were we called upon to follow the long horned steers, or mustangs on the trail, while the immense cattle ranges, stretching away in the distance as far as the eye could see, now began to be dotted with cities and towns and the cattle industry which once held a monopoly in the west, now had to give way to the industry of the farm and the mill. To us wild cowboys of the range, used to the wild and unrestricted life of the boundless plains, the new order of things did not appeal, and many of us became disgusted and quit the wild life for the pursuits of our more civilized brother. I was among that number and in 1890 I bid farewell to the life which I had followed for over twenty years.

It was with genuine regret that I left the long horn Texas cattle and the wild mustangs of the range, but the life had in a great measure lost its attractions and so I decided to quit it and try something else for a while. During my life so far I had no chance to secure an education, except the education of the plains and the cattle business. In this I recognize no superior being. Gifted with a splendid memory and quick observation I learned and remembered things that others passed by and forgot, and I have yet to meet the man who can give me instruction in the phases of a life in which I spent so long. After quitting the cowboy life I struck out for Denver. Here I met and married the present Mrs. Love, my second love. We were married August 22, 1889, and she is with me now a true and faithful partner, and says she is not one bit jealous of my first love, who lies buried in the city of Old Mexico.

One year later, in 1890, I accepted a position in the Pullman service on the Denver and Rio Grande Railroad, running between Denver and Salida, Colorado. The Pullman service was then in its infancy, so to speak, as there was as much difference between the Pullman sleeping cars of those days and the present as there is between the ox team and the automobile.

CHAPTER XVIII.

THE PULLMAN SERVICE. LIFE ON THE TRAIL. MY FIRST TRIP. A SLUMP IN TIPS. I BECOME DISGUSTED AND QUIT. A PERIOD OF HUSKING. MY NEXT TRIP ON THE PULLMAN. TIPS AND THE PEOPLE WHO GIVE THEM.

After my marriage in Denver, I rented a small cottage which I comfortably furnished and we, Mrs. Love and myself, started to housekeeping in a modest way. Then I began to look around for a job, but to a man who was used to the excitement and continual action of the range and the cattle ranches, the civilized and quiet life of the city is apt to prove stale and uninteresting. It was that way with me, and after passing up several jobs offered to me I thought I would try railroading for awhile, probably for the same reason that prompted me to leave home twenty years before; I still wanted to see the world. With that idea in mind, I went to the Pullman offices in Denver, and after making some inquiries I was directed to the office of Superintendent Rummels who was at that time superintendent of the Pullman service.

A Mr. Wright was his assistant. I found Superintendent Rummels in his office) and I asked him if he wanted to hire any more porters. He asked me if I had ever worked for the Pullman company. I told him no that I had been a cowboy ever since I was 16 years old. He then asked me if I had money enough to buy my Pullman uniform. I asked him how much it would cost and he said $22.00. I told him yes, I had the price. He asked me if I knew any one in Denver. I told him yes and gave him the name of Mr. Sprangler who had my money in his bank. Supt. Rummels told me to get a letter from Mr. Sprangler and he would put me on. So I went and got the letter and with it the money to pay for my uniform, after having my measure taken and sending for my suit. I borrowed a uniform from one of the other porters and the second day after I called on the superintendent I was sent on the run between Denver and Salida. One of the old men put me on to my duties and showed me how to make up my car and the general run of things.

On my first trip I found a kind friend in the Pullman conductor, a Mr. Keely, who helped me in many ways and I suppose I made many blunders as the difference between a Pullman car and the back of a Texas mustang is very great. However I managed to get around among the passengers in my car, and attend to their needs in some sort of a way.

My first trouble commenced when I succeeded in getting the shoes of passengers which had been given to me to polish, badly mixed up. The shoes of a portly red faced man whose berth was in the forward end of the car, I placed by the berth of a tall and slim western yankee at the other end of the car, while a number 7 and a number 9 shoe were placed decorously by the berth of a sour spinster from New York. This naturally caused a good sized rumpus the next morning. And sundry blessings were heaped on the head of yours truly. Nearly all the passengers were mad and the tips were conspicuous by their absence. That made me mad and thoroughly disgusted with the job. On returning to Denver I again called on Superintendent Rummels and told him that I had enough of the Pullman service, and would rather go back to the cattle and the range. Superintendent Rummels tried to persuade me to stay with it saying I had done all right, and would improve with experience but I was thoroughly disgusted and wanted no more of it, so I turned in my keys, got my uniform and walked out. So again I was without a job.

After going around Denver for several days, it struck me that there was money to be made selling fruit, vegetables, honey and chickens around the town. Accordingly I purchased a horse and wagon and an assorted stock and started out on my new vocation. This proved profitable from the start and I made good money which caused me to stay with it for nearly a year, when my natural restfulness caused me to become discontented and to yearn for more excitement and something a little faster so I disposed of my stock, horse and wagon, and started out to look for something else to do, but that something else was about as hard to find as the proverbial needle in the straw stack, at that particular time. Whether it was fate or the talk of the other porters whom I met I finally concluded to give the Pullman service another try. Accordingly I called on Mr. J. M. Smith who was now district superintendent of the Pullman service and asked him for a job. He asked me if I had been in the company's service before and I told him yes. He asked me how long and I told him one trip, and I told him why I quit, and that the tips were too slow for me. He asked me if I thought it was any better now, and I said I did not know whether it was any better or not but that I thought I could do better.

He told me the whole secret of success was in pleasing all my passengers. I told him I thought it was all right about pleasing two or three passengers but when it came to pleasing a whole car full of passengers, that was another matter. He said to try anyway. He than assigned me to a car running on the narrow gauge line between Denver and Alamosa, Creed and Durangro.

This was the real beginning of my Pullman service.

I ran on the Colorado roads under Superintendent Smith for a number of years and always found him courteous and obliging, always ready and willing to help us with advice and counsel, but what proved a mystery to me for a long time was how the superintendent managed to find out things that happened on my car when he was not present. Sometimes when I went to report or met him he would question me about things that happened on my run, such as pleasing the passengers and other things, which I did not suppose he knew a thing about and inquiries among the other trainmen only deepened the mystery.

I would ask the Pullman conductor if he told the superintendent such and such a thing and he would say no. Then I would ask him how the superintendent knew about them as he was not on the train. He would say he did not know. This kept up until finally I made up my mind that if there ever was a clairvoyant the superintendent certainly was one.

The fact that he was able to find out things that happened hundreds of miles away without any one telling him, kept me worked up for a long time until I finally tumbled to the special agents who are employed to travel as common passengers and report how things are going to the superintendent. That explained the whole mystery, but it did not in any way make me move easy in my mind, because if a special agent was along one trip, there was no reason to think that one was not along every trip. At least I made up my mind there was, and governed myself accordingly, but the increased attention given to my passengers as a result caused an increase in the tips, that came my way. With the increase in my earnings and the experience I was gaining I came to have a liking for the service, which is in no wise diminished at this time. I soon learned the knack of pleasing the greater number of my passengers, and this reported to the superintendent by the special agents raised me in the official's favor with the result that I was given more extensive and more profitable runs and soon became one of the most popular porters in Colorado. This brought with it increased responsibilities as well as increased profits and favors enjoyed.

When I started to work it was for $15.00 per month this has been increased from time to time until at present owing to my long service and having gained a thorough knowledge of my business, I am often made porter in charge. This position pays me as high as $40.00 per month. The difference between a porter and a porter in charge is that a porter generally has a car over which a Pullman conductor presides, which the porter in charge

owing to his long service and his knowledge of the business is placed in full charge of a car, making the services of a Pullman conductor unnecessary. A porter in the employ of the Pullman company for ten years and giving good service for that time receives from the company two suits of clothes per year, and other privileges not enjoyed by the beginner.

A porter just beginning in the service has to purchase his own uniform, the cost of which is never less than $20.00 for the summer suit or $22.00 for the winter suit. After five years of good service a porter is entitled to wear one white stripe on his coat sleeve to which one is added for every succeeding five years of good service. Naturally the porter that understands his business and gives his whole attention to the passengers in his car and to his work, will make more money than the porter who has not the patience to try and please his passengers. I have had porters complain to me about the small amount they were able to earn in the service and on questioning them I found it was wholly because they did not think it necessary to try and make friends of the people in their car. I early recognized the fact that if I expected to succeed in the Pullman service I must make all the friends I could on my runs, and the cases are very rare where I have failed to receive a tip of some kind from my passengers, although as it happens sometimes I have people in my car who are not very well blessed with this world's goods, and who can ill afford to spend money in tips. To such people I always give the same attention and care, as if I was sure to receive a $10 tip, and they rarely failed to give me a kind thank you, on leaving my car. In the course of our duties we naturally meet all manner of people, the business man out for business or pleasure, the drummers who nearly always give us a tip; the wife going to join her sick husband or the husband hurrying home to the bedside of his sick child; the invalid in search of health, or the family going home to attend the funeral of a loved one; the young man going to be married, and the young couple on their honeymoon; the capitalist, the miner, the sportsman and the vast army of people that go to make up the traveling public, who like the sands of the desert are forever shifting around from place to place, and with whom we porters are brought in closer contact perhaps than any one else on their travels. We must necessarily be good judges of human nature to be able to please the majority of the people who travel under our care. We nearly always receive a tip from those who ride with us for any distance. The size of the tip often depends on the mode of the passenger giving it. Even those who ride with us only a short distance often give us a tip of more generous proportions than will the man who has ridden with us several thousands of miles. The

superintendent himself when he rides in our car, we are sure to receive from him 25 cents or 50 cents for a day or a day's ride.

The smallest tip I have received from a passenger during my service was 2 cents. This amount I received from a rather cranky individual, who when I went to brush him off handed me two copper cents and followed them up with the remark that some of us porters needed calling down and some needed knocking down. My opinion if what he needed caused me to smile, wherein he wanted to know what I was smiling at. Needless to say I did not feel like wasting any more breath on him so I bundled his boxes and satchel out on the platform and left him to follow at his leisure.

The largest tips I ever received from a single traveler was $25.00 given me by one of the Rothschilds whom I brought from Chicago to Frisco, but this has been largely surpassed several times in car tips or trips. The Knights Templar one of whose cars I had charge of between Denver and Boston made, up a purse of $150.00 and presented it to me with the compliments of the passengers in recognition of the good service I had rendered them. While in charge of the private car of General Manager Fisher in a trip through California and Mexico, Mr. Fisher made up a purse of $75.00 for me, in recognition of my attentions to the members of his party. But the man who gave me 5 cents received as much attention from me as the man who gives me $5.00. It is perhaps all he can afford and the manner in which he gives it often makes up for the smallness of the tip.

CHAPTER XIX.

THE PULLMAN SLEEPING CAR. LONG TRIPS ON THE RAIL. THE WRECK. ONE TOUCH OF NATURE MAKES THE WHOLE WORLD KIN. A FEW OF THE RAILROADS OVER WHICH I HAVE TRAVELED. THE INVALID AND THE CARE WE GIVE THEM.

The modern Pullman sleeping car is a veritable palace on wheels furnished in the best materials, without regard to expense, comfort, convenience and the safety of the passengers being the main object. To say that the builders of the Pullman cars have succeeded in attaining this object is but a mild expression. Fine carpets cover the floors, the seats and chairs are upholstered in the best and softest of material, while every convenience is

provided for the use of the lucky mortal who is called across the continent on business or pleasure, and whose pleasure it is to travel and sleep in the Pullman sleeping car of the present day. The traveler of today when he has to go from Chicago to San Francisco, simply throws a few things in a grip, is driven to the Union terminal station in Chicago, where he secures a through ticket and a sleeping car berth. At the car steps he is met by the Pullman porter who relieves him of his grip and assists him on the train if necessary. From that time until four days later when he arrives in San Francisco, he has no more care. If he wishes to write letters there is a handy writing tablet with stationery and everything needful. He can write his letters and hand them to the porter to mail and continue his perusal of the morning paper. If he gets hungry he has but to step in the dining car, where he will find viands fit for a king. If he wants a shave or a haircut, the barber is in the next car. If he wants to view the scenery en route, the observation car is but a few steps away. When he gets sleepy and wishes to retire he presses the electric button at his elbow and the porter will do the rest, but if he prefers to lay in his luxurious bed and read, he has but to turn on the electric light at his bedside and he can read as long as he pleases, and when he arrives at San Francisco he will be cleanly shaven, nicely brushed, with his shoes freshly shined, and on the outside of a good breakfast, ready to tackle at once the business or the pleasure that brought him across the continent. Or, if the traveler prefers, he may swing aboard the magnificently equipped and royally appointed Los Angeles Limited, one of the finest through trains that this mundane sphere can boast. Catch this train in Chicago, which you may do any day in the year, and it will carry you with safety, speed and comfort over the fertile farms, meadows and plains; through the City of the Saints on the second day; then around the Great Dead Sea of America, over the sage brush plains and grazing ranges of southern Nevada, and into the Land of Sunshine and Flowers and the City of the Angels on the third day after leaving your home in Chicago.

What a contrast to the mode of travel our grandfathers were forced to adopt, a decade ago, when the old ox team and the prairie schooner wended its slow way over the mountains and plains, over trails in every turn of which lurked danger and death. "Verily the sun do move." During my service with the Pullman company I have traveled from the Atlantic to the Pacific and from the Gulf of Mexico to the borders of Canada, over nearly all the many different lines of railroad that makes the map of North America look like a spider had been crawling over it in search of a fly. I have visited all the prin-

cipal cities and towns where the sound of the bell and the whistle is heard, and I have in a great measure satisfied my desire to see the country. Among the great lines of railway over which I have traveled are the Union Pacific, whose overland limited, the Atlantic Express and the Portland-Chicago Special, are the acme of quick, safe and comfortable travel. The overland limited is electric lighted, steam heated and contains every known luxury and convenience of travel. The Denver and Rio Grande Railroad is noted the world over for its quick time, fine scenery, comfort and safety. The Southern Pacific, the Baltimore & Ohio Southwestern, the Missouri Pacific between St. Louis and all points east, all electric lighted trains with observation, parlor, cafe dining cars and Pullman sleeping cars; the Chicago & Northwestern, whose through train service to Chicago and the East from San Francisco, Los Angeles, Portland, Salt Lake, Ogden and Denver is not excelled in any land; the Illinois Central Railroad, whose eight track entrance to Chicago from the south along the lake front is one of the triumphs of Yankee railroading, and whose train service is elegant in the extreme. The Pennsylvania lines which will take you from Chicago to New York in eighteen hours and make you feel thoroughly comfortable while doing it. The Louisville and Nashville Railroad, whose lines reach every town and hamlet in the solid South. The Nickel Plate road, the direct line from Chicago to New York, Boston and all points east, all trains of the Nickel Plate road arrive and depart from the new LaSalle Street station, one of the finest railroad stations in the country. The Santa Fe, from whose trains you can view some of the finest scenery in the Rocky Mountains, including the Grand Canyon of Arizona, a mile deep, thirteen miles wide, two hundred and seventeen miles long and painted like a flower. The Lehigh Valley Railroad to Chicago, New York and Philadelphia, from whose car windows one may view the world-famous Niagara Falls. The Colorado & Southern, the Colorado road over which travel is one continuous delight. The San Pedro, Los Angeles and Salt Lake Railroad, one of the youngest but by no means the least of railroads, the road that lies as straight as the crow flies, linking together the City of the "Saints" and the City of the "Angels." The snow-capped Rocky Mountains and the sun-kissed shores of the Pacific Ocean, the dead sea and the live sea; the railroad that makes it possible to have a sleigh ride with your second wife in the City of the "Saints" on Sunday and pick flowers and eat oranges with your first wife in the City of the "Angels" on Tuesday. Over this line I am running at present, and while it has only been in operation a short time, yet the time and service equals and in some cases surpasses the time and service of the great Trunk Lines of the

east. We often make ninety miles an hour over the standard gauge roadbed, that equals any in this country. The cars are all new, the engines are the latest up-to-date kind. The cars are built for comfort and convenience, the trains are all electric lighted, steam heated and have every modern convenience for the safety and comfort of the passengers. This road, in common with some of the eastern roads employs chair car porters in addition to the Pullman porters. On all trains from Salt Lake to Los Angeles there are three or four Pullman porters and one chair car porter.

All trains have dining cars, which are in reality magnificent dining rooms, where three times a day the dainties of the season are prepared by a competent chef to satisfy the most discriminating inner man. The furnishings of these cars, the fine linen, the artistic glass (china and silverware), are guaranteed to make you enjoy your meal, even if you have got dyspepsia. Besides the dining car and the Pullman sleeping cars, there is attached to all overland trains on the Salt Lake route, a through tourist sleeper, which differs from the Pullman sleeper only in a slight difference in the furnishings. The service is the same, but the cost of a berth in them between Salt Lake and Los Angeles is just one-half that of the standard sleeper. I have never run on a road where better service, more courteous treatment or better time was made than on the S. P., L. A. & S. L. Railroad.

In these latter years, when progress is the watchword of the railroads in common with the other industries of the country, no expense or pains are spared by the railroad people to add to the comfort, enjoyments, safety and convenience of the traveling public, until now it is about as safe to travel as it is to stay at home, and not much if any more expensive. But in spite of all safeguards adopted by the railroads a wreck occurs once in a while the same as accidents occur at home.

The first wreck I was in the train struck a split switch with the result that the cars turned over and piled up in a ditch. That happened in Colorado. We were forced to crawl out through the windows, like a prairie dog out of his hole. No one was killed but the passengers were all pretty well shaken up and somewhat scared. As soon as the cars got comfortably piled up and the passengers were able to speak they all commenced yelling for the porter. But at that particular moment the porter was busy rubbing his shins and assuring himself there was nothing to be scared about. The passengers at such times are apt to forget that the porter is as scared as they are, and has forgotten all about tips and such commonplace matters as that, but after he gets his wits about him he loses no time in looking after his flock, and rendering assis-

tance to such of his passengers as need it, and most of them do need assistance of some kind if for no other reason than to be assured that they are not hurt. The Pullman porter of today must be a very versatile sort of a person, he must have plenty of patience, be a good judge of human nature, quick, kind and observant. Many are the times a gouty and crusty passenger has traveled in my car, who was in such a bad humor that it was next to impossible to please him, yet before he had ridden a hundred miles with me, I had him in good humor and laughing with the rest of the passengers. "Laugh and the whole world laughs with you."

It is by no means an uncommon thing for us porters to be called upon to turn nurse for sick or invalid passengers in our car, and often have I watched by the bedside of a sick passenger, feeding him, giving him medicine, bathing him and in fact becoming for the time being a hospital nurse, and many are the blessings I have received from my sick passengers, both men and women, whose pain I have eased, and their last moments on earth I have cheered. And this, dear reader, we do in the name of humanity and not in the name of tips.

CHAPTER XX.

THE TOURIST SLEEPING CAR. THE CHAIR CAR. THE SAFE-GUARDS OF MODERN RAILROADING. SEE AMERICA, THEN LET YOUR CHEST SWELL WITH PRIDE THAT YOU ARE AN AMERI-CAN.

The Pullman tourist sleeping car, which you can find on all through trains of the different railroads throughout the United States, are to the traveler of moderate means what the Pullman car is to the millionaire traveler. They are designed for the comfort and convenience of the traveling public to whom the expenditure of a dollar more or less is a matter of moment, and who cannot afford or do not care for the small extra show and tinsel of the Pullman sleeping car, but whose only desire is to make their journey pleasant, comfortable and safe. This they can do as well in the tourist as in the standard sleeping car.

There is a difference in price that will amount to a tidy sum in a long trip across the continent, but that fact does not always appeal to the traveling public, as I have had the poorest of passengers in the palace car and at other

times a millionaire and his family would be my passengers in the tourist cars. It seems to me a matter of fact and one which my long experience seems to verify, that the American traveler does not care so much about his comfort as his ability to get there, as the average American traveler is always in a hurry and in nine cases out of ten, he is thinking more about the speed of the train than he is about his immediate surroundings or the price he had paid for his ticket. The railroads, knowing this, have made and are continually making every effort to add to the speed and safety of their trains, but traveling long distances is a tiresome matter at the best and for that reason the railroads are continually making improvements with a view to add to the comfort, convenience and pleasure of the traveler, and in a journey such as one from Chicago to Los Angeles, for instance, there is no time to stop for meals and such trivial matters as a shave, as time is money lost to most of the passengers and to the railroad company also. For that reason the sleeping car is provided that you may sleep with as much comfort as if you were in your own home, the dining car is provided to furnish you a good meal on the fly and at a price that all can afford. The library and drawing room cars are provided, where you can make yourself as comfortable as you can in your own house. The porter will get your morning paper, furnish you with writing materials or your morning high ball, and look after you like a hen after her brood.

But on all railroads there are rules governing the passengers as well as the employees, the same as there are in all lines of business. A passenger may not, for instance, smoke in the body of the Pullman car, but must retire to the drawing room or his stateroom. As an instance in point, I had J. J. Corbett for a passenger in my car between Ogden and Chicago, a gentleman who was at that time in the height of his career and naturally thought he owned the earth or a large part of it, at any rate he came in the sleeper from the dining car, lit a cigar, propped his feet upon the opposite seat and prepared for a comfortable smoke. But it was against the rules to smoke in that part of the car, so I approached him and politely requested him not to smoke in that part of the car. He regarded me a few moments and with a sneer said, "So you are Mr. Pullman, are you?" I told him I was not Mr. Pullman, but I was in charge of one of Mr. Pullman's cars, and for that reason I was a representative of Mr. Pullman, and that it was strictly against the rules to smoke in that part of the car, and that if he wished to smoke he would have to go to the drawing room. He went, but the sleeping car conductor, who had watched the incident, told me I had better look out or Corbett would have

my scalp. I told the conductor I was not scared and that if Corbett hadn't gotten out I would have thrown him out, all of which I meant, but the conductor shook his head and said to look out. Sure enough the matter was reported to the superintendent, but that official on hearing the facts in the matter said I had done perfectly right, and what I was paid to do.

It is necessary that all passengers as well as all employees shall observe the rules of the company, for the benefit, safety and enjoyment of all the passengers and employees alike.

All the railroad men I have met from the president down have all proved themselves jolly good fellows, kind, considerate and always ready to render assistance and service to those in need, but at the same time they are strict about the rules and discipline. Thoroughly understanding their business themselves, they insist on the beginner obeying instructions and the laws of the road, because on that depends the lives of hundreds of people, and the value of thousands of dollars worth of property, and for the same reason they are expending thousands of dollars annually in new appliances, inventions and equipment, that will add to the saving of time or insure the safety of the traveler. Among the new inventions adopted by the modern railroads are the "Block" System, which makes collisions between two trains approaching each other on the same track almost an impossibility if the engineer is awake and attentive to business. Under this system when the trains approach a certain distance of each other a bell is rung in the cab of each locomotive simultaneously, and will continue to ring until the danger is over. This with the powerful electric headlights now used, with which the roadbed is lit up for a distance of five miles, makes a head-on collision almost impossible, while the air brakes, heavy rails, solid roadbed, doing away with the sharp curves and heavy grades, all add to the safety of the passengers and the saving of many miles in travel and many precious moments. It has always seemed strange to me that so many Americans rush off to Europe and foreign countries every year in search of health and pleasure, or to climb the Alps in Switzerland, and to view the scenery of the old world, when our own North America, the new world, offers so many better opportunities to study Dame Nature in all her phases, and I always say to the traveling American, "See America." How many of you have done so? Only those who have seen this grand country of ours can justly appreciate the grandeur of our mountains and rivers, valley and plain, canyon and gorge, lakes and springs, cities and towns, the grand evidences of God's handiwork scattered all over this fair land over which waves the stars and stripes. Go to New York and view the tall buildings, the

Brooklyn bridge, the subway, study the works of art to be found there, both in statuary and painting, ponder on the vast volume of commerce carried on with the outside world. Note the many different styles of architecture displayed in the palace of the millionaire and the house of the humble tradesman, view the magnificent Hudson river and the country homes along its grassy, tree-lined shores, note the ships from every clime riding at anchor in the East river. Then speculate on the changes that have been wrought in the course of the short time since Manhattan Island was purchased from the Indians by Pete Minuts for a few blankets and beads amounting in value to $24.00. Then board the Pennsylvania Limited, whose trains are the acme of modern railroading and go to Washington, the nation's capital city. Walk along Pennsylvania avenue and note its beauty. Visit the capitol and let your chest swell out with pride that you are an American. Visit the tomb of General Grant and the thousand and one magnificent statues scattered throughout the city. Visit Annapolis and West Point, where the leaders of the nation's navy and army are trained. Walk over the battlefields of Fredricksburg, Gettysburg and Lexington, and let your mind speculate on the events that made modern history.

Note the majestic Potomac and the Washington monument. Take a short trip north and see the great Niagara Falls, listen to what they tell you in their mighty roaring voice. Go to Pittsburg where the great steel works are located, and see how the steel pen and the steel cannon are made. Go to Chicago, that western hive of commerce. See the Great Lakes, or better still take a cruise on them. Note the great lumber industry of Michigan, and the traffic of the lakes. Go to Kansas City and Omaha and see the transformation of the Texas steer into the corned beef you ate at your last picnic, or was it chipped beef? See the immense stock yards with their thousands of cattle, hogs and sheep, and think of the thousands of people that they feed. Cross the Missouri river and enter on the plains of the great and recently unknown west. Think of the pioneer who in 1849 traversed these once barren stretches of prairie, walking beside his slow-moving ox team, seeking the promised breaking a trail for the generations that were to come after him as you are coming now in a Pullman car. Think of the dangers that beset him on every hand, then wonder at the nerve he had, then again let your chest swell with pride that you are an American, sprung from the same stock that men were composed of in those days. Note the grandeur of the Rocky Mountains as they rise from the plains, their peaks snow-capped, glistening in clear blue sky, breathe the pure essence of life, drink of the crystal streams twinkling

down their sides, then scorn the wine made by man. Listen to the salute of
the bells and the whistles as the trains approach and pass that strange mon-
ument of nature's handiwork, the Mount of the Holy Cross.

Go to the Yellowstone National Park and revel in the wonders thereof,
walk in the garden of the Gods and listen to the voice of the Giant Geyser as
it sends forth its torrents of boiling water. Bathe in the life-giving springs and
mud baths. Note the fantastic forms of the rocks and trees, carved by the
hand of nature, then go to Colorado Springs and climb Pikes Peak and
behold the world stretch out before you in valley, mountain and plain. Visit
the mines of Leadville and Cripple Creek, the store houses of a part of the
nation's wealth. Visit Denver and see the strides made in the improvement of
the west in a short time. Board the Denver & Rio Grande train and note the
magnificent scenery of mountain, canyons, gorges and the beautiful moun-
tain lakes and streams, note the Grand Canyon of the Colorado, the royal
gorge. Now note the great white expanse of the great Salt Lake, as it lies glis-
tening in the rays of the setting sun, and think of the stories you have heard
of it until the conductor brings you back to earth with the cry of "Ogden."

Note this bustling railroad center in the heart of the Rocky mountains,
and acknowledge our country's greatness. Visit Salt Lake City, the "City of
Zion," the Canaan of the new world. See the beautiful city nestling within
the protection of the Warsatch and Oquirrh range of mountains. Walk its
wide tree-lined streets, visit the tabernacle and hear the sweet strains of the
world's greatest organs. See the Mormon temple. Visit Saltair and sport in the
waves of the briny sea. Board the San Pedro, Los Angeles and Salt Lake west-
bound train and cross the end of this same lake, one of nature's wonders.

Cross the desert of Nevada, which was only a short time ago a desert
waste, on and on until you smell the orange blossoms of sunny California,
and the train emerges from the mountains and brings into view the grand
Pacific Ocean. See the big trees of California, the seals and the scenery of the
Yosemite valley. Visit the orange groves and the vineyards, and partake of the
orange and the grape. Visit Catalina Island in the Pacific Ocean, and try a
couple of hours fishing in its waters. Then take the Southern Pacific and
return to New York by way of Arizona, New Mexico, Texas, New Orleans,
Florida and other southern states. Then again let your chest swell with pride
that you are an American.

I think you will agree with me that this grand country of ours is the peer
of any in the world, and that volumes cannot begin to tell of the wonders of
it. Then after taking such a trip you will say with me, "See America." I have

seen a large part of America, and am still seeing it, but the life of a hundred years would be all too short to see our country. America, I love thee, Sweet land of Liberty, home of the brave and the free.

CHAPTER XXI.

A FEW OF THE RAILROAD MEN UNDER WHOM I HAVE SERVED. GEORGE M. PULLMAN. THE TOWN OF PULLMAN, ILL. AMERICAN RAILROADS LEAD THE WORLD. A FEW FIGURES.

Among the large number of railroad men I have served under and worked with during the fifteen years I have been on the road it gives me pleasure to recall the names of a few with whom I was more intimately acquainted and to whom I am indebted for many favors given and courtesies extended, and the pleasant duty devolves on me to mention the always courteous, obliging and most competent head of the Pullman department in Denver, Mr. Runnells, and his assistant, Mr. Wright, who sent me out on my first run in 1890. Next comes the well known name of District Superintendent J. M. Smith, who one year later sent me out on the run that marked the beginning of my Pullman service. To Mr. Smith more than to any other railroad man I am indebted for advice, counsel and countless favors shown me while I was in the service in the department over which he presided so long. I always found him courteous and obliging and never too busy to listen or to give a kind word of advice or counsel to all who approached him on company business or on the private affairs of the employees of the road. I had charge of a car for several years in his territory and many a time I have had him for a passenger and at such times he seemed more like an old friend than he did like the superintendent of the Pullman service.

I next transferred to the Ogden division. Here I met and came to know very well Superintendent Baker and his assistant, Johnnie Searce, and to these two gentlemen I am also indebted for many favors shown me, as they tried in every way possible to make my employment pleasant and profitable while I was in their territory. I was sent out on runs covered the greater portions of the United States, and while on some of my longer runs I often started from and returned to stations in different districts under different super-

intendents, but I always looked on Ogden as my home station and Superintendent Baker as my chief until another superintendent was given charge of the district and I transferred to Salt Lake and started to run on Senator Clark's new road, the S. P., L. A. & S. L. road, between Salt Lake and Los Angeles, under the superintendency of Mr. Twining and his assistant, Mr. Cotten, and these gentlemen also during the time I have been with them have shown me every favor and consideration, which goes far towards making my work a pleasure. In this connection also I mention the names of Jim Donohue, traveling engineer; W. H. Smith, trainmaster, and P. Randoff Morris and Jos. Jones, special agents, all jolly railroad men from A to Izard.

During my fifteen years' service I have met and served under many different superintendents and to mention the names of them all, would require a separate volume, but I will always hold them in kindly remembrance as they all have without exception been kindness itself to me.

Another old friend I have recently met on the steel road is William H. Blood, at present one of the popular conductors on the San Pedro, Los Angeles & Salt Lake Railroad. In the early seventies "Billy" was one of the best cowboys ranging over the western cattle country. He was with me on many of the old trails and in many a tight place, and like myself he always came out right side up with care and none the worse for wear.

E. W. Gillett, at present general passenger agent of the Salt Lake road, and one of the best known and most popular railroad men of the west, is another friend of the old days it is my pleasure to meet often now. I first met him under the following circumstances. I think it was in the year 1874 along in the fall, I had been up the trail with some cattle and was returning through Wyoming en route to Arizona. I had been riding hard all day and as it began to get dark I sighted a small station on the main line of the Union Pacific, and I concluded to give it a passing call out of curiosity. As I drew near I noticed several rough-looking customers hanging around in a suspicious manner, and I at once concluded that they were robbers there for the purpose of holding up the station. Events immediately following proved that I was right. They had not noticed me and they proceeded to hold up the agent in true western style, but that they had caught a tartar was evidenced by the rattle of the agent's artillery. Of course it was out of the question for me to miss such fun, so not waiting for an invitation I lost no time in getting my own forty-fives in active operation, and in less time than it takes to tell it what was left of those greasers were making tracks for the nearest state line, while a red-headed youngster with a smoking 45 in his fist was shaking hands

with me and trying to say something about my saving his life. I took a shine to him at once on account of his pluck and our friendship thus begun has lasted through the years until now time and fate have thrown us both together on the same line of railroad.

The railroad men as a class are the most jovial set of men one could find in any profession, well educated, broad minded, and always considerate of others and at the same time they know their business thoroughly, as they have to serve many years as apprentices, so to speak, in railroading, before they are given places of trust and responsibility, and the man who has reached the position of president or general manager of a railroad system, has learned pretty much all there is to be learned about the iron horse and the steel road, and they use that knowledge in providing for the safety and comfort of the millions of lives that are annually intrusted to their keeping.

The general manager is responsible not only for the lives of the traveling public, but of the army or railroad employee under him and he is supposed to know everything, and must always be prepared to do the right thing in the right place at the right time, and as in many cases life and death depend on it, he must know how.

A college education does not make a railroad manager, although it may help to do so. He in a great measure gets his education in the school of experience, and in some cases it is a hard school, and the most exacting of all schools, but at the same time it is a school in which one can learn anything under the sun, and learn it well, and in these days of the twentieth century's activity and progress, it is the man who knows how to do things that makes the world move. And after boiling everything down there is left in the pot two undisputable facts. They are that the railroad men cause the world to move by knowing how to do things, the other is that the railroad men move the people who live in the world, thus they move things' all around. And they are continually on the move themselves, which goes to prove that they are different from many other people inasmuch as they practice what they preach. And from these men of all classes from the president down I have received courtesies and the kindest of consideration, and these pleasant associations are pleasant memories to me and will always remain so.

It was my pleasure to meet and to chat with George M. Pullman, the father of the sleeping car, several times, and I found him to be a fine man, broad-minded in every sense of the word, always approachable and with always a kind word for every one of the large army of his employees that he met on his travels, and he always tried to meet them all. It was also my pleas-

ure to meet his two boys who are veritable chips of the old block.

One of the legends connected with the western mining history is that early in the As George M. Pullman was a poor prospector and had secured a lease on a piece of mining ground in Colorado, and that he formed the idea of the sleeping car from the tiers of bunks in the miners' lodging house, "bunk houses" they are called. However that may be Mr. Pullman has been the recipient of many a blessing from the weary traveler, and the idea, whatever it was, that led him to invent the sleeping car that has proved such a comfort to the traveler of today, deserves to go down in history as the greatest idea that ever came from the place where ideas come from.

It has been my pleasure to visit all the large shops of the Pullman company, including the town of Pullman, Ill., which is a good-sized city, named after Mr. Pullman, and was owned by him principally, and the large number of men employed in his shops there. The town contains fine churches and public buildings, a splendid library and reading rooms and amusement halls. And while I was there I failed to see a single saloon. It seems such places are tabooed there. The shops are the finest in this country, containing all the modern machinery of the finest kind and the men employed there are all past masters of their trades. Here are built all the finest sleeping cars and many of the finest special cars and railway cars seen on the railroads of this country. In addition there is also a very large amount of repairing done. As soon as anything goes wrong with a Pullman car it is at once sent into the shops for repair, and soon comes out in apple pie order. You may see the Pullman cars all over this country where there is a steel road, and other countries have their eyes on the mof late, and in the near future it will be possible to sleep in a Pullman car whether you are traveling in England, France, Sweden or China. They are a good thing and are sure to be pushed or rather pulled along.

In 1893 I went to Mr. Pullman and told him I was thinking of getting the porters of the Pullman Car Company to club together and contribute fifty cents per month apiece for the purpose of investing the proceeds in land, in view of eventually owning what we would call "The Porters' Home." Mr. Pullman told me he thought that a good idea, and said if we succeeded in buying one thousand acres of land, he would erect us a building on it, and signed a statement to that effect.

I then went to work and communicated with all the divisions of the Pullman Company, presenting this proposition to the porters of these different districts, but only succeeded in getting about twenty-five subscribers, the rest of them refusing to go into such a proposition, some of them saying all I

wanted was to get the money and make away with it. Inasmuch as this amount was to be sent to the main Pullman office in Chicago and I was to be there each month to see this money deposited. Others refused to go into it upon the ground that they were liable to be discharged from the Pullman service at any time, many other various excuses were offered. There were many of the Pullman conductors, however, who promised to contribute from one to five dollars toward this enterprise when we were ready to purchase the land.

My object was to have a Home and Hospital, with adjoining farming land, for the benefit of old and disabled porters who were not able to perform their duties as Pullman car porters. Had this been accomplished at that time, we would by now have had a large farm and a house and hospital connected therewith, and all the porters who are now unable to work would have had a good home and be cared for the rest of their lives. I hope to live long enough to yet see this plan become a reality.

At present the American railway leads the world. In no other country does the traveler find so much comfort, so many conveniences, so much pleasure, safety and speed as does the dweller in this robust young country belonging to our Uncle Samuel. At the present time there are in the United States upwards of two hundred and sixty thousand miles of railroad open and in operation, not to mention several thousand miles now building and projected. This immense mileage is divided between over one thousand different roads, while in 1851 there were only 149 different railroads with a total mileage of 9000 miles. The railroads today have a capital back of them amounting to over $14,000,000,000, and they pay their employees wages that foot up over $7,000,000 annually, while their earnings amount to the tidy sum of $2,500,000,000 in the same length of time. They carry somewhat more than 800,000,000 passengers every twelve months, and 2,200,000,000 tons of freight. These figures do not include the several million tons of trunks, sachets, grips, hat boxes and carpet bags that the average traveler considers it necessary to load him or herself down with on starting on a journey of any distance, and which comes in such large quantities sometimes as to make life a burden for us porters.

Read these figures again, dear reader, they are a conservative estimate of the business transacted by the railroads of this fair land of ours. You can count a million, can you count a billion? Immense, isn't it? It seems to show that the people of this country are great travelers, forever on the move, yet they tell us this is a country of homes and that the average American loves his home and home life above all things. These figures seem to show there

are a few people who havn't any home or if they have they are looking for one they like better, which, like the will of the wisp, evades them always, but they continue to shift around, always hopeful, never satisfied, and they will continue to shift around until Gabriel blows on his little tin horn.

But this class of people make but a small percentage of the traveling public. Business in this latter day of strife and competition makes long journeys necessary, and as the business of the world grows apace and the countries of the earth crowd closer together in the struggle for the almighty dollar, there will be need of more railroads to make the globe smaller and to cut off the hours and minutes of precious time that means money to the man of today. And as a man makes and saves money so will he spend it for the pleasure of himself and family, and as he must travel to find pleasure there must be railroads to carry him, and hence these figures I write now will look insignificant beside the magnificent total that will be put before the reader of that day, because if they increase in the next century as they have in the past, walking will be out of fashion and every body will ride and I hope sleep in a Pullman sleeping car.

CHAPTER XXII.

A FEW REMINISCENCES OF THE RANGE. SOME MEN I HAVE MET. BUFFALO BILL. THE JAMES BROTHERS. YELLOWSTONE KELLEY. THE MURDER OF BUCK CANNON BY BILL WOODS. THE SUICIDE OF JACK ZIMICK.

It has now been many years since I quit the range, and as my mind wanders back over those years as it often does, memories both pleasant and sad pass in review and it is but fitting that I record a few of them as a final to the history of my life which has been so full of action, which is but natural as the men of those days were men of action. They had to be, and probably their actions were not all good, that I freely admit, but while that is so, it is equally so that their actions were not all bad, far from it. And in the history of the frontier there is recorded countless heroic deeds performed, deeds and actions that required an iron nerve, self denial in all that these words imply, the sacrificing of one life to save the life of a stranger or a friend. Deeds that stamped the men of the western plains as men worthy to be called men, and

while not many of them would shine particularly in the polite society of today or among the 400 of Gotham, yet they did shine big and bright in the positions and at a time when men lived and died for a principle, and in the line of duty. A man who went to the far west or who claimed it as his home in the early days found there a life far different from that led by the dude of Fifth Avenue. There a man's work was to be done, and a man's life to be lived, and when death was to be met, he met it like a man. It was among such men and surroundings that I spent so many years of my life and there I met men some of whom are famous now, while others never lived long enough to reach the pinnacle of fame, but their memory is held no less sacred by the men who knew them well.

Some men I met in the cattle country are now known to the world as the baddest of bad men, yet I have seen these men perform deeds of valor, self sacrifice and kindness that would cause the deeds recorded as performed by gentlemen in "ye olden time when knighthood was in flower" to look insignificant in comparison, and yet these men lay no claim to the title of gentlemen. They were just plain men.

It was my pleasure to meet often during the early seventies the man who is now famous in the old world and the new world, Buffalo Bill (William F. Cody), cowboy, ranger, hunter, scout and showman, a man who carried his life in his hands day and night in the wild country where duty called, and has often bluffed the grim reaper Death to a standstill, and is living now, hale, hearty and famous.

Others who are equally famous but in another way are the James brothers, Jesse and Frank. I met them often in the old days on the range, and became very well acquainted with them and many others of their band. Their names are recorded in history as the most famous robbers of the new world, but to us cowboys of the cattle country who knew them well, they were true men, brave, kind, generous and considerate, and while they were robbers and bandits, yet what they took from the rich they gave to the poor. The James brothers band stole thousands of dollars; yet Jesse was a poor man when he fell a victim to the bullet of a cowardly, traitorous assassin, and Frank James is a poor man today. What then did they do with the thousands they stole? The answer is simple, they gave it away to those who were in need. That is why they had so many friends and the officers of the law found it so hard to capture them.

And if they were robbers, by what name are we to call some of the great trusts, corporations and brokers, who have for years been robbing the people

of this country, some of them, I am glad to say, are now behind prison bars, still others are even now piling up the dollars that they have been and are still stealing from the American people, and who on account of these same dollars are looked up to, respected and are honored members of society, and the only difference between them and the James brothers is that the James brothers stole from the rich and gave to the poor, while these respected members of society steal from the poor to make the rich richer, and which of them think you reader, will get the benefit of the judgment when the final day arrives and all men appear before the great white throne in final judgment?

Jessie James was a true man, a loving son and husband, true to his word, true to his principles and true to his comrads and his friends. I had the pleasure of meeting Frank James quite recently on the road while he was en route to the coast with his theatrical company and enjoyed a pleasant chat with him. He knew me and recalled many incidents of the old days and happenings in "no man's land."

Quite a different sort of man was Yellowstone Kelley government scout, hunter and trapper. He was one of the men who helped to make frontier history and open up the pathless wilds to the march of civilization. He was in the employ of the government as a scout and guide when I first met him, and thereafter during our many wanderings over the country, I with my cattle, he with Uncle Sam's soldiers or on a lone scout, we often bumped up against each other, and these meetings are among my treasured memories. He was a man who knew the country better than he knew his own mother, absolutely fearless, kind and generous to a fault. He was the sort of a man that once you meet him you could never forget him, and us boys who knew him well considered him the chief of all the government scouts of that day. I also had the pleasure of meeting Kit Carson in Arizona and nearly all the government scouts, hunters and trappers of the western country, and they can all be described in one sentence, they were men whom it was a pleasure and an honor to know.

"Billie the Kid" was another sort of a man and there has never been another man like him and I don't think there ever will be again. Writers claim that he was a man all bad. This I doubt as I knew him well and I have known him to do deeds of kindness. He had many traits that go to make a good man, but fate and circumstances were against the kid, yet I know he always remembered a kindness done him and he never forgave an enemy. I have rode by his side many a long mile, and it is hard to believe he was as bad as he is pictured to be, but the facts are against him, and when his career was

ended by the bullet from Sheriff Garrett's colt, the world was better off, likewise were some men who stood in mortal fear of the kid, and I suppose they had good reason to be afraid as the kid always kept his word.

During my employment with the Duval outfit and Pete Gallingan I often made trips on the trail with herds of cattle and horses belonging to other ranch owners, and on these trips many incidents occurred, amusing and sad. The following incident happened in the fall of 1878, when I went up the trail with the half circle box brand outfit, belonging to Arthur Gorman and company.

We had a small herd of horses to take to Dodge City, where we arrived after an uneventful trip, and after disposing of the horses we started out to do the town as usual. But in this we met an unexpected snag. Our bookkeeper, Jack Zimick, got into a poker game and lost all the money he had to pay the cowboys off with, which amounted to about two thousand dollars, and also about the same amount of the boss' money. The boys had about one and a half years' wages coming to them, and consequently they were in a rather bad humor when they heard this bit of news. They at once got after Zimick so hard that he took me and went to Kinsely, Kas., where Mr. Gorman was. Arriving there he went to the Smith saloon to get a room, as Smith ran a rooming house over his saloon, and it was the custom for all the cattle men to make it their headquarters when in the city. Here he met Mr. Gorman, and we were sitting around the room and Zimick had only told Mr. Gorman a few things, when all of a sudden Zimick drew his 45 colt revolver remarking as he did so, "Here is the last of Jack Zimick." He placed the gun to his head and before we could reach him he pulled the trigger, and his brains were scattered all over the room.

They arrested Mr. Gorman and myself and held up for a short time until things could be explained. Mr. Gorman was very much overcome by the act, as Jack was one of his best men, and had been with him a long time. Mr. Gorman had the body sent to Zimick's friends in Boston, and he personally paid off all the boys, taking the money out of his own pocket to do so, but when the boys heard of Jack's rash deed they said they would rather have lost every dollar they had, rather than have had Jack kill himself, as he was a favorite among all the cowboys, especially so among those in Mr. Gorman's employ. Zimick had been in the employ of Gorman and company for over ten years and he was Mr. Gorman's right hand man, and this was the first time he ever went wrong. Jack did not have the nerve to face his comrades again, and so I suppose he concluded that his colt 45 was the only friend he had to help him out of it.

In May 1882, I was in Durango, Colorado, and chanced' to be in a saloon on Main street where a lot of us boys were together, among them being Buck Cannon and Bill Woods. The drinks had been circulating around pretty freely when Cannon and Woods got into a dispute over Cannon's niece, to whom Woods had been paying attention, much against that young lady's wish. After some hot words between the men, Woods drew his 45 colt revolver, remarking as he did so, "I will kill you," and in raising it his finger must have slipped, as his gun went off and the bullet hit a glass of beer in the hand of a man who was in the act of raising it to his lips, scattering the broken glass all over the room, then passing through the ceiling of the saloon. In an instant Woods threw three bullets into Cannon, remarking as he did so, "I will kill you, for your niece is my heart's delight and I will die for her." Buck Cannon's dying words were, "Boys, don't let a good man die with his boots on."

Along in the spring of 1879 we sent to Dodge City, Kansas, with a herd of cattle for the market and after they were disposed of, we boys turned our attention to the search of amusement. Some of the boys made for the nearest saloon and card table, but I heard there was to be a dance at Bill Smith's dance hall and in company with some of the other boys decided to attend. There was always quite a large number of cowboys in Dodge City at this time of the year, so we were not surprised to find the dance hall crowded on our arrival there. Smith's place occupied a large, low frame building down by the railroad tracks on the south. We found many old acquaintances there, among them being Kiowa Bill, a colored cattle man and ranch owner of Kansas, whose ranch was on Kiowa creek. I had met him several times but this was the first time I had seen him in a couple of years, but as he was dancing with a young lady I could not get to speak with him at once. So I looked up a wall flower and proceeded to enjoy myself. We had not been dancing long when I became aware of a commotion over near the bar, and all eyes were turned in that direction. I soon ascertained the cause of the commotion to be a dispute between Kiowa Bill and Bill Smith, the proprietor of the place, who was behind the bar. Kiowa Bill, after finishing the dance with his fair partner, took her to the bar to treat her. Smith, who was tending bar refused to serve her saying she had enough already. Kiowa Bill told Smith he (Kiowa Bill) was paying for what she wanted to drink and that he wanted her to get what she wanted. Smith said no, she could not have anything more to drink as she had too much already. At this Kiowa Bill reached over the bar and struck Smith over the head with a whiskey bottle, partly stunning him, but he recovered

in an instant and grabbed his 45 Colt, Kiowa Bill doing the same and both guns spoke as one. Smith fell dead behind the bar with a bullet through his heart. Kiowa Bill rolled against the bar and slowly sank to the floor and was dead when we reached him.

The next day they were hauled to the cemetery, laying side by side in the same wagon, and were buried side by side in the same grave. Kiowa Bill had made his will a short time before and it was found on his body when he was killed.

I had known Kiowa Bill for several years and was present at a shooting scrape he had two years before, down in Texas, near the Arizona line. At one of the big round ups there, in 1877, myself and quite a crowd of the other boys were in camp eating our dinner when Kiowa Bill rode up. He had been looking after his own cattle as he owned over two thousand head himself. One of the boys in our party who did not like Bill, there being a feud between them for sometime, on noticing Bill approaching, remarked, "If that fellow comes here I will rope him." True to his word as Bill rode up, the cow-boy threw his lariat. Kiowa Bill, seeing the movement, threw the rope off at the same time springing down on the opposite side of his horse.

The cowboy, enraged at his failure to rope Bill, shouted, "I will fight you from the point of a jack knife, to the point of a 45," at the same time reaching for his 45 which was in the holster on his saddle, which was lying on the ground a short distance away. At that Kiowa Bill fired, striking the cowboy in the neck, breaking it. Bill then sprang in the saddle and put spurs to his horse in an effort to get away.

Several of the cowboys commenced shooting after Bill who returned the fire. One of the cowboys, squatting down and holding his 45 with both hands, in an effort to get a better aim on Bill, received a bullet in the leg from Bill's revolver that knocked him over backwards, and caused him to turn a couple of somersaults. Bill got away and went to New York. He was later arrested in St. Louis and brought back. At his trial he went free as it was shown that he killed the cowboy in self-defense. And his appearance at the dance was the first time I had seen him since the scrape in Texas.

Kiowa Bill was of a peaceful disposition and always refrained from bothering with others, but if others bothered with him they were liable to get killed as Kiowa Bill allowed no one to monkey with him. Such was life on the western ranges when I rode them, and such were my comrades and surroundings; humor and tragedy. In the midst of life we were in death, but above all shown the universal manhood. The wild and free life. The bound-

less plains. The countless thousands of long horn steers, the wild fleet footed mustangs. The buffalo and other game, the Indians, the delight of living, and the fights against death that caused every nerve to tingle, and the every day communion with men, whose minds were as broad as the plains they roamed, and whose creed was every man for himself and every friend for each other, and with each other till the end.

Another friend of the old times is Chas. R. Campbell, superintendent of the Kelso mines. Chats with these good whole-soured people of the cattle range bring back reminiscences of the past that would fill volumes but space and time in these days of hustle and bustle are but dreams and the world is full of them now.

I am at the present time connected with the General Securities Company in Los Angeles. Mr. A.A.C. Ames is president; Mr. James O. Butler, vice-president; Mr. Jacob E. Meyer, secretary, and Mr. Geo. W. Bishop, treasurer. These gentlemen are always extremely kind to me and the appreciation I feel for the kindnesses shown me will be fully rewarded.

As I stop to ponder over the days of old so full of adventure and excitement, health and happiness, love and sorrow, isn't it a wonder that some of us are alive to tell the tale. One moment we are rejoicing that we are alive; the next we are so near the jaws of death that it seems it would be almost a miracle that our lives be saved.

Life today on the cattle range is almost another epoch. Laws have been enacted in New Mexico and Arizona which forbid all the old-time sports and the cowboy is almost a being of the past. But, I, Nat Love, now in my 54th year, hale hearty and happy, will ever cherish a fond and loving feeling for the old days on the range, its exciting adventures, good horses, good and bad men, long venturesome rides, Indian fights and last but foremost the friends I have made and friends I have gained.

<div align="center">FINIS</div>

BOOKER T. WASHINGTON

(1856-1915)

ooker T. Washington was born in a slave hut in Franklin County, Virginia on April 5, 1856, and on the property of a plantation owner, James Burroughs. By the time of his death in 1915, Washington would become the nation's leading voice for blacks, be named an advisor to President Theodore Roosevelt, write a best–selling book, and become the founder of the Tuskegee Institute.

His life "had its beginning in the midst of the most miserable, desolate and discouraging surroundings," he wrote in *Up From Slavery*. He lived with his mother, Jane, a cook on the plantation, a brother, John and a sister, Amanda, and he was put to work in the salt mines at a very young age. He never knew his father, and slave ancestry and family records was not given much attention at the time, but Washington believed that his father was a white man who lived on one of the nearby plantations.

"Whoever he was," Washington wrote, "I never heard of his taking the least interest in me or providing in any way for my rearing." However, Washington blamed the system of slavery for this, and not the man. In fact, Washington is remarkable in his descriptions of his early life in *Up From Slavery*. He vividly describes the complex nature of human relationships within the world of slavery. When, during the Civil War, one of his young masters was killed, Washington recounts the deep feeling of sorrow among the slaves. "It was no sham sorrow," he wrote, "but real Some of the slaves would even beg for the privilege of sitting up at night to nurse their wounded masters."

When his family was freed from slavery, Washington remembers his mother kissing her children as tears ran down her cheeks, and the pity the slaves felt for their former owners, who, as Washington wrote, "did not at the moment seem to be sad because of the loss of property, but rather because of parting with those whom they had reared and who were in many ways very

close to them."

Washington also describes, in heartbreaking fashion, how celebration soon turned to gloom and resignation in the slave quarters shortly after their emancipation.

> To some it seemed that, now that they were in actual possession of it, freedom was a more serious thing than they had expected to find it. Some of the slaves were seventy or eighty years old; their best days were gone.
>
> They had no strength with which to earn a living in a strange place and among strange people, even if they had been sure where to find a new place of abode . . .
>
> Gradually, one by one, stealthily at first, the older slaves began to wander from the slave quarters back to the "big house," to have a whispered conversation with their former owners as to the future.

Soon after emancipation, Washington and his family moved to West Virginia, where his stepfather had secured a job in a salt-furnace in the town of Malden, where some of his new neighbors were "coloured people, and some were the poorest and most ignorant and degraded white people." Washington writes that it was here in Malden where he developed an intense longing to learn to read, and with the support of his illiterate mother, a neighborhood "home school" was established, with the only educated black man in the town, making rounds each day to homes on "teacher's day."

> The experience of a whole race beginning to go to school for the first time, presents one of the most interesting studies that has ever occurred in connection with the development of any race. Few people who were not right in the midst of the scenes can form any exact idea of the intense desire which the people of my race showed for an education . . . It was a whole race trying to go to school. Few were too young and none were too old, to make the attempt to learn . . . The great ambition of the older people was to try to learn to read the Bible before they died.

Washington's stepfather determined that the family could not do without young Booker's wages from the salt-furnace, and did not permit his stepson to attend a new school in Kanawha Valley—one of the "keenest disappoint-

ments that I ever experienced." However, his perseverance and agreement to attend school at 9:00 A.M., only if he put in several hours at the salt-furnace beforehand, enabled him to attend—though it was not an easy schedule to keep. Washington often resorted to moving the hands on the clock in the furnace office ahead a half hour so that he could make it to school on time!

This thirst for education would prove to be one of the dominant themes in Washington's life. Determined to better himself, he applied for and was accepted into the Hampton Normal and Agricultural Institute in Virginia in 1872, where he worked as a janitor to help pay the cost of his schooling. Upon graduation with honors in 1875, Washington returned to his hometown in Malden and spent the next few years teaching children in the day and adults at night.

Washington then studied at Wayland Seminary in Washington, D.C. in 1879 before joining the staff at Hampton, where he educated American Indians at the request of the school's founder and leader, General Samuel C. Armstrong.

Washington developed a very close relationship with the man he called, "the rarest, strongest most beautiful character that it has ever been my privilege to meet," and Armstrong thought so highly of Washington that he asked him, in 1881, to head a newly established Normal School for Blacks in Tuskegee, Alabama.

It was here that Washington established what would become a monument to his life's work. Arriving at an institution that consisted of two small converted buildings, no equipment and very little financial resources, Washington would eventually see the Tuskegee Normal and Industrial Institute consist of over 100 well-equipped buildings, more than 1,300 students, a faculty of nearly 200 teachers and an endowment of $2,000,000 by the time of his death in 1915.

Washington spent his early years at Tuskegee raising money for the institute, much of it coming from his speaking tours. He was able to raise a great deal of money from the white establishment who were impressed with his goals for the school, as well as the non-threatening racial views he espoused. Andrew Carnegie and John D. Rockefeller would become regular donors to the Tuskegee Institute, but Washington's message was not without controversy.

Washington believed that the best interests of blacks could be realized through education in crafts and industrial skills. He implored his fellow blacks, most of whom were poor, illiterate farm laborers, to put aside their goal of achieving civil rights and political power and put full force into cul-

tivating their industrial and farming skills to achieve economic independence and security. In essence, Washington wanted to abandon the battle for desegregation and against discrimination for the time being, so that blacks could acquire economic wealth and prosperity—which would ultimately win the respect and admiration of the white community.

Ultimately, Washington hoped this kind of economic parity would break down the divisions between the two races and create equal citizenship for blacks. In his epochal speech in 1895 to a racially mixed audience in Atlanta, Washington described his pragmatic vision with a sentence that would eventually be described as the "Atlanta Compromise" by critics:

> In all things that are purely social we can be separate as the fingers, yet one as the hand in all things essential to mutual progress.

The intellectual W.E.B. DuBois deplored Washington's message, especially his emphasis on vocational and craft-making skills taught at Tuskegee. DuBois felt this was detrimental to the academic development of blacks and the civil rights movement. When he released his bestselling autobiography, *Up From Slavery* in 1901, Washington's influence with both white and blacks grew. He became a special advisor to President Theodore Roosevelt, dining with him at the White House, but the visit was not without protest, as many whites felt it was a "breach of racial etiquette."

Washington's philosophy of black education and socioeconomic progress was comforting to whites and blacks alike; however, during the period of Washington's ascendancy, blacks were systematically excluded from any significant participation in political life. Discrimination and segregation became institutionalized in the south. Eventually, with the political clout of blacks stagnating, many came to believe that a more demanding approach would be needed in the battle for civil rights, and Washington's power began to wane.

Besides *Up From Slavery*, Washington wrote a dozen books, including *My Larger Education*. He would go on to receive honorary degrees from Harvard University and Dartmouth College. Though his critics might have argued that Washington's philosophy slowed the civil rights movement, no one could dispute his impact on American culture and the effect he had on education in the United States.

Up From Slavery,
An Autobiography

This volume is dedicated to my Wife
Margaret James Washington
And to my Brother
John H. Washington
Whose patience, fidelity, and hard work have gone far
to make the work at Tuskegee successful

PREFACE

This volume is the outgrowth of a series of articles, dealing with incidents in my life, which were published consecutively in the *Outlook*. While they were appearing in that magazine I was constantly surprised at the number of requests which came to me from all parts of the country, asking that the articles be permanently preserved in book form. I am most grateful to the *Outlook* for permission to gratify these requests.

I have tried to tell a simple, straightforward story, with no attempt at embellishment. My regret is that what I have attempted to do has been done so imperfectly. The greater part of my time and strength is required for the executive work connected with the Tuskegee Normal and Industrial Institute, and in securing the money necessary for the support of the institution. Much of what I have said has been written on board trains, or at hotels or railroad stations while I have been waiting for trains, or during the moments that I could spare from my work while at Tuskegee. With out the painstaking and generous assistance of Mr. Max Bennett Thrasher I could not have succeeded in any satisfactory degree.

CHAPTER I

A Slave Among Slaves

I was born a slave on a plantation in Franklin County, Virginia. I am not quite sure of the exact place or exact date of my birth, but at any rate I suspect I must have been born somewhere and at some time. As nearly as I have been able to learn, I was born near a cross-roads post-office called Hale's Ford, and the year was 1858 or 1859. I do not know the month or the day. The earliest impressions I can now recall are of the plantation and the slave quarters—the latter being the part of the plantation where the slaves had their cabins.

My life had its beginning in the midst of the most miserable, desolate, and discouraging surroundings. This was so, however, not because my owners were especially cruel, for they were not, as compared with many others. I was born in a typical log cabin, about fourteen by sixteen feet square. In this cabin I lived with my mother and a brother and sister till after the Civil War, when we were all declared free.

Of my ancestry I know almost nothing. In the slave quarters, and even later, I heard whispered conversations among the coloured people of the tortures which the slaves, including, no doubt, my ancestors on my mother's side, suffered in the middle passage of the slave ship while being conveyed from Africa to America. I have been unsuccessful in securing any information that would throw any accurate light upon the history of my family beyond my mother. She, I remember, had a half-brother and a half-sister. In the days of slavery not very much attention was given to family history and family records—that is, black family records. My mother, I suppose, attracted the attention of a purchaser who was afterward my owner and hers. Her addition to the slave family attracted about as much attention as the purchase of a new horse or cow. Of my father I know even less than of my mother. I do not even know his name. I have heard reports to the effect that he was a white man who lived on one of the near-by plantations. Whoever he was, I never heard of his taking the least interest in me or providing in any way for my rearing. But I do not find especial fault with him. He was simply another unfortunate victim of the institution which the Nation unhappily had engrafted upon it at that time.

The cabin was not only our living-place, but was also used as the kitchen for the plantation. My mother was the plantation cook. The cabin was with-

out glass windows; it had only openings in the side which let in the light, and also the cold, chilly air of winter. There was a door to the cabin—that is, something that was called a door—but the uncertain hinges by which it was hung, and the large cracks in it, to say nothing of the fact that it was too small, made the room a very uncomfortable one. In addition to these openings there was, in the lower right-hand corner of the room, the "cat-hole,"— a contrivance which almost every mansion or cabin in Virginia possessed during the ante-bellum period. The "cat-hole" was a square opening, about seven by eight inches, provided for the purpose of letting the cat pass in and out of the house at will during the night. In the case of our particular cabin I could never understand the necessity for this convenience, since there were at least a half-dozen other places in the cabin that would have accommodated the cats. There was no wooden floor in our cabin, the naked earth being used as a floor. In the centre of the earthen floor there was a large, deep opening covered with boards, which was used as a place in which to store sweet potatoes during the winter. An impression of this potato-hole is very distinctly engraved upon my memory, because I recall that during the process of putting the potatoes in or taking them out I would often come into possession of one or two, which I roasted and thoroughly enjoyed. There was no cooking-stove on our plantation, and all the cooking for the whites and slaves my mother had to do over an open fireplace, mostly in pots and "skillets." While the poorly built cabin caused us to suffer with cold in the winter, the heat from the open fire place in summer was equally trying.

The early years of my life, which were spent in the little cabin, were not very different from those of thousands of other slaves. My mother, of course, had little time in which to give attention to the training of her children during the day. She snatched a few moments for our care in the early morning before her work began, and at night after the day's work was done. One of my earliest recollections is that of my mother cooking a chicken late at night, and awakening her children for the purpose of feeding them. How or where she got it I do not know. I presume, however, it was procured from our owner's farm. Some people may call this theft. If such a thing were to happen now, I should condemn it as theft myself. But taking place at the time it did, and for the reason that it did, no one could ever make me believe that my mother was guilty of thieving. She was simply a victim of the system of slavery. I cannot remember having slept in a bed until after our family was declared free by the Emancipation Proclamation. Three children—John, my older brother, Amanda, my sister, and myself—had a pallet on the dirt floor,

or, to be more correct, we slept in and on a bundle of filthy rags laid upon the dirt floor.

I was asked not long ago to tell something about the sports and pastimes that I engaged in during my youth. Until that question was asked it had never occurred to me that there was no period of my life that was devoted to play. From the time that I can remember anything, almost every day of my life has been occupied in some kind of labour; though I think I would now be a more useful man if I had had time for sports. During the period that I spent in slavery I was not large enough to be of much service, still I was occupied most of the time in cleaning the yards, carrying water to the men in the fields, or going to the mill, to which I used to take the corn, once a week, to be ground. The mill was about three miles from the plantation. This work I always dreaded. The heavy bag of corn would be thrown across the back of the horse, and the corn divided about evenly on each side; but in some way, almost without exception, on these trips, the corn would so shift as to become unbalanced and would fall off the horse, and often I would fall with it. As I was not strong enough to reload the corn upon the horse, I would have to wait, sometimes for many hours, till a chance passer-by came along who would help me out of my trouble. The hours while waiting for some one were usually spent in crying. The time consumed in this way made me late in reaching the mill, and by the time I got my corn ground and reached home it would be far into the night. The road was a lonely one, and often led through dense forests. I was always frightened. The woods were said to be full of soldiers who had deserted from the army, and I had been told that the first thing a deserter did to a Negro boy when he found him alone was to cut off his ears. Besides, when I was late in getting home I knew I would always get a severe scolding or a flogging.

I had no schooling whatever while I was a slave, though I remember on several occasions I went as far as the schoolhouse door with one of my young mistresses to carry her books. The picture of several dozen boys and girls in a schoolroom engaged in study made a deep impression upon me, and I had the feeling that to get into a schoolhouse and study in this way would be about the same as getting into paradise.

So far as I can now recall, the first knowledge that I got of the fact that we were slaves, and that freedom of the slaves was being discussed, was early one morning before day, when I was awakened by my mother kneeling over her children and fervently praying that Lincoln and his armies might be successful, and that one day she and her children might be free. In this connec-

tion I have never been able to understand how the slaves throughout the South, completely ignorant as were the masses so far as books or newspapers were concerned, were able to keep themselves so accurately and completely informed about the great National questions that were agitating the country. From the time that Garrison, Lovejoy, and others began to agitate for freedom, the slaves throughout the South kept in close touch with the progress of the movement. Though I was a mere child during the preparation for the Civil War and during the war itself, I now recall the many late-at-night whispered discussions that I heard my mother and the other slaves on the plantation indulge in. These discussions showed that they understood the situation, and that they kept themselves informed of events by what was termed the "grape-vine" telegraph.

During the campaign when Lincoln was first a candidate for the Presidency, the slaves on our far-off plantation, miles from any railroad or large city or daily newspaper, knew what the issues involved were. When war was begun between the North and the South, every slave on our plantation felt and knew that, though other issues were discussed, the primal one was that of slavery. Even the most ignorant members of my race on the remote plantations felt in their hearts, with a certainty that admitted of no doubt, that the freedom of the slaves would be the one great result of the war, if the Northern armies conquered. Every success of the Federal armies and every defeat of the Confederate forces was watched with the keenest and most intense interest. Often the slaves got knowledge of the results of great battles before the white people received it. This news was usually gotten from the coloured man who was sent to the post-office for the mail. In our case the post-office was about three miles from the plantation and the mail came once or twice a week. The man who was sent to the office would linger about the place long enough to get the drift of the conversation from the group of white people who naturally congregated there, after receiving their mail, to discuss the latest news. The mail-carrier on his way back to our master's house would as naturally retail the news that he had secured among the slaves, and in this way they often heard of important events before the white people at the "big house," as the master's house was called.

I cannot remember a single instance during my childhood or early boyhood when our entire family sat down to the table together, and God's blessing was asked, and the family ate a meal in a civilized manner. On the plantation in Virginia, and even later, meals were gotten by the children very much as dumb animals get theirs. It was a piece of bread here and a scrap of

meat there. It was a cup of milk at one time and some potatoes at another. Sometimes a portion of our family would eat out of the skillet or pot, while some one else would eat from a tin plate held on the knees, and often using nothing but the hands with which to hold the food. When I had grown to sufficient size, I was required to go to the "big house" at meal-times to fan the flies from the table by means of a large set of paper fans operated by a pulley. Naturally much of the conversation of the white people turned upon the subject of freedom and the war, and I absorbed a good deal of it. I remember that at one time I saw two of my young mistresses and some lady visitors eating ginger-cakes, in the yard. At that time those cakes seemed to me to be absolutely the most tempting and desirable things that I had ever seen; and I then and there resolved that, if I ever got free, the height of my ambition would be reached if I could get to the point where I could secure and eat ginger-cakes in the way that I saw those ladies doing.

Of course as the war was prolonged the white people, in many cases, often found it difficult to secure food for themselves. I think the slaves felt the deprivation less than the whites, because the usual diet for the slaves was corn bread and pork, and these could be raised on the plantation; but coffee, tea, sugar, and other articles which the whites had been accustomed to use could not be raised on the plantation, and the conditions brought about by the war frequently made it impossible to secure these things. The whites were often in great straits. Parched corn was used for coffee, and a kind of black molasses was used instead of sugar. Many times nothing was used to sweeten the so-called tea and coffee.

The first pair of shoes that I recall wearing were wooden ones. They had rough leather on the top, but the bottoms, which were about an inch thick, were of wood. When I walked they made a fearful noise, and besides this they were very inconvenient, since there was no yielding to the natural pressure of the foot. In wearing them one presented an exceedingly awkward appearance. The most trying ordeal that I was forced to endure as a slave boy, however, was the wearing of a flax shirt. In the portion of Virginia where I lived it was common to use flax as part of the clothing for the slaves. That part of the flax from which our clothing was made was largely the refuse, which of course was the cheapest and roughest part. I can scarcely imagine any torture, except, perhaps, the pulling of tooth, that is equal to that caused by putting on a new flax shirt for the first time. It is almost equal to the feeling that one would experience if he had a dozen or more chestnut burrs, or a hundred small pin-points, in contact with his flesh. Even to this day I can recall accu-

rately the tortures that I underwent when putting on one of these garments. The fact that my flesh was soft and tender added to the pain. But I had no choice. I had to wear the flax shirt or none; and had it been left to me to choose, I should have chosen to wear no covering. In connection with the flax shirt, my brother John, who is several years older than I am, performed one of the most generous acts that I ever heard of one slave relative doing for another. On several occasions when I was being forced to wear a new flax shirt, he generously agreed to put it on in my stead and wear it for several days, till it was "broken in." Until I had grown to be quite a youth this single garment was all that I wore.

One may get the idea from what I have said, that there was bitter feeling toward the white people on the part of my race, because of the fact that most of the white population was away fighting in a war which would result in keeping the Negro in slavery if the South was successful. In the case of the slaves on our place this was not true, and it was not true of any large portion of the slave population in the South where the Negro was treated with anything like decency. During the Civil War one of my young masters was killed, and two were severely wounded. I recall the feeling of sorrow which existed among the slaves when they heard of the death of "Mars' Billy." It was no sham sorrow but real. Some of the slaves had nursed "Mars' Billy"; others had played with him when he was a child. "Mars' Billy" had begged for mercy in the case of others when the overseer or master was thrashing them. The sorrow in the slave quarter was only second to that in the "big house." When the two young masters were brought home wounded, the sympathy of the slaves was shown in many ways. They were just as anxious to assist in the nursing as the family relatives of the wounded. Some of the slaves would even beg for the privilege of sitting up at night to nurse their wounded masters. This tenderness and sympathy on the part of those held in bondage was a result of their kindly and generous nature. In order to defend and protect the women and children who were left on the plantations when the white males went to war, the slaves would have laid down their lives. The slave who was selected to sleep in the "big house" during the absence of the males was considered to have the place of honour. Any one attempting to harm "young Mistress" or "old Mistress" during the night would have had to cross the dead body of the slave to do so. I do not know how many have noticed it, but I think that it will be found to be true that there are few instances, either in slavery or freedom, in which a member of my race has been known to betray a specific trust.

As a rule, not only did the members of my race entertain no feelings of bitterness against the whites before and during the war, but there are many instances of Negroes tenderly caring for their former masters and mistresses who for some reason have become poor and dependent since the war. I know of instances where the former masters of slaves have for years been supplied with money by their former slaves to keep them from suffering. I have known of still other cases in which the former slaves have assisted in the education of the descendants of their former owners. I know of a case on a large plantation in the South in which a young white man, the son of the former owner of the estate, has become so reduced in purse and self-control by reason of drink that he is a pitiable creature; and yet, notwithstanding the poverty of the coloured people themselves on this plantation, they have for years supplied this young white man with the necessities of life. One sends him a little coffee or sugar, another a little meat, and so on. Nothing that the coloured people possess is too good for the son of "old Mars' Tom," who will perhaps never be permitted to suffer while any remain on the place who knew directly or indirectly of "old Mars' Tom."

I have said that there are few instances of a member of my race betraying a specific trust. One of the best illustrations of this which I know of is in the case of an ex-slave from Virginia whom I met not long ago in a little town in the state of Ohio. I found that this man had made a contract with his master, two or three years previous to the Emancipation Proclamation, to the effect that the slave was to be permitted to buy himself, by paying so much per year for his body; and while he was paying for himself, he was to be permitted to labour where and for whom he pleased. Finding that he could secure better wages in Ohio, he went there. When freedom came, he was still in debt to his master some three hundred dollars. Notwithstanding that the Emancipation Proclamation freed him from any obligation to his master, this black man walked the greater portion of the distance back to where his old master lived in Virginia, and placed the last dollar, with interest, in his hands. In talking to me about this, the man told me that he knew that he did not have to pay the debt, but that he had given his word to his master, and his word he had never broken. He felt that he could not enjoy his freedom till he had fulfilled his promise.

From some things that I have said one may get the idea that some of the slaves did not want freedom. This is not true. I have never seen one who did not want to be free, or one who would return to slavery.

I pity from the bottom of my heart any nation or body of people that is

so unfortunate as to get entangled in the net of slavery. I have long since ceased to cherish any spirit of bitterness against the Southern white people on account of the enslavement of my race. No one section of our country was wholly responsible for its introduction, and, besides, it was recognized and protected for years by the General Government. Having once got its tentacles fastened on to the economic and social life of the Republic, it was no easy matter for the country to relieve itself of the institution. Then, when we rid ourselves of prejudice, or racial feeling, and look facts in the face, we must acknowledge that, notwithstanding the cruelty and moral wrong of slavery, the ten million Negroes inhabiting this country, who themselves or whose ancestors went through the school of American slavery, are in a stronger and more hopeful condition, materially, intellectually, morally, and religiously, than is true of an equal number of black people in any other portion of the globe. This is so to such an extent that Negroes in this country, who themselves or whose forefathers went through the school of slavery, are constantly returning to Africa as missionaries to enlighten those who remained in the fatherland. This I say, not to justify slavery—on the other hand, I condemn it as an institution, as we all know that in America it was established for selfish and financial reasons, and not from a missionary motive—but to call attention to a fact, and to show how Providence so often uses men and institutions to accomplish a purpose. When persons ask me in these days how, in the midst of what sometimes seem hopelessly discouraging conditions, I can have such faith in the future of my race in this country, I remind them of the wilderness through which and out of which, a good Providence has already led us.

Ever since I have been old enough to think for myself, I have entertained the idea that, notwithstanding the cruel wrongs inflicted upon us, the black man got nearly as much out of slavery as the white man did. The hurtful influences of the institution were not by any means confined to the Negro. This was fully illustrated by the life upon our own plantation. The whole machinery of slavery was so constructed as to cause labour, as a rule, to be looked upon as a badge of degradation, of inferiority. Hence labour was something that both races on the slave plantation sought to escape. The slave system on our place, in a large measure, took the spirit of self-reliance and self-help out of the white people. My old master had many boys and girls, but not one, so far as I know, ever mastered a single trade or special line of productive industry. The girls were not taught to cook, sew, or to take care of the house. All of this was left to the slaves. The slaves, of course, had little

personal interest in the life of the plantation, and their ignorance prevented them from learning how to do things in the most improved and thorough manner. As a result of the system, fences were out of repair, gates were hanging half off the hinges, doors creaked, window-panes were out, plastering had fallen but was not replaced, weeds grew in the yard. As a rule, there was food for whites and blacks, but inside the house, and on the dining-room table, there was wanting that delicacy and refinement of touch and finish which can make a home the most convenient, comfortable, and attractive place in the world. Withal there was a waste of food and other materials which was sad. When freedom came, the slaves were almost as well fitted to begin life anew as the master, except in the matter of book-learning and ownership of property. The slave owner and his sons had mastered no special industry. They unconsciously had imbibed the feeling that manual labour was not the proper thing for them. On the other hand, the slaves, in many cases, had mastered some handicraft, and none were ashamed, and few unwilling, to labour.

Finally the war closed, and the day of freedom came. It was a momentous and eventful day to all upon our plantation. We had been expecting it. Freedom was in the air, and had been for months. Deserting soldiers returning to their homes were to be seen every day. Others who had been discharged, or whose regiments had been paroled, were constantly passing near our place. The "grape-vine telegraph" was kept busy night and day. The news and mutterings of great events were swiftly carried from one plantation to another. In the fear of "Yankee" invasions, the silverware and other valuables were taken from the "big house," buried in the woods, and guarded by trusted slaves. Woe be to any one who would have attempted to disturb the buried treasure. The slaves would give the Yankee soldiers food, drink, clothing—anything but that which had been specifically intrusted to their care and honour. As the great day drew nearer, there was more singing in the slave quarters than usual. It was bolder, had more ring, and lasted later into the night. Most of the verses of the plantation songs had some reference to freedom. True, they had sung those same verses before, but they had been careful to explain that the "freedom" in these songs referred to the next world, and had no connection with life in this world. Now they gradually threw off the mask, and were not afraid to let it be known that the "freedom" in their songs meant freedom of the body in this world. The night before the eventful day, word was sent to the slave quarters to the effect that something unusual was going to take place at the "big house" the next morning. There

was little, if any, sleep that night. All was excitement and expectancy. Early the next morning word was sent to all the slaves, old and young, to gather at the house. In company with my mother, brother, and sister, and a large number of other slaves, I went to the master's house. All of our master's family were either standing or seated on the veranda of the house, where they could see what was to take place and hear what was said. There was a feeling of deep interest, or perhaps sadness, on their faces, but not bitterness. As I now recall the impression they made upon me, they did not at the moment seem to be sad because of the loss of property, but rather because of parting with those whom they had reared and who were in many ways very close to them. The most distinct thing that I now recall in connection with the scene was that some man who seemed to be a stranger (a United States officer, I presume) made a little speech and then read a rather long paper—the Emancipation Proclamation, I think. After the reading we were told that we were all free, and could go when and where we pleased. My mother, who was standing by my side, leaned over and kissed her children, while tears of joy ran down her cheeks. She explained to us what it all meant, that this was the day for which she had been so long praying, but fearing that she would never live to see.

For some minutes there was great rejoicing, and thanksgiving, and wild scenes of ecstasy. But there was no feeling of bitterness. In fact, there was pity among the slaves for our former owners. The wild rejoicing on the part of the emancipated coloured people lasted but for a brief period, for I noticed that by the time they returned to their cabins there was a change in their feelings. The great responsibility of being free, of having charge of themselves, of having to think and plan for themselves and their children, seemed to take possession of them. It was very much like suddenly turning a youth of ten or twelve years out into the world to provide for himself. In a few hours the great questions with which the Anglo-Saxon race had been grappling for centuries had been thrown upon these people to be solved. These were the questions of a home, a living, the rearing of children, education, citizenship, and the establishment and support of churches. Was it any wonder that within a few hours the wild rejoicing ceased and a feeling of deep gloom seemed to pervade the slave quarters? To some it seemed that, now that they were in actual possession of it, freedom was a more serious thing than they had expected to find it. Some of the slaves were seventy or eighty years old; their best days were gone. They had no strength with which to earn a living in a strange place and among strange people, even if they had been sure where to find a new place of abode. To this class the problem seemed especially hard.

Besides, deep down in their hearts there was a strange and peculiar attachment to "old Marster" and "old Missus," and to their children, which they found it hard to think of breaking off. With these they had spent in some cases nearly a half-century, and it was no light thing to think of parting. Gradually, one by one, stealthily at first, the older slaves began to wander from the slave quarters back to the "big house" to have a whispered conversation with their former owners as to the future.

CHAPTER II

Boyhood Days

After the coming of freedom there were two points upon which practically all the people on our place were agreed, and I find that this was generally true throughout the South: that they must change their names, and that they must leave the old plantation for at least a few days or weeks in order that they might really feel sure that they were free.

In some way a feeling got among the coloured people that it was far from proper for them to bear the surname of their former owners, and a great many of them took other surnames. This was one of the first signs of freedom. When they were slaves, a coloured person was simply called "John" or "Susan." There was seldom occasion for more than the use of the one name. If "John" or "Susan" belonged to a white man by the name of "Hatcher," sometimes he was called "John Hatcher," or as often "Hatcher's John." But there was a feeling that "John Hatcher" or "Hatcher's John" was not the proper title by which to denote a freeman; and so in many cases "John Hatcher" was changed to "John S. Lincoln" or "John S. Sherman," the initial "S" standing for no name, it being simply a part of what the coloured man proudly called his "entitles."

As I have stated, most of the coloured people left the old plantation for a short while at least, so as to be sure, it seemed, that they could leave and try their freedom on to see how it felt. After they had remained away for a time, many of the older slaves, especially, returned to their old homes and made some kind of contract with their former owners by which they remained on the estate.

My mother's husband, who was the stepfather of my brother John and

myself, did not belong to the same owners as did my mother. In fact, he seldom came to our plantation. I remember seeing him there perhaps once a year, that being about Christmas time. In some way, during the war, by running away and following the Federal soldiers, it seems, he found his way into the new state of West Virginia. As soon as freedom was declared, he sent for my mother to come to the Kanawha Valley, in West Virginia. At that time a journey from Virginia over the mountains to West Virginia was rather a tedious and in some cases a painful undertaking. What little clothing and few household goods we had were placed in a cart, but the children walked the greater portion of the distance, which was several hundred miles.

I do not think any of us ever had been very far from the plantation, and the taking of a long journey into another state was quite an event. The parting from our former owners and the members of our own race on the plantation was a serious occasion. From the time of our parting till their death we kept up a correspondence with the older members of the family, and in later years we have kept in touch with those who were the younger members. We were several weeks making the trip, and most of the time we slept in the open air and did our cooking over a log fire out of doors. One night I recall that we camped near an abandoned log cabin, and my mother decided to build a fire in that for cooking, and afterward to make a "pallet" on the floor for our sleeping. Just as the fire had gotten well started a large black snake fully a yard and a half long dropped down the chimney and ran out on the floor. Of course we at once abandoned that cabin. Finally we reached our destination—a little town called Malden, which is about five miles from Charleston, the present capital of the state.

At that time salt-mining was the great industry in that part of West Virginia, and the little town of Malden was right in the midst of the salt-furnaces. My stepfather had already secured a job at a salt-furnace, and he had also secured a little cabin for us to live in. Our new house was no better than the one we had left on the old plantation in Virginia. In fact, in one respect it was worse. Notwithstanding the poor condition of our plantation cabin, we were at all times sure of pure air. Our new home was in the midst of a cluster of cabins crowded closely together, and as there were no sanitary regulations, the filth about the cabins was often intolerable. Some of our neighbours were coloured people, and some were the poorest and most ignorant and degraded white people. It was a motley mixture. Drinking, gambling, quarrels, fights, and shockingly immoral practices were frequent. All who lived in the little town were in one way or another connected with the salt

business. Though I was a mere child, my stepfather put me and my brother at work in one of the furnaces. Often I began work as early as four o'clock in the morning.

The first thing I ever learned in the way of book knowledge was while working in this salt-furnace. Each salt-packer had his barrels marked with a certain number. The number allotted to my stepfather was "18." At the close of the day's work the boss of the packers would come around and put "18" on each of our barrels, and I soon learned to recognize that figure wherever I saw it, and after while got to the point where I could make that figure, though I knew nothing about any other figures or letters.

From the time that I can remember having any thoughts about anything, I recall that I had an in tense longing to learn to read. I determined, when quite a small child, that, if I accomplished nothing else in life, I would in some way get enough education to enable me to read common books and newspapers. Soon after we got settled in some manner in our new cabin in West Virginia, I induced my mother to get hold of a book for me. How or where she got it I do not know, but in some way she procured an old copy of Webster's "blue-back" spelling-book, which contained the alphabet, followed by such meaningless words as "ab," "ba," "ca," "da." I began at once to devour this book, and I think that it was the first one I ever had in my hands. I had learned from somebody that the way to begin to read was to learn the alphabet, so I tried in all the ways I could think of to learn it,—all of course without a teacher, for I could find no one to teach me. At that time there was not a single member of my race anywhere near us who could read, and I was too timid to approach any of the white people. In some way, within a few weeks, I mastered the greater portion of the alphabet. In all my efforts to learn to read my mother shared fully my ambition, and sympathized with me and aided me in every way that she could. Though she was totally ignorant, so far as mere book knowledge was concerned, she had high ambitions for her children, and a large fund of good, hard, common sense which seemed to enable her to meet and master every situation. If I have done anything in life worth attention, I feel sure that I inherited the disposition from my mother.

In the midst of my struggles and longing for an education, a young coloured boy who had learned to read in the state of Ohio came to Malden. As soon as the coloured people found out that he could read, a newspaper was secured, and at the close of nearly every day's work this young man would be surrounded by a group of men and women who were anxious to

hear him read the news contained in the papers. How I used to envy this man! He seemed to me to be the one young man in all the world who ought to be satisfied with his attainments.

About this time the question of having some kind of a school opened for the coloured children in the village began to be discussed by members of the race. As it would be the first school for Negro children that had ever been opened in that part of Virginia, it was, of course, to be a great event, and the discussion excited the widest interest. The most perplexing question was where to find a teacher. The young man from Ohio who had learned to read the papers was considered, but his age was against him. In the midst of the discussion about a teacher another young coloured man from Ohio, who had been a soldier, in some way found his way into town. It was soon learned that he possessed considerable education, and he was engaged by the coloured people to teach their first school. As yet no free schools had been started for coloured people in that section, hence each family agreed to pay a certain amount per month, with the understanding that the teacher was to "board 'round"—that is, spend a day with each family. This was not bad for the teacher, for each family tried to provide the very best on the day the teacher was to be its guest. I recall that I looked forward with an anxious appetite to the "teacher's day" at our little cabin.

This experience of a whole race beginning to go to school for the first time, presents one of the most interesting studies that has ever occurred in connection with the development of any race. Few people who were not right in the midst of the scenes can form any exact idea of the intense desire which the people of my race showed for an education. As I have stated, it was a whole race trying to go to school. Few were too young, and none too old, to make the attempt to learn. As fast as any kind of teachers could be secured, not only were day-schools filled, but night-schools as well. The great ambition of the older people was to try to learn to read the Bible before they died. With this end in view, men and women who were fifty or seventy-five years old would often be found in the night-school. Sunday-schools were formed soon after freedom, but the principal book studied in the Sunday-school was the spelling-book. Day-school, night-school, Sunday-school, were always crowded, and often many had to be turned away for want of room.

The opening of the school in the Kanawha Valley, however, brought to me one of the keenest disappointments that I ever experienced. I had been working in a salt-furnace for several months, and my stepfather had discovered that I had a financial value, and so, when the school opened, he decid-

ed that he could not spare me from my work. This decision seemed to cloud my every ambition. The disappointment was made all the more severe by reason of the fact that my place of work was where I could see the happy children passing to and from school, mornings and afternoons. Despite this disappointment, however, I determined that I would learn something, anyway. I applied myself with greater earnestness than ever to the mastering of what was in the "blue-back" speller.

My mother sympathized with me in my disappointment, and sought to comfort me in all the ways she could, and to help me find a way to learn. After a while I succeeded in making arrangements with the teacher to give me some lessons at night, after the day's work was done. These night lessons were so welcome that I think I learned more at night than the other children did during the day. My own experiences in the night-school gave me faith in the night-school idea, with which, in after years, I had to do both at Hampton and Tuskegee. But my boyish heart was still set upon going to the day-school, and I let no opportunity slip to push my case. Finally I won, and was permitted to go to the school in the day for a few months, with the understanding that I was to rise early in the morning and work in the furnace till nine o'clock, and return immediately after school closed in the afternoon for at least two more hours of work.

The schoolhouse was some distance from the furnace, and as I had to work till nine o'clock, and the school opened at nine, I found myself in a difficulty. School would always be begun before I reached it, and sometimes my class had recited. To get around this difficulty I yielded to a temptation for which most people, I suppose, will condemn me; but since it is a fact, I might as well state it. I have great faith in the power and influence of facts. It is seldom that anything is permanently gained by holding back a fact. There was a large clock in a little office in the furnace. This clock, of course, all the hundred or more workmen depended upon to regulate their hours of beginning and ending the day's work. I got the idea that the way for me to reach school on time was to move the clock hands from half-past eight up to the nine o'clock mark. This I found myself doing morning after morning, till the furnace "boss" discovered that something was wrong, and locked the clock in a case. I did not mean to inconvenience any body. I simply meant to reach that schoolhouse in time.

When, however, I found myself at the school for the first time, I also found myself confronted with two other difficulties. In the first place, I found that all of the other children wore hats or caps on their heads, and I

had neither hat nor cap. In fact, I do not remember that up to the time of going to school I had ever worn any kind of covering upon my head, nor do I recall that either I or anybody else had even thought anything about the need of covering for my head. But, of course, when I saw how all the other boys were dressed, I began to feel quite uncomfortable. As usual, I put the case before my mother, and she explained to me that she had no money with which to buy a "store hat," which was a rather new institution at that time among the members of my race and was considered quite the thing for young and old to own, but that she would find a way to help me out of the difficulty. She accordingly got two pieces of "homespun" (jeans) and sewed them together, and I was soon the proud possessor of my first cap.

The lesson that my mother taught me in this has always remained with me, and I have tried as best I could to teach it to others. I have always felt proud, whenever I think of the incident, that my mother had strength of character enough not to be led into the temptation of seeming to be that which she was not—of trying to impress my schoolmates and others with the fact that she was able to buy me a "store hat" when she was not. I have always felt proud that she refused to go into debt for that which she did not have the money to pay for. Since that time I have owned many kinds of caps and hats, but never one of which I have felt so proud as of the cap made of the two pieces of cloth sewed together by my mother. I have noted the fact, but without satisfaction, I need not add, that several of the boys who began their careers with "store hats" and who were my schoolmates and used to join in the sport that was made of me because I had only a "homespun" cap, have ended their careers in the penitentiary, while others are not able now to buy any kind of hat.

My second difficulty was with regard to my name, or rather *a* name. From the time when I could remember anything, I had been called simply "Booker." Before going to school it had never occurred to me that it was needful or appropriate to have an additional name. When I heard the school-roll called, I noticed that all of the children had at least two names, and some of them indulged in what seemed to me the extravagance of having three. I was in deep perplexity, because I knew that the teacher would demand of me at least two names, and I had only one. By the time the occasion came for the enrolling of my name, an idea occurred to me which I thought would make me equal to the situation; and so, when the teacher asked me what my full name was, I calmly told him "Booker Washington," as if I had been called by that name all my life; and by that name I have since been known.

Later in my life I found that my mother had given me the name of "Booker Taliaferro" soon after I was born, but in some way that part of my name seemed to disappear, and for a long while was forgotten, but as soon as I found out about it I revived it, and made my full name "Booker Taliaferro Washington." I think there are not many men in our country who have had the privilege of naming themselves in the way that I have.

More than once I have tried to picture myself in the position of a boy or man with an honoured and distinguished ancestry which I could trace back through a period of hundreds of years, and who had not only inherited a name, but fortune and a proud family homestead; and yet I have sometimes had the feeling that if I had inherited these, and had been a member of a more popular race, I should have been inclined to yield to the temptation of depending upon my ancestry and my colour to do that for me which I should do for myself. Years ago I resolved that because I had no ancestry myself I would leave a record of which my children would be proud, and which might encourage them to still higher effort.

The world should not pass judgment upon the Negro, and especially the Negro youth, too quickly, or too harshly. The Negro boy has obstacles, discouragements, and temptations to battle with that are little known to those not situated as he is. When a white boy undertakes a task, it is taken for granted that he will succeed. On the other hand, people are usually surprised if the Negro boy does not fail. In a word, the Negro youth starts out with the presumption against him.

The influence of ancestry, however, is important in helping forward any individual or race, if too much reliance is not placed upon it. Those who constantly direct attention to the Negro youth's moral weaknesses, and compare his advancement with that of white youths, do not consider the influence of the memories which cling about the old family homesteads. I have no idea, as I have stated elsewhere, who my grandmother was. I have, or have had, uncles and aunts and cousins, but I have no knowledge as to where most of them are. My case will illustrate that of hundreds of thousands of black people in every part of our country. The very fact that the white boy is conscious that, if he fails in life, he will disgrace the whole family record, extending back through many generations, is of tremendous value in helping him to resist temptations. The fact that the individual has behind and surrounding him proud family history and connection serves as a stimulus to help him to overcome obstacles when striving for success.

The time that I was permitted to attend school during the day was short,

and my attendance was irregular. It was not long before I had to stop attending day-school altogether, and devote all of my time again to work. I resorted to the night school again. In fact, the greater part of the education I secured in my boyhood was gathered through the night-school after my day's work was done. I had difficulty often in securing a satisfactory teacher. Sometimes, after I had secured some one to teach me at night, I would find, much to my disappointment, that the teacher knew but little more than I did. Often I would have to walk several miles at night in order to recite my night-school lessons. There was never a time in my youth, no matter how dark and discouraging the days might be, when one resolve did not continually remain with me, and that was a determination to secure an education at any cost.

Soon after we moved to West Virginia, my mother accepted into our family, notwithstanding our poverty, an orphan boy, to whom afterward we I gave the name of James B. Washington. He has ever since remained a member of the family.

After I had worked in the salt-furnace for some time, work was secured for me in a coal-mine which was operated mainly for the purpose of securing fuel for the salt-furnace. Work in the coal-mine I always dreaded. One reason for this was that any one who worked in a coal-mine was always unclean, at least while at work, and it was a very hard job to get one's skin clean after the day's work was over. Then it was fully a mile from the opening of the coal-mine to the face of the coal, and all, of course, was in the blackest darkness. I do not believe that one ever experiences anywhere else such darkness as he does in a coal mine. The mine was divided into a large number of different "rooms" or departments, and, as I never was able to learn the location of all these "rooms," I many times found myself lost in the mine. To add to the horror of being lost, sometimes my light would go out, and then, if I did not happen to have a match, I would wander about in the darkness until by chance I found some one to give me a light. The work was not only hard, but it was dangerous. There was always the danger of being blown to pieces by a premature explosion of powder, or of being crushed by falling slate. Accidents from one or another of these causes were frequently occurring, and this kept me in constant fear. Many children of the tenderest years were compelled then, as is now true I fear, in most coal-mining districts, to spend a large part of their lives in these coal-mines, with little opportunity to get an education; and, what is worse, I have often noted that, as a rule, young boys who begin life in a coal-mine are often physically and mentally dwarfed.

They soon lose ambition to do anything else than to continue as a coal-miner.

In those days, and later as a young man, I used to try to picture in my imagination the feelings and ambitions of a white boy with absolutely no limit placed upon his aspirations and activities. I used to envy the white boy who had no obstacles placed in the way of his becoming a Congressman, Governor, Bishop, or President by reason of the accident of his birth or race. I used to picture the way that I would act under such circumstances; how I would begin at the bottom and keep rising until I reached the highest round of success.

In later years, I confess that I do not envy the white boy as I once did. I have learned that success is to be measured not so much by the position that one has reached in life as by the obstacles which he has overcome while try-ing to succeed. Looked at from this standpoint, I almost reach the conclu-sion that often the Negro boy's birth and connection with an unpopular race is an advantage, so far as real life is concerned. With few exceptions, the Negro youth must work harder and must perform his task even better than a white youth in order to secure recognition. But out of the hard and unusu-al struggle through which he is compelled to pass, he gets a strength, a con-fidence, that one misses whose pathway is comparatively smooth by reason of birth and race.

From any point of view, I had rather be what I am, a member of the Negro race, than be able to claim membership with the most favoured of any other race. I have always been made sad when I have heard members of any race claiming rights and privileges, or certain badges of distinction, on the ground simply that they were members of this or that race, regardless of their own individual worth or attainments. I have been made to feel sad for such persons because I am conscious of the fact that mere connection with what is known as a superior race will not permanently carry an individual forward unless he has individual worth, and mere connection with what is regarded as an inferior race will not finally hold an individual back if he possesses intrinsic, individual merit. Every persecuted individual and race should get much consolation out of the great human law, which is universal and eter-nal, that merit, no matter under what skin found, is in the long run, recog-nized and rewarded. This I have said here, not to call attention to myself as an individual, but to the race to which I am proud to belong.

CHAPTER III

The Struggle For An Education

One day, while at work in the coal-mine, I happened to overhear two miners talking about a great school for coloured people somewhere in Virginia. This was the first time that I had ever heard anything about any kind of school or college that was more pretentious than the little coloured school in our town.

In the darkness of the mine I noiselessly crept as close as I could to the two men who were talking. I heard one tell the other that not only was the school established for the members of my race, but that opportunities were provided by which poor but worthy students could work out all or a part of the cost of board, and at the same time be taught some trade or industry.

As they went on describing the school, it seemed to me that it must be the greatest place on earth, and not even Heaven presented more attractions for me at that time than did the Hampton Normal and Agricultural Institute in Virginia, about which these men were talking. I resolved at once to go to that school, although I had no idea where it was, or how many miles away, or how I was going to reach it; I remembered only that I was on fire constantly with one ambition, and that was to go to Hampton. This thought was with me day and night.

After hearing of the Hampton Institute, I continued to work for a few months longer in the coal mine. While at work there, I heard of a vacant position in the household of General Lewis Ruffner, the owner of the salt-furnace and coal-mine. Mrs. Viola Ruffner, the wife of General Ruffner, was a "Yankee" woman from Vermont. Mrs. Ruffner had a reputation all through the vicinity for being very strict with her servants, and especially with the boys who tried to serve her. Few of them had remained with her more than two or three weeks. They all left with the same excuse: she was too strict. I decided, however, that I would rather try Mrs. Ruffner's house than remain in the coal-mine, and so my mother applied to her for the vacant position. I was hired at a salary of $5 per month.

I had heard so much about Mrs. Ruffner's severity that I was almost afraid to see her, and trembled when I went into her presence. I had not lived with her many weeks, however, before I began to understand her. I soon began to learn that, first of all, she wanted everything kept clean about her, that she wanted things done promptly and systematically, and that at the bottom of

everything she wanted absolute honesty and frankness. Nothing must be sloven or slipshod; every door, every fence, must be kept in repair.

I cannot now recall how long I lived with Mrs. Ruffner before going to Hampton, but I think it must have been a year and a half. At any rate, I here repeat what I have said more than once before, that the lessons that I learned in the home of Mrs. Ruffner were as valuable to me as any education I have ever gotten anywhere since. Even to this day I never see bits of paper scattered around a house or in the street that I do not want to pick them up at once. I never see a filthy yard that I do not want to clean it, a paling off of a fence that I do not want to put it on, an unpainted or unwhitewashed house that I do not want to paint or whitewash it, or a button off one's clothes, or a grease-spot on them or on a floor, that I do not want to call attention to it.

From fearing Mrs. Ruffner I soon learned to look upon her as one of my best friends. When she found that she could trust me she did so implicitly. During the one or two winters that I was with her she gave me an opportunity to go to school for an hour in the day during a portion of the winter months, but most of my studying was done at night, sometimes alone, sometimes under some one whom I could hire to teach me. Mrs. Ruffner always encouraged and sympathized with me in all my efforts to get an education. It was while living with her that I began to get together my first library. I secured a dry-goods box, knocked out one side of it, put some shelves in it, and began putting into it every kind of book that I could get my hands upon, and called it my "library."

Notwithstanding my success at Mrs. Ruffner's I did not give up the idea of going to the Hampton Institute. In the fall of 1872 I determined to make an effort to get there, although, as I have stated, I had no definite idea of the direction in which Hampton was, or of what it would cost to go there. I do not think that any one thoroughly sympathized with me in my ambition to go to Hampton unless it was my mother, and she was troubled with a grave fear that I was starting out on a "wild-goose chase." At any rate, I got only a half-hearted consent from her that I might start. The small amount of money that I had earned had been consumed by my stepfather and the remainder of the family, with the exception of a very few dollars, and so I had very little with which to buy clothes and pay my travelling expenses. My brother John helped me all that he could, but of course that was not a great deal, for his work was in the coal-mine, where he did not earn much, and most of what he did earn went in the direction of paying the household expenses.

Perhaps the thing that touched and pleased me most in connection with

my starting for Hampton was the interest that many of the older coloured people took in the matter. They had spent the best days of their lives in slavery, and hardly expected to live to see the time when they would see a member of their race leave home to attend a boarding-school. Some of these older people would give me a nickel, others a quarter, or a handkerchief.

Finally the great day came, and I started for Hampton. I had only a small, cheap satchel that contained what few articles of clothing I could get. My mother at the time was rather weak and broken in health. I hardly expected to see her again, and thus our parting was all the more sad. She, however, was very brave through it all. At that time there were no through trains connecting that part of West Virginia with eastern Virginia. Trains ran only a portion of the way, and the remainder of the distance was travelled by stage-coaches.

The distance from Malden to Hampton is about five hundred miles. I had not been away from home many hours before it began to grow painfully evident that I did not have enough money to pay my fare to Hampton. One experience I shall long remember. I had been travelling over the mountains most of the afternoon in an old-fashioned stage-coach, when, late in the evening, the coach stopped for the night at a common, unpainted house called a hotel. All the other passengers except myself were whites. In my ignorance I supposed that the little hotel existed for the purpose of accommodating the passengers who travelled on the stage-coach. The difference that the colour of one's skin would make I had not thought anything about. After all the other passengers had been shown rooms and were getting ready for supper, I shyly presented myself before the man at the desk. It is true I had practically no money in my pocket with which to pay for bed or food, but I had hoped in some way to beg my way into the good graces of the landlord, for at that season in the mountains of Virginia the weather was cold, and I wanted to get indoors for the night. Without asking as to whether I had any money, the man at the desk firmly refused to even consider the matter of providing me with food or lodging. This was my first experience in finding out what the colour of my skin meant. In some way I managed to keep warm by walking about, and so got through the night. My whole soul was so bent upon reaching Hampton that I did not have time to cherish any bitterness toward the hotel-keeper.

By walking, begging rides both in wagons and in the cars, in some way, after a number of days, I reached the city of Richmond, Virginia, about eighty-two miles from Hampton. When I reached there, tired, hungry, and dirty, it was late in the night. I had never been in a large city, and this rather

added to my misery. When I reached Richmond, I was completely out of money. I had not a single acquaintance in the place, and, being unused to city ways, I did not know where to go. I applied at several places for lodging, but they all wanted money, and that was what I did not have. Knowing nothing else better to do, I walked the streets. In doing this I passed by many food-stands where fried chicken and half-moon apple pies were piled high and made to present a most tempting appearance. At that time it seemed to me that I would have promised all that I expected to possess in the future to have gotten hold of one of those chicken legs or one of those pies. But I could not get either of these, nor anything else to eat.

I must have walked the streets till after midnight. At last I became so exhausted that I could walk no longer. I was tired, I was hungry, I was everything but discouraged. Just about the time when I reached extreme physical exhaustion, I came upon a portion of a street where the board sidewalk was considerably elevated. I waited for a few minutes, till I was sure that no passers-by could see me, and then crept under the sidewalk and lay for the night upon the ground, with my satchel of clothing for a pillow. Nearly all night I could hear the tramp of feet over my head. The next morning I found myself somewhat refreshed, but I was extremely hungry, because it had been a long time since I had had sufficient food. As soon as it became light enough for me to see my surroundings I noticed that I was near a large ship, and that this ship seemed to be unloading a cargo of pig iron. I went at once to the vessel and asked the captain to permit me to help unload the vessel in order to get money for food. The captain, a white man, who seemed to be kind-hearted, consented. I worked long enough to earn money for my breakfast, and it seems to me, as I remember it now, to have been about the best breakfast that I have ever eaten.

My work pleased the captain so well that he told me if I desired I could continue working for a small amount per day. This I was very glad to do. I continued working on this vessel for a number of days. After buying food with the small wages I received there was not much left to add to the amount I must get to pay my way to Hampton. In order to economize in every way possible, so as to be sure to reach Hampton in a reasonable time, I continued to sleep under the same sidewalk that gave me shelter the first night I was in Richmond. Many years after that the coloured citizens of Richmond very kindly tendered me a reception at which there must have been two thousand people present. This reception was held not far from the spot where I slept the first night I spent in that city, and I must confess that my mind

was more upon the sidewalk that first gave me shelter than upon the reception, agreeable and cordial as it was.

When I had saved what I considered enough money with which to reach Hampton, I thanked the captain of the vessel for his kindness, and started again. Without any unusual occurrence I reached Hampton, with a surplus of exactly fifty cents with which to begin my education. To me it had been a long, eventful journey; but the first sight of the large, three-story brick school building seemed to have rewarded me for all that I had undergone in order to reach the place. If the people who gave the money to provide that building could appreciate the influence the sight of it had upon me, as well as upon thousands of other youths, they would feel all the more encouraged to make such gifts. It seemed to me to be the largest and most beautiful building I had ever seen. The sight of it seemed to give me new life. I felt that a new kind of existence had now begun—that life would now have a new meaning. I felt that I had reached the promised land, and I resolved to let no obstacle prevent me from putting forth the highest effort to fit myself to accomplish the most good in the world.

As soon as possible after reaching the grounds of the Hampton Institute, I presented myself before the head teacher for assignment to a class. Having been so long without proper food, a bath and change of clothing, I did not, of course, make a very favourable impression upon her, and I could see at once that there were doubts in her mind about the wisdom of admitting me as a student. I felt that I could hardly blame her if she got the idea that I was a worthless loafer or tramp. For some time she did not refuse to admit me, neither did she decide in my favour, and I continued to linger about her, and to impress her in all the ways I could with my worthiness. In the meantime I saw her admitting other students, and that added greatly to my discomfort, for I felt, deep down in my heart, that I could do as well as they, if I could only get a chance to show what was in me.

After some hours had passed, the head teacher said to me: "The adjoining recitation-room needs sweeping. Take the broom and sweep it."

It occurred to me at once that here was my chance. Never did I receive an order with more delight. I knew that I could sweep, for Mrs. Ruffner had thoroughly taught me how to do that when I lived with her.

I swept the recitation-room three times. Then I got a dusting-cloth and I dusted it four times. All the woodwork around the walls, every bench, table, and desk, I went over four times with my dusting-cloth. Besides, every piece of furniture had been moved and every closet and corner in the room had

been thoroughly cleaned. I had the feeling that in a large measure my future depended upon the impression I made upon the teacher in the cleaning of that room. When I was through, I reported to the head teacher. She was a "Yankee" woman who knew just where to look for dirt. She went into the room and inspected the floor and closets; then she took her handkerchief and rubbed it on the woodwork about the walls, and over the table and benches. When she was unable to find one bit of dirt on the floor, or a particle of dust on any of the furniture, she quietly remarked, "I guess you will do to enter this institution."

I was one of the happiest souls on earth. The sweeping of that room was my college examination, and never did any youth pass an examination for entrance into Harvard or Yale that gave him more genuine satisfaction. I have passed several examinations since then, but I have always felt that this was the best one I ever passed.

I have spoken of my own experience in entering the Hampton Institute. Perhaps few, if any, had anything like the same experience that I had, but about that same period there were hundreds who found their way to Hampton and other institutions after experiencing something of the same difficulties that I went through. The young men and women were determined to secure an education at any cost.

The sweeping of the recitation-room in the manner that I did it seems to have paved the way for me to get through Hampton. Miss Mary F. Mackie, the head teacher, offered me a position as janitor. This, of course, I gladly accepted, because it was a place where I could work out nearly all the cost of my board. The work was hard and taxing, but I stuck to it. I had a large number of rooms to care for, and had to work late into the night, while at the same time I had to rise by four o'clock in the morning, in order to build the fires and have a little time in which to prepare my lessons. In all my career at Hampton, and ever since I have been out in the world, Miss Mary F. Mackie, the head teacher to whom I have referred, proved one of my strongest and most helpful friends. Her advice and encouragement were always helpful and strengthening to me in the darkest hour.

I have spoken of the impression that was made upon me by the buildings and general appearance of the Hampton Institute, but I have not spoken of that which made the greatest and most lasting impression upon me, and that was a great man—the noblest, rarest human being that it has ever been my privilege to meet. I refer to the late General Samuel C. Armstrong.

It has been my fortune to meet personally many of what are called great

characters, both in Europe and America, but I do not hesitate to say that I never met any man who, in my estimation, was the equal of General Armstrong. Fresh from the degrading influences of the slave plantation and the coal-mines, it was a rare privilege for me to be permitted to come into direct contact with such a character as General Armstrong. I shall always remember that the first time I went into his presence he made the impression upon me of being a perfect man: I was made to feel that there was something about him that was superhuman. It was my privilege to know the General personally from the time I entered Hampton till he died, and the more I saw of him the greater he grew in my estimation. One might have removed from Hampton all the buildings, class-rooms, teachers, and industries, and given the men and women there the opportunity of coming into daily contact with General Armstrong, and that alone would have been a liberal education. The older I grow, the more I am convinced that there is no education which one can get from books and costly apparatus that is equal to that which can be gotten from contact with great men and women. Instead of studying books so constantly, how I wish that our schools and colleges might learn to study men and things!

General Armstrong spent two of the last six months of his life in my home at Tuskegee. At that time he was paralyzed to the extent that he had lost control of his body and voice in a very large degree. Notwithstanding his affliction, he worked almost constantly night and day for the cause to which he had given his life. I never saw a man who so completely lost sight of himself. I do not believe he ever had a selfish thought. He was just as happy in trying to assist some other institution in the South as he was when working for Hampton. Although he fought the Southern white man in the Civil War, I never heard him utter a bitter word against him afterward. On the other hand, he was constantly seeking to find ways by which he could be of service to the Southern whites.

It would be difficult to describe the hold that he had upon the students at Hampton, or the faith they had in him. In fact, he was worshipped by his students. It never occurred to me that General Armstrong could fail in anything that he undertook. There is almost no request that he could have made that would not have been complied with. When he was a guest at my home in Alabama, and was so badly paralyzed that he had to be wheeled about in an invalid's chair, I recall that one of the General's former students had occasion to push his chair up a long, steep hill that taxed his strength to the utmost. When the top of the hill was reached, the former pupil, with a glow

of happiness on his face, exclaimed, "I am so glad that I have been permitted to do something that was real hard for the General before he dies!" While I was a student at Hampton, the dormitories became so crowded that it was impossible to find room for all who wanted to be admitted. In order to help remedy the difficulty the General conceived the plan of putting up tents to be used as rooms. As soon as it became known that General Armstrong would be pleased if some of the older students would live in the tents during the winter, nearly every student in school volunteered to go.

I was one of the volunteers. The winter that we spent in those tents was an intensely cold one; and we suffered severely—how much I am sure General Armstrong never knew, because we made no complaints. It was enough for us to know that we were pleasing General Armstrong, and that we were making it possible for an additional number of students to secure an education. More than once, during a cold night, when a stiff gale would be blowing, our tent was lifted bodily, and we would find ourselves in the open air. The General would usually pay a visit to the tents early in the morning, and his earnest, cheerful, encouraging voice would dispel any feeling of despondency.

I have spoken of my admiration for General Armstrong, and yet he was but a type of that Christlike body of men and women who went into the Negro schools at the close of the war by the hundreds to assist in lifting up my race. The history of the world fails to show a higher, purer, and more unselfish class of men and women than those who found their way into those Negro schools.

Life at Hampton was a constant revelation to me; was constantly taking me into a new world. The matter of having meals at regular hours, of eating on a tablecloth, using a napkin, the use of the bath tub and of the toothbrush, as well as the use of sheets upon the bed, were all new to me.

I sometimes feel that almost the most valuable lesson I got at the Hampton Institute was in the use and value of the bath. I learned there for the first time some of its value, not only in keeping the body healthy, but in inspiring self-respect and promoting virtue. In all my travels in the South and elsewhere since leaving Hampton I have always in some way sought my daily bath. To get it sometimes when I have been the guest of my own people in a single-roomed cabin has not always been easy to do, except by slipping away to some stream in the woods. I have always tried to teach my people that some provision for bathing should be a part of every house.

For some time, while a student at Hampton I possessed but a single pair of socks, but when I had worn these till they became soiled, I would wash

them at night and hang them by the fire to dry, so that I might wear them again the next morning.

The charge for my board at Hampton was ten dollars per month. I was expected to pay a part of this in cash and to work out the remainder. To meet this cash payment, as I have stated, I had just fifty cents when I reached the institution. Aside from a very few dollars that my brother John was able to send me once in a while, I had no money with which to pay my board. I was determined from the first to make my work as janitor so valuable that my services would be indispensable. This I succeeded in doing to such an extent that I was soon informed that I would be allowed the full cost of my board in return for my work. The cost of tuition was seventy dollars a year. This, of course, was wholly beyond my ability to provide. If I had been compelled to pay the seventy dollars for tuition, in addition to providing for my board, I would have been compelled to leave the Hampton school. General Armstrong, however, very kindly got Mr. S. Griffitts Morgan, of New Bedford, Mass., to defray the cost of my tuition during the whole time that I was at Hampton. After I finished the course at Hampton and had entered upon my lifework at Tuskegee, I had the pleasure of visiting Mr. Morgan several times.

After having been for a while at Hampton, I found myself in difficulty because I did not have books and clothing. Usually, however, I got around the trouble about books by borrowing from those who were more fortunate than myself. As to clothes, when I reached Hampton I had practically nothing. Everything that I possessed was in a small hand satchel. My anxiety about clothing was increased because of the fact that General Armstrong made a personal inspection of the young men in ranks, to see that their clothes were clean. Shoes had to be polished, there must be no buttons off the clothing, and no grease-spots. To wear one suit of clothes continually, while at work and in the schoolroom, and at the same time keep it clean, was rather a hard problem for me to solve. In some way I managed to get on till the teachers learned that I was in earnest and meant to succeed, and then some of them were kind enough to see that I was partly supplied with second-hand clothing that had been sent in barrels from the North. These barrels proved a blessing to hundreds of poor but deserving students. Without them I question whether I should ever have gotten through Hampton.

When I first went to Hampton I do not recall that I had ever slept in a bed that had two sheets on it. In those days there were not many buildings there, and room was very precious. There were seven other boys in the same room with me; most of them, however, students who had been there for

some time. The sheets were quite a puzzle to me. The first night I slept under both of them, and the second night I slept on top of both of them; but by watching the other boys I learned my lesson in this, and have been trying to follow it ever since and to teach it to others.

I was among the youngest of the students who were in Hampton at that time. Most of the students were men and women—some as old as forty years of age. As I now recall the scene of my first year, I do not believe that one often has the opportunity of coming into contact with three or four hundred men and women who were so tremendously in earnest as these men and women were. Every hour was occupied in study or work. Nearly all had had enough actual contact with the world to teach them the need of education. Many of the older ones were, of course, too old to master the text-books very thoroughly, and it was often sad to watch their struggles; but they made up in earnestness much of what they lacked in books. Many of them were as poor as I was, and, besides having to wrestle with their books, they had to struggle with a poverty which prevented their having the necessities of life. Many of them had aged parents who were dependent upon them, and some of them were men who had wives whose support in some way they had to provide for.

The great and prevailing idea that seemed to take possession of every one was to prepare him self to lift up the people at his home. No one seemed to think of himself. And the officers and teachers, what a rare set of human beings they were! They worked for the students night and day, in season and out of season. They seemed happy only when they were helping the students in some manner. Whenever it is written—and I hope it will be—the part that the Yankee teachers played in the education of the Negroes immediately after the war will make one of the most thrilling parts of the history of this country. The time is not far distant when the whole South will appreciate this service in a way that it has not yet been able to do.

CHAPTER IV

Helping Others

At the end of my first year at Hampton I was confronted with another difficulty. Most of the students went home to spend their vacation. I

had no money with which to go home, but I had to go somewhere. In those days very few students were permitted to remain at the school during vacation. It made me feel very sad and homesick to see the other students preparing to leave and starting for home. I not only had no money with which to go home, but I had none with which to go anywhere.

In some way, however, I had gotten hold of an extra, second-hand coat which I thought was a pretty valuable coat. This I decided to sell, in order to get a little money for travelling expenses. I had a good deal of boyish pride, and I tried to hide, as far as I could, from the other students the fact that I had no money and nowhere to go. I made it known to a few people in the town of Hampton that I had this coat to sell, and, after a good deal of persuading, one coloured man promised to come to my room to look the coat over and consider the matter of buying it. This cheered my drooping spirits considerably. Early the next morning my prospective customer appeared. After looking the garment over carefully, he asked me how much I wanted for it. I told him I thought it was worth three dollars. He seemed to agree with me as to price, but remarked in the most matter-of-fact way: "I tell you what I will do; I will take the coat, and I will pay you five cents, cash down, and pay you the rest of the money just as soon as I can get it." It is not hard to imagine what my feelings were at the time.

With this disappointment I gave up all hope of getting out of the town of Hampton for my vacation work. I wanted very much to go where I might secure work that would at least pay me enough to purchase some much-needed clothing and other necessities. In a few days practically all the students and teachers had left for their homes, and this served to depress my spirits even more.

After trying for several days in and near the town of Hampton, I finally secured work in a restaurant at Fortress Monroe. The wages, however, were very little more than my board. At night, and between meals, I found considerable time for study and reading; and in this direction I improved myself very much during the summer.

When I left school at the end of my first year, I owed the institution sixteen dollars that I had not been able to work out. It was my greatest ambition during the summer to save money enough with which to pay this debt. I felt that this was a debt of honour, and that I could hardly bring myself to the point of even trying to enter school again till it was paid. I economized in every way that I could think of—did my own washing, and went without necessary garments—but still I found my summer vacation ending and I did

not have the sixteen dollars.

One day, during the last week of my stay in the restaurant, I found under one of the tables a crisp, new ten-dollar bill. I could hardly contain myself, I was so happy. As it was not my place of business I felt it to be the proper thing to show the money to the proprietor. This I did. He seemed as glad as I was, but he coolly explained to me that, as it was his place of business, he had a right to keep the money, and he proceeded to do so. This, I confess, was another pretty hard blow to me. I will not say that I became discouraged, for as I now look back over my life I do not recall that I ever became discouraged over anything that I set out to accomplish. I have begun everything with the idea that I could succeed, and I never had much patience with the multitudes of people who are always ready to explain why one cannot succeed. I have always had a high regard for the man who could tell me how to succeed. I determined to face the situation just as it was. At the end of the week I went to the treasurer of the Hampton Institute, General J. F. B. Marshall, and told him frankly my condition. To my gratification he told me that I could reenter the institution, and that he would trust me to pay the debt when I could. During the second year I continued to work as a janitor.

The education that I received at Hampton out of the text-books was but a small part of what I learned there. One of the things that impressed itself upon me deeply, the second year, was the unselfishness of the teachers. It was hard for me to understand how any individuals could bring themselves to the point where they could be so happy in working for others. Before the end of the year, I think I began learning that those who are happiest are those who do the most for others. This lesson I have tried to carry with me ever since.

I also learned a valuable lesson at Hampton by coming into contact with the best breeds of live stock and fowls. No student, I think, who has had the opportunity of doing this could go out into the world and content himself with the poorest grades.

Perhaps the most valuable thing that I got out of my second year was an understanding of the use and value of the Bible. Miss Nathalie Lord, one of the teachers, from Portland, Me., taught me how to use and love the Bible. Before this I had never cared a great deal about it, but now I learned to love to read the Bible, not only for the spiritual help which it gives, but on account of it as literature. The lessons taught me in this respect took such a hold upon me that at the present time, when I am at home, no matter how busy I am, I always make it a rule to read a chapter or a portion of a chapter in the morning, before beginning the work of the day.

Whatever ability I may have as a public speaker I owe in a measure to Miss Lord. When she found out that I had some inclination in this direction, she gave me private lessons in the matter of breathing, emphasis, and articulation. Simply to be able to talk in public for the sake of talking has never had the least attraction for me. In fact, I consider that there is nothing so empty and unsatisfactory as mere abstract public speaking; but from my early childhood I have had a desire to do something to make the world better, and then to be able to speak to the world about that thing.

The debating societies at Hampton were a constant source of delight to me. These were held on Saturday evening; and during my whole life at Hampton I do not recall that I missed a single meeting. I not only attended the weekly debating society, but was instrumental in organizing an additional society. I noticed that between the time when supper was over and the time to begin evening study there were about twenty minutes which the young men usually spent in idle gossip. About twenty of us formed a society for the purpose of utilizing this time in debate or in practice in public speaking. Few persons ever derived more happiness or benefit from the use of twenty minutes of time than we did in this way.

At the end of my second year at Hampton, by the help of some money sent me by my mother and brother John, supplemented by a small gift from one of the teachers at Hampton, I was enabled to return to my home in Malden, West Virginia, to spend my vacation. When I reached home I found that the salt-furnaces were not running, and that the coal-mine was not being operated on account of the miners being out on a "strike." This was something which, it seemed, usually occurred whenever the men got two or three months ahead in their savings. During the strike, of course, they spent all that they had saved, and would often return to work in debt at the same wages, or would move to another mine at considerable expense. In either case, my observations convinced me that the miners were worse off at the end of a strike. Before the days of strikes in that section of the country, I knew miners who had considerable money in the bank, but as soon as the professional labour agitators got control, the savings of even the more thrifty ones began disappearing.

My mother and the other members of the family were, of course, much rejoiced to see me and to note the improvement that I had made during my two years' absence. The rejoicing on the part of all classes of the coloured people, and especially the older ones, over my return, was almost pathetic. I had to pay a visit to each family and take a meal with each, and at each place

tell the story of my experiences at Hampton. In addition to this I had to speak before the church and Sunday-school, and at various other places. The thing that I was most in search of, though, work, I could not find. There was no work on account of the strike. I spent nearly the whole of the first month of my vacation in an effort to find something to do by which I could earn money to pay my way back to Hampton and save a little money to use after reaching there.

Toward the end of the first month, I went to a place a considerable distance from my home, to try to find employment. I did not succeed, and it was night before I got started on my return. When I had gotten within a mile or so of my home I was so completely tired out that I could not walk any farther, and I went into an old, abandoned house to spend the remainder of the night. About three o'clock in the morning my brother John found me asleep in this house, and broke to me, as gently as he could, the sad news that our dear mother had died during the night.

This seemed to me the saddest and blankest moment in my life. For several years my mother had not been in good health, but I had no idea, when I parted from her the previous day, that I should never see her alive again. Besides that, I had always had an intense desire to be with her when she did pass away. One of the chief ambitions which spurred me on at Hampton was that I might be able to get to be in a position in which I could better make my mother comfortable and happy. She had so often expressed the wish that she might be permitted to live to see her children educated and started out into the world.

In a very short time after the death of my mother our little home was in confusion. My sister Amanda, although she tried to do the best she could, was too young to know anything about keeping house, and my stepfather was not able to hire a housekeeper. Sometimes we had food cooked for us, and sometimes we did not. I remember that more than once a can of tomatoes and some crackers constituted a meal. Our clothing went uncared for, and everything about our home was soon in a tumble-down condition. It seems tome that this was the most dismal period of my life.

My good friend Mrs. Ruffner, to whom I have already referred, always made me welcome at her home, and assisted me in many ways during this trying period. Before the end of the vacation she gave me some work, and this, together with work in a coal-mine at some distance from my home, enabled me to earn a little money.

At one time it looked as if I would have to give up the idea of returning

to Hampton, but my heart was so set on returning that I determined not to give up going back without a struggle. I was very anxious to secure some clothes for the winter, but in this I was disappointed, except for a few garments which my brother John secured for me. Notwithstanding my need of money and clothing, I was very happy in the fact that I had secured enough money to pay my travelling expenses back to Hampton.

Once there, I knew that I could make myself so useful as a janitor that I could in some way get through the school year.

Three weeks before the time for the opening of the term at Hampton, I was pleasantly surprised to receive a letter from my good friend Miss Mary F. Mackie, the lady principal, asking me to return to Hampton two weeks before the opening of the school, in order that I might assist her in cleaning the buildings and getting things in order for the new school year. This was just the opportunity I wanted. It gave me a chance to secure a credit in the treasurer's office. I started for Hampton at once.

During these two weeks I was taught a lesson which I shall never forget. Miss Mackie was a member of one of the oldest and most cultured families of the North, and yet for two weeks she worked by my side cleaning windows, dusting rooms, putting beds in order, and what not. She felt that things would not be in condition for the opening of school unless every window-pane was perfectly clean, and she took the greatest satisfaction in helping to clean them herself. The work which I have described she did every year that I was at Hampton.

It was hard for me at this time to understand how a woman of her education and social standing could take such delight in performing such service, in order to assist in the elevation of an unfortunate race. Ever since then I have had no patience with any school for my race in the South which did not teach its students the dignity of labour.

During my last year at Hampton every minute of my time that was not occupied with my duties as janitor was devoted to hard study. I was determined, if possible, to make such a record in my class as would cause me to be placed on the "honour roll" of Commencement speakers. This I was successful in doing. It was June of 1875 when I finished the regular course of study at Hampton. The greatest benefits that I got out of my life at the Hampton Institute, perhaps, may be classified under two heads:—

First was contact with a great man, General S. C. Armstrong, who, I repeat, was, in my opinion, the rarest, strongest, and most beautiful character that it has ever been my privilege to meet.

Second, at Hampton, for the first time, I learned that education was expected to do for an individual. Before going there I had a good deal of the then rather prevalent idea among our people that to secure an education meant to have a good, easy time, free from all necessity for manual labour. At Hampton I not only learned that it was not a disgrace to labour, but learned to love labour, not alone for its financial value, but for labour's own sake and for the independence and self-reliance which the ability to do something which the world wants done brings. At that institution I got my first taste of what it meant to live a life of unselfishness, my first knowledge of the fact that the happiest individuals are those who do the most to make others useful and happy.

I was completely out of money when I graduated. In company with other Hampton students, I secured a place as a table waiter in a summer hotel in Connecticut, and managed to borrow enough money with which to get there. I had not been in this hotel long before I found out that I knew practically nothing about waiting on a hotel table. The head waiter, however, supposed that I was an accomplished waiter. He soon gave me charge of a table at which there sat four or five wealthy and rather aristocratic people. My ignorance of how to wait upon them was so apparent that they scolded me in such a severe manner that I became frightened and left their table, leaving them sitting there without food. As a result of this I was reduced from the position of waiter to that of a dish-carrier.

But I determined to learn the business of waiting, and did so within a few weeks and was restored to my former position. I have had the satisfaction of being a guest in this hotel several times since I was a waiter there.

At the close of the hotel season I returned to my former home in Malden, and was elected to teach the coloured school at that place. This was the beginning of one of the happiest periods of my life. I now felt that I had the opportunity to help the people of my home town to a higher life. I felt from the first that mere book education was not all that the young people of that town needed. I began my work at eight o'clock in the morning, and, as a rule, it did not end until ten o'clock at night. In addition to the usual routine of teaching, I taught the pupils to comb their hair, and to keep their hands and faces clean, as well as their clothing. I gave special attention to teaching them the proper use of the tooth-brush and the bath. In all my teaching I have watched carefully the influence of the tooth-brush, and I am convinced that there are few single agencies of civilization that are more far-reaching.

There were so many of the older boys and girls in the town, as well as men

and women, who had to work in the daytime but still were craving an opportunity for some education, that I soon opened a night-school. From the first, this was crowded every night, being about as large as the school that I taught in the day. The efforts of some of the men and women, who in many cases were over fifty years of age, to learn, were in some cases very pathetic.

My day and night school work was not all that I undertook. I established a small reading-room and a debating society. On Sundays I taught two Sunday-schools, one in the town of Malden in the afternoon, and the other in the morning at a place three miles distant from Malden. In addition to this, I gave private lessons to several young men whom I was fitting to send to the Hampton Institute. Without regard to pay and with little thought of it, I taught any one who wanted to learn any thing that I could teach him. I was supremely happy in the opportunity of being able to assist somebody else. I did receive, however, a small salary from the public fund, for my work as a public-school teacher.

During the time that I was a student at Hampton my older brother, John, not only assisted me all that lie could, but worked all of the time in the coal-mines in order to support the family. He willingly neglected his own education that he might help me. It was my earnest wish to help him to prepare to enter Hampton, and to save money to assist him in his expenses there. Both of these objects I was successful in accomplishing. In three years my brother finished the course at Hampton, and he is now holding the important position of Superintendent of Industries at Tuskegee. When he returned from Hampton, we both combined our efforts and savings to send our adopted brother, James, through the Hampton Institute. This we succeeded in doing, and he is now the postmaster at the Tuskegee Institute. The year 1877, which was my second year of teaching in Malden, I spent very much as I did the first.

It was while my home was at Malden that what was known as the "Ku Klux Klan" was in the height of its activity. The "Ku Klux" were bands of men who had joined themselves together for the purpose of regulating the conduct of the coloured people, especially with the object of preventing the members of the race from exercising any influence in politics. They corresponded somewhat to the "patrollers" of whom I used to hear a great deal during the days of slavery, when I was a small boy. The "patrollers" were bands of white men—usually young men—who were organized largely for the purpose of regulating the conduct of the slaves at night in such matters as preventing the slaves from going from one plantation to another without passes, and for pre-

venting them from holding any kind of meetings without permission and without the presence at these meetings of at least one white man.

Like the "patrollers" the "Ku Klux" operated almost wholly at night. They were, however, more cruel than the "patrollers." Their objects, in the main, were to crush out the political aspirations of the Negroes, but they did not confine themselves to this, because schoolhouses as well as churches were burned by them, and many innocent persons were made to suffer. During this period not a few coloured people lost their lives.

As a young man, the acts of these lawless bands made a great impression upon me. I saw one open battle take place at Malden between some of the coloured and white people. There must have been not far from a hundred persons engaged on each side; many on both sides were seriously injured, among them being General Lewis Ruffner, the husband of my friend Mrs. Viola Ruffner. General Ruffner tried to defend the coloured people, and for this he was knocked down and so seriously wounded that he never complete-ly recovered. It seemed to me as I watched this struggle between members of the two races, that there was no hope for our people in this country. The "Ku Klux" period was, I think, the darkest part of the Reconstruction days.

I have referred to this unpleasant part of the history of the South simply for the purpose of calling attention to the great change that has taken place since the days of the "Ku Klux." To-day there are no such organizations in the South, and the fact that such ever existed is almost forgotten by both races. There are few places in the South now where public sentiment would permit such organizations to exist.

CHAPTER V

The Reconstruction Period

The years from 1867 to 1878 I think may be called the period of Reconstruction. This included the time that I spent as a student at Hampton and as a teacher in West Virginia. During the whole of the Reconstruction period two ideas were constantly agitating the minds of the coloured people, or, at least, the minds of a large part of the race. One of these was the craze for Greek and Latin learning, and the other was a desire to hold office.

It could not have been expected that a people who had spent generations in slavery, and before that generations in the darkest heathenism, could at first form any proper conception of what an education meant. In every part of the South, during the Reconstruction period, schools, both day and night, were filled to overflowing with people of all ages and conditions, some being as far along in age as sixty and seventy years. The ambition to secure an education was most praiseworthy and encouraging. The idea, however, was too prevalent that, as soon as one secured a little education, in some unexplainable way he would be free from most of the hardships of the world, and, at any rate, could live without manual labour. There was a further feeling that a knowledge however little, of the Greek and Latin languages would make one a very superior human being, something bordering almost on the supernatural. I remember that the first coloured man whom I saw who knew, something about foreign languages impressed me at that time as being a man of all others to be envied.

Naturally, most of our people who received some little education became teachers or preachers. While among these two classes there were many capable, earnest, godly men and women, still a large proportion took up teaching or preaching as an easy way to make a living. Many became teachers who could do little more than write their names. I remember there came into our neighbourhood one of this class, who was in search of a school to teach, and the question arose while he was there as to the shape of the earth and how he would teach the children concerning this subject. He explained his position in the matter by saying that he was prepared to teach that the earth was either flat or round, according to the preference of a majority of his patrons.

The ministry was the profession that suffered most and still suffers, though there has been great improvement—on account of not only ignorant but in man, cases immoral men who claimed that they were "called to preach." In the earlier days of freedom almost every coloured man who learned to read would receive "a call to preach" within a few days after he began reading. At my home in West Virginia the process of being called to the ministry was a very interesting one. Usually the "call" came when the individual was sitting in church. Without warning the one called would fall upon the floor as if struck by a bullet, and would lie there for hours, speechless and motionless. Then the news would spread all through the neighbourhood that this individual had received a "call." If he were inclined to resist the summons, he would fall or be made to fall a second or third time. In the end he always yielded to the call. While I wanted an education badly, I confess that in my

youth I had a fear that when I had learned to read and write well I would receive one of these "calls"; but, for some reason, my call never came.

When we add the number of wholly ignorant men who preached or "exhorted" to that of those who possessed something of an education, it can be seen at a glance that the supply of ministers was large. In fact, some time ago I knew a certain church that had a total membership of about two hundred, and eighteen of that number were ministers. But, I repeat, in many communities in the South the character of the ministry is being improved, and I believe that within the next two or three decades a very large proportion of the unworthy ones will have disappeared. The "calls" to preach, I am glad to say, are not nearly so numerous now as they were formerly, and the calls to some industrial occupation are growing more numerous. The improvement that has taken place in the character of the teachers is even more marked than in the case of the ministers.

During the whole of the Reconstruction period our people throughout the South looked to the Federal Government for everything, very much as a child looks to its mother. This was not unnatural. The central government gave them freedom, and the whole Nation had been enriched for more than two centuries by the labour of the Negro. Even as a youth, and later in manhood, I had the feeling that was cruelly wrong in the central government, at the beginning of our freedom, to fail to make some provision for the general education of our people in addition to what the states might do, so that the people would be the better prepared for the duties of citizenship.

It is easy to find fault, to remark what might have been done, and perhaps, after all, and under all the circumstances, those in charge of the conduct of affairs did the only thing that could be done at the time. Still, as I look back now over the entire period of our freedom, I cannot help feeling that it would have been wiser if some plan could have been put in operation which would have made the possession of a certain amount of education or property, or both, a test for the exercise of the franchise, and a way provided by which this test should be made to apply honestly and squarely to both the white and black races.

Though I was but little more than a youth during the period of Reconstruction, I had the feeling that mistakes were being made, and that things could not remain in the condition that they were in then very long. I felt that the Reconstruction policy, so far as it related to my race, was in a large measure on a false foundation, was artificial and forced. In many cases it seemed to me that the ignorance of my race was being used as a tool with

which to help white men into office, and that there was an element in the North which wanted to punish the Southern white men by forcing the Negro into positions over the heads of the Southern whites. I felt that the Negro would be the one to suffer for this in the end. Besides, the general political agitation drew the attention of our people away from the more fundamental matters of perfecting themselves in the industries at their doors and in securing property.

The temptations to enter political life were so alluring that I came very near yielding to them at one time, but I was kept from doing so by the feeling that I would be helping in a more substantial way by assisting in the laying of the foundation of the race through a generous education of the hand, head, and heart. I saw coloured men who were members of the state legislatures, and county officers, who, in some cases, could not read or write, and whose morals were as weak as their education. Not long ago, when passing through the streets of a certain city in the South, I heard some brick-masons calling out, from the top of a two-story brick building on which they were working, for the "Governor" to "hurry up and bring up some more bricks." Several times I heard the command, "Hurry up, Governor!" "Hurry up, Governor!" My curiosity was aroused to such an extent that I made inquiry as to who the "Governor" was, and soon found that he was a coloured man who at one time had held the position of Lieutenant-Governor of his state.

But not all the coloured people who were in office during Reconstruction were unworthy of their positions, by any means. Some of them, like the late Senator B. K. Bruce, Governor Pinchback, and many others, were strong, upright, useful men. Neither were all the class designated as carpetbaggers dishonourable men. Some of them, like ex-Governor Bullock of Georgia, were men of high character and usefulness.

Of course the coloured people, so largely without education, and wholly without experience in government, made tremendous mistakes, just as any people similarly situated would have done. Many of the Southern whites have a feeling that, if the Negro is permitted to exercise his political rights now to any degree, the mistakes of the Reconstruction period will repeat themselves. I do not think this would be true, because the Negro is a much stronger and wiser man than he was thirty-five years ago, and he is fast learning the lesson that he cannot afford to act in a manner that will alienate his Southern white neighbours from him. More and more I am convinced that the final solution of the political end of our race problem will be for each state that finds it necessary to change the law bearing upon the franchise to

make the law apply with absolute honesty, and without opportunity for double dealing or evasion, to both races alike. Any other course my daily observation in the South convinces me, will be unjust to the Negro, unjust to the white man, and unfair to the rest of the states in the Union, and will be, like slavery, a sin that at some time we shall have to pay for.

In the fall of 1878, after having taught school in Malden for two years, and after I had succeeded in preparing several of the young men and women, besides my two brothers, to enter the Hampton Institute, I decided to spend some months in study at Washington, D. C. I remained there for eight months. I derived a great deal of benefit from the studies which I pursued, and I came into contact with some strong men and women. At the institution I attended there was no industrial training given to the students, and I had an opportunity of comparing the influence of an institution with no industrial training with that of one like the Hampton Institute, that emphasized the industries. At this school I found the students, in most cases, had more money, were better dressed, wore the latest style of all manner of clothing, and in some cases are more brilliant mentally. At Hampton it was a standing rule that, while the institution would be responsible for securing some one to pay the tuition for the students, the men and women themselves must provide for their own board, books, clothing, and room wholly by work, or partly by work and partly in cash. At the institution at which I now was, I found that a large proportion of the students by some means had their personal expenses paid for them. At Hampton the student was constantly making the effort through the industries to help himself, and that very effort was of immense value in character-building. The students at the other school seemed to be less self-dependent. They seemed to give more attention to mere outward appearances. In a word, they did not appear to me to be beginning at the bottom, on a real, solid foundation, to the extent that they were at Hampton. They knew more about Latin and Greek when they left school, but they seemed to know less about life and its conditions as they would meet it at their homes. Having lived for a number of years in the midst of comfortable surroundings, they were not as much inclined as the Hampton students to go into the country districts of the South, where there was little of comfort, to take up work for our people, and they were more inclined to yield to the temptation to become hot waiters and Pullman-car porters as their life-work.

During the time I was a student in Washington the city was crowded with coloured people, many of whom had recently come from the South. A large

proportion of these people had been drawn to Washington because they felt that they could lead a life of ease there. Others had secured minor government positions, and still another large class was there in the hope of securing Federal positions. A number of coloured men—some of them very strong and brilliant—were in the House of Representatives at that time, and one, the Hon. B. K. Bruce, was in the Senate. All this tended to make Washington an attractive place for members of the coloured race. Then, too, they knew that at all times they could have the protection of the law in the District of Columbia. The public schools in Washington for coloured people were better then than they were elsewhere. I took great interest in studying the life of our people there closely at that time. I found that while among them there was a large element of substantial, worthy citizens, there was also a superficiality about the life of a large class that greatly alarmed me. I saw young coloured men who were not earning more than four dollars a week spend two dollars or more for a buggy on Sunday to ride up and down Pennsylvania Avenue in order that they might try to convince the world that they were worth thousands. I saw other young men who received seventy-five or one hundred dollars per month from the Government, who were in debt at the end of every month. I saw men who but a few months previous were members of Congress, then without employment and in poverty. Among a large class there seemed to be a dependence upon the Government for every conceivable thing. The members of this class hat little ambition to create a position for themselves, but wanted the Federal officials to create one for them. How many times I wished then, and have often wished since, that by some power of magic I might remove the great bulk of these people into the country districts and plant them upon the soil, upon the solid and never deceptive foundation of Mother Nature, where all nations and races that have ever succeeded have gotten their start,—a start that at first may be slow and toilsome, but one that nevertheless is real.

In Washington I saw girls whose mothers were earning their living by laundrying. These girls were taught by their mothers, in rather a crude way it is true, the industry of laundrying. Later these girls entered the public schools and remained there perhaps six or eight years. When the public school course was finally finished, they wanted more costly dresses, more costly hats and shoes. In a word, while their wants had been increased, their ability to supply their wants had not been increased in the same degree. On the other hand, their six or eight years of book education had weaned them away from the occupation of their mothers. The result of this was in too

many cases that the girls went to the bad. I often thought how much wiser it would have been to give these girls the same amount of mental training—and I favour any kind of training, whether in the languages or mathematics, that gives strength and culture to the mind—but at the same time to give them the most thorough training in the latest and best methods of laundrying and other kindred occupations.

CHAPTER VI

Black Race And Red Race

During the year that I spent in Washington, and for some little time before this there had been considerable agitation in the state of West Virginia over the question of moving the capital of the state from Wheeling to some other central point. As a result of this, the Legislature designated three cities to be voted upon by the citizens of the state as the permanent seat of government. Among these cities was Charleston, only five miles from Malden, my home. At the close of my school year in Washington I was very pleasantly surprised to receive, from a committee of white people in Charleston, an invitation to canvass the state in the interests of that city. This invitation I accepted, and spent nearly three months in speaking in various parts of the state. Charleston was successful in winning the prize, and is now the permanent seat of government.

The reputation that I made as a speaker during this campaign induced a number of persons to make an earnest effort to get me to enter political life, but I refused, still believing that I could find other service which would prove of more permanent value to my race. Even then I had a strong feeling that what our people most needed was to get a foundation in education, industry, and property, and for this I felt that they could better afford to strive than for political preferment. As for my individual self, it appeared to me to be reasonably certain that I could succeed in political life, but I had a feeling that it would be a rather selfish kind of success—individual success at the cost of failing to do my duty in assisting in laying a foundation for the masses.

At this period in the progress of our race a very large proportion of the young men who went to school or to college did so with the expressed determination to prepare themselves to be great lawyers, or Congressmen, and

many of the women planned to become music teachers; but I had a reasonably fixed idea, even at that early period in my life, that there was need for something to be done to prepare the way for successful lawyers, Congressmen, and music teachers.

I felt that the conditions were a good deal like those of an old coloured man, during the days of slavery, who wanted to learn how to play on the guitar. In his desire to take guitar lessons he applied to one of his young masters to teach him, but the young man, not having much faith in the ability of the slave to master the guitar at his age, sought to discourage him by telling him: "Uncle Jake, I will give you guitar lessons; but, Jake, I will have to charge you three dollars for the first lesson, two dollars for the second lesson, and one dollar for the third lesson. But I will charge you only twenty-five cents for the last lesson."

Uncle Jake answered: "All right, boss, I hires you on dem terms. But boss! I wants yer to be sure an' give me dat las' lesson first."

Soon after my work in connection with the removal of the capital was finished, I received an invitation which gave me great joy and which at the same time was a very pleasant surprise. This was a letter from General Armstrong, inviting me to return to Hampton at the next Commencement to deliver what was called the "post-graduate address." This was an honour which I had not dreamed of receiving. With much care I prepared the best address that I was capable of. I chose for my subject "The Force That Wins."

As I returned to Hampton for the purpose of delivering this address, I went over much of the same ground—now, however, covered entirely by railroad—that I had traversed nearly six years before, when I first sought entrance into Hampton Institute as a student. Now I was able to ride the whole distance in the train. I was constantly contrasting this with my first journey to Hampton. I think I may say, without seeming egotism, that it is seldom that five years have wrought such a change in the life and aspirations of an individual.

At Hampton I received a warm welcome from teachers and students. I found that during my absence from Hampton the institute each year had been getting closer to the real needs and conditions of our people; that the industrial teaching, as well as that of the academic department, had greatly improved. The plan of the school was not modelled after that of any other institution then in existence, but every improvement was made under the magnificent leadership of General Armstrong solely with the view of meeting and helping the needs of our people as they presented themselves at the time. Too often, it seems to me, in missionary and educational work among

undeveloped races, people yield to the temptation of doing that which was done a hundred years before, or is being done in other communities a thousand miles away. The temptation often is to run each individual through a certain educational mould, regardless of the condition of the subject or the end to be accomplished. This was not so at Hampton Institute.

The address which I delivered on Commencement Day seems to have pleased every one, and many kind and encouraging words were spoken to me regarding it. Soon after my return to my home in West Virginia, where I had planned to continue teaching, I was again surprised to receive a letter from General Armstrong, asking me to return to Hampton, partly as a teacher and partly to pursue some supplementary studies. This was in the summer of 1879. Soon after I began my first teaching in West Virginia I had picked out four of the brightest and most promising of my pupils, in addition to my two brothers, to whom I have already referred, and had given them special attention, with the view of having them go to Hampton. They had gone there, and in each case the teachers had found them so well prepared that they entered advanced classes. This fact, it seen led to my being called back to Hampton as a teacher. One of the young men that I sent to Hampton in this way is now Dr. Samuel E. Courtney, a successful physician in Boston, and a member of the School Board of that city.

About this time the experiment was being tried for the first time, by General Armstrong, of educating Indians at Hampton. Few people then had any confidence in the ability of the Indians to receive education and to profit by it. General Armstrong was anxious to try the experiment systematically on a large scale. He secured from the reservations in the Western states over one hundred wild and for the most part perfectly ignorant Indians, the greater proportion of whom were young men. The special work which the General desired me to do was to be a sort of "house father" to the Indian young men—that is, I was to live in the building with them and have the charge of their discipline, clothing, rooms, and so on. This was a very tempting offer, but I had become so much absorbed in my work in West Virginia that I dreaded to give it up. However, I tore myself away from it. I did not know how to refuse to perform any service that General Armstrong ordered of me.

On going to Hampton, I took up my residence in a building with about seventy-five Indian youths. I was the only person in the building who was not a member of their race. At first I had a good deal of doubt about my ability to succeed. I knew that the average Indian felt himself above the white man, and, of course, he felt himself far above the Negro, largely on account

of the fact of the Negro having submitted to slavery—a thing which the Indian would never do. The Indians, in the Indian Territory, owned a large number of slaves during the days of slavery. Aside from this, there was a general feeling that the attempt to educate and civilize the red men at Hampton would be a failure. All this made me proceed very cautiously, for I felt keenly the great responsibility. But I was determined to succeed. It was not long before I had the complete confidence of the Indians, and not only this, but I think I am safe in saying that I had their love and respect. I found that they were about like any other human beings; that they responded to kind treatment and resented ill-treatment. They were continually planning to do something that would add to my happiness and comfort. The things that they disliked most, I think, were to have their long hair cut, to give up wearing their blankets, and to cease smoking; no white American ever thinks that any other race is wholly civilized until he wears the white man's clothes, eats the white man's food, speaks the white man's language, and professes the white man's religion.

When the difficulty of learning the English language was subtracted, I found that in the master of learning trades and in mastering academic studies there was little difference between the coloured and Indian students. It was a constant delight to me to note the interest which the coloured students took in trying to help the Indians in every way possible. There were a few of the coloured students who felt that the Indians ought not to be admitted to Hampton, but these were in the minority. Whenever they were asked to do so, the Negro students gladly took the Indians as room-mates, in order that they might teach them to speak English and to acquire civilized habits.

I have often wondered if there was a white institution in this country whose students would have welcomed the incoming of more than a hundred companions of another race in the cordial way that these black students at Hampton welcomed the red ones. How often I have wanted to say to white students that they lift themselves up in proportion as they help to lift others, and the more fortunate the race, and the lower in the scale of civilization, the more does one raise one's self by giving the assistance.

This reminds me of a conversation which I once had with the Hon. Frederick Douglass. At one time Mr. Douglass was travelling in the state of Pennsylvania, and was forced, on account of his colour, to ride in the baggage-car, in spite of the fact that he had paid the same price for his passage that the other passengers had paid. When some of the white passengers went into the baggage-car to console Mr. Douglass, and one of them said to him:

"I am sorry, Mr. Douglass, that you have been degraded in this manner," Mr. Douglass straightened himself up on the box upon which he was sitting, and replied: "They cannot degrade Frederick Douglass. The soul that is within me no man can degrade. I am not the one that is being degraded on account of this treatment, but those who are inflicting it upon me."

In one part of our country, where the law demands the separation of the races on the railroad trains, I saw at one time a rather amusing instance which showed how difficult it sometimes is to know where the black begins and the white ends.

There was a man who was well known in his community as a Negro, but who was so white that even an expert would have hard work to classify him as a black man. This man was riding in the part of the train set aside for the coloured passengers. When the train conductor reached him, he showed at once that he was perplexed. If the man was a Negro, the conductor did not want to send him into the white people's coach; at the same time, if he was a white man, the conductor did not want to insult him by asking him if he was a Negro. The official looked him over carefully, examining his hair, eyes, nose, and hands, but still seemed puzzled. Finally, to solve the difficulty, he stooped over and peeped at the man's feet. When I saw the conductor examining the feet of the man in question, I said to myself, "That will settle it"; and so it did, for the trainman promptly decided that the passenger was a Negro, and let him remain where he was. I congratulated myself that my race was fortunate in not losing one of its members.

My experience has been that the time to test a true gentleman is to observe him when he is in contact with individuals of a race that is less fortunate than his own. This is illustrated in no better way than by observing the conduct of the old-school type of Southern gentleman when he is in contact with his former slaves or their descendants.

An example of what I mean is shown in a story old of George Washington, who, meeting a coloured man in the road once, who politely lifted his hat, lifted his own in return. Some of his white friends who saw the incident criticised Washington for his action. In reply to their criticism George Washington said: "Do you suppose that I am going to permit a poor, ignorant, coloured man to be more polite than I am?"

While I was in charge of the Indian boys at Hampton, I had one or two experiences which illustrate the curious workings of caste in America. One of the Indian boys was taken ill, and it became my duty to take him to Washington, deliver him over to the Secretary of the Interior, and get a

receipt for him, in order that he might be returned to his Western reservation. At that time I was rather ignorant of the ways of the world. During my journey to Washington, on a steamboat, when the bell rang for dinner, I was careful to wait and not enter the dining room until after the greater part of the passengers had finished their meal. Then, with my charge, I went to the dining saloon. The man in charge politely informed me that the Indian could be served, but that I could not. I never could understand how he knew just where to draw the colour line, since the Indian and I were of about the same complexion. The steward, however, seemed to be an expert in this matter. I had been directed by the authorities at Hampton to stop at a certain hotel in Washington with my charge, but when I went to this hotel the clerk stated that he would be glad to receive the Indian into the house, but said that he could not accommodate me.

An illustration of something of this same feeling came under my observation afterward. I happened to find myself in a town in which so much excitement and indignation were being expressed that it seemed likely for a time that there would be a lynching. The occasion of the trouble was that a dark-skinned man had stopped at the local hotel. Investigation, however, developed the fact that this individual was a citizen of Morocco, and that while travelling in this country he spoke the English language. As soon as it was learned that he was not an American Negro, all the signs of indignation disappeared. The man who was the innocent cause of the excitement, though, found it prudent after that not to speak English.

At the end of my first year with the Indians there came another opening for me at Hampton, which, as I look back over my life now, seems to have come providentially, to help to prepare me for my work at Tuskegee later General Armstrong had found out that there was quite a number of young coloured men and women who were intensely in earnest in wishing to get an education, but who were prevented from entering Hampton Institute because they were too poor to be able to pay any portion of the cost of their board, or even to supply themselves with books. He conceived the idea of starting a night-school in connection with the Institute, into which a limited number of the most promising of these young men and women would be received, on condition that they were to work for ten hours during the day, and attend school for two hours at night. They were to be paid something above the cost of their board for their work. The greater part of their earnings was to be reserved in the school's treasury as a fund to be drawn on to pay their board when they had become students in the day-school, after they

had spent one or two years in the night-school. In this way they would obtain a start in their books and a knowledge of some trade or industry, in addition to the other far reaching benefits of the institution.

General Armstrong asked me to take charge of the night-school, and I did so. At the beginning; of this school there were about twelve strong, earnest men and women who entered the class. During the day the greater part of the young men worked in the school's sawmill, and the young women worked in the laundry. The work was not easy in either place, but in all my teaching I never taught pupils who gave me such genuine satisfaction as these did. They were good students, and mastered their work thoroughly. They were so much in earnest that only the ringing of the retiring-bell would make them stop studying, and often they would urge me to continue the lessons after the usual hour for going to bed had come.

These students showed so much earnestness both in their hard work during the day, as well as in their application to their studies at night, that I gave them the name of "The Plucky Class"—a name which soon grew popular and spread throughout the institution. After a student had been in the night-school long enough to prove what was in him, I gave him a printed certificate which read something like this:—

"This is to certify that James Smith is a member of The Plucky Class of the Hampton Institute, and is in good and regular standing."

The students prized these certificates highly, and they added greatly to the popularity of the night-school. Within a few weeks this department had grown to such an extent that there were about twenty-five students in attendance. I have followed the course of many of these twenty-five men and women ever since then, and they are now holding important and useful positions in nearly every part of the South. The night-school at Hampton, which started with only twelve students, now numbers between three and four hundred, and is one of the permanent and most important features of the institution.

CHAPTER VII

Early Days At Tuskegee

During the time that I had charge of the Indians and the night-school at Hampton, I pursued some studies myself, under the direction of the

instructors there. One of these instructors was the Rev. Dr. H. B. Frissell, the present Principal of the Hampton Institute, General Armstrong's successor.

In May, 1881, near the close of my first year in teaching the night-school, in a way that I had not dared expect, the opportunity opened for me to begin my life-work. One night in the chapel, after the usual chapel exercises were over, General Armstrong referred to the fact that he had received a letter from some gentlemen in Alabama asking him to recommend some one to take charge of what was to be a normal school for the coloured people in the little town of Tuskegee in that state. These gentlemen seemed to take it for granted that no coloured man suitable for the position could be secured, and they were expecting the General to recommend a white man for the place. The next day General Armstrong sent for me to come to his office, and, much to my surprise, asked me if I thought I could fill the position in Alabama. I told him that I would be willing to try. Accordingly, he wrote to the people who had applied to him for the information, that he did not know of any white man to suggest, but if they would be willing to take a coloured man, he had one whom he could recommend. In this letter he gave them my name.

Several days passed before anything more was heard about the matter. Some time afterward, one Sunday evening during the chapel exercises, a messenger came in and handed the general a telegram. At the end of the exercises he read the telegram to the school. In substance, these were its words: "Booker T. Washington will suit us. Send him at once."

There was a great deal of joy expressed among the students and teachers, and I received very hearty congratulations. I began to get ready at once to go to Tuskegee. I went by way of my old home in West Virginia, where I remained for several days, after which I proceeded to Tuskegee. I found Tuskegee to be a town of about two thousand inhabitants, nearly one-half of whom were coloured. It was in what was known as the Black Belt of the South. In the county in which Tuskegee is situated the coloured people outnumbered the whites by about three to one. In some of the adjoining and near-by counties the proportion was not far from six coloured persons to one white.

I have often been asked to define the term "Black Belt." So far as I can learn, the term was first used to designate a part of the country which was distinguished by the colour of the soil. The part of the country possessing this thick, dark, and naturally rich soil was, of course, the part of the South where the slaves were most profitable, and consequently they were taken there in the largest numbers. Later and especially since the war, the term

seems to be used wholly in a political sense—that is, to designate the counties where the black people outnumber the white.

Before going to Tuskegee I had expected to find there a building and all the necessary apparatus ready for me to begin teaching. To my disappointment, I found nothing of the kind. I did find, though, that which no costly building and apparatus can supply,—hundreds of hungry, earnest souls who wanted to secure knowledge.

Tuskegee seemed an ideal place for the school. It was in the midst of the great bulk of the Negro population, and was rather secluded, being five miles from the main line of railroad, with which it was connected by a short line. During the days of slavery, and since, the town had been a centre for the education of the white people. This was an added advantage, for the reason that I found the white people possessing a degree of culture and education that is not surpassed by many localities. While the coloured people were ignorant, they had not, as a rule degraded and weakened their bodies by vices such as are common to the lower class of people in the large cities. In general, I found the relations between the two races pleasant. For example, the largest, and I think at that time the only hardware store in the town was owned and operated jointly by a coloured man and a white man. This copartnership continued until the death of the white partner.

I found that about a year previous to my going to Tuskegee some of the coloured people who had heard something of the work of education being done at Hampton had applied to the state Legislature, through their representatives, for a small appropriation to be used in starting a normal school in Tuskegee. This request the Legislature had complied with to the extent of granting an annual appropriation of two thousand dollars. I soon learned however, that this money could be used only for the payment of the salaries of the instructors, and that there was no provision for securing land, buildings, or apparatus. The task before me did not seem a very encouraging one. It seemed much like making bricks without straw. The coloured people were overjoyed, and were constantly offering their services in any way in which they could be of assistance in getting the school started.

My first task was to find a place in which to open the school. After looking the town over with some care, the most suitable place that could be secured seemed to be a rather dilapidated shanty near the coloured Methodist church, together with the church itself as a sort of assembly-room. Both the church and the shanty were in about as bad condition as was possible. I recall that during the first months of school that I taught in this building it was in

such poor repair that, whenever it rained, one of the older students would very kindly leave his lessons and hold an umbrella over me while I heard the recitations of the others. I remember, also, that on more than one occasion my landlady held an umbrella over me while I ate breakfast.

At the time I went to Alabama the coloured people were taking considerable interest in politics, and they were very anxious that I should become one of them politically, in every respect. They seemed to have a little distrust of strangers in this regard. I recall that one man, who seemed to have been designated by the others to look after my political destiny, came to me on several occasions and said, with a good deal of earnestness: "We wants you to be sure to vote jes' like we votes. We can't read de newspapers very much, but we knows how to vote, an' we wants you to vote jes' like we votes." He added: "We watches de white man, and we keeps watching de white man till we finds out which way de white man's gwine to vote; an' when we finds out which way de white man's gwine to vote, den we votes 'xactly de other way. Den we knows we's right."

I am glad to add, however, that at the present time the disposition to vote against the white man merely because he is white is largely disappearing, and the race is learning to vote from principle, for what the voter considers to be for the best interests of both races.

I reached Tuskegee, as I have said, early in June, 1881. The first month I spent in finding accommodations for the school, and in travelling through Alabama, examining into the actual life of the people, especially in the country districts, and in getting the school advertised among the class of people that I wanted to have attend it. The most of my travelling was done over the country roads, with a mule and a cart or a mule and a buggy wagon for conveyance. I ate and slept with the people, in their little cabins. I saw their farms, their schools, their churches. Since, in the case of the most of these visits, there had been no notice given in advance that a stranger was expected, I had the advantage of seeing the real, everyday life of the people.

In the plantation districts I found that, as a rule the whole family slept in one room, and that in addition to the immediate family there sometimes were relatives, or others not related to the family, who slept in the same room. On more than one occasion I went outside the house to get ready for bed, or to wait until the family had gone to bed. They usually contrived some kind of a place for me to sleep, either on the floor or in a special part of another's bed. Rarely was there any place provided in the cabin where one could bathe even the face and hands, but usually some provision was made

for this outside the house, in the yard.

The common diet of the people was fat pork and corn bread. At times I have eaten in cabins where they had only corn bread and "black-eye peas" cooked in plain water. The people seemed to have no other idea than to live on this fat meat and corn bread,—the meat, and the meal of which the bread was made, having been bought at a high price at a store in town, notwithstanding the fact that the land all about the cabin homes could easily have been made to produce nearly every kind of garden vegetable that is raised anywhere in the country. Their one object seemed to be to plant nothing but cotton; and in many cases cotton was planted up to the very door of the cabin.

In these cabin homes I often found sewing-machines which had been bought, or were being bought, on instalments, frequently at a cost of as much as sixty dollars, or showy clocks for which the occupants of the cabins had paid twelve or fourteen dollars. I remember that on one occasion when I went into one of these cabins for dinner, when I sat down to the table for a meal with the four members of the family, I noticed that, while there were five of us at the table, there was but one fork for the five of us to use. Naturally there was an awkward pause on my part. In the opposite corner of that same cabin was an organ for which the people told me they were paying sixty dollars in monthly instalments. One fork, and a sixty-dollar organ!

In most cases the sewing-machine was not used, the clocks were so worthless that they did not keep correct time—and if they had, in nine cases out of ten there would have been no one in the family who could have told the time of day—while the organ, of course, was rarely used for want of a person who could play upon it.

In the case to which I have referred, where the family sat down to the table for the meal at which I was their guest, I could see plainly that this was an awkward and unusual proceeding, and was done in my honour. In most cases, when the family got up in the morning, for example, the wife would put a piece of meat in a frying-pan and put a lump of dough in a "skillet," as they called it. These utensils would be placed on the fire, and in ten or fifteen minutes breakfast would be ready. Frequently the husband would take his bread and meat in his hand and start for the field, eating as he walked. The mother would sit down in a corner and eat her breakfast, perhaps from a plate and perhaps directly from the "skillet" or frying-pan, while the children would eat their portion of the bread and meat while running about the yard. At certain seasons of the year, when meat was scarce, it was rarely that the children who were not old enough or strong enough to work in the fields

would have the luxury of meat.

The breakfast over, and with practically no attention given to the house, the whole family would, as a general thing, proceed to the cotton-field. Every child that was large enough to carry a hoe was put to work, and the baby—for usually there was at least one baby—would be laid down at the end of the cotton row, so that its mother could give it a certain amount of attention when she had finished chopping her row. The noon meal and the supper were taken in much the same way as the breakfast.

All the days of the family would be spent after much this same routine, except Saturday and Sunday. On Saturday the whole family would spend at least half a day, and often a whole day, in town. The idea in going to town was, I suppose, to do shopping, but all the shopping that the whole family had money for could have been attended to in ten minutes by one person. Still, the whole family remained in town for most of the day, spending the greater part of the time in standing on the streets, the women, too often, sitting about somewhere smoking or dipping snuff. Sunday was usually spent in going to some big meeting. With few exceptions, I found that the crops were mortgaged in the counties where I went, and that the most of the coloured farmers were in debt. The state had not been able to build schoolhouses in the country districts, and, as a rule, the schools were taught in churches or in log cabins. More than once, while on my journeys, I found that there was no provision made in the house used for school purposes for heating the building during the winter, and consequently a fire had to be built in the yard, and teacher and pupils passed in and out of the house as they got cold or warm. With few exceptions, I found the teachers in these country schools to be miserably poor in preparation for their work, and poor in moral character. The schools were in session from three to five months. There was practically no apparatus in the schoolhouses, except that occasionally there was a rough blackboard. I recall that one day I went into a schoolhouse—or rather into an abandoned log cabin that was being used as a schoolhouse—and found five pupils who were studying a lesson from one book. Two of these, on the front seat, were using the book between them; behind these were two others peeping over the shoulders of the first two, and behind the four was a fifth little fellow who was peeping over the shoulders of all four.

What I have said concerning the character of the schoolhouses and teachers will also apply quite accurately as a description of the church buildings and the ministers.

I met some very interesting characters during my travels. As illustrating the peculiar mental processes of the country people, I remember that I asked one coloured man, who was about sixty years old, to tell me something of his history. He said that he had been born in Virginia, and sold into Alabama in 1845. I asked him how many were sold at the same time. He said, "There were five of us; myself and brother and three mules."

In giving all these descriptions of what I saw during my month of travel in the country around Tuskegee, I wish my readers to keep in mind the fact that there were many encouraging exceptions to the conditions which I have described. I have stated in such plain words what I saw, mainly for the reason that later I want to emphasize the encouraging changes that have taken place in the community, not wholly by the work of the Tuskegee school, but by that of other institutions as well.

CHAPTER VIII

Teaching School In A Stable And A Hen-House

I confess that what I saw during my month of travel and investigation left me with a very heavy heart. The work to be done in order to lift these people up seemed almost beyond accomplishing. I was only one person, and it seemed to me that the little effort which I could put forth could go such a short distance toward bringing about results. I wondered if I could accomplish anything, and if it were worth while for me to try.

Of one thing I felt more strongly convinced than ever, after spending this month in seeing the actual life of the coloured people, and that was that, in order to lift them up, something must be done more than merely to imitate New England education as it then existed. I saw more clearly than ever the wisdom of the system which General Armstrong had inaugurated at Hampton. To take the children of such people as I had been among for a month, and each day give them a few hours of mere book education, I felt would be almost a waste of time.

After consultation with the citizens of Tuskegee, I set July 4, 1881, as the day for the opening of the school in the little shanty and church which had been secured for its accommodation. The white people, as well as the coloured, were greatly interested in the starting of the new school, and the

opening day was looked forward to with much earnest discussion. There were not a few white people in the vicinity of Tuskegee who looked with some disfavour upon the project. They questioned its value to the coloured people, and had a fear that it might result in bringing about trouble between the races. Some had the feeling that in proportion as the Negro received education, in the same proportion would his value decrease as an economic factor in the state. These people feared the result of education would be that the Negroes would leave the farms, and that it would be difficult to secure them for domestic service.

The white people who questioned the wisdom of starting this new school had in their minds pictures of what was called an educated Negro, with a high hat, imitation gold eye-glasses, a showy walking stick, kid gloves, fancy boots, and what not—in a word, a man who was determined to live by his wits. It was difficult for these people to see how education would produce any other kind of a coloured man.

In the midst of all the difficulties which I encountered in getting the little school started, and since then through a period of nineteen years, there are two men among all the many friends of the school in Tuskegee upon whom I have depended constantly for advice and guidance; and the success of the undertaking is largely due to these men, from whom I have never sought anything in vain. I mention them simply as types. One is a white man and an ex-slaveholder, Mr. George W. Campbell; the other is a black man and an ex-slave, Mr. Lewis Adams. These were the men who wrote to General Armstrong for a teacher.

Mr. Campbell is a merchant and banker, and had had little experience in dealing with matters pertaining to education. Mr. Adams was a mechanic, and had learned the trades of shoemaking, harness-making, and tinsmithing during the days of slavery. He had never been to school a day in his life, but in some way he had learned to read and write while a slave. From the first, these two men saw clearly what my plan of education was, sympathized with me, and supported me in every effort. In the days which were darkest financially for the school, Mr. Campbell was never appealed to when he was not willing to extend all the aid in his power. I do not know two men, one an ex-slaveholder, one an ex-slave, whose advice and judgment I would fed more like following in everything which concerns the life and development of the school at Tuskegee than those of these two men.

I have always felt that Mr. Adams, in a large degree, derived his unusual power of mind from the training given his hands in the process of mastering

well three trades during the days of slavery. If one goes to-day into any Southern town, and asks for the leading and most reliable coloured man in the community, I believe that in five cases out of ten he will be directed to a Negro who learned a trade during the days of slavery.

On the morning that the school opened, thirty students reported for admission. I was the only teacher. The students were about equally divided between the sexes. Most of them lived in Macon County, the county in which Tuskegee is situated, and of which it is the county-seat. A great many more students wanted to enter the school, but it had been decided to receive only those who were above fifteen years of age, and who had previously received some education. The greater part of the thirty were public-school teachers, and some of them were nearly forty years of age. With the teachers came some of their former pupils, and when they were examined it was amusing to note that in several cases the pupil entered a higher class than did his former teacher. It was also interesting to note how many big books some of them had studied, and how many high-sounding subjects some of them claimed to have mastered. The bigger the book and the longer the name of the subject, the prouder they felt of their accomplishment. Some had studied Latin, and one or two Greek. This they thought entitled them to special distinction.

In fact, one of the saddest things I saw during the month of travel which I have described was a young man, who had attended some high school, sitting down in a one-room cabin, with grease on his clothing, filth all around him, and weeds in the yard and garden, engaged in studying a French grammar.

The students who came first seemed to be fond of memorizing long and complicated "rules" in grammar and mathematics, but had little thought or knowledge of applying these rules to the everyday affairs of their life. One subject which they liked to talk about, and tell me that they had mastered, in arithmetic, was "banking and discount," but I soon found out that neither they nor almost any one in the neighbourhood in which they lived had ever had a bank account. In registering the names of the students, I found that almost every one of them had one or more middle initials. When I asked what the "J" stood for, in the name of John J. Jones, it was explained to me that this was a part of his "entitles." Most of the students wanted to get an education because they thought it would enable them to earn more money as school-teachers.

Notwithstanding what I have said about them in these respects, I have never seen a more earnest and willing company of young men and women

than these students were. They were all willing to learn the right thing as soon as it was shown them what was right. I was determined to start them off on a solid and thorough foundation, so far as their books were concerned. I soon learned that most of them had the merest smattering of the high-sounding things that they had studied. While they could locate the Desert of Sahara or the capital of China on an artificial globe, I found out that the girls could not locate the proper places for the knives and forks on an actual dinner-table, or the places on which the bread and meat should be set.

I had to summon a good deal of courage to take a student who had been studying cube root and "banking and discount," and explain to him that the wisest thing for him to do first was thoroughly to master the multiplication table.

The number of pupils increased each week, until by the end of the first month there were nearly fifty. Many of them, however, said that, as they could remain only for two or three months, they wanted to enter a high class and get a diploma the first year if possible.

At the end of the first six weeks a new and rare face entered the school as a co-teacher. This was Miss Olivia A. Davidson, who later became my wife. Miss Davidson was born in Ohio, and received her preparatory education in the public schools of that state. When little more than a girl, she heard of the need of teachers in the South. She went to the state of Mississippi and began teaching there. Later she taught in the city of Memphis. While teaching in Mississippi, one of her pupils be came ill with smallpox. Every one in the community was so frightened that no one would nurse the boy. Miss Davidson closed her school and remained by the bedside of the boy night and day until he recovered. While she was at her Ohio home on her vacation, the worst epidemic of yellow fever broke out in Memphis, Tenn., that perhaps has ever occurred in the South. When she heard of this, site at once telegraphed the Mayor of Memphis, offering her services as a yellow-fever nurse, although she had never had the disease.

Miss Davidson's experience in the South showed her that the people needed something more than mere book-learning. She heard of the Hampton system of education, and decided that this was what she wanted in order to prepare herself for better work: in the South. The attention of Mrs. Mary Hemenway, of Boston, was attracted to her rare ability. Through Mrs. Hemenway's kindness and generosity, Miss Davidson, after graduating at Hampton, received an opportunity to complete a two years' course of training at the Massachusetts State Normal School at Framingham.

Before she went to Framingham, some one suggested to Miss Davidson that, since she was so very light in colour, she might find it more comfortable not to be known as a coloured woman in this school in Massachusetts. She at once replied that under no circumstances and for no considerations would she consent to deceive any one in regard to her racial identity.

Soon after her graduation from the Framingham institution, Miss Davidson came to Tuskegee, bringing into the school many valuable and fresh ideas as to the best methods of teaching, as well as a rare character and a life of unselfishness that I think has seldom been equalled. No single individual did more toward laying the foundations of the Tuskegee Institute so as to insure the successful work that has been done there than Olivia A. Davidson.

Miss Davidson and I began consulting as to the future of the school from the first. The students were making progress in learning books and in developing their minds; but it became apparent at once that, if we were to make any permanent impression upon those who had come to us for training, we must do something besides teach them mere books. The students had come from homes where they had had no opportunities for lessons which would teach them how to care for their bodies. With few exceptions, the homes in Tuskegee in which the students boarded were but little improvement upon those from which they had come. We wanted to teach the students how to bathe; how to care for their teeth and clothing. We wanted to teach them what to eat, and how to eat it properly, and how to care for their rooms. Aside from this, we wanted to give them such a practical knowledge of some one industry, together with the spirit of industry, thrift, and economy, that they would be sure of knowing how to make a living after they had left us. We wanted to teach them to study actual things instead of mere books alone.

We found that the most of our students came from the country districts, where agriculture in some form or other was the main dependence of the people. We learned that about eighty-five per cent of the coloured people in the Gulf states depended upon agriculture for their living. Since this was true, we wanted to be careful not to educate our students out of sympathy with agricultural life, so that they would be attracted from the country to the cities, and yield to the temptation of trying to live by their wits. We wanted to give them such an education as would fit a large proportion of them to be teachers, and at the same time cause them to return to the plantation districts and show the people there how to put new energy and new ideas into farming, as well as into the intellectual and moral and religious life of the people.

All these ideas and needs crowded themselves upon us with a seriousness that seemed well-nigh overwhelming. What were we to do? We had only the little old shanty and the abandoned church which the good coloured people of the town of Tuskegee had kindly loaned us for the accommodation of the classes. The number of students was increasing daily. The more we saw of them and the more we travelled through the country districts, the more we saw that our efforts were reaching, to only a partial degree, the actual needs of the people whom we wanted to lift up through the medium of the students whom we should educate and send out as leaders.

The more we talked with the students, who were then coming to us from several parts of the state, the more we found that the chief ambition among a large proportion of them was to get an education so that they would not have to work any longer with their hands.

This is illustrated by a story told of a coloured man in Alabama, who, one hot day in July, while he was at work in a cotton-field, suddenly stopped, and, looking toward the skies, said: "O Lawd, de cotton am so grassy, de work am so hard, and the sun am so hot dat I b'lieve dis darky am called to preach!"

About three months after the opening of the school, and at the time when we were in the greatest anxiety about our work, there came into the market for sale an old and abandoned plantation which was situated about a mile from the town of Tuskegee. The mansion house—or "big house," as it would have been called—which had been occupied by the owners during slavery, had been burned. After making a careful examination of this place, it seemed to be just the location that we wanted in order to make our work effective and permanent.

But how were we to get it? The price asked for it was very little—only five hundred dollars—but we had no money, and we were strangers in the town and had no credit. The owner of the land agreed to let us occupy the place if we could make a payment of two hundred and fifty dollars down, with the understanding that the remaining two hundred and fifty dollars must be paid within a year. Although five hundred dollars was cheap for the land, it was a large sum when one did not have any part of it.

In the midst of the difficulty I summoned a great deal of courage and wrote to my friend General J. F. B. Marshall, the Treasurer of the Hampton Institute, putting the situation before him and beseeching him to lend me the two hundred and fifty dollars on my own personal responsibility. Within a few days a reply came to the effect that he had no authority to lend me

money belonging to the Hampton Institute, but that he would gladly lend me the amount needed from his own personal funds.

I confess that the securing of this money in this way was a great surprise to me, as well as a source of gratification. Up to that time I never had had in my possession so much money as one hundred dollars at a time, and the loan which I had asked General Marshall for seemed a tremendously large sum to me. The fact of my being responsible for the repaying of such a large amount of money weighed very heavily upon me.

I lost no time in getting ready to move the school on to the new farm. At the time we occupied the place there were standing upon it a cabin, formerly used as the dining room, an old kitchen, a stable, and an old hen-house. Within a few weeks we had all of these structures in use. The stable was repaired and used as a recitation-room, and very presently the hen-house was utilized for the same purpose.

I recall that one morning, when I told an old coloured man who lived near, and who sometimes helped me, that our school had grown so large that it would be necessary for us to use the hen-house for school purposes, and that I wanted him to help me give it a thorough cleaning out the next day, he replied, in the most earnest manner: "What you mean, boss? You sholy ain't gwine clean out de hen-house in de *day*-time?"

Nearly all the work of getting the new location ready for school purposes was done by the students after school was over in the afternoon. As soon as we got the cabins in condition to be used, I deter mined to clear up some land so that we could plant a crop. When I explained my plan to the young men, I noticed that they did not seem to take to it very kindly. It was hard for them to see the connection between clearing land and an education. Besides, many of them had been school-teachers, and they questioned whether or not clearing land would be in keeping with their dignity. In order to relieve them from any embarrassment, each afternoon after school I took my axe and led the way to the woods. When they saw that I was not afraid or ashamed to work, they began to assist with more enthusiasm. We kept at the work each afternoon, until we had cleared about twenty acres and had planted a crop.

In the meantime Miss Davidson was devising plans to repay the loan. Her first effort was made by holding festivals, or "suppers." She made a personal canvass among the white and coloured families in the town of Tuskegee, and got them to agree to give something, like a cake, a chicken, bread, or pies, that could be sold at the festival. Of course the coloured people were glad to

give anything that they could spare, but I want to add that Miss Davidson did not apply to a single white family, so far as I now remember, that failed to donate something; and in many ways the white families showed their interest in the school.

Several of these festivals were held, and quite a little sum of money was raised. A canvass was also made among the people of both races for direct gifts of money, and most of those applied to gave small sums. It was often pathetic to note the gifts of the older coloured people, most of whom had spent their best days in slavery. Sometimes they would give five cents, sometimes twenty-five cents. Sometimes the contribution was a quilt, or a quantity of sugarcane. I recall one old coloured woman, who was about seventy years of age, who came to see me when we were raising money to pay for the farm. She hobbled into the room where I was, leaning on a cane. She was clad in rags; but they were clean. She said: "Mr. Washin'ton, God knows I spent de bes' days of my life in slavery. God knows I's ignorant an' poor; but," she added, "I knows what you an' Miss Davidson is tryin' to do. I knows you is tryin' to make better men an' better women for de coloured race. I ain't got no money, but I wants you to take dese six eggs, what I's been savin' up, an' I wants you to put dese six eggs into de eddication of dese boys an' gals."

Since the work at Tuskegee started, it has been my privilege to receive many gifts for the benefit of the institution, but never any, I think, that touched me so deeply as this one.

CHAPTER IX

Anxious Days And Sleepless Nights

The coming of Christmas, that first year of our residence in Alabama, gave us an opportunity to get a farther insight into the real life of the people. The first thing that reminded us that Christmas had arrived was the "foreday" visits of scores of children rapping at our doors, asking for "Chris'mus gifts! Chris'mus gifts!" Between the hours of two o'clock and five o'clock in the morning I presume that we must have had a half-hundred such calls. This custom prevails throughout this portion of the South to-day.

During the days of slavery it was a custom quite generally observed throughout all the Southern states to give the coloured people a week of hol-

iday at Christmas, or to allow the holiday to continue as long as the "yule log" lasted. The male members of the race, and often the female members, were expected to get drunk. We found that for a whole week the coloured people in and around Tuskegee dropped work the day before Christmas, and that it was difficult to get any one to perform any service from the time they stopped work until after the New Year. Persons who at other times did not use strong drink thought it quite the proper thing to indulge in it rather freely during the Christmas week. There was a widespread hilarity, and a free use of guns, pistols, and gunpowder generally. The sacredness of the season seemed to have been almost wholly lost sight of.

During this first Christmas vacation I went some distance from the town to visit the people on one of the large plantations. In their poverty and ignorance it was pathetic to see their attempts to get joy out of the season that in most parts of the country is so sacred and so dear to the heart. In one cabin I noticed that all that the five children had to remind them of the coming of Christ was a single bunch of firecrackers, which they had divided among them. In another cabin, where there were at least a half-dozen persons, they had only ten cents' worth of ginger-cakes, which had been bought in the store the day before. In another family they had only a few pieces of sugar-cane. In still another cabin I found nothing but a new jug of cheap, mean whiskey, which the husband and wife were making free use of, notwithstanding the fact that the husband was one of the local ministers. In a few instances I found that the people had gotten hold of some bright-coloured cards that had been designed for advertising purposes, and were making the most of those. In other homes some member of the family had bought a new pistol. In the majority of cases there was nothing to be seen in the cabin to remind one of the coming of the Saviour, except that the people had ceased work in the fields and were lounging about their homes. At night, during Christmas week, they usually had what they called a "frolic," in some cabin on the plantation. This meant a kind of rough dance, where there was likely to be a good deal of whiskey used, and where there might be some shooting or cutting with razors.

While I was making this Christmas visit I met an old coloured man who was one of the numerous local preachers, who tried to convince me, from the experience Adam had in the Garden of Eden, that God had cursed all labour, and that, therefore, it was a sin for any man to work. For that reason this man sought to do as little work as possible. He seemed at that time to be supreme-ly happy, because he was living, as he expressed it, through one week that was

free from sin.

In the school we made a special effort to teach our students the meaning of Christmas, and to give them lessons in its proper observance. In this we have been successful to a degree that makes me feel safe in saying that the season now has a new meaning, not only through all that immediate region, but, in a measure, wherever our graduates have gone.

At the present time one of the most satisfactory features of the Christmas and Thanksgiving seasons at Tuskegee is the unselfish and beautiful way in which our graduates and students spend their time in administering to the comfort and happiness others, especially the unfortunate. Not long ago some of our young men spent a holiday in rebuilding a cabin for a helpless coloured woman who is about seventy-five years old. At another time I remember that I made it known in chapel, one night, that a very poor student was suffering from cold, because he needed a coat. The next morning two coats were sent to my office for him.

I have referred to the disposition on the part of the white people in the town of Tuskegee and vicinity to help the school. From the first, I resolved to make the school a real part of the community in which it was located. I was determined that no one should have the feeling that it was a foreign institution, dropped down in the midst of the people, for which they had no responsibility and in which they had no interest. I noticed that the very fact that they had been asked to contribute toward the purchase of the land made them begin to feel as if it was going to be their school, to a large degree. I noted that just in proportion as we made the white people feel that the institution was a part of the life of the community, and that, while we wanted to make friends in Boston, for example, we also wanted to make white friends in Tuskegee, and that we wanted to make the school of real service to all the people, their attitude toward the school became favourable.

Perhaps I might add right here, what I hope to demonstrate later, that, so far as I know, the Tuskegee school at the present time has no warmer and more enthusiastic friends anywhere than it has among the white citizens of Tuskegee and through out the state of Alabama and the entire South. From the first, I have advised our people in the South to make friends in every straightforward, manly way with their next-door neighbour, whether he be a black man or a white man. I have also advised them, where no principle is at stake, to consult the interests of their local communities, and to advise with their friends in regard to their voting.

For several months the work of securing the money with which to pay for

the farm went on without ceasing. At the end of three months enough was secured to repay the loan of two hundred and fifty dollars to General Marshall, and within two months more we had secured the entire five hundred dollars and had received a deed of the one hundred acres of land. This gave us a great deal of satisfaction. It was not only a source of satisfaction to secure a permanent location for the school, but it was equally satisfactory to know that the greater part of the money with which it was paid for had been gotten from the white and coloured people in the town of Tuskegee. The most of this money was obtained by holding festivals and concerts, and from small individual donations.

Our next effort was in the direction of increasing the cultivation of the land, so as to secure some return from it, and at the same time give the students training in agriculture. All the industries at Tuskegee have been started in natural and logical order, growing out of the needs of a community settlement. We began with farming, because we wanted something to eat.

Many of the students, also, were able to remain in school but a few weeks at a time, because they had so little money with which to pay their board. Thus another object which made it desirable to get an industrial system started was in order to mane it available as a means of helping the students to earn money enough so that they might be able to remain in school during the nine months' session of the school year.

The first animal that the school came into possession of was an old blind horse given us by one of the white citizens of Tuskegee. Perhaps I may add here that at the present time the school owns over two hundred horses, colts, mules, cows, calves, and oxen, and about seven hundred hogs and pigs, as well as a large number of sheep and goats.

The school was constantly growing in numbers, so much so that, after we had got the farm paid for, the cultivation of the land begun, and the old cabins which we had found on the place somewhat repaired, we turned our attention toward providing a large, substantial building. After having given a good deal of thought to the subject, we finally had the plans drawn for a building that was estimated to cost about six thousand dollars. This seemed to us a tremendous sum, but we knew that the school must go backward or forward, and that our work would mean little unless we could get hold of the students in their home life.

One incident which occurred about this time gave me a great deal of satisfaction as well as surprise. When it became known in the town that we were discussing the plans for a new, large building, a Southern white man who was

operating a sawmill not far from Tuskegee came to me and said that he would gladly put all the lumber necessary to erect the building on the grounds, with no other guarantee for payment than my word that it would be paid for when we secured some money. I told the man frankly that at the time we did not have in our hands one dollar of the money needed. Notwithstanding this, he insisted on being allowed to put the lumber on the grounds. After we had secured some portion of the money we permitted him to do this.

Miss Davidson again began the work of securing in various ways small contributions for the new building from the white and coloured people in and near Tuskegee. I think I never saw a community of people so happy over anything as were the coloured people over the prospect of this new building. One day, when we were holding a meeting to secure funds for its erection, an old, ante-bellum coloured man came a distance of twelve miles and brought in his ox-cart a large hog. When the meeting was in progress, he rose in the midst of the company and said that he had no money which he could give, but that he had raised two fine hogs, and that he had brought one of them as a contribution toward the expenses of the building. He closed his announcement by saying: "Any nigger that's got any love for his race, or any respect for himself, will bring a hog to the next meeting." Quite a number of men in the community also volunteered to give several days' work, each, toward the erection of the building.

After we had secured all the help that we could in Tuskegee, Miss Davidson decided to go North for the purpose of securing additional funds. For weeks she visited individuals and spoke in churches and before Sunday Schools and other organizations. She found this work quite trying, and often embarrassing. The school was not known, but she was not long in winning her way into the confidence of the best people in the North.

The first gift from any Northern person was received from a New York lady whom Miss David son met on the boat that was bringing her North. They fell into a conversation, and the Northern lady became so much interested in the effort being made at Tuskegee that before they parted Miss Davidson was handed a check for fifty dollars. For some time before our marriage, and also after it, Miss Davidson kept up the work of securing money in the North and in the South by interesting people by personal visits and through correspondence. At the same time she kept in close touch with the work at Tuskegee, as lady principal and classroom teacher. In addition to this, she worked among the older people in and near Tuskegee, and taught a Sunday school class in the town. She was never very strong, but never seemed

happy unless she was giving all of her strength to the cause which she loved. Often, at night, after spending the day in going from door to door trying to interest persons in the work at Tuskegee, she would be so exhausted that she could not undress herself. A lady upon whom she called, in Boston, afterward told me that at one time when Miss Davidson called to see her and sent up her card the lady was detained a little before she could see Miss Davidson, and when she entered the parlour she found Miss Davidson so exhausted that she had fallen asleep.

While putting up our first building, which was named Porter Hall, after Mr. A. H. Porter, of Brooklyn, N. Y., who gave a generous sum toward its erection, the need for money became acute. I had given one of our creditors a promise that upon a certain day he should be paid four hundred dollars. On the morning of that day we did not have a dollar. The mail arrived at the school at ten o'clock, and in this mail there was a check sent by Miss Davidson for exactly four hundred dollars. I could relate many instances of almost the same character. This four hundred dollars was given by two ladies in Boston. Two years later, when the worn at Tuskegee had grown considerably, and when we were in the midst of a season when we were so much in need of money that the future looked doubtful and gloomy, the same two Boston ladies sent us six thousand dollars. Words cannot describe our surprise, or the encouragement that the gift brought to us. Perhaps I might add here that for fourteen years these same friends have sent us six thousand dollars each year.

As soon as the plans were drawn for the new building, the students began digging out the earth where the foundations were to be laid, working after the regular classes were over. They had not fully outgrown the idea that it was hardly the proper thing for them to use their hands, since they had come there, as one of them expressed it, "to be educated, and not to work." Gradually, though, I noted with satisfaction that a sentiment in favour of work was gaining ground. After a few weeks of hard work the foundations were ready, and a day was appointed for the laying of the corner-stone.

When it is considered that the laying of this comer-stone took place in the heart of the South, in the "Black Belt," in the centre of that part of our country that was most devoted to slavery; that at that time slavery had been abolished only about sixteen years; that only sixteen years before that no Negro could be taught from books without the teacher receiving the condemnation of the law or of public sentiment—when all this is considered, the scene that was witnessed on that spring day at Tuskegee was a remarkable

one. I believe there are few places in the world where it could have taken place.

The principal address was delivered by the Hon. Waddy Thompson, the Superintendent of Education for the country. About the corner-stone were gathered the teachers, the students, their parents and friends, the county officials—who were white—and all the leading white men in that vicinity, together with many of the black men and women whom these same white people but a few years before had held a title to as property. The members of both races were anxious to exercise the privilege of placing under the corner-stone some memento.

Before the building was completed we passed through some very trying seasons. More than once our hearts were made to bleed, as it were, because bills were falling due that we did not have the money to meet. Perhaps no one who has not gone through the experience, month after month, of trying to erect buildings and provide equipment for a school when no one knew where the money was to come from, can properly appreciate the difficulties under which we laboured. During the first years at Tuskegee I recall that night after night I would roll and toss on my bed, without sleep, because of the anxiety and uncertainty which we were in regarding money. I knew that, in a large degree, we were trying an experiment—that of testing whether or not it was possible for Negroes to build up and control the affairs of a large educational institution. I knew that if we failed it would injure the whole race. I knew that the presumption was against us. I knew that in the case of white people beginning such an enterprise it would be taken for granted that they were going to succeed, but in our case I felt that people would be surprised if we succeeded. All this made a burden which pressed down on us, sometimes, it seemed, at the rate of a thousand pounds to the square inch.

In all our difficulties and anxieties, however, I never went to a white or a black person in the town of Tuskegee for any assistance that was in their power to render, without being helped according to their means. More than a dozen times, when bills figuring up into the hundreds of dollars were falling due, I applied to the white men of Tuskegee for small loans, often borrowing small amounts from as many as a half-dozen persons, to meet our obligations. One thing I was determined to do from the first, and that was to keep the credit of the school high, and this, I think I can say without boasting, we have done all through these years.

I shall always remember a bit of advice given me by Mr. George W. Campbell, the white man to whom I have referred as the one who induced

General Armstrong to send me to Tuskegee. Soon after I entered upon the work Mr. Campbell said to me, in his fatherly way: "Washington, always remember that credit is capital."

At one time when we were in the greatest distress for money that we ever experienced, I placed the situation frankly before General Armstrong. Without hesitation he gave me his personal check for all the money which he had saved for his own use. This was not the only time that General Armstrong helped Tuskegee in this way. I do not think I have ever made this fact public before.

During the summer of 1882, at the end of the first year's work of the school, I was married to Miss Fannie N. Smith, of Malden, W. Va. We began keeping house in Tuskegee early in the fall. This made a home for our teachers, who now had been increased to four in number. My wife was also a graduate of the Hampton Institute. After earnest and constant work in the interests of the school, together with her housekeeping duties, my wife passed away in May, 1884. One child, Portia M. Washington, was born during our marriage.

From the first, my wife most earnestly devoted her thoughts and time to the work of the school, and was completely one with me in every interest and ambition. She passed away, however, before she had an opportunity of seeing what the school was designed to be.

CHAPTER X

A Harder Task Than Making Bricks Without Straw

From the very beginning, at Tuskegee, I was determined to have the students do not only the agricultural and domestic work, but to have them erect their own buildings. My plan was to have them, while performing this service, taught the latest and best methods of labour, so that the school would not only get the benefit of their efforts, but the students themselves would be taught to see not only utility in labour, but beauty and dignity, would be taught, in fact, how to lift labour up from mere drudgery and toil, and would learn to love work for its own sake. My plan was not to teach them to work in the old way, but to show them how to make the forces of nature—air, water, steam, electricity, horse-power—assist them in their labour.

At first many advised against the experiment of having the buildings erected by the labour of the students, but I was determined to stick to it. I told those who doubted the wisdom of the plan that I knew that our first buildings would not be so comfortable or so complete in their finish as buildings erected by the experienced hands of outside work men, but that in the teaching of civilization, self-help, and self-reliance, the erection of the buildings by the students themselves would more than compensate for any lack of comfort or fine finish.

I further told those who doubted the wisdom of this plan, that the majority of our students came to us in poverty, from the cabins of the cotton, sugar, and rice plantations of the South, and that while I knew it would please the students very much to place them at once in finely constructed buildings, I felt that it would be following out a more natural process of development to teach them how to construct their own buildings. Mistakes I knew would be made, but these mistakes would teach us valuable lessons for the future.

During the now nineteen years' existence of the Tuskegee school, the plan of having the buildings erected by student labour has been adhered to. In this time forty buildings, counting small and large, have been built, and all except four are almost wholly the product of student labour. As an additional result, hundreds of men are now scattered throughout the South who received their knowledge of mechanics while being taught how to erect these buildings. Skill and knowledge are now handed down from one set of students to another in this way, until at the present time a building of any description or size can be constructed wholly by our instructors and students, from the drawing of the plans to the putting in of the electric fixtures without going off the grounds for a single workman.

Not a few times, when a new student has been led into the temptation of marring the looks of some building by lead-pencil marks or by the cuts of a jack-knife, I have heard an old student remind him: "Don't do that. That is our building. I helped put it up."

In the early days of the school I think my most trying experience was in the matter of brickmaking. As soon as we got the farm work reasonably well started, we directed our next efforts toward the industry of making bricks. We needed these for use in connection with the erection of our own buildings; but there was also another reason for establishing this industry. There was no brickyard in the town, and in addition to our own needs there was a demand for bricks in the general market.

I had always sympathized with the "Children of Israel," in their task of

"making bricks without straw," but ours was the task of making bricks with no money and no experience.

In the first place, the work was hard and dirty, and it was difficult to get the students to help. When it came to brickmaking, their distaste for manual labour in connection with book education became especially manifest. It was not a pleasant task for one to stand in the mud-pit for hours, with the mud up to his knees. More than one man became disgusted and left the school.

We tried several locations before we opened up a pit that furnished brick clay. I had always supposed that brickmaking was very simple, but I soon found out by bitter experience that it required special skill and knowledge, particularly in the burning of the bricks. After a good deal of effort we moulded about twenty-five thousand bricks, and put them into a kiln to be burned. This kiln turned out to be a failure, because it was not properly constructed or properly burned. We began at once, however, on a second kiln. This, for some reason, also proved a failure. The failure of this kiln made it still more difficult to get the students to take any part in the work. Several of the teachers, however, who had been trained in the industries at Hampton, volunteered their services, and in some way we succeeded in getting a third kiln ready for burning. The burning of a kiln required about a week. Toward the latter part of the week, when it seemed as if we were going to have a good many thousand bricks in a few hours, in the middle of the night the kiln fell. For the third time we had failed.

The failure of this last kiln left me without a single dollar with which to make another expert meet. Most of the teachers advised the abandoning of the effort to make bricks. In the midst of my troubles I thought of a watch which had come into my possession years before. I took this watch to the city of Montgomery, which was not far distant, and placed it in a pawn-shop. I secured cash upon it to the amount of fifteen dollars, with which to renew the brickmaking experiment. I returned to Tuskegee, and, with the help of the fifteen dollars, rallied our rather demoralized and discouraged forces and began a fourth attempt to make bricks. This time, I am glad to say, we were successful. Before I got hold of any money, the time-limit on my watch had expired, and I have never seen it since; but I have never regretted the loss of it.

Brickmaking has now become such an important industry at the school that last season our students manufactured twelve hundred thousand of first-class bricks, of a quality suitable to be sold in any market. Aside from this, scores of young men have mastered the brickmaking trade both the making

of bricks by hand and by machinery—and are now engaged in this industry in many parts of the South.

The making of these bricks taught me an important lesson in regard to the relations of the two races in the South. Many white people who had had no contact with the school, and perhaps no sympathy with it, came to us to buy bricks because they found out that ours were good bricks. They discovered that we were supplying a real want in the community. The making of these bricks caused many of the white residents of the neighbourhood to begin to feel that the education of the Negro was not making him worthless, but that in educating our students we were adding something to the wealth and comfort of the community. As the people of the neighbourhood came to us to buy bricks, we got acquainted with them; they traded with us and we with them. Our business interests became intermingled. We had something which they wanted; they had something which we wanted. This, in a large measure, helped to lay the foundation for the pleasant relations that have continued to exist between us and the white people in that section, and which now extend throughout the South.

Wherever one of our brickmakers has gone in the South, we find that he has something to contribute to the well-being of the community into which he has gone; something that has made the community feel that, in a degree, it is indebted to him, and perhaps, to a certain extent, dependent upon him. In this way pleasant relations between the races have been stimulated.

My experience is that there is something in human nature which always makes an individual recognize and reward merit, no matter under what colour of skin merit is found. I have found, too, that it is the visible, the tangible, that goes a long ways in softening prejudices. The actual sight of a first-class house that a Negro has built is ten times more potent than pages of discussion about a house that he ought to build, or perhaps could build.

The same principle of industrial education has been carried out in the building of our own wagons, carts, and buggies, from the first. We now own and use on our farm and about the school dozens of these vehicles, and every one of them has been built by the hands of the students. Aside from this, we help supply the local market with these vehicles. The supplying of them to the people in the community has had the same effect as the supplying of bricks, and the man who learns at Tuskegee to build and repair wagons and carts is regarded as a benefactor by both races in the community where he goes. The people with whom he lives and works are going to think twice before they part with such a man.

The individual who can do something that the world wants done will, in the end, make his way regardless of his race. One man may go into a community prepared to supply the people there with an analysis of Greek sentences. The community may not at that time be prepared for, or feel the need of, Greek analysis, but it may feel its need of bricks and houses and wagons. If the man can supply the need for those, then, it will lead eventually to a demand for the first product, and with the demand will come the ability to appreciate it and to profit by it.

About the time that we succeeded in burning our first kiln of bricks we began facing in an emphasized form the objection of the students to being taught to work. By this time it had gotten to be pretty well advertised throughout the state that every student who came to Tuskegee, no matter what his financial ability might be, must learn some industry. Quite a number of letters came from parents protesting against their children engaging in labour while they were in the school. Other parents came to the school to protest in person. Most of the new students brought a written or a verbal request from their parents to the effect that they wanted their children taught nothing but books. The more books, the larger they were, and the longer the titles printed upon them, the better pleased the students and their parents seemed to be.

I gave little heed to these protests, except that I lost no opportunity to go into as many parts of the state as I could, for the purpose of speaking to the parents, and showing them the value of industrial education. Besides, I talked to the students constantly on the subject. Notwithstanding the unpopularity of industrial work, the school continued to increase in numbers to such an extent that by the middle of the second year there was an attendance of about one hundred and fifty, representing almost all parts of the state of Alabama, and including a few from other states.

In the summer of 1882 Miss Davidson and I both went North and engaged in the work of raising funds for the completion of our new building. On my way North I stopped in New York to try to get a letter of recommendation from an officer of a missionary organization who had become somewhat acquainted with me a few years previous. This man not only refused to give me the letter, but advised me most earnestly to go back home at once, and not make an attempt to get money, for he was quite sure that I would never get more than enough to pay my travelling expenses. I thanked him for his advice, and proceeded on my journey.

The first place I went to in the North, was Northampton, Mass., where I

spent nearly a half-day in looking for a coloured family with whom I could board, never dreaming that any hotel would admit me. I was greatly surprised when I found that I would have no trouble in being accommodated at a hotel.

We were successful in getting money enough so that on Thanksgiving Day of that year we held our first service in the chapel of Porter Hall, although the building was not completed.

In looking about for some one to preach the Thanksgiving sermon, I found one of the rarest men that it has ever been my privilege to know. This was the Rev. Robert C. Bedford, a white man from Wisconsin, who was then pastor of a little coloured Congregational church in Montgomery, Ala. Before going to Montgomery to look for some one to preach this sermon I had never heard of Mr. Bedford. He had never heard of me. He gladly consented to come to Tuskegee and hold the Thanksgiving service. It was the first service of the kind that the coloured people there had ever observed, and what a deep interest they manifested in it! The sight of the new building made it a day of Thanksgiving for them never to be forgotten.

Mr. Bedford consented to become one of the trustees of the school, and in that capacity, and as a worker for it, he has been connected with it for eighteen years. During this time he has borne the school upon his heart night and day, and is never so happy as when he is performing some service, no matter how rumble, for it. He completely obliterates himself in everything, and looks only for per mission to serve where service is most disagreeable, and where others would not be attracted. In all my relations with him he has seemed to me to approach as nearly to the spirit of the Master as almost any man I ever met.

A little later there came into the service of the school another man, quite young at the time, and fresh from Hampton, without whose service the school never could have become what it is. This was Mr. Warren Logan, who now for seventeen years has been the treasurer of the Institute, and the acting principal during my absence. He has always shown a degree of unselfishness and an amount of business tact, coupled with a clear judgment, that has kept the school in good condition no matter how long I have been absent from it. During all the financial stress through which the school has passed, his patience and faith in our ultimate success have not left him.

As soon as our first building was near enough to completion so that we could occupy a portion of it—which was near the middle of the second year of the school—we opened a boarding department. Students had begun com-

ing from quite a distance, and in such increasing numbers that we felt more and more that we were merely skimming over the surface, in that we were not getting hold of the students in their home life.

We had nothing but the students and their appetites with which to begin a boarding department. No provision had been made in the new building for a kitchen and dining room; but we discovered that by digging out a large amount of earth from under the building we could make a partially lighted basement room that could be used for a kitchen and dining room. Again I called on the students to volunteer for work, this time to assist in digging out the basement. This they did, and in a few weeks we had a place to cook and eat in, although it was very rough and uncomfortable. Any one seeing the place now would never believe that it was once used for a dining room.

The most serious problem, though, was to get the boarding department started off in running order, with nothing to do with in the way of furniture, and with no money with which to buy anything. The merchants in the town would let us have what food we wanted on credit. In fact, in those earlier years I was constantly embarrassed because people seemed to have more faith in me than I had in myself. It was pretty hard to cook, however, without stoves, and awkward to eat without dishes. At first the cooking was done out-of-doors, in the old-fashioned, primitive style, in pots and skillets placed over a fire. Some of the carpenters' benches that had been used in the construction of the building were utilized for tables. As for dishes, there were too few to make it worth while to spend time in describing them.

No one connected with the boarding department seemed to have any idea that meals must be served at certain fixed and regular hours, and this was a source of great worry. Everything was so out of joint and so inconvenient that I feel safe in saying that for the first two weeks something was wrong at every meal. Either the meat was not done or had been burnt, or the salt had been left out of the bread, or the tea had been forgotten.

Early one morning I was standing near the dining-room door listening to the complaints of the students. The complaints that morning were especially emphatic and numerous, because the whole breakfast had been a failure. One of the girls who had failed to get any breakfast came out and went to the well to draw some water to drink to take the place of the breakfast which she had not been able to get. When she reached the well, she found that the rope was broken and that she could get no water. She turned from the well and said, in the most discouraged tone, not knowing that I was where I could hear her, "We can't even get water to drink at this school." I think no one

remark ever came so near discouraging me as that one.

At another time, when Mr. Bedford—whom I have already spoken of as one of our trustees, and a devoted friend of the institution—was visiting the school, he was given a bedroom immediately over the dining room. Early in the morning he was awakened by a rather animated discussion between two boys in the dining room below. The discussion was over the question as to whose turn it was to use the coffee-cup that morning. One boy won the case by proving that for three mornings he had not had an opportunity to use the cup at all.

But gradually, by patience and hard work, we brought order out of chaos, just as will be true of any problem if we stick to it with patience and wisdom and earnest effort.

As I look back now over that part of our struggle, I am glad that we had it. I am glad that we endured all those discomforts and inconveniences. I am glad that our students had to dig out the place for their kitchen and dining room. I am glad that our first boarding-place was in that dismal, ill-lighted, and damp basement. Had we started in a fine, attractive, convenient room, I fear we would have "lost our heads" and become "stuck up." It means a great deal, I think, to start off on a foundation which one has made for one's self.

When our old students return to Tuskegee now, as they often do, and go into our large, beautiful, well-ventilated, and well-lighted dining room, and see tempting, well-cooked food—largely grown by the students themselves—and see tables, neat tablecloths and napkins, and vases of flowers upon the tables, and hear singing birds, and note that each meal is served exactly upon the minute, with no disorder, and with almost no complaint coming from the hundreds that now fill our dining room, they, too, often say to me that they are glad that we started as we did, and built ourselves up year by year, by a slow and natural process of growth.

CHAPTER XI

Making Their Beds Before They Could Lie On Them

A little later in the history of the school we had a visit from General J. F. B. Marshall, the Treasurer of the Hampton Institute, who had had faith enough to lend us the first two hundred and fifty dollars with which to make

a payment down on the farm. He remained with us a week, and made a careful inspection of everything. He seemed well pleased with our progress, and wrote back interesting and encouraging reports to Hampton. A little later Miss Mary F. Mackie, the teacher who had given me the "sweeping" examination when I entered Hampton, came to see us, and still later General Armstrong himself came.

At the time of the visits of these Hampton friends the number of teachers at Tuskegee had increased considerably, and the most of the new teachers were graduates of the Hampton Institute. We gave our Hampton friends, especially General Armstrong, a cordial welcome. They were all surprised and pleased at the rapid progress that the school had made within so short a time. The coloured people from miles around came to the school to get a look at General Armstrong, about whom they had heard so much. The General was not only welcomed by the members of my own race, but by the Southern white people as well.

This first visit which General Armstrong made to Tuskegee gave me an opportunity to get an insight into his character such as I had not before had. I refer to his interest in the Southern white people. Before this, I had had the thought that General Armstrong, having fought the Southern: white man, rather cherished a feeling of bitterness toward the white South, and was interested in helping only the coloured man there. But this visit convinced me that I did not know the greatness and the generosity of the man. I soon learned, by his visits to the Southern white people, and from his conversations with them, that he was as anxious about the prosperity and the happiness of the white race as the black. He cherished no bitterness against the South, and was happy when an opportunity offered for manifesting his sympathy. In all my acquaintance with General Armstrong I never heard him speak, in public or in private, a single bitter word against the white man in the South. From his example in this respect I learned the lesson that great men cultivate love, and that only little men cherish a spirit of hatred. I learned that assistance given to the weak makes the one who gives it strong; and that oppression of the unfortunate makes one weak.

It is now long ago that I learned this lesson from General Armstrong, and resolved that I would permit no man, no matter what his colour might be, to narrow and degrade my soul by making me hate him. With God's help, I believe that I have completely rid myself of any ill feeling toward the Southern white man for any wrong that he may have inflicted upon my race. I am made to feel just as happy now when I am rendering service to Southern

white men as when the service is rendered to a member of my own race. I pity from the bottom of my heart any individual who is so unfortunate as to get into the habit of holding race prejudice.

The more I consider the subject, the more strongly I am convinced that the most harmful effect of the practice to which the people in certain sections of the South have felt themselves compelled to resort, in order to get rid of the force of the Negroes' ballot, is not wholly in the wrong done to the Negro, but in the permanent injury to the morals of the white man. The wrong to the Negro is temporary, but to the morals of the white man the injury is permanent. I have noted time and time again that when an individual perjures himself in order to break the force of the black man's ballot, he soon learns to practice dishonesty in other relations of life, not only where the Negro is concerned, but equally so where a white man is concerned. The white man who begins by cheating a Negro usually ends by cheating a white man. The white man who begins to break the law by lynching a Negro soon yields to the temptation to lynch a white man. All this, it seems to me, makes it important that the whole Nation lend a hand in trying to lift the burden of ignorance from the South.

Another thing that is becoming more apparent each year in the development of education in the South is the influence of General Armstrong's idea of education; and this not upon the blacks alone, but upon the whites also. At the present time there is almost no Southern state that is not putting forth efforts in the direction of securing industrial education for its white boys and girls, and in most cases it is easy to trace the history of these efforts back to General Armstrong.

Soon after the opening of our humble boarding department students began coming to us in still larger numbers. For weeks we not only had to contend with the difficulty of providing board, with no money, but also with that of providing sleeping accommodations. For this purpose we rented a number of cabins near the school. These cabins were in a dilapidated condition, and during the winter months the students who occupied them necessarily suffered from the cold. We charged the students eight dollars a month—all they were able to pay—for their board. This included, besides board, room, fuel, and washing. We also gave the students credit on their board bills for all the work which they did for the school which was of any value to the institution. The cost of tuition, which was fifty dollars a year for each student, we had to secure then, as now, wherever we could.

This small charge in cash gave us no capital with which to start a board-

ing department. The weather during the second winter of our work was very cold. We were not able to provide enough bed-clothes to keep the students warm. In fact, for some time we were not able to provide, except in a few cases, bedsteads and mattresses of any kind. During the coldest nights I was so troubled about the discomfort of the students that I could not sleep myself. I recall that on several occasions I went in the middle of the night to the shanties occupied by the young men, for the purpose of comforting them. Often I found some of them sitting huddled around a fire, with the one blanket which we had been able to provide wrapped around them, trying in this way to keep warm. During the whole night some of them did not attempt to lie down. One morning, when the night previous had been unusually cold, I asked those of the students in the chapel who thought that they had been frostbitten during the night to raise their hands. Three hands went up. Notwithstanding these experiences, there was almost no complaining on the part of the students. They knew that we were doing the best that we could for them. They were happy in the privilege of being permitted to enjoy any kind of opportunity that would enable them to improve their condition. They were constantly asking what they might do to lighten the burdens of the teachers.

I have heard it stated more than once, both in the North and in the South, that coloured people would not obey and respect each other when one member of the race is placed in a position of authority over others. In regard to this general belief and these statements, I can say that during the nineteen years of my experience at Tuskegee I never, either by word or act, have been treated with disrespect by any student or officer connected with the institution. On the other hand, I am constantly embarrassed by the many acts of thoughtful kindness. The students do not seem to want to see me carry a large book or a satchel or any kind of a burden through the grounds. In such cases more than one always offers to relieve me. I almost never go out of my office when the rain is falling that some student does not come to my side with an umbrella and ask to be allowed to hold it over me.

While writing upon this subject, it is a pleasure for me to add that in all my contact with the white people of the South I have never received a single personal insult. The white people in and near Tuskegee, to an especial degree, seem to count it a privilege to show me all the respect within their power, and often go out of their way to do this.

Not very long ago I was making a journey between Dallas (Texas) and Houston. In some way it became known in advance that I was on the train.

At nearly every station at which the train stopped, numbers of white people, including in most cases the officials of the town, came aboard and introduced themselves and thanked me heartily for the work that I was trying to do for the South.

On another occasion, when I was making a trip from Augusta, Georgia, to Atlanta, being rather tired from much travel, I rode in a Pullman sleeper. When I went into the car, I found there two ladies from Boston whom I knew well. These good ladies were perfectly ignorant, it seems, of the customs of the South, and in the goodness of their hearts insisted that I take a seat with them in their section. After some hesitation I consented. I had been there but a few minutes when one of them, without my knowledge, ordered supper to be served to the three of us. This embarrassed me still further. The car was full of Southern white men, most of whom had their eyes on our party. When I found that supper had been ordered, I tried to contrive some excuse that would permit me to leave the section, but the ladies insisted that I must eat with them. I finally settled back in my seat with a sigh, and said to myself, "I am in for it now, sure."

To add further to the embarrassment of the situation, soon after the supper was placed on the table one of the ladies remembered that she had in her satchel a special kind of tea which she wished served, and as she said she felt quite sure the porter did not know how to brew it properly, she insisted upon getting up and preparing and serving it herself. At last the meal was over; and it seemed the longest one that I had ever eaten. When we were through, I decided to get myself out of the embarrassing situation and go into the smoking-room, where most of the men were by that time, to see how the land lay. In the meantime, however, it had become known in some way throughout the car who I was. When I went into the smoking-room I was never more surprised in my life than when each man, nearly every one of them a citizen of Georgia, came up and introduced himself to me and thanked me earnestly for the work that I was trying to do for the whole South. This was not flattery, because each one of these individuals knew that he had nothing to gain by trying to flatter me.

From the first I have sought to impress the students with the idea that Tuskegee is not my institution, or that of the officers, but that it is their institution, and that they have as much interest in it as any of the trustees or instructors. I have further sought to have them feel that I am at the institution as their friend and adviser, and not as their overseer. It has been my aim to have them speak with directness and frankness about anything that con-

cerns the life of the school. Two or three times a year I ask the students to write me a letter criticising or making complaints or suggestions about anything connected with the institution. When this is not done, I have them meet me in the chapel for a heart-to-heart talk about the conduct of the school. There are no meetings with our students that I enjoy more than these, and none are more helpful to me in planning for the future. These meetings, it seems to me, enable me to get at the very heart of all that concerns the school. Few things help an individual more than to place responsibility upon him, and to let him know that you trust him. When I have read of labour troubles between employers and employees, I have often thought that many strikes and similar disturbances might be avoided if the employers would cultivate the habit of getting nearer to their employees, of consulting and advising with them, and letting them feel that the interests of the two are the same. Every individual responds to confidence, and this is not more true of any race than of the Negroes. Let them once understand that you are unselfishly interested in them, and you can lead them to any extent.

It was my aim from the first at Tuskegee to not only have the buildings erected by the students themselves, but to have them make their own furniture as far as was possible. I now marvel at the patience of the students while sleeping upon the floor while waiting for some kind of a bedstead to be constructed, or at their sleeping without any kind of a mattress while waiting for something that looked like a mattress to be made.

In the early days we had very few students who had been used to handling carpenter's tools, and the bedsteads made by the students then were very rough and very weak. Not unfrequently when I went into the students' rooms in the morning I would find at least two bedsteads lying about on the floor. The problem of providing mattresses was a difficult one to solve. We finally mastered this, however, by getting some cheap cloth and sewing pieces of this together so as to make large bags. These bags we filled with the pine straw—or, as it is sometimes called, pine needles—which we secured from the forests near by. I am glad to say that the industry of mattress-making has grown steadily since then, and has been improved to such an extent that at the present time it is an important branch of the work which is taught systematically to a number of our girls, and that the mattresses that now come out of the mattress shop at Tuskegee are about as good as those bought in the average store. For some time after the opening of the boarding department we had no chairs in the students' bedrooms or in the dining rooms. Instead of chairs we used stools which the students constructed by nailing together

three pieces of rough board. As a rule, the furniture in the students' rooms during the early days of the school consisted of a bed, some stools, and sometimes a rough table made by the students. The plan of having the students make the furniture is still followed, but the number of pieces in a room has been increased, and the workmanship has so improved that little fault can be found with the articles—now. One thing that I have always insisted upon at Tuskegee is that everywhere there should be absolute cleanliness. Over and over again the students were reminded it, those first years—and are reminded now—that people would excuse us for our poverty, for our lack of comforts and conveniences, but that they would not excuse us for dirt.

Another thing that has been insisted upon at the school is the use of the tooth-brush. "The gospel of the tooth-brush," as General Armstrong used to call it, is a part of our creed at Tuskegee. No student is permitted to remain who does not keep and use a tooth-brush. Several times, in recent years, students have come to us who brought with them almost no other article except a tooth-brush. They had heard from the lips of older students about our insisting upon the use of this, and so, to make a good impression, they brought at least a tooth brush with them. I remember that one morning, not long ago, I went with the lady principal on her usual morning tour of inspection of the girls' rooms. We found one room that contained three girls who had recently arrived at the school. When I asked them if they had tooth-brushes, one of the girls replied, pointing to a brush: "Yes, sir. That is our brush. We bought it together, yesterday." It did not take them long to learn a different lesson.

It has been interesting to note the effect that the use of the tooth-brush has had in bringing about a higher degree of civilization among the students. With few exceptions, I have noticed that, if we can get a student to the point where, when the first or second tooth-brush disappears, he of his own motion buys another, I have not been disappointed in the future of that individual. Absolute cleanliness of the body has been insisted upon from the first. The students have been taught to bathe as regularly as to take their meals. This lesson we began teaching before we had anything in the shape of a bath-house. Most of the students came from plantation districts, and often we had to teach them how to sleep at night; that is, whether between the two sheets—after we got to the point where we could provide them two sheets—or under both of them. Naturally I found it difficult to teach them to sleep between two sheets when we were able to supply but one. The importance of the use of the nightgown received the same attention.

For a long time one of the most difficult tasks was to teach the students that all the buttons were to be kept on their clothes, and that there must be no torn places and no grease-spots. This lesson, I am pleased to be able to say, has been so thoroughly learned and so faithfully handed down from year to year by one set of students to another that often at the present time, when the students march out of chapel in the evening and their dress is inspected, as it is every night, not one button is to be found missing.

CHAPTER XII

Raising Money

When we opened our boarding department, we provided rooms in the attic of Porter Hall, our first building, for a number of girls. But the number of students, of both sexes, continued to increase. We could find rooms outside the school grounds for many of the young men, but the girls we did not care to expose in this way. Very soon the problem of providing more rooms for the girls, as well as a larger boarding department for all the students, grew serious. As a result, we finally decided to undertake the construction of a still larger building—a building that would contain rooms for the girls and boarding accommodations for all.

After having had a preliminary sketch of the needed building made, we found that it would cost about ten thousand dollars. We had no money whatever with which to begin; still we decided to give the needed building a name. We knew we could name it, even though we were in doubt about our ability to secure the means for its construction. We decided to call the proposed building Alabama Hall, in honour of the state in which we were labouring. Again Miss Davidson began making efforts to enlist the interest and help of the coloured and white people in and near Tuskegee. They responded willingly, in proportion to their means. The students, as in the case of our first building, Porter Hall, began digging out the dirt in order to allow the laying of the foundations.

When we seemed at the end of our resources, so far as securing money was concerned, something occurred which showed the greatness of General Armstrong—something which proved how far he was above the ordinary individual. When we were in the midst of great anxiety as to where and how

we were to get funds for the new building, I received a telegram from General Armstrong asking me if could spend a month travelling with him through the North, and asking me, if I could do so, to come to Hampton at once. Of course I accepted General Armstrong's invitation, and went to Hampton immediately. On arriving there I found that the General had decided to take a quartette of singers through the North, and hold meetings for a month in important cities, at which meetings he and I were to speak. Imagine my surprise when the General told me, further, that these meetings were to be held, not in the interests of Hampton but in the interests of Tuskegee, and that the Hampton Institute was to be responsible for all the expenses.

Although he never told me so in so many words, I found out that General Armstrong took this method of introducing me to the people of the North, as well as for the sake of securing some immediate funds to be used in the erection of Alabama Hall. A weak and narrow man would have reasoned that all the money which came to Tuskegee in this way would be just so much taken from the Hampton Institute; but none of these selfish or short-sighted feelings ever entered the breast of General Armstrong. He was too big to be little, too good to be mean. He knew that the people in the North who gave money gave it for the purpose of helping the whole cause of Negro civilization, and not merely for the advancement of any one school. The General knew, too, that the way to strengthen Hampton was to make it a centre of unselfish power in the working out of the whole Southern problem.

In regard to the addresses which I was to make in the North, I recall just one piece of advice which the General gave me. He said: "Give them an idea for every word." I think it would be hard to improve upon this advice; and it might be made to apply to all public speaking From that time to the present I have always tried to keep his advice in mind.

Meetings were held in New York, Brooklyn, Boston, Philadelphia, and other large cities, and at all of these meetings General Armstrong pleaded, together with myself, for help, not for Hampton, but for Tuskegee. At these meetings an especial effort was made to secure help for the building of Alabama Hall, as well as to introduce the school to the attention of the general public. In both these respects the meetings proved successful.

After that kindly introduction I began going North alone to secure funds. During the last fifteen years I have been compelled to spend a large proportion of my time away from the school, in an effort to secure money to provide for the growing needs of the institution. In my efforts to get funds I have had some experiences that may be of interest to my readers. Time and time

again I have been asked, by people who are trying to secure money for phil-anthropic purposes, what rule or rules I followed to secure the interest and help of people who were able to contribute money to worthy objects. As far as the science of what is called begging can be reduced to rules, I would say that I have had but two rules. First, always to do my whole duty regarding making our work known to individuals and organizations; and, second, not to worry about the results. This second rule has been the hardest for me to live up to. When bills are on the eve of falling due, with not a dollar in hand with which to meet them, it is pretty difficult to learn not to worry, although I think I am learning more and more each year that all worry simply con-sumes, and to no purpose, just so much physical and mental strength that might otherwise be given to effective work. After considerable experience in coming into contact with wealthy and noted men, I have observed that those who have accomplished the greatest results are those who "keep under the body"; are those who never grow excited or lose self-control, but are always calm, self-possessed, patient, and polite. I think that President William McKinley is the best example of a man of this class that I have ever seen.

In order to be successful in any kind of undertaking, I think the main thing is for one to grow to the point where he completely forgets himself; that is, to lose himself in a great cause. In proportion as one loses himself in this way, in the same degree does he get the highest happiness out of his work.

My experience in getting money for Tuskegee has taught me to have no patience with those people who are always condemning the rich because they are rich, and because they do not give more to objects of charity. In the first place, those who are guilty of such sweeping criticisms do not know how many people would be made poor, and how much suffering would result, if wealthy people were to part all at once with any large proportion of their wealth in a way to disorganize and cripple great business enterprises. Then very few persons have any idea of the large number of applications for help that rich people are constantly being flooded with. I know wealthy people who receive as many as twenty calls a day for help. More than once, when I have gone into the offices of rich men, I have found half a dozen persons waiting to see them, and all come for the same purpose, that of securing money. And all these calls in person, to say nothing of the applications received through the mails. Very few people have any idea of the amount of money given away by persons who never permit their names to be known. I have often heard persons condemned for not giving away money, who, to my

own knowledge, were giving away thousands of dollars every year so quietly that the world knew nothing about it.

As an example of this, there are two ladies in New York, whose names rarely appear in print, but who, in a quiet way, have given us the means with which to erect three large and important buildings during the last eight years. Besides the gift of these buildings, they have made other generous donations to the school. And they not only help Tuskegee, but they are constantly seeking opportunities to help other worthy causes.

Although it has been my privilege to be the medium through which a good many hundred thousand dollars have been received for the work at Tuskegee, I have always avoided what the world calls "begging." I often tell people that I have never "begged" any money, and that I am not a "beggar." My experience and observation have convinced me that persistent asking outright for money from the rich does not, as a rule, secure help. I have usually proceeded on the principle that persons who possess sense enough to earn money have sense enough to know how to give it away, and that the mere making known of the facts regarding Tuskegee, and especially the facts regarding the work of the graduates, has been more effective than outright begging. I think that the presentation of facts, on a high, dignified plane, is all the begging that most rich people care for.

While the work of going from door to door and from office to office is hard, disagreeable, and costly in bodily strength, yet it has some compensations. Such work gives one a rare opportunity to study human nature. It also has its compensations in giving one an opportunity to meet some of the best people in the world—to be more correct, I think I should say the best people in the world. When one takes a broad survey of the country, he will find that the most useful and influential people in it are those who take the deepest interest in institutions that exist for the purpose of making the world better.

At one time, when I was in Boston, I called at the door of a rather wealthy lady, and was admitted to the vestibule and sent up my card. While I was waiting for an answer, her husband came in, and asked me in the most abrupt manner what I wanted. When I tried to explain the object of my call, he became still more ungentlemanly in his words and manner; and finally grew so excited that I left the house without waiting for a reply from the lady. A few blocks from that house I called to see a gentleman who received me in the most cordial manner. He wrote me his check for a generous sum, and then, before I had had an opportunity to thank him, said: "I am so grateful to you, Mr. Washington, for giving me the opportunity to help a good cause.

It is a privilege to have a share in it. We in Boston are constantly indebted to you for doing *our* work." My experience in securing money convinces me that the first type of man is growing more rare all the time, and that the latter type is increasing; that is, that, more and more, rich people are coming to regard men and women who apply to them for help for worthy objects, not as beggars, but as agents for doing their work.

In the city of Boston I have rarely called upon an individual for funds that I have not been thanked for calling, usually before I could get an opportunity to thank the donor for the money. In that city the donors seem to feel, in a large degree, that an honour is being conferred upon them in their being permitted to give. Nowhere else have I met with, in so large a measure, this fine and Christlike spirit as in the city of Boston, although there are many notable instances of it outside that city. I repeat my belief that the world is growing in the direction of giving. I repeat that the main rule by which I have been guided in collecting money is to do my full duty in regard to giving people who have money an opportunity to help.

In the early years of the Tuskegee school I walked the streets or travelled country roads in the North for days and days without receiving a dollar. Often it has happened, when during the week I had been disappointed in not getting a cent from the very individuals from whom I most expected help, and when I was almost broken down and discouraged, that generous help has come from someone who I had had little idea would give at all.

I recall that on one occasion I obtained information that led me to believe that a gentleman who lived about two miles out in the country from Stamford, Conn., might become interested in our efforts at Tuskegee if our conditions and needs were presented to him. On an unusually cold and stormy day I walked the two miles to see him. After some difficulty I succeeded in securing an interview with him. He listened with some degree of interest to what I had to say, but did not give me anything. I could not help having the feeling that, in a measure, the three hours that I had spent in seeing him had been thrown away. Still I had followed my usual rule of doing my duty. If I had not seen him, I should have felt unhappy over neglect of duty.

Two years after this visit a letter came to Tuskegee from this man, which read like this: "Enclosed I send you a New York draft for ten thousand dollars, to be used in furtherance of your work. I had placed this sum in my will for your school, but deem it wiser to give it to you while I live. I recall with pleasure your visit to me two years ago."

I can hardly imagine any occurrence which could have given me more

genuine satisfaction than the receipt of this draft. It was by far the largest single donation which up to that time the school had ever received. It came at a time when an unusually long period had passed since we had received any money. We were in great distress because of lack of funds, and the nervous strain was tremendous. It is difficult for me to think of any situation that is more trying on the nerves than that of conducting a large institution, with heavy financial obligations to meet, without knowing where the money is to come from to meet these obligations from month to month.

In our case I felt a double responsibility, and this made the anxiety all the more intense. If the institution had been officered by white persons, and had failed, it would have injured the cause of Negro education; but I knew that the failure of our institution, officered by Negroes, would not only mean the loss of a school, but would cause people, in a large degree, to lose faith in the ability of the entire race. The receipt of this draft for ten thousand dollars, under all these circumstances, partially lifted a burden that had been pressing down upon me for days.

From the beginning of our work to the present I have always had the feeling, and lose no opportunity to impress our teachers with the same idea, that the school will always be supported in proportion as the inside of the institution is kept clean and pure and wholesome.

The first time I ever saw the late Collis P. Huntington, the great railroad man, he gave me two dollars for our school. The last time I saw him, which was a few months before he died, he gave me fifty thousand dollars toward our endowment fund. Between these two gifts there were others of generous proportions which came every year from both Mr. and Mrs. Huntington.

Some people may say that it was Tuskegee's good luck that brought to us this gift of fifty thousand dollars. No, it was not luck. It was hard work. Nothing ever comes to one, that is worth having, except as a result of hard work. When Mr. Huntington gave me the first two dollars, I did not blame him for not giving me more, but made up my mind that I was going to convince him by tangible results that we were worthy of larger gifts. For a dozen years I made a strong effort to convince Mr. Huntington of the value of our work. I noted that just in proportion as the usefulness of the school grew, his donations in creased. Never did I meet an individual who took a more kindly and sympathetic interest in our school than did Mr. Huntington. He not only gave money to us, but took time in which to advise me, as a father would a son, about the general conduct of the school.

More than once I have found myself in some pretty tight places while col-

lecting money in the North. The following incident I have never related but once before, for the reason that I feared that people would not believe it. One morning I found myself in Providence, Rhode Island, without a cent of money with which to buy breakfast. In crossing the street to see a lady from whom I hoped to get some money, I found a bright new twenty-five-cent piece in the middle of the street car track. I not only had this twenty-five cents for my breakfast, but within a few minutes I had a donation from the lady on whom I had started to call.

At one of our Commencements I was bold enough to invite the Rev. E. Winchester Donald, D. D., rector of Trinity Church, Boston, to preach the Commencement sermon. As we then had no room large enough to accommodate all who would be present, the place of meeting was under a large, improvised arbour, built partly of brush and partly of rough boards. Soon after Dr. Donald had begun speaking, the rain came down in torrents, and he had to stop, while some one held an umbrella over him.

The boldness of what I had done never dawned upon me until I saw the picture made by the rector of Trinity Church standing before that large audience under an old umbrella, waiting for the rain to cease so that he could go on with his address.

It was not very long before the rain ceased and Dr. Donald finished his sermon; and an excellent sermon it was, too, in spite of the weather. After he had gone to his room, and had gotten the wet threads of his clothes dry. Dr. Donald ventured the remark that a large chapel at Tuskegee would not be out of place. The next day a letter came from two ladies who were then travelling in Italy, saying that they had decided to give us the money for such a chapel as we needed.

A short time ago we received twenty thousand dollars from Mr. Andrew Carnegie, to be used for the purpose of erecting a new library building. Our first library and reading-room were in a corner of a shanty, and the whole thing occupied a space about five by twelve feet. It required ten years of work before I was able to secure Mr. Carnegie's interest and help. The first time I saw him, ten years ago, he seemed to take but little interest in our school, but I was determined to show him that we were worthy of his help. After ten years of hard work I wrote him a letter reading as follows:

December 15, 1900.

Mr. Andrew Carnegie, 5 W. Fifty-First St., New York.

Dear Sir: Complying with the request which you made of me when I saw you at your residence a few days ago, I now submit in writing an appeal for a library building for our institution.

We have 1100 students, 86 officers and instructors, together with their families, and about 200 coloured people living near the school, all of whom would make use of the library building.

We have over 12,000 books, periodicals, etc., gifts from our friends, but we have no suitable place for them, and we have no suitable reading-room.

Our graduates go to work in every section of the South, and whatever knowledge might be obtained in the library would serve to assist in the elevation of the whole Negro race.

Such a building as we need could be erected for about $20,000. All of the work for the building, such as brickmaking, brick-masonry, carpentry, blacksmithing, etc., would be done by the students. The money which you would give would not only supply the building, but the erection of the building would give a large number of students an opportunity to learn the building trades, and the students would use the money paid to them to keep them selves in school. I do not believe that a similar amount of money often could be made go so far in uplifting a whole race.

If you wish further information, I shall be glad to furnish it.

Yours truly,
Booker T. Washington, Principal.

The next mail brought back the following reply:

"I will be very glad to pay the bills for the library building as they are incurred, to the extent of twenty thousand dollars, and I am glad of this opportunity to show the interest I have in your noble work."

I have found that strict business methods go a long way in securing the interest of rich people. It has been my constant aim at Tuskegee to carry out, in our financial and other operations, such business methods as would be approved of by any New York banking house.

I have spoken of several large gifts to the school; but by far the greater proportion of the money that has built up the institution has come in the form of small donations from persons of moderate means. It is upon these small gifts, which carry with them the interest of hundreds of donors, that any philanthropic work must depend largely for its support. In my efforts to get money I have often been surprised at the patience and deep interest of the ministers, who are besieged on every hand and at all hours of the day for help. If no other consideration had convinced me of the value of the Christian life, the Christlike work which the Church of all denominations in America has done during the last thirty-five years for the elevation of the black man would have made me a Christian. In a large degree it has been the pennies, the nickels, and the dimes which have come from the Sunday-schools, the Christian Endeavour societies, and the missionary societies, as well as from the Church proper, that have helped to elevate the Negro at so rapid a rate.

This speaking of small gifts reminds me to say that very few Tuskegee graduates fail to send us an annual contribution. These contributions range from twenty-five cents up to ten dollars.

Soon after beginning our third year's work we were surprised to receive money from three special, sources, and up to the present time we have continued to receive help from them. First, the State Legislature of Alabama increased its annual appropriation from two thousand dollars to three thousand dollars; I might add that still later it increased this sum to four thousand five hundred dollars a year. The effort to secure this increase was led by the Hon. M. F. Foster, the member of the Legislature from Tuskegee. Second, we received one thousand dollars from the John F. Slater Fund. Our work seemed to please the trustees of this fund, as they soon began increasing their annual grant. This has been added to from time to time until at present we receive eleven thousand dollars annually from this Fund. The other help to which I have referred came in the shape of an allowance from the Peabody Fund. This was at first five hundred dollars, but it has since been increased to fifteen hundred dollars.

The effort to secure help from the Slater and Peabody Funds brought me into contact with two rare men—men who have had much to do in shaping the policy for the education of the Negro. I refer to the Hon. J. L. M. Curry, of Washington, who is the general agent for these two funds, and Mr. Morris K. Jesup, of New York. Dr. Curry is a native of the South, an ex-Confederate soldier, yet I do not believe there is any man in the country who is more

deeply interested in the highest welfare of the Negro than Dr. Curry, or one who is more free from race prejudice. He enjoys the unique distinction of possessing to an equal degree the confidence of the black man and the Southern white man. I shall never forget the first time I met him. It was in Richmond, Va., where he was then living. I had heard much about him. When I first went into his presence, trembling because of my youth and inexperience, he took me by the hand so cordially, and spoke such encouraging words, and gave me such helpful advice regarding the proper course to pursue, that I came to know him then, as I have known him ever since, as a high example of one who is constantly and unselfishly at work for the betterment of humanity.

Mr. Morris K. Jesup, the treasurer of the Slater Fund, I refer to because I know of no man of wealth and large and complicated business responsibilities who gives not only money but his time and thought to the subject of the proper method of elevating the Negro to the extent that is true of Mr. Jesup. It is very largely through his effort and influence that during the last few years the subject of industrial education has assumed the importance that it has, and been placed on its present footing.

CHAPTER XIII

Two Thousand Miles For A Five-Minute Speech

Soon after the opening of our boarding department, quite a number of students who evidently were worthy, but who were so poor that they did not have any money to pay even the small charges at the school, began applying for admission. This class was composed of both men and women. It was a great trial to refuse admission to these applicants, and in 1884 we established a night-school to accommodate a few of them.

The night-school was organized on a plan similar to the one which I had helped to establish at Hampton. At first it was composed of about a dozen students. They were admitted to the night school only when they had no money with which to pay any part of their board in the regular day-school. It was further required that they must work for ten hours during the day at some trade or industry, and study academic branches for two hours during the evening. This was the requirement for the first one or two years of their

stay. They were to be paid something above the cost of their board, with the understanding that all of their earnings, except a very small part, were to be reserved in the school's treasury, to be used for paying their board in the regular day-school after they had entered that department. The night-school, started in this manner, has grown until there are at present four hundred and fifty-seven students enrolled in it alone.

There could hardly be a more severe test of a student's worth than this branch of the Institute's work. It is largely because it furnishes such a good opportunity to test the backbone of a student that I place such high value upon our night-school. Any one who is willing to work ten hours a day at the brick-yard, or in the laundry, through one or two years, in order that he or she may have the privilege of studying academic branches for two hours in the evening, has enough bottom to warrant being further educated.

After the student has left the night-school he enters the day-school, where he takes academic branches four days in a week, and works at his trade two days. Besides this he usually works at his trade during the three summer months. As a rule, after a student has succeeded in going through the night-school test, he finds a way to finish the regular course in industrial and academic training. No student, no matter how much money he may be able to command, is permitted to go through school without doing manual labour. In fact, the industrial work is now as popular as the academic branches. Some of the most successful men and women who have graduated from the institution obtained their start in the night-school.

While a great deal of stress is laid upon the industrial side of the work at Tuskegee, we do not neglect or overlook in any degree the religious and spiritual side. The school is strictly undenominational, but it is thoroughly Christian, and the spiritual training of the students is not neglected. Our preaching service, prayer-meetings, Sunday-school, Christian Endeavour Society, Young Men's Christian Association, and various missionary organizations, testify to this.

In 1885, Miss Olivia Davidson, to whom I have already referred as being largely responsible for the success of the school during its early history, and I were married. During our married life she continued to divide her time and strength between our home and the work for the school. She not only continued to work in the school at Tuskegee, but also kept up her habit of going North to secure funds. In 1889 she died, after four years of happy married life and eight years of hard and happy work for the school. She literally wore herself out in her never ceasing efforts in behalf of the work that she so dear-

ly loved. During our married life there were born to us two bright, beautiful boys, Booker and Ernest Davidson. The older of these, Booker, has already mastered the brickmaker's trade at Tuskegee.

I have often been asked how I began the practice of public speaking: In answer I would say that I never planned to give any large part of my life to speaking in public. I have always had more of an ambition to *do* things than merely to talk *about* doing them. It seems that when I went North with General Armstrong to speak at the series of public meetings to which I have referred, the President of the National Educational Association, the Hon. Thomas W. Bicknell, was present at one of those meetings and heard me speak. A few days afterward he sent me an invitation to deliver an address at the next meeting of the Educational Association. This meeting was to be held in Madison, Wis. I accepted the invitation. This was, in a sense, the beginning of my public-speaking career.

On the evening that I spoke before the Association there must have been not far from four thousand persons present. Without my knowing it, there were a large number of people present from Alabama, and some from the town of Tuskegee. These white people afterward frankly told me that they went to this meeting expecting to hear the South roundly abused, but were pleasantly surprised to find that there was no word of abuse in my address. On the contrary, the South was given credit for all the praiseworthy things that it had done. A white lady who was teacher in a college in Tuskegee wrote back to the local paper that she was gratified, as well as surprised, to note the credit which I gave the white people of Tuskegee for their help in get tiny the school started. This address at Madison was the first that I had delivered that in any large measure dealt with the general problem of the races. Those who heard it seemed to be pleased with what I said and with the general position that I took.

When I first came to Tuskegee, I determined that I would make it my home, that I would take as much pride in the right actions of the people of the town as any white man could do, and that I would, at the same time, deplore the wrong-doing of the people as much as any white man. I determined never to say anything in a public address in the North that I would not be willing to say in the South. I early learned that it is a hard matter to convert an individual by abusing him, and that this is more often accomplished by giving credit for all the praiseworthy actions performed than by calling attention alone to all the evil done.

While pursuing this policy I have not failed, at the proper time and in the

proper manner, to call attention, in no uncertain terms, to the wrongs which any part of the South has been guilty of. I have found that there is a large element in the South that is quick to respond to straightforward, honest criticism of any wrong policy. As a rule, the place to criticise the South, when criticism is necessary, is in the South—not in Boston. A Boston man who came to Alabama to criticise Boston would not effect so much good, I think, as one who had his word of criticism to say in Boston.

In this address at Madison I took the ground that the policy to be pursued with reference to the races was, by every honourable means, to bring them together and to encourage the cultivation of friendly relations, instead of doing that which would embitter. I further contended that, in relation to his vote, the Negro should more and more consider the interests of the community in which he lived, rather than seek alone to please some one who lived a thousand miles away from him and from his interests.

In this address I said that the whole future of the Negro rested largely upon the question as to whether or not he should make himself, through his skill, intelligence, and character, of such undeniable value to the community in which he lived that the community could not dispense with his presence. I said that any individual who learned to do something better than anybody else—learned to do a common thing in an uncommon manner—had solved his problem, regardless of the colour of his skin, and that in proportion as the Negro learned to produce what other people wanted and must have, in the same proportion would he be respected.

I spoke of an instance where one of our graduates had produced two hundred and sixty-six bushels of sweet potatoes from an acre of ground, in a community where the average production had been only forty-nine bushels to the acre. He had been able to do this by reason of his knowledge of the chemistry of the soil and by his knowledge of improved methods of agriculture. The white farmers in the neighbourhood respected him, and came to him for ideas regarding the raising of sweet potatoes. These white farmers honoured and respected him because he, by his skill and knowledge, had added something to the wealth and the comfort of the community in which he lived. I explained that my theory of education for the Negro would not, for example, confine him for all time to farm life—to the production of the best and the most sweet potatoes—but that, if he succeeded in this line of industry, he could lay the foundations upon which his children and grand children could grow to higher and more important things in life.

Such, in brief, were some of the views I advocated in this first address

dealing with the broad question of the relations of the two races, and since that time I have not found any reason for changing my views on any important point.

In my early life I used to cherish a feeling of ill will toward any one who spoke in bitter terms against the Negro, or who advocated measures that tended to oppress the black man or take from him opportunities for growth in the most complete manner. Now, whenever I hear any one advocating measures that are meant to curtail the development of another, I pity the individual who would do this. I pity him because I know that the one who makes this mistake does so because of his own lack of opportunity for the highest kind of growth. I pity him because I know that he is trying to stop the progress of the world, and because I know that in time the development and the ceaseless advance of humanity will make him ashamed of his weak and narrow position. One might as well try to stop the progress of a mighty railroad train by throwing his body across the track, as to try to stop the growth of the world in the direction of giving mankind more intelligence, more culture, more skill, more liberty, and in the direction of extending more sympathy and more brotherly kindness.

The address which I delivered at Madison, before the National Educational Association, gave me a rather wide introduction in the North, and soon after that opportunities began offering themselves for me to address audiences there.

I was anxious, however, that the way might also be opened for me to speak directly to a representative Southern white audience. A partial opportunity of this kind, one that seemed to me might serve as an entering wedge, presented itself in 1893, when the International meeting of Christian Workers was held at Atlanta, Ga. When this invitation came to me, I had engagements in Boston that seemed to make it impossible for me to speak in Atlanta. Still, after looking over my list of dates and places carefully, I found that I could take a train from Boston that would get me into Atlanta about thirty minutes before my address was to be delivered, and that I could remain in that city about sixty minutes before taking another train for Boston. My invitation to speak in Atlanta stipulated that I was to confine my address to five minutes. The question, then, was whether or not I could put enough into a five-minute address to make it worth while for me to make such a trip.

I knew that the audience would be largely composed of the most influential class of white men and women, and that it would be a rare opportunity for me to let them know what we were trying to do at Tuskegee, as well

as to speak to them about the relations of the races. So I decided to make the trip. I spoke for five minutes to an audience of two thousand people, composed mostly of Southern and Northern whites. What I said seemed to be received with favour and enthusiasm. The Atlanta papers of the next day commented in friendly terms on my address, and a good deal was said about it different parts of the country. I felt that I had in some degree accomplished my object—that of getting a hearing from the dominant class of the South.

The demands made upon me for public addresses continued to increase, coming in about equal numbers from my own people and from Northern whites. I gave as much time to these addresses as I could spare from the immediate work at Tuskegee. Most of the addresses in the North were made for the direct purpose of getting funds with which to support the school. Those delivered before the coloured people had for their main object the impressing upon them of the importance of industrial and technical education in addition to academic and religious training.

I now come to that one of the incidents in my life which seems to have excited the greatest amount of interest, and which perhaps went further than anything else in giving me a reputation that in a sense might be called National. I refer to the address which I delivered at the opening of the Atlanta Cotton states and International Exposition, at Atlanta, Gal, September 18, 1895.

So much has been said and written about this incident, and so many questions have been asked me concerning the address, that perhaps I may be excused for taking up the matter with some detail. The five-minute address in Atlanta, which I came from Boston to deliver, was possibly the prime cause for an opportunity being given me to make the second address there. In the spring of 1895 I received a telegram from prominent citizens in Atlanta asking me to accompany a committee from that city to Washington for the purpose of appearing before a committee of Congress in the interest of securing Government help for the Exposition. The committee was composed of about twenty-five of the most prominent and most influential white men of Georgia. All the members of this committee were white men except Bishop Grant, Bishop Gaines, and myself. The mayor and several other city and state officials spoke before the committee. They were followed by the two coloured bishops. My name was the last on the list of speakers. I had never before appeared before such a committee, nor had I ever delivered any address in the capital of the Nation. I had many misgivings as to what I ought to say, and as to the impression that my address would make. While I

cannot recall in detail what I said, I remember that I tried to impress upon the committee, with all the earnestness and plainness of any language that I could command, that if Congress wanted to do something which would assist in ridding the South of the race question and making friends between the two races, it should, in every proper way, encourage the material and intellectual growth of both races. I said that the Atlanta Exposition would present an opportunity for both races to show what advance they had made since freedom, and would at the same time afford encouragement to them to make still greater progress.

I tried to emphasize the fact that while the Negro should not be deprived by unfair means of the franchise, political agitation alone would not save him, and that back of the ballot he must have property, industry, skill, economy, intelligence, and character, and that no race without these elements could permanently succeed. I said that in granting the appropriation Congress could do something that would prove to be of real and lasting value to both races, and that it was the first great opportunity of the kind that had been presented since the close of the Civil War.

I spoke for fifteen or twenty minutes, and was surprised at the close of my address to receive the hearty congratulations of the Georgia committee and of the members of Congress who were present. The Committee was unanimous in making a favourable report, and in a few days the bill passes Congress. With the passing of this bill the success of the Atlanta Exposition was assured.

Soon after this trip to Washington the directors of the Exposition decided that it would be a fitting recognition of the coloured race to erect a large and attractive building which should be devoted wholly to showing the progress of the Negro since freedom. It was further decided to have the building designed and erected wholly by Negro mechanics. This plan was carried out. In design, beauty, and general finish the Negro Building was equal to the others on the grounds.

After it was decided to have a separate Negro exhibit, the question arose as to who should take charge of it. The officials of the Exposition were anxious that I should assume this responsibility, but I declined to do so, on the plea that the work at Tuskegee at that time demanded my time and strength. Largely at my suggestion, Mr. I. Garland Penn, of Lynchburg, Va., was selected to be at the head of the Negro department. I gave him all the aid that I could. The Negro exhibit, as a whole, was large and creditable. The two exhibits in this department which attracted the greatest amount of attention

were those from the Hampton Institute and the Tuskegee Institute. The people who seemed to be the most surprised, as well as pleased, at what they saw in the Negro Building were the Southern white people.

As the day for the opening of the Exposition drew near, the Board of Directors began preparing the programme for the opening exercises. In the discussion from day to day of the various features of this programme, the question came up as to the advisability of putting a member of the Negro race on for one of the opening addresses, since the Negroes had been asked to take such a prominent part in the Exposition. It was argued, further, that such recognition would mark the good feeling prevailing between the two races. Of course there were those who were opposed to any such recognition of the rights of the Negro, but the Board of Directors, composed of men who represented the best and most progressive element in the South, had their way, and voted to invite a black man to speak on the opening day. The next thing was to decide upon the person who was thus to represent the Negro race. After the question had been canvassed for several days, the directors voted unanimously to ask me to deliver one of the opening-day addresses, and in a few days after that I received the official invitation.

The receiving of this invitation brought to me sense of responsibility that it would be hard for any one not placed in my position to appreciate. What were my feelings when this invitation came to me? I remembered that I had been a slave; that my early years had been spent in the lowest depths of poverty and ignorance, and that I had had little opportunity to prepare me for such a responsibility as this. It was only a few years before that time mat any white man in the audience might have claimed me as his slave; and it was easily possible that some of my former owners might be present to hear me speak.

I knew, too, that this was the first time in the entire history of the Negro that a member of my race had been asked to speak from the same platform with white Southern men and women on any important National occasion. I was asked now to speak to an audience composed of the wealth and culture of the white South, the representatives of my former masters. I knew, too, that while the greater part of my audience would be composed of Southern people, yet there would be present a large number of Northern whites, as well as a great many men and women of my own race.

I was determined to say nothing that I did not feel from the bottom of my heart to be true and right. When the invitation came to me, there was not one word of intimation as to what I should say or as to what I should omit. In this I felt that the Board of Directors had paid a tribute to me. They

knew that by one sentence I could have blasted, in a large degree, the success of the Exposition. I was also painfully conscious of the fact that, while I must be true to my own race in my utterances, I had it in my power to make such an ill-timed ad dress as would result in preventing any similar invitation being extended to a black man again for years to come. I was equally determined to be true to the North, as well as to the best element of the white South, in what I had to say.

The papers, North and South, had taken up the discussion of my coming speech, and as the time for it drew near this discussion became more and more widespread. Not a few of the Southern white papers were unfriendly to the idea of my speaking. From my own race I received many suggestions as to what I ought to say. I prepared myself as best I could for the address, but as the eighteenth of September drew nearer, the heavier my heart be came, and the more I feared that my effort would prove a failure and a disappointment.

The invitation had come at a time when I was very busy with my school work, as it was the be ginning of our school year. After preparing my address, I went through it, as I usually do with all those utterances which I consider particularly important, with Mrs. Washington, and she approved of what I intended to say. On the sixteenth of September, the day before I was to start for Atlanta, so many of the Tuskegee teachers expressed a desire to hear my address that I consented to read it to them in a body. When I had done so, and had heard their criticisms and comments, I felt somewhat relieved, since they seemed to think well of what I had to say.

On the morning of September 17, together with Mrs. Washington and my three children, I started for Atlanta. I felt a good deal as I suppose a man feels when he is on his way to the gallows. In passing through the town of Tuskegee I met a white farmer who lived some distance out in the country. In a jesting manner this man said: "Washington, you have spoken before the Northern white people, the Negroes in the South, and to us country white people in the South; but in Atlanta, to-morrow, you will have before you the Northern whites, the Southern whites, and the Negroes all together. I am afraid that you have got yourself into a tight place." This farmer diagnosed the situation correctly, but his frank words did not add anything to my comfort.

In the course of the journey from Tuskegee to Atlanta both coloured and white people came to the train to point me out, and discussed with perfect freedom, in my hearing, what was going to take place the next day. We were met by a committee in Atlanta. Almost the first thing that I heard when I got off the train in that city was an expression something like this, from an old

coloured man near by: "Dat's de man of my race what's gwine to make a speech at de Exposition to-morrow. I'se sho' gwine to hear him."

Atlanta was literally packed, at the time, with people from all parts of this country, and with representatives of foreign governments, as well as with military and civic organizations. The after noon papers had forecasts of the next day's proceedings in flaring headlines. All this tended to add to my burden. I did not sleep much that night. The next morning, before day, I went carefully over what I intended to say. I also kneeled down and asked God's blessing upon my effort. Right here, perhaps, I ought to add that I make it a rule never to go before an audience, on any occasion, without asking the blessing of God upon what I want to say.

I always make it a rule to make especial preparation for each separate address. No two audiences are exactly alike. It is my aim to reach and talk to the heart of each individual audience, taking it into my confidence very much as I would a person. When I am speaking to an audience, I care little for how what I am saying is going to sound in the newspapers, or to another audience, or to an individual. At the time, the audience before me absorbs all my sympathy, thought, and energy.

Early in the morning a committee called to escort me to my place in the procession which was to march to the Exposition grounds. In this procession were prominent coloured citizens in carriages, as well as several Negro military organizations. I noted that the Exposition officials seemed to go out of their way to see that all of the coloured people in the procession were properly placed and properly treated. The procession was about three hours in reaching the Exposition grounds, and during all of this time the sun was shining down upon us disagreeably hot. When we reached the grounds, the heat, together with my nervous anxiety, made me feel as if I were about ready to collapse, and to feel that my address was not going to be a success. When I entered the audience-room, I found it packed with humanity from bottom to top, and there were thousands outside who could not get in.

The room was very large, and well suited to public speaking. When I entered the room, there were vigorous cheers from the coloured portion of the audience, and faint cheers from some of the white people. I had been told, while I had been in Atlanta, that while many white people were going to be present to hear me speak, simply out of curiosity, and that others who would be present would be in full sympathy with me, there was a still larger element of the audience which would consist of those who were going to be present for the purpose of hearing me make a fool of myself, or, at least, of

hearing me say some foolish thing, so that they could say to the officials who had invited me to speak, "I told you so!"

One of the trustees of the Tuskegee Institute, as well as my personal friend, Mr. William H. Baldwin, Jr. was at the time General Manager of the Southern Railroad, and happened to be in Atlanta on that day. He was so nervous about the kind of reception that I would have, and the effect that my speech would produce, that he could not persuade himself to go into the building, but walked back and forth in the grounds outside until the Opening exercises were over.

CHAPTER XIV

The Atlanta Exposition Address

The Atlanta Exposition, at which I had been asked to make an address as a representative of the Negro race, as stated in the last chapter, was opened with a short address from Governor Bullock. After other interesting exercises, including an invocation from Bishop Nelson, of Georgia, a dedicatory ode by Albert Howell, Jr., and addresses by the President of the Exposition and Mrs. Joseph Thompson, the President of the Woman's Board, Governor Bullock introduced me with the words, "We have with us to-day a representative of Negro enterprise and Negro civilization."

When I arose to speak, there was considerable cheering, especially from the coloured people. As I remember it now the thing that was uppermost in my mind was the desire to say something that would cement the friendship of the races and bring about hearty coöperation between them. So far as my outward surroundings were concerned, the only thing that I recall distinctly now is that when I got up, I saw thousands of eyes looking intently into my face. The following is the address which I delivered:—

MR. PRESIDENT AND GENTLEMEN OF THE BOARD
OF DIRECTORS AND CITIZENS.

One-third of the population of the South is of the Negro race. No enterprise seeking the material, civil, or moral welfare of this section can disregard this element of our population and reach the highest success. I but convey to

you, Mr. President and Directors, the sentiment of the masses of my race when I say that in no way have the value and manhood of the American Negro been more fittingly and generously recognized than by the managers of this magnificent Exposition at every stage of its progress. It is a recognition that will do more to cement the friendship of the two races than any occurrence since the dawn of our freedom.

Not only this, but the opportunity here afforded will awaken among us a new era of industrial progress. Ignorant and inexperienced, it is not strange that in the first years of our new life we began at the top instead of at the bottom; that a seat in Congress or the state legislature was more sought than real estate or industrial skill: that the convention of stump speaking had more attractions than starting a dairy farm or truck garden.

A ship lost at sea for many days suddenly sighted a friendly vessel. From the mast of the unfortunate vessel was seen a signal, "Water, water; we die of thirst!" The answer from the friendly vessel at once came back, "Cast down your bucket where you are." A second time the signal, "Water, water; send us water!" ran up from the distressed vessel, and was answered, "Cast down your bucket where you are." And a third and fourth signal for water was answered, "Cast down your bucket where you are." The captain of the distressed vessel, at last heeding the injunction, cast down his bucket, and it came up full of fresh, sparkling water from the mouth of the Amazon River. To those of my race who depend on bettering their condition in a foreign land or who underestimate the importance of cultivating friendly relations with the Southern white man, who is their next-door neighbour, I would say: "Cast down your bucket where you are"—cast it down in making friends in every manly way of the people of all races by whom we are surrounded.

Cast it down in agriculture, mechanics, in commerce, in domestic service, and in the professions. And in this connection it is well to bear in mind that whatever other sins the South may be called to bear, when it comes to business, pure and simple, it is in the South that the Negro is given a man's chance in the commercial world, and in nothing is this Exposition more eloquent than in emphasizing this chance. Our greatest danger is that in the great leap from slavery to freedom we may overlook the fact that the masses of us are to live by the productions of our hands, and fail to keep in mind that we shall prosper in proportion as we learn to dignify and glorify common labour and put brains and skill into the common occupations of life; shall prosper in proportion as we learn to draw the line between the superficial and the substantial, the ornamental gewgaws of life and the useful. No

race can prosper till it learns that there is as much dignity in tilling a field as in writing a poem. It is at the bottom of life we must begin, and not at the top. Nor should we permit our grievances to overshadow our opportunities.

To those of the white race who look to the incoming of those of foreign birth and strange tongue and habits for the prosperity of the South, were I permitted I would repeat what I say to my own race, "Cast down your bucket where you are." Cast it down among the eight millions of Negroes whose habits you know, whose fidelity and love you have tested in days when to have proved treacherous meant the ruin of your firesides. Cast down your bucket among these people who have, without strikes and labour wars, tilled your fields, cleared your forests, builded your railroads and cities, and brought forth treasures from the bowels of the earth, and helped make possible this magnificent representation of the progress of the South. Casting down your bucket among my people, helping and encouraging them as you are doing on these grounds, and to education of head, hand, and heart, you will find that they will buy your surplus land, make blossom the waste places in your fields, and run your factories. While doing this, you can be sure in the future, as in the past, that you and your families will be surrounded by the most patient, faithful, law-abiding, and unresentful people that the world has seen. As we have proved our loyalty to you in the past, in nursing your children, watching by the sick-bed of your mothers and fathers, and often following them with tear-dimmed eyes to their graves, so in the future, in our humble way, we shall stand by you with a devotion that no foreigner can approach, ready to lay down our lives, if need be, in defence of yours, interlacing our industrial, commercial, civil, and religious life with yours in a way that shall make the interests of both races one. In all things that are purely social we can be as separate as the fingers, yet one as the hand in all things essential to mutual progress.

There is no defence or security for any of us except in the highest intelligence and development of all. If anywhere there are efforts tending to curtail the fullest growth of the Negro, let these efforts be turned into stimulating, encouraging, and making him the most useful and intelligent citizen. Effort or means so invested will pay a thousand per cent. interest. These efforts will be twice blessed—"blessing him that gives and him that takes."
There is no escape through law of man or God from the inevitable:—

> The laws of changeless justice bind
> Oppressor with oppressed;

And close as sin and suffering joined
We march to fate abreast.

Nearly sixteen millions of hands will aid you in pulling the load upward, or they will pull against you the load downward. We shall constitute one-third and more of the ignorance and crime of the South, or one-third its intelligence and progress; we shall contribute one-third to the business and industrial prosperity of the South, or we shall prove a veritable body of death, stagnating, depressing, retarding every effort to advance the body politic.

Gentlemen of the Exposition, as we present to you our humble effort at an exhibition of our progress, you must not expect overmuch. Starting thirty years ago with ownership here and there in a few quilts and pumpkins and chickens (gathered from miscellaneous sources), remember the path that has led from these to the inventions and production of agricultural implements, buggies, steam-engines, newspapers, books, statuary, carving, paintings, the management of drug-stores and banks, has not been trodden without contact with thorns and thistles. While we take pride in what we exhibit as a result of our independent efforts, we do not for a moment forget that our part in this exhibition would fall far short of your expectations but for the constant help that has come to our educational life, not only from the Southern states, but especially from Northern philanthropists, who have made their gifts a constant stream of blessing and encouragement.

The wisest among my race understand that the agitation of questions of social equality is the extremest folly, and that progress in the enjoyment of all the privileges that will come to us must be the result of severe and constant struggle rather than of artificial forcing. No race that has anything to contribute to the markets of the world is long in any degree ostracized. It is important and right that all privileges of the law be ours, but it is vastly more important that we be prepared for the exercises of these privileges. The opportunity to earn a dollar in a factory just now is worth infinitely more than the opportunity to spend a dollar in an opera-house.

In conclusion, may I repeat that nothing in thirty years has given us more hope and encouragement, and drawn us so near to you of the white race, as this opportunity offered by the Exposition; and here bending, as it were, over the altar that represents the results of the struggles of your race and mine, both starting practically empty-handed three decades ago, I pledge that in your effort to work out the great and intricate problem which God has laid at the doors of the South, you shall have at all times the patient, sympathet-

ic help of my race; only let this be constantly in mind, that, while from representations in these buildings of the product of field, of forest, of mine, of factory, letters, and art, much good will come, yet far above and beyond material benefits will be that higher good, that, let us pray God, will come, in a blotting out of sectional differences and racial animosities and suspicions, in a determination to administer absolute justice, in a willing obedience among all classes to the mandates of law. This, this, coupled with our material prosperity, will bring into our beloved South a new heaven and a new earth.

The first thing that I remember, after I had finished speaking, was that Governor Bullock rushed across the platform and took me by the hand, and that others did the same. I received so many and such hearty congratulations that I found it difficult to get out of the building. I did not appreciate to any degree, however, the impression which my address seemed to have made, until the next morning, when I went into the business part of the city. As soon as I was recognized, I was surprised to find myself pointed out and surrounded by a crowd of men who wished to shake hands with me. This was kept up on every street on to which I went, to an extent which embarrassed me so much that I went back to my boarding-place. The next morning I returned to Tuskegee. At the station in Atlanta, and at almost all of the stations at which the train stopped between that city and Tuskegee, I found a crowd of people anxious to shake hands with me.

The papers in all parts of the United States pub fished the address in full, and for months afterward there were complimentary editorial references to it. Mr. Clark Howell, the editor of the Atlanta *Constitution*, telegraphed to a New York paper, among other words, the following, "I do not exaggerate when I say that Professor Booker T. Washington's address yesterday was one of the most notable speeches, both as to character and as to the warmth of its reception, ever delivered to a Southern audience. The address was a revelation. The whole speech is a platform upon which blacks and whites can stand with full justice to each other."

The Boston *Transcript* said editorially: "The speech of Booker T. Washington at the Atlanta Exposition, this week, seems to have dwarfed all the other proceedings and the Exposition itself. The sensation that it has caused in the press has never been equalled."

I very soon began receiving all kinds of propositions from lecture bureaus, and editors of magazines and papers, to take the lecture platform, and to

write articles. One lecture bureau offered me fifty thousand dollars, or two hundred dollars a night and expenses, if I would place my services at its disposal for a given period. To all these communications I replied that my life-work was at Tuskegee; and that whenever I spoke it must be in the interests of the Tuskegee school and my race, and that I would enter into no arrangements that seemed to place a mere commercial value upon my services.

Some days after its delivery I sent a copy of my address to the President of the United States, the Hon. Grover Cleveland. I received from him the following autograph reply:—

> Gray Gables, Buzzard's Bay, Mass.,
> October 6, 1895.
>
> Booker T. Washington, Esq.:
>
> My Dear Sir: I thank you for sending me a copy of your address delivered at the Atlanta Exposition.
>
> I thank you with much enthusiasm for making the address. I have read it with intense interest, and I think the Exposition would be fully justified if it did not do more than furnish the opportunity for its delivery. Your words cannot fail to delight and encourage all who wish well for your race; and if our coloured fellow-citizens do not from your utterances gather new hope and form new determinations to gain every valuable advantage offered them by their citizenship, it will be strange indeed.
>
> Yours very truly,
> Grover Cleveland.

Later I met Mr. Cleveland, for the first time, when, as President, he visited the Atlanta Exposition. At the request of myself and others he consented to spend an hour in the Negro Building, for the purpose of inspecting the Negro exhibit and of giving the coloured people in attendance an opportunity to shake hands with him. As soon as I met Mr. Cleveland I became impressed with his simplicity, greatness, and rugged honesty. I have met him many times since then, both at public functions and at his private residence in Princeton, and the more I see of him the more I admire him. When he visited the Negro Building in Atlanta he seemed to give himself up wholly, for that hour, to the coloured people. He seemed to be as careful to shake

hands with some old coloured "auntie" clad partially in rags, and to take as much pleasure in doing so, as if he were greeting some millionaire. Many of the coloured people took advantage of the occasion to get him to write his name in a book or on a slip of paper. He was as careful and patient in doing this as if he were putting his signature to some great state document.

Mr. Cleveland has not only shown his friendship for me in many personal ways, but has always consented to do anything I have asked of him for our school. This he has done, whether it was to make a personal donation or to use his influence in securing the donations of others. Judging from my personal acquaintance with Mr. Cleveland, I do not believe that he is conscious of possessing any colour prejudice. He is too great for that. In my contact with people I find that, as a rule, it is only the little, narrow people who live for themselves, who never read good books, who do not travel, who never open up their souls in a way to permit them to come into contact with other souls—with the great outside world. No man whose vision is bounded by colour can come into contact with what is highest and best in the world. In meeting men, in many places, I have found that the happiest people are those who do the most for others; the most miserable are those who do the least. I have also found that few things, if any, are capable of making one so blind and narrow as race prejudice. I often say to our students, in the course of my talks to them on Sunday evenings in the chapel, that the longer I live and the more experience I have of the world, the more I am convinced that, after all, the one thing that is most worth living for—and dying for, if need be—is the opportunity of making some one else more happy and more useful.

The coloured people and the coloured newspapers at first seemed to be greatly pleased with the character of my Atlanta address, as well as with its reception. But after the first burst of enthusiasm began to die away, and the coloured people began reading the speech in cold type, some of them seemed to feel that they had been hypnotized. They seemed to feel that I had been too liberal in my remarks toward the Southern whites, and that I had not spoken out strongly enough for what they termed the "rights" of the race. For a while there was a reaction, so far as a certain element of my own race was concerned, but later these reactionary ones seemed to have been won over to my way of believing and acting.

While speaking of changes in public sentiment, I recall that about ten years after the school at Tuskegee was established, I had an experience that I shall never forget. Dr. Lyman Abbott, then the pastor of Plymouth Church, and also editor of the *Outlook* (then the *Christian Union*), asked me to write

a letter for his paper giving my opinion of the exact condition, mental and moral, of the coloured ministers in the South, as based upon my observations. I wrote the letter, giving the exact facts as I conceived them to be. The picture painted was a rather black one—or, since I am black, shall I say "white?" It could not be otherwise with a race but a few years out of slavery, a race which had not had time or opportunity to produce a competent ministry.

What I said soon reached every Negro minister in the country, I think, and the letters of condemnation which I received from them were not few. I think that for a year after the publication of this article every association and every conference or religious body of any kind, of my race, that met, did not fail before adjourning to pass a resolution condemning me, or calling upon me to retract or modify what I had said. Many of these organizations went so far in their resolutions as to advise parents to cease sending their children to Tuskegee. One association even appointed a "missionary" whose duty it was to warn the people against sending their children to Tuskegee. This missionary had a son in the school, and I noticed that, what ever the "missionary" might have said or done with regard to others, he was careful not to take his son away from the institution. Many of the coloured papers, especially those that were the organs of religious bodies, joined in the general of condemnation or demands for retraction.

During the whole time of the excitement, and through all the criticism, I did not utter a word of explanation or retraction. I knew that I was right, and that time and the sober second thought of the people would vindicate me. It was not long before the bishops and other church leaders began to make a careful investigation of the conditions of the ministry, and they found out that I was right. In fact, the oldest and most influential bishop in one branch of the Methodist Church said that my words were far too mild. Very soon public sentiment began making itself felt, in demanding a purifying of the ministry. While this is not yet complete by any means, I think I may say, without egotism, and I have been told by many of our most influential ministers, that my words had much to do with starting a demand for the placing of a higher type of men in the pulpit. I have had the satisfaction of having many who once condemned me thank me heartily for my frank words.

The change of the attitude of the Negro ministry, so far as regards myself, is so complete that at the present time I have no warmer friends among any class than I have among the clergymen. The improvement in the character and life of the Negro ministers is one of the most gratifying evidences of the progress of the race. My experience with them, as well as other events in my

life, convince me that the thing to do, when one feels sure that he has said or done the right thing, and is condemned, is to stand still and keep quiet. If he is right, time will show it.

In the midst of the discussion which was going on concerning my Atlanta speech, I received the letter which I give below, from Dr. Gilman, the President of Johns Hopkins University, who had been made chairman of the judges of award in connection with the Atlanta Exposition:—

JOHNS HOPKINS UNIVERSITY, BALTIMORE,
President's Office, September 30, 1895.

DEAR MR. WASHINGTON: Would it be agreeable to you to be one of the Judges of Award in the Department of Education at Atlanta? If so, I shall be glad to place your name upon the list. A line by telegraph will be welcomed.
Yours very truly,
D. C. GILMAN.

I think I was even more surprised to receive this invitation than I had been to receive the invitation to speak at the opening of the Exposition. It was to be a part of my duty, as one of the jurors, to pass not only upon the exhibits of the coloured schools, but also upon those of the white schools. I accepted the position, and spent a month in Atlanta in performance of the duties which it entailed. The board of jurors was a large one, consisting in all of sixty members. It was about equally divided between Southern white people and Northern white people. Among them were college presidents, leading scientists and men of letters, and specialists in many subjects. When the group of jurors to which I was assigned met for organization, Mr. Thomas Nelson Page, who was one of the number, moved that I be made secretary of that division, and the motion was unanimously adopted. Nearly half of our division were Southern people. In performing my duties in the inspection of the exhibits of white schools I was in every case treated with respect, and at the close of our labours I parted from my associates with regret.

I am often asked to express myself more freely than I do upon the political condition and the political future of my race. These recollections of my experience in Atlanta give me the opportunity to do so briefly. My own belief is, although I have never before said so in so many words, that the time will come when the Negro in the South will be accorded all the political rights

which his ability, character, and material possessions entitle him to. I think, though, that the opportunity to freely exercise such political rights will not come in any large degree through outside or artificial forcing, but will be accorded to the Negro by the Southern white people themselves, and that they will protect him in the exercise of those rights. Just as soon as the South gets over the old feeling that it is being forced by "foreigners," or "aliens," to do something which it does not want to do, I believe that the change in the direction that I have indicated is going to begin. In fact, there are indications that it is already beginning in a slight degree.

Let me illustrate my meaning. Suppose that some months before the opening of the Atlanta Exposition there had been a general demand from the press and public platform outside the South that a Negro be given a place on the opening programme, and that a Negro be placed upon the board of jurors of award. Would any such recognition of the race have taken place? I do not think so. The Atlanta officials went as far as they did because they felt it to be a pleasure, as well as a duty, to reward what they considered merit in the Negro race. Say what we will, there is something in human nature which we cannot blot out, which makes one man, in the end, recognize and reward merit in another, regardless of colour or race.

I believe it is the duty of the Negro—as the greater part of the race is already doing—to deport himself modestly in regard to political claims, depending upon the slow but sure influences that proceed from the possession of property, intelligence, and high character for the full recognition of his political rights. I think that the according of the full exercise of political rights is going to be a matter of natural, slow growth, not an over night, gourd-vine affair. I do not believe that the Negro should cease voting, for a man cannot learn the exercise of self-government by ceasing to vote any more than a boy can learn to swim by keeping out of the water, but I do believe that in his voting he should more and more be influenced by those of intelligence and character who are his next-door neighbours.

I know coloured men who, through the encouragement, help, and advice of Southern white people, have accumulated thousands of dollars' worth of property, but who, at the same time, would never think of going to those same persons for advice concerning the casting of their ballots. This, it seems to me, is unwise and unreasonable, and should cease. In saying this I do not mean that the Negro should buckle, or not vote from principle, for the instant he ceases to vote from principle he loses the confidence and respect of the Southern white man even.

I do not believe that any state should make a law that permits an ignorant and poverty-stricken white man to vote, and prevents a black man in the same condition from voting. Such a law is not only unjust, but it will react, as all unjust laws do, in time; for the effect of such a law is to encourage the Negro to secure education and property, and at the same time it encourages the white man to remain in ignorance and poverty. I believe that in time, through the operation of intelligence and friendly race relations, all cheating at the ballot box in the South will cease. It will become apparent that the white man who begins by cheating a Negro out of his ballot soon learns to cheat a white man out of his, and that the man who does this ends his career of dishonesty by the theft of property or by some equally serious crime. In my opinion, the time will come when the South will encourage all of its citizens to vote. It will see that it pays better, from every standpoint, to have healthy, vigorous life than to have that political stagnation which always results when one-half of the population has no share and no interest in the Government.

As a rule, I believe in universal, free suffrage, but I believe that in the South we are confronted with peculiar conditions that justify the protection of the ballot in many of the states, for a while at least, either by an educational test, a property test, or by both combined; but whatever tests are required, they should be made to apply with equal and exact justice to both races.

CHAPTER XV

The Secret Of Success In Public Speaking

As to how my address at Atlanta was received by the audience in the Exposition building, I think I prefer to let Mr. James Creelman, the noted war correspondent, tell. Mr. Creelman was present, and telegraphed the following account to the New York *World*:—

> Atlanta, September 18.
> While President Cleveland was waiting at Gray Gables to-day, to send the electric spark that started the machinery of the Atlanta Exposition, a Negro Moses stood before great audience of white people and delivered an oration that marks a new

epoch in the history of the South; and a body of Negro troops marched in a procession with the citizen soldiery of Georgia and Louisiana. The whole city is thrilling to-night with a realization of the extraordinary significance of these two unprecedented events. Nothing has happened since Henry Grady's immortal speech before the New England society in New York that indicates so profoundly the spirit of the New South, except, perhaps, the opening of the Exposition itself.

When Professor Booker T. Washington, Principal of an industrial school for coloured people in Tuskegee, Ala., stood on the platform of the Auditorium, with the sun shining over the heads of his auditors into his eyes, and with his whole face lit up with the fire of prophecy, Clark Howell, the successor of Henry Grady, said to me, "That man's speech is the beginning of a moral revolution in America."

It is the first time that a Negro has made a speech in the South on any important occasion before an audience composed of white men and women. It electrified the audience, and the response was as if it had come from the throat of a whirlwind.

Mrs. Thompson had hardly taken her seat when all eyes were turned on a tall tawny Negro sitting in the front row of the platform. It was Professor Booker T. Washington, President of the Tuskegee (Alabama) Normal and Industrial Institute, who must rank from this time forth as the foremost man of his race in America. Gilmore's Band played the "Star-Spangled Banner," and the audience cheered. The tune changed to "Dixie" and the audience roared with shrill "hi-yis." Again the music changed, this time to "Yankee Doodle," and the clamour lessened.

All this time the eyes of the thousands present looked straight at the Negro orator. A strange thing was to happen. A black man was to speak for his people, with none to interrupt him. As Professor Washington strode to the edge of the stage, the low, descending sun shot fiery rays through the windows into his face. A great shout greeted him. He turned his head to avoid the blinding light, and moved about the platform for relief. Then he turned his wonderful countenance to the sun without a blink of the eyelids, and began to talk.

There was a remarkable figure; tall, bony, straight as a Sioux chief, high forehead, straight nose, heavy jaws, and strong, determined mouth, with big white teeth, piercing eyes, and a commanding manner. The sinews stood out on his bronzed neck, and his muscular right arm swung high in the air, with a lead-pencil grasped in the clinched brown fist. His big feet were planted squarely, with the heels together and the toes turned out. His voice rang out clear and true, and he paused impressively as he made each point. Within ten minutes the multitude was in an uproar of enthusiasm—handkerchiefs were waved, canes were flourished, hats were tossed in the air. The fairest women of Georgia stood up and cheered. It was as if the orator had bewitched them.

And when he held his dusky hand high above his head, with the fingers stretched wide apart, and said to the white people of the South on behalf of his race, "In all things that are purely social we can be as separate as the fingers, yet one as the hand in all things essential to mutual progress," the great wave of sound dashed itself against the walls, and the whole audience was on its feet in a delirium of applause, and I thought at that moment of the night when Henry Grady stood among the curling wreaths of tobacco-smoke in Delmonico's banquet-hall and said, "I am a Cavalier among Roundheads."

I have heard the great orators of many countries, but not even Gladstone himself could have pleaded a cause with more consummate power than did this angular Negro, standing in a nimbus of sunshine, surrounded by the men who once fought to keep his race in bondage. The roar might swell ever so high, but the expression of his earnest face never changed.

A ragged, ebony giant, squatted on the floor in one of the aisles, watched the orator with burning eyes and tremulous face until the supreme burst of applause came, and then the tears ran down his face. Most of the Negroes in the audience were crying, perhaps without knowing just why.

At the close of the speech Governor Bullock rushed across the stage and seized the orator's hand. Another shout greeted this demonstration, and for a few minutes the two men stood facing each other, hand in hand.

So far as I could spare the time from the immediate work at Tuskegee, after my Atlanta address, I accepted some of the invitations to speak in public which came to me, especially those that would take into territory where I thought it would pay to plead the cause of my race, but I always did this with the understanding that I was to be free to talk about my life-work and the needs of my people. I also had it understood that I was not to speak in the capacity of a professional lecturer, or for mere commercial gain.

In my efforts on the public platform I never have been able to understand why people come to hear me speak. This question I never can rid myself of. Time and time again, as I have stood in the street in front of a building and have seen men and women passing in large numbers into the audience-room where I was to speak, I have felt ashamed that I should be the cause of people—as it seemed to me—wasting a valuable hour of time. Some years ago I was to deliver an address before a literary society in Madison, Wis. An hour before the time set for me to speak, a fierce snow-storm began, and continued for several hours. I made up my mind that there would be no audience, and that I should not have to speak, but, as a matter of duty, I went to the church, and found it packed with people. The surprise gave me a shock that I did not recover from during the whole evening.

People often ask me if I feel nervous before speaking, or else they suggest that, since I speak so often, they suppose that I get used to it. In answer to this question I have to say that I always suffer intensely from nervousness before speaking. More than once, just before I was to make an important address, this nervous strain has been so great that I have resolved never again to speak in public. I not only feel nervous before speaking, but after I have finished I usually feel a sense of regret, because it seems to me as if I had left out of my address the main thing and the best thing that I had meant to say.

There is a great compensation, though, for this preliminary nervous suffering, that comes to me after I have been speaking for about ten minutes, and have come to feel that I have really mastered my audience, and that we have gotten into full and complete sympathy with each other. It seems to me that there is rarely such a combination of mental and physical delight in any effort as that which comes to a public speaker when he feels that he has a great audience completely within his control. There is a thread of sympathy and oneness that connects a public speaker with his audience, that is just as strong as though it was something tangible and visible. If in an audience of a thousand people there is one person who is not in sympathy with my views, or is inclined to be doubtful, cold, or critical, I can pick him out. When I

have found him I usually go straight at him, and it is a great satisfaction to watch the process of his thawing out. I find that the most effective medicine for such individuals is administered at first in the form of a story, although I never tell an anecdote simply for the sake of telling one. That kind of thing, I think, is empty and hollow, and an audience soon finds it out.

I believe that one always does himself and his audience an injustice when he speaks merely for the sake of speaking. I do not believe that one should speak unless, deep down in his heart, he feels convinced that he has a message to deliver. When one feels, from the bottom of his feet to the top of his head, that he has something to say that is going to help some individual or some cause, then let him say it; and in delivering his message I do not believe that many of the artificial rules of elocution can, under such circumstances, help him very much. Although there are certain things, such as pauses, breathing, and pitch of voice, that are very important, none of these can take the place of soul in an address. When I have an address to deliver, I like to forget all about the rules for the proper use of the English language, and all about rhetoric and that sort of thing, and I like to make the audience forget all about these things, too.

Nothing tends to throw me off my balance so quickly, when I am speaking, as to have some one leave the room. To prevent this, I make up my mind, as a rule, that I will try to make my address so interesting, will try to state so many interesting facts one after another, that no one can leave. The average audience, I have come to believe, wants facts rather than generalities or sermonizing. Most people, I think, are able to draw proper conclusions if they are given the facts in an interesting form on which to base them.

As to the kind of audience that I like best to talk to, I would put at the top of the list an organization of strong, wide-awake, business men, such, for example, as is found in Boston, New York, Chicago, and Buffalo. I have found no other audience so quick to see a point, and so responsive. Within the last few years I have had the privilege of speaking before most of the leading organizations of this kind in the large cities of the United States. The best time to get hold of an organization of business men is after a good dinner, although I think that one of the worst instruments of torture that was ever invented is the custom which makes it necessary for a speaker to sit through a fourteen-course dinner, every minute of the time feeling sure that his speech is going to prove a dismal failure and disappointment.

I rarely take part in one of these long dinners that I do not wish that I could put myself back in the little cabin where I was a slave boy, and again

go through the experience there—one that I shall never forget—of getting molasses to eat once a week from the "big house." Our usual diet on the plantation was corn bread and pork, but on Sunday morning my mother was permitted to bring down a little molasses from the "big house" for her three children, and when it was received how I did wish that every day was Sunday! I would get my tin plate and hold it up for the sweet morsel, but I would always shut my eyes while the molasses was being poured out into the plate, with the hope that when I opened them I would be surprised to see how much I had got. When I opened my eyes I would tip the plate in one direction and another, so as to make the molasses spread all over it, in the full belief that there would be more of it and that it would last longer if spread out in this way. So strong are my childish impressions of those Sunday morning feasts that it would be pretty hard for any one to convince me that there is not more molasses on a plate when it is spread all over the plate than when it occupies a little corner—if there is a corner in a plate. At any rate, I have never believed in "cornering" syrup. My share of the syrup was usually about two tablespoonfuls, and those two spoonfuls of molasses were much more enjoyable to me than is a fourteen-course dinner after which I am to speak.

Next to a company of business men, I prefer to speak to an audience of Southern people, of either race, together or taken separately. Their enthusiasm and responsiveness are a constant delight. The "amens" and "dat's de truf" that come spontaneously from the coloured individuals are calculated to spur any speaker on to his best efforts. I think that next in order of preference I would place a college audience. It has been my privilege to deliver addresses at many of our leading colleges, including Harvard, Yale, Williams, Amherst, Fisk University, the University of Pennsylvania, Wellesley, the University of Michigan, Trinity College in North Carolina, and many others.

It has been a matter of deep interest to me to note the number of people who have come to shake hands with me after an address, who say that this is the first time they have ever called a Negro "Mister."

When speaking directly in the interests of the Tuskegee Institute, I usually arrange, some time in advance, a series of meetings in important centres. This takes me before churches, Sunday-schools, Christian Endeavour Societies, and men's and women's clubs. When doing this I sometimes speak before as many as four organizations in a single day.

Three years ago, at the suggestion of Mr. Morris K. Jesup, of New York, and Dr. J. L. M. Curry, the general agent of the fund, the trustees of the John F. Slater Fund voted a sum of money to be used in paying the expenses of

Mrs. Washington and myself while holding a series of meetings among the coloured people in the large centres of Negro population, especially in the large cities of the ex-slaveholding states. Each year during the last three years we have devoted some weeks to this work. The plan that we have followed has been for me to speak in the morning to the ministers, teachers, and professional men. In the afternoon Mrs. Washington would speak to the women alone, and in the evening I spoke to a large mass-meeting. In almost every case the meetings have been attended not only by the coloured people in large numbers, but by the white people. In Chattanooga, Tenn., for example, there was present at the mass-meeting an audience of not less than three thousand persons, and I was informed that eight hundred of these were white. I have done no work that I really enjoyed more than this, or that I think has accomplished more good.

These meetings have given Mrs. Washington and myself an opportunity to get first-hand, accurate information as to the real condition of the race by seeing the people in their homes, their churches, their Sunday-schools, and their places of work, as well as in the prisons and dens of crime. These meetings also gave us an opportunity to see the relations that exist between the races. I never feel so hopeful about the race as I do after being engaged in a series of these meetings. I know that on such occasions there is much that comes to the surface that is superficial and deceptive, but I have had experience enough not to be deceived by mere signs and fleeting enthusiasms. I have taken pains to go to the bottom of things and get facts, in a cold, business-like manner.

I have seen the statement made lately, by one who claims to know what he is talking about, that, taking the whole Negro race into account, ninety per cent of the Negro women are not virtuous. There never was a baser falsehood uttered concerning a race, or a statement made that was less capable of being proved by actual facts.

No one can come into contact with the race for twenty years, as I have done in the heart of the South, without being convinced that the race is constantly making slow but sure progress materially, educationally, and morally. One might take up the life of the worst element in New York City, for example, and prove almost anything he wanted to prove concerning the white man, but all will agree that this is not a fair test.

Early in the year 1897 I received a letter inviting me to deliver an address at the dedication of the Robert Gould Shaw monument in Boston. I accepted the invitation. It is not necessary for me, I am sure, to explain who Robert

Gould Shaw was and what he did. The monument to his memory stands near the head of Boston Common, facing the State House. It is counted to be the most perfect piece of art of the kind to be found in the country.

The exercises connected with the dedication were held in Music Hall, in Boston, and the great hall was packed from top to bottom with one of the most distinguished audiences that ever assembled in the city. Among those present there were more persons representing the famous old anti-slavery element than it is likely will ever be brought together in the country again. The late Hon. Roger Wolcott, then Governor of Massachusetts, was the presiding officer, and on the platform with him were many other officials and hundreds of distinguished men. A report of the meeting which appeared in the Boston *Transcript* will describe it better than any words of mine could do:—

> The core and kernel of yesterday's great noon meeting in honour of the Brotherhood of Man, in Music Hall, was the superb address of the Negro President of Tuskegee. "Booker T. Washington received his Harvard A. M. last June, the first of his race," said Governor Wolcott, "to receive an honorary degree from the oldest university in the land, and this for the wise leadership of his people." When Mr. Washington rose in the flag-filled, enthusiasm-warmed, patriotic, and glowing atmosphere of Music Hall, people felt keenly that here was the civic justification of the old abolition spirit of Massachusetts; in his person the proof of her ancient and indomitable faith; in his strong thought and rich oratory, the crown and glory of the old war days of suffering and strife. The scene was full of historic beauty and deep significance. "Cold" Boston was alive with the fire that is always hot in her heart for righteousness and truth. Rows and rows of people who are seldom seen at any public function, whole families of those who are certain to be out of town on a holiday, crowded the place to overflowing. The city was at her birthright fête in the persons of hundreds of her best citizens, men and women whose names and lives stand for the virtues that make for honourable civic pride.
>
> Battle music had filled the air. Ovation after ovation, applause warm and prolonged, had greeted the officers and friends of Colonel Shaw, the sculptor, St. Gaudens, the memorial Committee, the Governor and his staff, and the Negro sol-

diers of the Fifty-fourth Massachusetts as they came upon the platform or entered the hall. Colonel Henry Lee, of Governor Andrew's old staff, had made a noble, simple presentation speech for the committee, paying tribute to Mr. John M. Forbes, in whose stead he served. Governor Wolcott had made his short, memorable speech, saying, "Fort Wagner marked an epoch in the history of a race, and called it into manhood." Mayor Quincy had received the monument for the city of Boston. The story of Colonel Shaw and his black regiment had been told in gallant words, and then, after the singing of

> Mine eyes have seen the glory
> Of the coming of the Lord,

Booker Washington arose. It was, of course, just the moment for him. The multitude, shaken out of its usual symphony-concert calm, quivered with an excitement that was not suppressed. A dozen times it had sprung to its feet to cheer and wave and hurrah, as one person. When this man of culture and voice and power, as well as a dark skin, began, and uttered the names of Stearns and of Andrew, feeling began to mount. You could see tears glisten in the eyes of soldiers and civilians. When the orator turned to the coloured soldiers on the platform, to the colour-bearer of Fort Wagner, who smilingly bore still the flag he had never lowered even when wounded, and said, "To you, to the scarred and scattered remnants of the Fifty-fourth, who, with empty sleeve and wanting leg, have honoured this occasion with your presence, to you, your commander is not dead. Though Boston erected no monument and history recorded no story, in you and in the loyal race which you represent, Robert Gould Shaw would have a monument which time could not wear away," then came the climax of the emotion of the day and the hour. It was Roger Wolcott, as well as the Governor of Massachusetts, the individual representative of the people's sympathy as well as the chief magistrate, who had sprung first to his feet and cried, "Three cheers to Booker T. Washington!"

Among those on the platform was Sergeant William H. Carney, of New Bedford, Mass., the brave coloured officer who was the colour-bearer at Fort Wagner and held the American flag. In spite of the fact that a large part of his regiment was killed, he escaped, and exclaimed, after the battle was over, "The old flag never touched the ground."

This flag Sergeant Carney held in his hands as he sat on the platform, and when I turned to address the survivors of the coloured regiment who were present, and referred to Sergeant Carney, he rose, as if by instinct, and raised the flag. It has been my privilege to witness a good many satisfactory and rather sensational demonstrations in connection with some of my public addresses, but in dramatic effect I have never seen or experienced anything which equalled this. For a number of minutes the audience seemed to entirely lose control of itself.

In the general rejoicing throughout the country which followed the close of the Spanish-American war, peace celebrations were arranged in several of the large cities. I was asked by President William R. Harper, of the University of Chicago, who was chairman of the committee of invitations for the celebration to be held in the city of Chicago, to deliver one of the addresses at the celebration there. I accepted the invitation, and delivered two addresses there during the Jubilee week. The first of these, and the principal one, was given in the Auditorium on the evening of Sunday, October 16. This was the largest audience that I have ever addressed, in any part of the country; and besides speaking in the main Auditorium, I also addressed, that same evening, two overflow audiences in other parts of the city.

It was said that there were sixteen thousand persons in the Auditorium, and it seemed to me as if there were as many more on the outside trying to get in. It was impossible for any one to get near the entrance without the aid of a policeman. President William McKinley attended this meeting, as did also the members of his Cabinet, many foreign ministers, and a large number of army and navy officers, many of whom had distinguished themselves in the war which had just closed. The speakers, besides myself, on Sunday evening, were Rabbi Emil G. Hirsch, Father Thomas P. Hodnett, and Dr. John H. Barrows.

The Chicago *Times-Herald*, in describing the meeting, said of my address:—

He pictured the Negro choosing slavery rather than extinction; recalled Crispus Attucks shedding his blood at the beginning

of the American Revolution, that white Americans might be free, while black Americans remained in slavery; rehearsed the conduct of the Negroes with Jackson at New Orleans; drew a vivid and pathetic picture of the Southern slaves protecting and supporting the families of their masters while the latter were fighting to perpetuate black slavery; recounted the bravery of coloured troops at Port Hudson and Forts Wagner and Pillow, and praised the heroism of the black regiments that stormed El Caney and Santiago to give freedom to the enslaved people of Cuba, forgetting, for the time being, the unjust discrimination that law and custom make against them in their own country.

In all of these things, the speaker declared, his race had chosen the better part. And then he made his eloquent appeal to the consciences of the white Americans: "When you have gotten the full story of the heroic conduct of the Negro in the Spanish-American war, have heard it from the lips of Northern soldier and Southern soldier, from ex-abolitionist and ex-masters, then decide within yourselves whether a race that is thus willing to die for its country should not be given the highest opportunity to live for its country."

The part of the speech which seemed to arouse the wildest and most sensational enthusiasm was that in which I thanked the President for his recognition of the Negro in his appointments during the Spanish-American war. The President was sitting in a box at the right of the stage. When I addressed him I turned toward the box, and as I finished the sentence thanking him for his generosity, the whole audience rose and cheered again and again, waving handkerchiefs and hats and canes, until the President arose in the box and bowed his acknowledgments. At that the enthusiasm broke out again, and the demonstration was almost indescribable.

One portion of my address at Chicago seemed to have been misunderstood by the Southern press, and some of the Southern papers took occasion to criticise me rather strongly. These criticisms continued for several weeks, until I finally received a letter from the editor of the *Age-Herald*, published in Birmingham, Ala., asking me if I would say just what I meant by this part of my address. I replied to him in a letter which seemed to satisfy my critics. In this letter I said that I had made it a rule never to say before a Northern audience anything that I would not say before an audience in the South. I

said that I did not think it was necessary for me to go into extended explanations; if my seventeen years of work in the heart of the South had not been explanation enough, I did not see how words could explain. I said that I made the same plea that I had made in my address at Atlanta, for the blotting out of race prejudice in "commercial and civil relations." I said that what is termed social recognition was a question which I never discussed, and then I quoted from my Atlanta address what I had said there in regard to that subject.

In meeting crowds of people at public gatherings, there is one type of individual that I dread. I mean the crank. I have become some accustomed to these people now that I can pick them out at a distance when I see them elbowing their way up to me. The average crank has a long beard, poorly cared for, a lean, narrow face, and wears a black coat. The front of his vest and coat are slick with grease, and his trousers bag at the knees.

In Chicago, after I had spoken at a meeting, I met one of these fellows. They usually have some process for curing all of the ills of the world at once. This Chicago specimen had a patent process by which, he said, Indian corn could be kept through a period of three or four years, and he felt sure that if the Negro race in the South would, as a whole, adopt his process, it would settle the whole race question. It mattered nothing that I tried to convince him that our present problem was to teach the Negroes how to produce enough corn to last them through one year. Another Chicago crank had a scheme by which he wanted me to join him in an effort to close up all the National banks in the country. If that was done, he felt sure it would put the Negro on his feet.

The number of people who stand ready to consume one's time, to no purpose, is almost countless. At one time I spoke before a large audience in Boston in the evening. The next morning I was awakened by having a card brought to my room, and with it a message that some one was anxious to see me. Thinking that it must be something very important, I dressed hastily and went down. When I reached the hotel office I found a blank and innocent-looking individual waiting for me, who coolly remarked: "I heard you talk at a meeting last night. I rather liked your talk, and so I came in this morning to hear you talk some more."

I am often asked how it is possible for me to superintend the work at Tuskegee and at the same time be so much away from the school. In partial answer to this I would say that I think I have learned, in some degree at least, to disregard the old maxim which says, "Do not get others to do that which you can do yourself." My motto, on the other hand, is, "Do not do that

which others can do as well."

One of the most encouraging signs in connection with the Tuskegee school is found in the fact that the organization is so thorough that the daily work of the school is not dependent upon the presence of any one individual. The whole executive force, including instructors and clerks, now numbers eighty-six. This force is so organized and subdivided that the machinery of the school goes on day by day like clockwork. Most of our teachers have been connected with the institution for a number of years, and are as much interested in it as I am. In my absence, Mr. Warren Logan, the treasurer, who has been at the school seventeen years, is the executive. He is efficiently sup ported by Mrs. Washington, and by my faithful secretary, Mr. Emmett J. Scott, who handles the bulk of my correspondence and keeps me in daily touch with the life of the school, and who also keeps me informed of whatever takes place in the South that concerns the race. I owe more to his tact, wisdom, and hard work than I can describe.

The main executive work of the school, whether I am at Tuskegee or not, centres in what we call the executive council. This council meets twice a week, and is composed of the nine persons who are at the head of the nine departments of the school. For example: Mrs. B. K. Bruce, the Lady Principal, the widow of the late ex-senator Bruce, is a member of the council, and represents in it all that pertains to the life of the girls at the school. In addition to the executive council there is a financial committee of six, that meets every week and decides upon the expenditures for the week. Once a month, and sometimes oftener, there is a general meeting of all the instructors. Aside from these there are innumerable smaller meetings, such as that of the instructors in the Phelps Hall Bible Training School, or of the instructors in the agricultural department.

In order that I may keep in constant touch with the life of the institution, I have a system of reports so arranged that a record of the school's work reaches me every day in the year, no matter in what part of the country I am. I know by these reports even what students are excused from school, and why they are excused-whether for reasons of ill health or otherwise. Through the medium of these reports I know each day what the income of the school in money is; I know how many gallons of milk and how many pounds of butter come from the dairy; what the bill of fare for the teachers and students is; whether a certain kind of meat was boiled or baked, and whether certain vegetables served in the dining room were bought from a store or procured from our own farm. Human nature I find to be very much the same the world

over, and it is sometimes not hard to yield to the temptation to go to a barrel of rice that has come from the store—with the grain all prepared to go into the pot—rather than to take the time and trouble to go to the field and dig and wash one's own sweet potatoes, which might be prepared in a manner to take the place of the rice.

I am often asked how, in the midst of so much work, a large part of which is before the public, I can find time for any rest or recreation, and what kind of recreation or sports I am fond of. This is rather a difficult question to answer. I have a strong feeling that every individual owes it to himself, and to the cause which he is serving, to keep a vigorous, healthy body, with the nerves steady and strong, prepared for great efforts and prepared for disappointments and trying positions. As far as I can, I make it a rule to plan for each day's work—not merely to go through with the same routine of daily duties, but to get rid of the routine work as early in the day as possible, and then to enter upon some new or advance work. I make it a rule to clear my desk every day, before leaving my office, of all correspondence and memoranda, so that on the morrow I can begin a new day of work. I make it a rule never to let my work drive me, but to so master it, and keep it in such complete control, and to keep so far ahead of it, that I will be the master instead of the servant. There is a physical and mental and spiritual enjoyment that comes from a consciousness of being the absolute master of one's work, in all its details, that is very satisfactory and inspiring. My experience teaches me that, if one learns to follow this plan, he gets a freshness of body and vigour of mind out of work that goes a long way toward keeping him strong and healthy. I believe that when one can grow to the point where he loves his work, this gives him a kind of strength that is most valuable.

When I begin my work in the morning, I expect to have a successful and pleasant day of it, but at the same time I prepare myself for unpleasant and unexpected hard places. I prepare myself to hear that one of our school buildings is on fire, or has burned, or that some disagreeable accident has occurred, or that some one has abused me in a public address or printed article, for something that I have done or omitted to do, or for something that he had heard that I had said—probably something that I had never thought of saying.

In nineteen years of continuous work I have taken but one vacation. That was two years ago, when some of my friends put the money into my hands and forced Mrs. Washington and myself to spend three months in Europe. I have said that I believe it is the duty of every one to keep his body in good condition. I try to look after the little ills, with the idea that if I take care of

the little ills the big ones will not come. When I find myself unable to sleep well, I know that something is wrong. If I find any part of my system the least weak, and not performing its duty, I consult a good physician. The ability to sleep well, at any time and in any place, I find of great advantage. I have so trained myself that I can lie down for a nap of fifteen or twenty minutes, and get up refreshed in body and mind.

I have said that I make it a rule to finish up each day's work before leaving it. There is, perhaps, one exception to this. When I have an unusually difficult question to decide—one that appeals strongly to the emotions—I find it a safe rule to sleep over it for a night, or to wait until I have had an opportunity to talk it over with my wife and friends.

As to my reading; the most time I get for solid reading is when I am on the cars. Newspapers are to me a constant source of delight and recreation. The only trouble is that I read too many of them. Fiction I care little for. Frequently I have to almost force myself to read a novel that is on every one's lips. The kind of reading that I have the greatest fondness for is biography. I like to be sure that I am reading about a real man or a real thing. I think I do not go too far when I say that I have read nearly every book and magazine article that has been written about Abraham Lincoln. In literature he is my patron saint.

Out of the twelve months in a year I suppose that, on an average, I spend six months away from Tuskegee. While my being absent from the school so much unquestionably has its disadvantages, yet there are at the same time some compensations. The change of work brings a certain kind of rest. I enjoy a ride of a long distance on the cars, when I am permitted to ride where I can be comfortable. I get rest on the cars, except when the inevitable individual who seems to be on every train approaches me with the now familiar phrase: "Isn't this Booker Washington? I want to introduce myself to you." Absence from the school enables me to lose sight of the unimportant details of the work, and study it in a broader and more comprehensive manner than I could do on the grounds. This absence also brings me into contact with the best work being done in educational lines, and into contact with the best educators in the land.

But, after all this is said, the time when I get the most solid rest and recreation is when I can be at Tuskegee, and, after our evening meal is over, can sit down, as is our custom, with my wife and Portia and Booker and Davidson, my three children, and read a story, or each take turns in telling a story. To me there is nothing on earth equal to that, although what is nearly

equal to it is to go with them for an hour or more as we like to do on Sunday afternoons, into the woods, where we can live for a while near the heart of nature, where no one can disturb or vex us, surrounded by pure air, the trees, the shrubbery, the flowers, and the sweet fragrance that springs from a hundred plants, enjoying the chirp of the crickets and the songs of the birds. This is solid rest.

My garden, also, what little time I can be at Tuskegee, is another source of rest and enjoyment. Somehow I like, as often as possible, to touch nature, not something that is artificial or an imitation, but the real thing. When I can leave my office in time so that I can spend thirty or forty minutes in spading the ground, in planting seeds, in digging about the plants, I feel that I am coming into contact with something that is giving me strength for the many duties and hard places that await me out in the big world. I pity the man or woman who has never learned to enjoy nature and to get strength and inspiration out of it.

Aside from the large number of fowls and animals kept by the school, I keep individually a number of pigs and fowls of the best grades, and in raising these I take a great deal of pleasure. I think the pig is my favourite animal. Few things are more satisfactory to me than a high-grade Berkshire or Poland China pig.

Games I care little for. I have never seen a game of football. In cards I do not know one card from another. A game of old-fashioned marbles with my two boys, once in a while, is all I care for in this direction. I suppose I would care for games now if I had had any time in my youth to give to them, but that was not possible.

CHAPTER XVI

Europe

In 1893 I was married to Miss Margaret James Murray, a native of Mississippi, and a graduate of Fisk University, in Nashville, Tenn., who had come to Tuskegee as a teacher several years before, and at the time we were married was filling the position of Lady Principal. Not only is Mrs. Washington completely one with me in the work directly connected with the school, relieving me of many burdens and perplexities, but aside from her

work on the school grounds, she carries on a mothers' meeting in the town of Tuskegee, and a plantation work among the women, children, and men who live in a settlement connected with a large plantation about eight miles from Tuskegee. Both the mothers' meeting and the plantation work are carried on, not only with a view to helping those who are directly reached, but also for the purpose of furnishing object-lessons in these two kinds of work that may be followed by our students when they go out into the world for their own life-work.

Aside from these two enterprises, Mrs. Washington is also largely responsible for a woman's club at the school which brings together, twice a month, the women who live on the school grounds and those who live near, for the discussion of some important topic. She is also the President of what is known as the Federation of Southern Coloured Women's Clubs, and is Chairman of the Executive Committee of the National Federation of Coloured Women's Clubs.

Portia, the oldest of my three children, has learned dressmaking. She has unusual ability in instrumental music. Aside from her studies at Tuskegee, she has already begun to teach there.

Baker Taliaferro is my next oldest child. Young as he is, he has already nearly mastered the brick mason's trade. He began working at this trade when he was quite small, dividing his time between this and class work; and he has developed great skill in the trade and a fondness for it. He says that he is going to be an architect and brickmason. One of the most satisfactory letters that I have ever received from any one came to me from Baker, last summer. When I left home for the summer, I told him that he must work at his trade half of each day, and that the other half of the day he could spend as he pleased. When I had been away from home two weeks, I received the following letter from him:

TUSKEGEE, ALABAMA.

MY DEAR PAPA: Before you left home you told me to work at my trade half of each day. I like my work so much that I want to work at my trade all day. Besides, I want to earn all the money I can, so that when I go to another school I shall have money to pay my expenses.

Your son,
BAKER.

My youngest child, Ernest Davidson Washington, says that he is going to be a physician. In addition to going to school, where he studies books and has manual training, he regularly spends a portion of his time in the office of our resident physician, and has already learned to do many of the duties which pertain to a doctor's office.

The thing in my life which brings me the keenest regret is that my work in connection with public affairs keeps me for so much of the time away from my family, where, of all places in the world, I delight to be. I always envy the individual whose life-work is so laid that he can spend his evenings at home. I have sometimes thought that people who have this rare privilege do not appreciate it as they should. It is such a rest and relief to get away from crowds of people, and handshaking, and travelling, and get home, even if it be for but a very brief while.

Another thing at Tuskegee out of which a great deal of pleasure and satisfaction is in the meeting with our students, and teachers, and their families, in the chapel for devotional exercises every evening at half-past eight, the last thing before retiring for the night. It is an inspiring sight when one stands on the platform there and sees before him eleven or twelve hundred earnest young men and women; and one cannot but feel that it is a privilege to help to guide them to a higher and more useful life.

In the spring of 1899 there came to me what I might describe as almost the greatest surprise of my life. Some good ladies in Boston arranged a public meeting in the interests of Tuskegee, to be held in the Hollis Street Theatre. This meeting was attended by large numbers of the best people of Boston, of both races. Bishop Lawrence presided. In addition to an address made by myself, Mr. Paul Lawrence Dunbar read from his poems, and Dr. W.E.B. DuBois read an original sketch.

Some of those who attended this meeting noticed that I seemed unusually tired, and some little time after the close of the meeting, one of the ladies who had been interested in it asked me in a casual way if I had ever been to Europe. I replied that I never had. She asked me if I had ever thought of going, and I told her no; that it was something entirely beyond me. This conversation soon passed out of my mind, but a few days afterward I was informed that some friends in Boston, including Mr. Francis J. Garrison, had raised a sum of money sufficient to pay all the expenses of Mrs. Washington and myself during a three or four months' trip to Europe. It was added with emphasis that we must go. A year previous to this Mr. Garrison had attempted to get me to promise to go to Europe for a summer's rest, with the under-

standing that he would be responsible for raising the money among his friends for the expenses of the trip. At that time such a journey seemed so entirely foreign to anything that I should ever be able to undertake that I confess I did not give the matter very serious attention; but later Mr. Garrison joined his efforts to those of the ladies whom I have mentioned, and when their plans were made known to me Mr. Garrison not only had the route mapped out, but had, I believe, selected the steamer upon which we were to sail.

The whole thing was so sudden and so unexpected that I was completely taken off my feet. I had been at work steadily for eighteen years in connection with Tuskegee, and I had never thought of anything else but ending my life in that way. Each day the school seemed to depend upon me more largely for its daily expenses, and I told these Boston friends that, while I thanked them sincerely for their thoughtfulness and generosity, I could not go to Europe, for the reason that the school could not live financially while I was absent. They then informed me that Mr. Henry L. Higginson, and some other good friends who I know do not want their names made public, were then raising a sum of money which would be sufficient to keep the school in operation while I was away. At this point I was compelled to surrender. Every avenue of escape had been closed.

Deep down in my heart the whole thing seemed more like a dream than like reality, and for a long time it was difficult for me to make myself believe that I was actually going to Europe. I had been born and largely reared in the lowest depths of slavery, ignorance, and poverty. In my childhood I had suffered for want of a place to sleep, for lack of food, clothing, and shelter. I had not had the privilege of sitting down to a dining-table until I was quite well grown. Luxuries had always seemed to me to be something meant for white people, not for my race. I had always regarded Europe, and London, and Paris, much as I regard heaven. And now could it be that I was actually going to Europe? Such thoughts as these were constantly with me.

Two other thoughts troubled me a good deal. I feared that people who heard that Mrs. Washington and I were going to Europe might not know all the circumstances, and might get the idea that we had become, as some might say, "stuck up," and were trying to "show off." I recalled that from my youth I had heard it said that too often, when people of my race reached any degree of success, they were inclined to unduly exalt themselves; to try and ape the wealthy, and in so doing to lose their heads. The fear that people might think this of us haunted me a good deal. Then, too, I could not see

how my conscience would permit me to spare the time from my work and be happy. It seemed mean and selfish in me to be taking a vacation while others were at work, and while there was so much that needed to be done. From the time I could remember, I had always been at work, and I did not see how I could spend three or four months in doing nothing. The fact was that I did not know how to take a vacation.

Mrs. Washington had much the same difficulty in getting away, but she was anxious to go because she thought that I needed the rest. There were many important National questions bearing upon the life of the race which were being agitated at that time, and this made it all the harder for us to decide to go. We finally gave our Boston friends our promise that we would go, and then they insisted that the date of our departure be set as soon as possible. So we decided upon May 10. My good friend Mr. Garrison kindly took charge of all the details necessary for the success of the trip, and he, as well as other friends, gave us a great number of letters of introduction to people in France and England, and made other arrangements for our comfort and convenience abroad. Good-bys were said at Tuskegee, and we were in New York May 9, ready to sail the next day. Our daughter Portia, who was then studying in South Framingham, Mass., came to New York to see us off. Mr. Scott, my secretary, came with me to New York, in order that I might clear up the last bit of business before I left. Other friends also came to New York to see us off. Just before we went on board the steamer another pleasant surprise came to us in the form of a letter from two generous ladies, stating that they had decided to give us the money with which to erect a new building to be used in properly housing all our industries for girls at Tuskegee.

We were to sail on the *Friesland,* of the Red Star Line, and a beautiful vessel she was. We went on board just before noon, the hour of sailing. I had never before been on board a large ocean steamer, and the feeling which took possession of me when I found myself there is rather hard to describe. It was a feeling, I think, of awe mingled with delight. We were agreeably surprised to find that the captain, as well as several of the other officers, not only knew who we were, but was expecting us and gave us a pleasant greeting. There were several passengers whom we knew, including Senator Sewell, of New Jersey, and Edward Marshall, the newspaper correspondent. I had just a little fear that we would not be treated civilly by some of the passengers. This fear was based upon what I had heard other people of my race, who had crossed the ocean, say about unpleasant experiences in crossing the ocean in American vessels. But in our case, from the captain down to the most hum-

ble servant, we were treated with the greatest kindness. Nor was this kindness confined to those who were connected with the steamer; it was shown by all the passengers also. There were not a few Southern men and women on board, and they were as cordial as those from other parts of the country.

As soon as the last good-bye were said, and the steamer had cut loose from the wharf, the load of care, anxiety, and responsibility which I had carried for eighteen years began to lift itself from my shoulders at the rate, it seemed to me, of a pound a minute. It was the first time in all those years that I had felt, even in a measure, free from care; and my feeling of relief it is hard to describe on paper. Added to this was the delightful anticipation of being in Europe soon. It all seemed more like a dream than like a reality.

Mr. Garrison had thoughtfully arranged to have us have one of the most comfortable rooms on the ship. The second or third day out I began to sleep, and I think that I slept at the rate of fifteen hours a day during the remainder of the ten days' passage. Then it was that I began to understand how tired I really was. These long sleeps I kept up for a month after we landed on the other side. It was such an unusual feeling to wake up in the morning and realize that I had no engagements; did not have to take a train at a certain hour: did not have an appointment to meet some one, or to make an address, at a certain hour. How different all this was from some of the experiences that I have been through when travelling, when I have sometimes slept in three different beds in a single night!

When Sunday came, the captain invited me to conduct the religious services, but, not being a minister, I declined. The passengers, however, began making requests that I deliver an address to them in the dining-saloon some time during the voyage, and this I consented to do. Senator Sewell presided at this meeting. After ten days of delightful weather, during which I was not seasick for a day, we landed at the interesting old city of Antwerp, in Belgium.

The next day after we landed happened to be one of those numberless holidays which the people of those countries are in the habit of observing. It was a bright, beautiful day. Our room in the hotel faced the main public square, and the sights there—the people coming in from the country with all kinds of beautiful flowers to sell, the women coming in with their dogs drawing large, brightly polished cans filled with milk, the people streaming into the cathedral—filled me with a sense of newness that I had never before experienced.

After spending some time in Antwerp, we were invited to go with a party

of a half-dozen persons on a trip through Holland. This party included Edward Marshall and some American artists who had come over on the same steamer with us. We accepted the invitation, and enjoyed the trip greatly. I think it was all the more interesting and instructive because we went for most of the way on one of the slow, old-fashioned canal-boats. This gave us an opportunity of seeing and studying the real life of the people in the country districts. We went in this way as far as Rotterdam, and later went to The Hague, where the Peace Conference was then in session, and where we were kindly received by the American representatives.

The thing that impressed itself most on me in Holland was the thoroughness of the agriculture and the excellence of the Holstein cattle. I never knew, before visiting Holland, how much it was possible for people to get out of a small plot of ground. It seemed to me that absolutely no land was wasted. It was worth a trip to Holland, too, just to get a sight of three or four hundred fine Holstein cows grazing in one of those intensely green fields.

From Holland we went to Belgium, and made a hasty trip through that country, stopping at Brussels, where we visited the battlefield of Waterloo. From Belgium we went direct to Paris, where we found that Mr. Theodore Stanton, the son of Mrs. Elizabeth Cady Stanton, had kindly provided accommodations for us. We had barely got settled in Paris before an invitation came to me from the University Club of Paris to be its guest at a banquet which was soon to be given. The other guests were ex-President Benjamin Harrison and Archbishop Ireland, who were in Paris at the time. The American Ambassador, General Horace Porter, presided at the banquet. My address on this occasion seemed to give satisfaction to those who heard it. General Harrison kindly devoted a large portion of his remarks at dinner to myself and to the influence of the work at Tuskegee on the American race question. After my address at this banquet other invitations came to me, but I declined the most of them, knowing that if I accepted them all, the object of my visit would be defeated. I did, however, consent to deliver an address in the American chapel the following Sunday morning, and at this meeting General Harrison, General Porter, and other distinguished Americans were present.

Later we received a formal call from the American Ambassador, and were invited to attend a reception at his residence. At this reception we met many Americans, among them Justices Fuller and Harlan, of the United States Supreme Court. During our entire stay of a month in Paris, both the American Ambassador and his wife, as well as several other Americans, were very kind to us.

While in Paris we saw a good deal of the now famous American Negro painter, Mr. Henry C. Tanner, whom we had formerly known in America. It was very satisfactory to find how well known Mr. Tanner was in the field of art, and to note the high standing which all classes accorded to him. When we told some Americans that we were going to the Luxembourg Palace to see a painting by an American Negro, it was hard to convince them that a Negro had been thus honoured. I do not believe that they were really convinced of the fact until they saw the picture for themselves. My acquaintance with Mr. Tanner reënforced in my mind the truth which I am constantly trying to impress upon our students at Tuskegee—and on our people throughout the country, as far as I can reach them with my voice—that any man, regardless of colour, will be recognized and rewarded just in proportion as he learns to do something well—learns to do it better than some one else—however humble the thing may be. As I have said, I believe that my race will succeed in proportion as it learns to do a common thing in an uncommon manner; learns to do a thing so thoroughly that no one can improve upon what it has done; learns to make its services of indispensable value. This was the spirit that inspired me in my first effort at Hampton, when I was given the opportunity to sweep and dust that schoolroom. In a degree I felt that my whole future life depended upon the thoroughness with which I cleaned that room, and I was determined to do it so well that no one could find any fault with the job. Few people ever stopped, I found, when looking at his pictures, to inquire whether Mr. Tanner was a Negro painter, a French painter, or a German painter. They simply knew that he was able to produce something which the world wanted—a great painting—and the matter of his colour did not enter into their minds. When a Negro girl learns to cook, to wash dishes, to sew, to write a book, or a Negro boy learns to groom horses, or to grow sweet potatoes, or to produce butter, or to build a house, or to be able to practice medicine, as well or better than some one else, they will be rewarded regardless of race or colour. In the long run, the world is going to have the best, and any difference in race, religion, or previous history will not long keep the world from what it wants.

I think that the whole future of my race hinges on the question as to whether or not it can make itself of such indispensable value that the people in the town and the state where we reside will feel that our presence is necessary to the happiness and well-being of the community. No man who continues to add something to the material, intellectual, and moral well-being of the place in which he lives is long left without proper reward. This is a great

human law which cannot be permanently nullified.

The love of pleasure and excitement which seems in a large measure to possess the French people impressed itself upon me. I think they are more noted in this respect than is true of the people of my own race. In point of morality and moral earnestness I do not believe that the French are ahead of my own race in America. Severe competition and the great stress of life have led them to learn to do things more thoroughly, and to exercise greater economy; but time, I think, will bring my race to the same point. In the matter of truth and high honour I do not believe that the average Frenchman is ahead of the American Negro; while so far as mercy and kindness to dumb animals go, I believe that my race is far ahead. In fact, when I left France, I had more faith in the future of the black man in America than I had ever possessed.

From Paris we went to London, and reached there early in July, just about the height of the London social season. Parliament was in session, and there was a great deal of gaiety. Mr. Garrison and other friends had provided us with a large number of letters of introduction, and they had also sent letters to other persons in different parts of the United Kingdom, apprising these people of our coming. Very soon after reaching London we were flooded with invitations to attend all manner of social functions, and a great many invitations came to me asking that I deliver public addresses. The most of these invitations I declined, for the reason that I wanted to rest. Neither were we able to accept more than a small proportion of the other invitations. The Rev. Dr. Brooke Herford and Mrs. Herford, whom I had known in Boston, consulted with the American Ambassador, the Hon. Joseph Choate, and arranged for me to speak at a public meeting to be held in Exeter Hall. Mr. Choate kindly consented to preside. The meeting was largely attended. There were many distinguished persons present, among them several members of Parliament, including Mr. James Bryce, who spoke at the meeting. What the American Ambassador said in introducing me, as well as a synopsis of what I said, was widely published in England and in the American papers at the time. Dr. and Mrs. Herford gave Mrs. Washington and myself a reception, at which we had the privilege of meeting some of the best people in England. Throughout our stay in London Ambassador Choate was most kind and attentive to us. At the Ambassador's reception I met, for the first time, Mark Twain.

We were the guests several times of Mrs. T. Fisher Unwin, the daughter of the English statesman, Richard Cobden. It seemed as if both Mr. and Mrs.

Unwin could not do enough for our comfort and happiness. Later, for nearly a week, we were the guests of the daughter of John Bright, now Mrs. Clark, of Street, England. Both Mr. and Mrs. Clark, with their daughter, visited us at Tuskegee the next year. In Birmingham, England, we were the guests for several days of Mr. Joseph Sturge, whose father was a great abolitionist and friend of Whittier and Garrison. It was a great privilege to meet throughout England those who had known and honoured the late William Lloyd Garrison, the Hon. Frederick Douglass, and other abolitionists. The English abolitionists with whom we came in contact never seemed to tire of talking about these two Americans. Before going to England I had had no proper conception of the deep interest displayed by the abolitionists of England in the cause of freedom, nor did I realize the amount of substantial help given by them.

In Bristol, England, both Mrs. Washington and I spoke at the Women's Liberal Club. I was also the principal speaker at the Commencement exercises of the Royal College for the Blind. These exercises were held in the Crystal Palace, and the presiding officer was the late Duke of Westminster, who was said to be, I believe, the richest man in England, if not in the world. The Duke, as well as his wife and their daughter, seemed to be pleased with what I said, and thanked me heartily. Through the kindness of Lady Aberdeen, my wife and I were enabled to go with a party of those who were attending the International Congress of Women, then in session in London, to see Queen Victoria, at Windsor Castle, where, afterward, we were all the guests of her Majesty at tea. In our party was Miss Susan B. Anthony, and I was deeply impressed with the fact that one did not often get an opportunity to see, during the same hour, two women so remarkable in different ways as Susan B. Anthony and Queen Victoria.

In the House of Commons, which we visited several times, we met Sir Henry M. Stanley. I talked with him about Africa and its relation to the American Negro, and after my interview with him I became more convinced than ever that there was no hope of the American Negro's improving his condition by emigrating to Africa.

On various occasions Mrs. Washington and I were the guests of Englishmen in their country homes, where, I think, one sees the Englishman at his best. In one thing, at least, I feel sure that the English are ahead of Americans, and that is, that they have learned how to get more out of life. The home life of the English seems to me to be about as perfect as anything can be. Everything moves like clockwork. I was impressed, too, with the def-

erence that the servants show to their "masters" and "mistresses,"—terms which I suppose would not be tolerated in America. The English servant expects, as a rule, to be nothing but a servant, and so he perfects himself in the art to a degree that no class of servants in America has yet reached. In our country, the servant expects to become, in a few years, a "master" himself. Which system is preferable? I will not venture an answer.

Another thing that impressed itself upon me throughout England was the high regard that all classes have for law and order, and the ease and thoroughness with which everything is done. The Englishmen, I found, took plenty of time for eating, as for everything else. I am not sure if, in the long run, they do not accomplish as much or more than rushing nervous Americans do.

My visit to England gave me a higher regard for the nobility than I had had. I had no idea that they were so generally loved and respected by the masses, nor had I any correct conception of how much time and money they spent in works of philanthropy, and how much real heart they put into this work. My impression had been that they merely spent money freely and had a "good time."

It was hard for me to get accustomed to speaking to English audiences. The average Englishman is so serious, and is so tremendously in earnest about everything, that when I told a story that would have made an American audience roar with laughter, the Englishmen simply looked me straight in the face without even cracking a smile.

When the Englishman takes you into his heart and friendship, he binds you there as with cords of steel, and I do not believe that there are many other friendships that are so lasting or so satisfactory. Perhaps I can illustrate this point in no better way than by relating the following incident. Mrs. Washington and I were invited to attend a reception given by the Duke and Duchess of Sutherland, at Stafford House—said to be the finest house in London; I may add that I believe the Duchess of Sutherland is said to be the most beautiful woman in England. There must have been at least three hundred persons at this reception. Twice during the evening the Duchess sought us out for a conversation, and she asked me to write her when we got home, and tell her more about the work at Tuskegee. This I did. When Christmas came we were surprised and delighted to receive her photograph with her autograph on it. The correspondence has continued, and we now feel that in the Duchess of Sutherland we have one of our warmest friends.

After three months in Europe we sailed from Southampton in the

steamship St. Louis. On this steamer there was a fine library that had been presented to the ship by the citizens of St. Louis, Mo. In this library I found a life of Frederick Douglass, which I began reading. I became especially interested in Mr. Douglass's description of the way he was treated on shipboard during his first or second visit to England. In this description he told how he was not permitted to enter the cabin, but had to confine himself to the deck of the ship. A few minutes after I had finished reading this description I was waited on by a committee of ladies and gentlemen with the request that I deliver an address at a concert which was to be given the following evening. And yet there are people who are bold enough to say that race feeling in America is not growing less intense! At this concert the Hon. Benjamin B. Odell, Jr., the present governor of New York, presided. I was never given a more cordial hearing anywhere. A large proportion of the passengers were Southern people. After the concert some of the passengers proposed that a subscription be raised to help the work at Tuskegee, and the money to support several scholarships was the result.

While we were in Paris I was very pleasantly surprised to receive the following invitation from the citizens of West Virginia and of the city near which I had spent my boyhood days:—

CHARLESTON, W. VA., MAY 16, 1899.
PROFESSOR BOOKER T. WASHINGTON, PARIS, FRANCE:

DEAR SIR: Many of the best citizens of West Virginia have united in liberal expressions of admiration and praise of your worth and work, and desire that on your return from Europe you should favour them with your presence and with the inspiration of your words. We most sincerely indorse this move, and on behalf of the citizens of Charleston extend to you our most cordial invitation to have you come to us, that we may honour you who have done so much by your life and work to honour us.

We are, Very truly yours,
THE COMMON COUNCIL OF THE CITY OF CHARLESTON,
By W. HERMAN SMITH, Mayor.

This invitation from the City Council of Charleston was accompanied by the following:—

PROFESSOR BOOKER T. WASHINGTON, PARIS, FRANCE:

Dear Sir: We, the citizens of Charleston and West Virginia, desire to express our pride in you and the splendid career that you have thus far accomplished, and ask that we be permitted to show our pride and interest in a substantial way.

Your recent visit to your old home in our midst awoke within us the keenest regret that we were not permitted to hear you and render some substantial aid to your work before you left for Europe.

In view of the foregoing, we earnestly invite you to share the hospitality of our city upon your return from Europe, and give us the opportunity to hear you and put ourselves in touch with your work in a way that will be most gratifying to yourself, and that we may receive the inspiration of your words and presence.

An early reply to this invitation, with an indication of the time you may reach our city, will greatly oblige,

Yours very respectfully,

The Charleston *Daily Gazette*; The Daily *Mail–Tribune*; G. W. Atkinson, Governor; E. L Boggs, Secretary to Governor; Wm. M. O. Dawson, Secretary of State; L. M. La Follette, Auditor; J. R Trotter, Superintendent of Schools; E. W. Wilson, ex-Governor; W. A. MacCorkle, ex-Governor; John Q. Dickinson, President Kanawha Valley Bank; L. Prichard, President Charleston National Bank; Geo. S. Couch, President Kanawha National Bank; Ed. Reid, Cashier Kanawha National Bank; Gen. S. Laidley, Superintendent City Schools; L. E. McWhorter, President Board of Education; Chas. K. Payne, wholesale merchant; and many others.

This invitation, coming as it did from the City Council, the state officers, and all the substantial citizens of both races of the community where I had spent my boyhood, and from which I had gone a few years before, unknown, in poverty and ignorance, in quest of an education, not only surprised me, but almost unmanned me. I could not understand what I had done to deserve it all.

I accepted the invitation, and at the appointee day was met at the railway station at Charleston by committee headed by ex-Governor W. A. MacCorkle, and composed of men of both races. The public reception was held in the Opera-House at Charleston. The Governor of the state, the Hon. George W. Atkinson, presided, and an address of welcome was made by ex-Governor MacCorkle. A prominent part in the reception was taken by the coloured citizens. The Opera-House was filled with citizens of both races, and among the white people were many for whom I had worked when a boy. The next day Governor and Mrs. Atkinson gave me a public reception at the State House, which was attended by all classes.

Not long after this the coloured people in Atlanta, Georgia, gave me a reception at which the Governor of the state presided, and a similar reception was given me in New Orleans, which was presided over by the Mayor of the city. Invitations came from many other places which I was not able to accept.

CHAPTER XVII

Last Words

Before going to Europe some events came I into my life which were great surprises to me. In fact, my whole life has largely been one of surprises. I believe that any man's life will be filled with constant, unexpected encouragements of this kind if he makes up his mind to do his level best each day of his life—that is, tries to make each day reach as nearly as possible the high-water mark of pure, unselfish, useful living. I pity the man, black or white, who has never experienced the joy and satisfaction that come to one by reason of an effort to assist in making some one else more useful and more happy.

Six months before he died, and nearly a year after he had been stricken with paralysis, General Armstrong expressed a wish to visit Tuskegee again before he passed away. Notwithstanding the fact that he had lost the use of his limbs to such extent that he was practically helpless, his wish was gratified, and he was brought to Tuskegee. The owners of the Tuskegee Railroad, white men living in the town, offered to run a special train without cost, out to the main station—Chehaw, five miles away—to meet him. He arrived on

the school grounds about nine o'clock in the evening. Some one had suggested that we give the General a "pine-knot torchlight reception." This plan was carried out, and the moment that his carriage entered the school grounds he began passing between two lines of lighted and waving "fat pine" wood knots held by over a thousand students and teachers. The whole thing was so novel and surprising that the General was completely overcome with happiness. He remained a guest in my home for nearly two months, and, although almost wholly without the use of voice or limb, he spent nearly every hour in devising ways and means to help the South. Time and time again he said to me, during this visit, that it was not only the duty of the country to assist in elevating the Negro of the South, but the poor white man as well. At the end of his visit I resolved anew to devote myself more earnestly than ever to the cause which was so near his heart. I said that if a man in his condition was willing to think, work, and act, I should not be wanting in furthering in every possible way the wish of his heart.

The death of General Armstrong, a few weeks later, gave me the privilege of getting acquainted with one of the finest, most unselfish, and most attractive men that I have ever come in contact with. I refer to the Rev. Dr. Hollis B. Frissell, now the Principal of the Hampton Institute, and General Armstrong's successor. Under the clear, strong, and almost perfect leadership of Dr. Frissell, Hampton has had a career of prosperity and usefulness that is all that the General could have wished for. It seems to be the constant effort of Dr. Frissell to hide his own great personality behind that of General Armstrong to make himself of "no reputation" for the sake of the cause.

More than once I have been asked what was the greatest surprise that ever came to me. I have little hesitation in answering that question. It was the following letter, which came to me one Sunday morning when I was sitting on the veranda of my home at Tuskegee, surrounded by my wife and three children:—

HARVARD UNIVERSITY, CAMBRIDGE, MAY 28, 1896.

PRESIDENT BOOKER T. WASHINGTON,

My Dear Sir: Harvard University desires to confer on you at the approaching Commencement an honorary degree; but it is our custom to confer degrees only on gentlemen who are present. Our Commencement occurs this year on June 24, and your presence would be desirable from about noon till

about five o'clock in the afternoon. Would it be possible for you to be in Cambridge on that day?

Believe me, with great regard,

Very truly yours,
CHARLES W. ELIOT.

This was a recognition that had never in the slightest manner entered into my mind, and it was hard for me to realize that I was to be honoured by a degree from the oldest and most renowned university in America. As I sat upon my veranda, with this letter in my hand, tears came into my eyes. My whole former life—my life as a slave on the plantation, my work in the coal-mine, the times when I was without food and clothing, when I made my bed under a sidewalk, my struggles for an education, the trying days I had had at Tuskegee, days when I did not know where to turn for a dollar to continue the work there, the ostracism and sometimes oppression of my race,—all this passed before me and nearly overcame me.

I had never sought or cared for what the world calls fame. I have always looked upon fame as something to be used in accomplishing good. I have often said to my friends that if I can use whatever prominence may have come to me as an instrument with which to do good, I am content to have it. I care for it only as a means to be used for doing good, just as wealth may be used. The more I come into contact with wealthy people, the more I believe that they are growing in the direction of looking upon their money simply as an instrument which God has placed in their hand for doing good with. I never go to the office of Mr. John D. Rockefeller, who more than once has been generous to Tuskegee, without being reminded of this. The close, careful, and minute investigation that he always makes in order to be sure that every dollar that he gives will do the most good—an investigation that is just as searching as if he were investing money in a business enter-prise—convinces me that the growth in this direction is most encouraging.

At nine o'clock, on the morning of June 24, I met President Eliot, the Board of Overseers of Harvard University, and the other guests, at the desig-nated place on the university grounds, for the purpose of being escorted to Sanders Theatre, where the Commencement exercises were to be held and degrees conferred. Among others invited to be present for the purpose of receiving a degree at this time were General Nelson A. Miles, Dr. Bell, the inventor of the Bell telephone, Bishop Vincent, and the Rev. Minot J. Savage. We were placed in fine immediately behind the President and the

Board of Overseers, and directly afterward the Governor of Massachusetts, escorted by the Lancers, arrived and took his place in the line of march by the side of President Eliot. In the line there were also various other officers and professors, clad in cap and gown. In this order we marched to Sanders Theatre, where, after the usual Commencement exercises, came the conferring of the honorary degrees. This, it seems, is always considered the most interesting feature at Harvard. It is not known, until the individuals appear, upon whom the honorary degrees are to be conferred, and those receiving these honours are cheered by the students and others in proportion to their popularity. During the conferring of the degrees excitement and enthusiasm are at the highest pitch.

When my name was called, I rose, and President Eliot, in beautiful and strong English, conferred upon me the degree of Master of Arts. After these exercises were over, those who had received honorary degrees were invited to lunch with the President. After the lunch we were formed in line again, and were escorted by the Marshal of the day, who that year happened to be Bishop William Lawrence, through the grounds, where, at different points, those who had been honoured were called by name and received the Harvard yell. This march ended at Memorial Hall, where the alumni dinner was served. To see over a thousand strong men, representing all that is best in State, Church, business, and education, with the glow and enthusiasm of college loyalty and college pride,—which has, I think, a peculiar Harvard flavour,—is a sight that does not easily fade from memory.

Among the speakers after dinner were President Eliot, Governor Roger Wolcott, General Miles, Dr. Minot J. Savage, the Hon. Henry Cabot Lodge, and myself. When I was called upon, I said, among other things:—

> It would in some measure relieve my embarrassment if I could, even in a slight degree, feel myself worthy of great honour which you do me to-day. Why you have called me from the Black Belt of the South, from among my humble people, to share in the honours of this occasion, is not for me to explain; and yet it may not be appropriate far me to suggest that it seems to me that one of the most vital questions that touch our American life is how to bring the strong, wealthy, and learned into helpful touch with the poorest, most ignorant, and humblest, and at the same time make one appreciate the vitalizing, strengthening influence of the other. How shall we make the

mansions on yon Beacon Street feel and see the need of the spirits in the lowliest cabin in Alabama cotton-fields or Louisiana sugar-bottoms? This problem Harvard University is solving, not by bringing itself down, but by bringing the masses up.

If my life in the past has meant anything in the lifting up of my people and the bringing about of better relations between your race and mine, I assure you from this day it will mean doubly more. In the economy of God there is but one standard by which an individual can succeed—there is but one for a race. This country demands that every race shall measure itself by the American standard. By it a race must rise or fall, succeed or fail, and in the last analysis mere sentiment counts for little. During the next half-century and more, my race must continue passing through the severe American crucible. We are to be tested in our patience, our forbearance, our perseverance, our power to endure wrong, to withstand temptations, to economize, to acquire and use skill; in our ability to compete, to succeed in commerce, to disregard the superficial for the real, the appearance for the substance, to be great and yet small, learned and yet simple, high and yet the servant of all.

As this was the first time that a New England university had conferred an honorary degree upon a Negro, it was the occasion of much newspaper comment throughout the country. A correspondent of a New York paper said:—

When the name of Booker T. Washington was called, and he arose to acknowledge and accept, there was such an outburst of applause as greeted no other name except that of the popular soldier patriot, General Miles. The applause was not studied and stiff, sympathetic and condoling; it was enthusiasm and admiration. Every part of the audience from pit to gallery joined in, and a glow covered the cheeks of those around me, proving sincere appreciation of the rising struggle of an ex-slave and the work he has accomplished for his race.

A Boston paper said, editorially:—

In conferring the honorary degree of Master of Arts

upon the Principal of Tuskegee Institute, Harvard University has honoured itself as well as the object of this distinction. The work which Professor Booker T. Washington has accomplished for the education, good citizenship and popular enlightenment in his chosen field of labour in the South entitles him to rank with our national benefactors. The university which can claim him on its list of sons, whether in regular course or *honoris causa*, may be proud.

It has been mentioned that Mr. Washington is the first of his race to receive an honorary degree from a New England university. This, in itself, is a distinction. But the degree was not conferred because Mr. Washington is a coloured man, or because he was born in slavery, but because has shown, by his work for the elevation of the people the Black Belt of the South, a genius and a broad humanity which count for greatness in any man, whether his skin be white or black.

Another Boston paper said:—

It is Harvard which, first among New England colleges, confers an honorary degree upon a black man. No one who has followed the history of Tuskegee and its work can to admire the courage, persistence, and splendid common sense of Booker T. Washington. Well may Harvard honour the ex-slave, the value of whose services, alike to his race and country, only the future can estimate.

The correspondent of the New York *Times* wrote:—

All the speeches were enthusiastically received, but the coloured man carried off the oratorical honours, and the applause which broke out when he had finished was vociferous and long-continued.

Soon after I began work at Tuskegee I formed a resolution, in the secret of my heart, that I would try to build up a school that would be of so much service to the country that the President of the United States would one day come to see it. This was, I confess, rather a bold resolution, and for a num-

ber of years I kept it hidden in my own thoughts, not daring to share it with any one.

In November, 1897, I made the first move in this direction, and that was in securing a visit from a member of President McKinley's Cabinet, the Hon. James Wilson, Secretary of Agriculture. He came to deliver an address at the formal opening of the Slater-Armstrong Agricultural Building, our first large building to be used for the purpose of giving training to our students in agriculture and kindred branches. In the fall of 1898 I heard that President McKinley was likely to visit Atlanta, Georgia, for the purpose of taking part in the Peace Jubilee exercises to be held there to commemorate the successful close of the Spanish-American war. At this time I had been hard at work, together with our teachers, for eighteen years, trying to build up a school that we thought would be of service to the Nation, and I determined to make a direct effort to secure a visit from the President and his Cabinet. I went to Washington, and I was not long in the city before I found my way to the White House. When I got there I found the waiting rooms full of people, and my heart began to sink, for I feared there would not be much chance of my seeing the President that day, if at all. But, at any rate, I got an opportunity to see Mr. J. Addison Porter, the secretary to the President, and explained to him my mission. Mr. Porter kindly sent my card directly to the President, and in a few minutes word came from Mr. McKinley that he would see me.

How any man can see so many people of all kinds, with all kinds of errands, and do so much hard work, and still keep himself calm, patient, and fresh for each visitor in the way that President McKinley does, I cannot understand. When I saw the President he kindly thanked me for the work which we were doing at Tuskegee for the interests of the country. I then told him, briefly, the object of my visit. I impressed upon him the fact that a visit from the Chief Executive of the Nation would not only encourage our students and teachers, but would help the entire race. He seemed interested, but did not make a promise to go to Tuskegee, for the reason that his plans about going to Atlanta were not then fully made; but he asked me to call the matter to his attention a few weeks later.

By the middle of the following month the President had definitely decided to attend the Peace Jubilee at Atlanta. I went to Washington again saw him, with a view of getting him to extend his trip to Tuskegee. On this second visit Mr. Charles W. Hare, a prominent white citizen of Tuskegee, kindly volunteered to accompany me, to reënforce my invitation with one from

the white people of Tuskegee and the vicinity.

Just previous to my going to Washington the second time, the country had been excited, and the coloured people greatly depressed, because of several severe race riots which had occurred at different points in the South. As soon as I saw the President, I perceived that his heart was greatly burdened by reason of these race disturbances. Although there were many people waiting to see him, he detained me for some time, discussing the condition and prospects of the race. He remarked several times that he was determined to show his interest and faith in the race, not merely in words, but by acts. When I told him that I thought that at that time scarcely anything would go farther in giving hope and encouragement to the race than the fact that the President of the Nation would be willing to travel one hundred and forty miles out of his way to spend a day at a Negro institution, he seemed deeply impressed.

While I was with the President, a white citizen of Atlanta, a Democrat and an ex-slaveholder, came into the room, and the President asked his opinion as to the wisdom of his going to Tuskegee. With hesitation the Atlanta man replied that it was proper thing for him to do. This opinion was reënforced by that friend of the race, Dr. J. L. M. Curry. The President promised that he would visit our school on the 16th of December.

When it became known that the President was going to visit our school, the white citizens of the town of Tuskegee—a mile distant from the school—were as much pleased as were our students and teachers. The white people of the town, including both men and women, began arranging to decorate the town, and to form themselves into committees for the purpose of coöperating with the officers of our school in order that the distinguished visitor might have a fitting reception. I think I never realized before this how much the white people of Tuskegee and vicinity thought of our institution. During the days when we were preparing for the President's reception, dozens of these people came to me and said that, while they did not want to push themselves into prominence, if there was anything they could do to help, or to relieve me personally, I had but to intimate it and they would be only too glad to assist. In fact, the thing that touched me almost as deeply as the visit of the President itself was the deep pride which all classes of citizens in Alabama seemed to take in our work.

The morning of December 16th brought to the little city of Tuskegee such a crowd as it had never seen before. With the President came Mrs. McKinley and all of the Cabinet officers but one; and most of them brought

their wives or some members of their families. Several prominent generals came, including General Shafter and General Joseph Wheeler, who were recently returned from the Spanish-American war. There was also a host of newspaper correspondents. The Alabama Legislature was in session at Montgomery at this time. This body passed a resolution to adjourn for the purpose of visiting Tuskegee. Just before the arrival of the President's party the Legislature arrived, headed by the governor and other state officials.

The citizens of Tuskegee had decorated the town from the station to the school in a generous manner. In order to economize in the matter of time, we arranged to have the whole school pass in review before the President. Each student carried a stalk of sugar-cane with some open bolls of cotton fastened to the end of it. Following the students the of all departments of the school passed in review, displayed on "floats" drawn by horses, mules, and oxen. On these floats we tried to exhibit not only the present work of the school, but to show the contrasts between the old methods of doing things and the new. As an example, we showed the old method of dairying in contrast with the improved methods, the old methods of tilling the soil in contrast with the new, the old methods of cooking and housekeeping in contrast with the new. These floats consumed an hour and a half of time in passing.

In his address in our large, new chapel, which the students had recently completed, the President said, among other things:—

> To meet you under such pleasant auspices and to have the opportunity of a personal observation of your work is indeed most gratifying. The Tuskegee Normal and Industrial Institute is ideal in its conception, and has already a large and growing reputation in the country, and is not unknown abroad. I congratulate all who are associated in this undertaking for the good work which it is doing in the education of its students to lead lives of honour and usefulness, thus exalting the race for which it was established.
>
> Nowhere, I think, could a more delightful location have been chosen for this unique educational experiment, which has attracted the attention and won the support even of conservative philanthropists in all sections of the country.
>
> To speak of Tuskegee without paying special tribute to Booker T. Washington's genius and perseverance would be impossible. The inception of this noble enterprise was his, and

he deserves high credit for it. His was the enthusiasm and enterprise which made its steady progress possible and established in the institution its present high standard of accomplishment. He has won a worthy reputation as one of the great leaders of his race, widely known and much respected at home and abroad as an accomplished educator, a great orator, and a true philanthropist.

The Hon. John D. Long, the Secretary of the Navy, said in part:—

I cannot make a speech to-day. My heart is too full—full of hope, admiration, and pride for my countrymen of both sections and both colours. I am filled with gratitude and admiration for your work, and from this time forward I shall have absolute confidence in your progress and in the solution of the problem in which you are engaged.

The problem, I say, has been solved. A picture has been presented to-day which should be put upon canvas with the pictures of Washington and Lincoln, and transmitted to future time and generations—a picture which the press of the country should spread broadcast over the land, a most dramatic picture, and that picture is this: The President of the United States standing on this platform on one side the Governor of Alabama, on the other, completing the trinity, a representative of a race only a few years ago in bondage, the coloured President of the Tuskegee Normal and Industrial Institute.

God bless the President under whose majesty such a scene as that is presented to the American people. Got bless the state of Alabama, which is showing that it can deal with this problem for itself. God bless the orator, philanthropist, and disciple of the Great Master—who, if he were on earth, would be doing the same work—Booker T. Washington.

Postmaster General Smith closed the address these words:—

We have witnessed many spectacles within the last few days. We have seen the magnificent grandeur and the magnificent achievements of one of the great metropolitan cities of

the South. We have seen heroes of the war pass by in procession. We have seen floral parades. But I am sure my colleagues will agree with me in saying that we have witnessed no spectacle more impressive and more encouraging, more inspiring for our future, than that which we have witnessed here this morning.

Some days after the President returned to Washington I received the letter which follows:—

EXECUTIVE MANSION, WASHINGTON, DEC. 23, 1899.

Dear Sir: By this mail I take pleasure in sending you engrossed copies of the souvenir of the visit of the President to your institution. These sheets bear the autographs of the President and the members of the Cabinet who accompanied him on the trip. Let me take this opportunity of congratulating you most heartily and sincerely upon the great success of the exercises provided for and entertainment furnished us under your auspices during our visit to Tuskegee. Every feature of the programme was perfectly executed and was viewed or participated in with the heartiest satisfaction by every visitor present. The unique exhibition which you gave of your pupils engaged in their industrial vocations was not only artistic but thoroughly impressive. The tribute paid by the President and his Cabinet to your work was none too high, and forms a most encouraging augury, I think, for the future prosperity of your institution. I cannot close without assuring you that the modesty shown by yourself in the exercises was most favourably commented upon by all the members of our party.

With best wishes for the continued advance of your most useful and patriotic undertaking, kind personal regards and the compliments of the season, believe me, always,
Very sincerely yours,
JOHN ADDISON PORTER.
Secretary to the President.

To PRESIDENT BOOKER T. WASHINGTON, Tuskegee Normal and Industrial Institute, Tuskegee, Ala.

Twenty years have now passed since I made the first humble effort at Tuskegee, in a broken-down shanty and an old hen-house, without owning a dollar's worth of property, and with but one teacher and thirty students. At the present time the institution owns twenty-three hundred acres of land, one thousand of which are under cultivation each year, entirely by student labour. There are now upon the grounds, counting large and small, sixty-six buildings; and all except four of these have been almost wholly erected by the labour of our students. While the students are at work upon the land and in erecting buildings, they are taught, by competent instructors, the latest methods of agriculture and the trades connected with building.

There are in constant operation at the school, in connection with thorough academic and religious training, thirty industrial departments. All of these teach industries at which our men and women can find immediate employment as soon as they leave the institution. The only difficulty now that the demand for our graduates from both white and black people in the South is so great that we cannot supply more than one-half the persons for whom applications come to us. Neither have we the buildings nor the money for current expenses to enable us to admit to the school more than one half the young men and women who apply to us for admission.

In our industrial teaching we keep three thin in mind: first, that the student shall be so educated that he shall be enabled to meet conditions as they exist now, in the part of the South where he lives—in a word, to be able to do the thing which the world wants done; second, that every student who graduates from the school shall have enough skill, coupled with intelligence and moral character, to enable him to make a living for himself and others; third, to send every graduate out feeling and knowing that labour is dignified and beautiful—to make each one love labour instead of trying to escape it. In addition to the agricultural training which we give to young men, and the training given to our girls in all the usual domestic employments, we now train a number of girls in agriculture each year. These girls are taught gardening, fruit-growing, dairying, bee-culture, and poultry-raising.

While the institution is in no sense denominational, we have a department known as the Phelps Hall Bible Training School, in which a number of students are prepared for the ministry and other forms of Christian work, especially work in the country districts. What is equally important, each one of these students works half of each day at some industry, in order to get skill and the love of work, so that when he goes out from the institution he is pre-

pared to set the people with whom he goes to labour a proper example in the matter of industry.

The value of our property is now over $700,000. If we add to this our endowment fund, which at present is $1,000,000, the value of the total property is now $1,700,000. Aside from the need for more buildings and for money for current expenses, the endowment fund should be increased at least $3,000,000. The annual current expenses are now about $150,000. The greater part of this I collect each year by going from door to door and from house to house. All of our property from mortgage, and is deeded to an undenominational board of trustees who have the control of the institution.

From thirty students the number has grown to hundred, coming from twenty-seven states and territories, from Africa, Cuba, Porto Rico, Jamaica, and other foreign countries. In our departments there are one hundred and ten officers and instructors; and if we add the families of our instructors, we have a constant population upon our grounds of not far from seventeen hundred people.

I have often been asked how we keep so large a body of people together, and at the same time keep them out of mischief. There are two answers: that the men and women who come to us for an education are in earnest; and that everybody is kept busy. The following outline of our daily work will testify to this:—

> 5 A.M., rising bell; 5.50 A.M., warning breakfast bell; 6 A.M., breakfast bell; 6.20 A.M., breakfast over; 6.20 to 6.50 A.M., rooms are cleaned; 6.50, work bell; 7.30, morning study hour; 8.00, morning school bell; 8.25, inspection of young men's toilet in ranks; 8.40, devotional exercises in chapel; 8.55, five minutes with the daily news; 9 A.M., class work begins; 12, class work closes; 12.15 P.M., dinner; 1 P.M., work bell; 1.30 P.M., class work begins; 3.30 P.M., class work ends; 5.30 P.M., bell to "knock off" work; 6 P.M., supper; 7.10 P.M., evening prayers; 7.30 P.M., evening study hour; 8.45 P.M., evening study hour closes; 9.20 P.M., warning retiring bell; 9.30 P.M., retiring bell.

We try to keep constantly in mind the fact that the worth of the school is to be judged by its graduates. Counting those who have finished the full course, together with those who have taken enough training to enable them

to do reasonably good work, we can safely say that at least six thousand men and women from Tuskegee are now at work in different parts of the South; men and women who, by their own example or by direct effort, are showing the masses of our race how to improve their material, educational, and moral and religious life. What is equally important, they are exhibiting a degree of common sense and self-control which is causing better relations to exist between the races and is causing the Southern white man to learn to believe in the value of educating the men and women of my race. Aside from this, there is the influence that is constantly being exerted through the mothers' meeting and the plantation work conducted by Mrs. Washington.

Wherever our graduates go, the changes which soon begin to appear in the buying of land, improving homes, saving money, in education, and in high moral character are remarkable. Whole communities are fast being revolutionized through the instrumentality of these men and women.

Ten years ago I organized at Tuskegee the first Negro Conference. This is an annual gathering which now brings to the school eight or nine hundred representative men and women of the race, who come to spend a day in finding out what the actual industrial, mental, and moral conditions of the people are, and in forming plans for improvement. Out from this central Negro Conference at Tuskegee have grown numerous state and local conferences which are doing the same kind of work. As a result of the influence of these gatherings, one delegate reported at the last annual meeting that ten families in his community had bought and paid homes. On the day following the annual Negro Conference, there is held the "Workers' Conference." This is composed of officers and teachers who are engaged in educational work in the larger institutions in the South. The Negro Conference furnishes a rare opportunity for these workers to study the real condition of the rank and file of the people.

In the summer of 1900, with the assistance of prominent coloured men as Mr. T. Thomas Fortune, who has always upheld my hands in every effort, I organized the National Negro Business League, which held its first meeting in Boston, and brought together for the first time a large number of the coloured men who are engaged in various types of trade or business in different parts of the United States. Thirty states were represented at our first meeting. Out of this national meeting grew state and local business leagues.

In addition to looking after the executive side of the work at Tuskegee, and raising the greater part of the money for the support of the school, I cannot seem to escape the duty of answering at least a part of the calls which

come to me unsought to address Southern white audiences and audiences of my own race, as well as frequent gatherings in the North. As to how much of my time is spent in this way, the following clipping from a Buffalo (N. Y.) paper will tell. This has reference to an occasion when I spoke before the National Educational Association in that city.

> Booker T. Washington, the foremost educator among the coloured people of the world, was a very busy man from the time he arrived in the city the other night from the West and registered at the Iroquois. He had hardly removed the stains of travel when it was time to partake of. Then he held a public levee in the parlours of the until eight o'clock. During that time he was greeted by over two hundred eminent teachers and educators from all parts of the United States. Shortly after eight o'clock he was driven in a carriage to Music Hall, and in one hour and a half he made two ringing addresses, as many as five thousand people, on Negro education. Then Mr. Washington was taken in charge by a delegation of coloured citizens, headed by the Rev. Mr. Watkins, and hustled off to a small informal reception, arranged in honour of the visitor by the people of his race.

Nor can I, in addition to making these addresses, escape the duty of calling the attention of the South and of the country in general, through the medium of the press, to matters that pertain to the interests of both races. This, for example, I have done in regard to the evil habit of lynching. When the Louisiana State Constitutional Convention was in session, I wrote an open letter to that body pleading for justice for the race. In all such efforts I have received warm and hearty support from the Southern newspapers, as well as from those in all other parts of the country.

Despite superficial and temporary signs which might lead one to entertain a contrary opinion, there was never a time when I felt more hopeful for the race than I do at the present. The great human law that in the end recognizes and rewards merit is everlasting and universal. The outside world does not know, neither can it appreciate, the struggle that is constantly going on in the hearts of both the Southern white people and their former slaves to free themselves from racial prejudice; and while both races are thus struggling they should have the sympathy, the support, and the forbearance of the rest

of the world.

As I write the closing words of this autobiography I find myself—not by design—in the city of Richmond, Virginia: the city which only a few decades ago was the capital of the Southern Confederacy, and where, about twenty-five years ago, because of my poverty I slept night after night under a sidewalk.

This time I am in Richmond as the guest of the coloured people of the city; and came at their request to deliver an address last night to both races in the Academy of Music, the largest and finest audience room in the city. This was the first time that the coloured people had ever been permitted to use this hall. The day before I came, the City Council passed a vote to attend the meeting in a body to hear me speak. The state Legislature, including the House of Delegates and the Senate, also passed a unanimous vote to attend in a body. In the presence of hundreds of coloured people, many distinguished white citizens, the City Council, the state Legislature, and state officials, I delivered my message, which was one of hope and cheer; and from the bottom of my heart I thanked both races for this welcome back to the state that gave me birth.

IDA B. WELLS

(1864-1931)

The daughter of slaves, Ida B. Wells was born on July 6, 1862 in Holly Springs, Mississippi, just months before the signing of the Emancipation Proclamation. Her parents went to work for their master after their emancipation, and were able to support Ida and her seven younger siblings, since her mother was a celebrated cook and her father was a highly skilled carpenter. Still, the Wells family was not without hardship. When Ida was just 14, an epidemic wave of Yellow Fever spread through Holly Springs and killed both her parents and her youngest sibling. True to the character that she would later in life become renowned for, Wells secured a teaching job in town to keep her family together, and still managed to continue her own education by attending nearby Rust College.

Already, the wheels were in motion for what would be a contentious and combative struggle by Wells for civil rights. On a train to Memphis, Tennessee, where she had just accepted a new teaching job for $25 a month, a conductor insisted she move from the parlor car to the smoking car—often called the "Jim Crow" car and reserved for blacks. Wells refused, and when the conductor grabbed her by the wrist, she bit him. At just 25 years old, she brought suit against the Chesapeake & Ohio Railroad Company and won. However, the state court eventually overturned the circuit court's decision.

The lawsuit against the railroad company, despite being legally unsuccessful, helped to ignite Wells' career as a journalist. Newspapers, which had been covering the fascinating story of this young black woman who dared to stand up to white supremacy in the courts, clamored to hear about her experiences. Soon, her writing career was in full bloom, and when she published a series of articles denouncing the quality of education provided to black children, her career as a teacher in Memphis was over.

In 1889, Wells became an editor and co-owner of a local black newspaper, *The Free Speech and Headlight*, where she also wrote editorials under the

pseudonym "Iola." Her columns championed black rights and caused quite a stir in the community. But the killing of one of her best friends in 1892 ignited a ceaseless campaign against lynching by Wells, which would impact the rest of her life.

Thomas Moss, Calvin McDowell and Henry Stewart were owners of People's Grocery Company, a small store which had begun to take customers away from competing white stores. A group of angry white men attempted to intimidate People's Grocery from doing business by attacking the store, but the owners resisted, shooting back at the attackers and injuring one. The owners of the store were subsequently arrested and jailed, but a lynch-mob stormed the jail, taking them away from town and hanging all three.

Wells began a crusade against the city of Memphis and encouraged the black townsmen to head west, railing against lynching and calling for a black boycott of the new streetcar line. In *The Free Speech and Headlight*, she wrote:

> The city of Memphis has demonstrated that neither character nor standing avails the Negro if he dares to protect himself against the white man or become his rival. There is nothing we can do about the lynching now, as we are out-numbered and without arms. The white mob could help itself to ammunition without pay, but the order is rigidly enforced against the selling of guns to Negroes. There is therefore only one thing left to do; save our money and leave a town which will neither protect our lives and property, nor give us a fair trial in the courts, but takes us out and murders us in cold blood when accused by white persons.

Many people acted on Wells' advice and left town, while others in the black community organized a boycott of white-owned businesses as a protest against the lynchings. But things did not quiet down in Memphis. While Wells was attending an editor's convention in New York, she received a warning not to return to Memphis because her life would be in danger. Her newspaper office was destroyed by an angry mob, and she stayed in New York, becoming a reporter for the *New York Age* newspaper before going on to England to gain support and hone her oratory skills.

When she returned to the United States in 1895, she met and married a lawyer and newspaper owner, Ferdinand Barnett. Together, they raised five children in Chicago, Illinois, and she used his newspaper, the *Chicago Conservator*, to call for equal rights. She also formed the Women's Era Club,

which was the first civic organization for African-American women, and the club was eventually renamed the Ida B. Wells club to honor her.

In 1895, Ida B. Wells-Barnett wrote *A Red Record*, which was one of the first published accounts of lynching episodes in the country—then at epidemic proportions in the years after Reconstruction. Although it was clear that Wells-Barnett had an agenda in her writings, she was very careful to present evidence that was factually accurate in her reports. She used white sources for most of her information, and used the statistics compiled by the *Chicago Tribune*. Her research showed that southern whites often defended the lynchings, citing they were the result of black men raping white women—though statistics showed that not even one in three lynchings even insinuated a rape charge, let alone proved one.

Wells-Barnett's language in *A Red Record* is fiery and provocative. She does not mince words or speak cautiously so as not to accuse, but rather she goes for the jugular of the southern white establishment:

> In considering the third reason assigned by the Southern white people for the butchery of blacks, the question must be asked, what the white man means when he charges the black man of rape? Does he mean the crime which the statutes of the civilized states describe as such? Not by any means. With the Southern white man, any misalliance existing between a white woman and a colored man is a sufficient foundation for the charge of rape. The Southern white man says that it is impossible for a voluntary alliance to exist between a white woman and a colored woman, and therefore, the fact of an alliance is a proof of force. In numerous instances where colored men have been lynched on the charge of rape, it was positively known at the time of lynching, and indisputably proven after the victim's death, that the relationship sustained between the man and woman was voluntary and clandestine, and that in no court of law could even the charge of assault have been successfully maintained.

From 1898 to 1902, Wells-Barnett became secretary of the National Afro-American Council, and in 1906, she joined with W.E.B. DuBois and others to further the Niagara Movement, Wells-Barnett was also one of two African-American women to sign "the call," to become a member of the "Committee of 40," which established the groundwork for what would eventually become the National Association for the Advancement of Colored

People in 1909, the oldest civil rights organization in the country.

In 1910, she founded and became the first president of the Negro Fellowship League. She was militant in her calls for justice and equality for African-Americans, and was a very vocal critic of Booker T. Washington, as well as a less radical N.A.A.C.P., which she later felt was not outspoken enough.

Continuing her anti-lynching crusade, Wells wrote *Southern Horrors: Lynch Law in All Its Phases*, and she became a tireless campaign worker for women's suffrage, establishing Chicago's Alpha Suffrage Club, and walking in the famous march for universal suffrage in Washington in 1913. By 1930, Wells-Barnett was still agitating, and she decided to run for the Illinois State legislature, making her one of the first black women to run for public office in America.

Ida B. Wells-Barnett was the most prestigious black female journalist in the country during her day. She died on March 25, 1931, and nearly forty years later, her autobiography, *Crusade for Justice* was published posthumously, insuring that her voice would be heard long after she was gone.

A Red Record

PREFACE.

Hon. Frederick Douglass' Letter. Dear Miss Wells:

Let me give you thanks for your faithful paper on the lynch abomination now generally practiced against colored people in the South. There has been no word equal to It in convincing power. I have spoken, but my word is feeble in comparison. You give us what you know and testify from actual knowledge. You have dealt with the facts with cool, painstaking fidelity, and left those naked and uncontradicted facts to speak for themselves.

Brave woman! you have done your people and mine a service which can neither be weighed nor measured. If the American conscience were only half alive, if the American church and clergy were only half Christianized, if American moral sensibility were not hardened by persistent Infliction of outrage and crime against colored people, a scream of horror, shame, and indignation would rise to Heaven wherever your pamphlet shall be read.

But alas! even crime has power to reproduce itself and create conditions favorable to its own existence. It sometimes seems we are deserted by earth and Heaven—yet we must still think, speak and work, and trust In the power of a merciful God for final deliverance

Very truly and gratefully yours,
FREDERICK DOUGLASS.
Cedar Hill, Anacostia, D. C.

CHAPTER I.

THE CASE STATED

The student of American sociology will find the year 1894 marked by a pronounced awakening of the public conscience to a system of anarchy and outlawry which had grown during a series of ten years to be so common, that scenes of unusual brutality failed to have any visible effect upon the humane sentiments of the people of our land.

Beginning with the emancipation of the Negro, the inevitable result of unbridled power exercised for two and a half centuries, by the white man over the Negro; began to show itself in acts of conscienceless outlawry. During the slave regime, the Southern white man owned the Negro body and soul. It was to his interest to dwarf the soul and preserve the body. Vested with unlimited power over his slave, to subject him to any and all kinds of physical punishment, the white man was still restrained from such punishment as tended to injure the slave by abating his physical powers and thereby reducing his financial worth. While slaves were scourged mercilessly, and in countless cases inhumanely treated in other respects, still the white owner rarely permitted his anger to go so far as to take a life, which would entail upon him a loss of several hundred dollars. The slave was rarely killed, he was too valuable; it was easier and quite as effective, for discipline or revenge, to sell him "Down South."

But Emancipation came and the vested interests of the white man in the Negro's body were lost. The white man had no right to scourge the emancipated Negro, still less has he a right to kill him. But the Southern white people had been educated so long in that school of practice, in which might makes right, that they disdained to draw strict lines of action in dealing with the Negro. In slave times the Negro was kept subservient and submissive by the frequency and severity of the scourging, but, with freedom, a new system of Intimidation came into vogue; the Negro was not only whipped and scourged; he was killed.

Not all nor nearly all of the murders done by white men, during the past thirty years in the South, have come to light, but the statistics as gathered and preserved by white men, and which have not been questioned, show that during these years more than ten thousand Negroes have been killed In cold blood, without the formality of Judicial trial and legal execution. And yet, as

evidence of the absolute impunity with which the white man dares to kill a Negro, the same record shows that during all these years, and for all these murders only three white men have been tried, convicted, and executed. As no white man has been lynched for the murder of colored people, these three executions are the only instances of the death penalty being visited upon white men for murdering Negroes.

Naturally enough the commission of these crimes began to tell upon the public conscience, and the Southern white man, as a tribute to the nineteenth century civilization, was in a manner compelled to give excuses for his barbarism. His excuses have adapted themselves to the emergency, and are aptly outlined by that greatest of all Negroes, Frederick Douglass, in an article of recent date, in which be shows that there have been three distinct eras of Southern barbarism, to account for which three distinct excuses have been made.

The first excuse given to the civilized world for the murder of unoffending Negroes was the necessity of the white man to repress and stamp out alleged "race riots." For years immediately succeeding the war there was an appalling slaughter of colored people, and the wires usually conveyed to northern people and the world the intelligence, first, that an insurrection was being planned by Negroes, which, a few hours later, would prove to have been vigorously resisted by white men, and controlled with a resulting loss of several killed and wounded. It was always a remarkable feature in these insurrections and riots that only Negroes were killed during the rioting, and that all the white men escaped unharmed.

From 1865 to 1872, hundreds of colored men and women were mercilessly murdered and the almost invariable reason assigned was that they met their death by being alleged participants in an insurrection or riot. But this story at last wore itself out. No insurrection ever materialized; no Negro rioter was ever apprehended and proven guilty, and no dynamite ever recorded the black man's protest against oppression and wrong. It was too much to ask thoughtful people to believe this transparent story, and the southern white people at last made up their minds that some other excuse must be bad.

Then came the second excuse, which had its birth during the turbulent times of reconstruction. By an amendment to the Constitution the right of franchise, and, theoretically at least, his ballot became his invaluable emblem of citizenship. In a government "of the people, for the people, and by the people," the Negro's vote became an important factor in all matters of state and national politics. But this did not last long. The southern white man

would not consider that the Negro had any right which a white man was bound to respect, and the idea of a republican form of government in the southern states grew into general contempt. It was maintained that "This is a white man's government," and regardless of numbers the white man should rule. "No Negro domination" became the new legend on the sanguinary banner of the sunny South, and under it rode the Ku Klux Klan, the Regulators, and the lawless mobs, which for any cause chose to murder one man or a dozen as suited their purpose best. It was a long, gory campaign; the blood chills and the heart almost loses faith in Christianity when one thinks of Yazoo, Hamburg, Edgefield, Copiah, and the countless massacres of defenseless Negroes, whose only crime was the attempt to exercise their right to vote.

But it was a bootless strife for colored people. The government which had made the Negro a citizen found itself unable to protect him. It gave him the right to vote, but denied him the protection which should have maintained that right. Scourged from his home; hunted through the swamps; hung by midnight raiders, and openly murdered in the light of day, the Negro clung to his right of franchise with a heroism which would have wrung admiration from the hearts of savages. He believed that in that small white ballot there was a subtle something which stood for manhood as well as citizenship, and thousands of brave black men went to their graves, exemplifying the one by dying for the other. The white man's victory soon became complete by fraud, violence, intimidation and murder. The franchise vouchsafed to the Negro grew to be a "barren ideality," and regardless of numbers, the colored people found themselves voiceless in the councils of those whose duty it was to rule. With no longer the fear of "Negro Domination" before their eyes, the white man's second excuse became valueless. With the Southern governments all subverted and the Negro actually eliminated from all participation in state and national elections, there could be no longer an excuse for killing Negroes to prevent "Negro Domination."

Brutality still continued; Negroes were whipped, scourged, exiled, shot and hung whenever and wherever it pleased the white man so to treat them, and as the civilized world with increasing persistency held the white people of the South to account for its outlawry, the murderers invented the third excuse—that Negroes had to be killed to avenge their assaults upon women. There could be framed no possible excuse more harmful to the Negro and more unanswerable if true in its sufficiency for the white man. Humanity abhors the assailant of womanhood, and this charge upon the Negro at once placed him beyond the pale of human sympathy. With such unanimity,

earnestness and apparent candor was this; charge made and reiterated that the world has accepted the story that the Negro is a monster which the Southern white man has painted him. And to-day, the Christian world feels, that while lynching a crime, and lawlessness and anarchy the certain precursors of a nation's fall, it can not by word or deed, extend sympathy or help to a race of outlaws, who might mistake their plea for justice and deem it an excuse for their continued wrongs.

The Negro has suffered much and is willing to suffer more. He recognizes that the wrongs of two centuries can not be righted in a day, and he tries to bear his burden with patience for to-day and be hopeful for to-morrow. But there comes a time when the veriest worm will turn, and the Negro feels to-day that after all the work he has done, all the sacrifices he has made, and all the suffering he has endured, if he did not, now, defend his name and manhood from this vile accusation, he would be unworthy even of the contempt of mankind. It is to this charge he now feels he must make answer.

If the Southern people in defense of their lawlessness, would tell the truth and admit that colored men and women are lynched for almost any offense, from murder to a misdemeanor, there would not now be the necessity for this defense. But when they intentionally, maliciously and constantly deny the record and bolster up these falsehoods by the words of legislators, preachers, governors and bishops, then the Negro must give to the world his side of the awful story. A word as to the charge itself. In considering the third reason assigned by the Southern white people for the butchery of blacks, the question must be asked, what the white man means when he charges the black man with rape. Does he mean the crime which the statutes of the civilized states describe as such? Not by any means. With the Southern white man, any misalliance existing between a white woman and a colored man is a sufficient foundation for the charge of rape. The Southern white man says that it is impossible for a voluntary alliance to exist between a white woman and a colored man, and therefore, the fact of an alliance is a proof of force. In numerous instances where colored men have been lynched on the charge of rape, it was positively known at the time of lynching, and indisputably proven after the victim's death, that the relationship sustained between the man and woman was voluntary and clandestine, and that in no court of law could even the charge of assault have been successfully maintained.

It was for the assertion of this fact, in the defense of her own race, that the writer hereof became an exile; her property destroyed and her return to her home forbidden under penalty of death, for writing the following edito-

rial which was printed in her paper, the Free Speech, in Memphis, Tenn., May 21, 1892:

"Eight Negroes lynched since last issue of the 'Free Speech' one at Little Rock, Ark., last Saturday morning where the citizens broke into the penitentiary and got their man; three near Anniston, Ala., one near New Orleans; and three at Clarksville, Ga., the last three for killing a white man, and live on the same old racket—the new alarm about raping white women. The same programme of hanging, then shooting bullets into the lifeless bodies was carried out to the letter. Nobody In this section of the country believes the old threadbare he that Negro men rape white women. If Southern white men are not careful, they will over-reach themselves and public sentiment will have a reaction; a conclusion will then be reached which will be very damaging to the moral reputation of their women."

But threats cannot suppress the truth, and while the Negro suffers the soul deformity, resultant from two and a half centuries of slavery, he is no more guilty of this vilest of all white charges than the white man who would blacken his name.

During all the years of slavery, no such charge was ever made, not even during the dark days of the rebellion, when the white man, following the fortunes of war went to do battle for the maintenance of slavery. While the master was away fighting to forge the fetters upon the slave, he left his wife and children with no protectors save the Negroes themselves. And yet during those years of trust and peril, no Negro proved recreant to his trust and no white man returned to a home that had been despoiled.

Likewise during the period of alleged "insurrection," and alarming "race riots," It never occurred to the white man, that his wife and children were in danger of assault. Nor in the Reconstruction era, when the hue and cry was against "Negro Domination," was there ever a thought that the domination would ever contaminate a fireside or strike to death the virtue of womanhood. It must appear strange indeed, to every thoughtful and candid man, that more than a quarter of a century elapsed before the Negro began to show signs of such infamous degeneration.

In his remarkable apology for lynching, Bishop Haygood, of Georgia, says: "No race, not the most savage, tolerates the rape of woman, but it may be said without reflection upon any other people that the Southern people are now and always have been most sensitive concerning the honor of their women their mothers, wives, sisters and daughters." It is not the purpose of this defense to say one word against the white women of the South. Such

need not be said, but it is their misfortune that the chivalrous white men of that section, in order to escape the deserved execration of the civilized world, should shield themselves by their cowardly and infamously false excuse, and call into question that very honor about which their distinguished priestly apologist claims they are most sensitive. To justify their own barbarism they assume a chivalry which they do not possess. True chivalry respects all womanhood and no one who reads the record, as it is written in the faces of the minion mulattos in the South, will for a minute conceive that the southern white man had a very chivalrous regard for the honor due the women of his own race or respect for the womanhood which circumstances placed in his power. That chivalry which is "most sensitive concerning the honor of women" can hope for but little respect from the civilized world, when it confines itself entirely to the women who happen to be white. Virtue knows no color line, and the chivalry which depends upon complexion of skill and texture of hair can command no honest respect.

When emancipation came to the Negroes, there arose in the northern part of the United States an almost divine sentiment among the noblest, purest and best white women of the North, who felt called to a mission to educate and Christianize the minions of southern ex-slaves. From every nook and corner of the North, brave young white women answered that call and left their cultured homes, their happy associations and their lives of ease, and with heroic determination went to the South to carry light and truth to the benighted blacks. It was a heroism no less than that which calls for volunteers for India, Africa and the Isles of the sea. To educate their unfortunate charges; to teach them the Christian virtues and to inspire in them the moral sentiments manifest in their own lives, these young women braved dangers whose record reads more like fiction than fact. They became social outlaws in the South. The peculiar sensitiveness of the southern white men for women, never shed its protecting influence about them. No friendly word from their own race cheered them in their work; no hospitable doors gave them the companionship like that from which they had come. No chivalrous white man doffed his hat in honor or respect. They were "Nigger teachers" unpardonable offenders in the social ethics of the South, and were insulted, persecuted and ostracized, not by Negroes, but by the white manhood which boasts of Its chivalry toward women.

And yet these northern women worked on, year after year, unselfishly, with a heroism which amounted almost to martyrdom. Threading their way through dense forests, working in schoolhouse, in the cabin and in the

church, thrown at all times and in all places among the unfortunate and lowly Negroes, whom they had come to find and to serve, these northern women, thousands and thousands of them, have spent more than a quarter of a century in giving to the colored people their splendid lessons for home and heart and soul. Without protection, save that which innocence gives to every good woman, they went about their work, fearing no assault and suffering none. Their chivalrous protectors were hundreds of miles away in their northern homes, and yet they never feared any "great dark faced mobs," they dared night or day to "go beyond their own roof trees." They never complained of assaults, and no mob was ever called into existence to avenge crimes against them. Before the world adjudges the Negro a moral monster, a vicious assailant of womanhood and a menace to the sacred precincts of home, the colored people ask the consideration of the silent record of gratitude, respect, protection and devotion of the minions of the race in the South, to the thousands of northern white women who have served as teachers and missionaries since the war.

The Negro may not have known what chivalry was, but he knew enough to preserve inviolate the womanhood of the South which was entrusted to his hands during the war. The finer sensibilities of his soul may have been crushed out by years of slavery, but his heart was full of gratitude to the white women of the North, who blessed his home and inspired his soul in all these years of freedom. Faithful to his trust in both of these instances, he should now have the impartial ear of the civilized world, when he dares to speak for himself as against the infamy wherewith he stands charged.

It is his regret, that, in his own defense, he must disclose to the world that degree of dehumanizing brutality which fixes upon America the blot of a national crime. Whatever faults and failings other nations may have in their dealings with their own subjects or with other people, no other civilized nation stands condemned before the world with a series of crimes so peculiarly national. It becomes a painful duty of the Negro to reproduce a record which shows that a large portion of the American people avow anarchy, condone murder and defy the contempt of civilization.

These pages are written in no spirit of vindictiveness, for all who give the subject consideration must concede that far too serious is the condition of that civilized government in which the spirit of unrestrained outlawry constantly increases in violence, and casts its blight over a continually growing area of territory. We plead not for the colored people alone, but for all victims of the terrible injustice which puts men and women to death without

form of law. During the year 1894, there were 132 persons executed in the United States by due form of law, while in the same year, 197 persons were put to death by mobs who gave the victims no opportunity to make a lawful defense.

No comment need be made upon a condition of public sentiment responsible for such alarming results.

The purpose of the pages which follow shall be to give the record which has been made, not by colored men, but that which is the result of compilations made by white men, of reports sent over the civilized world by white men in the South. Out of their own mouths shall the murderers be condemned. For a number of years the Chicago Tribune, admittedly one of the leading journals of America, has made a specialty of the compilation of statistics touching upon lynching. The data compiled by that journal and published to the world January 1st, 1894, up to the present time has not been disputed. In order to be safe from the charge of exaggeration, the incidents hereinafter reported have been confined to those vouched for by the Tribune.

CHAPTER II.

LYNCH LAW STATISTICS.

From the record published in the Chicago Tribune, January 1, 1894, the following computation of lynching statistics is made referring only to the colored victims of Lynch Law during the year 1893:

ARSON.

Sept. 15, Paul Hill, Carrollton, Ala.; Sept. 15, Paul Archer, Carrollton, Ala.; Sept. 15, William Archer, Carrollton, Ala.; Sept. 15, Emma Fair, Carrollton, Ala.

SUSPECTED ROBBERY.

Dec. 23, unknown negro, Fannin, Miss.

ASSAULT.

Dec. 25, Calvin Thomas, near Brainbridge, Ga.

ATTEMPTED ASSAULT.
Dec. 28, Tinman Green, Columbia, La.

INCENDIARISM.
Jan. 26, Patrick Wells, Quincy, Fla.; Feb. 9, Frank Harrell, Dickery, Miss.; Feb. 9, William Filder, Dickery, Miss.

ATTEMPTED RAPE.
Feb. 21, Richard Mays, Springville, Mo.; Aug. 14, Dug Hazleton, Carrollton, Ga.; Sept. 1, Judge McNeil, Cadiz, Ky.; Sept. 11, Frank Smith, Newton, Miss.; Sept. 16, William Jackson, Nevada, Mo.; Sept. 19, Riley Gulley, Pine Apple, Ala.; Oct. 9, John Davis, Shorterville, Ala.; Nov. 8, Robert Kennedy, Spartansburg, S. C.

BURGLARY.
Feb. 16, Richard Forman, Granada, Miss.

WIFE BEATING.
Oct. 14, David Jackson, Covington, La.

ATTEMPTED MURDER.
Sept. 21, Thomas Smith, Roanoke, Va.

ATTEMPTED ROBBERY.
Dec. 12, four unknown Negroes, near Selma, Ala.

RACE PREJUDICE.
Jan. 30, Thomas Carr, Kosciusko, Miss.; Feb. 7, William Butler, Hickory Creek, Texas; Aug. 27, Charles Tart, Lyons Station, Miss.; Dec. 7, Robert Greenwood, Cross county, Ark.; July 14, Allen Butler, Lawrenceville, Ill.

THIEVES.
Oct. 24, two unknown Negroes, Knox Point, La.

ALLEGED BARN BURNING.
Nov. 4, Edward Wagner, Lynchburg, Va.; Nov. 4, William Wagner, Lynchburg, Va.; Nov. 4, Samuel Motlow, Lynchburg, Va.; Nov. 4, Eliza Motlow, Lynchburg, Va.

ALLEGED MURDER.

Jan. 21, Robert Landry, St. James Parish, La.; Jan. 21, Chicken George, St. James Parish, La.; Jan. 21, Richard Davis, St. James Parish, La.; Dec. 8, Benjamin Menter, Berlin, Ala.; Dec. 8, Robert Wilkins, Berlin, Ala.; Dec. 8, Joseph Gevhens, Berlin, Ala.

ALLEGED COMPLICITY IN MURDER.

Sept. 16, Valsin Julian, Jefferson Parish, La.; Sept. 16, Basil Julian, Jefferson Parish, La.; Sept. 16, Paul Julian, Jefferson Parish, La.; Sept. 16, John Willis, Jefferson Parish, La.

MURDER.

June 29, Samuel Thorp, Savannah, Ga.; June 29, George S. Riechen, Waynesboro, Ga.; June 30, Joseph Bird, Wilberton, 1. T.; July 1, James Lamar, Darien, Ga.; July 28, Henry Miner, Dallas, Texas; July 28, Ada Hiers, Walterboro, S. C.; July 28, Alexander Brown, Bastrop, Texas; July 30, W. G. Jamison, Quincy, In.; Sept. 1, John Ferguson, Lawrens, S. C.; Sept. 1, Oscar Johnston, Berkeley, S. C.; Sept. 1, Henry Ewillg, Berkeley, S. C.; Sept. 8, William Smith, Camden, Ark.; Sept. 15, Staples Green, Livingston, Ala.; Sept. 29, Hiram Jacobs, Mount Vernon, Ga.; Sept. 29, Lucien Mannet, Mount Vernon, Ga.; Sept. 29, Hire Bevington, Mount Vernon, Ga.; Sept. 29, Weldon Gordon, Mount Vernon, Ga.; Sept. 29, Parse Strickland, Mount Vernon, Ga.; Oct. 20, William Dalton, Cartersville, Ga.; Oct. 27, M. D. Taylor, Wise Court House, Va.; Oct. 27, Isaac Williams, Madison, Ga.; Nov. 10, Miller Davis, Center Point, Ark.; Nov. 14, John Johnston, Auburn, N. Y.

Sept. 27, Calvin Stewart, Langley, S, C.; Sept 29, Henry Coleman, Benton, La.; Oct. 18, William Richards, Summerfield, Ga.; Oct. 18, James Dickson, Summerfield, Ga.; Oct. 27, Edward Jenkins, Clayton county, Ga.: Nov. 9, Henry Boggs, Fort White, Fla.; Nov. 14, three unknown negroes, Lake City Junction, Fla.; Nov. 14, D. T. Nelson, Varney, Ark.; Nov. 29, Newton Jones, Baxley, Ga.; Dec. 2, Lucius Holt, Concord, Ga.; Dec. 10, two unknown negroes, Richmond, Ala.; July 12, Henry Fleming, Columbus, Miss.; July 17, unknown negro, Briar Field, Ala.; July 18, Meredith Lewis, Roseland, La.; July 29, Edward Bin, Dresden, Tenn.; Aug. l, Henry Reynolds, Montgomery, Tenn.; Aug. 9, unknown negro, McCreery, Ark.; Aug. 12, unknown negro, Brantford, Fla.; Aug. 18, Charles Walton, Morganfield, Ky.; Aug. 21, Charles Tait, near Memphis, Tenn.; Aug. 28, Leonard Taylor, New Castle, Ky.; Sept. 8, Benjamin Jackson, Quincy, Miss.;

Sept. 14, John Williams, Jackson, Tenn.

SELF DEFENSE.

July 30, unknown negro Wingo, Ky.

POISONING WELLS.

Aug. 18, two unknown negroes, Franklin Parish, La.

ALLEGED WELL POISONING.

Sept. 15, Benjamin Jackson, Jackson, Miss.; Sept. 15, Mahala Jackson, Jackson, Miss; Sept. 16, Louisa Carter, Jackson, Miss.; Sept. 15, W. A. Haley, Jackson, Miss.; Sept. 15, Rufus Bigley, Jackson, Miss.

INSULTING WHITES.

Feb. 18, John Hughes, Moberly, Mo.; June 2, Isaac Lincoln, Fort Madison, S. C.

MURDEROUS ASSAULT.

April 20, Daniel Adams, Selina, Kan.

NO OFFENSE.

July 21, Charles Martin, Shelby Co., Tenn.; July 30, William Steen, Paris, Miss.; August 31, unknown negro, Yarborough, Tex.; Sept. 30, unknown negro, Houston, Tex.; Dec. 28, Mack Segars, Brantley, Ala.

ALLEGED RAPE.

July 7, Charles T. Miner, Bardwell, Ky.; Aug. 10, Daniel Lewis, Waycross, Ga.; Aug. 10, James Taylor, Waycross, Ga.; Aug. 10, John Chambers, Waycross, Ga.

ALLEGED STOCK POISONING.

Dec. 16, Henry G. Givens, Nebro, Ky.

SUSPECTED MURDER.

Dec. 23, Sloan Allen, West Mississippi.

SUSPICION OF RAPE.

Feb. 14, Andy Blount, Chattanooga, Tenn.

TURNING STATE'S EVIDENCE.

Dec. 19, William Ferguson, Adele, Ga.

RAPE.

Jan. 19, James Williams, Pickens Co., Ala.; Feb. 11, unknown negro, Forest Hill, Tenn.; Feb. 26, Joseph Hayne, or Paine, Jellico, Tenn.; Nov. 1, Abner Anthony, Hot Springs, Va., Nov. 1, Thomas Hill, Spring Place, Ga.; April 24, John Peterson, Denmark, S. C.; May 6, Samuel Gainard, S. C.; May 10, Haywood Banks, or Marksdale, Columbia, S. C.; May 12, Israel Halliway, Napolconvine, La.; May 12, unknown negro, Wythevine, Va.; May 31, John Wallace, Jefferson Springs, Ark.; June 3, Samuel Bush, Decatur, In.; June 8, L. C. Dumas, Gleason, Tenn., June 13, William Shorter, Winchester, Va.; June 14, George Williams, near Waco, Tex.; June 24, Daniel Edwards, Selina or Selma, Ala.; June 27, Ernest Murphy, Dalevine, Ala.; July 6, unknown negro, Poplar Head, La.; July 6, unknown negro, Poplar Head, La.; July 12, Robert Larkin, Oscola, Tex.; July 17, Warren Dean, Stone Creek, Ga.; July 21, unknown negro, Brantford, Fla.; July 17, John Cotton, Connersville, Ark.; July 22, Lee Walker, New Albany, Miss.: July 26, Handy, Suansea, S. C.; July 30, William Thompson, Columbia, S. C.; July 28, Isaac Harper, Calera, Ala.; July 30, Thomas Preston, Columbia, S. C.; July 30, Handy Kaigler, Columbia, S. C.; Aug. 13, Monroe Smith, Springfield, Ala.; Aug. 19, negro tramp, near Paducah, Ky.; Aug. 21, John Davis, Nilson, near Leavenworth, Kan., Aug. 23, Jacob Green Wood, S. C.; Sept. 2, William Arkinson, McKciiney, Ky.; Sept 16, unknown negro, Centerville, Ala.; Sept. 16, Jessie Mitchell, Amelia C. H., Va.; Sept 25, Perry Bratcher, New Boston, Tex.; Oct. 9, William Lacey, Jasper, Ala.; Oct. 22, John Gamble, Pikesville, Tenn.

OFFENSES CHARGED ARE AS FOLLOWS.

Rape, 39; attempted rape, 8; alleged rape, 4; suspicion of rape, 1; murder, 44; alleged murder, 6; alleged complicity in murder, 4: murderous assault, 1; attempted murder, 1; attempted robbery, 4; arson, 4; incendiarism, 3; alleged stock poisoning, 1; poisoning wells, 2; alleged poisoning wells, 5: burglary, 1; wife beating, 1; self defense, 1; suspected robbery, 1; assault and battery, 1; insulting whites, 2; malpractice, 1; alleged barn burning, 4; stealing, 2; unknown offense, 4; no offense, 1; race prejudice, 4; total, 159.

LYNCHINGS BY STATES.

Alabama, 25; Arkansas, 7; Florida, 7; Georgia, 24; Indian Territory, 1; Illinois, 3; Kansas, 2; Kentucky, 8; Louisiana, 18; Mississippi, 17; Missouri, 3; New York, 1; South Carolina, 15; Tennessee, 10; Texas, 8; Virginia, 10.

RECORD FOR THE YEAR 1892.

While it is intended that the record here presented shall Include specially the lynchings of 1893, it will not be amiss to give the record for the year preceding. The facts contended for will always appear manifest-that not one-third of the victims lynched were charged with rape, and further that the charges made embraced a range of offenses from murders to misdemeanors.

In 1892 there were 241 persons lynched. The entire number to divided among the following states:

Alabama, 22; Arkansas, 25; California, 3; Florida, Georgia, 17; Idaho, 8; Illinois, 1; Kansas, 3; Kentucky, 9; Louisiana, 29; Maryland, 1; Mississippi, 16; Missouri, 6; Montana, 4; New York, 1; North Carolina, 5; North Dakota, 1; Ohio, 3; South Carolina, 5; Tennessee, 28; Texas, 15; Virginia, 7; West Virginia, 6; Wyoming, 9; Arizona Territory, 3; Oklahoma, 2.

Of this number 190 were of Negro descent. Four of them were lynched in New York, Ohio and Kansas; the remainder were murdered in the South. Five of this number were females. The charges for which they were lynched cover a wide range. They are as follows:

Rape, 46; murder, 58; rioting, 3; race prejudice, 6; no cause given, 4; incendiarism, 6; robbery, 6; assault and battery, 1; attempted rape, 11; suspected robbery, 4; larceny, 1; self defense, 1; insulting women, 2; desperadoes, 6; fraud, 1; attempted murder, 2; no offense stated, boy and girl, 2.

In the case of the boy and girl above referred to, their father, named Hastings, was accused of the murder of a white man; his fourteen-year-old daughter and sixteen-year-old son were hanged and their bodies fined with bullets, then the father was also lynched. This was in November, 1892, at Jonesville, Louisiana.

CHAPTER III.

LYNCHING IMBECILS.
(An Arkansas Butchery.)

The only excuse which capital punishment attempts to find is upon the theory that the criminal is past the power of reformation and his life is a constant menace to the community. If, however, he is mentally unbalanced, irresponsible for his acts, there can be no more inhuman act conceived of

than the willful sacrifice of his life. So thoroughly is that principle grounded in the law, that all civilized society surrounds human life with a safeguard, which prevents the execution of a criminal who is insane, even if sane at the time of its criminal act. Should he become insane after its commission the law steps in and protects him during the period of his insanity. But Lynch Law has no such regard for human life. Assuming for itself an absolute supremacy over the law of the land, it has time and again dyed its hands in the blood of men who were imbeciles. Two or three noteworthy cases will suffice to show with what inhuman ferocity irresponsible men have been put to death by this system of injustice.

An instance occurred during the year 1892 in Arkansas, a report of which is given in full in the Arkansas Democrat, published at Little Rock, in that state, on the 11th day of February of that year. The paper mentioned is perhaps one of the leading weeklies in that state and the account given in detail have every mark of a careful and conscientious investigation. The victims of this tragedy were a colored man, named Hamp Biscoe, his wife and a thirteen year-old son. Hamp Biscoe, it appears, was a hard working, thrifty farmer, who lived near England, Arkansas, upon a small farm with his family. The investigation of the tragedy was conducted by a resident of Arkansas named R. B. Carlee, a white man, who furnished the account to the Arkansas Democrat over his own signature. He says the original trouble which led to the lynching was a quarrel between Biscoe and a white man about a debt About six years after Biscoe preempted his land, a white man made a demand of $100 upon him for services in showing him the land and making the sale. Biscoe denied the service and refused to pay the demand. The white man, however, brought suit, obtained judgment for the hundred dollars and Biscoe's farm was sold to pay the judgment.

The suit, judgment and subsequent legal proceedings appear to have driven Biscoe almost crazy and brooding over his wrongs he grew to be a confirmed imbecile. He would allow but few men, white or colored, to come upon his place, as he suspected every stranger to be planning to steal his farm. A week preceding the tragedy, a white man named Venable, whose farm adjoined Biscoe's, let down the fence and proceeded to drive through Biscoe's field. The latter saw him, grew very excited, cursed him and drove him from his farm with bitter oaths and violent threats. Venable went away and secured a warrant for Biscoe's arrest. This warrant was placed in the hands of a constable named John Ford, who took a colored deputy and two white men out to Biscoe's farm to make the arrest. When they arrived at the

house Biscoe refused to be arrested and warned them he would shoot if they persisted in their attempt to arrest him. The warning was unheeded by Ford, who entered upon the premises, when Biscoe, true to his word, fired upon him. The load tore a part of his clothes from his body, one shot going through his arm and entering his breast. After he had fallen, Ford drew his revolver and shot Biscoe in the head and his wife through the arm. The Negro deputy then began firing and struck Biscoe in the small of the back. Ford's wound was not dangerous and in a few days he was able to be around again. Biscoe, however, was so severely shot that he was unable to stand after the firing was over.

Two other white men hearing the exchange of shots went to the rescue of the officers, forced open the door of Biscoe's cabilland arrested him, his wife and thirteen-year old son, and took them, together with a babe at the breast, to a small frame house near the depot and put them under guard. The subsequent proceedings were briefly told by Mr. Carlee in the columns of the Arkansas Democrat above mentioned, from whose account the following excerpt is taken:

> "It was rumored here that the Negroes were to be lynched that night, but I do not think it was generally credited, as it was not believed that Ford was greatly hurt and the Negro was held to be fatally injured and crazy at that. But that night, about 8 o'clock, a party of perhaps twelve or fifteen men, a number of whom were known to the guards, came to the house and told the Negro guards they would take care of the prisoners now, and for them to leave; as they did not obey at once they were persuaded to leave with words that did not admit of delay.

> "The woman began to cry and said, 'You intend to kill us to get our money.' They told her to hush (she was heavy with child and had a child at her breast) as they intended to give her a nice present. The guards heard no more, but hastened to a Negro church near by and urged the preacher to go up and stop the mob. A few minutes after, the shooting began, perhaps about forty shots being fired. The white men then left rapidly and the Negroes went to the house. Hamp Biscoe and his wife were killed, the baby had a slight wound across the upper lip; the boy was still alive and lived until after

midnight, talking rationally and telling who did the shooting.

"He said when they came in and shot his father, he attempted to run out of doors and a young man shot him in the bowels and that he fell. He saw another man shoot his mother and a taller young man, whom he did not know, shoot his father. After they had killed them, the young man who had shot his mother pulled off her stockings and took $220 in currency that she had hid there. The men then came to the door where the boy was lying and one of them turned him over and put his pistol to his breast and shot him again. This if; the story the dying boy told as near as I can get it. It is quite singular that the guards and those who had conversed with him were not required to testify. The woman was known to have the money as she had exposed it that day. She also had $36 in silver, which the plunderer of the body did not get. The Negro was undoubtedly insane and had been for several years. The citizens of this community condemn the murder and have no sympathy with it. The Negro was a well to do farmer, but had become crazed because he was convinced some plot had been made to steal his land and only a few days ago declared that he expected to die in defense of his home In a short time and he did not care how soon. The killing of a woman with the child at her breast and In her condition, and also a young boy, was extremely brutal. As for Hamp Biscoe he was dangerous and should long have been confined in the Insane asylum. Such were the facts as near as I can get them and you can use them as you see it, but I would prefer you would suppress the names charged by the Negroes with the killing."

Perhaps the civilized world will think, that with all these facts laid before the public, by a writer who signs his name to his communication, in a land where grand juries are sworn to investigate, where judges and juries are sworn to administer the law and sheriffs are paid to execute the decrees of the courts, and where, in fact, every instrument of civilization to supposed to work for the common good of all citizens, that this matter was duty investigated, the criminals apprehended and the punishment meted out to the murderers. But this is a mistake; nothing of the kind was done or attempted. Six

months after the publication, above referred to, an investigator, writing to find out what had been done in the matter, received the following reply:

OFFICE OF
S. S. GLOVER, SHERIFF AND
COLLECTOR,
LONOKE COUNTY.
Lonoke, Ark., 9-12-1892.
Geo. Washington, Esq.,
Chicago, Ill.

DEAR SIR:—The parties who killed Hamp Briscoe February the 9th, have never been arrested. The parties are still in the county. It was done by some of the citizens, and those who know will not tell.
S. S. GLOVER, Sheriff.

Thus acts the mob with the victim of its fury, conscious that it will never be called to an account. Not only is this true, but the moral support of those who are chosen by the people to execute the law, is frequently given to the support of lawlessness and mob violence. The press and even the pulpit, In the main either by silence or open apology, have condoned and encouraged this state of anarchy.

TORTURED AND BURNED IN TEXAS

Never in the history of civilization has any Christian people stooped to such shocking brutality and Indescribable barbarism as that which characterized the people of Paris, Texas, and adjacent communities on the 1st of February, 1893. The cause of this awful outbreak of human passion was the murder of a four year old child, daughter of a man named Vance. This man, Vance, had been a police officer in Paris for years, and was known to be a man of bad temper, overbearing manner and given to harshly treating the prisoners under his care. He had arrested Smith and, it is said, cruelly mistreated him. Whether or not the murder of his child was an act of fiendish revenge, it has not been shown, but many persons who know of the incident have suggested that the secret of the attack on the child lay in a desire for revenge against its father.

In the same town there lived a Negro, named Henry Smith, a well known character, a kind of roustabout, who was generally considered a harmless, weak-minded fellow, not capable of doing any important work, but suffi-

ciently able to do chores and odd jobs around the houses of the white peo-
ple who cared to employ him. A few days before the final tragedy, this man,
Smith, was accused of murdering Myrtle Vance. The crime of murder was of
itself bad enough, and to prove that against Smith would have been amply
sufficient in Texas to have committed him to the gallows, but the finding of
the child so exasperated the father and his friends, that they at once shame-
fully exaggerated the facts and declared that the babe had been ruthlessly
assaulted and then killed. The truth was bad enough, but the white people
of the community made it a point to exaggerate every detail of the awful
affair, and to inflame the public mind so that nothing less than immediate
and violent death would satisfy the populace. As a matter of fact, the child
was not brutally assaulted as the world has been told in excuse for the awful
barbarism of that day. Persons who saw the child after its death, have stated,
under the most solemn pledge to truth, that there was no evidence of such
an assault as was published at that time, only a slight abrasion and discol-
oration was noticeable and that mostly about the neck. In spite of this fact,
so eminent a man as Bishop Haygood deliberately and, it must also appear,
maliciously falsified the fact by stating that the child was torn limb from
limb, or to quote his own words, "First outraged with demoniacal cruelty
and then taken by her heels and torn asunder in the mad wantonness of
gorilla ferocity."

Nothing is farther from the truth than that statement. It is a cold blood-
ed, deliberate, brutal falsehood which this Christian Bishop uses to bolster
up the Infamous plea that the people of Pairs were driven to insanity by
learning that the little child had been viciously assaulted, choked to death,
and then torn to pieces by a demon in human form. It was a brutal murder,
but no more brutal than hundreds of murders which occur in this country,
and which have been equalled every year in fiendishness and brutality, and
for which the death penalty is prescribed by law and inflicted only after the
person has been legally adjudged guilty of the crime. Those who knew Smith,
believe that Vance had at some time given him cause to seek revenge and that
this fearful crime was the outgrowth of his attempt to avenge himself of some
real or fancied wrong. That the murderer was known as an imbecile, had no
effect whatever upon the people who thirsted for his blood. They determined
to make an example of him and proceeded to carry out their purpose with
unspeakably greater ferocity than that which characterized the half crazy
object of their revenge.

For a day or so after the child was found in the woods, Smith remained

in the vicinity as if nothing had happened, and when finally becoming aware that he was suspected, he made an attempt to escape. He was apprehended, however, not far from the scene of his crime and the news flashed across the country that the white Christian people of Paris, Texas and the communities there about had deliberately determined to lay aside all forms of law and inaugurate an entirely new form of punishment for the murder. They absolutely refused to make any inquiry as to the sanity or insanity of their prisoner, but set the day and hour which in the presence of assembled thousands they put their helpless victim to the stake, tortured him, and then burned him to death for the delectation and satisfaction of Christian people.

Lest it might be charged that any description of the deeds of that day are exaggerated, a white man's description which was published in the white journals of this country is used. The *New York Sun* of February 2d, 1893, contains an account, from which we make the following excerpt:

> PARIS, Tex., Feb. 1, 1893.—Henry Smith, the negro ravished of 4-year-old Myrtle Vance, has expiated in part his awful crime by death at the stake. Ever since the perpetration of his awful crime this city and the entire surrounding country has been in a wild frenzy of excitement. When the news came last night that he had been captured at Hope, Ark., that he had been identified by B. B. Sturgeon, James T. Hicks, and many other of the Paris searching party, the city was wild with joy over the apprehension of the brute. Hundreds of people poured into the city from the adjoining country and the word passed from lip to lip that the punishment of the fiend should fit the crime—that death by fire was the penalty Smith should pay for the most atrocious murder and terrible outrage in Texas history. Curious and sympathizing alike, they came on train and wagons, on horse, and on foot to see if the frail mind of a man could think brought through Texarkana where 6,000 people awaited the train, anxious to aft a man who had received the fate of Ed. Coy. At that place speeches were made by prominent Parts citizens, who asked that the prisoner be not molested by Texarkana people, but that the guard be allowed to deliver him up to the outraged and Indignant citizens of Paris. Along the road the train gathered strength from the various towns, the people crowded upon the platforms and tops

of coaches anxious to see the lynching and the negro who was soon to be delivered to an infuriated mob.

BURNED AT THE STAKE.

Arriving here at 12 o'clock the train was met by a surging mass of humanity 10,000 strong. The negro was placed upon a carnival float in mockery of a king upon his throne, and, followed by an immense crowd, was escorted through the city so that all might see the most inhuman monster known in current history. The line of march was up Main street to the square, around the square down Clarksville street to Church street, thence to the open prairies about 300 yards from the Texas & Pacific depot. Here Smith was placed upon a scaffold, six feet square and ten feet high, securely bound, within the view of all beholders. Here the victim was tortured fifty minutes by red-hot iron brands thrust against his quivering body. Commencing at the feet the brands were placed against him inch by inch until they were thrust against the face. Then, being apparently dead, kerosene was poured upon him, cottonseed hulls placed beneath him and set on fire. In less time than it takes to relate it, the tortured man was wafted beyond the grave to another fire, hotter and more terrible than the one just experienced.

Curiosity seekers have carried away already all that was left of the memorable event, even to piece of charcoal. The cause of the crime was that Henry Vance when a deputy policeman, in the course of his duty was called to arrest Henry Smith for being drunk and disorderly. The Negro was unruly, and Vance was forced to use his club. The Negro swore vengeance, and several times assaulted Vance. In his greed for revenge, last Thursday, he grabbed up, the little girl and committed the crime. The father is prostrated with grief and the mother now lies at death's door, but she has lived to see the slayer of her innocent babe suffer the most horrible death that could be conceived.

TORTURE BEYOND DESCRIPTION.

Words to describe the awful torture inflicted upon Smith cannot be found. The Negro, for a long time after starting on the journey to Paris, did not realize his plight. At last when he was told that he must die by slow torture he begged for protection. His agony was awful. He pleaded and writhed in bodily and mental pain. Scarcely had the train reached Paris than this torture commenced. His clothes were torn off piecemeal and scattered to the crowd, people catching the shreds and putting them away as mementos. The

child's father, her brother, and two uncles then gathered about the Negro as he lay fastened to the torture platform and thrust hot irons into his quivering flesh. It was horrible—the man dying by slow torture in the midst of smoke from his own burning flesh. Every groan from the Bead, every contortion of his body was cheered by the thickly packed crowd of 10,000 persons. The mass of beings 600 yards in diameter, the scaffold being the center. After burning the feet and legs, the hot irons—plenty of fresh ones being at hand—were rolled up and down Smith's stomach, back, and arms. Then the eyes were burned out and irons were thrust down his throat.

The men of the Vance family having wreaked vengeance, the crowd piled all kinds of combustible stuff around the scaffold, poured oil on it and set it afire. The Negro rolled and tossed out of the mass, only to be pushed back by the people nearest him. He tossed out again, and was roped and pulled back. Hundreds of people turned away, but the vast crowd still looked calmly on. People were here from every part of this section. They came from Dallas, Fort Worth, Sherman, Denison, Bonham, Texarkana, Fort Smith, Ark., and the party of fifteen came from Hempstead county, Arkansas, where he was captured. Every train that came in was loaded to its utmost capacity, and there were demands at many points for special trains to bring the people here to see the unparalleled punishment for an unparalleled crime. When the news of the burning went over the country like wildfire, at every country town anvils boomed forth the announcement.

SHOULD HAVE BEEN IN AN ASYLUM.

It may not be amiss in connection with this awful affair, In proof of our assertion that Smith was an imbecile, to give the testimony of a well known colored minister, who lived at Paris, Texas, at the time of the lynching. He was a witness of the awful scenes there enacted, and attempted, in the name of God and humanity, to interfere in the programme. He barely escaped with his life, was driven out of the city and became an exile because of his actions. Reverend King was in New York about the middle of February, and he was there interviewed for a daily paper for that city, and we quote his account as an eye witness of the affair. Said he:

> "I was ridden out of Paris on a rail because I was the only man In Lamar county to raise my voice against the lynching of Smith. I opposed the illegal measures before the arrival of Henry Smith as a prisoner, and I was warned that I might

meet his fate it I was not careful; but the sense of Justice made me bold, and when I saw the poor wretch trembling with fear, and got so near him that I could hear his teeth chatter, I determined to stand by him to the last.

"I hated him for his crime, but two crimes do not make a virtue; and in the brief conversation I had with Smith I was more firmly convinced than ever that he was irresponsible.

"I had known Smith for years, and there were times when Smith was out of his head for weeks. Two years ago I made an effort to have him put in an asylum, hut the white people were trying to fasten the murder of a young colored girl upon him, and would not listen. For days before the murder of the little Vance girl, Smith was out of his head and dangerous. He had just undergone an attack of delirium tremens and was in no condition to be allowed at large. He realized his condition, for I spoke with him not three weeks ago, and in answer to my exhortations, he promised to reform. The next time I saw him was on the day of, his execution. "'Drink did it! drink did it;' he sobbed. Then bowing his face In his hands, he asked: 'Is it true, did I kill her? Oh, my God, my God!' For a moment he seemed to forget, the awful fate that awaited him, and his body swayed to and fro with grief. Some one seized me by the shoulder and hurled me back, and Smith fell writhing to the ground in terror as four men seized his arms to drag him to the Boat on which he has to be exhibited before he was finally burned at the stake. "I followed the procession and wept aloud as I saw little children of my own race follow the unfortunate man and taunt him with jeers. Even at the stake, children of both sexes and colors gathered in groups, and when the father of the murdered child raised the hissing iron with which he was about to torture the helpless victim, the children became as frantic as the grown people and struggled forward to obtain places of advantage.

"It was terrible. One little tot scarcely older than little Myrtle Vance clapped her baby hands as her father held her on his shoulders—above the heads of the people.

"'For God's sake,' I shouted, 'send the children home.'

"'No, no,' shouted a hundred maddened voices; 'let

them learn a lesson.' "I love children, but as I looked about the little faces distorted with passion and the bloodshot eyes of the cruel parents who held them high in their arms, I thanked God that I have none of my own.

"As the hot iron sank deep into poor Henry's flesh a hideous yell rent the air, and, with a sound as terrible as the cry of lost souls on judgment day, 20,000 maddened people took up the victim's cry of agony and a prolonged howl of maddened glee rent the air.

"No one wall himself now. Every man, woman and child in that awful crowd was worked up to a greater frenzy than that which actuated Smith's horrible crime. The people were capable of any new atrocity now, and as Smith's yells became more and more frequent, it was difficult hold the crowd back, so anxious were the savages to participate in the sickening tortures.

"For half and hour I tried to pray as the beads of agony rolled down my forehead and bathed my face.

"For an instant a hush spread over the people. I could stand no more, and with a superhuman effort dashed through the compact mass of humanity and stood at the toot of the burning scaffold.

"'In the name of God,' I cried, 'I command you to cease this torture.' "The heavy butt of a Winchester rifle descended on my head and I fell to the ground. Rough hands seized me and angry men bore me away, and I was thankful.

"At the outskirts of the crowd I was attacked again, and then several men, no doubt glad to get away from the fearful place, escorted me to my home, where I was allowed to take a small amount of clothing. A jeering crowd gathered without, and when I appeared at the door ready hands seized me and I was placed upon a rail and, with curses and oaths, taken to the railway station and placed upon a train. As the train moved out some one thrust a roll of bins into my hand and said, 'God bless you, but it was no use.'"

When asked if he should ever return to Paris, Mr. King said: "I shall never go south again. The impressions of that awful day will stay with me forever."

CHAPTER IV.

LYNCHING OF INNOCENT MEN.
(Lynched on Account of Relationship.)

If no other reason appealed to the sober sense of the American people to check the growth of Lynch Law, the absolute unreliability and recklessness of the mob in inflicting punishment for crimes done, should do so. Several instances of this spirit have occurred in the year past. In Louisiana, near New Orleans, in July, 1893, Roselius Julian, a colored man, shot and killed a white judge, named Victor Estopinal. The cause of the shooting has never been definitely ascertained. It is claimed that the Negro resented an insult to his wife, and the killing of the White man was an act of a Negro (who dared) to defend his home. The judge was killed In the court house, and Julian, heavily armed, made his escape to the swamps near the city. He has never been apprehended, and has any information ever been gleaned as to his whereabouts. A mob determined to secure the fugitive murderer and burn him alive. The swamps were hunted through and through In vain, when, being unable- to wreak their revenge upon the murderer, the mob turned its attention to his unfortunate relatives. Dispatches from New Orleans, dated September 19, 1893, described the affair as follows: "Posses were immediately organized and the surrounding country was scoured, but the search was fruitless so far as the real criminal was concerned. The mother, three brothers and two sisters of the Negro were arrested yesterday at the Black Ridge in the rear of the city by the police and taken to the little jail on Judge Estopinal's place about Southport, because of the belief that they were succoring the fugitive. "About 11 o'clock twenty-five men, some armed with rifles and shotguns, came up to the jail. They unlocked the door and held a conference among themselves as to what they should do. Some were in favor of hanging the five while others insisted that only two of the brothers should be strung up. This, was finally agreed to, and the two doomed Negroes were hurried to a pasture one hundred yards distant, and there asked to take their last chance of saving their lives by making a confession, but the Negroes made no reply. They were then told to kneel down and pray. One did so, the other remained standing, but both prayed fervently. The taller Negro was then hoisted up. The shorter Negro stood gazing at the horrible death of his brother without flinching. Five minutes later he was also hanged. The mob

decided to take the remaining brother out to Camp Parapet and hang him there. The other two were to be taken out and flogged, with an order to get out of the parish In less than half an hour. The third brother, Paul, was taken out to the camp, which is about a mile distant in the interior, and there he was hanged to a tree."

Another young man, who was in no way related to Julian, who perhaps did not even know the man and who was entirely innocent of any offense in connection therewith, was murdered by the same mob. The same paper says: "During the search for Julian on Saturday one branch of the posse visited the house of a Negro family in the neighborhood of Camp Parapet, and failing to find the object of their search, tried to induce John Willis, a young Negro, to disclose the whereabouts of Julian. He refused to do so, or could not do so, and was kicked to death by the gang."

AN INDIANA CASE.

Almost equal to the ferocity of the mob which killed the three brothers, Julian and the unoffending, John Willis, because of the murder of Judge Estopinal, was the action of a mob near Vincennes, Ind. In this case a wealthy colored man, named Allen Butler, who was well known in the community, and enjoyed the confidence and respect of the entire country, was made the victim of a mob and hung because his son had become unduly Intimate with a white girl who was a servant around his house. There was no pretense that the facts were otherwise than as here stated. The woman lived at Butler's house as a servant, and she and Butler's son fell in love with each other, and later it was found that the girl was In a delicate condition. It was claimed, but with how much truth no one has ever been able to tell, that the father had procured an abortion, or himself had operated on the girl, and that she had left the house to go back to her home. It was never claimed that the father was in any way responsible for the action of his son, but the authorities procured the arrest of both father and son, and at the preliminary examination the father gave bail to appear before the Grand Jury when it should convene. On the same night, however, the mob took the matter in hand and with the intention of hanging the son. It assembled near summer, while the boy, who had been unable to give bail, was lodged in jail at Lawrenceville. As it was impossible to reach Lawrenceville and hang the son, the leaders of the mob concluded they would go to Butler's house and hang him. Butler was found at his home, taken out by the mob and hung to a tree. This was in the law-abiding state of Indiana, which furnished the United

States its last president and which claims all the honor, pride and glory of northern civilization. None of the leaders of the mob were apprehended, and no steps whatever were taken to bring the murderers to justice.

KILLED FOR HIS STEPFATHER'S CRIME.

An account has been given of the cremation of Henry Smith, at Paris, Texas, for the murder, of the infant child of a man named Vince. It would appear that human ferocity was not sated when it vented itself upon a human being by burning his eyes out, by thrusting a red hot iron down his throat, and then by burning his body to ashes. Henry Smith, the victim of these savage orgies, was beyond all the power of torture, but a few miles outside of Paris, some members of the community concluded that it would be proper to kill a stepson named William Butler as a partial penalty for the original crime. This young man, against whom no word has ever been said, and who was in fact an orderly, peaceable boy, had been watched with the severest scrutiny by members of the mob who believed he knew something of the whereabouts of Smith. He declared from the very first that he did not know where his stepfather was, which statement was well proven to be a fact after the discovery of Smith in Arkansas, whence he had fled through swamps and woods and unfrequented places. Yet Butler was apprehended, placed under arrest, and on the night of February 6th, taken out on Hickory Creek, live miles southeast of Paris, and hung for his stepfather's crime. After his body was suspended in the air, the mob fined it with bullets.

LYNCHED BECAUSE THE JURY
ACQUITTED HIM.

The entire system of the judiciary of this country is in the hands of white people. To this add the fact of the inherent prejudice against colored people, and it will be clearly seen that a white jury is certain to find a Negro prisoner guilty if there is the least evidence to warrant such a finding.

Meredith Lewis was arrested in Roseland, La., in July of last year. A white jury found him not guilty of the crime of murder wherewith he stood charged. This did not suit the mob. A few nights after the verdict was rendered, and he declared to be innocent, a mob gathered in his vicinity and went to his house. He was allied, and suspecting nothing, went outside. He was seized and hurried off to a convenient spot and hanged by the neck until he was dead for the murder of a woman of which the jury had said he was innocent.

LYNCHED AS A SCAPEGOAT.

Wednesday, July 5th, about 10 o'clock in the morning, a terrible crime was committed within four miles of Wickliffe, Ky. Two girls, Mary and Ruby Ray, were found murdered a short distance from their home. The news of this terrible cowardly murder of two helpless young girls spread like wild fire, and searching parties scoured the territory surrounding Wickliffe and Bardwell. Two of the searching party, the Clark brothers, saw a man enter the Dupoyster cornfield; they got their guns and fired at the fleeing figure, but without effect; he got away, but they said he was a white man or nearly so. The search continued all day without effect, save the arrest of two or three strange Negroes. A bloodhound was brought from the penitentiary and put on the trail which he followed from the scene of the murder to the river and into the boat of a fisherman named Gordon. Gordon stated that he had ferried one man and only one across the river about half past six the evening of July 6th; that his passenger sat in front of him, and he was a white man or a very bright mulatto, who could not be told from a white man. The bloodhound was put across the river in the boat, and he struck a trail again at Bird's Point on the Missouri side, ran about three hundred yards to the cottage of a white farmer named Grant and there lay down refusing to go further.

Thursday morning a brakesman on a freight train going out of Sikeston, Mo., discovered a Negro stealing a ride; he ordered him off and had hot words which terminated in a fight. The brakesman had the Negro arrested. When arrested, between — and 12 o'clock, he had on a dark woolen shirt, light pants and coat, and no vest. He had twelve dollars in paper, two silver dollars and ninety-five cents in change; he had also four rings in his pockets, a knife and razor which were rusted and stained. The Sikeston authorities immediately jumped to the conclusion that this man was the murderer for whom the Kentuckians, across the river were searching. They telegraphed to Bardwell that their prisoner had on no coat, but wore a blue vest and pants which would perhaps correspond with the coat found at the scene of the murder, and that the names of the murdered girls were in the rings found in his possession.

As soon as this news was received, the sheriffs of Ballard and Carlisle counties and a posse of thirty well armed and determined Kentuckians, who had pledged their word the prisoner, should be taken back to the scene of the supposed crime, to be executed there if proved to be the guilty man, chartered a train and at nine o'clock Thursday night started for Sikeston. Arriving

there two hours later, the sheriff at Sikeston, who had no warrant for the prisoner's arrest and detention, delivered him into the hands of the mob without authority for so doing, and accompanied them to Bird's Point. The prisoner gave his name as Miner, his home at Springfield, and said he had never been in Kentucky in his life, but the sheriff turned him over to the mob to be taken to Wickliffe, that Frank Gordon, the fisherman, who had put a man across the river might identify him.

In other words, the protection of the law was withdrawn from C. J. Miner, and he was given to a mob by this sheriff at Sikeston, who knew that the prisoner's life depended on one man's word. After an altercation with the train men, who wanted another $50 for taking the train back to Bird's Point, the crowd arrived there at three o'clock, Friday morning. Here was anchored "The Three States," a ferry boat plying between Wickliffe, Ky., Cairo, Ill., and Bird's Point, Mo. This boat left Cairo at twelve o'clock, Thursday, with nearly three hundred of Cairo's best citizens and thirty kegs of beer on board. This was consumed while the crowd and the bloodhound waited for the prisoner.

When the prisoner was on board "The Three States" the dog was turned loose, and after moving aimlessly around, followed the crowd to where Miner sat handcuffed an 'there he stopped. The crowd closed in on the pair and insisted that the brute had identified him because of that action. When the boat reached Wickliffe, Gordon, the fisherman, was called on to say whether the prisoner was the man he ferried over the river the day of the murder.

The sheriff of Ballard county Informed him, sternly that if the prisoner was not the man, he (the fisherman) would be held responsible as knowing who the guilty man was. Gordon stated before, that the man he ferried across was a white man or a bright colored man; Miner was a dark brown skinned man, with kinky hair, "neither yellow nor black," says the Cairo Evening Telegram of Friday, July 7th. The fisherman went up to Miner from behind, looked at him without speaking for fully five minutes, then slowly said, "Yes, that's the man I crossed over." This was about six o'clock, Friday morning, and the crowd wished to hang Miner then and there. But Mr. Ray, the father of the girls, insisted that he be taken to Bardwell, the county seat of Ballard, and twelve miles inland. He said he thought a white man committed the crime, and that he was not satisfied that was the man. They took him to Bardwell and at ten o'clock, this same excited, unauthorized mob undertook to determine Miner's guilt. One of the Clark brothers who shot at a fleeing man in the Dupoyster cornfield, said the prisoner was the same man; the

other said he was not, but the testimony of the first was accepted. A colored woman who had said she gave breakfast to a colored man clad in a blue flannel suit the morning of the murder, said positively that she had never seen Miner before. The gold rings found in his possession had no names in them, as had been asserted, and Mr. Ray said they did not belong to his daughters. Meantime a funeral pyre for the purpose of burning Miner to death had been erected in the center of the village. While the crowd swayed by passion was clamoring that he be burnt, Miner stepped for Ward and made the following statement: "My name to C. J. Miner. I am from Springfield, Ill.; my wife lives at 716 N. 2d street. I am here among you today, looked upon as one of the most brutal men before the people. I stand here surrounded by men who are excited, men who are not willing to let the law take its course, and as far as the crime is concerned, I have committed no crime, and certainly no crime gross enough to deprive me of my life and liberty to walk upon the green earth."

A telegram was sent to the chief of the police at Springfield, Ill., asking if one C. J. Miner lived there. An answer in the negative was returned. A few hours after, it was ascertained that a man named Miner, and his wife, did live at the number the prisoner gave in his speech, but the information came to Bardwell too late to do the prisoner any good. Miner was taken to jail, every stitch of clothing literally torn from his body and examined again. On the lower left side of the bosom of his shirt was found a dark reddish spot about the size of a dime. Miner said it was paint which he had gotten on him at Jefferson Barracks. This spot was only, on the right side, and could not be seen from the under side at all, thus showing it had not gone through the cloth as blood or any liquid substance would do.

Chief-of-police Mahaney, of Cairo, Ill., was with the prisoner, and he took his knife and scraped at the spot, particles of which came off in his hand. Miner told them to take his clothes to any expert, and if the spot was shown to be blood, they might do anything they wished with him. They took his clothes away and were gone some time. After, a while they were brought back and thrown into the cell without a word. It is needless to say that If the spot had been found to be blood, that fact would have been announced, and the shirt retained as evidence. Meanwhile numbers of rough, drunken men crowded Into the cell and tried to force a confession of the deed from the prisoner's lips. He refused to talk save to reiterate his innocence. To Mr. Mahaney, who talked seriously and kindly to him, telling him the mob meant to burn and torture him at three o'clock, Miner said: "Burning and

torture here lasts but a little while, but if I die with a he on my soul, I shall be tortured forever. I am innocent." For more than three hours, all sorts of pressure in that way of threats, abuse and urging, was brought to bear to force him to confess to the murder and thus justify the mob in its deed of murder. Miner remained firm; but as the hour drew near, and the crowd became more impatient, he asked for a priest. As none could be procured, he then asked for a Methodist minister, who came, prayed with the doomed man, baptized him and exhorted Miner to confess. To keep up the flagging spirits of the dense crowd around the jail, the rumor went out more than once, that Miner had confessed. But the solemn assurance of the minister, chief-of-police, and leading editor who were with Miner all along-is that this rumor is absolutely false.

At three o'clock the mob rushed to the jail to secure the prisoner. Mr. Ray had changed his mind about the promised burning; he was still in doubt as to the prisoner's guilt. He again addressed the crowd to that effect, urging them not to burn Miner, and the mob heeded him so far, that they compromised on hanging instead of burning, which was agreed to by Mr. Ray. There was a loud yell, and a rush was made for the prisoner. He was stripped naked, his clothing literally torn from his body, and his shirt was tied around his loins. Some one declared the rope was a white man's death," and a log-chain, nearly a hundred feet in length, weighing over one hundred pounds, was placed round Miner's neck and body, and he was led and dragged through the streets of the village in that condition followed by thousands of people. He fainted from exhaustion several times, but was supported to the platform where they first intended burning him.

The chain was hooked around his neck, a man climbed the telegraph pole and the other end of the chain was passed up to him and made fast to the cross-arm. Others brought a long forked stick which Miner was made to straddle. By this means he was raised several feet from the ground and then let fall. The first fall broke his neck, but he was raised in this way and let fall a second time. Numberless shots were fired into the dangling body, for most of that crowd were heavily armed, and had been drinking all day. Miner's body hung thus exposed from three to five o'clock, during which time, several photographs of him as he hung dangling at the end of the chain were taken, and his toes and fingers were cut off. His body was taken down, placed on the platform, the torch applied, and in a few moments there was nothing left of C. J. Miner save a few bones and ashes. Thus perished another of the many victims of Lynch Law, but it is the honest and sober belief of many

who witnessed the scene that an innocent man has been barbarously and shockingly put to death In the glare of the 19th century civilization, by those who profess to believe In Christianity, law and order.

CHAPTER V.

LYNCHED FOR ANYTHING OR NOTHING.
(Lynched for Wife Beating.)

In nearly all communities wife beating is punishable with a fine, and in no community is it made a felony. Dave Jackson, of Abita, La., was a colored man who had beaten his wife. He had not killed her, nor seriously wounded her, but as Louisiana lynchers had not fined out their quota of crimes, his case was deemed of sufficient importance to apply the method of that barbarous people. He was in the custody of the officials, but the mob went to the jail and took him out in front of the prison and hanged him by the neck until he was dead. This was in Nov. 1893.

HANGED FOR STEALING HOGS.

Details are very meager of a lynching which occurred near Knox Point, La., on the 24th of October, 1893 upon one point, however, there was no uncertainty, and that is, that the persons lynched were Negroes. It was claimed that they had been stealing hogs, but even this claim had not been subjected to the investigation of a court. That matter was not considered necessary. A few of the neighbors who had lost hogs suspected these men were responsible for their loss, and made up their minds to furnish an example for others to be warned by. The two men were secured by a mob and hanged.

LYNCHED FOR NO OFFENSE.

Perhaps the most characteristic feature of this record of Lynch law for the year 1893, is the remarkable fact that five human beings were lynched and that the matter was considered of so little importance that the powerful press bureaus of the country did not consider the matter of enough importance to ascertain the causes for which they were hanged. It tells the world, with perhaps greater emphasis than any other feature of the record, that Lynch Law has become so common in the United States that the finding of the dead body of a Negro, suspended between heaven and earth to the limb of a tree,

is of so slight importance that neither the civil authorities nor press agencies consider the matter worth Investigating. July 21st, in Shelby county, Tenn., a colored man by the name of Charles Martin was lynched. July 30th, at Paris, Mo., a colored man named William Steen shared the same fate. December 28th, Mack Segars was announced to have been lynched at Brantley, Alabama. August 31st, at Yarborough, Texas, and on September 19th, at Houston, a colored man was found lynched, but so little attention was paid to the matter that not only was no record made as to why these last two men were lynched, but even their names were not given. The dispatches simply stated that an unknown Negro was found lynched in each case.

There are friends of humanity who feel their souls shrink from any compromise with murder, but whose deep and abiding reverence for womanhood causes them to hesitate in giving their support to this crusade against Lynch Law, out. of fear that they may encourage the miscreants whose deeds are worse than murder. But to these friends It must appear certain that these five men could not have been guilty of any terrible crime. They were simply lynched by parties of men who had it in their power to kill them, and who chose to avenge some fancied wrong by murder, rather than submit their grievances to court.

LYNCHED BECAUSE THEY WERE SAUCY.

At Moberly, Mo., February 18th and at Fort Madison, S. C., June 2d, both in 1892, a record was made in the line of lynching which should certainly appeal to every humanitarian who has any regard for the sacredness of human life. John Hughes, of Moberly, and Isaac Lincoln, of Fort Madison, and Will Lewis in Tullahoma, Tenn., suffered death for no more serious charge than that they "were saucy to white people." In the days of slavery it was held to be a very serious matter for a colored person to fail to yield the sidewalk at the demand of a white person, and it will not be surprising to find some evidence of this intolerance existing in the days of freedom. But the most that could be expected as a penalty for acting or speaking saucily to a white person would be a slight physical chastisement to make the Negro "know his place" or an arrest and fine. But Missouri, Tennessee and South Carolina chose to make precedents in their cases and as a result both men, after being charged with their offense and apprehended, were taken by a mob and lynched. The civil authorities who in either case would have been very quick to satisfy the aggrieved white people had they complained and brought the prisoners to court, by imposing proper penalty upon them, did not feel

it their duty to make any investigation after the Negroes were killed. They were dead and out of the way, and as no one would be called upon to render an account for their taking off, the matter was; dismissed from the public mind.

LYNCHED FOR A QUARREL.

One of the most notable instances of lynching for the year 1893, occurred about the 20th of September. It was notable for the fact that the mayor of the city exerted every available power to protect the victim of the lynching from the mob. In his splendid endeavor to uphold the law, the mayor called out the troops, and the result was a deadly fight between the militia and mob, nine of the mob being killed.

The trouble occurred at Roanoke, Va. It is frequently claimed that lynchings occur only in sparsely settled districts, and, in fact, it is a favorite plea of governors and reverend apologists to couple two arrant falsehoods, stating that lynchings occur only because of assaults upon white women, and that these assaults occur and the lynchings follow in thinly inhabited districts where the power of the law is entirely inadequate to meet the emergency. This Roanoke case is a double refutation, for it not only disproves the alleged charge that the Negro assaulted a white woman, as was telegraphed all over the county at the time, but it also shows conclusively that even in one of the largest cities of the old state of Virginia, one of the original thirteen colonies, which prides itself of being the mother of presidents, it was possible for a lynching to occur in broad daylight under circumstances of revolting savagery.

When the news first came from Roanoke of the contemplated lynching, it was stated that a big burly Negro had assaulted a white woman, that he had been apprehended and that the citizens were determined to summarily dispose of his case. Mayor Trout was a man who believed in maintaining the majesty of the law, and who at once gave notice that no lynching would be permitted in Roanoke, and that the Negro, whose name was Smith, being in the custody of the law, should be dealt with according to law; but the mob did not pay any attention to the brave words of the mayor. It evidently thought that it was only another case of swagger, such as frequently characterizes lynching episodes. Mayor Trout, finding immense crowds gathering about the city, and fearing an attempt to lynch Smith, called out the militia and stationed them at the jail.

It was known that the woman refused to accuse Smith of assaulting her,

and that his offense consisted in quarreling with her about the change of money in a transaction in which he bought something from her market booth. Both parties lost their temper, and the result was a row from which Smith had to make his escape. At once the old cry was sounded that the woman had been assaulted, and in a few hours all the town was wild with people thirsting for the assailant's blood. The further incidents of that day may well be told by a dispatch from Roanoke under date of the 21st of September and published in the Chicago Record. It says:

> "It is claimed by members of the military company that they frequently warned the mob to keep away from the Jail, under penalty of being shot. Capt. Bird told them he Was under orders to protect the prisoner whose life the mob so eagerly sought, and come what may he would not allow him to be taken by the mob. To this the crowd replied with hoots and derisive jeers. The rioters appeared to become frenzied at the determined stand taken by the men and Captain Bird, and finally a crowd of excited men made a rush for the side door of the jail. The captain directed his men to drive the would-be lynchers back.
>
> "At this moment the mob opened fire on the soldiers. This appeared for a moment to startle the captain and his men. But it was only for a moment. Then he coolly gave the command: 'Ready! aim! fire!' The company obeyed to the instant, and poured a volley of bullets into that part of the mob which was trying to batter down the side door of the jail.
>
> "The rioters fell back before the fire of the militia, leaving one man writhing in the agonies of death at the doorstep. There was a lull for a moment. Then the word was quickly passed through the throng in front of the jail and down the street that a man was killed. Then there was an awful rush toward the little band of soldiers. Excited men were yelling like demons.
>
> "The flight became general, and ere it was ended nine men were dead and more than forty wounded."

This stubborn stand on behalf of law and order disconcerted the crowd and it fell back in disorder. It did not long remain inactive but assembled again for a second assault.

Having only a small band of militia, and knowing they would be absolutely at the mercy of the thousands who were gathering to wreak vengeance upon them, the mayor ordered them to disperse and go to their homes, and he himself, having been wounded, was quietly conveyed out of the city.

The next day the mob grew in numbers and its rage increased in its intensity. There was no longer any doubt that Smith, innocent as he was of any crime, would be killed, for with the mayor out of the city and the governor of the state using no effort to control the mob, it was only a question of a few hours when the assault would be repeated and its victim put to death. All this happened as per programme. The description of that morning's carnival appeared in the paper above quoted and reads as follows:

"A squad of twenty men took the negro Smith from three policemen just before five o'clock this morning and hanged him to a hickory limb on Ninth avenue, in the residence section of the city. They riddled his body with bullets and put a placard on it saying: 'This is Mayor Trout's friend.' A coroner's jury of Bismel was summoned and viewed the body and rendered a verdict of death at the hands of unknown men. Thousands of persons visited the scene of the lynching between daylight and eight o'clock when the body was cut down. After the jury had completed its work the body was placed in the hands of officers, who were unable to keep back the mob. Three hundred men tried to drag the body through the streets of the town, but the Rev. Dr. Campbell of the First Presbyterian church and Capt. R. B. Moorman, with pleas and by force prevented them. Capt. Moorman hired a wagon and the body was put in it. It was then conveyed to the bank of the Roanoke, about two miles from the scene of the lynching. Here the body was dragged from the wagon by ropes for about 200 yards and burned. Piles of dry brushwood were brought, and the body was placed upon it, and more brushwood piled on the body, leaving only the head bare. The whole pile was then saturated with coal oil and a match was applied. The body was consumed within an hour. The cremation was witnessed by several thousand people. At one time the mob threatened to burn the

Negro in Mayor Trout's yard."

Thus did the people of Roanoke, Va., add this measure of proof to maintain our contention that it is only necessary to charge a Negro with a crime in order to secure his certain death. It was well known in the city before he was killed that he had not assaulted the woman with whom he had had the trouble, but he dared to have an altercation with a white woman, and he must pay the penalty. For an offense which would not in any civilized community have brought upon him a punishment greater than a fine of a few dollars, this unfortunate Negro was hung, shot and burned.

SUSPECTED, INNOCENT AND LYNCHED.

Five persons, Benjamin Jackson, his wife, Mahala Jackson, his mother-in-law, Lou Carter, Rufus Bigley, were lynched near Quincy, Miss., the charge against them being suspicion of well poisoning. It appears from the newspaper dispatches at that time that a family by the name of Woodruff was taken in, in September of 1892. As a result of their illness one or more of the family are said to have died, though that matter is not stated definitely. It was suspected that the cause of their illness was the existence of poison in the water, some miscreant having placed poison in the well. Suspicion pointed to a colored man named Benjamin Jackson who was at once arrested. With him also were arrested his wife and mother-in-law and all were held on the same charge.

The matter came up for judicial investigation, but as might have been expected, the white people concluded it was unnecessary to wait the result of the investigation that it was preferable to hang the accused first and try him afterward. By this method of procedure, the desired result was always obtained the accused was hanged. Accordingly Benjamin Jackson was taken from the officers a crowd of about two hundred people, while the inquest was being held, and hanged. After the killing of Jackson, the inquest was continued to ascertain the possible connection of the other persons charged with the crime. Against the wife and mother-in-law of the unfortunate man there was not the slightest evidence and the coroner's jury was fair enough to give them their liberty. They were declared innocent and returned, to their homes. But this did not protect the women from the demands of the Christian white people of that section of the country. In any other land and with any other people, the fact that these two accused persons were women would have pleaded in their favor for protection and fair play, but that had no weight with the Mississippi Christians nor the further fact that a jury of

white men had declared them innocent. The hanging of one victim on an unproven charge did not begin to satisfy the mob in Its bloodthirsty demands and the result was that even after the women had been discharged, they were at once taken in charge by a mob, which hung them by the neck until they were dead.

Still the mob was not satisfied. During the coroner's investigation the name of a fourth person, Rufus Bigley, was mentioned. He was acquainted with the Jacksons and that fact, together with some testimony adduced at the inquest, prompted the mob to decide that he should die also. Search was at once made for him and the next day he was apprehended. He was not given over into the hands of the civil authorities for trial nor did the coroner's inquest find that he was guilty, but the mob was quite sufficient in itself. After finding Bigley, he was strung up to a tree and his body left hanging, where it was found next day. It may be remarked here in passing that this instance of the moral degradation of the people of Mississippi did not excite any interest in the public at large. American Christianity beard of this awful affair and read of its details and neither press nor pulpit gave the matter more than a passing comment. Had it occurred in the wilds of interior Africa, there would have been an outcry from the humane people of this country against the savagery which would so mercilessly put men and women to death. But it was an evidence of American civilization to be passed by unnoticed, to be denied or condoned as the requirements of any future emergency might determine.

LYNCHED FOR AN ATTEMPTED ASSAULT.

With only a little more aggravation than that of Smith who quarreled at Roanoke with the market woman, was the assault which operated as the incentive to a most brutal lynching in Memphis, Tenn. Memphis is one of the queen cities of the south, with a population of about seventy thousand soul—easily one of the twenty largest, most progressive and wealthiest cities of the United States. And yet in its streets there occurred a scene of shocking savagery which would have disgraced the Congo. No woman was harmed, no serious indignity suffered. Two women driving to town in a wagon, were suddenly accosted by Lee Walker. He claimed that he demanded something to eat. The women claimed that he attempted to assault them. They gave such an alarm that he ran away. At once the dispatches spread over the country that a big, burly Negro had brutally assaulted two women. Crowds began to search for the alleged fiend. While hunting him they shot another Negro

dead in his tracks for refusing to stop when ordered to do so. After a few days Lee Walker was found, and put in jail in Memphis until the mob there was ready for him.

The Memphis Commercial of Sunday, July 23, contains a full account of the tragedy from which the following extracts are made:

> At 12 o'clock last night, Lee Walker, who attempted to outrage Miss Molhe McCadden, last Tuesday morning, was taken from the county jail and hanged to a telegraph pole just north of the prison. All day rumors were afloat that with night-fall an attack would be made upon the jail, and as everyone anticipated that a vigorous resistance would be made, a conflict between the mob and the authorities was feared.

> At 10 o'clock Capt. O'Haver, Sergt. Horan and several patrolmen were on hand, but they could do nothing with the crowd. An attack by the mob was made on the door in the south wall, and it yielded. Sheriff McLendon and several of its men threw themselves into the breach, but two or three of the storming party shoved by. They were seized by the police, but were not subdued, the officers refraining from using their clubs. The mob might at first have been dispersed by ten policemen who would use their clubs, but the sheriff insisted that no violence be done.

> The mob got an iron rail and used it as a battering ram against the lobby doors. Sheriff McLendon tried to stop them, and some one of the mob knocked him down with a chair. Still he counseled moderation and would not order his deputies and the police to disperse the crowd by force. The pacific policy of the sheriff impressed the mob with the idea that the officers were afraid, or at least would do them no harm, and they redoubled their efforts, urged on by a big switchman. At 12 o'clock the door of the prison was broken in with a rail.

> As soon as the rapist was brought out of the door calls were heard for a rope; then some one shouted, "Burn him!" But there was no time to make a fire. When Walker got into the lobby a dozen of the men began beating and stabbing him. He was half dragged, half carried to the corner of Front street and the alley between Sycamore and Min, and hung to a telegraph pole.

Walker made a desperate resistance. Two men entered his cell first and ordered him to come forth. He refused, and they failing to drag him out, others entered. He scratched and bit his assailants, wounding several of them severely with his teeth. The mob retaliated by striking and cutting him with fists and knives. When he reached the steps leading down to the door he made another stand and was stabbed again and again. By the time he reached the lobby his power to resist was gone, and he was shoved along through the mob of yelling, cursing men and boys, who beat, spat upon and slashed the wretch-like demon. One of the leaders of the mob fell, and the crowd walked ruthlessly over him. He was badly hurt-a jawbone fractured and internal injuries inflicted. After the lynching friends took charge of him.

The mob proceeded north on Front street with the victim, stopping at Sycamore street to get a rope from a grocery. "Take him to the iron bridge on Main street," yelled several men. The men who had hold of the Negro were in a hurry to finish the job, however, and when they reached the telephone pole at the corner of Front street and the first alley north of Sycamore they stopped. A hastily improvised noose was slipped over the Negro's head, and several young men mounted a pile of lumber near the pole and threw the rope over one of the Iron stepping pins. The Negro was lifted up until his feet were three feet above the ground, the rope was made taut, and a corpse dangled in midair. A big fellow who helped lead the mob pulled the Negro's legs until his neck cracked. The wretch's clothes had been torn off, and, as he swung, the man who pulled his legs mutilated the corpse.

One or two knife cuts more or less, made little difference in the appearance of the dead rapist, however, for before the rope was around his neck his skill was cut almost to ribbons. One pistol shot was fired while the corpse was hanging. A dozen voices protested against the use of firearms, and there was no more shooting. The body was permitted to hang for half an hour, then it was cut down and the rope divided among those who lingered around the scene of the tragedy. Then it was suggested that the corpse be burned, and it was done. The

performance, from the assault on the jail to the burning of the dead Negro was witness by a score or so of policemen and as many deputy sheriffs, but not a hand was lifted to stop the proceedings after the jail door yielded.

As the body hung to the telegraph pole, blood streaming down from the knife wounds in his neck, his hips and lower part of his legs also slashed with knives, the crowd hurled expletives at him, swung the body so that it was dashed against the pole, and, so far from the ghastly sight proving trying to the nerves, the crowd looked on with complaisance, if not with real pleasure. The Negro died hard. The neck was not broken, as the body was drawn up without being given a fall, and death came by strangulation. For fully ten minutes after he was strung up the chest heaved occasionally, and there were convulsive movements of the limbs. Finally he was pronounced dead, and a few minutes later Detective Richardson climbed on a pile of staves and cut the rope. The body fell in a ghastly heap, and the crowd laughed at the sound and crowded around the prostrate body, a few kicking the inanimate carcass.

Detective Richardson, who Is also a deputy coroner, then proceeded to Impanel the following jury of inquest: J. S. Moody, A. C. Waldran, B. J. Childs, J. N. House, Nelson Bins, T. L. Smith, and A. Newhouse. After viewing the body the inquest was adjourned without any testimony being taken until 9 o'clock this morning. The jury will meet at the coroner's office, 51 Beale street, up stairs, and decide on a verdict. If no witnesses are forthcoming, the jury will be able to arrive at a verdict just the same, as all members of it saw the lynching. Then some one raised the cry of "Burn him!" It was quickly taken up and soon resounded from a hundred throats. Detective Richardson, for a long time, single-handed, stood the crowd, off. He talked and begged the men not to bring disgrace on the city by burning the body, arguing that all the vengeance possible had been wrought.

While this was going on a small crowd was busy starting a fire in the middle of the street. The material was handy. Some bundles of staves were taken from the adjoining lumber yard for kindling. Heavier wood was obtained from the same

source, and coal oil from a neighboring grocery. Then the cries of "Burn him! Burn him!" were redoubled.

Half a dozen men seized the naked body. The crowd cheered. They marched to the fire, and giving the body a swing, it was landed in the middle of the fire. There was a cry for more wood, as the fire had begun to die owing to the long delay. Willing hands procured the wood, and it was piled up on the Negro, almost, for a time, obscuring him from view. The head was in plain view, as also were the limbs, and one arm which stood out high above the body, the elbow crooked, held in that position by a stick of wood. In a few moments the hands began to swell, then came great blisters over all the exposed parts of the body; then in places the flesh was burned away and the bones began to show through. It was a horrible sight, one which, perhaps, none there had ever witnessed before. It proved too much for a large part of the crowd and the majority of the mob left very shortly after the burning began.

But a large number stayed, and were not a bit set back by the sight of a human body being burned to ashes. Two or three white women, accompanied by their escorts, pushed to the front to obtain an unobstructed view, and looked on with astonishing coolness and nonchalance. One man and woman brought a little girl, not over 12 years old, apparently their daughter, to view a scene which was calculated to drive sleep from the child's eyes for many nights, if not to produce a permanent injury to her nervous system. The comments of the crowd were varied. Some remarked on the efficacy of this style of cure for rapists, others rejoiced that men's wives and daughters were now safe from this wretch. Some laughed as the flesh cracked and blistered, and while a large number pronounced the burning of a dead body as a useless episode, not in all that throng was a word of sympathy heard for the wretch himself.

The rope that was used to hang the Negro, and also that which was used to lead him from the jail, were eagerly so tight by relic hunters. They almost fought for a chance to cut off a piece of rope, and in an incredibly short time both ropes had disappeared and were scattered in the pockets of the crowd in sections of from an inch to six inches long. Others of the relic

hunters remained until the ashes cooled to obtain such ghastly relics as the teeth, nails, and bits of charred skill of the immolated victim of his own lust. After burning the body the mob tied a rope around the charred trunk and dragged it down Main street to the court house, where it was hanged to a center pole. The rope broke and the corpse dropped with a thud, but it was again hoisted, the charred legs barely touching the ground. The teeth were knocked out and the finger nails cut off as souvenirs. The crowd made so much noise that the police interfered. Undertaker Walsh was telephoned for, who took charge of the body and carried It to his establishment, where it will be prepared for burial in the potter's field today.

A prelude to this exhibition of 19th century barbarism was the following telegram received by the Chicago Inter Ocean, at 2 o'clock, Saturday afternoon—ten hours before the lynching:

"MEMPHIS, TENN., July 22, To Inter-Ocean, Chicago.
"Lee Walker, colored man, accused of raping white women, in jail here, will be taken out and burned by whites to-night. Can you send Miss Ida Wells to write it up? Answer. R. M. Martin, with Public Ledger."

The Public Ledger is one of the oldest evening daily papers in Memphis, and this telegram shows that the intentions of the mob were well known long before they were executed. The personnel of the mob is given by the Memphis Appeal-Avalanche. It says, "At first it seemed as if a crowd of roughs were the principals, but as it increased in size, men In all walks of life figured as leaders, although the majority were young men."

This was the punishment meted out to a Negro, charged, not with rape, but attempted assault, and without any proof as to his guilt, for the women were not given a chance to identify him. It was only a little less horrible than the burning alive of Henry Smith, at Parts, Texas, February 1st, 1893, or that of Edward Coy, in Texarkana, Texas, February 20, 1892. Both were charged with assault on white women, and both were tied to the stake and burned while yet alive, in the presence of ten thousand persons. In the case of Coy, the white woman in the case, applied the match, even while the victim protested his innocence.

The cut which is here given Is the exact reproduction of the photograph taken at the scene of the lynching at Clinton, Alabama, August, 1891. The cause for which the man was hanged is given in the words of the mob which were written on the back of the photograph, and they are also given. This photograph was sent to Judge A. W. Tourgee, of Mayville, N. Y.

In some of these cases the mob affects to believe in the Negro's guilt. The world is told that the white woman in the case identifies him, or the prisoner "confesses." But in the lynching which took place in Barnwell County, South Carolina, April 24, 1893, the mob's victim, John Peterson, escaped and placed himself under Governor Tillman's protection; not only did he declare his innocence, but offered to prove an alibi, by white witnesses. Before his witnesses could be brought, the mob arrived at the Governor's mansion, and demanded the prisoner. He was given up, and although the white woman in the case said he was not the man, he was hanged 24 hours after, and over a thousand bullets fired Into his body, on the declaration that "a crime had been committed and some one had to hang for it."

CHAPTER VI.

HISTORY OF SOME CASES OF RAPE.

It has been claimed that the Southern white women have been slandered because, in defending the Negro race from the charge that all colored men, who are lynched, only pay penalty for assaulting women. It is certain that lynching mobs have rot only refused to give the Negro a chance to defend himself, but have killed their victim with a full knowledge that the relationship of the alleged assailant with the woman who accused him, was voluntary and clandestine. As a matter of fact, one of the prime causes of the Lynch Law agitation has been a necessity for defending the Negro from this awful charge against him. This defense has been necessary because the apologists for outlawry insist that in no case has the accusing woman been a willing consort of her paramour, who is lynched because overtaken in wrong. It is well known, however, that such is the case. In July of this year, 1894, John Paul Bocock, a Southern white man living in New York, and assistant editor of the New York Tribune, took occasion to defy the publication of any instance where the lynched Negro was the victim of a white woman's falsehood. Such cases are not rare, but the press and people conversant with the facts, almost invariably suppress them.

The New York Sun of July 30th, 1894, contained a synopsis of interviews with leading congressmen and editors of the South. Speaker Crisp, of the House of Representative, who was recently a Judge of the Supreme Court of Georgia, led in declaring that lynching seldom or never took place, save for vile crime against women and children. Dr. Hoss, editor of the leading organ of the Methodist Church South, published In its columns that it was his belief that more than three hundred women had been assaulted by Negro men within three months. When asked to prove his charges, or give a single case upon which his "belief" was founded, he said that he could do so, but the details were unfit for publication. No other evidence but his "belief" could be adduced to substantiate this grave charge, yet Bishop Haygood, in the Forum of October, 1893, quotes this "belief" in apology for lynching, and voluntarily adds: "It is my opinion that this is an underestimate." The "opinion" of this man, based upon a "belief," had greater weight coming from a mail who has posed as a friend to "Our Brother in Black," and was accepted as authority. An interview of Miss Frances E. Willard, the great apostle of temperance, the daughter of abolitionists and a personal friend and helper of many individual colored people, has been quoted in support of the utterance of this calumny against a weak and defenseless race. In the New York Voice of October 23, 1890, after a tour in the South, where she was told all these things by the "best white people," she said: "The grogshop is the Negro's center of power. Better whisky and more of it is the rallying cry of great, dark-faced mobs. The colored race multiplies like the locusts of Egypt. The grogshop is its center of power. The safety of woman, of childhood, the home, is menaced in a thousand localities at this moment, so that men dare not go beyond the sight of their own roof-tree."

These charges so often reiterated, have had the effect of fastening the odium upon the face of a peculiar propensity for this foul crime. The Negro is thus forced to a defense of his good name, and this chapter will be devoted to the history of some of the cases where assault upon white women by Negroes is charged. He is not the aggressor in this fight, but the situation demands that the facts be given, and they will speak for themselves. Of the 1,115 Negro men, women and children hanged, shot and roasted alive from January 1st, 1882, to January 1st, 1894, inclusive, only 348 of that number were charged with rape. Nearly 700 of these persons were lynched for any other reason which could be manufactured by a mob wishing to indulge in a lynching bee.

A WHITE WOMAN'S FALSEHOOD.

The Cleveland, Ohio, Gazette, January 16, 1892, gives an account of one of these cases of "rape."

Mrs. J. C. Underwood, the wife of a minister of Elyria, Ohio, accused an Afro-American of rape. She told her husband that during his absence in 1888, stumping the state for the Prohibition Party, the man came to the kitchen door, forced his way In the house and insulted her. She tried to drive him out with a heavy poker, but he overpowered and chloroformed her, and when she revived her clothing was torn and she was in a horrible condition. She did not know the man, but could Identify him. She subsequently point-ed out William Offett, a married man, who was arrested, and, being In Ohio, was granted a trial.

The prisoner vehemently denied the charge of rape, but confessed he went to Mrs. Underwood's residence at her invitation and was criminally intimate with her at her request. This availed him nothing against the sworn testimony of a minister's wife, a lady of the highest respectability. He was found guilty, and entered the penitentiary, December 14, 1888, for fifteen years. Sometime afterwards the woman's remorse led her to confess to her husband that the man was innocent. These are her words: "I met Offett at the postoffice. It was raining. He was polite to me, and as I had several bun-dles In my arms he offered to carry them home for me, which he did. He had a strange fascination for me, and I invited him to call on me. He called, bringing chestnuts and candy for the children. By this means we got them to leave us alone in the room. Then I sat on his lap. He made a proposal to me and I readily consented. Why I did so I do not know, but that I did is true. He visited me several times after that and each time I was indiscreet. I did not care after the first time. In fact I could not have resisted, and had no desire to resist."

When asked by her husband why she told him she had been outraged, she said: "I had several reasons for telling you. One was the neighbors saw the fellow here, another was, I was afraid I had contracted a loathsome disease, and still another was that I feared I might give birth to a Negro baby. I hoped to save my reputation by telling you a deliberate lie." Her husband, horrified by the confession, had Offett, who had already served four years, released and secured a divorce. There have been many such cases throughout the South, with the difference that the Southern white men in insensate fury wreak their vengeance without intervention of law upon the Negro who consorts with their women.

TRIED TO MANUFACTURE AN OUTRAGE.

The Memphis (Tenn.) Ledger, of June 8, 1892, has the following: "If Lilhe Bailey, a rather pretty white girl, seventeen years of age, who is now at the city hospital, would be somewhat less reserved about her disgrace there would be some very nauseating details in the story of her life. She is the mother of a little coon. The truth might reveal fearful depravity or the evidence of a rank outrage. She will not divulge the name of the man who has left such black evidence of her disgrace, and in fact says it is a matter in which there can be no interest to the outside world. She came to Memphis nearly three months ago, and was taken in at the Woman's Refuge in the southern part of the city. She remained there until a few weeks ago when the child was born. The ladies in charge of the Refuge were horrified. The girl was at once sent to the city hospital, where she has been since May 30th. She is a country girl, she came to Memphis from her father's farm, a short distance from Hernando, Miss. Just when she left there she would not say. In fact she says she came to Memphis from Arkansas, and says her home is in that state. She is rather good looking, has blue eyes, a low forehead and dark red hair. The ladies at the Woman's Refuge do not know anything about the girl further than what they learned when she was an inmate of the institution; and she would not tell much. When the child was born an attempt was made to get the girl to reveal the name of the Negro who had disgraced her, she obstinately refused and it was impossible to elicit any information from her on the subject."

Note the wording: "The truth might reveal fearful depravity or rank outrage." If it had been a white child or if Lilhe Bailey had told a pitiful story of Negro outrage, it would have been a case of woman's weakness or assault and she could have remained at the Woman's Refuge. But a Negro child and to withhold Its father's name and thus prevent the killing of another Negro "rapist" was a case of "fearful depravity." Had she revealed the father's name, he would have been lynched and his taking off charged to an assault upon a white woman.

BURNED ALIVE FOR ADULTERY.

In Texarkana, Arkansas, Edward Coy was accused of assaulting a white woman. The press dispatches of February 18,1892, told in detail how he was tied to a tree, the flesh cut from his body by men and boys, and after coal oil was poured over him, the woman he had assaulted gladly set fire to him, and

15,000 persons saw him burn to death. October 1st, the Chicago Inter Ocean contained the following account of that horror from the pen of the "Bystander" Judge Albion W. Tourgee—as the result of his investigations:

> "1. The woman who was as victim of violence was of bad character; her husband was a drunkard and a gambler.
>
> "2. She was publicly reported and generally known to have been criminally intimate with Coy for more than a year previous.
>
> "3. She was compelled by threats, if not by violence, to make the charge against the victim.
>
> "4. When she came to apply the match Coy asked her if she would burn him after they had 'been sweethearting' so long.
>
> "5. A large majority of the 'superior' white men prominent in the affair are the reputed fathers of mulatto children.
>
> "These are not pleasant facts, but they are illustrative of the vital phase of the so-called 'race question,' which should properly be designated an earnest inquiry as to the best methods by which religion, science, law and political power may be employed to excuse injustice, barbarity and crime done to a people were inspired by any consuming zeal to vindicate God's law against miscregenationists of the most practical sort. The woman was a willing partner in the victim's guilt, and being of the 'superior' race must naturally have been more guilty."

NOT IDENTIFIED BUT LYNCHED.

February 11th, 1893, there occurred in Shelby county, Tennessee, the fourth Negro lynching within fifteen months. The three first were lynched in the city of Memphis for firing on white men in self-defense. This Negro, Richard Neal, was lynched a few miles front the city limits, and the following Is taken from the Memphis (Tenn..) Scimitar:

> "As the Scimitar stated on Saturday the Negro, Richard Neal, who raped Mrs. Jack White near Forest Hill, in this county, was lynched by a mob of about 200 white citizens or the neighborhood. Sheriff McLendon, accompanied by

Deputies Perkins, App and Harvey and a Scimitar reporter, arrived on the scene of the execution about 3:30 in the afternoon. The body was suspended from the first limb of a post oak tree by a new quarter inch grass rope. A hangman's knot, evidently tired by an expert, fitted snugly under the victim's arms behind him. His legs were not tied. The body was perfectly limber when the Sheriff's posse cut it down and retained enough heat to warm the feet of Deputy Perkins, whose road cart was converted into a hearse. On arriving with the body at Forest Hin the Sheriff made a bargain with a stalwart young man with a blond mustache and deep blue eyes, who told the Scimitar reporter that he was the leader of the mob, to haul the body to Germantown for $3.

"When within half-a-mile of Germantown the Sheriff end posse were overtaken by Squire McDonald of Collierville, who had come down to hold the inquest. The Squire had his jury with him, and it was agreed for the convenience of all parties that he should proceed with the corpse to Germantown and conduct the inquiry as to the cause of death. He did so, and a verdict of death from hanging by parties unknown was returned in due form.

"The execution of Neal was done deliberately and by the best people of the Collierville, Germantown and Forest Hill neighborhoods, without passion or exhibition of anger.

"He was arrested on Friday about ten o'clock, by Constable Bob Cash, who carried him before Mrs White. She said: 'I think he is the man. I am almost certain of it. If he isn't the man he is exactly like him.'

"The Negro's coat was torn also, and there were other circumstances against him. The committee returned and made its report, and the chairman put the question of guilt or innocence to a vote.

"All who thought the proof strong enough to warrant execution were invited to cross over to the other side of the road. Everybody but four or five Negroes crossed over. "The committee then placed Neal on a mule with his arms tied behind him, and proceeded to the scene of the crime, followed by the mob. The rope, with a noose already prepared, was tied

to the limb nearest the spot where the unpardonable sin was committed, and the doomed man's mule was brought to a standstill beneath it.

"Then Neal confessed. He said he was the right man, but denied that he used force or threats to accomplish his purpose. It was a matter of purchase, he claimed, and said the price paid was twenty-five cents. He warned the colored men present to beware of white women and resist temptation, for to yield to their blandishments or to the passions of men, meant death.

"While he was speaking, Mrs. White came from her home and calling Constable Cash to one side, asked if he could not save the Negro's life. The reply was, 'No,' and Mrs. White returned to the house.

"When all was in readiness, the husband of Neal's victim leaped upon the mile's back and adjusted the rope around the Negro's neck. No cap was used, and Neal showed no fear, nor did he beg for mercy. The mule was struck with a whip and bounded out from under Neal, leaving him suspended in the air with his feet about three feet from the ground."

DELIVERED TO THE MOB BY
THE GOVERNOR OF THE STATE.

John Peterson, near Denmark, S. C., was suspected of rape, but escaped, went to Columbia, and placed himself under Gov. Tillman's protection, declaring he too could prove an alibi by white witnesses. A white reporter hearing his declaration volunteered to find these witnesses, and telegraphed the governor that he would be in Columbia with them on Monday. In the meantime the mob at Denmark, learning Peterson's whereabouts, went to the governor and demanded the prisoner. Gov. Tinman, who had during his canvass for reselection the year before, declared that he would lead a mob to lynch a Negro that assaulted a white woman, gave Peterson up to the mob. He was taken back to Denmark, and the white girl in the case as positively declared that he was not the man. But the verdict of the mob was that "the crime had been committed and somebody had to hang for it, and if he, Peterson, was not guilty of that he was of some other crime," and he was hung, and his body riddled with 1,000 bullets.

LYNCHED AS A WARNING.

Alabama furnished a case in point. A colored man named Daniel Edwards, lived near Selma, Alabama, and worked for a family, of a farmer near that place. This resulted in an intimacy between the young man and a daughter of the householder, which finally developed in the disgrace of the girl. After the birth of the child, the mother disclosed the 'act that Edwards was its father. The relationship had been sustained for more than a year, and yet this colored man was apprehended, thrown into jail from whence he was taken by a mob of one hundred neighbors and hung to a tree and his body riddled with bullets. A dispatch which describes the lynching, ends as follows. "Upon his back was found pinned this morning the following: 'Warning to all Negroes that are too intimate with white girls. This the work of one hundred best citizens of the South Side.'"

There can be no doubt from the announcement made by this "one hundred best citizens" that they understood full well the character of the relationship which existed between Edwards and the girl, but when the dispatches were sent out, describing the affair, it was claimed that Edwards was lynched for rape.

SUPPRESSING THE TRUTH.

In a county in Mississippi during the month of July the Associated Press dispatches sent out a report that the sheriffs eight year old daughter had been assaulted by a big, black, burly brute who had been promptly lynched. The facts which have since been investigated show that the girl was more than eighteen year old and that she was discovered by her father in this young man's room who was a servant on the place. But these facts the Associated Press has not given to the world, nor did the same agency acquaint the world with the fact that a Negro youth who was lynched in Tuscumbia, Ala., the same year on the same charge told the white girl who accused him before the mob, that he had met her in the woods often by appointment. There is a young mulatto in one of the State prison of the South to-day who is there by charge of a young white woman to screen herself. He to a college graduate and had been corresponding with, and clandestinely visiting her until he was surprised and run out of her room en dishabille by her father. He was put in prison in another town to rave his life from the mob and his lawyer advised that it were better to save his life by pleading guilty to charges made and being sentenced for years, than to attempt a defense by exhibiting the letters

written him by this girl. In the latter event, the mob would surely murder him, while there was a chance for his life by adopting the former course. Names, places and dates are not given for the same reason.

The excuse has come to be so safe, it is not surprising that a Philadelphia girl, beautiful and well educated, and of good family, should make a confession published in all the daily papers of that city October, 1894, that she had been stealing for some time, and that to cover one of her thefts, she had said she had been bound and gagged in her father's house by a colored man, and money stolen therefrom by him. Had this been done in many localities, it would only have been necessary for her to "identify" the first Negro in that vicinity, to have brought about another lynching bee.

A VILE SLANDER WITH SCANT RETRACTION.

The following published in the Cleveland (Ohio) Leader of Oct. 23d, 1894, only emphasizes our demand that a fair trial shall be given those accused of crime, and the protection of the law be extended until time for a defense be granted.

> "The Sensational story sent out last night from Hicksville that a Negro had outraged a little four-year-old girl proves to be a base canard. The correspondents who went into the details should have taken the pains to investigate, and the officials should have known more of the matter before they gave out such grossly exaggerated information.
>
> "The Negro, Charles O'Neil, had been working for a couple of women and, it seems, had worked all winter without being remunerated. There is a little girl, and the girl's mother and grandmother evidently started the story with idea of frightening the Negro out of the country and thus balancing accounts. The town was considerably wrought up and for a time things looked serious. The accused had a preliminary hearing to-day and not an iota of evidence was produced to indicate that such a crime had been committed, or that he had even attempted such an outrage. The village marshal was frightened nearly out of his wits and did little to quiet the excitement last night. "The affair was an outrage on the Negro, at the expense of Innocent childhood, a brainless fabrication from start to finish."

The original story was sent throughout this country and England, but the

Cleveland Leader, so far as known, is the only journal which has published these facts in refutation of the slander so often published against the race.

Not only is it true that many of the alleged cases of rape against the Negro, are like the foregoing, but the same crime committed by white men against Negro women and girls, is never punished by mob or the law. A leading journal in South Carolina openly said some months ago that "it is not the same thing for a white man to assault a colored woman as for a colored man to assault a white woman, because the colored woman had no finer feelings nor virtue to be outraged!" Yet colored women have always had far more reason to complain of white men In this respect than ever white women have had of Negroes.

ILLINOIS HAS A LYNCHING.

In the month of June, 1893, the proud commonwealth of Illinois joined the ranks of Lynching States. Illinois, which gave to the world the immortal heroes, Lincoln, Grant and Logan, trailed its banner of justice in the dust-dyed its hands red in the blood of a man not proven guilty of crime. June 3, 1893, the country about Decatur, one of the largest cities of the state was startled with the cry that a white woman had been assaulted by a colored tramp. Three days later a colored man named Samuel Bush was arrested and put in jail. A white man testified that Bush, on the day of the assault, asked him where he could get a drink and he pointed to the house where the farmer's wife was subsequently said to have been assaulted. Bush said he went to the well but did not go near the house, and did not assault the woman. After he was arrested the alleged victim did not see him to identify him—he was presumed to be guilty.

The citizens determined to kill him. The mob gathered, went to the jail, met with no resistance, took the suspected man, dragged him out tearing every stitch of clothing from his body, then hanged him to a telegraph pole. The grand jury refused to indict the lynchers though the names of over twenty persons who were leaders in the mob were well known. In fact twenty-two persons were indicted, but the grand jurors and the prosecuting attorney disagreed as to the form of the indictments, which caused the jurors to change their minds. All indictments were reconsidered and the matter was dropped. Not one of the dozens of men prominent in that murder have suffered a whit more inconvenience for the butchery of that man, than they would have suffered for shooting a dog.

COLOR LINE JUSTICE.

In Baltimore, Maryland, a gang of white ruffians a respectable colored girl who was out walking with a young man of her own race. They held her escort and outraged the girl. It was a deed dastardly enough to arouse Southern blood, which gives its horror of rape as excuse for lawlessness, but she was a colored woman. The case went to the courts and they were acquitted.

In Nashville, Tennessee, there was a white man, Pat Hanifan, who outraged a little colored girl, and from the physical injuries received she was ruined for life. He was jailed for six months, discharged, and is now a detective in that city. In the same city, last May, a white man outraged a colored girl in a drug store. He was arrested and released on bail at the trial. It was rumored that five hundred colored men had organized to lynch him. Two hundred and fifty white citizens armed themselves with Winchesters and guarded him. A cannon was placed in front of his home, and the Buchanan Rifles (State Militia) ordered to the scene for his protection. The colored mob did not show up. Only two weeks before, Eph. Grizzard, who had only been charged with rape upon a white woman, had been taken from the jail, with Governor Buchanan and the police and militia standing by, dragged through the streets in broad daylight, knives plunged into him at every step, and with every fiendish cruelty that a frenzied mob could devise, he was at last swung out on the bridge with hands cut to pieces as he tried to climb up the stanchions. A naked, bloody example of the bloodthirstiness of the nineteenth century civilization of the Athens of the South! No cannon nor military were called out in his defense. He dared to visit a white woman.

At the very moment when these civilized whites were announcing their determination "to protect their wives and daughters," by murdering Grizzard, a white man was in the same jail for raping eight-year-old Maggie Reese, a colored girl. He was not harmed. The "honor" of grown women who were glad enough to be supported by the Grizzard boys and Ed Coy, as long as the liaison was not known, needed protection; they were white. The outrage upon helpless childhood needed no avenging in this case; she was black. A white man in Guthrie, Oklahoma Territory, two months after inflicted such injuries upon another colored girl that she died. He was not punished, but an attempt was made in the same town in the month of June to lynch a colored man who visited a white woman.

In Memphis, Tennessee, in the month of June, Ellerton L. Dorr, who is the husband of Russell Hancock's widow, was arrested for attempted rape on

Mattie Cole, a neighbor's cook; he was only prevented from accomplishing his purpose by the appearance of Mattie's employer. Dorr's friends say he was drunk and not responsible for his actions. The grand jury refused to indict him and he was discharged.

In Tallahassee, Florida, a colored girl, Charlotte Gilliam, was assaulted by white men. Her father went to have a warrant for their arrest issued, but the judge refused to issue it.

In Bowling Green, Virginia, Moses Christopher, a colored lad, was charged with assault, September 10. He was indicted, tried, convicted and sentenced to death in one day. In the same state at Danville, two weeks before August 29, Thomas J. Penn, a white man, committed a criminal assault upon Lina Hanna, a twelve-year-old colored girl, but he has not been tried, certainly not killed either by the law or the mob.

In Surrey county, Virginia, C. L. Brock, a white man, criminally assaulted a ten-year-old colored girl, and threatened to kill her if she told. Notwithstanding, she confessed to her aunt, Mrs. Alice Bates, and the white brute added further crime by killing Mrs. Bates when she upbraided him about his crime upon her niece. He emptied the contents of his revolver into her body as she lay. Brock has never been apprehended, and no effort has been made to do so by the legal authorities. But even when punishment is meted out by law to white villains for this horrible crime, it is seldom or never that capital punishment is invoked. Two cases just clipped from the daily papers will suffice to show how this crime is punished when committed by white offenders and black.

> LOUISVILLE, KY., October 19.—Smith Young, colored, was to day sentenced to be hanged. Young criminally assaulted a six-year old child about six months ago.
>
> Jacques Blucher, the Pontiac Frenchman who was arrested at that place for a criminal assault on his daughter Fanny on July 29 last, pleaded nolo contenders when placed on trial at East Greenwich, near Providence, R. I., Tuesday, and was sentenced to five years in State Prison.
>
> Charles Wilson was convicted of assault upon seven year-old Mamie Keys in Philadelphia, in October, and sentenced to ten years in prison. He was white. Indianapolis courts sentenced a white man in September to eight years in prison for assault upon a twelve year old white girl. April 24,

1893, a lynching was set for Denmark, S. C., on the charge of rape. A white girl accused a Negro of assault, and the mob was about to lynch him. A few hours before the lynching three reputable white men rode into the town and solemnly testified that the accused Negro was at work with them 25 miles away on the day and at the hour the crime had been committed. He was accordingly set free. A white person's word is taken as absolutely for as against a Negro.

CHAPTER VII.

THE CRUSADE JUSTIFIED.
(Appeal from America to the World.)

It has been urged in criticism of the movement appealing to the English people for sympathy and support in our crusade against Lynch Law that our action was unpatriotic, vindictive and useless. It is not a part of the plan of this pamphlet to make any defense for that crusade nor to indict any apology for the motives which led to the presentation of the facts of American lynchings to the world at large. To those who are not willfully blind and unjustly critical, the record of more than a thousand lynchings in ten years is enough to justify any peaceable movement tending to ameliorate the conditions which led to this unprecedented slaughter of human beings.

If America would not hear the cry of men, women and children whose dying groans ascended to heaven praying for relief, not only for them but for others who might soon be treated as they, then certainly no fair-minded person can charge disloyalty to those who make an appeal to the civilization of the world for such sympathy and help as it is possible to extend. If stating the facts of these lynchings, as they appeared from time to time in the white newspapers of America—the news gathered by white correspondents, compiled by white press bureaus and disseminated among white people shows any vindictiveness, then the mind which so charges is not amenable to argument.

But it is the desire of this pamphlet to urge that the crusade started and thus far continued has not been useless, but has been blessed with the most salutary results. The many evidences of the good results can not here be mentioned, but the thoughtful student of the situation can himself find ample

proof. There need not here be mentioned the fact that for the first time since lynching began, has there been any occasion for the governors of the several states to speak out in reference to these crimes against law and order. No matter how heinous the act of the lynchers may have been, it was discussed only for a day or so and then dismissed from the attention of the public. In one or two instances the governor has called attention to the crime, but the civil processes entirely failed to bring the murderers to justice. Since the crusade against lynching was started, however, governors of states, newspapers, senators and representatives and bishops of churches have all been compelled to take cognizance of the prevalence of this crime and to speak in one way or another in the defense of the charge against this barbarism in the United States. This has not been because there was any latent spirit of justice voluntarily asserting itself, especially in those who do the lynching, but because the American people now feel, both North and South, that they are objects in the gaze of the civilized world and that for every lynching asks that America render its account to civilization and itself.

AWFUL BARBARISM IGNORED.

Much has been said during the months of September and October of 1894 about the lynching of six colored men who on suspicion of incendiarism were made the victims of a most barbarous massacre. They were arrested, one by one, by officers of the law; they were handcuffed and chained together and by the officers of the law loaded in a wagon and deliberately driven into an ambush where a mob of lynchers awaited them. At the time and upon the chosen spot, in the darkness of the night and far removed from the habitation of any human soul, the wagon was halted and the mob fired upon the six manacled men, shooting them to death as no humane person would have shot dogs. Chained together as they were, in their awful struggles after the first volley, the victims tumbled out of the wagon upon the ground and there In the mud, struggling in their death throes, the victims were made the target of the murderous shotguns, which fired into the writhing, struggling, dying mass of humanity, until every spark of life was gone. Then the officers of the law who had them in charge, drove away to give the alarm and to tell the world that they had been waylaid and their prisoners forcibly taken from them and killed.

It has been claimed that the prompt, vigorous and highly commendable steps of the governor of the State of Tennessee and the judge having jurisdiction over the crime, and of the citizens of Memphis generally, was the nat-

ural revolt of the humane conscience in that section of the country, and the determination of honest and honorable men to rid the community of such men as those who were guilty of this terrible massacre. It has further been claimed that this vigorous uprising of the people and this most commendably prompt action of the civil authorities, is ample proof that the American people will not tolerate the lynching of innocent men, and that in cases where brutal lynchings not been promptly dealt with, the crimes on the part of the victims were such as to put them outside the pale of humanity and that the world considered their death a necessary sacrifice for the good of all.

But this line of argument can in no possible way be truthfully sustained. The lynching of the six men In 1894, barbarous as it was, was in no way more barbarous than took nothing more than a passing notice. It was only the other lynchings which preceded it, and of which the public fact that the attention of the civilized world has been called to lynching in America which made the people of Tennessee feel the absolute necessity for a prompt, vigorous and just arraignment of all the murderers connected with that crime. Lynching is no longer "Our Problem," it is the problem of the civilized world, and Tennessee could not afford to refuse the legal measure which Christianity demands shall be used for the punishment of crime.

MEMPHIS THEN AND NOW.

Only two years prior to the massacre of the six men near Memphis, that same city took part in a massacre in every way as bloody and brutal as that of September last it was the murder of three young colored men and who were known to be among the most honorable, reliable, worthy and peaceable colored citizens of the community. All of them were engaged in the mercantile business, being members of a corporation which conducted a large grocery store, and one of the three being a letter carrier in the employ of the government. These three men were arrested for restating an attack of a mob upon their store, in which melee none of the assailants, who had armed themselves for their devilish deeds by securing court processes, were killed or even seriously injured. But these three men were put in jail, and on three or four nights after their incarceration a mob of less than a dozen men, by collusion with the civil authorities, entered the jail, took the three men from the custody of the law and shot them to death. Memphis knew of this awful crime, knew then and knows today who the men were who committed it, and yet not the first step was ever taken to apprehend the guilty wretches who walk the streets today with the brand of murder upon their foreheads,

but as safe from harm as the most upright citizen of that community. Memphis would have been just as calm and complacent and self-satisfied over the murder of the six colored men in 1894 as it was over these three colored men in 1892, had it not recognized the fact that to escape the brand of barbarism it had not only to speak its denunciation but to act vigorously in vindication of its name.

AN ALABAMA HORROR IGNORED.

A further instance of this absolute disregard of every principle of justice and the indifference to the barbarism of Lynch Law may be cited here, and is furnished by white residents in the city of Carrolton, Alabama. Several cases of arson had been discovered, and in their search for the guilty parties, suspicion was found to rest upon three men and a woman. The four suspects were Paul Hill, Paul Archer, William Archer, his brother, and a woman named Emma Fair. The prisoners were apprehended, earnestly asserted their innocence, but went to jail without making any resistance. They claimed that they could easily prove their innocence upon trial.

One would suspect that the civilization which defends itself against the barbarisms of Lynch Law by stating that it lynches human beings only when they are guilty of awful attacks upon women and children, would have been very careful to have given these four prisoners, who were simply charged with arson, a fair trial, to which they were entitled upon every principle of law and humanity. Especially would this seem to be the case when it is considered that one of the prisoners charged was a woman, and if the Nineteenth Century has shown any advancement upon any lines of human action, it is pre-eminently shown in its reverence, respect and protection of its womanhood. But the people of Alabama failed to have any regard for womanhood whatever.

The three men and the woman were put in jail to await trial. A few days later it was rumored that they were to be subjects of Lynch Law, and, sure enough, at night a mob of lynchers went to the jail, not to avenge any awful crime against womanhood, but to kill four people who had been suspected of setting a house on fire. They were caged in their cells, helpless and defenseless, they were at the mercy of civilized white Americans, who, armed with shotguns, were there to maintain the majesty of American law. And most effectively was their duty done by these splendid representatives of Governor Fishback's brave and honorable white Southerners, who resent "outside interference." They lined themselves tip in the most effective manner and poured

volley after volley into the bodies of their helpless, pleading victims, who in their bolted prison cells could do nothing but suffer and die. Then these lynchers went quietly away and the bodies of the woman and three men were taken out and buried with as little ceremony as men would bury hogs.

No one will say that the massacre near Memphis in 1894 was any worse than this bloody crime of Alabama in 1892. The details of this shocking affair were given to the public by the press, but public sentiment was not moved to action in the least; it was only a matter of a day's notice and then went to swell the list of murders which stand charged against the noble, Christian people of Alabama.

AMERICA AWAKENED.

But there is now an awakened conscience throughout the land, and Lynch Law can not flourish in the future as it has in the past. The close of the year 1894 witnessed an aroused interest, an assertive humane principle which must tend to the extirpation of that crime. The awful butchery last mentioned failed to excite more than a passing comment in 1894, but far different is it today. Gov. Jones, of Alabama, in 1893 dared to speak out against the rule of the mob in no uncertain terms. His address indicated a most helpful result of the present agitation. In face of the many denials of the outrages on the one hand and apologies for lynchers on the other, Gov. Jones admits the awful lawlessness charged and refuses to join in the infamous plea made to condone the crime. No stronger nor more effective words have been said than those following from Gov. Jones.

"While the ability of the state to deal with open revolts against the supremacy of its laws has been ably demonstrated, I regret that deplorable acts of violence have been perpetrated, in at least four instances, within the past two years by mobs, whose sudden work and quick dispersions rendered it impossible to protect their victims. Within the past two years nine prisoners, who were either in jail or in the custody of the officers, been taken from them without resistance, and put to death. There was doubt of the guilt of the defendants in most of these cases, and few of them were charged with capital offenses. None of them involved the crime of rape. The largest rewards allowed by law were offered for the apprehension of the offenders, and officers were charged to a vigilant perform-

ance of their duties, and aided in some instances by the services of skinned detectives; but not a single arrest has been made and the grand juries in these counties have returned no bills of indictment. This would indicate either that local public sentiment approved these acts of violence or was too weak to punish them, or that the officers charged with that duty were in some way lacking in their performance. The evil cannot be cured or remedied by silence as to its existence. Unchecked, it will continue until it becomes a reproach to our good name, and a menace to our prosperity and peace: and it behooves you to exhaust all remedies within your power to find better preventives for such crimes."

A FRIENDLY WARNING.

From England comes a friendly voice which must give to every patriotic citizen food for earnest thought. Writing from London, to the Chicago Inter Ocean, Nov. 25, 1894, the distinguished compiler of our last census, Hon. Robert P. Porter, gives the American people a most interesting review of the anti-lynching crusade in England, submitting editorial opinions from all sections of England and Scotland, showing the consensus of British opinion on this subject. It hardly need be said, that without exception, the current of English thought deprecates the rule of mob law, and the conscience of England is shocked by the revelation made during the present crusade. In his letter Mr. Porter says:

"While some English Journals have joined certain American journals in ridiculing the well-meaning people who have formed the anti-lynching committee, there is a deep under current on this subject which is injuring the Southern States far more than those who have not been drawn into the question of English investment for the South as I have can surmise. This feeling is by no means all sentiment. An Englishman whose word and active cooperation could send a minion sterling to any legitimate Southern enterprise said the other day "I will not invest a farthing in States where these horrors occur. I have no particular sympathy with the anti-lynching committee, but such outrages indicate to my mind that where life is held to be of such little value there is even less assurance that

the laws will protect property. As I understand it the States, not the national government, control in such matters, and where those laws are strongest there is the best field for British capital."

Probably the most bitter attack on the anti-lynching committee has come from the London Times. Those Southern Governors; who had their bombastic letters published in the Times, with favorable editorial comment, may have had their laugh at the anti-lynchers here too soon. A few days ago, in commenting on an interesting communication from Richard H. Edmonds, editor of the Manufacturer's Record, setting forth the industrial advantages of the Southern States, which was published in its columns, the Times says:

> "Without in any way countenancing the impertinence of 'anti-lynching' committee, we may say that a state of things in which the killing of Negroes by bloodthirsty mobs is an incident of not infrequent occurrence is not conducive to success in industry. Its existence, however, is a serious obstacle to the success of the South in industry; for even now Negro labor, which means at best inefficient labor, must be largely relied on there, and its efficiency must be still further diminished by spasmodic terrorism.
>
> "Those interested in the development of the resources of the Southern States, and no one in proportion to his means has shown more faith in the progress of the South than the writer of this article, must take hold of this matter earnestly and intelligently. Sneering at the anti-lynching committee will do no good. Back of them, in fact, it not in form, is the public opinion of Great Britain. Even the Times cannot deny this. It may not be generally known in the United States, but while the Southern and some of the Northern newspapers are making a target of Miss Wells, the young colored woman who started this English movement, and cracking their jokes at the expense of Miss Florence Balbarnie, who, as honorable secretary, conducts the committee's correspondence, the strongest sort of sentiment is really at the back of the movement. Here we have crystallized every phase of political opinion. Extreme Unionists like the Duke of Argyll and advanced home rulers such as Justill McCartlly; Thomas Burt, the labor leader;

Herbert Burrows, the Socialist, and Tom Mann, representing all phases of the Labor party, are co-operating with conservatives like Sir T. Eldon Gorst. But the real strength of this committee is not visible to the casual observer. As a matter of fact it represents many of the leading and most powerful British journals. A. E. Fletcher is editor of the London Daily Chronicle; P. W. Clayden is prominent in the counsels of the London Daily News; Professor James Start is Gladstone's great friend and editor of the London Star; William Byles is editor and proprietor of the Bradford Observer; Sir Hugh Gilzen Reid is a leading Birmingham editor; in short, this committee has secured if not the leading editors, certainly important and warm friends. representing the Manchester Guardian, the Leeds Mercury, the Plymouth Western News, Newcastle Leader, the London Daily Graphic, the Westminster Gazette, the London Echo, a host of minor papers all over the kingdom, and practically the entire religious press of the kingdom.

"The greatest victory for the anti-lynchers comes this morning in the publication in the London Times of William Lloyd Garrison's letter. This letter will have immense effect here. It may have been printed in full in the United States, but nevertheless I will quote a paragraph which will strengthen the anti-lynchers greatly in their crusade here:

"'A year ago the South derided and resented Northern protests; to day it listens, explains and apologizes for its uncovered cruel ties. Surely a great triumph for a little woman to accomplish! It is the power of truth simply and unreservedly spoken, for her language was inadequate to describe the horrors exposed.'

"If the Southern states are wise, and I say this with the earnestness of a friend and one who has built a home in the mountain regions of the South and thrown his lot in with them, they will not only listen, but stop lawlessness of all kinds. If they do, and thus secure the confidence of Englishmen, we may in the next decade realize some of the hopes for the new South we have so fondly cherished."

CHAPTER VIII.

MISS WILLARD'S ATTITUDE.

No class of American citizens stands in greater need of the humane and thoughtful consideration of all sections of our country than do the colored people, nor does any class exceed us in the measure of grateful regard for acts of kindly interest in our behalf. It is, therefore, to us, a matter of keen regret that a Christian organization so large and influential as the Woman's Christian Temperance Union, should refuse to give its sympathy and support to our oppressed people who ask no further favor than the promotion of public sentiment which shall guarantee to every person accused of crime the safeguard of a fair and impartial trial, and protection from butchery by brutal mobs. Accustomed as we are to the indifference and apathy of Christian people, we would bear this instance of in fortune in silence, had not Miss Willard gone out of her way to antagonize the cause so near to our hearts by including in her Annual Address to the W.C.T.U. Convention at Cleveland, November 5, 1894, a studied, unjust and wholly unwarranted attack upon our work.

In her address Miss Willard said:

> The zeal for her race of Miss Ida B. Wells, a bright young colored woman, has, it seems to me, clouded her perception as to who were her friends and well-wishers in all high-minded and legitimate efforts to banish the abomination of lynching and torture from the land of the free and the home of the brave. It is my firm belief that in the statements made by Miss Wells concerning white women having taken the initiative in nameless acts between the races she has put an imputation upon half the white race in this country that is unjust, and, save in the rarest exceptional instances, wholly without foundation. This is the unanimous opinion of the most disinterested and observant leaders of opinion whom I have consulted on the subject, and I do not fear to say that the laudable efforts she is making are greatly handicapped by statements of this kind, nor to urge her as a friend and well-wisher to banish from her vocabulary all such allusions as a source of weakness to the cause she has at heart.

This paragraph, brief as it is, contains two statements which have not the slightest foundation in fact. At no time, nor in any place, have I made statements "concerning white women having taken the initiative in nameless acts between the races." Further, at no time, or place nor under any circumstance, have I directly or inferentially "put an imputation upon half the white race in this country" and I challenge this "friend and well-wisher" to give proof of the truth of her charge. Miss Willard protests against lynching In one paragraph and then, in the next, deliberately misrepresents my position in order that she may criticize a movements, whose only purpose is to protect our oppressed race from vindictive slander and Lynch Law.

What I have said and what I now repeat—in answer to her first charge—is, that colored men have been lynched for assault upon women, when the facts were plain that the relationship between the victim lynched and the alleged victim of his assault was voluntary, clandestine and illicit. For that very reason we maintain, that, in every section of our land, the accused should have a fair, impartial trial, so that a man who is colored shall not be hanged for an offense, which, if he were white, would not be adjudged a crime. Facts cited in another chapter—"History of Some Cases of Rape" amply maintain this position. The publication of these facts in defense of the good name of the race casts no "imputation upon half the white race in this country" and no such imputation can be inferred except by persons deliberately determined to be unjust.

But this is not the only injury which this cause has suffered at the hands of our "friend and well-wisher." It has been said that the Women's Christian Temperance Union, the most powerful organization of women in America, was misrepresented by me while I was in England. Miss Willard was in England at the time and knowing that no such misrepresentation came to her notice, she has permitted that impression to become fixed and widespread, when a word from her would have made the facts plain.

I never at any time or place or in any way misrepresented that organization. When asked what concerted action had been taken by churches and great moral agencies in America to put down Lynch Law, I was compelled in truth to say that no such action had occurred, that pulpit, press and moral agencies in the main were silent and for reasons known to themselves, ignored the awful conditions which to the English people appeared so abhorrent. Then the question was asked what the great moral reformers like Miss Frances Willard and Mr. Moody had done to suppress Lynch Law and again I answered—nothing. That Mr. Moody had never said a word against lynch-

ing in any of his trips to the South, or in the North either, so far as was known, and that Miss Willard's only public utterance on the situation had condoned lynching and other unjust practices of the South against the Negro. When proof of these statements was demanded, I sent a letter containing a copy of the New York Voice, Oct. 23, 1890, in which appeared Miss Willard's own words of wholesale slander against the colored race and condemnation of Southern white people's outrages against us. My letter in part reads as follows:

> But Miss Willard, the great temperance leader, went even further in putting the seal of her approval upon the southerners method of dealing with the Negro. In October, 1890, the Women's Christian Temperance Union held its national meeting at Atlanta, Georgia. It was the first time in the history of the organization that it had gone south for a national meeting, and met the Southerners in their own homes. They were welcomed with open arms. The governor of the state and the legislature gave special audiences in the halls of state legislation to the temperance workers. They set out to capture the northerners to their way of seeing things, and without troubling to hear the Negro side of the question, these temperance people accepted the white man's story of the problem with which he had to deal. State organizers were appointed that year, who had gone through the southern states since then, but in obedience to southern prejudices have confined their work to white persons only. It is only after Negroes are in prison for crimes that efforts of these temperance women are exerted without regard to "race, color, or previous condition." No "ounce of prevention" is used in their case; they are black, and it these women went among the Negroes for this work, the whites would not receive them. Except here and there, are found no temperance workers of the Negro race; "the great darkfaced mobs" are left the easy prey of the saloonkeepers.

There was pending in the National Congress at this time a Federal Election Bill, the object being to give the National Government control of the national elections in the several states. Had this bill become a law, the Negro, whose vote has been systematically suppressed since 1875 in the

southern states would have had the protection of the National Government, and his vote counted. The South would have been no longer "solid;" the Southerners saw that the balance of power which they unlawfully held in the House of Representatives and the Electoral College, based on the Negro population, would be wrested from them. So they nicknamed the pending elections law the "Force Bill" probably because it would force them to disgorge their in-gotten political gains—and defeated it. While it was being discussed, the question was submitted to Miss Willard: "What do you think of the race problem and the Force Bill?"

Said Miss Willard:

"Now, as to the 'race problem' in its minified, current meaning, I am a true lover of the southern people—have spoken and worked in, perhaps, 200 of their towns and cities; have been taken into their love and confidence at scores of hospitable firesides; have heard them pout out their hearts in the splendid frankness of their impetuous natures. And I have said to them at such times: 'When I go North there will be wafted to you no word from pen or voice that is not loyal to what we are saying here and now.' Going South, a woman, a temperance woman, and a Northern temperance woman--three great barriers to their good will yonder I was received by them with a confidence that was one of the most delightful surprises of my life. I think we have wronged the South, though we did not mean to do so. The reason was, in part, that we had irreparably wronged ourselves by putting no safeguards on the ballot box at the North that would sift out alien illiterates. They rule our cities today; the saloon is their palace, and the toddy stick their sceptre. It is not fair that they should vote, nor is it fair that a plantation Negro, who can neither read nor write, whose ideas are bounded by the fence of his own field and the price of his own mule, should be entrusted with the ballot. We ought to have put an educational test upon that ballot from the first. The Anglo-Saxon race will never submit to be dominated by the Negro so long as his altitude reaches no higher than the personal liberty of the saloon, and the power of appreciating the amount of liquor that a dollar will buy. New England would no more submit to this than South Carolina. 'Better

whisky and more of it' has been the rallying cry of great dark-faced mobs in the Southern localities where local option was snowed under by the colored vote. Temperance has no enemy like that, for it is unreasoning and unreasonable. Tonight it promises in a great congregation to vote for temperance at the Polls tomorrow; but tomorrow twenty-five cents changes that vote in favor of the liquor-seller.

"I pity the Southerners, and I believe the great mass of them are as conscientious and kindly-intentioned toward the colored man as an equal number of white church-members of the North. Would-be demagogues lead the colored people to destruction. Half-drunken white roughs murder them at the polls, or intimidate them so that they do not vote. But the better class of people must not be blamed for this, and a more thoroughly American population than the Christian people of the South does not exist. They have the traditions, the kindness, the probity, the courage of our forefathers. The problem on their hands is immeasurable. The colored race multiplies like the locusts of Egypt. The grog-shop is its center of power. 'The safety of woman, of childhood, of the home, is menaced in a thousand localities at this moment, so that the men dare not go beyond the sight of their own roof-tree.' How little we know of all this, seated in comfort and affluence here at the North, descanting upon the rights of every man to cast one vote and have it fairly counted; that well-worn shibboleth invoked once more to dodge a living issue.

"The fact is that illiterate colored men will not vote at the South until the white population chooses to have them do so; and under similar conditions they would not at the North."

Here we have Miss Willard's words in full, condoning fraud, violence, murder, at the ballot box; rapine, shooting, hanging and burning; for all these things are done and being done now by the Southern white people. She does not stop there, but goes a step further to aid them in blackening the good name of an the race, as shown by the sentences quoted in the paragraph above. These utterances, for which the colored people have never forgiven Miss Willard, and which Frederick Douglass has denounced as false, are to be found in full in the Voice of October 23, 1890, a temperance organ pub-

lished at New York city. This letter appeared in the May number of
Fraternity, the organ of the first Anti-Lynching society of Great Britain.
When Lady Henry Somerset learned through Miss Florence Balgarnie that
this letter had been published she informed me that if the interview was pub-
lished she would take steps to let the public know that my statements must
be received with caution. As I had no money to pay the printer to suppress
the edition which was already published and these ladies did not care to do
so, the May number of Fraternity was sent to its subscribers as usual. Three
days later there appeared in the daily Westminster Gazette an "interview"
with Miss Willard, written by Lady Henry Somerset, which was so subtly
unjust In its wording that I was forced to reply in my own defense. In that
reply I made only statements which, like those concerning Miss Willard's
Voice interview, have not been and cannot be denied. It was as follows:

LADY HENRY SOMERSET'S INTERVIEW
WITH MISS WILLARD.

To the Editor of the Westminster Gazette: Sir—The interview
published in your columns today hardly merits a reply, because
of the indifference to suffering manifested. Two ladies are rep-
resented sitting under a tree at Reigate, and, after some pre-
liminary remarks on the terrible subject of lynching, Miss
Willard laughingly replies by cracking a joke. And the conclud-
ing sentence of the interview shows the object is not to deter-
mine how best they may help the Negro who is being hanged,
shot and burned, but "to guard Miss Willard's reputation."

With me it is not myself nor my reputation, but the life
of my people, which is at stake, and I affirm that this is the first
time to my knowledge that Miss Willard has said a single word
in denunciation of lynching or demand for law. The year 1890,
the one in which the interview appears, had a larger lynching
record than any previous year, and the number and territory
have increased, to say nothing of the human beings burnt alive.

If so earnest as she would have the English public
believe her to be, why was she silent when five minutes were
give me to speak last June at Princes' Hall and in Holborn
Town Hall this May? I should say it was as President of the
Women's Christian Temperance Union of America she is

timid, because all these unions in the South emphasize the hatred of the Negro by excluding him. There is not a single colored woman admitted to the Southern W.C.T.U., but still Miss Willard blames the Negro for the defeat of Prohibition in the South. Miss Willard quotes from Fraternity, but forgets to add my immediate recognition of her presence on the platform at Holborn Town Hall, when, amidst many other resolutions on temperance and other subjects in which she is interested, time was granted to carry an anti-lynching resolution. I was so thankful for this crumb of her speechless presence that I hurried off to the editor of Fraternity and added a postscript to my article blazoning forth that fact.

Any statements I have made concerning, Miss Willard are confirmed by the Hon. Frederick Douglass (late United States minister to Haytii in a speech delivered by him in Washington in January of this year, which has since been published In a pamphlet. The fact is, Miss Willard is no better or worse than the great bulk of white Americans on the Negro questions. They are all afraid to speak out, and it is only British public opinion which will move them, as I am thankful to see it has already begun to move Miss Willard. I am, etc.,

May 21. IDA B. WELLS.

Unable to deny the truth of these assertions, the charge has been made that I have attacked Miss Willard and misrepresented the W.C.T.U. If to state facts is misrepresentation, then I plead guilty to the charge.

I said then and repeat now, that in all the ten terrible years of shooting, hanging and burning of men, women and children in America, the Women's Christian Temperance Union never suggested one plan or made one move to prevent those awful crimes. If this statement is untrue the records of that organization would disprove it before the ink is dry. It is clearly an issue of fact and in all fairness this charge of misrepresentation should either be substantiated or withdrawn.

It is not necessary, however, to make any representation concerning the W.C.T.U. and the lynching question. The record of that organization speaks for itself. During all the years prior to the agitation begun against Lynch Law, in which years men, women and children were scourged, hanged, shot and burned, the W.C.T.U had no word, either of pity or protest; its great heart,

which concerns itself about humanity the world over, was, toward our cause, pulseless as a stone. Let those who deny this speak by the record. Not until after the first British campaign, in 1893, was even a resolution passed by the body which is the self constituted guardian for "God, home and native land."

Nor need we go back to other years. The annual session of that organization held in Cleveland in November, 1894, made a record which confirms and emphasizes the silence charged against it. At that session, earnest efforts were made to secure the adoption of a resolution of protest against lynching. At that very time two men were being tried for the murder of six colored men who were arrested on charge of barn burning, chained together, and on pretense of being taken to jail, were driven into the woods where they were ambushed and all six shot to death. The six widows of the butchered men had just finished the most pathetic recital ever heard in any court room, and the mute appeal of twenty-seven orphans for justice touched the stoutest hearts. Only two weeks prior to the session, Gov. Jones of Alabama, in his last message to the retiring state legislature, cited the fact that in the two years just past, nine colored men had been taken from the legal authorities by lynching mobs and butchered in cold blood-and not one of these victims was even charged with an assault upon womanhood.

It was thought that this great organization, in face of these facts, would not hesitate to place itself on record in a resolution of protest against this awful brutality towards colored people. Miss Willard gave assurance that such a resolution would be adopted, and that assurance was relied on. The record of the session shows in what good faith that assurance was kept. After recommending an expression against Lynch Law, the President attacked the anti-lynching movement, deliberately misrepresenting my position, and in her annual address, charging me with a statement I never made.

Further than that, when the committee on resolutions reported their work, not a word was said against lynching. In the interest of the cause I smothered the resentment. I felt because of the unwarranted and unjust attack of the President, and labored with members to secure an expression of some kind, tending to abate the awful slaughter of my race. A resolution against lynching was introduced by Mrs. Fessenden and read, and then that great Christian body, which in Its resolutions had expressed itself in opposition to the social amusement of card playing, athletic sports and promiscuous dancing; had protested against the licensing of saloons, inveighed against tobacco, pledged its allegiance to the Prohibition party, and thanked the Populist party in Kansas, the Republican party in California and the

Democratic party in the South, wholly ignored the seven minions of colored people of this country whose plea was for a word of sympathy and support for the movement in their behalf. The resolution was not adopted, and the convention adjourned.

In the Union Signal Dec. 6, 1894, among the resolutions is found this one:

> Resolved, That the National W. C. T. U., which has for years counted among its departments that of peace and arbitration, is utterly opposed to all lawless acts in any and all parts of our common lands and it urges these principles upon the public, praying that the time may speedily come when no human being shall be condemned without due process of law; and when the unspeakable outrages which have so often provoked such lawlessness shall be banished from the world, and childhood, maidenhood and womanhood shall no more be the victims of atrocities worse than death.

This is not the resolution offered by Mrs. Fessenden. She offered the one passed last year by the W.C.T.U. which was a strong unequivocal denunciation of lynching. But she was told by the chairman of the committee on resolutions, Mrs. Rounds, that there was already a lynching resolution in the hands of the committee. Mrs. Fessenden yielded the floor on that assurance, and no resolution of any kind against lynching was submitted and none was voted upon, not even the one above, taken from the columns of the Union Signal, the organ of the national W.C.T.U.!

Even the wording of this resolution which was printed by the W.C.T.U., reiterates the false and unjust charge which has been so often made as an excuse for lynchers. Statistics show that less than one-third of the lynching victims are hanged, shot and burned alive for "unspeakable outrages against womanhood, maidenhood and childhood;" and that nearly a thousand, including women and children, have been lynched upon any pretext whatsoever; and that all have met death upon the unsupported word of white men and women. Despite these facts this resolution which was printed, cloaks an apology for lawlessness, in the same paragraph which affects to condemn it, where it speaks of "the unspeakable outrages which have so often provoked such lawlessness."

Miss Willard told me the day before the resolutions were offered that the Southern women present had held a caucus that day. This was after I, as fra-

ternal delegate from the Woman's Mite Missionary Society of the A.M.E. Church at Cleveland, O., had been Introduced to tender its greetings. In so doing I expressed the hope of the colored women that the W. C. T. U. would place itself on record as opposed to lynching which robbed them of husbands, fathers, brothers and sons and in many cases of women as well. No note was made either in the daily papers or the Union Signal of that introduction and greeting, although every other Incident of that morning was published. The failure to submit a lynching resolution and the wording of the one above appears to have been the result of that Southern caucus.

On the same day I had a private talk with Miss Willard and told her she had been unjust to me and the cause in her annual address, and asked that she correct the statement that I had misrepresented the W.C.T.U., or that I had "put an imputation on one-half the white race in this country." She said that somebody in England told her it was a pity that I attacked the white women of America. "Oh," said I, "then you went out of your way to prejudice me and my cause in youth annual address, not upon what you had heard me say, but what somebody had told you I said?" Her reply was that I must not blame her for her rhetorical expressions—that I had my way of expressing things and she had hers. I told her I most assuredly did blame her when those expressions were calculated to do such harm. I waited for an honest an unequivocal retraction of her statements based on "hearsay." Not a word of retraction or explanation was said in the convention and I remained misrepresented before that body through her connivance and consent.

The editorial notes in the Union Signal, Dec. 6, 1894, however, contains the following:

> "In her repudiation of the charges brought by Miss Ida Wells against white women as having taken the initiative In nameless crimes between the races, Miss Willard said in her annual address that this statement 'put an unjust imputation upon half the white race.' But as this expression has been misunderstood she desires to declare that she did not intend a literal interpretation to be given to the language used, but employed it to express a tendency that might ensue in public thought as a rebuilt of utterances so sweeping as some that have been made by Miss Wells."

Because this explanation is as unjust as the original offense, I am forced

in self-defense to submit this account of differences. I desire no quarrel with the W.C.T.U., but my love for the truth is greater than my regard for an alleged friend who, through ignorance or design misrepresents in the most harmful way the cause of a long suffering race, and then unable to maintain the truth of her attack excuses herself as it were by the wave of the hand, declaring that "she did not intend a literal interpretation to be given to the language used." When the lives of men, women and children are at stake, when the inhuman butchers of innocents attempt to justify their barbarism by fastening upon a whole race the oblique of the most infamous of crimes, It is little less than criminal to apologize for the butchers today and tomorrow to repudiate the apology by declaring it a figure of speech.

CHAPTER IX.

LYNCHING RECORD FOR 1894.

The following tables are based on statistics taken from the columns of the Chicago Tribune, Jan. 1, 1895. They are a valuable appendix to the foregoing pages. They show, among other things that in Louisiana, April 23-28, eight Negroes were lynched because one white man was killed by the Negro, the latter acting in self defense. Only seven of them are given in the list.

Near Memphis, Tenn., six Negroes were lynched—this time charged with burning barns. A trial of the indicted resulted in an acquittal, although it was shown on trial that the lynching was prearranged for them. Six widows and twenty-seven orphans are indebted to this mob for their condition, and this lynching swells the number to eleven Negroes lynched in and about Memphis since March 9, 1892.

In Brooks county, Ga., Dec. 23rd, while this Christian country was preparing for Christmas celebration, seven Negroes were lynched in twenty-four hours because they refused, or were unable to tell the whereabouts of a colored man named Pike, who killed a white man. The wives and daughters of these lynched men were horribly and brutally outraged by the murderers of their husbands and fathers. But the mob has not been punished and again women and children are robbed of their protectors whose blood cries unavenged to Heaven and humanity. Georgia heads the list of lynching states.

MURDER.

Jan. 9, Samuel Smith, Greenville, Ala.; Jan. 11, Sherman Wagoner, Mitchell, Ind.; Jan. 12, Roscoe Parker, West Union, Ohio; Feb. 7, Henry Bruce, Gulch Co., Ark.; March 5, Sylvester Rhodes, Collins, Ga.; March 15, Richard Puryea, Stroudsburg, Pa.; March 29, Oliver Jackson, Montgomery, Ala.; March 30, - Saybrick, Fisher's Ferry, Miss.; April 14, William Lewis, Lanison, Ala.; April 23, Jefferson Luggle, Cherokee, Kan.; April 23, Samuel Slaugate, Tallulah, La.; April 23, Thomas Claxton, Tallulah, La.; April 23, David Hawkins, Tallulah, La.; April 27, Thel Claxton, Tallulah, La.; April 27, Comp Claxton, Tallulah, La.; April 27, Scot Harvey, Tallulah, La.; April 27, Jerry McCly, Tallulah, La.; May 17, Henry Scott, Jefferson, Tex.; May 15, Coat Williams, Pine Grove, Fla.; June 2, Jefferson Crawford, Betliesda, S. C.; June 4, Thondo Underwood, Monroe, La.; June 8. Isaac Kemp, Cape Charles, Va.; June 13, Lon Hall, Sweethouse, Tex.; June 13, Bascom Cook, Sweethouse, Tex.; June 15, Luke Thomas, Biloxi, Miss.; June 29, John Williams, Sulphur, Tex.; June 29, Ulysses Hayden, Monett, Mo.; July 6, Hood, Amite, Miss.; July 7, James Bell, Charlotte, Tenn.; Sept. 2, Henderson Hollander, Elkhorn, W. Va.; Sept. 14, Robert Williams, Concordia Parish, La.; Sept. 22, Luke Washington, Meghee, Ark.; Sept. 22, Richard Washington, Meghee, Ark.; Sept. 22, Henry Crobyson, Meghee, Ark.; Nov. 10, Lawrence Younger, Lloyd, Va.; Dec. 17, unknown Negro, Williamston, S. C.; Dec. 23, Samuel Taylor, Brooks County, Ga.; Dec. 23, Charles Frazier, Brooks County, Ga.; Dec. 23, Samuel Oike, Brooks County, Ga.; Dec. 23, Harry Shcrard, Brooks County, Ga.; Dec. 23, unknown Negro, Brooks County, Ga.; Dec. 23, unknown Negro, Brooks County, Ga.; Dec. 23, unknown Negro, Brooks County, Ga.; Dec. 26, Daniel McDonald, Winston County, Miss.; Dec. 26, William Carter, Winston County, Miss.

RAPE.

Jan. 17, John Buckner, Valley Park, Mo.; Jan. 21, M. G. Cambell, Jellico Mines, Ky.; Jan. 27, unknown, Verona, Mo.; Feb. 11 Henry McCreeg, near Pioneer, Tenn.; April 6, Daniel Ahren, Greensboro, Ga.; April 15, Seymour Newland, Rushsylvania, Ohio; April 26, Robert Evarts, Jamaica, Ga.; April 27, James Robinson, Manassas, Va.; April 27, Benjamin White, Manassas, Va.; May 15, Nim Young, Ocala, Fla.; May 22, unknown, Miner County, Ga.; June 13, unknown, Blackshear, Ga.; June 18, Owen Opliltree, Forsyth, Ga.; June 22, Henry Capus, Magnolia, Ark.; June 26, Caleb Godly, Bowling Green, Ky.; June 28, Fayette Franklin, Mitchell, Ga.; July 2, Joseph Johnson,

Hiner's Creek, Mo.; July 6, Lewis Bankhead, Cooper, Ala.; July 16, Marion Howard, Scottsville, Ky.; July 20, William Griffith, Woodville, Tex.; Aug. 12, William Nershbread, Rossville, Tenn.; Aug. 14, Marshall Boston, Frankfort, Ky.; Sept. 19, David Gooseby, Atlanta, Ga.; Oct. 15, Willis Griffey, Princeton, Ky.; Nov. 8, Lee Lawrence, Jasper County, Ga.; Nov. 10, Needham Smith, Tipton County, Tenn.; Nov. 14, Robert Mosely, Dolinite, Ala.; Dec. 4, William Jackson, Ocala, Fla.; Dec. 18, unknown, Marion County, Fla.

UNKNOWN OFFENSES.

March 6, Lamsen Gregory. Bell's Depot, Tenn.; March 6, unknown woman, near Marche, Ark.; April 14, Alfred Brenn, Calhoun, Ga.; June 8, Harry Gin, West Lancaster, S. C.; Nov. 23, unknown, Landrum, S. C.; Dec. 5, Mrs. Teddy Arthur, Lincoln County, W. Va.

DESPERADO.

Jan. 14, Charles Willis, Ocala, Fla.

SUSPECTED INCENDIARISM.

Jan. 18, unknown, Bayou Sarah, La.

SUSPECTED ARSON.

June 14, J. H. Dave, Monroe, La.

ENTICING SERVANT AWAY.

Feb. 10, Collins, Athens, Ga.

TRAIN WRECKING.

Feb. 10, Jesse Diningham, Smokeyville, Tex.

HIGHWAY ROBBERY.

June 3, unknown, Dublin, Ga.

INCENDIARISM.

Nov. 8, Gabe Nalls, Blackford, Ky.; Nov. 8, Ulysses Nalls, Blackford, Ky.

ARSON

Dec. 20, James Allen, Brownsville, Tex.

ASSAULT.
Dec. 23, George King, New Orleans, La.

NO OFFENSE.
Dec. 28, Scott Sherman, Morehouse Parish

BURGLARY.
May 29, Henry Smith, Clinton, Miss.; May 29, William James, Clinton, Miss.

ALLEGED RAPE.
June 4, Ready Murdock, Yazoo, Miss.

ATTEMPTED RAPE.
July 14, unknown Negro, Biloxi, Miss.; July 26, Vance McClure, New Iberia, La.; July 26, William Tyler, Carlisle, Ky.; Sept. 14, James Smith, Stark, Fla.; Oct. 8, Henry Gibson, Fairfield, Tex.; Oct. 20, Williams, Upper Marlboro, Md.; June 9, Lewis Williams, Hewett Springs, Miss.; June 28, George Linton, Brookhaven, Miss.; June 28, Edward White, Hudson, Ala.; July 6, George Pond, Fulton, Miss.; July 7, Augustus Pond, Tupelo, Miss.

RACE PREJUDICE.
June 10, Mark Jacobs, Bienville, La.; July 24, unknown woman, Sampson County, Miss.

INTRODUCING SMALLPOX.
June 10, James Perry, Knoxville, Ark.

KIDNAPPING.
March 2, Lentige, Harland County, Ky.

CONSPIRACY.
May 29, J. T. Burgis, Palatka, Fla.

HORSE STEALING.
June 20, Archie Haynes, Mason County, Ky.; June 20, Burt Haynes, Mason County, Ky.; June 20, William Haynes, Mason County, Ky.

WRITING LETTER TO WHITE WOMAN.
May 9, unknown Negro, West Texas.

GIVING INFORMATION.
July 12, James Nelson, Abbeyville, S. C.

STEALING.
Jan. 5, Alfred Davis, Live Oak County, Ark.

LARCENY.
April 18, Henry Montgomery, Lewisburg, Tenn.

POLITICAL CAUSES.
July 19, John Brownlee, Oxford, Ala.

CONJURING.
July 20, Allen Myers, Rankill County, Miss.

ATTEMPTED MURDER.
June 1, Frank Ballard, Jackson, Tenn.

ALLEGED MURDER.
April 5, Negro, near Selma, Ala.; April 5, Negro, near Selma, Ala.

WITHOUT CAUSE.
May 17, Samuel Wood, Gates City, Va.

BARN BURNING.
April 22, Thomas Black, Tuscumbia, Ala.; April 22, John Williams, Tuscumbia, Ala.; April 22, Toney Johnson, Tuscumbia, Ala.; July 14, William Bell, Dixon, Tenn.; Sept. 1, Daniel Hawkins, Millington, Tenn.; Sept. 1, Robert Haynes, Millington, Tenn.; Sept. 1, Warner Williams, Millington, Tenn.; Sept. 1, Edward Hall, Millington, Tenn.; Sept. 1, John Haynes, Millington, Tenn.; Sept. 1, Graham White, Millington, Tenn.

ASKING WHITE WOMAN TO MARRY HIM.
May 23, William Brooks, Galesline, Ark.

OFFENSES CHARGED FOR LYNCHING.

Suspected arson, 2; stealing, 1; political causes, 1; murder, 45; rape, 29; desperado, 1; suspected incendiarism, 1; train wrecking, l; enticing servant away, 1; kidnapping, 1; unknown offense, 6; larceny, 1; barn burning, 10; writing letters to a white woman, l; without cause, 1; burglary, 1; asking white woman to marry, 1; conspiracy, l; attempted murder, 1; horse stealing, 3; highway robbery, 1; alleged rape, 1; attempted rape, 11; race prejudice, 2; introducing smallpox, 1; giving information, 1; conjuring, 1; incendiarism, 2; arson, 1; assault, 1; no offense, 1; alleged murder, 2; total (colored), 134.

LYNCHING STATES.

Mississippi, 15; Arkansas, 8; Virginia; 5; Tennessee, 15; Alabama, 12; Kentucky, 12; Texas, 9; Georgia, 19; South Carolina, 5; Florida, 7; Louisiana, 15; Missouri, 4; Ohio, 2; Maryland, l; West Virginia, 2; Indiana, l; Kansas, 1; Pennsylvania, 1.

LYNCHING BY THE MONTH.

January, 11; February, 17; March, 8; April, 36; May, 16; June, 31; July, 21; August, 4; September, 17; October, 7; November, 9; December, 20; total colored and white, 197.

WOMEN LYNCHED.

July 24, unknown woman, race prejudice, Sampson County, Miss.; March 6, unknown, woman, unknown offense, Marche, Ark.; Dec. 5, Mrs. Teddy Arthur, unknown cause, Lincoln County, W. Va.

CHAPTER X.

THE REMEDY.

It is a well established principle of law that every wrong has a remedy. Herein rests our respect for law. The Negro does not claim that all of the one thousand black men, women and children, who have been hanged, shot and burned alive during the past ten years, were innocent of the charges made against them. We have associated too long with the white man not to have copied his vices as well as his virtues. But we do insist that the punishment is not the same for both classes of criminals. In lynching, opportunity

to not given the Negro to defend himself against the unsupported accusations of white men and women. The word of the accuser is held to be true and the excited bloodthirsty mob demands that the rule of law be reversed and instead of proving the accused to be guilty, the victim of their hate and revenge must prove himself innocent. No evidence he can offer will satisfy the mob; he is bound hand and foot and swung into eternity. Then to excuse its infamy, the mob almost invariably reports the monstrous falsehood that its victim made a full confession before he was hanged.

With all military, legal and political power in their hands, only two of the lynching States have attempted a check by exercising the power which is theirs. Mayor Trout, of Roanoke, Virginia, called out the militia in 1893, to protect a Negro prisoner, and in so doing nine men were killed and a number wounded. Then the mayor and militia withdrew, left the Negro to his fate and he was promptly lynched. The business men realized the blow to the town's were given light sentences, the highest being one of twelve financial interests, called the mayor home, the grand jury indicted and prosecuted the ringleaders of the mob. They months in State prison. The day he arrived at the penitentiary, he was pardoned by the governor of the State.

The only other real attempt made by the authorities to protect a prisoner of the law, and which was more successful, was that of Gov. McKinley, of Ohio, who sent the militia to Washington Courthouse, O., in October, 1894, and live men were killed and twenty wounded in maintaining the principle that the law must be upheld.

In South Carolina, in April, 1893, Gov. Tinman aided the mob by yielding up to be killed, a prisoner of the law, who had voluntarily placed himself under the Governor's protection. Public sentiment by its representatives has encouraged Lynch Law, and upon the revolution of this sentiment we must depend for its abolition.

Therefore, we demand a fair trial by law for those accused of crime, and punishment by law after honest conviction. No maudlin sympathy for criminals is solicited, but we do ask that the law shall punish all alike. We earnestly desire those that control the forces which make public sentiment to join with us in the demand. Surely the humanitarian spirit of this country which reaches out to denounce the treatment of the Russian Jews, the Armenian Christians, the laboring poor of Europe, the Siberian exiles and the native women of India will not longer refuse to lift its voice on this subject. If it were known that the cannibals or the savage Indiana had burned three human beings alive in the past two years, the whole, of Christendom would

be roused, to devise ways and means to put a stop to it can you remain silent and inactive when such things are done in our own community and country? Is your duty to humanity in the United States less binding?

What can you do, reader, to prevent lynching, to thwart anarchy and promote law and order throughout our land?

1st. You can help disseminate the facts contained in this book by bringing them to the knowledge of every one with whom you come in contact, to the end that public sentiment may be revolutionized. Let the facts speak for themselves, with you as a medium.

2d. You can be instrumental in having churches, missionary societies, Y.M.C.A.'s, W.C.T.U.'s and all Christian and moral forces In connection with your religious and social life, pass resolutions of condemnation and protest every time a lynching takes place; and see that they are sent to the place where these outrages occur.

3d. Bring to the intelligent consideration of Southern people the refusal of capital to invest where lawlessness and mob violence hold sway. Many labor organizations have declared by resolution that they would avoid lynch infested localities as they would the pestilence when seeking new homes. If the South wishes to build up its waste places quickly, there is no better way than to uphold the majesty of the law by enforcing obedience to the same, and meting out the same punishment to all classes of criminals, white as well as black. "Equality before the law," must become a fact as well as a theory before America is truly the "land of the free and the home of the brave."

4th. Think and act on independent lines in this behalf, remembering that after all, it is the white man's civilization and the white man's government which are on trial. This crusade will determine whether that civilization can maintain itself by itself, or whether anarchy shall prevail; whether this Nation shall write itself down a success at self government, or in deepest humiliation admit its failure complete, whether the precepts and theories of Christianity are professed and practiced by American white people as Golden Rules of thought and action, or adopted as a system of morals to be preached to heathen until they attain to the intelligence which needs the system of Lynch Law.

5th. Congressman Blair offered a resolution In the House of Representatives, August, 1894. The organized life of the country can speedily make this a law by sending resolutions to Congress endorsing Mr. Blair's bill and asking Congress to create the commission. In no better way can the question be settled, and the Negro does not fear the issue. The following is the resolution:

"Resolved, By the House of Representatives and Senate In congress assembled, That the committee on labor be instructed to investigate and report the number, location and date of all alleged assaults by males upon females throughout the country during the ten years last preceding the passing of this Joint resolution, for or on account of which organized but unlawful violence has been inflicted or attempted to be inflicted. Also to ascertain and report all facts of organized but unlawful violence to the person, with the attendant facts and circumstances, which have been inflicted upon accused persons alleged to have been guilty of crimes punishable by due process of law which have taken place in any part of the country within the ten years last preceding the passage of this resolution. Such Investigation shall be made by the usual methods and agencies of the Department of Labor, and report made to Congress as soon as the work can be satisfactorily done, and the sum of $25,000, or so much thereof as may be necessary, is hereby appropriated to pay the expenses out of any money in the treasury not otherwise appropriated."

The belief has been constantly expressed in England that in the United States, which has produced Wm. Lloyd Garrison, Henry Ward Beecher, James Russell Lowell, John G. Whittier and Abraham Lincoln there must be those of their descendants who would take hold of the work of inaugurating an era of law and order. The colored people of this country who have been loyal to the flag believe the same, and strong in that belief have begun this crusade. To those who still feel they have no obligation in the matter, we commend the following lines of Lowell on "Freedom."

> Men! whose boast it is that ye
> Come of fathers brave and free,
> If there breathe on earth a slave
> Are ye truly free and brave?
> If ye do not feel the chain,
> When it works a brother's pain,
> Are ye not base slaves indeed,
> Slaves unworthy to be freed?

Women! who shall one day bear
Sons to breathe New England air,
If ye hear without a blush,
Deeds to make the roused blood rush
Like red lava through your veins,
For your sisters now in chains,
Answer! are ye fit to be
Mothers of the brave and free?

Is true freedom but to break
Fetters for our own dear sake,
And, with leathern hearts, forget
That we owe mankind a debt?
No! true freedom is to share
All the chains our brothers wear,
And, with heart and hand, to be
Earnest to make others free!
There are slaves who fear to speak
For the fallen and the weak;
They are slaves who will not choose
Hatred, scoffing, and abuse,
Rather than in silence shrink
From the truth they needs must think;
They are slaves who dare not be
In the right with two or three.

A FIELD FOR PRACTICAL WORK.

The very frequent inquiry made after my lectures by interested friends is, "What can I do to help the cause?" The answer always is, "Tell the world the facts." When the Christian world knows the alarming growth and extent of outlawry in our land, some means will be found to stop it.

The object of this publication is to tell the facts, and friends of the cause can lend a helping hand by aiding in the distribution of these books. When I present our cause to a minister, editor, lecturer, or representative of any moral agency, the first demand is for facts and figures. Plainly, I can not then hand out a book with a twenty-five sent tariff on the information contained. This would be only a new method in the book agents' art. In all such cases it is a pleasure to submit this book for investigation, with the certain assur-

ance of gaining a friend to the cause. There are many agencies which may be enlisted in our cause by the general circulation of the facts herein contained. The preachers, teachers, editors and humanitarians of the white race, at home and abroad, must have facts laid before them, and it is our duty to supply these facts. The Central Anti-Lynching League, Room 9, 128 Clark st., Chicago, has established a Free Distribution Fund, the work of which can be promoted by all who are interested in this work.

Anti-lynching leagues, societies and individuals can order books from this fund at agents' rates. The books will be sent to their order, or, if desired, will be distributed by the League among those whose co-operative aid we so greatly need. The writer hereof assures prompt distribution of books according to order, and public acknowledgment of all orders through the public press.

W.E.B. DUBOIS

(1864-1963)

ILLIAM EDWARD BURGHARDT DuBOIS WAS the most
influential voice for African-American protest in the first half
of the twentieth century in America. An intellectual, histori-
an and sociologist, he was one of the founders of the National Association
for the Advancement of Colored People, and edited its magazine *Crisis* for
twenty-four years. During his years at the magazine, DuBois was at the
height of his influence, and his views severely clashed with the philosophy of
Booker T. Washington, causing an ideological split between black Americans.
But DuBois was clearly the leading intellectual voice speaking out against
racial prejudice, and he devoted his entire life to the pursuit of civil rights.

Born in Great Barrington, Massachusetts on February 23, 1868, DuBois
was the son of Alfred and Mary Burghardt DuBois. Upon graduation from
high school in 1884, DuBois did his undergraduate studies at Fisk
University, in Nashville, Tennessee, receiving a Bachelor of Arts degree,
before moving on to Harvard University and acquiring another B.A., cum
laude in 1890. DuBois would go on to earn both his Masters and his Ph.D.
from Harvard, making him the first black person in American history to
obtain a doctorate degree in a secular subject. His dissertation, *The
Suppression of the African Slave Trade to the United States of America,
1638–1870*, was published in 1896, and marked the beginning of DuBois'
dedication to the study of black social science.

From 1892 to 1894, DuBois studied at the University of Berlin on a
Slater Fund Fellowship, which allowed him to travel all over Europe, virtual-
ly undeterred by racism. When he returned from Europe, DuBois began to
search for a teaching position, and his search was limited, by necessity, to
black schools only, until an offer from Wilberforce University in Ohio caught
his interest because it permitted him to teach "the classics." He became
Wilberforce's professor of Greek and Latin, earning a salary of $800 per year.

DuBois enjoyed the teaching aspects of his position, but felt the rigidity and obscurity of the school difficult to digest. Yet he did meet a woman, Nina Gomer, whom he'd marry, and the two would remain together until her death in 1950. They had two children, but only a daughter, Nina Yolande, would survive infancy.

Before long, an offer would arrive from the University of Pennsylvania, and DuBois was given the position of assistant instructor in sociology—infinitely more appealing to him because it took him away from language study and into the more dynamic issues of contemporary life. At a salary of $900, DuBois was delighted to be in Philadelphia, and since his duties at the university involved simply research rather than teaching, his productivity led to the publication of his second book, *The Philadelphia Negro*. This book represented a significant rebuttal to conventional American thought, since racism was widespread and was being disseminated in anatomical, historical and psychological contexts. DuBois argued that blacks deserved the full rights and dignities of American citizenship, making the point with the word "Negro" and how it should be capitalized "because I believe that eight million Americans are entitled to a capital letter."

DuBois was equally passionate when writing about racism's effect on "matters of life and death" in the Philadelphia ghettos. "How long," he wrote, "can a city teach its black children that the road to success is to have a white face? How long can a city do this and escape the inevitable penalty?" Racism running rampant in the city is "morally wrong, politically dangerous, industrially wasteful, and socially silly. It is the duty of whites to stop it, and to do so primarily for their own sakes."

The turn of the century found DuBois down south, as Atlanta University offered him a professorial position in economics and history. Here, DuBois was a full–time teacher from 1897-1910, and organized conferences for the University on "Negro Problems" and edited the proceedings for publication, enabling the public to read what the black intellectual community had discussed in the forums.

DuBois was also writing prolifically, and his famous book *The Souls of Black Folk* was published in 1903—with essays that took aim at Booker T. Washington, as well as conventional thought about the black role in American society. One article, first published in *Atlantic Monthly* in 1897 and later revised as part of "Of Our Spiritual Strivings" for *The Souls of Black Folk* includes one of DuBois' most renowned passages:

After the Egyptian and Indian, the Greek and Roman, the Teuton and Mongolian, the Negro is a sort of seventh son, born with a veil, and gifted with second-sight in this American world,—a world which yields him no true self-consciousness, but only lets him see himself through the revelation of the other world. It is a peculiar sensation, this double-consciousness, this sense of always looking at one's self through the eyes of others, of measuring one's soul by the tape of a world that looks on in amused contempt and pity. One ever feels his twoness,—an American, a Negro; two souls, two thoughts, two unreconciled strivings; two warring ideals in one dark body, whose dogged strength alone keeps it from being torn asunder.

In 1901, DuBois reviewed Booker T. Washington's autobiography, *Up From Slavery* in the Chicago literary journal, *Dial*. The article was later reprinted as part of *The Souls of Black Folk*, and it ignited the philosophical friction between two of the most prominent African American voices in history. To his credit, DuBois' essay dissented from Washington's book with deference and diplomacy, but was unwavering in making the point that Washington did not speak for all black people when he urged blacks to abandon an insistence on civil rights and political power. DuBois mentions black leaders such as Charles Waddell Chesnutt, Paul Laurence Dunbar and others who rebuffed Washington's Tuskegee movement, who "honor Mr. Washington for his attitude of conciliation toward the white South; they accept the 'Atlanta Compromise' in its broadest interpretation; they recognize, with him, many signs of promise, many men of high purpose and fair judgment . . . but at the same time . . . They do not expect that the free right to vote, to enjoy civic rights, and to be educated, will come in a moment; they do not expect to see the bias and prejudices of years disappear at the blast of a trumpet; but they are absolutely certain that the way for a people to gain their reasonable rights is not by voluntarily throwing them away and insisting that they do not want them; that the way for a people to gain respect is not by continually belittling and ridiculing themselves; that, on the contrary, Negroes must insist continually, in season and out of season, that voting is necessary to modern manhood, that color discrimination is barbarism, and that black boys need education as well as white boys.

WITH THE publication of *The Souls of Black Folk* in 1903, DuBois' prominence had been second only to Washington. The book was a landmark in American literature, making a social impact that would define the first half of the century. In 1905, DuBois helped found the Niagara Movement, a small organization which rebuked the platform of Washington. The organization ultimately disintegrated due to internal squabbles, but DuBois was beginning to emerge as the country's leading voice for blacks.

By 1910, he joined the executive board of the newly formed N.A.A.C.P., and became editor of the organization's organ, *Crisis*. Its first issue numbered 1,000 copies, and under DuBois' editorship, the circulation reached over 100,000 copies by 1917. At a time when 75 percent of America's ten million blacks were illiterate, the growth of *Crisis* must be considered one of the great achievements in American journalism. The magazine became a voice for the Black Renaissance of the early 1920s under DuBois' stewardship, and eventually gained a worldwide audience. He was in great demand as a lecturer, and traveled around the country with an agenda calling for educational excellence unencumbered by any religious, political or financial obligations. But unlike many fiery orators of his time, DuBois spoke in a very restrained manner and delivered his speech from his manuscript. Ultimately, DuBois came to believe that scholarly social studies were less effective tools in fighting racism, and organized agitation and propaganda were the only ways to bring about political change.

After World War I, DuBois became very active in the building of the Pan-African movement—a belief that all people of African descent had common interests and should work together in the struggle for freedom. By putting his voice behind this movement, DuBois articulated a surge in cultural nationalism. He began traveling abroad more frequently, sometimes representing the United States at presidential inaugurations oversees and conferring with world leaders on black issues. When his travels took him to the Soviet Union in 1926, DuBois saw a great deal of potential in the country and felt the Soviet system of socialism would succeed. The trip also served to strengthen the Marxist leanings he would maintain for the rest of his life.

He began to split from the N.A.A.C.P., and resigned from the editorship of *Crisis* in 1934 because he felt the organization had become dedicated to the interests of the black bourgeoisie and ignored the remaining black masses. At age 66, DuBois returned to Atlanta University and rekindled his love of education by teaching graduate students in sociology and economics. He continued to write, penning *Black Reconstruction: An Essay Toward a History*

of the Part Which Black Folk Played in the Attempt to Reconstruct Democracy in America, 1860–1880. Entering his 70th year, DuBois did not slow down. He stayed teaching at Atlanta University for ten more years, but in 1944, he eventually retuned to the N.A.A.C.P. to serve as the director of special research. If anyone thought DuBois would rest on his laurels and provide merely a consulting role, this was wrong. In fact, he began publishing articles and essays in many publications nationwide, and resumed speaking tours as well.

After World War II, he began identifying himself with left-leaning movements, joining Paul Robeson and W. Alphaeus Hunton in the Council on African Affairs to end colonialism. This cause got him involved in Henry Wallace's presidential campaign in 1948, and he continued to be a member of the Progressive Party, campaigning for U.S. senator from New York in 1950. The climate of McCarthyism led to DuBois' eventual indictment as an "unregistered foreign agent" and he was arraigned and tried in February 1951. His quick acquittal became one of the earliest victories against government witch-hunting cases.

DuBois continued to write, and the year after his wife died, he married Shirley Graham. He continued to write, but because of his leftist political leanings, his work did not garner much attention from the conventional media. The 1950s saw DuBois become completely disillusioned with the United States. In 1961, he joined the Communist Party, renounced his citizenship, and moved to Ghana, where he would die in exile two years later at the age of ninety-five.

The Souls
of
Black Folk

To
Burghardt And Yolande,
the Lost and the Found

THE FORETHOUGHT

HEREIN lie buried many things which if read with patience may show the strange meaning of being black here at the dawning of the Twentieth Century. This meaning is not without interest to you, Gentle Reader; for the problem of the Twentieth Century is the problem of the color-line.

I pray you, then, receive my little book in all charity, studying my words with me, forgiving mistake and foible for sake of the faith and passion that is in me, and seeking the grain of truth hidden there.

I have sought here to sketch, in vague, uncertain outline, the spiritual world in which ten thousand thousand Americans live and strive. First, in two chapters I have tried to show what Emancipation meant to them, and what was its aftermath. In a third chapter I have pointed out the slow rise of personal leadership, and criticised candidly the leader who bears the chief burden of his race to-day. Then, in two other chapters I have sketched in swift outline the two worlds within and without the Veil, and thus have come to the central problem of training men for life. Venturing now into deeper detail, I have in two chapters studied the struggles of the massed millions of the black peasantry, and in another have sought to make clear the present relations of the sons of master and man.

Leaving, then, the white world, I have stepped within the Veil, raising it that you may view faintly its deeper recesses,—the meaning of its religion,

the passion of its human sorrow, and the struggle of its greater souls. All this I have ended with a tale twice told but seldom written, and a chapter of song.

Some of these thoughts of mine have seen the light before in other guise. For kindly consenting to their republication here, in altered and extended form, I must thank the publishers of *The Atlantic Monthly, The World's Work, The Dial, The New World,* and the *Annals of the American Academy of Political and Social Science.*

Before each chapter, as now printed, stands a bar of the Sorrow Songs,— some echo of haunting melody from the only American music which welled up from black souls in the dark past. And, finally, need I add that I who speak here am bone of the bone and flesh of the flesh of them that live within the Veil?

W. E. B. Du B.
Atlanta, Ga., Feb. 1, 1903.

I

OF OUR SPIRITUAL STRIVINGS

O water, voice of my heart, crying in the sand,
 All night long crying with a mournful cry,
As I lie and listen, and cannot understand
 The voice of my heart in my side or the voice of the sea,
O water, crying for rest, is it I, is it I?
 All night long the water is crying to me.

Unresting water, there shall never be rest
 Till the last moon droop and the last tide fail,
And the fire of the end begin to burn in the west;
 And the heart shall be weary and wonder and cry like the sea,
All life long crying without avail,
 As the water all night long is crying to me.

<div align="right">Arthur Symons.</div>

B ETWEEN me and the other world there is ever an unasked question: unasked by some through feelings of delicacy; by others through the difficulty of rightly framing it. All, nevertheless, flutter round it. They approach me in a half-hesitant sort of way, eye me curiously or compassionately, and then, instead of saying directly, How does it feel to be a problem? they say, I know an excellent colored man in my town; or, I fought at Mechanicsville; or, Do not these Southern outrages make your blood boil? At these I smile, or am interested, or reduce the boiling to a simmer, as the occasion may require. To the real question, How does it feel to be a problem? I answer seldom a word.

And yet, being a problem is a strange experience—peculiar even for one who has never been anything else, save perhaps in babyhood and in Europe. It is in the early days of rollicking boyhood that the revelation first bursts upon one, all in a day, as it were I remember well when the shadow swept across me. I was a little thing, away up in the hills of New England, where the dark Housatonic winds between Hoosac and Taghkanic to the sea. In a wee wooden schoolhouse, something put it into the boys' and girls' heads to buy gorgeous visiting-cards—ten cents a package—and exchange. The exchange was merry, till one girl, a tall newcomer, refused my card,—refused it peremptorily, with a glance. Then it dawned upon me with a certain suddenness that I was different from the others; or like, mayhap, in heart and life and longing, but shut out from their world by a vast veil. I had thereafter no desire to tear down that veil, to creep through; I held all beyond it in common contempt, and lived above it in a region of blue sky and great wandering shadows. That sky was bluest when I could beat my mates at examination-time, or beat them at a foot-race, or even beat their stringy heads. Alas, with the years all this fine contempt began to fade; for the worlds I longed for, and all their dazzling opportunities, were theirs, not mine. But they should not keep these prizes, I said; some, all, I would wrest from them. Just how I would do it I could never decide: by reading law, by healing the sick, by telling the wonderful tales that swam in my head,—some way. With other black boys the strife was not so fiercely sunny: their youth shrunk into tasteless sycophancy, or into silent hatred of the pale world about them and mocking distrust of everything white; or wasted itself in a bitter cry, Why did God make me an outcast and a stranger in mine own house? The shades of the prison-house closed round about us all: walls strait and stubborn to the whitest, but relentlessly narrow, tall, and unscalable to sons of night who must plod darkly on in resignation, or beat unavailing palms against the stone, or steadily, half hopelessly, watch the streak of blue above.

After the Egyptian and Indian, the Greek and Roman, the Teuton and Mongolian, the Negro is a sort of seventh son, born with a veil, and gifted with second-sight in this American world,—a world which yields him no true self-consciousness, but only lets him see himself through the revelation of the other world. It is a peculiar sensation, this double-consciousness, this sense of always looking at one's self through the eyes of others, of measuring one's soul by the tape of a world that looks on in amused contempt and pity. One ever feels his two-ness,—an American, a Negro; two souls, two thoughts, two unreconciled strivings; two warring ideals in one dark body, whose dogged strength alone keeps it from being torn asunder.

The history of the American Negro is the history of this strife,—this longing to attain self-conscious manhood, to merge his double self into a better and truer self. In this merging he wishes neither of the older selves to be lost. He would not Africanize America, for America has too much to teach the world and Africa. He would not bleach his Negro soul in a flood of white Americanism, for he knows that Negro blood has a message for the world. He simply wishes to make it possible for a man to be both a Negro and an American, without being cursed and spit upon by his fellows, without having the doors of Opportunity closed roughly in his face.

This, then, is the end of his striving: to be a coworker in the kingdom of culture, to escape both death and isolation, to husband and use his best powers and his latent genius. These powers of body and mind have in the past been strangely wasted, dispersed, or forgotten. The shadow of a mighty Negro past flits through the tale of Ethiopia the Shadowy and of Egypt the Sphinx. Throughout history, the powers of single black men flash here and there like falling stars, and die sometimes before the world has rightly gauged their brightness. Here in America, in the few days since Emancipation, the black man's turning hither and thither in hesitant and doubtful striving has often made his very strength to lose effectiveness, to seem like absence of power, like weakness. And yet it is not weakness,—it is the contradiction of double aims. The double-aimed struggle of the black artisan—on the one hand to escape white contempt for a nation of mere hewers of wood and drawers of water, and on the other hand to plough and nail and dig for a poverty-stricken horde—could only result in making him a poor craftsman, for he had but half a heart in either cause. By the poverty and ignorance of his people, the Negro minister or doctor was tempted toward quackery and demagogy; and by the criticism of the other world, toward ideals that made him ashamed of his lowly tasks. The would-be black savant was confronted

by the paradox that the knowledge his people needed was a twice-told tale to his white neighbors, while the knowledge which would teach the white world was Greek to his own flesh and blood. The innate love of harmony and beauty that set the ruder souls of his people a-dancing and a-singing raised but confusion and doubt in the soul of the black artist; for the beauty revealed to him was the soul-beauty of a race which his larger audience despised, and he could not articulate the message of another people. This waste of double aims, this seeking to satisfy two unreconciled ideals, has wrought sad havoc with the courage and faith and deeds of ten thousand thousand people,—has sent them often wooing false gods and invoking false means of salvation, and at times has even seemed about to make them ashamed of themselves.

Away back in the days of bondage they thought to see in one divine event the end of all doubt and disappointment; few men ever worshipped Freedom with half such unquestioning faith as did the American Negro for two centuries. To him, so far as he thought and dreamed, slavery was indeed the sum of all villainies, the cause of all sorrow, the root of all prejudice; Emancipation was the key to a promised land of sweeter beauty than ever stretched before the eyes of wearied Israelites. In song and exhortation swelled one refrain—Liberty; in his tears and curses the God he implored had Freedom in his right hand. At last it came,—suddenly, fearfully, like a dream. With one wild carnival of blood and passion came the message in his own plaintive cadences:—

> "Shout, O children!
> Shout, you're free!
> For God has bought your liberty!"

Years have passed away since then,—ten, twenty, forty; forty years of national life, forty years of renewal and development, and yet the swarthy spectre sits in its accustomed seat at the Nation's feast. In vain do we cry to this our vastest social problem:—

> "Take any shape but that, and my firm nerves
> Shall never tremble!"

The Nation has not yet found peace from its sins; the freedman has not yet found in freedom his promised land. Whatever of good may have come in these years of change, the shadow of a deep disappointment rests upon the

Negro people,—a disappointment all the more bitter because the unattained ideal was unbounded save by the simple ignorance of a lowly people.

The first decade was merely a prolongation of the vain search for freedom, the boon that seemed ever barely to elude their grasp,—like a tantalizing will-o'-the-wisp, maddening and misleading the head-less host. The holocaust of war, the terrors of the Ku-Klux Klan, the lies of carpet-baggers, the disorganization of industry, and the contradictory advice of friends and foes, left the bewildered serf with no new watchword beyond the old cry for freedom. As the time flew, however, he began to grasp a new idea. The ideal of liberty demanded for its attainment powerful means, and these the Fifteenth Amendment gave him. The ballot, which before he had looked upon as a visible sign of freedom, he now regarded as the chief means of gaining and perfecting the liberty with which war had partially endowed him. And why not? Had not votes made war and emancipated millions? Had not votes enfranchised the freedmen? Was anything impossible to a power that had done all this? A million black men started with renewed zeal to vote themselves into the kingdom. So the decade flew away, the revolution of 1876 came, and left the half-free serf weary, wondering, but still inspired. Slowly but steadily, in the following years, a new vision began gradually to replace the dream of political power,—a powerful movement, the rise of another ideal to guide the unguided, another pillar of fire by night after a clouded day. It was the ideal of "book-learning"; the curiosity, born of compulsory ignorance, to know and test the power of the cabalistic letters of the white man, the longing to know. Here at last seemed to have been discovered the mountain path to Canaan; longer than the highway of Emancipation and law, steep and rugged, but straight, leading to heights high enough to overlook life.

Up the new path the advance guard toiled, slowly, heavily, doggedly; only those who have watched and guided the faltering feet, the misty minds, the dull understandings, of the dark pupils of these schools know how faithfully, how piteously, this people strove to learn. It was weary-work. The cold statistician wrote down the inches of progress here and there, noted also where here and there a foot had slipped or some one had fallen. To the tired climbers, the horizon was ever dark, the mists were often cold, the Canaan was always dim and far away. If, however, the vistas disclosed as yet no goal, no resting-place, little but flattery and criticism, the journey at least gave leisure for reflection and self-examination; it changed the child of Emancipation to the youth with dawning self-consciousness, self-realization,

self-respect. In those sombre forests of his striving his own soul rose before him, and he saw himself,—darkly as through a veil; and yet he saw in himself some faint revelation of his power, of his mission. He began to have a dim feeling that, to attain his place in the world, he must be himself, and not another. For the first time he sought to analyze the burden he bore upon his back, that dead-weight of social degradation partially masked behind a half-named Negro problem. He felt his poverty; without a cent, without a home, without land, tools, or savings, he had entered into competition with rich, landed, skilled neighbors. To be a poor man is hard, but to be a poor race in a land of dollars is the very bottom of hardships. He felt the weight of his ignorance,—not simply of letters, but of life, of business, of the humanities; the accumulated sloth and shirking and awkwardness of decades and centuries shackled his hands and feet. Nor was his burden all poverty and ignorance. The red stain of bastardy, which two centuries of systematic legal defilement of Negro women had stamped upon his race, meant not only the loss of ancient African chastity, but also the hereditary weight of a mass of corruption from white adulterers, threatening almost the obliteration of the Negro home.

A people thus handicapped ought not to be asked to race with the world, but rather allowed to give all its time and thought to its own social problems. But alas! while sociologists gleefully count his bastards and his prostitutes, the very soul of the toiling, sweating black man is darkened by the shadow of a vast despair. Men call the shadow prejudice, and learnedly explain it as the natural defence of culture against barbarism, learning against ignorance, purity against crime, the "higher" against the "lower" races. To which the Negro cries Amen! and swears that to so much of this strange prejudice as is founded on just homage to civilization, culture, righteousness, and progress, he humbly bows and meekly does obeisance. But before that nameless prejudice that leaps beyond all this he stands helpless, dismayed, and well-nigh speechless; before that personal disrespect and mockery, the ridicule and systematic humiliation, the distortion of fact and wanton license of fancy, the cynical ignoring of the better and the boisterous welcoming of the worse, the all-pervading desire to inculcate disdain for everything black, from Toussaint to the devil,—before this there rises a sickening despair that would disarm and discourage any nation save that black host to whom "discouragement" is an unwritten word.

But the facing of so vast a prejudice could not but bring the inevitable self-questioning, self-disparagement, and lowering of ideals which ever

accompany repression and breed in an atmosphere of contempt and hate. Whisperings and portents came borne upon the four winds: Lo! we are diseased and dying, cried the dark hosts; we cannot write, our voting is vain; what need of education, since we must always cook and serve? And the Nation echoed and enforced this self-criticism, saying: Be content to be servants, and nothing more; what need of higher culture for half-men? Away with the black man's ballot, by force or fraud,—and behold the suicide of a race! Nevertheless, out of the evil came something of good,—the more careful adjustment of education to real life, the clearer perception of the Negroes' social responsibilities, and the sobering realization of the meaning of progress.

So dawned the time of *Sturm und Drang:* storm and stress to-day rocks our little boat on the mad waters of the world-sea; there is within and without the sound of conflict, the burning of body and rending of soul; inspiration strives with doubt, and faith with vain questionings. The bright ideals of the past,—physical freedom, political power, the training of brains and the training of hands,—all these in turn have waxed and waned, until even the last grows dim and overcast. Are they all wrong,—all false? No, not that, but each alone was over-simple and incomplete,—the dreams of a credulous race—childhood, or the fond imaginings of the other world which does not know and does not want to know our power. To be really true, all these ideals must be melted and welded into one. The training of the schools we need to-day more than ever,—the training of deft hands, quick eyes and ears, and above all the broader, deeper, higher culture of gifted minds and pure hearts. The power of the ballot we need in sheer self-defence,—else what shall save us from a second slavery? Freedom, too, the long-sought, we still seek,—the freedom of life and limb, the freedom to work and think, the freedom to love and aspire. Work, culture, liberty,—all these we need, not singly but together, not successively but together, each growing and aiding each, and all striving toward that vaster ideal that swims before the Negro people, the ideal of human brotherhood, gained through the unifying ideal of Race; the ideal of fostering and developing the traits and talents of the Negro, not in opposition to or contempt for other races, but rather in large conformity to the greater ideals of the American Republic, in order that some day on American soil two world-races may give each to each those characteristics both so sadly lack. We the darker ones come even now not altogether empty-handed: there are to-day no truer exponents of the pure human spirit of the Declaration of Independence than the American Negroes; there is no true American music but the wild sweet melodies of the Negro slave; the American fairy tales and

folk-lore are Indian and African; and, all in all, we black men seem the sole oasis of simple faith and reverence in a dusty desert of dollars and smartness. Will America be poorer if she replace her brutal dyspeptic blundering with light-hearted but determined Negro humility? or her coarse and cruel wit with loving jovial good-humor? or her vulgar music with the soul of the Sorrow Songs?

Merely a concrete test of the underlying principles of the great republic is the Negro Problem, and the spiritual striving of the freedmen's sons is the travail of souls whose burden is almost beyond the measure of their strength, but who bear it in the name of an historic race, in the name of this the land of their fathers' fathers, and in the name of human opportunity.

And now what I have briefly sketched in large outline let me on coming pages tell again in many ways, with loving emphasis and deeper detail, that men may listen to the striving in the souls of black folk.

II

OF THE DAWN OF FREEDOM

Careless seems the great Avenger;
 History's lessons but record
One death-grapple in the darkness
 'Twixt old systems and the Word;
Truth forever on the scaffold,
 Wrong forever on the throne;
Yet that scaffold sways the future,
 And behind the dim unknown
Standeth God within the shadow
 Keeping watch above His own.
 Lowell.

THE problem of the twentieth century is the problem of the color-line,—the relation of the darker to the lighter races of men in Asia and Africa, in America and the islands of the sea. It was a phase of this problem that caused the Civil War; and however much they who marched South and North in 1861 may have fixed on the technical points of union and local autonomy as a shibboleth, all nevertheless knew, as we know, that the question of Negro slavery was the real cause of the conflict. Curious it was, too, how this deeper question ever forced itself to the surface despite effort and disclaimer. No sooner had Northern armies touched Southern soil than this old question, newly guised, sprang from the earth,—What shall be done with Negroes? Peremptory military commands, this way and that, could not answer the query; the Emancipation Proclamation seemed but to broaden and intensify the difficulties; and the War Amendments made the Negro problems of to-day.

It is the aim of this essay to study the period of history from 1861 to 1872 so far as it relates to the American Negro. In effect, this tale of the dawn of Freedom is an account of that government of men called the Freedmen's Bureau,—one of the most singular and interesting of the attempts made by great nation to grapple with vast problems of race and social condition.

The war has naught to do with slaves, cried Congress, the President, and the Nation; and yet no sooner had the armies, East and West, penetrated Virginia and Tennessee than fugitive slaves appeared within their lines. They came at night, when the flickering camp-fires shone like vast unsteady stars along the black horizon: old men and thin, with gray and tufted hair; women, with frightened eyes, dragging whimpering hungry children; men and girls, stalwart and gaunt,—a horde of starving vagabonds, homeless, helpless, and pitiable, in their dark distress. Two methods of treating these newcomers seemed equally logical to opposite sorts of minds. Ben Butler, in Virginia, quickly declared slave property contraband of war, and put the fugitives to work; while Fremont, in Missouri, declared the slaves free under martial law. Butler's action was approved, but Fremont's was hastily counter-manded, and his successor, Halleck, saw things differently. "Hereafter," he commanded, "no slaves should be allowed to come into your lines at all; if any come without your knowledge, when owners call for them deliver them." Such a policy was difficult to enforce; some of the black refugees declared themselves freemen, others showed that their masters had deserted them, and still others were captured with forts and plantations. Evidently, too, slaves were a source of strength to the Confederacy, and were being used as labor-

ers and producers. "They constitute a military resource," wrote Secretary Cameron, late in 1861; "and being such, that they should not be turned over to the enemy is too plain to discuss." So gradually the tone of the army chiefs changed; Congress forbade the rendition of fugitives, and Butler's "contrabands" were welcomed as military laborers. This complicated rather than solved the problem, for now the scattering fugitives became a steady stream, which flowed faster as the armies marched.

Then the long-headed man with care-chiselled face who sat in the White House saw the inevitable, and emancipated the slaves of rebels on New Year's, 1863. A month later Congress called earnestly for the Negro soldiers whom the act of July, 1862, had half grudgingly allowed to enlist. Thus the barriers were levelled and the deed was done. The stream of fugitives swelled to a flood, and anxious army officers kept inquiring: "What must be done with slaves, arriving almost daily? Are we to find food and shelter for women and children?"

It was a Pierce of Boston who pointed out the way, and thus became in a sense the founder of the Freedmen's Bureau. He was a firm friend of Secretary Chase; and when, in 1861, the care of slaves and abandoned lands devolved upon the Treasury officials, Pierce was specially detailed from the ranks to study the conditions. First, he cared for the refugees at Fortress Monroe; and then, after Sherman had captured Hilton Head, Pierce was sent there to found his Port Royal experiment of making free workingmen out of slaves. Before his experiment was barely started, however, the problem of the fugitives had assumed such proportions that it was taken from the hands of the over-burdened Treasury Department and given to the army officials. Already centres of massed freedmen were forming at Fortress Monroe, Washington, New Orleans, Vicksburg and Corinth, Columbus, Ky., and Cairo, Ill., as well as at Port Royal. Army chaplains found here new and fruitful fields; "superintendents of contrabands" multiplied, and some attempt at systematic work was made by enlisting the able-bodied men and giving work to the others.

Then came the Freedmen's Aid societies, born of the touching appeals from Pierce and from these other centres of distress. There was the American Missionary Association, sprung from the Amistad, and now full-grown for work; the various church organizations, the National Freedmen's Relief Association, the American Freedmen's Union, the Western Freedmen's Aid Commission,—in all fifty or more active organizations, which sent clothes, money, school-books, and teachers southward. All they did was needed, for

the destitution of the freedmen was often reported as "too appalling for belief," and the situation was daily growing worse rather than better.

And daily, too, it seemed more plain that this was no ordinary matter of temporary relief, but a national crisis; for here loomed a labor problem of vast dimensions. Masses of Negroes stood idle, or, if they worked spasmodically, were never sure of pay, and if perchance they received pay, squandered the new thing thoughtlessly. In these and other ways were camp-life and the new liberty demoralizing the freedmen. The broader economic organization thus clearly demanded sprang up here and there as accident and local conditions determined. Here it was that Pierce's Port Royal plan of leased plantations and guided workmen pointed out the rough way. In Washington the military governor, at the urgent appeal of the superintendent, opened confiscated estates to the cultivation of the fugitives, and there in the shadow of the dome gathered black farm villages. General Dix gave over estates to the freedmen of Fortress Monroe, and so on, South and West. The government and benevolent societies furnished the means of cultivation, and the Negro turned again slowly to work. The systems of control, thus started, rapidly grew, here and there, into strange little governments, like that of General Banks in Louisiana, with its ninety thousand black subjects, its fifty thousand guided laborers, and its annual budget of one hundred thousand dollars and more. It made out four thousand pay-rolls a year, registered all freedmen, inquired into grievances and redressed them, laid and collected taxes, and established a system of public schools. So, too, Colonel Eaton, the superintendent of Tennessee and Arkansas, ruled over one hundred thousand freedmen, leased and cultivated seven thousand acres of cotton land, and fed ten thousand paupers a year. In South Carolina was General Saxton, with his deep interest in black folk. He succeeded Pierce and the Treasury officials, and sold forfeited estates, leased abandoned plantations, encouraged schools, and received from Sherman, after that terribly picturesque march to the sea, thousands of the wretched camp followers.

Three characteristic things one might have seen in Sherman's raid through Georgia, which threw the new situation in shadowy relief: the Conqueror, the Conquered, and the Negro. Some see all significance in the grim front of the destroyer, and some in the bitter sufferers of the Lost Cause. But to me neither soldier nor fugitive speaks with so deep a meaning as that dark human cloud that clung like remorse on the rear of those swift columns, swelling at times to half their size, almost engulfing and choking them. In vain were they ordered back, in vain were bridges hewn from beneath their

feet; on they trudged and writhed and surged, until they rolled into Savannah, a starved and naked horde of tens of thousands. There too came the characteristic military remedy: "The islands from Charleston south, the abandoned rice-fields along the rivers for thirty miles back from the sea, and the country bordering the St. John's River, Florida, are reserved and set apart for the settlement of Negroes now made free by act of war." So read the celebrated "Field-order Number Fifteen."

All these experiments, orders, and systems were bound to attract and perplex the government and the nation. Directly after the Emancipation Proclamation, Representative Eliot had introduced a bill creating a Bureau of Emancipation; but it was never reported. The following June a committee of inquiry, appointed by the Secretary of War, reported in favor of a temporary bureau for the "improvement, protection, and employment of refugee freedmen," on much the same lines as were afterwards followed. Petitions came in to President Lincoln from distinguished citizens and organizations, strongly urging a comprehensive and unified plan of dealing with the freedmen, under a bureau which should be "charged with the study of plans and execution of measures for easily guiding, and in every way judiciously and humanely aiding, the passage of our emancipated and yet to be emancipated blacks from the old condition of forced labor to their new state of voluntary industry."

Some half-hearted steps were taken to accomplish this, in part, by putting the whole matter again in charge of the special Treasury agents. Laws of 1863 and 1864 directed them to take charge of and lease abandoned lands for periods not exceeding twelve months, and to "provide in such leases, or otherwise for the employment and general welfare" of the freedmen. Most of the army officers greeted this as a welcome relief from perplexing "Negro affairs," and Secretary Fessenden, July 29,1864, issued an excellent system of regulations, which were afterward closely followed by General Howard. Under Treasury agents, large quantities of land were leased in the Mississippi Valley, and many Negroes were employed; but in August, 1864, the new regulations were suspended for reasons of "public policy," and the army was again in control.

Meanwhile Congress had turned its attention to the subject; and in March the House passed a bill by a majority of two establishing a Bureau for Freedmen in the War Department. Charles Sumner, who had charge of the bill in the Senate, argued that freedmen and abandoned lands ought to be under the same department, and reported a substitute for the House bill attaching the Bureau to the Treasury Department. This bill passed, but too

late for action by the House. The debates wandered over the whole policy of the administration and the general question of slavery, without touching very closely the specific merits of the measure in hand. Then the national election took place; and the administration, with a vote of renewed confidence from the country, addressed itself to the matter more seriously. A conference between the two branches of Congress agreed upon a carefully drawn measure which contained the chief provisions of Sumner's bill, but made the proposed organization; a department independent of both the War and the Treasury officials. The bill was conservative, giving the new department "general superintendence of all freedmen." Its purpose was to "establish regulations" for them, protect them, lease them lands, adjust their wages, and appear in civil and military courts as their "next friend." There were many limitations attached to the powers thus granted, and the organization was made permanent. Nevertheless, the Senate defeated the bill, and a new conference committee was appointed. This committee reported a new bill, February 28, which was whirled through just as the session closed, and became the act of 1865 establishing in the War Department a "Bureau of Refugees, Freedmen, and Abandoned Lands."

This last compromise was a hasty bit of legislation, vague and uncertain in outline. A Bureau was created, "to continue during the present War of Rebellion, and for one year thereafter," to which was given "the supervision and management of all abandoned lands and the control of all subjects relating to refugees and freedmen," under "such rules and regulations as may be presented by the head of the Bureau and approved by the President." A Commissioner, appointed by the President and Senate, was to control the Bureau, with an office force not exceeding ten clerks. The President might also appoint assistant commissioners in the seceded States, and to all these offices military officials might be detailed at regular pay. The Secretary of War could issue rations, clothing, and fuel to the destitute, and all abandoned property was placed in the hands of the Bureau for eventual lease and sale to ex-slaves in forty-acre parcels.

Thus did the United States government definitely assume charge of the emancipated Negro as the ward of the nation. It was a tremendous undertaking. Here at a stroke of the pen was erected a government of millions of men,—and not ordinary men either, but black men emasculated by a peculiarly complete system of slavery, centuries old; and now, suddenly, violently, they come into a new birthright, at a time of war and passion, in the midst of the stricken and embittered population of their former masters. Any man

might well have hesitated to assume charge of such a work, with vast responsibilities, indefinite powers, and limited resources. Probably no one but a soldier would have answered such a call promptly; and, indeed, no one but a soldier could be called, for Congress had appropriated no money for salaries and expenses.

Less than a month after the weary Emancipator passed to his rest, his successor assigned Major-Gen. Oliver O. Howard to duty as Commissioner of the new Bureau. He was a Maine man, then only thirty-five years of age. He had marched with Sherman to the sea, had fought well at Gettysburg, and but the year before had been assigned to the command of the Department of Tennessee. An honest man, with too much faith in human nature, little aptitude for business and intricate detail, he had had large opportunity of becoming acquainted at first hand with much of the work before him. And of that work it has been truly said that "no approximately correct history of civilization can ever be written which does not throw out in bold relief, as one of the great landmarks of political and social progress, the organization and administration of the Freedmen's Bureau."

On May 12, 1865, Howard was appointed; and he assumed the duties of his office promptly on the 15th and began examining the field of work. A curious mess he looked upon: little despotisms, communistic experiments, slavery, peonage, business speculations, organized charity, unorganized almsgiving,—all reeling on under the guise of helping the freedmen, and all enshrined in the smoke and blood of war and the cursing and silence of angry men. On May 19 the new government—for a government it really was—issued its constitution; commissioners were to be appointed in each of the seceded States, who were to take charge of "all subjects relating to refugees and freedmen," and all relief and rations were to be given by their consent alone. The Bureau invited continued cooperation with benevolent societies, and declared: "It will be the object of all commissioners to introduce practicable systems of compensated labor," and to establish schools. Forthwith nine assistant commissioners were appointed. They were to hasten to their fields of work; seek gradually to close relief establishments, and make the destitute self-supporting; act as courts of law where there were no courts, or where Negroes were not recognized in them as free; establish the institution of marriage among ex-slaves, and keep records; see that freedmen were free to choose their employers, and help in making fair contracts for them; and finally, the circular said: "Simple good faith, for which we hope on all hands for those concerned in the passing away of slavery, will especially

relieve the assistant commissioners in the discharge of their duties toward the freedmen, as well as promote the general welfare."

No sooner was the work thus started, and the general system and local organization in some measure begun, than two grave difficulties appeared which changed largely the theory and outcome of Bureau work. First, there were the abandoned lands of the South. It had long been the more or less definitely expressed theory of the North that all the chief problems of Emancipation might be settled by establishing the slaves on the forfeited lands of their masters,—a sort of poetic justice, said some. But this poetry done into solemn prose meant either wholesale confiscation of private property in the South, or vast appropriations. Now Congress had not appropriated a cent, and no sooner did the proclamations of general amnesty appear than the eight hundred thousand acres of abandoned lands in the hands of the Freedmen's Bureau melted quickly away. The second difficulty lay in perfecting the local organization of the Bureau throughout the wide field of work. Making a new machine and sending out officials of duly ascertained fitness for a great work of social reform is no child's task; but this task was even harder, for a new central organization had to be fitted on a heterogeneous and confused but already existing system of relief and control of ex-slaves; and the agents available for this work must be sought for in an army still busy with war operations,—men in the very nature of the case ill fitted for delicate social work,—or among the questionable camp followers of an invading host. Thus, after a year's work, vigorously as it was pushed, the problem looked even more difficult to grasp and solve than at the beginning. Nevertheless, three things that year's work did, well worth the doing: it relieved a vast amount of physical suffering; it transported seven thousand fugitives from congested centres back to the farm; and, best of all it inaugurated the crusade of the New England schoolma'am.

The annals of this Ninth Crusade are yet to be written,—the tale of a mission that seemed to our age far more quixotic than the quest of St. Louis seemed to his. Behind the mists of ruin and rapine waved the calico dresses of women who dared, and after the hoarse mouthings of the field guns rang the rhythm of the alphabet. Rich and poor they were, serious and curious. Bereaved now of a father, now of a brother, now of more than these, they came seeking a life work in planting New England school houses among the white and black of the South. They did their work well. In that first year they taught one hundred thousand souls, and more.

Evidently, Congress must soon legislate again on the hastily organized

Bureau, which had so quickly grown into wide significance and vast possibilities. An institution such as that was well-nigh as difficult to end as to begin. Early in 1866 Congress took up the matter, when Senator Trumbull, of Illinois, introduced a bill to extend the Bureau and enlarge its powers. This measure received, at the hands of Congress, far more thorough discussion and attention than its predecessor. The war cloud had thinned enough to allow a clearer conception of the work of Emancipation. The champions of the bill argued that the strengthening of the Freedmen's Bureau was still a military necessity; that it was needed for the proper carrying out of the Thirteenth Amendment, and was a work of sheer justice to the ex-slave, at a trifling cost to the government. The opponents of the measure declared that the war was over, and the necessity for war measures past; that the Bureau, by reason of its extraordinary powers, was clearly unconstitutional in time of peace, and was destined to irritate the South and pauperize the freedmen, at a final cost of possibly hundreds of millions. These two arguments were unanswered, and indeed unanswerable: the one that the extraordinary powers of the Bureau threatened the civil rights of all citizens; and the other that the government must have power to do what manifestly must be done, and that present abandonment of the freedmen meant their practical re-enslavement. The bill which finally passed enlarged and made permanent the Freedmen's Bureau. It was promptly vetoed by President Johnson as "unconstitutional," "unnecessary," and "extrajudicial," and failed of passage over the veto. Meantime, however, the breach between Congress and the President began to broaden, and a modified form of the lost bill was finally passed over the President's second veto, July 16.

The act of 1866 gave the Freedmen's Bureau its final form,—the form by which it will be known to posterity and judged of men. It extended the existence of the Bureau to July, 1868; it authorized additional assistant commissioners, the retention of army officers mustered out of regular service, the sale of certain forfeited lands to freedmen on nominal terms, the sale of Confederate public property for Negro schools, and a wider field of judicial interpretation and cognizance. The government of the unreconstructed South was thus put very largely in the hands of the Freedmen's Bureau, especially as in many cases the departmental military commander was now made also assistant commissioner. It was thus that the Freedmen's Bureau became a full-fledged government of men. It made laws, executed them and interpreted them; it laid and collected taxes, defined and punished crime, maintained and used military force, and dictated such measures as it thought necessary

and proper for the accomplishment of its varied ends. Naturally, all these powers were not exercised continuously nor to their fullest extent; and yet, as General Howard has said, "scarcely any subject that has to be legislated upon in civil society" failed, at one time or another, to demand the action of this singular Bureau.

To understand and criticise intelligently so vast a work, one must not forget an instant the drift of things in the later sixties. Lee had surrendered, Lincoln was dead, and Johnson and Congress were at loggerheads; the Thirteenth Amendment was adopted, the Fourteenth pending, and the Fifteenth declared in force in 1870. Guerrilla raiding, the ever-present flickering after-flame of war, was spending its force against the Negroes, and all the Southern land was awakening as from some wild dream to poverty and social revolution. In a time of perfect calm, amid willing neighbors and streaming wealth, the social uplifting of four million slaves to an assured and self-sustaining place in the body politic and economic would have been a herculean task; but when to the inherent difficulties of so delicate and nice a social operation were added the spite and hate of conflict, the hell of war; when suspicion and cruelty were rife, and gaunt Hunger wept beside Bereavement,—in such a case, the work of any instrument of social regeneration was in large part foredoomed to failure. The very name of the Bureau stood for a thing in the South which for two centuries and better men had refused even to argue,—that life amid free Negroes was simply unthinkable, the maddest of experiments.

The agents that the Bureau could command varied all the way from unselfish philanthropists to narrow-minded busybodies and thieves; and even though it be true that the average was far better than the worst, it was the occasional fly that helped spoil the ointment.

Then amid all crouched the freed slave, bewildered between friend and foe. He had emerged from slavery,—not the worst slavery in the world, not a slavery that made all life unbearable, rather a slavery that had here and there something of kindliness, fidelity, and happiness,—but withal slavery, which, so far as human aspiration and desert were concerned, classed the black man and the ox together. And the Negro knew full well that, whatever their deeper convictions may have been, Southern men had fought with desperate energy to perpetuate this slavery under which the black masses, with half-articulate thought, had writhed and shivered. They welcomed freedom with a cry. They shrank from the master who still strove for their chains; they fled to the friends that had freed them, even though those friends stood ready to use

them as a club for driving the recalcitrant South back into loyalty. So the cleft between the white and black South grew. Idle to say it never should have been; it was as inevitable as its results were pitiable. Curiously incongruous elements were left arrayed against each other,—the North, the government, the carpet-bagger, and the slave, here and there, all the South that was white, whether gentleman or vagabond, honest man or rascal, lawless murderer or martyr to duty.

Thus it is doubly difficult to write of this period calmly, so intense was the feeling, so mighty the human passions that swayed and blinded men. Amid it all, two figures ever stand to typify that day to coming ages,—the one, a gray-haired gentleman, whose fathers had quit themselves like men, whose sons lay in nameless graves; who bowed to the evil of slavery because its abolition threatened untold ill to all; who stood at last, in the evening of life, a blighted, ruined form, with hate in his eyes;—and the other, a form hovering dark and mother-like, her awful face black with the mists of centuries, had aforetime quailed at that white master's command, had bent in love over the cradles of his sons and daughters, and closed in death the sunken eyes of his wife,—aye, too, at his behest had laid herself low to his lust, and borne a tawny man-child to the world, only to see her dark boy's limbs scattered to the winds by midnight marauders riding after "damned Niggers." These were the saddest sights of that woful day; and no man clasped the hands of these two passing figures of the present-past; but, hating, they went to their long home, and, hating, their children's children live to-day.

Here, then, was the field of work for the Freedmen's Bureau; and since, with some hesitation, it was continued by the act of 1868 until 1869, let us look upon four years of its work as a whole. There were, in 1868, nine hundred Bureau officials scattered from Washington to Texas, ruling, directly and indirectly, many millions of men. The deeds of these rulers fall mainly under seven heads: the relief of physical suffering, the overseeing of the beginnings of free labor, the buying and selling of land, the establishment of schools, the paying of bounties, the administration of justice, and the financiering of all these activities.

Up to June, 1869, over half a million patients had been treated by Bureau physicians and surgeons, and sixty hospitals and asylums had been in operation. In fifty months twenty-one million free rations were distributed at a cost of over four million dollars. Next came the difficult question of labor. First, thirty thousand black men were transported from the refuges and relief

stations back to the farms, back to the critical trial of a new way of working. Plain instructions went out from Washington: the laborers must be free to choose their employers, no fixed rate of wages was prescribed, and there was to be no peonage or forced labor. So far, so good; but where local agents differed *toto cælo* in capacity and character, where the *personnel* was continually changing, the outcome was necessarily varied. The largest element of success lay in the fact that the majority of the freedmen were willing, even eager, to work. So labor contracts were written,—fifty thousand in a single State,—laborers advised, wages guaranteed, and employers supplied. In truth, the organization became a vast labor bureau,—not perfect, indeed, notably defective here and there, but on the whole successful beyond the dreams of thoughtful men. The two great obstacles which confronted the officials were the tyrant and the idler,—the slaveholder who was determined to perpetuate slavery under another name; and the freedman who regarded freedom as perpetual rest,—the Devil and the Deep Sea.

In the work of establishing the Negroes as peasant proprietors, the Bureau was from the first handicapped and at last absolutely checked. Something was done, and larger things were planned; abandoned lands were leased so long as they remained in the hands of the Bureau, and a total revenue of nearly half a million dollars derived from black tenants. Some other lands to which the nation had gained title were sold on easy terms, and public lands were opened for settlement to the very few freedmen who had tools and capital. But the vision of "forty acres and a mule"—the righteous and reasonable ambition to become a landholder, which the nation had all but categorically promised the freedmen—was destined in most cases to bitter disappointment. And those men of marvellous hindsight who are to-day seeking to preach the Negro back to the present peonage of the soil know well, or ought to know, that the opportunity of binding the Negro peasant willingly to the soil was lost on that day when the Commissioner of the Freedmen's Bureau had to go to South Carolina and tell the weeping freedmen, after their years of toil, that their land was not theirs, that there was a mistake—somewhere. If by 1874 the Georgia Negro alone owned three hundred and fifty thousand acres of land, it was by grace of his thrift rather than by bounty of the government.

The greatest success of the Freedmen's Bureau lay in the planting of the free school among Negroes, and the idea of free elementary education among all classes in the South. It not only called the schoolmistresses through the benevolent agencies and built them schoolhouses, but it helped discover and

support such apostles of human culture as Edmund Ware, Samuel Armstrong, and Erastus Cravath. The opposition to Negro education in the South was at first bitter, and showed itself in ashes, insult, and blood; for the South believed an educated Negro to be a dangerous Negro. And the South was not wholly wrong; for education among all kinds of men always has had, and always will have, an element of danger and revolution, of dissatisfaction and discontent. Nevertheless, men strive to know. Perhaps some inkling of this paradox, even in the unquiet days of the Bureau, helped the bayonets allay an opposition to human training which still to-day lies smouldering in the South, but not flaming. Fisk, Atlanta, Howard, and Hampton were founded in these days, and six million dollars were expended for educational work, seven hundred and fifty thousand dollars of which the freedmen themselves gave of their poverty.

Such contributions, together with the buying of land and various other enterprises, showed that the ex-slave was handling some free capital already. The chief initial source of this was labor in the army, and his pay and bounty as a soldier. Payments to Negro soldiers were at first complicated by the ignorance of the recipients, and the fact that the quotas of colored regiments from Northern States were largely filled by recruits from the South, unknown to their fellow soldiers. Consequently, payments were accompanied by such frauds that Congress, by joint resolution in 1867, put the whole matter in the hands of the Freedmen's Bureau. In two years six million dollars was thus distributed to five thousand claimants, and in the end the sum exceeded eight million dollars. Even in this system fraud was frequent; but still the work put needed capital in the hands of practical paupers, and some, at least, was well spent.

The most perplexing and least successful part of the Bureau's work lay in the exercise of its judicial functions. The regular Bureau court consisted of one representative of the employer, one of the Negro, and one of the Bureau. If the Bureau could have maintained a perfectly judicial attitude, this arrangement would have been ideal, and must in time have gained confidence; but the nature of its other activities and the character of its personnel prejudiced the Bureau in favor of the black litigants, and led without doubt to much injustice and annoyance. On the other hand, to leave the Negro in the hands of Southern courts was impossible. In a distracted land where slavery had hardly fallen, to keep the strong from wanton abuse of the weak, and the weak from gloating insolently over the half-shorn strength of the strong, was a thankless, hopeless task. The former masters of the land were peremp-

torily ordered about, seized, and imprisoned, and punished over and again, with scant courtesy from army officers. The former slaves were intimidated, beaten, raped, and butchered by angry and revengeful men. Bureau courts tended to become centres simply for punishing whites, while the regular civil courts tended to become solely institutions for perpetuating the slavery of blacks. Almost every law and method ingenuity could devise was employed by the legislatures to reduce the Negroes to serfdom,—to make them the slaves of the State, if not of individual owners; while the Bureau officials too often were found striving to put the "bottom rail on top," and give the freedmen a power and independence which they could not yet use. It is all well enough for us of another generation to wax wise with advice to those who bore the burden in the heat of the day. It is full easy now to see that the man who lost home, fortune, and family at a stroke, and saw his land ruled by "mules and niggers," was really benefited by the passing of slavery. It is not difficult now to say to the young freedman, cheated and cuffed about, who has seen his father's head beaten to a jelly and his own mother namelessly assaulted, that the meek shall inherit the earth. Above all, nothing is more convenient than to heap on the Freedmen's Bureau all the evils of that evil day, and damn it utterly for every mistake and blunder that was made.

All this is easy, but it is neither sensible nor just. Some one had blundered, but that was long before Oliver Howard was born; there was criminal aggression and heedless neglect, but without some system of control there would have been far more than there was. Had that control been from within, the Negro would have been re-enslaved, to all intents and purposes. Coming as the control did from without, perfect men and methods would have bettered all things; and even with imperfect agents and questionable methods, the work accomplished was not undeserving of commendation.

Such was the dawn of Freedom; such was the work of the Freedmen's Bureau, which, summed up in brief, may be epitomized thus: For some fifteen million dollars, beside the sums spent before 1865, and the dole of benevolent societies, this Bureau set going a system of free labor, established a beginning of peasant proprietorship, secured the recognition of black freedmen before courts of law, and founded the free common school in the South. On the other hand, it failed to begin the establishment of good-will between ex-masters and freedmen, to guard its work wholly from paternalistic methods which discouraged self-reliance, and to carry out to any considerable extent its implied promises to furnish the freedmen with land. Its successes were the result of hard work, supplemented by the aid of philanthropists and

the eager striving of black men. Its failures were the result of bad local agents, the inherent difficulties of the work, and national neglect.

Such an institution, from its wide powers, great responsibilities, large control of moneys, and generally conspicuous position, was naturally open to repeated and bitter attack. It sustained a searching Congressional investigation at the instance of Fernando Wood in 1870. Its archives and few remaining functions were with blunt discourtesy transferred from Howard's control, in his absence, to the supervision of Secretary of War Belknap in 1872, on the Secretary's recommendation. Finally, in consequence of grave intimations of wrong-doing made by the Secretary and his subordinates, General Howard was court-martialed in 1874. In both of these trials the Commissioner of the Freedmen's Bureau was officially exonerated from any wilful misdoing, and his work commended. Nevertheless, many unpleasant things were brought to light,—the methods of transacting the business of the Bureau were faulty; several cases of defalcation were proved, and other frauds strongly suspected; there were some business transactions which savored of dangerous speculation, if not dishonesty; and around it all lay the smirch of the Freedmen's Bank.

Morally and practically, the Freedmen's Bank was part of the Freedmen's Bureau, although it had no legal connection with it. With the prestige of the government back of it, and a directing board of unusual respectability and national reputation, this banking institution had made a remarkable start in the development of that thrift among black folk which slavery had kept them from knowing. Then in one sad day came the crash,—all the hard-earned dollars of the freedmen disappeared; but that was the least of the loss,—all the faith in saving went too, and much of the faith in men; and that was a loss that a Nation which to-day sneers at Negro shiftlessness has never yet made good. Not even ten additional years of slavery could have done so much to throttle the thrift of the freedmen as the mismanagement and bankruptcy of the series of savings banks chartered by the Nation for their especial aid. Where all the blame should rest, it is hard to say; whether the Bureau and the Bank died chiefly by reason of the blows of its selfish friends or the dark machinations of its foes, perhaps even time will never reveal for here lies unwritten history.

Of the foes without the Bureau, the bitterest were those who attacked not so much its conduct or policy under the law as the necessity for any such institution at all. Such attacks came primarily from the Border States and the South; and they were summed up by Senator Davis, of Kentucky, when he

moved to entitle the act of 1866 a bill "to promote strife and conflict between the white and black races . . . by a grant of unconstitutional power." The argument gathered tremendous strength South and North; but its very strength was its weakness. For, argued the plain common-sense of the nation, if it is unconstitutional, unpractical, and futile for the nation to stand guardian over its helpless wards, then there is left but one alternative,—to make those wards their own guardians by arming them with the ballot. Moreover, the path of the practical politician pointed the same way; for, argued this opportunist, if we cannot peacefully reconstruct the South with white votes, we certainly can with black votes. So justice and force joined hands.

The alternative thus offered the nation was not between full and restricted Negro suffrage; else every sensible man, black and white, would easily have chosen the latter. It was rather a choice between suffrage and slavery, after endless blood and gold had flowed to sweep human bondage away. Not a single Southern legislature stood ready to admit a Negro, under any conditions, to the polls; not a single Southern legislature believed free Negro labor was possible without a system of restrictions that took all its freedom away; there was scarcely a white man in the South who did not honestly regard Emancipation as a crime, and its practical nullification as a duty. In such a situation, the granting of the ballot to the black man was a necessity, the very least a guilty nation could grant a wronged race, and the only method of compelling the South to accept the results of the war. Thus Negro suffrage ended a civil war by beginning a race feud. And some felt gratitude toward the race thus sacrificed in its swaddling clothes on the altar of national integrity; and some felt and feel only indifference and contempt.

Had political exigencies been less pressing, the opposition to government guardianship of Negroes less bitter, and the attachment to the slave system less strong, the social seer can well imagine a far better policy,—a permanent Freedmen's Bureau, with a national system of Negro schools; a carefully supervised employment and labor office; a system of impartial protection before the regular courts; and such institutions for social betterment as savings-banks, land and building associations, and social settlements. All this vast expenditure of money and brains might have formed a great school of prospective citizenship, and solved in a way we have not yet solved the most perplexing and persistent of the Negro problems.

That such an institution was unthinkable in 1870 was due in part to certain acts of the Freedmen's Bureau itself. It came to regard its work as mere-

ly temporary, and Negro suffrage as a final answer to all present perplexities. The political ambition of many of its agents and protégés led it far afield into questionable activities, until the South, nursing its own deep prejudices, came easily to ignore all the good deeds of the Bureau and hate its very name with perfect hatred. So the Freedmen's Bureau died, and its child was the Fifteenth Amendment.

The passing of a great human institution before its work is done, like the untimely passing of a single soul, but leaves a legacy of striving for other men. The legacy of the Freedmen's Bureau is the heavy heritage of this generation. To-day, when new and vaster problems are destined to strain every fibre of the national mind and soul, would it not be well to count this legacy honestly and carefully? For this much all men know: despite compromise, war, and struggle, the Negro is not free. In the backwoods of the Gulf States, for miles and miles, he may not leave the plantation of his birth; in well-nigh the whole rural South the black farmers are peons, bound by law and custom to an economic slavery, from which the only escape is death or the penitentiary. In the most cultured sections and cities of the South the Negroes are a segregated servile caste, with restricted rights and privileges. Before the courts, both in law and custom, they stand on a different and peculiar basis. Taxation without representation is the rule of their political life. And the result of all this is, and in nature must have been, lawlessness and crime. That is the large legacy of the Freedmen's Bureau, the work it did not do because it could not.

I have seen a land right merry with the sun, where children sing, and rolling hills lie like passioned women wanton with harvest. And there in the King's Highway sat and sits a figure veiled and bowed, by which the traveller's footsteps hasten as they go. On the tainted air broods fear. Three centuries' thought has been the raising and unveiling of that bowed human heart, and now behold a century new for the duty and the deed. The problem of the Twentieth Century is the problem of the color-line.

III

OF MR. BOOKER T. WASHINGTON AND OTHERS

From birth till death enslaved; in word, in deed, unmanned!

* * * * * * * * * *

Hereditary bondsmen! Know ye not
Who would be free themselves must strike the blow?
<div align="right">Byron.</div>

E ASILY the most striking thing in the history of the American Negro
since 1876 is the ascendancy of Mr. Booker T. Washington. It began at
the time when war memories and ideals were rapidly passing; a day of aston-
ishing commercial development was dawning; a sense of doubt and hesita-
tion overtook the freedmen's sons,—then it was that his leading began. Mr.
Washington came, with a simple definite programme, at the psychological
moment when the nation was a little ashamed of having bestowed so much
sentiment on Negroes, and was concentrating its energies on Dollars. His
programme of industrial education, conciliation of the South, and submis-
sion and silence as to civil and political rights, was not wholly original; the
Free Negroes from 1830 up to war-time had striven to build industrial
schools, and the American Missionary Association had from the first taught
various trades; and Price and others had sought a way of honorable alliance
with the best of the Southerners. But Mr. Washington first indissolubly
linked these things; he put enthusiasm, unlimited energy, and perfect faith
into this programme, and changed it from a by-path into a veritable Way of
Life. And the tale of the methods by which he did this is a fascinating study
of human life.

It startled the nation to hear a Negro advocating such a programme after
many decades of bitter complaint; it startled and won the applause of the
South, it interested and won the admiration of the North; and after a confused
murmur of protest, it silenced if it did not convert the Negroes themselves.

To gain the sympathy and coöperation of the various elements compris-
ing the white South was Mr. Washington's first task; and this, at the time
Tuskegee was founded, seemed, for a black man, well-nigh impossible. And
yet ten years later it was done in the word spoken at Atlanta: "In all things
purely social we can be as separate as the five fingers, and yet one as the hand

in all things essential to mutual progress." This "Atlanta Compromise" is by all odds the most notable thing in Mr. Washington's career. The South interpreted it in different ways: the radicals received it as a complete surrender of the demand for civil and political equality; the conservatives, as a generously conceived working basis for mutual understanding. So both approved it, and to-day its author is certainly the most distinguished Southerner since Jefferson Davis and the one with the largest personal following.

Next to this achievement comes Mr. Washington's work in gaining place and consideration in the North. Others less shrewd and tactful had formerly essayed to sit on these two stools and had fallen between them; but as Mr. Washington knew the heart of the South from birth and training, so by singular insight he intuitively grasped the spirit of the age which was dominating the North. And so thoroughly did he learn the speech and thought of triumphant commercialism, and the ideals of material prosperity, that the picture of a lone black boy poring over a French grammar amid the weeds and dirt of a neglected home soon seemed to him the acme of absurdities. One wonders what Socrates and St. Francis of Assisi would say to this.

And yet this very singleness of vision and thorough oneness with his age is a mark of the successful man. It is as though Nature must needs make men narrow in order to give them force. So Mr. Washington's cult has gained unquestioning followers, his work has wonderfully prospered, his friends are legion, and his enemies are confounded. To-day he stands as the one recognized spokesman of his ten million fellows, and one of the most notable figures in a nation of seventy millions. One hesitates, therefore, to criticise a life which, beginning with so little, has done so much. And yet the time is come when one may speak in all sincerity and utter courtesy of the mistakes and shortcomings of Mr. Washington's career, as well as of his triumphs, without being thought captious or envious, and without forgetting that it is easier to do ill than well in the world.

The criticism that has hitherto met Mr. Washington has not always been of this broad character. In the South especially has he had to walk warily to avoid the harshest judgments,—and naturally so, for he is dealing with the one subject of deepest sensitiveness to that section. Twice—once when at the Chicago celebration of the Spanish-American War he alluded to the color-prejudice that is "eating away the vitals of the South," and once when he dined with President Roosevelt—has the resulting Southern criticism been violent enough to threaten seriously his popularity. In the North the feeling has several times forced itself into words, that Mr. Washington's counsels of

submission overlooked certain elements of true manhood, and that his educational programme was unnecessarily narrow. Usually, however, such criticism has not found open expression, although, too, the spiritual sons of the Abolitionists have not been prepared to acknowledge that the schools founded before Tuskegee, by men of broad ideals and self-sacrificing spirit, were wholly failures or worthy of ridicule. While, then, criticism has not failed to follow Mr. Washington, yet the prevailing public opinion of the land has been but too willing to deliver the solution of a wearisome problem into his hands, and say, "If that is all you and your race ask, take it."

Among his own people, however, Mr. Washington has encountered the strongest and most lasting opposition, amounting at times to bitterness, and even to-day continuing strong and insistent even though largely silenced in outward expression by the public opinion of the nation. Some of this opposition is, of course, mere envy; the disappointment of displaced demagogues and the spite of narrow minds. But aside from this, there is among educated and thoughtful colored men in all parts of the land a feeling of deep regret, sorrow, and apprehension at the wide currency and ascendancy which some of Mr. Washington's theories have gained. These same men admire his sincerity of purpose, and are willing to forgive much to honest endeavor which is doing something worth the doing. They cooperate with Mr. Washington as far as they conscientiously can; and, indeed, it is no ordinary tribute to this man's tact and power that, steering as he must between so many diverse interests and opinions, he so largely retains the respect of all.

But the hushing of the criticism of honest opponents is a dangerous thing. It leads some of the best of the critics to unfortunate silence and paralysis of effort, and others to burst into speech so passionately and intemperately as to lose listeners. Honest and earnest criticism from those whose interests are most nearly touched,—criticism of writers by readers, of government by those governed, of leaders by those led,—this is the soul of democracy and the safeguard of modern society. If the best of the American Negroes receive by outer pressure a leader whom they had not recognized before, manifestly there is here a certain palpable gain. Yet there is also irreparable loss,—a loss of that peculiarly valuable education which a group receives when by search and criticism it finds and commissions its own leaders. The way in which this is done is at once the most elementary and the nicest problem of social growth. History is but the record of such group-leadership; and yet how infinitely changeful is its type and character! And of all types and kinds, what can be more instructive than the leadership of a group within a group?—that

curious double movement where real progress may be negative and actual advance be relative retrogression. All this is the social student's inspiration and despair.

Now in the past the American Negro has had instructive experience in the choosing of group leaders, founding thus a peculiar dynasty which in the light of present conditions is worth while studying. When sticks and stones and beasts form the sole environment of a people, their attitude is largely one of determined opposition to and conquest of natural forces. But when to earth and brute is added an environment of men and ideas, then the attitude of the imprisoned group may take three main forms,—a feeling of revolt and revenge; an attempt to adjust all thought and action to the will of the greater group; or, finally, a determined effort at self-realization and self-development despite environing opinion. The influence of all of these attitudes at various times can be traced in the history of the American Negro, and in the evolution of his successive leaders.

Before 1750, while the fire of African freedom still burned in the veins of the slaves, there was in all leadership or attempted leadership but the one motive of revolt and revenge,—typified in the terrible Maroons, the Danish blacks, and Cato of Stono, and veiling all the Americas in fear of insurrection. The liberalizing tendencies of the latter half of the eighteenth century brought, along with kindlier relations between black and white, thoughts of ultimate adjustment and assimilation. Such aspiration was especially voiced in the earnest songs of Phyllis, in the martyrdom of Attucks, the fighting of Salem and Poor, the intellectual accomplishments of Banneker and Derham, and the political demands of the Cuffes.

Stern financial and social stress after the war cooled much of the previous humanitarian ardor. The disappointment and impatience of the Negroes at the persistence of slavery and serfdom voiced itself in two movements. The slaves in the South, aroused undoubtedly by vague rumors of the Haytian revolt, made three fierce attempts at insurrection,—in 1800 under Gabriel in Virginia, in 1822 under Vesey in Carolina, and in 1831 again in Virginia under the terrible Nat Turner. In the Free States, on the other hand, a new and curious attempt at self-development was made. In Philadelphia and New York color-prescription led to a withdrawal of Negro communicants from white churches and the formation of a peculiar socio-religious institution among the Negroes known as the African Church,—an organization still living and controlling in its various branches over a million of men.

Walker's wild appeal against the trend of the times showed how the world

was changing after the coming of the cotton-gin. By 1830 slavery seemed hopelessly fastened on the South, and the slaves thoroughly cowed into submission. The free Negroes of the North, inspired by the mulatto immigrants from the West Indies, began to change the basis of their demands; they recognized the slavery of slaves, but insisted that they themselves were freemen, and sought assimilation and amalgamation with the nation on the same terms with other men. Thus, Forten and Purvis of Philadelphia, Shad of Wilmington, Du Bois of New Haven, Barbadoes of Boston, and others, strove singly and together as men, they said, not as slaves; as "people of color," not as "Negroes." The trend of the times, however, refused them recognition save in individual and exceptional cases, considered them as one with all the despised blacks, and they soon found themselves striving to keep even the rights they formerly had of voting and working and moving as freemen. Schemes of migration and colonization arose among them; but these they refused to entertain, and they eventually turned to the Abolition movement as a final refuge.

Here, led by Remond, Nell, Wells-Brown, and Douglass, a new period of self-assertion and self-development dawned. To be sure, ultimate freedom and assimilation was the ideal before the leaders, but the assertion of the manhood rights of the Negro by himself was the main reliance, and John Brown's raid was the extreme of its logic. After the war and emancipation, the great form of Frederick Douglass, the greatest of American Negro leaders, still led the host. Self-assertion, especially in political lines, was the main programme, and behind Douglass came Elliot, Bruce, and Langston, and the Reconstruction politicians, and, less conspicuous but of greater social significance Alexander Crummell and Bishop Daniel Payne.

Then came the Revolution of 1876, the suppression of the Negro votes, the changing and shifting of ideals, and the seeking of new lights in the great night. Douglass, in his old age, still bravely stood for the ideals of his early manhood,—ultimate assimilation through self-assertion, and on no other terms. For a time Price arose as a new leader, destined, it seemed, not to give up, but to re-state the old ideals in a form less repugnant to the white South. But he passed away in his prime. Then came the new leader. Nearly all the former ones had become leaders by the silent suffrage of their fellows, had sought to lead their own people alone, and were usually, save Douglass, little known outside their race. But Booker T. Washington arose as essentially the leader not of one race but of two,—a compromiser between the South, the North, and the Negro. Naturally the Negroes resented, at first bitterly, signs

of compromise which surrendered their civil and political rights, even though this was to be exchanged for larger chances of economic development. The rich and dominating North, however, was not only weary of the race problem, but was investing largely in Southern enterprises, and welcomed any method of peaceful coöperation. Thus, by national opinion, the Negroes began to recognize Mr. Washington's leadership; and the voice of criticism was hushed.

Mr. Washington represents in Negro thought the old attitude of adjustment and submission; but adjustment at such a peculiar time as to make his programme unique. This is an age of unusual economic development, and Mr. Washington's programme naturally takes an economic cast, becoming a gospel of Work and Money to such an extent as apparently almost completely to overshadow the higher aims of life. Moreover, this is an age when the more advanced races are coming in closer contact with the less developed races, and the race-feeling is therefore intensified; and Mr. Washington's programme practically accepts the alleged inferiority of the Negro races. Again, in our own land, the reaction from the sentiment of war time has given impetus to race-prejudice against Negroes, and Mr. Washington withdraws many of the high demands of Negroes as men and American citizens. In other periods of intensified prejudice all the Negro's tendency to self-assertion has been called forth; at this period a policy of submission is advocated. In the history of nearly all other races and peoples the doctrine preached at such crises has been that manly self-respect is worth more than lands and houses, and that a people who voluntarily surrender such respect, or cease striving for it, are not worth civilizing.

In answer to this, it has been claimed that the Negro can survive only through submission. Mr. Washington distinctly asks that black people give up, at least for the present, three things,—

First, political power,

Second, insistence on civil rights,

Third, higher education of Negro youth,—

and concentrate all their energies on industrial education, the accumulation of wealth, and the conciliation of the South. This policy has been courageously and insistently advocated for over fifteen years, and has been triumphant for perhaps ten years. As a result of this tender of the palm-branch, what has been the return? In these years there have occurred:

1. The disfranchisement of the Negro.

2. The legal creation of a distinct status of civil inferiority for the Negro.

3. The steady withdrawal of aid from institutions for the higher training of the Negro.

These movements are not, to be sure, direct results of Mr. Washington's teachings; but his propaganda has, without a shadow of doubt, helped their speedier accomplishment. The question then comes: Is it possible, and probable, that nine millions of men can make effective progress in economic lines if they are deprived of political rights, made a servile caste, and allowed only the most meagre chance for developing their exceptional men? If history and reason give any distinct answer to these questions, it is an emphatic No. And Mr. Washington thus faces the triple paradox of his career:

> 1. He is striving nobly to make Negro artisans business men and property-owners; but it is utterly impossible, under modern competitive methods, for workingmen and property-owners to defend their rights and exist without the right of suffrage.
> 2. He insists on thrift and self-respect, but at the same time counsels a silent submission to civic inferiority such as is bound to sap the manhood of any race in the long run.
> 3. He advocates common-school and industrial training, and depreciates institutions of higher learning; but neither the Negro common-schools, nor Tuskegee itself, could remain open a day were it not for teachers trained in Negro colleges, or trained by their graduates.

This triple paradox in Mr. Washington's position is the object of criticism by two classes of colored Americans. One class is spiritually descended from Toussaint the Savior, through Gabriel, Vesey, and Turner, and they represent the attitude of revolt and revenge; they hate the white South blindly and distrust the white race generally, and so far as they agree on definite action, think that the Negro's only hope lies in emigration beyond the borders of the United States. And yet, by the irony of fate, nothing has more effectually made this programme seem hopeless than the recent course of the United States toward weaker and darker peoples in the West Indies, Hawaii, and the Philippines,—for where in the world may we go and be safe from lying and brute force?

The other class of Negroes who cannot agree with Mr. Washington has hitherto said little aloud. They deprecate the sight of scattered counsels, of

internal disagreement; and especially they dislike making their just criticism of a useful and earnest man an excuse for a general discharge of venom from small-minded opponents. Nevertheless, the questions involved are so fundamental and serious that it is difficult to see how men like the Grimkes, Kelly Miller, J.W.E. Bowen, and other representatives of this group, can much longer be silent. Such men feel in conscience bound to ask of this nation three things:

1. The right to vote.
2. Civic equality.
3. The education of youth according to ability.

They acknowledge Mr. Washington's invaluable service in counselling patience and courtesy in such demands; they do not ask that ignorant black men vote when ignorant whites are debarred, or that any reasonable restrictions in the suffrage should not be applied; they know that the low social level of the mass of the race is responsible for much discrimination against it, but they also know, and the nation knows, that relentless color-prejudice is more often a cause than a result of the Negro's degradation; they seek the abatement of this relic of barbarism, and not its systematic encouragement and pampering by all agencies of social power from the Associated Press to the Church of Christ. They advocate, with Mr. Washington, a broad system of Negro common schools supplemented by thorough industrial training; but they are surprised that a man of Mr. Washington's insight cannot see that no such educational system ever has rested or can rest on any other basis than that of the well-equipped college and university, and they insist that there is a demand for a few such institutions throughout the South to train the best of the Negro youth as teachers, professional men, and leaders.

This group of men honor Mr. Washington for his attitude of conciliation toward the white South; they accept the "Atlanta Compromise" in its broadest interpretation; they recognize, with him, many signs of promise, many men of high purpose and fair judgment, in this section; they know that no easy task has been laid upon a region already tottering under heavy burdens. But, nevertheless, they insist that the way to truth and right lies in straightforward honesty, not in indiscriminate flattery; in praising those of the South who do well and criticising uncompromisingly those who do ill; in taking advantage of the opportunities at hand and urging their fellows to do the same, but at the same time in remembering that only a firm adherence to their higher ideals and aspirations will ever keep those ideals within the realm of possibility. They do not expect that the free right to vote, to enjoy civic

rights, and to be educated, will come in a moment; they do not expect to see the bias and prejudices of years disappear at the blast of a trumpet; but they are absolutely certain that the way for a people to gain their reasonable rights is not by voluntarily throwing them away and insisting that they do not want them; that the way for a people to gain respect is not by continually belittling and ridiculing themselves; that, on the contrary, Negroes must insist continually, in season and out of season, that voting is necessary to modern manhood, that color discrimination is barbarism, and that black boys need education as well as white boys.

In failing thus to state plainly and unequivocally the legitimate demands of their people, even at the cost of opposing an honored leader, the thinking classes of American Negroes would shirk a heavy responsibility,—a responsibility to themselves, a responsibility to the struggling masses, a responsibility to the darker races of men whose future depends so largely on this American experiment, but especially a responsibility to this nation,—this common Fatherland. It is wrong to encourage a man or a people in evildoing; it is wrong to aid and abet a national crime simply because it is unpopular not to do so. The growing spirit of kindliness and reconciliation between the North and South after the frightful differences of a generation ago ought to be a source of deep congratulation to all, and especially to those whose mistreatment caused the war; but if that reconciliation is to be marked by the industrial slavery and civic death of those same black men, with permanent legislation into a position of inferiority, then those black men, if they are really men, are called upon by every consideration of patriotism and loyalty to oppose such a course by all civilized methods, even though such opposition involves disagreement with Mr. Booker T. Washington. We have no right to sit silently by while the inevitable seeds are sown for a harvest of disaster to our children, black and white.

First, it is the duty of black men to judge the South discriminatingly. The present generation of Southerners are not responsible for the past, and they should not be blindly hated or blamed for it. Furthermore, to no class is the indiscriminate endorsement of the recent course of the South toward Negroes more nauseating than to the best thought of the South. The South is not "solid"; it is a land in the ferment of social change, wherein forces of all kinds are fighting for supremacy; and to praise the ill the South is to-day perpetrating is just as wrong as to condemn the good. Discriminating and broad-minded criticism is what the South needs,—needs it for the sake of her own white sons and daughters, and for the insurance of robust, healthy

mental and moral development.

To-day even the attitude of the Southern whites toward the blacks is not, as so many assume, in all cases the same; the ignorant Southerner hates the Negro, the workingmen fear his competition, the money-makers wish to use him as a laborer, some of the educated see a menace in his upward development, while others—usually the sons of the masters—wish to help him to rise. National opinion has enabled this last class to maintain the Negro common schools, and to protect the Negro partially in property, life, and limb. Through the pressure of the money-makers the Negro is in danger of being reduced to semi-slavery, especially in the country districts; the workingmen, and those of the educated who fear the Negro, have united to disfranchise him, and some have urged his deportation; while the passions of the ignorant are easily aroused to lynch and abuse any black man. To praise this intricate whirl of thought and prejudice is nonsense; to inveigh indiscriminately against "the South" is unjust; but to use the same breath in praising Governor Aycock, exposing Senator Morgan, arguing with Mr. Thomas Nelson Page, and denouncing Senator Ben Tillman, is not only sane, but the imperative duty of thinking black men.

It would be unjust to Mr. Washington not to acknowledge that in several instances he has opposed movements in the South which were unjust to the Negro; he sent memorials to the Louisiana and Alabama constitutional conventions, he has spoken against lynching, and in other ways has openly or silently set his influence against sinister schemes and unfortunate happenings. Notwithstanding this, it is equally true to assert that on the whole the distinct impression left by Mr. Washington's propaganda is, first, that the South is justified in its present attitude toward the Negro because of the Negro's degradation; secondly, that the prime cause of the Negro's failure to rise more quickly is his wrong education in the past; and, thirdly, that his future rise depends primarily on his own efforts. Each of these propositions is a dangerous half-truth. The supplementary truths must never be lost sight of: first, slavery and race-prejudice are potent if not sufficient causes of the Negro's position; second, industrial and common-school training were necessarily slow in planting because they had to await the black teachers trained by higher institutions,—it being extremely doubtful if any essentially different development was possible, and certainly a Tuskegee was unthinkable before 1880; and, third, while it is a great truth to say that the Negro must strive and strive mightily to help himself, it is equally true that unless his striving be not simply seconded, but rather aroused and encouraged, by the initiative

of the richer and wiser environing group, he cannot hope for great success.

In his failure to realize and impress this last point, Mr. Washington is especially to be criticised. His doctrine has tended to make the whites, North and South, shift the burden of the Negro problem to the Negro's shoulders and stand aside as critical and rather pessimistic spectators; when in fact the burden belongs to the nation, and the hands of none of us are clean if we bend not our energies to righting these great wrongs.

The South ought to be led, by candid and honest criticism, to assert her better self and do her full duty to the race she has cruelly wronged and is still wronging. The North—her co-partner in guilt—cannot salve her conscience by plastering it with gold. We cannot settle this problem by diplomacy and suaveness, by "policy" alone. If worse come to worst, can the moral fibre of this country survive the slow throttling and murder of nine millions of men?

The black men of America have a duty to perform, a duty stern and delicate,—a forward movement to oppose a part of the work of their greatest leader. So far as Mr. Washington preaches Thrift, Patience, and Industrial Training for the masses, we must hold up his hands and strive with him, rejoicing in his honors and glorying in the strength of this Joshua called of God and of man to lead the headless host. But so far as Mr. Washington apologizes for injustice, North or South, does not rightly value the privilege and duty of voting, belittles the emasculating effects of caste distinctions, and opposes the higher training and ambition of our brighter minds,—so far as he, the South, or the Nation, does this,—we must unceasingly and firmly oppose them. By every civilized and peaceful method we must strive for the rights which the world accords to men, clinging unwaveringly to those great words which the sons of the Fathers would fain forget: "We hold these truths to be self-evident: That all men are created equal; that they are endowed by their Creator with certain unalienable rights; that among these are life, liberty, and the pursuit of happiness."

IV

OF THE MEANING OF PROGRESS

Willst Du Deine Macht verkünden,
Wähle sie die frei von Sünden,

Steh'n in Deinem ew'gen Haus!
Deine Geister sende aus!
Die Unsterblichen, die Reinen,
Die nicht fühlen, die nicht weinen!
Nicht die zarte Jungfrau wähle,
Nicht der Hirtin weiche Seele!

Schiller.

ONCE upon a time I taught school in the hills of Tennessee, where the broad dark vale of the Mississippi begins to roll and crumple to greet the Alleghanies. I was a Fisk student then, and all Fisk men thought that Tennessee—beyond the Veil—was theirs alone, and in vacation time they sallied forth in lusty bands to meet the county school-commissioners. Young and happy, I too went, and I shall not soon forget that summer, seventeen years ago.

First, there was a Teachers' Institute at the county-seat; and there distinguished guests of the superintendent taught the teachers fractions and spelling and other mysteries,—white teachers in the morning, Negroes at night. A picnic now and then, and a supper, and the rough world was softened by laughter and song. I remember how— But I wander.

There came a day when all the teachers left the Institute and began the hunt for schools. I learn from hearsay (for my mother was mortally afraid of fire-arms) that the hunting of ducks and bears and men is wonderfully interesting, but I am sure that the man who has never hunted a country school has something to learn of the pleasures of the chase. I see now the white, hot roads lazily rise and fall and wind before me under the burning July sun; I feel the deep weariness of heart and limb as ten, eight, six miles stretch relentlessly ahead; I feel my heart sink heavily as I hear again and again, "Got a teacher? Yes." So I walked on and on—horses were too expensive—until I had wandered beyond railways, beyond stage lines, to a land of "varmints" and rattlesnakes, where the coming of a stranger was an event, and men lived

and died in the shadow of one blue hill.

Sprinkled over hill and dale lay cabins and farmhouses, shut out from the world by the forests and the rolling hills toward the east. There I found at last a little school. Josie told me of it; she was a thin, homely girl of twenty, with a dark-brown face and thick, hard hair. I had crossed the stream at Watertown, and rested under the great willows; then I had gone to the little cabin in the lot where Josie was resting on her way to town. The gaunt farmer made me welcome, and Josie, hearing my errand, told me anxiously that they wanted a school over the hill; that but once since the war had a teacher been there; that she herself longed to learn,—and thus she ran on, talking fast and loud, with much earnestness and energy.

Next morning I crossed the tall round hill, lingered to look at the blue and yellow mountains stretching toward the Carolinas, then plunged into the wood, and came out at Josie's home. It was a dull frame cottage with four rooms, perched just below the brow of the hill, amid peach-trees. The father was a quiet simple soul, calmly ignorant, with no touch of vulgarity. The mother was different,—strong, bustling, and energetic, with a quick, restless tongue, and an ambition to live "like folks." There was a crowd of children. Two boys had gone away. There remained two growing girls; a shy midget of eight; John, tall, awkward, and eighteen; Jim, younger, quicker, and better looking; and two babies of indefinite age. Then there was Josie herself. She seemed to be the centre of the family: always busy at service, or at home, or berry-picking; a little nervous and inclined to scold, like her mother, yet faithful, too, like her father. She had about her a certain fineness, the shadow of an unconscious moral heroism that would willingly give all of life to make life broader, deeper, and fuller for her and hers. I saw much of this family afterwards, and grew to love them for their honest efforts to be decent and comfortable, and for their knowledge of their own ignorance. There was with them no affectation. The mother would scold the father for being so "easy"; Josie would roundly berate the boys for carelessness; and all knew that it was a hard thing to dig a living out of a rocky side-hill.

I secured the school. I remember the day I rode horseback out to the commissioner's house with a pleasant young white fellow who wanted the white school. The road ran down the bed of a stream; the sun laughed and the water jingled, and we rode on. "Come in," said the commissioner,— "come in. Have a seat. Yes, that certificate will do. Stay to dinner. What do you want a month?" "Oh," thought I, "this is lucky"; but even then fell the awful shadow of the Veil, for they ate first, then I—alone.

The schoolhouse was a log hut, where Colonel Wheeler used to shelter his corn. It sat in a lot behind a rail fence and thorn bushes, near the sweetest of springs. There was an entrance where a door once was, and within, a massive rickety fireplace; great chinks between the logs served as windows. Furniture was scarce. A pale blackboard crouched in the corner. My desk was made of three boards, reinforced at critical points, and my chair, borrowed from the landlady, had to be returned every night. Seats for the children— these puzzled me much. I was haunted by a New England vision of neat little desks and chairs, but, alas! the reality was rough plank benches without backs, and at times without legs. They had the one virtue of making naps dangerous,—possibly fatal, for the floor was not to be trusted.

It was a hot morning late in July when the school opened. I trembled when I heard the patter of little feet down the dusty road, and saw the growing row of dark solemn faces and bright eager eyes facing me. First came Josie and her brothers and sisters. The longing to know, to be a student in the great school at Nashville, hovered like a star above this child-woman amid her work and worry, and she studied doggedly. There were the Dowells from their farm over toward Alexandria,—Fanny, with her smooth black face and wondering eyes; Martha, brown and dull; the pretty girl—wife of a brother, and the younger brood.

There were the Burkes,—two brown and yellow lads, and a tiny haughty-eyed girl. Fat Reuben's little chubby girl came, with golden face and old-gold hair, faithful and solemn. 'Thenie was on hand early,—a jolly, ugly, good-hearted girl, who slyly dipped snuff and looked after her little bow-legged brother. When her mother could spare her, 'Tildy came,—a midnight beauty, with starry eyes and tapering limbs; and her brother, correspondingly homely. And then the big boys,—the hulking Lawrences; the lazy Neills, unfathered sons of mother and daughter; Hickman, with a stoop in his shoulders; and the rest.

There they sat, nearly thirty of them, on the rough benches, their faces shading from a pale cream to a deep brown, the little feet bare and swinging, the eyes full of expectation, with here and there a twinkle of mischief, and the hands grasping Webster's blue-back spelling-book. I loved my school, and the fine faith the children had in the wisdom of their teacher was truly marvellous. We read and spelled together, wrote a little, picked flowers, sang, and listened to stories of the world beyond the hill. At times the school would dwindle away, and I would start out. I would visit Mun Eddings, who lived in two very dirty rooms, and ask why little Lugene, whose flaming face

seemed ever ablaze with the dark-red hair uncombed, was absent all last week, or why I missed so often the inimitable rags of Mack and Ed. Then the father, who worked Colonel Wheeler's farm on shares, would tell me how the crops needed the boys; and the thin, slovenly mother, whose face was pretty when washed, assured me that Lugene must mind the baby. "But we'll start them again next week." When the Lawrences stopped, I knew that the doubts of the old folks about book-learning had conquered again, and so, toiling up the hill, and getting as far into the cabin as possible, I put Cicero "pro Archia Poeta" into the simplest English with local applications, and usually convinced them—for a week or so.

On Friday nights I often went home with some of the children,—sometimes to Doc Burke's farm. He was a great, loud, thin Black, ever working, and trying to buy the seventy-five acres of hill and dale where he lived; but people said that he would surely fail, and the "white folks would get it all." His wife was a magnificent Amazon, with saffron face and shining hair, uncorseted and barefooted, and the children were strong and beautiful. They lived in a one-and-a-half-room cabin in the hollow of the farm, near the spring. The front room was full of great fat white beds, scrupulously neat; and there were bad chromos on the walls, and a tired centre-table. In the tiny back kitchen I was often invited to "take out and help" myself to fried chicken and wheat biscuit, "meat" and corn pone, string-beans and berries. At first I used to be a little alarmed at the approach of bedtime in the one lone bedroom, but embarrassment was very deftly avoided. First, all the children nodded and slept, and were stowed away in one great pile of goose feathers; next, the mother and the father discreetly slipped away to the kitchen while I went to bed; then, blowing out the dim light, they retired in the dark. In the morning all were up and away before I thought of awaking. Across the road, where fat Reuben lived, they all went outdoors while the teacher retired, because they did not boast the luxury of a kitchen.

I liked to stay with the Dowells, for they had four rooms and plenty of good country fare. Uncle Bird had a small, rough farm, all woods and hills, miles from the big road; but he was full of tales,—he preached now and then,—and with his children, berries, horses, and wheat he was happy and prosperous. Often, to keep the peace, I must go where life was less lovely; for instance, 'Tildy's mother was incorrigibly dirty, Reuben's larder was limited seriously, and herds of untamed insects wandered over the Eddingses' beds. Best of all I loved to go to Josie's, and sit on the porch, eating peaches, while the mother bustled and talked: how Josie had bought the sewing-machine;

how Josie worked at service in winter, but that four dollars a month was "mighty little" wages; how Josie longed to go away to school, but that it "looked like" they never could get far enough ahead to let her; how the crops failed and the well was yet unfinished; and, finally, how "mean" some of the white folks were.

For two summers I lived in this little world; it was dull and humdrum. The girls looked at the hill in wistful longing, and the boys fretted and haunted Alexandria. Alexandria was "town,"—a straggling, lazy village of houses, churches, and shops, and an aristocracy of Toms, Dicks, and Captains. Cuddled on the hill to the north was the village of the colored folks, who lived in three- or four-room unpainted cottages, some neat and homelike, and some dirty. The dwellings were scattered rather aimlessly, but they centred about the twin temples of the hamlet, the Methodist, and the Hard-Shell Baptist churches. These, in turn, leaned gingerly on a sad-colored schoolhouse. Hither my little world wended its crooked way on Sunday to meet other worlds, and gossip, and wonder, and make the weekly sacrifice with frenzied priest at the altar of the "old-time religion." Then the soft melody and mighty cadences of Negro song cluttered and thundered.

I have called my tiny community a world, and so its isolation made it; and yet there was among us but a half-awakened common consciousness, sprung from common joy and grief, at burial, birth, or wedding; from a common hardship in poverty, poor land, and low wages; and, above all, from the sight of the Veil that hung between us and Opportunity. All this caused us to think some thoughts together; but these, when ripe for speech, were spoken in various languages. Those whose eyes twenty-five and more years before had seen "the glory of the coming of the Lord," saw in every present hindrance or help a dark fatalism bound to bring all things right in His own good time. The mass of those to whom slavery was a dim recollection of childhood found the world a puzzling thing: it asked little of them, and they answered with little, and yet it ridiculed their offering. Such a paradox they could not understand, and therefore sank into listless indifference, or shiftlessness, or reckless bravado. There were, however, some—such as Josie, Jim, and Ben—to whom War, Hell, and Slavery were but childhood tales, whose young appetites had been whetted to an edge by school and story and half-awakened thought. Ill could they be content, born without and beyond the World. And their weak wings beat against their barriers,—barriers of caste, of youth, of life; at last, in dangerous moments, against everything that opposed even a whim.

The ten years that follow youth, the years when first the realization comes that life is leading somewhere,—these were the years that passed after I left my little school. When they were past, I came by chance once more to the walls of Fisk University, to the halls of the chapel of melody. As I lingered there in the joy and pain of meeting old school friends, there swept over me a sudden longing to pass again beyond the blue hill, and to see the homes and the school of other days, and to learn how life had gone with my school-children; and I went.

Josie was dead, and the gray-haired mother said simply, "We've had a heap of trouble since you've been away." I had feared for Jim. With a cultured parentage and a social caste to uphold him, he might have made a venture-some merchant or a West Point cadet. But here he was, angry with life and reckless; and when Farmer Durham charged him with stealing wheat, the old man had to ride fast to escape the stones which the furious fool hurled after him. They told Jim to run away; but he would not run, and the constable came that afternoon. It grieved Josie, and great awkward John walked nine miles every day to see his little brother through the bars of Lebanon jail. At last the two came back together in the dark night. The mother cooked sup-per, and Josie emptied her purse, and the boys stole away. Josie grew thin and silent, yet worked the more. The hill became steep for the quiet old father, and with the boys away there was little to do in the valley. Josie helped them to sell the old farm, and they moved nearer town. Brother Dennis, the car-penter, built a new house with six rooms; Josie toiled a year in Nashville, and brought back ninety dollars to furnish the house and change it to a home.

When the spring came, and the birds twittered, and the stream ran proud and full, little sister Lizzie, bold and thoughtless, flushed with the passion of youth, bestowed herself on the tempter, and brought home a nameless child. Josie shivered and worked on, with the vision of schooldays all fled, with a face wan and tired,—worked until, on a summer's day, some one married another; then Josie crept to her mother like a hurt child, and slept—and sleeps.

I paused to scent the breeze as I entered the valley. The Lawrences have gone,—father and son forever,—and the other son lazily digs in the earth to live. A new young widow rents out their cabin to fat Reuben. Reuben is a Baptist preacher now, but I fear as lazy as ever, though his cabin has three rooms; and little Ella has grown into a bouncing woman, and is ploughing corn on the hot hillside. There are babies a-plenty, and one half-witted girl. Across the valley is a house I did not know before, and there I found, rock-

ing one baby and expecting another, one of my schoolgirls, a daughter of Uncle Bird Dowell. She looked somewhat worried with her new duties, but soon bristled into pride over her neat cabin and the tale of her thrifty husband, the horse and cow, and the farm they were planning to buy.

My log schoolhouse was gone. In its place stood Progress; and Progress, I understand, is necessarily ugly. The crazy foundation stones still marked the former site of my poor little cabin, and not far away, on six weary boulders, perched a jaunty board house, perhaps twenty by thirty feet, with three windows and a door that locked. Some of the window-glass was broken, and part of an old iron stove lay mournfully under the house. I peeped through the window half reverently, and found things that were more familiar. The blackboard had grown by about two feet, and the seats were still without backs. The county owns the lot now, I hear, and every year there is a session of school. As I sat by the spring and looked on the Old and the New I felt glad, very glad, and yet—

After two long drinks I started on. There was the great double log-house on the corner. I remembered the broken, blighted family that used to live there. The strong, hard face of the mother, with its wilderness of hair, rose before me. She had driven her husband away, and while I taught school a strange man lived there, big and jovial, and people talked. I felt sure that Ben and 'Tildy would come to naught from such a home. But this is an odd world; for Ben is a busy farmer in Smith County, "doing well, too," they say, and he had cared for little 'Tildy until last spring, when a lover married her. A hard life the lad had led, toiling for meat, and laughed at because he was homely and crooked. There was Sam Carlon, an impudent old skinflint, who had definite notions about "niggers," and hired Ben a summer and would not pay him. Then the hungry boy gathered his sacks together, and in broad daylight went into Carlon's corn; and when the hard-fisted farmer set upon him, the angry boy flew at him like a beast. Doc Burke saved a murder and a lynching that day.

The story reminded me again of the Burkes, and an impatience seized me to know who won in the battle, Doc or the seventy-five acres. For it is a hard thing to make a farm out of nothing, even in fifteen years. So I hurried on, thinking of the Burkes. They used to have a certain magnificent barbarism about them that I liked. They were never vulgar, never immoral, but rather rough and primitive, with an unconventionality that spent itself in loud guffaws, slaps on the back, and naps in the corner. I hurried by the cottage of the misborn Neill boys. It was empty, and they were grown into fat, lazy

farm-hands. I saw the home of the Hickmans, but Albert, with his stooping shoulders, had passed from the world. Then I came to the Burkes' gate and peered through; the inclosure looked rough and untrimmed, and yet there were the same fences around the old farm save to the left, where lay twenty-five other acres. And lo! the cabin in the hollow had climbed the hill and swollen to a half-finished six-room cottage.

The Burkes held a hundred acres, but they were still in debt. Indeed, the gaunt father who toiled night and day would scarcely be happy out of debt, being so used to it. Some day he must stop, for his massive frame is showing decline. The mother wore shoes, but the lion-like physique of other days was broken. The children had grown up. Rob, the image of his father, was loud and rough with laughter. Birdie, my school baby of six, had grown to a picture of maiden beauty, tall and tawny. "Edgar is gone," said the mother, with head half bowed,—"gone to work in Nashville; he and his father couldn't agree."

Little Doc, the boy born since the time of my school, took me horseback down the creek next morning toward Farmer Dowell's. The road and the stream were battling for mastery, and the stream had the better of it. We splashed and waded, and the merry boy, perched behind me, chattered and laughed. He showed me where Simon Thompson had bought a bit of ground and a home; but his daughter Lana, a plump, brown, slow girl, was not there. She had married a man and a farm twenty miles away. We wound on down the stream till we came to a gate that I did not recognize, but the boy insisted that it was "Uncle Bird's." The farm was fat with the growing crop. In that little valley was a strange stillness as I rode up; for death and marriage had stolen youth and left age and childhood there. We sat and talked that night after the chores were done. Uncle Bird was grayer, and his eyes did not see so well, but he was still jovial. We talked of the acres bought,—one hundred and twenty-five,—of the new guest-chamber added, of Martha's marrying. Then we talked of death: Fanny and Fred were gone; a shadow hung over the other daughter, and when it lifted she was to go to Nashville to school. At last we spoke of the neighbors, and as night fell, Uncle Bird told me how, on a night like that, 'Thenie came wandering back to her home over yonder, to escape the blows of her husband. And next morning she died in the home that her little bow-legged brother, working and saving, had bought for their widowed mother.

My journey was done, and behind me lay hill and dale, and Life and Death. How shall man measure Progress there where the dark-faced Josie lies? How many heartfuls of sorrow shall balance a bushel of wheat? How

hard a thing is life to the lowly, and yet how human and real! And all this life and love and strife and failure,—is it the twilight of nightfall or the flush of some faint-dawning day?

Thus sadly musing, I rode to Nashville in the Jim Crow car.

V

OF THE WINGS OF ATALANTA

O black boy of Atlanta
 But half was spoken;
The slave's chains and the master's
 Alike are broken;
The one curse of the races
 Held both in tether;
They are rising-all are rising—
 The black and white together.
 Whittier.

S OUTH of the North, yet north of the South, lies the City of a Hundred Hills, peering out from the shadows of the past into the promise of the future. I have seen her in the morning, when the first flush of day had half-roused her; she lay gray and still on the crimson soil of Georgia; then the blue smoke began to curl from her chimneys, the tinkle of bell and scream of whistle broke the silence, the rattle and roar of busy life slowly gathered and swelled, until the seething whirl of the city seemed a strange thing in a sleepy land.

Once, they say, even Atlanta slept dull and drowsy at the foot-hills of the Alleghanies, until the iron baptism of war awakened her with its sullen waters, aroused and maddened her, and left her listening to the sea. And the sea cried to the hills and the hills answered the sea, till the city rose like a

widow and cast away her weeds, and toiled for her daily bread; toiled steadily, toiled cunningly,—perhaps with some bitterness, with a touch of réclame,—and yet with real earnestness, and real sweat.

It is a hard thing to live haunted by the ghost of an untrue dream; to see the wide vision of empire fade into real ashes and dirt; to feel the pang of the conquered, and yet know that with all the Bad that fell on one black day, something was vanquished that deserved to live, something killed that in justice had not dared to die; to know that with the Right that triumphed, triumphed something of Wrong, something sordid and mean, something less than the broadest and best. All this is bitter hard; and many a man and city and people have found in it excuse for sulking and brooding, and listless waiting.

Such are not men of the sturdier make; they of Atlanta turned resolutely toward the future; and that future held aloft vistas of purple and gold:— Atlanta, Queen of the cotton kingdom; Atlanta, Gateway to the Land of the Sun; Atlanta, the new Lachesis, spinner of web and woof for the world. So the city crowned her hundred hills with factories, and stored her shops with cunning handiwork, and stretched long iron ways to greet the busy Mercury in his coming. And the Nation talked of her striving.

Perhaps Atlanta was not christened for the winged maiden of dull Bœotia; you know the tale,—how swarthy Atalanta, tall and wild, would marry only him who out-raced her; and how the wily Hippomenes laid three apples of gold in the way. She fled like a shadow, paused, startled over the first apple, but even as he stretched his hand, fled again; hovered over the second, then, slipping from his hot grasp, flew over river, vale, and hill; but as she lingered over the third, his arms fell round her, and looking on each other, the blazing passion of their love profaned the sanctuary of Love, and they were cursed. If Atlanta be not named for Atalanta, she ought to have been.

Atalanta is not the first or the last maiden whom greed of gold has led to defile the temple of Love; and not maids alone, but men in the race of life, sink from the high and generous ideals of youth to the gambler's code of the Bourse; and in all our Nation's striving is not the Gospel of Work befouled by the Gospel of Pay? So common is this that one-half think it normal; so unquestioned, that we almost fear to question if the end of racing is not gold, if the aim of man is not rightly to be rich. And if this is the fault of America, how dire a danger lies before a new land and a new city, lest Atlanta, stooping for mere gold, shall find that gold accursed!

It was no maiden's idle whim that started this hard racing; a fearful wilderness lay about the feet of that city after the War,—feudalism, poverty,

the rise of the Third Estate, serfdom, the re-birth of Law and Order, and above and between all, the Veil of Race. How heavy a journey for weary feet! what wings must Atalanta have to flit over all this hollow and hill, through sour wood and sullen water, and by the red waste of sun-baked clay! How fleet must Atalanta be if she will not be tempted by gold to profane the Sanctuary!

The Sanctuary of our fathers has, to be sure, few Gods,—some sneer, "all too few." There is the thrifty Mercury of New England, Pluto of the North, and Ceres of the West; and there, too, is the half-forgotten Apollo of the South, under whose ægis the maiden ran,—and as she ran she forgot him, even as there in Bœotia Venus was forgot. She forgot the old ideal of the Southern gentleman,—that new-world-heir of the grace and courtliness of patrician, knight, and noble; forgot his honor with his foibles, his kindliness with his carelessness, and stooped to apples of gold,—to men busier and sharper, thriftier and more unscrupulous. Golden apples are beautiful—I remember the lawless days of boyhood, when orchards in crimson and gold tempted me over fence and field—and, too, the merchant who has dethroned the planter is no despicable parvenu. Work and wealth are the mighty levers to lift this old new land; thrift and toil and saving are the highways to new hopes and new possibilities; and yet the warning is needed lest the wily Hippomenes tempt Atalanta to thinking that golden apples are the goal of racing, and not mere incidents by the way.

Atlanta must not lead the South to dream of material prosperity as the touchstone of all success; already the fatal might of this idea is beginning to spread; it is replacing the finer type of Southerner with vulgar money-getters; it is burying the sweeter beauties of Southern life beneath presence and ostentation. For every social ill the panacea of Wealth has been urged,—wealth to overthrow the remains of the slave feudalism; wealth to raise the "cracker" Third Estate; wealth to employ the black serfs, and the prospect of wealth to keep them working; wealth as the end and aim of politics, and as the legal tender for law and order; and, finally, instead of Truth, Beauty, and Goodness, wealth as the ideal of the Public School.

Not only is this true in the world which Atlanta typifies, but it is threatening to be true of a world beneath and beyond that world,—the Black World beyond the Veil. To-day it makes little difference to Atlanta, to the South, what the Negro thinks or dreams or wills. In the soul-life of the land he is to-day, and naturally will long remain, unthought of, half forgotten; and yet when he does come to think and will and do for himself,—and let

no man dream that day will never come,—then the part he plays will not be one of sudden learning, but words and thoughts he has been taught to lisp in his race-childhood. To-day the ferment of his striving toward self-realization is to the strife of the white world like a wheel within a wheel: beyond the Veil are smaller but like problems of ideals, of leaders and the led, of serfdom, of poverty, of order and subordination, and, through all, the Veil of Race. Few know of these problems, few who know notice them; and yet there they are, awaiting student, artist, and seer,—a field for somebody sometime to discover. Hither has the temptation of Hippomenes penetrated; already in this smaller world, which now indirectly and anon directly must influence the larger for good or ill, the habit is forming of interpreting the world in dollars. The old leaders of Negro opinion, in the little groups where there is a Negro social consciousness, are being replaced by new; neither the black preacher nor the black teacher leads as he did two decades ago. Into their places are pushing the farmers and gardeners, the well-paid porters and artisans, the businessmen,—all those with property and money. And with all this change, so curiously parallel to that of the Other-world, goes too the same inevitable change in ideals. The South laments to-day the slow, steady disappearance of a certain type of Negro,—the faithful, courteous slave of other days, with his incorruptible honesty and dignified humility. He is passing away just as surely as the old type of Southern gentleman is passing, and from not dissimilar causes,—the sudden transformation of a fair far-off ideal of Freedom into the hard reality of bread-winning and the consequent deification of Bread.

In the Black World, the Preacher and Teacher embodied once the ideals of this people,—the strife for another and a juster world, the vague dream of righteousness, the mystery of knowing; but to-day the danger is that these ideals, with their simple beauty and weird inspiration, will suddenly sink to a question of cash and a lust for gold. Here stands this black young Atalanta, girding herself for the race that must be run; and if her eyes be still toward the hills and sky as in the days of old, then we may look for noble running; but what if some ruthless or wily or even thoughtless Hippomenes lay golden apples before her? What if the Negro people be wooed from a strife for righteousness, from a love of knowing, to regard dollars as the be-all and end-all of life? What if to the Mammonism of America be added the rising Mammonism of the re-born South, and the Mammonism of this South be reinforced by the budding Mammonism of its half-awakened black millions? Whither, then, is the new-world quest of Goodness and Beauty and Truth

gone glimmering? Must this, and that fair flower of Freedom which, despite the jeers of latter-day striplings, sprung from our fathers' blood, must that too degenerate into a dusty quest of gold,—into lawless lust with Hippomenes?

The hundred hills of Atlanta are not all crowned with factories. On one, toward the west, the setting sun throws three buildings in bold relief against the sky. The beauty of the group lies in its simple unity:—a broad lawn of green rising from the red street with mingled roses and peaches; north and south, two plain and stately halls; and in the midst, half hidden in ivy, a larger building, boldly graceful, sparingly decorated, and with one low spire. It is a restful group,—one never looks for more; it is all here, all intelligible. There I live, and there I hear from day to day the low hum of restful life. In winter's twilight, when the red sun glows, I can see the dark figures pass between the halls to the music of the night-bell. In the morning, when the sun is golden, the clang of the day-bell brings the hurry and laughter of three hundred young hearts from hall and street, and from the busy city below,— children all dark and heavy-haired,—to join their clear young voices in the music of the morning sacrifice. In a half-dozen class-rooms they gather then,—here to follow the love-song of Dido, here to listen to the tale of Troy divine; there to wander among the stars, there to wander among men and nations,—and elsewhere other well-worn ways of knowing this queer world. Nothing new, no timesaving devices,—simply old time—glorified methods of delving for Truth, and searching out the hidden beauties of life, and learning the good of living. The riddle of existence is the college curriculum that was laid before the Pharaohs, that was taught in the groves by Plato, that formed the trivium and quadrivium, and is to-day laid before the freedmen's sons by Atlanta University. And this course of study will not change; its methods will grow more deft and effectual, its content richer by toil of scholar and sight of seer; but the true college will ever have one goal,—not to earn meat, but to know the end and aim of that life which meat nourishes.

The vision of life that rises before these dark eyes has in it nothing mean or selfish. Not at Oxford or at Leipsic, not at Yale or Columbia, is there an air of higher resolve or more unfettered striving; the determination to realize for men, both black and white, the broadest possibilities of life, to seek the better and the best, to spread with their own hands the Gospel of Sacrifice,— all this is the burden of their talk and dream. Here, amid a wide desert of caste and proscription, amid the heart-hurting slights and jars and vagaries

of a deep race-dislike, lies this green oasis, where hot anger cools, and the bitterness of disappointment is sweetened by the springs and breezes of Parnassus; and here men may lie and listen, and learn of a future fuller than the past, and hear the voice of Time:

"Entbehren sollst du, sollst entbehren."

They made their mistakes, those who planted Fisk and Howard and Atlanta before the smoke of battle had lifted; they made their mistakes, but those mistakes were not the things at which we lately laughed somewhat uproariously. They were right when they sought to found a new educational system upon the University: where, forsooth, shall we ground knowledge save on the broadest and deepest knowledge? The roots of the tree, rather than the leaves, are the sources of its life; and from the dawn of history, from Academus to Cambridge, the culture of the University has been the broad foundation-stone on which is built the kindergarten's A B C.

But these builders did make a mistake in minimizing the gravity of the problem before them; in thinking it a matter of years and decades; in therefore building quickly and laying their foundation carelessly, and lowering the standard of knowing, until they had scattered haphazard through the South some dozen poorly equipped high schools and miscalled them universities. They forgot, too, just as their successors are forgetting, the rule of inequality:—that of the million black youth, some were fitted to know and some to dig; that some had the talent and capacity of university men, and some the talent and capacity of blacksmiths; and that true training meant neither that all should be college men nor all artisans, but that the one should be made a missionary of culture to an untaught people, and the other a free workman among serfs. And to seek to make the blacksmith a scholar is almost as silly as the more modern scheme of making the scholar a blacksmith; almost, but not quite.

The function of the university is not simply to teach bread-winning, or to furnish teachers for the public schools, or to be a centre of polite society; it is, above all, to be the organ of that fine adjustment between real life and the growing knowledge of life, an adjustment which forms the secret of civilization. Such an institution the South of to-day sorely needs. She has religion, earnest, bigoted:—religion that on both sides the Veil often omits the sixth, seventh, and eighth commandments, but substitutes a dozen sup-

plementary ones. She has, as Atlanta shows, growing thrift and love of toil; but she lacks that broad knowledge of what the world knows and knew of human living and doing, which she may apply to the thousand problems of real life to-day confronting her. The need of the South is knowledge and culture,—not in dainty limited quantity, as before the war, but in broad busy abundance in the world of work; and until she has this, not all the Apples of Hesperides, be they golden and bejewelled, can save her from the curse of the Bœotian lovers.

The Wings of Atalanta are the coming universities of the South. They alone can bear the maiden past the temptation of golden fruit. They will not guide her flying feet away from the cotton and gold; for—ah, thoughtful Hippomenes!—do not the apples lie in the very Way of Life? But they will guide her over and beyond them, and leave her kneeling in the Sanctuary of Truth and Freedom and broad Humanity, virgin and undefiled. Sadly did the Old South err in human education, despising the education of the masses, and niggardly in the support of colleges. Her ancient university foundations dwindled and withered under the foul breath of slavery; and even since the war they have fought a failing fight for life in the tainted air of social unrest and commercial selfishness, stunted by the death of criticism, and starving for lack of broadly cultured men. And if this is the white South's need and danger, how much heavier the danger and need of the freedmen's sons! how pressing here the need of broad ideals and true culture, the conservation of soul from sordid aims and petty passions! Let us build the Southern university—William and Mary, Trinity, Georgia, Texas, Tulane, Vanderbilt, and the others—fit to live; let us build, too, the Negro universities:—Fisk, whose foundation was ever broad; Howard, at the heart of the Nation; Atlanta at Atlanta, whose ideal of scholarship has been held above the temptation of numbers. Why not here, and perhaps elsewhere, plant deeply and for all time centres of learning and living, colleges that yearly would send into the life of the South a few white men and a few black men of broad culture, catholic tolerance, and trained ability, joining their hands to other hands, and giving to this squabble of the Races a decent and dignified peace?

Patience, Humility, Manners, and Taste, common schools and kinder-gartens, industrial and technical schools, literature and tolerance,—all these spring from knowledge and culture, the children of the university. So must men and nations build, not otherwise, not upside down.

Teach workers to work,—a wise saying; wise when applied to German

boys and American girls; wiser when said of Negro boys, for they have less knowledge of working and none to teach them. Teach thinkers to think,—a needed knowledge in a day of loose and careless logic; and they whose lot is gravest must have the carefulest training to think aright. If these things are so, how foolish to ask what is the best education for one or seven or sixty million souls! shall we teach them trades, or train them in liberal arts? Neither and both: teach the workers to work and the thinkers to think; make carpenters of carpenters, and philosophers of philosophers, and fops of fools. Nor can we pause here. We are training not isolated men but a living group of men,—nay, a group within a group. And the final product of our training must be neither a psychologist nor a brickmason, but a man. And to make men, we must have ideals, broad, pure, and inspiring ends of living,—not sordid money-getting, not apples of gold. The worker must work for the glory of his handiwork, not simply for pay; the thinker must think for truth, not for fame. And all this is gained only by human strife and longing; by ceaseless training and education; by founding Right on righteousness and Truth on the unhampered search for Truth; by founding the common school on the university, and the industrial school on the common school; and weaving thus a system, not a distortion, and bringing a birth, not an abortion.

When night falls on the City of a Hundred Hills, a wind gathers itself from the seas and comes murmuring westward. And at its bidding, the smoke of the drowsy factories sweeps down upon the mighty city and covers it like a pall, while yonder at the University the stars twinkle above Stone Hall. And they say that yon gray mist is the tunic of Atalanta pausing over her golden apples. Fly, my maiden, fly, for yonder comes Hippomenes!

VI

OF THE TRAINING OF BLACK MEN

Why, if the Soul can fling the Dust aside,
And naked on the Air of Heaven ride,
　Were 't not a Shame—were 't not a Shame for him
In this clay carcase crippled to abide?
　　　　　Omar Khayyám (Fitzgerald).

From the shimmering swirl of waters where many, many thoughts ago the slave-ship first saw the square tower of Jamestown, have flowed down to our day three streams of thinking: one swollen from the larger world here and over-seas, saying, the multiplying of human wants in culture-lands calls for the world-wide coöperation of men in satisfying them. Hence arises a new human unity, pulling the ends of earth nearer, and all men, black, yellow, and white. The larger humanity strives to feel in this contact of living Nations and sleeping hordes a thrill of new life in the world, crying, "If the contact of Life and Sleep be Death, shame on such Life." To be sure, behind this thought lurks the afterthought of force and dominion,—the making of brown men to delve when the temptation of beads and red calico cloys.

The second thought streaming from the death-ship and the curving river is the thought of the older South,—the sincere and passionate belief that somewhere between men and cattle, God created a tertium quid, and called it a Negro,—a clownish, simple creature, at times even lovable within its limitations, but straitly foreordained to walk within the Veil. To be sure, behind the thought lurks the afterthought,—some of them with favoring chance might become men, but in sheer self-defence we dare not let them, and we build about them walls so high, and hang between them and the light a veil so thick, that they shall not even think of breaking through.

And last of all there trickles down that third and darker thought,—the thought of the things themselves, the confused, half-conscious mutter of men who are black and whitened, crying "Liberty, Freedom, Opportunity— vouchsafe to us, O boastful World, the chance of living men!" To be sure, behind the thought lurks the afterthought,—suppose, after all, the World is right and we are less than men? Suppose this mad impulse within is all wrong, some mock mirage from the untrue?

So here we stand among thoughts of human unity, even through conquest and slavery; the inferiority of black men, even if forced by fraud; a shriek in the night for the freedom of men who themselves are not yet sure of their right to demand it. This is the tangle of thought and afterthought

wherein we are called to solve the problem of training men for life.

Behind all its curiousness, so attractive alike to sage and dilettante, lie its dim dangers, throwing across us shadows at once grotesque and awful. Plain it is to us that what the world seeks through desert and wild we have within our threshold,—a stalwart laboring force, suited to the semi-tropics; if, deaf to the voice of the Zeitgeist, we refuse to use and develop these men, we risk poverty and loss. If, on the other hand, seized by the brutal afterthought, we debauch the race thus caught in our talons, selfishly sucking their blood and brains in the future as in the past, what shall save us from national decadence? Only that saner selfishness, which Education teaches men, can find the rights of all in the whirl of work.

Again, we may decry the color-prejudice of the South, yet it remains a heavy fact. Such curious kinks of the human mind exist and must be reckoned with soberly. They cannot be laughed away, nor always successfully stormed at, nor easily abolished by act of legislature. And yet they must not be encouraged by being let alone. They must be recognized as facts, but unpleasant facts; things that stand in the way of civilization and religion and common decency. They can be met in but one way,—by the breadth and broadening of human reason, by catholicity of taste and culture. And so, too, the native ambition and aspiration of men, even though they be black, backward, and ungraceful, must not lightly be dealt with. To stimulate wildly weak and untrained minds is to play with mighty fires; to flout their striving idly is to welcome a harvest of brutish crime and shameless lethargy in our very laps. The guiding of thought and the deft coordination of deed is at once the path of honor and humanity.

And so, in this great question of reconciling three vast and partially contradictory streams of thought, the one panacea of Education leaps to the lips of all:—such human training as will best use the labor of all men without enslaving or brutalizing; such training as will give us poise to encourage the prejudices that bulwark society, and to stamp out those that in sheer barbarity deafen us to the wail of prisoned souls within the Veil, and the mounting fury of shackled men.

But when we have vaguely said that Education will set this tangle straight, what have we uttered but a truism? Training for life teaches living; but what training for the profitable living together of black men and white? A hundred and fifty years ago our task would have seemed easier. Then Dr. Johnson blandly assured us that education was needful solely for the embellishments of life, and was useless for ordinary vermin. To-day we have climbed to

heights where we would open at least the outer courts of knowledge to all, display its treasures to many, and select the few to whom its mystery of Truth is revealed, not wholly by birth or the accidents of the stock market, but at least in part according to deftness and aim, talent and character. This programme, however, we are sorely puzzled in carrying out through that part of the land where the blight of slavery fell hardest, and where we are dealing with two backward peoples. To make here in human education that ever necessary combination of the permanent and the contingent—of the ideal and the practical in workable equilibrium—has been there, as it ever must be in every age and place, a matter of infinite experiment and frequent mistakes.

In rough approximation we may point out four varying decades of work in Southern education since the Civil War. From the close of the war until 1876 was the period of uncertain groping and temporary relief. There were army schools, mission schools and schools of the Freedman's Bureau in chaotic disarrangement seeking system and cooperation. Then followed ten years of constructive definite effort toward the building of complete school systems in the South. Normal schools and colleges were founded for the freedmen, and teachers trained there to man the public schools. There was the inevitable tendency of war to underestimate the prejudices of the master and the ignorance of the slave, and all seemed clear sailing out of the wreckage of the storm. Meantime, starting in this decade yet especially developing from 1885 to 1895, began the industrial revolution of the South. The land saw glimpses of a new destiny and the stirring of new ideals. The educational system striving to complete itself saw new obstacles and a field of work ever broader and deeper. The Negro colleges, hurriedly founded, were inadequately equipped, illogically distributed, and of varying efficiency and grade; the normal and high schools were doing little more than common-school work, and the common schools were training but a third of the children who ought to be in them, and training these too often poorly. At the same time the white South, by reason of its sudden conversion from the slavery ideal, by so much the more became set and strengthened in its racial prejudice, and crystallized it into harsh law and harsher custom; while the marvellous pushing forward of the poor white daily threatened to take even bread and butter from the mouths of the heavily handicapped sons of the freedmen. In the midst, then, of the larger problem of Negro education sprang up the more practical question of work, the inevitable economic quandary that faces a people in the transition from slavery to freedom, and especially those who make that change amid hate and prejudice, lawlessness and ruthless competition.

The industrial school springing to notice in this decade, but coming to full recognition in the decade beginning with 1895, was the proffered answer to this combined educational and economic crisis, and an answer of singular wisdom and timeliness. From the very first in nearly all the schools some attention had been given to training in handiwork, but now was this training first raised to a dignity that brought it in direct touch with the South's magnificent industrial development, and given an emphasis which reminded black folk that before the Temple of Knowledge swing the Gates of Toil.

Yet after all they are but gates, and when turning our eyes from the temporary and the contingent in the Negro problem to the broader question of the permanent uplifting and civilization of black men in America, we have a right to inquire, as this enthusiasm for material advancement mounts to its height, if after all the industrial school is the final and sufficient answer in the training of the Negro race; and to ask gently, but in all sincerity, the ever-recurring query of the ages, Is not life more than meat, and the body more than raiment? And men ask this to-day all the more eagerly because of sinister signs in recent educational movements. The tendency is here, born of slavery and quickened to renewed life by the crazy imperialism of the day, to regard human beings as among the material resources of a land to be trained with an eye single to future dividends. Race-prejudices, which keep brown and black men in their "places," we are coming to regard as useful allies with such a theory, no matter how much they may dull the ambition and sicken the hearts of struggling human beings. And above all, we daily hear that an education that encourages aspiration, that sets the loftiest of ideals and seeks as an end culture and character rather than bread-winning, is the privilege of white men and the danger and delusion of black.

Especially has criticism been directed against the former educational efforts to aid the Negro. In the four periods I have mentioned, we find first, boundless, planless enthusiasm and sacrifice; then the preparation of teachers for a vast public-school system; then the launching and expansion of that school system amid increasing difficulties; and finally the training of workmen for the new and growing industries. This development has been sharply ridiculed as a logical anomaly and flat reversal of nature. Soothly we have been told that first industrial and manual training should have taught the Negro to work, then simple schools should have taught him to read and write, and finally, after years, high and normal schools could have completed the system, as intelligence and wealth demanded.

That a system logically so complete was historically impossible, it needs

but a little thought to prove. Progress in human affairs is more often a pull than a push, a surging forward of the exceptional man, and the lifting of his duller brethren slowly and painfully to his vantage-ground. Thus it was no accident that gave birth to universities centuries before the common schools, that made fair Harvard the first flower of our wilderness. So in the South: the mass of the freedmen at the end of the war lacked the intelligence so necessary to modern workingmen. They must first have the common school to teach them to read, write, and cipher; and they must have higher schools to teach teachers for the common schools. The white teachers who flocked South went to establish such a common-school system. Few held the idea of founding colleges; most of them at first would have laughed at the idea. But they faced, as all men since them have faced, that central paradox of the South,—the social separation of the races. At that time it was the sudden volcanic rupture of nearly all relations between black and white, in work and government and family life. Since then a new adjustment of relations in economic and political affairs has grown up,—an adjustment subtle and difficult to grasp, yet singularly ingenious, which leaves still that frightful chasm at the color-line across which men pass at their peril. Thus, then and now, there stand in the South two separate worlds; and separate not simply in the higher realms of social intercourse, but also in church and school on railway and street-car, in hotels and theatres, in streets and city sections, in books and newspapers in asylums and jails, in hospitals and graveyards. There is still enough of contact for large economic and group cooperation, but the separation is so thorough and deep that it absolutely precludes for the present between the races anything like that sympathetic and effective group-training and leadership of the one by the other, such as the American Negro and all backward peoples must have for effectual progress.

This the missionaries of '68 soon saw; and if effective industrial and trade schools were impracticable before the establishment of a common-school system, just as certainly no adequate common schools could be founded until there were teachers to teach them Southern whites would not teach them; Northern whites in sufficient numbers could not be had. If the Negro was to learn, he must teach himself, and the most effective help that could be given him was the establishment of schools to train Negro teachers. This conclusion was slowly but surely reached by every student of the situation until simultaneously, in widely separated regions, without consultation or systematic plan, there arose a series of institutions designed to furnish teachers for the untaught. Above the sneers of critics at the obvious defects of this

procedure must ever stand its one crushing rejoinder: in a single generation they put thirty thousand black teachers in the South; they wiped out the illiteracy of the majority of the black people of the land, and they made Tuskegee possible.

Such higher training-schools tended naturally to deepen broader development: at first they were common and grammar schools, then some became high schools. And finally, by 1900, some thirty-four had one year or more of studies of college grade. This development was reached with different degrees of speed in different institutions: Hampton is still a high school, while Fisk University started her college in 1871, and Spelman Seminary about 1896. In all cases the aim was identical,—to maintain the standards of the lower training by giving teachers and leaders the best practicable training; and above all, to furnish the black world with adequate standards of human culture and lofty ideals of life. It was not enough that the teachers of teachers should be trained in technical normal methods; they must also, so far as possible, be broad-minded, cultured men and women, to scatter civilization among a people whose ignorance was not simply of letters, but of life itself.

It can thus be seen that the work of education in the South began with higher institutions of training, which threw off as their foliage common schools, and later industrial schools, and at the same time strove to shoot their roots ever deeper toward college and university training. That this was an inevitable and necessary development, sooner or later, goes without saying; but there has been, and still is, a question in many minds if the natural growth was not forced, and if the higher training was not either overdone or done with cheap and unsound methods. Among white Southerners this feeling is widespread and positive. A prominent Southern journal voiced this in a recent editorial.

> "The experiment that has been made to give the colored students classical training has not been satisfactory. Even though many were able to pursue the course, most of them did so in a parrot-like way, learning what was taught, but not seeming to appropriate the truth and import of their instruction, and graduating without sensible aim or valuable occupation for their future. The whole scheme has proved a waste of time, efforts, and the money of the state."

While most fair-minded men would recognize this as extreme and over-

drawn, still without doubt many are asking, Are there a sufficient number of Negroes ready for college training to warrant the undertaking? Are not too many students prematurely forced into this work? Does it not have the effect of dissatisfying the young Negro with his environment? And do these graduates succeed in real life? Such natural questions cannot be evaded, nor on the other hand must a Nation naturally skeptical as to Negro ability assume an unfavorable answer without careful inquiry and patient openness to conviction. We must not forget that most Americans answer all queries regarding the Negro *a priori*, and that the least that human courtesy can do is to listen to evidence.

The advocates of the higher education of the Negro would be the last to deny the incompleteness and glaring defects of the present system: too many institutions have attempted to do college work, the work in some cases has not been thoroughly done, and quantity rather than quality has sometimes been sought. But all this can be said of higher education throughout the land; it is the almost inevitable incident of educational growth, and leaves the deeper question of the legitimate demand for the higher training of Negroes untouched. And this latter question can be settled in but one way,—by a firsthand study of the facts. If we leave out of view all institutions which have not actually graduated students from a course higher than that of a New England high school, even though they be called colleges; if then we take the thirty-four remaining institutions, we may clear up many misapprehensions by asking searchingly, What kind of institutions are they? what do they teach? and what sort of men do they graduate?

And first we may say that this type of college, including Atlanta, Fisk, and Howard, Wilberforce and Claflin, Biddle, Shaw, and the rest, is peculiar, almost unique. Through the shining trees that whisper before me as I write, I catch glimpses of a boulder of New England granite, covering a grave, which graduates of Atlanta University have placed there,—

"IN GRATEFUL MEMORY OF THEIR FORMER TEACHER AND FRIEND AND OF THE UNSELFISH LIFE HE LIVED, AND THE NOBLE WORK HE WROUGHT; THAT THEY, THEIR CHILDREN, AND THEIR CHILDREN'S CHILDREN MIGHT BE BLESSED."

This was the gift of New England to the freed Negro: not alms, but a friend; not cash, but character. It was not and is not money these seething millions want, but love and sympathy, the pulse of hearts beating with red blood;—a gift which to-day only their own kindred and race can bring to the masses, but which once saintly souls brought to their favored children in the crusade of the sixties, that finest thing in American history, and one of the few things untainted by sordid greed and cheap vainglory. The teachers in these institutions came not to keep the Negroes in their place, but to raise them out of the defilement of the places where slavery had wallowed them. The colleges they founded were social settlements; homes where the best of the sons of the freedmen came in close and sympathetic touch with the best traditions of New England. They lived and ate together, studied and worked, hoped and harkened in the dawning light. In actual formal content their curriculum was doubtless old-fashioned, but in educational power it was supreme, for it was the contact of living souls.

From such schools about two thousand Negroes have gone forth with the bachelor's degree. The number in itself is enough to put at rest the argument that too large a proportion of Negroes are receiving higher training. If the ratio to population of all Negro students throughout the land, in both college and secondary training, be counted, Commissioner Harris assures us "it must be increased to five times its present average" to equal the average of the land.

Fifty years ago the ability of Negro students in any appreciable numbers to master a modern college course would have been difficult to prove. To-day it is proved by the fact that four hundred Negroes, many of whom have been reported as brilliant students, have received the bachelor's degree from Harvard, Yale, Oberlin, and seventy other leading colleges. Here we have, then, nearly twenty-five hundred Negro graduates, of whom the crucial query must be made, How far did their training fit them for life? It is of course extremely difficult to collect satisfactory data on such a point,— difficult to reach the men, to get trustworthy testimony, and to gauge that testimony by any generally acceptable criterion of success. In 1900, the Conference at Atlanta University undertook to study these graduates, and published the results. First they sought to know what these graduates were doing, and succeeded in getting answers from nearly two-thirds of the living. The direct testimony was in almost all cases corroborated by the reports of the colleges where they graduated, so that in the main the reports were wor-

thy of credence. Fifty-three per cent of these graduates were teachers,—presidents of institutions, heads of normal schools, principals of city school-systems, and the like. Seventeen per cent were clergymen; another seventeen per cent were in the professions, chiefly as physicians. Over six per cent were merchants farmers, and artisans, and four per cent were in the government civil-service. Granting even that a considerable proportion of the third unheard from are unsuccessful, this is a record of usefulness. Personally I know many hundreds of these graduates, and have corresponded with more than a thousand; through others I have followed carefully the life-work of scores; I have taught some of them and some of the pupils whom they have taught, lived in homes which they have builded, and looked at life through their eyes. Comparing them as a class with my fellow students in New England and in Europe, I cannot hesitate in saying that nowhere have I met men and women with a broader spirit of helpfulness, with deeper devotion to their life-work, or with more consecrated determination to succeed in the face of bitter difficulties than among Negro college-bred men. They have, to be sure, their proportion of ne'er-do-weels, their pedants and lettered fools, but they have a surprisingly small proportion of them; they have not that culture of manner which we instinctively associate with university men, forgetting that in reality it is the heritage from cultured homes, and that no people a generation removed from slavery can escape a certain unpleasant rawness and gaucherie, despite the best of training.

With all their larger vision and deeper sensibility, these men have usually been conservative, careful leaders. They have seldom been agitators, have withstood the temptation to head the mob, and have worked steadily and faithfully in a thousand communities in the South. As teachers, they have given the South a commendable system of city schools and large numbers of private normal-schools and academies. Colored college-bred men have worked side by side with white college graduates at Hampton; almost from the beginning the backbone of Tuskegee's teaching force has been formed of graduates from Fisk and Atlanta. And to-day the institute is filled with college graduates, from the energetic wife of the principal down to the teacher of agriculture, including nearly half of the executive council and a majority of the heads of departments. In the professions, college men are slowly but surely leavening the Negro church, are healing and preventing the devastations of disease, and beginning to furnish legal protection for the liberty and property of the toiling masses. All this is needful work. Who would do it if

Negroes did not? How could Negroes do it if they were not trained carefully for it? If white people need colleges to furnish teachers, ministers, lawyers, and doctors, do black people need nothing of the sort?

If it is true that there are an appreciable number of Negro youth in the land capable by character and talent to receive that higher training, the end of which is culture, and if the two and a half thousand who have had something of this training in the past have in the main proved themselves useful to their race and generation, the question then comes, What place in the future development of the South ought the Negro college and college-bred man to occupy? That the present social separation and acute race-sensitiveness must eventually yield to the influences of culture, as the South grows civilized, is clear. But such transformation calls for singular wisdom and patience. If, while the healing of this vast sore is progressing, the races are to live for many years side by side, united in economic effort, obeying a common government, sensitive to mutual thought and feeling, yet subtly and silently separate in many matters of deeper human intimacy,—if this unusual and dangerous development is to progress amid peace and order, mutual respect and growing intelligence, it will call for social surgery at once the delicatest and nicest in modern history. It will demand broad-minded, upright men, both white and black, and in its final accomplishment American civilization will triumph. So far as white men are concerned, this fact is to-day being recognized in the South, and a happy renaissance of university education seems imminent. But the very voices that cry hail to this good work are, strange to relate, largely silent or antagonistic to the higher education of the Negro.

Strange to relate! for this is certain, no secure civilization can be built in the South with the Negro as an ignorant, turbulent proletariat. Suppose we seek to remedy this by making them laborers and nothing more: they are not fools, they have tasted of the Tree of Life, and they will not cease to think, will not cease attempting to read the riddle of the world. By taking away their best equipped teachers and leaders, by slamming the door of opportunity in the faces of their bolder and brighter minds, will you make them satisfied with their lot? or will you not rather transfer their leading from the hands of men taught to think to the hands of untrained demagogues? We ought not to forget that despite the pressure of poverty, and despite the active discouragement and even ridicule of friends, the demand for higher training steadily increases among Negro youth: there were, in the years from 1875 to 1880, 22 Negro graduates from Northern colleges; from 1885 to 1890 there were

43, and from 1895 to 1900, nearly 100 graduates. From Southern Negro colleges there were, in the same three periods, 143, 413, and over 500 graduates. Here, then, is the plain thirst for training; by refusing to give this Talented Tenth the key to knowledge, can any sane man imagine that they will lightly lay aside their yearning and contentedly become hewers of wood and drawers of water?

No. The dangerously clear logic of the Negro's position will more and more loudly assert itself in that day when increasing wealth and more intricate social organization preclude the South from being, as it so largely is, simply an armed camp for intimidating black folk. Such waste of energy cannot be spared if the South is to catch up with civilization. And as the black third of the land grows in thrift and skill, unless skilfully guided in its larger philosophy, it must more and more brood over the red past and the creeping, crooked present, until it grasps a gospel of revolt and revenge and throws its new-found energies athwart the current of advance. Even to-day the masses of the Negroes see all too clearly the anomalies of their position and the moral crookedness of yours. You may marshal strong indictments against them, but their counter-cries, lacking though they be in formal logic, have burning truths within them which you may not wholly ignore, O Southern Gentlemen! If you deplore their presence here, they ask, Who brought us? When you cry, Deliver us from the vision of intermarriage, they answer that legal marriage is infinitely better than systematic concubinage and prostitution. And if in just fury you accuse their vagabonds of violating women, they also in fury quite as just may reply: The rape which your gentlemen have done against helpless black women in defiance of your own laws is written on the foreheads of two millions of mulattoes, and written in ineffaceable blood. And finally, when you fasten crime upon this race as its peculiar trait, they answer that slavery was the arch-crime, and lynching and lawlessness its twin abortion; that color and race are not crimes, and yet they it is which in this land receives most unceasing condemnation, North, East, South, and West.

I will not say such arguments are wholly justified,—I will not insist that there is no other side to the shield; but I do say that of the nine millions of Negroes in this nation, there is scarcely one out of the cradle to whom these arguments do not daily present themselves in the guise of terrible truth. I insist that the question of the future is how best to keep these millions from brooding over the wrongs of the past and the difficulties of the present, so that all their energies may be bent toward a cheerful striving and co-opera-

tion with their white neighbors toward a larger, juster, and fuller future. That one wise method of doing this lies in the closer knitting of the Negro to the great industrial possibilities of the South is a great truth. And this the common schools and the manual training and trade schools are working to accomplish. But these alone are not enough. The foundations of knowledge in this race, as in others, must be sunk deep in the college and university if we would build a solid, permanent structure. Internal problems of social advance must inevitably come,—problems of work and wages, of families and homes, of morals and the true valuing of the things of life; and all these and other inevitable problems of civilization the Negro must meet and solve largely for himself, by reason of his isolation; and can there be any possible solution other than by study and thought and an appeal to the rich experience of the past? Is there not, with such a group and in such a crisis, infinitely more danger to be apprehended from half trained minds and shallow thinking than from over-education and over-refinement? Surely we have wit enough to found a Negro college so manned and equipped as to steer successfully between the dilettante and the fool. We shall hardly induce black men to believe that if their stomachs be full, it matters little about their brains. They already dimly perceive that the paths of peace winding between honest toil and dignified manhood call for the guidance of skilled thinkers, the loving, reverent comradeship between the black lowly and the black men emancipated by training and culture.

The function of the Negro college, then, is clear: it must maintain the standards of popular education, it must seek the social regeneration of the Negro, and it must help in the solution of problems of race contact and cooperation. And finally, beyond all this, It must develop men. Above our modern socialism, and out of the worship of the mass, must persist and evolve that higher individualism which the centres of culture protect; there must come a loftier respect for the sovereign human soul that seeks to know itself and the world about it; that seeks a freedom for expansion and self-development; that will love and hate and labor in its own way, untrammeled alike by old and new. Such souls aforetime have inspired and guided worlds, and if we be not wholly bewitched by our Rhine-gold, they shall again. Herein the longing of black men must have respect: the rich and bitter depth of their experience, the unknown treasures of their inner life, the strange rendings of nature they have seen, may give the world new points of view and make their loving, living, and doing precious to all human hearts. And to themselves in these the days that try their souls, the chance to soar in the dim blue air above

the smoke is to their finer spirits boon and guerdon for what they lose on earth by being black.

I sit with Shakespeare and he winces not. Across the color line I move arm in arm with Balzac and Dumas, where smiling men and welcoming women glide in gilded halls. From out the caves of evening that swing between the strong-limbed earth and the tracery of the stars, I summon Aristotle and Aurelius and what soul I will, and they come all graciously with no scorn nor condescension. So, wed with Truth, I dwell above the Veil. Is this the life you grudge us, O knightly America? Is this the life you long to change into the dull red hideousness of Georgia? Are you so afraid lest peering from this high Pisgah, between Philistine and Amalekite, we sight the Promised Land?

VII

OF THE BLACK BELT

I am black but comely, O ye daughters of Jerusalem,
As the tents of Kedar, as the curtains of Solomon.
Look not upon me, because I am black,
Because the sun hath looked upon me:
My mother's children were angry with me;
They made me the keeper of the vineyards;
But mine own vineyard have I not kept.
 The Song Of Solomon.

Out of the North the train thundered, and we woke to see the crimson soil of Georgia stretching away bare and monotonous right and left. Here and there lay straggling, unlovely villages, and lean men loafed leisurely at the depots; then again came the stretch of pines and clay. Yet we did not nod, nor weary of the scene; for this is historic ground. Right across our track, three hundred and sixty years ago, wandered the cavalcade of Hernando de Soto, looking for gold and the Great Sea; and he and his footsore captives disappeared yonder in the grim forests to the west. Here sits Atlanta, the city of a hundred hills, with something Western, something Southern, and something quite its own, in its busy life. Just this side Atlanta is the land of the Cherokees and to the southwest, not far from where Sam Hose was crucified, you may stand on a spot which is to-day the centre of the Negro problem,—the centre of those nine million men who are America's dark heritage from slavery and the slave-trade.

Not only is Georgia thus the geographical focus of our Negro population, but in many other respects, both now and yesterday, the Negro problems have seemed to be centered in this State. No other State in the Union can count a million Negroes among its citizens,—a population as large as the slave population of the whole Union in 1800; no other State fought so long and strenuously to gather this host of Africans. Oglethorpe thought slavery against law and gospel; but the circumstances which gave Georgia its first inhabitants were not calculated to furnish citizens over-nice in their ideas about rum and slaves. Despite the prohibitions of the trustees, these Georgians, like some of their descendants, proceeded to take the law into their own hands; and so pliant were the judges, and so flagrant the smuggling, and so earnest were the prayers of Whitefield, that by the middle of the eighteenth century all restrictions were swept away, and the slave-trade went merrily on for fifty years and more.

Down in Darien, where the Delegal riots took place some summers ago, there used to come a strong protest against slavery from the Scotch Highlanders; and the Moravians of Ebenezer did not like the system. But not till the Haytian Terror of Toussaint was the trade in men even checked; while the national statute of 1808 did not suffice to stop it. How the Africans poured in!—fifty thousand between 1790 and 1810, and then, from Virginia and from smugglers, two thousand a year for many years more. So the thirty thousand Negroes of Georgia in 1790 were doubled in a decade,—were over a hundred thousand in 1810, had reached two hundred thousand in 1820, and half a million at the time of the war. Thus like a snake the black

population writhed upward.

But we must hasten on our journey. This that we pass as we near Atlanta is the ancient land of the Cherokees,—that brave Indian nation which strove so long for its fatherland, until Fate and the United States Government drove them beyond the Mississippi. If you wish to ride with me you must come into the "Jim Crow Car." There will be no objection,—already four other white men, and a little white girl with her nurse, are in there. Usually the races are mixed in there; but the white coach is all white. Of course this car is not so good as the other, but it is fairly clean and comfortable. The discomfort lies chiefly in the hearts of those four black men yonder—and in mine.

We rumble south in quite a business-like way. The bare red clay and pines of Northern Georgia begin to disappear, and in their place appears a rich rolling land, luxuriant, and here and there well tilled. This is the land of the Creek Indians; and a hard time the Georgians had to seize it. The towns grow more frequent and more interesting, and brand-new cotton mills rise on every side. Below Macon the world grows darker; for now we approach the Black Belt,—that strange land of shadows, at which even slaves paled in the past, and whence come now only faint and half-intelligible murmurs to the world beyond. The "Jim Crow Car" grows larger and a shade better; three rough field-hands and two or three white loafers accompany us, and the newsboy still spreads his wares at one end. The sun is setting, but we can see the great cotton country as we enter it,—the soil now dark and fertile, now thin and gray, with fruit-trees and dilapidated buildings,—all the way to Albany.

At Albany, in the heart of the Black Belt, we stop. Two hundred miles south of Atlanta, two hundred miles west of the Atlantic, and one hundred miles north of the Great Gulf lies Dougherty County, with ten thousand Negroes and two thousand whites. The Flint River winds down from Andersonville, and, turning suddenly at Albany, the county-seat, hurries on to join the Chattahoochee and the sea. Andrew Jackson knew the Flint well, and marched across it once to avenge the Indian Massacre at Fort Mims. That was in 1814, not long before the battle of New Orleans; and by the Creek treaty that followed this campaign, all Dougherty County, and much other rich land, was ceded to Georgia. Still, settlers fought shy of this land, for the Indians were all about, and they were unpleasant neighbors in those days. The panic of 1837, which Jackson bequeathed to Van Buren, turned the planters from the impoverished lands of Virginia, the Carolinas, and east

Georgia, toward the West. The Indians were removed to Indian Territory, and settlers poured into these coveted lands to retrieve their broken fortunes. For a radius of a hundred miles about Albany, stretched a great fertile land, luxuriant with forests of pine, oak, ash, hickory, and poplar; hot with the sun and damp with the rich black swamp-land; and here the corner-stone of the Cotton Kingdom was laid.

Albany is to-day a wide-streeted, placid, Southern town, with a broad sweep of stores and saloons, and flanking rows of homes,—whites usually to the north, and blacks to the south. Six days in the week the town looks decidedly too small for itself, and takes frequent and prolonged naps. But on Saturday suddenly the whole county disgorges itself upon the place, and a perfect flood of black peasantry pours through the streets, fills the stores, blocks the sidewalks, chokes the thoroughfares, and takes full possession of the town. They are black, sturdy, uncouth country folk, good-natured and simple, talkative to a degree, and yet far more silent and brooding than the crowds of the Rhine-pfalz, or Naples, or Cracow. They drink considerable quantities of whiskey, but do not get very drunk; they talk and laugh loudly at times, but seldom quarrel or fight. They walk up and down the streets, meet and gossip with friends, stare at the shop windows, buy coffee, cheap candy, and clothes, and at dusk drive home—happy? well no, not exactly happy, but much happier than as though they had not come.

Thus Albany is a real capital,—a typical Southern county town, the centre of the life of ten thousand souls; their point of contact with the outer world, their centre of news and gossip, their market for buying and selling, borrowing and lending, their fountain of justice and law. Once upon a time we knew country life so well and city life so little, that we illustrated city life as that of a closely crowded country district. Now the world has well-nigh forgotten what the country is, and we must imagine a little city of black people scattered far and wide over three hundred lonesome square miles of land, without train or trolley, in the midst of cotton and corn, and wide patches of sand and gloomy soil.

It gets pretty hot in Southern Georgia in July,—a sort of dull, determined heat that seems quite independent of the sun; so it took us some days to muster courage enough to leave the porch and venture out on the long country roads, that we might see this unknown world. Finally we started. It was about ten in the morning, bright with a faint breeze, and we jogged leisurely southward in the valley of the Flint. We passed the scattered box-like cabins of the brick-yard hands, and the long tenement-row facetiously called

"The Ark," and were soon in the open country, and on the confines of the great plantations of other days. There is the "Joe Fields place"; a rough old fellow was he, and had killed many a "nigger" in his day. Twelve miles his plantation used to run,—a regular barony. It is nearly all gone now; only straggling bits belong to the family, and the rest has passed to Jews and Negroes. Even the bits which are left are heavily mortgaged, and, like the rest of the land, tilled by tenants. Here is one of them now,—a tall brown man, a hard worker and a hard drinker, illiterate, but versed in farm-lore as his nodding crops declare. This distressingly new board house is his, and he has just moved out of yonder moss-grown cabin with its one square room.

From the curtains in Benton's house, down the road, a dark comely face is staring at the strangers; for passing carriages are not every-day occurrences here. Benton is an intelligent yellow man with a good-sized family, and manages a plantation blasted by the war and now the broken staff of the widow. He might be well-to-do, they say; but he carouses too much in Albany. And the half-desolate spirit of neglect born of the very soil seems to have settled on these acres. In times past there were cotton-gins and machinery here; but they have rotted away.

The whole land seems forlorn and forsaken. Here are the remnants of the vast plantations of the Sheldons, the Pellots, and the Rensons; but the souls of them are passed. The houses lie in half ruin, or have wholly disappeared; the fences have flown, and the families are wandering in the world. Strange vicissitudes have met these whilom masters. Yonder stretch the wide acres of Bildad Reasor; he died in war-time, but the upstart overseer hastened to wed the widow. Then he went, and his neighbors too, and now only the black tenant remains; but the shadow-hand of the master's grand-nephew or cousin or creditor stretches out of the gray distance to collect the rack-rent remorselessly, and so the land is uncared-for and poor. Only black tenants can stand such a system, and they only because they must. Ten miles we have ridden to-day and have seen no white face.

A resistless feeling of depression falls slowly upon us, despite the gaudy sunshine and the green cotton-fields. This, then, is the Cotton Kingdom,— the shadow of a marvellous dream. And where is the King? Perhaps this is he,—the sweating plough-man, tilling his eighty acres with two lean mules, and fighting a hard battle with debt. So we sit musing, until, as we turn a corner on the sandy road, there comes a fairer scene suddenly in view,—a neat cottage snugly ensconced by the road, and near it a little store. A tall bronzed man rises from the porch as we hail him, and comes out to our car-

riage. He is six feet in height, with a sober face that smiles gravely. He walks too straight to be a tenant,—yes, he owns two hundred and forty acres. "The land is run down since the boom—days of eighteen hundred and fifty," he explains, and cotton is low. Three black tenants live on his place, and in his little store he keeps a small stock of tobacco, snuff, soap, and soda, for the neighborhood. Here is his gin-house with new machinery just installed. Three hundred bales of cotton went through it last year. Two children he has sent away to school. Yes, he says sadly, he is getting on, but cotton is down to four cents; I know how Debt sits staring at him.

Wherever the King may be, the parks and palaces of the Cotton Kingdom have not wholly disappeared. We plunge even now into great groves of oak and towering pine, with an undergrowth of myrtle and shrubbery. This was the "home-house" of the Thompsons,—slave-barons who drove their coach and four in the merry past. All is silence now, and ashes, and tangled weeds. The owner put his whole fortune into the rising cotton industry of the fifties, and with the falling prices of the eighties he packed up and stole away. Yonder is another grove, with unkempt lawn, great magnolias, and grass-grown paths. The Big House stands in half-ruin, its great front door staring blankly at the street, and the back part grotesquely restored for its black tenant. A shabby, well-built Negro he is, unlucky and irresolute. He digs hard to pay rent to the white girl who owns the remnant of the place. She married a policeman, and lives in Savannah.

Now and again we come to churches. Here is one now,—Shepherd's, they call it,—a great whitewashed barn of a thing, perched on stilts of stone, and looking for all the world as though it were just resting here a moment and might be expected to waddle off down the road at almost any time. And yet it is the centre of a hundred cabin homes; and sometimes, of a Sunday, five hundred persons from far and near gather here and talk and eat and sing. There is a school house near, a very airy, empty shed; but even this is an improvement, for usually the school is held in the church. The churches vary from log-huts to those like Shepherd's, and the schools from nothing to this little house that sits demurely on the county line. It is a tiny plank-house, perhaps ten by twenty, and has within a double row of rough unplaned benches, resting mostly on legs, sometimes on boxes. Opposite the door is a square home-made desk. In one corner are the ruins of a stove, and in the other a dim blackboard. It is the cheerfulest schoolhouse I have seen in Dougherty, save in town. Back of the schoolhouse is a lodgehouse two stories high and not quite finished. Societies meet there,—societies "to care for

the sick and bury the dead"; and these societies grow and flourish.

We had come to the boundaries of Dougherty, and were about to turn west along the county-line, when all these sights were pointed out to us by a kindly old man, black, white-haired, and seventy. Forty-five years he had lived here, and now supports himself and his old wife by the help of the steer tethered yonder and the charity of his black neighbors. He shows us the farm of the Hills just across the county line in Baker,—a widow and two strapping sons, who raised ten bales (one need not add "cotton" down here) last year. There are fences and pigs and cows, and the soft-voiced, velvet-skinned young Memnon, who sauntered half-bashfully over to greet the strangers, is proud of his home. We turn now to the west along the county line. Great dismantled trunks of pines tower above the green cotton-fields, cracking their naked gnarled fingers toward the border of living forest beyond. There is little beauty in this region, only a sort of crude abandon that suggests power,— a naked graudeur, as it were. The houses are bare and straight; there are no hammocks or easy-chairs, and few flowers. So when, as here at Rawdon's, one sees a vine clinging to a little porch, and home-like windows peeping over the fences, one takes a long breath. I think I never before quite realized the place of the Fence in civilization. This is the Land of the Unfenced, where crouch on either hand scores of ugly one-room cabins, cheerless and dirty. Here lies the Negro problem in its naked dirt and penury. And here are no fences. But now and then the cries-cross rails or straight palings break into view, and then we know a touch of culture is near. Of course Harrison Gohagen,—a quiet yellow man, young, smooth-faced, and diligent,—of course he is lord of some hundred acres, and we expect to see a vision of well-kept rooms and fat beds and laughing children. For has he not fine fences? And those over yonder, why should they build fences on the rack-rented land? It will only increase their rent.

On we wind, through sand and pines and glimpses of old plantations, till there creeps into sight a cluster of buildings,—wood and brick, mills and houses, and scattered cabins. It seemed quite a village. As it came nearer and nearer, however, the aspect changed: the buildings were rotten, the bricks were falling out, the mills were silent, and the store was closed. Only in the cabins appeared now and then a bit of lazy life. I could imagine the place under some weird spell, and was half-minded to search out the princess. An old ragged black man, honest, simple, and improvident, told us the tale. The Wizard of the North—the Capitalist—had rushed down in the seventies to woo this coy dark soil. He bought a square mile or more, and for a time the

field-hands sang, the gins groaned, and the mills buzzed. Then came a change. The agent's son embezzled the funds and ran off with them. Then the agent himself disappeared. Finally the new agent stole even the books, and the company in wrath closed its business and its houses, refused to sell, and let houses and furniture and machinery rust and rot. So the Waters-Loring plantation was stilled by the spell of dishonesty, and stands like some gaunt rebuke to a scarred land.

Somehow that plantation ended our day's journey; for I could not shake off the influence of that silent scene. Back toward town we glided, past the straight and thread-like pines, past a dark tree-dotted pond where the air was heavy with a dead sweet perfume. White slender-legged curlews flitted by us, and the garnet blooms of the cotton looked gay against the green and purple stalks. A peasant girl was hoeing in the field, white-turbaned and black-limbed. All this we saw, but the spell still lay upon us.

How curious a land is this,—how full of untold story, of tragedy and laughter, and the rich legacy of human life; shadowed with a tragic past, and big with future promise! This is the Black Belt of Georgia. Dougherty County is the west end of the Black Belt, and men once called it the Egypt of the Confederacy. It is full of historic interest. First there is the Swamp, to the west, where the Chickasawhatchee flows sullenly southward. The shadow of an old plantation lies at its edge, forlorn and dark. Then comes the pool; pendent gray moss and brackish waters appear, and forests filled with wild-fowl. In one place the wood is on fire, smouldering in dull red anger; but nobody minds. Then the swamp grows beautiful; a raised road, built by chained Negro convicts, dips down into it, and forms a way walled and almost covered in living green. Spreading trees spring from a prodigal luxu-riance of undergrowth; great dark green shadows fade into the black back-ground, until all is one mass of tangled semi-tropical foliage, marvellous in its weird savage splendor. Once we crossed a black silent stream, where the sad trees and writhing creepers, all glinting fiery yellow and green, seemed like some vast cathedral,—some green Milan builded of wildwood. And as I crossed, I seemed to see again that fierce tragedy of seventy years ago. Osceola, the Indian-Negro chieftain, had risen in the swamps of Florida, vowing vengeance. His war-cry reached the red Creeks of Dougherty, and their war-cry rang from the Chattahoochee to the sea. Men and women and children fled and fell before them as they swept into Dougherty. In yonder shadows a dark and hideously painted warrior glided stealthily on,—anoth-er and another, until three hundred had crept into the treacherous swamp.

Then the false slime closing about them called the white men from the east. Waist-deep, they fought beneath the tall trees, until the war-cry was hushed and the Indians glided back into the west. Small wonder the wood is red.

Then came the black slaves. Day after day the clank of chained feet marching from Virginia and Carolina to Georgia was heard in these rich swamp lands. Day after day the songs of the callous, the wail of the mother-less, and the muttered curses of the wretched echoed from the Flint to the Chickasawhatchee, until by 1860 there had risen in West Dougherty perhaps the richest slave kingdom the modern world ever knew. A hundred and fifty barons commanded the labor of nearly six thousand negroes, held sway over farms with ninety thousand acres of tilled land, valued even in times of cheap soil at three millions of dollars. Twenty thousand bales of ginned cotton went yearly to England, New and Old; and men that came there bankrupt made money and grew rich. In a single decade the cotton output increased four-fold and the value of lands was tripled. It was the heyday of the nouveau riche, and a life of careless extravagance reigned among the masters. Four and six bob-tailed thoroughbreds rolled their coaches to town; open hospitality and gay entertainment were the rule. Parks and groves were laid out, rich with flower and vine, and in the midst stood the low wide-halled "big house," with its porch and columns and great fire-places.

And yet with all this there was something sordid, something forced,—a certain feverish unrest and recklessness; for was not all this show and tinsel built upon a groan? "This land was a little Hell," said a ragged, brown, and grave-faced man to me. We were seated near a roadside blacksmith-shop, and behind was the bare ruin of some master's home. "I've seen niggers drop dead in the furrow, but they were kicked aside, and the plough never stopped. And down in the guard-house, there's where the blood ran."

With such foundations a kingdom must in time sway and fall. The mas-ters moved to Macon and Augusta, and left only the irresponsible overseers on the land. And the result is such ruin as this, the Lloyd "home-place":— great waving oaks, a spread of lawn, myrtles and chestnuts, all ragged and wild; a solitary gate-post standing where once was a castle entrance; an old rusty anvil lying amid rotting bellows and wood in the ruins of a blacksmith shop; a wide rambling old mansion, brown and dingy, filled now with the grandchildren of the slaves who once waited on its tables while the family of the master has dwindled to two lone women, who live in Macon and feed hungrily off the remnants of an earldom. So we ride on, past phantom gates and falling homes,—past the once flourishing farms of the Smiths, the

Gandys, and the Lagores,—and find all dilapidated and half ruined, even there where a solitary white woman, a relic of other days, sits alone in state among miles of Negroes and rides to town in her ancient coach each day.

This was indeed the Egypt of the Confederacy,—the rich granary whence potatoes and corn and cotton poured out to the famished and ragged Confederate troops as they battled for a cause lost long before 1861. Sheltered and secure, it became the place of refuge for families, wealth, and slaves. Yet even then the hard ruthless rape of the land began to tell. The red-clay sub-soil already had begun to peer above the loam. The harder the slaves were driven the more careless and fatal was their farming. Then came the revolution of war and Emancipation, the bewilderment of Reconstruction,—and now, what is the Egypt of the Confederacy, and what meaning has it for the nation's weal or woe?

It is a land of rapid contrasts and of curiously mingled hope and pain. Here sits a pretty blue-eyed quadroon hiding her bare feet; she was married only last week, and yonder in the field is her dark young husband, hoeing to support her, at thirty cents a day without board. Across the way is Gatesby, brown and tall, lord of two thousand acres shrewdly won and held. There is a store conducted by his black son, a blacksmith shop, and a ginnery. Five miles below here is a town owned and controlled by one white New Englander. He owns almost a Rhode Island county, with thousands of acres and hundreds of black laborers. Their cabins look better than most, and the farm, with machinery and fertilizers, is much more business-like than any in the county, although the manager drives hard bargains in wages. When now we turn and look five miles above, there on the edge of town are five houses of prostitutes, two of blacks and three of whites; and In one of the houses of the whites a worthless black boy was harbored too openly two years ago; so he was hanged for rape. And here, too, is the high whitewashed fence of the "stockade," as the county prison is called; the white folks say it is ever full of black criminals,—the black folks say that only colored boys are sent to jail, and they not because they are guilty, but because the State needs criminals to eke out its income by their forced labor.

The Jew is the heir of the slave-baron in Dougherty; and as we ride westward, by wide stretching cornfields and stubby orchards of peach and pear, we see on all sides within the circle of dark forest a Land of Canaan. Here and there are tales of projects for money-getting, born in the swift days of Reconstruction,—"improvement" companies, wine companies, mills and factories; nearly all failed, and the Jew fell heir. It is a beautiful land, this

Dougherty, west of the Flint. The forests are wonderful, the solemn pines have disappeared, and this is the "Oakey Woods," with its wealth of hickories, beeches, oaks, and palmettos. But a pall of debt hangs over the beautiful land; the merchants are in debt to the wholesalers, the planters are in debt to the merchants, the tenants owe the planters, and laborers bow and bend beneath the burden of it all. Here and there a man has raised his head above these murky waters. We passed one fenced stock-farm, with grass and grazing cattle, that looked very homelike after endless corn and cotton. Here and there are black freeholders: there is the gaunt dull-black Jackson, with his hundred acres. "I says, 'Look up! If you don't look up you can't get up,'" remarks Jackson, philosophically. And he's gotten up. Dark Carter's neat barns would do credit to New England. His master helped him to get a start, but when the black man died last fall the master's sons immediately laid claim to the estate. "And them white folks will get it, too," said my yellow gossip.

I turn from these well-tended acres with a comfortable feeling that the Negro is rising. Even then, however, the fields, as we proceed, begin to redden and the trees disappear. Rows of old cabins appear filled with renters and laborers,—cheerless, bare, and dirty, for the most part, although here and there the very age and decay makes the scene picturesque. A young black fellow greets us. He is twenty-two, and just married. Until last year he had good luck renting; then cotton fell, and the sheriff seized and sold all he had. So he moved here, where the rent is higher, the land poorer, and the owner inflexible; he rents a forty-dollar mule for twenty dollars a year. Poor lad!— a slave at twenty-two. This plantation, owned now by a Russian Jew, was a part of the famous Bolton estate. After the war it was for many years worked by gangs of Negro convicts,—and black convicts then were even more plentiful than now; it was a way of making Negroes work, and the question of guilt was a minor one. Hard tales of cruelty and mistreatment of the chained freemen are told, but the county authorities were deaf until the free-labor market was nearly ruined by wholesale migration. Then they took the convicts from the plantations, but not until one of the fairest regions of the "Oakey Woods" had been ruined and ravished into a red waste, out of which only a Yankee or a Jew could squeeze more blood from debt-cursed tenants.

No wonder that Luke Black, slow, dull, and discouraged, shuffles to our carriage and talks hopelessly. Why should he strive? Every year finds him deeper in debt. How strange that Georgia, the world-heralded refuge of poor debtors, should bind her own to sloth and misfortune as ruthlessly as ever

England did! The poor land groans with its birth-pains, and brings forth scarcely a hundred pounds of cotton to the acre, where fifty years ago it yielded eight times as much. Of this meagre yield the tenant pays from a quarter to a third in rent, and most of the rest in interest on food and supplies bought on credit. Twenty years yonder sunken-checked, old black man has labored under that system, and now, turned day-laborer, is supporting his wife and boarding himself on his wages of a dollar and a half a week, received only part of the year.

The Bolton convict farm formerly included the neighboring plantation. Here it was that the convicts were lodged in the great log prison still standing. A dismal place it still remains, with rows of ugly huts filled with surly ignorant tenants. "What rent do you pay here?" I inquired. "I don't know,—what is it, Sam?" "All we make," answered Sam. It is a depressing place,—bare, unshaded, with no charm of past association, only a memory of forced human toil,—now, then, and before the war. They are not happy, these black men whom we meet throughout this region. There is little of the joyous abandon and playfulness which we are wont to associate with the plantation Negro. At best, the natural good-nature is edged with complaint or has changed into sullenness and gloom. And now and then it blazes forth in veiled but hot anger. I remember one big red-eyed black whom we met by the roadside. Forty-five years he had labored on this farm, beginning with nothing, and still having nothing. To be sure, he had given four children a common-school training, and perhaps if the new fence-law had not allowed unfenced crops in West Dougherty he might have raised a little stock and kept ahead. As it is, he is hopelessly in debt, disappointed, and embittered. He stopped us to inquire after the black boy in Albany, whom it was said a policeman had shot and killed for loud talking on the sidewalk. And then he said slowly: "Let a white man touch me, and he dies; I don't boast this,—I don't say it around loud, or before the children,—but I mean it. I've seen them whip my father and my old mother in them cotton-rows till the blood ran; by—" and we passed on.

Now Sears, whom we met next lolling under the chubby oak-trees, was of quite different fibre. Happy?—Well, yes; he laughed and flipped pebbles, and thought the world was as it was. He had worked here twelve years and has nothing but a mortgaged mule. Children? Yes, seven; but they hadn't been to school this year,—couldn't afford books and clothes, and couldn't spare their work. There go part of them to the fields now,—three big boys astride mules, and a strapping girl with bare brown legs. Careless ignorance

and laziness here, fierce hate and vindictiveness there;—these are the extremes of the Negro problem which we met that day, and we scarce knew which we preferred.

Here and there we meet distinct characters quite out of the ordinary. One came out of a piece of newly cleared ground, making a wide detour to avoid the snakes. He was an old, hollow-cheeked man, with a drawn and characterful brown face. He had a sort of self-contained quaintness and rough humor impossible to describe; a certain cynical earnestness that puzzled one. "The niggers were jealous of me over on the other place," he said, "and so me and the old woman begged this piece of woods, and I cleared it up myself. Made nothing for two years, but I reckon I've got a crop now." The cotton looked tall and rich, and we praised it. He curtsied low, and then bowed almost to the ground, with an imperturbable gravity that seemed almost suspicious. Then he continued, "My mule died last week,"—a calamity in this land equal to a devastating fire in town,—"but a white man loaned me another." Then he added, eyeing us, "Oh, I gets along with white folks." We turned the conversation. "Bears? deer?" he answered, "well, I should say there were," and he let out a string of brave oaths, as be told hunting-tales of the swamp. We left him standing still in the middle of the road looking after us, and yet apparently not noticing us.

The Whistle place, which includes his bit of land, was bought soon after the war by an English syndicate, the "Dixie Cotton and Corn Company." A marvellous deal of style their factor put on, with his servants, and coach-and-six; so much so that the concern soon landed in inextricable bankruptcy. Nobody lives in the old house now, but a man comes each winter out of the North and collects his high rents. I know not which are the more touching,—such old empty houses, or the homes of the masters' sons. Sad and bitter tales lie hidden back of those white doors,—tales of poverty, of struggle, of disappointment. A revolution such as that of '63 is a terrible thing; they that rose rich in the morning often slept in paupers' beds. Beggars and vulgar speculators rose to rule over them, and their children went astray. See yonder sad-colored house, with its cabins and fences and glad crops! It is not glad within; last month the prodigal son of the struggling father wrote home from the city for money. Money! Where was it to come from? And so the son rose in the night and killed his baby, and killed his wife, and shot himself dead. And the world passed on.

I remember wheeling around a bend in the road beside a graceful bit of forest and a singing brook. A long low house faced us, with porch and flying

pillars, great oaken door, and a broad lawn shining in the evening sun. But the window-panes were gone, the pillars were worm-eaten, and the moss-grown roof was falling in. Half curiously I peered through the unhinged door, and saw where, on the wall across the hall, was written in once gay letters a faded "Welcome."

Quite a contrast to the southwestern part of Dougherty County is the northwest. Soberly timbered in oak and pine, it has none of that half tropical luxuriance of the southwest. Then, too, there are fewer signs of a romantic past, and more of systematic modern land-grabbing and money-getting. White people are more in evidence here, and farmer and hired labor replace to some extent the absentee landlord and rack-rented tenant. The crops have neither the luxuriance of the richer land nor the signs of neglect so often seen, and there were fences and meadows here and there. Most of this land was poor, and beneath the notice of the slave-baron, before the war. Since then his nephews and the poor whites and the Jews have seized it. The returns of the farmer are too small to allow much for wages, and yet he will not sell off small farms. There is the Negro Sanford; he has worked fourteen years as overseer on the Ladson place, and "paid out enough for fertilizers to have bought a farm," but the owner will not sell off a few acres.

Two children—a boy and a girl—are hoeing sturdily in the fields on the farm where Corliss works. He is smooth-faced and brown, and is fencing up his pigs. He used to run a successful cotton-gin, but the Cotton Seed Oil Trust has forced the price of ginning so low that he says it hardly pays him. He points out a stately old house over the way as the home of "Pa Willis." We eagerly ride over, for "Pa Willis" was the tall and powerful black Moses who led the Negroes for a generation, and led them well. He was a Baptist preacher, and when he died two thousand black people followed him to the grave; and now they preach his funeral sermon each year. His widow lives here,—a weazened, sharp-featured little woman, who curtsied quaintly as we greeted her. Further on lives Jack Delson, the most prosperous Negro farmer in the county. It is a joy to meet him,—a great broad-shouldered, handsome black man, intelligent and jovial. Six hundred and fifty acres he owns, and has eleven black tenants. A neat and tidy home nestled in a flower-garden, and a little store stands beside it.

We pass the Munson place, where a plucky white widow is renting and struggling; and the eleven hundred acres of the Sennet plantation, with its Negro overseer. Then the character of the farms begins to change. Nearly all the lands belong to Russian Jews; the overseers are white, and the cabins are

bare board-houses scattered here and there. The rents are high, and day-laborers and "contract" hands abound. It is a keen, hard struggle for living here, and few have time to talk. Tired with the long ride, we gladly drive into Gillonsville. It is a silent cluster of farm-houses standing on the crossroads, with one of its stores closed and tile other kept by a Negro preacher. They tell great tales of busy times at Gillonsville before all the railroads came to Albany; now it is chiefly a memory. Riding down the street, we stop at the preacher's and seat ourselves before the door. It was one of those scenes one cannot soon forget:—a wide, low, little house, whose motherly roof reached over and sheltered a snug little porch. There we sat, after the long hot drive, drinking cool water,—the talkative little storekeeper who is my daily companion; the silent old black woman patching pantaloons and saying never a word; the ragged picture of helpless misfortune who called in just to see the preacher; and finally the neat matronly preacher's wife, plump, yellow, and intelligent. "Own land?" said the wife; "well, only this house." Then she added quietly, "We did buy seven hundred acres up yonder, and paid for it; but they cheated us out of it. Sells was the owner." "Sells!" echoed the ragged misfortune, who was leaning against the balustrade and listening, "he's a regular cheat. I worked for him thirty-seven days this spring, and he paid me in cardboard checks which were to be cashed at the end of the month. But he never cashed them,—kept putting me off. Then the sheriff came and took my mule and corn and furniture—" "Furniture?" I asked; "but furniture is exempt from seizure by law." "Well, he took it just the same," said the hard-faced man.

VIII

OF THE QUEST OF THE GOLDEN FLEECE

But the Brute said in his breast, "Till the mills I grind have ceased,
The riches shall be dust of dust, dry ashes be the feast!

 "On the strong and cunning few
 Cynic favors I will strew;
I will stuff their maw with overplus until their spirit dies;
 From the patient and the low

I will take the joys they know;
They shall hunger after vanities and still an-hungered go.
Madness shall be on the people, ghastly jealousies arise;
Brother's blood shall cry on brother up the dead and empty skies."
William Vaughn Moody.

HAVE you ever seen a cotton-field white with the harvest,—its golden fleece hovering above the black earth like a silvery cloud edged with dark green, its bold white signals waving like the foam of billows from Carolina to Texas across that Black and human Sea? I have sometimes half suspected that here the winged ram Chrysomallus left that Fleece after which Jason and his Argonauts went vaguely wandering into the shadowy East three thousand years ago; and certainly one might frame a pretty and not far-fetched analogy of witchery and dragon's teeth, and blood and armed men, between the ancient and the modern Quest of the Golden Fleece in the Black Sea.

And now the golden fleece is found; not only found, but, in its birth place, woven. For the hum of the cotton-mills is the newest and most significant thing in the New South to-day. All through the Carolinas and Georgia, away down to Mexico, rise these gaunt red buildings, bare and homely, and yet so busy and noisy withal that they scarce seem to belong to the slow and sleepy land. Perhaps they sprang from dragons' teeth. So the Cotton Kingdom still lives; the world still bows beneath her sceptre. Even the markets that once defied the parvenu have crept one by one across the seas, and then slowly and reluctantly, but surely, have started toward the Black Belt.

To be sure, there are those who wag their heads knowingly and tell us that the capital of the Cotton Kingdom has moved from the Black to the White Belt,—that the Negro of to-day raises not more than half of the cotton crop. Such men forget that the cotton crop has doubled, and more than doubled, since the era of slavery, and that, even granting their contention, the Negro is still supreme in a Cotton Kingdom larger than that on which the

Confederacy builded its hopes. So the Negro forms to-day one of the chief figures in a great world-industry; and this, for its own sake, and in the light of historic interest, makes the field-hands of the cotton country worth studying.

We seldom study the condition of the Negro to-day honestly and carefully. It is so much easier to assume that we know it all. Or perhaps, having already reached conclusions in our own minds, we are loth to have them disturbed by facts. And yet how little we really know of these millions,—of their daily lives and longings, of their homely joys and sorrows, of their real shortcomings and the meaning of their crimes! All this we can only learn by intimate contact with the masses, and not by wholesale arguments covering millions separate in time and space, and differing widely in training and culture. To-day, then, my reader, let us turn our faces to the Black Belt of Georgia and seek simply to know the condition of the black farm-laborers of one county there.

Here in 1890 lived ten thousand Negroes and two thousand whites. The country is rich, yet the people are poor. The keynote of the Black Belt is debt; not commercial credit, but debt in the sense of continued inability on the part of the mass of the population to make income cover expense. This is the direct heritage of the South from the wasteful economies of the slave régime; but it was emphasized and brought to a crisis by the Emancipation of the slaves. In 1860, Dougherty County had six thousand slaves, worth at least two and a half millions of dollars; its farms were estimated at three millions,—making five and a half millions of property, the value of which depended largely on the slave system, and on the speculative demand for land once marvellously rich but already partially devitalized by careless and exhaustive culture. The war then meant a financial crash; in place of the five and a half millions of 1860, there remained in 1870 only farms valued at less than two millions. With this came increased competition in cotton culture from the rich lands of Texas; a steady fall in the normal price of cotton followed, from about fourteen cents a pound in 1860 until it reached four cents in 1898. Such a financial revolution was it that involved the owners of the cotton-belt in debt. And if things went ill with the master, how fared it with the man?

The plantations of Dougherty County in slavery days were not as imposing and aristocratic as those of Virginia. The Big House was smaller and usually one-storied, and sat very near the slave cabins. Sometimes these cabins stretched off on either side like wings; sometimes only on one side, forming a double row, or edging the road that turned into the plantation from the

main thoroughfare. The form and disposition of the laborers' cabins throughout the Black Belt is to-day the same as in slavery days. Some live in the self-same cabins, others in cabins rebuilt on the sites of the old. All are sprinkled in little groups over the face of the land, centering about some dilapidated Big House where the head-tenant or agent lives. The general character and arrangement of these dwellings remains on the whole unaltered. There were in the county, outside the corporate town of Albany, about fifteen hundred Negro families in 1898. Out of all these, only a single family occupied a house with seven rooms; only fourteen have five rooms or more. The mass live in one- and two-room homes.

The size and arrangements of a people's homes are no unfair index of their condition. If, then, we inquire more carefully into these Negro homes, we find much that is unsatisfactory. All over the face of the land is the one-room cabin,—now standing in the shadow of the Big House, now staring at the dusty road, now rising dark and sombre amid the green of the cotton-fields. It is nearly always old and bare, built of rough boards, and neither plastered nor ceiled. Light and ventilation are supplied by the single door and by the square hole in the wall with its wooden shutter. There is no glass, porch, or ornamentation without. Within is a fireplace, black and smoky, and usually unsteady with age. A bed or two, a table, a wooden chest, and a few chairs compose the furniture; while a stray show-bill or a newspaper makes up the decorations for the walls. Now and then one may find such a cabin kept scrupulously neat, with merry steaming fireplace and hospitable door; but the majority are dirty and dilapidated, smelling of eating and sleeping, poorly ventilated, and anything-but homes.

Above all, the cabins are crowded. We have come to associate crowding with homes in cities almost exclusively. This is primarily because we have so little accurate knowledge of country life. Here in Dougherty County one may find families of eight and ten occupying one or two rooms, and for every ten rooms of house accommodation for the Negroes there are twenty-five persons. The worst tenement abominations of New York do not have above twenty-two persons for every ten rooms. Of course, one small, close room in a city, without a yard, is in many respects worse than the larger single country room. In other respects it is better; it has glass windows, a decent chimney, and a trustworthy floor. The single great advantage of the Negro peasant is that he may spend most of his life outside his hovel, in the open fields.

There are four chief causes of these wretched homes: First, long custom born of slavery has assigned such homes to Negroes; white laborers would be

offered better accommodations, and might, for that and similar reasons, give better work. Secondly, the Negroes, used to such accommodations, do not as a rule demand better; they do not know what better houses mean. Thirdly, the landlords as a class have not yet come to realize that it is a good business investment to raise the standard of living among labor by slow and judicious methods; that a Negro laborer who demands three rooms and fifty cents a day would give more efficient work and leave a larger profit than a discouraged toiler herding his family in one room and working for thirty cents. Lastly, among such conditions of life there are few incentives to make the laborer become a better farmer. If he is ambitious, he moves to town or tries other labor; as a tenant-farmer his outlook is almost hopeless, and following it as a makeshift, he takes the house that is given him without protest.

In such homes, then, these Negro peasants live. The families are both small and large; there are many single tenants,—widows and bachelors, and remnants of broken groups. The system of labor and the size of the houses both tend to the breaking up of family groups: the grown children go away as contract hands or migrate to town, the sister goes into service; and so one finds many families with hosts of babies, and many newly married couples, but comparatively few families with half-grown and grown sons and daughters. The average size of Negro families has undoubtedly decreased since the war, primarily from economic stress. In Russia over a third of the bridegrooms and over half the brides are under twenty; the same was true of the ante-bellum Negroes. To-day, however, very few of the boys and less than a fifth of the Negro girls under twenty are married. The young men marry between the ages of twenty-five and thirty-five; the young women between twenty and thirty. Such postponement is due to the difficulty of earning sufficient to rear and support a family; and it undoubtedly leads, in the country districts, to sexual immorality. The form of this immorality, however, is very seldom that of prostitution, and less frequently that of illegitimacy than one would imagine. Rather, it takes the form of separation and desertion after a family group has been formed. The number of separated persons is thirty-five to the thousand,—a very large number. It would of course be unfair to compare this number with divorce statistics, for many of these separated women are in reality widowed, were the truth known, and in other cases the separation is not permanent.

Nevertheless, here lies the seat of greatest moral danger. There is little or no prostitution among these Negroes, and over three-fourths of the families, as found by house-to-house investigation, deserve to be classed as decent

people with considerable regard for female chastity. To be sure, the ideas of the mass would not suit New England, and there are many loose habits and notions. Yet the rate of illegitimacy is undoubtedly lower than in Austria or Italy, and the women as a class are modest. The plague-spot in sexual relations is easy marriage and easy separation. This is no sudden development, nor the fruit of Emancipation. It is the plain heritage from slavery. In those days Sam, with his master's consent, "took up" with Mary. No ceremony was necessary, and in the busy life of the great plantations of the Black Belt it was usually dispensed with. If now the master needed Sam's work in another plantation or in another part of the same plantation, or if he took a notion to sell the slave, Sam's married life with Mary was usually unceremoniously broken, and then it was clearly to the master's interest to have both of them take new mates. This widespread custom of two centuries has not been eradicated in thirty years. To-day Sam's grandson "takes up" with a woman without license or ceremony; they live together decently and honestly, and are, to all intents and purposes, man and wife. Sometimes these unions are never broken until death; but in too many cases family quarrels, a roving spirit, a rival suitor, or perhaps more frequently the hopeless battle to support a family, lead to separation, and a broken household is the result. The Negro church has done much to stop this practice, and now most marriage ceremonies are performed by the pastors. Nevertheless, the evil is still deep seated, and only a general raising of the standard of living will finally cure it.

Looking now at the county black population as a whole, it is fair to characterize it as poor and ignorant. Perhaps ten per cent compose the well-to-do and the best of the laborers, while at least nine per cent are thoroughly lewd and vicious. The rest, over eighty per cent, are poor and ignorant, fairly honest and well meaning, plodding, and to a degree shiftless, with some but not great sexual looseness. Such class lines are by no means fixed; they vary, one might almost say, with the price of cotton. The degree of ignorance cannot easily be expressed. We may say, for instance, that nearly two-thirds of them cannot read or write. This but partially expresses the fact. They are ignorant of the world about them, of modern economic organization, of the function of government, of individual worth and possibilities,—of nearly all those things which slavery in self-defence had to keep them from learning. Much that the white boy imbibes from his earliest social atmosphere forms the puzzling problems of the black boy's mature years. America is not another word for Opportunity to *all* her sons.

It is easy for us to lose ourselves in details in endeavoring to grasp and

comprehend the real condition of a mass of human beings. We often forget that each unit in the mass is a throbbing human soul. Ignorant it may be, and poverty stricken, black and curious in limb and ways and thought; and yet it loves and hates, it toils and tires, it laughs and weeps its bitter tears, and looks in vague and awful longing at the grim horizon of its life,—all this, even as you and I. These black thousands are not in reality lazy; they are improvident and careless; they insist on breaking the monotony of toil with a glimpse at the great town-world on Saturday; they have their loafers and their rascals; but the great mass of them work continuously and faithfully for a return, and under circumstances that would call forth equal voluntary effort from few if any other modern laboring class. Over eighty-eight per cent of them—men, women, and children—are farmers. Indeed, this is almost the only industry. Most of the children get their schooling after the "crops are laid by," and very few there are that stay in school after the spring work has begun. Child-labor is to be found here in some of its worst phases, as fostering ignorance and stunting physical development. With the grown men of the county there is little variety in work: thirteen hundred are farmers, and two hundred are laborers, teamsters, etc., including twenty-four artisans, ten merchants, twenty-one preachers, and four teachers. This narrowness of life reaches its maximum among the women: thirteen hundred and fifty of these are farm laborers, one hundred are servants and washerwomen, leaving sixty-five housewives, eight teachers, and six seamstresses.

Among this people there is no leisure class. We often forget that in the United States over half of the youth and adults are not in the world earning incomes, but are making homes, learning of the world, or resting after the heat of the strife. But here ninety six per cent are toiling; no one with leisure to turn the bare and cheerless cabin into a home, no old folks to sit beside the fire and hand down traditions of the past; little of careless happy childhood and dreaming youth. The dull monotony of daily toil is broken only by the gayety of the thoughtless and the Saturday trip to town. The toil, like all farm toil, is monotonous, and here there are little machinery and few tools to relieve its burdensome drudgery. But with all this, it is work in the pure open air, and this is something in a day when fresh air is scarce.

The land on the whole is still fertile, despite long abuse. For nine or ten months in succession the crops will come if asked: garden vegetables in April, grain in May, melons in June and July, hay in August, sweet potatoes in September, and cotton from then to Christmas. And yet on two-thirds of the land there is but one crop, and that leaves the toilers in debt. Why is this?

Away down the Baysan road, where the broad flat fields are flanked by great oak forests, is a plantation; many thousands of acres it used to run, here and there, and beyond the great wood. Thirteen hundred human beings here obeyed the call of one,—were his in body, and largely in soul. One of them lives there yet,—a short, stocky man, his dull-brown face seamed and drawn, and his tightly curled hair gray-white. The crops? Just tolerable, he said; just tolerable. Getting on? No—he wasn't getting on at all. Smith of Albany "furnishes" him, and his rent is eight hundred pounds of cotton. Can't make anything at that. Why didn't he buy land? Humph! Takes money to buy land. And he turns away. Free! The most piteous thing amid all the black ruin of war-time, amid the broken fortunes of the masters, the blighted hopes of mothers and maidens, and the fall of an empire,—the most piteous thing amid all this was the black freedman who threw down his hoe because the world called him free. What did such a mockery of freedom mean? Not a cent of money, not an inch of land, not a mouthful of victuals,—not even ownership of the rags on his back. Free! On Saturday, once or twice a month, the old master, before the war, used to dole out bacon and meal to his Negroes. And after the first flush of freedom wore off, and his true helplessness dawned on the freedman, he came back and picked up his hoe, and old master still doled out his bacon and meal. The legal form of service was theoretically far different; in practice, task-work or "cropping" was substituted for daily toil in gangs; and the slave gradually became a metayer, or tenant on shares, in name, but a laborer with indeterminate wages in fact.

Still the price of cotton fell, and gradually the landlords deserted their plantations, and the reign of the merchant began. The merchant of the Black Belt is a curious institution,—part banker, part landlord, part contractor, and part despot. His store, which used most frequently to stand at the cross-roads and become the centre of a weekly village, has now moved to town; and thither the Negro tenant follows him. The merchant keeps everything,—clothes and shoes, coffee and sugar, pork and meal, canned and dried goods, wagons and ploughs, seed and fertilizer,—and what he has not in stock he can give you an order for at the store across the way. Here, then, comes the tenant, Sam Scott, after he has contracted with some absent landlord's agent for hiring forty acres of land; he fingers his hat nervously until the merchant finishes his morning chat with Colonel Sanders, and calls out, "Well, Sam, what do you want?" Sam wants him to "furnish" him,—i.e., to advance him food and clothing for the year, and perhaps seed and tools, until his crop is raised and sold. If Sam seems a favorable subject, he and the merchant go to

a lawyer, and Sam executes a chattel mortgage on his mule and wagon in return for seed and a week's rations. As soon as the green cotton-leaves appear above the ground, another mortgage is given on the "crop." Every Saturday, or at longer intervals, Sam calls upon the merchant for his "rations"; a family of five usually gets about thirty pounds of fat side-pork and a couple of bushels of corn-meal a month. Besides this, clothing and shoes must be furnished; if Sam or his family is sick, there are orders on the druggist and doctor; if the mule wants shoeing, an order on the blacksmith, etc. If Sam is a hard worker and crops promise well, he is often encouraged to buy more,—sugar, extra clothes, perhaps a buggy. But he is seldom encouraged to save. When cotton rose to ten cents last fall, the shrewd merchants of Dougherty County sold a thousand buggies in one season, mostly to black men.

The security offered for such transactions—a crop and chattel mortgage—may at first seem slight. And, indeed, the merchants tell many a true tale of shiftlessness and cheating; of cotton picked at night, mules disappearing, and tenants absconding. But on the whole the merchant of the Black Belt is the most prosperous man in the section. So skilfully and so closely has he drawn the bonds of the law about the tenant, that the black man has often simply to choose between pauperism and crime; he "waives" all homestead exemptions in his contract; he cannot touch his own mortgaged crop, which the laws put almost in the full control of the land-owner and of the merchant. When the crop is growing the merchant watches it like a hawk; as soon as it is ready for market he takes possession of it, sells it, pays the land-owner his rent, subtracts his bill for supplies, and if, as sometimes happens, there is anything left, he hands it over to the black serf for his Christmas celebration.

The direct result of this system is an all-cotton scheme of agriculture and the continued bankruptcy of the tenant. The currency of the Black Belt is cotton. It is a crop always salable for ready money, not usually subject to great yearly fluctuations in price, and one which the Negroes know how to raise. The landlord therefore demands his rent in cotton, and the merchant will accept mortgages on no other crop. There is no use asking the black tenant, then, to diversify his crops,—he cannot under this system. Moreover, the system is bound to bankrupt the tenant. I remember once meeting a little one-mule wagon on the River road. A young black fellow sat in it driving listlessly, his elbows on his knees. His dark-faced wife sat beside him, stolid, silent.

"Hello!" cried my driver,—he has a most impudent way of addressing these people, though they seem used to it,—"what have you got there?"

"Meat and meal," answered the man, stopping. The meat lay uncovered

in the bottom of the wagon,—a great thin side of fat pork covered with salt; the meal was in a white bushel bag.

"What did you pay for that meat?"

"Ten cents a pound." It could have been bought for six or seven cents cash.

"And the meal?"

"Two dollars." One dollar and ten cents is the cash price in town. Here was a man paying five dollars for goods which he could have bought for three dollars cash, and raised for one dollar or one dollar and a half.

Yet it is not wholly his fault. The Negro farmer started behind,—started in debt. This was not his choosing, but the crime of this happy-go-lucky nation which goes blundering along with its Reconstruction tragedies, its Spanish war interludes and Philippine matinees, just as though God really were dead. Once in debt, it is no easy matter for a whole race to emerge.

In the year of low-priced cotton, 1898, out of three hundred tenant families one hundred and seventy five ended their year's work in debt to the extent of fourteen thousand dollars; fifty cleared nothing, and the remaining seventy-five made a total profit of sixteen hundred dollars. The net indebtedness of the black tenant families of the whole county must have been at least sixty thousand dollars. In a more prosperous year the situation is far better; but on the average the majority of tenants end the year even, or in debt, which means that they work for board and clothes. Such an economic organization is radically wrong. Whose is the blame?

The underlying causes of this situation are complicated but discernible. And one of the chief, outside the carelessness of the nation in letting the slave start with nothing, is the widespread opinion among the merchants and employers of the Black Belt that only by the slavery of debt can the Negro be kept at work. Without doubt, some pressure was necessary at the beginning of the free-labor system to keep the listless and lazy at work; and even to-day the mass of the Negro laborers need stricter guardianship than most Northern laborers. Behind this honest and widespread opinion dishonesty and cheating of the ignorant laborers have a good chance to take refuge. And to all this must be added the obvious fact that a slave ancestry and a system of unrequited toil has not improved the efficiency or temper of the mass of black laborers. Nor is this peculiar to Sambo; it has in history been just as true of John and Hans, of Jacques and Pat, of all ground-down peasantries. Such is the situation of the mass of the Negroes in the Black Belt to-day; and they are thinking about it. Crime, and a cheap and dangerous socialism, are

the inevitable results of this pondering. I see now that ragged black man sitting on a log, aimlessly whittling a stick. He muttered to me with the murmur of many ages, when he said: "White man sit down whole year; Nigger work day and night and make crop; Nigger hardly gits bread and meat; white man sittin' down gits all. *It's wrong.*" And what do the better classes of Negroes do to improve their situation? One of two things: if any way possible, they buy land; if not, they migrate to town. Just as centuries ago it was no easy thing for the serf to escape into the freedom of town-life, even so today there are hindrances laid in the way of county laborers. In considerable parts of all the Gulf States, and especially in Mississippi, Louisiana, and Arkansas, the Negroes on the plantations in the back-country districts are still held at forced labor practically without wages. Especially is this true in districts where the farmers are composed of the more ignorant class of poor whites, and the Negroes are beyond the reach of schools and intercourse with their advancing fellows. If such a peon should run away, the sheriff, elected by white suffrage, can usually be depended on to catch the fugitive, return him, and ask no questions. If he escape to another county, a charge of petty thieving, easily true, can be depended upon to secure his return. Even if some unduly officious person insist upon a trial, neighborly comity will probably make his conviction sure, and then the labor due the county can easily be bought by the master. Such a system is impossible in the more civilized parts of the South, or near the large towns and cities; but in those vast stretches of land beyond the telegraph and the newspaper the spirit of the Thirteenth Amendment is sadly broken. This represents the lowest economic depths of the black American peasant; and in a study of the rise and condition of the Negro freeholder we must trace his economic progress from this modern serfdom.

Even in the better-ordered country districts of the South the free movement of agricultural laborers is hindered by the migration-agent laws. The "Associated Press" recently informed the world of the arrest of a young white man in Southern Georgia who represented the "Atlantic Naval Supplies Company," and who "was caught in the act of enticing hands from the turpentine farm of Mr. John Greer." The crime for which this young man was arrested is taxed five hundred dollars for each county in which the employment agent proposes to gather laborers for work outside the State. Thus the Negroes' ignorance of the labor-market outside his own vicinity is increased rather than diminished by the laws of nearly every Southern State.

Similar to such measures is the unwritten law of the back districts and small towns of the South, that the character of all Negroes unknown to the

mass of the community must be vouched for by some white man. This is really a revival of the old Roman idea of the patron under whose protection the new-made freedman was put. In many instances this system has been of great good to the Negro, and very often under the protection and guidance of the former master's family, or other white friends, the freedman progressed in wealth and morality. But the same system has in other cases resulted in the refusal of whole communities to recognize the right of a Negro to change his habitation and to be master of his own fortunes. A black stranger in Baker County, Georgia, for instance, is liable to be stopped anywhere on the public highway and made to state his business to the satisfaction of any white interrogator. If he fails to give a suitable answer, or seems too independent or "sassy," he may be arrested or summarily driven away.

Thus it is that in the country districts of the South, by written or unwritten law, peonage, hindrances to the migration of labor, and a system of white patronage exists over large areas. Besides this, the chance for lawless oppression and illegal exactions is vastly greater in the country than in the city, and nearly all the more serious race disturbances of the last decade have arisen from disputes in the county between master and man,—as, for instance, the Sam Hose affair. As a result of such a situation, there arose, first, the Black Belt; and, second, the Migration to Town. The Black Belt was not, as many assumed, a movement toward fields of labor under more genial climatic conditions; it was primarily a huddling for self-protection,—a massing of the black population for mutual defence in order to secure the peace and tranquillity necessary to economic advance. This movement took place between Emancipation and 1880, and only partially accomplished the desired results. The rush to town since 1880 is the counter-movement of men disappointed in the economic opportunities of the Black Belt.

In Dougherty County, Georgia, one can see easily the results of this experiment in huddling for protection. Only ten per cent of the adult population was born in the county, and yet the blacks outnumber the whites four or five to one. There is undoubtedly a security to the blacks in their very numbers,—a personal freedom from arbitrary treatment, which makes hundreds of laborers cling to Dougherty in spite of low wages and economic distress. But a change is coming, and slowly but surely even here the agricultural laborers are drifting to town and leaving the broad acres behind. Why is this? Why do not the Negroes become land-owners, and build up the black landed peasantry, which has for a generation and more been the dream of philanthropist and statesman?

To the car-window sociologist, to the man who seeks to understand and know the South by devoting the few leisure hours of a holiday trip to unravelling the snarl of centuries,—to such men very often the whole trouble with the black field-hand may be summed up by Aunt Ophelia's word, "Shiftless!" They have noted repeatedly scenes like one I saw last summer. We were riding along the highroad to town at the close of a long hot day. A couple of young black fellows passed us in a mule-team, with several bushels of loose corn in the ear. One was driving, listlessly bent forward, his elbows on his knees,—a happy-go-lucky, careless picture of irresponsibility. The other was fast asleep in the bottom of the wagon. As we passed we noticed an ear of corn fall from the wagon. They never saw it,—not they. A rod farther on we noted another ear on the ground; and between that creeping mule and town we counted twenty-six ears of corn. Shiftless? Yes, the personification of shiftlessness. And yet follow those boys: they are not lazy; to-morrow morning they'll be up with the sun; they work hard when they do work, and they work willingly. They have no sordid, selfish, money-getting ways, but rather a fine disdain for mere cash. They'll loaf before your face and work behind your back with good-natured honesty. They'll steal a watermelon, and hand you back your lost purse intact. Their great defect as laborers lies in their lack of incentive to work beyond the mere pleasure of physical exertion. They are careless because they have not found that it pays to be careful; they are improvident because the improvident ones of their acquaintance get on about as well as the provident. Above all, they cannot see why they should take unusual pains to make the white man's land better, or to fatten his mule, or save his corn. On the other hand, the white land-owner argues that any attempt to improve these laborers by increased responsibility, or higher wages, or better homes, or land of their own, would be sure to result in failure. He shows his Northern visitor the scarred and wretched land; the ruined mansions, the worn-out soil and mortgaged acres, and says, This is Negro freedom!

Now it happens that both master and man have just enough argument on their respective sides to make it difficult for them to understand each other The Negro dimly personifies in the white man all his ills and misfortunes; if he is poor, it is because the white man seizes the fruit of his toil; if he is ignorant, it is because the white man gives him neither time nor facilities to learn; and, indeed, if any misfortune happens to him, it is because of some hidden machinations of "white folks." On the other hand, the masters and the masters' sons have never been able to see why the Negro, instead of settling down to be day-laborers for bread and clothes, are infected with a silly desire to rise

in the world, and why they are sulky, dissatisfied, and careless, where their fathers were happy and dumb and faithful. "Why, you niggers have an easier time than I do," said a puzzled Albany merchant to his black customer. "Yes," he replied, "and so does yo' hogs."

Taking, then, the dissatisfied and shiftless field-hand as a starting-point, let us inquire how the black thousands of Dougherty have struggled from him up toward their ideal, and what that ideal is. All social struggle is evidenced by the rise, first of economic, then of social classes, among a homogeneous population. To-day the following economic classes are plainly differentiated among these Negroes.

A "submerged tenth" of croppers, with a few paupers; forty per cent who are metayers and thirty-nine per cent of semi-metayers and wage-laborers. There are left five per cent of money-renters and six per cent of freeholders,—the "Upper Ten" of the land. The croppers are entirely without capital, even in the limited sense of food or money to keep them from seed-time to harvest. All they furnish is their labor; the land-owner furnishes land, stock, tools, seed, and house; and at the end of the year the laborer gets from a third to a half of the crop. Out of his share, however, comes pay and interest for food and clothing advanced him during the year. Thus we have a laborer without capital and without wages, and an employer whose capital is largely his employees' wages. It is an unsatisfactory arrangement, both for hirer and hired, and is usually in vogue on poor land with hard-pressed owners.

Above the croppers come the great mass of the black population who work the land on their own responsibility, paying rent in cotton and supported by the crop-mortgage system. After the war this system was attractive to the freedmen on account of its larger freedom and its possibilities for making a surplus. But with the carrying out of the crop-lien system, the deterioration of the land, and the slavery of debt, the position of the metayers has sunk to a dead level of practically unrewarded toil. Formerly all tenants had some capital, and often considerable; but absentee landlordism, rising rack-rent, and falling cotton have stripped them well-nigh of all, and probably not over half of them to-day own their mules. The change from cropper to tenant was accomplished by fixing the rent. If, now, the rent fixed was reasonable, this was an incentive to the tenant to strive. On the other hand, if the rent was too high, or if the land deteriorated, the result was to discourage and check the efforts of the black peasantry. There is no doubt that the latter case is true; that in Dougherty County every economic advantage of the price of cotton in market and of the strivings of the tenant has been taken advantage

of by the landlords and merchants, and swallowed up in rent and interest. If cotton rose in price, the rent rose even higher; if cotton fell, the rent remained or followed reluctantly. If a tenant worked hard and raised a large crop, his rent was raised the next year; if that year the crop failed, his corn was confiscated and his mule sold for debt. There were, of course, exceptions to this,—cases of personal kindness and forbearance; but in the vast majority of cases the rule was to extract the uttermost farthing from the mass of the black farm laborers.

The average metayer pays from twenty to thirty per cent of his crop in rent. The result of such rack-rent can only be evil,—abuse and neglect of the soil, deterioration in the character of the laborers, and a widespread sense of in justice. "Wherever the country is poor," cried Arthur Young, "it is in the hands of metayers," and "their condition is more wretched than that of day-laborers." He was talking of Italy a century ago; but he might have been talking of Dougherty County to-day. And especially is that true to-day which he declares was true in France before the Revolution: "The metayers are considered as little better than menial servants, removable at pleasure, and obliged to conform in all things to the will of the landlords." On this low plane half the black population of Dougherty County—perhaps more than half the black millions of this land—are to-day struggling.

A degree above these we may place those laborers who receive money wages for their work. Some receive a house with perhaps a garden-spot; then supplies of food and clothing are advanced, and certain fixed wages are given at the end of the year, varying from thirty to sixty dollars, out of which the supplies must be paid for, with interest. About eighteen per cent of the population belong to this class of semi-metayers, while twenty-two per cent are laborers paid by the month or year, and are either "furnished" by their own savings or perhaps more usually by some merchant who takes his chances of payment. Such laborers receive from thirty-five to fifty cents a day during the working season. They are usually young unmarried persons, some being women; and when they marry they sink to the class of metayers, or, more seldom, become renters.

The renters for fixed money rentals are the first of the emerging classes, and form five per cent of the families. The sole advantage of this small class is their freedom to choose their crops, and the increased responsibility which comes through having money transactions. While some of the renters differ little in condition from the metayers, yet on the whole they are more intelligent and responsible persons, and are the ones who eventually become land-

owners. Their better character and greater shrewdness enable them to gain, perhaps to demand, better terms in rents; rented farms, varying from forty to a hundred acres, bear an average rental of about fifty-four dollars a year. The men who conduct such farms do not long remain renters; either they sink to metayers, or with a successful series of harvests rise to be land-owners.

In 1870 the tax-books of Dougherty report no Negroes as landholders. If there were any such at that time,—and there may have been a few,—their land was probably held in the name of some white patron,—a method not uncommon during slavery. In 1875 ownership of land had begun with seven hundred and fifty acres; ten years later this had increased to over sixty-five hundred acres, to nine thousand acres in 1890 and ten thousand in 1900. The total assessed property has in this same period risen from eighty thousand dollars in 1875 to two hundred and forty thousand dollars in 1900.

Two circumstances complicate this development and make it in some respects difficult to be sure of the real tendencies; they are the panic of 1893, and the low price of cotton in 1898. Besides this, the system of assessing property in the country districts of Georgia is somewhat antiquated and of uncertain statistical value; there are no assessors, and each man makes a sworn return to a tax-receiver. Thus public opinion plays a large part, and the returns vary strangely from year to year. Certainly these figures show the small amount of accumulated capital among the Negroes, and the consequent large dependence of their property on temporary prosperity. They have little to tide over a few years of economic depression, and are at the mercy of the cotton-market far more than the whites. And thus the land-owners, despite their marvellous efforts, are really a transient class, continually being depleted by those who fall back into the class of renters or metayers, and augmented by newcomers from the masses. Of the one hundred land-owners in 1898, half had bought their land since 1893, a fourth between 1890 and 1893, a fifth between 1884 and 1890, and the rest between 1870 and 1884. In all, one hundred and eighty-five Negroes have owned land in this county since 1875.

If all the black land-owners who had ever held and here had kept it or left it in the hands of black men, the Negroes would have owned nearer thirty thousand acres than the fifteen thousand they now hold. And yet these fifteen thousand acres are a creditable showing,—a proof of no little weight of the worth and ability of the Negro people. If they had been given an economic start at Emancipation, if they had been in an enlightened and rich community which really desired their best good, then we might perhaps call

such a result small or even insignificant. But for a few thousand poor igno-
rant field-hands, in the face of poverty, a falling market, and social stress, to
save and capitalize two hundred thousand dollars in a generation has meant
a tremendous effort. The rise of a nation, the pressing forward of a social
class, means a bitter struggle, a hard and soul-sickening battle with the world
such as few of the more favored classes know or appreciate.

Out of the hard economic conditions of this portion of the Black Belt,
only six per cent of the population have succeeded in emerging into peasant
proprietorship; and these are not all firmly fixed, but grow and shrink in
number with the wavering or the cotton-market. Fully ninety-four per cent
have struggled for land and failed, and half of them sit in hopeless serfdom.
For these there is one other avenue of escape toward which they have turned
in increasing numbers, namely, migration to town. A glance at the distribu-
tion of land among the black owners curiously reveals this fact. In 1898 the
holdings were as follows: Under forty acres, forty-nine families; forty to two
hundred and fifty acres, seventeen families; two hundred and fifty to one
thousand acres, thirteen families; one thousand or more acres, two families.
Now in 1890 there were forty-four holdings, but only nine of these were
under forty acres. The great increase of holdings, then, has come in the buy-
ing of small homesteads near town, where their owners really share in the
town life; this is a part of the rush to town. And for every land-owner who
has thus hurried away from the narrow and hard conditions of country life,
how many field-hands, how many tenants, how many ruined renters, have
joined that long procession? Is it not strange compensation? The sin of the
country districts is visited on the town, and the social sores of city life to-day
may, here in Dougherty County, and perhaps in many places near and far,
look for their final healing without the city walls.

IX

OF THE SONS OF MASTER AND MAN

> Life treads on life, and heart on heart;
> We press too close in church and mart
> To keep a dream or grave apart.
> <div align="right">Mrs. Browning.</div>

THE world-old phenomenon of the contact of diverse races of men is to have new exemplification during the new century. Indeed, the characteristic of our age is the contact of European civilization with the world's undeveloped peoples. Whatever we may say of the results of such contact in the past, it certainly forms a chapter in human action not pleasant to look back upon. War, murder, slavery, extermination, and debauchery,—this has again and again been the result of carrying civilization and the blessed gospel to the isles of the sea and the heathen without the law. Nor does it altogether satisfy the conscience of the modern world to be told complacently that all this has been right and proper, the fated triumph of strength over weakness, of righteousness over evil, of superiors over inferiors. It would certainly be soothing if one could readily believe all this; and yet there are too many ugly facts for everything to be thus easily explained away. We feel and know that there are many delicate differences in race psychology, numberless changes that our crude social measurements are not yet able to follow minutely, which explain much of history and social development. At the same time, too, we know that these considerations have never adequately explained or excused the triumph of brute force and cunning over weakness and innocence.

It is, then, the strife of all honorable men of the twentieth century to see that in the future competition of races the survival of the fittest shall mean the triumph of the good, the beautiful, and the true; that we may be able to preserve for future civilization all that is really fine and noble and strong, and not continue to put a premium on greed and impudence and cruelty. To bring this hope to fruition, we are compelled daily to turn more and more to a conscientious study of the phenomena of race-contact,—to a study frank and fair, and not falsified and colored by our wishes or our fears. And we have in the South as fine a field for such a study as the world affords,—a field, to be sure, which the average American scientist deems somewhat beneath his dignity, and which the average man who is not a scientist knows

all about, but nevertheless a line of study which by reason of the enormous race complications with which God seems about to punish this nation must increasingly claim our sober attention, study, and thought, we must ask, what are the actual relations of whites and blacks in the South? and we must be answered, not by apology or faultfinding, but by a plain, unvarnished tale.

In the civilized life of to-day the contact of men and their relations to each other fall in a few main lines of action and communication: there is, first, the physical proximity of homes and dwelling-places, the way in which neighborhoods group themselves, and the contiguity of neighborhoods. Secondly, and in our age chiefest, there are the economic relations,—the methods by which individuals coöperate for earning a living, for the mutual satisfaction of wants, for the production of wealth. Next, there are the political relations, the coöperation in social control, in group government, in laying and paying the burden of taxation. In the fourth place there are the less tangible but highly important forms of intellectual contact and commerce, the interchange of ideas through conversation and conference, through periodicals and libraries; and, above all, the gradual formation for each community of that curious *tertium quid* which we call public opinion. Closely allied with this come the various forms of social contact in everyday life, in travel, in theatres, in house gatherings, in marrying and giving in marriage. Finally, there are the varying forms of religious enterprise, of moral teaching and benevolent endeavor. These are the principal ways in which men living in the same communities are brought into contact with each other. It is my present task, therefore, to indicate, from my point of view, how the black race in the South meet and mingle with the whites in these matters of everyday life.

First, as to physical dwelling. It is usually possible to draw in nearly every Southern community a physical color-line on the map, on the one side of which whites dwell and on the other Negroes. The winding and intricacy of the geographical color line varies, of course, in different communities. I know some towns where a straight line drawn through the middle of the main street separates nine-tenths of the whites from nine-tenths of the blacks. In other towns the older settlement of whites has been encircled by a broad band of blacks; in still other cases little settlements or nuclei of blacks have sprung up amid surrounding whites. Usually in cities each street has its distinctive color, and only now and then do the colors meet in close proximity. Even in the country something of this segregation is manifest in the smaller areas, and of course in the larger phenomena of the Black Belt.

All this segregation by color is largely independent of that natural clus-

tering by social grades common to all communities. A Negro slum may be in dangerous proximity to a white residence quarter, while it is quite common to find a white slum planted in the heart of a respectable Negro district. One thing, however, seldom occurs: the best of the whites and the best of the Negroes almost never live in anything like close proximity. It thus happens that in nearly every Southern town and city, both whites and blacks see commonly the worst of each other. This is a vast change from the situation in the past, when, through the close contact of master and house-servant in the patriarchal big house, one found the best of both races in close contact and sympathy, while at the same time the squalor and dull round of toil among the field-hands was removed from the sight and hearing of the family. One can easily see how a person who saw slavery thus from his father's parlors, and sees freedom on the streets of a great city, fails to grasp or comprehend the whole of the new picture. On the other hand, the settled belief of the mass of the Negroes that the Southern white people do not have the black man's best interests at heart has been intensified in later years by this continual daily contact of the better class of blacks with the worst representatives of the white race.

Coming now to the economic relations of the races, we are on ground made familiar by study, much discussion, and no little philanthropic effort. And yet with all this there are many essential elements in the cooperation of Negroes and whites for work and wealth that are too readily overlooked or not thoroughly understood. The average American can easily conceive of a rich land awaiting development and filled with black laborers. To him the Southern problem is simply that of making efficient workingmen out of this material, by giving them the requisite technical skill and the help of invested capital. The problem, however, is by no means as simple as this, from the obvious fact that these workingmen have been trained for centuries as slaves. They exhibit, therefore, all the advantages and defects of such training; they are willing and good-natured, but not self-reliant, provident, or careful. If now the economic development of the South is to be pushed to the verge of exploitation, as seems probable, then we have a mass of workingmen thrown into relentless competition with the workingmen of the world, but handicapped by a training the very opposite to that of the modern self-reliant democratic laborer. What the black laborer needs is careful personal guidance, group leadership of men with hearts in their bosoms, to train them to foresight, carefulness, and honesty. Nor does it require any fine-spun theories of racial differences to prove the necessity of such group training after the brains

of the race have been knocked out by two hundred and fifty years of assiduous education in submission, carelessness, and stealing. After Emancipation, it was the plain duty of some one to assume this group leadership and training of the Negro laborer. I will not stop here to inquire whose duty it was,—whether that of the white ex-master who had profited by unpaid toil, or the Northern philanthropist whose persistence brought on the crisis, or the National Government whose edict freed the bondmen; I will not stop to ask whose duty it was, but I insist it was the duty of some one to see that these workingmen were not left alone and unguided, without capital, without land, without skill, without economic organization, without even the bald protection of law, order, and decency,—left in a great land, not to settle down to slow and careful internal development, but destined to be thrown almost immediately into relentless and sharp competition with the best of modern workingmen under an economic system where every participant is fighting for himself, and too often utterly regardless of the rights or welfare of his neighbor.

For we must never forget that the economic system of the South to-day which has succeeded the old régime is not the same system as that of the old industrial North, of England, or of France, with their trades-unions, their restrictive laws, their written and unwritten commercial customs, and their long experience. It is, rather, a copy of that England of the early nineteenth century, before the factory acts,—the England that wrung pity from thinkers and fired the wrath of Carlyle. The rod of empire that passed from the hands of Southern gentlemen in 1865, partly by force, partly by their own petulance, has never returned to them. Rather it has passed to those men who have come to take charge of the industrial exploitation of the New South,—the sons of poor whites fired with a new thirst for wealth and power, thrifty and avaricious Yankees, shrewd and unscrupulous Jews. Into the hands of these men the Southern laborers, white and black, have fallen; and this to their sorrow. For the laborers as such there is in these new captains of industry neither love nor hate, neither sympathy nor romance; it is a cold question of dollars and dividends. Under such a system all labor is bound to suffer. Even the white laborers are not yet intelligent, thrifty, and well trained enough to maintain themselves against the powerful inroads of organized capital. The results among them, even, are long hours of toil, low wages, child labor, and lack of protection against usury and cheating. But among the black laborers all this is aggravated, first, by a race prejudice which varies from a doubt and distrust among the best element of whites to a frenzied

hatred among the worst; and, secondly, it is aggravated, as I have said before, by the wretched economic heritage of the freedmen from slavery. With this training it is difficult for the freedman to learn to grasp the opportunities already opened to him, and the new opportunities are seldom given him, but go by favor to the whites.

Left by the best elements of the South with little protection or oversight, he has been made in law and custom the victim of the worst and most unscrupulous men in each community. The crop-lien system which is depopulating the fields of the South is not simply the result of shiftlessness on the part of Negroes, but is also the result of cunningly devised laws as to mortgages, liens, and misdemeanors, which can be made by conscienceless men to entrap and snare the unwary until escape is impossible, further toil a farce, and protest a crime. I have seen, in the Black Belt of Georgia, an ignorant, honest Negro buy and pay for a farm in installments three separate times, and then in the face of law and decency the enterprising Russian Jew who sold it to him pocketed money and deed and left the black man landless, to labor on his own land at thirty cents a day. I have seen a black farmer fall in debt to a white storekeeper, and that storekeeper go to his farm and strip it of every single marketable article,—mules, ploughs, stored crops, tools, furniture, bedding, clocks, looking-glass,—and all this without a warrant, without process of law, without a sheriff or officer, in the face of the law for homestead exemptions, and without rendering to a single responsible person any account or reckoning. And such proceedings can happen, and will happen, in any community where a class of ignorant toilers are placed by custom and race-prejudice beyond the pale of sympathy and race-brotherhood. So long as the best elements of a community do not feel in duty bound to protect and train and care for the weaker members of their group, they leave them to be preyed upon by these swindlers and rascals.

This unfortunate economic situation does not mean the hindrance of all advance in the black South, or the absence of a class of black landlords and mechanics who, in spite of disadvantages, are accumulating property and making good citizens. But it does mean that this class is not nearly so large as a fairer economic system might easily make it, that those who survive in the competition are handicapped so as to accomplish much less than they deserve to, and that, above all, the personnel of the successful class is left to chance and accident, and not to any intelligent culling or reasonable methods of selection. As a remedy for this, there is but one possible procedure. We must accept some of the race prejudice in the South as a fact,—deplorable in

its intensity, unfortunate in results, and dangerous for the future, but nevertheless a hard fact which only time can efface. We cannot hope, then, in this generation, or for several generations, that the mass of the whites can be brought to assume that close sympathetic and self-sacrificing leadership of the blacks which their present situation so eloquently demands. Such leadership, such social teaching and example, must come from the blacks themselves. For some time men doubted as to whether the Negro could develop such leaders; but to-day no one seriously disputes the capability of individual Negroes to assimilate the culture and common sense of modern civilization, and to pass it on, to some extent at least, to their fellows. If this is true, then here is the path out of the economic situation, and here is the imperative demand for trained Negro leaders of character and intelligence,—men of skill, men of light and leading, college-bred men, black captains of industry, and missionaries of culture; men who thoroughly comprehend and know modern civilization, and can take hold of Negro communities and raise and train them by force of precept and example, deep sympathy, and the inspiration of common blood and ideals. But if such men are to be effective they must have some power,—they must be backed by the best public opinion of these communities, and able to wield for their objects and aims such weapons as the experience of the world has taught are indispensable to human progress.

Of such weapons the greatest, perhaps, in the modern world is the power of the ballot; and this brings me to a consideration of the third form of contact between whites and blacks in the South,—political activity.

In the attitude of the American mind toward Negro suffrage can be traced with unusual accuracy the prevalent conceptions of government. In the fifties we were near enough the echoes of the French Revolution to believe pretty thoroughly in universal suffrage. We argued, as we thought then rather logically, that no social class was so good, so true, and so disinterested as to be trusted wholly with the political destiny of its neighbors; that in every state the best arbiters of their own welfare are the persons directly affected; consequently that it is only by arming every hand with a ballot,—with the right to have a voice in the policy of the state,—that the greatest good to the greatest number could be attained. To be sure, there were objections to these arguments, but we thought we had answered them tersely and convincingly; if some one complained of the ignorance of voters, we answered, "Educate them." If another complained of their venality, we replied "Disfranchise them or put them in jail." And, finally, to the men who feared demagogues

and the natural perversity of some human beings we insisted that time and bitter experience would teach the most hardheaded. It was at this time that the question of Negro suffrage in the South was raised. Here was a defenceless people suddenly made free. How were they to be protected from those who did not believe in their freedom and were determined to thwart it? Not by force, said the North; not by government guardianship, said the South; then by the ballot, the sole and legitimate defence of a free people, said the Common Sense of the Nation. No one thought, at the time, that the exslaves could use the ballot intelligently or very effectively; but they did think that the possession of so great power by a great class in the nation would compel their fellows to educate this class to its intelligent use.

Meantime, new thoughts came to the nation: the inevitable period of moral retrogression and political trickery that ever follows in the wake of war overtook us. So flagrant became the political scandals that reputable men began to leave politics alone, and politics consequently became disreputable. Men began to pride themselves on having nothing to do with their own government, and to agree tacitly with those who regarded public office as a private perquisite. In this state of mind it became easy to wink at the suppression of the Negro vote in the South, and to advise self-respecting Negroes to leave politics entirely alone. The decent and reputable citizens of the North who neglected their own civic duties grew hilarious over the exaggerated importance with which the Negro regarded the franchise. Thus it easily happened that more and more the better class of Negroes followed the advice from abroad and the pressure from home, and took no further interest in politics, leaving to the careless and the venal of their race the exercise of their rights as voters. The black vote that still remained was not trained and educated, but further debauched by open and unblushing bribery, or force and fraud; until the Negro voter was thoroughly inoculated with the idea that politics was a method of private gain by disreputable means.

And finally, now, to-day, when we are awakening to the fact that the perpetuity of republican institutions on this continent depends on the purification of the ballot, the civic training of voters, and the raising of voting to the plane of a solemn duty which a patriotic citizen neglects to his peril and to the peril of his children's children,—in this day, when we are striving for a renaissance of civic virtue, what are we going to say to the black voter of the South? Are we going to tell him still that politics is a disreputable and useless form of human activity? Are we going to induce the best class of Negroes to take less and less interest in government, and to give up their right to take

such an interest, without a protest? I am not saying a word against all legitimate efforts to purge the ballot of ignorance, pauperism, and crime. But few have pretended that the present movement for disfranchisement in the South is for such a purpose; it has been plainly and frankly declared in nearly every case that the object of the disfranchising laws is the elimination of the black man from politics.

Now, is this a minor matter which has no influence on the main question of the industrial and intellectual development of the Negro? Can we establish a mass of black laborers and artisans and landholders in the South who, by law and public opinion, have absolutely no voice in shaping the laws under which they live and work? Can the modern organization of industry, assuming as it does free democratic government and the power and ability of the laboring classes to compel respect for their welfare,—can this system be carried out in the South when half its laboring force is voiceless in the public councils and powerless in its own defence? To-day the black man of the South has almost nothing to say as to how much he shall be taxed, or how those taxes shall be expended; as to who shall execute the laws, and how they shall do it; as to who shall make the laws, and how they shall be made. It is pitiable that frantic efforts must be made at critical times to get law-makers in some States even to listen to the respectful presentation of the black man's side of a current controversy. Daily the Negro is coming more and more to look upon law and justice, not as protecting safeguards, but as sources of humiliation and oppression. The laws are made by men who have little interest in him; they are executed by men who have absolutely no motive for treating the black people with courtesy or consideration; and, finally, the accused law-breaker is tried, not by his peers, but too often by men who would rather punish ten innocent Negroes than let one guilty one escape.

I should be the last one to deny the patent weaknesses and shortcomings of the Negro people; I should be the last to withhold sympathy from the white South in its efforts to solve its intricate social problems. I freely acknowledge that it is possible, and sometimes best, that a partially undeveloped people should be ruled by the best of their stronger and better neighbors for their own good, until such time as they can start and fight the world's battles alone. I have already pointed out how sorely in need of such economic and spiritual guidance the emancipated Negro was, and I am quite willing to admit that if the representatives of the best white Southern public opinion were the ruling and guiding powers in the South to-day the conditions indicated would be fairly well fulfilled. But the point I have insisted

upon, and now emphasize again, is that the best opinion of the South to-day is not the ruling opinion. That to leave the Negro helpless and without a ballot to-day is to leave him, not to the guidance of the best, but rather to the exploitation and debauchment of the worst; that this is no truer of the South than of the North,—of the North than of Europe: in any land, in any country under modern free competition, to lay any class of weak and despised people, be they white, black, or blue, at the political mercy of their stronger, richer, and more resourceful fellows, is a temptation which human nature seldom has withstood and seldom will withstand.

Moreover, the political status of the Negro in the South is closely connected with the question of Negro crime. There can be no doubt that crime among Negroes has sensibly increased in the last thirty years, and that there has appeared in the slums of great cities a distinct criminal class among the blacks. In explaining this unfortunate development, we must note two things: (1) that the inevitable result of Emancipation was to increase crime and criminals, and (2) that the police system of the South was primarily designed to control slaves. As to the first point, we must not forget that under a strict slave system there can scarcely be such a thing as crime. But when these variously constituted human particles are suddenly thrown broadcast on the sea of life, some swim, some sink, and some hang suspended, to be forced up or down by the chance currents of a busy hurrying world. So great an economic and social revolution as swept the South in '63 meant a weeding out among the Negroes of the incompetents and vicious, the beginning of a differentiation of social grades. Now a rising group of people are not lifted bodily from the ground like an inert solid mass, but rather stretch upward like a living plant with its roots still clinging in the mould. The appearance, therefore, of the Negro criminal was a phenomenon to be awaited; and while it causes anxiety, it should not occasion surprise.

Here again the hope for the future depended peculiarly on careful and delicate dealing with these criminals. Their offences at first were those of laziness, carelessness, and impulse, rather than of malignity or ungoverned viciousness. Such misdemeanors needed discriminating treatment, firm but reformatory, with no hint of injustice, and full proof of guilt. For such dealing with criminals, white or black, the South had no machinery, no adequate jails or reformatories; its police system was arranged to deal with blacks alone, and tacitly assumed that every white man was ipso facto a member of that police. Thus grew up a double system of justice, which erred on the white side by undue leniency and the practical immunity of red-handed

criminals, and erred on the black side by undue severity, injustice, and lack of discrimination. For, as I have said, the police system of the South was originally designed to keep track of all Negroes, not simply of criminals; and when the Negroes were freed and the whole South was convinced of the impossibility of free Negro labor, the first and almost universal device was to use the courts as a means of reënslaving the blacks. It was not then a question of crime, but rather one of color, that settled a man's conviction on almost any charge. Thus Negroes came to look upon courts as instruments of injustice and oppression, and upon those convicted in them as martyrs and victims.

When, now, the real Negro criminal appeared, and instead of petty stealing and vagrancy we began to have highway robbery, burglary, murder, and rape, there was a curious effect on both sides the color-line: the Negroes refused to believe the evidence of white witnesses or the fairness of white juries, so that the greatest deterrent to crime, the public opinion of one's own social caste, was lost, and the criminal was looked upon as crucified rather than hanged. On the other hand, the whites, used to being careless as to the guilt or innocence of accused Negroes, were swept in moments of passion beyond law, reason, and decency. Such a situation is bound to increase crime, and has increased it. To natural viciousness and vagrancy are being daily added motives of revolt and revenge which stir up all the latent savagery of both races and make peaceful attention to economic development often impossible.

But the chief problem in any community cursed with crime is not the punishment of the criminals, but the preventing of the young from being trained to crime. And here again the peculiar conditions of the South have prevented proper precautions. I have seen twelve-year-old boys working in chains on the public streets of Atlanta, directly in front of the schools, in company with old and hardened criminals; and this indiscriminate mingling of men and women and children makes the chain-gangs perfect schools of crime and debauchery. The struggle for reformatories, which has gone on in Virginia, Georgia, and other States, is the one encouraging sign of the awakening of some communities to the suicidal results of this policy.

It is the public schools, however, which can be made, outside the homes, the greatest means of training decent self-respecting citizens. We have been so hotly engaged recently in discussing trade-schools and the higher education that the pitiable plight of the public-school system in the South has almost dropped from view. Of every five dollars spent for public education in the State of Georgia, the white schools get four dollars and the Negro one dollar; and even then the white public-school system, save in the cities, is bad

and cries for reform. If this is true of the whites, what of the blacks? I am becoming more and more convinced, as I look upon the system of common-school training in the South, that the national government must soon step in and aid popular education in some way. To-day it has been only by the most strenuous efforts on the part of the thinking men of the South that the Negro's share of the school fund has not been cut down to a pittance in some half-dozen States; and that movement not only is not dead, but in many communities is gaining strength. What in the name of reason does this nation expect of a people, poorly trained and hard pressed in severe economic competition, without political rights, and with ludicrously inadequate common-school facilities? What can it expect but crime and listlessness, offset here and there by the dogged struggles of the fortunate and more determined who are themselves buoyed by the hope that in due time the country will come to its senses?

I have thus far sought to make clear the physical, economic, and political relations of the Negroes and whites in the South, as I have conceived them, including, for the reasons set forth, crime and education. But after all that has been said on these more tangible matters of human contact, there still remains a part essential to a proper description of the South which it is difficult to describe or fix in terms easily understood by strangers. It is, in fine, the atmosphere of the land, the thought and feeling, the thousand and one little actions which go to make up life. In any community or nation it is these little things which are most elusive to the grasp and yet most essential to any clear conception of the group life taken as a whole. What is thus true of all communities is peculiarly true of the South, where, outside of written history and outside of printed law, there has been going on for a generation as deep a storm and stress of human souls, as intense a ferment of feeling, as intricate a writhing of spirit, as ever a people experienced. Within and without the sombre veil of color vast social forces have been at work,—efforts for human betterment, movements toward disintegration and despair, tragedies and comedies in social and economic life, and a swaying and lifting and sinking of human hearts which have made this land a land of mingled sorrow and joy, of change and excitement and unrest.

The centre of this spiritual turmoil has ever been the millions of black freedmen and their sons, whose destiny is so fatefully bound up with that of the nation. And yet the casual observer visiting the South sees at first little of this. He notes the growing frequency of dark faces as he rides along,—but otherwise the days slip lazily on, the sun shines, and this little world seems

as happy and contented as other worlds he has visited. Indeed, on the question of questions—the Negro problem—he hears so little that there almost seems to be a conspiracy of silence; the morning papers seldom mention it, and then usually in a far-fetched academic way, and indeed almost every one seems to forget and ignore the darker half of the land, until the astonished visitor is inclined to ask if after all there is any problem here. But if he lingers long enough there comes the awakening: perhaps in a sudden whirl of passion which leaves him gasping at its bitter intensity; more likely in a gradually dawning sense of things he had not at first noticed. Slowly but surely his eyes begin to catch the shadows of the color-line: here he meets crowds of Negroes and whites; then he is suddenly aware that he cannot discover a single dark face; or again at the close of a day's wandering he may find himself in some strange assembly, where all faces are tinged brown or black, and where he has the vague, uncomfortable feeling of the stranger. He realizes at last that silently, resistlessly, the world about flows by him in two great streams: they ripple on in the same sunshine, they approach and mingle their waters in seeming carelessness,—then they divide and flow wide apart. It is done quietly; no mistakes are made, or if one occurs, the swift arm of the law and of public opinion swings down for a moment, as when the other day a black man and a white woman were arrested for talking together on Whitehall Street in Atlanta.

Now if one notices carefully one will see that between these two worlds, despite much physical contact and daily intermingling, there is almost no community of intellectual life or point of transference where the thoughts and feelings of one race can come into direct contact and sympathy with the thoughts and feelings of the other. Before and directly after the war, when all the best of the Negroes were domestic servants in the best of the white families, there were bonds of intimacy, affection, and sometimes blood relationship, between the races. They lived in the same home, shared in the family life, often attended the same church, and talked and conversed with each other. But the increasing civilization of the Negro since then has naturally meant the development of higher classes: there are increasing numbers of ministers, teachers, physicians, merchants, mechanics, and independent farmers, who by nature and training are the aristocracy and leaders of the blacks. Between them, however, and the best element of the whites, there is little or no intellectual commerce. They go to separate churches, they live in separate sections, they are strictly separated in all public gatherings, they travel separately, and they are beginning to read different papers and books. To

most libraries, lectures, concerts, and museums, Negroes are either not admitted at all, or on terms peculiarly galling to the pride of the very classes who might otherwise be attracted. The daily paper chronicles the doings of the black world from afar with no great regard for accuracy; and so on, throughout the category of means for intellectual communication,—schools, conferences, efforts for social betterment, and the like,—it is usually true that the very representatives of the two races, who for mutual benefit and the welfare of the land ought to be in complete understanding and sympathy, are so far strangers that one side thinks all whites are narrow and prejudiced, and the other thinks educated Negroes dangerous and insolent. Moreover, in a land where the tyranny of public opinion and the intolerance of criticism is for obvious historical reasons so strong as in the South, such a situation is extremely difficult to correct. The white man, as well as the Negro, is bound and barred by the color-line, and many a scheme of friendliness and philanthropy, of broad-minded sympathy and generous fellowship between the two has dropped still-born because some busybody has forced the color-question to the front and brought the tremendous force of unwritten law against the innovators.

It is hardly necessary for me to add very much in regard to the social contact between the races. Nothing has come to replace that finer sympathy and love between some masters and house servants which the radical and more uncompromising drawing of the color-line in recent years has caused almost completely to disappear. In a world where it means so much to take a man by the hand and sit beside him, to look frankly into his eyes and feel his heart beating with red blood; in a world where a social cigar or a cup of tea together means more than legislative halls and magazine articles and speeches,— one can imagine the consequences of the almost utter absence of such social amenities between estranged races, whose separation extends even to parks and streetcars.

Here there can be none of that social going down to the people,—the opening of heart and hand of the best to the worst, in generous acknowledgment of a common humanity and a common destiny. On the other hand, in matters of simple almsgiving, where there can be no question of social contact, and in the succor of the aged and sick, the South, as if stirred by a feeling of its unfortunate limitations, is generous to a fault. The black beggar is never turned away without a good deal more than a crust, and a call for help for the unfortunate meets quick response. I remember, one cold winter, in Atlanta, when I refrained from contributing to a public relief fund lest

Negroes should be discriminated against, I afterward inquired of a friend: "Were any black people receiving aid?" "Why," said he, "they were *all* black."

And yet this does not touch the kernel of the problem. Human advancement is not a mere question of almsgiving, but rather of sympathy and cooperation among classes who would scorn charity. And here is a land where, in the higher walks of life, in all the higher striving for the good and noble and true, the color-line comes to separate natural friends and co-workers; while at the bottom of the social group, in the saloon, the gambling-hell, and the brothel, that same line wavers and disappears.

I have sought to paint an average picture of real relations between the sons of master and man in the South. I have not glossed over matters for policy's sake, for I fear we have already gone too far in that sort of thing. On the other hand, I have sincerely sought to let no unfair exaggerations creep in. I do not doubt that in some Southern communities conditions are better than those I have indicated; while I am no less certain that in other communities they are far worse.

Nor does the paradox and danger of this situation fail to interest and perplex the best conscience of the South. Deeply religious and intensely democratic as are the mass of the whites, they feel acutely the false position in which the Negro problems place them. Such an essentially honest-hearted and generous people cannot cite the caste-levelling precepts of Christianity, or believe in equality of opportunity for all men, without coming to feel more and more with each generation that the present drawing of the color-line is a flat contradiction to their beliefs and professions. But just as often as they come to this point, the present social condition of the Negro stands as a menace and a portent before even the most open-minded: if there were nothing to charge against the Negro but his blackness or other physical peculiarities, they argue, the problem would be comparatively simple; but what can we say to his ignorance, shiftlessness, poverty, and crime? can a self-respecting group hold anything but the least possible fellowship with such persons and survive? and shall we let a mawkish sentiment sweep away the culture of our fathers or the hope of our children? The argument so put is of great strength, but it is not a whit stronger than the argument of thinking Negroes: granted, they reply, that the condition of our masses is bad; there is certainly on the one hand adequate historical cause for this, and unmistakable evidence that no small number have, in spite of tremendous disadvantages, risen to the level of American civilization. And when, by proscription

and prejudice, these same Negroes are classed with and treated like the lowest of their people, simply because they are Negroes, such a policy not only discourages thrift and intelligence among black men, but puts a direct premium on the very things you complain of,—inefficiency and crime. Draw lines of crime, of incompetency, of vice, as tightly and uncompromisingly as you will, for these things must be proscribed; but a color-line not only does not accomplish this purpose, but thwarts it.

In the face of two such arguments, the future of the South depends on the ability of the representatives of these opposing views to see and appreciate and sympathize with each other's position,—for the Negro to realize more deeply than he does at present the need of uplifting the masses of his people, for the white people to realize more vividly than they have yet done the deadening and disastrous effect of a color-prejudice that classes Phillis Wheatley and Sam Hose in the same despised class.

It is not enough for the Negroes to declare that color-prejudice is the sole cause of their social condition, nor for the white South to reply that their social condition is the main cause of prejudice. They both act as reciprocal cause and effect, and a change in neither alone will bring the desired effect. Both must change, or neither can improve to any great extent. The Negro cannot stand the present reactionary tendencies and unreasoning drawing of the color-line indefinitely without discouragement and retrogression. And the condition of the Negro is ever the excuse for further discrimination. Only by a union of intelligence and sympathy across the color-line in this critical period of the Republic shall justice and right triumph,—

> "That mind and soul according well,
> May make one music as before,
> But vaster."

X

OF THE FAITH OF THE FATHERS

> Dim face of Beauty haunting all the world,
> Fair face of Beauty all too fair to see,
> Where the lost stars adown the heavens are hurled,—

There, there alone for thee
May white peace be.

 * * * * * * * *

Beauty, sad face of Beauty, Mystery, Wonder,
 What are these dreams to foolish babbling men
Who cry with little noises 'neath the thunder
 Of Ages ground to sand,
 To a little sand.

 Fiona Macleod

I T was out in the country, far from home, far from my foster home, on a dark Sunday night. The road wandered from our rambling log-house up the stony bed of a creek, past wheat and corn, until we could hear dimly across the fields a rhythmic cadence of song,—soft, thrilling, powerful, that swelled and died sorrowfully in our ears. I was a country school-teacher then, fresh from the East, and had never seen a Southern Negro revival. To be sure, we in Berkshire were not perhaps as stiff and formal as they in Suffolk of olden time; yet we were very quiet and subdued, and I know not what would have happened those clear Sabbath mornings had some one punctuated the sermon with a wild scream, or interrupted the long prayer with a loud Amen! And so most striking to me, as I approached the village and the little plain church perched aloft, was the air of intense excitement that possessed that mass of black folk. A sort of suppressed terror hung in the air and seemed to seize us,—a pythian madness, a demoniac possession, that lent terrible reality to song and word. The black and massive form of the preacher swayed and quivered as the words crowded to his lips and flew at us in singular eloquence. The people moaned and fluttered, and then the gaunt-checked brown woman beside me suddenly leaped straight into the air and shrieked like a lost soul, while round about came wail and groan and outcry, and a scene of human passion such as I had never conceived before.

Those who have not thus witnessed the frenzy of a Negro revival in the untouched backwoods of the South can but dimly realize the religious feeling of the slave; as described, such scenes appear grotesque and funny, but as seen they are awful. Three things characterized this religion of the slave,—

the Preacher, the Music, and the Frenzy. The Preacher is the most unique personality developed by the Negro on American soil. A leader, a politician, an orator, a "boss," an intriguer, an idealist,—all these he is, and ever, too, the centre of a group of men, now twenty, now a thousand in number. The combination of a certain adroitness with deep-seated earnestness, of tact with consummate ability, gave him his preeminence, and helps him maintain it. The type, of course, varies according to time and place, from the West Indies in the sixteenth century to New England in the nineteenth, and from the Mississippi bottoms to cities like New Orleans or New York.

The Music of Negro religion is that plaintive rhythmic melody, with its touching minor cadences, which, despite caricature and defilement, still remains the most original and beautiful expression of human life and long- ing yet born on American soil. Sprung from the African forests, where its counterpart can still be heard, it was adapted, changed, and intensified by the tragic soul-life of the slave, until, under the stress of law and whip, it became the one true expression of a people's sorrow, despair, and hope.

Finally the Frenzy or "Shouting," when the Spirit of the Lord passed by, and, seizing the devotee, made him mad with supernatural joy, was the last essential of Negro religion and the one more devoutly believed in than all the rest. It varied in expression from the silent rapt countenance or the low mur- mur and moan to the mad abandon of physical fervor,—the stamping, shrieking, and shouting, the rushing to and fro and wild waving of arms, the weeping and laughing, the vision and the trance. All this is nothing new in the world, but old as religion, as Delphi and Endor. And so firm a hold did it have on the Negro, that many generations firmly believed that without this visible manifestation of the God there could be no true communion with the Invisible.

These were the characteristics of Negro religious life as developed up to the time of Emancipation. Since under the peculiar circumstances of the black man's environment they were the one expression of his higher life, they are of deep interest to the student of his development, both socially and psy- chologically. Numerous are the attractive lines of inquiry that here group themselves. What did slavery mean to the African savage? What was his atti- tude toward the World and Life? What seemed to him good and evil,—God and Devil? Whither went his longings and strivings, and wherefore were his heart-burnings and disappointments? Answers to such questions can come only from a study of Negro religion as a development, through its gradual changes from the heathenism of the Gold Coast to the institutional Negro

church of Chicago.

Moreover, the religious growth of millions of men, even though they be slaves, cannot be without potent influence upon their contemporaries. The Methodists and Baptists of America owe much of their condition to the silent but potent influence of their millions of Negro converts. Especially is this noticeable in the South, where theology and religious philosophy are on this account a long way behind the North, and where the religion of the poor whites is a plain copy of Negro thought and methods. The mass of "gospel" hymns which has swept through American churches and well-nigh ruined our sense of song consists largely of debased imitations of Negro melodies made by ears that caught the jingle but not the music, the body but not the soul, of the Jubilee songs. It is thus clear that the study of Negro religion is not only a vital part of the history of the Negro in America, but no uninteresting part of American history.

The Negro church of to-day is the social centre of Negro life in the United States, and the most characteristic expression of African character. Take a typical church in a small Virginian town: it is the "First Baptist"—a roomy brick edifice seating five hundred or more persons, tastefully finished in Georgia pine, with a carpet, a small organ, and stained-glass windows. Underneath is a large assembly room with benches. This building is the central club-house of a community of a thousand or more Negroes. Various organizations meet here,—the church proper, the Sunday-school, two or three insurance societies, women's societies, secret societies, and mass meetings of various kinds. Entertainments, suppers, and lectures are held beside the five or six regular weekly religious services. Considerable sums of money are collected and expended here, employment is found for the idle, strangers are introduced, news is disseminated and charity distributed. At the same time this social, intellectual, and economic centre is a religious centre of great power. Depravity, Sin, Redemption, Heaven, Hell, and Damnation are preached twice a Sunday with much fervor, and revivals take place every year after the crops are laid by; and few indeed of the community have the hardihood to withstand conversion. Back of this more formal religion, the Church often stands as a real conserver of morals, a strengthener of family life, and the final authority on what is Good and Right.

Thus one can see in the Negro church to-day, reproduced in microcosm, all that great world from which the Negro is cut off by color-prejudice and social condition. In the great city churches the same tendency is noticeable and in many respects emphasized. A great church like the Bethel of

Philadelphia has over eleven hundred members, an edifice seating fifteen hundred persons and valued at one hundred thousand dollars, an annual budget of five thousand dollars, and a government consisting of a pastor with several assisting local preachers, an executive and legislative board, financial boards and tax collectors; general church meetings for making laws; subdivided groups led by class leaders, a company of militia, and twenty-four auxiliary societies. The activity of a church like this is immense and far-reaching, and the bishops who preside over these organizations throughout the land are among the most powerful Negro rulers in the world.

Such churches are really governments of men, and consequently a little investigation reveals the curious fact that, in the South, at least, practically every American Negro is a church member. Some, to be sure, are not regularly enrolled, and a few do not habitually attend services; but, practically, a proscribed people must have a social centre, and that centre for this people is the Negro church. The census of 1890 showed nearly twenty-four thousand Negro churches in the country, with a total enrolled membership of over two and a half millions, or ten actual church members to every twenty-eight persons, and in some Southern States one in every two persons. Besides these there is the large number who, while not enrolled as members, attend and take part in many of the activities of the church. There is an organized Negro church for every sixty black families in the nation, and in some States for every forty families, owning, on an average, a thousand dollars' worth of property each, or nearly twenty-six million dollars in all.

Such, then, is the large development of the Negro church since Emancipation. The question now is, What have been the successive steps of this social history and what are the present tendencies? First, we must realize that no such institution as the Negro church could rear itself without definite historical foundations. These foundations we can find if we remember that the social history of the Negro did not start in America. He was brought from a definite social environment,—the polygamous clan life under the headship of the chief and the potent influence of the priest. His religion was nature-worship, with profound belief in invisible surrounding influences, good and bad, and his worship was through incantation and sacrifice. The first rude change in this life was the slave ship and the West Indian sugarfields. The plantation organization replaced the clan and tribe, and the white master replaced the chief with far greater and more despotic powers. Forced and long-continued toil became the rule of life, the old ties of blood relationship and kinship disappeared, and instead of the family appeared a new

polygamy and polyandry, which, in some cases, almost reached promiscuity. It was a terrific social revolution, and yet some traces were retained of the former group life, and the chief remaining institution was the Priest or Medicine-man. He early appeared on the plantation and found his function as the healer of the sick, the interpreter of the Unknown, the comforter of the sorrowing, the supernatural avenger of wrong, and the one who rudely but picturesquely expressed the longing, disappointment, and resentment of a stolen and oppressed people. Thus, as bard, physician, judge, and priest, within the narrow limits allowed by the slave system, rose the Negro preacher, and under him the first Afro-American institution the Negro church. This church was not at first by any means Christian nor definitely organized; rather it was an adaptation and mingling of heathen rites among the members of each plantation, and roughly designated as Voodooism. Association with the masters, missionary effort and motives of expediency gave these rites an early veneer of Christianity, and after the lapse of many generations the Negro church became Christian.

Two characteristic things must be noticed in regard to this church. First, it became almost entirely Baptist and Methodist in faith; secondly, as a social institution it antedated by many decades the monogamic Negro home. From the very circumstances of its beginning, the church was confined to the plantation, and consisted primarily of a series of disconnected units; although, later on, some freedom of movement was allowed, still this geographical limitation was always important and was one cause of the spread of the decentralized and democratic Baptist faith among the slaves. At the same time, the visible rite of baptism appealed strongly to their mystic temperament. To-day the Baptist Church is still largest in membership among Negroes, and has a million and a half communicants. Next in popularity came the churches organized in connection with the white neighboring churches, chiefly Baptist and Methodist, with a few Episcopalian and others. The Methodists still form the second greatest denomination, with nearly a million members. The faith of these two leading denominations was more suited to the slave church from the prominence they gave to religious feeling and fervor. The Negro membership in other denominations has always been small and relatively unimportant, although the Episcopalians and Presbyterians are gaining among the more intelligent classes to-day, and the Catholic Church is making headway in certain sections. After Emancipation, and still earlier in the North, the Negro churches largely severed such affiliations as they had had with the white churches, either by choice or by compulsion. The Baptist

churches became independent, but the Methodists were compelled early to unite for purposes of episcopal government. This gave rise to the great African Methodist Church, the greatest Negro organization in the world, to the Zion Church and the Colored Methodist, and to the black conferences and churches in this and other denominations.

The second fact noted, namely, that the Negro church antedates the Negro home, leads to an explanation of much that is paradoxical in this communistic institution and in the morals of its members. But especially it leads us to regard this institution as peculiarly the expression of the inner ethical life of a people in a sense seldom true elsewhere. Let us turn, then, from the outer physical development of the church to the more important inner ethical life of the people who compose it. The Negro has already been pointed out many times as a religious animal,—a being of that deep emotional nature which turns instinctively toward the supernatural. Endowed with a rich tropical imagination and a keen, delicate appreciation of Nature, the transplanted African lived in a world animate with gods and devils, elves and witches; full of strange influences,—of Good to be implored, of Evil to be propitiated. Slavery, then, was to him the dark triumph of Evil over him. All the hateful powers of the Under-world were striving against him, and a spirit of revolt and revenge filled his heart. He called up all the resources of heathenism to aid,—exorcism and witchcraft, the mysterious Obi worship with its barbarous rites, spells, and blood-sacrifice even, now and then, of human victims. Weird midnight orgies and mystic conjurations were invoked, the witch-woman and the voodoo-priest became the centre of Negro group life, and that vein of vague superstition which characterizes the unlettered Negro even to-day was deepened and strengthened.

In spite, however, of such success as that of the fierce Maroons, the Danish blacks, and others, the spirit of revolt gradually died away under the untiring energy and superior strength of the slave masters. By the middle of the eighteenth century the black slave had sunk, with hushed murmurs, to his place at the bottom of a new economic system, and was unconsciously ripe for a new philosophy of life. Nothing suited his condition then better than the doctrines of passive submission embodied in the newly learned Christianity. Slave masters early realized this, and cheerfully aided religious propaganda within certain bounds. The long system of repression and degradation of the Negro tended to emphasize the elements in his character which made him a valuable chattel: courtesy became humility, moral strength degenerated into submission, and the exquisite native appreciation of the

beautiful became an infinite capacity for dumb suffering. The Negro, losing the joy of this world, eagerly seized upon the offered conceptions of the next; the avenging Spirit of the Lord enjoining patience in this world, under sorrow and tribulation until the Great Day when He should lead His dark children home,—this became his comforting dream. His preacher repeated the prophecy, and his bards sang,—

> "Children, we all shall be free
> When the Lord shall appear!"

This deep religious fatalism, painted so beautifully in "Uncle Tom," came soon to breed, as all fatalistic faiths will, the sensualist side by side with the martyr. Under the lax moral life of the plantation, where marriage was a farce, laziness a virtue, and property a theft, a religion of resignation and submission degenerated easily, in less strenuous minds, into a philosophy of indulgence and crime. Many of the worst characteristics of the Negro masses of to-day had their seed in this period of the slave's ethical growth. Here it was that the Home was ruined under the very shadow of the Church, white and black; here habits of shiftlessness took root, and sullen hopelessness replaced hopeful strife.

With the beginning of the abolition movement and the gradual growth of a class of free Negroes came a change. We often neglect the influence of the freedman before the war, because of the paucity of his numbers and the small weight he had in the history of the nation. But we must not forget that his chief influence was internal,—was exerted on the black world; and that there he was the ethical and social leader. Huddled as he was in a few centres like Philadelphia, New York, and New Orleans, the masses of the freedmen sank into poverty and listlessness; but not all of them. The free Negro leader early arose and his chief characteristic was intense earnestness and deep feeling on the slavery question. Freedom became to him a real thing and not a dream. His religion became darker and more intense, and into his ethics crept a note of revenge, into his songs a day of reckoning close at hand. The "Coming of the Lord" swept this side of Death, and came to be a thing to be hoped for in this day. Through fugitive slaves and irrepressible discussion this desire for freedom seized the black millions still in bondage, and became their one ideal of life. The black bards caught new notes, and sometimes even dared to sing,—

"O Freedom, O Freedom, O Freedom over me!
Before I'll be a slave
I'll be buried in my grave,
And go home to my Lord
And be free."

For fifty years Negro religion thus transformed itself and identified itself with the dream of Abolition, until that which was a radical fad in the white North and an anarchistic plot in the white South had become a religion to the black world. Thus, when Emancipation finally came, it seemed to the freedman a literal Coming of the Lord. His fervid imagination was stirred as never before, by the tramp of armies, the blood and dust of battle, and the wail and whirl of social upheaval. He stood dumb and motionless before the whirlwind: what had he to do with it? Was it not the Lord's doing, and marvellous in his eyes? Joyed and bewildered with what came, he stood awaiting new wonders till the inevitable Age of Reaction swept over the nation and brought the crisis of to-day.

It is difficult to explain clearly the present critical stage of Negro religion. First, we must remember that living as the blacks do in close contact with a great modern nation, and sharing, although imperfectly, the soul-life of that nation, they must necessarily be affected more or less directly by all the religious and ethical forces that are to-day moving the United States. These questions and movements are, however, overshadowed and dwarfed by the (to them) all-important question of their civil, political, and economic status. They must perpetually discuss the "Negro Problem,"—must live, move, and have their being in it, and interpret all else in its light or darkness. With this come, too, peculiar problems of their inner life,—of the status of women, the maintenance of Home, the training of children, the accumulation of wealth, and the prevention of crime. All this must mean a time of intense ethical ferment, of religious heart-searching and intellectual unrest. From the double life every American Negro must live, as a Negro and as an American, as swept on by the current of the nineteenth while yet struggling in the eddies of the fifteenth century,—from this must arise a painful self-consciousness, an almost morbid sense of personality and a moral hesitancy which is fatal to self-confidence. The worlds within and without the Veil of Color are changing, and changing rapidly, but not at the same rate, not in the same way; and this must produce a peculiar wrenching of the soul, a peculiar sense of doubt and bewilderment. Such a double life, with double thoughts, double duties,

and double social classes, must give rise to double words and double ideals, and tempt the mind to presence or to revolt, to hypocrisy or to radicalism.

In some such doubtful words and phrases can one perhaps most clearly picture the peculiar ethical paradox that faces the Negro of to-day and is tingeing and changing his religious life. Feeling that his rights and his dearest ideals are being trampled upon, that the public conscience is ever more deaf to his righteous appeal, and that all the reactionary forces of prejudice, greed, and revenge are daily gaining new strength and fresh allies, the Negro faces no enviable dilemma. Conscious of his impotence, and pessimistic, he often becomes bitter and vindictive; and his religion, instead of a worship, is a complaint and a curse, a wail rather than a hope, a sneer rather than a faith. On the other hand, another type of mind, shrewder and keener and more tortuous too, sees in the very strength of the anti-Negro movement its patent weaknesses, and with Jesuitic casuistry is deterred by no ethical considerations in the endeavor to turn this weakness to the black man's strength. Thus we have two great and hardly reconcilable streams of thought and ethical strivings; the danger of the one lies in anarchy, that of the other in hypocrisy. The one type of Negro stands almost ready to curse God and die, and the other is too often found a traitor to right and a coward before force; the one is wedded to ideals remote, whimsical, perhaps impossible of realization; the other forgets that life is more than meat and the body more than raiment. But, after all, is not this simply the writhing of the age translated into black,—the triumph of the Lie which to-day, with its false culture, faces the hideousness of the anarchist assassin?

To-day the two groups of Negroes, the one in the North, the other in the South, represent these divergent ethical tendencies, the first tending toward radicalism, the other toward hypocritical compromise. It is no idle regret with which the white South mourns the loss of the old-time Negro,—the frank, honest, simple old servant who stood for the earlier religious age of submission and humility. With all his laziness and lack of many elements of true manhood, he was at least open-hearted, faithful, and sincere. To-day he is gone, but who is to blame for his going? Is it not those very persons who mourn for him? Is it not the tendency, born of Reconstruction and Reaction, to found a society on lawlessness and deception, to tamper with the moral fibre of a naturally honest and straightforward people until the whites threaten to become ungovernable tyrants and the blacks criminals and hypocrites? Deception is the natural defence of the weak against the strong, and the South used it for many years against its conquerors; to-day it must be prepared to see its black

proletariat turn that same two-edged weapon against itself. And how natural this is! The death of Denmark Vesey and Nat Turner proved long since to the Negro the present hopelessness of physical defence. Political defence is becoming less and less available, and economic defence is still only partially effective. But there is a patent defence at hand,—the defence of deception and flattery, of cajoling and lying. It is the same defence which the Jews of the Middle Age used and which left its stamp on their character for centuries. To-day the young Negro of the South who would succeed cannot be frank and outspoken, honest and self-assertive, but rather he is daily tempted to be silent and wary, politic and sly; he must flatter and be pleasant, endure petty insults with a smile, shut his eyes to wrong; in too many cases he sees positive personal advantage in deception and lying. His real thoughts, his real aspirations, must be guarded in whispers; he must not criticise, he must not complain. Patience, humility, and adroitness must, in these growing black youth, replace impulse, manliness, and courage. With this sacrifice there is an economic opening, and perhaps peace and some prosperity. Without this there is riot, migration, or crime. Nor is this situation peculiar to the Southern United States,—is it not rather the only method by which undeveloped races have gained the right to share modern culture? The price of culture is a Lie.

On the other hand, in the North the tendency is to emphasize the radicalism of the Negro. Driven from his birthright in the South by a situation at which every fibre of his more outspoken and assertive nature revolts, he finds himself in a land where he can scarcely earn a decent living amid the harsh competition and the color discrimination. At the same time, through schools and periodicals, discussions and lectures, he is intellectually quickened and awakened. The soul, long pent up and dwarfed, suddenly expands in new-found freedom. What wonder that every tendency is to excess,—radical complaint, radical remedies, bitter denunciation or angry silence. Some sink, some rise. The criminal and the sensualist leave the church for the gambling-hell and the brothel, and fill the slums of Chicago and Baltimore; the better classes segregate themselves from the group-life of both white and black, and form an aristocracy, cultured but pessimistic, whose bitter criticism stings while it points out no way of escape. They despise the submission and subserviency of the Southern Negroes, but offer no other means by which a poor and oppressed minority can exist side by side with its masters. Feeling deeply and keenly the tendencies and opportunities of the age in which they live, their souls are bitter at the fate which drops the Veil between; and the very fact that this bitterness is natural and justifiable only serves to

intensify it and make it more maddening.

Between the two extreme types of ethical attitude which I have thus sought to make clear wavers the mass of the millions of Negroes, North and South; and their religious life and activity partake of this social conflict within their ranks. Their churches are differentiating,—now into groups of cold, fashionable devotees, in no way distinguishable from similar white groups save in color of skin; now into large social and business institutions catering to the desire for information and amusement of their members, warily avoiding unpleasant questions both within and without the black world, and preaching in effect if not in word: *Dum vivimus, vivamus.*

But back of this still broods silently the deep religious feeling of the real Negro heart, the stirring, unguided might of powerful human souls who have lost the guiding star of the past and are seeking in the great night a new religious ideal. Some day the Awakening will come, when the pent-up vigor of ten million souls shall sweep irresistibly toward the Goal, out of the Valley of the Shadow of Death, where all that makes life worth living—Liberty, Justice, and Right—is marked "For White People Only."

XI

OF THE PASSING OF THE FIRST-BORN

O sister, sister, thy first-begotten,
The hands that cling and the feet that follow,
The voice of the child's blood crying yet,
Who hath remembered me? who hath forgotten?
Thou hast forgotten, O summer swallow,
But the world shall end when I forget.

<div align="right">Swinburne.</div>

Unto you a child is born," sang the bit of yellow paper that fluttered into my room one brown October morning. Then the fear of fatherhood mingled wildly with the joy of creation; I wondered how it looked and how it felt,—what were its eyes, and how its hair curled and crumpled itself. And I thought in awe of her,—she who had slept with Death to tear a man-child from underneath her heart, while I was unconsciously wandering. I fled to my wife and child, repeating the while to myself half wonderingly, "Wife and child? Wife and child?"—fled fast and faster than boat and steam-car, and yet must ever impatiently await them; away from the hard-voiced city, away from the flickering sea into my own Berkshire Hills that sit all sadly guarding the gates of Massachusetts.

Up the stairs I ran to the wan mother and whimpering babe, to the sanctuary on whose altar a life at my bidding had offered itself to win a life, and won. What is this tiny formless thing, this newborn wail from an unknown world,—all head and voice? I handle it curiously, and watch perplexed its winking, breathing, and sneezing. I did not love it then; it seemed a ludicrous thing to love; but her I loved, my girl-mother, she whom now I saw unfolding like the glory of the morning—the transfigured woman.

Through her I came to love the wee thing, as it grew and waxed strong; as its little soul unfolded itself in twitter and cry and half-formed word, and as its eyes caught the gleam and flash of life. How beautiful he was, with his olive-tinted flesh and dark gold ringlets, his eyes of mingled blue and brown, his perfect little limbs, and the soft voluptuous roll which the blood of Africa had moulded into his features! I held him in my arms, after we had sped far away to our Southern home,—held him, and glanced at the hot red soil of Georgia and the breathless city of a hundred hills, and felt a vague unrest. Why was his hair tinted with gold? An evil omen was golden hair in my life. Why had not the brown of his eyes crushed out and killed the blue?—for brown were his father's eyes, and his father's father's. And thus in the Land of the Color-line I saw, as it fell across my baby, the shadow of the Veil.

Within the Veil was he born, said I; and there within shall he live,—a Negro and a Negro's son. Holding in that little head—ah, bitterly!—the unbowed pride of a hunted race, clinging with that tiny dimpled hand—ah, wearily!—to a hope not hopeless but unhopeful, and seeing with those bright wondering eyes that peer into my soul a land whose freedom is to us a mockery and whose liberty a lie. I saw the shadow of the Veil as it passed over my baby, I saw the cold city towering above the blood-red land. I held my face beside his little cheek, showed him the star-children and the twinkling lights as they began

to flash, and stilled with an even-song the unvoiced terror of my life.

So sturdy and masterful he grew, so filled with bubbling life, so tremulous with the unspoken wisdom of a life but eighteen months distant from the All-life,—we were not far from worshipping this revelation of the divine, my wife and I. Her own life builded and moulded itself upon the child; he tinged her every dream and idealized her every effort. No hands but hers must touch and garnish those little limbs; no dress or frill must touch them that had not wearied her fingers; no voice but hers could coax him off to Dreamland, and she and he together spoke some soft and unknown tongue and in it held communion. I too mused above his little white bed; saw the strength of my own arm stretched onward through the ages through the newer strength of his; saw the dream of my black fathers stagger a step onward in the wild phantasm of the world; heard in his baby voice the voice of the Prophet that was to rise within the Veil.

And so we dreamed and loved and planned by fall and winter, and the full flush of the long Southern spring, till the hot winds rolled from the fetid Gulf, till the roses shivered and the still stern sun quivered its awful light over the hills of Atlanta. And then one night the little feet pattered wearily to the wee white bed, and the tiny hands trembled; and a warm flushed face tossed on the pillow, and we knew baby was sick. Ten days he lay there,—a swift week and three endless days, wasting, wasting away. Cheerily the mother nursed him the first days, and laughed into the little eyes that smiled again. Tenderly then she hovered round him, till the smile fled away and Fear crouched beside the little bed.

Then the day ended not, and night was a dreamless terror, and joy and sleep slipped away. I hear now that Voice at midnight calling me from dull and dreamless trance,—crying, "The Shadow of Death! The Shadow of Death!" Out into the starlight I crept, to rouse the gray physician,—the Shadow of Death, the Shadow of Death. The hours trembled on; the night listened; the ghastly dawn glided like a tired thing across the lamplight. Then we two alone looked upon the child as he turned toward us with great eyes, and stretched his string-like hands,—the Shadow of Death! And we spoke no word, and turned away.

He died at eventide, when the sun lay like a brooding sorrow above the western hills, veiling its face; when the winds spoke not, and the trees, the great green trees he loved, stood motionless. I saw his breath beat quicker and quicker, pause, and then his little soul leapt like a star that travels in the night and left a world of darkness in its train. The day changed not; the same tall

trees peeped in at the windows, the same green grass glinted in the setting sun. Only in the chamber of death writhed the world's most piteous thing—a childless mother.

I shirk not. I long for work. I pant for a life full of striving. I am no coward, to shrink before, the rugged rush of the storm, nor even quail before the awful shadow of the Veil. But hearken, O Death! Is not this my life hard enough,—is not that dull land that stretches its sneering web about me cold enough,—is not all the world beyond these four little walls pitiless enough, but that thou must needs enter here,—thou, O Death? About my head the thundering storm beat like a heartless voice, and the crazy forest pulsed with the curses of the weak; but what cared I, within my home beside my wife and baby boy? Wast thou so jealous of one little coign of happiness that thou must needs enter there,—thou, O Death?

A perfect life was his, all joy and love, with tears to make it brighter,—sweet as a summer's day beside the Housatonic. The world loved him; the women kissed his curls, the men looked gravely into his wonderful eyes, and the children hovered and fluttered about him. I can see him now, changing like the sky from sparkling laughter to darkening frowns, and then to wondering thoughtfulness as he watched the world. He knew no color-line, poor dear,—and the Veil, though it shadowed him, had not yet darkened half his sun. He loved the white matron, he loved his black nurse; and in his little world walked souls alone, uncolored and unclothed. I—yea, all men—are larger and purer by the infinite breadth of that one little life. She who in simple clearness of vision sees beyond the stars said when he had flown, "He will be happy There; he ever loved beautiful things." And I, far more ignorant, and blind by the web of mine own weaving, sit alone winding words and muttering, "If still he be, and he be There, and there be a There, let him be happy, O Fate!"

Blithe was the morning of his burial, with bird and song and sweet-smelling flowers. The trees whispered to the grass, but the children sat with hushed faces. And yet it seemed a ghostly unreal day,—the wraith of Life. We seemed to rumble down an unknown street behind a little white bundle of posies, with the shadow of a song in our ears. The busy city dinned about us; they did not say much, those pale-faced hurrying men and women; they did not say much,—they only glanced and said, "Niggers!"

We could not lay him in the ground there in Georgia, for the earth there is strangely red; so we bore him away to the northward, with his flowers and his little folded hands. In vain, in vain!—for where, O God I beneath thy

broad blue sky shall my dark baby rest in peace,—where Reverence dwells, and Goodness, and a Freedom that is free?

All that day and all that night there sat an awful gladness in my heart,— nay, blame me not if I see the world thus darkly through the Veil,—and my soul whispers ever to me, saying, "Not dead, not dead, but escaped; not bond, but free." No bitter meanness now shall sicken his baby heart till it die a living death, no taunt shall madden his happy boyhood. Fool that I was to think or wish that this little soul should grow choked and deformed within the Veil! I might have known that yonder deep unworldly look that ever and anon floated past his eyes was peering far beyond this narrow Now. In the poise of his little curl-crowned head did there not sit all that wild pride of being which his father had hardly crushed in his own heart? For what, forsooth, shall a Negro want with pride amid the studied humiliations of fifty million fellows? Well sped, my boy, before the world had dubbed your ambition inso-lence, had held your ideals unattainable, and taught you to cringe and bow. Better far this nameless void than stops my life than a sea of sorrow for you.

Idle words; he might have borne his burden more bravely than we,—aye, and found it lighter too, some day; for surely, surely this is not the end. Surely there shall yet dawn some mighty morning to lift the Veil and set the prisoned free. Not for me,—I shall die in my bonds,—but for fresh young souls who have not known the night and waken to the morning; a morning when men ask of the workman, not "Is he white?" but "Can he work?" When men ask artists, not "Are they black?" but "Do they know?" Some morning this may be, long, long years to come. But now there wails, on that dark shore within the Veil, the same deep voice, *Thou shalt forego!* And all have I foregone at that command, and with small complaint,—all save that fair young form that lies so coldly wed with death in the nest I had builded.

If one must have gone, why not I? Why may I not rest me from this rest-lessness and sleep from this wide waking? Was not the world's alembic, Time, in his young hands, and is not my time waning? Are there so many workers in the vineyard that the fair promise of this little body could lightly be tossed away? The wretched of my race that line the alleys of the nation sit fatherless and unmothered; but Love sat beside his cradle, and in his ear Wisdom wait-ed to speak. Perhaps now he knows the All-love, and needs not to be wise. Sleep, then, child,—sleep till I sleep and waken to a baby voice and the cease-less patter of little feet—above the Veil.

XII

OF ALEXANDER CRUMMELL

Then from the Dawn it seemed there came, but faint
As from beyond the limit of the world,
Like the last echo born of a great cry,
Sounds, as if some fair city were one voice
Around a king returning from his wars.

<div align="right">Tennyson.</div>

T HIS is the history of a human heart,—the tale of a black boy who many
long years ago began to struggle with life that he might know the world
and know himself. Three temptations he met on those dark dunes that lay
gray and dismal before the wonder-eyes of the child: the temptation of Hate,
that stood out against the red dawn; the temptation of Despair, that dark-
ened noonday; and the temptation of Doubt, that ever steals along with twi-
light. Above all, you must hear of the vales he crossed,—the Valley of
Humiliation and the Valley of the Shadow of Death.

I saw Alexander Crummell first at a Wilberforce commencement season,
amid its bustle and crush. Tall, frail, and black he stood, with simple digni-
ty and an unmistakable air of good breeding. I talked with him apart, where
the storming of the lusty young orators could not harm us. I spoke to him
politely, then curiously, then eagerly, as I began to feel the fineness of his
character,—his calm courtesy, the sweetness of his strength, and his fair
blending of the hope and truth of life. Instinctively I bowed before this man,
as one bows before the prophets of the world. Some seer he seemed, that
came not from the crimson Past or the gray To-come, but from the pulsing
Now,—that mocking world which seemed to me at once so light and dark,
so splendid and sordid. Four-score years had he wandered in this same world

of mine, within the Veil.

He was born with the Missouri Compromise and lay a-dying amid the echoes of Manila and El Caney: stirring times for living, times dark to look back upon, darker to look forward to. The black-faced lad that paused over his mud and marbles seventy years ago saw puzzling vistas as he looked down the world. The slave-ship still groaned across the Atlantic, faint cries burdened the Southern breeze, and the great black father whispered mad tales of cruelty into those young ears. From the low doorway the mother silently watched her boy at play, and at nightfall sought him eagerly lest the shadows bear him away to the land of slaves.

So his young mind worked and winced and shaped curiously a vision of Life; and in the midst of that vision ever stood one dark figure alone,—ever with the hard, thick countenance of that bitter father, and a form that fell in vast and shapeless folds. Thus the temptation of Hate grew and shadowed the growing child,—gliding stealthily into his laughter, fading into his play, and seizing his dreams by day and night with rough, rude turbulence. So the black boy asked of sky and sun and flower the never-answered Why? and loved, as he grew, neither the world nor the world's rough ways.

Strange temptation for a child, you may think; and yet in this wide land to-day a thousand thousand dark children brood before this same temptation, and feel its cold and shuddering arms. For them, perhaps, some one will some day lift the Veil,—will come tenderly and cheerily into those sad little lives and brush the brooding hate away, just as Beriah Green strode in upon the life of Alexander Crummell. And before the bluff, kind-hearted man the shadow seemed less dark. Beriah Green had a school in Oneida County, New York, with a score of mischievous boys. "I'm going to bring a black boy here to educate," said Beriah Green, as only a crank and an abolitionist would have dared to say. "Oho!" laughed the boys. "Ye-es," said his wife; and Alexander came. Once before, the black boy had sought a school, had travelled, cold and hungry, four hundred miles up into free New Hampshire, to Canaan. But the godly farmers hitched ninety yoke of oxen to the abolition schoolhouse and dragged it into the middle of the swamp. The black boy trudged away.

The nineteenth was the first century of human sympathy,—the age when half wonderingly we began to descry in others that transfigured spark of divinity which we call Myself; when clodhoppers and peasants, and tramps and thieves, and millionaires and—sometimes—Negroes, became throbbing souls whose warm pulsing life touched us so nearly that we half gasped with

surprise, crying, "Thou too! Hast Thou seen Sorrow and the dull waters of Hopelessness? Hast Thou known Life?" And then all helplessly we peered into those Other-worlds, and wailed, "O World of Worlds, how shall man make you one?"

So in that little Oneida school there came to those schoolboys a revelation of thought and longing beneath one black skin, of which they had not dreamed before. And to the lonely boy came a new dawn of sympathy and inspiration. The shadowy, formless thing—the temptation of Hate, that hovered between him and the world—grew fainter and less sinister. It did not wholly fade away, but diffused itself and lingered thick at the edges. Through it the child now first saw the blue and gold of life,—the sun-swept road that ran 'twixt heaven and earth until in one far-off wan wavering line they met and kissed. A vision of life came to the growing boy,—mystic, wonderful. He raised his head, stretched himself, breathed deep of the fresh new air. Yonder, behind the forests, he heard strange sounds; then glinting through the trees he saw, far, far away, the bronzed hosts of a nation calling,—calling faintly, calling loudly. He heard the hateful clank of their chains, he felt them cringe and grovel, and there rose within him a protest and a prophecy. And he girded himself to walk down the world.

A voice and vision called him to be a priest,—a seer to lead the uncalled out of the house of bondage. He saw the headless host turn toward him like the whirling of mad waters,—he stretched forth his hands eagerly, and then, even as he stretched them, suddenly there swept across the vision the temptation of Despair.

They were not wicked men,—the problem of life is not the problem of the wicked, they were calm, good men, Bishops of the Apostolic Church of God, and strove toward righteousness. They said slowly, "It is all very natural—it is even commendable; but the General Theological Seminary of the Episcopal Church cannot admit a Negro." And when that thin, half-grotesque figure still haunted their doors, they put their hands kindly, half sorrowfully, on his shoulders, and said, "Now,—of course, we—we know how *you* feel about it; but you see it is impossible,—that is—well—it is premature. Sometime, we trust—sincerely trust—all such distinctions will fade away; but now the world is as it is."

This was the temptation of Despair; and the young man fought it doggedly. Like some grave shadow he flitted by those halls, pleading, arguing, half angrily demanding admittance, until there came the final No; until men hustled the disturber away, marked him as foolish, unreasonable, and

injudicious, a vain rebel against God's law. And then from that Vision Splendid all the glory faded slowly away, and left an earth gray and stern rolling on beneath a dark despair. Even the kind hands that stretched themselves toward him from out the depths of that dull morning seemed but parts of the purple shadows. He saw them coldly, and asked, "Why should I strive by special grace when the way of the world is closed to me?" All gently yet, the hands urged him on,—the hands of young John Jay, that daring father's daring son; the hands of the good folk of Boston, that free city. And yet, with a way to the priesthood of the Church open at last before him, the cloud lingered there; and even when in old St. Paul's the venerable Bishop raised his white arms above the Negro deacon—even then the burden had not lifted from that heart, for there had passed a glory from the earth.

And yet the fire through which Alexander Crummell went did not burn in vain. Slowly and more soberly he took up again his plan of life. More critically he studied the situation. Deep down below the slavery and servitude of the Negro people he saw their fatal weaknesses, which long years of mistreatment had emphasized. The dearth of strong moral character, of unbending righteousness, he felt, was their great shortcoming, and here he would begin. He would gather the best of his people into some little Episcopal chapel and there lead, teach, and inspire them, till the leaven spread, till the children grew, till the world hearkened, till—till—and then across his dream gleamed some faint after-glow of that first fair vision of youth—only an after-glow, for there had passed a glory from the earth.

One day—it was in 1842, and the springtide was struggling merrily with the May winds of New England—he stood at last in his own chapel in Providence, a priest of the Church. The days sped by, and the dark young clergyman labored; he wrote his sermons carefully; he intoned his prayers with a soft, earnest voice; he haunted the streets and accosted the wayfarers; he visited the sick, and knelt beside the dying. He worked and toiled, week by week, day by day, month by month. And yet month by month the congregation dwindled, week by week the hollow walls echoed more sharply, day by day the calls came fewer and fewer, and day by day the third temptation sat clearer and still more clearly within the Veil; a temptation, as it were, bland and smiling, with just a shade of mockery in its smooth tones. First it came casually, in the cadence of a voice: "Oh, colored folks? Yes." Or perhaps more definitely: "What do you expect?" In voice and gesture lay the doubt— the temptation of Doubt. How he hated it, and stormed at it furiously! "Of course they are capable," he cried; "of course they can learn and strive and

achieve—" and "Of course," added the temptation softly, "they do nothing of the sort." Of all the three temptations, this one struck the deepest. Hate? He had outgrown so childish a thing. Despair? He had steeled his right arm against it, and fought it with the vigor of determination. But to doubt the worth of his life-work,—to doubt the destiny and capability of the race his soul loved because it was his; to find listless squalor instead of eager endeavor; to hear his own lips whispering, "They do not care; they cannot know; they are dumb driven cattle,—why cast your pearls before swine?"—this, this seemed more than man could bear; and he closed the door, and sank upon the steps of the chancel, and cast his robe upon the floor and writhed.

The evening sunbeams had set the dust to dancing in the gloomy chapel when he arose. He folded his vestments, put away the hymn-books, and closed the great Bible. He stepped out into the twilight, looked back upon the narrow little pulpit with a weary smile, and locked the door. Then he walked briskly to the Bishop, and told the Bishop what the Bishop already knew. "I have failed," he said simply. And gaining courage by the confession, he added: "What I need is a larger constituency. There are comparatively few Negroes here, and perhaps they are not of the best. I must go where the field is wider, and try again." So the Bishop sent him to Philadelphia, with a letter to Bishop Onderdonk.

Bishop Onderdonk lived at the head of six white steps,—corpulent, red-faced, and the author of several thrilling tracts on Apostolic Succession. It was after dinner, and the Bishop had settled himself for a pleasant season of contemplation, when the bell must needs ring, and there must burst in upon the Bishop a letter and a thin, ungainly Negro. Bishop Onderdonk read the letter hastily and frowned. Fortunately, his mind was already clear on this point; and he cleared his brow and looked at Crummell. Then he said, slowly and impressively: "I will receive you into this diocese on one condition: no Negro priest can sit in my church convention, and no Negro church must ask for representation there."

I sometimes fancy I can see that tableau: the frail black figure, nervously twitching his hat before the massive abdomen of Bishop Onderdonk; his threadbare coat thrown against the dark woodwork of the book-cases, where Fox's "Lives of the Martyrs" nestled happily beside "The Whole Duty of Man." I seem to see the wide eyes of the Negro wander past the Bishop's broadcloth to where the swinging glass doors of the cabinet glow in the sunlight. A little blue fly is trying to cross the yawning keyhole. He marches briskly up to it, peers into the chasm in a surprised sort of way, and rubs his

feelers reflectively; then he essays its depths, and, finding it bottomless, draws back again. The dark-faced priest finds himself wondering if the fly too has faced its Valley of Humiliation, and if it will plunge into it,—when lo! it spreads its tiny wings and buzzes merrily across, leaving the watcher wingless and alone.

Then the full weight of his burden fell upon him. The rich walls wheeled away, and before him lay the cold rough moor winding on through life, cut in twain by one thick granite ridge,—here, the Valley of Humiliation; yonder, the Valley of the Shadow of Death. And I know not which be darker,—no, not I. But this I know: in yonder Vale of the Humble stand to-day a million swarthy men, who willingly would

> ". . . bear the whips and scorns of time,
> The oppressor's wrong, the proud man's contumely,
> The pangs of despised love, the law's delay,
> The insolence of office, and the spurns
> That patient merit of the unworthy takes,"—

all this and more would they bear did they but know that this were sacrifice and not a meaner thing. So surged the thought within that lone black breast. The Bishop cleared his throat suggestively; then, recollecting that there was really nothing to say, considerately said nothing, only sat tapping his foot impatiently. But Alexander Crummell said, slowly and heavily: "I will never enter your diocese on such terms." And saying this, he turned and passed into the Valley of the Shadow of Death. You might have noted only the physical dying, the shattered frame and hacking cough; but in that soul lay deeper death than that. He found a chapel in New York,—the church of his father; he labored for it in poverty and starvation, scorned by his fellow priests. Half in despair, he wandered across the sea, a beggar with outstretched hands. Englishmen clasped them,—Wilberforce and Stanley, Thirwell and Ingles, and even Froude and Macaulay; Sir Benjamin Brodie bade him rest awhile at Queen's College in Cambridge, and there he lingered, struggling for health of body and mind, until he took his degree in '53. Restless still and unsatisfied he turned toward Africa, and for long years, amid the spawn of the slave-smugglers, sought a new heaven and a new earth.

So the man groped for light; all this was not Life,—it was the world-wandering of a soul in search of itself, the striving of one who vainly sought his

place in the world, ever haunted by the shadow of a death that is more than death,—the passing of a soul that has missed its duty. Twenty years he wandered,—twenty years and more; and yet the hard rasping question kept gnawing within him, "What, in God's name, am I on earth for?" In the narrow New York parish his soul seemed cramped and smothered. In the fine old air of the English University he heard the millions wailing over the sea. In the wild fever-cursed swamps of West Africa he stood helpless and alone.

You will not wonder at his weird pilgrimage,—you who in the swift whirl of living, amid its cold paradox and marvellous vision, have fronted life and asked its riddle face to face. And if you find that riddle hard to read, remember that yonder black boy finds it just a little harder; if it is difficult for you to find and face your duty, it is a shade more difficult for him; if your heart sickens in the blood and dust of battle, remember that to him the dust is thicker and the battle fiercer. No wonder the wanderers fall! No wonder we point to thief and murderer, and haunting prostitute, and the never-ending throng of unhearsed dead! The Valley of the Shadow of Death gives few of its pilgrims back to the world.

But Alexander Crummell it gave back. Out of the temptation of Hate, and burned by the fire of Despair, triumphant over Doubt, and steeled by Sacrifice against Humiliation, he turned at last home across the waters, humble and strong, gentle and determined. He bent to all the gibes and prejudices, to all hatred and discrimination, with that rare courtesy which is the armor of pure souls. He fought among his own, the low, the grasping, and the wicked, with that unbending righteousness which is the sword of the just. He never faltered, he seldom complained; he simply worked, inspiring the young, rebuking the old, helping the weak, guiding the strong.

So he grew, and brought within his wide influence all that was best of those who walk within the Veil. They who live without knew not nor dreamed of that full power within, that mighty inspiration which the dull gauze of caste decreed that most men should not know. And now that he is gone, I sweep the Veil away and cry, Lo! the soul to whose dear memory I bring this little tribute. I can see his face still, dark and heavy-lined beneath his snowy hair; lighting and shading, now with inspiration for the future, now in innocent pain at some human wickedness, now with sorrow at some hard memory from the past. The more I met Alexander Crummell, the more I felt how much that world was losing which knew so little of him. In another age he might have sat among the elders of the land in

purple-bordered toga; in another country mothers might have sung him to the cradles.

He did his work,—he did it nobly and well; and yet I sorrow that here he worked alone, with so little human sympathy. His name to-day, in this broad land, means little, and comes to fifty million ears laden with no incense of memory or emulation. And herein lies the tragedy of the age: not that men are poor,—all men know something of poverty; not that men are wicked,— who is good? not that men are ignorant,—what is Truth? Nay, but that men know so little of men.

He sat one morning gazing toward the sea. He smiled and said, "The gate is rusty on the hinges." That night at star-rise a wind came moaning out of the west to blow the gate ajar, and then the soul I loved fled like a flame across the Seas, and in its seat sat Death.

I wonder where he is to-day? I wonder if in that dim world beyond, as he came gliding in, there rose on some wan throne a King,—a dark and pierced Jew, who knows the writhings of the earthly damned, saying, as he laid those heart-wrung talents down, "Well done!" while round about the morning stare, sat singing.

XIII

OF THE COMING OF JOHN

What bring they 'neath the midnight,
Beside the River-sea?
They bring the human heart wherein
No nightly calm can be;
That droppeth never with the wind,
Nor drieth with the dew;
O calm it; God; thy calm is broad
To cover spirits too.
The river floweth on.

 Mrs. Browning.

CARLISLE Street runs westward from the centre of Johnstown, across a great black bridge, down a hill and up again, by little shops and meat-markets, past single-storied homes, until suddenly it stops against a wide green lawn. It is a broad, restful place, with two large buildings outlined against the west. When at evening the winds come swelling from the east, and the great pall of the city's smoke hangs wearily above the valley, then the red west glows like a dreamland down Carlisle Street, and, at the tolling of the supper-bell, throws the passing forms of students in dark silhouette against the sky. Tall and black, they move slowly by, and seem in the sinister light to flit before the city like dim warning ghosts. Perhaps they are; for this is Wells Institute, and these black students have few dealings with the white city below.

And if you will notice, night after night, there is one dark form that ever hurries last and late toward the twinkling lights of Swain Hall,—for Jones is never on time. A long, straggling fellow he is, brown and hard-haired, who seems to be growing straight out of his clothes, and walks with a half-apologetic roll. He used perpetually to set the quiet dining room into waves of merriment, as he stole to his place after the bell had tapped for prayers; he seemed so perfectly awkward. And yet one glance at his face made one forgive him much,—that broad, good-natured smile in which lay no bit of art or artifice, but seemed just bubbling good-nature and genuine satisfaction with the world.

He came to us from Altamaha, away down there beneath the gnarled oaks of Southeastern Georgia, where the sea croons to the sands and the sands listen till they sink half drowned beneath the waters, rising only here and there in long, low islands. The white folk of Altamaha voted John a good boy,— fine plough-hand, good in the rice-fields, handy everywhere, and always good-natured and respectful. But they shook their heads when his mother wanted to send him off to school. "It'll spoil him,—ruin him," they said; and

they talked as though they knew. But full half the black folk followed him proudly to the station, and carried his queer little trunk and many bundles. And there they shook and shook hands, and the girls kissed him shyly and the boys clapped him on the back. So the train came and he pinched his little sister lovingly, and put his great arms about his mother's neck, and then was away with a puff and a roar into the great yellow world that flamed and flared about the doubtful pilgrim. Up the coast they hurried, past the squares and palmettos of Savannah, through the cotton-fields and through the weary night, to Millville, and came with the morning to the noise and bustle of Johnstown.

And they that stood behind, that morning in Altamaha, and watched the train as it noisily bore playmate and brother and son away to the world, had thereafter one ever-recurring word,—"When John comes." Then what parties were to be, and what speakings in the churches; what new furniture in the front room,—perhaps even a new front room; and there would be a new schoolhouse, with John as teacher; and then perhaps a big wedding; all this and more—when John comes. But the white people shook their heads.

At first he was coming at Christmas-time,—but the vacation proved too short; and then, the next summer,—but times were hard and schooling costly, and so, instead, he worked in Johnstown. And so it drifted to the next summer, and the next,—till playmates scattered, and mother grew gray, and sister went up to the Judge's kitchen to work. And still the legend lingered,— "When John comes."

Up at the Judge's they rather liked this refrain; for they too had a John— a fair-haired, smooth-faced boy, who had played many a long summer's day to its close with his darker namesake. "Yes, sir! John is at Princeton, sir," said the broad-shouldered gray-haired Judge every morning as he marched down to the post-office. "Showing the Yankees what a Southern gentleman can do," he added; and strode home again with his letters and papers. Up at the great pillared house they lingered long over the Princeton letter,—the Judge and his frail wife, his sister and growing daughters. "It'll make a man of him," said the Judge, "college is the place." And then he asked the shy little waitress, "Well, Jennie, how's your John?" and added reflectively, "Too bad, too bad your mother sent him off,—it will spoil him." And the waitress wondered.

Thus in the far-away Southern village the world lay waiting, half consciously, the coming of two young men, and dreamed in an inarticulate way of new things that would be done and new thoughts that all would think.

And yet it was singular that few thought of two Johns,—for the black folk thought of one John, and he was black; and the white folk thought of another John, and he was white. And neither world thought the other world's thought, save with a vague unrest.

Up in Johnstown, at the Institute, we were long puzzled at the case of John Jones. For a long time the clay seemed unfit for any sort of moulding. He was loud and boisterous, always laughing and singing, and never able to work consecutively at anything. He did not know how to study; he had no idea of thoroughness; and with his tardiness, carelessness, and appalling good-humor, we were sore perplexed. One night we sat in faculty-meeting, worried and serious; for Jones was in trouble again. This last escapade was too much, and so we solemnly voted "that Jones, on account of repeated disorder and inattention to work, be suspended for the rest of the term."

It seemed to us that the first time life ever struck Jones as a really serious thing was when the Dean told him he must leave school. He stared at the gray-haired man blankly, with great eyes. "Why,—why," he faltered, "but— I have n't graduated!" Then the Dean slowly and clearly explained, reminding him of the tardiness and the carelessness, of the poor lessons and neglected work, of the noise and disorder, until the fellow hung his head in confusion. Then he said quickly, "But you won't tell mammy and sister,—you won't write mammy, now will you? For if you won't I'll go out into the city and work, and come back next term and show you something." So the Dean promised faithfully, and John shouldered his little trunk, giving neither word nor look to the giggling boys, and walked down Carlisle Street to the great city, with sober eyes and a set and serious face.

Perhaps we imagined it, but someway it seemed to us that the serious look that crept over his boyish face that afternoon never left it again. When he came back to us he went to work with all his rugged strength. It was a hard struggle, for things did not come easily to him,—few crowding memories of early life and teaching came to help him on his new way; but all the world toward which he strove was of his own building, and he builded slow and hard. As the light dawned lingeringly on his new creations, he sat rapt and silent before the vision, or wandered alone over the green campus peering through and beyond the world of men into a world of thought. And the thoughts at times puzzled him sorely; he could not see just why the circle was not square, and carried it out fifty-six decimal places one midnight,—would have gone further, indeed, had not the matron rapped for lights out. He caught terrible colds lying on his back in the meadows of nights, trying to

think out the solar system; he had grave doubts as to the ethics of the Fall of Rome, and strongly suspected the Germans of being thieves and rascals, despite his text-books; he pondered long over every new Greek word, and wondered why this meant that and why it couldn't mean something else, and how it must have felt to think all things in Greek. So he thought and puzzled along for himself,—pausing perplexed where others skipped merrily, and walking steadily through the difficulties where the rest stopped and surrendered.

Thus he grew in body and soul, and with him his clothes seemed to grow and arrange themselves; coat sleeves got longer, cuffs appeared, and collars got less soiled. Now and then his boots shone, and a new dignity crept into his walk. And we who saw daily a new thoughtfulness growing in his eyes began to expect something of this plodding boy. Thus he passed out of the preparatory school into college, and we who watched him felt four more years of change, which almost transformed the tall, grave man who bowed to us commencement morning. He had left his queer thought-world and come back to a world of motion and of men. He looked now for the first time sharply about him, and wondered he had seen so little before. He grew slowly to feel almost for the first time the Veil that lay between him and the white world; he first noticed now the oppression that had not seemed oppression before, differences that erstwhile seemed natural, restraints and slights that in his boyhood days had gone unnoticed or been greeted with a laugh. He felt angry now when men did not call him "Mister," he clenched his hands at the "Jim Crow" cars, and chafed at the color-line that hemmed in him and his. A tinge of sarcasm crept into his speech, and a vague bitterness into his life; and he sat long hours wondering and planning a way around these crooked things. Daily he found himself shrinking from the choked and narrow life of his native town. And yet he always planned to go back to Altamaha,—always planned to work there. Still, more and more as the day approached he hesitated with a nameless dread; and even the day after graduation he seized with eagerness the offer of the Dean to send him North with the quartette during the summer vacation, to sing for the Institute. A breath of air before the plunge, he said to himself in half apology.

It was a bright September afternoon, and the streets of New York were brilliant with moving men. They reminded John of the sea, as he sat in the square and watched them, so changelessly changing, so bright and dark, so grave and gay. He scanned their rich and faultless clothes, the way they carried their hands, the shape of their hats; he peered into the hurrying car-

riages. Then, leaning back with a sigh, he said, "This is the World." The notion suddenly seized him to see where the world was going; since many of the richer and brighter seemed hurrying all one way. So when a tall, light-haired young man and a little talkative lady came by, he rose half hesitating-ly and followed them. Up the street they went, past stores and gay shops, across a broad square, until with a hundred others they entered the high por-tal of a great building.

He was pushed toward the ticket-office with the others, and felt in his pocket for the new five-dollar bill he had hoarded. There seemed really no time for hesitation, so he drew it bravely out, passed it to the busy clerk, and received simply a ticket but no change. When at last he realized that he had paid five dollars to enter he knew not what, he stood stock-still amazed. "Be careful," said a low voice behind him; "you must not lynch the colored gen-tleman simply because he's in your way," and a girl looked up roguishly into the eyes of her fair-haired escort. A shade of annoyance passed over the escort's face. "You will not understand us at the South," he said half impa-tiently, as if continuing an argument. "With all your professions, one never sees in the North so cordial and intimate relations between white and black as are everyday occurrences with us. Why, I remember my closest playfellow in boyhood was a little Negro named after me, and surely no two,—well!" The man stopped short and flushed to the roots of his hair, for there direct-ly beside his reserved orchestra chairs sat the Negro he had stumbled over in the hallway. He hesitated and grew pale with anger, called the usher and gave him his card, with a few peremptory words, and slowly sat down. The lady deftly changed the subject.

All this John did not see, for he sat in a half maze minding the scene about him; the delicate beauty of the hall, the faint perfume, the moving myriad of men, the rich clothing and low hum of talking seemed all a part of a world so different from his, so strangely more beautiful than anything he had known, that he sat in dreamland, and started when, after a hush, rose high and clear the music of Lohengrin's swan. The infinite beauty of the wail lingered and swept through every muscle of his frame, and put it all a-tune. He closed his eyes and grasped the elbows of the chair, touching unwitting-ly the lady's arm. And the lady drew away. A deep longing swelled in all his heart to rise with that clear music out of the dirt and dust of that low life that held him prisoned and befouled. If he could only live up in the free air where birds sang and setting suns had no touch of blood! Who had called him to be the slave and butt of all? And if he had called, what right had he to call

when a world like this lay open before men?

Then the movement changed, and fuller, mightier harmony swelled away. He looked thoughtfully across the hall, and wondered why the beautiful gray-haired woman looked so listless, and what the little man could be whispering about. He would not like to be listless and idle, he thought, for he felt with the music the movement of power within him. If he but had some master-work, some life-service, hard,—aye, bitter hard, but without the cringing and sickening servility, without the cruel hurt that hardened his heart and soul. When at last a soft sorrow crept across the violins, there came to him the vision of a far-off home,—the great eyes of his sister, and the dark drawn face of his mother. And his heart sank below the waters, even as the sea-sand sinks by the shores of Altamaha, only to be lifted aloft again with that last ethereal wail of the swan that quivered and faded away into the sky.

It left John sitting so silent and rapt that he did not for some time notice the usher tapping him lightly on the shoulder and saying politely, "Will you step this way, please, sir?" A little surprised, he arose quickly at the last tap, and, turning to leave his seat, looked full into the face of the fair-haired young man. For the first time the young man recognized his dark boyhood playmate, and John knew that it was the Judge's son. The white John started, lifted his hand, and then froze into his chair; the black John smiled lightly, then grimly, and followed the usher down the aisle. The manager was sorry, very, very sorry,—but he explained that some mistake had been made in selling the gentleman a seat already disposed of; he would refund the money, of course,—and indeed felt the matter keenly, and so forth, and— before he had finished John was gone, walking hurriedly across the square and down the broad streets, and as he passed the park he buttoned his coat and said, "John Jones, you're a natural-born fool." Then he went to his lodgings and wrote a letter, and tore it up; he wrote another, and threw it in the fire. Then he seized a scrap of paper and wrote: "Dear Mother and Sister—I am coming—John."

"Perhaps," said John, as he settled himself on the train, "perhaps I am to blame myself in struggling against my manifest destiny simply because it looks hard and unpleasant. Here is my duty to Altamaha plain before me; perhaps they'll let me help settle the Negro problems there,—perhaps they won't. 'I will go in to the King, which is not according to the law; and if I perish, I perish.'" And then he mused and dreamed, and planned a life-work; and the train flew south.

Down in Altamaha, after seven long years, all the world knew John was

coming. The homes were scrubbed and scoured,—above all, one; the gardens and yards had an unwonted trimness, and Jennie bought a new gingham. With some finesse and negotiation, all the dark Methodists and Presbyterians were induced to join in a monster welcome at the Baptist Church; and as the day drew near, warm discussions arose on every corner as to the exact extent and nature of John's accomplishments. It was noontide on a gray and cloudy day when he came. The black town flocked to the depot, with a little of the white at the edges,—a happy throng, with "Good-mawnings" and "Howdys" and laughing and joking and jostling. Mother sat yonder in the window watching; but sister Jennie stood on the platform, nervously fingering her dress,—tall and lithe, with soft brown skin and loving eyes peering from out a tangled wilderness of hair. John rose gloomily as the train stopped, for he was thinking of the "Jim Crow" car; he stepped to the platform, and paused: a little dingy station, a black crowd gaudy and dirty, a half-mile of dilapidated shanties along a straggling ditch of mud. An overwhelming sense of the sordidness and narrowness of it all seized him; he looked in vain for his mother, kissed coldly the tall, strange girl who called him brother, spoke a short, dry word here and there; then, lingering neither for hand-shaking nor gossip, started silently up the street, raising his hat merely to the last eager old aunty, to her open-mouthed astonishment. The people were distinctly bewildered. This silent, cold man,—was this John? Where was his smile and hearty hand-grasp? "'Peared kind o' down in the mouf," said the Methodist preacher thoughtfully. "Seemed monstus stuck up," complained a Baptist sister. But the white postmaster from the edge of the crowd expressed the opinion of his folks plainly. "That damn Nigger," said he, as he shouldered the mail and arranged his tobacco, "has gone North and got plum full o' fool notions; but they won't work in Altamaha." And the crowd melted away.

The meeting of welcome at the Baptist Church was a failure. Rain spoiled the barbecue, and thunder turned the milk in the ice-cream. When the speaking came at night, the house was crowded to overflowing. The three preachers had especially prepared themselves, but somehow John's manner seemed to throw a blanket over everything,—he seemed so cold and preoccupied, and had so strange an air of restraint that the Methodist brother could not warm up to his theme and elicited not a single "Amen"; the Presbyterian prayer was but feebly responded to, and even the Baptist preacher, though he wakened faint enthusiasm, got so mixed up in his favorite sentence that he had to close it by stopping fully fifteen minutes sooner than he meant. The people moved uneasily in their seats as John rose to reply. He

spoke slowly and methodically. The age, he said, demanded new ideas; we were far different from those men of the seventeenth and eighteenth centuries,—with broader ideas of human brotherhood and destiny. Then he spoke of the rise of charity and popular education, and particularly of the spread of wealth and work. The question was, then, he added reflectively, looking at the low discolored ceiling, what part the Negroes of this land would take in the striving of the new century. He sketched in vague outline the new Industrial School that might rise among these pines, he spoke in detail of the charitable and philanthropic work that might be organized, of money that might be saved for banks and business. Finally he urged unity, and deprecated especially religious and denominational bickering. "To-day," he said, with a smile, "the world cares little whether a man be Baptist or Methodist, or indeed a churchman at all, so long as he is good and true. What difference does it make whether a man be baptized in river or wash-bowl, or not at all? Let's leave all that littleness, and look higher." Then, thinking of nothing else, he slowly sat down. A painful hush seized that crowded mass. Little had they understood of what he said, for he spoke an unknown tongue, save the last word about baptism; that they knew, and they sat very still while the clock ticked. Then at last a low suppressed snarl came from the Amen corner, and an old bent man arose, walked over the seats and climbed straight up into the pulpit. He was wrinkled and black, with scant gray and tufted hair; his voice and hands shook as with palsy; but on his face lay the intense rapt look of the religious fanatic. He seized the Bible with his rough, huge hands; twice he raised it inarticulate, and then fairly burst into words, with rude and awful eloquence. He quivered, swayed, and bent; then rose aloft in perfect majesty, till the people moaned and wept, wailed and shouted, and a wild shrieking arose from the corners where all the pent-up feeling of the hour gathered itself and rushed into the air. John never knew clearly what the old man said; he only felt himself held up to scorn and scathing denunciation for trampling on the true Religion, and he realized with amazement that all unknowingly he had put rough, rude hands on something this little world held sacred. He arose silently, and passed out into the night. Down toward the sea he went, in the fitful starlight, half conscious of the girl who followed timidly after him. When at last he stood upon the bluff, he turned to his little sister and looked upon her sorrowfully, remembering with sudden pain how little thought he had given her. He put his arm about her and let her passion of tears spend itself on his shoulder.

Long they stood together, peering over the gray unresting water.

"John," she said, "does it make every one—unhappy when they study and learn lots of things?"

He paused and smiled. "I am afraid it does," he said.

"And, John, are you glad you studied?"

"Yes," came the answer, slowly but positively.

She watched the flickering lights upon the sea, and said thoughtfully, "I wish I was unhappy,—and—and," putting both arms about his neck, "I think I am, a little, John."

It was several days later that John walked up to the Judge's house to ask for the privilege of teaching the Negro school. The Judge himself met him at the front door, stared a little hard at him, and said brusquely, "Go 'round to the kitchen door, John, and wait." Sitting on the kitchen steps, John stared at the corn, thoroughly perplexed. What on earth had come over him? Every step he made offended some one. He had come to save his people, and before he left the depot he had hurt them. He sought to teach them at the church, and had outraged their deepest feelings. He had schooled himself to be respectful to the Judge, and then blundered into his front door. And all the time he had meant right,—and yet, and yet, somehow he found it so hard and strange to fit his old surroundings again, to find his place in the world about him. He could not remember that he used to have any difficulty in the past, when life was glad and gay. The world seemed smooth and easy then. Perhaps,—but his sister came to the kitchen door just then and said the Judge awaited him.

The Judge sat in the dining-room amid his morning's mail, and he did not ask John to sit down. He plunged squarely into the business. "You've come for the school, I suppose. Well, John, I want to speak to you plainly. You know I'm a friend to your people. I've helped you and your family, and would have done more if you hadn't got the notion of going off. Now I like the colored people, and sympathize with all their reasonable aspirations; but you and I both know, John, that in this country the Negro must remain subordinate, and can never expect to be the equal of white men. In their place, your people can be honest and respectful; and God knows, I'll do what I can to help them. But when they want to reverse nature, and rule white men, and marry white women, and sit in my parlor, then, by God! we'll hold them under if we have to lynch every Nigger in the land. Now, John, the question is, are you, with your education and Northern notions, going to accept the situation and teach the darkies to be faithful servants and laborers as your fathers were,—I knew your father, John, he belonged to my brother, and he

was a good Nigger. Well—well, are you going to be like him, or are you going to try to put fool ideas of rising and equality into these folks' heads, and make them discontented and unhappy?"

"I am going to accept the situation, Judge Henderson," answered John, with a brevity that did not escape the keen old man. He hesitated a moment, and then said shortly, "very well,—we'll try you awhile. Good-morning."

It was a full month after the opening of the Negro school that the other John came home, tall, gay, and headstrong. The mother wept, the sisters sang. The whole white town was glad. A proud man was the Judge, and it was a goodly sight to see the two swinging down Main Street together. And yet all did not go smoothly between them, for the younger man could not and did not veil his contempt for the little town, and plainly had his heart set on New York. Now the one cherished ambition of the Judge was to see his son mayor of Altamaha, representative to the legislature, and—who could say?—governor of Georgia. So the argument often waxed hot between them. "Good heavens, father," the younger man would say after dinner, as he light-ed a cigar and stood by the fireplace, "you surely don't expect a young fellow like me to settle down permanently in this—this God-forgotten town with nothing but mud and Negroes?" "I did," the Judge would answer laconical-ly; and on this particular day it seemed from the gathering scowl that he was about to add something more emphatic, but neighbors had already begun to drop in to admire his son, and the conversation drifted.

"Heah that John is livenin' things up at the darky school," volunteered the postmaster, after a pause.

"What now?" asked the Judge, sharply.

"Oh, nothin' in particulah,—just his almighty air and uppish ways. B'lieve I did heah somethin' about his givin' talks on the French Revolution, equality, and such like. He's what I call a dangerous Nigger."

"Have you heard him say anything out of the way?"

"Why, no,—but Sally, our girl, told my wife a lot of rot. Then, too, I don's need to heah: a Nigger what won't say 'sir' to a white man, or—"

"Who is this John?" interrupted the son.

"Why, it's little black John, Peggy's son,—your old playfellow."

The young man's face flushed angrily, and then he laughed.

"Oh," said he, "it's the darky that tried to force himself into a seat beside the lady I was escorting—"

But Judge Henderson waited to hear no more. He had been nettled all day, and now at this he rose with a half-smothered oath, took his hat and

cane, and walked straight to the schoolhouse.

For John, it had been a long, hard pull to get things started in the rickety old shanty that sheltered his school. The Negroes were rent into factions for and against him, the parents were careless, the children irregular and dirty, and books, pencils, and slates largely missing. Nevertheless, he struggled hopefully on, and seemed to see at last some glimmering of dawn. The attendance was larger and the children were a shade cleaner this week. Even the booby class in reading showed a little comforting progress. So John settled himself with renewed patience this afternoon.

"Now, Mandy," he said cheerfully, "that's better; but you mustn't chop your words up so: 'If the—man—goes.' Why, your little brother even wouldn't tell a story that way, now would he?"

"Naw, suh, he cain't talk."

"All right; now let's try again: 'If the man—'"

"John!"

The whole school started in surprise, and the teacher half arose, as the red, angry face of the Judge appeared in the open doorway.

"John, this school is closed. You children can go home and get to work. The white people of Altamaha are not spending their money on black folks to have their heads crammed with impudence and lies. Clear out! I'll lock the door myself."

Up at the great pillared house the tall young son wandered aimlessly about after his father's abrupt departure. In the house there was little to interest him; the books were old and stale, the local newspaper flat, and the women had retired with headaches and sewing. He tried a nap, but it was too warm. So he sauntered out into the fields, complaining disconsolately, "Good Lord! how long will this imprisonment last!" He was not a bad fellow,—just a little spoiled and self-indulgent, and as headstrong as his proud father. He seemed a young man pleasant to look upon, as he sat on the great black stump at the edge of the pines idly swinging his legs and smoking. "Why, there isn't even a girl worth getting up a respectable flirtation with," he growled. Just then his eye caught a tall, willowy figure hurrying toward him on the narrow path. He looked with interest at first, and then burst into a laugh as he said, "Well, I declare, if it isn't Jennie, the little brown kitchen-maid! Why, I never noticed before what a trim little body she is. Hello, Jennie! Why, you haven't kissed me since I came home," he said gaily. The young girl stared at him in surprise and confusion,—faltered something inarticulate, and attempted to pass. But a wilful mood had seized the young idler,

and he caught at her arm. Frightened, she slipped by; and half mischievously he turned and ran after her through the tall pines.

Yonder, toward the sea, at the end of the path, came John slowly, with his head down. He had turned wearily homeward from the schoolhouse; then, thinking to shield his mother from the blow, started to meet his sister as she came from work and break the news of his dismissal to her. "I'll go away," he said slowly; "I'll go away and find work, and send for them. I cannot live here longer." And then the fierce, buried anger surged up into his throat. He waved his arms and hurried wildly up the path.

The great brown sea lay silent. The air scarce breathed. The dying day bathed the twisted oaks and mighty pines in black and gold. There came from the wind no warning, not a whisper from the cloudless sky. There was only a black man hurrying on with an ache in his heart, seeing neither sun nor sea, but starting as from a dream at the frightened cry that woke the pines, to see his dark sister struggling in the arms of a tall and fair-haired man.

He said not a word, but, seizing a fallen limb, struck him with all the pent-up hatred of his great black arm; and the body lay white and still beneath the pines, all bathed in sunshine and in blood. John looked at it dreamily, then walked back to the house briskly, and said in a soft voice, "Mammy, I'm going away,—I'm going to be free."

She gazed at him dimly and faltered, "No'th, honey, is yo' gwine No'th agin?"

He looked out where the North Star glistened pale above the waters, and said, "Yes, mammy, I'm going—North."

Then, without another word, he went out into the narrow lane, up by the straight pines, to the same winding path, and seated himself on the great black stump, looking at the blood where the body had lain. Yonder in the gray past he had played with that dead boy, romping together under the solemn trees. The night deepened; he thought of the boys at Johnstown. He wondered how Brown had turned out, and Carey? And Jones,—Jones? Why, he was Jones, and he wondered what they would all say when they knew, when they knew, in that great long dining-room with its hundreds of merry eyes. Then as the sheen of the starlight stole over him, he thought of the gilded ceiling of that vast concert hall, and heard stealing toward him the faint sweet music of the swan. Hark! was it music, or the hurry and shouting of men? Yes, surely! Clear and high the faint sweet melody rose and fluttered like a living thing, so that the very earth trembled as with the tramp of horses and murmur of angry men.

He leaned back and smiled toward the sea, whence rose the strange

melody, away from the dark shadows where lay the noise of horses galloping, galloping on. With an effort he roused himself, bent forward, and looked steadily down the pathway, softly humming the "Song of the Bride,"—

"Freudig geführt, ziehet dahin."

Amid the trees in the dim morning twilight he watched their shadows dancing and heard their horses thundering toward him, until at last they came sweeping like a storm, and he saw in front that haggard white-haired man, whose eyes flashed red with fury. Oh, how he pitied him,—pitied him,— and wondered if he had the coiling twisted rope. Then, as the storm burst round him, he rose slowly to his feet and turned his closed eyes toward the Sea.

And the world whistled in his ears.

XIV

OF THE SORROW SONGS

> I walk through the churchyard
> To lay this body down;
> I know moon-rise, I know star-rise;
> I walk in the moonlight, I walk in the starlight;
> I'll lie in the grave and stretch out my arms,
> I'll go to judgment in the evening of the day,
> And my soul and thy soul shall meet that day,
> When I lay this body down.
> Negro Song.

THEY that walked in darkness sang songs in the olden days—Sorrow Songs—for they were weary at heart. And so before each thought that

1014 ᴄ⁄ɔ MY SOUL HAS GROWN DEEP

I have written in this book I have set a phrase, a haunting echo of these weird old songs in which the soul of the black slave spoke to men. Ever since I was a child these songs have stirred me strangely. They came out of the South unknown to me, one by one, and yet at once I knew them as of me and of mine. Then in after years when I came to Nashville I saw the great temple builded of these songs towering over the pale city. To me Jubilee Hall seemed ever made of the songs themselves, and its bricks were red with the blood and dust of toil. Out of them rose for me morning, noon, and night, bursts of wonderful melody, full of the voices of my brothers and sisters, full of the voices of the past.

Little of beauty has America given the world save the rude grandeur God himself stamped on her bosom; the human spirit in this new world has expressed itself in vigor and ingenuity rather than in beauty. And so by fateful chance the Negro folk-song—the rhythmic cry of the slave—stands today not simply as the sole American music, but as the most beautiful expression of human experience born this side the seas. It has been neglected, it has been, and is, half despised, and above all it has been persistently mistaken and misunderstood; but notwithstanding, it still remains as the singular spiritual heritage of the nation and the greatest gift of the Negro people.

Away back in the thirties the melody of these slave songs stirred the nation, but the songs were soon half forgotten. Some, like "Near the lake where drooped the willow," passed into current airs and their source was forgotten; others were caricatured on the "minstrel" stage and their memory died away. Then in war-time came the singular Port Royal experiment after the capture of Hilton Head, and perhaps for the first time the North met the Southern slave face to face and heart to heart with no third witness. The Sea Islands of the Carolinas, where they met, were filled with a black folk of primitive type, touched and moulded less by the world about them than any others outside the Black Belt. Their appearance was uncouth, their language funny, but their hearts were human and their singing stirred men with a mighty power. Thomas Wentworth Higginson hastened to tell of these songs, and Miss McKim and others urged upon the world their rare beauty. But the world listened only half credulously until the Fisk Jubilee Singers sang the slave songs so deeply into the world's heart that it can never wholly forget them again.

There was once a blacksmith's son born at Cadiz, New York, who in the changes of time taught school in Ohio and helped defend Cincinnati from Kirby Smith. Then he fought at Chancellorsville and Gettysburg and finally

served in the Freedman's Bureau at Nashville. Here he formed a Sunday-school class of black children in 1866, and sang with them and taught them to sing. And then they taught him to sing, and when once the glory of the Jubilee songs passed into the soul of George L. White, he knew his life-work was to let those Negroes sing to the world as they had sung to him. So in 1871 the pilgrimage of the Fisk Jubilee Singers began. North to Cincinnati they rode,—four half-clothed black boys and five girl-women,—led by a man with a cause and a purpose. They stopped at Wilberforce, the oldest of Negro schools, where a black bishop blessed them. Then they went, fighting cold and starvation, shut out of hotels, and cheerfully sneered at, ever northward; and ever the magic of their song kept thrilling hearts, until a burst of applause in the Congregational Council at Oberlin revealed them to the world. They came to New York and Henry Ward Beecher dared to welcome them, even though the metropolitan dailies sneered at his "Nigger Minstrels." So their songs conquered till they sang across the land and across the sea, before Queen and Kaiser, in Scotland and Ireland, Holland and Switzerland. Seven years they sang, and brought back a hundred and fifty thousand dollars to found Fisk University.

Since their day they have been imitated—sometimes well, by the singers of Hampton and Atlanta, sometimes ill, by straggling quartettes. Caricature has sought again to spoil the quaint beauty of the music, and has filled the air with many debased melodies which vulgar ears scarce know from the real. But the true Negro folk-song still lives in the hearts of those who have heard them truly sung and in the hearts of the Negro people.

What are these songs, and what do they mean? I know little of music and can say nothing in technical phrase, but I know something of men, and knowing them, I know that these songs are the articulate message of the slave to the world. They tell us in these eager days that life was joyous to the black slave, careless and happy. I can easily believe this of some, of many. But not all the past South, though it rose from the dead, can gainsay the heart-touching witness of these songs. They are the music of an unhappy people, of the children of disappointment; they tell of death and suffering and unvoiced longing toward a truer world, of misty wanderings and hidden ways.

The songs are indeed the siftings of centuries; the music is far more ancient than the words, and in it we can trace here and there signs of development. My grandfather's grandmother was seized by an evil Dutch trader two centuries ago; and coming to the valleys of the Hudson and Housatonic, black, little, and lithe, she shivered and shrank in the harsh north winds,

looked longingly at the hills, and often crooned a heathen melody to the child between her knees, thus:

The child sang it to his children and they to their children's children, and so two hundred years it has travelled down to us and we sing it to our children, knowing as little as our fathers what its words may mean, but knowing well the meaning of its music.

This was primitive African music; it may be seen in larger form in the strange chant which heralds "The Coming of John":

> "You may bury me in the East,
> You may bury me in the West,
> But I'll hear the trumpet sound in that morning,"

—the voice of exile.

Ten master songs, more or less, one may pluck from this forest of melody—songs of undoubted Negro origin and wide popular currency, and songs peculiarly characteristic of the slave. One of these I have just mentioned. Another whose strains begin this book is "Nobody knows the trouble I've seen." When, struck with a sudden poverty, the United States refused to fulfil its promises of land to the freedmen, a brigadier-general went down to the Sea Islands to carry the news. An old woman on the outskirts of the throng began singing this song; all the mass joined with her, swaying. And the soldier wept.

The third song is the cradle-song of death which all men know,—"Swing low, sweet chariot,"—whose bars begin the life story of "Alexander

Crummell." Then there is the song of many waters, "Roll, Jordan, roll," a mighty chorus with minor cadences. There were many songs of the fugitive like that which opens "The Wings of Atalanta," and the more familiar "Been a-listening." The seventh is the song of the End and the Beginning—"My Lord, what a mourning! when the stars begin to fall"; a strain of this is placed before "The Dawn of Freedom." The song of groping—"My way's cloudy"— begins "The Meaning of Progress"; the ninth is the song of this chapter— "Wrestlin' Jacob, the day is a-breaking,"—a pæan of hopeful strife. The last master song is the song of songs—"Steal away,"—sprung from "The Faith of the Fathers."

There are many others of the Negro folk-songs as striking and character-istic as these, as, for instance, the three strains in the third, eighth, and ninth chapters; and others I am sure could easily make a selection on more scien-tific principles. There are, too, songs that seem to me a step removed from the more primitive types: there is the maze-like medley, "Bright sparkles," one phrase of which heads "The Black Belt"; the Easter carol, "Dust, dust and ashes"; the dirge, "My mother's took her flight and gone home"; and that burst of melody hovering over "The Passing of the First-Born"—"I hope my mother will be there in that beautiful world on high."

These represent a third step in the development of the slave song, of which "You may bury me in the East" is the first, and songs like "March on" (chapter six) and "Steal away" are the second. The first is African music, the second Afro-American, while the third is a blending of Negro music with the music heard in the foster land. The result is still distinctively Negro and the method of blending original, but the elements are both Negro and Cau-casian. One might go further and find a fourth step in this development, where the songs of white America have been distinctively influenced by the slave songs or have incorporated whole phrases of Negro melody, as "Swanee River" and "Old Black Joe." Side by side, too, with the growth has gone the debasements and imitations—the Negro "minstrel" songs, many of the "gospel" hymns, and some of the contemporary "coon" songs,—a mass of music in which the novice may easily lose himself and never find the real Negro melodies.

In these songs, I have said, the slave spoke to the world. Such a message is naturally veiled and half articulate. Words and music have lost each other and new and cant phrases of a dimly understood theology have displaced the older sentiment. Once in a while we catch a strange word of an unknown tongue, as the "Mighty Myo," which figures as a river of death, more often

slight words or mere doggerel are joined to music of singular sweetness. Purely secular songs are few in number, partly because many of them were turned into hymns by a change of words, partly because the frolics were seldom heard by the stranger, and the music less often caught. Of nearly all the songs, however, the music is distinctly sorrowful. The ten master songs I have mentioned tell in word and music of trouble and exile, of strife and hiding; they grope toward some unseen power and sigh for rest in the End.

The words that are left to us are not without interest, and, cleared of evident dross, they conceal much of real poetry and meaning beneath conventional theology and unmeaning rhapsody. Like all primitive folk, the slave stood near to Nature's heart. Life was a "rough and rolling sea" like the brown Atlantic of the Sea Islands; the "Wilderness" was the home of God, and the "lonesome valley" led to the way of life. "Winter'll soon be over," was the picture of life and death to a tropical imagination. The sudden wild thunder-storms of the South awed and impressed the Negroes,—at times the rumbling seemed to them "mournful," at times imperious:

> "My Lord calls me,
> He calls me by the thunder,
> The trumpet sounds it in my soul."

The monotonous toil and exposure is painted in many words. One sees the ploughmen in the hot, moist furrow, singing:

> "Dere's no rain to wet you,
> Dere's no sun to burn you,
> Oh, push along, believer,
> I want to go home."

The bowed and bent old man cries, with thrice-repeated wail:

> "O Lord, keep me from sinking down,"

and he rebukes the devil of doubt who can whisper:

> "Jesus is dead and God's gone away."

Yet the soul-hunger is there, the restlessness of the savage, the wail of the wanderer, and the plaint is put in one little phrase:

Over the inner thoughts of the slaves and their relations one with another the shadow of fear ever hung, so that we get but glimpses here and there, and also with them, eloquent omissions and silences. Mother and child are sung, but seldom father; fugitive and weary wanderer call for pity and affection, but there is little of wooing and wedding; the rocks and the mountains are well known, but home is unknown. Strange blending of love and helplessness sings through the refrain:

> "Yonder's my ole mudder,
> Been waggin' at de hill so long;
> 'Bout time she cross over,
> Git home bime-by."

Elsewhere comes the cry of the "motherless" and the "Farewell, farewell, my only child."

Love-songs are scarce and fall into two categories—the frivolous and light, and the sad. Of deep successful love there is ominous silence, and in one of the oldest of these songs there is a depth of history and meaning:

A black woman said of the song, "It can't be sung without a full heart and a troubled sperrit." The same voice sings here that sings in the German folk-song:

"Jetz Geh i' an's brunele, trink' aber net."

Of death the Negro showed little fear, but talked of it familiarly and even fondly as simply a crossing of the waters, perhaps—who knows?—back to his ancient forests again. Later days transfigured his fatalism, and amid the dust and dirt the toiler sang:

"Dust, dust and ashes, fly over my grave,
But the Lord shall bear my spirit home."

The things evidently borrowed from the surrounding world undergo characteristic change when they enter the mouth of the slave. Especially is this true of Bible phrases. "Weep, O captive daughter of Zion," is quaintly turned into "Zion, weep-a-low," and the wheels of Ezekiel are turned every way in the mystic dreaming of the slave, till he says:

"There's a little wheel a-turnin' in-a-my heart."

As in olden time, the words of these hymns were improvised by some leading minstrel of the religious band. The circumstances of the gathering, however, the rhythm of the songs, and the limitations of allowable thought, confined the poetry for the most part to single or double lines, and they seldom were expanded to quatrains or longer tales, although there are some few examples of sustained efforts, chiefly paraphrases of the Bible. Three short series of verses have always attracted me,—the one that heads this chapter, of one line of which Thomas Wentworth Higginson has fittingly said, "Never, it seems to me, since man first lived and suffered was his infinite longing for peace uttered more plaintively." The second and third are descriptions of the Last Judgment,—the one a late improvisation, with some traces of outside influence:

"Oh, the stars in the elements are falling,
And the moon drips away into blood,
And the ransomed of the Lord are returning unto God,

Blessed be the name of the Lord."
And the other earlier and homelier picture from the low coast lands:

> "Michael, haul the boat ashore,
> Then you'll hear the horn they blow,
> Then you'll hear the trumpet sound,
> Trumpet sound the world around,
> Trumpet sound for rich and poor,
> Trumpet sound the Jubilee,
> Trumpet sound for you and me."

Through all the sorrow of the Sorrow Songs there breathes a hope—a faith in the ultimate justice of things. The minor cadences of despair change often to triumph and calm confidence. Sometimes it is faith in life, sometimes a faith in death, sometimes assurance of boundless justice in some fair world beyond. But whichever it is, the meaning is always clear: that sometime, somewhere, men will judge men by their souls and not by their skins. Is such a hope justified? Do the Sorrow Songs sing true?

The silently growing assumption of this age is that the probation of races is past, and that the backward races of to-day are of proven inefficiency and not worth the saving. Such an assumption is the arrogance of peoples irreverent toward Time and ignorant of the deeds of men. A thousand years ago such an assumption, easily possible, would have made it difficult for the Teuton to prove his right to life. Two thousand years ago such dogmatism, readily welcome, would have scouted the idea of blond races ever leading civilization. So wofully unorganized is sociological knowledge that the meaning of progress, the meaning of "swift" and "slow" in human doing, and the limits of human perfectability, are veiled, unanswered sphinxes on the shores of science. Why should Æschylus have sung two thousand years before Shakespeare was born? Why has civilization flourished in Europe, and flickered, flamed, and died in Africa? So long as the world stands meekly dumb before such questions, shall this nation proclaim its ignorance and unhallowed prejudices by denying freedom of opportunity to those who brought the Sorrow Songs to the Seats of the Mighty?

Your country? How came it yours? Before the Pilgrims landed we were here. Here we have brought our three gifts and mingled them with yours: a gift of story and song-soft, stirring melody in an ill-harmonized and unmelodious land; the gift of sweat and brawn to beat back the wilderness, conquer

the soil, and lay the foundations of this vast economic empire two hundred years earlier than your weak hands could have done it; the third, a gift of the Spirit. Around us the history of the land has centred for thrice a hundred years; out of the nation's heart we have called all that was best to throttle and subdue all that was worst; fire and blood, prayer and sacrifice, have billowed over this people, and they have found peace only in the altars of the God of Right. Nor has our gift of the Spirit been merely passive. Actively we have woven ourselves with the very warp and woof of this nation,—we fought their battles, shared their sorrow, mingled our blood with theirs, and generation after generation have pleaded with a headstrong, careless people to despise not Justice, Mercy, and Truth, lest the nation be smitten with a curse. Our song, our toil, our cheer, and warning have been given to this nation in blood-brotherhood. Are not these gifts worth the giving? Is not this work and striving? Would America have been America without her Negro people?

Even so is the hope that sang in the songs of my fathers well sung. If somewhere in this whirl and chaos of things there dwells Eternal Good, pitiful yet masterful, then anon in His good time America shall rend the Veil and the prisoned shall go free. Free, free as the sunshine trickling down the morning into these high windows of mine, free as yonder fresh young voices welling up to me from the caverns of brick and mortar below-swelling with song, instinct with life, tremulous treble and darkening bass. My children, my little children, are singing to the sunshine, and thus they sing:

And the traveller girds himself, and sets his face toward the Morning, and goes his way.

THE AFTER-THOUGHT

Hear my cry, O God the Reader; vouchsafe that this my book fall not still-born into the world wilderness. Let there spring, Gentle One, from out its leaves vigor of thought and thoughtful deed to reap the harvest wonderful. Let the ears of a guilty people tingle with truth, and seventy millions sigh for the righteousness which exalteth nations, in this drear day when human brotherhood is mockery and a snare. Thus in Thy good time may infinite reason turn the tangle straight, and these crooked marks on a fragile leaf be not indeed.

THE END

JAMES WELDON JOHNSON
(1871-1938)

ames Weldon Johnson may be best known for writing the lyrics to the song, "Lift Every Voice and Sing," which is often referred to as the black national anthem. Johnson wrote the song in 1899 with his brother, John, an accomplished composer, and his early fame rested largely on his songwriting accomplishments. But Johnson was also known as "Harlem's Renaissance Man," because of his great many talents and abilities. His contributions as an attorney, an intellectual, a poet, novelist, educator, diplomat and social historian all earned him a prominent place in the political and literary spectrum of his time. But it was his novel, *The Autobiography of an Ex-Colored Man* that may indeed be his most important work.

Johnson was born in 1871 in Jacksonville, Florida, and his family was fortunate enough to provide the economic security and public-mindedness that enabled him to succeed in his career. His father was a headwaiter and his mother was a teacher, and the importance of education was instilled in Johnson at a very early age. He attended Atlanta University, receiving a Bachelor of Arts degree in 1894. (He would receive his Masters degree there in 1904.) As an undergraduate student, Johnson began his prolific writing career, composing over 30 poems, beginning a lifelong passion for poetry and the African-American experience.

Upon his graduation, Johnson returned to the Stanton School, which he attended in Jacksonville, and became a teacher in the lower school before ultimately moving up to the high school and eventually becoming principal at the age of twenty-three. In 1895, he founded the *Daily American*, a newspaper covering issues of relevance to the black community. The paper preached a self-help philosophy, similar to the message of Booker T. Washington, but would only live for a year. Johnson practically ran the paper as a one-man operation, thanks to financial constraints, and the paper's death

was a heartbreaking one for its founder.

But Johnson was not one to wallow in defeat. While at the Stanton School, he was captivated by the study of law and deeply felt that skills associated with obtaining a law degree would be extraordinarily useful in his career. The result—in 1897, Johnson became the first black admitted to the bar in the state of Florida. He set up and maintained a successful practice in Jacksonville with friend who was able to pass as white, and the experiences he gathered through his friend would ultimately become the seeds of inspiration for his novel, *The Autobiography of an Ex-Colored Man.*

Despite the success of his practice, Johnson soon tired of law—mainly because it interfered with his responsibilities as principal of the Stanton School. His younger brother, John Rosamond, returned to Jacksonville in 1897 after graduating from the New England Conservatory of Music, and together, the two collaborated on compositions so successfully that the brothers found themselves in New York by the end of the decade, writing music for Broadway musicals.

The two brothers traveled back and forth between Jacksonville and New York for several years, but the lure of Harlem and Broadway finally convinced them both to settle in New York. They joined Bob Cole, and became successful writers of "Coon Songs," and black musical reviews, as well as over 200 songs for Broadway musicals, including "The Sleeping Beauty" and "Humpty Dumpty." But it was a song they wrote for the Stanton School's celebration of Lincoln's birthday that would ultimately prove their greatest.

"Lift Every Voice and Sing," written in 1900, was not a song the Johnson brothers thought much about after it was published. But the students at Stanton remembered it, and the song spread around the south until twenty years later, it was adopted by the N.A.A.C.P. as the "Negro National Hymn." It would turn out to be the perfect metaphor for Johnson's life—a mix of his art and his politics, and a theme that would define his career.

After the turn of the century, Johnson began to become more interested in literature. In 1904, he studied under the tutelage of critic and novelist Brander Matthews, who was teaching at Columbia University, and he began to withdraw from his songwriting business. But in 1906, his political connections with the Roosevelt administration helped him secure a position as U.S. Ambassador to Venezuela, and by 1909, Johnson would secure the same post in Nicaragua. However, his years as a foreign consul did not diminish his desire to write. In 1912, he published his only novel, *The Autobiography of an Ex-Colored Man*, anonymously. It was one of the earliest accounts of a

black man exploring American society while "passing" as white, and served as a sociological composition as well as a work of fiction. Although the novel did not sell well, Johnson was quickly establishing himself as a writer of influence when he became a contributing editor of the *New York Age* in 1914, where he used his column as a voice against racial inequality.

In 1916, his activism was in full gear, and he served as an official for the N.A.A.C.P., responsible for building up the organization in the South and the West. He investigated America's misrule in Haiti in 1920, and in what many believe was his finest hour as a racial leader, Johnson lobbied for the successful passage of the Dyer Anti-Lynching Bill in Congress in 1921. Eventually, he would become the N.A.A.C.P.'s executive secretary.

In 1927, Johnson announced that he was the author of *The Autobiography of an Ex-Colored Man*, and the novel finally gained the popular appeal many critics thought it deserved. In it, Johnson writes of a mixed-race hero of exceptional ability and an ambiguous appearance, affording him a unique social perspective. Early in the book, his protagonist recounts an occasion when he discovers he's not actually a Caucasian. He is at school when the principal enters the class, asking all white children to stand up. He rises, along with the other white children, but the principal asks him to be seated and "rise with the others." Dazed, he takes his seat and the first thing he does when he gets home is confront his mother, who had shielded him from his true racial identity.

> I ran downstairs to where my mother was sitting with a piece of work in her hands. I buried my head in her lap and blurted out, "Mother, mother, tell me, am I a nigger?" I could not see her face, but I knew the piece of work dropped to the floor, and I felt her hands on my head. I looked up into her face and repeated, "Tell me, mother, am I a nigger?" There were tears in her eyes, and I could see that she was suffering for me.
>
> And then it was that I looked at her critically for the first time. I had thought of her in a childish way only as the most beautiful woman in the world; now I looked at her searching for defects.

So strong was the clamor to equate the novel's protagonist with Johnson himself, that he was propelled to write his own autobiography, published in 1933, and titled, *Along This Way*. By this time, Johnson had become a central figure in the Harlem Renaissance. He edited several books on Negro

poetry and Negro spirituals, as well as writing his own essays on African-American contributions to the New York music scene. He also returned to poetry, writing *God's Trombones, Seven Negro Sermons in Verse*, and was a key voice in encouraging more ambitious literary aspirations among black writers.

The 1930s saw Johnson take on an even more visible role, lecturing widely on civil rights and guiding the N.A.A.C.P. to new levels of membership and influence. He ultimately went into semi-retirement, accepting a position as Professor of Creative Literature and Writing at Fisk University. Here, Johnson wrote *Negro Americans, What Now?* (1934), a book that some critics believe was the blueprint for the black revolution of the 1960s.

On June 26, 1938, a train struck a car Johnson was riding in a heavy thunderstorm in Wiscasset, Maine. Johnson was killed, and his body was transported to Harlem for a funeral that attracted over 2,000 people. New York Mayor Fiorello La Guardia eulogized Johnsons life and work: "Greatness in a man is a quality that does not know the boundaries of race or creed."

James Weldon Johnson was laid to rest in Brooklyn, New York, a copy of his favorite poems, *God's Trombones,* in his hands.

The Autobiography of an Ex-Colored Man

CHAPTER I

I KNOW that in writing the following pages I am divulging the great secret of my life, the secret which for some years I have guarded far more carefully than any of my earthly possessions; and it is a curious study to me to analyze the motives which prompt me to do it. I feel that I am led by the same impulse which forces the unfound-out criminal to take somebody into his confidence, although he knows that the act is liable, even almost certain, to lead to his undoing. I know that I am playing with fire, and I feel the thrill which accompanies that most fascinating pastime; and, back of it all, I think I find a sort of savage and diabolical desire to gather up all the little tragedies of my life, and turn them into a practical joke on society.

And, too, I suffer a vague feeling of unsatisfaction, of regret, of almost remorse from which I am seeking relief, and of which I shall speak in the last paragraph of this account.

I was born in a little town of Georgia a few years after the close of the Civil War. I shall not mention the name of the town, because there are people still living there who could be connected with this narrative. I have only a faint recollection of the place of my birth. At times I can close my eyes, and call up in a dream—like way things that seem to have happened ages ago in some other world. I can see in this half vision a little house,—I am quite sure it was not a large one;—I can remember that flowers grew in the front yard, and that around each bed of flowers was a hedge of vari-colored glass bottles stuck in the ground neck down. I remember that once, while playing around in the sand, I became curious to know whether or not the bottles grew as the flowers did, and I proceeded to dig them up to find out; the investigation brought me a terrific spanking which indelibly fixed the incident in my mind. I can remember, too, that behind the house was a shed under which

stood two or three wooden wash-tubs. These tubs were the earliest aversion of my life, for regularly on certain evenings I was plunged into one of them, and scrubbed until my skin ached. I can remember to this day the pain caused by the strong, rank soap getting into my eyes.

Back from the house a vegetable garden ran, perhaps, seventy-five or one hundred feet; but to my childish fancy it was an endless territory. I can still recall the thrill of joy, excitement and wonder it gave me to go on an exploring expedition through it, to find the blackberries, both ripe and green, that grew along the edge of the fence.

I remember with what pleasure I used to arrive at, and stand before, a little enclosure in which stood a patient cow chewing her cud, how I would occasionally offer her through the bars a piece of my bread and molasses, and how I would jerk back my hand in half fright if she made any motion to accept my offer.

I have a dim recollection of several people who moved in and about this little house, but I have a distinct mental image of only two; one, my mother, and the other, a tall man with a small, dark mustache. I remember that his shoes or boots were always shiny, and that he wore a gold chain and a great gold watch with which he was always willing to let me play. My admiration was almost equally divided between the watch and chain and the shoes. He used to come to the house evenings, perhaps two or three times a week; and it became my appointed duty whenever he came to bring him a pair of slippers, and to put the shiny shoes in a particular corner; he often gave me in return for this service a bright coin which my mother taught me to promptly drop in a little tin bank. I remember distinctly the last time this tall man came to the little house in Georgia; that evening before I went to bed he took me up in his arms, and squeezed me very tightly; my mother stood behind his chair wiping tears from her eyes. I remember how I sat upon his knee, and watched him laboriously drill a hole through a ten-dollar gold piece, and then tie the coin around my neck with a string. I have worn that gold piece around my neck the greater part of my life, and still possess it, but more than once I have wished that some other way had been found of attaching it to me besides putting a hole through it.

On the day after the coin was put around my neck my mother and I started on what seemed to me an endless journey. I knelt on the seat and watched through the train window the corn and cotton fields pass swiftly by until I fell asleep. When I fully awoke we were being driven through the streets of a large city—Savannah. I sat up and blinked at the bright lights. At Savannah

we boarded a steamer which finally landed us in New York. From New York we went to a town in Connecticut, which became the home of my boyhood.

My mother and I lived together in a little cottage which seemed to me to be fitted up almost luxuriously; there were horse-hair covered chairs in the parlor, and a little square piano; there was a stairway with red carpet on it leading to a half second story; there were pictures on the walls, and a few books in a glass-doored case. My mother dressed me very neatly, and I developed that pride which well-dressed boys generally have. She was careful about my associates, and I myself was quite particular. As I look back now I can see that I was a perfect little aristocrat. My mother rarely went to anyone's house, but she did sewing, and there were a great many ladies coming to our cottage. If I were around they would generally call me, and ask me my name and age and tell my mother what a pretty boy I was. Some of them would pat me on the head and kiss me.

My mother was kept very busy with her sewing; sometimes she would have another woman helping her. I think she must have derived a fair income from her work. I know, too, that at least once each month she received a letter; I used to watch for the postman, get the letter, and run to her with it; whether she was busy or not she would take it and instantly thrust it into her bosom. I never saw her read one of them. I knew later that these letters contained money and, what was to her, more than money. As busy as she generally was she, however, found time to teach me my letters and figures and how to spell a number of easy words. Always on Sunday evenings she opened the little square piano, and picked out hymns. I can recall now that whenever she played hymns from the book her tempos were always decidedly largo. Sometimes on other evenings when she was not sewing she would play simple accompaniments to some old southern songs which she sang. In these songs she was freer, because she played them by ear. Those evenings on which she opened the little piano were the happiest hours of my childhood. Whenever she started toward the instrument I used to follow her with all the interest and irrepressible joy that a pampered pet dog shows when a package is opened in which he knows there is a sweet bit for him. I used to stand by her side, and often interrupt and annoy her by chiming in with strange harmonies which I found either on the high keys of the treble or low keys of the bass. I remember that I had a particular fondness for the black keys. Always on such evenings, when the music was over, my mother would sit with me in her arms often for a very long time. She would hold me close, softly crooning some old melody without words, all the while gently stroking her face

against my head; many and many a night I thus fell asleep. I can see her now, her great dark eyes looking into the fire, to where? No one knew but she. The memory of that picture has more than once kept me from straying too far from the place of purity and safety in which her arms held me.

At a very early age I began to thump on the piano alone, and it was not long before I was able to pick out a few tunes. When I was seven years old I could play by ear all of the hymns and songs that my mother knew. I had also learned the names of the notes in both clefs, but I preferred not to be hampered by notes. About this time several ladies for whom my mother sewed heard me play, and they persuaded her that I should at once be put under a teacher; so arrangements were made for me to study the piano with a lady who was a fairly good musician; at the same time arrangements were made for me to study my books with this lady's daughter. My music teacher had no small difficulty at first in pinning me down to the notes. If she played my lesson over for me I invariably attempted to reproduce the required sounds without the slightest recourse to the written characters. Her daughter, my other teacher, also had her worries. She found that, in reading, whenever I came to words that were difficult or unfamiliar I was prone to bring my imagination to the rescue and read from the picture. She has laughingly told me, since then, that I would sometimes substitute whole sentences and even paragraphs from what meaning I thought the illustrations conveyed. She said she sometimes was not only amused at the fresh treatment I would give an author's subject, but that when I gave some new and sudden turn to the plot of the story she often grew interested and even excited in listening to hear what kind of a denouement I would bring about. But I am sure this was not due to dullness, for I made rapid progress in both my music and my books.

And so, for a couple of years my life was divided between my music and my school books. Music took up the greater part of my time. I had no playmates, but amused myself with games—some of them my own invention-which could be played alone. I knew a few boys whom I had met at the church which I attended with my mother, but I had formed no close friendships with any of them. Then, when I was nine years old, my mother decided to enter me in the public school, so all at once I found myself thrown among a crowd of boys of all sizes and kinds; some of them seemed to me like savages. I shall never forget the bewilderment, the pain, the heart-sickness of that first day at school. I seemed to be the only stranger in the place; every other boy seemed to know every other boy. I was fortunate enough, however, to be assigned to a teacher who knew me; my mother made her

dresses. She was one of the ladies who used to pat me on the head and kiss me. She had the tact to address a few words directly to me; this gave me a certain sort of standing in the class, and put me somewhat at ease.

Within a few days I had made one staunch friend, and was on fairly good terms with most of the boys. I was shy of the girls, and remained so; even now, a word or look from a pretty woman sets me all a-tremble. This friend I bound to me with hooks of steel in a very simple way. He was a big awkward boy with a face full of freckles and a head full of very red hair. He was perhaps fourteen years of age; that is, four or five years older than any other boy in the class. This seniority was due to the fact that he had spent twice the required amount of time in several of the preceding classes. I had not been at school many hours before I felt that "Red Head"—as I involuntarily called him—and I were to be friends. I do not doubt that this feeling was strengthened by the fact that I had been quick enough to see that a big, strong boy was a friend to be desired at a public school; and, perhaps, in spite of his dullness, "Red Head" had been able to discern that I could be of service to him. At any rate there was a simultaneous mutual attraction.

The teacher had strung the class promiscuously round the walls of the room for a sort of trial heat for places of rank, when the line was straightened out I found that by skillful maneuvering I had placed myself third, and had piloted "Red Head" to the place next to me. The teacher began by giving us to spell the words corresponding to our order in the line. "Spell first." "Spell second." "Spell third." I rattled off, "t-h-i-r-d, third," in a way which said, "Why don't you give us something hard?" As the words went down the line I could see how lucky I had been to get a good place together with an easy word. As young as I was I felt impressed with the unfairness of the whole proceeding when I saw the tailenders going down before "twelfth" and "twentieth," and I felt sorry for those who had to spell such words in order to hold a low position. "Spell fourth." "Red Head," with his hands clutched tightly behind his back, began bravely, "f-o-r-t-h." Like a flash a score of hands went up, and the teacher began saying, "No snapping of fingers, no snapping of fingers." This was the first word missed, and it seemed to me that some of the scholars were about to lose their senses; some were dancing up and down on one foot with a hand above their heads, the fingers working furiously, and joy beaming all over their faces; others stood still, their hands raised not so high, their fingers working less rapidly, and their faces expressing not quite so much happiness; there were still others who did not move nor raise their hands, but stood with great wrinkles on their foreheads,

looking very thoughtful.

The whole thing was new to me, and I did not raise my hand, but slyly whispered the letter "u" to "Red Head" several times. "Second chance," said the teacher. The hands went down and the class became quiet. "Red Head," his face now red, after looking beseechingly at the ceiling, then pitiably at the floor, began very haltingly, "f-u-." Immediately an impulse to raise hands went through the class, but the teacher checked it, and poor "Red Head," though he knew that each letter he added only took him farther out of the way, went doggedly on and finished, "r-t-h." The hand raising was now repeated with more hubbub and excitement than at first. Those who before had not moved a finger were now waving their hands above their heads. "Red Head" felt that he was lost. He looked very big and foolish, and some of the scholars began to snicker. His helpless condition went straight to my heart, and gripped my sympathies. I felt that if he failed it would in some way be my failure. I raised my hand, and under cover of the excitement and the teacher's attempts to regain order, I hurriedly shot up into his ear twice, quite distinctly, "f-o-u-r-t-h," "f-o-u-r-t-h." The teacher tapped on her desk and said, "Third and last chance." The hands came down, the silence became oppressive. "Red Head" began, "f"—Since that day I have waited anxiously for many a turn of the wheel of fortune, but never under greater tension than I watched for the order in which those letters would fall from "Red's" lips— "o-u-r-t-h." A sigh of relief and disappointment went up from the class. Afterwards, through all our school days, "Red Head" shared my wit and quickness and I benefited by his strength and dogged faithfulness.

There were some black and brown boys and girls in the school, and several of them were in my class. One of the boys strongly attracted my attention from the first day I saw him. His face was as black as night, but shone as though it was polished; he had sparkling eyes, and when he opened his mouth he displayed glistening white teeth. It struck me at once as appropriate to call him "Shiny face," or "Shiny eyes," or "Shiny teeth," and I spoke of him often by one of these names to the other boys. These terms were finally merged into "Shiny," and to that name he answered good naturedly during the balance of his public school days.

"Shiny" was considered without question to be the best speller, the best reader, the best penman, in a word, the best scholar, in the class. He was very quick to catch anything; but, nevertheless, studied hard; thus he possessed two powers very rarely combined in one boy. I saw him year after year, on up into the high school, win the majority of the prizes for punctuality,

deportment, essay writing and declamation. Yet it did not take me long to discover that, in spite of his standing as a scholar, he was in some way looked down upon.

The other black boys and girls were still more looked down upon. Some of the boys often spoke of them as "niggers." Sometimes on the way home from school a crowd would walk behind them repeating:

> "Nigger, nigger, never die,
> Black face and shiny eye."

On one such afternoon one of the black boys turned suddenly on his tormentors, and hurled a slate; it struck one of the white boys in the mouth, cutting a slight gash in his lip. At sight of the blood the boy who had thrown the slate ran, and his companions quickly followed. We ran after them pelting them with stones until they separated in several directions. I was very much wrought up over the affair, and went home and told my mother how one of the "niggers" had struck a boy with a slate. I shall never forget how she turned on me. "Don't you ever use that word again," she said, "and don't you ever bother the colored children at school. You ought to be ashamed of yourself." I did hang my head in shame, but not because she had convinced me that I had done wrong, but because I was hurt by the first sharp word she had ever given me.

My school days ran along very pleasantly. I stood well in my studies, not always so well with regard to my behavior. I was never guilty of any serious misconduct, but my love of fun sometimes got me into trouble. I remember, however, that my sense of humor was so sly that most of the trouble usually fell on the head of the other fellow. My ability to play on the piano at school exercises was looked upon as little short of marvelous in a boy of my age. I was not chummy with many of my mates, but, on the whole, was about as popular as it is good for a boy to be.

One day near the end of my second term at school the principal came into our room, and after talking to the teacher, for some reason said, "I wish all of the white scholars to stand for a moment." I rose with the others. The teacher looked at me, and calling my name said, "You sit down for the present, and rise with the others." I did not quite understand her, and questioned, "Ma'm?" She repeated with a softer tone in her voice, "You sit down now, and rise with the others." I sat down dazed. I saw and heard nothing. When the others were asked to rise I did not know it. When school was dis-

missed I went out in a kind of stupor. A few of the white boys jeered me, say-ing, "Oh, you're a nigger too." I heard some black children say, "We knew he was colored." "Shiny" said to them, "Come along, don't tease him," and thereby won my undying gratitude.

I hurried on as fast as I could, and had gone some distance before I per-ceived that "Red Head" was walking by my side. After a while he said to me, "Le' me carry your books." I gave him my strap without being able to answer. When we got to my gate he said as he handed me my books, "Say, you know my big red agate? I can't shoot with it any more. I'm going to bring it to school for you to-morrow." I took my books and ran into the house. As I passed through the hallway I saw that my mother was busy with one of her customers; I rushed up into my own little room, shut the door, and went quickly to where my looking-glass hung on the wall. For an instant I was afraid to look, but when I did I looked long and earnestly. I had often heard people say to my mother, "What a pretty boy you have." I was accustomed to hear remarks about my beauty; but, now, for the first time, I became con-scious of it, and recognized it. I noticed the ivory whiteness of my skin, the beauty of my mouth, the size and liquid darkness of my eyes, and how the long black lashes that fringed and shaded them produced an effect that was strangely fascinating even to me. I noticed the softness and glossiness of my dark hair that fell in waves over my temples, making my forehead appear whiter than it really was. How long I stood there gazing at my image I do not know. When I came out and reached the head of the stairs, I heard the lady who had been with my mother going out. I ran downstairs, and rushed to where my mother was sitting with a piece of work in her hands. I buried my head in her lap and blurted out, "Mother, mother, tell me, am I a nigger?" I could not see her face, but I knew the piece of work dropped to the floor, and I felt her hands on my head. I looked up into her face and repeated, "Tell me, mother, am I a nigger?" There were tears in her eyes, and I could see that she was suffering for me. And then it was that I looked at her critically for the first time. I had thought of her in a childish way only as the most beau-tiful woman in the world; now I looked at her searching for defects. I could see that her skin was almost brown, that her hair was not so soft as mine, and that she did differ in some way from the other ladies who came to the house; yet, even so, I could see that she was very beautiful, more beautiful than any of them. She must have felt that I was examining her, for she hid her face in my hair, and said with difficulty, "No, my darling, you are not a nigger." She went on, "You are as good as anybody; if anyone calls you a nigger don't

notice them." But the more she talked the less was I reassured, and I stopped her by asking, "Well, mother, am I white? Are you white?" She answered tremblingly, "No, I am not white, but you—your father is one of the greatest men in the country—the best blood of the South is in you—" This suddenly opened up in my heart a fresh chasm of misgiving and fear, and I almost fiercely demanded, "Who is my father? Where is he?" She stroked my hair and said, "I'll tell you about him some day." I sobbed, "I want to know now." She answered, "No, not now."

Perhaps it had to be done, but I have never forgiven the woman who did it so cruelly. It may be that she never knew that she gave me a sword-thrust that day in school which was years in healing.

CHAPTER II

S INCE I have grown older I have often gone back and tried to analyze the change that came into my life after that fateful day in school. There did come a radical change, and, young as I was, I felt fully conscious of it, though I did not fully comprehend it. Like my first spanking, it is one of the few incidents in my life that I can remember clearly. In the life of every one there is a limited number of unhappy experiences which are not written upon the memory, but stamped there with a die; and in long years after they can be called up in detail, and every emotion that was stirred by them can be lived through anew; these are the tragedies of life. We may grow to include some of them among the trivial incidents of childhood—a broken toy, a promise made to us which was not kept, a harsh, heart-piercing word—but these, too, as well as the bitter experiences and disappointments of mature years, are the tragedies of life.

And so I have often lived through that hour, that day, that week in which was wrought the miracle of my transition from one world into another; for I did indeed pass into another world. From that time I looked out through other eyes, my thoughts were colored, my words dictated, my actions limited by one dominating, all-pervading idea which constantly increased in force and weight until I finally realized in it a great, tangible fact.

And this is the dwarfing, warping, distorting influence which operates upon each colored man in the United States. He is forced to take his outlook on all things, not from the viewpoint of a citizen, or a man, nor even a

human being, but from the viewpoint of a colored man. It is wonderful to me that the race has progressed so broadly as it has, since most of its thought and all of its activity must run through the narrow neck of one funnel.

And it is this, too, which makes the colored people of this country, in reality, a mystery to the whites. It is a difficult thing for a white man to learn what a colored man really thinks; because, generally, with the latter an additional and different light must be brought to bear on what he thinks; and his thoughts are often influenced by considerations so delicate and subtle that it would be impossible for him to confess or explain them to one of the opposite race. This gives to every colored man, in proportion to his intellectuality, a sort of dual personality; there is one phase of him which is disclosed only in the freemasonry of his own race. I have often watched with interest and sometimes with amazement even ignorant colored men under cover of broad grins and minstrel antics maintain this dualism in the presence of white men.

I believe it to be a fact that the colored people of this country know and understand the white people better than the white people know and understand them.

I now think that this change which came into my life was at first more subjective than objective. I do not think my friends at school changed so much toward me as I did toward them. I grew reserved, I might say suspicious. I grew constantly more and more afraid of laying myself open to some injury to my feelings or my pride. I frequently saw or fancied some slight where, I am sure, none was intended. On the other hand, my friends and teachers were, if anything different, more considerate of me; but I can remember that it was against this very attitude in particular that my sensitiveness revolted. "Red" was the only one who did not so wound me; up to this day I recall with a swelling heart his clumsy efforts to make me understand that nothing could change his love for me.

I am sure that at this time the majority of my white schoolmates did not understand or appreciate any differences between me and themselves; but there were a few who had evidently received instructions at home on the matter, and more than once they displayed their knowledge in word and action. As the years passed I noticed that the most innocent and ignorant among the others grew in wisdom.

I, myself, would not have so clearly understood this difference had it not been for the presence of the other colored children at school; I had learned what their status was, and now I learned that theirs was mine. I had had no particular like or dislike for these black and brown boys and girls; in fact,

with the exception of "Shiny," they had occupied very little of my thought, but I do know that when the blow fell I had a very strong aversion to being classed with them. So I became something of a solitary. "Red" and I remained inseparable,—and there was between "Shiny" and me a sort of sympathetic bond, but my intercourse with the others was never entirely free from a feeling of constraint. But I must add that this feeling was confined almost entirely to my intercourse with boys and girls of about my own age; I did not experience it with my seniors. And when I grew to manhood I found myself freer with elderly white people than with those near my own age.

I was now about eleven years old, but these emotions and impressions which I have just described could not have been stronger or more distinct at an older age. There were two immediate results of my forced loneliness; I began to find company in books, and greater pleasure in music. I made the former discovery through a big, gilt-bound, illustrated copy of the Bible, which used to lie in splendid neglect on the center table in our little parlor. On top of the Bible lay a photograph album. I had often looked at the pictures in the album, and one day after taking the larger book down, and opening it on the floor, I was overjoyed to find that it contained what seemed to be an inexhaustible supply of pictures. I looked at these pictures many times; in fact, so often that I knew the story of each one without having to read the subject, and then, somehow, I picked up the thread of history on which is strung the trials and tribulations of the Hebrew children; this I followed with feverish interest and excitement. For a long time King David, with Samson a close second, stood at the head of my list of heroes; he was not displaced until I came to know Robert the Bruce. I read a good portion of the Old Testament, all that part treating of wars and rumors of wars, and then started in on the New. I became interested in the life of Christ, but became impatient and disappointed when I found that, notwithstanding the great power he possessed, he did not make use of it when, in my judgment, he most needed to do so. And so my first general impression of the Bible was what my later impression has been of a number of modern books, that the authors put their best work in the first part, and grew either exhausted or careless toward the end.

After reading the Bible, or those parts which held my attention, I began to explore the glass-doored book-case which I have already mentioned. I found there "Pilgrim's Progress," "Peter Parley's History of the United States," Grimm's "Household Stories," "Tales of a Grandfather," a bound vol-

ume of an old English publication, I think it was called "The Mirror," a lit-
tle volume called "Familiar Science," and somebody's "Natural Theology,"
which latter, of course, I could not read, but which, nevertheless, I tackled,
with the result of gaining a permanent dislike for all kinds of theology. There
were several other books of no particular name or merit, such as agents sell
to people who know nothing of buying books. How my mother came by this
little library which, considering all things, was so well suited to me, I never
sought to know. But she was far from being an ignorant woman, and had
herself, very likely, read the majority of these books, though I do not remem-
ber ever having seen her with a book in her hand, with the exception of the
Episcopal Prayerbook. At any rate she encouraged in me the habit of read-
ing, and when I had about exhausted those books in the little library which
interested me, she began to buy books for me. She also regularly gave me
money to buy a weekly paper which was then very popular for boys.

At this time I went in for music with an earnestness worthy of maturer
years a change of teachers was largely responsible for this. I began now to take
lessons of the organist of the church which I attended with my mother; he
was a good teacher and quite a thorough musician. He was so skillful in his
instruction, and filled me with such enthusiasm that my progress—these are
his words—was marvelous. I remember that when I was barely twelve years
old I appeared on a program with a number of adults at an entertainment
given for some charitable purpose, and carried off the honors. I did more, I
brought upon myself through the local newspapers the handicapping title of
"Infant prodigy."

I can believe that I did astonish my audience, for I never played the piano
like a child, that is, in the "one-two-three" style with accelerated motion.
Neither did I depend upon mere brilliancy of technic, a trick by which chil-
dren often surprise their listeners, but I always tried to interpret a piece of
music; I always played with feeling. Very early I acquired that knack of using
the pedals which makes the piano a sympathetic, singing instrument; quite a
different thing from the source of hard or blurred sounds it so generally is. I
think this was due not entirely to natural artistic temperament, but largely to
the fact that I did not begin to learn the piano by counting out exercises, but
by trying to reproduce the quaint songs which my mother used to sing, with
all their pathetic turns and cadences.

Even at a tender age, in playing, I helped to express what I felt by some
of the mannerisms which I afterwards observed in great performers; I had not
copied them. I have often heard people speak of the mannerisms of musi-

cians as affectations adopted for mere effect; in some cases this may be so; but a true artist can no more play upon the piano or violin without putting his whole body in accord with the emotions he is striving to express than a swallow can fly without being graceful. Often when playing I could not keep the tears which formed in my eyes from rolling down my cheeks. Sometimes at the end or even in the midst of a composition, as big a boy as I was, I would jump from the piano, and throw myself sobbing into my mother's arms. She, by her caresses and often her tears, only encouraged these fits of sentimental hysteria. Of course, to counteract this tendency to temperamental excesses I should have been out playing ball or in swimming with other boys of my age; but my mother didn't know that. There was only once when she was really firm with me, making me do what she considered was best, I did not want to return to school after the unpleasant episode which I have related, and she was inflexible.

I began my third term, and the days ran along as I have already indicated. I had been promoted twice, and had managed each time to pull "Red" along with me. I think the teachers came to consider me the only hope of his ever getting through school, and I believe they secretly conspired with me to bring about the desired end. At any rate, I know it became easier in each succeeding examination for me not only to assist "Red," but absolutely to do his work. It is strange how in some things honest people can be dishonest without the slightest compunction. I knew boys at school who were too honorable to tell a fib even when one would have been just the right thing, but could not resist the temptation to assist or receive assistance in an examination. I have long considered it the highest proof of honesty in a man to hand his street-car fare to the conductor who had overlooked it.

One afternoon after school, during my third term, I rushed home in a great hurry to get my dinner, and go to my music teacher's. I was never reluctant about going there, but on this particular afternoon I was impetuous. The reason of this was, I had been asked to play the accompaniment for a young lady who was to play a violin solo at a concert given by the young people of the church, and on this afternoon we were to have our first rehearsal. At that time playing accompaniments was the only thing in music I did not enjoy; later this feeling grew into positive dislike. I have never been a really good accompanist because my ideas of interpretation were always too strongly individual. I constantly forced my accelerandos and rubatos upon the soloist, often throwing the duet entirely out of gear.

Perhaps the reader has already guessed why I was so willing and anxious

to play the accompaniment to this violin solo; if not,—the violinist was a girl of seventeen or eighteen whom I had first heard play a short time before on a Sunday afternoon at a special service of some kind, and who had moved me to a degree which now I can hardly think of as possible. At present I do not think it was due to her wonderful playing, though I judge she must have been a very fair performer, but there was just the proper setting to produce the effect upon a boy such as I was; the half dim church, the air of devotion on the part of the listeners the heaving tremor of the organ under the clear wail of the violin, and she, her eyes almost closing, the escaping strands of her dark hair wildly framing her pale face, and her slender body swaying to the tones she called forth, all combined to fire my imagination and my heart with a passion though boyish, yet strong and, somehow, lasting. I have tried to describe the scene; if I have succeeded it is only half success, for words can only partially express what I would wish to convey. Always in recalling that Sunday afternoon I am subconscious of a faint but distinct fragrance which, like some old memory-awakening perfume, rises and suffuses my whole imagination, inducing a state of reverie so airy as to just evade the powers of expression.

She was my first love, and I loved her as only a boy loves. I dreamed of her, I built air castles for her, she was the incarnation of each beautiful heroine I knew; when I played the piano it was to her, not even did music furnish an adequate outlet for my passion; I bought a new notebook, and, to sing her praises, made my first and last attempts at poetry. I remember one day at school, after having given in our note-books to have some exercises corrected, the teacher called me to her desk and said, "I couldn't correct your exercises because I found nothing in your book but a rhapsody on somebody's brown eyes." I had passed in the wrong note-book. I don't think I have felt greater embarrassment in my whole life than I did at that moment. I was not only ashamed that my teacher should see this nakedness of my heart, but that she should find out that I had any knowledge of such affairs. It did not then occur to me to be ashamed of the kind of poetry I had written.

Of course, the reader must know that all of this adoration was in secret; next to my great love for this young lady was the dread that in some way she would find it out. I did not know what some men never find out, that the woman who cannot discern when she is loved has never lived. It makes me laugh to think how successful I was in concealing it all; within a short time after our duet all of the friends of my dear one were referring to me as her "little sweetheart," or her "little beau," and she laughingly encouraged it.

This did not entirely satisfy me, I wanted to be taken seriously. I had definitely made up my mind that I should never love another woman, and that if she deceived me I should do something desperate—the great difficulty was to think of something sufficiently desperate—and the heartless jade, how she led me on!

So I hurried home that afternoon, humming snatches of the violin part of the duet, my heart beating with pleasurable excitement over the fact that I was going to be near her, to have her attention placed directly upon me; that I was going to be of service to her, and in a way in which I could show myself to advantage—this last consideration has much to do with cheerful service.—The anticipation produced in me a sensation somewhat between bliss and fear. I rushed through the gate, took the three steps to the house at one bound, threw open the door, and was about to hang my cap on its accustomed peg of the hall rack when I noticed that that particular peg was occupied by a black derby hat. I stopped suddenly, and gazed at this hat as though I had never seen an object of its description. I was still looking at it in open-eyed wonder when my mother, coming out of the parlor into the hallway, called me, and said there was someone inside who wanted to see me. Feeling that I was being made a party to some kind of mystery I went in with her, and there I saw a man standing leaning with one elbow on the mantel, his back partly turned toward the door. As I entered he turned, and I saw a tall, handsome, well dressed gentleman of perhaps thirty-five; he advanced a step toward me with a smile on his face. I stopped and I him with the same feelings with which I had looked at the derby hat, except that they were greatly magnified. I looked at him from head to foot, but he was an absolute blank to me until my eyes rested on his slender, elegant, polished shoes; then it seemed that indistinct and partly obliterated films of memory began at first slowly then rapidly to unroll, forming a vague panorama of my childhood days in Georgia.

My mother broke the spell by calling me by name, and saying, "This is your father."

"Father, Father," that was the word which had been to me a source of doubt and perplexity ever since the interview with my mother on the subject. How often I had wondered about my father, who he was, what he was like, whether alive or dead, and above all, why she would not tell me about him. More than once I had been on the point of recalling to her the promise she had made me, but I instinctively felt that she was happier for not telling me and that I was happier for not being told; yet I had not the slight-

est idea what the real truth was. And here he stood before me, just the kind of looking father I had wishfully pictured him to be; but I made no advance toward him; I stood there feeling embarrassed and foolish, not knowing what to say or do. I am not sure but that he felt pretty much the same. My mother stood at my side with one hand on my shoulder almost pushing me forward, but I did not move. I can well remember the look of disappointment, even pain, on her face, and I can now understand that she could expect nothing else but that at the name "father" I should throw myself into his arms. But I could not rise to this dramatic or, better, melodramatic climax. Somehow I could not arouse any considerable feeling of need for a father. He broke the awkward tableau by saying, "Well, boy, aren't you glad to see me?" He evidently meant the words kindly enough, but I don't know what he could have said that would have had a worse effect; however, my good breeding came to my rescue, and I answered, "Yes, sir," and went to him and offered him my hand. He took my hand into one of his, and, with the other, stroked my head saying that I had grown into a fine youngster. He asked me how old I was; which, of course, he must have done merely to say something more, or perhaps he did so as a test of my intelligence. I replied, "Twelve, sir." He then made the trite observation about the flight of time, and we lapsed into another awkward pause.

My mother was all in smiles; I believe that was one of the happiest moments of her life. Either to put me more at ease or to show me off, she asked me to play something for my father. There is only one thing in the world that can make music, at all times and under all circumstances, up to its general standard, that is a hand-organ, or one of its variations. I went to the piano and played something in a listless, half-hearted way. I simply was not in the mood. I was wondering, while playing, when my mother would dismiss me and let me go; but my father was so enthusiastic in his praise that he touched my vanity—which was great—and more than that; he displayed that sincere appreciation which always arouses an artist to his best effort, and, too, in an unexplainable manner makes him feel like shedding tears. I showed my gratitude by playing for him a Chopin waltz with all the feeling that was in me. When I had finished my mother's eyes were glistening with tears; my father stepped across the room, seized me in his arms, and squeezed me to his breast. I am certain that for that moment he was proud to be my father. He sat and held me standing between his knees while he talked to my mother. I, in the meantime, examined him with more curiosity, perhaps, than politeness. I interrupted the conversation by asking, "Mother, is he

going to stay with us now?" I found it impossible to frame the word "father"; it was too new to me; so I asked the question through my mother. Without waiting for her to speak, my father answered, "I've got to go back to New York this afternoon, but I'm coming to see you again." I turned abruptly and went over to my mother, and almost in a whisper reminded her that I had an appointment which I should not miss, to my pleasant surprise she said that she would give me something to eat at once so that I might go. She went out of the room, and I began to gather from off the piano the music I needed. When I had finished, my father, who had been watching me, asked, "Are you going?" I replied, "Yes, sir, I've got to go to practice for a concert." He spoke some words of advice to me about being a good boy and taking care of my mother when I grew tip, and added that he was going to send me something nice from New York. My mother called, and I said good-by to him, and went out. I saw him only once after that.

I quickly swallowed down what my mother had put on the table for me, seized my cap and music, and hurried off to my teacher's house. On the way I could think of nothing but this new father, where he came from, where he had been, why he was here, and why he would not stay. In my mind I ran over the whole list of fathers I had become acquainted with in my reading, but I could not classify him. The thought did not cross my mind that he was different from me, and even if it had the mystery would not thereby have been explained; for notwithstanding my changed relations with most of my schoolmates, I had only a faint knowledge of prejudice and no idea at all how it ramified and affected the entire social organism. I felt, however, that there was something about the whole affair which had to be hid.

When I arrived I found that she of the brown eyes had been rehearsing with my teacher, and was on the point of leaving. My teacher with some expressions of surprise asked why I was late, and I stammered out the first deliberate lie of which I have any recollection. I told him that when I reached home from school I found my mother quite sick, and that I had stayed with her a while before coming. Then unnecessarily and gratuitously, to give my words force of conviction, I suppose, I added, "I don't think she'll be with us very long." In speaking these words I must have been comical; for I noticed that my teacher, instead of showing signs of anxiety or sorrow, half hid a smile. But how little did I know that in that lie I was speaking a prophecy.

She of the brown eyes unpacked her violin, and we went through the duet several times. I was soon lost to all other thoughts in the delights of music and love. I say delights of love without reservation; for at no time of life is

love so pure, so delicious, so poetic, so romantic, as it is in boyhood. A great deal has been said about the heart of a girl when she stands "where the brook and river meet," but what she feels is negative; more interesting is the heart of a boy when just at the budding dawn of manhood he stands looking wide-eyed into the long vistas opening before him; when he first becomes conscious of the awakening and quickening of strange desires and unknown powers when what he sees and feels is still shadowy and mystical enough to be intangible, and, so, more beautiful; when his imagination is unsullied, and his faith new and whole—then it is that love wears a halo—the man who has not loved before he was fourteen has missed a fore-taste of Elysium.

When I reached home it was quite dark, and I found my mother without a light, sitting rocking in a chair as she so often used to do in my childhood days, looking into the fire and singing softly to herself. I nestled close to her, and with her arms around me she haltingly told me who my father was,—a great man, a fine gentleman,—he loved me and loved her very much; he was going to make a great man of me. All she said was so limited by reserve and so colored by her feelings that it was but half truth; and so, I did not yet fully understand.

CHAPTER III

PERHAPS I ought not pass on this narrative without mentioning that the duet was a great success; so great that we were obliged to respond with two encores. It seemed to me that life could hold no greater joy than it contained when I took her hand and we stepped down to the front of the stage bowing to our enthusiastic audience. When we reached the little dressing-room, where the other performers were applauding as wildly as the audience, she impulsively threw both her arms around me, and kissed me, while I struggled to get away.

One day a couple of weeks after my father had been to see us a wagon drove up to our cottage loaded with a big box. I was about to tell the man on the wagon that they had made a mistake, when my mother, acting dark-ly wise, told them to bring their load in; she had them to unpack the box, and quickly there was evolved from the boards, paper and other packing material, a beautiful, brand new, upright piano. Then she informed me that it was a present to me from my father. I at once sat down and ran my fingers

over the keys; the full, mellow tone of the instrument was ravishing. I thought, almost remorsefully, of how I had left my father; but, even so, there momentarily crossed my mind a feeling of disappointment that the piano was not a grand. The new instrument greatly increased the pleasure of my hours of study and practice at home.

Shortly after this I was made a member of the boys' choir, it being found that I possessed a clear, strong soprano voice. I enjoyed the singing very much. About a year later I began the study of the pipe organ and the theory of music; and before I finished the grammar school I had written out several simple preludes for organ which won the admiration of my teacher, and which he did me the honor to play at services.

The older I grew the more thought I gave to the question of my and my mother's position, and what was our exact relation to the world in general. My idea of the whole matter was rather hazy. My study of United States history had been confined to those periods which were designated in my book as "Discovery," "Colonial," "Revolutionary," and "Constitutional." I now began to study about the Civil War, but the story was told in such a condensed and skipping style that I gained from it very little real information. It is a marvel how children ever learn any history out of books of that sort. And, too, I began now to read the newspapers; I often saw articles which aroused my curiosity, but did not enlighten me. But, one day, I drew from the circulating library a book that cleared the whole mystery, a book that I read with the same feverish intensity with which I had read the old Bible stories, a book that gave me my first perspective of the life I was entering; that book was "Uncle Tom's Cabin."

This work of Harriet Beecher Stowe has been the object of much unfavorable criticism. It has been assailed, not only as fiction of the most imaginative sort, but as being a direct misrepresentation. Several successful attempts have lately been made to displace the book from northern school libraries. Its critics would brush it aside with that remark there never was a Negro as good as Uncle Tom, nor a slave-holder as bad as Lagree. For my part, I was never an admirer of Uncle Tom, nor of his type of goodness; but I believe that there were lots of old Negroes as foolishly good as he; the proof of which is that they knowingly stayed and worked the plantations that furnished sinews for the army which was fighting to keep them enslaved. But, in these later years, several cases have come to my personal knowledge in which old Negroes have died and left what was a considerable fortune to the descendants of their former masters. I do not think it takes any great stretch

of the imagination to believe there was a fairly large class of slave holders typ-ified in Lagree. And we must also remember that the author depicted a num-ber of worthless if not vicious Negroes, and a slave holder who was as much of a Christian and a gentleman as it was possible for one in his position to be; that she pictured the happy, singing, shuffling darkey as well as the moth-er waiting for her child sold "down river."

I do not think it is claiming too much to say that "Uncle Tom's Cabin" was a fair and truthful panorama of slavery; however that may be, it opened my eyes as to who and what I was and what my country considered me; in fact, it gave me my bearing. But there was no shock; I took the whole reve-lation in a kind of stoical way. One of the greatest benefits I derived from reading the book was that I could afterwards talk frankly with my mother on all the questions which had been vaguely troubling my mind. As a result, she was entirely freed from reserve, and often herself brought up the subject, talking of things directly touching her life and mine and of things which had come down to her through the "old folks." What she told me interested and even fascinated me; and, what may seem strange, kindled in me a strong desire to see the South. She spoke to me quite frankly about herself, my father and myself; she, the sewing girl of my father's mother; he, an impetu-ous young man home from college; I, the child of this unsanctioned love. She told me even the principal reason for our coming North. My father was about to be married to a young lady of another great Southern family. She did not neglect to add that another reason for our being in Connecticut was that he intended to give me an education, and make a man of me. In none of her talks did she ever utter one word of complaint against my father. She always endeavored to impress upon me how good he had been and still was, and that he was all to us that custom and the law would allow. She loved him; more, she worshiped him, and she died firmly believing that he loved her more than any other woman in the world. Perhaps she was right. Who knows?

All of these newly awakened ideas and thoughts took the form of a defi-nite aspiration on the day I graduated from the grammar school. And what a day that was! The girls in white dresses with fresh ribbons in their hair; the boys in new suits and creaky shoes; the great crowd of parents and friends, the flowers, the prizes and congratulations, made the day seem to me one of the greatest importance. I was on the programme and played a piano solo which was received by the audience with that amount of applause which I had come to look upon as being only the just due to my talent.

But the real enthusiasm was aroused by "Shiny." He was the principal speaker of the day, and well did he measure up to the honor. He made a striking picture, that thin little black boy standing on the platform, dressed in clothes that did not fit him any too well, his eyes burning with excitement, his shrill, musical voice vibrating in tones of appealing defiance, and his black face alight with such great intelligence and earnestness as to be positively handsome. What were his thoughts when he stepped forward and looked into that crowd of faces all white with the exception of a score or so that were lost to view. I do not know, but I fancy he felt his loneliness. I think there must have rushed over him a feeling akin to that of a gladiator tossed into the arena and bade to fight for his life. I think that solitary little black figure standing there felt that for the particular time and place he bore the weight and responsibility of his race; that for him to fail meant general defeat; but he won, and nobly. His oration was Wendell Phillips' "Toussaint L'Ouverture," a speech which may now be classed as rhetorical, even, perhaps, bombastic, but as the words fell from "Shiny's" lips their effect was magical. How so young an orator could stir so great enthusiasm was to be wondered at. When in the famous peroration, his voice trembling with suppressed emotion rose higher and higher and then rested on the name Toussaint L'Ouverture, it was like touching an electric button which loosed the pent-up feelings of his listeners. They actually rose to him.

I have since known of colored men who have been chosen as class orators in our leading universities, of others who have played on the 'Varsity football and base-ball teams, of colored speakers who have addressed great white audiences. In each of these instances I believe the men were stirred by the same emotions which actuated "Shiny" on the day of his graduation; and, too, in each case where the efforts have reached any high standard of excellence they have been followed by the same phenomenon of enthusiasm. I think the explanation of the latter lies in what is a basic, though often dormant, principle of the Anglo-Saxon heart, love of fair play. "Shiny," it is true, was what is so common in his race, a natural orator; but I doubt that any white boy of equal talent could have wrought the same effect. The sight of that boy gallantly waging with puny, black arms, so unequal a battle touched the deep springs in the hearts of his audience, and they were swept by a wave of sympathy and admiration.

But the effect upon me of "Shiny's" speech was double; I not only shared the enthusiasm of his audience, but he imparted to me some of his own enthusiasm. I felt leap within me pride that I was colored; and I began to

form wild dreams of bringing glory and honor to the Negro race. For days I could talk of nothing else with my mother except my ambitions to be a great man, a great colored man, to reflect credit on the race, and gain fame for myself. It was not until years after that I formulated a definite and feasible plan for realizing my dreams.

I entered the high school with my class, and still continued my study of the piano, the pipe organ and the theory of music. I had to drop out of the boys' choir on account of a changing voice; this I regretted very much. As I grew older my love for reading grew stronger. I read with studious interest everything I could find relating to colored men who had gained prominence. My heroes had been King David, then Robert the Bruce; now Frederick Douglass was enshrined in the place of honor. When I learned that Alexander Dumas was a colored man, I re-read "Monte Cristo" and "The Three Guardsmen" with magnified pleasure. I lived between my music and books, on the whole a rather unwholesome life for a boy to lead. I dwelt in a world of imagination, of dreams and air castles,—the kind of atmosphere that sometimes nourishes a genius, more often men unfitted for the practical struggles of life. I never played a game of ball, never went fishing or learned to swim; in fact, the only outdoor exercise in which I took any interest was skating. Nevertheless, though slender, I grew well-formed and in perfect health. After I entered the high school I began to notice the change in my mother's health, which I suppose had been going on for some years. She began to complain a little and to cough a great deal; she tried several reme- dies, and finally went to see a doctor; but though she was failing in health she kept her spirits up. She still did a great deal of sewing, and in the busy seasons hired two women to help her. The purpose she had formed of hav- ing me go through college without financial worries kept her at work when she was not fit for it. I was so fortunate as to be able to organize a class of eight or ten beginners on the piano, and so start a separate little fund of my own. As the time for my graduation from the high school grew nearer, the plans for my college career became the chief subject of our talks. I sent for catalogues of all the prominent schools in the East, and eagerly gathered all the information I could concerning them from different sources. My mother told me that my father wanted me to go to Harvard or Yale; she herself had a half desire for me to go to Atlanta University, and even had me write for a cat- alogue of that school. There were two reasons, however, that inclined her to my father's choice: the first, that at Harvard or Yale I should be near her; the second, that my father had promised to pay a part of my college education.

Both "Shiny" and "Red" came to my house quite often of evenings, and we used to talk over our plans and prospects for the future. Sometimes I would play for them, and they seemed to enjoy the music very much. My mother often prepared sundry southern dishes for them, which I am not sure but they enjoyed more. "Shiny" had an uncle in Amherst, Mass., and he expected to live with him and work his way through Amherst College. "Red" declared that he had enough of school and that after he got his high school diploma he would get a position in a bank. It was his ambition to become a banker, and he felt sure of getting the opportunity through certain members of his family.

My mother barely had strength to attend the closing exercises of the high school when I graduated; and after that day she was seldom out of bed. She could no longer direct her work, and under the expense of medicines, doctors, and someone to look after her, our college fund began to diminish rapidly. Many of her customers and some of the neighbors were very kind, and frequently brought her nourishment of one kind or another. My mother realized what I did not, that she was mortally ill, and she had me write a long letter to my father. For some time past she had heard from him only at irregular intervals; we never received an answer. In those last days I often sat at her bedside and read to her until she fell asleep. Sometimes I would leave the parlor door open and play on the piano, just loud enough for the music to reach her. This she always enjoyed.

One night, near the end of July, after I had been watching beside her for some hours, I went into the parlor, and throwing myself into the big arm chair dozed off into a fitful sleep. I was suddenly aroused by one of the neighbors, who had come in to sit with her that night. She said, "Come to your mother at once." I hurried upstairs, and at the bedroom door met the woman who was acting as nurse. I noted with a dissolving heart the strange look of awe on her face. From my first glance at my mother, I discerned the light of death upon her countenance. I fell upon my knees beside the bed, and burying my face in the sheets sobbed convulsively. She died with the fingers of her left hand entwined in my hair.

I will not rake over this, one of the two sacred sorrows of my life; nor could I describe the feeling of unutterable loneliness that fell upon me. After the funeral I went to the house of my music teacher; he had kindly offered me the hospitality of his home for so long as I might need it. A few days later I moved my trunk, piano, my music and most of my books to his home; the rest of my books I divided between "Shiny" and "Red." Some of the house-

hold effects I gave to "Shiny's" mother and to two or three of the neighbors who had been kind to us during my mother's illness; the others I sold. After settling up my little estate I found that besides a good supply of clothes, a piano, some books and other trinkets, I had about two hundred dollars in cash.

The question of what I was to do now confronted me. My teacher suggested a concert tour; but both of us realized that I was too old to be exploited as an infant prodigy and too young and inexperienced to go before the public as a finished artist. He, however, insisted that the people of the town would generously patronize a benefit concert, so took up the matter, and made arrangements for such an entertainment. A more than sufficient number of people with musical and elocutionary talent volunteered their services to make a programme. Among these was my brown-eyed violinist. But our relations were not the same as they were when we had played our first duet together. A year or so after that time she had dealt me a crushing blow by getting married. I was partially avenged, however, by the fact that, though she was growing more beautiful, she was losing her ability to play the violin.

I was down on the programme for one number. My selection might have appeared at that particular time as a bit of affectation, but I considered it deeply appropriate; I played Beethoven's "Sonata Pathétique." When I sat down at the piano, and glanced into the faces of the several hundreds of people who were there solely on account of love or sympathy for me, emotions swelled in my heart which enabled me to play the "Pathétique" as I could never again play it. When the last tone died away the few who began to applaud were hushed by the silence of the others; and for once I played without receiving an encore.

The benefit yielded me a little more than two hundred dollars, thus raising my cash capital to about four hundred dollars. I still held to my determination of going to college; so it was now a question of trying to squeeze through a year at Harvard or going to Atlanta where the money I had would pay my actual expenses for at least two years. The peculiar fascination which the South held over my imagination and my limited capital decided me in favor of Atlanta University; so about the last of September I bade farewell to the friends and scenes of my boyhood, and boarded a train for the South.

CHAPTER IV

T HE FARTHER I got below Washington the more disappointed I became in the appearance of the country. I peered through the car windows, looking in vain for the luxuriant semi-tropical scenery which I had pictured in my mind. I did not find the grass so green, nor the woods so beautiful, nor the flowers so plentiful, as they were in Connecticut. Instead, the red earth partly covered by tough, scrawny grass, the muddy straggling roads, the cottages of unpainted pine boards, and the clay daubed huts imparted a "burnt up" impression. Occasionally we ran through a little white and green village that was like an oasis in a desert.

When I reached Atlanta my steadily increasing disappointment was not lessened. I found it a big, dull, red town. This dull red color of that part of the South I was then seeing had much, I think, to do with the extreme depression of my spirits—no public squares, no fountains, dingy street-cars and, with the exception of three or four principal thoroughfares, unpaved streets. It was raining when I arrived and some of these unpaved streets were absolutely impassable. Wheels sank to the hubs in red mire, and I actually stood for an hour and watched four or five men work to save a mule, which had stepped into a deep sink, from drowning, or, rather, suffocating in the mud. The Atlanta of to-day is a new city.

On the train I had talked with one of the Pullman car porters, a bright young fellow who was himself a student, and told him that I was going to Atlanta to attend school. I had also asked him to tell me where I might stop for a day or two until the University opened. He said I might go with him to the place where he stopped during his "layovers" in Atlanta. I gladly accepted his offer, and went with him along one of those muddy streets until we came to a rather rickety looking frame house, which we entered. The proprietor of the house was a big, fat, greasy looking brown-skinned man. When I asked him if he could give me accommodation he wanted to know how long I would stay. I told him perhaps two days, not more than three. In reply he said, "Oh, dat's all right den," at the same time leading the way up a pair of creaky stairs. I followed him and the porter to a room, the door of which the proprietor opened while continuing, it seemed, his remark, "Oh, dat's all right den," by adding, "You kin sleep in dat cot in de corner der. Fifty cents please." The porter interrupted by saying, "You needn't collect from him now, he's got a trunk." This seemed to satisfy the man, and he went down

leaving me and my porter friend in the room. I glanced around the apartment and saw that it contained a double bed and two cots, two wash-stands, three chairs, and a time-worn bureau with a looking-glass that would have made Adonis appear hideous. I looked at the cot in which I was to sleep and suspected, not without good reasons, that I should not be the first to use the sheets and pillow-case since they had last come from the wash. When I thought of the clean, tidy, comfortable surroundings in which I had been reared, a wave of homesickness swept over me that made me feel faint. Had it not been for the presence of my companion, and that I knew this much of his history,—that he was not yet quite twenty, just three years older than myself, and that he had been fighting his own way in the world, earning his own living and providing for his own education since he was fourteen, I should not have been able to stop the tears that were welling up in my eyes.

I asked him why it was that the proprietor of the house seemed unwilling to accommodate me for more than a couple of days. He informed me that the man ran a lodging house especially for Pullman porters, and as their stays in town were not longer than one or two nights it would interfere with his arrangements to have anyone stay longer. He went on to say, "You see this room is fixed up to accommodate four men at a time. Well, by keeping a sort of table of trips, in and out, of the men, and working them like checkers, he can accommodate fifteen or sixteen in each week, and generally avoid having an empty bed. You happen to catch a bed that would have been empty for a couple of nights." I asked him where he was going to sleep. He answered, "I sleep in that other cot to-night; to-morrow night I go out." He went on to tell me that the man who kept the house did not serve meals, and that if I was hungry we would go out and get something to eat.

We went into the street, and in passing the railroad station I hired a wagon to take my trunk to my lodging place. We passed along until, finally, we turned into a street that stretched away, up and down hill, for a mile or two; and here I caught my first sight of colored people in large numbers. I had seen little squads around the railroad stations on my way south; but here I saw a street crowded with them. They filled the shops and thronged the sidewalks and lined the curb. I asked my companion if all the colored people in Atlanta lived in this street. He said they did not, and assured me that the ones I saw were of the lower class. I felt relieved, in spite of the size of the lower class. The unkempt appearance, the shambling, slouching gait and loud talk and laughter of these people aroused in me a feeling of almost repulsion. Only one thing about them awoke a feeling of interest; that was

their dialect. I had read some Negro dialect and had heard snatches of it on my journey down from Washington; but here I heard it in all of its fullness and freedom. I was particularly struck by the way in which it was punctuated by such exclamatory phrases as "Lawd a mussy!" "G'wan man!" "Bless ma soul!" "Look heah chile!" These people talked and laughed without restraint. In fact, they talked straight from their lungs, and laughed from the pits of their stomachs. And this hearty laughter was often justified by the droll humor of some remark. I paused long enough to hear one man say to another, "W'at's de mattah wid you an' yo' fr'en' Sam?" and the other came back like a flash, "Ma fr'en? He ma fr'en? Man! I'd go to his funeral jes de same as I'd go to a minstrel show." I have since learned that this ability to laugh heartily is, in part, the salvation of the American Negro; it does much to keep him from going the way of the Indian.

The business places of the street along which we were passing consisted chiefly of low bars, cheap dry-goods and notion stores, barber shops, and fish and bread restaurants. We, at length, turned down a pair of stairs that led to a basement, and I found myself in an eating-house somewhat better than those I had seen in passing; but that did not mean much for its excellence. The place was smoky, the tables were covered with oil-cloth, the floor covered with sawdust, and from the kitchen came a rancid odor of fish fried over several times, which almost nauseated me. I asked my companion if this were the place where we were to eat. He informed me that it was the best place in town where a colored man could get a meal. I then wanted to know why somebody didn't open a place where respectable colored people who had money could be accommodated. He answered, "It wouldn't pay, all the respectable colored people eat at home, and the few who travel generally have friends in the towns to which they go, who entertain them." He added "Of course, you could go in any place in the city; they wouldn't know you from white."

I sat down with the porter at one of the tables, but was not hungry enough to eat with any relish what was put before me. The food was not badly cooked; but the iron knives and forks needed to be scrubbed, the plates and dishes and glasses needed to be washed and well dried. I minced over what I took on my plate while my companion ate. When we finished we paid the waiter twenty cents each and went out. We walked around until the lights of the city were lit. Then the porter said that he must get to bed and have some rest, as he had not had six hours' sleep since he left Jersey City. I went back to our lodging-house with him.

When I awoke in the morning there were, besides my new found friend, two other men in the room, asleep in the double bed. I got up and dressed myself very quietly, so as not to awake anyone. I then drew from under the pillow my precious roll of greenbacks, took out a ten dollar bill, and very softly unlocking my trunk, put the remainder, about three hundred dollars, in the inside pocket of a coat near the bottom; glad of the opportunity to put it unobserved in a place of safety. When I had carefully locked my trunk, I tiptoed toward the door with the intention of going out to look for a decent restaurant where I might get something fit to eat. As I was easing the door open, my porter friend said with a yawn, "Hello! You're going out?" I answered him, "Yes." "Oh!" he yawned again, "I guess I've had enough sleep; wait a minute, I'll go with you." For the instant his friendship bored and embarrassed me. I had visions of another meal in the greasy restaurant of the day before. He must have divined my thoughts; for he went on to say, "I know a woman across town who takes a few boarders; I think we can go over there and get a good breakfast." With a feeling of mingled fears and doubts regarding what the breakfast might be, I waited until he had dressed himself.

When I saw the neat appearance of the cottage we entered my fears vanished, and when I saw the woman who kept it my doubts followed the same course. Scrupulously clean, in a spotless white apron and colored head handkerchief, her round face beaming with motherly kindness, she was picturesquely beautiful. She impressed me as one broad expanse of happiness and good nature. In a few minutes she was addressing me as "chile" and "honey." She made me feel as though I should like to lay my head on her capacious bosom and go to sleep.

And the breakfast, simple as it was, I could not have had at any restaurant in Atlanta at any price. There was fried chicken, as it is fried only in the South, hominy boiled to the consistency where it could be eaten with a fork, and biscuits so light and flaky that a fellow with any appetite at all would have no difficulty in disposing of eight or ten. When I had finished I felt that I had experienced the realization of, at least, one of my dreams of Southern life.

During the meal we found out from our hostess, who had two boys in school, that Atlanta University opened on that very day. I had somehow mixed my dates. My friend the porter suggested that I go out to the University at once and offered to walk over and show me the way. We had to walk because, although the University was not more than twenty minutes distance from the center of the city, there were no street-cars running in that direction. My first sight of the school grounds made me feel that I was not

far from home; here the red hills had been terraced and covered with green grass; clean gravel walks, well shaded, lead up to the buildings; indeed, it was a bit of New England transplanted. At the gate my companion said he would bid me good-by, because it was likely that he would not see me again before his car went out. He told me that he would make two more trips to Atlanta, and that he would come out and see me; that after his second trip he would leave the Pullman service for the winter and return to school in Nashville. We shook hands, I thanked him for all his kindness, and we said good-by.

I walked up to a group of students and made some inquiries. They directed me to the president's office in the main building. The president gave me a cordial welcome; it was more than cordial; he talked to me, not as the official head of a college, but as though he were adopting me into what was his large family, to personally look after my general welfare as well as my education. He seemed especially pleased with the fact that I had come to them all the way from the North. He told me that I could have come to the school as soon as I had reached the city, and that I had better move my trunk out at once. I gladly promised him that I would do so. He then called a boy and directed him to take me to the matron, and to show me around afterwards. I found the matron even more motherly than the president was fatherly. She had me to register, which was in effect to sign a pledge to abstain from the use of intoxicating beverages, tobacco, and profane language, while I was a student in the school. This act caused me no sacrifice; as, up to that time, I was free from either habit. The boy who was with me then showed me about the grounds. I was especially interested in the industrial building.

The sounding of a bell, he told me, was the signal for the students to gather in the general assembly hall, and he asked me if I would go. Of course I would. There were between three and four hundred students and perhaps all of the teachers gathered in the room. I noticed that several of the latter were colored. The president gave a talk addressed principally to new comers; but I scarcely heard what he said, I was so much occupied in looking at those around me. They were of all types and colors, the more intelligent types predominating. The colors ranged from jet black to pure white, with light hair and eyes. Among the girls especially there were many so fair that it was difficult to believe that they had Negro blood in them. And, too, I could not help but notice that many of the girls, particularly those of the delicate brown shades, with black eyes and wavy dark hair, were decidedly pretty. Among the boys, many of the blackest were fine specimens of young manhood, tall, straight, and muscular, with magnificent heads; these were the kind of boys

who developed into the patriarchal "uncles" of the old slave régime.

When I left the University it was with the determination to get my trunk, and move out to the school before night. I walked back across the city with a light step and a light heart. I felt perfectly satisfied with life for the first time since my mother's death. In passing the railroad station I hired a wagon and rode with the driver as far as my stopping place. I settled with my landlord and went upstairs to put away several articles I had left out. As soon as I opened my trunk a dart of suspicion shot through my heart; the arrangement of things did not look familiar. I began to dig down excitedly to the bottom till I reached the coat in which I had concealed my treasure. My money was gone! Every single bill of it. I knew it was useless to do so, but I searched through every other coat, every pair of trousers, every vest, and even into each pair of socks. When I had finished my fruitless search I sat down dazed and heartsick. I called the landlord up, and informed him of my loss, he comforted me by saying that I ought to have better sense than to keep money in a trunk, and that he was not responsible for his lodgers' personal effects. His cooling words brought me enough to my senses to cause me to look and see if anything else was missing. Several small articles were gone, among them a black and gray necktie of odd design upon which my heart was set; almost as much as the loss of my money, I felt the loss of my tie.

After thinking for awhile as best I could, I wisely decided to go at once back to the University and lay my troubles before the president. I rushed breathlessly back to the school. As I neared the grounds the thought came across me, would not my story sound fishy? Would it not place me in the position of an impostor or beggar? What right had I to worry these busy people with the results of my carelessness? If the money could not be recovered, and I doubted that it could, what good would it do to tell them about it. The shame and embarrassment which the whole situation gave me caused me to stop at the gate. I paused, undecided, for a moment; then turned and slowly retraced my steps, and so changed the whole course of my life.

If the reader has never been in a strange city without money or friends, it is useless to try to describe what my feelings were, he could not understand. If he has been, it is equally useless, for he understands more than words could convey. When I reached my lodgings I found in the room one of the porters who had slept there the night before. When he heard what misfortune had befallen me he offered many words of sympathy and advice. He asked me how much money I had left, I told him that I had ten or twelve dollars in my pocket. He said, "That won't last you very long here, and you will hardly be

able to find anything to do in Atlanta. I'll tell you what you do, go down to Jacksonville and you won't have any trouble to get a job in one of the big hotels there, or in St. Augustine." I thanked him, but intimated my doubts of being able to get to Jacksonville on the money I had. He reassured me by saying, "Oh that's all right. You express your trunk on through, and I'll take you down in my closet." I thanked him again, not knowing then, what it was to travel in a Pullman porter's closet. He put me under a deeper debt of gratitude by lending me fifteen dollars, which he said I could pay back after I had secured work. His generosity brought tears to my eyes, and I concluded that, after all, there were some kind hearts in the world.

I now forgot my troubles in the hurry and excitement of getting my trunk off in time to catch the train, which went out at seven o'clock. I even forgot that I hadn't eaten anything since morning. We got a wagon—the porter went with me—and took my trunk to the express office. My new friend then told me to come to the station at about a quarter of seven, and walk straight to the car where I should see him standing, and not to lose my nerve. I found my rôle not so difficult to play as I thought it would be, because the train did not leave from the central station, but from a smaller one, where there were no gates and guards to pass. I followed directions, and the porter took me on his car, and locked me in his closet. In a few minutes the train pulled out for Jacksonville.

I may live to be a hundred years old, but I shall never forget the agonies I suffered that night. I spent twelve hours doubled up in the porter's basket for soiled linen, not being able to straighten up on account of the shelves for clean linen just over my head. The air was hot and suffocating and the smell of damp towels and used linen was sickening. At each lurch of the car over the none too smooth track, I was bumped and bruised against the narrow walls of my narrow compartment. I became acutely conscious of the fact that I had not eaten for hours. Then nausea took possession of me, and at one time I had grave doubts about reaching my destination alive. If I had the trip to make again, I should prefer to walk.

CHAPTER V

T HE NEXT morning I got out of the car at Jacksonville with a stiff and aching body. I determined to ask no more porters, not even my bene-

factor, about stopping places; so I found myself on the street not knowing where to go. I walked along listlessly until I met a colored man who had the appearance of a preacher. I asked him if he could direct me to a respectable boarding-house for colored people. He said that if I walked along with him in the direction he was going he would show me such a place. I turned and walked at his side. He proved to be a minister, and asked me a great many direct questions about myself. I answered as many as I saw fit to answer; the others I evaded or ignored. At length we stopped in front of a frame house, and my guide informed me that it was the place. A woman was standing in the doorway, and he called to her saying that he had brought her a new boarder. I thanked him for his trouble, and after he had urged upon me to attend his church while I was in the city, he went on his way.

I went in and found the house neat and not uncomfortable. The parlor was furnished with cane-bottomed chairs, each of which was adorned with a white crocheted tidy. The mantel over the fireplace had a white crocheted cover, a marble-topped center table held a lamp, a photograph album and several trinkets, each of which was set upon a white crocheted mat. There was a cottage organ in a corner of the room, and I noted that the lamp-racks upon it were covered with white crocheted mats. There was a matting on the floor, but a white crocheted carpet would not have been out of keeping. I made arrangements with the landlady for my board and lodging; the amount was, I think, three dollars and a half a week. She was a rather fine looking, stout, brown-skinned woman of about forty years of age. Her husband was a light colored Cuban, a man about one half her size, and one whose age could not be guessed from his appearance. He was small in size, but a handsome black mustache and typical Spanish eyes redeemed him from insignificance.

I was in time for breakfast, and at the table I had the opportunity to see my fellow-boarders. There were eight or ten of them. Two, as I afterwards learned, were colored Americans. All of them were cigar makers and worked in one of the large factories-cigar making is the one trade in which the color-line is not drawn. The conversation was carried on entirely in Spanish, and my ignorance of the language subjected me more to alarm than embarrassment. I had never heard such uproarious conversation; everybody talked at once, loud exclamations, rolling "carambas," menacing gesticulations with knives, forks, and spoons. I looked every moment for the clash of blows. One man was emphasizing his remarks by flourishing a cup in his hand, seemingly forgetful of the fact that it was nearly full of hot coffee. He ended by empty-ing it over what was, relatively, the only quiet man at the table excepting

myself, bringing from him a volley of language which made the others appear dumb by comparison. I soon learned that in all of this clatter of voices and table utensils they were discussing purely ordinary affairs and arguing about mere trifles, and that not the least ill-feeling was aroused. It was not long before I enjoyed the spirited chatter and badinage at the table as much as I did my meals,—and the meals were not bad.

I spent the afternoon in looking around the town. The streets were sandy, but were well shaded by fine oak trees, and far preferable to the clay roads of Atlanta. One or two public squares with green grass and trees gave the city a touch of freshness. That night after supper I spoke to my landlady and her husband about my intentions. They told me that the big winter hotels would not open within two months. It can easily be imagined what effect this news had on me. I spoke to them frankly about my financial condition and related the main fact of my misfortune in Atlanta. I modestly mentioned my ability to teach music and asked if there was any likelihood of my being able to get some scholars. My landlady suggested that I speak to the preacher who had shown me her house; she felt sure that through his influence I should be able to get up a class in piano. She added, however, that the colored people were poor, and that the general price for music lessons was only twenty-five cents. I noticed that the thought of my teaching white pupils did not even remotely enter her mind. None of this information made my prospects look much brighter.

The husband, who up to this time had allowed the woman to do most of the talking, gave me the first bit of tangible hope; he said that he could get me a job as a "stripper" in the factory where he worked, and that if I succeeded in getting some music pupils I could teach a couple of them every night, and so make a living until something better turned up. He went on to say that it would not be a bad thing for me to stay at the factory and learn my trade as a cigar maker, and impressed on me that, for a young man knocking about the country, a trade was a handy thing to have. I determined to accept his offer and thanked him heartily. In fact, I became enthusiastic, not only because I saw a way out of my financial troubles, but also because I was eager and curious over the new experience I was about to enter. I wanted to know all about the cigar making business. This narrowed the conversation down to the husband and myself, so the wife went in and left us talking.

He was what is called a *regaliá* workman, and earned from thirty-five to forty dollars a week. He generally worked a sixty dollar job; that is, he made cigars for which he was paid at the rate of sixty dollars per thousand. It was

impossible for him to make a thousand in a week because he had to work very carefully and slowly. Each cigar was made entirely by hand. Each piece of filler and each wrapper had to be selected with care. He was able to make a bundle of one hundred cigars in a day, not one of which could be told from the others by any difference in size or shape, or even by any appreciable difference in weight. This was the acme of artistic skill in cigar making. Workmen of this class were rare, never more than three or four of them in one factory, and it was never necessary for them to remain out of work. There were men who made two, three, and four hundred cigars of the cheaper grades in a day; they had to be very fast in order to make decent week's wages. Cigar making was a rather independent trade; the men went to work when they pleased and knocked off when they felt like doing so. As a class the workmen were careless and improvident; some very rapid makers would not work more than three or four days out of the week, and there were others who never showed up at the factory on Mondays. "Strippers" were the boys who pulled the long stems from the tobacco leaves. After they had served at that work for a certain time they were given tables as apprentices.

All of this was interesting to me; and we drifted along in conversation until my companion struck the subject nearest his heart, the independence of Cuba. He was an exile from the island, and a prominent member of the Jacksonville *Junta*. Every week sums of money were collected from *juntas* all over the country. This money went to buy arms and ammunition for the insurgents. As the man sat there nervously smoking his long, "green" cigar, and telling me of the Gomezes, both the white one and the black one, of Maceo and Bandera, he grew positively eloquent. He also showed that he was a man of considerable education and reading. He spoke English excellently, and frequently surprised me by using words one would hardly expect from a foreigner. The first one of this class of words he employed almost shocked me, and I never forgot it, 'twas "ramify." We sat on the piazza until after ten o'clock. When we arose to go in to bed it was with the understanding that I should start in the factory on the next day.

I began work the next morning seated at a barrel with another boy, who showed me how to strip the stems from the leaves, to smooth out each half leaf, and to put the "rights" together in one pile, and the "lefts" together in another pile on the edge of the barrel. My fingers, strong and sensitive from their long training, were well adapted to this kind of work; and within two weeks I was accounted the fastest "stripper" in the factory. At first the heavy odor of the tobacco almost sickened me; but when I became accustomed to

it I liked the smell. I was now earning four dollars a week, and was soon able to pick up a couple more by teaching a few scholars at night, whom I had secured through the good offices of the preacher I had met on my first morning in Jacksonville.

At the end of about three months, through my skill as a "stripper" and the influence of my landlord, I was advanced to a table, and began to learn my trade; in fact, more than my trade; for I learned not only to make cigars, but also to smoke, to swear, and to speak Spanish. I discovered that I had a talent for languages as well as for music. The rapidity and ease with which I acquired Spanish astonished my associates. In a short time I was able not only to understand most of what was said at the table during meals, but to join in the conversation. I bought a method for learning the Spanish language, and with the aid of my landlord as a teacher, by constant practice with my fellow workmen, and by regularly reading the Cuban newspapers, and finally some books of standard Spanish literature which were at the house, I was able in less than a year to speak like a native. In fact, it was my pride that I spoke better Spanish than many of the Cuban workmen at the factory.

After I had been in the factory a little over a year, I was repaid for all the effort I had put forth to learn Spanish by being selected as "reader." The "reader" is quite an institution in all cigar factories which employ Spanish-speaking workmen. He sits in the center of the large room in which the cigar makers work and reads to them for a certain number of hours each day all the important news from the papers and whatever else he may consider would be interesting. He often selects an exciting novel, and reads it in daily installments. He must, of course, have a good voice, but he must also have a reputation among the men for intelligence, for being well posted and having in his head a stock of varied information. He is generally the final authority on all arguments which arise; and, in a cigar factory, these arguments are many and frequent, ranging from discussions on the respective and relative merits of rival baseball clubs to the duration of the sun's light and energy-cigar-making is a trade in which talk does not interfere with work. My position as "reader" not only released me from the rather monotonous work of rolling cigars, and gave me something more in accord with my tastes, but also added considerably to my income. I was now earning about twenty-five dollars a week, and was able to give up my peripatetic method of giving music lessons. I hired a piano and taught only those who could arrange to take their lessons where I lived. I finally gave up teaching entirely; as what I made scarcely paid for my time and trouble. I kept the piano, however, in order to

keep up my own studies, and occasionally I played at some church concert or other charitable entertainment.

Through my music teaching and my not absolutely irregular attendance at church I became acquainted with the best class of colored people in Jacksonville. This was really my entrance into the race. It was my initiation into what I have termed the freemasonry of the race. I had formulated a theory of what it was to be colored, now I was getting the practice. The novelty of my position caused me to observe and consider things which, I think, entirely escaped the young men I associated with; or, at least, were so commonplace to them as not to attract their attention. And of many of the impressions which came to me then I have realized the full import only within the past few years, since I have had a broader knowledge of men and history, and a fuller comprehension of the tremendous struggle which is going on between the races in the South.

It is a struggle; for though the black man fights passively he nevertheless fights; and his passive resistance is more effective at present than active resistance could possibly be. He bears the fury of the storm as does the willow tree.

It is a struggle; for though the white man of the South may be too proud to admit it, he is, nevertheless, using in the contest his best energies; he is devoting to it the greater part of his thought and much of his endeavor. The South to-day stands panting and almost breathless from its exertions.

And how the scene of the struggle has shifted! The battle was first waged over the right of the Negro to be classed as a human being with a soul; later, as to whether he had sufficient intellect to master even the rudiments of learning; and to-day it is being fought out over his social recognition.

I said somewhere in the early part of this narrative that because the colored man looked at everything through the prism of his relationship to society as a colored man, and because most of his mental efforts ran through the narrow channel bounded by his rights and his wrongs, it was to be wondered at that he has progressed so broadly as he has. The same thing may be said of the white man of the South; most of his mental efforts run through one narrow channel; his life as a man and a citizen, many of his financial activities and all of his political activities are impassably limited by the ever present "Negro question." I am sure it would be safe to wager that no group of Southern white men could get together and talk for sixty minutes without bringing up the "race question." If a Northern white man happened to be in the group the time could be safely cut to thirty minutes. In this respect I consider the condition of the whites more to be deplored than that of the blacks.

Here, a truly great people, a people that produced a majority of the great historic Americans from Washington to Lincoln now forced to use up its energies in a conflict as lamentable as it is violent.

I shall give the observations I made in Jacksonville as seen through the light of after years; and they apply generally to every Southern community. The colored people may be said to be roughly divided into three classes, not so much in respect to themselves as in respect to their relations with the whites. There are those constituting what might be called the desperate class,—the men who work in the lumber and turpentine camps, the ex-convicts, the bar-room loafers are all in this class. These men conform to the requirements of civilization much as a trained lion with low muttered growls goes through his stunts under the crack of the trainer's whip. They cherish a sullen hatred for all white men, and they value life as cheap. I have heard more than one of them say, "I'll go to hell for the first white man that bothers me." Many who have expressed that sentiment have kept their word; and it is that fact which gives such prominence to this class; for in numbers it is but a small proportion of the colored people, but it often dominates public opinion concerning the whole race. Happily, this class represents the black people of the South far below their normal physical and moral condition, but in its increase lies the possibility of grave dangers. I am sure there is no more urgent work before the white South, not only for its present happiness, but its future safety, than the decreasing of this class of blacks. And it is not at all a hopeless class; for these men are but the creatures of conditions, as much so as the slum and criminal elements of all the great cities of the world are creatures of conditions. Decreasing their number by shooting and burning them of will not be successful, for these men are truly desperate, and thoughts of death, however terrible, have little effect in deterring them from acts the result of hatred or degeneracy. This class of blacks hate everything covered by a white skin, and in return they are loathed by the whites. The whites regard them just about as a man would a vicious mule, a thing to be worked, driven and beaten, and killed for kicking.

The second class, as regards the relation between blacks and whites, comprises the servants, the washer-women, the waiters, the cooks, the coachmen, and all who are connected with the whites by domestic service. These may be generally characterized as simple, kindhearted and faithful; not over fine in their moral deductions, but intensely religious, and relatively,—such matters can be judged only relatively,—about as honest and wholesome in their lives as any other grade of society. Any white person is "good" who treats them

kindly, and they love them for that kindness. In return, the white people with whom they have to do regard them with indulgent affection. They come into close daily contact with the whites, and may be called the connecting link between whites and blacks; in fact, it is through them that the whites know the rest of their colored neighbors. Between this class of the blacks and the whites there is little or no friction.

The third class is composed of the independent workmen and tradesmen, and of the well-to-do and educated colored people; and, strange to say, for a directly opposite reason they are as far removed from the whites as the members of the first class I mentioned. These people live in a little world of their own; in fact, I concluded that if a colored man wanted to separate himself from his white neighbors he had but to acquire some money, education and culture, and to live in accordance. For example the proudest and fairest lady in the South could with propriety—and it is what she would most likely do—go to the cabin of Aunt Mary, her cook, if Aunt Mary were sick, and minister to her comfort with her own hands; but if Mary's daughter, Eliza, a girl who used to run around my lady's kitchen, but who has received an education and married a prosperous young colored man, were at death's door, my lady would no more think of crossing the threshold of Eliza's cottage than she would of going into a bar-room for a drink.

I was walking down the street one day with a young man who was born in Jacksonville, but had been away to prepare himself for a professional life. We passed a young white man, and my companion said to me, "You see that young man? We grew up together, we have played, hunted, and fished together, we have even eaten and slept together, and now since I have come back home he barely speaks to me." The fact that the whites of the South despise and ill-treat the desperate class of blacks is not only explainable according to the ancient laws of human nature, but it is not nearly so serious or important as the fact that as the progressive colored people advance they constantly widen the gulf between themselves and their white neighbors. I think that the white people somehow feel that colored people who have education and money, who wear good clothes and live in comfortable houses, are "putting on airs," that they do these things for the sole purpose of "spiting the white folks," or are, at best, going through a sort of monkey-like imitation. Of course, such feelings can only cause irritation or breed disgust. It seems that the whites have not yet been able to realize and understand that these people in striving to better their physical and social surroundings in accordance with their financial and intellectual progress are simply obeying

an impulse which is common to human nature the world over. I am in grave doubt as to whether the greater part of the friction in the South is caused by the whites having a natural antipathy to Negroes as a race, or an acquired antipathy to Negroes in certain relations to themselves. However that may be, there is to my mind no more pathetic side of this many sided question than the isolated position into which are forced the very colored people who most need and who could best appreciate sympathetic coöperation; and their position grows tragic when the effort is made to couple them, whether or no, with the Negroes of the first class I mentioned.

This latter class of colored people are well disposed towards the whites, and always willing to meet them more than half way. They, however, feel keenly any injustice or gross discrimination, and generally show their resentment. The effort is sometimes made to convey the impression that the better class of colored people fight against riding in "jim crow" cars because they want to ride with white people or object to being with humbler members of their own race. The truth is they object to the humiliation of being forced to ride in a *particular* car, aside from the fact that that car is distinctly inferior, and that they are required to pay full first-class fare. To say that the whites are forced to ride in the superior car is less than a joke. And, too, odd as it may sound, refined colored people get no more pleasure out of riding with offensive Negroes than anybody else would get.

I can realize more fully than I could years ago that the position of the advanced element of the colored race is often very trying. They are the ones among the blacks who carry the entire weight of the race question; it worries the others very little, and I believe the only thing which at times sustains them is that they know that they are in the right. On the other hand, this class of colored people get a good deal of pleasure out of life; their existence is far from being one long groan about their condition. Out of a chaos of ignorance and poverty they have evolved a social life of which they need not be ashamed. In cities where the professional and well-to-do class is large, they have formed society,—society as discriminating as the actual conditions will allow it to be; I should say, perhaps, society possessing discriminating tendencies which become rules as fast as actual conditions allow. This statement will, I know, sound preposterous, even ridiculous, to some persons, but as this class of colored people is the least known of the race it is not surprising. These social circles are connected throughout the country, and a person in good standing in one city is readily accepted in another. One who is on the outside will often find it a difficult matter to get in. I know of one case per-

sonally in which money to the extent of thirty or forty thousand dollars and a fine house, not backed up by a good reputation, after several years of repeated effort, failed to gain entry for the possessor. These people have their dances and dinners and card parties, their musicals and their literary societies. The women attend social affairs dressed in good taste, and the men in evening dress-suits which they own; and the reader will make a mistake to confound these entertainments with the "Bellman's Balls" and "White-washers' Picnics" and "Lime Kiln Clubs" with which the humorous press of the country illustrates "Cullud Sassiety."

Jacksonville, when I was there, was a small town, and the number of educated and well-to-do colored people was few; so this society phase of life did not equal what I have since seen in Boston, Washington, Richmond, and Nashville; and it is upon what I have more recently seen in these cities that I have made the observations just above. However, there were many comfortable and pleasant homes in Jacksonville to which I was often invited. I belonged to the literary society—at which we generally discussed the race question—and attended all of the church festivals and other charitable entertainments. In this way I passed three years which were not at all the least enjoyable of my life. In fact, my joy took such an exuberant turn that I fell in love with a young school teacher and began to have dreams of matrimonial bliss; but another turn in the course of my life brought these dreams to an end.

I do not wish to mislead my readers into thinking that I led a life in Jacksonville which would make copy as the hero of a Sunday School library book. I was a hail fellow well met with all of the workmen at the factory, most of whom knew little and cared less about social distinctions. From their example I learned to be careless about money; and for that reason I constantly postponed and finally abandoned resuming to Atlanta University. It seemed impossible for me to save as much as two hundred dollars. Several of the men at the factory were my intimate friends, and I frequently joined them in their pleasures. During the summer months we went almost every Monday on an excursion to a seaside resort called Pablo Beach. These excursions were always crowded. There was a dancing pavilion, a great deal of drinking and generally a fight or two to add to the excitement. I also contracted the cigar-maker's habit of riding around in a hack on Sunday afternoons. I sometimes went with my cigar-maker friends to public balls that were given at a large hall on one of the main streets. I learned to take a drink occasionally and paid for quite a number that my friends took; but strong

liquors never appealed to my appetite. I drank them only when the company I was in required it, and suffered for it afterwards. On the whole, though I was a bit wild, I can't remember that I ever did anything disgraceful, or, as the usual standard for young men goes, anything to forfeit my claim to respectability.

At one of the first public balls I attended I saw the Pullman car porter who had so kindly assisted me in getting to Jacksonville. I went immediately to one of my factory friends and borrowed fifteen dollars with which to repay the loan my benefactor had made me. After I had given him the money, and was thanking him, I noticed that he wore what was, at least, an exact duplicate of my lamented black and gray tie. It was somewhat worn, but distinct enough for me to trace the same odd design which had first attracted my eye. This was enough to arouse my strongest suspicions, but whether it was sufficient for the law to take cognizance of I did not consider. My astonishment and the ironical humor of the situation drove everything else out of my mind.

These balls were attended by a great variety of people. They were generally given by the waiters of some one of the big hotels and were often patronized by a number of hotel guests who came to "see the sights." The crowd was always noisy, but good-natured; there was much quadrille dancing, and a strong-lunged man called figures in a voice which did not confine itself to the limits of the hall. It is not worth the while for me to describe in detail how these people acted; they conducted themselves in about the same manner as I have seen other people at similar balls conduct themselves. When one has seen something of the world and human nature he must conclude, after all, that between people in like stations of life there is very little difference the world over.

However, it was at one of these balls that I first saw the cake-walk. There was a contest for a gold watch, to be awarded to the hotel headwaiter receiving the greatest number of votes. There was some dancing while the votes were being counted. Then the floor was cleared for the cake-walk. A half-dozen guests from some of the hotels took seats on the stage to act as judges, and twelve or fourteen couples began to walk for a "sure enough" highly decorated cake, which was in plain evidence. The spectators crowded about the space reserved for the contestants and watched them with interest and excitement. The couples did not walk around in a circle, but in a square, with the men on the inside. The fine points to be considered were the bearing of the men, the precision with which they turned the corners, the grace of the

women, and the ease with which they swung around the pivots. The men walked with stately and soldierly step, and the women with considerable grace. The judges arrived at their decision by a process of elimination. The music and the walk continued for some minutes; then both were stopped while the judges conferred, when the walk began again several couples were left out. In this way the contest was finally narrowed down to three or four couples. Then the excitement became intense; there was much partisan cheering as one couple or another would execute a turn in extra elegant style. When the cake was finally awarded the spectators were about evenly divided between those who cheered the winners and those who muttered about the unfairness of the judges. This was the cake-walk in its original form, and it is what the colored performers on the theatrical stage developed into the prancing movements now known all over the world, and which some Parisian critics pronounced the acme of poetic motion.

There are a great many colored people who are ashamed of the cake-walk, but I think they ought to be proud of it. It is my opinion that the colored people of this country have done four things which refute the oft advanced theory that they are an absolutely inferior race, which demonstrate that they have originality and artistic conception; and, what is more, the power of creating that which can influence and appeal universally. The first two of these are the Uncle Remus stories, collected by Joel Chandler Harris, and the Jubilee songs, to which the Fisk singers made the public and the skilled musicians of both America and Europe listen. The other two are ragtime music and the cake-walk. No one who has traveled can question the world-conquering influence of ragtime and I do not think it would be an exaggeration to say that in Europe the United States is popularly known better by ragtime than by anything else it has produced in a generation. In Paris they call it American music. The newspapers have already told how the practice of intricate cake walk steps has taken up the time of European royalty and nobility. These are lower forms of art, but they give evidence of a power that will some day be applied to the higher forms. In this measure, at least, and aside from the number of prominent individuals the colored people of the United States have produced, the race has been a world influence, and all of the Indians between Alaska and Patagonia haven't done as much.

Just when I was beginning to look upon Jacksonville as my permanent home, and was beginning to plan about marrying the young school teacher, raising a family, and working in a cigar factory the rest of my life, for some reason, which I do not now remember, the factory at which I worked was

indefinitely shut down. Some of the men got work in other factories in town, some decided to go to Key West and Tampa others made up their minds to go to New York for work. All at once a desire like a fever seized me to see the North again, and I cast my lot with those bound for New York.

CHAPTER VI

W E STEAMED up into New York harbor late one afternoon in spring. The last efforts of the sun were being put forth in turning the waters of the bay to glistening gold; the green islands on either side, in spite of their warlike mountings, looked calm and peaceful; the buildings of the town shone out in a reflected light which gave the city an air of enchantment; and, truly, it is an enchanted spot. New York City is the most fatally fascinating thing in America. She sits like a great witch at the gate of the country, showing her alluring white face, and hiding her crooked hands and feet under the folds of her wide garments,—constantly enticing thousands from far within, and tempting those who come from across the seas to go no farther. And all these become the victims of her caprice. Some she at once crushes beneath her cruel feet others she condemns to a fate like that of galley slaves, a few she favors and fondles, riding them high on the bubbles of fortune, then with a sudden breath she blows the bubbles out and laughs mockingly as she watches them fall.

Twice I had passed through it; but this was really my first visit to New York, and as I walked about that evening I began to feel the dread power of the city; the crowds, the lights, the excitement, the gayety and all its subtler stimulating influences began to take effect upon me. My blood ran quicker, and I felt that I was just beginning to live. To some natures this stimulant of life in a great city becomes a thing as binding and necessary as opium is to one addicted to the habit. It becomes their breath of life; they cannot exist outside of it; rather than be deprived of it they are content to suffer hunger, want, pain and misery; they would not exchange even a ragged and wretched condition among the great crowd for any degree of comfort away from it.

As soon as we landed, four of us went directly to a lodging-house in 27th Street, just west of Sixth Avenue. The house was run by a short stout mulatto man, who was exceedingly talkative and inquisitive. In fifteen minutes he not only knew the history of the past life of each one of us, but had a clear-

er idea of what we intended to do in the future than we ourselves. He sought this information so much with an air of being very particular as to whom he admitted into his house that we tremblingly answered every question that he asked. When we had become located we went out and got supper, then walked around until about ten o'clock. At that hour we met a couple of young fellows who lived in New York and were known to one of the members of our party. It was suggested we go to a certain place which was known by the proprietor's name. We turned into one of the cross streets and mounted the stoop of a house in about the middle of a block between Sixth and Seventh Avenues. One of the young men whom we had met rang a bell, and a man on the inside cracked the door a couple of inches; then opened it and let us in. We found ourselves in the hallway of what had once been a residence. The front parlor had been converted into a bar, and a half dozen or so of well dressed men were in the room. We went in, and after a general introduction had several rounds of beer. In the back parlor a crowd was sitting and standing around the walls of the room watching an exciting and noisy game of pool. I walked back and joined this crowd to watch the game, and principally to get away from the drinking party. The game was really interesting, the players being quite expert, and the excitement was heightened by the bets which were being made on the result. At times the antics and remarks of both players and spectators were amusing. When, at a critical point, a player missed a shot he was deluged by those financially interested in his making it with a flood of epithets synonymous to "chump"; while from the others he would be jeered by such remarks as "Nigger, dat cue ain't no hoe-handle." I noticed that among this class of colored men the word "nigger" was freely used in about the same sense as the word "fellow," and sometimes as a term of almost endearment; but I soon learned that its use was positively and absolutely prohibited to white men.

I stood watching this pool game until I was called by my friends, who were still in the bar-room, to go upstairs. On the second floor there were two large rooms. From the hall I looked into the one on the front. There was a large, round table in the center, at which five or six men were seated playing poker. The air and conduct here were greatly in contrast to what I had just seen in the pool-room; these men were evidently the aristocrats of the place; they were well, perhaps a bit flashily, dressed and spoke in low modulated voices, frequently using the word "gentlemen"; in fact, they seemed to be practicing a sort of Chesterfieldian politeness towards each other. I was watching these men with a great deal of interest and some degree of admira-

tion, when I was again called by the members of our party, and I followed them on to the back room. There was a door-keeper at this room, and we were admitted only after inspection. When we got inside I saw a crowd of men of all ages and kinds grouped about an old billiard table, regarding some of whom, in supposing them to be white, I made no mistake. At first I did not know what these men were doing; they were using terms that were strange to me. I could hear only a confusion of voices exclaiming, "Shoot the two!" "Shoot the four!" "Fate me!" "Fate me!" "I've got you fated!" "Twenty-five cents he don't turn!" This was the ancient and terribly fascinating game of dice, popularly known as "craps." I, myself, had played pool in Jacksonville; it is a favorite game among cigar-makers, and I had seen others play cards; but here was something new. I edged my way in to the table and stood between one of my new-found New York friends and a tall, slender, black fellow, who was making side bets while the dice were at the other end of the table. My companion explained to me the principles of the game; and they are so simple that they hardly need to be explained twice. The dice came around the table until they reached the man on the other side of the tall, black fellow. He lost, and the latter said, "Gimme the bones." He threw a dollar on the table and said, "Shoot the dollar." His style of play was so stren-uous that he had to be allowed plenty of room. He shook the dice high above his head, and each time he threw them on the table he emitted a grunt such as men give when they are putting forth physical exertion with a rhythmic regularity. He frequently whirled completely around on his heels, throwing the dice the entire length of the table, and talking to them as though they were trained animals. He appealed to them in short singsong phrases. "Come dice," he would say. "Little Phoebe," "Little Joe," "'Way down yonder in the cornfield." Whether these mystic incantations were efficacious or not I could not say, but, at any rate, his luck was great, and he had what gamblers term "nerve." "Shoot the dollar!" "Shoot the two!" "Shoot the four!" "Shoot the eight!" came from his lips as quickly as the dice turned to his advantage. My companion asked me if I had ever played. I told him no. He said that I ought to try my luck; that everybody won at first. The tall man at my side was wav-ing his arms in the air exclaiming "Shoot the sixteen!" "Shoot the sixteen!" "Fate me!" Whether it was my companion's suggestion or some latent dare-devil strain in my blood which suddenly sprang into activity I do not know; but with a thrill of excitement which went through my whole body I threw a twenty dollar bill on the table and said in a trembling voice, "I fate you."

I could feel that I had gained the attention and respect of everybody in

the room, every eye was fixed on me, and the widespread question "Who is he?" went around. This was gratifying to a certain sense of vanity of which I have never been able to rid myself, and I felt that it was worth the money even if I lost. The tall man with a whirl on his heels and a double grunt threw the dice, four was the number which turned up. This is considered as a hard "point" to make. He redoubled his contortions and his grunts and his pleadings to the dice; but on his third or fourth throw the fateful seven turned up, and I had won. My companion and all my friends shouted to me to follow up my luck. The fever was on me. I seized the dice. My hands were so hot that the bits of bone felt like pieces of ice. I shouted as loudly as I could, "Shoot it all!" but the blood was tingling so about my ears that I could not hear my own voice. I was soon "fated." I threw the dice—seven—I had won. "Shoot it all!" I cried again. There was a pause; the stake was more than one man cared to or could cover. I was finally "fated" by several men taking "a part" of it. I then threw the dice again. Seven. I had won. "Shoot it all!" I shouted excitedly. After a short delay I was "fated." Again I rolled the dice. Eleven. Again I had won. My friends now surrounded me and, much against my inclination, forced me to take down all of the money except five dollars. I tried my luck once more, and threw some small "Point" which I failed to make, and the dice passed on to the next man.

In less than three minutes I had won more than two hundred dollars, a sum which afterwards cost me dearly. I was the hero of the moment, and was soon surrounded by a group of men who expressed admiration for my "nerve" and predicted for me a brilliant future as a gambler. Although at the time I had no thought of becoming a gambler I felt proud of my success. I felt a bit ashamed, too, that I had allowed my friends to persuade me to take down my money so soon. Another set of men also got around me, and begged me for twenty-five or fifty cents to put them back into the game. I gave each of them something. I saw that several of them had on linen dusters, and as I looked about I noticed that there were perhaps a dozen men in the room similarly clad. I asked the fellow who had been my prompter at the dice table why they dressed in such a manner. He told me that men who had lost all the money and jewelry they possessed, frequently, in an effort to recoup their losses would gamble away all their outer clothing and even their shoes; and that the proprietor kept on hand a supply of linen dusters for all who were so unfortunate. My informant went on to say that sometimes a fellow would become almost completely dressed and then, by a turn of the dice, would be thrown back into a state of semi-nakedness. Some of them were vir-

tually prisoners and unable to get into the streets for days at a time. They ate at the lunch counter, where their credit was good so long as they were fair gamblers and did not attempt to jump their debts, and they slept around in chairs. They importuned friends and winners to put them back in the game, and kept at it until fortune again smiled on them. I laughed heartily at this, not thinking the day was coming which would find me in the same ludicrous predicament.

On passing downstairs I was told that the third and top floor of the house was occupied by the proprietor. When we passed through the bar I treated everybody in the room,—and that was no small number, for eight or ten had followed us down. Then our party went out. It was now about half-past twelve, but my nerves were at such a tension that I could not endure the mere thought of going to bed. I asked if there was no other place to which we could go; our guides said yes, and suggested that we go to the "Club." We went to Sixth Avenue, walked two blocks, and turned to the west into another street. We stopped in front of a house with three stories and a basement. In the basement was a Chinese Chop-suey restaurant. There was a red lantern at the iron gate to the areaway, inside of which the Chinaman's name was printed. We went up the steps of the stoop, rang the bell, and were admitted without any delay. From the outside the house bore a rather gloomy aspect, the windows being absolutely dark, but within it was a veritable house of mirth. When we had passed through a small vestibule and reached the hallway we heard mingled sounds of music and laughter, the clink of glasses and the pop of bottles. We went into the main room, and I was little prepared for what I saw. The brilliancy of the place, the display of diamond rings, scarf-pins, ear-rings and breast-pins, the big rolls of money that were brought into evidence when drinks were paid for, and the air of gayety that pervaded, all completely dazzled and dazed me. I felt positively giddy, and it was several minutes before I was able to make any clear and definite observations.

We at length secured places at a table in a corner of the room, and as soon as we could attract the attention of one of the busy waiters ordered a round of drinks. When I had somewhat collected my senses I realized that in a large back room into which the main room opened, there was a young fellow singing a song, accompanied on the piano by a short, thickset, dark man. Between each verse he did some dance steps, which brought forth great applause and a shower of small coins at his feet. After the singer had responded to a rousing encore, the stout man at the piano began to run his fingers

up and down the keyboard. This he did in a manner which indicated that he was master of a good deal of technic. Then he began to play; and such playing! I stopped talking to listen. It was music of a kind I had never heard before. It was music that demanded physical response, patting of the feet, drumming of the fingers, or nodding of the head in time with the beat. The barbaric harmonies, the audacious resolutions often consisting of an abrupt jump from one key to another, the intricate rhythms in which the accents fell in the most unexpected places, but in which the beat was never lost, produced a most curious effect. And, too, the player,—the dexterity of his left hand in making rapid octave runs and jumps was little short of marvelous; and, with his right hand, he frequently swept half the keyboard with clean cut chromatics which he fitted in so nicely as never to fail to arouse in his listeners a sort of pleasant surprise at the accomplishment of the feat.

This was ragtime music, then a novelty in New York, and just growing to be a rage which has not yet subsided. It was originated in the questionable resorts about Memphis and St. Louis by Negro piano players, who knew no more of the theory of music than they did of the theory of the universe, but were guided by natural musical instinct and talent. It made its way to Chicago, where it was popular some time before it reached New York. These players often improvised crude and, at times, vulgar words to fit the melodies. This was the beginning of the ragtime song. Several of these improvisations were taken down by white men, the words slightly altered, and published under the names of the arrangers. They sprang into immediate popularity and earned small fortunes, of which the Negro originators got only a few dollars. But I have learned that since that time a number of colored men, of not only musical talent, but training, are writing out their own melodies and words and reaping the reward of their work. I have learned also that they have a large number of white imitators and adulterators.

American musicians, instead of investigating ragtime, attempt to ignore it or dismiss it with a contemptuous word. But that has always been the course of scholasticism in every branch of art. Whatever new thing the *people* like is pooh-poohed, whatever is *popular* is spoken of as not worth the while. The fact is, nothing great or enduring, especially in music, has ever sprung full-fledged and unprecedented from the brain of any master; the best that he gives to the world he gathers from the hearts of the people, and runs it through the alembic of his genius. In spite of the bans which musicians and music teachers have placed upon it, the people still demand and enjoy ragtime. One thing cannot be denied; it is music which possesses at least one

strong element of greatness; it appeals universally; not only the American, but the English, the French, and even the German people, find delight in it. In fact, there is not a corner of the civilized world in which it is not known, and this proves its originality; for if it were an imitation, the people of Europe, anyhow, would not have found it a novelty. Anyone who doubts that there is a peculiar heel-tickling, smile-provoking, joy-awakening charm in ragtime needs only to hear a skillful performer play the genuine article to be convinced. I believe that it has its place as well as the music which draws from us sighs and tears.

I became so interested in both the music and the player that I left the table where I was sitting, and made my way through the hall into the back room, where I could see as well as hear. I talked to the piano player between the musical numbers, and found out that he was just a natural musician, never having taken a lesson in his life. Not only could he play almost anything he heard, but could accompany singers in songs he had never heard. He had by ear alone, composed some pieces, several of which he played over for me; each of them was properly proportioned and balanced. I began to wonder what this man with such a lavish natural endowment would have done had he been trained. Perhaps he wouldn't have done anything at all; he might have become, at best, a mediocre imitator of the great masters in what they have already done to a finish, or one of the modern innovators who strive after originality by seeing how cleverly they can dodge about through the rules of harmony, and at the same time avoid melody. It is certain that he would not have been so delightful as he was in ragtime.

I sat by watching and listening to this man until I was dragged away by my friends. The place was now almost deserted; only a few stragglers hung on, and they were all the worse for drink. My friends were well up in this class. We passed into the street; the lamps were pale against the sky; day was just breaking. We went home and got into bed. I fell into a fitful sort of sleep with ragtime music ringing continually in my ears.

CHAPTER VII

I SHALL take advantage of this pause in my narrative to more closely describe the "Club" spoken of in the latter part of the preceding chapter,—to describe it, as I afterwards came to know it, as an habitue. I shall do

this, not only because of the direct influence it had on my life, but also because it was at that time the most famous place of its kind in New York, and was well known to both white and colored people of certain classes.

I have already stated that in the basement of the house there was a Chinese restaurant. The Chinaman who kept it did an exceptionally good business; for chop-suey was a favorite dish among the frequenters of the place. It is a food that, somehow, has the power of absorbing alcoholic liquors that have been taken into the stomach. I have heard men claim that they could sober up on chop-suey. Perhaps that accounted, in some degree, for its popularity. On the main floor there were two large rooms, a parlor about thirty feet in length and a large square back room into which the parlor opened. The floor of the parlor was carpeted; small tables and chairs were arranged about the room; the windows were draped with lace curtains, and the walls were literally covered with photographs or lithographs of every colored man in America who had ever "done anything." There were pictures of Frederick Douglass and of Peter Jackson, of all the lesser lights of the prize-fighting ring, of all the famous jockeys and the stage celebrities, down to the newest song and dance team. The most of these photographs were autographed and, in a sense, made a really valuable collection. In the back room there was a piano; and tables were placed around the wall. The floor was bare and the center was left vacant for singers, dancers and others who entertained the patrons. In a closet in this room which jutted out into the hall the proprietor kept his buffet. There was no open bar, because the place had no liquor license. In this back room the tables were sometimes pushed aside, and the floor given over to general dancing. The front room on the next floor was a sort of private party room; a back room on the same floor contained no furniture, and was devoted to the use of new and ambitious performers. In this room song and dance teams practiced their steps, acrobatic teams practiced their tumbles, and many other kinds of "acts" rehearsed their "turns." The other rooms of the house were used as sleeping apartments.

No gambling was allowed, and the conduct of the place was surprisingly orderly. It was, in short, a center of colored bohemians and sports. Here the great prize fighters were wont to come, the famous jockeys, the noted minstrels, whose names and faces were familiar on every bill-board in the country; and these drew a multitude of those who love to dwell in the shadow of greatness. There were then no organizations giving performances of such order as are now given by several colored companies; that was because no manager could imagine that audiences would pay to see Negro performers in

any other rôle than that of Mississippi River roustabouts; but there was lots of talent and ambition. I often heard the younger and brighter men discussing the time when they would compel the public to recognize that they could do something more than grin and cut pigeon wings.

Sometimes one or two of the visiting stage professionals, after being sufficiently urged, would go into the back room, and take the places of the regular amateur entertainers, but they were very sparing with these favors, and the patrons regarded them as special treats. There was one man, a minstrel, who, whenever he responded to a request to "do something," never essayed anything below a reading from Shakespeare. How well he read I do not know, but he greatly impressed me; and I can, at least, say that he had a voice which strangely stirred those who heard it. Here was a man who made people laugh at the size of his mouth, while he carried in his heart a burning ambition to be a tragedian; and so after all he did play a part in a tragedy.

These notables of the ring, the turf and the stage, drew to the place crowds of admirers, both white and colored. Whenever one of them came in there were awe-inspired whispers from those who knew him by sight, in which they enlightened those around them as to his identity, and hinted darkly at their great intimacy with the noted one. Those who were on terms of approach immediately showed their privilege over others less fortunate by gathering around their divinity. I was, at first, among those who dwelt in darkness. Most of these celebrities I had never heard of. This made me an object of pity among many of my new associates. I, however, soon learned to fake a knowledge for the benefit of those who were greener than I; and, finally, I became personally acquainted with the majority of the famous personages who came to the "Club."

A great deal of money was spent here; so many of the patrons were men who earned large sums. I remember one night a dapper little brown-skinned fellow was pointed out to me, and I was told that he was the most popular jockey of the day, and that he earned $12,000 a year. This latter statement I couldn't doubt, for with my own eyes I saw him spending at about that rate. For his friends and those who were introduced to him he bought nothing but wine;-in the sporting circle, "wine" means champagne-and paid for it at five dollars a quart. He sent a quart to every table in the place with his compliments; and on the table at which he and his party were seated there were more than a dozen bottles. It was the custom at the "Club" for the waiter not to remove the bottles when champagne was being drunk until the party had finished. There were reasons for this; it advertised the brand of wine, it adver-

tised that the party was drinking wine, and advertised how much they had bought. This jockey had won a great race that day, and he was rewarding his admirers for the homage they paid him, all of which he accepted with a fine air of condescension.

Besides the people I have just been describing there was at the place almost every night one or two parties of white people, men and women, who were out sight-seeing, or slumming. They generally came in cabs; some of them would stay only for a few minutes, while others sometimes stayed until morning. There was also another set of white people who came frequently; it was made up of variety performers and others who delineated darky characters; they came to get their imitations first hand from the Negro entertainers they saw there.

There was still another set of white patrons, composed of women; these were not occasional visitors, but five or six of them were regular habitues. When I first saw them I was not sure that they were white. In the first place, among the many colored women who came to the "Club" there were several just as fair; and, secondly, I always saw these women in company with colored men. They were all good-looking and well dressed, and seemed to be women of some education. One of these in particular attracted my attention; she was an exceedingly beautiful woman of perhaps thirty-five; she had glistening copper-colored hair, very white skin and eyes very much like Du Maurier's conception of Trilby's "twin gray stars." When I came to know her I found that she was a woman of considerable culture; she had traveled in Europe, spoke French, and played the piano well. She was always dressed elegantly, but in absolute good taste. She always came to the "Club" in a cab, and was soon joined by a well set up, very black young fellow. He was always faultlessly dressed; one of the most exclusive tailors in New York made his clothes, and he wore a number of diamonds in about as good taste as they could be worn by a man. I learned that she paid for his clothes and his diamonds. I learned, too, that he was not the only one of his kind. More that I learned would be better suited to a book on social phenomena than to a narrative of my life.

This woman was known at the "Club" as the rich widow. She went by a very aristocratic sounding name, which corresponded to her appearance. I shall never forget how hard it was for me to get over my feelings of surprise, perhaps more than surprise, at seeing her with her black companion; somehow I never exactly enjoyed the sight. I have devoted so much time to this pair, the "widow" and her companion, because it was through them that

another decided turn was brought about in my life.

CHAPTER VIII

O N THE day following our night at the "Club" we slept until late in the afternoon, so late that beginning of search for work was entirely out of the question. This did not cause me much worry, for I had more than three hundred dollars, and New York had impressed me as a place where there was lots of money and not much difficulty in getting it. It is needless to inform my readers that I did not long hold this opinion. We got out of the house about dark, went round to a restaurant on Sixth Avenue and ate something, then walked around for a couple of hours. I finally suggested that we visit the same places we had been in the night before. Following my suggestion we started first to the gambling house. The man on the door let us in without any question; I accredited this to my success of the night before. We went straight to the "crap" room, and I at once made my way to a table, where I was rather flattered by the murmur of recognition which went around. I played in up and down luck for three or four hours; then, worn with nervous excitement, quit, having lost about fifty dollars. But I was so strongly possessed with the thought that I would make up my losses the next time I played that I left the place with a light heart.

When we got into the street our party was divided against itself; two were for going home at once and getting to bed. They gave as a reason that we were to get up early and look for jobs. I think the real reason was that they had each lost several dollars in the game. I lived to learn that in the world of sport all men win alike but lose differently; and so gamblers are rated, not by the way in which they win, but by the way in which they lose. Some men lose with a careless smile, recognizing that losing is a part of the game; others curse their luck and rail at fortune; and others, still, lose sadly; after each such experience they are swept by a wave of reform; they resolve to stop gambling and be good. When in this frame of mind it would take very little persuasion to lead them into a prayer-meeting. Those in the first class are looked upon with admiration, those in the second class are merely commonplace; while those in the third are regarded with contempt. I believe these distinctions hold good in all the ventures of life. After some minutes one of my friends and I succeeded in convincing the other two that a while at the

"Club" would put us all in better spirits; and they consented to go on our promise not to stay longer than an hour. We found the place crowded, and the same sort of thing going on which we had seen the night before. I took a seat at once by the side of the piano player, and was soon lost to everything else except the novel charm of the music. I watched the performer with the idea of catching the trick; and, during one of his intermissions, I took his place at the piano and made an attempt to imitate him, but even my quick ear and ready fingers were unequal to the task on first trial.

We did not stay at the "Club" very long, but went home to bed in order to be up early the next day. We had no difficulty in finding work, and my third morning in New York found me at a table rolling cigars. I worked steadily for some weeks, at the same time spending my earnings between the "crap" game and the "Club." Making cigars became more and more irksome to me; perhaps my more congenial work as a "reader" had unfitted me for work at the table. And, too, the late hours I was keeping made such a sedentary occupation almost beyond the powers of will and endurance. I often found it hard to keep my eyes open and sometimes had to get up and move around to keep from falling asleep. I began to miss whole days from the factory, days on which I was compelled to stay at home and sleep.

My luck at the gambling table was varied; sometimes I was fifty to a hundred dollars ahead, and at other times I had to borrow money from my fellow workmen to settle my room rent and pay for my meals. Each night after leaving the dice game I went to the "Club" to hear the music and watch the gayety. If I had won, this was in accord with my mood, if I had lost, it made me forget. I at last realized that making cigars for a living and gambling for a living could not both be carried on at the same time, and I resolved to give up the cigar-making. This resolution led me into a life which held me bound more than a year. During that period my regular time for going to bed was somewhere between four and six o'clock in the mornings. I got up late in the afternoons, walked about a little, then went to the gambling house or the "Club." My New York was limited to ten blocks; the boundaries were Sixth Avenue from Twenty-third to Thirty-third Streets, with the cross streets one block to the west. Central Park was a distant forest, and the lower part of the city a foreign land. I look back upon the life I then led with a shudder when I think what would have been had I not escaped it. But had I not escaped it, I would have been no more unfortunate than are many young colored men who come to New York. During that dark period I became acquainted with a score of bright, intelligent young fellows who had come up to the great city

with high hopes and ambitions, and who had fallen under the spell of this under life, a spell they could not throw off. There was one popularly known as "the doctor"; he had had two years in the Harvard Medical School; but here he was, living this gas-light life, his will and moral sense so enervated and deadened that it was impossible for him to break away. I do not doubt that the same thing is going on now, but I have rather sympathy than censure for these victims, for I know how easy it is to slip into a slough from which it takes a herculean effort to leap.

I regret that I cannot contrast my views of life among colored people of New York; but the truth is, during my entire stay in this city I did not become acquainted with a single respectable family. I knew that there were several colored men worth a hundred or so thousand dollars each, and some families who proudly dated their free ancestry back a half-dozen generations. I also learned that in Brooklyn there lived quite a large colony in comfortable homes, most of which they owned; but at no point did my life come in contact with theirs.

In my gambling experiences I passed through all the states and conditions that a gambler is heir to. Some days found me able to peel ten and twenty dollar bills from a roll, and others found me clad in a linen duster and carpet slippers. I finally caught up another method of earning money, and so did not have to depend entirely upon the caprices of fortune at the gaming table. Through continually listening to the music at the "Club," and through my own previous training, my natural talent and perseverance, I developed into a remarkable player of ragtime; indeed, I had the name at that time of being the best ragtime player in New York. I brought all my knowledge of classic music to bear and, in so doing, achieved some novelties which pleased and even astonished my listeners. It was I who first made ragtime transcriptions of familiar classic selections. I used to play Mendelssohn's "Wedding March" in a manner that never failed to arouse enthusiasm among the patrons of the "Club." Very few nights passed during which I was not asked to play it. It was no secret that the great increase in slumming visitors was due to my playing. By mastering ragtime I gained several things; first of all, I gained the title of professor. I was known as the "professor" as long as I remained in that world. Then, too, I gained the means of earning a rather fair livelihood. This work took up much of my time and kept me almost entirely away from the gambling table. Through it I also gained a friend who was the means by which I escaped from this lower world. And, finally, I secured a wedge which has opened to me more doors and made me a welcome guest than my play-

ing of Beethoven and Chopin could ever have done.

The greater part of the money I now began to earn came through the friend to whom I alluded in the foregoing paragraph. Among the other white "slummers" there came into the "Club" one night a clean cut slender, but athletic looking man, who would have been taken for a youth had it not been for the tinge of gray about his temples. He was clean shaven, had regular features, and all of his movements bore the indefinable but unmistakable stamp of culture. He spoke to no one, but sat languidly puffing cigarettes and sipping a glass of beer. He was the center of a great deal of attention, all of the old timers were wondering who he was. When I had finished playing he called a waiter and by him sent me a five-dollar bill. For about a month after that he was at the "Club" one or two nights each week, and each time after I had played he gave me five dollars. One night he sent for me to come to his table; he asked me several questions about myself; then told me that he had an engagement which he wanted me to fill. He gave me a card containing his address and asked me to be there on a certain night.

I was on hand promptly, and found that he was giving a dinner in his own apartments to a party of ladies and gentlemen, and that I was expected to furnish the musical entertainment. When the grave, dignified man at the door let me in, the place struck me as being almost dark my eyes had been so accustomed to the garish light of the "Club." He took my coat and hat, bade me take a seat, and went to tell his master that I had come. When my eyes were adjusted to the soft light I saw that I was in the midst of elegance and luxury in such a degree as I had never seen; but not the elegance which makes one ill at ease. As I sank into a great chair the subdued tone, the delicately sensuous harmony of my surroundings drew from me a deep sigh of relief and comfort. How long the man was gone I do not know; but I was startled by a voice saying "Come this way, if you please, sir," and I saw him standing by my chair. I had been asleep; and I awoke very much confused and a little ashamed because I did not know how many times he may have called me. I followed him through into the dining-room, where the butler was putting the finishing touches to a table which already looked like a big jewel. The doorman turned me over to the butler, and I passed with the butler on back to where several waiters were busy polishing and assorting table utensils. Without being asked whether I was hungry or not, I was placed at a table and given something to eat. Before I had finished eating I heard the laughter and talk of the guests who were arriving. Soon afterwards I was called in to begin my work.

I passed in to where the company was gathered, and went directly to the piano. According to a suggestion from the host I began with classic music. During the first number there was absolute quiet and appreciative attention, and when I had finished I was given a round of generous applause. After that the talk and the laughter began to grow until the music was only an accompaniment to the chatter. This, however, did not disconcert me as it once would have done, for I had become accustomed to playing in the midst of uproarious noise. As the guests began to pay less attention to me I was enabled to pay more to them. There were about a dozen of them. The men ranged in appearance from a girlish looking youth to a big grizzled man whom everybody addressed as "Judge." None of the women appeared to be under thirty, but each of them struck me as being handsome. I was not long in finding out that they were all decidedly blasé. Several of the women smoked cigarettes, and with a careless grace which showed they were used to the habit. Occasionally a "damn it!" escaped from the lips of some one of them, but in such a charming way as to rob it of all vulgarity. The most notable thing which I observed was that the reserve of the host increased in direct proportion with the hilarity of his guests. I thought that there was something going wrong which displeased him. I afterwards reamed that it was his habitual manner on such occasions. He seemed to take cynical delight in watching and studying others indulging in excess. His guests were evidently accustomed to his rather non-participating attitude, for it did not seem in any degree to dampen their spirits.

When dinner was served the piano was moved and the door left open, so that the company might hear the music while eating. At a word from the host I struck up one of my liveliest ragtime pieces. The effect was perhaps surprising, even to the host; the ragtime music came very near spoiling the party so far as eating the dinner was concerned. As soon as I began the conversation stopped suddenly. It was a pleasure to me to watch the expression of astonishment and delight that grew on the faces of everybody. These were people,—and they represented a large class,—who were ever expecting to find happiness in novelty, each day restlessly exploring and exhausting every resource of this great city that might possibly furnish a new sensation or awaken a fresh emotion, and who were always grateful to anyone who aided them in their quest. Several of the women left the table and gathered about the piano. They watched my fingers, asked what kind of music it was that I was playing, where I had learned it and a host of other questions. It was only by being repeatedly called back to the table that they were induced to finish

their dinner. When the guests arose I struck up my ragtime transcription of Mendelssohn's "Wedding March," playing it with terrific chromatic octave runs in the base. This raised everybody's spirits to the highest point of gayety, and the whole company involuntarily and unconsciously did an impromptu cake-walk. From that time on until the time of leaving they kept me so busy that my arms ached. I obtained a little respite when the girlish looking youth and one or two of the ladies sang several songs, but after each of these it was, "back to ragtime."

In leaving, the guests were enthusiastic in telling the host that he had furnished them the most unique entertainment they had "ever" enjoyed. When they had gone, my millionaire friend,—for he was reported to be a millionaire,—said to me with a smile, "Well, I have given them something they've never had before." After I had put on my coat and was ready to leave he made me take a glass of wine; he then gave me a cigar and twenty dollars in bills. He told me that he would give me lots of work, his only stipulation being that I should not play any engagements such as I had just filled for him, except by his instructions. I readily accepted the proposition, for I was sure that I could not be the loser by such a contract.

I afterwards played for him at many dinners and parties of one kind or another. Occasionally he "loaned" me to some of his friends. And, too, I often played for him alone at his apartments. At such times he was quite a puzzle to me until I became accustomed to his manners. He would sometimes sit for three or four hours hearing me play, his eyes almost closed, making scarcely a motion except to light a fresh cigarette, and never commenting one way or another on the music. At first, I used sometimes to think that he had fallen asleep and would pause in playing. The stopping of the music always aroused him enough to tell me to play this or that; and I soon learned that my task was not to be considered finished until he got up from his chair and said, "That will do." The man's powers of endurance in listening often exceeded mine in performing—yet I am not sure that he was always listening. At times I became so oppressed with fatigue and sleepiness that it took almost superhuman effort to keep my fingers going; in fact I believe I sometimes did so while dozing. During such moments, this man sitting there so mysteriously silent, almost hid in a cloud of heavy-scented smoke, filled me with a sort of unearthly terror. He seemed to be some grim, mute, but relentless tyrant, possessing over me a supernatural power which he used to drive me on mercilessly to exhaustion. But these feelings came very rarely; besides, he paid me so liberally I could forget much. There at length grew between us

a familiar and warm relationship; and I am sure he had a decided personal liking for me. On my part, I looked upon him at that time as about all a man could wish to be.

The "Club" still remained my headquarters, and when I was not playing for my good patron I was generally to be found there. However, I no longer depended on playing at the "Club" to earn my living; I rather took rank with the visiting celebrities and, occasionally, after being sufficiently urged, would favor my old and new admirers with a number or two. I say, without any egotistic pride, that among my admirers were several of the best looking women who frequented the place and who made no secret of the fact that they admired me as much as they did my playing. Among these was the "widow"; indeed, her attentions became so marked that one of my friends warned me to beware of her black companion, who was generally known as a "bad man." He said there was much more reason to be careful because the pair had lately quarreled, and had not been together at the "Club" for some nights. This warning greatly impressed me and I resolved to stop the affair before it should go any further; but the woman was so beautiful that my native gallantry and delicacy would not allow me to repulse her; my finer feelings entirely overcame my judgment. The warning also opened my eyes sufficiently to see that though my artistic temperament and skill made me interesting and attractive to the woman, she was, after all, using me only to excite the jealousy of her companion—and revenge herself upon him. It was this surly black despot who held sway over her deepest emotions.

One night, shortly afterwards, I went into the "Club" and saw the "widow" sitting at a table in company with another woman. She at once beckoned for me to come to her. I went, knowing that I was committing worse than folly. She ordered a quart of champagne and insisted that I sit down and drink with her. I took a chair on the opposite side of the table and began to sip a glass of the wine. Suddenly I noticed by an expression on the "widow's" face that something had occurred. I instinctively glanced around and saw that her companion had just entered. His ugly look completely frightened me. My back was turned to him, but by watching the "widow's" eyes I judged that he was pacing back and forth across the room. My feelings were far from being comfortable, I expected every moment to feel a blow on my head. She, too, was very nervous; she was trying hard to appear unconcerned, but could not succeed in hiding her real feelings. I decided that it was best to get out of such a predicament even at the expense of appearing cowardly, and I made a motion to rise. Just as I partly turned in my chair, I saw

the black fellow approaching; he walked directly to our table and leaned over. The "Widow" evidently feared he was going to strike her, and she threw back her head. Instead of striking her he whipped out a revolver and fired; the first shot went straight into her throat. There were other shots fired, but how many I do not know; for the first knowledge I had of my surroundings and actions was that I was rushing through the chop-suey restaurant into the street. Just which streets I followed when I got outside I do not know, but I think I must have gone towards Eighth Avenue, then down towards Twenty-third Street and across towards Fifth Avenue. I traveled not by sight, but instinctively. I felt like one fleeing in a horrible nightmare.

How long and far I walked I cannot tell; but on Fifth Avenue, under a light, I passed a cab containing a solitary occupant, who called to me, and I recognized the voice and face of my millionaire friend. He stopped the cab and asked, "What on earth are you doing strolling in this part of the town?" For answer I got into the cab and related to him all that had happened. He reassured me by saying that no charge of any kind could be brought against me; then added, "But, of course, you don't want to be mixed up in such an affair." He directed the driver to turn around and go into the park, and then went on to say, "I decided last night that I'd go to Europe to-morrow. I think I'll take you along instead of Walter." Walter was his valet. It was settled that I should go to his apartments for the rest of the night and sail with him in the morning.

We drove around through the park, exchanging only an occasional word. The cool air somewhat calmed my nerves and I lay back and closed my eyes; but still I could see that beautiful white throat with the ugly wound. The jet of blood pulsing from it had placed an indelible red stain on my memory.

CHAPTER IX

I DID not feel at ease until the ship was well out of New York harbor; and, notwithstanding the repeated reassurances of my millionaire friend and my own knowledge of the facts in the case, I somehow could not rid myself of the sentiment that I was, in a great degree, responsible for the widow's tragic end. We had brought most of the morning papers aboard with us, but my great fear of seeing my name in connection with the killing would not permit me to read the accounts, although, in one of the papers, I did look at

the picture of the victim, which did not in the least resemble her. This morbid state of mind, together with seasickness kept me miserable for three or four days. At the end of that time my spirits began to revive, and I took an interest in the ship, my fellow passengers, and the voyage in general. On the second or third day out we passed several spouting whales; but I could not arouse myself to make the effort to go to the other side of the ship to see them. A little later we ran in close proximity to a large iceberg. I was curious enough to get up and look at it, and I was fully repaid for my pains. The sun was shining full upon it, and it glistened like a mammoth diamond, cut with a million facets. As we passed it constantly changed its shape; at each different angle of vision it assumed new and astonishing forms of beauty. I watched it through a pair of glasses, seeking to verify my early conception of an iceberg—in the geographies of my grammar-school days the pictures of icebergs always included a stranded polar bear, standing desolately upon one of the snowy crags. I looked for the bear, but if he was there he refused to put himself on exhibition.

It was not, however, until the morning that we entered the harbor of Havre that I was able to shake off my gloom. Then the strange sights, the chatter in an unfamiliar tongue and the excitement of landing and passing the customs officials caused me to forget completely the events of a few days before. Indeed, I grew so light-hearted that when I caught my first sight of the train which was to take us to Paris, I enjoyed a hearty laugh. The toy-looking engine, the stuffy little compartment cars with tiny, old-fashioned wheels, struck me as being extremely funny. But before we reached Paris my respect for our train rose considerably. I found that the "tiny" engine made remarkably fast time, and that the old fashioned wheels ran very smoothly. I even began to appreciate the "stuffy" cars for their privacy. As I watched the passing scenery from the car window it seemed too beautiful to be real. The bright-colored houses against the green background impressed me as the work of some idealistic painter. Before we arrived in Paris there was awakened in my heart a love for France which continued to grow stronger, a love which to-day makes that country for me the one above all others to be desired.

We rolled into the station Saint Lazare about four o'clock in the afternoon, and drove immediately to the Hotel Continental. My benefactor, humoring my curiosity and enthusiasm, which seemed to please him very much, suggested that we take a short walk before dinner. We stepped out of the hotel and turned to the right into the Rue de Rivoli. When the vista of

the Place de la Concorde and the Champs Elysées suddenly burst on me I could hardly credit my own eyes. I shall attempt no such superogatory task as a description of Paris. I wish only to give briefly the impressions which that wonderful city made upon me. It impressed me as the perfect and perfectly beautiful city; and even after I had been there for some time, and seen not only its avenues and palaces, but its most squalid alleys and hovels, this impression was not weakened. Paris became for me a charmed spot, and whenever I have returned there I have fallen under the spell, a spell which compels admiration for all of its manners and customs and justification of even its follies and sins.

We walked a short distance up the Champs Elysées and sat for a while in chairs along the sidewalk, watching the passing crowds on foot and in carriages. It was with reluctance that I went back to the hotel for dinner. After dinner we went to one of the summer theaters, and after the performance my friend took me to a large café on one of the grand boulevards. Here it was that I had my first glimpse of the French life of popular literature, so different from real French life. There were several hundred people, men and women, in the place drinking, smoking, talking, and listening to the music. My millionaire friend and I took seats at a table where we sat smoking and watching the crowd. It was not long before we were joined by two or three good-looking, well-dressed young women. My friend talked to them in French and bought drinks for the whole party. I tried to recall my high school French, but the effort availed me little. I could stammer out a few phrases, but, very naturally, could not understand a word that was said to me. We stayed at the café a couple of hours, then went back to the hotel. The next day we spent several hours in the shops and at the tailors. I had no clothes except what I had been able to gather together at my benefactor's apartments the night before we sailed. He bought me the same kind of clothes which he himself wore, and that was the best; and he treated me in every way as he dressed me, as an equal, not as a servant. In fact, I don't think anyone could have guessed that such a relation existed. My duties were light and few, and he was a man full of life and vigor, who rather enjoyed doing things for himself. He kept me supplied with money far beyond what ordinary wages would have amounted to. For the first two weeks we were together almost constantly, seeing the sights, sights old to him, but from which he seemed to get new pleasure in showing them to me. During the day we took in the places of interest, and at night the theaters and cafés. This sort of life appealed to me as ideal, and I asked him one day how long he intended to stay in Paris.

He answered, "Oh, until I get tired of it." I could not understand how that could ever happen. As it was, including several short trips to the Mediterranean, to Spain, to Brussels, and to Ostend, we did remain there fourteen or fifteen months. We stayed at the Hotel Continental about two months of this time. Then my millionaire took apartments, hired a piano, and lived almost the same life he lived in New York. He entertained a great deal, some of the parties being a good deal more blasé than the New York ones. I played for the guests at all of them with an effect which to relate would be but a tiresome repetition to the reader. I played not only for the guests, but continued, as I used to do in New York, to play often for the host when he was alone. This man of the world, who grew weary of everything, and was always searching for something new, appeared never to grow tired of my music; he seemed to take it as a drug. He fell into a habit which caused me no little annoyance; sometimes he would come in during the early hours of the morning, and finding me in bed asleep, would wake me up and ask me to play something. This, so far as I can remember, was my only hardship during my whole stay with him in Europe.

After the first few weeks spent in sight-seeing, I had a great deal of time left to myself; my friend was often I did not know where. When not with him I spent the day nosing about all the curious nooks and corners of Paris; of this I never grew tired. At night I usually went to some theater, but always ended up at the big café on the Grand Boulevards. I wish the reader to know that it was not alone the gayety which drew me there; aside from that I had a laudable purpose. I had purchased an English-French conversational dictionary, and I went there every night to take a language lesson. I used to get three or four of the young women who frequented the place at a table and buy beer and cigarettes for them. In return I received my lesson. I got more than my money's worth; for they actually compelled me to speak the language. This, together with reading the papers every day, enabled me within a few months to express myself fairly well, and, before I left Paris, to have more than an ordinary command of French. Of course, every person who goes to Paris could not dare to learn French in this manner, but I can think of no easier or quicker way of doing it. The acquiring of another foreign language awoke me to the fact that with a little effort I could secure an added accomplishment as fine and as valuable as music; so I determined to make myself as much of a linguist as possible. I bought a Spanish newspaper every day in order to freshen my memory on that language, and, for French, devised what was, so far as I knew, an original system of study. I compiled a

list which I termed "Three hundred necessary words." These I thoroughly committed to memory, also the conjugation of the verbs which were included in the list. I studied these words over and over, much like children of a couple of generations ago studied the alphabet. I also practiced a set of phrases like the following: "How?" "What did you say?" "What does the word — — mean?" "I understand all you say except —— ." "Please repeat." "What do you call —— ?" "How do you say —— ?" These I called my working sentences. In an astonishingly short time I reached the point where the language taught itself,—where I learned to speak merely by speaking. This point is the place which students taught foreign languages in our schools and colleges find great difficulty in reaching. I think the main trouble is that they learn too much of a language at a time. A French child with a vocabulary of two hundred words can express more spoken ideas than a student of French can with a knowledge of two thousand. A small vocabulary, the smaller the better, which embraces the common, everyday—used ideas, thoroughly mastered, is the key to a language. When that much is acquired the vocabulary can be increased simply by talking. And it is easy. Who cannot commit three hundred words to memory? Later I tried my method, if I may so term it, with German, and found that it worked in the same way.

I spent a good many evenings at the Grand Opera. The music there made me strangely reminiscent of my life in Connecticut, it was an atmosphere in which I caught a fresh breath of my boyhood days and early youth. Generally, in the morning, after I had attended a performance, I would sit at the piano and for a couple of hours play the music which I used to play in my mother's little parlor.

One night I went to hear "Faust." I got into my seat just as the lights went down for the first act. At the end of the act I noticed that my neighbor on the left was a young girl. I cannot describe her either as to feature, color of her hair, or of her eyes; she was so young, so fair, so ethereal, that I felt to stare at her would be a violation; yet I was distinctly conscious of her beauty. During the intermission she spoke English in a low voice to a gentleman and a lady who sat in the seats to her left, addressing them as father and mother. I held my programme as though studying it, but listened to catch every sound of her voice. Her observations on the performance and the audience were so fresh and naive as to be almost amusing. I gathered that she was just out of school, and that this was her first trip to Paris. I occasionally stole a glance at her, and each time I did so my heart leaped into my throat. Once I glanced beyond to the gentleman who sat next to her. My glance immedi-

ately turned into a stare. Yes, there he was, unmistakably, my father! looking hardly a day older than when I had seen him some ten years before. What a strange coincidence! What should I say to him? What would he say to me? Before I had recovered from my first surprise there came another shock in the realization that the beautiful, tender girl at my side was my sister. Then all the springs of affection in my heart, stopped since my mother's death, burst out in fresh and terrible torrents, and I could have fallen at her feet and worshiped her. They were singing the second act, but I did not hear the music. Slowly the desolate loneliness of my position became clear to me. I knew that I could not speak, but I would have given a part of my life to touch her hand with mine and call her sister. I sat through the opera until I could stand it no longer. I felt that I was suffocating. Valentine's love seemed like mockery, and I felt an almost uncontrollable impulse to rise up and scream to the audience, "Here, here in your very midst, is a tragedy, a real tragedy!" This impulse grew so strong that I became afraid of myself, and in the darkness of one of the scenes I stumbled out of the theater. I walked aimlessly about for an hour or so, my feelings divided between a desire to weep and a desire to curse. I finally took a cab and went from café to café, and for one of the very few times in my life drank myself into a stupor.

It was unwelcome news for me when my benefactor—I could not think of him as employer—informed me that he was at last tired of Paris. This news gave me, I think, a passing doubt as to his sanity. I had enjoyed life in Paris, and, taking all things into consideration, enjoyed it wholesomely. One thing which greatly contributed to my enjoyment was the fact that I was an American. Americans are immensely popular in Paris; and this is not due solely to the fact that they spend lots of money there; for they spend just as much or more in London, and in the latter city they are merely tolerated because they do spend. The Londoner seems to think that Americans are people whose only claim to be classed as civilized is that they have money, and the regrettable thing about that is that the money is not English. But the French are more logical and freer from prejudices than the British; so the difference of attitude is easily explained. Only once in Paris did I have cause to blush for my American citizenship. I had become quite friendly with a young man from Luxembourg whom I had met at the big café. He was a stolid, slow-witted fellow, but, as we say, with a heart of gold. He and I grew attached to each other and were together frequently. He was a great admirer of the United States and never grew tired of talking to me about the country and asking for information. It was his intention to try his fortune there some

day. One night he asked me in a tone of voice which indicated that he expect-
ed an authoritative denial of an ugly rumor, "Did they really burn a man alive
in the United States?" I never knew what I stammered out to him as an
answer. I should have felt relieved if I could even have said to him, "Well,
only one."

When we arrived in London my sadness at leaving Paris was turned into
despair. After my long stay in the French capital, huge, ponderous, massive
London seemed to me as ugly a thing as man could contrive to make. I
thought of Paris as a beauty spot on the face of the earth, and of London as
a big freckle. But soon London's massiveness, I might say its very ugliness,
began to impress me. I began to experience that sense of grandeur which one
feels when he looks at a great mountain or a mighty river. Beside London
Paris becomes a toy, a pretty plaything. And I must own that before I left the
world's metropolis I discovered much there that was beautiful. The beauty in
and about London is entirely different from that in and about Paris; and I
could not but admit that the beauty of the French city seemed hand-made,
artificial, as though set up for the photographer's camera, everything nicely
adjusted so as not to spoil the picture; while that of the English city was
rugged, natural and fresh.

How these two cities typify the two peoples who built them! Even the
sound of their names express a certain racial difference. Paris is the concrete
expression of the gayety, regard for symmetry, love of art and, I might well
add, of the morality of the French people. London stands for the conser-
vatism, the solidarity, the utilitarianism and, I might well add, the hypocrisy
of the Anglo-Saxon. It may sound odd to speak of the morality of the French,
if not of the hypocrisy of the English; but this seeming paradox impressed
me as a deep truth. I saw many things in Paris which were immoral accord-
ing to English standards, but the absence of hypocrisy, the absence of the
spirit to do the thing if it might only be done in secret, robbed these very
immoralities of the damning influence of the same evils in London. I have
walked along the terrace cafés of Paris and seen hundreds of men and women
sipping their wine and beer, without observing a sign of drunkenness. As
they drank, they chatted and laughed and watched the passing crowds; the
drinking seemed to be a secondary thing. This I have witnessed, not only in
the cafés along the Grand Boulevards, but in the out-of-way places patron-
ized by the working classes. In London I have seen in the "Pubs" men and
women crowded in stuffy little compartments, drinking seemingly only for
the pleasure of swallowing as much as they could hold. I have seen there

women from eighteen to eighty, some in tatters, and some clutching babes in their arms, drinking the heavy English ales and whiskies served to them by women. In the whole scene, not one ray of brightness, not one flash of gayety, only maudlin joviality or grim despair. And I have thought, if some men and women will drink—and it is certain that some will—is it not better that they do so under the open sky, in the fresh air, than huddled together in some close, smoky room? There is a sort of frankness about the evils of Paris which robs them of much of the seductiveness of things forbidden, and with that frankness goes a certain cleanliness of thought belonging to things not hidden. London will do whatever Paris does, provided exterior morals are not shocked. As a result, Paris has the appearance only of being the more immoral city. The difference may be summed up in this: Paris practices its sins as lightly as it does its religion, while London practices both very seriously.

I should not neglect to mention what impressed me most forcibly during my stay in London. It was not St. Paul's nor the British Museum nor Westminster Abbey. It was nothing more or less than the simple phrase "Thank you," or sometimes more elaborated, "Thank you very kindly, sir." I was continually surprised by the varied uses to which it was put; and, strange to say, its use as an expression of politeness seemed more limited than any other. One night I was in a cheap music hall and accidentally bumped into a waiter who was carrying a tray-load of beer, almost bringing him to several shillings' worth of grief. To my amazement he righted himself and said, "Thank ye, sir," and left me wondering whether he meant that he thanked me for not completely spilling his beer, or that he would thank me for keeping out of his way.

I also found cause to wonder upon what ground the English accuse Americans of corrupting the language by introducing slang words. I think I heard more and more different kinds of slang during my few weeks' stay in London than in my whole "tenderloin" life in New York. But I suppose the English feel that the language is theirs, and that they may do with it as they please without at the same time allowing that privilege to others.

My "millionaire" was not so long in growing tired of London as of Paris. After a stay of six or eight weeks we went across into Holland. Amsterdam was a great surprise to me. I had always thought of Venice as the city of canals; but it had never entered my mind that I should find similar conditions in a Dutch town. I don't suppose the comparison goes far beyond the fact that there are canals in both cities—I have never seen Venice—but

Amsterdam struck me as being extremely picturesque. From Holland we went to Germany, where we spent five or six months, most of the time in Berlin. I found Berlin more to my taste than London, and occasionally I had to admit that in some things it was superior to Paris.

In Berlin I especially enjoyed the orchestral concerts, and I attended a large number of them. I formed the acquaintance of a good many musicians, several of whom spoke of my playing in high terms. It was in Berlin that my inspiration was renewed. One night my "millionaire" entertained a party of men composed of artists, musicians, writers and, for aught I know, a count or two. They drank and smoked a great deal talked art and music, and discussed, it seemed to me, everything that ever entered man's mind. I could only follow the general drift of what they were saying. When they discussed music it was more interesting to me; for then some fellow would run excitedly to the piano and give a demonstration of his opinions, and another would follow quickly doing the same. In this way, I learned that; regardless of what his specialty might be, every man in the party was a musician. I was at the same time impressed with the falsity of the general idea that Frenchmen are excitable and emotional, and that Germans are calm and phlegmatic. Frenchmen are merely gay and never overwhelmed by their emotions. When they talk loud and fast it is merely talk, while Germans get worked up and red in the face when sustaining an opinion; and in heated discussions are likely to allow their emotions to sweep them off their feet.

My "millionaire" planned, in the midst of the discussion on music, to have me play the "new American music" and astonish everybody present. The result was that I was more astonished than anyone else. I went to the piano and played the most intricate ragtime piece I knew. Before there was time for anybody to express an opinion on what I had done, a big be-spectacled, bushy-headed man rushed over, and, shoving me out of the chair, exclaimed, "Get up! Get up!" He seated himself at the piano, and taking the theme of my ragtime, played it through first in straight chords; then varied and developed it through every known musical form. I sat amazed. I had been turning classic music into ragtime, a comparatively easy task; and this man had taken ragtime and made it classic. The thought came across me like a flash.—It can be done, why can't I do it? From that moment my mind was made up. I clearly saw the way of carrying out the ambition I had formed when a boy.

I now lost interest in our trip. I thought, here I am a man, no longer a boy, and what am I doing but wasting my time and abusing my talent. What

use am I making of my gifts? What future have I before me following my present course? These thoughts made me feel remorseful, and put me in a fever to get to work, to begin to do something. Of course I know now that I was not wasting time; that there was nothing I could have done at that age which would have benefited me more than going to Europe as I did. The desire to begin work grew stronger each day. I could think of nothing else. I made up my mind to go back into the very heart of the South, to live among the people, and drink in my inspiration first-hand. I gloated over the immense amount of material I had to work with, not only modern ragtime, but also the old slave songs,—material which no one had yet touched.

The more decided and anxious I became to return to the United States, the more I dreaded the ordeal of breaking with my "millionaire." Between this peculiar man and me there had grown a very strong bond of affection, backed up by a debt which each owed to the other. He had taken me from a terrible life in New York and by giving me the opportunity of traveling and of coming in contact with the people with whom he associated, had made me a polished man of the world. On the other hand, I was his chief means of disposing of the thing which seemed to sum up all in life that he dreaded—Time. As I remember him now, I can see that time was what he was always endeavoring to escape, to bridge over, to blot out, and it is not strange that some years later he did escape it forever, by leaping into eternity.

For some weeks I waited for just the right moment in which to tell my patron of my decision. Those weeks were a trying time to me. I felt that I was playing the part of a traitor to my best friend. At length, one day, he said to me, "Well, get ready for a long trip; we are going to Egypt, and then to Japan." The temptation was for an instant almost overwhelming, but I summoned determination enough to say, "I don't think I want to go." "What!" he exclaimed, "you want to go back to your dear Paris? You still think that the only spot on earth? Wait until you see Cairo and Tokio, you may change your mind." "No," I stammered, "it is not because I want to go back to Paris. I want to go back to the United States." He wished to know my reason, and I told him, as best I could, my dreams, my ambition, and my decision. While I was talking he watched me with a curious, almost cynical, smile growing on his lips. When I had finished he put his hand on my shoulder.—This was the first physical expression of tender regard he had ever shown me—and looking at me in a big-brotherly way, said, "My boy, you are by blood, by appearance, by education and by tastes, a white man. Now why do you want to throw your life away amidst the poverty and ignorance, in the hopeless

struggle of the black people of the United States? Then look at the terrible handicap you are placing on yourself by going home and working as a Negro composer; you can never be able to get the hearing for your work which it might deserve. I doubt that even a white musician of recognized ability could succeed there by working on the theory that American music should be based on Negro themes. Music is a universal art; anybody's music belongs to everybody; you can't limit it to race or country. Now, if you want to become a composer, why not stay right here in Europe? I will put you under the best teachers on the continent. Then if you want to write music on Negro themes, why, go ahead and do it."

We talked for some time on music and the race question. On the latter subject I had never before heard him express any opinion. Between him and me no suggestion of racial differences had ever come up. I found that he was a man entirely free from prejudice, but he recognized that prejudice was a big stubborn entity which had to be taken into account. He went on to say, "This idea you have of making a Negro out of yourself is nothing more than a sentiment, and you do not realize the fearful import of what you intend to do. What kind of a Negro would you make now, especially in the South? If you had remained there, or perhaps even in your club in New York, you might have succeeded very well; but now you would be miserable. I can imagine no more dissatisfied human being than an educated, cultured and refined colored man in the United States. I have given more study to the race question in the United States than you may suppose, and I sympathize with the Negroes there; but what's the use? I can't right their wrongs, and neither can you; they must do that themselves. They are unfortunate in having wrongs to right, and you would be foolish to unnecessarily take their wrongs on your shoulders. Perhaps some day, through study and observation, you will come to see that evil is a force and, like the physical and chemical forces, we cannot annihilate it; we may only change its form. We light upon one evil and hit it with all the might of our civilization, but only succeed in scattering it into a dozen of other forms. We hit slavery through a great civil war. Did we destroy it? No, we only changed it into hatred between sections of the country: in the South, into political corruption and chicanery, the degradation of the blacks through peonage, unjust laws, unfair and cruel treatment; and the degradation of the whites by their resorting to these practices; the paralyzation of the public conscience, and the ever overhanging dread of what the future may bring. Modern civilization hit ignorance of the masses through the means of popular education. What has it done but turn igno-

rance into anarchy, socialism, strikes, hatred between poor and rich, and universal discontent. In like manner, modem philanthropy hit at suffering and disease through asylums and hospitals; it prolongs the sufferers' lives, it is true; but is, at the same time, sending down strains of insanity and weakness into future generations. My philosophy of life is this: make yourself as happy as possible, and try to make those happy whose lives come into touch with yours; but to attempt to right the wrongs and ease the sufferings of the world in general, is a waste of effort. You had just as well try to bail the Atlantic by pouring the water into the Pacific."

This tremendous flow of serious talk from a man I was accustomed to see either gay or taciturn so surprised and overwhelmed me that I could not frame a reply. He left me thinking over what he had said. Whatever was the soundness of his logic or the moral tone of his philosophy, his argument greatly impressed me. I could see, in spite of the absolute selfishness upon which it was based, that there was reason and common sense in it. I began to analyze my own motives, and found that they, too, were very largely mixed with selfishness. Was it more a desire to help those I considered my people or more a desire to distinguish myself, which was leading me back to the United States? That is a question I have never definitely answered.

For several weeks longer I was in a troubled state of mind. Added to the fact that I was loath to leave my good friend, was the weight of the question he had aroused in my mind, whether I was not making a fatal mistake. I suffered more than one sleepless night during that time. Finally, I settled the question on purely selfish grounds, in accordance with my "millionaire's" philosophy. I argued that music offered me a better future than anything else I had any knowledge of, and, In opposition to my friend's opinion, that I should have greater chances of attracting attention as a colored composer than as a white one. But I must own that I also felt stirred by an unselfish desire to voice all the joys and sorrows, the hopes and ambitions, of the American Negro, in classic musical form.

When my mind was fully made up I told my friend. He asked me when I intended to start. I replied that I would do so at once. He then asked me how much money I had. I told him that I had saved several hundred dollars out of sums he had given me. He gave me a check for $500, told me to write to him care of his Paris bankers if I ever needed his help, wished me good luck, and bade me good-by. Ail this he did almost coldly; and I often wondered whether he was in a hurry to get rid of what he considered a fool, or whether he was striving to hide deeper feelings of sorrow.

And so I separated from the man who was, all in all, the best friend I ever had, except my mother, the man who exerted the greatest influence ever brought into my life, except that exerted by my mother. My affection for him was so strong, my recollections of him are so distinct; he was such a peculiar and striking character, that I could easily fill several chapters with reminiscences of him; but for fear of tiring the reader I shall go on with my narration.

I decided to go to Liverpool and take ship for Boston. I still had an uneasy feeling about returning to New York, and in a few days I found myself aboard ship headed for home.

CHAPTER X

Aᴍᴏɴɢ the first of my fellow passengers of whom I took any particular notice, was a tall, broad-shouldered, almost gigantic, colored man. His dark-brown face was clean shaven; he was well dressed and bore a decidedly distinguished air. In fact, if he was not handsome, he at least compelled admiration for his fine physical proportions. He attracted general attention as he strode the deck in a sort of majestic loneliness. I became curious to know who he was and determined to strike up an acquaintance with him at the first opportune moment. The chance came a day or two later. He was sitting in the smoking-room, with a cigar in his mouth which had gone out, reading a novel. I sat down beside him and, offering him a fresh cigar, said, "You don't mind my telling you something unpleasant, do you?" He looked at me with a smile, accepted the proffered cigar, and replied in a voice which comported perfectly with his size and appearance, "I think my curiosity overcomes any objections I might have." "Well," I said, "have you noticed that the man who sat at your right in the saloon during the first meal has not sat there since?" He frowned slightly without answering my question. "Well," I continued, "he asked the steward to remove him; and not only that, he attempted to persuade a number of the passengers to protest against your presence in the dining-saloon." The big man at my side took a long draw from his cigar, threw his head back and slowly blew a great cloud of smoke toward the ceiling. Then turning to me he said, "Do you know, I don't object to anyone having prejudices so long as those prejudices don't interfere with my personal liberty. Now, the man you are speaking of had a perfect right to change his seat if I in any way interfered with his appetite or his digestion. I

would have no reason to complain if he removed to the farthest corner of the saloon, or even if he got off the ship; but when his prejudice attempts to move me one foot, one inch, out of the place where I am comfortably located, then I object." On the word "object" he brought his great fist down on the table in front of us with such a crash that everyone in the room turned to look. We both covered up the slight embarrassment with a laugh, and strolled out on the deck.

We walked the deck for an hour or more, discussing different phases of the Negro question. I, in referring to the race, used the personal pronoun "we"; my companion made no comment about it, nor evinced any surprise, except to slightly raise his eyebrows the first time he caught the significance of the word. He was the broadest minded colored man I have ever talked with on the Negro question. He even went so far as to sympathize with and offer excuses for some white Southern points of view. I asked him what were his main reasons for being so hopeful. He replied, "In spite of all that is written, said and done, this great, big, incontrovertible fact stands out,—the Negro is progressing, and that disproves all the arguments in the world that he is incapable of progress. I was born in slavery, and at emancipation was set adrift a ragged penniless bit of humanity. I have seen the Negro in every grade, and I know what I am talking about. Our detractors point to the increase of crime as evidence against us; certainly we have progressed in crime as in other things; what less could be expected? And yet, in this respect, we are far from the point which has been reached by the more highly civilized white race. As we continue to progress, crime among us will gradually lose much of its brutal, vulgar, I might say healthy, aspect, and become more delicate, refined and subtle. Then it will be less shocking and noticeable, although more dangerous to society." Then dropping his tone of irony, he continued with some show of eloquence, "But, above all, when I am discouraged and disheartened, I have this to fall back on: if there is a principle of right in the world, which finally prevails, and I believe that there is; if there is a merciful but justice-loving God in heaven, and I believe that there is, we shall win; for we have right on our side; while those who oppose us can defend themselves by nothing in the moral law, nor even by anything in the enlightened thought of the present age."

For several days, together with other topics, we discussed the race problem, not only of the United States, but the race problem as it affected native Africans and Jews. Finally, before we reached Boston, our conversation had grown familiar and personal. I had told him something of my past and much

about my intentions for the future. I learned that he was a physician, a graduate of Howard University Washington, and had done post-graduate work in Philadelphia; and this was his second trip abroad to attend professional courses. He had practiced for some years in the city of Washington, and though he did not say so, I gathered that his practice was a lucrative one. Before we left the ship he had made me promise that I would stop two or three days in Washington before going on South.

We put up at a hotel in Boston for a couple of days, and visited several of my new friend's acquaintances; they were all people of education and culture and, apparently, of means. I could not but help being struck by the great difference between them and the same class of colored people in the South. In speech and thought they were genuine Yankees. The difference was especially noticeable in their speech. There was none of that heavy-tongued enunciation which characterizes even the best educated colored people of the South. It is remarkable, after all, what an adaptable creature the Negro is. I have seen the black West India gentleman in London, and he is in speech and manners a perfect Englishman. I have seen natives of Haiti and Martinique in Paris, and they are more Frenchy than a Frenchman. I have no doubt that the Negro would make a good Chinaman, with exception of the pigtail.

My stay in Washington, instead of being two or three days, was two or three weeks. This was my first visit to the National Capital, and I was, of course, interested in seeing the public buildings and something of the working of the government; but most of my time I spent with the doctor among his friends and acquaintances. The social phase of life among colored people, which I spoke of in an earlier chapter, is more developed in Washington than in any other city in the country. This is on account of the large number of individuals earning good salaries and having a reasonable amount of leisure time to be drawn from. There are dozens of physicians and lawyers, scores of school teachers and hundreds of clerks in the departments. As to the colored department clerks, I think it fair to say that in educational equipment they average above the white clerks of the same grade; for, whereas a colored college graduate will seek such a job, the white university man goes into one of the many higher vocations which are open to him.

In a previous chapter I spoke of social life among colored people; so there is no need to take it up again here. But there is one thing I did not mention: among Negroes themselves there is the peculiar inconsistency of a color question. Its existence is rarely admitted and hardly ever mentioned; it may not be too strong a statement to say that the greater portion of the race is uncon-

scious of its influence; yet this influence, though silent, is constant. It is evidenced most plainly in marriage selection; thus the black men generally marry women fairer than themselves; while, on the other hand, the dark women of stronger mental endowment are very often married to light-complexioned men, the effect is a tendency toward lighter complexions, especially among the more active elements in the race. Some might claim that this is a tacit admission of colored people among themselves of their own inferiority judged by the color line. I do not think so. What I have termed an inconsistency is, after all, most natural, it is, in fact, a tendency in accordance with what might be called an economic necessity. So far as racial differences go, the United States puts a greater premium on color or better, lack of color, than upon anything else in the world. To paraphrase, "Have a white skin, and all things else may be added unto you." I have seen advertisements in newspapers for waiters, bell boys or elevator men, which read, "Light colored man wanted." It is this tremendous pressure which the sentiment of the country exerts that is operating on the race. There is involved not only the question of higher opportunity, but often the question of earning a livelihood, and so I say it is not strange, but a natural tendency. Nor is it any more a sacrifice of self respect that a black man should give to his children every advantage he can which complexion of the skin carries, than that the new or vulgar rich should purchase for their children the advantages which ancestry aristocracy, and social position carry. I once heard a colored man sum it up in these words, "It's no disgrace to be black, but it's often very inconvenient."

Washington shows the Negro not only at his best, but also at his worst. As I drove around with the doctor, he commented rather harshly on those of the latter class which we saw. He remarked: "You see those lazy loafing, good-for-nothing darkies, they're not worth digging graves for, yet they are the ones who create impressions of the race for the casual observer. It's because they are always in evidence on the street corners, while the rest of us are hard at work, and you know a dozen loafing darkies make a bigger crowd and a worse impression in this country than fifty white men of the same class. But they ought not to represent the race. We are the race, and the race ought to be judged by us, not by them. Every race and every nation is judged by the best it has been able to produce, not by the worst."

The recollection of my stay in Washington is a pleasure to me now. In company with the doctor I visited Howard University, the public schools, the excellent colored hospital, with which he was in some way connected, if I remember correctly, and many comfortable and even elegant homes. It was

with some reluctance that I continued my journey south. The doctor was very kind in giving me letters to people in Richmond and Nashville when I told him that I intended to stop in both of these cities. In Richmond a man who was then editing a very creditable colored newspaper, gave me a great deal of his time, and made my stay there of three or four days very pleasant. In Nashville I spent a whole day at Fisk University, the home of the "Jubilee Singers," and was more than repaid for my time. Among my letters of introduction was one to a very prosperous physician. He drove me about the city and introduced me to a number of people. From Nashville I went to Atlanta, where I stayed long enough to gratify an old desire to see Atlanta University again. I then continued my journey to Macon.

During the trip from Nashville to Atlanta I went into the smoking compartment of the car to smoke a cigar. I was traveling in a Pullman, not because of an abundance of funds, but because through my experience with my "millionaire," a certain amount of comfort and luxury had become a necessity to me whenever it was obtainable. When I entered the car I found only a couple of men there; but in a half hour there were half a dozen or more. From the general conversation I learned that a fat Jewish looking man was a cigar manufacturer, and was experimenting in growing Havana tobacco in Florida; that a slender be-spectacled young man was from Ohio and a professor in some State institution in Alabama; that a white-mustached, well dressed man was an old Union soldier who had fought through the Civil War; and that a tall, raw-boned, red-faced man, who seemed bent on leaving nobody in ignorance of the fact that he was from Texas, was a cotton planter.

In the North men may ride together for hours in a "smoker" and unless they are acquainted with each other never exchange a word; in the South, men thrown together in such manner are friends in fifteen minutes. There is always present a warm-hearted cordiality which will melt down the most frigid reserve. It may be because Southerners are very much like Frenchmen in that they must talk; and not only must they talk, but they must express their opinions.

The talk in the car was for a while miscellaneous,—on the weather, crops, business prospects—the old Union soldier had invested capital in Atlanta, and he predicted that that city would soon be one of the greatest in the country—finally the conversation drifted to politics; then, as a natural sequence, turned upon the Negro question.

In the discussion of the race question, the diplomacy of the Jew was something to be admired; he had the faculty of agreeing with everybody

without losing his allegiance to any side. He knew that to sanction Negro oppression would be to sanction Jewish oppression, and would expose him to a shot along that line from the old soldier, who stood firmly on the ground of equal rights and opportunity to all men; yet long traditions and business instincts told him, when in Rome to act as a Roman. Altogether his position was a delicate one, and I gave him credit for the skill he displayed in maintaining it. The young professor was apologetic. He had had the same views as the G. A. R. man; but a year in the South had opened his eyes, and he had to confess that the problem could hardly be handled any better than it was being handled by the Southern whites. To which the G. A. R. man responded somewhat rudely that he had spent ten times as many years in the South as his young friend, and that he could easily understand how holding a position in a State institution in Alabama would bring about a change of views. The professor turned very red and had very little more to say. The Texan was fierce, eloquent and profane in his argument and, in a lower sense, there was a direct logic in what he said, which was convincing; it was only by taking higher ground, by dealing in what Southerners call "theories" that he could be combatted. Occasionally some one of the several other men in the "smoker" would throw in a remark to reinforce what he said, but he really didn't need any help; he was sufficient in himself.

In the course of a short time the controversy narrowed itself down to an argument between the old soldier and the Texan. The latter maintained hotly that the Civil War was a criminal mistake on the part of the North, and that the humiliation which the South suffered during Reconstruction could never be forgotten. The Union man retorted just as hotly that the South was responsible for the war, and that the spirit of unforgetfulness on its part was the greatest cause of present friction; that it seemed to be the one great aim of the South to convince the North that the latter made a mistake in fighting to preserve the Union and liberate the slaves. "Can you imagine," he went on to say, "what would have been the condition of things eventually if there had been no war, and the South had been allowed to follow its course? Instead of one great, prosperous country with nothing before it but the conquests of peace, a score of petty republics, as in Central and South America, wasting their energies in war with each other or in revolutions."

"Well," replied the Texan, "anything—no country at all is better than having niggers over you. But anyhow, the war was fought and the niggers were freed; for it's no use beating around the bush, the niggers, and not the Union, was the cause of it; and now do you believe that all the niggers on

earth are worth the good white blood that was spilt? You freed the nigger and you gave him the ballot, but you couldn't make a citizen out of him. He don't know what he's voting for, and we buy 'em like so many hogs. You're giving 'em education, but that only makes slick rascals out of 'em."

"Don't fancy for a moment," said the Northern man, "that you have any monopoly in buying ignorant votes. The same thing is done on a larger scale in New York and Boston, and in Chicago and San Francisco; and they are not black votes either. As to education making the Negro worse, you had just as well tell me that religion does the same thing. And, by the way, how many educated colored men do you know personally?"

The Texan admitted that he knew only one, and added that he was in the penitentiary. "But," he said, "do you mean to claim, ballot or no ballot, education or no education, that niggers are the equals of white men?"

"That's not the question," answered the other, "but if the Negro is so distinctly inferior, it is a strange thing to me that it takes such tremendous effort on the part of the white man to make him realize it, and to keep him in the same place into which inferior men naturally fall. However, let us grant for sake of argument that the Negro is inferior in every respect to the white man; that fact only increases our moral responsibility in regard to our actions toward him. Inequalities of numbers, wealth and power, even of intelligence and morals, should make no difference in the essential rights of men."

"If he's inferior and weaker, and is shoved to the wall, that's his own look out," said the Texan. "That's the law of nature; and he's bound to go to the wall; for no race in the world has ever been able to stand competition with the Anglo-Saxon. The Anglo-Saxon race has always been and always will be the masters of the world, and the niggers in the South ain't going to change all the records of history."

"My friend," said the old soldier slowly, "if you have studied history will you tell me, as confidentially between white men, what the Anglo-Saxon has ever done?"

The Texan was too much astonished by the question to venture any reply.

His opponent continued, "Can you name a single one of the great fundamental and original intellectual achievements which have raised man in the scale of civilization that may be credited to the Anglo-Saxon? The art of letters, of poetry, of music, of sculpture, of painting, of the drama, of architecture; the science of mathematics, of astronomy, of philosophy, of logic, of physics, of chemistry, the use of the metals and the principles of mechanics, were all invented or discovered by darker and what we now call inferior races

and nations. We have carried many of these to their highest point of perfection, but the foundation was laid by others. Do you know the only original contribution to civilization we can claim is what we have done in steam and electricity and in making implements of war more deadly; and there we worked largely on principles which we did not discover. Why, we didn't even originate the religion we use. We are a great race, the greatest in the world today, but we ought to remember that we are standing on a pile of past races, and enjoy our position with a little less show of arrogance. We are simply having our turn at the game, and we were a long time getting to it. After all, racial supremacy is merely a matter of dates in history. The man here who belongs to what is, all in all, the greatest race the world ever produced, is almost ashamed to own it. If the Anglo-Saxon is the source of everything good and great in the human race from the beginning, why wasn't the German forest the birthplace of civilization?"

The Texan was somewhat disconcerted, for the argument had passed a little beyond his limits, but he swung it back to where he was sure of his ground by saying, "All that may be true, but it hasn't got much to do with us and the niggers here in the South. We've got 'em here, and we've got 'em to live with, and it's a question of white man or nigger, no middle ground. You want us to treat niggers as equals. Do you want to see 'em sitting around in our parlors? Do you want to see a mulatto South? To bring it right home to you, would you let your daughter marry a nigger?"

"No, I wouldn't consent to my daughter's marrying a nigger, but that doesn't prevent my treating a black man fairly. And I don't see what fair treatment has to do with niggers sitting around in your parlors; they can't come there unless they're invited. Out of all the white men I know, only a hundred or so have the privilege of sitting around in my parlor. As to the mulatto South, if you Southerners have one boast that is stronger than another, it is your women; you put them on a pinnacle of purity and virtue and bow down in a chivalric worship before them; yet you talk and act as though, should you treat the Negro fairly and take the anti-intermarriage laws off your statute books, these same women would rush into the arms of black lovers and husbands. It's a wonder to me that they don't rise up and resent the insult."

"Colonel," said the Texan, as he reached into his handbag and brought out a large flask of whiskey, "you might argue from now until hell freezes over, and you might convince me that you're right, but you'll never convince me that I'm wrong. All you say sounds very good, but it's got nothing to do

with facts. You can say what men ought to be, but they ain't that; so there you are. Down here in the South we're up against facts, and we're meeting 'em like facts. We don't believe the nigger is or ever will be the equal of the white man, and we ain't going to treat him as an equal; I'll be damned if we will. Have a drink." Everybody, except the professor, partook of the generous Texan's flask, and the argument closed in a general laugh and good feeling.

I went back into the main part of the car with the conversation on my mind. Here I had before me the bald, raw, naked aspects of the race question in the South; and, in consideration of the step I was just taking, it was far from encouraging. The sentiments of the Texan—and he expressed the sentiments of the South—fell upon me like a chill. I was sick at heart. Yet, I must confess that underneath it all I felt a certain sort of admiration for the man who could not be swayed from what he held as his principles. Contrasted with him, the young Ohio professor was indeed a pitiable character. And all along, in spite of myself, I have been compelled to accord the same kind of admiration to the Southern white man for the manner in which he defends not only his virtues but his vices. He knows, that judged by a high standard, he is narrow and prejudiced, that he is guilty of unfairness, oppression and cruelty, but this he defends as stoutly as he would his better qualities. This same spirit obtains in a great degree among the blacks; they, too, defend their faults and failings. This spirit carries them so far at times as to make them sympathizers with members of their race who are perpetrators of crime. And, yet, among themselves they are their own most merciless critics. I have never heard the race so terribly arraigned as I have by colored speakers to strictly colored audiences. It is the spirit of the South to defend everything belonging to it. The North is too cosmopolitan and tolerant for such a spirit. If you should say to an Easterner that Paris is a gayer city than New York he would be likely to agree with you, or at least to let you have your way; but to suggest to a South Carolinian that Boston is a nicer city to live in than Charleston would be to stir his greatest depths of argument and eloquence.

But, to-day, as I think over that smoking-car argument, I can see it in a different light. The Texan's position does not render things so hopeless, for it indicates that the main difficulty of the race question does not lie so much in the actual condition of the blacks as it does in the mental attitude of the whites; and a mental attitude, especially one not based on truth, can be changed more easily than actual conditions. That is to say, the burden of the question is not that the whites are struggling to save ten million despondent

and moribund people from sinking into a hopeless slough of ignorance, poverty and barbarity in their very midst, but that they are unwilling to open certain doors of opportunity and to accord certain treatment to ten million aspiring, education-and-property-acquiring people. In a word, the difficulty of the problem is not so much due to the facts presented, as to the hypothesis assumed for its solution. In this it is similar to the problem of the Solar System. By a complex, confusing and almost contradictory mathematical process, by the use of zigzags instead of straight lines, the earth can be proven to be the center of things celestial; but by an operation so simple that it can be comprehended by a schoolboy, its position can be verified among the other worlds which revolve about the sun, and its movements harmonized with the laws of the universe. So, when the white race assumes as a hypothesis that it is the main object of creation, and that all things else are merely subsidiary to its well being, sophism, subterfuge, perversion of conscience, arrogance, injustice, oppression, cruelty, sacrifice of human blood, all are required to maintain the position, and its dealings with other races become indeed a problem, a problem which, if based on a hypothesis of common humanity, could be solved by the simple rules of justice.

When I reached Macon I decided to leave my trunk and all my surplus belongings, to pack my bag, and strike out into the interior. This I did; and by train, by mule and ox-cart, I traveled through many counties. This was my first real experience among rural colored people, and all that I saw was interesting to me; but there was a great deal which does not require description at my hands; for log cabins and plantations and dialect-speaking darkies are perhaps better known in American literature than any other single picture of our national life. Indeed, they form an ideal and exclusive literary concept of the American Negro to such an extent that it is almost impossible to get the reading public to recognize him in any other setting; but I shall endeavor to avoid giving the reader any already overworked and hackneyed descriptions. This generally accepted literary ideal of the American Negro constitutes what is really an obstacle in the way of the thoughtful and progressive element of the race. His character has been established as a happy-go-lucky, laughing, shuffling, banjo-picking being, and the reading public has not yet been prevailed upon to take him seriously. His efforts to elevate himself socially are looked upon as a sort of absurd caricature of "white civilization." A novel dealing with colored people who lived in respectable homes and amidst a fair degree of culture and who naturally acted "just like white folks" would be taken in a comic opera sense. In this respect the Negro

is much in the position of a great comedian who gives up the lighter rôles to play tragedy. No matter how well he may portray the deeper passions, the public is loth to give him up in his old character; they even conspire to make him a failure in serious work, in order to force him back into comedy. In the same respect, the public is not too much to be blamed, for great comedians are far more scarce than mediocre tragedians; every amateur actor is a tragedian. However, this very fact constitutes the opportunity of the future Negro novelist and poet to give the country something new and unknown, in depicting the life, the ambitions, the struggles and the passions of those of their race who are striving to break the narrow limits of traditions. A beginning has already been made in that remarkable book by Dr. Du Bois, "The Souls of Black Folk."

Much, too, that I saw while on this trip, in spite of my enthusiasm, was disheartening. Often I thought of what my "millionaire" had said to me, and wished myself back in Europe. The houses in which I had to stay were generally uncomfortable, sometimes worse. I often had to sleep in a division or compartment with several other people. Once or twice I was not so fortunate as to find divisions; everybody slept on pallets on the floor. Frequently I was able to lie down and contemplate the stars which were in their zenith. The food was at times so distasteful and poorly cooked that I could not eat it. I remember that once I lived for a week or more on buttermilk, on account of not being able to stomach the fat bacon, the rank turnip tops and the heavy damp mixture of meal, salt and water, which was called corn bread. It was only my ambition to do the work which I had planned that kept me steadfast to my purpose. Occasionally I would meet with some signs of progress and uplift in even one of these backwood settlements—houses built of boards, with windows, and divided into rooms, decent food and a fair standard of living. This condition was due to the fact that there was in the community some exceptionally capable Negro farmer whose thrift served as an example. As I went about among these dull, simple people, the great majority of them hard working; in their relations with the whites, submissive, faithful, and often affectionate, negatively content with their lot, and contrasted them with those of the race who had been quickened by the forces of thought, I could not but appreciate the logic of the position held by those Southern leaders who have been bold enough to proclaim against the education of the Negro. They are consistent in their public speech with Southern sentiment and desires. Those public men of the South who have not been daring or heedless enough to defy the ideals of twentieth century civilization

and of modern humanitarianism and philanthropy, find themselves in the embarrassing situation of preaching one thing and praying for another. They are in the position of the fashionable woman who is compelled by the laws of polite society to say to her dearest enemy, "How happy I am to see you."

And yet in this respect how perplexing is Southern character; for in opposition to the above, it may be said that the claim of the Southern whites that they love the Negro better than the Northern whites do, is in a manner true. Northern white people love the Negro in a sort of abstract way, as a race; through a sense of justice, charity and philanthropy, they will liberally assist in his elevation. A number of them have heroically spent their lives in this effort (and just here I wish to say that when the colored people reach the monument building stage, they should not forget the men and women who went South after the war and founded schools for them). Yet, generally speaking, they have no particular liking for individuals of the race. Southern white people despise the Negro as a race, and will do nothing to aid in his elevation as such; but for certain individuals they have a strong affection, and are helpful to them in many ways. With these individual members of the race they live on terms of the greatest intimacy; they intrust to them their children, their family treasures and their family secrets; in trouble they often go to them for comfort and counsel; in sickness they often rely upon their care. This affectionate relation between the Southern whites and those blacks who come into close touch with them has not been overdrawn even in fiction.

This perplexity of Southern character extends even to the mixture of the races. That is spoken of as though it were dreaded worse than smallpox, leprosy or the plague. Yet, when I was in Jacksonville I knew several prominent families there with large colored branches, which went by the same name and were known and acknowledged as blood relatives. And what is more, there seemed to exist between these black brothers and sisters and uncles and aunts a decided friendly feeling.

I said above that Southern whites would do nothing for the Negro as a race. I know the South claims that it has spent millions for the education of the blacks, and that it has of its own free will shouldered this awful burden. It seems to be forgetful of the fact that these millions have been taken from the public tax funds for education, and that the law of political economy which recognizes the land owner as the one who really pays the taxes is not tenable. It would be just as reasonable for the relatively few land-owners of Manhattan to complain that they had to stand the financial burden of the education of the thousands and thousands of children whose parents pay rent

for tenements and flats. Let the millions of producing and consuming Negroes be taken out of the South, and it would be quickly seen how much less of public funds there would be to appropriate for education or any other purpose.

In thus traveling about through the country, I was sometimes amused on arriving at some little railroad-station town to be taken for and treated as a white man, and six hours later, when it was learned that I was stopping at the house of the colored preacher or school teacher, to note the attitude of the whole town change. At times this led even to embarrassment. Yet it cannot be so embarrassing for a colored man to be taken for white as for a white man to be taken for colored; and I have heard of several cases of the latter kind.

All this while I was gathering material for work, jotting down in my notebook themes and melodies, and trying to catch the spirit of the Negro in his relatively primitive state. I began to feel the necessity of hurrying so that I might get back to some city like Nashville to begin my compositions, and at the same time earn at least a living by teaching and performing before my funds gave out. At the last settlement in which I stopped I found a mine of material. This was due to the fact that "big meeting" was in progress. "Big meeting" is an institution something like camp-meeting; the difference being that it is held in a permanent church, and not in a temporary structure. All the churches of some one denomination—of course, either Methodist or Baptist—in a county or, perhaps, in several adjoining counties, are closed, and the congregations unite at some centrally located church for a series of meetings lasting a week. It is really a social as well as a religious function. The people come in great numbers, making the trip, according to their financial status, in buggies drawn by sleek, fleet-footed mules, in ox-teams, or on foot. It was amusing to see some of the latter class trudging down the hot and dusty road with their shoes, which were brand new, strung across their shoulders. When they got near the church they sat on the side of the road and, with many grimaces, tenderly packed their feet into those instruments of torture. This furnished, indeed, a trying test of their religion. The famous preachers come from near and far, and take turns in warning sinners of the day of wrath. Food, in the form of those two Southern luxuries, fried chicken and roast pork, is plentiful, and no one need go hungry. On the opening Sunday the women are immaculate in starched stiff white dresses adorned with ribbons either red or blue. Even a great many of the men wear streamers of vari-colored ribbons in the buttonholes of their coats. A few of them carefully cultivate a fore lock of hair by wrapping it in twine, and on such

festive occasions decorate it with a narrow ribbon streamer. Big meetings afford a fine opportunity to the younger people to meet each other dressed in their Sunday clothes, and much rustic courting, which is as enjoyable as any other kind, is indulged in.

This big meeting which I was lucky enough to catch was particularly well attended; the extra large attendance was due principally to two attractions, a man by name of John Brown, who was renowned as the most powerful preacher for miles around; and a wonderful leader of singing, who was known as "Singing Johnson." These two men were a study and a revelation to me. They caused me to reflect upon how great an influence their types have been in the development of the Negro in America. Both these types are now looked upon generally with condescension or contempt by the progressive element among the colored people; but it should never be forgotten that it was they who led the race from paganism, and kept it steadfast to Christianity through all the long, dark years of slavery.

John Brown was a jet black man of medium size, with a strikingly intelligent head and face, and a voice like an organ peal. He preached each night after several lesser lights successively held the pulpit during an hour or so. As far as subject matter is concerned, all of the sermons were alike; each began with the fall of man, ran through various trials and tribulations of the Hebrew children, on to the redemption by Christ, and ended with a fervid picture of the judgment day and the fate of the damned. But John Brown possessed magnetism and an imagination so free and daring that he was able to carry through what the other preachers would not attempt. He knew all the arts and tricks of oratory, the modulation of the voice to almost a whisper, the pause for effect, the rise through light, rapid fire sentences to the terrific, thundering outburst of an electrifying climax. In addition, he had the intuition of a born theatrical manager. Night after night this man held me fascinated. He convinced me that, after all, eloquence consists more in the manlier of saying than in what is said. It is largely a matter of tone pictures.

The most striking example of John Brown's magnetism and imagination was his "heavenly march"; I shall never forget how it impressed me when I heard it. He opened his sermon in the usual way; then proclaiming to his listeners that he was going to take them on the heavenly march, he seized the Bible under his arm and began to pace up and down the pulpit platform. The congregation immediately began with their feet a tramp, tramp, tramp, in time with the preacher's march in the pulpit, all the while singing in an undertone a hymn about marching to Zion. Suddenly he cried, "Halt!" Every

foot stopped with the precision of a company of well drilled soldiers, and the singing ceased. The morning star had been reached. Here the preacher described the beauties of that celestial body. Then the march, the tramp, tramp, tramp, and the singing was again taken up. Another "Halt!" They had reached the evening star. And so on, past the sun and the moon—the intensity of religious emotion all the time increasing—along the milky way, on up to the gates of heaven. Here the halt was longer, and the preacher described at length the gates and walls of the New Jerusalem. Then he took his hearers through the pearly gates, along the golden streets, pointing out the glories of the City, pausing occasionally to greet some patriarchal members of the church, well known to most of his listeners in life, who had had "the tears wiped from their eyes, were clad in robes of spotless white, with crowns of gold upon their heads and harps within their hands," and ended his march before the great white throne. To the reader this may sound ridiculous, but listened to under the circumstances, it was highly and effectively dramatic. I was a more or less sophisticated and non-religious man of the world but the torrent of the preacher's words, moving with the rhythm and glowing with the eloquence of primitive poetry swept me along, and I, too, felt like joining in the shouts of "Amen! Hallelujah!"

John Brown's powers in describing the delights of heaven were no greater than those in depicting the horrors of hell. I saw great, strapping fellows, trembling and weeping like children at the "mourners' bench." His warnings to sinners were truly terrible. I shall never forget one expression that he used, which for originality and aptness could not be excelled. In my opinion, it is more graphic and, for us, far more expressive than St. Paul's "It is hard to kick against the pricks." He struck the attitude of a pugilist and thundered out, "Young man, yo' arm's too short to box wid God!"

As interesting as was John Brown to me, the other man, "Singing Johnson," was more so. He was a small, dark-brown, one-eyed man, with a clear, strong, high-pitched voice, a leader of singing, a maker of songs, a man who could improvise at the moment lines to fit the occasion. Not so striking a figure as John Brown, but, at "big meetings," equally important. It is indispensable to the success of the singing, when the congregation is a large one made up of people from different communities, to have someone with a strong voice who knows just what hymn to sing and when to sing it, who can pitch it in the right key, and who has all the leading lines committed to memory. Sometimes it devolves upon the leader to "sing down" a long-winded, or uninteresting speaker. Committing to memory the leading lines of all the

Negro spiritual songs is no easy task, for they run up into the hundreds. But the accomplished leader must know them all, because the congregation sings only the refrains and repeats; every ear in the church is fixed upon him, and if he becomes mixed in his lines or forgets them, the responsibility falls directly on his shoulders.

For example, most of these hymns are constructed to be sung in the following manner:

> Leader— "Swing low, sweet chariot."
> Congregation—"Coming for to carry me home."
> Leader— "Swing low, sweet chariot."
> Congregation—"Coming for to carry me home."
> Leader— "I look over yonder, what do I see?"
> Congregation—"Coming for to carry me home."
> Leader— "Two little angels coming after me."
> Congregation—"Coming for to carry me home."
> — etc., etc., etc.

The solitary and plaintive voice of the leader is answered by a sound like the roll of the sea, producing a most curious effect.

In only a few of these songs do the leader and the congregation start off together. Such a song is the well known "Steal away to Jesus."

The leader and the congregation begin:

> "Steal away, steal away,
> Steal away to Jesus;
> Steal away, steal away home,
> I ain't got long to stay here."

Then the leader alone:

> "My Lord he calls me,
> He calls me by the thunder,
> The trumpet sounds within-a my soul."

Then all together:

> "I ain't got long to stay here."

The leader and the congregation again take up the opening refrain then the leader sings three more leading lines alone, and so on almost ad infinitum. It will be seen that even here most of the work falls upon the leader, for the congregation sings the same lines over and over, while his memory and ingenuity are taxed to keep the songs going.

Generally, the parts taken up by the congregation are sung in a three-part harmony, the women singing the soprano and a transposed tenor, the men with high voices singing the melody, and those with low voices, a thundering bass. In a few of these songs, however, the leading part is sung in unison by the whole congregation, down to the last line, which is harmonized. The effect of this is intensely thrilling. Such a hymn is "Go down Moses." It stirs the heart like a trumpet call.

"Singing Johnson" was an ideal leader; and his services were in great demand. He spent his time going about the country from one church to another. He received his support in much the same way as the preachers,—part of a collection, food and lodging. All of his leisure time he devoted to originating new words and melodies and new lines for old songs. He always sang with his eyes,—or to be more exact—his eye closed, indicating the tempo by swinging his head to and fro. He was a great judge of the proper hymn to sing at a particular moment; and I noticed several times, when the preacher reached a certain climax, or expressed a certain sentiment, that Johnson broke in with a line or two of some appropriate hymn. The speaker understood, and would pause until the singing ceased.

As I listened to the singing of these songs, the wonder of their production grew upon me more and more. How did the men who originated them manage to do it? The sentiments are easily accounted for; they are mostly taken from the Bible; but the melodies, where did they come from? Some of them so weirdly sweet, and others so wonderfully strong. Take, for instance, "Go down Moses." I doubt that there is a stronger theme in the whole musical literature of the world. And so many of these songs contain more than mere melody; there is sounded in them that elusive undertone, the note in music which is not heard with the ears. I sat often with the tears rolling down my cheeks and my heart melted within me. Any musical person who has never heard a Negro congregation under the spell of religious fervor sing these old songs, has missed one of the most thrilling emotions which the human heart may experience. Anyone who can listen to Negroes sing, "Nobody knows de trouble I see, Nobody knows but Jesus," without shedding tears, must indeed have a heart of stone.

As yet, the Negroes themselves do not fully appreciate these old slave songs. The educated classes are rather ashamed of them, and prefer to sing hymns from books. This feeling is natural; they are still too close to the conditions under which the songs were produced; but the day will come when this slave music will be the most treasured heritage of the American Negro.

At the close of the "big meeting" I left the settlement where it was being held, full of enthusiasm. I was in that frame of mind which, in the artistic temperament, amounts to inspiration. I was now ready and anxious to get to some place where I might settle down to work, and give expression the ideas which were teeming in my head; but I strayed into another deviation from my path of life as I had it marked out which led me into an entirely different road. Instead of going to the nearest and most convenient railroad station, I accepted the invitation of a young man who had been present the closing Sunday at the meeting, to drive with him some miles farther to the town in which he taught school, and there take the train. My conversation with this young man as we drove along through the country was extremely interesting. He had been a student in one of the Negro colleges,—strange coincidence, in the very college, as I learned through him, in which "Shiny" was now a professor. I was, of course, curious to hear about my boyhood friend; and had it not been vacation time, and that I was not sure that I would find him, I should have gone out of my way to pay him a visit; but I determined to write to him as soon as the school opened. My companion talked to me about his work among the people, of his hopes and his discouragements. He was tremendously in earnest; I might say, too much so. In fact, it may be said that the majority of intelligent colored people are, in some degree, too much in earnest over the race question. They assume and carry so much that their progress is at times impeded, and they are unable to see things in their proper proportions. In many instances, a slight exercise of the sense of humor would save much anxiety of soul. Anyone who marks the general tone of editorials in colored newspapers is apt to be impressed with this idea. If the mass of Negroes took their present and future as seriously as do the most of their leaders, the race would be in no mental condition to sustain the terrible pressure which it undergoes, it would sink of its own weight. Yet, it must be acknowledged that in the making of a race over-seriousness is a far lesser failing than its reverse, and even the faults resulting from it lean toward the right.

We drove into the town just before dark. As we passed a large unpainted church, my companion pointed it out as the place where he held his school. I promised that I would go there with him the next morning and stay a

while. The town was of that kind which hardly requires or deserves descrip-
tion; a straggling line of brick and wooden stores on one side of the railroad
track and some cottages of various sizes on the other side constituted about
the whole of it. The young school teacher boarded at the best house in the
place owned by a colored man. It was painted, had glass windows, contained
"store bought" furniture, an organ, and lamps with chimneys. The owner
held a job of some kind on the railroad. After supper it was not long before
everybody was sleepy. I occupied the room with the school teacher. In a few
minutes after we got into the room he was in bed and asleep; but I took
advantage of the unusual luxury of a lamp which gave light, and sat looking
over my notes and jotting down some ideas which were still fresh in my
mind. Suddenly I became conscious of that sense of alarm which is always
aroused by the sound of hurrying footsteps on the silence of the night. I
stopped work, and looked at my watch. It was after eleven. I listened, strain-
ing every nerve to hear above the tumult of my quickening pulse. I caught
the murmur of voices, then the gallop of a horse, then of another and anoth-
er. Now thoroughly alarmed, I woke my companion, and together we both
listened. After a moment he put out the light, softly opened the window-
blind, and we cautiously peeped out. We saw men moving in one direction,
and from the mutterings we vaguely caught the rumor that some terrible
crime had been committed, murder! rape! I put on my coat and hat. My
friend did all in his power to dissuade me from venturing out; but it was
impossible for me to remain in the house under such tense excitement. My
nerves would not have stood it. Perhaps what bravery I exercised in going out
was due to the fact that I felt sure my identity as a colored man had not yet
become known in the town.

I went out, and, following the drift, reached the railroad station. There
was gathered there a crowd of men, all white, and others were steadily arriv-
ing, seemingly from all the surrounding country. How did the news spread
so quickly? I watched these men moving under the yellow glare of the
kerosene lamps about the station, stern, comparatively silent, all of them
armed, some of them in boots and spurs; fierce determined men. I had come
to know the type well, blond, tall and lean, with ragged mustache and beard,
and glittering gray eyes. At the first suggestion of daylight they began to dis-
perse in groups, going in several directions. There was no extra noise or
excitement, no loud talking, only swift, sharp words of command given by
those who seemed to be accepted as leaders by mutual understanding. In fact,
the impression made upon me was that everything was being done in quite

an orderly manner. In spite of so many leaving, the crowd around the station continued to grow; at sunrise there were a great many women and children. By this time I also noticed some colored people; a few seemed to be going about customary tasks, several were standing on the outskirts of the crowd; but the gathering of Negroes usually seen in such towns was missing.

Before noon they brought him in. Two horsemen rode abreast; between them, half dragged, the poor wretch made his way through the dust. His hands were tied behind him, and ropes around his body were fastened to the saddle horns of his double guard. The men who at midnight had been stern and silent were now emitting that terror instilling sound known as the "rebel yell." A space was quickly cleared in the crowd, and a rope placed about his neck, when from somewhere came the suggestion, "Burn him!" It ran like an electric current. Have you ever witnessed the transformation of human beings into savage beasts? Nothing can be more terrible. A railroad tie was sunk into the ground, the rope was removed and a chain brought and securely coiled around the victim and the stake. There he stood, a man only in form and stature, every sign of degeneracy stamped upon his countenance. His eyes were dull and vacant, indicating not a single ray of thought. Evidently the realization of his fearful fate had robbed him of whatever reasoning power he had ever possessed. He was too stunned and stupefied even to tremble. Fuel was brought from everywhere, oil, the torch; the flames crouched for an instant as though to gather strength, then leaped up as high as their victim's head. He squirmed, he writhed, strained at his chains, then gave out cries and groans that I shall always hear. The cries and groans were choked off by the fire and smoke; but his eyes bulging from their sockets, rolled from side to side, appealing in vain for help. Some of the crowd yelled and cheered, others seemed appalled at what they had done, and there were those who turned away sickened at the sight. I was fixed to the spot where I stood, powerless to take my eyes from what I did not want to see.

It was over before I realized that time had elapsed. Before I could make myself believe that what I saw was really happening, I was looking at a scorched post, a smoldering fire, blackened bones, charred fragments sifting down through coils of chain, and the smell of burnt flesh—human flesh—was in my nostrils.

I walked a short distance away, and sat down in order to clear my dazed mind. A great wave of humiliation and shame swept over me. Shame that I belonged to a race that could be so dealt with; and shame for my country, that it, the great example of democracy to the world, should be the only civ-

ilized, if not the only state on earth, where a human being would be burned alive. My heart turned bitter within me. I could understand why Negroes are led to sympathize with even their worst criminals, and to protect them when possible. By all the impulses of normal human nature they can and should do nothing less.

Whenever I hear protests from the South that it should be left alone to deal with the Negro question, my thoughts go back to that scene of brutality and savagery. I do not see how a people that can find in its conscience any excuse whatever for slowly burning to death a human being, or to tolerate such an act, can be entrusted with the salvation of a race. Of course, there are in the South men of liberal thought who do not approve lynching; but I wonder how long they will endure the limits which are placed upon free speech. They still cower and tremble before "Southern opinion." Even so late as the recent Atlanta riot, those men who were brave enough to speak a word in behalf of justice and humanity felt called upon, by way of apology, to preface what they said with a glowing rhetorical tribute to the Anglo-Saxon's superiority, and to refer to the "great and impassable gulf" between the races "fixed by the Creator at the foundation of the world." The question of the relative qualities of the two races is still an open one. The reference to the "great gulf" loses force in face of the fact that there are in this country perhaps three or four million people with the blood of both races in their veins; but I fail to see the pertinency of either statement, subsequent to the beating and murdering of scores of innocent people in the streets of a civilized and Christian city.

The Southern whites are in many respects a great people. Looked at from a certain point of view, they are picturesque. If one will put himself in a romantic frame of mind, he can admire their notions of chivalry and bravery and justice. In this same frame of mind an intelligent man can go to the theater and applaud the impossible hero, who with his single sword slays everybody in the play except the equally impossible heroine. So can an ordinary peace-loving citizen sit by a comfortable fire and read with enjoyment of the bloody deeds of pirates and the fierce brutality of Vikings. This is the way in which we gratify the old, underlying animal instincts and passions; but we should shudder with horror at the mere idea of such practices being realities in this day of enlightened and humanitarianized thought. The Southern whites are not yet living quite in the present age, many of their general ideas hark back to a former century, some of them to the Dark Ages. In the light of other days, they are sometimes magnificent. To-day they are often ludi-

crous and cruel.

How long I sat with bitter thoughts running through my mind, I do not know; perhaps an hour or more. When I decided to get up and go back to the house I found that I could hardly stand on my feet. I was as weak as a man who had lost blood. However, I dragged myself along, with the central idea of a general plan well fixed in my mind. I did not find my school teacher friend at home, so did not see him again. I swallowed a few mouthfuls of food, packed my bag, and caught the afternoon train.

When I reached Macon, I stopped only long enough to get the main part of my luggage, and to buy a ticket for New York. All along the journey I was occupied in debating with myself the step which I had decided to take. I argued that to forsake one's race to better one's condition was no less worthy an action than to forsake one's country for the same purpose. I finally made up my mind that I would neither disclaim the black race nor claim the white race; but that I would change my name, raise a mustache, and let the world take me for what it would; that it was not necessary for me to go about with a label of inferiority pasted across my forehead. All the while, I understood that it was not discouragement, or fear, or search for a larger field of action and opportunity, that was driving me out of the Negro race. I knew that it was shame, unbearable shame. Shame at being identified with a people that could with impunity be treated worse than animals. For certainly the law would restrain and punish the malicious burning alive of animals.

So once again, I found myself gazing at the towers of New York, and wondering what future that city held in store for me.

CHAPTER XI

I HAVE now reached that part of my narrative where I must be brief, and touch only lightly on important facts; therefore, the reader must make up his mind to pardon skips and jumps and meager details.

When I reached New York I was completely lost. I could not have felt more a stranger had I been suddenly dropped into Constantinople. I knew not where to turn or how to strike out. I was so oppressed by a feeling of loneliness that the temptation to visit my old home in Connecticut was well nigh irresistible. I reasoned, however, that unless I found my old music teacher, I should be, after so many years of absence, as much of a stranger

there as in New York; and, furthermore, that in view of the step which I had decided to take, such a visit would be injudicious. I remembered, too, that I had some property there in the shape of a piano and a few books, but decided that it would not be worth what it might cost me to take possession.

By reason of the fact that my living expenses in the South had been very small, I still had nearly four hundred dollars of my capital left. In contemplation of this, my natural and acquired Bohemian tastes asserted themselves, and I decided to have a couple of weeks' good time before worrying seriously about the future. I went to Coney Island and the other resorts, took in the pre-season shows along Broadway, and ate at first class restaurants; but I shunned the old Sixth Avenue district as though it were pest infected. My few days of pleasure made appalling inroads upon what cash I had, and caused me to see that it required a good deal of money to live in New York as I wished to live, and that I should have to find, very soon, some more or less profitable employment. I was sure that unknown, without friends or prestige, it would be useless to try to establish myself as a teacher of music; so I gave that means of earning a livelihood scarcely any consideration. And even had I considered it possible to secure pupils, as I then felt, I should have hesitated about taking up a work in which the chances for any considerable financial success are necessarily so small. I had made up my mind that since I was not going to be a Negro, I would avail myself of every possible opportunity to make a white man's success; and that, if it can be summed up in any one word, means "money."

I watched the "want" columns in the newspapers and answered a number of advertisements; but in each case found the positions were such as I could not fill or did not want. I also spent several dollars for "ads" which brought me no replies. In this way I came to know the hopes and disappointments of a large and pitiable class of humanity in this great city, the people who look for work through the newspapers. After some days of this sort of experience, I concluded that the main difficulty with me was that I was not prepared for what I wanted to do. I then decided upon a course which, for an artist, showed an uncommon amount of practical sense and judgment. I made up my mind to enter a business college. I took a small room, ate at lunch counters, in order to economize, and pursued my studies with the zeal that I have always been able to put into any work upon which I set my heart. Yet, in spite of all my economy, when I had been at the school for several months, my funds gave out completely. I reached the point where I could not afford sufficient food for each day. In this plight, I was glad to get, through one of the

teachers, a job as an ordinary clerk in a downtown wholesale house. I did my work faithfully, and received a raise of salary before I expected it. I even managed to save a little money out of my modest earnings. In fact, I began then to contract the money fever, which later took strong possession of me. I kept my eyes open, watching for a chance to better my condition. It finally came in the form of a position with a house which was at the time establishing a South American department. My knowledge of Spanish was, of course, the principal cause of my good luck; and it did more for me; it placed me where the other clerks were practically put out of competition with me. I was not slow in taking advantage of the opportunity to make myself indispensable to the firm.

What an interesting and absorbing game is money making! After each deposit at my savings-bank, I used to sit and figure out, all over again, my principal and interest, and make calculations on what the increase would be in such and such time. Out of this I derived a great deal of pleasure. I denied myself as much as possible in order to swell my savings. Even so much as I enjoyed smoking, I limited myself to an occasional cigar, and that was generally of a variety which in my old days at the "Club" was known as a "Henry Mud." Drinking I cut out altogether, but that was no great sacrifice.

The day on which I was able to figure up $1,000.00 marked an epoch in my life. And this was not because I had never before had money. In my gambling days and while I was with my "millionaire" I handled sums running high up into the hundreds; but they had come to me like fairy god-mother's gifts, and at a time when my conception of money was that it was made only to spend. Here, on the other hand, was a thousand dollars which I had earned by days of honest and patient work, a thousand dollars which I had carefully watched grow from the first dollar; and I experienced, in owning them, a pride and satisfaction which to me was an entirely new sensation. As my capital went over the thousand dollar mark, I was puzzled to know what to do with it, how to put it to the most advantageous use. I turned down first one scheme and then another, as though they had been devised for the sole purpose of gobbling up my money. I finally listened to a friend who advised me to put all I had in New York real estate; and under his guidance I took equity in a piece of property on which stood a rickety old tenement-house. I did not regret following this friend's advice, for in something like six months I disposed of my equity for more than double my investment. From that time on I devoted myself to the study of New York real estate, and watched for opportunities to make similar investments. In spite of two or three specula-

tions which did not turn out well, I have been remarkably successful. To-day I am the owner and part-owner of several flat-houses. I have changed my place of employment four times since resuming to New York, and each change has been a decided advancement. Concerning the position which I now hold, I shall say nothing except that it pays extremely well.

As my outlook on the world grew brighter, I began to mingle in the social circles of the men with whom I came in contact; and gradually, by a process of elimination, I reached a grade of society of no small degree of culture. My appearance was always good and my ability to play on the piano, especially ragtime, which was then at the height of its vogue, made me a welcome guest. The anomaly of my social position often appealed strongly to my sense of humor. I frequently smiled inwardly at some remark not altogether complimentary to people of color; and more than once I felt like declaiming, "I am a colored man. Do I not disprove the theory that one drop of Negro blood renders a man unfit?" Many a night when I returned to my room after an enjoyable evening, I laughed heartily over what struck me as the capital joke I was playing.

Then I met her, and what I had regarded as a joke was gradually changed into the most serious question of my life. I first saw her at a musical which was given one evening at a house to which I was frequently invited. I did not notice her among the other guests before she came forward and sang two sad little songs. When she began I was out in the hallway where many of the men were gathered; but with the first few notes I crowded with others into the doorway to see who the singer was. When I saw the girl, the surprise which I had felt at the first sound of her voice was heightened; she was almost tall and quite slender, with lustrous yellow hair and eyes so blue as to appear almost black. She was as white as a lily, and she was dressed in white. Indeed, she seemed to me the most dazzlingly white thing I had ever seen. But it was not her delicate beauty which attracted me most; it was her voice, a voice which made one wonder how tones of such passionate color could come from so fragile a body.

I determined that when the programme was over I would seek an introduction to her; but at the moment, instead of being the easy man of the world, I became again the bashful boy of fourteen, and my courage failed me. I contented myself with hovering as near her as politeness would permit; near enough to hear her voice, which in conversation was low, yet thrilling, like the deeper middle tones of a flute. I watched the men gather around her talking and laughing in an easy manner, and wondered how it was possible for

them to do it. But destiny, my special destiny, was at work. I was standing near, talking with affected gayety to several young ladies, who, however, must have remarked my preoccupation; for my second sense of hearing was alert to what was being said by the group of which the girl in white was the center, when I heard her say "I think his playing of Chopin is exquisite." And one of my friends in the group replied, "You haven't met him? Allow me—" then turning to me, "Old man, when you have a moment I wish you to meet Miss ——." I don't know what she said to me or what I said to her. I can remember that I tried to be clever, and experienced a growing conviction that I was making myself appear more and more idiotic. I am certain, too, that, in spite of my Italian-like complexion, I was as red as a beet.

Instead of taking the car I walked home. I needed the air and exercise as a sort of sedative. I am not sure whether my troubled condition of mind was due to the fact that I had been struck by love or to the feeling that I had made a bad impression upon her.

As the weeks went by, and when I had met her several more times, I came to know that I was seriously in love; and then began for me days of worry, for I had more than the usual doubts and fears of a young man in love to contend with.

Up to this time I had assumed and played my rôle as a white man with a certain degree of nonchalance, a carelessness as to the outcome, which made the whole thing more amusing to me than serious; but now I ceased to regard "being a white man" as a sort of practical joke. My acting had called for mere external effects. Now I began to doubt my ability to play the part. I watched her to see if she was scrutinizing me, to see if she was looking for anything in me which made me differ from the other men she knew. In place of an old inward feeling of superiority over many of my friends, I began to doubt myself. I began even to wonder if I really was like the men I associated with; if there was not, after all, an indefinable something which marked a difference.

But, in spite of my doubts and timidity, my affair progressed, and I finally felt sufficiently encouraged to decide to ask her to marry me. Then began the hardest struggle of my life, whether to ask her to marry me under false colors or to tell her the whole truth. My sense of what was exigent made me feel there was no necessity of saying anything; but my inborn sense of honor rebelled at even indirect deception in this case. But however much I moralized on the question, I found it more and more difficult to reach the point of confession. The dread that I might lose her took possession of me each time I sought to speak, and rendered it impossible for me to do so. That

moral courage requires more than physical courage is no mere poetic fancy. I am sure I would have found it easier to take the place of a gladiator, no matter how fierce the Numidian lion, than to tell that slender girl that I had Negro blood in my veins. The fact which I had at times wished to cry out, I now wished to hide forever.

During this time we were drawn together a great deal by the mutual bond of music. She loved to hear me play Chopin, and was herself far from being a poor performer of his compositions. I think I carried her every new song that was published which I thought suitable to her voice, and played the accompaniment for her. Over these songs we were like two innocent children with new toys. She had never been anything but innocent; but my innocence was a transformation wrought by my love for her, love which melted away my cynicism and whitened my sullied soul and gave me back the wholesome dreams of my boyhood. There is nothing better in all the world that a man can do for his moral welfare than to love a good woman.

My artistic temperament also underwent an awakening. I spent many hours at my piano, playing over old and new composers. I also wrote several little pieces in a more or less Chopinesque style, which I dedicated to her. And so the weeks and months went by. Often words of love trembled on my lips, but I dared not utter them, because I knew they would have to be followed by other words which I had not the courage to frame. There might have been some other woman in my set with whom I could have fallen in love and asked to marry me without a word of explanation; but the more I knew this girl, the less could I find it in my heart to deceive her. And yet, in spite of this specter that was constantly looming up before me, I could never have believed that life held such happiness as was contained in those dream days of love.

One Saturday afternoon, in early June, I was coming up Fifth Avenue, and at the corner of Twenty-third Street I met her. She had been shopping. We stopped to chat for a moment, and I suggested that we spend half an hour at the Eden Musée. We were standing leaning on the rail in front of a group of figures, more interested in what we had to say to each other than in the group, when my attention became fixed upon a man who stood at my side studying his catalogue. It took me only an instant to recognize in him my old friend "Shiny." My first impulse was to change my position at once. As quick as a flash I considered all the risks I might run in speaking to him, and most especially the delicate question of introducing him to her. I must confess that in my embarrassment and confusion I felt small and mean. But

before I could decide what to do he looked around at me and, after an instant, said, "Pardon me; but isn't this ——?" The nobler part in me responded to the sound of his voice, and I took his hand in a hearty clasp. Whatever fears I had felt were quickly banished, for he seemed, at a glance, to divine my situation, and let drop no word that would have aroused suspicion as to the truth. With a slight misgiving I presented him to her, and was again relieved of fear. She received the introduction in her usual gracious manner, and without the least hesitancy or embarrassment joined in the conversation. An amusing part about the introduction was that I was upon the point of introducing him as "Shiny," and stammered a second or two before I could recall his name. We chatted for some fifteen minutes. He was spending his vacation North, with the intention of doing four or six weeks' work in one of the summer schools; he was also going to take a bride back with him in the fall. He asked me about myself, but in so diplomatic a way that I found no difficulty in answering him. The polish of his language and the unpedantic manner in which he revealed his culture greatly impressed her; and after we had left the Musée she showed it by questioning me about him. I was surprised at the amount of interest a refined black man could arouse. Even after changes in the conversation she reverted several times to the subject of "Shiny." Whether it was more than mere curiosity I could not tell, but I was convinced that she herself knew very little about prejudice.

Just why it should have done so I do not know, but somehow the "Shiny" incident gave me encouragement and confidence to cast the die of my fate; but I reasoned that since I wanted to marry her only, and since it concerned her alone, I would divulge my secret to no one else, not even her parents.

One evening, a few days afterwards, at her home, we were going over some new songs and compositions, when she asked me, as she often did, to play the "13th Nocturne." When I began she drew a chair near to my right, and sat leaning with her elbow on the end of the piano, her chin resting on her hand, and her eyes reflecting the emotions which the music awoke in her. An impulse which I could not control rushed over me, a wave of exaltation, the music under my fingers sank almost to a whisper, and calling her for the first time by her Christian name, but without daring to look at her, I said, "I love you, I love you, I love you." My fingers were trembling, so that I ceased playing. I felt her hand creep to mine, and when I looked at her her eyes were glistening with tears. I understood, and could scarcely resist the longing to take her in my arms; but I remembered, remembered that which has been the sacrificial altar of so much happiness—Duty and bending over her hand in

mind, I said, "Yes, I love you; but there is something more, too, that I must tell you." Then I told her, in what words I do not know, the truth. I felt her hand grow cold, and when I looked up she was gazing at me with a wild, fixed stare as though I was some object she had never seen. Under the strange light in her eyes I felt that I was growing black and thick-featured and crimp-haired. She appeared not to have comprehended what I had said. Her lips trembled and she attempted to say something to me; but the words stuck in her throat. Then dropping her head on the piano she began to weep with great sobs that shook her frail body. I tried to console her, and blurted out incoherent words of love; but this seemed only to increase her distress, and when I left her she was still weeping.

When I got into the street I felt very much as I did the night after meeting my father and sister at the opera in Paris, even a similar desperate inclination to get drunk; but my self-control was stronger. This was the only time in my life that I ever felt absolute regret at being colored, that I cursed the drops of African blood in my veins, and wished that I were really white. When I reached my rooms I sat and smoked several cigars while I tried to think out the significance of what had occurred. I reviewed the whole history of our acquaintance, recalled each smile she had given me, each word she had said to me that nourished my hope. I went over the scene we had just gone through, trying to draw from it what was in my favor and what was against me. I was rewarded by feeling confident that she loved me, but I could not estimate what was the effect upon her of my confession. At last, nervous and unhappy, I wrote her a letter, which I dropped into the mailbox before going to bed, in which I said:

> "I understand, understand even better than you, and so I suffer even more than you. But why should either of us suffer for what neither of us is to blame? If there is any blame, it belongs to me, and I can only make the old, yet strongest plea that can be offered, I love you; and I know that my love, my great love, infinitely overbalances that blame, and blots it out. What is it that stands in the way of our happiness? It is not what you feel or what I feel; it is not what you are or what I am. It is what others feel and are. But, oh! is that a fair price? In all the endeavors and struggles of life in all our strivings and longings there is only one thing worth seeking, only one thing worth winning, and that is love. It is not always found, but

when it is, there is nothing in all the world for which it can be
profitably exchanged."

The second morning after, I received a note from her which stated briefly
that she was going up in New Hampshire to spend the summer with relatives
there. She made no reference to what had passed between us; nor did she say
exactly when she would leave the city. The note contained no single word
that gave me any clue to her feelings. I could only gather hope from the fact
that she had written at all. On the same evening, with a degree of trepidation
which rendered me almost frightened, I went to her house.

I met her mother, who told me that she had left for the country that very
afternoon. Her mother treated me in her usual pleasant manner, which fact
greatly reassured me; and I left the house with a vague sense of hope stirring
in my breast, which sprang from the conviction that she had not yet divulged
my secret. But that hope did not remain with me long. I waited one, two,
three weeks, nervously examining my mail every day, looking for some word
from her. All of the letters received by me seemed so insignificant, so worth-
less, because there was none from her. The slight buoyancy of spirit which I
had felt gradually dissolved into gloomy heartsickness. I became preoccu-
pied, I lost appetite, lost sleep, and lost ambition. Several of my friends inti-
mated to me that perhaps I was working too hard.

She stayed away the whole summer. I did not go to the house, but saw
her father at various times, and he was as friendly as ever. Even after I knew
that she was back in town I did not go to see her. I determined to wait for
some word or sign. I had finally taken refuge and comfort in my pride, pride
which, I suppose, I came by naturally enough.

The first time I saw her after her return was one night at the theater. She
and her mother sat in company with a young man whom I knew slightly, not
many seats away from me. Never did she appear more beautiful; and yet, it
may have been my fancy, she seemed a trifle paler and there was a suggestion
of haggardness in her countenance. But that only heightened her beauty; the
very delicacy of her charm melted down the strength of my pride. My situa-
tion made me feel weak and powerless, like a man trying with his bare hands
to break the iron bars of his prison cell. When the performance was over I
hurried out and placed myself where, unobserved, I could see her as she
passed out. The haughtiness of spirit in which I had sought relief was all
gone, and I was willing and ready to undergo any humiliation.

Shortly afterward we met at a progressive card party, and during the

evening we were thrown together at one of the tables as partners. This was really our first meeting since the eventful night at her house. Strangely enough, in spite of our mutual nervousness, we won every trick of the game, and one of our opponents jokingly quoted the old saw, "Lucky at cards, unlucky in love." Our eyes met, and I am sure that in the momentary glance my whole soul went out to her in one great plea. She lowered her eyes and uttered a nervous little laugh. During the rest of the game I fully merited the unexpressed and expressed abuse of my various partners; for my eyes followed her wherever she was, and I played whatever card my fingers happened to touch.

Later in the evening she went to the piano and began to play very softly, as to herself, the opening bars of the 13th Nocturne. I felt that the psychic moment of my life had come, a moment which if lost could never be called back; and, in as careless a manner as I could assume, I sauntered over to the piano and stood almost bending over her. She continued playing; but, in a voice that was almost a whisper, she called me by my Christian name and said, "I love you, I love you, I love you." I took her place at the piano and played the Nocturne in a manner that silenced the chatter of the company both in and out of the room; involuntarily closing it with the major triad.

We were married the following spring, and went to Europe for several months. It was a double joy for me to be in France again under such conditions.

First there came to us a little girl, with hair and eyes dark like mine, but who is growing to have ways like her mother. Two years later there came a boy, who has my temperament, but is fair like his mother, a little golden-headed god, a face and head that would have delighted the heart of an old Italian master. And this boy, with his mother's eyes and features, occupies an inner sanctuary of my heart; for it was for him that she gave all; and that is the second sacred sorrow of my life.

The few years of our married life were supremely happy, and, perhaps she was even happier than I; for after our marriage, in spite of all the wealth of her love which she lavished upon me, there came a new dread to haunt me, a dread which I cannot explain and which was unfounded, but one that never left me. I was in constant fear that she would discover in me some short-coming which she would unconsciously attribute to my blood rather than to a failing of human nature. But no cloud ever came to mar our life together; her loss to me is irreparable. My children need a mother's care, but I shall never marry again. It is to my children that I have devoted my life. I no

longer have the same fear for myself of my secret being found out; for since my wife's death I have gradually dropped out of social life; but there is nothing I would not suffer to keep the "brand" from being placed upon them.

It is difficult for me to analyze my feelings concerning my present position in the world. Sometimes it seems to me that I have never really been a Negro, that I have been only a privileged spectator of their inner life; at other times I feel that I have been a coward, a deserter, and I am possessed by a strange longing for my mother's people.

Several years ago I attended a great meeting in the interest of Hampton Institute at Carnegie Hall. The Hampton students sang the old songs and awoke memories that left me sad. Among the speakers were R. C. Ogden, Ex-Ambassador Choate, and Mark Twain; but the greatest interest of the audience was centered in Booker T. Washington, and not because he so much surpassed the others in eloquence but because of what he represented with so much earnestness and faith. And it is this that all of that small but gallant band of colored men who are publicly fighting the cause of their race have behind them. Even those who oppose them know that these men have the eternal principles of right on their side, and they will be victors even though they should go down in defeat. Beside them I feel small and selfish. I am an ordinarily successful white man who has made a little money. They are men who are making history and a race. I, too, might have taken part in a work so glorious.

My love for my children makes me glad that I am what I am, and keeps me from desiring to be otherwise; and yet, when I sometimes open a little box in which I still keep my fast yellowing manuscripts the only tangible remnants of a vanished dream, a dead ambition, a sacrificed talent, I cannot repress the thought, that, after all, I have chosen the lesser part, that I have sold my birthright for a mess of pottage.

PAUL LAURENCE DUNBAR

(1872-1906)

*I*n his brief life, Paul Laurence Dunbar managed to achieve international fame for his poetry and short stories, and at just 21 years of age, his work prompted Frederick Douglass to declare Dunbar "the most promising young colored man in America." Though his rise to fame is a remarkable story in itself, critics and scholars have often pointed out that Dunbar's poetry was deserving of the praise it garnered based solely on its quality, and not for reasons of the author's race, origin and condition.

When *Lyrics of Lowly Life* was published in 1896, Dunbar was only 24 years old. He would not live another ten years, but his large body of work exemplified the prolific nature and diligence of the young man whose gift for poetry enabled him to travel the world and become friends with some of the most prominent Americans of the time.

Dunbar was born in 1872 in Dayton, Ohio, the son of former slaves. His father, Joshua Dunbar escaped slavery and fled to Canada, only to return and serve in the Fifty-fifth Massachusetts Infantry Regiment and the 5th Massachusetts Colored Cavalry Regiment during the Civil War. Paul was fascinated with the stories of his mother's slavery and his father's experiences on the battlefields. He demonstrated an early interest in writing, and composed his first poem at the age of six. Before he finished high school, his poetry had been published in local newspapers.

Coincidentally, two of Dunbar's schoolmates were Orville and Wilbur Wright, who helped Dunbar publish his first book of poetry, *Oak and Ivy* in 1892 at the age of twenty. He quickly established a reputation around Dayton as a poet, and began to recite his work at various clubs and organizations in town. But after his graduation from high school, the only work Dunbar could find was that of an elevator operator, working for four dollars a week. Dunbar used this opportunity to sell volumes of his poetry to elevator passengers for one dollar each, and used the money to repay the cost of

publishing the book.

Dunbar was invited to join the Western Association of Writers when the organization coincidentally met in Dayton that year, and with the World's Columbian Exposition opening in 1893, he left for Chicago to seek work. There, he met several influential blacks, including Frederick Douglass, who was then the Consul General to the Republic of Haiti, and Douglass hired him to work in the Haitian Pavilion. Dunbar's time in Chicago at the Exposition led to some lasting friendships, but when the Exposition left Chicago, he returned to Dayton, his elevator job and his writing.

Shortly after his return, the playwright and actor James A. Herne did a public recital of a Dunbar poem and was moved enough to introduce the young poet's work to William Dean Howells, who reviewed Dunbar's *Majors and Minors* in *Harper's Weekly* in 1896, and then convinced Dodd, Mead to publish more of Dunbar's verse. Howell's glowing review made Paul Laurence Dunbar a prominent national figure overnight.

Dodd, Mead would end up combining Dunbar's first two volumes of poetry into one volume titled, *Lyrics of Lowly Life*, and Howell himself wrote an introduction that asks the reader not to read Dunbar's poems because he is black or because he is the son of slaves. Rather, he implores the reader to simply enjoy the poems as they stand alone. He writes:

> I cannot undertake to prophesy concerning this; but if he (Dunbar) should do nothing more than he has done, I should feel that he had made the strongest claim for the negro in English literature that the negro has yet made. He has at least produced something that, however we may critically disagree about it, we cannot well refuse to enjoy; in more than one piece he has produced a work of art.

Soon after the publication of *Lyrics of Lowly Life*, Dunbar's fame blossomed, and he struck out on a recital tour in England. There, he met the African-English composer, Samuel Coleridge-Taylor, and the two collaborated on a collection of choral pieces entitled *Seven African Romances*, as well an opera, *Dream Lovers*.

Dunbar had achieved the kind of critical acclaim that few writers achieve after a lifetime of writing, but despite his success, some critics spoke out against what they believed were Dunbar's use of negative racial stereotypes.

James Weldon Johnson, the Harlem intellectual and poet had a conversation with Dunbar, and claimed the young poet was depressed that the pub-

lic and many of his critics wanted nothing but the dialect pieces of southern plantation life. Other critics, such as Howells, actually preferred the dialect poems, and was particularly impressed with "The Party," which, he said, "opened vistas into the simple, sensuous, joyous nature of his race."

However innocuous Dunbar's poetry may have seemed to some, he was not beyond writing about the black condition and civil rights issues. In his poem, "We Wear the Mask," Dunbar writes of the suppressed pain of blacks:

> We wear the mask that grins and lies,
> It hides our cheeks and shades our eyes,—
> This debt we pay to human guile;
> With torn and bleeding hearts we smile,
> And mouth with myriad subtleties.
>
> Why should the world be over-wise,
> In counting all our tears and sighs?
> Nay, let them only see us, while
> We wear the mask.
>
> We smile, but, O great Christ, our cries
> To thee from tortured souls arise.
> We sing, but oh the clay is vile
> Beneath our feet, and long the mile;
> But let the world dream otherwise,
> We wear the mask!

Like his friends Booker T. Washington and W.E.B. DuBois, Dunbar had become a voice symbolic of the black struggle for justice and equal rights in America. When he returned from England, he married a young writer, teacher and proponent of racial and gender equality with a graduate degree from Cornell University. They lived in Washington, D.C., and Dunbar took a job in the reading room of the Library of Congress. However, less than a year after taking the job, Dunbar quit, finding the work tiresome, and he felt the accumulation of dust was contributing to his languishing tuberculosis. Under doctor's orders to rest, Dunbar continued to write and give recitals of his work.

His fame continued to increase, and he was invited to ride in William McKinley's inaugural parade in January of 1901, and McKinley's successor,

Theodore Roosevelt, presented Dunbar with a ceremonial sword. But the following year, Dunbar separated from his wife, and depression from his declining health, his broken marriage, and alcoholism began to take its toll. He continued to write, however, right up until his death at the age of 33, in the arms of his mother at her home in Dayton, Ohio in 1906. Dunbar's legacy, many critics believe, is that of an innovative and brave artist who stretched dialect into serious social ideas. He is considered by many the father of black poetry in the twentieth century.

Lyrics of Lowly Life

ERE SLEEP COMES DOWN
TO SOOTHE THE WEARY EYES.

Ere sleep comes down to soothe the weary eyes,
 Which all the day with ceaseless care have sought
The magic gold which from the seeker flies;
 Ere dreams put on the gown and cap of thought,
And make the waking world a world of lies,—
 Of lies most palpable, uncouth, forlorn,
That say life's full of aches and tears and sighs,—
 Oh, how with more than dreams the soul is torn,
Ere sleep comes down to soothe the weary eyes.

Ere sleep comes down to soothe the weary eyes,
 How all the griefs and heartaches we have known
Come up like pois'nous vapors that arise
 From some base witch's caldron, when the crone,
To work some potent spell, her magic plies.
 The past which held its share of bitter pain,
Whose ghost we prayed that Time might exorcise,
 Comes up, is lived and suffered o'er again,
Ere sleep comes down to soothe the weary eyes.

Ere sleep comes down to soothe the weary eyes,
 What phantoms fill the dimly lighted room;
What ghostly shades in awe-creating guise
 Are bodied forth within the teeming gloom.
What echoes faint of sad and soul-sick cries,

 And pangs of vague inexplicable pain
That pay the spirit's ceaseless enterprise,
 Come thronging through the chambers of the brain,
Ere sleep comes down to soothe the weary eyes.

Ere sleep comes down to soothe the weary eyes,
 Where ranges forth the spirit far and free?
Through what strange realms and unfamiliar skies
 Tends her far course to lands of mystery?
To lands unspeakable—beyond surmise,
 Where shapes unknowable to being spring,
Till, faint of wing, the Fancy fails and dies
 Much wearied with the spirit's journeying,
Ere sleep comes down to soothe the weary eyes.

Ere sleep comes down to soothe the weary eyes,
 How questioneth the soul that other soul,—
The inner sense which neither cheats nor lies,
 But self exposes unto self, a scroll
Full writ with all life's acts unwise or wise,
 In characters indelible and known;
So, trembling with the shock of sad surprise,
 The soul doth view its awful self alone,
Ere sleep comes down to soothe the weary eyes.

When sleep comes down to seal the weary eyes,
 The last dear sleep whose soft embrace is balm,
And whom sad sorrow teaches us to prize
 For kissing all our passions into calm,
Ah, then, no more we heed the sad world's cries,
 Or seek to probe th' eternal mystery,
Or fret our souls at long-withheld replies,
 At glooms through which our visions cannot see,
When sleep comes down to seal the weary eyes.

THE POET AND HIS SONG.

A song is but a little thing,
And yet what joy it is to sing!
In hours of toil it gives me zest,
And when at eve I long for rest;
When cows come home along the bars,
 And in the fold I hear the bell,
As Night, the shepherd, herds his stars,
 I sing my song, and all is well.

There are no ears to hear my lays,
No lips to lift a word of praise;
But still, with faith unfaltering,
I live and laugh and love and sing.
What matters yon unheeding throng?
 They cannot feel my spirit's spell,
Since life is sweet and love is long,
 I sing my song, and all is well.

My days are never days of ease;
I till my ground and prune my trees.
When ripened gold is all the plain,
I put my sickle to the grain.
I labor hard, and toil and sweat,
 While others dream within the dell;
But even while my brow is wet,
 I sing my song, and all is well.

Sometimes the sun, unkindly hot,
My garden makes a desert spot;
Sometimes a blight upon the tree
Takes all my fruit away from me;
And then with throes of bitter pain
 Rebellious passions rise and swell;
But—life is more than fruit or grain,
 And so I sing, and all is well.

RETORT.

"Thou art a fool," said my head to my heart,
"Indeed, the greatest of fools thou art,
 To be led astray by the trick of a tress,
By a smiling face or a ribbon smart;"
 And my heart was in sore distress.

Then Phyllis came by, and her face was fair,
The light gleamed soft on her raven hair;
 And her lips were blooming a rosy red.
Then my heart spoke out with a right bold air:
 "Thou art worse than a fool, O head!"

ACCOUNTABILITY.

Folks ain't got no right to censuah othah folks about dey habits;
Him dat giv' de squir'ls de bushtails made de bobtails fu' de rabbits.
Him dat built de gread big mountains hollered out de little valleys,
Him dat made de streets an' driveways was n't shamed to make de
alleys.

We is all constructed diff'ent, d'ain't no two of us de same;
We cain't he'p ouah likes an' dislikes, ef we 'se bad we ain't to blame.
Ef we 'se good, we need n't show off, case you bet it ain't ouah doin'
We gits into su'ttain channels dat we jes' cain't he'p pu'suin'.

But we all fits into places dat no othah ones could fill,
An' we does the things we has to, big er little, good er ill.
John cain't tek de place o' Henry, Su an' Sally ain't alike;
Bass ain't nuthin' like a suckah, chub ain't nuthin' like a pike.

When you come to think about it, how it's all planned out
it's splendid.
Nuthin 's done er evah happens, 'dout hit 's somefin' dat's intended;
Don't keer whut you does, you has to, an' hit sholy beats de dick-
ens,—
Viney, go put on de kittle, I got one o' mastah's chickens.

FREDERICK DOUGLASS.

A hush is over all the teeming lists,
 And there is pause, a breath-space in the strife;
A spirit brave has passed beyond the mists
 And vapors that obscure the sun of life.
And Ethiopia, with bosom torn,
Laments the passing of her noblest born.

She weeps for him a mother's burning tears—
 She loved him with a mother's deepest love.
He was her champion thro' direful years,
 And held her weal all other ends above.
When Bondage held her bleeding in the dust,
He raised her up and whispered, "Hope and Trust."

For her his voice, a fearless clarion, rung
 That broke in warning on the ears of men;
For her the strong bow of his power he strung,
 And sent his arrows to the very den
Where grim Oppression held his bloody place
And gloated o'er the mis'ries of a race.

And he was no soft-tongued apologist;
 He spoke straightforward, fearlessly uncowed;
The sunlight of his truth dispelled the mist,
 And set in bold relief each dark-hued cloud;
To sin and crime he gave their proper hue,

And hurled at evil what was evil's due.

Through good and ill report he cleaved his way
 Right onward, with his face set toward the heights,
Nor feared to face the foeman's dread array,—
 The lash of scorn, the sting of petty spites.
He dared the lightning in the lightning's track,
And answered thunder with his thunder back.

When men maligned him, and their torrent wrath
 In furious imprecations o'er him broke,
He kept' his counsel as he kept his path;
 'T was for his race, not for himself, he spoke.
He knew the import of his Master's call,
And felt himself too mighty to be small.

No miser in the good he held was he,—
 His kindness followed his horizon's rim.
His heart, his talents, and his hands were free
 To all who truly needed aught of him.
Where poverty and ignorance were rife,
He gave his bounty as he gave his life.

The place and cause that first aroused his might
 Still proved its power until his latest day.
In Freedom's lists and for the aid of Right
 Still in the foremost rank he waged the fray;
Wrong lived; his occupation was not gone.
He died in action with his armor on!

We weep for him, but we have touched his hand,
 And felt the magic of his presence nigh,
The current that he sent throughout the land,
 The kindling spirit of his battle-cry.
O'er all that holds us we shall triumph yet,
And place our banner where his hopes were set!

Oh, Douglass, thou hast passed beyond the shore,

But still thy voice is ringing o'er the gale!
Thou'st taught thy race how high her hopes may soar,
 And bade her seek the heights, nor faint, nor fail.
She will not fail, she heeds thy stirring cry,
She knows thy guardian spirit will be nigh,
And, rising from beneath the chast'ning rod,
She stretches out her bleeding hands to God!

LIFE.

A crust of bread and a corner to sleep in,
A minute to smile and an hour to weep in,
A pint of joy to a peck of trouble,
And never a laugh but the moans come double;
 And that is life!

A crust and a corner that love makes precious,
With the smile to warm and the tears to refresh us;
And joy seems sweeter when cares come after,
And a moan is the finest of foils for laughter;
 And that is life!

THE LESSON.

My cot was down by a cypress grove,
 And I sat by my window the whole night long,
And heard well up from the deep dark wood
 A mocking-bird's passionate song.

And I thought of myself so sad and lone,
 And my life's cold winter that knew no spring;
Of my mind so weary and sick and wild,
 Of my heart too sad to sing.

But e'en as I listened the mock-bird's song,
 A thought stole into my saddened heart,
And I said, "I can cheer some other soul
 By a carol's simple art."

For oft from the darkness of hearts and lives
 Come songs that brim with joy and light,
As out of the gloom of the cypress grove
 The mocking-bird sings at night.

So I sang a lay for a brother's ear
 In a strain to soothe his bleeding heart,
And he smiled at the sound of my voice and lyre,
 Though mine was a feeble art.

But at his smile I smiled in turn,
 And into my soul there came a ray:
In trying to soothe another's woes
 Mine own had passed away.

THE RISING OF THE STORM.

 The lake's dark breast
 Is all unrest,
It heaves with a sob and a sigh.
 Like a tremulous bird,
 From its slumber stirred,
The moon is a-tilt in the sky.

 From the silent deep
 The waters sweep,
But faint on the cold white stones,
 And the wavelets fly
 With a plaintive cry
O'er the old earth's bare, bleak bones.

And the spray upsprings
On its ghost-white wings,
And tosses a kiss at the stars;
While a water-sprite,
In sea-pearls dight,
Hums a sea-hymn's solemn bars.

Far out in the night,
On the wavering sight
I see a dark hull loom;
And its light on high,
Like a Cyclops' eye,
Shines out through the mist and gloom.

Now the winds well up
From the earth's deep cup,
And fall on the sea and shore,
And against the pier
The waters rear
And break with a sullen roar.

Up comes the gale,
And the mist-wrought veil
Gives way to the lightning's glare,
And the cloud-drifts fall,
A sombre pall,
O'er water, earth, and air.

The storm-king flies,
His whip he plies,
And bellows down the wind.
The lightning rash
With blinding flash
Comes pricking on behind.

Rise, waters, rise,
And taunt the skies
With your swift-flitting form.

Sweep, wild winds, sweep,
 And tear the deep
To atoms in the storm.

 And the waters leapt,
 And the wild winds swept,
And blew out the moon in the sky,
 And I laughed with glee,
 It was joy to me
As the storm went raging by!

SUNSET.

The river sleeps beneath the sky,
 And clasps the shadows to its breast;
The crescent moon shines dim on high;
 And in the lately radiant west
 The gold is fading into gray.
 Now stills the lark his festive lay,
 And mourns with me the dying day.

While in the south the first faint star
 Lifts to the night its silver face,
And twinkles to the moon afar
 Across the heaven's graying space,
 Low murmurs reach me from the town,
 As Day puts on her sombre crown,
 And shakes her mantle darkly down.

THE OLD APPLE-TREE.

There 's a memory keeps a-runnin'
 Through my weary head to-night,
An' I see a picture dancin'

In the fire-flames' ruddy light;
'Tis the picture of an orchard
 Wrapped in autumn's purple haze,
With the tender light about it
 That I loved in other days.
An' a-standin' in a corner
 Once again I seem to see
The verdant leaves an' branches
 Of an old apple-tree.

You perhaps would call it ugly,
 An' I don't know but it 's so,
When you look the tree all over
 Unadorned by memory's glow;
For its boughs are gnarled an' crooked,
 An' its leaves are gettin' thin,
An' the apples of its bearin'
 Would n't fill so large a bin
As they used to. But I tell you,
 When it comes to pleasin' me,
It 's the dearest in the orchard,—
 Is that old apple-tree.

I would hide within its shelter,
 Settlin' in some cosy nook,
Where no calls nor threats could stir me
 From the pages o' my book.
Oh, that quiet, sweet seclusion
 In its fulness passeth words!
It was deeper than the deepest
 That my sanctum now affords.
Why, the jaybirds an' the robins,
 They was hand in glove with me,
As they winked at me an' warbled
 In that old apple-tree.

It was on its sturdy branches
 That in summers long ago

I would tie my swing an' dangle
 In contentment to an' fro,
Idly dreamin' childish fancies,
 Buildin' castles in the air,
Makin' o' myself a hero
 Of romances rich an' rare.
I kin shet my eyes an' see it
 Jest as plain as plain kin be,
That same old swing a-danglin'
 To the old apple-tree.

There 's a rustic seat beneath it
 That I never kin forget.
It 's the place where me an' Hallie—
 Little sweetheart—used to set,
When we 'd wander to the orchard
 So 's no listenin' ones could hear
As I whispered sugared nonsense
 Into her little willin' ear.
Now my gray old wife is Hallie,
 An' I'm grayer still than she,
But I 'll not forget our courtin'
 'Neath the old apple-tree.

Life for us ain't all been summer,
 But I guess we've had our share
Of its flittin' joys an' pleasures,
 An' a sprinklin' of its care.
Oft the skies have smiled upon us;
 Then again we've seen 'em frown,
Though our load was ne'er so heavy
 That we longed to lay it down.
But when death does come a-callin',
 This my last request shall be,—
That they 'll bury me an' Hallie
 'Neath the old apple-tree.

A PRAYER.

O Lord, the hard-won miles
 Have worn my stumbling feet:
Oh, soothe me with thy smiles,
 And make my life complete.

The thorns were thick and keen
 Where'er I trembling trod;
The way was long between
 My wounded feet and God.

Where healing waters flow
 Do thou my footsteps lead.
My heart is aching so;
 Thy gracious balm I need.

PASSION AND LOVE.

A maiden wept and, as a comforter,
Came one who cried, "I love thee," and he seized
Her in his arms and kissed her with hot breath,
That dried the tears upon her flaming cheeks.
While evermore his boldly blazing eye
Burned into hers; but she uncomforted
Shrank from his arms and only wept the more.

Then one came and gazed mutely in her face
With wide and wistful eyes; but still aloof
He held himself; as with a reverent fear,
As one who knows some sacred presence nigh.
And as she wept he mingled tear with tear,
That cheered her soul like dew a dusty flower,—
Until she smiled, approached, and touched his hand!

THE SEEDLING.

As a quiet little seedling
 Lay within its darksome bed,
To itself it fell a-talking,
 And this is what it said:

"I am not so very robust,
 But I 'll do the best I can;"
And the seedling from that moment
 Its work of life began.

So it pushed a little leaflet
 Up into the light of day,
To examine the surroundings
 And show the rest the way.

The leaflet liked the prospect,
 So it called its brother, Stem;
Then two other leaflets heard it,
 And quickly followed them.

To be sure, the haste and hurry
 Made the seedling sweat and pant;
But almost before it knew it
 It found itself a plant.

The sunshine poured upon it,
 And the clouds they gave a shower;
And the little plant kept growing
 Till it found itself a flower.

Little folks, be like the seedling,
 Always do the best you can;
Every child must share life's labor
 Just as well as every man.

And the sun and showers will help you
 Through the lonesome, struggling hours,
Till you raise to light and beauty
 Virtue's fair, unfading flowers.

PROMISE.

I grew a rose within a garden fair,
And, tending it with more than loving care,
I thought how, with the glory of its bloom,
I should the darkness of my life illume;
And, watching, ever smiled to see the lusty bud
Drink freely in the summer sun to tinct its blood.

My rose began to open, and its hue
Was sweet to me as to it sun and dew;
I watched it taking on its ruddy flame
Until the day of perfect blooming came,
Then hasted I with smiles to find it blushing red—
Too late! Some thoughtless child had plucked my rose and fled!

FULFILMENT.

I grew a rose once more to please mine eyes.
All things to aid it—dew, sun, wind, fair skies—
Were kindly; and to shield it from despoil,
I fenced it safely in with grateful toil.
No other hand than mine shall pluck this flower, said I,
And I was jealous of the bee that hovered nigh.
It grew for days; I stood hour after hour
To watch the slow unfolding of the flower,
And then I did not leave its side at all,
Lest some mischance my flower should befall.
At last, oh joy! the central petals burst apart.

It blossomed—but, alas! a worm was at its heart!

SONG.

MY heart to thy heart,
　　My hand to thine;
My lips to thy lips,
　　Kisses are wine
Brewed for the lover in sunshine and shade;
Let me drink deep, then, my African maid.

Lily to lily,
　　Rose unto rose;
My love to thy love
　　Tenderly grows.
Rend not the oak and the ivy in twain,
Nor the swart maid from her swarthier swain.

AN ANTE-BELLUM SERMON.

We is gathahed hyeah, my brothahs,
　　In dis howlin' wildaness,
Fu' to speak some words of comfo't
　　To each othah in distress.
An' we chooses fu' ouah subjic'
　　Dis—we 'll 'splain it by an' by;
"An' de Lawd said, 'Moses, Moses,'
　　An' de man said, 'Hyeah am I.'"

Now ole Pher'oh, down in Egypt,
　　Was de wuss man evah bo'n,
An' he had de Hebrew chillun
　　Down dah wukin' in his co'n;
'T well de Lawd got tiahed o' his foolin',
　　An' sez he: "I 'll let him know—

Look hyeah, Moses, go tell Pher'oh
 Fu' to let dem chillun go."

"An' ef he refuse to do it,
 I will make him rue de houah,
Fu' I 'll empty down on Egypt
 All de vials of my powah."
Yes, he did—an' Pher'oh's ahmy
 Was n't wuth a ha'f a dime;
Fu' de Lawd will he'p his chillun,
 You kin trust him evah time.

An' yo' enemies may 'sail you
 In de back an' in de front;
But de Lawd is all aroun' you,
 Fu' to ba' de battle's brunt.
Dey kin fo'ge yo' chains an' shackles
 F'om de mountains to de sea;
But de Lawd will sen' some Moses
 Fu' to set his chillun free.

An' de lan' shall hyeah his thundah,
 Lak a blas' f'om Gab'el's ho'n,
Fu' de Lawd of hosts is mighty
 When he girds his ahmor on.
But fu' feah some one mistakes me,
 I will pause right hyeah to say,
Dat I'm still a-preachin' ancient,
 I ain't talkin' 'bout to-day.

But I tell you, fellah christuns,
 Things 'll happen mighty strange;
Now, de Lawd done dis fu' Isrul,
 An' his ways don't nevah change,
An' de love he showed to Isrul
 Was n't all on Isrul spent;
Now don't run an' tell yo' mastahs
 Dat I 's preachin' discontent.

'Cause I is n't; I 'se a-judgin'
 Bible people by deir ac's;
I'se a-givin' you de Scriptuah,
 I'se a-handin' you de fac's.
Cose ole Pher'oh b'lieved in slav'ry,
 But de Lawd he let him see,
Dat de people he put bref in,—
 Evah mothah's son was free.

An' dahs othahs thinks lak Pher'oh,
 But dey calls de Scriptuah liar,
Fu' de Bible says "a servant
 Is a-worthy of his hire."
An' you cain't git roun' nor thoo dat,
 An' you cain't git ovah it,
Fu' whatevah place you git in,
 Dis hyeah Bible too 'll fit.

So you see de Lawd's intention,
 Evah sence de worl' began,
Was dat His almighty freedom
 Should belong to evah man,
But I think it would be bettah,
 Ef I'd pause agin to say,
Dat I 'm talkin' 'bout ouah freedom
 In a Bibleistic way.

But de Moses is a-comin',
 An' he 's comin', suah and fas'
We kin hyeah his feet a-trompin',
 We kin hyeah his trumpit blas'.
But I want to wa'n you people,
 Don't you git too brigity;
An' don't you git to braggin'
 'Bout dese things, you wait an' see.

But when Moses wif his powah
 Comes an' sets us chillun free,
We will praise de gracious Mastah
 Dat has gin us liberty;
An' we 'll shout ouah halleluyahs,
 On dat mighty reck'nin' day,
When we 'se reco'nised ez citiz'—
 Huh uh! Chillun, let us pray!

ODE TO ETHIOPIA.

O Mother Race! to thee I bring
This pledge of faith unwavering,
 This tribute to thy glory.
I know the pangs which thou didst feel,
When Slavery crushed thee with its heel,
 With thy dear blood all gory.

Sad days were those—ah, sad indeed!
But through the land the fruitful seed
 Of better times was growing.
The plant of freedom upward sprung,
And spread its leaves so fresh and young—
 Its blossoms now are blowing.

On every hand in this fair land,
Proud Ethiope's swarthy children stand
 Beside their fairer neighbor;
The forests flee before their stroke,
Their hammers ring, their forges smoke,—
 They stir in honest labour.

They tread the fields where honour calls;
Their voices sound through senate halls

In majesty and power.
To right they cling; the hymns they sing
Up to the skies in beauty ring,
 And bolder grow each hour.

Be proud, my Race, in mind and soul;
Thy name is writ on Glory's scroll
 In characters of fire.
High 'mid the clouds of Fame's bright sky
Thy banner's blazoned folds now fly,
 And truth shall lift them higher.

Thou hast the right to noble pride,
Whose spotless robes were purified
 By blood's severe baptism.
Upon thy brow the cross was laid,
And labour's painful sweat-beads made
 A consecrating chrism.

No other race, or white or black,
When bound as thou wert, to the rack,
 So seldom stooped to grieving;
No other race, when free again,
Forgot the past and proved them men
 So noble in forgiving.

Go on and up! Our souls and eyes
Shall follow thy continuous rise;
 Our ears shall list thy story
From bards who from thy root shall spring,
And proudly tune their lyres to sing
 Of Ethiopia's glory.

THE CORN-STALK FIDDLE.

When the corn 's all cut and the bright stalks shine

Like the burnished spears of a field of gold;
When the field-mice rich on the nubbins dine,
 And the frost comes white and the wind blows cold;
Then it's heigho! fellows and hi-diddle-diddle,
For the time is ripe for the corn-stalk fiddle.

And you take a stalk that is straight and long,
 With an expert eye to its worthy points,
And you think of the bubbling strains of song
 That are bound between its pithy joints—
Then you cut out strings, with a bridge in the middle,
With a corn-stalk bow for a corn-stalk fiddle.

Then the strains that grow as you draw the bow
 O'er the yielding strings with a practiced hand!
And the music's flow never loud but low
 Is the concert note of a fairy band.
Oh, your dainty songs are a misty riddle
To the simple sweets of the corn-stalk fiddle.

When the eve comes on, and our work is done,
 And the sun drops down with a tender glance,
With their hearts all prime for the harmless fun,
 Come the neighbor girls for the evening's dance,
And they wait for the well-known twist and twiddle—
More time than tune—from the corn-stalk fiddle.

Then brother Jabez takes the bow,
 While Ned stands off with Susan Bland,
Then Henry stops by Milly Snow,
 And John takes Nellie Jones's hand,
While I pair off with Mandy Biddle,
And scrape, scrape, scrape goes the corn-stalk fiddle.

"Salute your partners," comes the call,
 "All join hands and circle round,"
"Grand train back," and "Balance all,"
 Footsteps lightly spurn the ground.

"Take your lady and balance down the middle"
To the merry strains of the corn-stalk fiddle.
So the night goes on and the dance is o'er,
 And the merry girls are homeward gone,
But I see it all in my sleep once more,
 And I dream till the very break of dawn
Of an impish dance on a red-hot griddle
To the screech and scrape of a corn-stalk fiddle.

THE MASTER-PLAYER.

An old, worn harp that had been played
Till all its strings were loose and frayed,
Joy, Hate, and Fear, each one essayed,
To play. But each in turn had found
No sweet responsiveness of sound.

Then Love the Master-Player came
With heaving breast and eyes aflame;
The Harp he took all undismayed,
Smote on its strings, still strange to song,
And brought forth music sweet and strong.

THE MYSTERY.

I was not; now I am—a few days hence
I shall not be; I fain would look before
And after, but can neither do; some Power
Or lack of power says "no" to all I would.
I stand upon a wide and sunless plain,
Nor chart nor steel to guide my steps aright.
Whene'er, o'ercoming fear, I dare to move,
I grope without direction and by chance.
Some feign to hear a voice and feel a hand

That draws them ever upward thro' the gloom.
But I—I hear no voice and touch no hand,
Tho' oft thro' silence infinite I list,

And strain my hearing to supernal sounds;
Tho' oft thro' fateful darkness do I reach,
And stretch my hand to find that other hand.
I question of th' eternal bending skies
That seem to neighbor with the novice earth;
But they roll on, and daily shut their eyes
On me, as I one day shall do on them,
And tell me not the secret that I ask.

NOT THEY WHO SOAR.

Not they who soar, but they who plod
Their rugged way, unhelped, to God
Are heroes; they who higher fare,
And, flying, fan the upper air,
Miss all the toil that hugs the sod.
'Tis they whose backs have felt the rod,
Whose feet have pressed the path unshod,
May smile upon defeated care,
 Not they who soar.

High up there are no thorns to prod,
Nor boulders lurking 'neath the clod
To turn the keenness of the share,
For flight is ever free and rare;
But heroes they the soil who 've trod,
 Not they who soar!

WHITTIER.

Not o'er thy dust let there be spent
The gush of maudlin sentiment;
Such drift as that is not for thee,
Whose life and deeds and songs agree,
Sublime in their simplicity.

Nor shall the sorrowing tear be shed.
O singer sweet, thou art not dead!
In spite of time's malignant chill,
With living fire thy songs shall thrill,
And men shall say, "He liveth still!"

Great poets never die, for Earth
Doth count their lives of too great worth
To lose them from her treasured store;
So shalt thou live for evermore—
Though far thy form from mortal ken—
Deep in the hearts and minds of men.

TWO SONGS.

A bee that was searching for sweets one day
Through the gate of a rose garden happened to stray.
In the heart of a rose he hid away,
And forgot in his bliss the light of day,
As sipping his honey he buzzed in song;
Though day was waning, he lingered long,
 For the rose was sweet, so sweet.

A robin sits pluming his ruddy breast,
And a madrigal sings to his love in her nest:
"Oh, the skies they are blue, the fields are green,
And the birds in your nest will soon be seen!"

She hangs on his words with a thrill of love,
And chirps to him as he sits above,
 For the song is sweet, so sweet.
A maiden was out on a summer's day
With the winds and the waves and the flowers at play;
And she met with a youth of gentle air,
With the light of the sunshine on his hair.
Together they wandered the flowers among;
They loved, and loving they lingered long,
 For to love is sweet, so sweet.

Bird of my lady's bower,
 Sing her a song;
Tell her that every hour,
 All the day long,
Thoughts of her come to me,
 Filling my brain
With the warm ecstasy
 Of love's refrain.

Little bird! happy bird!
 Being so near,
Where e'en her slightest word
 Thou mayest hear,
Seeing her glancing eyes,
 Sheen of her hair,
Thou art in paradise,—
 Would I were there.

I am so far away,
 Thou art so near;
Plead with her, birdling gay,
 Plead with my dear.
Rich be thy recompense,
 Fine be thy fee,
If through shine eloquence
 She hearken me.

A BANJO SONG.

Oh, dere's lots o' keer an' trouble
 In dis world to swaller down;
An' ol' Sorrer's purty lively
 In her way o' gittin' roun'.
Yet dere 's times when I furgit 'em,—
 Aches an' pains an' troubles all,—
An' it's when I tek at ebenin'
 My ol' banjo f'om de wall.

'Bout de time dat night is fallin'
 An' my daily wu'k is done,
An' above de shady hilltops
 I kin see de settin' sun;
When de quiet, restful shadders
 Is beginnin' jes' to fall,—
Den I take de little banjo
 F'om its place upon de wall.

Den my fam'ly gadders roun' me
 In de fadin' o' de light,
Ez I strike de strings to try 'em
 Ef dey all is tuned er-right.
An' it seems we're so nigh heaben
 We kin hyeah de angels sing
When de music o' dat banjo
 Sets my cabin all er-ring.

An' my wife an' all de othahs,—
 Male an' female, small an' big,—
Even up to gray-haired granny,
 Seem jes' boun' to do a jig;
'Twell I change de style o' music,
 Change de movement an' de time,
An' de ringin' little banjo
 Plays an ol' hea't-feelin' hime.

An' somehow my th'oat gits choky,
 An' a lump keeps tryin' to rise
Lak it wan'ed to ketch de water
 Dat was flowin' to my eyes;
An' I feel dat I could sorter
 Knock de socks clean off o' sin
Ez I hyeah my po' ol' granny
 Wif huh tremblin' voice jine in.

Den we all th'ow in our voices
 Fu' to he'p de chune out too,
Lak a big camp-meetin' choiry
 Tryin' to sing a mou'nah th'oo.
An' our th'oahts let out de music,
 Sweet an' solemn, loud an' free,
'Twell de raftahs o' my cabin
 Echo wif de melody.

Oh, de music o' de banjo,
 Quick an' deb'lish, solemn, slow,
Is de greates' joy an' solace
 Dat a weary slave kin know!
So jes' let me hyeah it ringin',
 Dough de chune be po' an' rough,
It 's a pleasure; an' de pleasures
 O' dis life is few enough.

Now, de blessed little angels
 Up in heaben, we are told,
Don't do nothin' all dere lifetime
 'Ceptin' play on ha'ps o' gold.
Now I think heaben'd be mo' homelike
 Ef we 'd hyeah some music fall
F'om a real ol'-fashioned banjo,
 Like dat one upon de wall.

LONGING.

If you could sit with me beside the sea to-day,
And whisper with me sweetest dreamings o'er and o'er;
I think I should not find the clouds so dim and gray,
And not so loud the waves complaining at the shore.

If you could sit with me upon the shore to-day,
And hold my hand in yours as in the days of old,
I think I should not mind the chill baptismal spray,
Nor find my hand and heart and all the world so cold.

If you could walk with me upon the strand to-day,
And tell me that my longing love had won your own,
I think all my sad thoughts would then be put away,
And I could give back laughter for the Ocean's moan!

THE PATH.

There are no beaten paths to Glory's height,
There are no rules to compass greatness known;
Each for himself must cleave a path alone,
And press his own way forward in the fight.
Smooth is the way to ease and calm delight,
And soft the road Sloth chooseth for her own;
But he who craves the flower of life full-blown,
Must struggle up in all his armor dight!
What though the burden bear him sorely down
And crush to dust the mountain of his pride,
Oh, then, with strong heart let him still abide;
For rugged is the roadway to renown,
Nor may he hope to gain the envied crown
Till he hath thrust the looming rocks aside.

THE LAWYERS' WAYS.

I've been list'nin' to them lawyers
 In the court house up the street,
An' I 've come to the conclusion
 That I'm most completely beat.
Fust one feller riz to argy,
 An' he boldly waded in
As he dressed the tremblin' pris'ner
 In a coat o' deep-dyed sin.

Why, he painted him all over
 In a hue o' blackest crime,
An' he smeared his reputation
 With the thickest kind o' grime,
Tell I found myself a-wond'rin',
 In a misty way and dim,
How the Lord had come to fashion
 Sich an awful man as him.
Then the other lawyer started,
 An', with brimmin', tearful eyes,
Said his client was a martyr
 That was brought to sacrifice.
An' he give to that same pris'ner
 Every blessed human grace,
Tell I saw the light o' virtue
 Fairly shinin' from his face.

Then I own 'at I was puzzled
 How sich things could rightly be;
An' this aggervatin' question
 Seems to keep a-puzzlin' me.
So, will some one please inform me,
 An' this mystery unroll—
How an angel an' a devil
 Can persess the self-same soul?

ODE FOR MEMORIAL DAY.

Done are the toils and the wearisome marches,
 Done is the summons of bugle and drum.
Softly and sweetly the sky overarches,
 Shelt'ring a land where Rebellion is dumb.
Dark were the days of the country's derangement,
 Sad were the hours when the conflict was on,
But through the gloom of fraternal estrangement
 God sent his light, and we welcome the dawn.
O'er the expanse of our mighty dominions,
 Sweeping away to the uttermost parts,
Peace, the wide-flying, on untiring pinions,
 Bringeth her message of joy to our hearts.

Ah, but this joy which our minds cannot measure,
 What did it cost for our fathers to gain!
Bought at the price of the heart's dearest treasure,
 Born out of travail and sorrow and pain;
Born in the battle where fleet Death was flying,
 Slaying with satire-stroke bloody and fell;
Born where the heroes and martyrs were dying,
 Torn by the fury of bullet and shell.
Ah, but the day is past: silent the rattle,
 And the confusion that followed the fight.
Peace to the heroes who died in the battle,
 Martyrs to truth and the crowning of Right!

Out of the blood of a conflict fraternal,
 Out of the dust and the dimness of death,
Burst into blossoms of glory eternal
 Flowers that sweeten the world with their breath.
Flowers of charity, peace, and devotion
 Bloom in the hearts that are empty of strife;
Love that is boundless and broad as the ocean
 Leaps into beauty and fulness of life.
So, with the singing of pæans and chorale,
 And with the flag flashing high in the sun,

Place on the graves of our heroes the laurels
 Which their unfaltering valor has won!

PREMONITION.

D EAR heart, good-night!
 Nay, list awhile that sweet voice singing
 When the world is all so bright,
And the sound of song sets the heart a-ringing,
 Oh, love, it is not right—
 Not then to say, "Good-night."

 Dear heart, good-night!
The late winds in the lake weeds shiver,
 And the spray flies cold and white.
And the voice that sings gives a telltale quiver—
 "Ah, yes, the world is bright,
 But, dearest heart, good-night!"

 Dear heart, good-night!
And do not longer seek to hold me!
 For my soul is in affright
As the fearful glooms in their pall enfold me.
 See him who sang how white
 And still; so, dear, good-night.

 Dear heart, good-night!
Thy hand I'll press no more forever,
 And mine eyes shall lose the light;
For the great white wraith by the winding river
 Shall check my steps with might.
 So, dear, good-night, good-night!

RETROSPECTION.

When you and I were young, the days
　　　Were filled with scent of pink and rose,
　　　And full of joy from dawn till close,
From morning's mist till evening's haze.
　　　And when the robin sung his song
　　　The verdant woodland ways along,
　　　　We whistled louder than he sung.
And school was joy, and work was sport
For which the hours were all too short,
　　　When you and I were young, my boy,
　　　When you and I were young.

When you and I were young, the woods
　　　Brimmed bravely o'er with every joy
　　　To charm the happy-hearted boy.
The quail turned out her timid broods;
　　　The prickly copse, a hostess fine,
　　　Held high black cups of harmless wine;
　　　　And low the laden grape-vine swung
With beads of night-kissed amethyst
Where buzzing lovers held their tryst,
　　　When you and I were young, my boy,
　　　When you and I were young.

When you and I were young, the cool
　　　And fresh wind fanned our fevered brows
　　　When tumbling o'er the scented mows,
Or stripping by the dimpling pool,
　　　Sedge-fringed about its shimmering face,
　　　Save where we 'd worn an ent'ring place.
　　　　How with our shouts the calm banks rung!
How flashed the spray as we plunged in,—
Pure gems that never caused a sin!
　　　When you and I were young, my boy,
　　　When you and I were young.

When you and I were young, we heard
 All sounds of Nature with delight,—
 The whirr of wing in sudden flight,
The chirping of the baby-bird.
 The columbine's red bells were rung;
 The locust's vested chorus sung;
 While every wind his zithern strung
To high and holy-sounding keys,
And played sonatas in the trees—
 When you and I were young, my boy,
 When you and I were young.

When you and I were young, we knew
 To shout and laugh, to work and play,
 And night was partner to the day
In all our joys. So swift time flew
 On silent wings that, ere we wist,
 The fleeting years had fled unmissed;
 And from our hearts this cry was wrung—
To fill with fond regret and tears
The days of our remaining years—
 "When you and I were young, my boy,
 When you and I were young."

UNEXPRESSED.

Deep in my heart that aches with the repression,
 And strives with plenitude of bitter pain,
There lives a thought that clamors for expression,
 And spends its undelivered force in vain.

What boots it that some other may have thought it?
 The right of thoughts' expression is divine;
The price of pain I pay for it has bought it,
 I care not who lays claim to it—'t is mine!

And yet not mine until it be delivered;
 The manner of its birth shall prove the test.
Alas, alas, my rock of pride is shivered—
 I beat my brow—the thought still unexpressed.

SONG OF SUMMER.

Dis is gospel weathah sho'—
 Hills is sawt o' hazy.
Meddahs level ez a flo'
 Callin' to de lazy.
Sky all white wif streaks o' blue,
 Sunshine softly gleamin',
D'ain't no wuk hit's right to do,
 Nothin' 's right but dreamin'.

Dreamin' by de rivah side
 Wif de watahs glist'nin',
Feelin' good an' satisfied
 Ez you lay a-list'nin'
To the little nakid boys
 Splashin' in de watah,
Hollerin' fu' to spress deir joys
 Jes' lak youngsters ought to.

Squir'l a-tippin' on his toes,
 So 's to hide an' view you;
Whole flocks o' camp-meetin' crows
 Shoutin' hallelujah.
Peckahwood erpon de tree
 Tappin' lak a hammah;
Jaybird chattin' wif a bee,
 Tryin' to teach him grammah.

Breeze is blowin' wif perfume,
 Jes' enough to tease you;

Hollyhocks is all in bloom,
 Smellin' fu' to please you.
Go 'way, folks, an' let me 'lone,
 Times is gettin' dearah—
Summah 's settin' on de th'one,
 An' I'm a-layin' neah huh!

SPRING SONG.

A blue-bell springs upon the ledge,
A lark sits singing in the hedge;
Sweet perfumes scent the balmy air,
And life is brimming everywhere.
What lark and breeze and bluebird sing,
 Is Spring, Spring, Spring!

No more the air is sharp and cold;
The planter wends across the word,
And, glad, beneath the shining sky
We wander forth, my love and I.
And ever in our hearts doth ring
 This song of Spring, Spring!

For life is life and love is love,
'Twixt maid and man or dove and dove.
Life may be short, life may be long,
But love will come, and to its song
Shall this refrain for ever cling
 Of Spring, Spring, Spring!

TO LOUISE.

Oh, the poets may sing of their Lady Irenes,
And may rave in their rhymes about wonderful queens;

But I throw my poetical wings to the breeze,
And soar in a song to my Lady Louise.
A sweet little maid, who is dearer, I ween,
Than any fair duchess, or even a queen.
When speaking of her I can't plod in my prose,
For she 's the wee lassie who gave me a rose.

Since poets, from seeing a lady's lip curled,
Have written fair verse that has sweetened the world;
Why, then, should not I give the space of an hour
To making a song in return for a flower?
I have found in my life—it has not been so long—
There are too few of flowers—too little of song.
So out of that blossom, this lay of mine grows,
For the dear little lady who gave me the rose.

I thank God for innocence, dearer than Art,
That lights on a by-way which leads to the heart,
And led by an impulse no less than divine,
Walks into the temple and sits at the shrine.
I would rather pluck daisies that grow in the wild,
Or take one simple rose from the hand of a child,
Than to breathe the rich fragrance of flowers that bide
In the gardens of luxury, passion, and pride.

I know not, my wee one, how came you to know
Which way to my heart was the right way to go;
Unless in your purity, soul-clean and clear,
God whispers his messages into your ear.
You have now had my song, let me end with a prayer
That your life may be always sweet, happy, and fair;
That your joys may be many, and absent your woes,
O dear little lady who gave me the rose!

THE RIVALS.

'Twas three an' thirty year ago,
When I was ruther young, you know,
I had my last an' only fight
About a gal one summer night.
'T was me an' Zekel Johnson; Zeke
'N' me 'd be'n spattin' 'bout a week,
Each of us tryin' his best to show
That he was Liza Jones's beau.
We could n't neither prove the thing,
Fur she was fur too sharp to fling
One over fur the other one
An' by so doin' stop the fun
That we chaps did n't have the sense
To see she got at our expense,
But that 's the way a feller does,
Fur boys is fools an' allus was.
An' when they 's females in the game
I reckon men 's about the same.
Well, Zeke an' me went on that way
An' fussed an' quarrelled day by day;
While Liza, mindin' not the fuss,
Jest kep' a-goin' with both of us,
Tell we pore chaps, that's Zeke an' me,
Was jest plum mad with jealousy.
Well, fur a time we kep' our places,
An' only showed by frownin' faces
An' looks 'at well our meanin' boded
How full o' fight we both was loaded.
At last it come, the thing broke out,
An' this is how it come about.
One night ('twas fair, you 'll all agree)
I got Eliza's company,
An' leavin' Zekel in the lurch,
Went trottin' off with her to church.
An' jest as we had took our seat

(Eliza lookin' fair an' sweet),
Why, I jest could n't help but grin
When Zekel come a-bouncin' in
As furious as the law allows.
He 'd jest be'n up to Liza's house,
To find her gone, then come to church
To have this end put to his search.
I guess I laffed that meetin' through,
An' not a mortal word I knew
Of what the preacher preached er read
Er what the choir sung er said.
Fur every time I 'd turn my head
I could n't skeercely help but see
'At Zekel had his eye on me.
An' he 'ud sort o' turn an' twist
An' grind his teeth an' shake his fist.
I laughed, fur la! the hull church seen us,
An' knowed that suthin' was between us.
Well, meetin' out, we started hum,
I sorter feelin' what would come.
We 'd jest got out, when up stepped Zeke,
An' said, "Scuse me, I 'd like to speak
To you a minute." "Cert," said I—
A-nudgin' Liza on the sly
An' laughin' in my sleeve with glee,
I asked her, please, to pardon me.
We walked away a step er two,
Jest to git out o' Liza's view,
An' then Zeke said, "I want to know
Ef you think you're Eliza's beau,
An' 'at I'm goin' to let her go
Hum with sich a chap as you?"
An' I said bold, "You bet I do."
Then Zekel, sneerin', said 'at he
Did n't want to hender me.
But then he 'lowed the gal was his
An' 'at he guessed he knowed his biz,
An' was n't feared o' all my kin

With all my friends an' chums throwed in.
Some other things he mentioned there
That no born man could no ways bear
Er think o' ca'mly tryin' to stan'
Ef Zeke had be'n the bigges' man
In town, an' not the leanest runt
'At time an' labor ever stunt.
An' so I let my fist go "bim,"
I thought I'd mos' nigh finished him.
But Zekel did n't take it so.
He jest ducked down an' dodged my blow
An' then come back at me so hard,
I guess I must 'a' hurt the yard,
Er spilet the grass plot where I fell,
An' sakes alive it hurt me; well,
It would n't be'n so bad, you see,
But he jest kep' a-hittin' me.
An' I hit back an' kicked an' pawed,
But 't seemed 't was mostly air I clawed,
While Zekel used his science well
A-makin' every motion tell.
He punched an' hit, why, goodness lands,
Seemed like he had a dozen hands.
Well, afterwhile they stopped the fuss,
An' some one kindly parted us.
All beat an' cuffed an' clawed an' scratched,
An' needin' both our faces patched,
Each started hum a different way;
An' what o' Liza, do you say,
Why, Liza—little humbug—dern her,
Why, she'd gone home with Hiram Turner.

THE LOVER AND THE MOON.

A lover whom duty called over the wave,
 With himself communed: "Will my love be true

If left to herself? Had I better not sue
Some friend to watch over her, good and grave?
 But my friend might fail in my need," he said,
 "And I return to find love dead.
 Since friendships fade like the flow'rs of June,
 I will leave her in charge of the stable moon."

Then he said to the moon: "O dear old moon,
 Who for years and years from thy throne above
 Hast nurtured and guarded young lovers and love,
My heart has but come to its waiting June,
 And the promise time of the budding vine;
 Oh, guard thee well this love of mine."
 And he harked him then while all was still,
 And the pale moon answered and said, "I will."

And he sailed in his ship o'er many seas,
 And he wandered wide o'er strange far strands:
 In isles of the south and in Orient lands,
Where pestilence lurks in the breath of the breeze.
 But his star was high, so he braved the main,
 And sailed him blithely home again;
 And with joy he bended his footsteps soon
 To learn of his love from the matron moon.

She sat as of yore, in her olden place,
 Serene as death, in her silver chair.
 A white rose gleamed in her whiter hair,
And the tint of a blush was on her face.
 At sight of the youth she sadly bowed
 And hid her face 'neath a gracious cloud.
 She faltered faint on the night's dim marge,
 But "How," spoke the youth, "have you kept your charge?"

The moon was sad at a trust ill-kept;
 The blush went out in her blanching cheek,
 And her voice was timid and low and weak,
As she made her plea and sighed and wept.

"Oh, another prayed and another plead,
 And I could n't resist," she answering said;
"But love still grows in the hearts of men;
 Go forth, dear youth, and love again."

But he turned him away from her proffered grace.
 "Thou art false, O moon, as the hearts of men,
 I will not, will not love again."
And he turned sheer 'round with a soul-sick face
 To the sea, and cried: "Sea, curse the moon,
 Who makes her vows and forgets so soon."
 And the awful sea with anger stirred,
 And his breast heaved hard as he lay and heard.

And ever the moon wept down in rain,
 And ever her sighs rose high in wind;
 But the earth and sea were deaf and blind,
And she wept and sighed her griefs in vain.
 And ever at night, when the storm is fierce,
 The cries of a wraith through the thunder pierce;
 And the waves strain their awful hands on high
 To tear the false moon from the sky.

CONSCIENCE AND REMORSE.

"Good-Bye," I said to my conscience—
 "Good-bye for aye and aye,"
And I put her hands off harshly,
 And turned my face away;
And conscience smitten sorely
 Returned not from that day.

But a time came when my spirit
 Grew weary of its pace;
And I cried: "Come back, my conscience;
 I long to see thy face."

But conscience cried: "I cannot;
 Remorse sits in my place."

IONE.

I.

Ah, yes, 't is sweet still to remember,
 Though 't were less painful to forget;
For while my heart glows like an ember,
 Mine eyes with sorrow's drops are wet,
 And, oh, my heart is aching yet.
It is a law of mortal pain
 That old wounds, long accounted well,
 Beneath the memory's potent spell,
Will wake to life and bleed again.

So 't is with me; it might be better
 If I should turn no look behind,—
If I could curb my heart, and fetter
 From reminiscent gaze my mind,
 Or let my soul go blind—go blind!
But would I do it if I could?
 Nay! ease at such a price were spurned;
 For, since my love was once returned,
All that I suffer seemeth good.

I know, I know it is the fashion,
 When love has left some heart distressed,
To weight the air with wordful passion;
 But I am glad that in my breast
 I ever held so dear a guest.
Love does not come at every nod,
 Or every voice that calleth "hasten;"
 He seeketh out some heart to chasten,
And whips it, wailing, up to God!

Love is no random road wayfarer
 Who where he may must sip his glass.
Love is the King, the Purple-Wearer,
 Whose guard recks not of tree or grass
 To blaze the way that he may pass.
What if my heart be in the blast
 That heralds his triumphant way;
 Shall I repine, shall I not say:
"Rejoice, my heart, the King has passed!"

In life, each heart holds some sad story—
 The saddest ones are never told.
I, too, have dreamed of fame and glory,
 And viewed the future bright with gold;
 But that is as a tale long told.
Mine eyes have lost their youthful flash,
 My cunning hand has lost its art;
 I am not old, but in my heart
The ember lies beneath the ash.

I loved! Why not? My heart was youthful,
 My mind was filled with healthy thought.
He doubts not whose own self is truthful,
 Doubt by dishonesty is taught;
 So loved I boldly, fearing naught.
I did not walk this lowly earth;
 Mine was a newer, higher sphere,
 Where youth was long and life was dear,
And all save love was little worth.

Her likeness! Would that I might limn it,
 As Love did, with enduring art;
Nor dust of days nor death may dim it,
 Where it lies graven on my heart,
 Of this sad fabric of my life a part.
I would that I might paint her now
 As I beheld her in that day,
 Ere her first bloom had passed away,

And left the lines upon her brow.
A face serene that, beaming brightly,
 Disarmed the hot sun's glances bold.
A foot that kissed the ground so lightly,
 He frowned in wrath and deemed her cold,
 But loved her still though he was old.
A form where every maiden grace
 Bloomed to perfection's richest flower,—
 The statued pose of conscious power,
Like lithe-limbed Dian's of the chase.

Beneath a brow too fair for frowning,
 Like moon-lit deeps that glass the skies
Till all the hosts above seem drowning,
 Looked forth her steadfast hazel eyes,
 With gaze serene and purely wise.
And over all, her tresses rare,
 Which, when, with his desire grown weak,
 The Night bent down to kiss her cheek,
Entrapped and held him captive there.

This was Ione; a spirit finer
 Ne'er burned to ash its house of clay;
A soul instinct with fire diviner
 Ne'er fled athwart the face of day,
 And tempted Time with earthly stay.
Her loveliness was not alone
 Of face and form and tresses' hue;
 For aye a pure, high soul shone through
Her every act: this was Ione.

II.

'Twas in the radiant summer weather,
 When God looked, smiling, from the sky;
And we went wand'ring much together
 By wood and lane, Ione and I,
 Attracted by the subtle tie
Of common thoughts and common tastes,

Of eyes whose vision saw the same,
And freely granted beauty's claim
Where others found but worthless wastes.

We paused to hear the far bells ringing
Across the distance, sweet and clear.
We listened to the wild bird's singing
The song he meant for his mate's ear,
And deemed our chance to do so dear.
We loved to watch the warrior Sun,
With flaming shield and flaunting crest,
Go striding down the gory West,
When Day's long fight was fought and won.

And life became a different story;
Where'er I looked, I saw new light.
Earth's self assumed a greater glory,
Mine eyes were cleared to fuller sight.
Then first I saw the need and might
Of that fair band, the singing throng,
Who, gifted with the skill divine,
Take up the threads of life, spun fine,
And weave them into soulful song.

They sung for me, whose passion pressing
My soul, found vent in song nor line.
They bore the burden of expressing
All that I felt, with art's design,
And every word of theirs was mine.
I read them to Ione, ofttimes,
By hill and shore, beneath fair skies,
And she looked deeply in mine eyes,
And knew my love spoke through their rhymes.

Her life was like the stream that floweth,
And mine was like the waiting sea;
Her love was like the flower that bloweth,
And mine was like the searching bee—

I found her sweetness all for me.
God plied him in the mint of time,
 And coined for us a golden day,
 And rolled it ringing down life's way
With love's sweet music in its chime.

And God unclasped the Book of Ages,
 And laid it open to our sight;
Upon the dimness of its pages,
 So long consigned to rayless night,
 He shed the glory of his light.
We read them well, we read them long,
 And ever thrilling did we see
 That love ruled all humanity,—
The master passion, pure and strong.

III.

To-day my skies are bare and ashen,
 And bend on me without a beam.
Since love is held the master-passion,
 Its loss must be the pain supreme—
 And grinning Fate has wrecked my dream.
But pardon, dear departed Guest,
 I will not rant, I will not rail;
 For good the grain must feel the flail;
There are whom love has never blessed.

I had and have a younger brother,
 One whom I loved and love to-day
As never fond and doting mother
 Adored the babe who found its way
 From heavenly scenes into her day.
Oh, he was full of youth's new wine,—
 A man on life's ascending slope,
 Flushed with ambition, full of hope;
And every wish of his was mine.

A kingly youth; the way before him
 Was thronged with victories to be won;
So joyous, too, the heavens o'er him
 Were bright with an unchanging sun,—
 His days with rhyme were overrun.
Toil had not taught him Nature's prose,
 Tears had not dimmed his brilliant eyes,
 And sorrow had not made him wise;
His life was in the budding rose.

I know not how I came to waken,
 Some instinct pricked my soul to sight;
My heart by some vague thrill was shaken,—
 A thrill so true and yet so slight,
 I hardly deemed I read aright.
As when a sleeper, ign'rant why,
 Not knowing what mysterious hand
 Has called him out of slumberland,
Starts up to find some danger nigh.

Love is a guest that comes, unbidden,
 But, having come, asserts his right;
He will not be repressed nor hidden.
 And so my brother's dawning plight
 Became uncovered to my sight.
Some sound-mote in his passing tone
 Caught in the meshes of my ear;
 Some little glance, a shade too dear,
Betrayed the love he bore Ione.

What could I do? He was my brother,
 And young, and full of hope and trust;
I could not, dared not try to smother
 His flame, and turn his heart to dust.
 I knew how oft life gives a crust
To starving men who cry for bread;
 But he was young, so few his days,
 He had not learned the great world's ways,
Nor Disappointment's volumes read.

However fair and rich the booty,
 I could not make his loss my gain.
For love is dear, but dearer, duty,
 And here my way was clear and plain.
 I saw how I could save him pain.
And so, with all my day grown dim,
 That this loved brother's sun might shine,
 I joined his suit, gave over mine,
And sought Ione, to plead for him.

I found her in an eastern bower,
 Where all day long the am'rous sun
Lay by to woo a timid flower.
 This day his course was well-nigh run,
 But still with lingering art he spun
Gold fancies on the shadowed wall.
 The vines waved soft and green above,
 And there where one might tell his love,
I told my griefs—I told her all!

I told her all, and as she hearkened,
 A tear-drop fell upon her dress.
With grief her flushing brow was darkened;
 One sob that she could not repress
 Betrayed the depths of her distress.
Upon her grief my sorrow fed,
 And I was bowed with unlived years,
 My heart swelled with a sea of tears,
The tears my manhood could not shed.

The world is Rome, and Fate is Nero,
 Disporting in the hour of doom.
God made us men; times make the hero—
 But in that awful space of gloom
 I gave no thought but sorrow's room.
All—all was dim within that bower,
 What time the sun divorced the day;

And all the shadows, glooming gray,
Proclaimed the sadness of the hour.

She could not speak—no word was needed;
 Her look, half strength and half despair,
Told me I had not vainly pleaded,
 That she would not ignore my prayer.
 And so she turned and left me there,
And as she went, so passed my bliss;
 She loved me, I could not mistake—
 But for her own and my love's sake,
Her womanhood could rise to this!

My wounded heart fled swift to cover,
 And life at times seemed very drear.
My brother proved an ardent lover—
 What had so young a man to fear?
 He wed Ione within the year.
No shadow clouds her tranquil brow,
 Men speak her husband's name with pride,
 While she sits honored at his side—
She is—she must be happy now!

I doubt the course I took no longer,
 Since those I love seem satisfied.
The bond between them will grow stronger
 As they go forward side by side;
 Then will my pains be justified.
Their joy is mine, and that is best—
 I am not totally bereft;
 For I have still the mem'ry left—
Love stopped with me—a Royal Guest!

RELIGION.

I am no priest of crooks nor creeds,

For human wants and human needs
Are more to me than prophets' deeds;
And human tears and human cares
Affect me more than human prayers.

Go, cease your wail, lugubrious saint!
You fret high Heaven with your plaint.
Is this the "Christian's joy" you paint?
Is this the Christian's boasted bliss?
Avails your faith no more than this?

Take up your arms, come out with me,
Let Heav'n alone; humanity
Needs more and Heaven less from thee.
With pity for mankind look 'round;
Help them to rise—and Heaven is found.

DEACON JONES' GRIEVANCE.

I've been watchin' of 'em, parson,
 An' I'm sorry fur to say
'At my mind is not contented
 With the loose an' keerless way
'At the young folks treat the music;
 'T ain't the proper sort o' choir.
Then I don't believe in Christuns
 A-singin' hymns for hire.

But I never would 'a' murmured
 An' the matter might 'a' gone
Ef it was n't fur the antics
 'At I've seen 'em kerry on;
So I thought it was my dooty
 Fur to come to you an' ask
Ef you would n't sort o' gently
 Take them singin' folks to task.

Fust, the music they 've be'n singin'
 Will disgrace us mighty soon;
It's a cross between a opry
 An' a ol' cotillion tune.
With its dashes an' its quavers
 An' its hifalutin style—
Why, it sets my head to swimmin'
 When I 'm comin' down the aisle.

Now it might be almost decent
 Ef it was n't fur the way
'At they git up there an' sing it,
 Hey dum diddle, loud and gay.
Why, it shames the name o' sacred
 In its brazen worldliness,
An' they've even got "Ol' Hundred"
 In a bold, new-fangled dress.
You'll excuse me, Mr. Parson,
 Ef I seem a little sore;
But I 've sung the songs of Isr'el
 For threescore years an' more,
An' it sort o' hurts my feelin's
 Fur to see 'em put away
Fur these harum-scarum ditties
 'At is capturin' the day.

There 's anuther little happ'nin'
 'At I'll mention while I'm here,
Jes' to show 'at my objections
 All is offered sound and clear.
It was one day they was singin'
 An' was doin' well enough—
Singin' good as people could sing
 Sich an awful mess o' stuff—

When the choir give a holler,
 An' the organ give a groan,

An' they left one weak-voiced feller
 A-singin' there alone!
But he stuck right to the music,
 Tho' 't was tryin' as could be;
An' when I tried to help him,
 Why, the hull church scowled at me.

You say that 's so-low singin',
 Well, I pray the Lord that I
Growed up when folks was willin'
 To sing their hymns so high.
Why, we never had sich doin's
 In the good ol' Bethel days,
When the folks was all contented
 With the simple songs of praise.

Now I may have spoke too open,
 But 't was too hard to keep still,
An' I hope you'll tell the singers
 'At I bear 'em no ill-will.
'At they all may git to glory
 Is my wish an' my desire,
But they'll need some extry trainin'
 'Fore they jine the heavenly choir.

ALICE.

Know you, winds that blow your course
 Down the verdant valleys,
That somewhere you must, perforce,
 Kiss the brow of Alice?
When her gentle face you find,
Kiss it softly, naughty wind.

Roses waving fair and sweet
 Thro' the garden alleys,

Grow into a glory meet
 For the eye of Alice;
Let the wind your offering bear
Of sweet perfume, faint and rare.

Lily holding crystal dew
 In your pure white chalice,
Nature kind hath fashioned you
 Like the soul of Alice;
It of purest white is wrought,
Filled with gems of crystal thought.

AFTER THE QUARREL.

So we, who 've supped the self-same cup,
 To-night must lay our friendship by;
Your wrath has burned your judgment up,
 Hot breath has blown the ashes high.
You say that you are wronged—ah, well,
 I count that friendship poor, at best
A bauble, a mere bagatelle,
 That cannot stand so slight a test.

I fain would still have been your friend,
 And talked and laughed and loved with you;
But since it must, why, let it end;
 The false but dies, 't is not the true.
So we are favored, you and I,
 Who only want the living truth.
It was not good to nurse the lie;
 'Tis well it died in harmless youth.

I go from you to-night to sleep.
 Why, what 's the odds? why should I grieve?
I have no fund of tears to weep
 For happenings that undeceive.

The days shall come, the days shall go
 Just as they came and went before.
The sun shall shine, the streams shall flow
 Though you and I are friends no more.

And in the volume of my years,
 Where all my thoughts and acts shall be,
The page whereon your name appears
 Shall be forever sealed to me.
Not that I hate you over-much,
 'Tis less of hate than love defied;
Howe'er, our hands no more shall touch,
 We 'll go our ways, the world is wide.

BEYOND THE YEARS.

I.

Beyond the years the answer lies,
Beyond where brood the grieving skies
 And Night drops tears.
Where Faith rod-chastened smiles to rise
 And doff its fears,
And carping Sorrow pines and dies—
 Beyond the years.

II.

Beyond the years the prayer for rest
Shall beat no more within the breast;
 The darkness clears,
And Morn perched on the mountain's crest
 Her form uprears—
The day that is to come is best,
 Beyond the years.

III.

Beyond the years the soul shall find
That endless peace for which it pined,
 For light appears,
And to the eyes that still were blind
 With blood and tears,
Their sight shall come all unconfined
 Beyond the years.

AFTER A VISIT.

I be'n down in ole Kentucky
 Fur a week er two, an' say,
'T wuz ez hard ez breakin' oxen
 Fur to tear myse'f away.
Allus argerin' 'bout fren'ship
 An' yer hospitality—
Y' ain't no right to talk about it
 Tell you be'n down there to see.

See jest how they give you welcome
 To the best that's in the land,
Feel the sort o' grip they give you
 When they take you by the hand.
Hear 'em say, "We're glad to have you,
 Better stay a week er two;"
An' the way they treat you makes you
 Feel that ev'ry word is true.

Feed you tell you hear the buttons
 Crackin' on yore Sunday vest;
Haul you roun' to see the wonders
 Tell you have to cry for rest.
Drink yer health an' pet an' praise you
 Tell you git to feel ez great

Ez the Sheriff o' the county
 Er the Gov'ner o' the State.

Wife, she sez I must be crazy
 'Cause I go on so, an' Nelse
He 'lows, "Goodness gracious! daddy,
 Cain't you talk about nuthin' else?"
Well, pleg-gone it, I'm jes' tickled,
 Bein' tickled ain't no sin;
I be'n down in ole Kentucky,
 An' I want o' go ag'in.

CURTAIN.

Villain shows his indiscretion,
Villain's partner makes confession.
Juvenile, with golden tresses,
Finds her pa and dons long dresses.
Scapegrace comes home money-laden,
Hero comforts tearful maiden,
Soubrette marries loyal chappie,
Villain skips, and all are happy.

THE SPELLIN'-BEE.

I never shall furgit that night when father hitched up Dobbin,
An' all us youngsters clambered in an' down the road went bobbin'
To school where we was kep' at work in every kind o' weather,
But where that night a spellin'-bee was callin' us together.
'Twas one o' Heaven's banner nights, the stars was all a glitter,
The moon was shinin' like the hand o' God had jest then lit her.
The ground was white with spotless snow, the blast was sort o' stin-
gin';
But underneath our round-abouts, you bet our hearts was singin'.
That spellin'-bee had be'n the talk o' many a precious moment,
The youngsters all was wild to see jes' what the precious show

meant,
An' we whose years was in their teens was little less desirous
O' gittin' to the meetin' so 's our sweethearts could admire us.
So on we went so anxious fur to satisfy our mission
That father had to box our ears, to smother our ambition.
But boxin' ears was too short work to hinder our arrivin',
He jest turned roun' an' smacked us all, an' kep' right on a-drivin'.
Well, soon the schoolhouse hove in sight, the winders beamin'
brightly;
The sound o' talkin' reached our ears, and voices laffin' lightly.
It puffed us up so full an' big 'at I 'll jest bet a dollar,
There wa'n't a feller there but felt the strain upon his collar.
So down we jumped an' in we went ez sprightly ez you make 'em,
But somethin' grabbed us by the knees an' straight began to shake
'em.
Fur once within that lighted room, our feelin's took a canter,
An' scurried to the zero mark ez quick ez Tam O'Shanter.
'Cause there was crowds o' people there, both sexes an' all stations;
It looked like all the town had come an' brought all their relations.
The first I saw was Nettie Gray, I thought that girl was dearer
'N' gold; an' when I got a chance, you bet I aidged up near her.
An' Farmer Dobbs's girl was there, the one 'at Jim was sweet on,
An' Cyrus Jones an' Mandy Smith an' Faith an' Patience Deaton.
Then Parson Brown an' Lawyer Jones were present—all attention,
An' piles on piles of other folks too numerous to mention.
The master rose an' briefly said: "Good friends, dear brother
Crawford,
To spur the pupils' minds along, a little prize has offered.
To him who spells the best to-night-or 't may be 'her'—no tellin'—
He offers ez a jest reward, this precious work on spellin'."
A little blue-backed spellin'-book with fancy scarlet trimmin',
We boys devoured it with our eyes—so did the girls an' women.
He held it up where all could see, then on the table set it,
An' ev'ry speller in the house felt mortal bound to get it.
At his command we fell in line, prepared to do our dooty,
Outspell the rest an' set 'em down, an' carry home the booty.
'T was then the merry times began, the blunders, an' the laffin',
The nudges an' the nods an' winks an' stale good-natured chaffin'.

Ole Uncle Hiram Dane was there, the clostest man a-livin',
Whose only bugbear seemed to be the dreadful fear o' givin'.
His beard was long, his hair uncut, his clothes all bare an' dingy;
It was n't 'cause the man was pore, but jest so mortal stingy.
An' there he sot by Sally Riggs a-smilin' an' a-smirkin',
An' all his childern lef' to home a diggin' an' a-workin'.
A widower he was, an' Sal was thinkin' 'at she'd wing him;
I reckon he was wond'rin' what them rings o' hern would bring him.
An' when the spellin'-test commenced, he up an' took his station,
A-spellin' with the best o' them to beat the very nation.
An' when he 'd spell some youngster down, he 'd turn to look at Sally,
An' say: "The teachin' nowadays can't be o' no great vally."
But true enough the adage says, "Pride walks in slipp'ry places,"
Fur soon a thing occurred that put a smile on all our faces.
The laffter jest kep' ripplin' 'roun' an' teacher could n't quell it,
Fur when he give out "charity" ole Hiram could n't spell it.
But laffin' 's ketchin' an' it throwed some others off their bases,
An' folks 'u'd miss the very word that seemed to fit their cases.
Why, fickle little Jessie Lee come near the house upsettin'
By puttin' in a double "kay" to spell the word "coquettin'."
An' when it come to Cyrus Jones, it tickled me all over—
Him settin' up to Mandy Smith an' got sot down on "lover."
But Lawyer Jones of all gone men did shorely look the gonest,
When he found out that he'd furgot to put the "h" in "honest."
An' Parson Brown, whose sermons were too long fur toleration,
Caused lots o' smiles by missin' when they give out "condensation."
So one by one they giv' it up—the big words kep' a-landin',
Till me an' Nettie Gray was left, the only ones a-standin',
An' then my inward strife began—I guess my mind was petty—
I did so want that spellin'-book; but then to spell down Nettie
Jest sort o' went ag'in my grain—I somehow could n't do it,
An' when I git a notion fixed, I'm great on stickin' to it.
So when they giv' the next word out—I had n't orter tell it,
But then 't was all fur Nettie's sake—I missed so 's she could spell it.
She spelt the word, then looked at me so lovin'-like an' mello',
I tell you 't sent a hunderd pins a-shootin' through a fello'.
O' course I had to stand the jokes an' chaffin' of the fello's,
But when they handed her the book I vow I was n't jealous.

We sung a hymn, an' Parson Brown dismissed us like he orter,
Fur, la! he 'd learned a thing er two an' made his blessin' shorter.
'Twas late an' cold when we got out, but Nettie liked cold weather,
An' so did I, so we agreed we 'd jest walk home together.
We both wuz silent, fur of words we nuther had a surplus,
'Till she spoke out quite sudden like, "You missed that word on pur-
pose."
Well, I declare it frightened me; at first I tried denyin',
But Nettie, she jest smiled an' smiled, she knowed that I was lyin'.
Sez she: "That book is yourn by right;" sez I: "It never could be—
I—I—you—ah—" an' there I stuck, an' well she understood me.
So we agreed that later on when age had giv' us tether,
We'd jine our lots an' settle down to own that book together.

KEEP A-PLUGGIN' AWAY

I've a humble little motto
That is homely, though it 's true,—
 Keep a-pluggin' away.
It 's a thing when I 've an object
That I always try to do,—
 Keep a-pluggin' away.
When you 've rising storms to quell,
When opposing waters swell,
It will never fail to tell,—
 Keep a-pluggin' away.

If the hills are high before
And the paths are hard to climb,
 Keep a-pluggin' away.
And remember that successes
Come to him who bides his time,—
 Keep a-pluggin' away.
From the greatest to the least
None are from the rule released.
Be thou toiler, poet, priest,

Keep a-pluggin' away.
Delve away beneath the surface,
There is treasure farther down,—
 Keep a-pluggin' away.
Let the rain come down in torrents,
Let the threat'ning heavens frown,
 Keep a-pluggin' away.
When the clouds have rolled away,
There will come a brighter day
All your labor to repay,—
 Keep a-pluggin' away.

There 'll be lots of sneers to swallow,
There 'll be lots of pain to bear,—
 Keep a-pluggin' away.
If you 've got your eye on heaven,
Some bright day you'll wake up there,—
 Keep a-pluggin' away.
Perseverance still is king;
Time its sure reward will bring;
Work and wait unwearying,—
 Keep a-pluggin' away.

NIGHT OF LOVE.

The moon has left the sky, love,
 The stars are hiding now,
And frowning on the world, love,
 Night bares her sable brow.
The snow is on the ground, love,
 And cold and keen the air is.
I 'm singing here to you, love;
 You're dreaming there in Paris.

But this is Nature's law, love,
 Though just it may not seem,

That men should wake to sing, love,
 While maidens sleep and dream.
Them care may not molest, love,
 Nor stir them from their slumbers,
Though midnight find the swain, love,
 Still halting o'er his numbers.

I watch the rosy dawn, love,
 Come stealing up the east,
While all things round rejoice, love,
 That Night her reign has ceased.
The lark will soon be heard, love,
 And on his way be winging;
When Nature's poets wake, love,
 Why should a man be singing?

COLUMBIAN ODE.

I.

Four hundred years ago a tangled waste
 Lay sleeping on the west Atlantic's side;
Their devious ways the Old World's millions traced
 Content, and loved, and labored, dared and died,
While students still believed the charts they conned,
 And revelled in their thriftless ignorance,
Nor dreamed of other lands that lay beyond
 Old Ocean's dense, indefinite expanse.

II.

But deep within her heart old Nature knew
 That she had once arrayed, at Earth's behest,
Another offspring, fine and fair to view,—
 The chosen suckling of the mother's breast.
The child was wrapped in vestments soft and fine,

Each fold a work of Nature's matchless art;
The mother looked on it with love divine,
And strained the loved one closely to her heart.
And there it lay, and with the warmth grew strong
And hearty, by the salt sea breezes fanned,
Till Time with mellowing touches passed along,
And changed the infant to a mighty land.

III.

But men knew naught of this, till there arose
That mighty mariner, the Genoese,
Who dared to try, in spite of fears and foes,
The unknown fortunes of unsounded seas.
O noblest of Italia's sons, thy bark
Went not alone into that shrouding night!
O dauntless darer of the rayless dark,
The world sailed with thee to eternal light!
The deer-haunts that with game were crowded then
To-day are tilled and cultivated lands;
The schoolhouse tow'rs where Bruin had his den,
And where the wigwam stood the chapel stands;
The place that nurtured men of savage mien
Now teems with men of Nature's noblest types;
Where moved the forest-foliage banner green,
Now flutters in the breeze the stars and stripes!

A BORDER BALLAD.

Oh, I have n't got long to live, for we all
Die soon, e'en those who live longest;
And the poorest and weakest are taking their chance
Along with the richest and strongest.
So it 's heigho for a glass and a song,
And a bright eye over the table,
And a dog for the hunt when the game is flush,

And the pick of a gentleman's stable.
There is Dimmock o' Dune, he was here yesternight,
 But he 's rotting to-day on Glen Arragh;
'Twas the hand o' MacPherson that gave him the blow,
 And the vultures shall feast on his marrow.
But it 's heigho for a brave old song
 And a glass while we are able;
Here 's a health to death and another cup
 To the bright eye over the table.

I can show a broad back and a jolly deep chest,
 But who argues now on appearance?
A blow or a thrust or a stumble at best
 May send me to-day to my clearance.
Then it 's heigho for the things I love,
 My mother 'll be soon wearing sable,
But give me my horse and my dog and my glass,
 And a bright eye over the table.

AN EASY-GOIN' FELLER.

Ther' ain't no use in all this strife,
An' hurryin', pell-mell, right thro' life.
I don't believe in goin' too fast
To see what kind o' road you 've passed.
It ain't no mortal kind o' good,
'N' I would n't hurry ef I could.
I like to jest go joggin' 'long,
To limber up my soul with song;
To stop awhile 'n' chat the men,
'N' drink some cider now an' then.

Do' want no boss a-standin' by
To see me work; I allus try
To do my dooty right straight up,
An' earn what fills my plate an' cup.

An' ez fur boss, I 'll be my own,
I like to jest be let alone,
To plough my strip an' tend my bees,
An' do jest like I doggoned please.
My head 's all right, an' my heart 's meller,
But I 'm a easy-goin' feller.

A NEGRO LOVE SONG.

Seen my lady home las' night,
 Jump back, honey, jump back.
Hel' huh han' an' sque'z it tight,
 Jump back, honey, jump back.
Hyeahd huh sigh a little sigh,
Seen a light gleam f'om huh eye,
An' a smile go flittin' by—
 Jump back, honey, jump back.

Hyeahd de win' blow thoo de pine,
 Jump back, honey, jump back.
Mockin'-bird was singin' fine,
 Jump back, honey, jump back.
An' my hea't was beatin' so,
When I reached my lady's do',
 Dat I could n't ba' to go—
 Jump back, honey, jump back.

Put my ahm aroun' huh wais',
 Jump back, honey, jump back.
Raised huh lips an' took a tase,
 Jump back, honey, jump back.
Love me, honey, love me true?
Love me well ez I love you?
 An' she answe'd, "'Cose I do"—
 Jump back, honey, jump back.

THE DILETTANTE: A MODERN TYPE.

He scribbles some in prose and verse,
 And now and then he prints it;
He paints a little,—gathers some
 Of Nature's gold and mints it.

He plays a little, sings a song,
 Acts tragic rôles, or funny;
He does, because his love is strong,
 But not, oh, not for money!

He studies almost everything
 From social art to science;
A thirsty mind, a flowing spring,
 Demand and swift compliance.

He looms above the sordid crowd—
 At least through friendly lenses;
While his mamma looks pleased and proud,
 And kindly pays expenses.

BY THE STREAM.

By the stream I dream in calm delight, and watch as in a glass,
How the clouds like crowds of snowy-hued and white-robed
maidens pass,
And the water into ripples breaks and sparkles as it spreads,
Like a host of armored knights with silver helmets on their heads.
And I deem the stream an emblem fit of human life may go,
For I find a mind may sparkle much and yet but shallows show,
And a soul may glow with myriad lights and wondrous mysteries,
When it only lies a dormant thing and mirrors what it sees.

THE COLORED SOLDIERS.

If the muse were mine to tempt it
 And my feeble voice were strong,
If my tongue were trained to measures,
 I would sing a stirring song.
I would sing a song heroic
 Of those noble sons of Ham,
Of the gallant colored soldiers
 Who fought for Uncle Sam!

In the early days you scorned them,
 And with many a flip and flout
Said "These battles are the white man's,
 And the whites will fight them out."
Up the hills you fought and faltered,
 In the vales you strove and bled,
While your ears still heard the thunder
 Of the foes' advancing tread.

Then distress fell on the nation,
 And the flag was drooping low;
Should the dust pollute your banner?
 No! the nation shouted, No!
So when War, in savage triumph,
 Spread abroad his funeral pall—
Then you called the colored soldiers,
 And they answered to your call.

And like hounds unleashed and eager
 For the life blood of the prey,
Sprung they forth and bore them bravely
 In the thickest of the fray.
And where'er the fight was hottest,
 Where the bullets fastest fell,
There they pressed unblanched and fearless
 At the very mouth of hell.

Ah, they rallied to the standard
 To uphold it by their might;
None were stronger in the labors,
 None were braver in the fight.
From the blazing breach of Wagner
 To the plains of Olustee,
They were foremost in the fight
 Of the battles of the free.

And at Pillow! God have mercy
 On the deeds committed there,
And the souls of those poor victims
 Sent to Thee without a prayer.
Let the fulness of Thy pity
 O'er the hot wrought spirits sway
Of the gallant colored soldiers
 Who fell fighting on that day!

Yes, the Blacks enjoy their freedom,
 And they won it dearly, too;
For the life blood of their thousands
 Did the southern fields bedew.
In the darkness of their bondage,
 In the depths of slavery's night,
Their muskets flashed the dawning,
 And they fought their way to light.

They were comrades then and brothers,
 Are they more or less to-day?
They were good to stop a bullet
 And to front the fearful fray.
They were citizens and soldiers,
 When rebellion raised its head;
And the traits that made them worthy,—
 Ah! those virtues are not dead.

They have shared your nightly vigils,
 They have shared your daily toil;

And their blood with yours commingling
 Has enriched the Southern soil.
They have slept and marched and suffered
 'Neath the same dark skies as you,
They have met as fierce a foeman,
 And have been as brave and true.

And their deeds shall find a record
 In the registry of Fame;
For their blood has cleansed completely
 Every blot of Slavery's shame.
So all honor and all glory
 To those noble sons of Ham—
The gallant colored soldiers
 Who fought for Uncle Sam!

NATURE AND ART.

TO MY FRIEND CHARLES BOOTH NETTLETON.

I.

The young queen Nature, ever sweet and fair,
 Once on a time fell upon evil days.
 From hearing oft herself discussed with praise,
There grew within her heart the longing rare
To see herself; and every passing air
 The warm desire fanned into lusty blaze.
 Full oft she sought this end by devious ways,
But sought in vain, so fell she in despair.
For none within her train nor by her side
 Could solve the task or give the envied boon.
 So day and night, beneath the sun and moon,
She wandered to and fro unsatisfied,
 Till Art came by, a blithe inventive elf,
 And made a glass wherein she saw herself.

II.

Enrapt, the queen gazed on her glorious self,
　　Then trembling with the thrill of sudden thought,
　　Commanded that the skilful wight be brought
That she might dower him with lands and pelf.
Then out upon the silent sea-lapt shelf
　　And up the hills and on the downs they sought
　　Him who so well and wondrously had wrought;
And with much search found and brought home the elf.
　　But he put by all gifts with sad replies,
And from his lips these words flowed forth like wine:
　　"O queen, I want no gift but thee," he said.
She heard and looked on him with love-lit eyes,
Gave him her hand, low murmuring, "I am shine,"
　　And at the morrow's dawning they were wed.

AFTER WHILE.

A POEM OF FAITH.

I think that though the clouds be dark,
That though the waves dash o'er the bark,
Yet after while the light will come,
And in calm waters safe at home
　　The bark will anchor.
Weep not, my sad-eyed, gray-robed maid,
Because your fairest blossoms fade,
That sorrow still o'erruns your cup,
And even though you root them up,
　　The weeds grow ranker.

For after while your tears shall cease,
And sorrow shall give way to peace;
The flowers shall bloom, the weeds shall die,
And in that faith seen, by and by

Thy woes shall perish.
Smile at old Fortune's adverse tide,
Smile when the scoffers sneer and chide.
Oh, not for you the gems that pale,
And not for you the flowers that fail;
 Let this thought cherish:

That after while the clouds will part,
And then with joy the waiting heart
Shall feel the light come stealing in,
That drives away the cloud of sin
 And breaks its power.
And you shall burst your chrysalis,
And wing away to realms of bliss,
Untrammelled, pure, divinely free,
Above all earth's anxiety
 From that same hour.

THE OL' TUNES.

You kin talk about yer anthems
 An' yer arias an' sich,
An' yer modern choir-singin'
 That you think so awful rich;
But you orter heerd us youngsters
 In the times now far away,
A-singin' o' the ol' tunes
 In the ol'-fashioned way.

There was some of us sung treble
 An' a few of us growled bass,
An' the tide o' song flowed smoothly
 With its 'comp'niment o' grace;
There was spirit in that music,
 An' a kind o' solemn sway,
A-singin' o' the ol' tunes

In the ol'-fashioned way.

I remember oft o' standin'
 In my homespun pantaloons—
On my face the bronze an' freckles
 O' the suns o' youthful Junes—
Thinkin' that no mortal minstrel
 Ever chanted sich a lay
As the ol' tunes we was singin'
 In the ol'-fashioned way.

The boys 'ud always lead us,
 An' the girls 'ud all chime in,
Till the sweetness o' the singin'
 Robbed the list'nin' soul o' sin;
An' I used to tell the parson
 'Twas as good to sing as pray,
When the people sung the ol' tunes
 In the ol'-fashioned way.

How I long ag'in to hear 'em
 Pourin' forth from soul to soul,
With the treble high an' meller,
 An' the bass's mighty roll;
But the times is very diff'rent,
 An' the music heerd to-day
Ain't the singin' o' the ol' tunes
 In the ol'-fashioned way.

Little screechin' by a woman,
 Little squawkin' by a man,
Then the organ's twiddle-twaddle,
 Jest the empty space to span,—
An' ef you should even think it,
 'T is n't proper fur to say
That you want to hear the ol' tunes
 In the ol'-fashioned way.

But I think that some bright mornin',
 When the toils of life air o'er,
An' the sun o' heaven arisin'
 Glads with light the happy shore,
I shall hear the angel chorus,
 In the realms of endless day,
A-singin' o' the ol' tunes
 In the ol'-fashioned way.

MELANCHOLIA.

Silently without my window,
 Tapping gently at the pane,
 Falls the rain.
Through the trees sighs the breeze
 Like a soul in pain.
Here alone I sit and weep;
Thought hath banished sleep.

Wearily I sit and listen
 To the water's ceaseless drip.
 To my lip
Fate turns up the bitter cup,
 Forcing me to sip;
'T is a bitter, bitter drink,
Thus I sit and think,—

Thinking things unknown and awful,
 Thoughts on wild, uncanny themes,
 Waking dreams.
Spectres dark, corpses stark,
 Show the gaping seams
Whence the cold and cruel knife
Stole away their life.

Bloodshot eyes all strained and staring,

 Gazing ghastly into mine;
 Blood like wine
On the brow-clotted now—
 Shows death's dreadful sign.
Lonely vigil still I keep;
Would that I might sleep!

Still, oh, still, my brain is whirling!
 Still runs on my stream of thought;
 I am caught
In the net fate hath set.
 Mind and soul are brought
To destruction's very brink;
Yet I can but think!

Eyes that look into the future,—
 Peeping forth from out my mind,
 They will find
Some new weight, soon or late,
 On my soul to bind,
Crushing all its courage out,—
Heavier than doubt.

Dawn, the Eastern monarch's daughter,
 Rising from her dewy bed,
 Lays her head
'Gainst the clouds' sombre shrouds
 Now half fringed with red.
O'er the land she 'gins to peep;
Come, O gentle Sleep!

Hark! the morning cock is crowing;
 Dreams, like ghosts, must hie away;
 'T is the day.
Rosy morn now is born:
 Dark thoughts may not stay.
Day my brain from foes will keep;
Now, my soul, I sleep.

THE WOOING.

A youth went faring up and down,
 Alack and well-a-day.
He fared him to the market town,
 Alack and well-a-day.
And there he met a maiden fair,
With hazel eyes and auburn hair;
His heart went from him then and there,
 Alack and well-a-day.

She posies sold right merrily,
 Alack and well-a-day;
But not a flower was fair as she,
 Alack and well-a-day.
He bought a rose and sighed a sigh,
"Ah, dearest maiden, would that I
Might dare the seller too to buy!"
 Alack and well-a-day.

She tossed her head, the coy coquette,
 Alack and well-a-day.
"I'm not, sir, in the market yet,"
 Alack and well-a-day.
"Your love must cool upon a shelf;
Tho' much I sell for gold and pelf,
I'm yet too young to sell myself,"
 Alack and well-a-day.

The youth was filled with sorrow sore,
 Alack and well-a-day;
And looked he at the maid once more,
 Alack and well-a-day.
Then loud he cried, "Fair maiden, if
Too young to sell, now as I live,
You're not too young yourself to give,"
 Alack and well-a-day.

The little maid cast down her eye,
 Alack and well-a-day,
And many a flush began to rise,
 Alack and well-a-day.
"Why, since you are so bold," she said,
"I doubt not you are highly bred,
So take me!" and the twain were wed,
 Alack and well-a-day.

MERRY AUTUMN.

It's all a farce,—these tales they tell
 About the breezes sighing,
And moans astir o'er field and dell,
 Because the year is dying.

Such principles are most absurd,—
 I care not who first taught 'em;
There 's nothing known to beast or bird
 To make a solemn autumn.

In solemn times, when grief holds sway
 With countenance distressing,
You'll note the more of black and gray
 Will then be used in dressing.

Now purple tints are all around;
 The sky is blue and mellow;
And e'en the grasses turn the ground
 From modest green to yellow.

The seed burrs all with laughter crack
 On featherweed and jimson;
And leaves that should be dressed in black
 Are all decked out in crimson.

A butterfly goes winging by;
 A singing bird comes after;
And Nature, all from earth to sky,
 Is bubbling o'er with laughter.

The ripples wimple on the rills,
 Like sparkling little lasses;
The sunlight runs along the hills,
 And laughs among the grasses.

The earth is just so full of fun
 It really can't contain it;
And streams of mirth so freely run
 The heavens seem to rain it.

Don't talk to me of solemn days
 In autumn's time of splendor,
Because the sun shows fewer rays,
 And these grow slant and slender.

Why, it 's the climax of the year,—
 The highest time of living!—
Till naturally its bursting cheer
 Just melts into thanksgiving.

WHEN DE CO'N PONE'S HOT.

Dey is times in life when Nature
 Seems to slip a cog an' go,
Jes' a-rattlin' down creation,
 Lak an ocean's overflow;
When de worl' jes' stahts a-spinnin'
 Lak a picaninny's top,
An' yo' cup o' joy is brimmin'
 'Twell it seems about to slop,
An' you feel jes' lak a racah,

Dat is trainin' fu' to trot—
When yo' mammy says de blessin'
 An' de co'n pone 's hot.

When you set down at de table,
 Kin' o' weary lak an' sad,
An' you'se jes' a little tiahed
 An' purhaps a little mad;
How yo' gloom tu'ns into gladness,
 How yo' joy drives out de doubt
When de oven do' is opened,
 An' de smell comes po'in' out;
Why, de 'lectric light o' Heaven
 Seems to settle on de spot,
When yo' mammy says de blessin'
 An' de co'n pone's hot.

When de cabbage pot is steamin'
 An' de bacon good an' fat,
When de chittlins is a-sputter'n'
 So's to show you whah dey's at;
Tek away yo' sody biscuit,
 Tek away yo' cake an' pie,
Fu' de glory time is comin',
 An' it's 'proachin' mighty nigh,
An' you want to jump an' hollah,
 Dough you know you'd bettah not,
When yo' mammy says de blessin',
 An' de co'n pone's hot.

I have hyeahd o' lots o' sermons,
 An' I 've hyeahd o' lots o' prayers,
An' I 've listened to some singin'
 Dat has tuck me up de stairs
Of de Glory-Lan' an' set me
 Jes' below de Mahstah's th'one,
An' have lef' my hea't a-singin'
 In a happy aftah tone;

But dem wu'ds so sweetly murmured
 Seem to tech de softes' spot,
When my mammy says de blessin',
 An' de co'n pone 's hot.

BALLAD.

I know my love is true,
 And oh the day is fair.
The sky is clear and blue,
The flowers are rich of hue,
 The air I breathe is rare,
 I have no grief or care;
For my own love is true,
 And oh the day is fair.

My love is false I find,
 And oh the day is dark.
Blows sadly down the wind,
While sorrow holds my mind;
 I do not hear the lark,
 For quenched is life's dear spark,—
My love is false I find,
 And oh the day is dark!

For love doth make the day
 Or dark or doubly bright;
Her beams along the way
Dispel the gloom and gray.
 She lives and all is bright,
 She dies and life is night.
For love doth make the day,
 Or dark or doubly bright.

THE CHANGE HAS COME.

THE change has come, and Helen sleeps—
 Not sleeps; but wakes to greater deeps
Of wisdom, glory, truth, and light,
Than ever blessed her seeking sight,
In this low, long, lethargic night,
 Worn out with strife
 Which men call life.

The change has come, and who would say
"I would it were not come to-day"?
 What were the respite till to-morrow?
 Postponement of a certain sorrow,
 From which each passing day would borrow
 Let grief be dumb,
 The change has come.

COMPARISON.

The sky of brightest gray seems dark
 To one whose sky was ever white.
To one who never knew a spark,
 Thro' all his life, of love or light,
 The grayest cloud seems over-bright.

The robin sounds a beggar's note
 Where one the nightingale has heard,
But he for whom no silver throat
 Its liquid music ever stirred,
 Deems robin still the sweetest bird.

A CORN-SONG.

On the wide veranda white,
In the purple failing light,
Sits the master while the sun is lowly burning;
And his dreamy thoughts are drowned
In the softly flowing sound
Of the corn-songs of the field-hands slow returning.

> Oh, we hoe de co'n
> Since de ehly mo'n;
> Now de sinkin' sun
> Says de day is done.

O'er the fields with heavy tread,
Light of heart and high of head,
Though the halting steps be labored, slow, and weary;
Still the spirits brave and strong
Find a comforter in song,
And their corn-song rises ever loud and cheery.

> Oh, we hoe de co'n
> Since de ehly mo'n;
> Now de sinkin' sun
> Says de day is done.

To the master in his seat,
Comes the burden, full and sweet,
Of the mellow minor music growing clearer,
As the toilers raise the hymn,
Thro' the silence dusk and dim,
To the cabin's restful shelter drawing nearer.

> Oh, we hoe de co'n
> Since de ehly mo'n;
> Now de sinkin' sun
> Says de day is done.

And a tear is in the eye
Of the master sitting by,
As he listens to the echoes low-replying
To the music's fading calls
As it faints away and falls
Into silence, deep within the cabin dying.

> Oh, we hoe de co'n
> Since de ehly mo'n;
> Now de sinkin' sun
> Says de day is done.

DISCOVERED.

Seen you down at chu'ch las' night,
 Nevah min', Miss Lucy.
What I mean? oh, dat 's all right,
 Nevah min', Miss Lucy.
You was smatt ez sma't could be,
But you could n't hide f'om me.
Ain't I got two eyes to see!
 Nevah min', Miss Lucy.

Guess you thought you's awful keen;
 Nevah min', Miss Lucy.
Evahthing you done, I seen;
 Nevah min', Miss Lucy.
Seen him tek yo' ahm jes' so,
When he got outside de do'—
Oh, I know dat man's yo' beau!
 Nevah min', Miss Lucy.

Say now, honey, wha 'd he say?—
 Nevah min', Miss Lucy!
Keep yo' secrets-dat 's yo' way—
 Nevah min', Miss Lucy.

Won't tell me an' I'm yo' pal—
I'm gwine tell his othah gal,—
Know huh, too, huh name is Sal;
 Nevah min', Miss Lucy!

DISAPPOINTED.

An old man planted and dug and tended,
 Toiling in joy from dew to dew;
The sun was kind, and the rain befriended;
 Fine grew his orchard and fair to view.
Then he said: "I will quiet my thrifty fears,
For here is fruit for my failing years."

But even then the storm-clouds gathered,
 Swallowing up the azure sky;
The sweeping winds into white foam lathered
 The placid breast of the bay, hard by;
Then the spirits that raged in the darkened air
Swept o'er his orchard and left it bare.

The old man stood in the rain, uncaring,
 Viewing the place the storm had swept;
And then with a cry from his soul despairing,
 He bowed him down to the earth and wept.
But a voice cried aloud from the driving rain;
"Arise, old man, and plant again!"

INVITATION TO LOVE.

Come when the nights are bright with stars
 Or when the moon is mellow;
Come when the sun his golden bars
 Drops on the hay-field yellow.

Come in the twilight soft and gray,
Come in the night or come in the day,
Come, O Love, whene'er you may,
 And you are welcome, welcome.

You are sweet, O Love, dear Love,
You are soft as the nesting dove.
Come to my heart and bring it rest
As the bird flies home to its welcome nest.

Come when my heart is full of grief
 Or when my heart is merry;
Come with the falling of the leaf
 Or with the redd'ning cherry.

Come when the year's first blossom blows,
Come when the summer gleams and glows,
Come with the winter's drifting snows,
 And you are welcome, welcome.

HE HAD HIS DREAM.

He had his dream, and all through life,
Worked up to it through toil and strife.
Afloat fore'er before his eyes,
It colored for him all his skies:
 The storm-cloud dark
 Above his bark,
The calm and listless vault of blue
Took on its hopeful hue,
It tinctured every passing beam—
 He had his dream.

He labored hard and failed at last,
His sails too weak to bear the blast,
The raging tempests tore away

And sent his beating bark astray.
>> But what cared he
>> For wind or sea!
He said, "The tempest will be short,
My bark will come to port."
He saw through every cloud a gleam—
>> He had his dream.

GOOD-NIGHT.

The lark is silent in his nest,
>> The breeze is sighing in its flight,
Sleep, Love, and peaceful be thy rest.
>> Good-night, my love, good-night, good-night.

Sweet dreams attend thee in thy sleep,
>> To soothe thy rest till morning's light,
And angels round thee vigil keep.
>> Good-night, my love, good-night, good-night.

Sleep well, my love, on night's dark breast,
>> And ease thy soul with slumber bright;
Be joy but shine and I am blest.
>> Good-night, my love, good-night, good-night,

A COQUETTE CONQUERED.

Yes, my ha't 's ez ha'd ez stone—
Go 'way, Sam, an' lemme 'lone.
No; I ain't gwine change my min'—
Ain't gwine ma'y you—nuffin' de kin'.

Phiny loves you true an' deah?
Go ma'y Phiny; whut I keer?

Oh, you need n't mou'n an' cry—
I don't keer how soon you die.

Got a present! Whut you got?
Somef'n fu' de pan er pot!
Huh! yo' sass do sholy beat—
Think I don't git 'nough to eat?

Whut 's dat un'neaf yo' coat?
Looks des lak a little shoat.
'T ain't no possum! Bless de Lamb!
Yes, it is, you rascal, Sam!

Gin it to me; whut you say?
Ain't you sma't now! Oh, go 'way!
Possum do look mighty nice,
But you ax too big a price.

Tell me, is you talkin' true,
Dat 's de gal's whut ma'ies you?
Come back, Sam; now whah 's you gwine?
Co'se you knows dat possum's mine!

NORA: A SERENADE.

Ah, Nora, my Nora, the light fades away,
 While Night like a spirit steals up o'er the hills;
The thrush from his tree where he chanted all day,
 No longer his music in ecstasy trills.
Then, Nora, be near me; thy presence doth cheer me,
 Thine eye hath a gleam that is truer than gold.
I cannot but love thee; so do not reprove me,
 If the strength of my passion should make me too bold.

Nora, pride of my heart,—
 Rosy cheeks, cherry lips, sparkling with glee,—

Wake from thy slumbers, wherever thou art;
 Wake from thy slumbers to me.

Ah, Nora, my Nora, there 's love in the air,—
 It stirs in the numbers that thrill in my brain;
Oh, sweet, sweet is love with its mingling of care,
 Though joy travels only a step before pain.
Be roused from thy slumbers and list to my numbers;
 My heart is poured out in this song unto thee.
Oh, be thou not cruel, thou treasure, thou jewel;
 Turn thine ear to my pleading and hearken to me.

OCTOBER.

October is the treasurer of the year,
 And all the months pay bounty to her store;
The fields and orchards still their tribute bear,
 And fill her brimming coffers more and more.
But she, with youthful lavishness,
Spends all her wealth in gaudy dress,
 And decks herself in garments bold
 Of scarlet, purple, red, and gold.

She heedeth not how swift the hours fly,
 But smiles and sings her happy life along;
She only sees above a shining sky;
 She only hears the breezes' voice in song.
Her garments trail the woodlands through,
And gather pearls of early dew
 That sparkle, till the roguish Sun
 Creeps up and steals them every one.

But what cares she that jewels should be lost,
 When all of Nature's bounteous wealth is hers?
Though princely fortunes may have been their cost,
 Not one regret her calm demeanor stirs.

Whole-hearted, happy, careless, free,
She lives her life out joyously,
 Nor cares when Frost stalks o'er her way
 And turns her auburn locks to gray.

A SUMMER'S NIGHT.

The night is dewy as a maiden's mouth,
 The skies are bright as are a maiden's eyes,
 Soft as a maiden's breath the wind that flies
Up from the perfumed bosom of the South.

Like sentinels, the pines stand in the park;
 And hither hastening, like rakes that roam,
 With lamps to light their wayward footsteps home,
The fireflies come stagg'ring down the dark.

SHIPS THAT PASS IN THE NIGHT.

Out in the sky the great dark clouds are massing;
 I look far out into the pregnant night,
Where I can hear a solemn booming gun
 And catch the gleaming of a random light,
That tells me that the ship I seek is passing, passing.

My tearful eyes my soul's deep hurt are glassing;
 For I would hail and check that ship of ships.
I stretch my hands imploring, cry aloud,
 My voice falls dead a foot from mine own lips,
And but its ghost doth reach that vessel, passing, passing.

O Earth, O Sky, O Ocean, both surpassing,
 O heart of mine, O soul that dreads the dark!
Is there no hope for me? Is there no way

That I may sight and check that speeding bark
Which out of sight and sound is passing, passing?

THE DELINQUENT.

Goo'-by, Jinks, I got to hump,
Got to mek dis pony jump;
See dat sun a—goin' down
'N' me a-foolin' hyeah in town!
　　Git up, Suke—go long!

Guess Mirandy 'll think I 's tight,
Me not home an' comin' on night.
What's dat stan'in' by de fence?
Pshaw! why don't I lu'n some sense?
　　Git up, Suke—go long!

Guess I spent down dah at Jinks'
Mos' a dollah fur de drinks.
Bless yo'r soul, you see dat star?
Lawd, but won't Mirandy rar?
　　Git up, Suke—go long!

Went dis mo'nin', hyeah it 's night,
Dah 's de cabin dah in sight.
Who 's dat stan'in' in de do'?
Dat must be Mirandy, sho',
　　Git up, Suke—go long!

Got de close-stick in huh han',
Dat look funny, goodness lan',
Sakes alibe, but she look glum!
Hyeah, Mirandy, hyeah I come!
　　Git up, Suke—go long!
　Ef 't had n't a be'n fur you, you slow ole fool,
I'd a' be'n home long fo' now!

DAWN.

An angel, robed in spotless white,
Bent down and kissed the sleeping Night.
Night woke to blush; the sprite was gone.
Men saw the blush and called it Dawn.

A DROWSY DAY.

The air is dark, the sky is gray,
 The misty shadows come and go,
And here within my dusky room
Each chair looks ghostly in the gloom.
 Outside the rain falls cold and slow—
Half-stinging drops, half-blinding spray.

Each slightest sound is magnified,
 For drowsy quiet holds her reign;
The burnt stick in the fireplace breaks,
The nodding cat with start awakes,
 And then to sleep drops off again,
Unheeding Towser at her side.

I look far out across the lawn,
 Where huddled stand the silly sheep;
My work lies idle at my hands,
My thoughts fly out like scattered strands
 Of thread, and on the verge of sleep—
Still half awake—I dream and yawn.

What spirits rise before my eyes!
 How various of kind and form!
Sweet memories of days long past,
The dreams of youth that could not last,
 Each smiling calm, each raging storm,
That swept across my early skies.

Half seen, the bare, gaunt-fingered boughs
 Before my window sweep and sway,
And chafe in tortures of unrest.
My chin sinks down upon my breast;
 I cannot work on such a day,
But only sit and dream and drowse.

DIRGE.

Place this bunch of mignonette
 In her cold, dead hand;
When the golden sun is set,
 Where the poplars stand,
Bury her from sun and day,
Lay my little love away
 From my sight.

She was like a modest flower
 Blown in sunny June,
Warm as sun at noon's high hour,
 Chaster than the moon.
Ah, her day was brief and bright,
Earth has lost a star of light;
 She is dead.

Softly breathe her name to me,—
 Ah, I loved her so.
Gentle let your tribute be;
 None may better know
Her true worth than I who weep
O'er her as she lies asleep—
 Soft asleep.

Lay these lilies on her breast,
 They are not more white
Than the soul of her, at rest

'Neath their petals bright.
Chant your aves soft and low,
Solemn be your tread and slow,—
 She is dead.

Lay her here beneath the grass,
 Cool and green and sweet,
Where the gentle brook may pass
 Crooning at her feet.
Nature's bards shall come and sing,
And the fairest flowers shall spring
 Where she lies.

Safe above the water's swirl,
 She has crossed the bar;
Earth has lost a precious pearl,
 Heaven has gained a star,
That shall ever sing and shine,
Till it quells this grief of mine
 For my love.

HYMN.

When storms arise
And dark'ning skies
 About me threat'ning lower,
To thee, O Lord, I raise mine eyes,
To thee my tortured spirit flies
 For solace in that hour.
Thy mighty arm
Will let no harm
 Come near me nor befall me;
Thy voice shall quiet my alarm,
When life's great battle waxeth warm—
 No foeman shall appall me.

Upon thy breast
Secure I rest,
From sorrow and vexation;
No more by sinful cares oppressed,
But in thy presence ever blest,
O God of my salvation.

PREPARATION.

The little bird sits in the nest and sings
A shy, soft song to the morning light;
And it flutters a little and prunes its wings.
The song is halting and poor and brief,
And the fluttering wings scarce stir a leaf;
But the note is a prelude to sweeter things,
And the busy bill and the flutter slight
Are proving the wings for a bolder flight!

THE DESERTED PLANTATION.

Oh, de grubbin'-hoe 's a-rustin' in de co'nah,
An' de plow 's a-tumblin' down in de fiel',
While de whippo'will 's a-wailin' lak a mou'nah
When his stubbo'n hea't is tryin' ha'd to yiel'.

In de furrers whah de co'n was allus wavin',
Now de weeds is growin' green an' rank an' tall;
An' de swallers roun' de whole place is a-bravin'
Lak dey thought deir folks had allus owned it all.

An' de big house stan's all quiet lak an' solemn,
Not a blessed soul in pa'lor, po'ch, er lawn;
Not a guest, ner not a ca'iage lef' to haul 'em,
Fu' de ones dat tu'ned de latch-string out air gone.

An' de banjo's voice is silent in de qua'ters,
 D'ain't a hymn ner co'n-song ringin' in de air;
But de murmur of a branch's passin' waters
 Is de only soun' dat breks de stillness dere.

Whah 's de da'kies, dem dat used to be a-dancin'
 Evry night befo' de ole cabin do'?
Whah 's de chillun, dem dat used to be a-prancin'
 Er a-rollin' in de san' er on de flo'?

Whah 's ole Uncle Mordecai an' Uncle Aaron?
 Whah 's Aunt Doshy, Sam, an' Kit, an' all de res'
Whah 's ole Tom de da'ky fiddlah, how's he farin'?
 Whah 's de gals dat used to sing an' dance de bes'?

Gone! not one o' dem is lef' to tell de story;
 Dey have lef' de deah ole place to fall away.
Could n't one o' dem dat seed it in its glory
 Stay to watch it in de hour of decay?

Dey have lef' de ole plantation to de swallers,
 But it hol's in me a lover till de las';
Fu' I fin' hyeah in de memory dat follers
 All dat loved me an' dat I loved in de pas'.

So I'll stay an' watch de deah ole place an' tend it
 Ez I used to in de happy days gone by.
'Twell de othah Mastah thinks it 's time to end it,
 An' calls me to my qua'ters in de sky.

THE SECRET.

What says the wind to the waving trees?
 What says the wave to the river?
What means the sigh in the passing breeze?
 Why do the rushes quiver?

Have you not heard the fainting cry
Of the flowers that said "Good-bye, good-bye"?

List how the gray dove moans and grieves
 Under the woodland cover;
List to the drift of the falling leaves,
 List to the wail of the lover.
Have you not caught the message heard
Already by wave and breeze and bird?

Come, come away to the river's bank,
 Come in the early morning;
Come when the grass with dew is dank,
 There you will find the warning—
A hint in the kiss of the quickening air
Of the secret that birds and breezes bear.

THE WIND AND THE SEA.

I stood by the shore at the death of day,
 As the sun sank flaming red;
And the face of the waters that spread away
 Was as gray as the face of the dead.

And I heard the cry of the wanton sea
 And the moan of the wailing wind;
For love's sweet pain in his heart had he,
 But the gray old sea had sinned.

The wind was young and the sea was old,
 But their cries went up together;
The wind was warm and the sea was cold,
 For age makes wintry weather.

So they cried aloud and they wept amain,
 Till the sky grew dark to hear it;

And out of its folds crept the misty rain,
 In its shroud, like a troubled spirit.

For the wind was wild with a hopeless love,
 And the sea was sad at heart
At many a crime that he wot of,
 Wherein he had played his part.

He thought of the gallant ships gone down
 By the will of his wicked waves;
And he thought how the churchyard in the town
 Held the sea-made widows' graves.

The wild wind thought of the love he had left
 Afar in an Eastern land,
And he longed, as long the much bereft,
 For the touch of her perfumed hand.

In his winding wail and his deep-heaved sigh
 His aching grief found vent;
While the sea looked up at the bending sky
 And murmured: "I repent."

But e'en as he spoke, a ship came by,
 That bravely ploughed the main,
And a light came into the sea's green eye,
 And his heart grew hard again.

Then he spoke to the wind: "Friend, seest thou not
 Yon vessel is eastward bound?
Pray speed with it to the happy spot
 Where thy loved one may be found."

And the wind rose up in a dear delight,
 And after the good ship sped;
But the crafty sea by his wicked might
 Kept the vessel ever ahead.

Till the wind grew fierce in his despair,
 And white on the brow and lip.
He tore his garments and tore his hair,
 And fell on the flying ship.

And the ship went down, for a rock was there,
 And the sailless sea loomed black;
While burdened again with dole and care,
 The wind came moaning back.

And still he moans from his bosom hot
 Where his raging grief lies pent,
And ever when the ships come not,
 The sea says: "I repent."

RIDING TO TOWN.

When labor is light and the morning is
I find it a pleasure beyond all compare
To hitch up my nag and go hurrying down
And take Katie May for a ride into town;
 For bumpety-bump goes the wagon,
 But tra-la-la-la our lay,
There's joy in a song as we rattle along
 In the light of the glorious day.

A coach would be fine, but a spring wagon 's good;
My jeans are a match for Kate's gingham and hood;
The hills take us up and the vales take us down,
But what matters that? we are riding to town,
 And bumpety-bump goes the wagon,
 But tra-la-la-la sing we.
There's never a care may live in the air
 That is filled with the breath of our glee.

And after we've started, there's naught can repress

The thrill of our hearts in their wild happiness;
The heavens may smile or the heavens may frown,
And it's all one to us when we 're riding to town.
 For bumpety-bump goes the wagon,
 But tra-la-la-la we shout,
For our hearts they are clear and there's nothing to fear,
 And we've never a pain nor a doubt.

The wagon is weak and the roadway is rough,
And tho' it is long it is not long enough,
For mid all my ecstasies this is the crown
To sit beside Katie and ride into town,
 When bumpety-bump goes the wagon,
 But tra-la-la-la our song;
And if I had my way, I'd be willing to pay
 If the road could be made twice as long.

WE WEAR THE MASK.

We wear the mask that grins and lies,
It hides our cheeks and shades our eyes,—
This debt we pay to human guile;
With torn and bleeding hearts we smile,
And mouth with myriad subtleties.

Why should the world be over-wise,
In counting all our tears and sighs?
Nay, let them only see us, while
 We wear the mask.

We smile, but, O great Christ, our cries
To thee from tortured souls arise.
We sing, but oh the clay is vile
Beneath our feet, and long the mile;
But let the world dream otherwise,
 We wear the mask!

THE MEADOW LARK.

THOUGH the winds be dank,
 And the sky be sober,
 And the grieving Day
 In a mantle gray
 Hath let her waiting maiden robe her,—
 All the fields along
 I can hear the song
Of the meadow lark,
 As she flits and flutters,
 And laughs at the thunder when it mutters.
 O happy bird, of heart most gay
 To sing when skies are gray!

When the clouds are full,
 And the tempest master
 Lets the loud winds sweep
 From his bosom deep
 Like heralds of some dire disaster,
 Then the heart alone
 To itself makes moan;
And the songs come slow,
 While the tears fall fleeter,
 And silence than song by far seems sweeter
 Oh, few are they along the way
 Who sing when skies are gray!

ONE LIFE.

Oh, I am hurt to death, my Love;
 The shafts of Fate have pierced my striving heart,
And I am sick and weary of
 The endless pain and smart.
My soul is weary of the strife,

And chafes at life, and chafes at life.

Time mocks me with fair promises,
 A blooming future grows a barren past,
Like rain my fair full-blossomed trees
 Unburden in the blast.
The harvest fails on grain and tree,
Nor comes to me, nor comes to me.

The stream that bears my hopes abreast
 Turns ever from my way its pregnant tide.
My laden boat, torn from its rest,
 Drifts to the other side.
So all my hopes are set astray,
And drift away, and drift away.

The lark sings to me at the morn,
 And near me wings her skyward-soaring flight;
But pleasure dies as soon as born,
 The owl takes up the night,
And night seems long and doubly dark;
I miss the lark, I miss the lark.

Let others labor as they may,
 I 'll sing and sigh alone, and write my line.
Their fate is theirs, or grave or gay,
 And mine shall still be mine.
I know the world holds joy and glee,
But not for me,—'t is not for me.

CHANGING TIME.

The cloud looked in at the window,
 And said to the day, "Be dark!"
And the roguish rain tapped hard on the pane,
 To stifle the song of the lark.

The wind sprang up in the tree tops
 And shrieked with a voice of death,
But the rough-voiced breeze, that shook the trees,
 Was touched with a violet's breath.

DEAD.

A knock is at her door, but she is weak;
Strange dews have washed the paint streaks from her cheek;
She does not rise, but, ah, this friend is known,
And knows that he will find her all alone.
So opens he the door, and with soft tread
Goes straightway to the richly curtained bed.
His soft hand on her dewy head he lays.
A strange white light she gives him for his gaze.
Then, looking on the glory of her charms,
He crushes her resistless in his arms.

Stand back! look not upon this bold embrace,
Nor view the calmness of the wanton's face;
With joy unspeakable and 'bated breath,
She keeps her last, long liaison with death!

A CONFIDENCE.

Uncle John, he makes me tired;
Thinks 'at he's jest so all-fired
Smart, 'at he kin pick up, so,
Ever'thing he wants to know.
Tried to ketch me up last night,
But you bet I would n't bite.
I jest kep' the smoothes' face,
But I led him sich a chase,

Could n't corner me, you bet—
I skipped all the traps he set.
Makin' out he wanted to know
Who was this an' that girl's beau;
So 's he'd find out, don't you see,
Who was goin' 'long with me.
But I answers jest ez sly,
An' I never winks my eye,
Tell he hollers with a whirl,
"Look here, ain't you got a girl?"
Y' ought 'o seen me spread my eyes,
Like he 'd took me by surprise,
An' I said, "Oh, Uncle John,
Never thought o' havin' one."
An' somehow that seemed to tickle
Him an' he shelled out a nickel.
Then you ought to seen me leave
Jest a-laffin' in my sleeve.
Fool him—well, I guess I did;
He ain't on to this here kid.
Got a girl! well, I guess yes,
Got a dozen more or less,
But I got one reely one,
Not no foolin' ner no fun;
Fur I 'm sweet on her, you see,
An' I rusher guess 'at she
Must be kinder sweet on me,
So we 're keepin' company.
Honest Injun! this is true,
Ever' word I'm tellin' you!
But you won't be sich a scab
Ez to run aroun' an' blab.
Mebbe 't ain't the way with you,
But you know some fellers do.
Spoils a girl to let her know
'At you talk about her so.
Don't you know her? her name 's Liz,
Nicest girl in town she is.

Purty? ah, git out, you gilly—
Liz 'ud purt 'nigh knock you silly.
Y' ought 'o see her when she's dressed
All up in her Sunday best,
All the fellers nudgin' me,
An' a-whisperin', gemunee!
Betcher life 'at I feel proud
When she passes by the crowd.
'T 's kinder nice to be a-goin'
With a girl 'at makes some showin'—
One you know 'at hadn't no snide,
Makes you feel so satisfied.
An' I 'll tell you she's a trump,
Never even seen her jump
Like some silly girls 'ud do,
When I'd hide and holler "Boo!"
She 'd jest laff an' say "Git out!
What you hollerin' about?"
When some girls 'ud have a fit
That 'un don't git skeered a bit,
Never makes a bit o' row
When she sees a worm er cow.
Them kind 's few an' far between;
Bravest girl I ever seen.
Tell you 'nuther thing she 'll do,
Mebbe you won't think it 's true,
But if she 's jest got a dime
She 'll go halvers ever' time.
Ah, you goose, you need n't laff;
That 's the kinder girl to have.
If you knowed her like I do,
Guess you 'd kinder like her too.
Tell you somep'n' if you'll swear
You won't tell it anywhere.
Oh, you got to cross yer heart
Earnest, truly, 'fore I start.
Well, one day I kissed her cheek;
Gee, but I felt cheap an' weak,

'Cause at first she kinder flared,
'N', gracious goodness! I was scared.
But I need n't been, fer la!
Why, she never told her ma.
That 's what I call grit, don't you?
Sich a girl 's worth stickin' to.

PHYLLIS.

Phyllis, ah, Phyllis, my life is a gray day,
 Few are my years, but my griefs are not few,
Ever to youth should each day be a May-day,
 Warm wind and rose-breath and diamonded dew—
Phyllis, ah, Phyllis, my life is a gray day.

Oh for the sunlight that shines on a May-day!
 Only the cloud hangeth over my life.
Love that should bring me youth's happiest heyday
 Brings me but seasons of sorrow and strife;
Phyllis, ah, Phyllis, my life is a gray day.

Sunshine or shadow, or gold day or gray day,
 Life must be lived as our destinies rule;
Leisure or labor or work day or play day—
 Feasts for the famous and fun for the fool;
Phyllis, ah, Phyllis, my life is a gray day.

RIGHT'S SECURITY.

What if the wind do howl without,
And turn the creaking weather-vane;
What if the arrows of the rain
Do beat against the window-pane?
Art thou not armored strong and fast

Against the sallies of the blast?
Art thou not sheltered safe and well
Against the flood's insistent swell?

What boots it, that thou stand'st alone,
And laughest in the battle's face
When all the weak have fled the place
And let their feet and fears keep pace?
Thou wavest still shine ensign, high,
And shoutest thy loud battle-cry;
Higher than e'er the tempest roared,
It cleaves the silence like a sword.

Right arms and armors, too, that man
Who will not compromise with wrong;
Though single, he must front the throng
And wage the battle hard and long.
Minorities, since time began,
Have shown the better side of man;
And often in the lists of Time
One man has made a cause sublime!

IF.

If life were but a dream, my Love,
 And death the waking time;
If day had not a beam, my Love,
 And night had not a rhyme,—
 A barren, barren world were this
 Without one saving gleam;
 I 'd only ask that with a kiss
 You 'd wake me from the dream.

If dreaming were the sum of days,
 And loving were the bane;
If battling for a wreath of bays

Could soothe a heart in pain,—
 I 'd scorn the meed of battle's might,
 All other aims above
 I 'd choose the human's higher right,
 To suffer and to love!

THE SONG.

My soul, lost in the music's mist,
Roamed, rapt, 'neath skies of amethyst.
The cheerless streets grew summer meads,
The Son of Phoebus spurred his steeds,
And, wand'ring down the mazy tune,
December lost its way in June,
While from a verdant vale I heard
The piping of a love-lorn bird.

A something in the tender strain
Revived an old, long-conquered pain,
And as in depths of many seas,
My heart was drowned in memories.
The tears came welling to my eyes,
Nor could I ask it otherwise;
For, oh! a sweetness seems to last
Amid the dregs of sorrows past.

It stirred a chord that here of late
I 'd grown to think could not vibrate.
It brought me back the trust of youth,
The world again was joy and truth.
And Avice, blooming like a bride,
Once more stood trusting at my side.
But still, with bosom desolate,
The 'lorn bird sang to find his mate.

Then there are trees, and lights and stars,

The silv'ry tinkle of guitars;
And throbs again as throbbed that waltz,
Before I knew that hearts were false.
Then like a cold wave on a shore,
Comes silence and she sings no more.
I wake, I breathe, I think again,
And walk the sordid ways of men.

SIGNS OF THE TIMES.

Air a-gittin' cool an' coolah,
 Frost a-comin' in de night,
Hicka' nuts an' wa'nuts fallin',
 Possum keepin' out o' sight.
Tu'key struttin' in de ba'nya'd,
 Nary step so proud ez his;
Keep on struttin', Mistah Tu'key,
 Yo' do' know whut time it is.

Cidah press commence a-squeakin'
 Eatin' apples sto'ed away,
Chillun swa'min' 'roun' lak hotness,
 Huntin' aigs ermung de hay.
Mistah Tu'key keep on gobblin'
 At de geese a-flyin' souf,
Oomph! dat bird do' know whut's comin';
 Ef he did he'd shet his mouf.

Pumpkin gittin' good an' yallah
 Mek me open up my eyes;
Seems lak it's a-lookin' at me
 Jes' a-la'in' dah sayin' "Pies."
Tu'key gobbler gwine 'roun' blowin',
 Gwine 'roun' gibbin' sass an' slack;
Keep on talkin', Mistah Tu'key,
 You ain't seed no almanac.

Fa'mer walkin' th'oo de ba'nya'd
Seein' how things is comin' on,
Sees ef all de fowls is fatt'nin—
Good times comin' sho 's you bo'n.
Hyeahs dat tu'key gobbler braggin',
Den his face break in a smile—
Nebbah min', you sassy rascal,
He 's gwine nab you atter while.

Choppin' suet in de kitchen,
Stonin' raisins in de hall,
Beef a-cookie' fu' de mince meat,
Spices groun'—I smell 'em all.
Look hyeah, Tu'key, stop dat gobblin',
You ain' luned de sense ob feah,
You ol' fool, yo' naik 's in dangah,
Do' you know Thanksgibbin 's hyeah?

WHY FADES A DREAM?

Why fades a dream?
 An iridescent ray
Flecked in between the tryst
 Of night and day.
 Why fades a dream?—
Of consciousness the shade
Wrought out by lack of light and made
 Upon life's stream.
 Why fades a dream?

That thought may thrive,
 So fades the fleshless dream;
Lest men should learn to trust
 The things that seem.
 So fades a dream,

That living thought may grow
And like a waxing star-beam glow
 Upon life's stream—
 So fades a dream.

THE SPARROW.

A little bird, with plumage brown,
Beside my window flutters down,
A moment chirps its little strain,
Then taps upon my window-pane,
And chirps again, and hops along,
To call my notice to its song;
But I work on, nor heed its lay,
Till, in neglect, it flies away.

So birds of peace and hope and love
Come fluttering earthward from above,
To settle on life's window-sills,
And ease our load of earthly ills;
But we, in traffic's rush and din
Too deep engaged to let them in,
With deadened heart and sense plod on,
Nor know our loss till they are gone.

SPEAKIN' O' CHRISTMAS.

Breezes blowin' middlin' brisk,
Snow-flakes thro' the air a-whisk,
Fallin' kind o' soft an' light,
Not enough to make things white,
But jest sorter siftin' down
So 's to cover up the brown
Of the dark world's rugged ways

'N' make things look like holidays.
Not smoothed over, but jest specked,
Sorter strainin' fur effect,
An' not quite a-gittin' through
What it started in to do.
Mercy sakes! it does seem queer
Christmas day is 'most nigh here.
Somehow it don't seem to me
Christmas like it used to be,—
Christmas with its ice an' snow,
Christmas of the long ago.
You could feel its stir an' hum
Weeks an' weeks before it come;
Somethin' in the atmosphere
Told you when the day was near,
Did n't need no almanacs;
That was one o' Nature's fac's.
Every cottage decked out gay—
Cedar wreaths an' holly spray—
An' the stores, how they were drest,
Tinsel tell you could n't rest;
Every winder fixed up pat,
Candy canes, an' things like that;
Noah's arks, an' guns, an' dolls,
An' all kinds o' fol-de-rols.
Then with frosty bells a-chime,
Slidin' down the hills o' time,
Right amidst the fun an' din
Christmas come a-bustlin' in,
Raised his cheery voice to call
Out a welcome to us all
Hale and hearty, strong an' bluff,
That was Christmas, sure enough.
Snow knee-deep an' coastin' fine,
Frozen mill-ponds all ashine,
Seemin' jest to lay in wait,
Beggin' you to come an' skate.
An' you 'd git your gal an' go

Stumpin' cheerily thro' the snow,
Feelin' pleased an' skeert an' warm
'Cause she had a-holt yore arm.
Why, when Christmas come in, we
Spent the whole glad day in glee,
Havin' fun an' feastin' high
An' some courtin' on the sly.
Bustin' in some neighbor's door
An' then suddenly, before
He could give his voice a lift,
Yellin' at him, "Christmas gift."
Now sich things are never heard,
"Merry Christmas" is the word.
But it 's only change o' name,
An' means givin' jest the same.
There 's too many new-styled ways
Now about the holidays.
I 'd jest like once more to see
Christmas like it used to be!

LONESOME.

Mother 's gone a-visitin' to spend a month er two,
An', oh, the house is lonesome ez a nest whose birds has flew
To other trees to build ag'in; the rooms seem jest so bare
That the echoes run like sperrits from the kitchen to the stair.
The shelters flap more lazy-like 'n what they used to do,
Sence mother 's gone a-visitin' to spend a month er two.

We 've killed the fattest chicken an' we 've cooked her to a turn;
We 've made the richest gravy, but I jest don't give a durn
Fur nothin' 'at I drink er eat, er nothin' 'at I see.
The food ain't got the pleasant taste it used to have to me.
They 's somep'n' stickin' in my throat ez tight ez hardened glue,
Sence mother 's gone a-visitin' to spend a month er two.

The hollyhocks air jest ez pink, they 're double ones at that,
An' I wuz prouder of 'em than a baby of a cat.
But now I don't go near 'em, though they nod an' blush at me,
Fur they 's somep'n' seems to gall me in their keerless sort o' glee
An' all their fren'ly noddin' an' their blushin' seems to say:
"You're purty lonesome, John, old boy, sence mother 's gone away."

The neighbors ain't so fren'ly ez it seems they 'd ort to be;
They seem to be a-lookin' kinder sideways like at me,
A-kinder feared they 'd tech me off ez ef I wuz a match,
An' all because 'at mother's gone an' I'm a-keepin' batch!
I 'm shore I don't do nothin' worse 'n what I used to do
'Fore mother went a-visitin' to spend a month er two.

The sparrers ac's more fearsome like an' won't hop quite so near,
The cricket's chirp is sadder, an' the sky ain't ha'f so clear;
When ev'nin' comes, I set an' smoke tell my eyes begin to swim,
An' things aroun' commence to look all blurred an' faint an' dim.
Well, I guess I'll have to own up 'at I 'm feelin' purty blue
Sence mother's gone a-visitin' to spend a month er two.

GROWIN' GRAY.

Hello, ole man, you 're a-gittin' gray,
An' it beats ole Ned to see the way
'At the crow's feet 's a-getherin' aroun' yore eyes;
Tho' it ought n't to cause me no su'prise,
Fur there 's many a sun 'at you 've seen rise
An' many a one you 've seen go down
Sence yore step was light an' yore hair was brown,
An' storms an' snows have had their way—
Hello, ole man, you 're a-gittin' gray.

Hello, ole man, you 're a-gittin' gray,
An' the youthful pranks 'at you used to play
Are dreams of a far past long ago

That lie in a heart where the fires burn low—
That has lost the flame though it kept the glow,
An' spite of drivin' snow an' storm,
Beats bravely on forever warm.
December holds the place of May—
Hello, ole man, you're a-gittin' gray.

Hello, ole man, you're a-gittin' gray—
Who cares what the carpin' youngsters say?
For, after all, when the tale is told,
Love proves if a man is young or old!
Old age can't make the heart grow cold
When it does the will of an honest mind;
When it beats with love fur all mankind;
Then the night but leads to a fairer day—
Hello, ole man, you 're a-gittin' gray!

TO THE MEMORY OF MARY YOUNG.

God has his plans, and what if we
With our sight be too blind to see
Their full fruition; cannot he,
Who made it, solve the mystery?
One whom we loved has fall'n asleep,
Not died; although her calm be deep,
Some new, unknown, and strange surprise
In Heaven holds enrapt her eyes.

And can you blame her that her gaze
Is turned away from earthly ways,
When to her eyes God's light and love
Have giv'n the view of things above?
A gentle spirit sweetly good,
The pearl of precious womanhood;
Who heard the voice of duty clear,
And found her mission soon and near.

She loved all nature, flowers fair,
The warmth of sun, the kiss of air,
The birds that filled the sky with song,
The stream that laughed its way along.
Her home to her was shrine and throne,
But one love held her not alone;
She sought out poverty and grief,
Who touched her robe and found relief.

So sped she in her Master's work,
Too busy and too brave to shirk,
When through the silence, dusk and dim,
God called her and she fled to him.
We wonder at the early call,
And tears of sorrow can but fall
For her o'er whom we spread the pall;
But faith, sweet faith, is over all.

The house is dust, the voice is dumb,
But through undying years to come,
The spark that glowed within her soul
Shall light our footsteps to the goal.
She went her way; but oh, she trod
The path that led her straight to God.
Such lives as this put death to scorn;
They lose our day to find God's morn.

WHEN MALINDY SINGS.

G'way an' quit dat noise, Miss Lucy—
 Put dat music book away;
What 's de use to keep on tryin'?
 Ef you practice swell you 're gray,
You cain't sta't no notes a-flyin'
 Lak de ones dat rants and rings

F'om de kitchen to de big woods
 When Malindy sings.

You ain't got de nachel o'gans
 Fu' to make de soun' come right,
You ain't got de tu'ns an' twistin's
 Fu' to make it sweet an' light.
Tell you one thing now, Miss Lucy,
 An' I'm tellin' you fu' true,
When hit comes to real right singin',
 'T ain't no easy thing to do.

Easy 'nough fu' folks to hollah,
 Lookin' at de lines an' dots,
When dey ain't no one kin sence it,
 An' de chune comes in, in spots;
But fu' real melojous music,
 Dat jes' strikes yo' hea't and clings,
Jes' you stan' an' listen wif me
 When Malindy sings.

Ain't you nevah hyeahd Malindy?
 Blessed soul, tek up de cross!
Look hyeah, ain't you jokin', honey?
 Well, you don't know whut you los'.
Y' ought to hyeah dat gal a-wa'blin',
 Robins, la'ks, an' all dem things,
Heish dey moues an' hides dey faces
 When Malindy sings.

Fiddlin' man jes' stop his fiddlin',
 Lay his fiddle on de she'f;
Mockin'-bird quit tryin' to whistle,
 'Cause he jes' so shamed hisse'f.
Folks a-playin' on de banjo
 Draps dey fingahs on de strings—
Bless yo' soul—fu'gits to move 'em,
 When Malindy sings.

She jes' spreads huh mouf and hollahs,
 "Come to Jesus," twell you hyeah
Sinnahs' tremblin' steps and voices,
 Timid-lak a-drawin' neah;
Den she tu'ns to "Rock of Ages,"
 Simply to de cross she clings,
An' you fin' yo' teahs a-drappin'
 When Malindy sings.

Who dat says dat humble praises
 Wif de Master nevah counts?
Heish yo' mouf, I hyeah dat music,
 Ez hit rises up an' mounts—
Floatin' by de hills an' valleys,
 Way above dis buryin' sod,
Ez hit makes its way in glory
 To de very gates of God!

Oh, hit 's sweetah den de music
 Of an edicated band;
An' hit 's dearah dan de battle's
 Song o' triumph in de lan'.
It seems holier den evenin'
 When de solemn chu'ch bell rings,
Ez I sit an' ca'mly listen
 While Malindy sings.

Towsah, stop dat ba'kin', hyeah me!
 Mandy, mek dat chile keep still;
Don't you hyeah de echoes callin'
 F'om de valley to de hill?
Let me listen, I can hyeah it,
 Th'oo de bresh of angel's wings,
Sof' an' sweet, "Swing Low, Sweet Chariot,"
 Ez Malindy sings.

THE PARTY.

Dey had a gread big pahty down to Tom's de othah night;
Was I dah? You bet! I nevah in my life see sich a sight;
All de folks f'om fou' plantations was invited, an' dey come,
Dey come troopin' thick ez chillun when dey hyeahs a fife an' drum.
Evahbody dressed deir fines'—Heish yo' mouf an' git away,
Ain't seen no sich fancy dressin' sence las' quah'tly meetin' day;
Gals all dressed in silks an' satins, not a wrinkle ner a crease,
Eyes a-battin', teeth a-shinin', haih breshed back ez slick ez grease;
Sku'ts all tucked an' puffed an' ruffled, evah blessed seam an' stitch;
Ef you 'd seen 'em wif deir mistus, could n't swahed to which was
which.
Men all dressed up in Prince Alberts, swallertails 'u'd tek yo' bref!
I cain't tell you nothin' 'bout it, y' ought to seen it fu' yo'se'f.
Who was dah? Now who you askin'? How you 'spect I gwine to
know?
You mus' think I stood an' counted evahbody at de do'.
Ole man Babah's house-boy Isaac, brung dat gal, Malindy Jane,
Huh a-hangin' to his elbow, him a-struttin' wif a cane;
My, but Hahvey Jones was jealous! seemed to stick him lak a tho'n;
But he laughed with Viney Cahteh, tryin' ha'd to not let on,
But a pusson would 'a' noticed f'om de d'rection of his look,
Dat he was watchin' ev'ry step dat Ike an' Lindy took.
Ike he foun' a cheer an' asked huh: "Won't you set down?" wif a
smile,
An' she answe'd up a-bowin', "Oh, I reckon 't ain't wuth while."
Dat was jes' fu' style, I reckon, 'cause she sot down jes' de same,
An' she stayed dah 'twell he fetched huh fu' to jine some so't o'
game;
Den I hyeahd huh sayin' propah, ez she riz to go away,
"Oh, you raly mus' excuse me, fu' I hardly keers to play."
But I seen huh in a minute wif de othahs on de flo',
An' dah was n't any one o' dem a-playin' any mo';
Comin' down de flo' a-bowin' an' a-swayin' an' a-swingin',
Puttin' on huh high-toned mannahs all de time dat she was singin':
"Oh, swing Johnny up an' down, swing him all aroun',
Swing Johnny up an' down, swing him all aroun',

Oh, swing Johnny up an' down, swing him all aroun',
Fa' you well, my dahlin'."
Had to laff at ole man Johnson, he's a caution now, you bet—
Hittin' clost onto a hunderd, but he 's spry an' nimble yet;
He 'lowed how a-so't o'gigglin', "I ain't ole, I'll let you see,
D'ain't no use in gittin' feeble, now you youngstahs jes' watch me,"
An' he grabbed ole Aunt Marier—weighs th'ee hunderd mo' er less,
An' he spun huh 'roun' de cabin swingin' Johnny lak de res'.
Evahbody laffed an' hollahed: "Go it! Swing huh, Uncle Jim!"
An' he swung huh too, I reckon, lak a youngstah, who but him.
Dat was bettah 'n young Scott Thomas, tryin' to be so awful smaht.
You know when dey gits to singin' an' dey comes to dat ere paht:

 "In some lady's new brick house,
 In some lady's gyahden.
 Ef you don't let me out, I will jump out,
 So fa' you well, my dahlin'."

Den dey 's got a circle 'roun' you, an' you 's got to break de line;
Well, dat dahky was so anxious, lak to bust hisse'f a-tryin';
Kep' on blund'rin' 'roun' an' foolin' 'twell he giv' one gread big
jump,
Broke de line, an' lit head-fo'most in de fiahplace right plump;
Hit 'ad fiah in it, mind you; well, I thought my soul I'd bust,
Tried my best to keep f'om laffin', but hit seemed like die I must!
Y' ought to seen dat man a-scramblin' f'om de ashes an' de grime.
Did it bu'n him! Sich a question, why he did n't give it time;
Th'ow'd dem ashes and dem cindahs evah which-a-way I guess,
An' you nevah did, I reckon, clap yo' eyes on sich a mess;
Fu' he sholy made a picter an' a funny one to boot,
Wif his clothes all full o' ashes an' his face all full o' soot.
Well, hit laked to stopped de pahty, an' I reckon lak ez not
Dat it would ef Tom's wife, Mandy, hadn't happened on de spot,
To invite us out to suppah—well, we scrambled to de table,
An' I 'd lak to tell you 'bout it—what we had—but I ain't able,
Mention jes' a few things, dough I know I had n't orter,
Fu' I know 't will staht a hank'rin' an' yo' mouf 'll 'mence to worter.
We had wheat bread white ez cotton an' a egg pone jes like gol',
Hog jole, bilin' hot an' steamin' roasted shoat an' ham sliced cold—
Look out! What's de mattah wif you? Don't be fallin' on de flo';

Ef it 's go'n' to 'fect you dat way, I won't tell you nothin' mo'.
Dah now—well, we had hot chittlin's—now you 's tryin' ag'in to
fall,Cain't you stan' to hyeah about it? S'pose you 'd been an' seed it
all; Seed dem gread big sweet pertaters, layin' by de possum's side,
Seed dat coon in all his gravy, reckon den you'd up and died!
Mandy 'lowed "you all mus' 'scuse me, d' wa'n't much upon my
she'ves,
But I 's done my bes' to suit you, so set down an' he'p yo'se'ves."
Tom, he 'lowed: "I don't b'lieve in 'pologisin' an' perfessin',
Let 'em tek it lak dey ketch it. Eldah Thompson, ask de blessin'."
Wish you'd seed dat colo'ed preachah cleah his th'oat an' bow his
head;
One eye shet, an' one eye open,—dis is evah wud he said:
"Lawd, look down in tendah mussy on sich generous hea'ts ez dese;
Make us truly thankful, amen. Pass dat possum, ef you please!"
Well, we eat and drunk ouah po'tion, 'twell dah was n't nothin' lef,
An' we felt jes' like new sausage, we was mos' nigh stuffed to def!
Tom, he knowed how we'd be feelin', so he had de fiddlah 'roun',
An' he made us cleah de cabin fu' to dance dat suppah down.
Jim, de fiddlah, chuned his fiddle, put some rosum on his bow,
Set a pine box on de table, mounted it an' let huh go!
He 's a fiddlah, now I tell you, an' he made dat fiddle ring,
'Twell de ol'est an' de lamest had to give deir feet a fling.
Jigs, cotillions, reels an' break-downs, cordrills an' a waltz er two;
Bless yo' soul, dat music winged 'em an' dem people lak to flew.
Cripple Joe, de ole rheumatic, danced dat flo' f'om side to middle,
Th'owed away his crutch an' hopped it, what's rheumatics 'ginst a
fiddle?
Eldah Thompson got so tickled dat he lak to los' his grace,
Had to tek bofe feet an' hol' dem so 's to keep 'em in deir place.
An' de Christuns an' de sinnahs got so mixed up on dat flo',
Dat I don't see how dey 'd pahted ef de trump had chanced to blow.
Well, we danced dat way an' capahed in de mos' redic'lous way,
'Twell de roostahs in de bahnyard cleahed deir th'oats an' crowed fu'
day.
Y' ought to been dah, fu' I tell you evahthing was rich an' prime,
An' dey ain't no use in talkin', we jes had one scrumptious time!

Acknowledgments

This book would not have been possible without the help of a number of talented people who made many different contributions at various stages of the book's development. Among those deserving special thanks are:

Gil King, Professor Houston Baker, Professor Nellie McKay, Professor William Andrews, Lawrence Otis Graham, Valerie Miller and the Library Company of Philadelphia, Jean Currie Church and the Moorland-Spingarn Research Center at Howard University, Elaine Maruhn and the University of Nebraska Press, Sylvia Snape of the University of Massachusetts Department of English.

Thanks are also due to several past and present members of the staff of Running Press: Serrin Bodmer, Carlo DeVito, Bill Jones, Danielle McCole, Catherine Sweeney, and Michael Washburn.

The first author ever to win two PEN/Faulkner Awards for literature, **John Edgar Wideman** has built his literary reputation with eleven works of fiction as well as two personal memoirs. A chronicler of black urban life, the acclaim for Wideman and his work includes his characterization by the *Los Angeles Times Book Review* as "our most powerful and accomplished artist of the black urban world," and by the *New York Times* as "a writer who belongs in our permanent library." Two of his books, *Brothers and Keepers* and *Philadelphia Fire*, were *New York Times* bestsellers. The latter novel won Wideman the PEN/Faulkner Award in 1994, the other winner being *Sent for You Yesterday* in 1984. Wideman's most recent novel is *Two Cities*. The scion of a working-class Pittsburgh family who became a Rhodes scholar and famed athlete, Wideman's life, no less than his literary career, has put him in the spotlight. (The memoir *Brothers and Keepers* deals with Wideman's complex relationship with his brother Robby, a convicted felon.) A leading expert on the African-American contribution to American literature and thought, Wideman is currently one of the most valued members of the faculty of the University of Massachusetts at Amherst.